MyBcommLab

Do you get the connection between communication skills and career success? Do you need a better way to practice writing skills and grammar content outside of class? Do you want to become a polished communicator? MyBcommLab can help. Go to **www.mybcommlab.com** — where *Practice Makes Polished* — to access the following interactive tools.

PRE-TEST, POST-TEST, AND CUSTOMIZED STUDY PLANS

Complete a pre-test, and the results generate a customized study plan with remediation activities. Study plans tag incorrect questions from the pre-test to the appropriate textbook learning objective, enabling you to concentrate on only the topics where you need more help. Study plans include flash cards, eBook reading assignments, sample documents, and Interactive Lectures. Customized study plans keep you on track throughout the semester. Conclude with the post-test to verify chapter mastery.

GRAMMAR DIAGNOSTIC STUDY PLAN

Complete the Grammar Diagnostic test to see what areas require more support. This customized study plan provides you with a self-paced learning method designed to improve your grammar skills.

BUSINESS COMMUNICATION MINI-SIMS

The brand new Business Communication Mini-Sims are interactive real-world scenarios that invite you to take on the role of a company decision-maker and apply the concepts you have just learned. You are scored on the brief simulation and directed to the eBook, quizzes, and other learning aids to reinforce the concepts.

DOCUMENT MAKEOVERS

Practice identifying communication errors and revising actual documents with Document Makeovers, which are based on chapter objectives.

STUDENT PRESENTATIONS

Learn the ins and outs of delivering an effective presentation by watching these short videos. The Student Presentations incorporate tips on voice, tone, stance, hand gestures, and much more.

ALWAYS LEARNING

PEARSON

Business Communication Today

Eleventh Edition

Business Communication Today

Courtland L. Bovée

Professor of Business Communication
C. Allen Paul Distinguished Chair
Grossmont College

John V. Thill

Chairman and Chief Executive Officer
Global Communication Strategies

PEARSON

Boston   Columbus   Indianapolis   New York   San Francisco   Upper Saddle River
Amsterdam   Cape Town   Dubai   London   Madrid   Milan   Munich   Paris   Montreal
Toronto   Delhi   Mexico City   São Paulo   Sydney   Hong Kong   Seoul   Singapore   Taipei   Tokyo

Editorial Director: Sally Yagan
Editor in Chief: Erin Svendsen
Acquisitions Editor: James Heine
Editorial Project Manager: Karin Williams
Editorial Assistant: Ashlee Bradbury
Director of Marketing: Patrice Lumumba Jones
Marketing Manager: Nikki Ayana Jones
Marketing Assistant: Ian Gold
Senior Managing Editor: Judy Leale
Senior Production Project Manager: Karalyn Holland
Senior Operations Supervisor: Arnold Vila
Operations Specialist: Cathleen Petersen
Creative Director: Blair Brown
Senior Art Director: Kenny Beck
Cover Designer: Kenny Beck

Interior Designer: Laura C. Ierardi
Manager, Rights and Permissions: Hessa Albader
Cover Art: Pearson Image Specialist, Corin Skidds;
   Pearson Image Photographer, Shayle Keating;
   Additional Images from Shutterstock/ Kaya Altay,
   Irina Tischenko, Velychko, Carlos E. Santa Maria,
   PhotoHappiness, Mashe
Media Project Manager, Editorial: Denise Vaughn
Media Project Manager, Production: Lisa Rinaldi
Full-Service Project Management: Heather Willison,
   S4Carlisle Publishing Services
Composition: S4Carlisle Publishing Services
Printer/Binder: Quebecor World Color/Versailles
Cover Printer: Lehigh-Phoenix Color/Hagerstown
Text Font: 10.5/12 Minion

Credits and acknowledgments borrowed from other sources and reproduced, with permission, in this textbook appear on the appropriate page within text or on page ACK-1.

Microsoft® and Windows® are registered trademarks of the Microsoft Corporation in the U.S.A. and other countries. Screen shots and icons reprinted with permission from the Microsoft Corporation. This book is not sponsored or endorsed by or affiliated with the Microsoft Corporation.

Library of Congress Cataloging-in-Publication Data
Bovée, Courtland L.
   Business communication today / Courtland L. Bovée, John V. Thill. — 11th ed.
      p. cm.
   Includes bibliographical references and index.
   ISBN 978-0-13-253955-5 (alk. paper)
   1. Business communication—United States—Case studies.   2. Communication
in organizations—United States—Case studies.   I. Thill, John V.   II. Title.
   HF5718.B66 2011
   658.4′5—dc23

                                                         2011022339

10 9 8 7 6 5 4 3 2 1

ISBN 10:   0-13-253955-1
ISBN 13: 978-0-13-253955-5

Contents in Brief

Contents

CHAPTER 19

Applying and Interviewing for Employment   548

Real-Time Updates—Learn More

Real-Time Updates "Learn More" is a unique feature that you will see strategically located throughout the text, connecting them with dozens of carefully selected online media items. These elements—categorized by the icons shown below representing podcasts, PDF files, articles/websites, online videos, and PowerPoint presentations—complement the text's coverage by providing contemporary examples and valuable insights from successful professionals.

REAL-TIME UPDATES
Learn More by Reading This Article

REAL-TIME UPDATES
Learn More by Listening to This Podcast

REAL-TIME UPDATES
Learn More by Watching This Video

REAL-TIME UPDATES
Learn More by Reading This PDF

REAL-TIME UPDATES
Learn More by Watching This
PowerPoint Presentation

Preface

Major Changes and Improvements in This Edition

Bovée and Thill texts have long set the benchmark in this field for rigorous, high-value revisions that make sure instructors and students have the most comprehensive, realistic, and contemporary materials available. The following table identifies the major changes and improvements in the eleventh edition of *Business Communication Today*.

Significant Content Additions and Upgrades	In addition to numerous updates and streamlining rewrites throughout, the following sections are all new or substantially revised with new material: • *Understanding Why Communication Matters* (in Chapter 1) • *The Social Communication Model* (in Chapter 1) • *Committing to Ethical and Legal Communication* (in Chapter 1; new coverage of transparency) • *Distinguishing Ethical Dilemmas from Ethical Lapses* (in Chapter 1; revised and streamlined) • *Business Communication 2.0: Who's Responsible Here?* (in Chapter 1; updated) • *Communicating Effectively in Teams* (in Chapter 2; new coverage of collaboration) • *Using Meeting Technologies* (in Chapter 2; updated) • *Communicating Across Cultures: Whose Skin Is This, Anyway?* (in Chapter 2) • *Business Etiquette Online* (in Chapter 2; updated) • *Developing Cultural Competency* (in Chapter 3) • *Communicating Across Cultures: Us Versus Them: Generational Conflict in the Workplace* (in Chapter 3) • *Speaking and Listening Carefully* (in Chapter 3; updated with accommodation strategies) • *Analyzing the Situation* (in Chapter 4) • *Building Reader Interest with Storytelling Techniques* (in Chapter 4) • *Emphasizing the Positive* (in Chapter 5; new coverage of euphemisms) • *Business Communication 2.0: Walking Around with the Entire Internet in Your Hands* (in Chapter 7) • *Compositional Modes for Electronic Media* (in Chapter 7) • *Managing Communication in a Social Media Environment* (in Chapter 7)

(continued)

Significant Content Additions and Upgrades (Continued)	• *Social Networking and Community Participation Websites* (in Chapter 7)

      Social Networks

         Business Communication Uses of Social Networks

         Strategies for Business Communication on Social Networks

      User-Generated Content Sites

      Community Q&A Sites

      Community Participation Websites

• *Microblogging* (in Chapter 7)

• New two-page highlight feature: *Business Communicators Innovating with Social Media* (in Chapter 7)

• *Closing on a Respectful Note* (in Chapter 9)

• *Making Negative Announcements on Routine Business Matters* (in Chapter 9)

• *Rejecting Suggestions and Proposals* (in Chapter 9)

• *Refusing Social Networking Recommendation Requests* (in Chapter 9)

• *Rejecting Job Applications* (in Chapter 9)

• *Giving Negative Performance Reviews* (in Chapter 9; substantially revised)

• *Business Communication 2.0: We're Under Attack! Responding to Rumors and Criticism in a Social Media Environment* (in Chapter 9; substantially revised)

• *Writing Promotional Messages for Social Media* (in Chapter 10; revised)

• *Online Monitoring Tools* (in Chapter 11)

• *Creating Successful Business Plans* (in Chapter 13; revised)

• *Business Communication 2.0: Hey You! Hands Off My Content!* (in Chapter 14)

• *Presentation Close* (in Chapter 16)

• *Ending with Clarity and Confidence* (in Chapter 16)

• *Embracing the Backchannel* (in Chapter 16)

• *Designing Effective Slides* (in Chapter 17)

• *Creating Effective Slide Content* (in Chapter 17)

• *Creating Effective Handouts* (in Chapter 17)

• *Finding the Ideal Opportunity in Today's Job Market* (in Chapter 18)

      Writing the Story of You

      Learning to Think Like an Employer

      Translating Your General Potential into a Specific Solution for Each Employer

      Taking the Initiative to Find Opportunities

      Building Your Network

      Avoiding Mistakes

• *Composing Your Résumé* (in Chapter 18; revised with the latest advice on keywords)

• *Printing a Scannable Résumé* (in Chapter 18; updated to reflect the decline of this format)

Significant Content Additions and Upgrades (Continued)	• *Creating an Online Résumé* (in Chapter 18) • *Following Up After Submitting a Résumé* (in Chapter 19) • *Learning About the Organization and Your Interviewers* (in Chapter 19)
The Social Media Revolution	This edition includes up-to-date coverage of the social communication model that is redefining business communication and reshaping the relationships between companies and their stakeholders. Social media concepts and techniques are integrated throughout the book, from career planning to presentations. Here are some examples: • Social media questions, activities, and cases appear throughout the book, using Twitter, Facebook, LinkedIn, and other media that have taken the business world by storm in the past couple of years. • Three dozen examples of business applications of social media show students how a variety of companies use these tools. • The social communication model is now covered in Chapter 1. • A new two-page, magazine-style feature in Chapter 7 highlights the innovative uses of social media by a variety of companies. • Social networking sites are now covered as a brief-message medium in Chapter 7. • The Twitter-enabled *backchannel*, which is revolutionizing electronic presentations, is covered in Chapter 16. • Social media tools are covered extensively in the career-planning Prologue and the two employment communication Chapters (18 and 19).
Compositional Modes for Electronic Media	For all the benefits they offer, social media and other innovations place new demands on business communicators. This edition introduces you to nine important modes of writing for electronic media.
Personal Branding	As the workforce continues to evolve and with employment likely to remain unstable for some time to come, it is more important than ever for you to take control of your career. An important first step is to clarify and communicate your *personal brand*, a topic that is now addressed in the Prologue and carried through to the employment-message chapters.
Storytelling Techniques	Some of the most effective business messages, from advertising to proposals to personal branding, rely on storytelling techniques. This edition offers hands-on advice and multiple activities to help you develop "business-class" narrative techniques.
Full Implementation of Objective-Driven Learning	Every aspect of this new edition is organized by learning objectives, from the chapter content to the student activities in the textbook and online at mybcommlab.com. This structure makes it easier for you to study, practice, check your progress, and focus on those areas where you need a little extra work.
Deeper Integration with MyBcommLab	This essential online resource now offers even more ways to test your understanding of the concepts presented in every chapter, practice vital skills, and create customized study plans.
Multimedia Resources	Extend your learning experience with unique *Real-Time Updates* "Learn More" media elements that connect you with dozens of handpicked videos, podcasts, and other items that complement chapter content.

(continued)

New Communication Close-ups (Chapter-Opening Vignette and Chapter-Ending Projects)	Chapter 1: Toyota's Auto-Biography user-generated content program Chapter 6: Noted web designer Jefferson Rabb's user-focused design principles Chapter 9: Chargify's communication errors regarding a price increase Chapter 13: MyCityWay's winning business plan Chapter 15: Garage Technology Ventures's advice for writing executive summaries Chapter 16: Comedy super-agent Peter Principato's techniques for effective presentations Chapter 17: Garr Reynolds's revolutionary Zen-inspired slide designs Chapter 18: Alliant Techsystems and cutting-edge workforce analytics Chapter 19: Zappos's free-spirited approach to recruiting free-spirited employees
New Review and Analysis Questions and Skills-Development Projects	More than 110 new questions and activities are offered in Test Your Knowledge, Apply Your Knowledge, and Practice Your Skills categories.
New Communication Cases	Communication cases give you the opportunity to solve real-world communication challenges using the media skills you'll be expected to have in tomorrow's workplace; one-third of the 145 cases are new in this edition.
New Figures and More Annotated Model Documents	The eleventh edition offers an unmatched portfolio of business communication exhibits. Here are the highlights: • More than 60 new figures provide examples of the latest trends in business communication. • More than 90 annotated model documents, ranging from printed letters and reports to websites, blogs, and social networking sites, show you in detail how successful business messages work. • Nearly 80 exhibits feature communication examples from real companies, including Bigelow Tea, Delicious, Google, IBM, Microsoft Bing, Patagonia, Red Bull, Segway, Southwest Airlines, and Zappos. • More than 110 illustrated examples of communication technologies help you grasp the wide range of tools and media formats you will encounter on the job.
Critique the Professionals	This new activity invites you to analyze an example of professional communication using the principles learned in each chapter.
Quick Learning Guide	This convenient review tool at the end of every chapter summarizes the learning objectives, lists essential terminology from the chapter, and collects the checklists in one handy place. Start here when it's time to study for a test.

Extend the Value of Your Textbook with Free Multimedia Content

Business Communication Today's unique Real-Time Updates system automatically provides weekly content updates, including podcasts, PowerPoint presentations, online videos, PDF files, and articles. You can subscribe to updates chapter by chapter, so you get only the material that applies to the chapter you are studying. You can access Real-Time Updates through MyBcommLab or by visiting http://real-timeupdates.com/bct11.

1 Read messages from the authors and access special assignment materials and "Learn More" media items.

2 Click on any chapter to see the updates and media items for that chapter.

3 Scan headlines and click on any item of interest to read the article or download the media item.

Every item is personally selected by the authors to complement the text and support in-class activities.

4 Subscribe via RSS to individual chapters to get updates automatically for the chapter you're currently studying.

5 Media items are categorized by type so you can quickly find podcasts, videos, PowerPoints, and more.

What Is the Single Most Important Step You Can Take to Enhance Your Career Prospects?

No matter what profession you want to pursue, the ability to communicate will be an essential skill—and a skill that employers expect you to have when you enter the workforce. This course introduces you to the fundamental principles of business communication and gives you the opportunity to develop your communication skills. You'll discover how business communication differs from personal and social communication, and you'll see how today's companies are using blogs, social networks, podcasts, virtual worlds, wikis, and other technologies. You'll learn a simple three-step writing process that works for all types of writing and speaking projects, both in college and on the job. Along the way, you'll gain valuable insights into ethics, etiquette, listening, teamwork, and nonverbal communication. Plus, you'll learn effective strategies for the many types of communication challenges you'll face on the job, from routine messages about transactions to complex reports and websites.

Colleges and universities vary in the prerequisites established for the business communication course, but we advise taking at least one course in English composition before enrolling in this class. Some coursework in business studies will also give you a better perspective on communication challenges in the workplace. However, we have taken special care not to assume any in-depth business experience, so you can use *Business Communication Today* successfully even if you have limited on-the-job experience or business coursework.

HOW THIS COURSE WILL HELP YOU

Few courses can offer the three-for-the-price-of-one value you get from a business communication class. Check out these benefits:

- **In your other classes.** The communication skills you learn in this class can help you in every other course you will take in college. From simple homework assignments to complicated team projects to class presentations, you'll be able to communicate more effectively with less time and effort.
- **During your job search.** You can reduce the stress of searching for a job and stand out from the competition. As you'll see in Chapters 18 and 19, every activity in the job search process relies on communication. The better you can communicate, the more successful you'll be in landing interesting and rewarding work.
- **On the job.** After you get that great job, the time and energy you have invested in this course will continue to yield benefits year after year. As you tackle each project and every new challenge, influential company leaders—the people who decide how quickly you'll get promoted and how much you'll earn—will be paying close attention to how well you communicate. They will observe your interactions with colleagues, customers, and business partners. They'll take note of how well you can collect data, find the essential ideas buried under mountains of information, and convey those points to other people. They'll observe your ability to adapt to different audiences and circumstances. They'll be watching when you encounter tough situations that require careful attention to ethics and etiquette. The good news: Every insight you gain and every skill you develop in this course will help you shine in your career.

HOW TO SUCCEED IN THIS COURSE

Although this course explores a wide range of message types and appears to cover quite a lot of territory, the underlying structure of the course is actually rather simple. You'll learn a few basic concepts, identify some key skills to use and procedures to follow—and then practice, practice, practice. Whether you're writing a blog posting in response to one of the real-company cases or drafting your own résumé, you'll be practicing the same skills again and again. With feedback and reinforcement from your instructor and your classmates, your confidence will grow and the work will become easier and more enjoyable.

The following sections offer advice on approaching each assignment, using your textbook, and taking advantage of some other helpful resources.

Approaching Each Assignment

In the spirit of practice and improvement, you will have a number of writing (and possibly speaking) assignments throughout this course. These suggestions will help you produce better results with less effort:

- **First, don't panic!** If the thought of writing a report or giving a speech sends a chill up your spine, you're not alone. Everybody feels that way when first learning business communication skills, and even experienced professionals can feel nervous about major projects. Keeping three points in mind will help. First, every project can be broken down into a series of small, manageable tasks. Don't let a big project overwhelm you; it's nothing more than a bunch of smaller tasks. Second, remind yourself that you have the skills you need to accomplish each task. As you move through the course, the assignments are carefully designed to match the skills you've developed up to that point. Third, if you feel panic creeping up on you, take a break and regain your perspective.

- **Focus on one task at a time.** A common mistake writers make is trying to organize and express their ideas while simultaneously worrying about audience reactions, grammar, spelling, formatting, page design, and a dozen other factors. Fight the temptation to do everything at once; otherwise, your frustration will soar and your productivity will plummet. In particular, don't worry about grammar, spelling, and word choices during your first draft. Concentrate on the organization of your ideas first, then the way you express those ideas, and then the presentation and production of your messages. Following the three-step writing process is an ideal way to focus on one task at a time in a logical sequence.

- **Give yourself plenty of time.** As with every other school project, putting things off to the last minute creates unnecessary stress. Writing and speaking projects in particular are much easier if you tackle them in small stages with breaks in between, rather than trying to get everything done in one frantic blast. Moreover, there will be instances when you simply get stuck on a project, and the best thing to do is walk away and give your mind a break. If you allow room for breaks in your schedule, you'll minimize the frustration and spend less time overall on your homework, too.

- **Step back and assess each project before you start.** The writing and speaking projects you'll have in this course cover a wide range of communication scenarios, and it's essential that you adapt your approach to each new challenge. Resist the urge to dive in and start writing without a plan. Ponder the assignment for a while, consider the various approaches you might take, and think carefully about your objectives before you start writing. Nothing is more frustrating than getting stuck halfway through because you're not sure what you're trying to say or you've wandered off track. Spend a little time planning, and you'll spend a lot less time writing.

- **Use the three-step writing process.** Those essential planning tasks are the first step in the three-step writing process, which you'll learn about in Chapter 4 and use throughout the course. This process has been developed and refined by professional writers with decades of experience and thousands of projects ranging from short blog posts to 500-page textbooks. It works, so take advantage of it.

- **Learn from the examples and model documents.** This textbook offers dozens of realistic examples of business messages, many with notes along the sides that explain strong and weak points (see the FreshBooks example on the next page). Study these and any other examples that your instructor provides. Learn what works and what doesn't work, then apply these lessons to your own writing.

- **Learn from experience.** Finally, learn from the feedback you get from your instructor and from other students. Don't take the criticism personally; your instructor and your classmates are commenting about the work, not about you. View every bit of feedback as an opportunity to improve.

Using This Textbook Package

This book and its accompanying online resources introduce you to the key concepts in business communication while helping you develop essential skills. As you read each chapter, start by studying the learning objectives. They will help you identify the most

The headline doesn't try to be clever or cute; instead, it instantly conveys important information to readers.

The graph shows which terms generated the fastest payments (shortest blue bars) and highest percentage paid (orange dots).

This bold header quickly summarizes the nature of the analysis.

These clearly written paragraphs explain the two aspects of the analysis, and they speak the same language as business accounting professionals.

The article continues beyond here, but notice again the concise, straightforward wording of this subheading (the section explains that polite wording on invoices improves customer responsiveness).

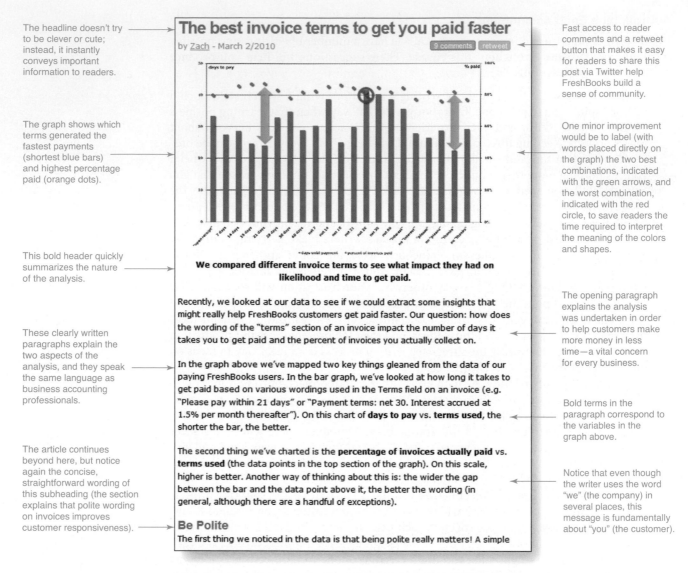

Fast access to reader comments and a retweet button that makes it easy for readers to share this post via Twitter help FreshBooks build a sense of community.

One minor improvement would be to label (with words placed directly on the graph) the two best combinations, indicated with the green arrows, and the worst combination, indicated with the red circle, to save readers the time required to interpret the meaning of the colors and shapes.

The opening paragraph explains the analysis was undertaken in order to help customers make more money in less time—a vital concern for every business.

Bold terms in the paragraph correspond to the variables in the graph above.

Notice that even though the writer uses the word "we" (the company) in several places, this message is fundamentally about "you" (the customer).

Here is one of more than 90 annotated model documents that point out what works (and sometimes, what doesn't work) in a variety of professional messages and documents. Used with permission of FreshBooks.

important concepts in the chapter and give you a feel for what you'll be learning. Following the learning objectives, the Communication Close-up vignette features a successful professional role model who uses the same skills you will be learning in the chapter.

As you work your way through the chapter, compare the advice given with the various examples, both the brief in-text examples and the standalone model documents. Also, keep an eye out for the Real-Time Updates elements in each chapter. The authors have selected these videos, podcasts, presentations, and other online media to provide informative and entertaining enhancements to the text material.

At the end of each chapter, the Quick Learning Guide gives you the chance to quickly verify your grasp of important concepts. Following that, you'll see two sets of questions that help you test and apply your knowledge, and two sets of projects that help you practice and expand your skills. Many chapters also feature communication cases, which are more involved projects that require you to plan and complete a variety of messages and documents. All these activities are tagged by learning objective, so if you have any questions about the concepts you need to apply, just revisit that part of the chapter.

Several chapters have activities with downloadable media such as presentations and podcasts or the use of the Bovée-Thill wiki simulator. If your instructor assigns these activities, follow the instructions in the text to locate the correct files. And if you'd like some help getting started with Facebook, Twitter, or LinkedIn, we have created screencasts with helpful advice on these topics.

In addition to the 19 chapters of the text itself, here are some special features that will help you succeed in the course and on the job:

- **Prologue: Building a Career with Your Communication Skills.** This section (immediately following this Preface) helps you understand today's dynamic workplace, the steps you can take to adapt to the job market, and the importance of creating an employment portfolio and building your personal brand.
- **Handbook.** The Handbook of Grammar, Mechanics, and Usage (see page H-1) serves as a convenient reference of essential business English.
- **MyBcommLab.** If your course includes MyBcommLab, you can take advantage of this unique resource to test your understanding of the concepts presented in every chapter. Each MyBcommLab chapter offers assessment resources that include study plans, videos, interactive lectures, flashcards, mini-simulations, PowerPoints, Document Makeovers, and critical thinking questions to reinforce chapter concepts.
- **Real-Time Updates.** You can use this unique newsfeed service to make sure you're always kept up to date on important topics. Plus, at strategic points in every chapter, you will be directed to the Real-Time Updates website to get the latest information about specific subjects. To sign up, visit http://real-timeupdates.com/bct11. You can also access Real-Time Updates through MyBcommLab.
- **Business Communication Web Search.** With our unique web search approach, you can quickly access more than 325 search engines. The tool uses a simple and intuitive interface engineered to help you find precisely what you want, whether it's Power-Point files, Adobe Acrobat PDF files, Microsoft Word documents, Excel files, videos, or podcasts. Check it out at http://businesscommunicationblog.com/websearch.
- **CourseSmart eTextbooks Online.** CourseSmart is an exciting new choice for students looking to save money. As an alternative to purchasing the print textbook, you can purchase an electronic version of the same content and receive a significant discount off the suggested list price of the print text. With a CourseSmart eTextbook, you can search the text, make notes online, print out reading assignments that incorporate lecture notes and bookmark important passages for later review. For more information or to purchase access to the CourseSmart eTextbook, visit www.coursesmart.com.

FEEDBACK

We would appreciate hearing from you! Let us know what you think about this textbook by writing to college_marketing@prenhall.com. Please include "Feedback About Bovee/Thill BCT 11e" in the subject line. We review every comment we receive from students and use this feedback to make sure that future editions meet student needs in every way possible.

About the Authors

Courtland L. Bovée and John V. Thill have been leading textbook authors for more than two decades, introducing millions of students to the fields of business and business communication. Their award-winning texts are distinguished by proven pedagogical features, extensive selections of contemporary case studies, hundreds of real-life examples, engaging writing, thorough research, and the unique integration of print and electronic resources. Each new edition reflects the authors' commitment to continuous refinement and improvement, particularly in terms of modeling the latest practices in business and the use of technology.

Professor Bovée has 22 years of teaching experience at Grossmont College in San Diego, where he has received teaching honors and was accorded that institution's C. Allen Paul Distinguished Chair. Mr. Thill is a prominent communications consultant who has worked with organizations ranging from Fortune 500 multinationals to entrepreneurial start-ups. He formerly held positions with Pacific Bell and Texaco.

Courtland Bovée and John Thill were recently awarded proclamations from the Governor of Massachusetts for their lifelong contributions to education and for their commitment to the summer youth baseball program that is sponsored by the Boston Red Sox.

Acknowledgments

The eleventh edition of *Business Communication Today* reflects the professional experience of a large team of contributors and advisors. We express our thanks to the many individuals whose valuable suggestions and constructive comments influenced the success of this book.

Michelle Boucher, *Southwestern College*
Nicole A. Buzzetto-More, *University of Maryland–Eastern Shore*
Lana W. Carnes, *Eastern Kentucky University*
Rebecca Cline, *Middle Georgia College*
Steven Deeley, *Santiago Canyon College*
Cynthia Evans, *University of Northern Colorado*
Duane Franceschi, *Canyon College*
Jeffrey Goddin, *Indiana University*
Roxanne B. Hamilton, *Landmark College*
Hal P. Kingsley, *Trocaire College*
Lisa B. Martin, *Piedmont Technical College*
Mabry M. O'Donnell, *Marietta College*
Brenda Rhodes, *Northeastern Junior College*
Sarah K. Rodgers, *Owens Community College*
Karen J. Roush, *Independence Community College*
Jessica Stoudenmire, *El Camino College*
Tracy K. Tunwall, *Mount Mercy College*
Joyce W. Twing, *Vermont Technical College*
Kathi Vosevich, *Shorter College*
Mark C. Zorn, *Butler County Community College*

REVIEWERS OF PREVIOUS EDITIONS

We especially want to thank these reviewers, whose detailed and perceptive comments resulted in excellent refinements:

Timothy Alder, *Pennsylvania State University–University Park*
Heather Allman, *University of West Florida*
Patricia Boyd, *Arizona State University*
Janice Cooke, *University of New Orleans*
Terry Engebretsen, *Idaho State University*
Fernando Ganivet, *Florida International University*
Bonnie Garrity, *D'Youville College*
Susanne Hartl, *Nyack College*
Joyce Hicks, *Valparaiso University*
Lynda Hodge, *Guilford Technical Community College*
Mary Humphrys, *University of Toledo*
Iris Johnson, *Virginia Commonwealth University*
Sharon Kobritz, *Husson University*
Marsha Kruger, *University of Nebraska–Omaha*
Marianna Larsen, *Utah State University*
Anita Leffel, *University of Texas–San Antonio*
Paul Lewellan, *Augustana College*
Richard Malamud, *California State University–Dominguez Hills*
Thomas Marshall, *Robert Morris University*
Leanne Maunu, *Palomar College*
Michael McLane, *University of Texas–San Antonio*
Bronna McNeely, *Midwestern State University*
Margaret O'Connor, *Bloomsburg University of Pennsylvania*

Holly Payne, *University of Southern Indiana*
Kathy Peacock, *Utah State University*
Folke Person, *Idaho State University*
Betty Robbins, *University of Oklahoma*
Drew Sabol, *SUNY Institute of Technology*
Diza Sauers, *University of Arizona*
Nicola Scott, *George Mason University*
Lucinda Sinclair, *Longwood University*
Rodney Smith, *University of Dubuque*
Natalie Stillman-Webb, *The University of Utah*
Bruce Strom, *University of Indianapolis*
Dana Swensen, *Utah State University*
Timothy Thorpe, *Sterling College*
Dennielle True, *Florida Gulf Coast University*
Robyn Walker, *University of Arizona*
Rosemary Walker, *University of Illinois at Chicago*
Judy Walton, *Howard University*
Thomas Watkins, *Solano Community College*
Patricia Wyatt, *Bossier Parrish Community College*

REVIEWERS OF DOCUMENT MAKEOVERS

We sincerely thank the following reviewers for their assistance with the Document Makeovers:

Lisa Barley, *Eastern Michigan University*
Marcia Bordman, *Gallaudet University*
Jean Bush-Bacelis, *Eastern Michigan University*
Bobbye Davis, *Southern Louisiana University*
Cynthia Drexel, *Western State College*
Kenneth Gibbs, *Worcester State College*
Ellen Leathers, *Bradley University*
Diana McKowen, *Indiana University*
Bobbie Nicholson, *Mars Hill College*
Andrew Smith, *Holyoke Community College*
Jay Stubblefield, *North Carolina Wesleyan College*
Dawn Wallace, *Southeastern Louisiana University*

REVIEWERS OF MODEL DOCUMENTS

The many model documents in the text and their accompanying annotations received invaluable review from

Diane Todd Bucci, *Robert Morris University*
Dacia Charlesworth, *Indiana University–Purdue University, Fort Wayne*
Avon Crismore, *Indiana University*
Nancy Goehring, *Monterey Peninsula College*
James Hatfield, *Florida Community College at Jacksonville*
Estelle Kochis, *Suffolk County Community College*
Sherry Robertson, *Arizona State University*

PERSONAL ACKNOWLEDGMENTS

We wish to extend a heartfelt thanks to our many friends, acquaintances, and business associates who provided materials or agreed to be interviewed so that we could bring the real world into the classroom.

A very special acknowledgment goes to George Dovel, whose superb writing skills, distinguished background, and wealth of business experience assured this project of clarity and completeness. Also, recognition and thanks to Jackie Estrada for her outstanding skills and excellent attention to details. Her creation of the "Peak Performance Grammar and Mechanics" material is especially noteworthy. Jill Gardner's professionalism and keen eye for quality were invaluable.

We also feel it is important to acknowledge and thank the Association for Business Communication, an organization whose meetings and publications provide a valuable forum for the exchange of ideas and for professional growth.

Additionally, we would like to thank the supplement authors who prepared material for this new edition. They include Gina Genova, University of California, Santa Barbara; Lori Cerreto; Myles Hassell, University of New Orleans; and Jay Stubblefield, North Carolina Wesleyan College.

Dedication

This book is dedicated to you and the millions of other students who have helped make *Business Communication Today* a market leader. We appreciate the opportunity to play a role in your education, and we wish you success and satisfaction in your studies and in your career.

Courtland L. Bovée

John V. Thill

Prologue

Building a Career with Your Communication Skills

Using This Course to Help Launch Your Career

This course will help you develop vital communication skills that you'll use throughout your career—and those skills can help you launch an interesting and rewarding career, too. This brief prologue sets the stage by helping you understand today's dynamic workplace, the steps you can take to adapt to the job market, and the importance of creating an employment portfolio and building your personal brand. Take a few minutes to read it while you think about the career you hope to create for yourself.

Understanding Today's Dynamic Workplace

Social, political, and financial events continue to change workplace conditions from year to year, so the job market you read about this year might not be the same market you try to enter a year or two from now. However, you can count on a few forces that are likely to affect your entry into the job market and your career success in years to come:[1]

- **Unpredictability.** Your career probably won't be as stable as careers were in your parents' generation. In today's business world, your career will likely be affected by globalization, mergers and acquisitions, short-term mentality driven by the demands of stockholders, ethical upheavals, and the relentless quest for lower costs. On the plus side, new opportunities, new companies, and even entire industries can appear almost overnight. So while your career might not be as predictable as careers used to be, it could well be more of an adventure.
- **Flexibility.** As companies try to become more agile in a globalized economy, many employees—sometimes of their choice and sometimes not—are going solo and setting up shop as independent contractors. Innovations in electronic communication and social media will continue to spur the growth of *virtual organizations* and *virtual teams*, in which independent contractors and companies of various sizes join forces for long- or short-term projects, often without formal employment arrangements.
- **Economic globalization.** Commerce across borders has been going on for thousands of years, but the volume of international business has roughly tripled in the past 30 years. One significant result is *economic globalization*, the increasing integration and interdependence of national economies around the world. Just as companies now compete across borders, as an employee or independent contractor you also compete globally. This situation can be disruptive and traumatic in some instances, but it also creates opportunities.
- **Growth of small business.** Small businesses employ about half of the private-sector workforce in this country and create somewhere between two-thirds and three-quarters of new jobs, so chances are good that you'll work for a small firm at some point.

What do all these forces mean to you? First, take charge of your career—and stay in charge of it. Understand your options, have a plan, and don't count on others to watch out for your future. Second, as you will learn throughout this course, understanding your audience is key to successful communication, so it is essential for you to understand how employers view today's job market.

HOW EMPLOYERS VIEW TODAY'S JOB MARKET

From an employer's perspective, the employment process is always a question of balance. Maintaining a stable workforce can improve practically every aspect of business performance, yet many employers want the flexibility to shrink and expand payrolls as business conditions change. Employers obviously want to attract the best talent, but the best talent is more expensive and more vulnerable to offers from competitors, so there are always financial trade-offs to consider.

Employers also struggle with the ups and downs of the economy. When unemployment is low, the balance of power shifts to employees, and employers have to compete in order to attract and keep top talent. When unemployment is high, the power shifts back to employers, who can afford to be more selective and less accommodating. In other words, pay attention to the economy; at times you can be more aggressive in your demands, but, at other times, you need to be more accommodating.

Many employers now fill some labor needs by hiring temporary workers or engaging contractors on a project-by-project basis. Many U.S. employers are now also more willing to move jobs to cheaper labor markets outside the country and to recruit globally to fill positions in the United States. Both trends have stirred controversy, especially in the technology sector, as U.S. firms recruit top engineers and scientists from other countries while shifting mid- and low-range jobs to India, China, Russia, the Philippines, and other countries with lower wage structures.[2]

In summary, companies view employment as a complex business decision with lots of variables to consider. To make the most of your potential, regardless of the career path you pursue, you need to view employment in the same way.

WHAT EMPLOYERS LOOK FOR IN JOB APPLICANTS

Given the complex forces in the contemporary workplace and the unrelenting pressure of global competition, what are employers looking for in the candidates they hire? The short answer: a lot. Like all "buyers," companies want to get as much as they can for the money they spend. The closer you can present yourself as the ideal candidate, the better your chances are of getting a crack at the most exciting opportunities.

Specific expectations vary by profession and position, of course, but virtually all employers look for the following general skills and attributes:[3]

- **Communication skills.** The reason this item is listed first isn't that you're reading a business communication textbook. Communication is listed first because it is far and away the most commonly mentioned skill set when employers are asked about what they look for in employees. Improving your communication skills will help in every aspect of your professional life.
- **Interpersonal and team skills.** You will have many individual responsibilities on the job, but chances are you won't work all alone very often. Learn to work with others—and help them succeed as you succeed.
- **Intercultural and international awareness and sensitivity.** Successful employers tend to be responsive to diverse workforces, markets, and communities, and they look for employees with the same outlook.
- **Data collection, analysis, and decision-making skills.** Employers want people who know how to identify information needs, find the necessary data, convert the data into useful knowledge, and make sound decisions.
- **Computer and electronic media skills.** Today's workers need to know how to use common office software and to communicate using a wide range of electronic media.
- **Time and resource management.** If you've had to juggle multiple priorities during college, consider that great training for the business world. Your ability to plan

projects and manage the time and resources available to you will make a big difference on the job.

- **Flexibility and adaptability.** Stuff happens, as they say. Employees who can roll with the punches and adapt to changing business priorities and circumstances will go further (and be happier) than employees who resist change.
- **Professionalism.** Professionalism is the quality of performing at the highest possible level and conducting oneself with confidence, purpose, and pride. True professionals strive to excel, continue to hone their skills and build their knowledge, are dependable and accountable, demonstrate a sense of business etiquette, make ethical decisions, show loyalty and commitment, don't give up when things get tough, and maintain a positive outlook.

Adapting to Today's Job Market

Adapting to the workplace is a lifelong process of seeking the best fit between what you want to do and what employers (or clients, if you work independently) are willing to pay you to do. It's important to know what you want to do, what you have to offer, and how to make yourself more attractive to employers.

WHAT DO YOU WANT TO DO?

Economic necessities and the vagaries of the marketplace will influence much of what happens in your career, of course; nevertheless, it's wise to start your employment search by examining your values and interests. Identify what you want to do first, then see whether you can find a position that satisfies you at a personal level while also meeting your financial needs. Consider these questions:

- **What would you like to do every day?** Research occupations that interest you. Find out what people really do every day. Ask friends, relatives, alumni from your school, and contacts in your social networks. Read interviews with people in various professions to get a sense of what their careers are like.
- **How would you like to work?** Consider how much independence you want on the job, how much variety you like, and whether you prefer to work with products, machines, people, ideas, figures, or some combination thereof.
- **How do your financial goals fit with your other priorities?** For instance, many high-paying jobs involve a lot of stress, sacrifices of time with family and friends, and frequent travel or relocation. If location, lifestyle, intriguing work, or other factors are more important to you, you may well have to sacrifice some level of pay to achieve them.
- **Have you established some general career goals?** For example, do you want to pursue a career specialty such as finance or manufacturing, or do you want to gain experience in multiple areas with an eye toward upper management?
- **What sort of corporate culture are you most comfortable with?** Would you be happy in a formal hierarchy with clear reporting relationships? Or do you prefer less structure? Teamwork or individualism? Do you like a competitive environment?

Filling out the assessment in Table 1 might help you get a clearer picture of the nature of work you would like to pursue in your career.

WHAT DO YOU HAVE TO OFFER?

Knowing what you want to do is one thing. Knowing what a company is willing to pay you to do is another thing entirely. You may already have a good idea of what you can offer employers. If not, some brainstorming can help you identify your skills, interests, and characteristics. Start by jotting down 10 achievements you're proud of, and think carefully about what specific skills these achievements demanded of you. For example, leadership skills, speaking ability, and artistic talent may have helped you coordinate a successful class

TABLE 1	Career Self-Assessment				
Activity or Situation	No Preference	Strongly Agree	Agree	Disagree
1. I want to work independently.				
2. I want variety in my work.				
3. I want to work with people.				
4. I want to work with technology.				
5. I want physical work.				
6. I want mental work.				
7. I want to work for a large organization.				
8. I want to work for a nonprofit organization.				
9. I want to work for a small business.				
10. I want to work for a service business.				
11. I want to start or buy a business someday.				
12. I want regular, predictable work hours.				
13. I want to work in a city location.				
14. I want to work in a small town or suburb.				
15. I want to work in another country.				
16. I want to work outdoors.				
17. I want to work in a structured environment.				
18. I want to avoid risk as much as possible.				
19. I want to enjoy my work, even if that means making less money.				
20. I want to become a high-level corporate manager.				

project. As you analyze your achievements, you may well begin to recognize a pattern of skills. Which of them might be valuable to potential employers?

Next, look at your educational preparation, work experience, and extracurricular activities. What do your knowledge and experience qualify you to do? What have you learned from volunteer work or class projects that could benefit you on the job? Have you held any offices, won any awards or scholarships, mastered a second language? What skills have you developed in nonbusiness situations that could transfer to a business position?

Take stock of your personal characteristics. Are you aggressive, a born leader? Or would you rather follow? Are you outgoing, articulate, great with people? Or do you prefer working alone? Make a list of what you believe are your four or five most important qualities. Ask a relative or friend to rate your traits as well.

If you're having difficulty figuring out your interests, characteristics, or capabilities, consult your college career center. Many campuses administer a variety of tests that can help you identify interests, aptitudes, and personality traits. These tests won't reveal your "perfect" job, but they'll help you focus on the types of work best suited to your personality.

HOW CAN YOU MAKE YOURSELF MORE VALUABLE?

While you're figuring out what you want from a job and what you can offer an employer, you can take positive steps now toward building your career. First, look for volunteer projects, temporary jobs, freelance work, or internships that will help expand your experience base and skill set.[4] You can look for freelance projects on Craigslist (www.craigslist .org) and numerous other websites; some of these jobs have only nominal pay, but they do provide an opportunity for you to display your skills.

Also consider applying your talents to *crowdsourcing* projects, in which companies and nonprofit organizations invite the public to contribute solutions to various challenges. For example, Fellowforce (www.fellowforce.com) posts projects involving advertising, business writing, photography, graphic design, programming, strategy development, and other skills.[5] Even if your contributions aren't chosen, you still have developed solutions to real business problems that you can show to potential employers as examples of your work.

These opportunities help you gain valuable experience and relevant contacts, provide you with important references and work samples for your *employment portfolio*, and help you establish your *personal brand* (see the following sections).

Second, learn more about the industry or industries in which you want to work and stay on top of new developments. Join networks of professional colleagues and friends who can help you keep up with trends and events. Many professional societies have student chapters or offer students discounted memberships. Take courses and pursue other educational or life experiences that would be difficult while working full time.

For more ideas and advice on planning your career, check out the resources listed in Table 2.

BUILDING AN EMPLOYMENT PORTFOLIO

Employers want proof that you have the skills to succeed on the job, but even if you don't have much relevant work experience, you can use your college classes to assemble that proof. Simply create and maintain an *employment portfolio*, which is a collection of projects that demonstrate your skills and knowledge. You can create a *print portfolio* and an *e-portfolio*; both can help with your career effort. A print portfolio gives you something tangible to bring to interviews, and it lets you collect project results that might not be easy to show online, such as a handsomely bound report.

An e-portfolio is a multimedia presentation of your skills and experiences.[6] Think of it as a website that contains your résumé, work samples, letters of recommendation, relevant videos or podcasts you have recorded, blog posts and articles you may have written, and other information about you and your skills. If you have set up a *lifestream* (a real-time aggregation of your content creation, online interests, and social media interactions) that is professionally focused, consider adding that to your e-portfolio. Be creative. For example, a student who was pursuing a degree in meteorology added a video clip of himself delivering a weather forecast.[7] The portfolio can be burned on a CD or DVD for physical distribution or, more commonly, it can be posted online—whether it's a personal website, your college's site (if student pages are available), a specialized portfolio hosting site such as Behance (www.behance.com), or a résumé hosting site such as VisualCV (www.visualcv.com) that offers multimedia résumés. To see a selection of student e-portfolios from colleges around the United States, go to http://real-timeupdates.com/bct11, click on "Student Assignments," and then click on "Prologue" to locate the link to student e-portfolios.

TABLE 2	Career Planning Resources
Resource	**URL**
Career Rocketeer	www.careerrocketeer.com
The Creative Career	http://thecreativecareer.com
Brazen Careerist	www.brazencareerist.com
Daily Career Connection	http://dailycareerconnection.com
The Career Key	http://careerkey.blogspot.com
Rise Smart	www.risesmart.com/risesmart/blog
Women's Leadership Blog	http://blog.futurewomenleaders.net/blog
The Career Doctor	www.careerdoctor.org/career-doctor-blog

Throughout this course, pay close attention to the assignments marked "Portfolio Builder" (they start in Chapter 7). These items will make particularly good samples of not only your communication skills but also your ability to understand and solve business-related challenges. By combining these projects with samples from your other courses, you can create a compelling portfolio by the time you're ready to start interviewing. Your portfolio is also a great resource for writing your résumé because it reminds you of all the great work you've done over the years. Moreover, you can continue to refine and expand your portfolio throughout your career; many professionals use e-portfolios to advertise their services. For example, Evan Eckard, a specialist in web design, marketing, and branding, promotes his capabilities by showing a range of successful projects in his online portfolio, which you can view at www.evaneckard.com.

As you assemble your portfolio, collect anything that shows your ability to perform, whether it's in school, on the job, or in other venues. However, you *must* check with employers before including any items that you created while you were an employee and check with clients before including any *work products* (anything you wrote, designed, programmed, and so on) they purchased from you. Many business documents contain confidential information that companies don't want distributed to outside audiences.

For each item you add to your portfolio, write a brief description that helps other people understand the meaning and significance of the project. Include such items as these:

- **Background.** Why did you undertake this project? Was it a school project, a work assignment, or something you did on your own initiative?
- **Project objectives.** Explain the project's goals, if relevant.
- **Collaborators.** If you worked with others, be sure to mention that and discuss team dynamics if appropriate. For instance, if you led the team or worked with others long distance as a virtual team, point that out.
- **Constraints.** Sometimes the most impressive thing about a project is the time or budget constraints under which it was created. If such constraints apply to a project, consider mentioning them in a way that doesn't sound like an excuse for poor quality. If you had only one week to create a website, for example, you might say that "One of the intriguing challenges of this project was the deadline; I had only one week to design, compose, test, and publish this material."
- **Outcomes.** If the project's goals were measurable, what was the result? For example, if you wrote a letter soliciting donations for a charitable cause, how much money did you raise?
- **Learning experience.** If appropriate, describe what you learned during the course of the project.

Keep in mind that the portfolio itself is a communication project too, so be sure to apply everything you'll learn in this course about effective communication and good design. Assume that every potential employer will find your e-portfolio site (even if you don't tell them about it), so don't include anything that could come back to haunt you. Also, if you have anything embarrassing on Facebook, MySpace, or any other social networking site, remove it immediately.

To get started, first check with the career center at your college; many schools now offer e-portfolio systems for their students. (Some schools now require e-portfolios, so you may already be building one.) You can also find plenty of advice online; search for "e-portfolio," "student portfolio," or "professional portfolio." Finally, consider a book such as *Portfolios for Technical and Professional Communicators*, by Herb J. Smith and Kim Haimes-Korn. This book is intended for communication specialists, but it offers great advice for anyone wanting to create a compelling employment portfolio.

BUILDING YOUR PERSONAL BRAND

Products and companies have brands that represent collections of certain attributes, such as the safety emphasis of Volvo cars, the performance emphasis of BMW, or the luxury emphasis of Cadillac. Similarly, when people who know you think about you, they have a particular set of qualities in mind based on your professionalism, your priorities, and the

Figure 1   **Personal Branding on LinkedIn**

various skills and attributes you have developed over the years. Perhaps without even being conscious of it, you have created a personal brand for yourself (see Figure 1).

As you plan the next stage of your career, start managing your personal brand deliberately. Branding specialist Mohammed Al-Taee defines personal branding succinctly as "a way of clarifying and communicating what makes you different and special."[8]

You can learn more about personal branding from the sources listed in Table 3, and you will have multiple opportunities to plan and refine your personal brand during this course. For example, Chapter 7 offers tips on business applications of social media, which are key to personal branding, and Chapters 18 and 19 guide you through the process of creating a résumé, building your network, and presenting yourself in interviews. To get you started, here are the basics of a successful personal branding strategy:[9]

- **Figure out the "story of you."** Simply put, where have you been in life, and where are you going? Every good story has dramatic tension that pulls readers in and makes them wonder what will happen next. Where is your story going next?

TABLE 3	Personal Branding Resources
Resource	**URL**
Personal Branding Blog	www.personalbrandingblog.com
Mohammed Al-Taee	http://altaeeblog.com
Brand Yourself	http://blog.brand-yourself.com
Krishna De	www.krishnade.com/blog
Cube Rules	http://cuberules.com
Jibber Jobber	www.jibberjobber.com/blog
The Engaging Brand	http://theengagingbrand.typepad.com
Brand-Yourself	http://blog.brand-yourself.com

- **Clarify your professional theme.** Volvos, BMWs, and Cadillacs can all get you from Point A to Point B in safety, comfort, and style—but each brand emphasizes some attributes more than others to create a specific image in the minds of potential buyers. Similarly, you want to be seen as something more than just an accountant, a supervisor, a salesperson. What will your theme be? Brilliant strategist? Hard-nosed, get-it-done tactician? Technical guru? Problem solver? Creative genius? Inspirational leader?

- **Reach out and connect.** Major corporations spread the word about their brands with multimillion-dollar advertising campaigns. You can promote your brand for free or close to it. The secret is networking, which you'll learn more about in Chapter 18. You will build your brand by connecting with like-minded people, sharing information, demonstrating skills and knowledge, and helping others succeed.

- **Deliver on your brand's promise—every time, all the time.** When you promote a brand, you make a promise—a promise that whoever buys that brand will get the benefits you are promoting. All of this planning and communication is of no value if you fail to deliver on the promises that your branding efforts make. Conversely, when you deliver quality results time after time, your talents and your professionalism will speak for you.

We wish you great success in this course and in your career!

PART 1

Understanding the Foundations of Business Communication

CHAPTER 1	Achieving Success Through Effective Business Communication
CHAPTER 2	Mastering Team Skills and Interpersonal Communication
CHAPTER 3	Communicating in a World of Diversity

No other skill can help your career in as many ways as communication. Discover what business communication is all about, why communication skills are essential to your career, and how to adapt your communication experiences in life and college to the business world. Improve your skills in such vital areas as team interaction, etiquette, listening, and nonverbal communication. Explore the advantages and the challenges of a diverse workforce and develop the skills that every communicator needs to succeed in today's multicultural business environment.

Achieving Success Through Effective Business Communication

LEARNING OBJECTIVES   After studying this chapter, you will be able to

1 Explain the importance of effective communication to your career and to the companies where you will work

2 Describe the communication skills employers will expect you to have and the nature of communicating in an organization by using an audience-centered approach

3 Describe the communication process model and the ways that social media are changing the nature of business communication

4 List four general guidelines for using communication technology effectively

5 Define *ethics*, explain the difference between an ethical dilemma and an ethical lapse, and list six guidelines for making ethical communication choices

MyBcommLab Test your mastery of this chapter and its Learning Objectives. Visit mybcommlab.com to apply what you've learned in Document Makeovers and interactive simulation scenarios.

COMMUNICATION CLOSE-UP AT **TOYOTA**

Toyota's user-generated content campaign, Auto-Biography, invited owners to submit stories, photos, and videos that describe their favorite moments and memories with their Toyota vehicles.

www.facebook.com/toyota

Imagine that you're in the market for a new car and need to learn about the various models, options, dealers, and other factors involved in this important purchase. Fortunately, a friend has just gone through this process and can provide valuable information from a consumer's perspective.

Now imagine that you have a hundred or a thousand or ten thousand friends who have recently purchased cars. Imagine how much information you could get from all these people—and all you need to do is jump on Facebook, Epinions, or another social media website.

Consumers have been sharing information online for as long as computers have been connected, but the rapid growth of social media has merged these isolated conversations into a global phenomenon that has permanently changed the nature of business communication. The Japanese automaker Toyota is one of the millions of companies around the world using social media to supplement or even replace traditional forms of customer communication.

Toyota was looking for some positive communication in 2010, after concerns about sticking gas pedals led to the recall of millions of vehicles and prompted the company to halt sales of eight models while it investigated the problem. The situation was potentially serious, to be sure, but Toyota executive Bob Zeinstra said loyal Toyota owners responded with an "outpouring of support and care."

To capitalize on this goodwill, built up through years of delivering safe, dependable vehicles, Toyota invited owners to tell their stories through a Facebook campaign it called "Auto-Biography." The program featured a customized Facebook application that encouraged owners to "Showcase your most memorable moments [with your Toyota] and get inspired by the stories of other loyal Toyota owners."

Thousands of Toyota owners contributed, sharing everything from the pet names they gave their cars to how they use their cars for work or play to the way their families passed down a Toyota from one generation to the next. Many listed the number of miles they had on their cars, some up to 300,000 or more, making strong statements to support the Toyota message of reliability. Many owners also personalized their stories with photos or videos of themselves and their cars. Toyota highlighted a small number of the stories through professionally produced animated or live videos, which it then featured prominently on the Auto-Biography page and used in print and television advertising.

By inviting satisfied customers to the tell their own stories through *user-generated content* (which you'll read more about in Chapter 7), the campaign helped Toyota repair its reputation among potential car buyers and respond to negative stories in the news media. Moreover, Zeinstra says the Facebook initiative also reminded current Toyota owners "why they love their cars so much."[1]

Understanding Why Communication Matters

Whether it's as simple as a smile or as ambitious as a Facebook campaign, **communication** is the process of transferring information and meaning between *senders* and *receivers*, using one or more written, oral, visual, or electronic media. The essence of communication is sharing—providing data, information, insights, and inspiration in an exchange that benefits both you and the people with whom you are communicating.[2]

You will invest a lot of time and energy in this course to develop your communication skills, so it's fair to ask whether it will be worthwhile. This section outlines the many ways in which good communication skills are critical for your career and for any company you join.

COMMUNICATION IS IMPORTANT TO YOUR CAREER

Improving your communication skills may be the single most important step you can take in your career. You can have the greatest ideas in the world, but they're no good to your company or your career if you can't express them clearly and persuasively. Some jobs, such as sales and customer support, are primarily about communicating. In fields such as engineering or finance, you often need to share complex ideas with executives, customers, and colleagues, and your ability to connect with people outside your field can be as important as your technical expertise. If you have the entrepreneurial urge, you will need to communicate with a wide range of audiences, from investors, bankers, and government regulators to employees, customers, and business partners.

As you take on leadership and management roles, communication becomes even more important. The higher you rise in an organization, the less time you will spend using the technical skills of your particular profession and the more time you will spend communicating. Top executives spend most of their time communicating, and businesspeople who can't communicate well don't stand much chance of reaching the top.

Many employers express frustration at the poor communication skills of many employees—particularly recent college graduates who haven't yet learned how to adapt their communication styles to a professional business environment. If you learn to write well, speak well, listen well, and recognize the appropriate way to communicate in any situation, you'll gain a major advantage that will serve you throughout your career.[3]

This course teaches you how to send and receive information more effectively and helps you improve your communication skills through practice in an environment that provides honest, constructive criticism. You will discover how to collaborate in teams, listen effectively, master nonverbal communication, and participate in productive meetings. You'll learn about communicating across cultural boundaries. You'll learn a three-step process that helps you write effective business messages, and you'll get specific tips for crafting a

1 LEARNING OBJECTIVE

Explain the importance of effective communication to your career and to the companies where you will work.

Communication is the process of transferring information and meaning between senders and receivers.

Ambition and great ideas aren't enough; you need to be able to communicate with people in order to succeed in business.

Strong communication skills give you an advantage in the job market.

MyBcommLab

● Access this chapter's simulation entitled Successful Business Communication, located at mybcommlab.com.

variety of business messages using a wide range of media, from social networks to blogs to online presentations. Develop these skills, and you'll start your business career with a clear competitive advantage.

COMMUNICATION IS IMPORTANT TO YOUR COMPANY

Effective communication yields numerous business benefits.

Aside from the personal benefits, communication should be important to you because it is important to your company. Effective communication helps businesses in numerous ways. It provides[4]

- Closer ties with important communities in the marketplace
- Opportunities to influence conversations, perceptions, and trends
- Increased productivity and faster problem solving
- Better financial results and higher return for investors
- Earlier warning of potential problems, from rising business costs to critical safety issues
- Stronger decision making based on timely, reliable information
- Clearer and more persuasive marketing messages
- Greater employee engagement with their work, leading to higher employee satisfaction and lower employee turnover

WHAT MAKES BUSINESS COMMUNICATION EFFECTIVE?

Effective messages are *practical, factual, concise, clear,* and *persuasive*.

Effective communication strengthens the connections between a company and all of its **stakeholders**, those groups affected in some way by the company's actions: customers, employees, shareholders, suppliers, neighbors, the community, the nation, and the world as a whole.[5] Conversely, when communication breaks down, the results can range from time wasting to tragic.

To make your communication efforts as effective as possible, focus on making them practical, factual, concise, clear, and persuasive:

- **Provide practical information.** Give recipients useful information, whether it's to help them perform a desired action or understand a new company policy.
- **Give facts rather than vague impressions.** Use concrete language, specific detail, and information that is clear, convincing, accurate, and ethical. Even when an opinion is called for, present compelling evidence to support your conclusion.
- **Present information in a concise, efficient manner.** Concise messages show respect for people's time, and they increase the chances of a positive response.
- **Clarify expectations and responsibilities.** Craft messages to generate a specific response from a specific audience. When appropriate, clearly state what you expect from audience members or what you can do for them.
- **Offer compelling, persuasive arguments and recommendations.** Show your readers precisely how they will benefit from responding to your message the way you want them to.

Keep these five important characteristics in mind as you review Figure 1.1 on page 5 and Figure 1.2 on page 6. At first glance, both emails appear to be well constructed, but Figure 1.2 is far more effective, as the comments in blue explain.

Communicating in Today's Global Business Environment

2 LEARNING OBJECTIVE

Describe the communication skills employers will expect you to have and the nature of communicating in an organization by using an audience-centered approach.

You've been communicating your entire life, of course, but if you don't have a lot of work experience yet, meeting the expectations of a professional environment might require some adjustment. This section offers a brief look at the unique challenges of business communication, the skills that employers will expect you to have, the nature of communication in an organizational environment, and the importance of adopting an audience-centered approach.

By using a vague subject line, fails to alert people to the upcoming meeting

Opens with a cold, somewhat off-putting greeting

Puts reader on the defense with a negative, accusatory tone

Assumes that people who won't attend don't want to, which might not be true

Lacks a close (such as "thank you"), which contributes to the harsh, abrupt tone

Doesn't provide necessary background information for anyone who missed the meeting

Fails to clarify who needs to do what by when

Specifies the day but not the date, which could lead to confusion

Fails to provide alternative contact information or invite questions about the meeting, making it difficult for team members to clarify their assignments or raise concerns

Figure 1.1 Ineffective Business Communication
At first glance, this email message looks like a reasonable attempt at communicating with the members of a project team. However, review the blue annotations to see just how many problems the message really has.

MyBcommLab

Apply Figure 1.1's key concepts by revising a new document. Go to Chapter 1 in mybcommlab.com and select Document Makeovers.

UNDERSTANDING THE UNIQUE CHALLENGES OF BUSINESS COMMUNICATION

Although you have been communicating with some success your entire life, business communication is often more complicated and demanding than the social communication you typically engage in with family, friends, and school associates. This section highlights five issues that illustrate why business communication requires a high level of skill and attention.

You will need to adjust your communication habits to the more formal demands of business and the unique environment of your company.

The Globalization of Business and the Increase in Workforce Diversity

Today's businesses increasingly reach across international borders to market their products, partner with other businesses, and employ workers and executives—an effort known as **globalization**. Many U.S. companies rely on exports for a significant portion of their sales, sometimes up to 50 percent or more, and managers and employees in these firms need to communicate with many other cultures. Moreover, thousands of companies from all around the world vie for a share of the massive U.S. market, so chances are you'll do business with or even work for a company based in another country at some point in your career.

Businesses are paying more attention to **workforce diversity**—all the differences among people who work together, including differences in age, gender, sexual orientation, education, cultural background, religion, ability, and life experience. As Chapter 3 discusses, successful companies realize that a diverse workforce can yield a significant competitive advantage, but it also requires a more conscientious approach to communication.

Smart employers recognize the benefits of a more diverse workforce—and the additional challenges of ensuring smooth communication between people from diverse backgrounds.

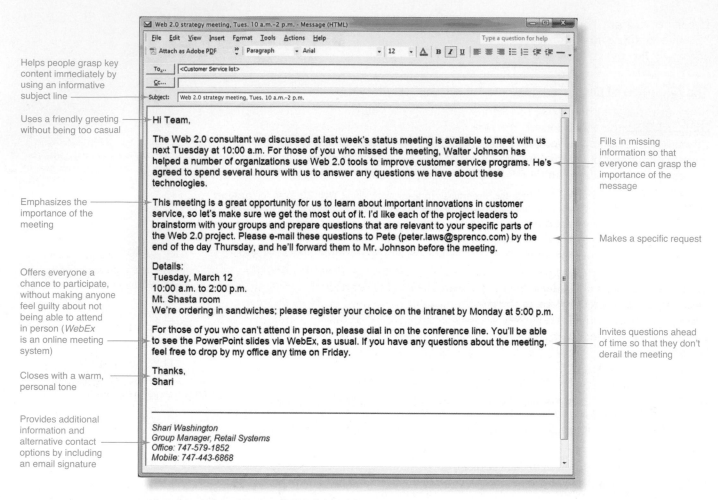

Helps people grasp key content immediately by using an informative subject line

Uses a friendly greeting without being too casual

Emphasizes the importance of the meeting

Offers everyone a chance to participate, without making anyone feel guilty about not being able to attend in person (*WebEx* is an online meeting system)

Closes with a warm, personal tone

Provides additional information and alternative contact options by including an email signature

Fills in missing information so that everyone can grasp the importance of the message

Makes a specific request

Invites questions ahead of time so that they don't derail the meeting

Figure 1.2   Effective Business Communication
This improved version of the email message from Figure 1.1 does a much better job of communicating the essential information these team members need in order to effectively prepare for the meeting.

The Increasing Value of Business Information

As global competition for talent, customers, and resources continues to grow, the importance of information continues to escalate as well. Companies in virtually every industry rely heavily on **knowledge workers**, employees at all levels of an organization who specialize in acquiring, processing, and communicating information. Three examples help to illustrate the value of information in today's economy:

- **Competitive insights.** The more a company knows about its competitors and their plans, the better able it will be to adjust its own business plans.
- **Customer needs.** Information about customer needs is analyzed and summarized in order to develop goods and services that better satisfy customer demands.
- **Regulations and guidelines.** Today's businesses must understand and follow a wide range of government regulations and guidelines covering such areas as employment, environment, taxes, and accounting.

Information has become one of the most important resources in business today.

No matter what the specific type of information, the better you are able to understand it, use it, and communicate it to others, the more competitive you and your company will be.

The Pervasiveness of Technology

Business communication today is heavily dependent on a growing array of technologies.

Technology influences virtually every aspect of business communication today. To benefit from these tools, however, you need to have at least a basic level of skills. If your level of technical expertise doesn't keep up with that of your colleagues and coworkers, the imbalance can put you at a disadvantage and complicate the communication process. Throughout this course, you'll gain insights into using numerous tools and systems more effectively.

The Evolution of Organizational Structures and Leadership Styles

Every firm has a particular structure that defines the relationships among units in the company, and these relationships influence the nature and quality of communication throughout the organization. *Tall structures* have many layers of management between the lowest and highest positions, and they can suffer communication breakdowns and delays as messages are passed up and down through multiple layers.[6]

> Organizations with tall structures may unintentionally restrict the flow of information; flatter structures can make it easier to communicate effectively.

To overcome such problems, many businesses have adopted *flat structures* that reduce the number of layers and promote more open and direct communication. However, with fewer formal lines of control and communication in these organizations, individual employees are expected to assume more responsibility for communication.

Specific types of organization structures present unique communication challenges. In a *matrix structure*, for example, employees report to two managers at the same time, such as a project manager and a department manager. The need to coordinate workloads, schedules, and other matters increases the communication burden on everyone involved. In a *network structure*, sometimes known as a *virtual organization*, a company supplements the talents of its employees with services from one or more external partners, such as a design lab, a manufacturing firm, or a sales and distribution company.

> Newer types of organization structures such as matrices and networks present new communication challenges.

Regardless of the particular structure a company uses, your communication efforts will also be influenced by the organization's **corporate culture**: the mixture of values, traditions, and habits that gives a company its atmosphere and personality. Many successful companies encourage employee contributions by fostering *open climates* that promote candor and honesty, helping employees feel free enough to admit their mistakes, disagree with the boss, and share negative or unwelcome information.

> Open corporate cultures benefit from free-flowing information and employee input.

A Heavy Reliance on Teamwork

Both traditional and innovative company structures can rely heavily on teamwork, and you will probably find yourself on dozens of teams throughout your career. Teams are commonly used in business today, but they're not always successful—and a key reason that teams fail to meet their objectives is poor communication. Chapter 2 offers insights into the complex dynamics of team communication and identifies skills you need in order to be an effective communicator in group settings.

> Working in a team makes you even more responsible for communicating effectively.

UNDERSTANDING WHAT EMPLOYERS EXPECT FROM YOU

Today's employers expect you to be competent at a wide range of communication tasks. Fortunately, the skills that employers expect from you are the same skills that will help you advance in your career:[7]

- Organizing ideas and information logically and completely
- Expressing ideas and information coherently and persuasively
- Actively listening to others
- Communicating effectively with people from diverse backgrounds and experiences
- Using communication technologies effectively and efficiently
- Following accepted standards of grammar, spelling, and other aspects of high-quality writing and speaking

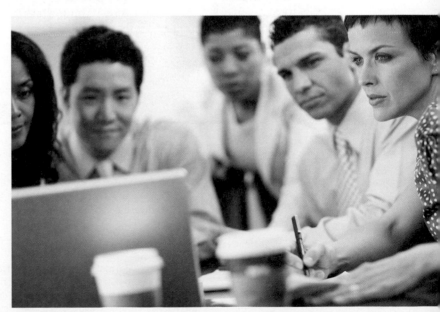

The ability to work effectively in teams will help you at every stage of your career.

- Communicating in a civilized manner that reflects contemporary expectations of business etiquette, even when dealing with indifferent or hostile audiences
- Communicating ethically, even when choices aren't crystal clear
- Managing your time wisely and using resources efficiently

You'll have the opportunity to practice these skills throughout this course—but don't stop there. Successful professionals continue to hone communication skills throughout their careers.

COMMUNICATING IN AN ORGANIZATIONAL CONTEXT

In addition to having the proper skills, you need to learn how to apply those skills in the business environment, which can be quite different from the social and scholastic environments you are accustomed to. Every organization has a **formal communication network**, in which ideas and information flow along the lines of command (the hierarchical levels) in the company's organization structure (see Figure 1.3). Throughout the formal network, information flows in three directions. *Downward communication* flows from executives to employees, conveying executive decisions and providing information that helps employees do their jobs. *Upward communication* flows from employees to executives, providing insight into problems, trends, opportunities, grievances, and performance—thus allowing executives to solve problems and make intelligent decisions. *Horizontal communication* flows between departments to help employees share information, coordinate tasks, and solve complex problems.[8]

Every organization also has an **informal communication network**, often referred to as the *grapevine* or the *rumor mill*, that encompasses all communication that occurs outside the formal network. Some of this informal communication takes place naturally as a result of employee interaction both on the job and in social settings, and some of it takes place when the formal network doesn't provide information that employees want. In fact, the inherent limitations of formal communication networks helped spur the growth of social media in the business environment.

> The formal communication network mirrors the company's organizational structure.

> Social media play an increasingly important role in the informal communication network.

Figure 1.3   Formal Communication Network
The formal communication network is defined by the relationships between the various job positions in the organization. Messages can flow *upward* (from a lower-level employee to a higher-level employee), *downward* (from a higher-level employee to a lower-level employee), and *horizontally* (across the organization, between employees at the same or similar levels).

ADOPTING AN AUDIENCE-CENTERED APPROACH

An **audience-centered approach** involves understanding and respecting the members of your audience and making every effort to get your message across in a way that is meaningful to them (see Figure 1.4). This approach is also known as adopting the **"you" attitude**, in contrast to messages that are about "me." Learn as much as possible about the biases, education, age, status, style, and personal and professional concerns of your receivers. If you're addressing people you don't know and you're unable to find out more about them, try to project yourself into their position by using common sense and imagination. This ability to relate to the needs of others is a key part of *emotional intelligence*, which is widely considered to be a vital characteristic of successful managers and leaders.[9] The more you know about the people you're communicating with, the easier it will be to concentrate on

An audience-centered approach involves understanding, respecting, and meeting the needs of your audience members.

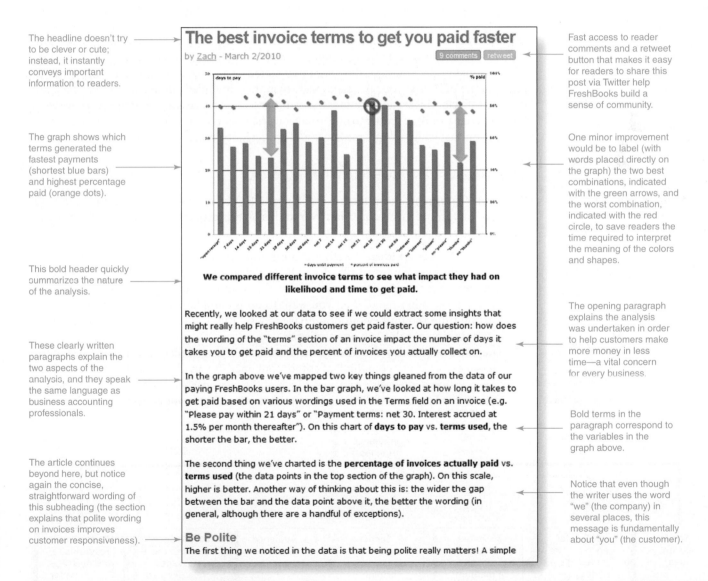

The headline doesn't try to be clever or cute; instead, it instantly conveys important information to readers.

The graph shows which terms generated the fastest payments (shortest blue bars) and highest percentage paid (orange dots).

This bold header quickly summarizes the nature of the analysis.

These clearly written paragraphs explain the two aspects of the analysis, and they speak the same language as business accounting professionals.

The article continues beyond here, but notice again the concise, straightforward wording of this subheading (the section explains that polite wording on invoices improves customer responsiveness).

Fast access to reader comments and a retweet button that makes it easy for readers to share this post via Twitter help FreshBooks build a sense of community.

One minor improvement would be to label (with words placed directly on the graph) the two best combinations, indicated with the green arrows, and the worst combination, indicated with the red circle, to save readers the time required to interpret the meaning of the colors and shapes.

The opening paragraph explains the analysis was undertaken in order to help customers make more money in less time—a vital concern for every business.

Bold terms in the paragraph correspond to the variables in the graph above.

Notice that even though the writer uses the word "we" (the company) in several places, this message is fundamentally about "you" (the customer).

The best invoice terms to get you paid faster
by Zach - March 2/2010

We compared different invoice terms to see what impact they had on likelihood and time to get paid.

Recently, we looked at our data to see if we could extract some insights that might really help FreshBooks customers get paid faster. Our question: how does the wording of the "terms" section of an invoice impact the number of days it takes you to get paid and the percent of invoices you actually collect on.

In the graph above we've mapped two key things gleaned from the data of our paying FreshBooks users. In the bar graph, we've looked at how long it takes to get paid based on various wordings used in the Terms field on an invoice (e.g. "Please pay within 21 days" or "Payment terms: net 30. Interest accrued at 1.5% per month thereafter"). On this chart of **days to pay** vs. **terms used**, the shorter the bar, the better.

The second thing we've charted is the **percentage of invoices actually paid** vs. **terms used** (the data points in the top section of the graph). On this scale, higher is better. Another way of thinking about this is: the wider the gap between the bar and the data point above it, the better the wording (in general, although there are a handful of exceptions).

Be Polite
The first thing we noticed in the data is that being polite really matters! A simple

Figure 1.4   Audience-Centered Communication
This blog post from the developers of the FreshBooks online business accounting system demonstrates audience focus in multiple ways, starting with the effort behind the message. Every company worries about how quickly customers will pay their bills, so FreshBooks analyzed the customer data it had on hand to see which payment terms and invoice messages generated the quickest responses. This alone is remarkable customer service; the audience-focused presentation of the information makes it that much better.

MyBcommLab

Apply Figure 1.4's key concepts by revising a new document. Go to Chapter 1 in mybcommlab.com and select Document Makeovers.

Etiquette, the expected norms of behavior in any particular situation, can have a profound influence on your company's success and your career.

their needs—which, in turn, will make it easier for them to hear your message, understand it, and respond positively.

A vital element of audience-centered communication is **etiquette**, the expected norms of behavior in any particular situation. In today's hectic, competitive world, etiquette might seem a quaint and outdated notion. However, the way you conduct yourself and interact with others can have a profound influence on your company's success and your career. When executives hire and promote you, they expect your behavior to protect the company's reputation. The more you understand such expectations, the better chance you have of avoiding career-damaging mistakes. The principles of etiquette discussed in Chapter 2 will help you communicate with an audience-centered approach in a variety of business settings.

Exploring the Communication Process

Describe the communication process model and the ways that social media are changing the nature of business communication.

As you no doubt know from your personal interactions over the years, even well-intentioned communication efforts can fail. Messages can get lost or simply ignored. The receiver of a message can interpret it in ways the sender never imagined. In fact, two people receiving the same information can reach different conclusions about what it means.

Fortunately, by understanding communication as a process with distinct steps, you can improve the odds that your messages will reach their intended audiences and produce their intended effects. This section explores the communication process in two stages: first by following a message from one sender to one receiver in the basic communication model, and then expanding on that with multiple messages and participants in the social communication model.

THE BASIC COMMUNICATION MODEL

Viewing communication as a process helps you identify steps you can take to improve your success as a communicator.

By viewing communication as a process (Figure 1.5), you can identify and improve the skills you need to be more successful. Many variations on this process model exist, but these eight steps provide a practical overview:

1. **The sender has an idea.** Whether a communication effort will ultimately be effective starts right here. For example, if you have a clear idea about a procedure change that will save your company time and money, the communication process is off to a strong start. On the other hand, if all you want to do is complain about how the company is wasting time and money but don't have any solutions, you probably won't communicate anything of value to your audience.

2. **The sender encodes the idea as a message.** When someone puts an idea into a **message**—which you can think of as the "container" for an idea—he or she is **encoding** it, or expressing it in words or images. Much of the focus of this course is on developing the skills needed to successfully encode your ideas into effective messages.

Figure 1.5 A Model of the Communication Process
These eight steps illustrate how an idea travels from a sender to a receiver. After you explore the process in more detail in the following pages, refer to Figure 1.7 on page 15 for advice on improving your skills at each step. This diagram offers a simplified view of a process that is both complex and subtle, but it provides a good foundation on which to build your understanding of communication.

3. **The sender produces the message in a transmittable medium.** With the appropriate message to express an idea, the sender now needs a **communication medium** to present that message to the intended audience. As you'll read in Chapter 4, media for transmitting messages can be divided into *oral, written, visual,* and *electronic* forms.

4. **The sender transmits the message through a channel.** Just as technology continues to increase the number of media options at your disposal, it continues to provide new **communication channels** you can use to transmit your messages. The distinction between medium and channel can get a bit murky, but think of the medium as the *form* a message takes and the channel as the system used to *deliver* the message. The channel can be a face-to-face conversation, the Internet, another company—any method or system capable of delivering messages.

5. **The audience receives the message.** If the channel functions properly, the message reaches its intended audience. However, mere arrival at the destination is no guarantee that the message will be noticed or understood correctly. As "How Audiences Receive Messages" (page 12) explains, many messages are either ignored or misinterpreted as noise.

6. **The audience decodes the message.** After a message is received, the receiver needs to extract the idea from the message, a step known as **decoding**. "How Audiences Decode Messages" (page 13) takes a closer look at this complex and subtle step in the process.

7. **The audience responds to the message.** By crafting messages in ways that show the benefits of responding, senders can increase the chances that recipients will respond in positive ways. However, as "How Audiences Respond to Messages" (page 14) points out, whether a receiver responds as the sender hopes depends on the receiver (a) *remembering* the message long enough to act on it, (b) being *able* to act on it, and (c) being *motivated* to respond.

8. **The audience provides feedback to sender.** In addition to responding (or not responding) to the message, audience members may give **feedback** that helps the sender evaluate the effectiveness of the communication effort. Feedback can be verbal (using written or spoken words), nonverbal (using gestures, facial expressions, or other signals), or both. Just like the original message, however, this feedback from the receiver also needs to be decoded carefully. A smile, for example, can have many meanings.

Considering the complexity of this process—and the barriers and distractions that often stand between sender and receiver—it should come as no surprise that communication efforts often fail to achieve the sender's objective. Fortunately, the better you understand the process, the more successful you'll be.

The following sections take a closer look at two important aspects of the process: environmental barriers that can block or distort messages and the steps audiences take to receive, decode, and respond to messages.

Barriers in the Communication Environment

Within any communication environment, messages can be disrupted by a variety of **communication barriers**. These include noise and distractions, competing messages, filters, and channel breakdowns:

- **Noise and distractions.** External distractions range from uncomfortable meeting rooms to crowded computer screens with instant messages and reminders popping up all over the place. Internal distractions are thoughts and emotions that prevent audiences from focusing on incoming messages. The common habit of *multitasking*, attempting more than one task at a time, is practically guaranteed to create communication distractions. Moreover, research suggests that "chronic multitasking" can reduce productivity and increase errors.[10]

- **Competing messages.** Having your audience's undivided attention is a rare luxury. In most cases, you must compete with other messages that are trying to reach your audience at the same time, which is why it is so essential to craft messages that your audience will care about.

The medium is the *form* a message takes and the channel is the system used to *deliver* the message.

A number of barriers can block or distort messages before they reach the intended audience.

REAL-TIME UPDATES
Learn More by Watching This Video

Are you damaging yourself with noise?

Sound expert Julian Treasure highlights the serious problems associated with noisy environments and offers insights into improving your work and personal lives through careful attention to sound. Go to http://real-timeupdates.com/bct11 and click on "Learn More." If you are using MyBcommLab, you can access Real-Time Updates within each chapter or under Student Study Tools.

- **Filters.** Messages can be blocked or distorted by *filters*, any human or technological interventions between the sender and the receiver. Filtering can be both intentional (such as automatically filing incoming messages based on sender or content) or unintentional (such as an overly aggressive spam filter that deletes legitimate emails). As you read earlier, the structure and culture of an organization can also inhibit the flow of vital messages. And, in some cases, the people or companies you rely on to deliver your message can distort it or filter it to meet their own needs.

- **Channel breakdowns.** Sometimes the channel simply breaks down and fails to deliver your message at all. A colleague you were counting on to deliver a message to your boss might have forgotten to do so, or a computer server might have crashed and prevented your blog from updating.

> Minimizing barriers and distractions in the communication environment is everyone's responsibility.

Everyone in an organization can help minimize barriers and distractions. As a communicator, try to be aware of any barriers that could prevent your messages from reaching their intended audiences. As a manager, keep an eye out for any organizational barriers that could be inhibiting the flow of information. In any situation, a small dose of common sense and courtesy goes a long way. Turn off that mobile phone before you step into a meeting. Don't talk across the tops of other people's cubicles. Be sensitive to personal differences, too; for instance, some people enjoy working with music on, but music is a huge distraction for others.[11]

Take steps to insulate yourself from distractions, too. Don't let messages interrupt you every minute of the day. Set aside time to attend to messages all at once so that you can focus the rest of the time.

Inside the Mind of Your Audience

After a message works its way through the communication channel and reaches the intended audience, it encounters a whole new set of challenges. Understanding how audiences receive, decode, and respond to messages will help you create more effective messages.

> To actually receive a message, audience members need to sense it, select it, then perceive it as a message.

How Audiences Receive Messages   For an audience member to receive a message, three events need to occur: The receiver has to *sense* the presence of a message, *select* it from all the other messages clamoring for attention, and *perceive* it as an actual message (as opposed to random, pointless noise).[12] You can appreciate the magnitude of this challenge by driving down any busy street in a commercial section of town. You'll encounter literally hundreds of messages—billboards, posters, store window displays, car stereos, pedestrians waving or talking on mobile phones, car horns, street signs, traffic lights, and so on. However, you sense, select, and perceive only a small fraction of these messages.

Today's business audiences are much like drivers on busy streets. They are inundated with so many messages and so much noise that they can miss or ignore many of the messages intended for them. Through this course, you will learn a variety of techniques to craft messages that get noticed. In general, follow these five principles to increase your chances of success:

- **Consider audience expectations.** Deliver messages using the media and channels that the audience expects. If colleagues expect meeting notices to be delivered by email, don't suddenly switch gears and start delivering the

Message overload is a constant challenge in contemporary life; your messages must compete with many others clamoring for the audience's attention.

notices via blog postings without telling anyone. Of course, sometimes going *against* expectations can stimulate audience attention, which is why advertisers sometimes do wacky and creative things to get your attention. However, for most business communication efforts, following the expectations of your audience is the most efficient way to get your message across.

- **Ensure ease of use.** Even if audiences are actively looking for your messages, they probably won't see the messages if you make them hard to find, hard to access, or hard to read. Poorly designed websites with confusing navigation are common culprits in this respect.
- **Emphasize familiarity.** Use words, images, and designs that are familiar to your audience. For example, most visitors to company websites expect to see information about the company on a page called "About" or "About Us."
- **Practice empathy.** Make sure your messages speak to the audience by clearly addressing *their* wants and needs—not yours. People are inclined to notice messages that relate to their individual concerns.[13]
- **Design for compatibility.** For the many messages delivered electronically these days, be sure to verify technological compatibility with your audience. For instance, if your website requires visitors to have a particular video capability in their browsers, you won't reach those audience members who don't have that software installed.

How Audiences Decode Messages   A received message doesn't "mean" anything until the recipient decodes it and assigns meaning to it, and there is no guarantee that the receiver will assign the same meaning that the sender intended. Even well-crafted, well-intentioned communication efforts can fail at this stage because assigning meaning through decoding is a highly personal process that is influenced by culture, individual experience, learning and thinking styles, hopes, fears, and even temporary moods. Moreover, audiences tend to extract the meaning they expect to get from a message, even if it's the opposite of what the sender intended.[14] In fact, rather than "extract" your meaning, it's more accurate to say that your audience members re-create their own meaning—or meanings—from the message.

As you'll discover in Chapter 3, culture shapes people's views of the world in profound ways, from determinations of right and wrong to details such as the symbolic meanings attached to specific colors. For instance, because U.S. culture celebrates youth and individual accomplishment, it is "natural" for many people raised in this country to admire young, independent-minded leaders who rebel against older, established ways of doing business. A culture such as Japan's, however, generally places a higher value on respect for older colleagues, consensus decision making, and group accomplishment. Given these differences, a younger colleague's bold proposal to radically reshape business strategy could be interpreted more positively in one culture than in the other—quite independent of the proposal's merits alone.

At an individual level, beliefs and biases influence the meaning that audiences extract from messages. For instance, the human brain organizes incoming sensations into a mental "map" that represents each person's individual **perception** of reality. If a detail doesn't fit for any reason, people are often inclined to distort the information to make it fit rather than rearrange their mental map—a phenomenon known as **selective perception**.[15] For example, an executive who has staked her reputation on a particular business strategy might distort or ignore evidence that suggests the strategy is failing.

Differences in language and usage also influence received meaning. If you ask an employee to send you a report on sales figures "as soon as possible," does that mean within 10 seconds, 10 minutes, or 10 days? By clarifying expectations and resolving potential ambiguities in your messages, you can minimize such uncertainties. In general, the more experiences you share with another person, the more likely you are to share perception and thus share meaning (see Figure 1.6 on the next page).

Individual thinking styles are another important factor in message decoding. For example, someone who places a high value on objective analysis and clear logic might interpret a message differently than someone who values emotion or intuition (reaching conclusions without using rational processes).

Sidebar notes:

To improve the odds that your messages will be successfully perceived by your audience, pay close attention to expectations, ease of use, familiarity, empathy, and technical compatibility.

Decoding is a complex process; receivers often extract different meanings from messages than the senders intended.

Selective perception occurs when people ignore or distort incoming information to fit their preconceived notions of reality.

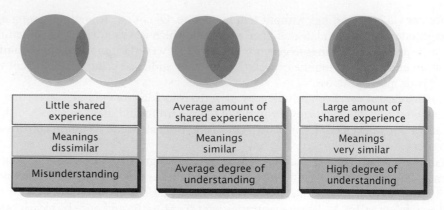

Figure 1.6   How Shared Experience Affects Understanding
The more that two people or two groups of people share experiences—personal, professional, and cultural—the more likely it is that receivers will extract the intended meanings that senders encode into the messages.

How Audiences Respond to Messages   Your message has been delivered, received, and correctly decoded. Now what? Will audience members respond in the way you'd like them to? Only if three events occur.

First, the recipient has to *remember* the message long enough to act on it. Simplifying greatly, memory works in several stages: *Sensory memory* momentarily captures incoming data from the senses; then, whatever the recipient pays attention to is transferred to *short-term memory*. Information in short-term memory will quickly disappear if it isn't transferred to *long-term memory*, which can be done either actively (such as when a person memorizes a list of items) or passively (such as when a new piece of information connects with something else the recipient already has stored in long-term memory). Finally, the information needs to be *retrieved* when the recipient wants to act on it.[16] In general, people find it easier to remember and retrieve information that is important to them personally or professionally. Consequently, by communicating in ways that are sensitive to your audience's wants and needs, you greatly increase the chance that your messages will be remembered and retrieved.

Second, the recipient has to be *able* to respond as you wish. Obviously, if recipients simply cannot do what you want them to do, they will not respond according to your plan. By understanding your audience (you'll learn more about audience analysis in Chapter 4), you can work to minimize these unsuccessful outcomes.

Third, the recipient has to be *motivated* to respond. You'll encounter many situations in which your audience has the option of responding but isn't required to. For instance, a record company may or may not offer your band a contract, or your boss may or may not respond to your request for a raise. Throughout this course, you'll learn techniques for crafting messages that can help motivate readers to respond.

Now that you have some additional insights into what makes communication succeed, take another look at the communication process model. Figure 1.7 identifies the key challenges in the process and summarizes the steps you can take along the way to become a more effective communicator.

THE SOCIAL COMMUNICATION MODEL

The basic model presented in Figure 1.5 shows how a single idea moves from one sender to one receiver. In a larger sense, it also helps represent the traditional nature of much business communication, which was primarily defined by a *publishing* or *broadcasting* mindset. Externally, a company issued carefully scripted messages to a mass audience that often had few options for responding to those messages or initiating messages of their own. Customers and other interested parties had few ways to connect with one another to ask questions, share information, or offer support. Internally, communication tended to follow the same "we talk, you listen" model, with upper managers issuing directives to lower-level supervisors and employees.

Audiences will likely respond to a message if they remember it, if they're able to respond, and if they're properly motivated to respond.

By explaining how audiences will benefit by responding to your messages, you'll increase their motivation to respond.

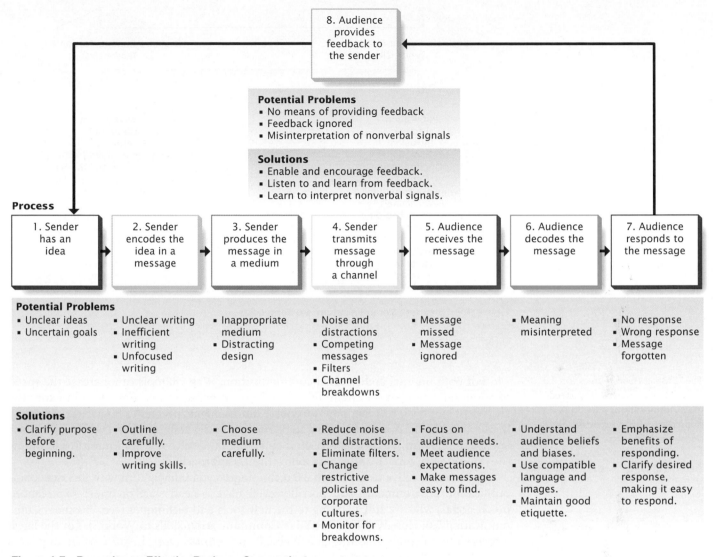

Figure 1.7   Becoming an Effective Business Communicator
The communication process presents many opportunities for messages to get lost, distorted, or misinterpreted as they travel from sender to receiver. Fortunately, you can take action at every step in the process to increase your chances of success.

However, a variety of technologies have enabled and inspired a new approach to business communication. In contrast to the publishing mindset, this new **social communication model** is *interactive* and *conversational*. Customers and other groups are now empowered through **social media**, electronic media that transform passive audiences into active participants in the communication process by allowing them to share content, revise content, respond to content, or contribute new content. Just as **Web 2.0** signifies this second generation of World Wide Web technologies (social networks, blogs, and other tools that you'll read about in Chapter 7), **Business Communication 2.0** is a convenient label for this new approach to business communication.

On the surface, this approach might look like it's just added some new media tools. However, as Figure 1.8 on the next page shows, the changes are much deeper and more profound. In a typical 1.0 approach, messages are scripted by designated communicators, approved by someone in authority, distributed through selected channels, and delivered without modification to a passive audience that is not invited or even expected to respond. In the 2.0 approach, the rules change dramatically. Customers and other stakeholders participate in, influence, and often take control of conversations in the marketplace. They rely on each other for information about products, offer technical support, and even participate in group buying using social tools.[17]

The social communication model is interactive, conversational, and usually open to all who wish to participate.

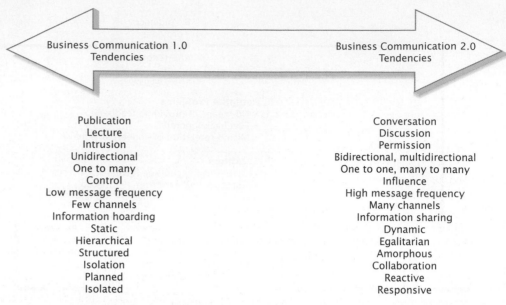

Business Communication 1.0 Tendencies	Business Communication 2.0 Tendencies
Publication	Conversation
Lecture	Discussion
Intrusion	Permission
Unidirectional	Bidirectional, multidirectional
One to many	One to one, many to many
Control	Influence
Low message frequency	High message frequency
Few channels	Many channels
Information hoarding	Information sharing
Static	Dynamic
Hierarchical	Egalitarian
Structured	Amorphous
Isolation	Collaboration
Planned	Reactive
Isolated	Responsive

Figure 1.8 Business Communication: 1.0 Versus 2.0
Business Communication 2.0 differs from conventional communication strategies and practices in a number of significant ways.

The "Business Communication 2.0" approach can increase the speed of communication, lower cost, improve access to expertise, and boost employee satisfaction.

For both internal and external communication, Web 2.0 tools can increase the speed of communication, lower communication costs, improve access to pockets of expertise, and boost employee satisfaction.[18] Of course, no company, no matter how enthusiastically it embraces the 2.0 mindset, is going to be run as a social club in which everyone has a say and a vote. Instead, a hybrid approach is emerging in which some communications follow the traditional approach and others follow the 2.0 approach.[19]

If you're an active user of Web 2.0 technologies, you'll fit right in with this new communication environment—and possibly even have a head start on more experienced professionals who are still adapting to the new tools and techniques (see "Business Communication 2.0: How Will You Put Your Communication Skills to Work?"). For the latest information on communicating in a Web 2.0 environment, visit **http://real-timeupdates .com/bct11** and select Chapter 1.

Using Technology to Improve Business Communication

4 LEARNING OBJECTIVE

List four general guidelines for using communication technology effectively.

Today's businesses rely heavily on technology to enhance communication. In fact, many of the technologies you might use in your personal life, from microblogs to video games to virtual worlds, are also used in business. You will find technology discussed extensively throughout this book, with specific advice on using both common and emerging tools. The four-page photo essay "Powerful Tools for Communicating Efficiently" (see pages 18–21) provides an overview of the technologies that connect people in offices, factories, and other business settings.

Anyone who has used a computer, a smartphone, or other advanced gadget knows that the benefits of technology are not automatic. Poorly designed or inappropriately used technology can hinder communication more than it helps. To communicate effectively, learn to keep technology in perspective, guard against information overload and information addiction, use technological tools productively, and disengage from the computer frequently to communicate in person.

KEEPING TECHNOLOGY IN PERSPECTIVE

Don't rely too much on technology or let it overwhelm the communication process.

Perhaps the single most important point to remember about technology is that it is simply a tool, a means by which you can accomplish certain tasks. Technology is an aid to

BUSINESS COMMUNICATION 2.0 — How Will You Put Your Communication Skills to Work?

The authors have recently met a number of young professionals who use the latest media tools to improve communication in their work. Here are a few of their stories:

- Meg Stivison (University of Massachusetts–Amherst) writes a blog and maintains a Flickr photo-sharing collection for the Stickley Museum at Craftsman Farms in Cary, North Carolina.
- Aga Westfall (Northern Arizona University) of the Santy Agency, an advertising firm in Phoenix, Arizona, uses the Twitter microblogging tool for research and networking.
- Melissa Popp (Millersville University), who is employed by Best Buy in Dover, Delaware, uses YouTube to educate her customers about electronic products.
- Matthew Nederlanden (Palm Beach Atlantic University) of Pompano Beach, Florida, just launched a new *crowdsourcing* advertising agency that allows anyone to create a concept for a commercial, post it on YouTube, and get paid based on how many people view it.
- Jerrold Thompson (Evergreen State College) of Clinton, Washington, launched In My Life Video, a service that produces personal autobiographies. The skills he honed in class helped him write content for his website and a script for a promotional video he posted on YouTube.
- Philip Beech (Brooks Institute of Photography) of Portland, Oregon, uses Facebook to communicate with other Home Video Studio franchise owners and to promote his business to prospective clients.

- Chris Millichap (University of Wisconsin–Madison) of Chicago, Illinois, uses Facebook to promote Boosh Magazine, an online college entertainment publication.
- Matthew Meyer (Indiana University) of Oakland, California, is an e-learning developer for the employee services firm Adecco who has written and produced a series of training podcasts for a major pharmaceutical client.
- Liz Wise (Art Institute of Colorado) and her colleagues at Drillspot.com, a tools and hardware website based in Boulder, Colorado, use a wiki to minimize the number of meetings held and to store and share instructions for tasks and procedures.
- Ted Rubin (SUNY Purchase) of Atlanta, Georgia, is a remote server support analyst for Career Connection who uses Really Simple Syndication (RSS) newsfeeds to receive updates from vendors and to track the continuous results from his searches on Google News.

CAREER APPLICATIONS

1. If you are currently working, how could you use electronic media to improve the way you communicate with customers or colleagues? (If you're not currently working, think about a job you had in the past or think about a friend's or classmate's job for this exercise.)
2. In what ways have you used electronic media in your college classes? Can you identify any disadvantages of using these media to communicate with instructors and classmates?

interpersonal communication, not a replacement for it. Technology can't think for you or communicate for you, and if you lack some essential skills, technology can't fill in the gaps.

While this advice might sound obvious, it is easy to get caught up in the "gee whiz" factor, particularly with new technologies. No matter how exotic or entertaining it may be, technology has business value only if it helps deliver the right information to the right people at the right time.

GUARDING AGAINST INFORMATION OVERLOAD AND INFORMATION ADDICTION

The overuse or misuse of communication technology can lead to **information overload**, in which people receive more information than they can effectively process. Information overload makes it difficult to discriminate between useful and useless information, lowers productivity, and amplifies employee stress both on the job and at home—even to the point of causing health and relationship problems.[20]

As a recipient, you often have some level of control over the number and types of messages you choose to receive. Use the filtering features of your communication systems to isolate high-priority messages that deserve your attention.

Information overload results when people receive more information than they can effectively process.

REAL-TIME UPDATES
Learn More by Reading This PDF

Steps you can take to help reduce information overload

Everyone needs to play a part in reducing the burden of too much data and information in the work environment; this document has plenty of helpful tips. Go to http://real-timeupdates.com/bct11 and click on "Learn More." If you are using MyBcommLab, you can access Real-Time Updates within each chapter or under Student Study Tools.

(continued on page 21)

Powerful Tools for Communicating Effectively

The tools of business communication evolve with every new generation of digital technology. Selecting the right tool for each situation can enhance your business communication in many ways. In today's flexible office settings, communication technology helps people keep in touch and stay productive. When coworkers in different cities or countries need to collaborate, they can meet and share ideas without costly travel. Companies use communication technology to keep track of parts, orders, and shipments—and to keep customers well-informed. Those same customers can also communicate with companies in many ways at any time of day or night. For a closer look at the latest business uses of social media tools in particular, see pages 180–187 in Chapter 7.

Electronic Presentations

Electronic presentations, both on-site and online, are a mainstay of business communication.

Wireless Networks

Many business professionals today have only part-time offices or no offices at all, relying on wireless networks to stay connected with colleagues and customers.

REDEFINING THE OFFICE

Technology makes it easier for business professionals to stay connected with customers and colleagues, wherever their work takes them. Electronic presentations, shared workspaces, and virtual meeting spaces can bring professionals together at the same time or give them access to vital resources on their own schedules. Wireless networks and mobile-phone data services let workers "cut the wire" from the home office and move around as they need to.

Shared Workspaces

Online workspaces such as Documentum eRoom and Share Point Workspace make it easy for far-flung team members to access shared files anywhere at any time. The workspace can control which team members can read, edit, and save specific files.

Virtual Meeting Spaces

A number of companies (such as Cranial Tap, whose virtual headquarters is shown here) now hold meetings, host conferences, and demonstrate products and services in virtual worlds such as Second Life.

Unified Communications

Many workers can now access their voice and electronic communication (including email and instant messaging) through a single portal. *Follow-me phone service* automatically forwards incoming calls. *Text-to-speech* features using voice synthesis can convert email and IM to voice messages.

Wikis

Wikis promote collaboration by simplifying the process of creating and editing online content. Anyone with access (some wikis are private; some are public) can add and modify pages as new information becomes available.

Reprint Courtesy of International Business Machines Corporation, © 2011 International Business Machines Corporation.

Social Networking

Businesses use a variety of social networks as specialized networks to engage customers, find new employees, attract investors, and share ideas and challenges with peers.

Crowdsourcing and Collaboration Platforms

Crowdsourcing, inviting input from groups of people inside or outside the organization, can give companies access to a much wider range of ideas, solutions to problems, and insights into market trends.

COLLABORATING

Working in teams is essential in almost every business. Teamwork can become complicated, however, when team members work in different parts of the company, in different time zones, or even for different companies. Technology helps bridge the distance by making it possible to brainstorm, attend virtual meetings, share files, meet new business partners, and collaborate with experts outside the company from widely separated locations.

Web-Based Meetings

Web-based meetings allow team members from all over the world to collaborate online. Various systems support instant messaging, video, real-time editing tools, and more.

Videoconferencing and Telepresence

Video conferencing provides many of the benefits of in-person meetings at a fraction of the cost. Advanced systems feature *telepresence,* in which the video images are life-sized and extremely realistic.

RSS Newsfeeds and Aggregators

Aggregators, sometimes called *newsreaders*, automatically collect information about new blogposts, podcasts, and other content via Really Simple Syndication (RSS) newsfeeds, giving audiences more control over the content they receive.

Social Tagging and Bookmarking

Audiences become part of the communication channel when they find and recommend online content through tagging and bookmarking sites such as Delicious and Digg.

SHARING INFORMATION

Companies use a variety of communication technologies to create products and services, deliver them to customers, and support users with vital information. The ability to easily access and share the latest information improves the flow and timing of supplies, lowers operating costs, improves customer satisfaction, and boosts financial performance. Easy information access also helps companies respond to customer needs by providing them accurate information and timely product deliveries.

Interactive Data Visualization

A stunning array of new tools helps business professionals analyze, display, and share vast quantities of data and nonnumeric information.

Community Q&A

Many companies now rely heavily on communities of customers to help each other with product questions and other routine matters.

Supply Chain Management Software

Manufacturers, distributors, and retailers now automatically share information that used to require labor-intensive manual reporting. Improved information flow increases report accuracy and helps each company in the supply chain manage inventory.

Online Customer Support

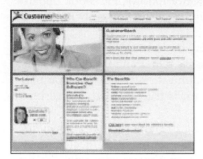

For online shoppers who need instant help, many retail websites make it easy to connect with a live sales rep via phone or instant messaging. Alternatively, software tools known as *virtual agents* or *bots* can answer simple questions and respond to requests for electronic documents.

Podcast

With the portability and convenience of downloadable audio and video recordings, podcasts have quickly become a popular means of delivering everything from college lectures to marketing messages. Podcasts are also used for internal communication, replacing conference calls, newsletters, and other media.

Microblogs

Microblogging services (of which Twitter is by far the best known) are a great way to share ideas, solicit feedback, monitor market trends, and announce special deals and events.

User-Generated Content

User-generated content sites let businesses host photos, videos, software programs, technical solutions, and other valuable content for their customer communities.

INTERACTING WITH CUSTOMERS

Maintaining an open dialog is essential to finding, engaging, and supporting customers. Today's communication technologies, particularly the ever-evolving field of social media, make it easier for customers to interact with a company whenever, wherever, and however they wish. Companies that take the lead in fostering a conversation with their markets have a big advantage over companies that don't.

Blogs

Blogs let companies connect with customers and other audiences in a fast and informal way. Commenting features let readers participate in the conversation, too.

Also, be wary of subscribing to too many blog feeds, Twitter follows, Facebook updates, and other sources of recurring messages. Focus on the information you truly need to do your job.

An important step in reducing information overload is to avoid sending unnecessary messages.

As a sender, you can help reduce information overload by making sure you don't send unnecessary messages. In addition, when you send messages that aren't urgent or crucial, let people know so they can prioritize. Also, most communication systems let you mark messages as urgent; however, use this feature only when it is truly needed. Overusing it leads to annoyance and anxiety, not action.

Beyond simple overload, some workers are beginning to show signs of *information technology addiction*—to the point of craving the stimulation of being connected practically around the clock, even while on vacation. Although employees who refuse to disconnect from their work might sound like a manager's dream, being constantly "plugged in" often does more harm than good. As Rutgers University professor Gayle Porter puts it, "Employers rightfully provide programs to help workers with chemical or substance addictions. Addiction to technology can be equally damaging to the mental health of the worker."[21]

USING TECHNOLOGICAL TOOLS PRODUCTIVELY

Facebook, Twitter, YouTube, IM, and other technologies are key parts of what has been called the "information technology paradox," in which information tools can waste as much time as they save. Concerns over inappropriate use of social networking sites, for example, have led many companies to ban employees from accessing them during work hours.[22]

Inappropriate web use not only distracts employees from work responsibilities but can leave employers open to lawsuits for sexual harassment if inappropriate images are displayed in or transmitted around the company.[23] Social media have created another set of managerial challenges, given the risk that employee blogs or social networking pages can expose confidential information or damage a firm's reputation in the marketplace. With all these technologies, the best solution lies in developing clear policies that are enforced evenly for all employees.[24]

Managers need to guide their employees in productive use of information tools because the speed and simplicity of these tools is also one of their greatest weaknesses. The flood of messages from an expanding array of electronic sources can significantly affect employees' ability to focus on their work. In one study, workers exposed to a constant barrage of email, IM, and phone calls experienced an average 10-point drop in their functioning intelligence quotient (IQ).[25]

In addition to using your tools appropriately, knowing how to use them efficiently can make a big difference in your productivity. You don't have to become an expert in most cases, but you need to be familiar with the basic features and functions of the tools you are expected to use on the job. As a manager, you also need to ensure that your employees have sufficient training to productively use the tools you expect them to use.

RECONNECTING WITH PEOPLE

Let's say you IM a colleague asking how she did with her sales presentation to an important client, and her answer comes back simply as "Fine." What does *fine* mean? Is an order expected soon? Or did she lose the sale and doesn't want to talk about it? If you visit with her in person, or at least talk over the phone, she might provide additional information, or you might be able to offer advice or support during a difficult time.

Moreover, even the best technologies cannot truly match the rich experience of person-to-person contact. For example, *telepresence* videoconferencing systems (discussed in Chapter 2) can create a convincing illusion of people thousands of miles apart being in the same room. However, even enthusiastic users know that this technology has limits. Jill Smart, an executive with the consulting firm Accenture, often takes advantage of the company's advanced telepresence facilities but still travels

As businesses increasingly rely on technology for communication, personal interaction becomes even more important because even the best technologies can't replace the human element.

frequently to meet with clients—particularly clients in other countries and cultures. "You get things from being there, over breakfast and dinner, building relationships face to face."[26]

Committing to Ethical and Legal Communication

Ethics are the accepted principles of conduct that govern behavior within a society. Ethical behavior is a company-wide concern, but because communication efforts are the public face of a company, they are subjected to particularly rigorous scrutiny from regulators, legislators, investors, consumer groups, environmental groups, labor organizations, and anyone else affected by business activities. **Ethical communication** includes all relevant information, is true in every sense, and is not deceptive in any way. In contrast, unethical communication can distort the truth or manipulate audiences in a variety of ways:[27]

- **Plagiarism.** Plagiarism is presenting someone else's words or other creative product as your own. Note that plagiarism can be illegal if it violates a **copyright**, which is a form of legal protection for the expression of creative ideas.[28]
- **Omitting essential information.** Information is essential if your audience needs it to make an intelligent, objective decision.
- **Selective misquoting.** Distorting or hiding the true intent of someone else's words is unethical.
- **Misrepresenting numbers.** Statistics and other data can be unethically manipulated by increasing or decreasing numbers, exaggerating, altering statistics, or omitting numeric data.
- **Distorting visuals.** Images can be manipulated in unethical ways, such as making a product seem bigger than it really is or changing the scale of graphs and charts to exaggerate or conceal differences.
- **Failing to respect privacy or information security needs.** Failing to respect the privacy of others or failing to adequately protect information entrusted to your care can also be considered unethical (and is sometimes illegal).

The widespread adoption of social media has increased the attention given to the issue of **transparency**, which in this context refers to a sense of openness, of giving all participants in a conversation access to the information they need to accurately process the messages they are receiving. A key aspect of transparency is knowing who is behind the messages one receives. Consider the promotional event that Netflix staged in Toronto to announce the launch of its streaming video service in Canada. The outdoor news conference seemed to attract dozens of curious people who were excited about the availability of Netflix. However, many of these people who "spontaneously" showed up were actually paid actors with instructions to "look really excited, particularly if asked by media to do any interviews about the prospect of Netflix in Canada." The company apologized when the stunt was exposed.[29]

A major issue in business communication transparency is **stealth marketing**, which involves attempting to promote products and services to customers who don't know they're being marketed to. A common stealth marketing technique is rewarding someone to promote products to his or her friends without telling them it's a form of advertising. Critics—including the U.S. Federal Trade Commission (FTC) and the Word of Mouth Marketing Association—assert that such techniques are deceptive because they don't give their targets the opportunity to raise their instinctive defenses against the persuasive powers of marketing messages.[30]

Aside from ethical concerns, trying to fool the public is simply bad for business. As LaSalle University communication professor Michael Smith puts it, "The public backlash can be long, deep, and damaging to a company's reputation."[31]

REAL-TIME UPDATES
Learn More by Reading This Article

Will your social media habits kill your career?

Follow these tips to make sure your social media habits don't keep you from getting a job or derail your career after it has begun. Go to http://real-timeupdates.com/bct11 and click on "Learn More." If you are using MyBcommLab, you can access Real-Time Updates within each chapter or under Student Study Tools.

5 LEARNING OBJECTIVE

Define *ethics*, explain the difference between an ethical dilemma and an ethical lapse, and list six guidelines for making ethical communication choices.

Any time you try to mislead your audience, the result is unethical communication.

Transparency gives audience members access to all the information they need in order to process messages accurately.

The controversial practice of stealth marketing involves marketing to people without their knowledge.

DISTINGUISHING ETHICAL DILEMMAS FROM ETHICAL LAPSES

An ethical dilemma is a choice between alternatives that may all be ethical and valid.

Some ethical questions are easy to recognize and resolve, but others are not. Deciding what is ethical can be a considerable challenge in complex business situations. An **ethical dilemma** involves choosing among alternatives that aren't clear-cut. Perhaps two conflicting alternatives are both ethical and valid, or perhaps the alternatives lie somewhere in the gray area between clearly right and clearly wrong. Every company has responsibilities to multiple groups of people inside and outside the firm, and those various groups often have competing interests. For instance, employees generally want higher wages and more benefits, but investors who have risked their money in the company want management to keep costs low so that profits are strong enough to drive up the stock price. Both sides have a valid ethical position.

An ethical lapse is making a choice that you know to be unethical.

In contrast, an **ethical lapse** is a clearly unethical choice. For example, homebuyers in an Orlando, Florida, housing development were sold houses without being told that the area was once a U.S. Army firing range and that live bombs and ammunition were still buried in multiple locations around the neighborhood.[32] With both internal and external communication efforts, the pressure to produce results or justify decisions can make unethical communication a tempting choice. (Compare the messages in Figures 1.9 and 1.10.)

ENSURING ETHICAL COMMUNICATION

Ensuring ethical business communication requires three elements: ethical individuals, ethical company leadership, and the appropriate policies and structures to support employees' efforts to make ethical choices.[33] Moreover, these three elements need to work in harmony. If employees see company executives making unethical decisions and flouting company guidelines, they might conclude that the guidelines are meaningless and emulate their bosses' unethical behavior.

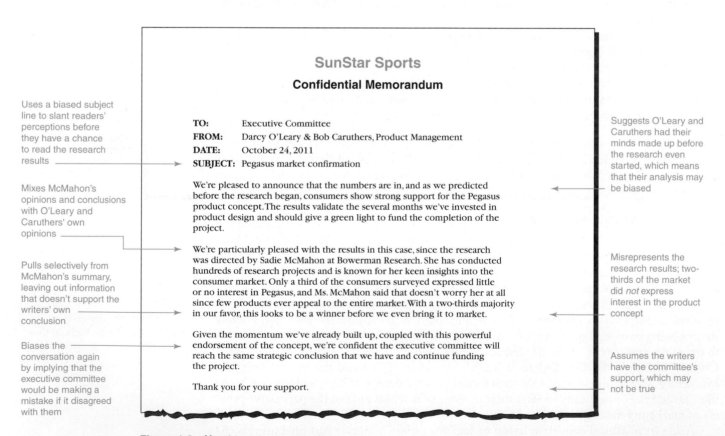

Figure 1.9   Unethical Communication
The writers of this memo clearly want the company to continue funding their pet project, even though the marketing research doesn't support such a decision. By comparing this memo with the version shown in Figure 1.10, you can see how the writers twisted the truth and omitted evidence in order to put a positive "spin" on the research.

Tries not to "sell" the conclusion ahead of time, using an even-handed subject line

Offers full disclosure of all the background information

Provides the complete text of the researcher's summary

Separates the researcher's observations and opinions from the writers' own

Invites further discussion of the situation

SunStar Sports
Confidential Memorandum

TO:	Executive Committee
FROM:	Darcy O'Leary & Bob Caruthers, Product Management
DATE:	October 24, 2011
SUBJECT:	Market research summary for Pegasus project

The market research for the Pegasus Project concluded last week with phone interviews of 236 sporting goods buyers in 18 states. As in the past, we used Bowerman Research to conduct the interviews, under the guidance of Bowerman's survey supervisor, Sadie McMahon. Ms. McMahon has directed surveys on more than 200 consumer products, and we've learned to place a great deal of confidence in her market insights.

A complete report, including all raw data and verbatim quotes, will be available for downloading on the Engineering Department intranet by the end of next week. However, in light of the project-funding discussions going on this week, we believe the conclusions from the research warrant your immediate attention.

Sadie McMahon's research summary

Consumer interest in the new product code-named Pegasus is decidedly mixed, with 34% expressing little or no interest in the product but 37% expressing moderate to strong interest. The remaining 29% expressed confusion about the basic product concept and were therefore unable to specify their level of interest. The segment expressing little or no interest is not a cause for concern in most cases; few products appeal to the entire consumer market.

However, the portion of the market expressing confusion about the fundamental design of the product is definitely cause for concern. We rarely see more than 10 or 15% confusion at this stage of the design process. A 29% confusion figure suggests that the product design does not fit many consumers' expectations and that it might be difficult to sell if SunStar goes ahead with production.

Our recommendations

At $7.6 million, the development costs for Pegasus are too high to proceed with this much uncertainty. The business case we prepared at the beginning of the project indicated that at least 50% consumer acceptance would be needed in order to generate enough sales to produce an acceptable return on the engineering investment. We would need to convince nearly half of the "confused" segment in order to reach that threshold. We recommend that further development be put on hold until the design can be clarified and validated with another round of consumer testing.

Please contact Darcy at ext. 2354 or Bob at ext. 2360 if you have any questions or concerns.

Emphasizes the skills of the researcher without biasing the readers regarding her conclusions

Explains that more in-depth information will be available soon but emphasizes the importance of reviewing this summary right now

Illustrates clearly that the market expert is concerned about the project

States clearly and honestly that the project will not live up to original hopes

Figure 1.10 Ethical Communication
This version of the memo shown in Figure 1.9 presents the evidence in a more honest and ethical manner.

Employers have a responsibility to establish clear guidelines for ethical behavior, including ethical business communication. Many companies establish an explicit ethics policy by using a written **code of ethics** to help employees determine what is acceptable. For example, Gap Inc. (the owner of the Gap, Banana Republic, and Old Navy retail chains), publishes a detailed Code of Business Conduct for its employees, addressing such areas as conflicts of interest, product integrity, health and safety, protection of company assets and information, and political activities by employees.[34] A code is often part of a larger program of employee training and communication channels that allow employees to ask questions and report instances of questionable ethics. To ensure ongoing compliance with their codes of ethics, many companies also conduct **ethics audits** to monitor ethical progress and to point out any weaknesses that need to be addressed.

Responsible employers establish clear ethical guidelines for their employees to follow.

If you can't decide whether a choice is ethical, picture yourself explaining your decision to someone whose opinion you value.

However, whether or not formal guidelines are in place, every employee has a responsibility to communicate in an ethical manner. In the absence of clear guidelines, ask yourself the following questions about your business communications:[35]

- Have you defined the situation fairly and accurately?
- What is your intention in communicating this message?
- What impact will this message have on the people who receive it, or who might be affected by it?
- Will the message achieve the greatest possible good while doing the least possible harm?
- Will the assumptions you've made change over time? That is, will a decision that seems ethical now seem unethical in the future?
- Are you comfortable with your decision? Would you be embarrassed if it were printed in tomorrow's newspaper or spread across the Internet? Think about a person whom you admire and ask yourself what he or she would think of your decision.

BUSINESS COMMUNICATION 2.0

Who's Responsible Here?

When companies engage in *comparative advertising*, making explicit comparisons between their products and those of competitors, complaints of false statements and defamation are fairly common. In that sense, a lawsuit that Subway recently filed against Quiznos is not in itself unusual. Subway claimed that Quiznos made unfair and untrue comparisons about the size and meat content of one of its sandwiches and failed to disclose the fact that the larger Quiznos sandwich cost nearly twice as much as the Subway sandwich.

What made this case unusual—and gave it potentially far-reaching impact for business communication—is the Web 2.0 angle of *user-generated content* (UGC). As part of its efforts to promote this particular sandwich, Quiznos sponsored a contest in which members of the public were invited to create their own commercials. The contest encouraged people to highlight the "meat, no meat" theme, suggesting that the Quiznos sandwich had copious amounts of beef, while the Subway sandwich had far less. More than 100 people submitted videos, which were posted to a Quiznos website and to iFilm, a now-defunct video clip website owned by the media giant Viacom.

Subway's lawsuit claimed that some of the videos contained false and disparaging content for which Quiznos and iFilm should be held liable. Subway asserted that Quiznos specifically encouraged contestants to promote one product at the expense of the other, so it should not be immune from responsibility. Quiznos's lawyers responded by pointing out that the company did not create these videos and is therefore not liable. "We're just facilitating consumers who go out and create their own expression in the form of a commercial."

Quiznos first tried to have the UGC part of the lawsuit dismissed by claiming the same immunity that YouTube and similar services have regarding the content that members of the public post on their websites. However, a judge refused, saying the law protecting YouTube (the Communications Decency Act, or CDA) doesn't necessarily protect Quiznos in this case. Quiznos subsequently asked for a summary judgment to avoid going to trial. When that request was also denied, the two companies settled out of court.

That private settlement closed the dispute between the two sandwich chains, but it left the matter of legal responsibility for UGC campaigns wide open. The central question is how much involvement a company sponsoring a UGC contest has in the content of the submissions. The court indicated that by sponsoring the contest and presenting the contest guidelines in a particular way, Quiznos played *some* role in the creation of the videos. However, because the case didn't go to trial, the question of whether that role was significant enough to strip the company of legal immunity under the CDA is still unresolved. Until clear legal guidelines are established, companies running UGC programs, such as Toyota's Auto-Biography campaign, will need to tread carefully to avoid legal problems.

CAREER APPLICATIONS

1. Legal issues aside, in your opinion, is Quiznos ethically responsible for any false or misleading information that may be found in the user-generated videos? Why or why not?
2. Most consumers lack the skills and equipment needed to produce professional-quality video commercials. Why would companies such as Quiznos invite them to create commercials?

ENSURING LEGAL COMMUNICATION

In addition to ethical guidelines, business communication is also bound by a wide variety of laws and regulations, including the following areas:

- **Promotional communication.** Marketing specialists need to be aware of the many laws that govern truth and accuracy in advertising. These laws address such issues as product reviews written by bloggers who receive compensation from the companies involved, false and deceptive advertising, misleading or inaccurate labels on product packages, and "bait and switch" tactics in which a store advertises a lower-priced product to lure consumers into a store but then tries to sell them a more expensive item.[36] Chapter 10 explores this area in more detail.

- **Contracts.** A **contract** is a legally binding promise between two parties, in which one party makes a specified offer and the other party accepts. Contracts are fundamental to virtually every aspect of business, from product sales to property rental to credit cards and loans to professional service agreements.[37]

- **Employment communication.** A variety of local, state, and federal laws govern communication between employers and both potential and current employees. For example, job descriptions must be written in a way that doesn't intentionally or unintentionally discriminate against women, minorities, or people with disabilities.[38]

- **Intellectual property.** In an age when instant global connectivity makes copying and retransmitting electronic files effortless, the protection of intellectual property (IP) has become a widespread concern. **Intellectual property** includes patents, copyrighted materials, trade secrets, and even Internet domain names.[39] Bloggers in particular need to be careful about IP protection, given the carefree way that some post the work of others without offering proper credit. For guidelines on this hot topic, get the free *Legal Guide for Bloggers* at www.eff.org/bloggers/legal.

- **Financial reporting.** Finance and accounting professionals who work for publicly traded companies (those that sell stock to the public) must adhere to stringent reporting laws. For instance, a number of corporations have recently been targets of both government investigations and shareholder lawsuits for offering misleading descriptions of financial results and revenue forecasts.

- **Defamation.** Negative comments about another party raise the possibility of **defamation**, the intentional communication of false statements that damage character or reputation.[40] (Written defamation is called *libel*; spoken defamation is called *slander*.) Someone suing for defamation must prove (1) that the statement is false, (2) that the language is injurious to the person's reputation, and (3) that the statement has been published.

- **Transparency requirements.** Governments around the world are taking steps to help ensure that consumers and other parties know who is behind the information they receive, particularly from online sources. The European Union, for instance, outlaws a number of online marketing tactics, including "flogs," short for "fake blogs," in which an employee or a paid agent posing as an independent consumer posts positive stories about a company's products.[41] In the United States, the FTC recently adopted a requirement that product-review bloggers disclose any relationship—such as receiving payments or free goods—they have with the companies whose products they discuss in their blogs.[42]

If you have any doubts about the legality of a message you intend to distribute, ask for advice from your company's legal department. A small dose of caution can prevent huge legal headaches and protect your company's reputation in the marketplace.

For the latest information on ethical and legal issues in business communication, visit http://real-timeupdates.com/bct11 and click on Chapter 1.

Business communication is governed by a wide variety of laws designed to ensure accurate, complete messages.

REAL-TIME UPDATES
Learn More by Reading This Article

Learn how intellectual property protection promotes sustainable growth

The mission of the International Intellectual Property Institute is promoting sustainable growth through economic and regulatory environments that encourage innovation and creativity. Go to http://real-timeupdates.com/bct11 and click on "Learn More." If you are using MyBcommLab, you can access Real-Time Updates within each chapter or under Student Study Tools.

Quick Learning Guide

MyBcommLab

If your course uses MyBcommLab, log on to www.mybcommlab.com to access the following study and assessment aids associated with this chapter:

- Video applications
- Personalized study plan
- Real-Time Updates
- Model documents
- Peer review activity
- Sample presentations
- Pre/post test

If you are not using MyBcommLab, you can access Real-Time Updates through http://real-timeupdates.com/bct11.

CHAPTER OUTLINE

Understanding Why Communication Matters
Communication Is Important to Your Career
Communication Is Important to Your Company
What Makes Business Communication Effective?

Communicating in Today's Global Business Environment
Understanding the Unique Challenges of Business Communication
Understanding What Employers Expect from You
Communicating in an Organizational Context
Adopting an Audience-Centered Approach

Exploring the Communication Process
The Basic Communication Model
The Social Communication Model

Using Technology to Improve Business Communication
Keeping Technology in Perspective
Guarding Against Information Overload and Information Addiction
Using Technological Tools Productively
Reconnecting with People

Committing to Ethical and Legal Communication
Distinguishing Ethical Dilemmas from Ethical Lapses
Ensuring Ethical Communication
Ensuring Legal Communication

SUMMARY OF LEARNING OBJECTIVES

1 **Explain the importance of effective communication to your career and to the companies where you will work.** Effective communication is important to your career because no matter what line of work you pursue, you need to be able to share information with other people. You can have the greatest business ideas in the world, but they're no good to you if you can't express them clearly and persuasively. In addition to benefiting you personally, your communication skills will help your company in multiple ways, offering (1) closer ties with important communities in the marketplace; (2) opportunities to influence conversations, perceptions, and trends; (3) increased productivity and faster problem solving; (4) better financial results; (5) earlier warning of potential problems; (6) stronger decision making; (7) clearer and more persuasive marketing messages; and (8) greater employee engagement with work.

2 **Describe the communication skills employers will expect you to have and the nature of communicating in an organization using an audience-centered approach.** Employers expect you to have a wide range of communication skills, including (1) organizing ideas and information logically and completely; (2) expressing yourself coherently and persuasively; (3) actively listening to others; (4) communicating effectively with people from diverse backgrounds; (5) using communication technologies effectively and efficiently; (6) following accepted standards of grammar, spelling, and style; (7) communicating in a civilized manner; (8) communicating ethically; and (9) using time and resources wisely.

Applying these skills effectively in a business environment involves learning how to use both the *formal* and *informal* communication networks in your organization. The formal network mirrors the official hierarchy and structure of the organization; the informal network involves all the communication among members of the organization, regardless of their job positions. Adopting an *audience-centered approach* involves understanding and respecting the members of your audience and making every effort to get your message across in a way that is meaningful to them. This approach is also known as adopting the *"you" attitude* (where "you" is the recipient of the message you are sending).

3 **Describe the communication process model and the ways that social media are changing the nature of business communication.** Communication is a complex and subtle process, and any attempt to model it will involve some simplification, but it is helpful to view the process as eight steps: (1) the sender starts with an *idea* to share; (2) the sender *encodes* the meaning of that idea as a *message*; (3) the sender produces the message in a transmittable *medium*; (4) the sender transmits the message through a *channel*; (5) the audience receives the message; (6) the audience *decodes* the message to extract its meaning; (7) The audience responds to the message; and (8) the audience provides *feedback* to sender.

Social media are transforming the practice of business communication and changing the nature of the relationships between companies and their stakeholders. Traditional business communication can be thought of as having a "publishing" mindset, in which a company produces carefully scripted messages and distributes them to an audience that has few options for responding to the company or interacting with one another. In contrast, the "Business Communication 2.0" approach uses Web 2.0 social media tools to create an interactive and participative environment in which all parties have a chance to join the conversation. Many of the old rules and expectations, including tight control of the content and distribution of the message, no longer apply in this new environment.

4 **List four general guidelines for using communication technology effectively.** First, keep technology in perspective. Make sure that it supports the communication effort rather than overwhelming or disrupting it. Second, guard against information overload and information technology addiction. Third, learn how to use technological tools productively—and avoid using them in deliberately unproductive ways. Fourth, reconnect in person from time to time to ensure that communication is successful and that technology doesn't come between you and the people you need to reach.

5 **Define *ethics*, explain the difference between an ethical dilemma and an ethical lapse, and list six guidelines for making ethical communication choices.** *Ethics* are the accepted principles of conduct that govern behavior within a society. Ethical communication is particularly important in business because communication is the public face of a company, which is why communication efforts are intensely scrutinized by company stakeholders. The difference between an ethical dilemma and an ethical lapse is a question of clarity. An ethical dilemma occurs when the choice is unclear because two or more alternatives seem equally right or equally wrong. In contrast, an ethical lapse occurs when a person makes a conscious choice that is clearly unethical.

To make ethical choices in any situation, ask yourself these six questions: (1) Have I defined the situation fairly and accurately? (2) What is my intention in communicating this message? (3) What impact will this message have on the people who receive it, or who might be affected by it? (4) Will the message achieve the greatest possible good while doing the least possible harm? (5) Will the assumptions I've made change over time? That is, will a decision that seems ethical now seem unethical in the future? (6) Am I truly comfortable with my decision?

KEY TERMS

audience-centered approach Understanding and respecting the members of your audience and making every effort to get your message across in a way that is meaningful to them

Business Communication 2.0 A new approach to business communication based on social communication

code of ethics A written set of ethical guidelines that companies expect their employees to follow

communication The process of transferring information and meaning using one or more written, oral, visual, or electronic media

communication barriers Forces or events that can disrupt communication, including noise and distractions, competing messages, filters, and channel breakdowns

communication channels Systems used to deliver messages

communication medium The form in which a message is presented; the four categories of media are oral, written, visual, and electronic

contract A legally binding promise between two parties, in which one party makes a specified offer and the other party accepts

copyright A form of legal protection for the expression of creative ideas

corporate culture The mixture of values, traditions, and habits that give a company its atmosphere and personality

decoding Extracting the idea from a message

defamation The intentional communication of false statements that damage character or reputation

encoding Putting an idea into a message (words, images, or a combination of both)

ethical communication Communication that includes all relevant information, is

true in every sense, and is not deceptive in any way

ethical dilemma Situation that involves making a choice when the alternatives aren't completely wrong or completely right

ethical lapse A clearly unethical choice

ethics The accepted principles of conduct that govern behavior within a society

ethics audits Ongoing efforts to monitor ethical progress and to point out any weaknesses that need to be addressed

etiquette The expected norms of behavior in any particular situation

feedback Information from receivers regarding the quality and effectiveness of a message

formal communication network Communication channels that flow along the lines of command

globalization Efforts by businesses to reach across international borders to market their products, partner with other businesses, and employ workers and executives

informal communication network All communication that takes place outside the formal network; often referred to as the grapevine or the rumor mill

information overload Condition in which people receive more information than they can effectively process

intellectual property Assets including patents, copyrighted materials, trade secrets, and even Internet domain names

knowledge workers Employees at all levels of an organization who specialize in acquiring, processing, and communicating information

message The "container" for an idea to be transmitted from a sender to a receiver

perception A person's awareness or view of reality; also, the process of detecting incoming messages

selective perception The inclination to distort or ignore incoming information rather than change one's beliefs

social communication model An interactive, conversational approach to communication in which formerly passive audience members are empowered to participate fully

social media Electronic media such as social networks and blogs that transform passive audiences into active participants in the communication process by allowing them to share content, revise content, respond to content, or contribute new content

stakeholders Groups affected by a company's actions: customers, employees, shareholders, suppliers, neighbors, the community, and the world at large

stealth marketing Attempts to promote products and services to customers who don't know they're being marketed to

transparency Giving all participants in a conversation access to the information they need to accurately process the messages they are receiving

Web 2.0 The second generation of World Wide Web technologies, which emphasize social media and interactivity

workforce diversity All the differences among the people who work together, including differences in age, gender, sexual orientation, education, cultural background, religion, ability, and life experience

"you" attitude Communicating with an audience-centered approach; creating messages that are about "you," the receiver, rather than "me," the sender

COMMUNICATION CHALLENGES AT **TOYOTA**

You've recently joined the staff of Bob Zeinstra, the executive in charge of product management, advertising, and communication strategy at Toyota Motor Sales, USA. In your role as a social media specialist, you look for opportunities to help Toyota build positive relationships with all its stakeholders. Use what you've learned in this chapter to address the following challenges.

INDIVIDUAL CHALLENGE: Review the customer stories submitted to the Auto-Biography campaign at **www.facebook .com/toyota**. Select two stories that present Toyota in a positive light, with one story that emphasizes product reliability and other practical matters and one story that conveys the emotional bond that an owner has developed with his or her vehicle. In an email message to your instructor or a post on your class blog, summarize the two stories you chose and explain your reasons for choosing them.

TEAM CHALLENGE: As the Quiznos–Subway conflict described on page 26 emphasizes, user-generated content can expose a company to a variety of legal and public relations risks. With a team assigned by your instructor, brainstorm general guidelines that Toyota could use to protect itself while still taking advantage of the potential of user-generated content. For example, should the company accept user-submitted videos that show images of risky driving behavior or stories that include critical comments about Toyota products or dealers? Summarize your recommendations in a class presentation or other format as your instructor directs.

TEST YOUR KNOWLEDGE

To review chapter content related to each question, refer to the indicated Learning Objective.

1. What benefits does effective communication give you and your organization? [LO-1]
2. What are the five attributes of effective business communication? [LO-1]
3. How does formal communication differ from informal communication? [LO-2]
4. Why should communicators take an audience-centered approach to communication? [LO-2]
5. What steps have to occur before an audience member perceives the presence of an incoming message? [LO-3]
6. What are the most common barriers in any communication environment? [LO-3]
7. How does the social communication model differ from traditional business communication practices? [LO-3]
8. How is communication affected by information overload? [LO-4]
9. What is an ethical dilemma? [LO-5]
10. What is an ethical lapse? [LO-5]

APPLY YOUR KNOWLEDGE

To review chapter content related to each question, refer to the indicated Learning Objective.

1. If you are an acknowledged expert in your field, do you really need to care about communication skills? Why or why not? [LO-1]
2. How does the presence of a reader comments feature on a corporate blog reflect audience-centered communication? [LO-2]

3. How are social networks, wikis, and other Web 2.0 technologies changing the practice of business communication? [LO-3]
4. Is it possible for companies to be too dependent on communication technology? Explain briefly. [LO-4]
5. Because of your excellent communication skills, your boss always asks you to write his reports for him. When you overhear the CEO complimenting him on his logical organization and clear writing style, your boss responds as if he'd written all those reports himself. What kind of ethical choice does your boss's response represent? What can you do in this situation? Briefly explain your solution and your reasoning. [LO-5]

PRACTICE YOUR SKILLS

Message for Analysis: Analyzing Communication Effectiveness [LO-1]

Read the following blog posting and then (1) analyze whether the message is effective or ineffective (be sure to explain why) and (2) revise the message so that it follows this chapter's guidelines.

> It has come to my attention that many of you are lying on your time cards. If you come in late, you should not put 8:00 on your card. If you take a long lunch, you should not put 1:00 on your time card. I will not stand for this type of cheating. I simply have no choice but to institute an employee monitoring system. Beginning next Monday, video cameras will be installed at all entrances to the building, and your entry and exit times will be logged each time you use electronic key cards to enter or leave.
>
> Anyone who is late for work or late coming back from lunch more than three times will have to answer to me. I don't care

if you had to take a nap or if you girls had to shop. This is a place of business, and we do not want to be taken advantage of by slackers who are cheaters to boot.

It is too bad that a few bad apples always have to spoil things for everyone.

Exercises

Active links for all websites in this chapter can be found on MyBcommLab; see your User Guide for instructions on accessing the content for this chapter. Each activity is labeled according to the primary skill or skills you will need to use. To review relevant chapter content, you can refer to the indicated Learning Objective. In some instances, supporting information will be found in another chapter, as indicated.

1. **Writing: Compositional Modes: Summaries [LO-1], Chapter 4** Write a paragraph introducing yourself to your instructor and your class. Address such areas as your background, interests, achievements, and goals. Submit your paragraph using email, blog, or social network, as indicated by your instructor.

2. **Media Skills: Microblogging [LO-1], Chapter 6** Write four effective messages of no more than 140 characters each (short enough to work as Twitter tweets, in other words) to persuade other college students to take the business communication course. Think of the first message as the "headline" of an advertisement that makes a bold promise regarding the value this course offers every aspiring business professional. The next three messages should be support points that provide evidence to back up the promise made in the first message.[43]

3. **Fundamentals: Analyzing Communication Effectiveness [LO-1]** Bring to class a sales message that you received in the mail or via email. Comment on how well the communication
   a. provides practical information
   b. gives facts rather than impressions
   c. clarifies and condenses information
   d. states precise responsibilities
   e. persuades others and offers recommendations

4. **Planning: Assessing Audience Needs [LO-2], Chapter 3** Choose a business career that sounds interesting to you and imagine that you are getting ready to apply for jobs in that field. Naturally, you want to create a compelling, audience-focused résumé that answers the key questions a hiring manager is most likely to have. Identify three personal or professional qualities you have that would be important for someone in this career field. Write a brief statement (one or two sentences) regarding each quality, describing in audience-focused terms how you can contribute to a company in this respect. Submit your statements via email or class blog.

5. **Communication Etiquette: Communicating with Sensitivity and Tact [LO-2]** Potential customers frequently visit your production facility before making purchase decisions. You and the people who report to you in the sales department have received extensive training in etiquette issues because you deal with high-profile clients so often. However, the rest of the workforce has not received such

training, and you worry that someone might inadvertently say or do something that would offend one of these potential customers. In a two-paragraph email, explain to the general manager why you think anyone who might come in contact with customers should receive basic etiquette training.

6. **Collaboration: Team Project; Planning: Assessing Audience Needs [LO-2], Chapter 2, Chapter 4** Your boss has asked your work group to research and report on corporate child-care facilities. Of course, you'll want to know who (besides your boss) will be reading your report. Working with two team members, list four or five other things you'll want to know about the situation and about your audience before starting your research. Briefly explain why each of the items on your list is important.

7. **Planning: Constructing a Persuasive Argument [LO-3], Chapter 10** You are the customer service manager for a company that sells a software package used by not-for-profit organizations to plan and manage fundraising campaigns. The powerful software is complicated enough to require a fairly extensive user's manual, and the company has always provided a printed manual to customers. Customers frequently email your department with questions about using the software and suggestions for using the software to maximize fundraising efforts. You know that many customers could benefit from the answers to those questions and the suggestions from fellow customers, but with a printed manual issued once every couple years, you don't have any way to collect and distribute this information in a timely fashion.

   You've been researching wikis and believe this would be a great way to let customers participate in an ongoing conversation about using the software. In fact, you'd like to convert the printed manual to a wiki on which any registered customer could add or edit pages. Rather than spend thousands of dollars printing a manual that is difficult to expand or update, the wiki would be a "living" document that continually evolves as people ask and answer questions and offer suggestions. The rest of the management team is extremely nervous, however. "We're the experts—not the customer," one says. Another asks, "How can we ensure the quality of the information if any customer can change it?" They don't deny that customers have valuable information to add; they just don't want customers to have control of an important company document. Making up any information you need, write a brief email to your colleagues, explaining the benefits of letting customers contribute to a wiki-based user manual. (You can refer to pages 413–415 to learn more about wikis.)

8. **Planning: Constructing a Persuasive Argument [LO-3], Chapter 10** Blogging has become a popular way for employees to communicate with customers and other parties outside the company. In some cases, employee blogs have been quite beneficial for both companies and their customers by providing helpful information and "putting a human face" on other formal and imposing corporations. However, in some other cases, employees have been fired for posting information that their employers said was inappropriate. One particular area of concern is criticism of the company or individual managers. Should employees be allowed to criticize their employers in a public forum such as a blog?

In a brief email message, argue for or against company policies that prohibit critical information in employee blogs.

9. **Fundamentals: Analyzing Communication Effectiveness [LO-3]** Use the eight phases of the communication process to analyze a miscommunication you've recently had with a co-worker, supervisor, classmate, teacher, friend, or family member. What idea were you trying to share? How did you encode and transmit it? Did the receiver get the message? Did the receiver correctly decode the message? How do you know? Based on your analysis, identify and explain the barriers that prevented your successful communication in this instance.

10. **Technology: Using Communication Tools [LO-4]** Find a free online communication service that you have no experience using as a content creator or contributor. Services to consider include blogging (such as Blogger), microblogging (such as Twitter), community Q&A sites (such as Yahoo! Answers), and user-generated content sites (such as Flickr). Perform a basic task such as opening an account or setting up a blog. Was the task easy to perform? Were the instructions clear? Could you find help online if you needed it? Is there anything about the experience that could be improved? Summarize your conclusions in a brief email message to your instructor.

11. **Communication Ethics: Distinguishing Ethical Dilemmas and Ethical Lapses [LO-5]** Knowing that you have numerous friends throughout the company, your boss relies on you for feedback concerning employee morale and other issues affecting the staff. She recently asked you to start reporting any behavior that might violate company policies, from taking home office supplies to making personal long-distance calls. List the issues you'd like to discuss with her before you respond to her request.

12. **Communication Ethics: Distinguishing Ethical Dilemmas and Ethical Lapses [LO-5]** In less than a page, explain why you think each of the following is or is not ethical.
    a. Keeping quiet about a possible environmental hazard you've just discovered in your company's processing plant
    b. Overselling the benefits of instant messaging to your company's managers; they never seem to understand the benefits of technology, so you believe it's the only way to convince them to make the right choice

c. Telling an associate and close friend that she needs to pay more attention to her work responsibilities, or management will fire her
d. Recommending the purchase of equipment your department doesn't really need in order to use up your allocated funds before the end of the fiscal year so that your budget won't be cut next year—when you might have a real need for the money

13. **Communication Ethics: Providing Ethical Leadership [LO-5]** Cisco, a leading manufacturer of equipment for the Internet and corporate networks, has developed a code of ethics that it expects employees to abide by. Visit the company's website, at www.cisco.com, and find its *code of conduct*. In a brief paragraph, describe three specific examples of things you could do that would violate these provisions; then list at least three opportunities that Cisco provides its employees to report ethics violations or ask questions regarding ethical dilemmas.

EXPAND YOUR SKILLS

Critique the Professionals

Locate an example of professional communication from a reputable online source. It can reflect any aspect of business communication, from an advertisement or a press release to a company blog or website. Evaluate this communication effort in light of any aspect of this chapter that is relevant to the sample and interesting to you. For example, is the piece effective? Audience-centered? Ethical? Using whatever medium your instructor requests, write a brief analysis of the piece (no more than one page), citing specific elements from the piece and support from the chapter.

Sharpening Your Career Skills Online

Bovée and Thill's Business Communication Web Search, at http://businesscommunicationblog.com/websearch, is a unique research tool designed specifically for business communication research. Use the Web Search function to find an online video, a podcast, or a PowerPoint presentation that explains at least one essential business communication skill. Write a brief email message to your instructor or a post for your class blog, describing the item that you found and summarizing the career skills information you learned from it.

Mastering Team Skills and Interpersonal Communication

2

LEARNING OBJECTIVES After studying this chapter, you will be able to

1 List the advantages and disadvantages of working in teams, describe the characteristics of effective teams, and highlight four key issues of group dynamics

2 Offer guidelines for collaborative communication, identify major collaboration technologies, and explain how to give constructive feedback

3 List the key steps needed to ensure productive team meetings

4 Identify the major technologies used to enhance or replace in-person meetings

5 Identify three major modes of listening, describe the listening process, and explain the problem of selective listening

6 Explain the importance of nonverbal communication and identify six major categories of nonverbal expression

7 Explain the importance of business etiquette and identify three key areas in which good etiquette is essential

MyBcommLab Test your mastery of this chapter and its Learning Objectives. Visit mybcommlab.com to apply what you've learned in Document Makeovers and interactive simulation scenarios.

COMMUNICATION CLOSE-UP AT ROSEN LAW FIRM

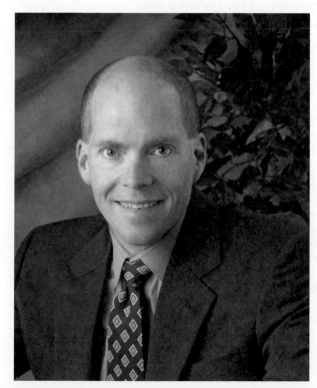

Lee Rosen's law firm uses a wiki to manage thousands of documents while boosting teamwork and collaboration.

www.rosen.com

When communication tools function at their best, they can go beyond mere facilitation to transformation. Such was the case at Rosen Law Firm, based in Raleigh, North Carolina. Lee Rosen, the firm's owner and chief executive, wanted to replace an expensive, complicated, and inflexible computer system that employees relied on for everything from contact lists to appointment calendars to document storage. The solution he chose was a wiki, the same technology that enables nearly 100,000 people around the world to contribute to Wikipedia.

The wiki certainly helped cut costs, and it did much more. Besides handling much of the firm's document storage and formal communication, the wiki introduced an informal social element that is helping employees bond as a community. Many have added personal pages with information about themselves, helping employees get to know their colleagues on a more intimate level.

In implementing the wiki, Rosen faced a common challenge with new communication tools: getting people to give up familiar ways of doing things and embrace change. Knowing that the value of a company wiki depends on the level of employee contribution—and that having some of the staff switch while others cling to old ways would seriously disrupt communication—he encouraged use of the new wiki with a friendly competition. For each page an employee created during

33

the three-month competition, he or she was given one possible combination to the company safe, which contained a $1,000 cash prize. From time to time, Rosen also forced use of the wiki by publishing important information only on the wiki.

As often happens when companies face significant changes, the move to the wiki did cause some turmoil. Two camps of employees argued over the best way to organize information and got caught up in an "edit war," repeatedly undoing each other's decisions. They eventually reached a compromise that resolved the disagreement and had lasting benefits for teamwork and interpersonal communication across the firm. According to Rosen, "It forced everybody to learn about each other's job."[1]

Communicating Effectively in Teams

The teamwork interactions among the employees at Rosen Law Firm (profiled in the chapter-opening Communication Close-up) represent one of the most essential elements of interpersonal communication. **Collaboration**—working together to meet complex challenges—has become a core job responsibility for roughly half the U.S. workforce.[2] No matter what career path you pursue, it's a virtual guarantee that you will be expected to collaborate in at least some of your work activities. Your communication skills will pay off handsomely in these interactions, because the productivity and quality of collaborative efforts depend heavily on the communication skills of the professionals involved.

A **team** is a unit of two or more people who share a mission and the responsibility for working to achieve a common goal.[3] **Problem-solving teams** and **task forces** assemble to resolve specific issues and then disband when their goals have been accomplished. Such teams are often *cross-functional*, pulling together people from a variety of departments who have different areas of expertise and responsibility. The diversity of opinions and experiences can lead to better decisions, but competing interests can lead to tensions that highlight the need for effective communication. **Committees** are formal teams that usually have a long life span and can become a permanent part of the organizational structure. Committees typically deal with regularly recurring tasks, such as an executive committee that meets monthly to plan strategies and review results.

ADVANTAGES AND DISADVANTAGES OF TEAMS

When teams are successful, they can improve productivity, creativity, employee involvement, and even job security.[4] Teams are often at the core of **participative management**,

---

ETHICS DETECTIVE   ## Solving the Case of the Missing Team

Your entire team has been looking forward to this meeting for weeks. When the company president assembled this team to find creative solutions to the company's cash flow problems, few people thought it would succeed. However, through plenty of hard work, you and your colleagues have found new sources of investment capital. Now it's time to present your accomplishments to the board of directors. Because exposure in front of the board can be a major career boost, the team planned to present the results together, giving each person a few minutes in the limelight.

However, Jackson Mueller, the chief financial officer and the leader of your team, had a surprise for you this morning. He said he'd received word at the last minute that the board wants a short, concise presentation, and he said the only way to do so was with a single presenter. No one was happy about the change, but Mueller is the highest-ranking employee on the team and the only one with experience presenting to the board.

Disappointment turned to dismay as you and your teammates watched from the back of the conference room. Mueller deftly compressed your 60-minute presentation down to 20 minutes, and the board showered him with praise. However, he never introduced any of the other team members, so your potential moment in the sun passed without recognition.

ANALYSIS

Did Mueller behave unethically by not introducing you and your colleagues to the board? Explain your answer.

Later on, you complain to a colleague that by stressing "my team" so often, Mueller actually made the presentation all about him, not the team. But one of your colleagues argues that the team's assignment was to solve the problem, not to score career points with the board, so that goal shouldn't have been such a top priority. Explain why you agree or disagree.

the effort to involve employees in the company's decision making. A successful team can provide a number of advantages:[5]

- **Increased information and knowledge.** By pooling the experience of several individuals, a team has access to more information in the decision-making process.
- **Increased diversity of views.** Team members can bring a variety of perspectives to the decision-making process—as long as these diverse viewpoints are guided by a shared goal.[6]
- **Increased acceptance of a solution.** Those who participate in making a decision are more likely to support it and encourage others to accept it.
- **Higher performance levels.** Working in teams can unleash new levels of creativity and energy in workers who share a sense of purpose and mutual accountability. Effective teams can be better than top-performing individuals at solving complex problems.[7]

> Effective teams can pool knowledge, take advantage of diverse viewpoints, and increase acceptance of solutions the team proposes.

Although teamwork has many advantages, it also has a number of potential disadvantages. At the worst, working in teams can be a frustrating waste of time. Teams need to be aware of and work to counter the following potential disadvantages:

- **Groupthink.** Like other social structures, business teams can generate tremendous pressures to conform with accepted norms of behavior. **Groupthink** occurs when peer pressures cause individual team members to withhold contrary or unpopular opinions. The result can be decisions that are worse than the choices the team members might have made individually.
- **Hidden agendas.** Some team members may have a **hidden agenda**—private, counter-productive motives, such as a desire to take control of the group, to undermine someone else on the team, or to pursue a business goal that runs counter to the team's mission.
- **Cost.** Aligning schedules, arranging meetings, and coordinating individual parts of a project can eat up a lot of time and money.

> Teams need to avoid the negative impact of groupthink, hidden agendas, and excessive costs.

CHARACTERISTICS OF EFFECTIVE TEAMS

The most effective teams have a clear objective and shared sense of purpose, have a strong sense of trust, communicate openly and honestly, reach decisions by consensus, think creatively, and know how to resolve conflict.[8] Teams that have these attributes can focus their time and energy on their work, without being disrupted by destructive conflict (see page 37).

In contrast, teams that lack one or more of these attributes can get bogged down in conflict or waste time and resources pursuing unclear goals. Two of the most common reasons cited for unsuccessful teamwork are a lack of trust and poor communication. A lack of trust can result from team members being suspicious of one another's motives or ability to contribute.[9] Communication breakdowns are most likely to occur when teams operate across cultures, countries, or time zones.[10]

> Effective teams have a clear sense of purpose, open and honest communication, consensus-based decision making, creativity, and effective conflict resolution.

GROUP DYNAMICS

The interactions and processes that take place among the members of a team are called **group dynamics**. Productive teams tend to develop clear **norms**, informal standards of conduct that members share and that guide member behavior. Group dynamics are influenced by several factors: the roles that team members assume, the current phase of team development, the team's success in resolving conflict, and the team's success in overcoming resistance.

> Group dynamics are the interactions and processes that take place in a team.

Assuming Team Roles

Members of a team can play various roles, which fall into three categories (see Table 2.1 on the following page). Members who assume **self-oriented roles** are motivated mainly to fulfill personal needs, so they tend to be less productive than other members. "Dream teams" composed of multiple superstars often don't perform as well as one might expect because high-performing individuals can have trouble putting the team's needs ahead of their own.[11] In addition, highly skilled and experienced people with difficult personalities might not contribute for the simple reason that other team members may avoid interacting with them.[12]

> Each member of a group plays a role that affects the outcome of the group's activities.

TABLE 2.1	Team Roles—Functional and Dysfunctional	
Dysfunctional: Self-Oriented Roles	**Functional: Team-Maintenance Roles**	**Functional: Task-Facilitating Roles**
Controlling: Dominating others by exhibiting superiority or authority	**Encouraging:** Drawing out other members by showing verbal and nonverbal support, praise, or agreement	**Initiating:** Getting the team started on a line of inquiry
Withdrawing: Retiring from the team either by becoming silent or by refusing to deal with a particular aspect of the team's work	**Harmonizing:** Reconciling differences among team members through mediation or by using humor to relieve tension	**Information giving or seeking:** Offering (or seeking) information relevant to questions facing the team
Attention seeking: Calling attention to oneself and demanding recognition from others	**Compromising:** Offering to yield on a point in the interest of reaching a mutually acceptable decision	**Coordinating:** Showing relationships among ideas, clarifying issues, summarizing what the team has done
Diverting: Focusing the team's discussion on topics of interest to the individual rather than on those relevant to the task		**Procedure setting:** Suggesting decision-making procedures that will move the team toward a goal

Far more likely to contribute to team goals are members who assume **team-maintenance roles** to help everyone work well together and those who assume **task-oriented roles** to help the team reach its goals.[13]

Allowing for Team Evolution

Teams typically evolve through a variety of phases, such as orientation, conflict, brainstorming, emergence, and reinforcement.

Teams typically evolve through a number of phases on their way to becoming productive (see Figure 2.1). A variety of models have been proposed to describe the evolution toward becoming a productive team. Here is how one commonly used model identifies the phases a problem-solving team goes through as it evolves:[14]

1. **Orientation.** Team members socialize, establish their roles, and begin to define their task or purpose. Team-building exercises and activities can help teams break down barriers and develop a sense of shared purpose.[15] For geographically dispersed virtual teams, creating a "team operating agreement" that sets expectations for online meetings, communication processes, and decision making can help overcome the disadvantages of distance.[16]
2. **Conflict.** Team members begin to discuss their positions and become more assertive in establishing their roles. Disagreements and uncertainties are natural in this phase.
3. **Brainstorming.** Team members air all the options and fully discuss the pros and cons. At the end of this phase, members begin to settle on a single solution to the problem. Note that while group brainstorming remains a highly popular activity in today's companies, it may not always be the most productive way to generate new ideas. Some research indicates that having people brainstorm individually and then bring their ideas to a group meeting is more successful.[17]
4. **Emergence.** Consensus is reached when the team finds a solution that all members are willing to support (even if they have reservations).
5. **Reinforcement.** The team clarifies and summarizes the agreed-upon solution. Members receive their assignments for carrying out the group's decision, and they make arrangements for following up on those assignments.

Figure 2.1   Phases of Group Development
Groups generally progress through several stages on their way to becoming productive and reaching their objectives.

You may also hear the process defined as *forming*, *storming*, *norming*, *performing*, and *adjourning*, the phases identified by researcher Bruce Tuckman when he proposed one of the earliest models of group development.[18] Regardless of the model you consider, these stages are a general framework for team development. Some teams may move forward and backward through several stages before they become productive, and other teams may be productive right away, even while some or all members are in a state of conflict.[19]

Resolving Conflict

Conflict in team activities can arise for a number of reasons: competition for resources, disagreement over goals or responsibilities, poor communication, power struggles, or fundamental differences in values, attitudes, and personalities.[20] Although the term *conflict* sounds negative, conflict isn't necessarily bad. Conflict can be *constructive* if it forces important issues into the open, increases the involvement of team members, and generates creative ideas for solving a problem. Teamwork isn't necessarily about happiness and harmony; even teams that have some interpersonal friction can excel with effective leadership and team players committed to strong results. As teamwork experts Andy Boynton and Bill Fischer put it, "Virtuoso teams are not about getting polite results."[21]

In contrast, conflict is *destructive* if it diverts energy from more important issues, destroys the morale of teams or individual team members, or polarizes or divides the team.[22] Destructive conflict can lead to *win-lose* or *lose-lose* outcomes, in which one or both sides lose, to the detriment of the entire team. If you approach conflict with the idea that both sides can satisfy their goals to at least some extent (a *win-win* strategy), you can minimize losses for everyone. For a win-win strategy to work, everybody must believe that (1) it's possible to find a solution that both parties can accept, (2) cooperation is better for the organization than competition, (3) the other party can be trusted, and (4) greater power or status doesn't entitle one party to impose a solution.

The following seven measures can help team members successfully resolve conflict:

- **Proactive behavior.** Deal with minor conflict before it becomes major conflict.
- **Communication.** Get those directly involved in a conflict to participate in resolving it.
- **Openness.** Get feelings out in the open before dealing with the main issues.
- **Research.** Seek factual reasons for a problem before seeking solutions.
- **Flexibility.** Don't let anyone lock into a position before considering other solutions.
- **Fair play.** Insist on fair outcomes and don't let anyone avoid a fair solution by hiding behind the rules.
- **Alliance.** Get opponents to fight together against an "outside force" instead of against each other.

Overcoming Resistance

One particular type of conflict that can affect team progress is resistance to change. Sometimes this resistance is clearly irrational, such as when people resist any kind of change, whether it makes sense or not. Sometimes, however, resistance is perfectly logical. A change may require someone to relinquish authority or give up comfortable ways of doing things. If someone is resisting change, you can be persuasive with calm, reasonable communication:

- **Express understanding.** You might say, "I understand that this change might be difficult, and if I were in your position, I might be reluctant myself." Help the other person relax and talk about his or her anxiety so that you have a chance to offer reassurance.[23]
- **Bring resistance out into the open.** When people are noncommittal and silent, they may be tuning you out without even knowing why. Continuing with your argument is futile. Deal directly with the resistance, without accusing. You might say, "You seem to have reservations about this idea. Have I made some faulty assumptions?" Such questions force people to face and define their resistance.[24]
- **Evaluate others' objections fairly.** Use active listening to focus on what the other person is expressing, both the words and the feelings. Get the person to open up so that you can understand the basis for the resistance. Others' objections may raise legitimate

Conflict in teams can be either constructive or destructive.

Destructive conflict can lead to win-lose or lose-lose outcomes.

When you encounter resistance or hostility, try to maintain your composure and address the other person's emotional needs.

REAL-TIME UPDATES
Learn More by Watching This Video

Use negotiation skills to resolve conflicts

Learn how to resolve conflicts through the win-win strategies of empathetic negotiation. Go to http://real-timeupdates.com/bct11 and click on "Learn More." If you are using MyBcommLab, you can access Real-Time Updates within each chapter or under Student Study Tools.

points that you'll need to discuss, or they may reveal problems that you'll need to minimize.[25]

Hold your arguments until the other person is ready for them. Getting your point across depends as much on the other person's frame of mind as it does on your arguments. You can't assume that a strong argument will speak for itself. By becoming more audience centered, you will learn to address the other person's emotional needs first.

Collaborating on Communication Efforts

2   LEARNING OBJECTIVE

Offer guidelines for collaborative communication, identify major collaboration technologies, and explain how to give constructive feedback.

You should expect to collaborate on a wide variety of research, writing, design, and presentation projects in your career. When teams collaborate, the collective energy and expertise of the various members can lead to results that transcend what each individual could do otherwise.[26] However, collaborating on team messages requires special effort; the following section offers a number of helpful guidelines.

GUIDELINES FOR COLLABORATIVE WRITING

In any collaborative effort, team members coming from different backgrounds may have different work habits or priorities: A technical expert may focus on accuracy and scientific standards, an editor may be more concerned about organization and coherence, and a manager may focus on schedules, cost, and corporate goals. In addition, team members differ in writing styles, work habits, and personality traits.

To collaborate effectively, everyone involved must be flexible and open to other opinions, focusing on team objectives rather than on individual priorities.[27] Successful writers know that most ideas can be expressed in many ways, so they avoid the "my way is best" attitude. The following guidelines will help you collaborate more successfully:[28]

Successful collaboration on writing projects requires a number of steps, from selecting the right partners and agreeing on project goals to establishing clear processes and avoiding writing as a group.

- **Select collaborators carefully.** Whenever possible, choose a combination of people who together have the experience, information, and talent needed for each project.
- **Agree on project goals before you start.** Starting without a clear idea of what the team hopes to accomplish inevitably leads to frustration and wasted time.
- **Give your team time to bond before diving in.** If people haven't had the opportunity to work together before, make sure they can get to know each other before being asked to collaborate.
- **Clarify individual responsibilities.** Because members will be depending on each other, make sure individual responsibilities are clear.
- **Establish clear processes.** Make sure everyone knows how the work will be managed from start to finish.
- **Avoid composing as a group.** The actual composition is the only part of developing team messages that usually does not benefit from group participation. Brainstorming the wording of short pieces of text, particularly headlines, slogans, and other high-visibility elements, can be an effective way to stimulate creative word choices. However, for longer projects, you will usually find it more efficient to plan, research, and outline together but assign the task of writing to one person or divide larger projects among multiple writers. If you divide the writing, try to have one person do a final revision pass to ensure a consistent style.
- **Make sure tools and techniques are ready and compatible across the team.** Even minor details such as different versions of software can delay projects.
- **Check to see how things are going along the way.** Don't assume that everything is working just because you don't hear anything negative.

A wide variety of collaboration tools now exist to help professionals work on reports, presentations, and other communication efforts.

TECHNOLOGIES FOR COLLABORATIVE WRITING

A variety of collaboration tools exist to help teams write together. Among the simpler tools are group review and editing features in word processing software and the Adobe Acrobat electronic document system (PDF files) and web-based document systems such as Google

Teams can use a variety of analysis, planning, and decision-making tools, including agenda, cost-benefit tables, and quick polls.

Participants can add to this diagram as the team brainstorms (a SWOT diagram is a planning tool that identifies strengths, weaknesses, opportunities, and threats).

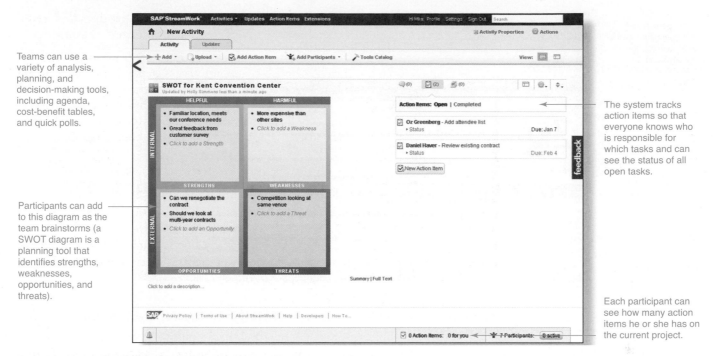

The system tracks action items so that everyone knows who is responsible for which tasks and can see the status of all open tasks.

Each participant can see how many action items he or she has on the current project.

Figure 2.2   Collaboration Technologies
Collaboration technologies such as SAP's StreamWork system help team members work together in real time, with documents, decisions, messages, and other vital project elements accessible to everyone.

Docs. More complex solutions include **content management systems** that organize and control the content for many websites (particularly larger corporate sites). A **wiki**, from the Hawaiian word for *quick*, is a website that allows anyone with access to add new material and edit existing material (see Figure 2.2). Chapter 14 offers guidelines for effective wiki collaboration.

The key benefits of wikis include simple operation—writers don't need to know any of the techniques normally required to create web content—and the freedom to post new or revised material without prior approval. This approach is quite different from a content management system, in which both the organization of the website and the *work flow* (the rules for creating, editing, reviewing, and approving content) are tightly controlled.[29] A content management system is a great tool for maintaining consistent presentation on a company's primary public website, whereas a wiki allows a team to collaborate with speed and flexibility.

Enterprise wiki systems extend the wiki concept with additional features for business use that ensure information quality and confidentiality and also provide the speed and flexibility of a wiki. For instance, *access control* lets a team leader identify who is allowed to read and modify a wiki. *Change monitoring* alerts team members when significant changes or additions are made. And *rollback* allows a team to "travel back in time" to see all previous versions of pages.[30]

Groupware is a general term for computer-based systems that let people communicate, share files, review previous message threads, work on documents simultaneously, and connect using social networking tools. These systems help companies capture and share knowledge from multiple experts, bringing greater insights to bear on tough challenges.[31] **Shared workspaces** are online "virtual offices" that give everyone on a team access to the same set of resources and information: databases, calendars, project plans, pertinent messaging and exchanges, reference materials, and team-created documents (see Figure 2.3 on the following page). You may see some of these workspaces referred to as *intranets* (restricted-access websites that are open to employees only) or *extranets* (restricted sites that are available to employees and to outside parties by invitation only).

In the coming years, keep an eye out for emerging technologies that can help teams collaborate in new ways. For example, *cloud computing*, a somewhat vague term for

Wiki benefits include simple operation and the ability to post new or revised material instantly without a formal review process.

 Give wiki writing a try using the unique Bovée-Thill wiki simulator. Visit http://real-timeupdates.com/bct11, click on "Student Assignments," and then click on any of the wiki exercises.

Each project and program gets its own workspace, which can be shared with designated users inside or outside the company.

Within each workspace, the system organizes tasks, links, messages, project assignments, message archives, and all the other resources a team needs.

The system tracks all recent activity on a project, creating a searchable record of messages, task assignments, and other important details.

Figure 2.3   Shared Workspaces
Zig Marketing uses the WizeHive platform to create shared online workspaces for its employees, business partners, and clients.

"on-demand" software capabilities delivered over the Internet, promises to expand the ways in which geographically dispersed teams can collaborate quickly and inexpensively.[32]

SOCIAL NETWORKS AND VIRTUAL COMMUNITIES

Social networking technologies are becoming vital communication links in many companies.

Chapter 1 explains how social media and the Web 2.0 approach are redefining business communication. Within that context, **social networking technologies** are redefining teamwork and team communication by helping erase the constraints of geographic and organization boundaries. In addition to enabling and enhancing teamwork, social networks have numerous other business applications and benefits; see Table 7.1 on page 184 for more information.

The two fundamental elements of any social networking technology are *profiles* (the information stored about each member of the network) and *connections* (mechanisms for finding and communicating with other members).[33] If you're familiar with Facebook, you have a basic idea of how social networks function. Thousands of companies now use Facebook, but you may also encounter networks created specifically for business use, the most significant being LinkedIn (www.linkedin.com). Others include Ryze (www.ryze.com), Spoke (www.spoke.com), and Xing (www.xing.com).

A *community of practice* links professionals with similar job interests; a key benefit is accumulating long-term organizational knowledge.

Some companies use social networking technologies to form *virtual communities* or *communities of practice* that link employees with similar professional interests throughout the company and sometimes with customers and suppliers as well. The huge advantage that social networking brings to these team efforts is in identifying the best people to collaborate on each problem or project, no matter where they are around the world or what their official roles are in the organization. Such communities are similar to teams in many respects, but one major difference is in the responsibility for accumulating organizational knowledge over the long term. For example, the pharmaceutical company Pfizer has a number of permanent product safety communities that provide specialized advice on drug safety issues to researchers all across the company.[34]

Social networking can also help a company maintain a sense of community even as it grows beyond the size that normally permits a lot of daily interaction. At the online retailer Zappos, fostering a supportive work environment is the company's top priority. To encourage the sense of community among its expanding workforce, Zappos uses social networking tools to track employee connections and encourage workers to reach out and build relationships.[35]

TABLE 2.2	**Giving Constructive Feedback**
How to Be Constructive	**Explanation**
Think through your suggested changes carefully.	Many business documents must illustrate complex relationships between ideas and other information, so isolated and superficial edits can do more harm than good.
Discuss improvements rather than flaws.	Instead of saying "this is confusing," for instance, explain how the writing can be improved to make it clearer.
Focus on controllable behavior.	The writer may not have control over every variable that affected the quality of the message, so focus on those aspects the writer can control.
Be specific.	Comments such as "I don't get this" or "Make this clearer" don't give the writer much direction.
Keep feedback impersonal.	Focus comments on the message, not on the person who created it.
Verify understanding.	If in doubt, ask for confirmation from the recipient to make sure that the person understood your feedback.
Time your feedback carefully.	Respond in a timely fashion so that the writer will have sufficient time to implement the changes you suggest.
Highlight any limitations your feedback may have.	If you didn't have time to give the document a thorough edit, or if you're not an expert in some aspect of the content, let the writer know so that he or she can handle your comments appropriately.

GIVING—AND RESPONDING TO—CONSTRUCTIVE FEEDBACK

Aside from processes and tools, collaborative communication often involves giving and receiving feedback about writing efforts. **Constructive feedback**, sometimes called *constructive criticism*, focuses on the process and outcomes of communication, not on the people involved (see Table 2.2). In contrast, **destructive feedback** delivers criticism with no guidance to stimulate improvement.[36] For example, "This proposal is a confusing mess, and you failed to convince me of anything" is destructive feedback. Your goal is to be more constructive: "Your proposal could be more effective with a clearer description of the manufacturing process and a well-organized explanation of why the positives outweigh the negatives." When giving feedback, avoid personal attacks and give the person clear guidelines for improvement.

When you give writing feedback, make it constructive by focusing on how the material can be improved.

When you receive constructive feedback, resist the understandable urge to defend your work or deny the validity of the feedback. Remaining open to criticism isn't easy when you've poured your heart and soul into a project, but good feedback provides a valuable opportunity to learn and to improve the quality of your work.

When you receive constructive feedback on your writing, keep your emotions in check and view it as an opportunity to improve.

Making Your Meetings More Productive

Much of your workplace communication will occur during in-person or online meetings, so to a large degree, your ability to contribute to the company—and to be recognized for your contributions—will depend on your meeting skills. Well-run meetings can help companies solve problems, develop ideas, and identify opportunities. Meetings can also be a great way to promote team building through the experience of social interaction.[37] As useful as meetings can be, though, they can be a waste of time if they aren't planned and managed well. You can help ensure productive meetings by preparing carefully, conducting meetings efficiently, and using meeting technologies wisely.

3 | LEARNING OBJECTIVE

List the key steps needed to ensure productive team meetings.

Much of the communication you'll participate in will take place in meetings.

PREPARING FOR MEETINGS

The first step in preparing for a meeting is to make sure the meeting is really necessary. Meetings can consume hundreds or thousands of dollars of productive time while taking people away from other work, so don't hold a meeting if some other form of communication

To ensure a successful meeting, decide on your purpose ahead of time, select the right participants, choose the venue and time, and set a clear agenda.

(such as a blog post) can serve the purpose as effectively.[38] If a meeting is truly necessary, proceed with these four planning tasks:

- **Identify your purpose.** Meetings can focus on exchanging information, reaching decisions, or collaborating to solve problems or identify opportunities. Whatever your purpose, identify what the best possible result of the meeting would be (such as "we carefully evaluated all three product ideas and decided which one to invest in"). Use this hoped-for result to shape the direction and content of the meeting.[39]

- **Select participants for the meeting.** The rule here is simple: Invite everyone who really needs to be involved, and don't invite anyone who doesn't. For decision-making meetings, for example, invite only those people who are in a direct position to help the meeting reach its objective. The more people you have, the longer it will take to reach consensus. Meetings with more than 10 or 12 people can become unmanageable if everyone is expected to participate in the discussion and decision making.

- **Choose the venue and the time.** Online meetings (see page 43) are often the best way and sometimes the only way to connect people in multiple locations or to reach large audiences. For onsite meetings, review the facility and the seating arrangements. Are rows of chairs suitable, or do you need a conference table or some other arrangement? Pay attention to room temperature, lighting, ventilation, acoustics, and refreshments; these details can make or break a meeting. If you have control over the timing, morning meetings are often more productive because people are generally more alert and not yet engaged with the work of the day.

- **Set the agenda.** The success of a meeting depends on the preparation of the participants. Distribute a carefully written agenda to participants, giving them enough time to prepare as needed (see Figure 2.4). A productive agenda answers three key questions: (1) What do we need to do in this meeting to accomplish our goals? (2) What issues will be of greatest importance to all participants? (3) What information must be available in order to discuss these issues?[40]

MyBcommLab

Apply Figure 2.4's key concepts by revising a new document. Go to Chapter 2 in mybcommlab.com and select Document Makeovers.

Figure 2.4   Typical Meeting Agenda
Agenda formats vary widely, depending on the complexity of the meeting and the presentation technologies that will be used. For an online meeting, for instance, a good approach is to first send a detailed planning agenda in advance of the meeting so that presenters know what they need to prepare, then create a simpler display agenda such as this to guide the progress of the meeting.

CONDUCTING AND CONTRIBUTING TO EFFICIENT MEETINGS

Everyone in a meeting shares the responsibility for making the meeting productive. If you're the designated leader of a meeting, however, you have an extra degree of responsibility and accountability. The following guidelines will help leaders and participants contribute to more effective meetings:

- **Keep the discussion on track.** A good meeting leader draws out the best ideas the group has to offer and resolves differences of opinion while maintaining progress toward achieving the meeting's purpose and staying on schedule.
- **Follow agreed-upon rules.** The larger the meeting, the more formal you need to be to maintain order. Formal meetings use **parliamentary procedure**, a time-tested method for planning and running effective meetings. The best-known guide to this procedure is *Robert's Rules of Order* (www.robertsrules.com).
- **Encourage participation.** On occasion, some participants will be too quiet and others too talkative. The quiet participants may be shy, they may be expressing disagreement or resistance, or they may be working on unrelated tasks. Draw them out by asking for their input on issues that pertain to them.
- **Participate actively.** If you're a meeting participant, look for opportunities to contribute to both the subject of the meeting and the smooth interaction of the group. Speak up if you have something useful to say but don't monopolize the discussion or talk simply to bring attention to yourself.
- **Close effectively.** At the conclusion of the meeting, verify that the objectives have been met or arrange for follow-up work, if needed. Either summarize the general conclusion of the discussion or the actions to be taken. Make sure all participants have a chance to clear up any misunderstandings.

To review the tasks that contribute to productive meetings, refer to "Checklist: Improving Meeting Productivity."

For formal meetings, it's good practice to appoint one person to record the **minutes**, a summary of the important information presented and the decisions made during a meeting. In smaller or informal meetings, attendees often make their own notes on their copies of the agenda. In either case, a clear record of the decisions made and the people responsible for follow-up action is essential. If your company doesn't have a specific format for minutes, follow the generic format shown in Figure 2.5 on the following page.

Everyone shares the responsibility for successful meetings.

Using Meeting Technologies

A growing array of technologies enables professionals to enhance or even replace traditional meetings. Replacing in-person meetings with long-distance, virtual interaction can dramatically reduce costs and resource usage, reduce wear and tear on employees, and give teams access to a wider pool of expertise. For example, by meeting customers and business partners online instead of in person, during a recent 18-month period Cisco Systems cut its travel-related costs by $100 million, reduced its carbon footprint by millions of tons, and improved employee productivity and satisfaction.[41]

Meeting-replacement technologies have helped spur the emergence of **virtual teams**, whose members work in different locations and interact electronically through **virtual meetings**. Instant messaging (IM) and teleconferencing are the simplest forms of virtual meetings.

4 LEARNING OBJECTIVE

Identify the major technologies used to enhance or replace in-person meetings.

✓ **Checklist** | Improving Meeting Productivity

A. Prepare carefully.
- Make sure the meeting is necessary.
- Decide on your purpose.
- Select participants carefully.
- Choose the venue and the time.
- Establish and distribute a clear agenda.

B. Lead effectively and participate fully.
- Keep the meeting on track.
- Follow agreed-upon rules.
- Encourage participation.
- Participate actively.
- Close effectively.

Figure 2.5   Typical Minutes of a Meeting
Intranet and blog postings are a common way to distribute meeting minutes. The specific format of the minutes is less important than making sure you record all the key information, particularly regarding responsibilities that were assigned during the meeting. Key elements include a list of those present and a list of those who were invited but didn't attend, followed by the times the meeting started and ended, all major decisions reached at the meeting, all assignments of tasks to meeting participants, and all subjects that were deferred to a later meeting. In addition, the minutes objectively summarize important discussions, noting the names of those who contributed major points. Outlines, subheadings, and lists help organize the minutes; additional documentation (such as tables or charts submitted by meeting participants) is noted in the minutes and attached. Many companies now post meeting minutes on internal websites for easy reference.

MyBcommLab

Apply Figure 2.5's key concepts by revising a new document. Go to Chapter 2 in mybcommlab.com and select Document Makeovers.

Videoconferencing lets participants see and hear each other, demonstrate products, and transmit other visual information. *Telepresence* technologies (see Figure 2.6) enable realistic conferences in which participants thousands of miles apart almost seem to be in the same room.[42] The ability to convey nonverbal subtleties such as facial expressions and hand gestures makes these systems particularly good for negotiations, collaborative problem solving, and other complex discussions.[43]

The most sophisticated web-based meeting systems combine the best of real-time communication, shared workspaces, and videoconferencing with other tools, such as *virtual whiteboards*, that let teams collaborate in real time. Such systems are used for everything from spontaneous discussions among small groups to carefully planned, formal events such as customer training seminars or press conferences.[44]

Virtual meeting technologies connect people spread around the country or around the world.

Technology continues to create intriguing opportunities for online interaction. For instance, one of the newest virtual tools is online brainstorming, in which a company can conduct "idea campaigns" to generate new ideas from people across the organization. These range from small team meetings to huge events such as IBM's giant InnovationJam, in which 100,000 IBM employees, family members, and customers from 160 countries were invited to brainstorm online for three days.[45]

Companies are also beginning to experiment with virtual meetings and other communication activities in virtual worlds that range from realistic-looking environments that represent offices and conference rooms (see Figure 2.7) to the otherworldly environment of Second Life (www.secondlife.com). In Second Life, professionals can create online *avatars* to represent themselves in meetings, training sessions, sales presentations, and even casual conversations with customers they happen to bump into (see page 18 for an example of business communication in Second Life).

Conducting successful meetings over the phone or online requires extra planning before the meeting and more diligence during the meeting. Because virtual meetings offer less visual contact and nonverbal communication than in-person meetings, leaders need to make sure everyone stays engaged and has the opportunity to contribute. Paying attention during online meetings takes greater effort as well. Participants need to stay committed to the meeting and resist the temptation to work on unrelated tasks.[46]

For the latest information on meeting technologies, visit http://real-timeupdates.com/bct11 and click on Chapter 2.

Figure 2.6   Telepresence
How many people are in this conference room in Chicago? Only the two people in the foreground are in the conference room; the other six are in Atlanta and London. Virtual meeting technologies such as this telepresence system connect people spread across the country or around the world.

The virtual environment is made up of offices, conference rooms, and other spaces where people can interact through IM chat, voice conferencing, and document sharing.

Informal meeting spaces can also be created, such as the "courtyard" shown here.

Colleagues are available at the click of a mouse.

Here is the transcript of an IM conversation taking place in the courtyard.

Figure 2.7   Virtual Meetings
Virtual meeting technologies offer a variety of ways to interact online. The Team Space system from Sococo mimics the layout of an office building, allowing users to click into offices, conference rooms, and other spaces to initiate virtual meetings and presentations.

Improving Your Listening Skills

5   LEARNING OBJECTIVE

Identify three major modes of listening, describe the listening process, and explain the problem of selective listening.

Your long-term career prospects are closely tied to your ability and willingness to listen. Effective listening strengthens organizational relationships, alerts an organization to opportunities for innovation, and allows an organization to manage diversity both in the workforce and in the customers it serves.[47] Companies whose employees and managers listen effectively stay in touch, up to date, and out of trouble. Some 80 percent of top executives say that listening is the most important skill needed to get things done in the workplace.[48] Plus, today's younger employees place a high premium on being heard, so listening is becoming even more vital for managers.[49] In fact, many of the leading business schools in the United States have begun retooling their curricula in recent years to put more emphasis on "soft skills" such as listening.[50]

RECOGNIZING VARIOUS TYPES OF LISTENING

To be a good listener, adapt the way you listen to suit the situation.

Effective listeners adapt their listening approaches to different situations. The primary goal of **content listening** is to understand and retain the information in the speaker's message. Because you're not evaluating the information at this point, it doesn't matter whether you agree or disagree, approve or disapprove—only that you understand. Try to overlook the speaker's style and any limitations in the presentation; just focus on the information.[51]

The goal of **critical listening** is to understand and evaluate the meaning of the speaker's message on several levels: the logic of the argument, the strength of the evidence, the validity of the conclusions, the implications of the message, the speaker's intentions and motives, and the omission of any important or relevant points. If you're skeptical, ask questions to explore the speaker's point of view and credibility. Be on the lookout for bias that could color the way the information is presented and be careful to separate opinions from facts.[52]

The goal of **empathic listening** is to understand the speaker's feelings, needs, and wants so that you can appreciate his or her point of view, regardless of whether you share that perspective. By listening with empathy, you help the individual vent the emotions that prevent a calm, clear-headed approach to the subject. Avoid the temptation to jump in with advice unless the person specifically asks for it. Also, don't judge the speaker's feelings and don't try to tell people they shouldn't feel this or that emotion. Instead, let the speaker know that you appreciate his or her feelings and understand the situation. After you establish that connection, you can help the speaker move on to search for a solution.[53]

Listening actively means making the effort to turn off your internal filters and biases to truly hear and understand what the other person is saying.

No matter what mode they are using at any given time, effective listeners try to engage in **active listening**, making a conscious effort to turn off their own filters and biases to truly hear and understand what the other party is saying. They ask questions to verify key points and encourage the speaker through positive body language.[54]

UNDERSTANDING THE LISTENING PROCESS

Listening involves five steps: receiving, decoding, remembering, evaluating, and responding.

Listening is a far more complex process than most people think—and most of us aren't very good at it. People typically listen at no better than a 25 percent efficiency rate, remember only about half of what's said during a 10-minute conversation, and forget half of that within 48 hours.[55] Furthermore, when questioned about material they've just heard, they are likely to get the facts mixed up.[56]

Listening follows the same sequence as the general communication process model described in Chapter 1 (page 10), with the added challenge that it happens in real time. To listen effectively, you need to successfully complete five separate steps:[57]

1. **Receiving.** You start by physically hearing the message and acknowledging it. Physical reception can be blocked by noise, impaired hearing, or inattention. Some experts also include nonverbal messages as part of this stage because these factors influence the listening process as well.

2. **Decoding.** Your next step is to assign meaning to sounds, which you do according to your own values, beliefs, ideas, expectations, roles, needs, and personal history.

REAL-TIME UPDATES
Learn More by Watching
This PowerPoint Presentation

Take a fast course in listening skills

This brief online course will help make you a better listener on the job and in every other aspect of life. Go to http://real-timeupdates.com/bct11 and click on "Learn More." If you are using MyBcommLab, you can access Real-Time Updates within each chapter or under Student Study Tools.

3. **Remembering.** Before you can act on the information, you need to store it for future processing. As you learned in Chapter 1, incoming messages must first be captured in short-term memory before being transferred to long-term memory for more permanent storage.
4. **Evaluating.** Your next step is to evaluate the message by applying critical thinking skills to separate fact from opinion and evaluate the quality of the evidence.
5. **Responding.** After you've evaluated the speaker's message, you react. If you're communicating one-on-one or in a small group, the initial response generally takes the form of verbal feedback. If you're one of many in an audience, your initial response may take the form of applause, laughter, or silence. Later on, you may act on what you have heard.

REAL-TIME UPDATES
Learn More by Watching This Video

Are you a good listener?

Most of us believe we are good listeners, but the constant communication breakdowns in business and personal settings is evidence that we could all improve. Go to http://real-timeupdates .com/bct11 and click on "Learn More." If you are using MyBcommLab, you can access Real-Time Updates within each chapter or under Student Study Tools.

If any one of these steps breaks down, the listening process becomes less effective or even fails entirely. As both a sender and a receiver, you can reduce the failure rate by recognizing and overcoming a variety of physical and mental barriers to effective listening.

OVERCOMING BARRIERS TO EFFECTIVE LISTENING

Good listeners look for ways to overcome potential barriers throughout the listening process (see Table 2.3). Some factors you may not be able to control, such as conference room acoustics or poor phone reception. However, you can control other factors, such as not interrupting speakers and not creating distractions that make it difficult for others to pay attention. And don't think that you're not interrupting just because you're not talking. Such actions as texting or checking your watch can interrupt a speaker and lead to communication breakdowns.

Selective listening is one of the most common barriers to effective listening. If your mind wanders, you may stay tuned out until you hear a word or phrase that gets your attention again. But by that time, you're unable to recall what the speaker *actually* said; instead, you remember what you think the speaker *probably* said.[58]

One reason listeners' minds tend to wander is that people think faster than they speak. Most people speak at about 120 to 150 words per minute, but listeners can process audio information at up to 500 words per minute or more.[59] Consequently, your brain has a lot of free time whenever you're listening, and if left unsupervised, it will find a thousand other things to think

Good listeners actively try to overcome the barriers to successful listening.

Your mind can process information much faster than most speakers talk, so you need to focus to listen effectively.

TABLE 2.3	**What Makes an Effective Listener?**
Effective Listeners	**Ineffective Listeners**
• Listen actively.	• Listen passively.
• Take careful and complete notes, when applicable.	• Take no notes or ineffective notes.
• Make frequent eye contact with the speaker (depends on culture to some extent).	• Make little or no eye contact—or inappropriate eye contact.
• Stay focused on the speaker and the content.	• Allow their minds to wander, are easily distracted, work on unrelated tasks.
• Mentally paraphrase key points to maintain attention level and ensure comprehension.	• Fail to paraphrase.
• Adjust listening style to the situation.	• Listen with the same style, regardless of the situation.
• Give the speaker nonverbal cues (such as nodding to show agreement or raising eyebrows to show surprise or skepticism).	• Fail to give the speaker nonverbal feedback.
• Save questions or points of disagreement until an appropriate time.	• Interrupt whenever they disagree or don't understand.
• Overlook stylistic differences and focus on the speaker's message.	• Are distracted by or unduly influenced by stylistic differences; are judgmental.
• Make distinctions between main points and supporting details.	• Unable to distinguish main points from details.
• Look for opportunities to learn.	• Assume they already know everything that's important to know.

✓ **Checklist** | **Overcoming Barriers to Effective Listening**

- Lower barriers to physical reception whenever you can (such as avoiding interrupting speakers by asking questions or by exhibiting disruptive nonverbal behaviors).
- Avoid selective listening by focusing on the speaker and carefully analyzing what you hear.
- Keep an open mind by avoiding any prejudgment and by not listening defensively.

- Don't count on your memory; write down or record important information.
- Improve your short-term memory by repeating information or breaking it into shorter lists.
- Improve your long-term memory by using association, categorization, visualization, and mnemonics.

about. Make the effort to focus on the speaker and use the extra time to analyze and paraphrase what you hear or to take relevant notes.

Overcoming interpretation barriers can be difficult because you may not even be aware of them. As Chapter 1 notes, selective perception leads listeners to mold messages to fit their own conceptual frameworks. Listeners sometimes make up their minds before fully hearing the speaker's message, or they engage in *defensive listening*—protecting their egos by tuning out anything that doesn't confirm their beliefs or their view of themselves.

Even when your intentions are good, you can still misinterpret incoming messages if you and the speaker don't share enough language or experience. When listening to a speaker whose native language or life experience is different from yours, try to paraphrase that person's ideas. Give the speaker a chance to confirm what you think you heard or to correct any misinterpretation.

> When information is crucial, don't count on your memory—record the information mechanically or electronically.

If the information you hear will be important to use later, write it down or otherwise record it. Don't rely on your memory. If you do need to memorize, you can hold information in short-term memory by repeating it silently or organizing a long list of items into several shorter lists. To store information in long-term memory, four techniques can help: (1) Associate new information with something closely related (such as the restaurant in which you met a new client), (2) categorize the new information into logical groups (such as alphabetizing a list of names), (3) visualize words and ideas as pictures, and (4) create mnemonics such as acronyms or rhymes.

For a reminder of the steps you can take to overcome listening barriers, see "Checklist: Overcoming Barriers to Effective Listening."

Improving Your Nonverbal Communication Skills

> **6** | **LEARNING OBJECTIVE**
>
> Explain the importance of nonverbal communication, and identify six major categories of nonverbal expression.

> Nonverbal communication can supplement or even replace verbal messages (those that use words).

Nonverbal communication is the interpersonal process of sending and receiving information, both intentionally and unintentionally, without using written or spoken language. Nonverbal signals play a vital role in communication because they can strengthen a verbal message (when the nonverbal signals match the spoken words), weaken a verbal message (when nonverbal signals don't match the words), or replace words entirely. For example, you might tell a client that a project is coming along nicely, but your forced smile and nervous glances will send an entirely different message.

RECOGNIZING NONVERBAL COMMUNICATION

Paying special attention to nonverbal signals in the workplace will enhance your ability to communicate successfully. The range and variety of nonverbal signals are almost endless, but you can grasp the basics by studying six general categories:

> Nonverbal signals include facial expression, gesture and posture, vocal characteristics, personal appearance, touch, and time and space.

- **Facial expression.** Your face is the primary vehicle for expressing your emotions; it reveals both the type and the intensity of your feelings.[60] Your eyes are especially effective for indicating attention and interest, influencing others, regulating interaction, and establishing dominance.[61]
- **Gesture and posture.** The way you position and move your body expresses both specific and general messages, some voluntary and some involuntary. Many gestures—a wave of the hand, for example—have specific and intentional meanings. Other types of body movement are unintentional and express more general messages. Slouching, leaning forward,

fidgeting, and walking briskly are all unconscious signals that can reveal whether you feel confident or nervous, friendly or hostile, assertive or passive, powerful or powerless.

- **Vocal characteristics.** Voice carries both intentional and unintentional messages. A speaker can intentionally control pitch, pace, and stress to convey a specific message. For instance, compare "*What* are you doing?" and "What are *you* doing?" Unintentional vocal characteristics can convey happiness, surprise, fear, and other emotions (for example, fear often increases the pitch and the pace of your speaking voice).
- **Personal appearance.** Although an individual's body type and facial features impose limitations, you can control grooming, clothing, accessories, piercings, tattoos, and hairstyle. To make a good impression, adopt the style of the people you want to impress.
- **Touch.** Touch is governed by cultural customs that establish who can touch whom and how in various circumstances. In the United States and Great Britain, for instance, people usually touch less frequently than people in France or Costa Rica do. Even within each culture's norms, however, individual attitudes toward touch vary widely. A manager might be comfortable using hugs to express support or congratulations, but his or her subordinates could interpret those hugs as a show of dominance or sexual interest.[62] Touch is a complex subject. The best advice: When in doubt, don't touch.
- **Time and space.** Like touch, time and space can be used to assert authority, imply intimacy, and send other nonverbal messages. For instance, some people try to demonstrate their own importance or disregard for others by making other people wait; others show respect by being on time. Similarly, taking care not to invade private space, such as standing too close when talking, is a way to show respect for others. Keep in mind that expectations regarding both time and space vary by culture.

USING NONVERBAL COMMUNICATION EFFECTIVELY

Paying attention to nonverbal cues will make you both a better speaker and a better listener. When you're talking, be more conscious of the nonverbal cues you could be sending. Are they effective without being manipulative? Consider a situation in which an employee has come to you to talk about a raise. This situation is stressful for the employee, so don't say you're interested in what she has to tell you and then spend your time glancing at your computer or checking your watch. Conversely, if you already know you won't be able to give her the raise, be honest in your expression of emotions. Don't overcompensate for your own stress by smiling too broadly or shaking her hand too vigorously. Both nonverbal signals would raise her hopes without justification. In either case, match your nonverbal cues to the tone of the situation.

Also consider the nonverbal signals you send when you're not talking—the clothes you wear, the way you sit, the way you walk. Are you talking like a serious business professional but dressing like you belong in a dance club or a frat house? (Appropriate clothing for work situations is discussed in the next section, on business etiquette.)

When you listen, be sure to pay attention to the speaker's nonverbal cues. Do they amplify the spoken words or contradict them? Is the speaker intentionally using nonverbal signals to send you a message that he or she can't put into words? Be observant but don't assume that you can "read someone like a book." Nonverbal signals are powerful, but they aren't infallible, particularly if you don't know a person's normal behavioral patterns.[63] For example, contrary to popular belief, avoiding eye contact and covering one's face while

Work to make sure your nonverbal signals match the tone and content of your spoken communication.

What signals does your personal appearance send?

✓ Checklist   Improving Nonverbal Communication Skills

- Understand the roles that nonverbal signals play in communication, complementing verbal language by strengthening, weakening, or replacing words.
- Note that facial expressions (especially eye contact) reveal the type and intensity of a speaker's feelings.
- Watch for cues from gestures and posture.
- Listen for vocal characteristics that can signal the emotions underlying the speaker's words.

- Recognize that listeners are influenced by physical appearance.
- Be careful with physical contact; touch can convey positive attributes but can also be interpreted as dominance or sexual interest.
- Pay attention to the use of time and space.

talking are not reliable clues that someone is lying. Even when telling the truth, most people don't make uninterrupted eye contact with the listeners, and various gestures such as touching one's face might be normal behavior for particular people.[64] Moreover, these and other behaviors may be influenced by culture (in some cultures, sustained eye contact can be interpreted as a sign of disrespect) or might just be ways of coping with stressful situations.[65]

If something doesn't feel right, ask the speaker an honest and respectful question; doing so may clear everything up, or it may uncover issues you need to explore further. See "Checklist: Improving Nonverbal Communication Skills" for a summary of key ideas regarding nonverbal skills.

Developing Your Business Etiquette

Etiquette is an essential element of every aspect of business communication.

You may have noticed a common thread running through the topics of successful teamwork, productive meetings, effective listening, and nonverbal communication: All these activities depend on mutual respect and consideration among all participants. As Chapter 1 notes, etiquette is now considered an essential business skill. Nobody wants to work with someone who is rude to colleagues or an embarrassment to the company. Moreover, shabby treatment of others in the workplace can be a huge drain on morale and productivity.[66] Poor etiquette can drive away customers, investors, and other critical audiences—and it can limit your career potential.

This section addresses some key etiquette points to remember when you're in the workplace, out in public, and online. Long lists of etiquette rules can be difficult to remember, but you can get by in most every situation by being aware of your effect on others, treating everyone with respect, and keeping in mind that the impressions you leave behind can have a lasting effect on you and your company—so make sure to leave positive impressions wherever you go.

BUSINESS ETIQUETTE IN THE WORKPLACE

Personal appearance can have considerable impact on your success in business.

Workplace etiquette includes a variety of behaviors, habits, and aspects of nonverbal communication. Although it isn't always thought of as an element of etiquette, your personal appearance in the workplace sends a strong signal to managers, colleagues, and customers. Pay attention

---

COMMUNICATING ACROSS CULTURES

Whose Skin Is This, Anyway?

Generational differences abound in the workplace, but few are quite as visible as *body art*: tattoos, piercings (other than ear lobes), and hair dyes in unconventional colors. According to survey data from the Pew Research Center, people younger than 40 are much more inclined than those over 40 to display some form of body art. For example, people 26 to 40 years old are four times more likely to have tattoos than people who are 41 to 64 years old.

With such profound differences, it's no surprise that body art has become a contentious issue in many workplaces, between employees wanting to express themselves and employers wanting to maintain particular standards of professional appearance. As employment law attorney Danielle S. Urban notes, the issue gets even more complicated when religious symbolism is involved.

Who is likely to win this battle? Will the body art aficionados who continue to join the workforce and who are now rising up the managerial ranks force a change in what is considered acceptable appearance in the workplace? Or will they be forced to cover up in order to meet traditional standards?

So far, most companies appear to be relying on the judgment of their employees and managers, rather than enforcing strict guidelines. Many seem to accept that tastes and norms are changing and that body art has become a widespread form of self-expression rather than a mode of rebellion. Job seekers are still advised to be discrete, however, particularly with facial piercings and large, visible tattoos. The nonverbal signals you think you are sending might not be the signals a hiring manager receives.

CAREER APPLICATIONS

1. Should companies have stricter standards of appearance for "customer-facing" employees than for employees who do not interact with customers? Why or why not?

2. Should companies allow their employees the same freedom of expression and appearance latitude as their customers exhibit? For example, if a firm's clientele tends to be heavily tattooed, should employees be allowed the same freedom? Why or why not?

TABLE 2.4	Assembling a Business Wardrobe		
1 **Smooth and Finished** **(Start with This)**	**2** **Elegant and Refined** **(To Column 1, Add This)**	**3** **Crisp and Starchy** **(To Column 2, Add This)**	**4** **Up-to-the-Minute Trendy** **(To Column 3, Add This)**
1. Choose well-tailored clothing that fits well; it doesn't have to be expensive, but it does have to fit and be appropriate for business.	1. Choose form-fitting (but not skin-tight) clothing—not swinging or flowing fabrics, frills, or fussy trimmings.	1. Wear blouses or shirts that are or appear starched.	1. Supplement your foundation with pieces that reflect the latest styles.
2. Keep buttons, zippers, and hemlines in good repair.	2. Choose muted tones and soft colors or classics, such as a dark blue suit or a basic black dress.	2. Choose closed top-button shirts or button-down shirt collars, higher-neckline blouses, or long sleeves with French cuffs and cuff links.	2. Add a few pieces in bold colors but wear them sparingly to avoid a garish appearance.
3. Select shoes that are comfortable enough for long days but neither too casual nor too dressy for the office; keep shoes clean and in good condition.	3. If possible, select a few classic pieces of jewelry (such as a string of pearls or diamond cuff links) for formal occasions.	3. Wear creased trousers or a longer skirt hemline.	3. Embellish your look with the latest jewelry and hairstyles but keep the overall effect looking professional.
4. Make sure the fabrics you wear are clean, are carefully pressed, and do not wrinkle easily.	4. Wear jackets that complement an outfit and lend an air of formality to your appearance. Avoid jackets with more than two tones; one color should dominate.		
5. Choose colors that flatter your height, weight, skin tone, and style; sales advisors in good clothing stores can help you choose.			

to the style of dress where you work and adjust your style to match. Expectations for specific jobs, companies, and industries can vary widely. The financial industries tend to be more formal than high technology, for instance, and sales and executive positions usually involve more formal expectations than positions in engineering or manufacturing. Observe others, and don't be afraid to ask for advice. If you're not sure, dress modestly and simply—earn a reputation for what you can do, not for what you can wear. Table 2.4 offers some general guidelines on assembling a business wardrobe that's cost-effective and flexible.

Grooming is as important as attire. Pay close attention to cleanliness and avoid using products with powerful scents, such as perfumed soaps, colognes, shampoos, and after-shave lotions (many people are bothered by these products, and some are allergic to them). Shampoo your hair frequently, keep your hands and nails neatly manicured, use mouthwash and deodorant, and make regular trips to a barber or hair stylist.[67]

If you work in an office setting, you'll spend as much time with your officemates as you do with family and friends. Personal demeanor is therefore a vital element of workplace harmony. No one expects (or wants) you to be artificially upbeat and bubbly every second of the day, but a single negative personality can make an entire office miserable. Rude behavior is more than an etiquette issue, too; it can have serious financial costs through lower productivity and lost business opportunities.[68] Every person in the company has a responsibility to contribute to a positive, energetic work environment.

Given the telephone's central role in business communication, phone skills are essential in most professions. Because phone calls lack the visual richness of face-to-face conversations, you have to rely on your attitude and tone of voice to convey confidence and professionalism. Table 2.5 on the next page summarizes helpful tips for placing and receiving phone calls in a confident, professional manner.

Mobile phones are a contentious point of etiquette in today's workplace. They can boost productivity if used mindfully, but they can be a productivity- and morale-draining disruption when used carelessly. Be aware that attitudes about mobile phones vary widely, and don't be surprised if you encounter policies restricting their use in offices or meeting rooms. Nearly half of U.S. companies already have such policies.[69]

Mobile phones are a frequent source of etiquette blunders.

TABLE 2.5	Quick Tips for Improving Your Phone Skills		
General Tips	**Placing Calls**	**Receiving Calls**	**Using Voice Mail**
Use frequent verbal responses that show you're listening ("Oh yes," "I see," "That's right").	Be ready before you call so that you don't waste the other person's time.	Answer promptly and with a smile so that you sound friendly and positive.	When recording your own outgoing message, make it brief and professional.
Increase your volume just slightly to convey your confidence.	Minimize the noise level in your environment as much as possible to avoid distracting the other party.	Identify yourself and your company (some companies have specific instructions for what to say when you answer).	If you can, record temporary greetings on days when you are unavailable all day so that callers will know you're gone for the day.
Don't speak in a monotone; vary your pitch and inflections so people know you're interested.	Identify yourself and your organization, briefly describe why you're calling, and verify that you've called at a good time.	Establish the needs of your caller by asking, "How may I help you?" If you know the caller's name, use it.	Check your voice-mail messages regularly and return all necessary calls within 24 hours.
Slow down when conversing with people whose native language isn't the same as yours.	Don't take up too much time. Speak quickly and clearly, and get right to the point of the call.	If you can, answer questions promptly and efficiently; if you can't help, tell them what you can do for them.	Leave simple, clear messages with your name, number (don't assume the recipient has caller ID), purpose for calling, and times when you can be reached.
Stay focused on the call throughout; others can easily tell when you're not paying attention.	Close in a friendly, positive manner and double-check all vital information such as meeting times and dates.	If you must forward a call or put someone one hold, explain what you are doing first.	State your name and telephone number slowly so that the other person can easily write them down; repeat both if the other person doesn't know you.
		If you forward a call to someone else, try to speak with that person first to verify that he or she is available and to introduce the caller.	Be careful what you say; most voice-mail systems allow users to forward messages to anyone else in the system.
		If you take a message for someone else, be complete and accurate, including the caller's name, number, and organization.	Replay your message before leaving the system to make sure it is clear and complete.

Like every other aspect of communication, your phone habits say a lot about how much respect you have for the people around you. Selecting obnoxious ring tones, talking loudly in open offices or public places, using your phone right next to someone else, making excessive or unnecessary personal calls during work hours, invading someone's privacy by using your camera phone without permission, taking or making calls in restrooms and other inappropriate places, texting while someone is talking to you, allowing incoming calls to interrupt meetings or discussions—all are disrespectful choices that will reflect negatively on you.[70]

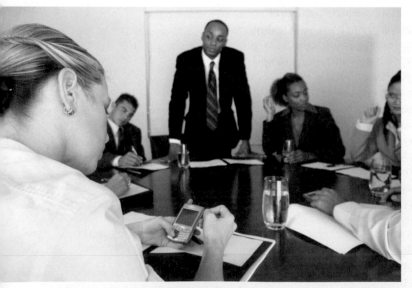

Inappropriate use of mobile phones and other devices is a sign of disrespect.

BUSINESS ETIQUETTE IN SOCIAL SETTINGS

From business lunches to industry conferences, you may represent your company when you're out in public. Make sure your appearance and actions are appropriate to the situation. Get to know the customs of the culture when you meet new people. For example, in North America, a firm handshake is expected when two people meet, whereas a respectful bow of the head is more appropriate in Japan. If you are expected to shake hands, be aware that the passive "dead fish" handshake creates an extremely negative impression. If you are physically able, always stand when shaking someone's hand.

When introducing yourself, include a brief description of your role in the company. When introducing two other people, speak their first and last names clearly and then try to offer some information (perhaps a shared professional interest) to help the two people ease into a conversation.[71] Generally speaking, the lower-ranking person is introduced to the senior-ranking person, without regard to gender.[72]

Business is often conducted over meals, and knowing the basics of dining etiquette will make you more effective in these situations.[73] Start by choosing foods that are easy to eat. Avoid alcoholic beverages in most instances, but if drinking one is appropriate, save it for the end of the meal. Leave business documents under your chair until entrée plates have been removed; the business aspect of the meal doesn't usually begin until then.

Just as in the office, when you use your mobile phone around other people in public, you send the message that people around you aren't as important as your call and that you don't respect your caller's privacy.[74] If it's not a matter of life and death, or at least an urgent request from your boss or a customer, wait until you're back in the office.

Finally, always remember that business meals are a forum for business, period. Don't get on your soapbox about politics, religion, or any other topic that's likely to stir up emotions. Don't complain about work, don't ask deeply personal questions, avoid profanity, and be careful with humor—a joke that entertains some people could easily offend others.

REAL-TIME UPDATES
Learn More by Watching
This PowerPoint Presentation

Don't let etiquette blunders derail your career

Get great advice on developing professional telephone skills, making a positive impression while dining, and dressing for success in any career environment (including great tips on buying business suits). Go to http://real-timeupdates.com/bct11 and click on "Learn More." If you are using MyBcommLab, you can access Real-Time Updates within each chapter or under Student Study Tools.

BUSINESS ETIQUETTE ONLINE

Electronic media seem to be a breeding ground for poor etiquette. Learn the basics of professional online behavior to avoid mistakes that could hurt your company or your career. Here are some guidelines to follow whenever you are representing your company while using electronic media:[75]

- **Avoid personal attacks.** The anonymous and instantaneous nature of online communication can cause even level-headed people to strike out in blog postings, social networks, and other media.
- **Stay focused on the original topic.** If you want to change the subject of an email exchange, a forum discussion, or a blog comment thread, start a new message.
- **Don't present opinions as facts, and support facts with evidence.** This guideline applies to all communication, of course, but online venues in particular seem to tempt people into presenting their beliefs and opinions as unassailable truths.
- **Follow basic expectations of spelling, punctuation, and capitalization.** Sending careless, acronym-filled messages that look like you're texting your high school buddies makes you look like an amateur.
- **Use virus protection and keep it up to date.** Sending or posting a file that contains a computer virus is rude.
- **Ask if this is a good time for an IM chat.** Don't assume that just because a person is showing as "available" on your IM system that he or she wants to chat with you right this instant.
- **Watch your language and keep your emotions under control.** A moment of indiscretion could haunt you forever.
- **Avoid multitasking while using IM and other tools.** You might think you're saving time by doing a dozen things at once, but you're probably making the other person wait while you bounce back and forth between IM and your other tasks.
- **Never assume privacy.** Assume that anything you type will be stored forever, could be forwarded to other people, and might be read by your boss or the company's security staff.
- **Don't use "reply all" in email unless everyone can benefit from your reply.** If one or more recipients of an email message don't need the information in your reply, remove their addresses before you send.
- **Don't waste others' time with sloppy, confusing, or incomplete messages.** Doing so is disrespectful.
- **Respect boundaries of time and virtual space.** For instance, don't start using an employee's personal Facebook page for business messages unless you've discussed it beforehand, and don't assume people are available to discuss work matters around the clock, even if you do find them online in the middle of the night.

When you represent your company online, you must adhere to a high standard of etiquette and respect for others.

Respect personal and professional boundaries when using Facebook and other social networking tools.

Quick Learning Guide

MyBcommLab

If your course uses MyBcommLab, log on to www.mybcommlab.com to access the following study and assessment aids associated with this chapter:

- Video applications
- Real-Time Updates
- Peer review activity
- Pre/post test
- Personalized study plan
- Model documents
- Sample presentations

If you are not using MyBcommLab, you can access Real-Time Updates through http://real-timeupdates.com/bct11.

SUMMARY OF LEARNING OBJECTIVES

1 **List the advantages and disadvantages of working in teams, describe the characteristics of effective teams, and highlight four key issues of group dynamics.** Teams can achieve a higher level of performance than individuals because of the combined intelligence and energy of the group. Motivation and creativity can flourish in team settings. Moreover, individuals tend to perform better because they achieve a sense of purpose by belonging to a group. Teams also bring more input and a greater diversity of views, which tends to result in better decisions. And because team members participate in the decision process, they are more committed to seeing the team succeed. Teams are not without disadvantages, however. Poorly managed teams can be a waste of everyone's time. For example, if members are pressured to conform, they may develop groupthink, which can lead to poor-quality decisions and ill-advised actions. Some members may let their private motives get in the way.

Four important aspects of group dynamics are assuming team roles, allowing for team evolution, resolving conflict, and overcoming resistance.

2 **Offer guidelines for collaborative communication, identify major collaboration technologies, and explain how to give constructive feedback.** Key guidelines for collaborative writing include (1) selecting collaborators carefully, (2) agreeing on project goals before starting, (3) giving the team time to bond before starting the work, (4) clarifying individual responsibilities, (5) establishing clear processes, (6) avoiding composing as a group, (7) making sure tools and techniques are ready and compatible, and (8) checking to see how things are going along the way.

Major collaboration technologies include web content management systems, wikis, groupware, and shared workspaces.

To give constructive feedback, focus on the work and how it can be improved, rather than on the person and the mistakes.

3 **List the key steps needed to ensure productive team meetings.** The most important step in planning a meeting is to make sure that a meeting is necessary and is the best way to accomplish the given objective. If it is, proceed by identifying the purpose of the meeting, selecting the right mix of participants to accomplish the goal, choosing the venue and time carefully, and setting a clear agenda.

Once the meeting is underway, work to keep the discussion on track, follow agreed-upon rules, encourage participation, participate actively yourself, and close the meeting effectively to make sure all decisions and action items are clearly understood.

4 **Identify the major technologies used to enhance or replace in-person meetings.** Meeting enhancement and replacement technologies range from simple audio teleconferencing and IM chat sessions to videoconferences, telepresence systems, web-based meetings, and virtual worlds that range from realistic-looking conference rooms to the otherworldly environment of Second Life.

5 **Identify three major modes of listening, describe the listening process, and explain the problem of selective listening.** *Content listening* is listening to understand and retain the information in the speaker's message. *Critical listening* is listening to understand and evaluate the meaning of the speaker's message on several levels, including the logic of the argument and the strength of the speaker's evidence. *Empathic listening* is listening to understand the speaker's feelings, needs, and wants. Regardless of the mode used, effective listeners try to engage in *active listening*, making a conscious effort to turn off their own filters and biases to truly hear and understand what the other party is saying.

The listening process involves five activities: (1) receiving (physically hearing the message), (2) decoding (assigning meaning to what you hear), (3) remembering (storing the message for future reference), (4) evaluating (thinking about the message), and (5) responding (reacting to the message, taking action, or giving feedback).

The listening process can be hampered by a variety of barriers, one of the most common of which is selective listening. When people listen selectively, they hear only parts of the speaker's message, either because they allow their minds to wander or engage in defensive listening by tuning out information that threatens their beliefs or egos.

6 **Explain the importance of nonverbal communication, and identify six major categories of nonverbal expression.** *Nonverbal communication* is important because nonverbal signals can strengthen, weaken, or even replace verbal messages. The major categories of nonverbal signals are facial expression, gestures and posture, vocal characteristics, personal appearance, touch, and the use of time and space.

7 **Explain the importance of business etiquette, and identify three key areas in which good etiquette is essential.** Attention to etiquette is essential to success in every form of business communication—so much so that etiquette is considered an important business skill. Poor etiquette can hinder team efforts, drain morale and productivity, drive away customers and investors, and limit your career potential. Three key areas in which good etiquette is essential are the workplace, social settings in which you represent your employer, and online interactions in which you represent your employer.

KEY TERMS

active listening Making a conscious effort to turn off filters and biases to truly hear and understand what someone is saying

collaboration Working together to meet complex challenges

committees Formal teams that usually have a long life span and can become a permanent part of the organizational structure

constructive feedback Focuses on the process and outcomes of communication, not on the people involved

content listening Listening to understand and retain the speaker's message

content management systems Computer systems that organize and control the content for websites

critical listening Listening to understand and evaluate the meaning of the speaker's message

destructive feedback Delivers criticism with no guidance to stimulate improvement

empathic listening Listening to understand the speaker's feelings, needs, and wants so that you can appreciate his or her point of view

group dynamics The interactions and processes that take place among the members of a team

groupthink Situation in which peer pressure causes individual team members to withhold contrary or unpopular opinions

groupware Computer-based systems that let people communicate, share files, present materials, and work on documents simultaneously

hidden agenda Private, counterproductive motives, such as a desire to take control of the group

minutes Written summary of the important information presented and the decisions made during a meeting

nonverbal communication Sending and receiving information, both intentionally and unintentionally, without using written or spoken language

norms Informal standards of conduct that members share and that guide member behavior

parliamentary procedure A time-tested method for planning and running effective meetings; the best-known guide to this procedure is *Robert's Rules of Order*

participative management The effort to involve employees in the company's decision making

problem-solving teams Teams that assemble to resolve specific issues and then disband when their goals have been accomplished

selective listening Listening to only part of what a speaker is saying; ignoring the parts one doesn't agree with or find interesting

self-oriented roles Unproductive team roles in which people are motivated mainly to fulfill personal needs

shared workspaces Online "virtual offices" that give everyone on a team access to the same set of resources and information

social networking technologies Online technologies such as LinkedIn and Facebook that help erase the constraints of geographic and organization boundaries

task forces Another form of problem-solving teams, often with members from more than one organization

task-oriented roles Productive team roles directed toward helping the team reach its goals

team A unit of two or more people who share a mission and the responsibility for working to achieve a common goal

team-maintenance roles Productive team roles directed toward helping everyone work well together

virtual meetings Meetings that take place online rather than in person

virtual teams Teams whose members work in different locations and interact electronically

wiki Special type of website that allows anyone with access to add new material and edit existing material

✓ Checklist

Improving Meeting Productivity

A. **Prepare carefully.**
   - Make sure the meeting is necessary.
   - Decide on your purpose.
   - Select participants carefully.
   - Choose the venue and the time.
   - Establish and distribute a clear agenda.

B. **Lead effectively and participate fully.**
   - Keep the meeting on track.
   - Follow agreed-upon rules.
   - Encourage participation.
   - Participate actively.
   - Close effectively.

✓ Checklist

Overcoming Barriers to Effective Listening

- Lower barriers to physical reception whenever you can (such as avoiding interrupting speakers by asking questions or by exhibiting disruptive nonverbal behaviors).
- Avoid selective listening by focusing on the speaker and carefully analyzing what you hear.
- Keep an open mind by avoiding any prejudgment and by not listening defensively.
- Don't count on your memory; write down or record important information.
- Improve your short-term memory by repeating information or breaking it into shorter lists.
- Improve your long-term memory by using association, categorization, visualization, and mnemonics.

✓ Checklist

Improving Nonverbal Communication Skills

- Understand the roles that nonverbal signals play in communication, complementing verbal language by strengthening, weakening, or replacing words.
- Note that facial expressions (especially eye contact) reveal the type and intensity of a speaker's feelings.
- Watch for cues from gestures and posture.
- Listen for vocal characteristics that can signal the emotions underlying the speaker's words.
- Recognize that listeners are influenced by physical appearance.
- Be careful with physical contact; touch can convey positive attributes but can also be interpreted as dominance or sexual interest.
- Pay attention to the use of time and space.

COMMUNICATION CHALLENGES AT **ROSEN LAW FIRM**

You recently joined Rosen Law Firm and quickly became an enthusiastic user of the company's internal wiki. In your brief time being involved with the wiki, you have observed some behavior that runs counter to the spirit of collaborative writing. Study these two scenarios and decide how to respond.

INDIVIDUAL CHALLENGE:
One particular employee keeps editing your pages on the wiki, often making changes that appear to add no value, as far as you can see. She doesn't seem to be editing other employees' pages nearly so often, so you are beginning to wonder if she has a personal grudge against you. You want to address this uncomfortable situation without dragging your boss into it. First, decide how to approach your contentious colleague. Should you drop by her office unannounced, call her on the phone, send her an email message, or perhaps insert a sarcastic comment about excessive editing on one of her wiki pages? Second, whichever mode of communication you've chosen, outline the message you think you should share with her.

TEAM CHALLENGE: A common dilemma in every form of collaborative writing is deciding how soon to share early drafts with your colleagues in order to get their feedback and contributions. Should you send out an unpolished rough draft for the team's input before investing a lot of time in polishing and formatting, or should you do a second or third draft to enhance readability—knowing that the team might delete entire sections that you've worked hard to polish? On the Rosen wiki, some contributors seem to go into "grammar attack mode" whenever a rough draft appears. They seem to ignore the message and content altogether and instead focus on punctuation, grammar, and formatting concerns. With a small team of fellow students, draft some brief guidelines for wiki contributors, conveying these three points: (1) Punctuation, grammar, and formatting are definitely important, but worrying about them too early in the writing process can hamper the free exploration of ideas and information; (2) when reviewing early drafts, wiki users need to make a conscious effort to look past the presentation and focus on the information; and (3) contributors who post rough drafts seeking input should make the pages at least minimally readable so that reviewers can focus on the content and ideas. (To learn more about editing and working with wikis, you can peek ahead to page 147 in Chapter 6 and page 413 in Chapter 14.)

TEST YOUR KNOWLEDGE

To review chapter content related to each question, refer to the indicated Learning Objective.

1. How can organizations and employees benefit from successful teamwork? [LO-1]
2. What is groupthink, and how can it affect an organization? [LO-1]
3. How can employees and companies take advantage of social networking technologies to promote teamwork? [LO-2]
4. Why would a company use a wiki to support team collaboration rather than a content management system? [LO-2]
5. As a team or department leader, what steps can you take to ensure that your meetings are successful and efficient? [LO-3]
6. What are the advantages of virtual meetings? [LO-4]
7. What are the main activities that make up the listening process? [LO-5]
8. How does content listening differ from critical listening and empathic listening? [LO-5]
9. What are the six major categories of nonverbal communication? [LO-6]
10. Why is etiquette an important business skill? [LO-7]

APPLY YOUR KNOWLEDGE

To review chapter content related to each question, refer to the indicated Learning Objective.

1. You head up the interdepartmental design review team for a manufacturer of high-performance motorcycles, and things are not going well at the moment. The design engineers and marketing strategists keep arguing about which should be a higher priority, performance or aesthetics, and the accountants say both groups are driving the cost of the new model through the roof by adding too many new features. Everyone has valid points to make, but the team is bogging down in conflict. Explain how you could go about resolving the stalemate. [LO-1]
2. You and another manager in your company disagree about whether employees should be encouraged to create online profiles on LinkedIn and other business-oriented social networking websites. You say these connections can be valuable to employees by helping them meet their peers throughout the industry and valuable to the company by identifying potential sales leads and business partners. The other manager says that encouraging employees to become better known

in the industry will only make it easier for competitors to lure them away with enticing job offers. Write a brief email message that outlines your argument. (Make up any information you need about the company and its industry.) [LO-2]

3. How can nonverbal communication help you run a meeting? How can it help you call a meeting to order, emphasize important topics, show approval, express reservations, regulate the flow of conversation, and invite a colleague to continue with a comment? [LO-3], [LO-6]

4. Considering what you've learned about nonverbal communication, what are some of the ways in which communication might break down during an online meeting in which the participants can see video images of only the person presenting at any given time—and then only his or her head? [LO-6]

5. Why do you think people are more likely to engage in rude behaviors during online communication than during in-person communication? [LO-7]

PRACTICE YOUR SKILLS

Message for Analysis: Planning Meetings [LO-3]

A project leader has made notes about covering the following items at the quarterly budget meeting. Prepare a formal agenda by putting these items into a logical order and rewriting, where necessary, to give phrases a more consistent sound.

- Budget Committee Meeting to be held on December 12, 2011, at 9:30 a.m., and we have allotted one hour for the meeting
- I will call the meeting to order.
- Real estate director's report: A closer look at cost overruns on Greentree site. (10 minutes)
- The group will review and approve the minutes from last quarter's meeting. (5 minutes)
- I will ask the finance director to report on actual versus projected quarterly revenues and expenses. (15 minutes)
- I will distribute copies of the overall divisional budget and announce the date of the next budget meeting.
- Discussion: How can we do a better job of anticipating and preventing cost overruns? (20 minutes)
- Meeting will take place in Conference Room 3, with WebEx active for remote employees.
- What additional budget issues must be considered during this quarter?

Exercises

Active links for all websites in this chapter can be found on MyBcommLab; see your User Guide for instructions on accessing the content for this chapter. Each activity is labeled according to the primary skill or skills you will need to use. To review relevant chapter content, you can refer to the indicated Learning Objective. In some instances, supporting information will be found in another chapter, as indicated.

1. **Collaboration: Working in Teams [LO-1], [LO-2]** In teams assigned by your instructor, prepare a 10-minute presentation on the potential disadvantages of using social media for business communication. When the presentation is ready, discuss how effective the team was using the criteria of (1) having a clear objective and a shared sense of purpose, (2) communicating openly and honestly, (3) reaching decisions by consensus, (4) thinking creatively, and (5) knowing how to resolve conflict. Be prepared to discuss your findings with the rest of the class.

2. **Collaboration: Working in Teams [LO-1]** In teams of four or five classmates, role play a scenario in which the team is to decide which department at your college will receive a $1 million gift from an anonymous donor. The catch: Each member of the team will advocate for a different department (decide among yourselves who represents which departments), which means that all but one member will "lose" in the final decision. Working as a team, decide which department will receive the donation and discuss the results to help everyone on the team support the decision. Be prepared to present your choice and your justification for it to the rest of the class.

3. **Negotiation and Conflict Resolution: Resolving Conflicts; Communication Ethics: Providing Ethical Leadership [LO-1], Chapter 1** During team meetings, one member constantly calls for votes or decisions before all the members have voiced their views. As the leader, you asked this member privately about his behavior. He replied that he was trying to move the team toward its goals, but you are concerned that he is really trying to take control. How can you deal with this situation without removing the member from the group?

4. **Collaboration: Collaborating on Writing Projects; Media Skills: Blogging [LO-2]** In this project, you will conduct research on your own and then merge your results with those of the rest of your team. Search Twitter for messages on the subject of workplace safety. (You can use Twitter's advanced search page at http://search.twitter.com/advanced or use the "site: twitter.com" qualifier on a regular search engine.) Compile at least five general safety tips that apply to any office setting, and then meet with your team to select the five best tips from all those the team has collected. Collaborate on a blog post that lists the team's top five tips.

 Learn how to use Twitter search. Visit http://real-timeupdates .com/bct11, click on "Students Assignments," and then click on "Twitter Screencast."

5. **Communication Etiquette: Etiquette in the Workplace, Participating in Meetings [LO-3], [LO-7]** In group meetings, some of your colleagues have a habit of interrupting and arguing with the speaker, taking credit for ideas that aren't theirs, and shooting down ideas they don't agree with. You're the newest person in the group and not sure if this is accepted behavior in this company, but it concerns you both personally and professionally. Should you go with the flow and adopt their behavior or stick with your own communication style, even though you might get lost in the noise? In a two-paragraph email message or post for your class blog, explain the pros and cons of both approaches.

6. **Collaboration: Participating in Meetings [LO-3]** With a classmate, attend a local community or campus meeting where you can observe a group discussion, vote, or take other group action. During the meeting, take notes individually and, afterward, work together to answer the following questions.

   a. What is your evaluation of this meeting? In your answer, consider (1) the leader's ability to articulate the meeting's goals clearly, (2) the leader's ability to engage members in a meaningful discussion, (3) the group's dynamics, and (4) the group's listening skills.

   b. How did group members make decisions? Did they vote? Did they reach decisions by consensus? Did those with dissenting opinions get an opportunity to voice their objections?

   c. How well did the individual participants listen? How could you tell?

   d. Did any participants change their expressed views or their votes during the meeting? Why might that have happened?

   e. Did you observe any of the communication barriers discussed in Chapter 1? Identify them.

   f. Compare the notes you took during the meeting with those of your classmate. What differences do you notice? How do you account for these differences?

7. **Collaboration: Leading Meetings [LO-3], Chapter 3** Every month, each employee in your department is expected to give a brief oral presentation on the status of his or her project. However, your department has recently hired an employee who has a severe speech impediment that prevents people from understanding most of what he has to say. As department manager, how will you resolve this dilemma? Please explain.

8. **Collaboration: Using Collaboration Technologies [LO-4]** In a team assigned by your instructor, use Zoho (www.zoho .com; free for personal use), Google Docs (http://docs .google.com), or a comparable system to collaborate on a set of directions that out-of-town visitors could use to reach a specific point on your campus, such as a stadium or dorm. The team should choose the location and the mode(s) of transportation involved. Be creative—brainstorm the best ways to guide first-time visitors to the selected location using all the media at your disposal.

9. **Interpersonal Communication: Listening Actively [LO-5]** For the next several days, take notes on your listening performance during at least a half-dozen situations in class, during social activities, and at work, if applicable. Referring to the traits of effective listeners in Table 2.3 (page 47), rate yourself using *always, frequently, occasionally,* or *never* on these positive listening habits. In a report no longer than one page, summarize your analysis and identify specific areas in which you can improve your listening skills.

10. **Interpersonal Communication: Listening to Empathize [LO-5]** Think back over conversations you have had with friends, family members, coworkers, or classmates in the past week. Select a conversation in which the other person wanted to talk about something that was troubling him or her—a bad situation at work, a scary exam on the horizon, difficulties with a professor, a health problem, financial concerns, or the like. As you replay this conversation in your mind, think about how well you did in terms of empathic listening (see page 46). For example, did you find yourself being critical when the person really just needed someone to listen? Did you let the person know, by your words or actions, that you cared about his or her dilemma, even if you were not able to help in any other way? Analyze your listening performance in a brief email message to your instructor. *Note:* Do not disclose any private information in your message; you can change the names of the people involved or the circumstances as needed to maintain privacy.

11. **Nonverbal Communication: Analyzing Nonverbal Signals [LO-6]** Select a business letter and envelope that you have received at work or home. Analyze their appearance. What nonverbal messages do they send? Are these messages consistent with the content of the letter? If not, what could the sender have done to make the nonverbal communication consistent with the verbal communication? Summarize your findings in a post on your class blog or in an email message to your instructor.

12. **Nonverbal Communication: Analyzing Nonverbal Signals [LO-6]** Describe what the following body movements suggest when someone exhibits them during a conversation. How do such movements influence your interpretation of spoken words? Summarize your findings in a post on your class blog or in an email message to your instructor.

    a. Shifting one's body continuously while seated

    b. Twirling and playing with one's hair

    c. Sitting in a sprawled position

    d. Rolling one's eyes

    e. Extending a weak handshake

13. **Communication Etiquette: Telephone Skills [LO-7]** Late on a Friday afternoon, you learn that the facilities department is going to move you—and your computer, your desk, and all your files—to another office first thing Monday morning. However, you have an important client meeting scheduled in your office for Monday afternoon, and you need to finalize some contract details on Monday morning. You simply can't lose access to your office at this point, and you're more than a little annoyed that your boss didn't ask you before approving the move. He has already left for the day, but you know he usually checks his voice mail over the weekend, so you decide to leave a message, asking him to cancel the move or at least call you at home as soon as possible. Using the voice-mail guidelines listed in Table 2.5 (page 52), plan your message (use an imaginary phone number as your contact number and make up any other details you need for the call). As directed by your instructor, submit either a written script of the message or a podcast recording of the actual message.

14. **Communication Etiquette: Etiquette in the Workplace [LO-7]** As the local manager of an international accounting firm, you place high priority on professional etiquette. Not only does it communicate respect to your clients, it also instills confidence in your firm by showing that you and your staff are aware of and able to meet the expectations of

almost any audience. Earlier today, you took four recently hired college graduates to lunch with an important client. You've done this for years, and it's usually an upbeat experience for everyone, but today's lunch was a disaster. One of the new employees made not one, not two, but three calls on his mobile phone during lunch. Another interrupted the client several times and even got into a mild argument. The third employee kept making sarcastic jokes about politics, making everyone at the table uncomfortable. And the fourth showed up dressed like she was expecting to bale hay or work in a coal mine, not have a business lunch in a posh restaurant. You've already called the client to apologize, but now you need to coach these employees on proper business etiquette. Draft a brief memo to these employees, explaining why etiquette is so important to the company's success—and to their individual careers.

EXPAND YOUR SKILLS

Critique the Professionals

Celebrities can learn from successful businesses when it comes to managing their careers, but businesses can learn from successful celebrities, too—particularly when it comes to building communities online using social media. For instance, social media guru Dan Schawbel cites Vin Diesel, Ashton Kutcher, Lady Gaga, Lenny Kravitz, and Michael Phelps as celebrities who have used Facebook to build their personal brands.[76] Locate three celebrities (musicians, actors, authors, or athletes) who have sizable fan bases on Facebook and analyze how they use the social network. Using whatever medium your instructor requests, write a brief analysis (no more than one page) of the lessons, positive or negative, that a business could learn from these celebrities. Be sure to cite specific elements from the Facebook pages you've chosen, and if you think any of the celebrities have made mistakes in their use of Facebook, describe those as well.

Sharpening Your Career Skills Online

Bovée and Thill's Business Communication Web Search, at http://businesscommunicationblog.com/websearch, is a unique research tool designed specifically for business communication research. Use the Web Search function to find an online video, a podcast, or a PowerPoint presentation that offers advice on improving your active listening skills in business situations. Write a brief email message to your instructor, describing the item that you found and summarizing the career skills information you learned from it.

3 | Communicating in a World of Diversity

LEARNING OBJECTIVES After studying this chapter, you will be able to

1 Discuss the opportunities and challenges of intercultural communication

2 Define *culture*, explain how culture is learned, and define *ethnocentrism* and *stereotyping*

3 Explain the importance of recognizing cultural variations, and list eight categories of cultural differences

4 List four general guidelines for adapting to any business culture

5 Identify seven steps you can take to improve your intercultural communication skills

MyBcommLab Test your mastery of this chapter and its Learning Objectives. Visit mybcommlab.com to apply what you've learned in Document Makeovers and interactive simulation scenarios.

COMMUNICATION CLOSE-UP AT IBM

Ron Glover oversees IBM's efforts to build a competitive advantage by capitalizing on the benefits of a diverse workforce.

www.ibm.com

The *I* in IBM stands for *International*, but it could just as easily stand for *Intercultural*, as a testament to the computer giant's long-standing commitment to embracing diversity. Ron Glover, IBM's vice president of global workforce diversity, knows from years of experience that communicating successfully across cultures is no simple task, however—particularly in a company that employs more than 350,000 people and sells to customers in roughly 175 countries around the world.

Language presents a formidable barrier to communication when you consider that IBM's employees speak more than 165 languages. But language is just one of many elements that play a role in communication between cultures. Differences in age, ethnic background, gender, sexual orientation, physical ability, and economic status can all affect the communication process. Glover emphasizes that "to operate successfully, we must be especially mindful of how we respect and value differences among people in countries and regions." He recognizes that these differences represent both a challenge and an opportunity, and a key part of his job is helping IBM executives and employees work together in a way that transforms their cultural differences into a critical business strength. Diversity, he explains, is "an essential aspect of IBM's broader business strategy." To emphasize this fact, managers cannot receive a top performance ranking unless they can demonstrate that they are practicing IBM's diversity values.

Throughout its long history of employing and working with people from a variety of cultures, IBM has learned some powerful lessons. Perhaps the most significant is its conclusion that successfully managing a diverse workforce and competing in a diverse marketplace starts with embracing those differences, not trying to ignore them or pretending they don't affect interpersonal communication. Take Ron Glover's advice when he says that even if your company never does business internationally, "you will need to effectively engage differences to remain viable in the economy of the future."[1]

Understanding the Opportunities and Challenges of Communication in a Diverse World

IBM's experience (profiled in the chapter-opening Communication Close-up) illustrates the opportunities and the challenges for business professionals who know how to communicate with diverse audiences. Although the concept is often framed in terms of ethnic background, a broader and more useful definition of **diversity** includes "all the characteristics and experiences that define each of us as individuals."[2] As one example, the pharmaceutical company Merck identifies 19 separate dimensions of diversity in its discussions of workforce diversity, including race, age, military experience, parental status, marital status, and thinking style.[3] As you'll learn in this chapter, these characteristics and experiences can have a profound effect on the way businesspeople communicate.

Intercultural communication is the process of sending and receiving messages between people whose cultural backgrounds could lead them to interpret verbal and non-verbal signs differently. Every attempt to send and receive messages is influenced by culture, so to communicate successfully, you need a basic grasp of the cultural differences you may encounter and how you should handle them. Your efforts to recognize and bridge cultural differences will open up business opportunities throughout the world and maximize the contributions of all the employees in a diverse workforce.

THE OPPORTUNITIES IN A GLOBAL MARKETPLACE

Thanks to communication and transportation technologies, natural boundaries and national borders are no longer the impassable barriers they once were. Local markets are opening to worldwide competition as businesses of all sizes look for new growth opportunities outside their own countries. Thousands of U.S. businesses depend on exports for significant portions of their revenues. Every year, these companies export hundreds of billions of dollars worth of

1 **LEARNING OBJECTIVE**

Discuss the opportunities and challenges of intercultural communication.

Diversity includes all the characteristics that define people as individuals.

MyBcommLab

● Access this chapter's simulation entitled Communicating in a World of Diversity, located at mybcommlab.com.

You will communicate with people from other cultures throughout your career.

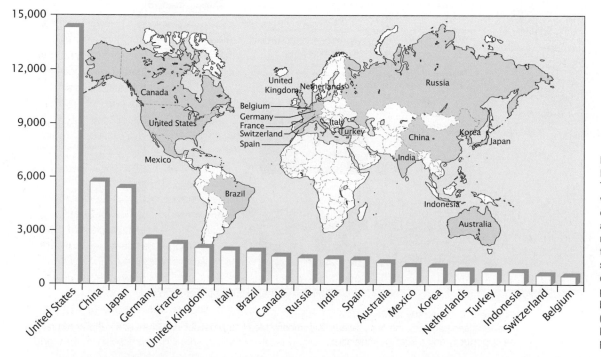

Figure 3.1 World's Biggest Economies This snapshot of the world's twenty largest economies gives you an idea of the global nature of business today. Figures shown are estimates of gross domestic product (GDP) in billions of U.S. dollars. (2010 data from the International Monetary Fund)

materials and merchandise, along with billions more in personal and professional services. If you work in one of these companies, you may well be called on to visit or at least communicate with a wide variety of people who speak languages other than English and who live in cultures quite different from what you're used to (see Figure 3.1 on the previous page). Of the top 10 export markets for U.S. products, only two, Canada and Great Britain, have English as an official language—and Canada also has French as an official language.[4]

THE ADVANTAGES OF A DIVERSE WORKFORCE

The diversity of today's workforce brings distinct advantages to businesses:

- A broader range of views and ideas
- A better understanding of diverse, fragmented markets
- A broader pool of talent from which to recruit

Even if you never visit another country or transact business on a global scale, you will interact with colleagues from a variety of cultures, with a wide range of characteristics and life experiences. Over the past few decades, many innovative companies have changed the way they approach diversity, from seeing it as a legal requirement (providing equal opportunities for all) to seeing it as a strategic opportunity to connect with customers and take advantage of the broadest possible pool of talent.[5] Smart business leaders recognize the competitive advantages of a diverse workforce that offers a broader spectrum of viewpoints and ideas, helps companies understand and identify with diverse markets, and enables companies to benefit from a wider range of employee talents (see Figure 3.2). "It just makes good business sense," says Gord Nixon, CEO of Royal Bank of Canada.[6] According to IBM's Ron Glover, more diverse teams tend to be more innovative over the long term than more homogeneous teams (those on which team members tend to have similar backgrounds).[7]

Merck's top-line message about diversity acknowledges the strategic advantages available to companies that embrace diversity in their hiring and management practices.

Specific supporting points back up the high-level message about the company's commitment to embracing diversity in all facets of its business.

In addition to developing and supporting a diverse workforce, Merck also works closely with a diverse base of suppliers to its various business units.

This diagram lists the 19 dimensions of diversity that Merck takes into account in its management philosophy.

Significant awards and recognitions let potential employers and business partners know that Merck is serious about inclusivity.

Figure 3.2 Diversity at Merck
Like IBM (see page 60), the pharmaceutical company Merck approaches employee and supplier diversity as an opportunity and a strategy imperative.

Diversity is simply a fact of life for all companies. The United States has been a nation of immigrants from the beginning, and that trend continues today. The western and northern Europeans who made up the bulk of immigrants during the nation's early years now share space with people from across Asia, Africa, Eastern Europe, and other parts of the world. Even the term *minority*, as it applies to nonwhite residents, makes less and less sense every year: In two states (California and New Mexico), in several dozen large cities, and about 10 percent of the counties across the United States, Caucasian Americans make up less than half the population.[8] This pattern of immigration isn't unique to the United States. For example, workers from Africa, Asia, and the Middle East are moving to Europe in search of new opportunities, while workers from India, the Philippines, and Southeast Asia contribute to the employment base of the Middle East.[9]

However, you and your colleagues don't need to be recent immigrants to constitute a diverse workforce. Differences in everything from age and gender to religion and ethnic heritage to geography and military experience enrich the workplace. Both immigration and workforce diversity create advantages—and challenges—for business communicators throughout the world.

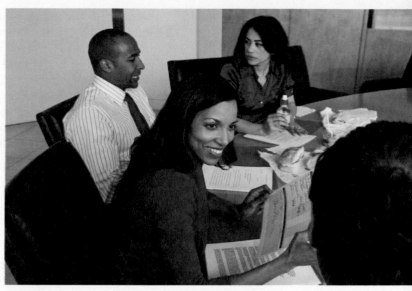

Communication among people of diverse cultural backgrounds and life experiences is not always easy, but doing it successfully can create tremendous strategic advantages.

THE CHALLENGES OF INTERCULTURAL COMMUNICATION

Today's increasingly diverse workforce encompasses a wide range of skills, traditions, backgrounds, experiences, outlooks, and attitudes toward work—all of which can affect communication in the workplace. Supervisors face the challenge of connecting with these diverse employees, motivating them, and fostering cooperation and harmony among them. Teams face the challenge of working together closely, and companies are challenged to coexist peacefully with business partners and with the community as a whole.

The interaction of culture and communication is so pervasive that separating the two is virtually impossible. The way you communicate is deeply influenced by the culture in which you were raised. The meaning of words, the significance of gestures, the importance of time and space, the rules of human relationships—these and many other aspects of communication are defined by culture. To a large degree, your culture influences the way you think, which naturally affects the way you communicate as both a sender and a receiver.[10] Intercultural communication is much more complicated than simply matching language between sender and receiver—it goes beyond mere words to beliefs, values, and emotions.

Elements of human diversity can affect communication at every stage of the communication process (see page 10), from the ideas a person deems important enough to share to the habits and expectations of giving feedback. In particular, your instinct is to encode your message using the assumptions of *your* culture. However, members of your audience decode your message according to the assumptions of *their* culture. The greater the difference between cultures, the greater the chance for misunderstanding.[11]

Throughout this chapter, you'll see examples of how communication styles and habits vary from one culture to another. These examples are intended to illustrate the major themes of intercultural communication, not to give an exhaustive list of styles and habits of any particular culture. With an understanding of these major themes, you'll be prepared to explore the specifics of any culture.

A company's cultural diversity affects how its business messages are conceived, composed, delivered, received, and interpreted.

Culture influences everything about communication, including
- Language
- Nonverbal signals
- Word meaning
- Time and space issues
- Rules of human relationships

Developing Cultural Competency

Cultural competency includes an appreciation for cultural differences that affect communication and the ability to adjust one's communication style to ensure that efforts to send

2 LEARNING OBJECTIVE

Define *culture*, explain how culture is learned, and define *ethnocentrism* and *stereotyping*.

Cultural competency requires a combination of attitude, knowledge, and skills.

and receive messages across cultural boundaries are successful. In other words, it requires a combination of attitude, knowledge, and skills.[12]

The good news is that you're already an expert in culture, at least in the culture in which you grew up. You understand how your society works, how people are expected to communicate, what common gestures and facial expressions mean, and so on. The bad news is that because you're such an expert in your own culture, your communication is largely automatic; that is, you rarely stop to think about the communication rules you're following. An important step toward successful intercultural communication is becoming more aware of these rules and of the way they influence your communication.

UNDERSTANDING THE CONCEPT OF CULTURE

Culture is a shared system of symbols, beliefs, attitudes, values, expectations, and behavior norms.

Culture is a shared system of symbols, beliefs, attitudes, values, expectations, and norms for behavior. Your cultural background influences the way you prioritize what is important in life, helps define your attitude toward what is appropriate in a situation, and establishes rules of behavior.[13]

You belong to several cultures, each of which affects the way you communicate.

Actually, you belong to several cultures. In addition to the culture you share with all the people who live in your own country, you belong to other cultural groups, including an ethnic group, possibly a religious group, and perhaps a profession that has its own special language and customs. With its large population and long history of immigration, the United States is home to a vast array of cultures. As one indication of this diversity, the inhabitants of this country now speak more than 170 languages.[14] In contrast, Japan is much more homogeneous, having only a few distinct cultural groups.[15]

Members of a given culture tend to have similar assumptions about how people should think, behave, and communicate, and they all tend to act on those assumptions in much the same way. Cultures can differ widely and vary in their rate of change, degree of complexity, and tolerance toward outsiders. These differences affect the level of trust and openness that you can achieve when communicating with people of other cultures.

You learn culture both directly (by being instructed) and indirectly (by observing others).

People learn culture directly and indirectly from other members of their group. As you grow up in a culture, you are taught by the group's members who you are and how best to function in that culture. Sometimes you are explicitly told which behaviors are acceptable; at other times you learn by observing which values work best in a particular group. In these ways, culture is passed on from person to person and from generation to generation.[16]

Cultures tend to offer views of life that are both coherent (internally logical) and complete (able to answer all of life's big questions).

In addition to being automatic, culture tends to be *coherent*; that is, a culture appears to be fairly logical and consistent when viewed from the inside. Certain norms within a culture may not make sense to someone outside the culture, but they probably make sense to those inside. Such coherence generally helps a culture function more smoothly internally, but it can create disharmony between cultures that don't view the world in the same way.

Finally, cultures tend to be complete; that is, they provide most of their members with most of the answers to life's big questions. This idea of completeness dulls or even suppresses curiosity about life in other cultures. Not surprisingly, such completeness can complicate communication with other cultures.[17]

OVERCOMING ETHNOCENTRISM AND STEREOTYPING

Ethnocentrism is the tendency to judge all other groups according to the standards, behaviors, and customs of one's own group.

Ethnocentrism is the tendency to judge other groups according to the standards, behaviors, and customs of one's own group. Given the automatic influence of one's own culture, when people compare their culture to others, they often conclude that their own group is superior.[18] An even more extreme reaction is **xenophobia**, a fear of strangers and foreigners. Clearly, businesspeople who take these views are not likely to communicate successfully across cultures.

Stereotyping is assigning generalized attributes to an individual on the basis of membership in a particular group.

Distorted views of other cultures or groups also result from **stereotyping**, assigning a wide range of generalized attributes to an individual on the basis of membership in a particular culture or social group. For instance, assuming that an older colleague will be out of touch with the youth market or that a younger colleague can't be an inspiring leader are examples of stereotyping age groups.

Cultural pluralism is the acceptance of multiple cultures on their own terms.

Those who want to show respect for other people and to communicate effectively in business need to adopt a more positive viewpoint, in the form of **cultural pluralism**— the practice of accepting multiple cultures on their own terms. When crossing cultural boundaries, you'll be even more effective if you move beyond simple acceptance and adapt your communication style to that of the new cultures you encounter—even integrating aspects of those cultures into your own.[19] A few simple habits can help:

- **Avoid assumptions.** Don't assume that others will act the same way you do, use language and symbols the same way you do, or even operate from the same values and beliefs. For instance, in a comparison of the 10 most important values in three cultures, people from the United States had *no* values in common with people from Japanese or Arab cultures.[20]
- **Avoid judgments.** When people act differently, don't conclude that they are in error or that their way is invalid or inferior.
- **Acknowledge distinctions.** Don't ignore the differences between another person's culture and your own.

> You can avoid ethnocentrism and stereotyping by avoiding assumptions and judgments and by accepting differences.

Unfortunately, overcoming ethnocentrism and stereotyping is not a simple task, even for people who are highly motivated to do so. Moreover, research suggests that people often have beliefs and biases that they're not even aware of—and that may even conflict with the beliefs they *think* they have. (To see if you have some of these *implicit beliefs*, visit the Project Implicit website, at https://implicit.harvard.edu/implicit, and take some of the simple online tests.)[21]

Recognizing Variations in a Diverse World

3 **LEARNING OBJECTIVE**

Explain the importance of recognizing cultural variations, and list eight categories of cultural differences.

You can begin to learn how people in other cultures want to be treated by recognizing and accommodating eight main types of cultural differences: contextual, legal and ethical, social, nonverbal, age, gender, religious, and ability.

CONTEXTUAL DIFFERENCES

Every attempt at communication occurs within a **cultural context**, the pattern of physical cues, environmental stimuli, and implicit understanding that convey meaning between two members of the same culture. However, cultures around the world vary widely in the role that context plays in communication.

> Cultural context is the pattern of physical cues, environmental stimuli, and implicit understanding that conveys meaning between members of the same culture.

In a **high-context culture**, people rely less on verbal communication and more on the context of nonverbal actions and environmental setting to convey meaning. For instance, a Chinese speaker expects the receiver to discover the essence of a message and uses indirectness and metaphor to provide a web of meaning.[22] The indirect style can be a source of confusion during discussions with people from low-context cultures, who are more accustomed to receiving direct answers. Also, in high-context cultures, the rules of everyday life are rarely explicit; instead, as individuals grow up, they learn how to recognize situational cues (such as gestures and tone of voice) and how to respond as expected.[23] The primary role of communication in high-context cultures is building relationships, not exchanging information.[24]

> High-context cultures rely heavily on nonverbal actions and environmental setting to convey meaning; low-context cultures rely more on explicit verbal communication.

In a **low-context culture** such as the United States, people rely more on verbal communication and less on circumstances and cues to convey meaning. In such cultures, rules and expectations are usually spelled out through explicit statements such as "Please wait until I'm finished" or "You're welcome to browse."[25] The primary task of communication in low-context cultures is exchanging information.[26]

Contextual differences are apparent in the way businesspeople approach situations such as decision making, problem solving, negotiating, interaction among levels in the organizational hierarchy, and socializing outside the workplace.[27] For instance, in low-context cultures, businesspeople tend to focus on the results of the decisions they face, a reflection of the cultural emphasis on logic and progress (for example, "Will this be good for our

Negotiations between businesspeople in low-context and high-context cultures can be hampered by the different communication styles of the two cultures.

REAL-TIME UPDATES
Learn More by Reading This PDF

International etiquette tips

These quick etiquette tips will smooth the way for working in major business centers around the world. Go to http://real-timeupdates.com/bct11 and click on "Learn More." If you are using MyBcommLab, you can access Real-Time Updates within each chapter or under Student Study Tools.

company? For my career?"). In comparison, higher-context cultures emphasize the means or the method by which a decision will be made. Building or protecting relationships can be as important as the facts and information used in making the decisions.[28] Consequently, negotiators working on business deals in such cultures may spend most of their time together building relationships rather than hammering out contractual details.

The distinctions between high and low context are generalizations, of course, but they are important to keep in mind as guidelines. Communication tactics that work well in a high-context culture may backfire in a low-context culture and vice versa.

LEGAL AND ETHICAL DIFFERENCES

Cultural context influences legal and ethical behavior, which in turn can affect communication. For example, the meaning of business contracts can vary from culture to culture. While a manager from a U.S. company would tend to view a signed contract as the end of the negotiating process, with all the details hammered out, his or her counterpart in many Asian cultures might view the signed contract as an agreement to do business—and only then begin to negotiate the details of the deal.[29]

Honesty and respect are cornerstones of ethical communication, regardless of culture.

As you conduct business around the world, you'll find that both legal systems and ethical standards differ from culture to culture. Making ethical choices across cultures can seem complicated, but you can keep your messages ethical by applying four basic principles:[30]

- **Actively seek mutual ground.** To allow the clearest possible exchange of information, both parties must be flexible and avoid insisting that an interaction take place strictly in terms of one culture or another.
- **Send and receive messages without judgment.** To allow information to flow freely, both parties must recognize that values vary from culture to culture, and they must trust each other.
- **Send messages that are honest.** To ensure that information is true, both parties must see things as they are—not as they would like them to be. Both parties must be fully aware of their personal and cultural biases.
- **Show respect for cultural differences.** To protect the basic human rights of both parties, each must understand and acknowledge the other's needs and preserve each other's dignity by communicating without deception.

SOCIAL DIFFERENCES

Formal rules of etiquette are explicit and well defined, but informal rules are learned through observation and imitation.

The nature of social behavior varies among cultures, sometimes dramatically. Some behavioral rules are formal and specifically articulated (table manners are a good example), and others are informal and learned over time (such as the comfortable distance to stand from a colleague during a discussion). The combination of formal and informal rules influences the overall behavior of most people in a society most of the time. In addition to the factors already discussed, social norms can vary from culture to culture in the following areas:

- **Attitudes toward work and success.** In the United States, for instance, a widespread view is that material comfort earned by individual effort is a sign of superiority and that people who work hard are better than those who don't.

Respect and rank are reflected differently from culture to culture in the way people are addressed and in their working environment.

- **Roles and status.** Culture influences the roles that people play, including who communicates with whom, what they communicate, and in what way. For example, in some countries women still don't play a prominent role in business, so women executives who visit these countries may find that they're not taken seriously as businesspeople.[31] Culture also dictates how people show respect and signify rank. For example, people in the United States show respect by addressing top managers as "Mr. Roberts" or "Ms. Gutierrez." However, people in China are addressed according to their official titles, such as "President" or "Manager."[32]

- **Use of manners.** What is polite in one culture may be considered rude in another. For instance, asking a colleague "How was your weekend?" is a common way of making small talk in the United States, but the question sounds intrusive to people in cultures in which business and private lives are seen as separate spheres. Research a country's expectations before you visit, and watch carefully and learn after you arrive.

REAL-TIME UPDATES
Learn More by Watching This Video

Video guide puts culture in context

Enjoy a pictorial tour of cultures around the world as you learn more about communication across the spectrum of cultural context. Go to http://real-timeupdates.com/bct11 and click on "Learn More." If you are using MyBcommLab, you can access Real-Time Updates within each chapter or under Student Study Tools.

- **Concepts of time.** People in low-context cultures see time as a way to plan the business day efficiently, often focusing on only one task during each scheduled period and viewing time as a limited resource. However, executives from high-context cultures often see time as more flexible. Meeting a deadline is less important than building a business relationship.[33] Commenting on the culture shock that many U.S. professionals experience when going to work in China, one veteran observer explained that "in the West, there is such a premium on getting things done quickly, but when you come to work in China, you need to work on listening and being more patient and understanding of local ways of doing business."[34]

The rules of polite behavior vary from country to country.

Attitudes toward time, such as strict adherence to meeting schedules, can vary throughout the world.

- **Future orientation.** Successful companies tend to have a strong *future orientation,* planning for and investing in the future, but national cultures around the world vary widely in this viewpoint. Some societies encourage a long-term outlook that emphasizes planning and investing—making sacrifices in the short term for the promise of better outcomes in the future. Others are oriented more toward the present, even to the point of viewing the future as hopelessly remote and not worth planning for.[35]

- **Openness and inclusiveness.** At both the national level and within smaller groups, cultures vary on how open they are to accepting people from other cultures and people who don't necessarily fit the prevailing norms within the culture. An unwillingness to accommodate others can range from outright exclusion to subtle pressures to conform to majority expectations. IBM has long been a leader in the effort to create an inclusive environment that ensures fair opportunities for both employees and external business partners. Executive-led task forces at the company represent women; Asian American, African American, Hispanic American, and Native American people; people with disabilities; and gay, lesbian, bisexual, and transgender employees. Diversity is embraced at the employee level through more than 100 networking groups that unite people who have a variety of talents and interests.[36]

Cultures around the world exhibit varying degrees of openness toward both outsiders and people whose personal identities don't align with prevailing social norms.

NONVERBAL DIFFERENCES

As discussed in Chapter 2, nonverbal communication can be a reliable guide to determining the meaning of a message—but this situation holds true only if the sender and receiver assign the same meaning to nonverbal signals. For instance, the simplest hand gestures have different meanings in different cultures. A gesture that communicates good luck in Brazil is the equivalent of giving someone "the finger" in Colombia.[37] Don't assume that the gestures you grew up with will translate to another culture; doing so could lead to embarrassing mistakes.

The meaning of nonverbal signals can vary widely from culture to culture, so you can't rely on assumptions.

When you have the opportunity to interact with people in another culture, the best advice is to study the culture in advance and then observe the way people behave in the following areas:

- **Greetings.** Do people shake hands, bow, or kiss lightly (on one side of the face or both)? Do people shake hands only when first introduced and every time they say hello or good-bye?

- **Personal space.** When people are conversing, do they stand closer together or farther away than you are accustomed to?

- **Touching.** Do people touch each other on the arm to emphasize a point or slap each other on the back to show congratulations? Or do they refrain from touching altogether?

Communication styles and expectations can vary widely among age groups, putting extra demands on teams that include workers of varying ages.

A culture's views on youth and aging affect how people communicate with one another.

- **Facial expressions.** Do people shake their heads to indicate "no" and nod them to indicate "yes"? This is what people are accustomed to in the United States, but it is not universal.
- **Eye contact.** Do people make frequent eye contact or avoid it? Frequent eye contact is often taken as a sign of honesty and openness in the United States, but in other cultures it can be a sign of aggressiveness or disrespect.
- **Posture.** Do people slouch and relax in the office and in public, or do they sit up and stand up straight?
- **Formality.** In general, does the culture seem more or less formal than yours?

Following the lead of people who grew up in the culture is not only a great way to learn but a good way to show respect as well.

AGE DIFFERENCES

In U.S. culture, youth is often associated with strength, energy, possibilities, and freedom, and age is sometimes associated with declining powers and the inability to keep pace. However, older workers can offer broader experience, the benefits of important business relationships nurtured over many years, and high degrees of "practical intelligence"—the ability to solve complex, poorly defined problems.[38]

In contrast, in cultures that value age and seniority, longevity earns respect and increasing power and freedom. For instance, in many Asian societies, the oldest employees hold the most powerful jobs, the most impressive titles, and the greatest degrees of freedom and decision-making authority. If a younger employee disagrees with one of these senior executives, the discussion is never conducted in public. The notion of "saving face," of avoiding public embarrassment, is too strong. Instead, if a senior person seems to be in error about something, other employees will find a quiet, private way to communicate whatever information they feel is necessary.[39]

In addition to cultural values associated with various life stages, the multiple generations within a culture present another dimension of diversity. Today's workplaces can have three or even four generations working side by side. Each of these generations has been shaped by dramatically different world events, social trends, and technological advances, so it is not surprising that they often have different values, expectations, and communication habits. For instance, Generation Y workers (see "Us Versus Them: Generational Conflict in the Workplace") have a strong preference for communicating via short electronic messages, but Baby Boomers and Generation Xers sometimes find these brief messages abrupt and impersonal.[40]

GENDER DIFFERENCES

The perception of men and women in business varies from culture to culture, and these differences can affect communication efforts. In some cultures, men hold most or all positions of authority, and women are expected to play a more subservient role. Female executives who visit these cultures may not be taken seriously until they successfully handle challenges to their knowledge, capabilities, and patience.[41]

As more women take on positions of greater responsibility, enlightened company leaders are making a point to examine past assumptions and practices.[42] For instance, company cultures that have been dominated by men for years may have adopted communication habits that some women have difficulty relating to—such as the frequent use of certain sports metaphors or the acceptance of coarse language.

Broadly speaking, men tend to emphasize content in their messages, while women tend to emphasize relationship maintenance.

Whatever the culture, evidence suggests that men and women tend to have slightly different communication styles. Broadly speaking, men tend to emphasize content in their communication efforts, whereas women place a higher premium on relationship maintenance.[43] This difference can create friction when two parties in a conversation have different needs and expectations from the interchange. Again, these are broad generalizations that do not apply to every person in every situation, but keeping them in mind can help men and women overcome communication hurdles in the workplace.

<table>
<tr><td>**COMMUNICATING ACROSS CULTURES**</td><td>Us Versus Them: Generational Conflict in the Workplace</td></tr>
</table>

The way people view the world as adults is profoundly shaped by the social and technological trends they experienced while growing up, so it's no surprise that each generation entering the workforce has a different perspective than the generations already at work. Throw in the human tendencies to resist change and to assume that whatever way one is doing something must be the best way to do it, and you have a recipe for conflict. Moreover, generations in a workplace sometimes feel themselves competing for jobs, resources, influence, and control. The result can be tension, mistrust, and communication breakdowns.

Lumping people into generations is an imprecise science at best, but it helps to know the labels commonly applied to various age groups and to have some idea of their broad characteristics. These labels are not official, and there is no general agreement on when some generations start and end, but you will see and hear references to the following groups (approximate years of birth shown in parentheses):

- **The Radio Generation** (1925 to 1945). People in this group are beyond what was once considered the traditional retirement age of 65, but many want or need to continue working.
- **Baby Boomers** (1946 to 1964). This large segment of the workforce, which now occupies many mid- and upper-level managerial positions, got its name from the population boom in the years following World War II. The older members of this generation are just now reaching retirement age, but many will continue to work beyond age 65—meaning that younger workers waiting for some of these management spots to open up might have to wait a while longer.
- **Generation X** (1965 to 1980). This relatively smaller "MTV generation" is responsible for many of the innovations that have shaped communication habits today but sometimes feels caught between the large mass of Baby Boomers ahead of them and the younger Generation Y employees entering the workforce. When Generation X does finally get the

chance to take over starting in 2015 or 2020, it will be managing in a vastly different business landscape, one in which virtual organizations and networks of independent contractors replace much of the hierarchy inherited from the Baby Boomers.

- **Generation Y** (1981 to 1995). Also known as *millennials*, this youngest generation currently in the workforce is noted for its entrepreneurial instincts and technological savvy. This generation's comfort level with social networks and other Web 2.0 tools is helping to change business communication practices—but is also a source of concern for managers worried about information leaks and employee productivity.
- **Generation Z** (after 1996). If you're a member of Generation Y, those footsteps you hear behind you are coming from Generation Z, also known as *Generation I* (for Internet) or the *Net Generation*. The first full generation to be born after the World Wide Web was invented will be entering the workforce soon.

These brief summaries can hardly do justice to entire generations of workers, but they give you some idea of the different generational perspectives and the potential for communication problems. As with all cultural conflicts, successful communication starts with recognizing and understanding these differences.

CAREER APPLICATIONS

1. How would you resolve a conflict between a Baby Boomer manager who worries about the privacy and productivity aspects of social networking and a Generation Y employee who wants to use these tools on the job?
2. Consider the range of labels from the Radio Generation to the Net Generation. What does this tell you about the possible influence of technology on business communication habits?

RELIGIOUS DIFFERENCES

Religion is a dominant force in many cultures and the source of many differences between cultures.[44] The effort to accommodate employees' life interests on a broader scale has led a number of companies to address the issue of religion in the workplace. As one of the most personal and influential aspects of life, religion brings potential for controversy in a work setting. On the one hand, some employees feel they should be able to express their beliefs in the workplace and not be forced to "check their faith at the door" when they come to work. On the other hand, companies want to avoid situations in which openly expressed religious differences cause friction between employees or distract employees from their responsibilities. To help address such concerns, firms such as Ford, Intel, Texas Instruments, and American Airlines allow employees to form faith-based employee support groups as part of their diversity strategies. In contrast, Procter & Gamble is among the companies that don't allow organized religious activities at their facilities.[45]

Religion in the workplace is a complex and contentious issue—and it's getting more so every year, at least as measured by a significant rise in the number of religious discrimination

U.S. law requires employers to accommodate employees' religious beliefs to a reasonable degree.

lawsuits.[46] Beyond accommodating individual beliefs to a reasonable degree, as required by U.S. law, companies occasionally need to resolve situations that pit one group of employees against another or against the company's policies.[47] As more companies work to establish inclusive workplaces, and as more employees seek to integrate religious convictions into their daily work, you can expect this issue to be increasingly discussed at many companies in the coming years.

ABILITY DIFFERENCES

Colleagues and customers with disabilities that affect communication represent an important aspect of the diversity picture. People whose hearing, vision, cognitive ability, or physical ability to operate electronic devices is impaired can be at a significant disadvantage in today's workplace. As with other elements of diversity, success starts with respect for individuals and sensitivity to differences.

Assistive technologies help employers create more inclusive workplaces and benefit from the contribution of people with physical or cognitive impairments.

Employers can also invest in a variety of *assistive technologies* that help people with disabilities perform activities that might otherwise be difficult or impossible. These technologies include devices and systems that help workers communicate orally and visually, interact with computers and other equipment, and enjoy greater mobility in the workplace. For example, designers can emphasize *web accessibility*, taking steps to make websites more accessible to people whose vision is limited. Assistive technologies create a vital link for thousands of employees with disabilities, giving them opportunities to pursue a greater range of career paths and giving employers access to a broader base of talent. With the United States possibly heading for a serious shortage of workers in a few years, the economy will need all the workers who can make a contribution, and assistive technologies will be an important part of the solution.[48]

Adapting to Other Business Cultures

4 LEARNING OBJECTIVE

List four general guidelines for adapting to any business culture.

Whether you're trying to work productively with members of another generation in your own office or with a business partner on the other side of the world, adapting your approach is essential to successful communication. This section offers general advice on adapting to any business culture and specific advice for professionals from other cultures on adapting to U.S. business culture.

GUIDELINES FOR ADAPTING TO ANY BUSINESS CULTURE

You'll find a variety of specific tips in "Improving Intercultural Communication Skills," starting on the next page, but here are four general guidelines that can help all business communicators improve their cultural competency:

An important step in understanding and adapting to other cultures is to recognize the influences that your own culture has on your communication habits.

- **Become aware of your own biases.** Successful intercultural communication requires more than just an understanding of the other party's culture; you need to understand your own culture and the way it shapes your communication habits.[49] For instance, knowing that you value independence and individual accomplishment will help you communicate more successfully in a culture that values consensus and group harmony.
- **Ignore the "Golden Rule."** You probably heard this growing up: "Treat people the way you want to be treated." The problem with the Golden Rule is that other people don't always want to be treated the same way you want to be treated, particularly across cultural boundaries. The best approach: Treat people the way *they* want to be treated.
- **Exercise tolerance, flexibility, and respect.** As IBM's Ron Glover puts it, "To the greatest extent possible, we try to manage our people and our practices in ways that are respectful of the core principles of any given country or organization or culture."[50]
- **Practice patience and maintain a sense of humor.** Even the most committed and attuned business professionals can make mistakes in intercultural communication, so it is vital for all parties to be patient with one another. As business becomes ever more global, even people in the most tradition-bound cultures are learning to deal

with outsiders more patiently and overlook occasional cultural blunders.[51] A sense of humor is a helpful asset as well, allowing people to move past awkward and embarrassing moments. When you make a mistake, simply apologize and, if appropriate, ask the other person to explain the accepted way; then move on.

GUIDELINES FOR ADAPTING TO U.S. BUSINESS CULTURE

If you are a recent immigrant to the United States or grew up in a culture outside the U.S. mainstream, you can apply all the concepts and skills in this chapter to help adapt to U.S. business culture. Here are some key points to remember as you become accustomed to business communication in this country:[52]

- **Individualism.** In contrast to cultures that value group harmony and group success, U.S. culture generally expects individuals to succeed by their own efforts, and it rewards individual success. Even though teamwork is emphasized in many companies, competition between individuals is expected and even encouraged in many cases.
- **Equality.** Although the country's historical record on equality has not always been positive and some inequalities still exist, equality is considered a core American value. This principle applies to race, gender, social background, and even age. To a greater degree than people in many other cultures, Americans believe that every person should be given the opportunity to pursue whatever dreams and goals he or she has in life.
- **Privacy and personal space.** Although this appears to be changing somewhat with the popularity of social networking and other personal media, people in the United States are accustomed to a fair amount of privacy. That also applies to their "personal space" at work. For example, they expect you to knock before entering a closed office and to avoid asking questions about personal beliefs or activities until they get to know you well.
- **Time and schedules.** U.S. businesses value punctuality and the efficient use of time. For instance, meetings are expected to start and end at designated times.
- **Religion.** The United States does not have an official state religion. Many religions are practiced throughout the country, and people are expected to respect each other's beliefs.
- **Communication style.** Communication tends to be direct and focused more on content and transactions than on relationships or group harmony.

As with all observations about culture, these are generalizations, of course. Any nation of more than 300 million people will exhibit a wide variety of behaviors. However, following these guidelines will help you succeed in most business communication situations.

Improving Intercultural Communication Skills

Communicating successfully between cultures requires a variety of skills (see Figure 3.3 on the next page). You can improve your intercultural skills throughout your career by studying other cultures and languages, respecting preferences for communication styles, learning to write and speak clearly, listening carefully, knowing when to use interpreters and translators, and helping others adapt to your culture.

STUDYING OTHER CULTURES

Effectively adapting your communication efforts to another culture requires not only knowledge about the culture but also the ability and motivation to change your personal habits as needed.[53] Fortunately, you don't need to learn about the whole world all at once. Many companies appoint specialists for specific countries or regions, giving employees a chance

REAL-TIME UPDATES
Learn More by Watching This Video

Overcoming culture shock

This entertaining five-part video series shares the experience of an Israeli journalist undergoing culture shock when coming to graduate school in New York City, and it offers help and encouragement to anyone living in a new culture for the first time. Go to http://real-timeupdates.com/bct11 and click on "Learn More." If you are using MyBcommLab, you can access Real-Time Updates within each chapter or under Student Study Tools.

The values espoused by American culture include individualism, equality, and privacy.

5 **LEARNING OBJECTIVE**

Identify seven steps you can take to improve your intercultural communication skills.

REAL-TIME UPDATES
Learn More by Watching This PowerPoint Presentation

Essential guidelines for adapting to other business cultures

Learn great etiquette tips for doing business in France, Germany, Japan, Mexico, and Russia. Go to http://real-timeupdates.com/bct11 and click on "Learn More." If you are using MyBcommLab, you can access Real-Time Updates within each chapter or under Student Study Tools.

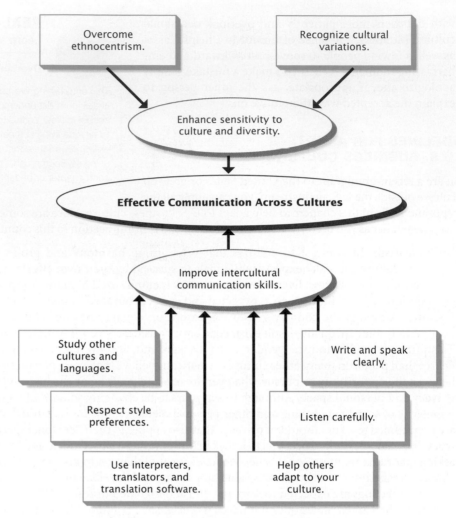

Figure 3.3   Components of Successful Intercultural Communication
Communicating in a diverse business environment is not always an easy task, but you can continue to improve your sensitivity and build your skills as you progress in your career.

Successful intercultural communication can require the modification of personal communication habits.

Making an effort to learn about another person's culture is a sign of respect.

to focus on just one culture at a time. Some firms also provide resources to help employees prepare for interaction with other cultures. On IBM's Global Workforce Diversity intranet site, for instance, employees can click on the "GoingGlobal" link to learn about customs in specific cultures.[54]

Even a small amount of research and practice will help you get through many business situations. In addition, most people respond positively to honest effort and good intentions, and many business associates will help you along if you show an interest in learning more about their cultures. Don't be afraid to ask questions, either. People will respect your concern and curiosity. You will gradually accumulate considerable knowledge, which will help you feel comfortable and be effective in a wide range of business situations.

Numerous websites (such as www.kwintessential.co.uk) and books offer advice on traveling to and working in specific cultures. Also try to sample newspapers, magazines, and even the music and movies of another country. For instance, a movie can demonstrate nonverbal customs even if you don't grasp the language. (However, be careful not to rely solely on entertainment products. If people in other countries based their opinions of U.S. culture only on the silly teen flicks and violent action movies that the United States exports around the globe, what sort of impression do you imagine they'd get?) For some of the key issues to research before doing business in another country, refer to Table 3.1.

TABLE 3.1	Doing Business in Other Cultures
Action	**Details to Consider**
Understand social customs	• How do people react to strangers? Are they friendly? Hostile? Reserved? • How do people greet each other? Should you bow? Nod? Shake hands? • How do you express appreciation for an invitation to lunch, dinner, or someone's home? Should you bring a gift? Send flowers? Write a thank-you note? • Are any phrases, facial expressions, or hand gestures considered rude? • How do you attract the attention of a waiter? Do you tip the waiter? • When is it rude to refuse an invitation? How do you refuse politely? • What topics may or may not be discussed in a social setting? In a business setting? • How do social customs dictate interaction between men and women? Between younger people and older people?
Learn about clothing and food preferences	• What occasions require special attire? • What colors are associated with mourning? Love? Joy? • Are some types of clothing considered taboo for one gender or the other? • How many times a day do people eat? • How are hands or utensils used when eating? • Where is the seat of honor at a table?
Assess political patterns	• How stable is the political situation? • Does the political situation affect businesses in and out of the country? • Is it appropriate to talk politics in social or business situations?
Understand religious and social beliefs	• To which religious groups do people belong? • Which places, objects, actions, and events are sacred? • Do religious beliefs affect communication between men and women or between any other groups? • Is there a tolerance for minority religions? • How do religious holidays affect business and government activities? • Does religion require or prohibit eating specific foods? At specific times?
Learn about economic and business institutions	• Is the society homogeneous or heterogeneous? • What languages are spoken? • What are the primary resources and principal products? • Are businesses generally large? Family controlled? Government controlled? • What are the generally accepted working hours? • How do people view scheduled appointments? • Are people expected to socialize before conducting business?
Appraise the nature of ethics, values, and laws	• Is money or a gift expected in exchange for arranging business transactions? • Do people value competitiveness or cooperation? • What are the attitudes toward work? Toward money? • Is politeness more important than factual honesty?

STUDYING OTHER LANGUAGES

Consider what it must be like to work at IBM, where the global workforce speaks more than 165 languages. Without the ability to communicate in more than one language, how could this diverse group of people ever conduct business? As commerce continues to become more globalized and many countries become more linguistically diverse, the demand for multilingual communicators continues to grow as well. The ability to communicate in more than one language can make you a more competitive job candidate and open up a wider variety of career opportunities (see "The Web 2.0 Way to Learn a New Language").

Even if your colleagues or customers in another country speak your language, it's worth the time and energy to learn common phrases in theirs. Learning the basics not only helps you get through everyday business and social situations but also demonstrates your commitment to the business relationship. After all, the other person probably spent years learning your language.

Finally, don't assume that people from two countries who speak the same language speak it the same way. The French spoken in Quebec and other parts of Canada is often noticeably different from the French spoken in France. Similarly, it's often said that the United States and the United Kingdom are two countries divided by a common language.

English is the most prevalent language in international business, but don't assume that everyone understands it or speaks it the same way.

| BUSINESS COMMUNICATION 2.0 | The Web 2.0 Way to Learn a New Language |

Taking classes with a skilled teacher and getting real-life practice while living in another country are proven ways to learn a new language, but what if neither of these options is available to you? Thanks to the growth of social networking technology and other Web 2.0 communication tools, independent language learners now have a multitude of online learning options.

Palabea (www.palabea.net) is a great example of the possibilities of the Web 2.0 approach to learning. By adapting social networking concepts for the unique demands of language learning, this service offers numerous helpful features:

- **Online chat with other language learners.** No matter what language you're trying to learn, someone somewhere in the world speaks it—and is trying to learn your language. Palabea lets you connect and help each other with text, audio, or video chat.
- **Connections to native speakers in your local area.** Palabea can connect you with nearby native speakers of the language you're trying to learn.

- **User-generated content.** Palabea offers a growing collection of podcasts, video lectures, documents, and other learning tools, all contributed by members.
- **Virtual classrooms.** Just as online meeting systems let business colleagues collaborate in real time on reports and other documents, Palabea's virtual classrooms let members meet online to review and correct translations and other projects.

Palabea is just one of many online resources that can help language learners. For example, the Free Language website (http://freelanguage.org) offers links to free resources for several dozen languages.

CAREER APPLICATIONS

1. How could a multinational company such as IBM benefit from the capabilities offered by Palabea and similar websites?
2. As a manager, would you be comfortable having employees use a free service such as Palabea before sending them on important overseas assignments? Why or why not?

For instance, *period* (punctuation), *elevator*, and *gasoline* in the United States are *full stop*, *lift*, and *petrol* in the United Kingdom.

RESPECTING PREFERENCES FOR COMMUNICATION STYLE

Communication style—including the level of directness, the degree of formality, media preferences, and other factors—varies widely from culture to culture. Knowing what your communication partners expect can help you adapt to their particular style. Once again, watching and learning are the best ways to improve your skills. However, you can infer some generalities by learning more about the culture. For instance, U.S. workers typically prefer an open and direct communication style; they find other styles frustrating or suspect. Directness is also valued in Sweden as a sign of efficiency; but, unlike with discussions in the United States, heated debates and confrontations are unusual. Italian, German, and French executives don't put colleagues at ease with praise before they criticize—doing so seems manipulative to them. However, professionals from high-context cultures, such as Japan or China, tend to be less direct.[55] Finally, in general, business correspondence in other countries is often more formal than the style used by U.S. businesspeople (see Figure 3.4).

WRITING CLEARLY

Clarity and simplicity are essential when writing to or speaking with people who don't share your native language.

Writing clearly is always important, of course, but it is essential when you are writing to people whose first language is not English. Follow these recommendations to make sure your message can be understood:[56]

- **Choose words carefully.** Use precise words that don't have the potential to confuse with multiple meanings. For instance, the word *right* has several dozen different meanings and usages, so look for a synonym that conveys the specific meaning you intend, such as *correct, appropriate, desirable, moral, authentic,* or *privilege.*[57]

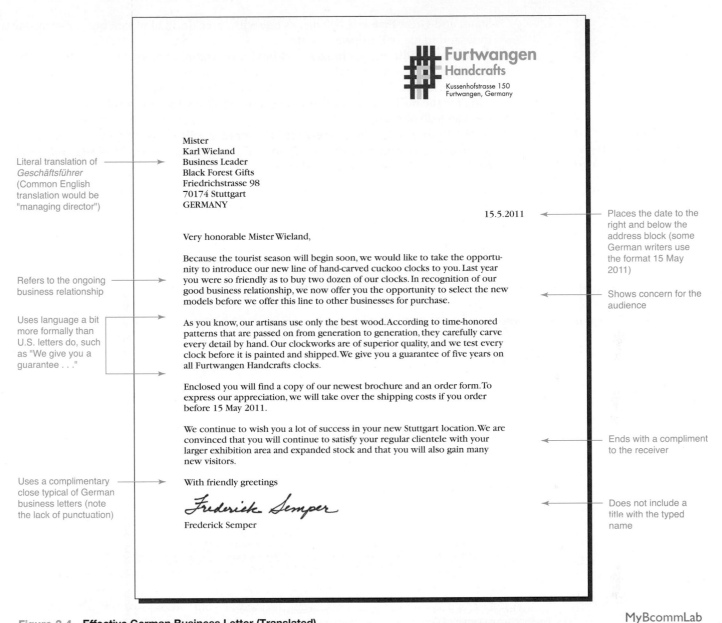

Figure 3.4   Effective German Business Letter (Translated)
In Germany, business letters usually open with a reference to the business relationship and close with a compliment to the recipient. In this letter written by a supplier to a nearby retailer, you can see that the tone is more formal than would typically be used in the United States.

MyBcommLab

Apply Figure 3.4's key concepts by revising a new document. Go to Chapter 3 in mybcommlab.com and select Document Makeovers.

- **Be brief.** Use simple sentences and short paragraphs, breaking information into smaller chunks that are easier for readers to process.
- **Use plenty of transitions.** Help readers follow your train of thought by using transitional words and phrases (see page 133). For example, tie related points together with expressions such as *in addition* and *first, second,* and *third.*
- **Address international correspondence properly.** Refer to Tables A.1 through A.5 for an explanation of different address elements and salutations commonly used in various countries.
- **Cite numbers and dates carefully.** In the United States, 12-05-11 means December 5, 2011, but in many other countries, it means May 12, 2011. Dates in Japan and China are usually expressed with the year first, followed by the month and then the day; therefore, to write December 5, 2011, in Japan, write it as 2011-12-05. Similarly, in the United

States and Great Britain 1.000 means one with three decimal places, but it means one thousand in many European countries.

- **Avoid slang, idiomatic phrases, and business jargon.** Everyday speech and writing are full of slang and **idiomatic phrases**—phrases that mean more than the sum of their literal parts. Examples from U.S. English include "Off the top of my head" and "More bang for the buck." Your audience may have no idea what you're talking about when you use such phrases.

- **Avoid humor and other references to popular culture.** Jokes and references to popular entertainment usually rely on culture-specific information that might be completely unknown to your audience.

Humor does not "travel well" because it usually relies on intimate knowledge of a particular culture.

Although some of these differences may seem trivial, meeting the expectations of an international audience illustrates both knowledge of and respect for the other cultures (see Figure 3.5 and Figure 3.6).

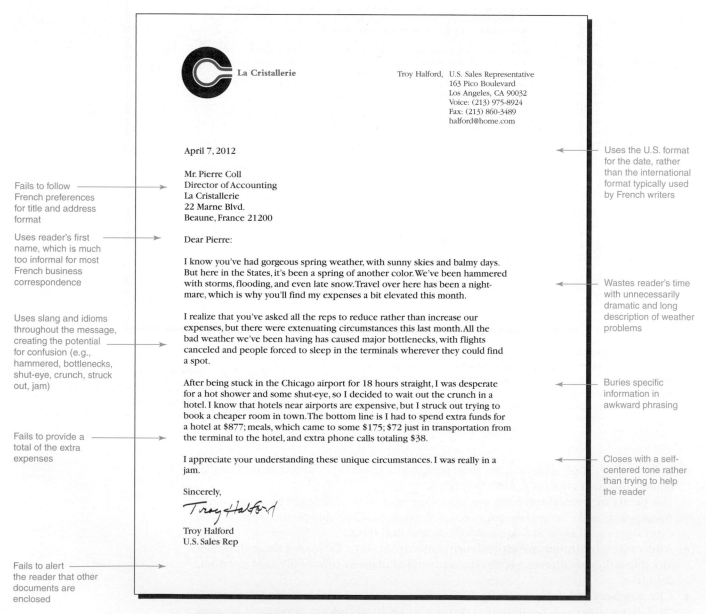

Figure 3.5 Ineffective Intercultural Letter
This letter from a U.S. sales representative to a manager in France exhibits several intercultural mistakes, including the informal tone and use of U.S. slang. Compare this with the improved version in Figure 3.6.

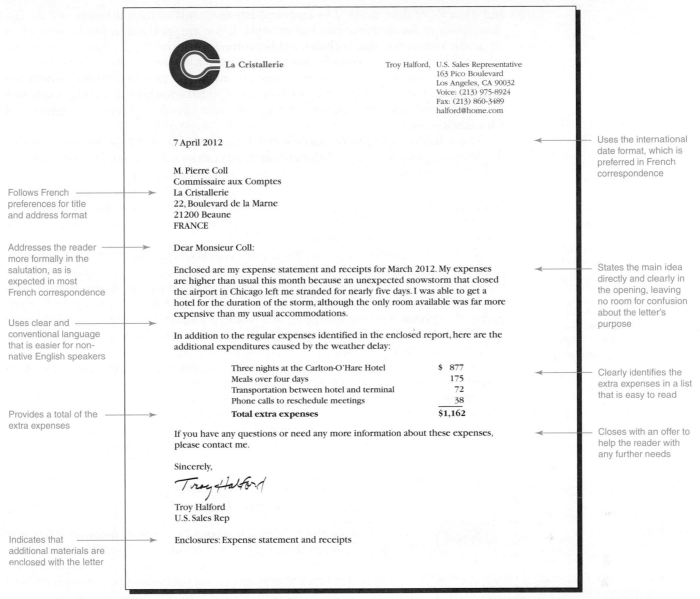

Follows French preferences for title and address format

Addresses the reader more formally in the salutation, as is expected in most French correspondence

Uses clear and conventional language that is easier for non-native English speakers

Provides a total of the extra expenses

Indicates that additional materials are enclosed with the letter

Uses the international date format, which is preferred in French correspondence

States the main idea directly and clearly in the opening, leaving no room for confusion about the letter's purpose

Clearly identifies the extra expenses in a list that is easy to read

Closes with an offer to help the reader with any further needs

Figure 3.6   Effective Intercultural Letter
This version of the letter in Figure 3.5 follows French standards for correspondence and is also easier to read and to scan.

MyBcommLab

Apply Figure 3.6's key concepts by revising a new document. Go to Chapter 3 in mybcommlab.com and select Document Makeovers.

SPEAKING AND LISTENING CAREFULLY

Languages vary considerably in the significance of tone, pitch, speed, and volume, which can create challenges for people trying to interpret the explicit meaning of words themselves as well as the overall nuance of a message. The English word *progress* can be a noun or a verb, depending on which syllable you accent. In Chinese, the meaning of the word *mà* changes depending on the speaker's tone; it can mean *mother, pileup, horse,* or *scold.* And routine Arabic speech can sound excited or angry to an English-speaking U.S. listener.[58]

To ensure successful conversations between parties who speak different native languages or even regional variations of the same language, speakers and listeners alike need to make accommodations.[59] Speakers should adjust the content of their messages and the style of their delivery to accommodate the needs of their listeners and the circumstances of the conversation. For example, if you are speaking in person or over an electronic connection that includes a video component, you can use hand gestures and other nonverbal signals to clarify your spoken message. However, when you don't have a visual connection, you must take extra care to convey your meaning through words and vocal characteristics alone. Conversely, listeners need to be tolerant of accents, vocabulary choices, gestures, and other factors that might distract them from hearing the meaning of a speaker's message.

When talking with people whose native language is different from yours, remember that the processing of even everyday conversations can be difficult. For instance, speakers from the United States are notorious for stringing together multiple words into a single, mystifying pseudoword, such as turning "Did you eat yet?" into "Jeetyet?" The French language uses a concept known as *liaison*, in which one word is intentionally joined with the next. Without a lot of practice, new French speakers have a hard time telling when one word ends and the next one begins.

To be more effective in intercultural conversations, remember these tips: (1) Speak slowly and clearly; (2) don't rephrase until it's obviously necessary (immediately rephrasing something you've just said doubles the translation workload for the listener); (3) look for and ask for feedback to make sure your message is getting through; (4) don't talk down to the other person by overenunciating words or oversimplifying sentences; and (5) at the end of the conversation, double-check to make sure you and the listener agree on what has been said and decided.

As a listener, you'll need some practice to get a sense of vocal patterns. The key is simply to accept what you hear first, without jumping to conclusions about meaning or motivation. Let other people finish what they have to say. If you interrupt, you may miss something important. You'll also show a lack of respect. If you do not understand a comment, ask the person to repeat it. Any momentary awkwardness you might feel in asking for extra help is less important than the risk of unsuccessful communication.

Speaking clearly and getting plenty of feedback are two of the keys to successful intercultural conversations.

To listen more effectively in intercultural situations, accept what you hear without judgment and let people finish what they have to say.

For important business communication, use a professional interpreter (for oral communication) or translator (for written communication).

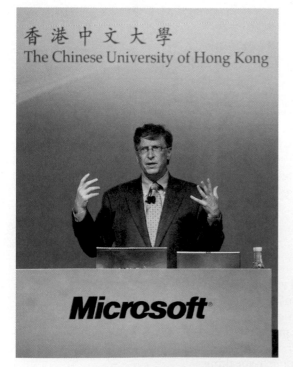

Experienced international speakers, such as Microsoft chairman Bill Gates, are careful to incorporate culture and language variations into their communication efforts.

USING INTERPRETERS, TRANSLATORS, AND TRANSLATION SOFTWARE

You may encounter business situations that require using an *interpreter* (for spoken communication) or a *translator* (for written communication). Interpreters and translators can be expensive, but skilled professionals provide invaluable assistance for communicating in other cultural contexts.[60] Keeping up with current language usage in a given country or culture is also critical in order to avoid embarrassing blunders. For example, the marketing agency Landor Associates usually engages three native-language speakers to review translated materials to make sure the sense of the message is compatible with current usage and slang in a given country.[61] Some companies use *back-translation* to ensure accuracy. Once a translator encodes a message into another language, a different translator retranslates the same message into the original language. This back-translation is then compared with the original message to discover any errors or discrepancies.

The time and cost required for professional translation has encouraged the development of **machine translation**, any form of computerized intelligence used to translate one language to another. Dedicated software tools and online services such as WorldLingo (www.worldlingo.com) offer various forms of automated translation. Major search engines let you request translated versions of the websites you find. Although none of these tools can translate as well as human translators, they can be quite useful with individual words and short phrases, and they can often give you the overall gist of a message.[62]

✔ Checklist | Improving Intercultural Communication Skills

- Understand your own culture so that you can recognize its influences on your communication habits.
- Study other cultures so that you can appreciate cultural variations.
- Study the languages of people with whom you communicate, even if you can learn only a few basic words and phrases.
- Help nonnative speakers learn your language.
- Respect cultural preferences for communication style.
- Write clearly, using brief messages, simple language, generous transitions, and appropriate international conventions.

- Avoid slang, humor, and references to popular culture.
- Speak clearly and slowly, giving listeners time to translate your words.
- Ask for feedback to verify that communication was successful.
- Listen carefully and ask speakers to repeat anything you don't understand.
- Use interpreters and translators for important messages.

HELPING OTHERS ADAPT TO YOUR CULTURE

Everyone can contribute to successful intercultural communication. Whether a younger person is unaccustomed to the formalities of a large corporation or a colleague from another country is working on a team with you, look for opportunities to help people fit in and adapt their communication style. For example, if a nonnative English speaker is making mistakes that could hurt his or her credibility, you can offer advice on the appropriate words and phrases to use. Most language learners truly appreciate this sort of assistance, as long as it is offered in a respectful manner. Moreover, chances are that while you're helping, you'll learn something about the other person's culture and language, too.

> Help others adapt to your culture; it will create a more productive workplace and teach you about their cultures as well.

You can also take steps to simplify the communication process. For instance, oral communication in a second language is usually more difficult than written forms of communication, so instead of asking a foreign colleague to provide information in a conference call, you could ask for a written response instead of or in addition to the live conversation.

For a brief summary of ideas to improve intercultural communication in the workplace, see "Checklist: Improving Intercultural Communication Skills." For additional information on communicating in a world of diversity, visit http://real-timeupdates.com/bct11 and click on Chapter 3.

COMMUNICATION CHALLENGES AT IBM

Ron Glover is responsible for overall diversity planning and strategy at IBM, but every manager throughout the company is expected to foster a climate of inclusion and support for employees of every cultural background. As a team leader in one of IBM's software development labs, you're learning to exercise sound business judgment and use good listening skills to help resolve situations that arise within your diverse group of employees. How would you address these challenges?

INDIVIDUAL CHALLENGE: Vasily Pevsner, a Russian immigrant, has worked in the department for five years. He works well alone, but he resists working with other employees, even in team settings where collaboration is expected. Given the importance that you place on teamwork, how should you handle the situation? List several alternatives for addressing this dilemma, identify which one you would choose, and explain why you would choose this one.

TEAM CHALLENGE: Your employees are breaking into ethnically based cliques. Members of ethnic groups eat together, socialize together, and often chat in their native languages while they work. You appreciate how these groups give their members a sense of community, but you worry that these informal communication channels are alienating nonmembers and fragmenting the flow of information. How can you encourage a stronger sense of community and teamwork across your department? Brainstorm at least three steps you can take to encourage better cross-cultural communication in your group.

Quick Learning Guide

MyBcommLab

If your course uses MyBcommLab, log on to www.mybcommlab.com to access the following study and assessment aids associated with this chapter:

- Video applications
- Real-Time Updates
- Peer review activity
- Pre/post test
- Personalized study plan
- Model documents
- Sample presentations

If you are not using MyBcommLab, you can access Real-Time Updates through http://real-timeupdates.com/bct11.

SUMMARY OF LEARNING OBJECTIVES

1. **Discuss the opportunities and challenges of intercultural communication.** The global marketplace spans natural boundaries and national borders, allowing worldwide competition between businesses of all sizes. Therefore, today's businesspeople are likely to communicate across international borders with people who live in different cultures. Moreover, even domestic workforces are becoming more and more diverse, with employees having different national, religious, and ethnic backgrounds. In this environment, companies can benefit from a broad range of viewpoints and ideas, get a good understanding of diverse markets, and recruit workers from the broadest possible pool of talent. However, intercultural communication presents challenges as well, including motivating diverse employees to cooperate and to work together in teams as well as understanding enough about how culture affects language to prevent miscommunication.

2. **Define** *culture*, **explain how culture is learned, and define** *ethnocentrism* **and** *stereotyping*. Culture is a shared system of symbols, beliefs, attitudes, values, expectations, and norms for behavior. Culture is learned by listening to advice from other members of a society and by observing their behaviors. This double-edged method uses direct and indirect learning to ensure that culture is passed from person to person and from generation to generation.

    Ethnocentrism is the tendency to judge other groups according to the standards, behaviors, and customs of one's own group. Stereotyping is assigning a wide range of generalized attributes to individuals on the basis of their membership in a particular culture or social group, without considering an individual's unique characteristics. To overcome ethnocentrism and stereotyping, work to avoid assumptions, avoid judgments, and acknowledge distinctions.

3. **Explain the importance of recognizing cultural variations, and list eight categories of cultural differences.** People from different cultures encode and decode messages differently, increasing the chances of misunderstanding. By recognizing and accommodating cultural differences, we avoid automatically assuming that everyone's thoughts and actions are just like ours. Begin by focusing on eight categories of differences: contextual differences (the degree to which a culture relies on verbal or nonverbal actions to convey meaning), legal and ethical differences (the degree to which laws and ethics are regarded and obeyed), social differences (how members value work and success, recognize status, define manners, and think about time), nonverbal differences (differing attitudes toward greetings, personal space, touching, facial expression, eye contact, posture, and formality), age differences (how members think about youth, seniority, and longevity), gender differences (how men and women communicate), religious differences (how beliefs affect workplace relationships), and ability differences (inclusive strategies that enable people with disabilities to more fully communicate with the rest of the workforce).

4. **List four general guidelines for adapting to any business culture.** You can adapt to any business culture by (1) becoming aware of your own cultural biases so that you can understand how these forces shape your communication habits; (2) ignoring the Golden Rule (treating people the way you want them to treat you) and instead treating them the way they want to be treated; (3) exercising tolerance, flexibility, and respect; and (4) practicing patience and maintaining a sense of humor to get you through the bumpy spots.

5. **Identify seven steps you can take to improve your intercultural communication skills.** Communicating successfully between cultures requires a variety of skills, all of which you can continue to improve throughout your career. Make your intercultural communication effective by (1) studying other cultures; (2) studying other languages; (3) respecting your audience's preferences for communication style; (4) writing as clearly as possible; (5) speaking as clearly as you can; (6) listening carefully; using interpreters, translators, and translation software when necessary; and (7) helping others adapt to your own culture.

cultural competency An appreciation for cultural differences that affect communication and the ability to adjust one's communication style to ensure that efforts to send and receive messages across cultural boundaries are successful

cultural context The pattern of physical cues, environmental stimuli, and implicit understanding that convey meaning between two members of the same culture

cultural pluralism The practice of accepting multiple cultures on their own terms

culture A shared system of symbols, beliefs, attitudes, values, expectations, and norms for behavior

diversity All the characteristics and experiences that define each of us as individuals

ethnocentrism The tendency to judge other groups according to the standards, behaviors, and customs of one's own group

high-context culture Culture in which people rely less on verbal communication and more on the context of nonverbal actions and environmental setting to convey meaning

idiomatic phrases Phrases that mean more than the sum of their literal parts; such phrases can be difficult for nonnative speakers to understand

intercultural communication The process of sending and receiving messages between people whose cultural backgrounds could lead them to interpret verbal and nonverbal signs differently

low-context culture Culture in which people rely more on verbal communication and less on circumstances and cues to convey meaning

machine translation Any form of computerized intelligence used to translate one language to another

stereotyping Assigning a wide range of generalized attributes to an individual on the basis of membership in a particular culture or social group

xenophobia Fear of strangers and foreigners

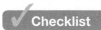 **Checklist**

Improving Intercultural Communication Skills

- Understand your own culture so that you can recognize its influences on your communication habits.
- Study other cultures so that you can appreciate cultural variations.
- Study the languages of people with whom you communicate, even if you can learn only a few basic words and phrases.
- Help nonnative speakers learn your language.
- Respect cultural preferences for communication style.
- Write clearly, using brief messages, simple language, generous transitions, and appropriate international conventions.
- Avoid slang, humor, and references to popular culture.
- Speak clearly and slowly, giving listeners time to translate your words.
- Ask for feedback to verify that communication was successful.
- Listen carefully and ask speakers to repeat anything you don't understand.
- Use interpreters and translators for important messages.

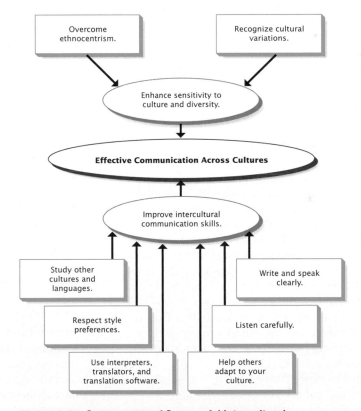

Figure 3.3 Components of Successful Intercultural Communication

Communicating in a diverse business environment is not always an easy task, but you can continue to improve your sensitivity and build your skills as you progress in your career.

TEST YOUR KNOWLEDGE

To review chapter content related to each question, refer to the indicated Learning Objective.

1. How have market globalization and cultural diversity contributed to the increased importance of intercultural communication? [LO-1]
2. What are the potential advantages of a diverse workforce? [LO-1]
3. How do high-context cultures differ from low-context cultures? [LO-2]
4. What is ethnocentrism, and how can it be overcome in communication? [LO-2]
5. In addition to contextual differences, what other categories of cultural differences exist? [LO-3]
6. What four principles apply to ethical intercultural communication? [LO-3]
7. How does a sense of humor come in handy during intercultural communication? [LO-4]
8. How can the Golden Rule cause problems in intercultural communication? [LO-4]
9. What are the risks of using computerized translation when you need to read a document written in another language? [LO-5]
10. What steps can you take to help someone from another culture adapt to your culture? [LO-5]

APPLY YOUR KNOWLEDGE

To review chapter content related to each question, refer to the indicated Learning Objective.

1. Does a company that had no business dealings outside the United States need to concern itself with intercultural communication issues? Explain you answer. [LO-1]
2. Make a list of the top five priorities in your life (for example, fame, wealth, family, spirituality, peace of mind, individuality, artistic expression). Compare your list with the priorities that appear to be valued in the culture in which you are currently living. (You can be as broad or as narrow as you like in defining *culture* for this exercise, such as overall U.S. culture or culture in your college or university.) Do your personal priorities align with the culture's priorities? If not, how might this disparity affect your communication with other members of the culture? [LO-2]
3. How does making an effort to avoid assumptions contribute to the practice of cultural pluralism? [LO-3]
4. Why is it important to understand your own culture when attempting to communicate with people from other cultures? [LO-4]
5. Think about the last three movies or television shows set in the United States that you've watched. In what ways would these entertainment products be helpful or unhelpful for people from other countries trying to learn about U.S. culture? [LO-5]

PRACTICE YOUR SKILLS

Message for Analysis:
Adapting to Cultural Differences [LO-5]

Your boss wants to send a brief email message, welcoming employees recently transferred to your department from the company's Hong Kong branch. These employees, all of whom are Hong Kong natives, speak English, but your boss asks you to review his message for clarity. What would you suggest your boss change in the following email message—and why? Would you consider this message to be audience centered? Why or why not? (Hint: Do some quick research on Hong Kong to identify the style of English that people in Hong Kong are likely to speak.)

> I wanted to welcome you ASAP to our little family here in the States. It's high time we shook hands in person and not just across the sea. I'm pleased as punch about getting to know you all, and I for one will do my level best to sell you on America.

Exercises

Active links for all websites in this chapter can be found on MyBcommLab; see your User Guide for instructions on accessing the content for this chapter. Each activity is labeled according to the primary skill or skills you will need to use. To review relevant chapter content, you can refer to the indicated Learning Objective. In some instances, supporting information will be found in another chapter, as indicated.

1. **Intercultural Communication: Recognizing Cultural Variations [LO-1], [LO-3], [LO-4]** Review the definitions of the generations on page 69. Based on your year of birth, in which generation do you belong? Do you feel a part of this generation? Why or why not? If you were born outside the United States, do the generational boundaries seem accurate to you? Now consider the biases that you might have regarding other generations. For example, if you are a member of Generation Y, what do you think about the Baby Boomers and their willingness to embrace new ideas? Identify several of your generational biases that could create friction in the workplace. Summarize your responses to these questions in a post on your class blog or an email message to your instructor.

2. **Intercultural Communication: Adapting to Cultural Variations [LO-2]** You are a new manager at K & J Brick, a masonry products company that is now run by the two sons of the man who founded it 50 years ago. For years, the co-owners have invited the management team to a wilderness lodge for a combination of outdoor sports and annual business planning meetings. You don't want to miss the event, but you know that the outdoor activities weren't designed for someone like you, whose physical impairments prevent participation in the sporting events. Draft a short email message to the rest of the management team, suggesting changes to the annual event that will allow all managers to participate.

3. **Intercultural Communication: Recognizing Cultural Variations [LO-2]** Differences in gender, age, and physical abilities contribute to the diversity of today's workforce. Working with a classmate, role-play a conversation in which

   a. a woman is being interviewed for a job by a male personnel manager.
   b. an older person is being interviewed for a job by a younger personnel manager.
   c. an employee who is a native speaker of English is being interviewed for a job by a hiring manager who is a recent immigrant with relatively poor English skills.

   How did differences between the applicant and the interviewer shape the communication? What can you do to improve communication in such situations?

4. **Intercultural Communication: Recognizing Cultural Variations [LO-3]** You represent a Canadian toy company that's negotiating to buy miniature truck wheels from a manufacturer in Osaka, Japan. In your first meeting, you explain that your company expects to control the design of the wheels as well as the materials that are used to make them. The manufacturer's representative looks down and says softly, "Perhaps that will be difficult." You press for agreement, and to emphasize your willingness to buy, you show the prepared contract you've brought with you. However, the manufacturer seems increasingly vague and uninterested. What cultural differences may be interfering with effective communication in this situation? (Canada is considered a low-context culture; Japan is high-context.) In a brief email message to your instructor or a post on your class blog, share your analysis.

5. **Intercultural Communication: Writing for Multiple-Language Audiences [LO-5]** Reading English-language content written by nonnative speakers of English can be a good reminder of the challenges of communicating in another language. The writing can be confusing or even amusing at first glance, but the key to remember here is that your writing might sound just as confusing or amusing to someone else if your roles were reversed.

   Identify a company that is based in a non-English speaking country but that includes English-language text on its website. (The "Advanced" search capabilities of your favorite search engine can help you locate websites from a particular country.) Study the language on this site. Does it sound as though it was written by someone adept at English? If the first site you've found does have writing that sounds natural to a native U.S. English speaker, find another company whose website doesn't. Select a section of text, at least several sentences long, and rewrite it to sound more "American." Submit the original text and your rewritten version to your instructor.

6. **Intercultural Communication: Writing for Multiple-Language Audiences; Collaboration: Team Projects [LO-5], Chapter 2** With a team assigned by your instructor,

review the Facebook pages of five companies, looking for words and phrases that might be confusing to a nonnative speaker of English. If you (or someone on the team) is a nonnative speaker, explain to the team why those word choices could be confusing. Choose three sentences, headlines, company slogans, or other pieces of text that contain potentially confusing words and rewrite them to minimize the chances of misinterpretation. As much as possible, try to retain the tone of the original—although you may find that this is impossible in some instances. Use Google Docs to compile the original selections and your revised versions, then email the documents to your instructor.

7. **Intercultural Communication: Speaking with Multiple-Language Audiences; Collaboration: Team Projects [LO-5], Chapter 2** Working with two other students, prepare a list of 10 examples of slang (in your own language) that might be misinterpreted or misunderstood during a business conversation with someone from another culture. Next to each example, suggest other words you might use to convey the same message. Do the alternatives mean *exactly* the same as the original slang or idiom? Submit your list of original words and suggested replacements, with an explanation of why each replacement is better than the original.

8. **Intercultural Communication: Studying Cultures [LO-5]** Choose a specific country, such as India, Portugal, Bolivia, Thailand, or Nigeria, with which you are not familiar. Research the culture and write a brief summary for your class blog of what a U.S. manager would need to know about concepts of personal space and rules of social behavior in order to conduct business successfully in that country.

9. **Intercultural Communication: Writing for Multiple-Language Audiences [LO-5]** Explore the powers and limitations of free online translation services such as Yahoo! Babel Fish (http://babelfish.yahoo.com) or Google Translate (http://translate.google.com). Enter a sentence from this chapter, such as "Local markets are opening to worldwide competition as businesses of all sizes look for new growth opportunities outside their own countries." First, translate the sentence from English to Spanish and click to complete the translation. Next, copy the Spanish version and paste it into the translation entry box and back-translate it from Spanish to English. Now repeat this test for German, French, Italian, or another language. Did the sentence survive the round trip? Does it still sound like normal business writing when translated back into English?

   (1) What are the implications for the use of automated translation services for international correspondence? (2) Would you feel comfortable using an online tool such as this to translate an important business message? (3) How might you use this website to sharpen your intercultural communication skills? Summarize your findings in a brief report.

10. **Intercultural Communication: Speaking with Multiple-Language Audiences; Media Skills: Podcasting [LO-5], Chapter 7** Your company was one of the first to use podcasting as a business communication tool. Executives frequently record messages (such as monthly sales summaries) and post them on the company's intranet site; employees from the 14 offices in Europe, Asia, and North America then download the files to their music players or other devices and listen to the messages while riding the train to work, eating lunch at their desks, and so on. Your boss asks you to draft the opening statement for a podcast that will announce a revenue drop caused by intensive competitive pressure. She reviews your script and hands it back with a gentle explanation that it needs to be revised for international listeners. Improve the following statement in as many ways as you can:

Howdy, comrades. Shouldn't surprise anyone that we took a beating this year, given the insane pricing moves our knucklehead competitors have been making. I mean, how those clowns can keep turning a profit is beyond me, what with steel costs still going through the roof and labor costs heating up—even in countries where everybody goes to find cheap labor—and hazardous waste disposal regs adding to operating costs, too.

EXPAND YOUR SKILLS

Critique the Professionals

Find an online business document—such as a company webpage, blog post, Facebook Info tab, or LinkedIn profile—that you believe commits an intercultural communication blunder by failing to consider the needs of at least some of its target readers. For example, a website might use slang or idiomatic language that could confuse some readers, or it might use language that offends some readers. In a post on your class blog, share the text you found and explain why you think it does not succeed as effective intercultural communication. Be sure to include a link back to the original material.

Sharpening Your Career Skills Online

Bovée and Thill's Business Communication Web Search, at http://businesscommunicationblog.com/websearch, is a unique research tool designed specifically for business communication research. Use the Web Search function to find a website, video, podcast, or PowerPoint presentation that offers advice on communicating with business contacts in another country or culture. Write a brief email message to your instructor, describing the item that you found and summarizing the career skills information you learned from it.

CHAPTER 4	**Planning Business Messages**
CHAPTER 5	**Writing Business Messages**
CHAPTER 6	**Completing Business Messages**

Every professional can learn to write more effectively while spending less time and energy creating effective messages. Discover a proven writing process that divides the challenge of communicating into three simple steps: planning, writing, and completing messages. The process works for everything from blog posts to formal reports to your résumé. With a bit of practice, you'll be using the process to write more effectively without even thinking about it.

4 Planning Business Messages

LEARNING OBJECTIVES   After studying this chapter, you will be able to

1 Describe the three-step writing process

2 Explain why it's important to analyze a communication situation in order to define your purpose and profile your audience before writing a message

3 Discuss information-gathering options for simple messages and identify three attributes of quality information

4 List the factors to consider when choosing the most appropriate medium for a message

5 Explain why good organization is important to both you and your audience and list the tasks involved in organizing a message

MyBcommLab Test your mastery of this chapter and its Learning Objectives. Visit mybcommlab.com to apply what you've learned in Document Makeovers and interactive simulation scenarios.

COMMUNICATION CLOSE-UP AT **H&R BLOCK**

The tax services giant H&R Block uses social media extensively to build relationships with clients and customers. The company's YouTube channel, for example, offers videos with tax tips and gives H&R Block employees the opportunity to answer questions from viewers.

www.hrblock.com

Many U.S. taxpayers don't think about their taxes until they absolutely have to, and then they want to think about taxes as little as possible. In this context of extreme apathy, H&R Block certainly has a challenge on its hands when it wants to communicate with taxpayers about tax preparation products and services.

H&R Block is the leading tax-preparation firm in the United States, with a range of options for virtually every class of taxpayer. Those who want to avoid the laborious chore of doing their own taxes can hand the job over to a tax professional in one of the company's 13,000 offices nationwide. In contrast, those taxpayers who are willing to do most or all of the work themselves can choose from a variety of digital alternatives, including both PC software and web-based solutions.

Although tax preparation is one of the least exciting consumer experiences, H&R Block has developed a reputation for creative communication efforts that make use of the latest innovations in social media. For example, in a recent product launch that noted media expert Shel Israel characterized as "among the most extensive business-to-consumer social media campaigns in history," the company used a variety of techniques to connect with potential customers: videos on YouTube (including a contest for user-created videos), profiles on MySpace and Facebook, Twitter microblogging, and "H&R Block Island" in the virtual world Second Life.

The innovations aren't simply about technology, however. In the spirit of Business Communication 2.0 (see Chapter 1), the company emphasizes a conversational, two-way approach in which the company listens as carefully as it speaks. For example, staffers follow a large number of Twitter users who have asked tax questions in the past, with the goal of maintaining an open channel of communication.

Particularly coming from a company that has a stodgy, old-school image in the minds of many people, this cutting-edge communication has surprised more than a few social media observers. Perhaps even more amazing is that H&R Block has actually generated some public interest in the field of tax preparation.[1]

Understanding the Three-Step Writing Process

1 LEARNING OBJECTIVE

Describe the three-step writing process.

The three-step writing process consists of planning, writing, and completing your message.

The emphasis that H&R Block (profiled in the chapter-opening Communication Close-up) puts on connecting with customers is a lesson that applies to business messages for all stakeholders. Fortunately, by following the process introduced in this chapter, you can learn to create successful messages that meet audience needs and highlight your skills as a perceptive business professional.

The three-step writing process (see Figure 4.1) helps ensure that your messages are both *effective* (meeting your audience's needs and getting your points across) and *efficient* (making the best use of your time and your audience's time):

- **Step 1: Planning business messages.** To plan any message, first *analyze the situation* by defining your purpose and developing a profile of your audience. When you're sure what you need to accomplish with your message, *gather information* that will meet your audience's needs. Next, *select the right medium* (oral, written, visual, or electronic) to deliver your message. Then *organize the information* by defining your main idea, limiting your scope, selecting the direct or indirect approach, and outlining your content. Planning messages is the focus of this chapter.
- **Step 2: Writing business messages.** After you've planned your message, *adapt to your audience* with sensitivity, relationship skills, and an appropriate writing style. Then you're ready to *compose your message* by choosing strong words, creating effective

MyBcommLab

- Access this chapter's simulation entitled The Communication Process, located at mybcommlab.com.

1 Plan →	**2 Write** →	**3 Complete**
Analyze the Situation Define your purpose and develop an audience profile.	**Adapt to Your Audience** Be sensitive to audience needs by using a "you" attitude, politeness, positive emphasis, and unbiased language. Build a strong relationship with your audience by establishing your credibility and projecting your company's preferred image. Control your style with a conversational tone, plain English, and appropriate voice.	**Revise the Message** Evaluate content and review readability, edit and rewrite for conciseness and clarity.
Gather Information Determine audience needs and obtain the information necessary to satisfy those needs.		**Produce the Message** Use effective design elements and suitable layout for a clean, professional appearance.
Select the Right Medium Select the best medium for delivering your message.		**Proofread the Message** Review for errors in layout, spelling, and mechanics.
Organize the Information Define your main idea, limit your scope, select a direct or an indirect approach, and outline your content.	**Compose the Message** Choose strong words that will help you create effective sentences and coherent paragraphs.	**Distribute the Message** Deliver your message using the chosen medium; make sure all documents and all relevant files are distributed successfully.

Figure 4.1 The Three-Step Writing Process
This three-step process will help you create more effective messages in any medium. As you get more practice with the process, it will become easier and more automatic.

sentences, and developing coherent paragraphs. Writing business messages is discussed in Chapter 5.

- **Step 3: Completing business messages.** After writing your first draft, *revise your message* by evaluating the content, reviewing readability, and editing and rewriting until your message comes across concisely and clearly, with correct grammar, proper punctuation, and effective format. Next, *produce your message*. Put it into the form that your audience will receive and review all design and layout decisions for an attractive, professional appearance. *Proofread* the final product to ensure high quality and then *distribute your message*. Completing business messages is discussed in Chapter 6.

Throughout this book, you'll learn how to apply these steps to a wide variety of business messages: short messages such as social network and blog posts (Chapters 7 through 10), longer messages such as reports and wikis (Chapters 13 through 15), oral presentations (Chapters 16 and 17), and the employment messages you can use to build a great career (Chapters 18 and 19).

OPTIMIZING YOUR WRITING TIME

As a starting point, allot half your available time for planning, one-quarter for writing, and one-quarter for completing your messages—but adjust these percentages for each project.

The more you use the three-step writing process, the more intuitive and automatic it will become. You'll also get better at allotting your time for each task during a writing project. Start by figuring out how much time you have to spend on a given project. Then, as a general rule, set aside roughly 50 percent of that time for planning, 25 percent for writing, and 25 percent for completing.

Allotting half your time for planning might seem excessive, but as the next section explains, careful planning usually saves time overall by focusing your writing and reducing rework. Of course, the ideal time split varies from project to project. Simpler and shorter messages require less planning than long reports, websites, and other complex projects. Also, the time required to produce and distribute messages can vary widely, depending on the media, the size of the audience, and other factors. However, start with the 50–25–25 split as a guideline and use your best judgment for each project.

PLANNING EFFECTIVELY

Trying to save time by skimping on planning usually costs you more time in the long run.

As soon as the need to create a message appears, inexperienced communicators are often tempted to dive directly into writing. However, skipping or shortchanging the planning stage often creates extra work and stress later in the process. First, thoughtful planning is necessary to make sure you provide the right information in the right format to the right people. Taking the time to understand your audience members and their needs helps you find and assemble the facts they're looking for and deliver that information in a concise and compelling way. Second, with careful planning, the writing stage is faster, easier, and a lot less stressful. Third, planning can save you from embarrassing blunders that could hurt your company or your career.

Analyzing the Situation

Every communication effort takes place in a particular situation, meaning you have a specific message to send a specific audience under a specific set of circumstances. For example, describing your professional qualifications in an email message to an executive in your own company differs significantly from describing your qualifications in your LinkedIn profile. The email message is likely to be focused on one specific goal, such as explaining why you would be a good choice to head up a major project, and you have the luxury of focusing on the needs of a single, personally identifiable reader. In contrast, your social networking profile could have multiple goals, such as connecting with your peers in other companies and presenting your qualifications to potential employers, and it might be viewed by hundreds or thousands of readers, each with his or her own needs.

The underlying information for these two messages could be roughly the same, but the level of detail to include, the tone of the writing, the specific word choices—these and other choices you need to make will differ from one situation to another. Making the right choices starts with defining your purpose clearly and understanding your audience's needs.

DEFINING YOUR PURPOSE

All business messages have a **general purpose**: to inform, to persuade, or to collaborate with the audience. This purpose helps define the overall approach you'll need to take, from gathering information to organizing your message. Within the scope of its general purpose, each message also has a **specific purpose**, which identifies what you hope to accomplish with your message and what your audience should do or think after receiving your message. For instance, is your goal simply to update your audience about some upcoming event, or do you want people to take immediate action? State your specific purpose as precisely as possible, even to the point of identifying which audience members should respond, how they should respond, and when.

After you have defined your specific purpose, take a moment for a reality check. Decide whether that purpose merits the time and effort required for you to prepare and send the message—and for your audience to spend the time required to read it, view it, or listen to it. Test your purpose by asking these four questions:

- **Will anything change as a result of your message?** Don't contribute to information overload by sending messages that won't change anything. For instance, if you don't like your company's latest advertising campaign but you're not in a position to influence it, sending a critical message to your colleagues won't change anything and won't benefit anyone.
- **Is your purpose realistic?** Recognizing whether a goal is realistic is an important part of having good business sense. For example, if you request a raise while the company is struggling, you might send the message that you're not tuned into the situation around you.
- **Is the time right?** People who are busy or distracted when they receive your message are less likely to pay attention to it. Many professions and departments have recurring cycles in their workloads, for instance, and messages sent during peak times may be ignored.
- **Is your purpose acceptable to your organization?** Your company's business objectives and policies, and even laws that apply to your particular industry, may dictate whether a particular purpose is acceptable.

When you are satisfied that you have a clear and meaningful purpose and that this is a smart time to proceed, your next step is to understand the members of your audience and their needs.

DEVELOPING AN AUDIENCE PROFILE

The more you know about your audience members, their needs, and their expectations, the more effectively you'll be able to communicate with them. Follow these steps to conduct a thorough audience analysis (see Figure 4.2 on page 90):

- **Identify your primary audience.** For some messages, certain audience members may be more important than others. Don't ignore the needs of less influential members, but make sure you address the concerns of the key decision makers.
- **Determine audience size and geographic distribution.** A message aimed at 10,000 people spread around the globe will probably require a different approach than one aimed at a dozen people down the hall.
- **Determine audience composition.** Look for similarities and differences in culture, language, age, education, organizational rank and status, attitudes, experience, motivations, and any other factors that could affect the successful reception and decoding of your message.

> Your general purpose may be to inform, to persuade, or to collaborate.
>
> Your specific purpose is what you hope to accomplish with your message and what your audience should do or think after receiving your message.

> Wait to send a message, or do not send it at all, if
> - Nothing will change as a result of sending
> - The purpose is not realistic
> - The timing is not right
> - The purpose is not acceptable to your organization

REAL-TIME UPDATES
Learn More by Reading This PDF

Dig deep into audience needs with this planning tool

This in-depth audience analysis tool can help you analyze audience needs for even the most complex communication scenarios. Go to http://real-timeupdates.com/bct11 and click on "Learn More." If you are using MyBcommLab, you can access Real-Time Updates within each chapter or under Student Study Tools.

Audience analysis notes

Project: A report recommending that we close down the on-site exercise facility and subsidize private memberships at local health clubs.

- **Primary audience:** Nicole Perazzo, vice president of operations, and her supervisory team.

- **Size and geographic distribution:** Nine managers total; Nicole and five of her staff are here on site; three other supervisors are based in Hong Kong.

- **Composition:** All have experience in operations management, but several are new to the company.

- **Level of understanding:** All will no doubt understand the financial considerations, but the newer managers may not understand the importance of the on-site exercise facility to many of our employees.

- **Expectations and preferences.** They're expecting a firm recommendation, backed up with well-thought-out financial rationale and suggestions for communicating the bad news to employees. For a decision of this magnitude, a formal report is appropriate; email distribution is expected.

- **Probable reaction.** From one-on-one discussions, I know that several of the managers receiving this report are active users of the on-site facility and won't welcome the suggestion that we should shut it down. However, some nonexercisers generally think it's a luxury the company can't afford. Audience reactions will range from highly positive to highly negative; the report should focus on overcoming the highly negative reactions since they're the ones I need to convince.

Figure 4.2   Example of Using Audience Analysis to Plan a Message
For simple, routine messages, you usually don't need to analyze your audience in depth. However, for complex messages or messages for indifferent or hostile audiences, take the time to study their information needs and potential reactions to your message.

If audience members have different levels of understanding of the topic, aim your message at the most influential decision makers.

- **Gauge audience members' level of understanding.** If audience members share your general background, they'll probably understand your material without difficulty. If not, your message will need an element of education to help people understand your message.
- **Understand audience expectations and preferences.** For example, will members of your audience expect complete details or just a summary of the main points? In general, for internal communication, the higher up the organization your message goes, the fewer details people want to see.

To win over a skeptical audience, use a gradual approach and plenty of evidence.

- **Forecast probable audience reaction.** As you'll read later in the chapter, potential audience reaction affects message organization. If you expect a favorable response, you can state conclusions and recommendations up front and offer minimal supporting evidence. If you expect skepticism, you can introduce conclusions gradually and with more proof.

Gathering Information

3 **LEARNING OBJECTIVE**

Discuss information-gathering options for simple messages, and identify three attributes of quality information.

When you have a clear picture of your audience, your next step is to assemble the information that you will include in your message. For simple messages, you may already have all the information at hand, but for more complex messages, you may need to do considerable research and analysis before you're ready to begin writing. Chapter 11 explores formal techniques for finding, evaluating, and processing information. Meanwhile, you can often use a variety of informal techniques to gather insights and guide your research efforts:

- **Consider the audience's perspective.** Put yourself in the audience's position; what are these people thinking, feeling, or planning? What information do they need to move in the direction you would like them to move?

- **Read reports and other company documents.** Annual reports, financial statements, news releases, blogs by industry experts, marketing reports, and customer surveys are just a few of the many potential sources. Find out whether your company has a *knowledge-management system*, a centralized database that collects the experiences and insights of employees throughout the organization.
- **Ask supervisors, colleagues, customers, or people in your online networks.** Fellow workers and customers may have information you need, or they may know what your audience will be interested in. And one of the huge advantages of social media is the ability to quickly locate experts and sources of vital information.
- **Ask your audience for input.** If you're unsure what audience members need from your message, ask them. Admitting you don't know but want to meet their needs will impress an audience more than guessing and getting it wrong.

UNCOVERING AUDIENCE NEEDS

In many situations, your audience's information needs will be obvious, or readers will be able to tell you what they need. In other situations, though, people may be unable to articulate exactly what is needed. If someone makes a vague or broad request, ask questions to narrow the focus. If your boss says, "Find out everything you can about Interscope Records," narrow the investigation by asking which aspect of the company and its business is most important. Asking a question or two often forces the person to think through the request and define more precisely what is required.

If you're given a vague request, ask questions to clarify it before you plan a response.

In addition, try to think of relevant information needs that your audience may not have expressed. Suppose you've been asked to compare two health insurance plans for your firm's employees, but your research has uncovered a third alternative that might be even better. You could then expand your report to include a brief explanation of why the third plan should be considered and compare it to the two original plans. Use judgment, however; in some situations you need to provide only what the audience expects and nothing more.

If appropriate, include additional information that might be helpful, even though the requester didn't specifically ask for it.

FINDING YOUR FOCUS

You may encounter situations in which the assignment or objective is so vague that you have no idea how to get started in determining what the audience needs to know. In such cases, you can use some *discovery techniques* to help generate ideas and uncover possible avenues to research. One popular technique is **free writing**, in which you write whatever comes to mind, without stopping to make any corrections, for a set period of time. The big advantage of free writing is that you silence your "inner critic" and just express ideas as they come to you. You might end up with a rambling mess by any conventional measure, but that's not important. Within that tangle of expressions, you might also find some useful ideas and angles that hadn't occurred to you yet—perhaps the crucial idea that will jumpstart the entire project.

If you're stuck for ideas, try free writing or sketching ideas instead of writing them.

The best discovery option in some cases might not be writing at all, but rather *sketching*. If you're unable to come up with any words, grab a sketchpad and start drawing. While you're thinking visually, your brain might release some great ideas that were trapped behind words.

The techniques listed under "Defining Your Main Idea" on page 100 can also be helpful if you don't know where to start.

PROVIDING REQUIRED INFORMATION

After you've defined your audience's information needs, be ready to satisfy those needs completely. One good way to test the thoroughness of your message is to use the **journalistic approach:** Check to see whether your message answers *who, what, when, where, why,* and *how.* Using this method, you can

REAL-TIME UPDATES
Learn More by Reading This Article

Need some fresh creative inspiration?

If you're stuck on a project and your brain could use a little spark, try these unusual, creative techniques to break through tough problems. Go to http://real-timeupdates.com/bct11 and click on "Learn More." If you are using MyBcommLab, you can access Real-Time Updates within each chapter or under Student Study Tools.

Test the completeness of your document by making sure it answers all six journalistic questions: *who, what, when, where, why,* and *how.*

quickly tell whether a message fails to deliver. For example, consider this message requesting information from employees:

> We are exploring ways to reduce our office space leasing costs and would like your input on a proposed plan in which employees who telecommute on alternate days could share offices. Please let me know what you think of this proposal.

The message fails to tell employees everything they need to know in order to provide meaningful responses. The *what* could be improved by identifying the specific information points the writer needs from employees (such as whether individual telecommuting patterns are predictable enough to allow scheduling of shared offices). The writer also doesn't specify *when* the responses are needed or *how* the employees should respond. By failing to address such points, the request is likely to generate a variety of responses, some possibly helpful but some probably not.

Be Sure the Information Is Accurate

Be certain that the information you provide is accurate and that the commitments you make can be kept.

The *quality* of the information you provide is every bit as important as the *quantity*. Inaccurate information in business messages can cause a host of problems, from embarrassment and lost productivity to serious safety and legal issues. You may commit the organization to promises it isn't able to keep—and the error could harm your reputation as a reliable businessperson. Thanks to the Internet, inaccurate information may persist for years after you distribute it.

You can minimize mistakes by double-checking every piece of information you collect. If you are consulting sources outside the organization, ask yourself whether the information is current and reliable. You must be particularly careful when using sources you find online. As you'll read in Chapter 11, the simplicity of online publishing and the frequent lack of editorial oversight call for extra care in using online information. Be sure to review any mathematical or financial calculations. Check all dates and schedules and examine your own assumptions and conclusions to be certain they are valid.

Be Sure the Information Is Ethical

A clear sense of ethics should guide your decisions when determining how much detail to include in your message.

By working hard to ensure the accuracy of the information you gather, you'll also avoid many ethical problems in your messages. If you do make an honest mistake, such as

---

| **ETHICS DETECTIVE** | Solving the Case of the Missing Safety Warning |

Your company, Furniture Formations, creates a variety of home furniture products, with extensive use of fine woods. To preserve the look and feel of the wood, your craftspeople use an oil-based finish that you purchase from a local building products wholesaler. The workers apply the finish with rags, which are thrown away after each project. After a news report about spontaneous combustion of waste rags in other furniture shops, you grow concerned enough to contact the wholesaler and ask for verification of the product's safety. The wholesaler knows that you've been considering a nonflammable, water-based alternative from another source but tries to assure you with the following message:

> Seal the rags in an approved container and dispose of it according to local regulations. As you probably already know, county regulations require all commercial users of solvent-based materials to dispose of leftover finishes at the county's hazardous waste facility.

You're still not satisfied. You visit the website of the oil's manufacturer, Minwax, and find the following cautionary statement about the product you're currently using:

> For some products, when oil-soaked rags and other porous waste are improperly discarded, heat can build up which may result in flames that immediately feed on the oil-soaked material. This phenomenon is known as spontaneous combustion and can be avoided simply by immersing all wood-finishing materials, including rags, steel wool and other waste, in a water-filled, metal container. Seal the container and dispose of in accordance with local regulations.

ANALYSIS

Was the wholesaler guilty of an ethical lapse in this case? If yes, explain what you think the lapse is and why you believe it is unethical. If no, explain why you think the statement qualifies as ethical.

delivering information you initially thought to be true but later found to be false, contact the recipients of the message immediately and correct the error. No one can reasonably fault you in such circumstances, and people will respect your honesty.

Messages can also be unethical if important information is omitted (see "Ethics Detective: Solving the Case of the Missing Safety Warning"). Of course, as a business professional, you may have legal or other sound business reasons for not including every detail about every matter. Just how much detail should you include? Make sure you include enough detail to avoid misleading your audience. If you're unsure how much information your audience needs, offer as much as you believe best fits your definition of complete and then offer to provide more upon request.

Be Sure the Information Is Pertinent

When gathering information for your message, remember that some points will be more important to your audience than others. Audience members will appreciate your efforts to prioritize the information they need and filter out the information they don't. Moreover, by focusing on the information that concerns your audience the most, you increase your chances of accomplishing your own communication goals.

If you don't know your audience or if you're communicating with a large group of people who have diverse interests, use common sense to identify points of interest. Audience factors such as age, job, location, income, and education can give you a clue. If you're trying to sell memberships in a health club, you might adjust your message for athletes, busy professionals, families, and people in different locations or in different income brackets. The comprehensive facilities and professional trainers would appeal to athletes, whereas the low monthly rates would appeal to college students on tight budgets.

Some messages necessarily reach audiences with a diverse mix of educational levels, subject awareness, and other variables. In these cases, your only choice is to try to accommodate the likely range of audience members.

> Audiences respond best to information that has been filtered and prioritized to meet their needs.

> Rely on common sense if you don't know enough about your audience to know exactly what will interest them.

Selecting the Right Medium

A **medium** is the form through which you choose to communicate a message. You may choose to talk with someone face to face, post to a blog, send an email message, or create a webcast. The range of media possibilities is wide and growing wider all the time. In fact, with so many options now available, selecting the best medium for a given message is itself an important communication skill (see Figure 4.3).

4 LEARNING OBJECTIVE

List the factors to consider when choosing the most appropriate medium for a message.

Figure 4.3 Media Choices
Online video has become one of the most important media for business communication. On its branded YouTube channel, Burton Snowboards offers numerous short videos that portray the excitement of snowboarding.

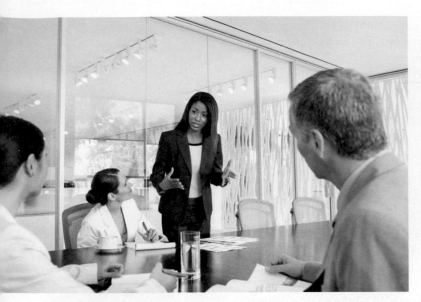

The higher you rise in an organization, the more time you'll spend talking and listening. Your ability to communicate with people from virtually any background will be key to your success.

Although media categories have become increasingly blurred in recent years, for the sake of discussion, you can think of media as being *oral*, *written*, *visual*, or *electronic* (which often combines several media types).

ORAL MEDIA

Oral media include face-to-face conversations, interviews, speeches, and in-person presentations and meetings. By giving communicators the ability to see, hear, and react to each other, oral media are useful for encouraging people to ask questions, make comments, and work together to reach a consensus or decision. For example, experts recommend that managers engage in frequent "walk-arounds," chatting with employees to get input, answer their questions, and interpret important business events and trends.[2]

Of course, if you don't want a lot of questions or interaction, using oral media can be an unwise choice. However, consider your audience carefully before deciding to limit interaction by choosing a different medium. As a manager, you will encounter unpleasant situations (declining an employee's request for a raise, for example)

Oral communication is best when you need to encourage interaction, express emotions, or monitor emotional responses.

for which sending an email message or otherwise avoiding personal contact will seem appealing to you. In many such cases, though, you owe the other party the opportunity to ask questions or express concerns. Moreover, facing the tough situations in person will earn you a reputation as an honest, caring manager.

WRITTEN MEDIA

Nonelectronic written messages have been replaced in many instances by electronic media, although printed messages still have a place in business today.

Written messages take many forms, from traditional memos to glossy reports that rival magazines in production quality. **Memos** are brief printed documents traditionally used for the routine, day-to-day exchange of information within an organization. In many organizations, social networking, IM, email, blogs, and other electronic media have largely replaced paper memos.

Letters are brief written messages generally sent to recipients outside the organization. In addition to conveying a particular message, they perform an important public relations function in fostering good working relationships with customers, suppliers, and others. Many organizations save time and money on routine communication with *form letters*, in which a standard message is personalized as needed for each recipient.

Reports and proposals are usually longer than memos and letters, although both can be created in memo or letter format. These documents come in a variety of lengths, ranging from a few pages to several hundred, and are usually fairly formal in tone. Chapters 13 through 15 discuss reports and proposals in detail.

VISUAL MEDIA

In some situations, a message that is predominantly visual, with text used to support the illustration, can be more effective than a message that relies primarily on text.

Although you probably won't work with many messages that are purely visual (with no text), the importance of visual elements in business communication continues to grow. Traditional business messages rely primarily on text, with occasional support from graphical elements such as charts, graphs, or diagrams to help illustrate points discussed in the text. However, many business communicators are discovering the power of messages in which the visual element is dominant and supported by small amounts of text. For the purposes of this discussion, you can think of *visual media* as any format in which one or more visual elements play a central role in conveying the message content (see Figure 4.4).

Messages that combine powerful visuals with supporting text, sometimes known as *infographics*, can be effective for a number of reasons. Today's audiences are pressed for time and bombarded with messages, so anything that communicates quickly is welcome. Visuals are also effective at describing complex ideas and processes because they can

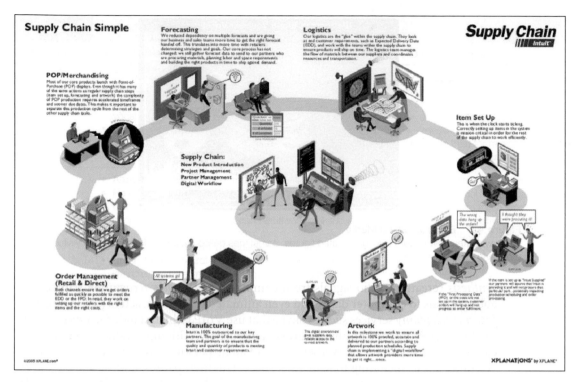

Figure 4.4 Visual Media
In traditional business messages, visual elements usually support the text. However, in some instances, the message can be presented more effectively by reversing that relationship—basing the message on a dominant visual and using text to support that image.

reduce the work required for an audience to identify the parts and relationships that make up the whole. Also, in a multilingual business world, diagrams, symbols, and other images can lower communication barriers by requiring less language processing. Finally, visual depictions can be easier to remember than purely textual descriptions or explanations. Chapter 12 offers more information on visual design.

ELECTRONIC MEDIA

The range of electronic media is broad and continues to grow even broader, from phone calls and podcasts to blogs and wikis to email and text messaging. When you want to make a powerful impression, using electronic media can increase the excitement and visual appeal with interactivity, animation, audio, and video.

> In general, use electronic media to deliver messages quickly, to reach widely dispersed audiences, and to take advantage of rich multimedia formats.

The growth of electronic communication options is both a blessing and a curse for business communicators. On the one hand, you have more tools than ever before to choose from, with more ways to deliver rational and emotional content. On the other hand, the sheer range of choices can complicate your job, because you often need to choose among multiple media and you need to know how to use each medium successfully.

From the audience's perspective, a common frustration with electronic media is lack of integration, with people being forced to use an ever-growing arsenal of separate but overlapping media options in order to stay informed.[3] As the options multiply, the struggle to monitor multiple sources of information can consume considerable time and energy. To minimize frustration and maximize productivity, company managers should establish clear expectations for the use of electronic media and carefully integrate—or officially choose *not* to use—each new media innovation.

> Today's audiences can get frustrated with the sheer number of electronic media in the workplace.

You'll learn more about using electronic media throughout this book (in Chapter 7, in particular), but for now, here is a quick overview of the major electronic media being used in business:

- **Electronic versions of oral media.** These media include telephone calls, teleconferencing, voice-mail messages, audio recordings such as compact discs and podcasts, *voice*

Leaner:
fewer cues,
no interactivity,
no personal focus

Standard reports	Custom reports	Telephone calls	Face-to-face
Static webpages	Letters & memos	Teleconferencing	conversations
Mass media	Email & IM	Video (including	Multimedia
Posters & signs	Wikis	vodcasts,	presentations
	Blogs	vlogs,	Multimedia
	Podcasts	video IM)	webpages
			Virtual reality

Richer:
multiple cues,
interactive,
personalized

Figure 4.6 Media Richness
Business media vary widely in terms of *richness*, which is the number of informational cues available, their ability to incorporate feedback, and the degree to which they can be personalized.

members' time and workloads. If a message isn't urgent and doesn't require immediate feedback, choose a medium such as email that allows people to respond at their convenience.

- **Cost.** Cost is both a real financial factor and a perceived nonverbal signal. For example, depending on the context, extravagant (and expensive) video or multimedia presentations can send a nonverbal signal of sophistication and professionalism—or careless disregard for company budgets.

When choosing the appropriate medium, don't forget to consider your audience's preferences and expectations.

- **Audience preferences.** Be sure to consider which medium or media your audience expects or prefers.[9] For instance, businesspeople in the United States, Canada, and Germany emphasize written messages, whereas in Japan professionals tend to emphasize oral messages—perhaps because Japan's high-context culture carries so much of the message in nonverbal cues and "between-the-lines" interpretation.[10]

Organizing Your Information

Organization can make the difference between success and failure. Compare the two versions of the message in Figure 4.7. The ineffective version exhibits several common organization mistakes: taking too long to get to the point, including irrelevant material, getting ideas mixed up, and leaving out necessary information.

Explain why good organization is important to both you and your audience, and list the tasks involved in organizing a message.

RECOGNIZING THE IMPORTANCE OF GOOD ORGANIZATION

Good organization helps audience members understand your message, accept your message, and save time.

Good organization helps your readers or listeners in three key ways. First, it helps them understand your message. In a well-organized message, you make the main point clear at the outset, present additional points to support that main idea, and satisfy all the information needs of the audience. But if your message is poorly organized, your meaning can be obscured, and your audiences may form inaccurate conclusions about what you've written or said.

Second, good organization helps receivers accept your message. If your writing appears confused and disorganized, people will likely conclude that the *thinking* behind the writing is also confused and disorganized. Moreover, effective messages often require a bit more than simple, clear logic. A diplomatic approach helps receivers accept your message, even if it's not exactly what they want to hear. In contrast, a poorly organized message on an emotionally charged topic can alienate the audience before you have the chance to get your point across.

Good organization saves you time and energy in the writing and completing phases.

Third, good organization saves your audience time. Well-organized messages are efficient. They contain only relevant ideas, and they are brief. Moreover, each piece of information is located in a logical place in the overall flow; each section builds on the one before to create a coherent whole, without forcing people to look for missing pieces.

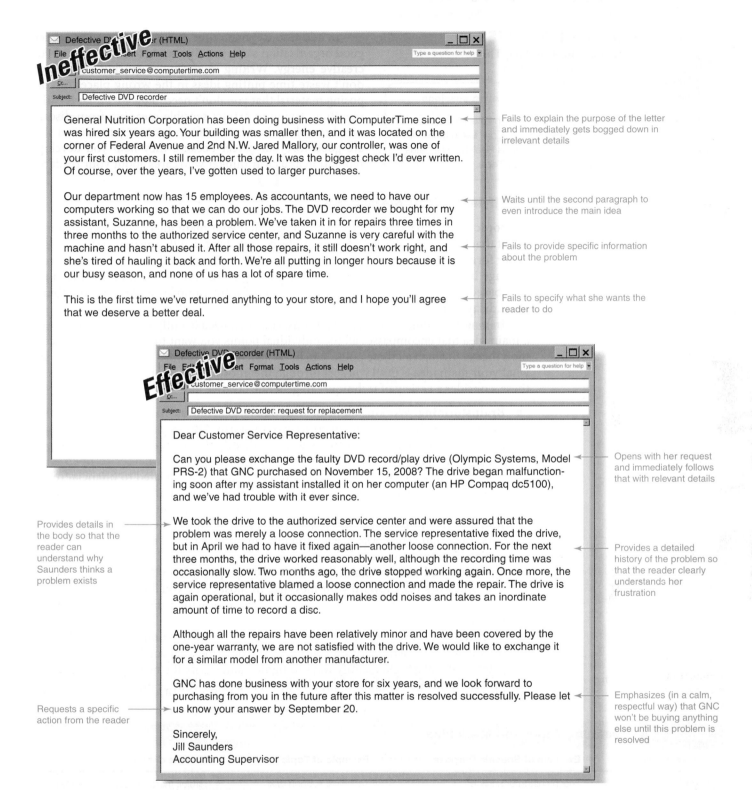

Better brokers
Willing to pay more

Figure 4.8 U
Mind mapping
that a complex
create graphica
insights into the

• **Mind m**
   mind m
   related i
   mapping

LIMITING

The **scope** of
the level of d
business me
you're using.
don't have a
main idea—a
   Whateve
to half a doz
Listing 20 or
being thorou
detail as ram
supporting p
customers, c
ate for your
points so tha
   The nur
communicat
topic, your a
their recepti

Ineffective

Defective D   r (HTML)

File   ert Format Tools Actions Help   Type a question for help

customer_service@computertime.com

Cc...

Subject: Defective DVD recorder

General Nutrition Corporation has been doing business with ComputerTime since I
was hired six years ago. Your building was smaller then, and it was located on the
corner of Federal Avenue and 2nd N.W. Jared Mallory, our controller, was one of
your first customers. I still remember the day. It was the biggest check I'd ever written.
Of course, over the years, I've gotten used to larger purchases.

Our department now has 15 employees. As accountants, we need to have our
computers working so that we can do our jobs. The DVD recorder we bought for my
assistant, Suzanne, has been a problem. We've taken it in for repairs three times in
three months to the authorized service center, and Suzanne is very careful with the
machine and hasn't abused it. After all those repairs, it still doesn't work right, and
she's tired of hauling it back and forth. We're all putting in longer hours because it is
our busy season, and none of us has a lot of spare time.

This is the first time we've returned anything to your store, and I hope you'll agree
that we deserve a better deal.

- Fails to explain the purpose of the letter and immediately gets bogged down in irrelevant details

- Waits until the second paragraph to even introduce the main idea

- Fails to provide specific information about the problem

- Fails to specify what she wants the reader to do

Effective

Defective DVD recorder (HTML)

File Edit   ert Format Tools Actions Help   Type a question for help

customer_service@computertime.com

Cc...

Subject: Defective DVD recorder: request for replacement

Dear Customer Service Representative:

Can you please exchange the faulty DVD record/play drive (Olympic Systems, Model
PRS-2) that GNC purchased on November 15, 2008? The drive began malfunctioning soon after my assistant installed it on her computer (an HP Compaq dc5100),
and we've had trouble with it ever since.

We took the drive to the authorized service center and were assured that the
problem was merely a loose connection. The service representative fixed the drive,
but in April we had to have it fixed again—another loose connection. For the next
three months, the drive worked reasonably well, although the recording time was
occasionally slow. Two months ago, the drive stopped working again. Once more, the
service representative blamed a loose connection and made the repair. The drive is
again operational, but it occasionally makes odd noises and takes an inordinate
amount of time to record a disc.

Although all the repairs have been relatively minor and have been covered by the
one-year warranty, we are not satisfied with the drive. We would like to exchange it
for a similar model from another manufacturer.

GNC has done business with your store for six years, and we look forward to
purchasing from you in the future after this matter is resolved successfully. Please let
us know your answer by September 20.

Sincerely,
Jill Saunders
Accounting Supervisor

- Provides details in the body so that the reader can understand why Saunders thinks a problem exists

- Requests a specific action from the reader

- Opens with her request and immediately follows that with relevant details

- Provides a detailed history of the problem so that the reader clearly understands her frustration

- Emphasizes (in a calm, respectful way) that GNC won't be buying anything else until this problem is resolved

Figure 4.7 Improving the Organization of a Message
The improved version of this email message is clear and efficient,
presenting only the necessary information in a logical sequence.

MyBcommLab

Apply Figure 4.7's key concepts by revising a new document. Go to
Chapter 4 in mybcommlab.com and select Document Makeovers.

The site's navigation is designed to let individual audience segments (in this case, content providers), find messages that address their unique concerns.

The first paragraph states the main idea, that Blu-ray is the ideal format for high-definition media content.

Each of the next four paragraphs focuses on one major supporting point, with carefully chosen details to back up each supporting point— without overloading the reader with too much detail or irrelevant information.

Figure 4.9   Limiting the Scope of a Message
The Blu-ray Disc Association is the industry consortium that oversees the technical standards and other matters related to Blu-ray discs used for movies, music, and data storage. In this section of its website, the association describes the benefits of the Blu-ray format, with a separate message for each of four stakeholder groups. This particular screen describes the benefits for one of those groups (*content providers*, such as movie studios). Notice how the scope of the message is limited to supporting a single main idea—the business benefits of Blu-ray for this specific audience.

You'll need fewer words to present routine information to a knowledgeable audience that already knows and respects you. You'll need more words to build a consensus about a complex and controversial subject, especially if the members of your audience are skeptical or hostile strangers.

CHOOSING BETWEEN DIRECT AND INDIRECT APPROACHES

After you've defined your main idea and supporting points, you're ready to decide on the sequence you will use to present your information. You have two basic options:

Use the direct approach if the audience's reaction is likely to be positive and the indirect approach if it is likely to be negative.

- **The direct approach.** When you know your audience will be receptive to your message, use the **direct approach**: Start with the main idea (such as a recommendation, a conclusion, or a request) and follow that with your supporting evidence.
- **The indirect approach.** When your audience will be skeptical about or even resistant to your message, use the **indirect approach**: Start with the evidence first and build your case before presenting the main idea.

To choose between these two alternatives, analyze your audience's likely reaction to your purpose and message (see Figure 4.10). Bear in mind, however, that Figure 4.10 presents only general guidelines; always consider the unique circumstances of each message and audience situation. The following sections offer more insight on choosing the best approach for routine and positive messages, negative messages, and persuasive messages.

The type of message also influences the choice of the direct or indirect approach. In the coming chapters, you'll get specific advice on choosing the best approach for a variety of communication challenges.

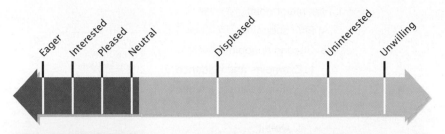

	Direct Approach	Indirect Approach	
Audience Reaction	Eager/interested/ pleased/neutral	Displeased	Uninterested/unwilling
Message Opening	Start with the main idea, the request, or the good news.	Start with a neutral statement that acts as a transition to the reasons for the bad news.	Start with a statement or question that captures attention.
Message Body	Provide necessary details.	Give reasons to justify a negative answer. State or imply the bad news, and make a positive suggestion.	Arouse the audience's interest in the subject. Build the audience's desire to comply.
Message Close	Close with a cordial comment, a reference to the good news, or a statement about the specific action desired.	Close cordially.	Request action.

Figure 4.10 Choosing Between the Direct and Indirect Approaches
Think about the way your audience is likely to respond before choosing your approach.

OUTLINING YOUR CONTENT

After you have chosen the best approach, it's time to figure out the most logical and effective way to present your major points and supporting details. Get into the habit of creating outlines when you're preparing business messages. You'll save time, get better results, and do a better job of navigating through complicated business situations. Even if you're just jotting down three or four key points, making an outline will help you organize your thoughts for faster writing. When you're preparing a longer, more complex message, an outline is indispensable because it helps you visualize the relationships among the various parts.

You're no doubt familiar with the basic outline formats that identify each point with a number or letter and that indent certain points to show which ones are of equal status. A good outline divides a topic into at least two parts, restricts each subdivision to one category, and ensures that each subdivision is separate and distinct (see Figure 4.11 on page 104).

Another way to visualize the outline of your message is to create an organization chart similar to the charts used to show a company's management structure (see Figure 4.12 on page 104). Put the main idea, like the top executive in a company, in the highest-level box to establish the big picture. The lower-level ideas, like lower-level employees, provide the details. All the ideas should be logically organized into divisions of thought, just as a company is organized into divisions and departments.[11] Using a visual chart instead of a traditional outline has many benefits. Charts help you (1) see the various levels of ideas and how the parts fit together, (2) develop new ideas, and (3) restructure your information flow. The mind-mapping technique used to generate ideas works in a similar way.

Whichever outlining or organizing scheme you use, start your message with the main idea, follow that with major supporting points, and then illustrate these points with evidence.

Start with the Main Idea

The main idea helps you establish the goals and general strategy of the message, and it summarizes two vital considerations: (1) *what* you want your audience members to do or think

You may want to experiment with other organizational schemes in addition to traditional outlines.

The main idea is a specific statement about your topic.

Figure 4.11   **Organizing Your Thoughts with a Clear Outline**
No matter what outlining format you use, think through your major supporting points and the examples and evidence that can support each point.

and (2) *why* they should do so. Everything in your message should either support the main idea or explain its implications. As discussed earlier, the direct approach states the main idea quickly and directly, whereas the indirect approach delays the main idea until after the evidence is presented.

State the Major Points

Major supporting points clarify and explain your main idea.

You need to support your main idea with major points that clarify and explain the main idea in concrete terms. If your purpose is to inform and the material is factual, your major points may be based on something physical or financial—something you can visualize or measure, such as activities to be performed, functional units, spatial or chronological relationships, or parts of a whole. When you're describing a process, the major points are almost inevitably steps in the process. When you're describing an object, the major points often correspond to the parts of the object. When you're giving a historical account, major points represent events in the chronological chain of events. If your purpose is to persuade or to collaborate, select major points that develop a line of reasoning or a logical argument that proves your central message and motivates your audience to act.

Figure 4.12   **Organization Chart Method for Outlining**
The organization chart approach is helpful when you're faced with a large variety of facts, figures, and other bits of information and aren't quite sure how they all might relate to one another. When you gather pieces of evidence together under major points, a clearer picture of the main idea will emerge.

Provide Examples and Evidence

After you've defined the main idea and identified major supporting points, think about examples and evidence that can confirm, illuminate, or expand on your supporting points. Choose examples and evidence carefully so that these elements support your overall message without distracting or overwhelming your audience. One good example, particularly if it is conveyed through a compelling story (see the next section), is usually more powerful than several weaker examples. Similarly, a few strong points of evidence are usually more persuasive than a large collection of minor details. Keep in mind that you can back up your major supporting points in a variety of ways, depending on the subject material and the available examples and evidence (see Table 4.3).

Back up your supporting points with carefully selected examples and evidence.

If your schedule permits, put your outline aside for a day or two before you begin composing your first draft. Then review it with a fresh eye, looking for opportunities to improve the flow of ideas.

BUILDING READER INTEREST WITH STORYTELLING TECHNIQUES

Storytelling might seem like an odd subject for a business course, but narrative techniques can be an effective way to organize messages in a surprising number of business communication situations, from recruiting and training employees to enticing investors and customers. Storytelling is such a vital means of communicating that, in the words of management consultant Steve Tobak, "It's hard to imagine your career going anywhere if you can't tell a story."[12] Fortunately, you've been telling stories all your life, so narrative techniques already come naturally to you; now it's just a matter of adapting those techniques to business situations.

You've already been on the receiving end of thousands of business stories—storytelling is one of the most common structures used in television commercials and other advertisements (see Figure 4.13 on page 106). People love to share stories about themselves and

TABLE 4.3	Six Types of Detail	
Type of Detail	**Example**	**Comment**
Facts and figures	Sales are strong this month. We have two new contracts worth $5 million and a good chance of winning another worth $2.5 million.	Enhances credibility more than any other type. Can become boring if used excessively. Most common type used in business.
Example or illustration	We've spent four months trying to hire recent accounting graduates, but so far, only one person has joined our firm. One candidate told me that she would love to work for us, but she can get $10,000 more a year elsewhere.	Adds life to a message, but one example does not prove a point. Idea must be supported by other evidence as well.
Description	Upscale hamburger restaurants target burger lovers who want more than the convenience and low prices of a McDonald's burger. These places feature wine and beer, half-pound burgers, and generous side dishes (nachos, potato skins). Atmosphere is key.	Helps audience visualize the subject by creating a sensory impression. Does not prove a point but clarifies it and makes it memorable. Begins with an overview of the function; defines its purpose, lists major parts, and explains how it operates.
Narration (storytelling)	When Rita Longworth took over as CEO, she faced a tough choice: shut down the tablet PC division entirely or outsource manufacturing as a way to lower costs while keeping the division alive. As her first step, she convened a meeting with all the managers in the division to get their input on the two options. (Story continues from there.)	Stimulates audience interest throughout dramatic tension. In many instances, must be supplemented with statistical data in order to prove a point convincingly.
Reference to authority	I discussed this idea with Jackie Loman in the Chicago plant, and she was very supportive. As you know, Jackie has been in charge of that plant for the past six years. She is confident that we can speed up the number 2 line by 150 units an hour if we add another worker.	Bolsters a case while adding variety and credibility. Works only if authority is recognized and respected by audience.
Visual aids	Graphs, charts, tables, infographics, data visualization	Helps audience grasp the key points about sets of data or visualize connections between ideas.

Figure 4.13 Storytelling at Patagonia
Patagonia's Tin Shed website serves two storytelling functions. The tin shed (Patagonia's first building) plays a key role in the story of the company's founding and early years, and the online image of the shed offers gateways to a growing collection of stories on such topics as how various Patagonia products came into being, how outdoor enthusiasts use the company's products, and how Patagonia is engaged with various causes related to the outdoors.

others, too, which makes social media ideal for storytelling.[13] User-generated content, such as Toyota's Auto-Biography campaign highlighted in Chapter 1, is usually all about storytelling.

Career-related stories, such as how someone sought and found the opportunity to work on projects he or she is passionate about, can entice skilled employees to consider joining a firm. Entrepreneurs use stories to help investors see how their new ideas have the potential to affect people's lives (and therefore generate lots of sales). Stories can be cautionary tales as well, dramatizing the consequences of career blunders, ethical mistakes, and strategic missteps.

A key reason storytelling can be so effective is that stories help readers and listeners imagine themselves living through the experience of the person in the story. Chip Heath of Stanford University and his brother, Dan Heath of Duke University, have spent years exploring the question of why some ideas "stick" and others disappear. One of their conclusions is that ideas conveyed through storytelling tend to thrive because stories "put knowledge into a framework that is more lifelike, more true to our day-to-day existence."[14]

In addition, stories can demonstrate cause-and-effect relationships in a compelling fashion.[15] Imagine attending a new employee orientation and listening to the trainer read off a list of ethics rules and guidelines. Now imagine the trainer telling the story of someone who sounded a lot like you in the very near future, fresh out of college and full of energy and ambition. Desperate to hit demanding sales targets, the person in the story began entering transactions before customers had actually agreed to purchase, hoping the sales would eventually come through and no one would be the wiser. However, the scheme was exposed during a routine audit, and the rising star was booted out of the company with an ethical stain that would haunt him for years. You may not remember all the rules and guidelines, but chances are you will remember what happened to that person who sounded a lot like you. This ability to share organizational values is one of the major benefits of using storytelling in business communication, particularly across diverse workforces.[16]

A classic story has three basic parts. The beginning of the story presents someone whom the audience can identify with in some way, and this person has a dream to pursue or a problem to solve. (Think of how movies and novels often start by introducing a likable character who immediately gets into danger, for example.) The middle of the story shows this character taking action and making decisions as he or she pursues the goal or tries to solve the problem. The storyteller's objective here is to build the audience's interest by increasing the tension: Will the "hero" overcome the obstacles in his or her path and eventually succeed or fail? The end of the story answers that question and usually offers a lesson to be learned about the outcome as well.

By the way, even though these are "stories," these must not be made-up tales. Telling stories that didn't happen to people who don't exist while presenting them as real-life events is a serious breach of ethics that damages a company's credibility.[17]

Consider adding an element of storytelling whenever your main idea involves the opportunity to inspire, to persuade, to teach, or to warn readers or listeners about the potential outcomes of a particular course of action.

For fresh ideas and media materials on planning messages, visit http://real-timeupdates .com/bct11 and click on Chapter 4. For a quick refresher on message-planning tasks, see "Checklist: Planning Business Messages."

> Storytelling is an effective way to organize many business messages because it helps readers personalize the message and understand causes and consequences.

> Organize stories in three parts: a beginning that introduces a sympathetic person with a dream or a challenge, a middle that shows the complications to be overcome, and an ending that resolves the situation and shows the moral or message of the story.

✓ Checklist Planning Business Messages

A. Analyze the situation.
- Determine whether the purpose of your message is to inform, persuade, or collaborate.
- Identify what you want your audience to think or do after receiving the message.
- Make sure your purpose is worthwhile and realistic.
- Make sure the time is right for your message.
- Make sure your purpose is acceptable to your organization.
- Identify the primary audience.
- Determine the size and composition of your audience.
- Estimate your audience's level of understanding and probable reaction to your message.

B. Gather information.
- Decide whether to use formal or informal techniques for gathering information.

- Find out what your audience needs to know.
- Provide all required information and make sure it's accurate, ethical, and pertinent.

C. Select the best medium for your message.
- Understand the advantages and disadvantages of oral, written, visual, and electronic media.
- Consider media richness, formality, media limitations, urgency, cost, and audience preference.

D. Organize your information.
- Define your main idea.
- Limit your scope.
- Choose the direct or indirect approach.
- Outline content by starting with the main idea, adding major points, and illustrating with evidence.
- Look for opportunities to use storytelling to build audience interest.

Quick Learning Guide

MyBcommLab

If your course uses MyBcommLab, log on to **www.mybcommlab.com** to access the following study and assessment aids associated with this chapter:

- Video applications
- Real-Time Updates
- Peer review activity
- Pre/post test
- Personalized study plan
- Model documents
- Sample presentations

If you are not using MyBcommLab, you can access Real-Time Updates through **http://real-timeupdates.com/bct11**.

SUMMARY OF LEARNING OBJECTIVES

1 **Describe the three-step writing process.** (1) Planning consists of four tasks: analyzing the situation (defining your purpose and profiling your audience), gathering the information to meet your audience's needs, selecting the best medium for the message and the situation, and organizing the information (defining your main idea, limiting your scope, selecting an approach, and outlining your content). (2) The writing step consists of two tasks: adapting to your audience and composing the message. Adapt your message to your audience by being sensitive to audience needs, building a strong relationship with your audience, and controlling your style. Compose your message by drafting your thoughts with strong words, effective sentences, and coherent paragraphs. (3) Completing your message consists of four tasks: revising your message by evaluating content and then rewriting and editing for clarity and conciseness, producing your message by using effective design elements and suitable delivery methods, proofreading your message for mistakes in spelling and mechanics, and distributing it in a way that meets both your needs and your audience's needs.

2 **Explain why it's important to analyze a communication situation in order to define your purpose and profile your audience before writing a message.** You must know enough about your purpose to shape your message in a way that will achieve your goal. Moreover, without a clear purpose to guide you, you are bound to waste time and energy. To decide whether you should proceed with your message, answer four questions: (1) Will anything change as a result of this message? (2) Is my purpose realistic? (3) Is this the right time for this message? (4) Is the purpose acceptable to my organization? Developing an audience profile is essential as well because doing so helps you identify the information you need to include in your message and is the most effective way to structure your message.

3 **Discuss information-gathering options for simple messages, and identify three attributes of quality information.** Gathering the information that will fulfill your audience's needs is a vital step before you attempt to organize your content. For more complex documents, you may need to plan a research project to acquire all the necessary information. However, for simple messages, if you don't already have all the information you need, you can gather it by using other methods, such as considering the audience's perspective, reading existing reports and other company documents, talking with supervisors and others who have information and insight, and asking your audience members directly for their input. To determine whether the information you've gathered is good enough, verify that it is accurate, ethical, and pertinent to the audience's needs.

4 **List the factors to consider when choosing the most appropriate medium for a message.** The first factor to consider is media richness. Richness is determined by the medium's ability to (1) convey a message using more than one informational cue, such as sound, motion, nonverbal cues, and so on; (2) facilitate feedback; and (3) establish personal focus. Other factors to consider when selecting media include the level of formality, the specific limitations of each medium, the level of urgency, the cost of various media options, and your audience's preferences.

5 **Explain why good organization is important to both you and your audience, and list the tasks involved in organizing a message.** When you organize messages carefully, you save time and conserve creative energy because the writing process is quicker and you spend less time rewriting. Good organization also helps your audience members understand your message, it helps them accept your message, and it saves them time as well. The tasks involved in organizing your message include defining your main idea, limiting your scope to the information needed to convey and support that main idea, choosing the direct or indirect approach, and then outlining your content.

KEY TERMS

direct approach Message organization that starts with the main idea (such as a recommendation, a conclusion, or a request) and follows that with your supporting evidence

free writing An exploratory technique in which you write whatever comes to mind, without stopping to make any corrections, for a set period of time

general purpose The broad intent of a message—to inform, to persuade, or to collaborate with the audience

indirect approach Message organization that starts with the evidence and builds your case before presenting the main idea

journalistic approach Verifying the completeness of a message by making sure it answers the *who, what, when, where, why,* and *how* questions

letters Brief written messages generally sent to recipients outside the organization

main idea A specific statement about the topic

medium The form through which you choose to communicate a message

memos Brief printed documents traditionally used for the routine, day-to-day exchange of information within an organization; most have been replaced by electronic media

multimedia Refers to the use of two or more media to deliver a message, typically some combination of audio, video, text, and visual graphics

scope The range of information presented in a message, its overall length, and the level of detail provided

specific purpose Identifies what you hope to accomplish with your message and what your audience should do or think after receiving your message

topic The overall subject of a message

Planning Business Messages

A. Analyze the situation.
- Determine whether the purpose of your message is to inform, persuade, or collaborate.
- Identify what you want your audience to think or do after receiving the message.
- Make sure your purpose is worthwhile and realistic.
- Make sure the time is right for your message.
- Make sure your purpose is acceptable to your organization.
- Identify the primary audience.
- Determine the size and composition of your audience.
- Estimate your audience's level of understanding and probable reaction to your message.

B. Gather information.
- Decide whether to use formal or informal techniques for gathering information.
- Find out what your audience needs to know.
- Provide all required information and make sure it's accurate, ethical, and pertinent.

C. Select the best medium for your message.
- Understand the advantages and disadvantages of oral, written, visual, and electronic media.
- Consider media richness, formality, media limitations, urgency, cost, and audience preference.

D. Organize your information.
- Define your main idea.
- Limit your scope.
- Choose the direct or indirect approach.
- Outline content by starting with the main idea, adding major points, and illustrating with evidence.
- Look for opportunities to use storytelling to build audience interest.

1 Plan →	**2** Write →	**3** Complete
Analyze the Situation Define your purpose and develop an audience profile. **Gather Information** Determine audience needs and obtain the information necessary to satisfy those needs. **Select the Right Medium** Select the best medium for delivering your message. **Organize the Information** Define your main idea, limit your scope, select a direct or an indirect approach, and outline your content.	**Adapt to Your Audience** Be sensitive to audience needs by using a "you" attitude, politeness, positive emphasis, and unbiased language. Build a strong relationship with your audience by establishing your credibility and projecting your company's preferred image. Control your style with a conversational tone, plain English, and appropriate voice. **Compose the Message** Choose strong words that will help you create effective sentences and coherent paragraphs.	**Revise the Message** Evaluate content and review readability, edit and rewrite for conciseness and clarity. **Produce the Message** Use effective design elements and suitable layout for a clean, professional appearance. **Proofread the Message** Review for errors in layout, spelling, and mechanics. **Distribute the Message** Deliver your message using the chosen medium; make sure all documents and all relevant files are distributed successfully.

Figure 4.1 The Three-Step Writing Process
This three-step process will help you create more effective messages in any medium. As you get more practice with the process, it will become easier and more automatic.

COMMUNICATION CHALLENGES AT H&R BLOCK

Robert Turtledove, H&R Block's chief marketing officer, was impressed enough with your communication skills and social media experience to add you to the team that markets H&R Block's digital tax-preparation solutions. Using the insights you gained in this chapter, address these two communication challenges.

INDIVIDUAL CHALLENGE: Your first assignment is to write a 50-word introduction to the H&R Block At Home tax software (formerly known as TaxCut) that can be used whenever the company needs a concise summary. For example, your text will be loaded into the IM chat system so that whenever anyone asks about the software, customer service representatives can send your text with just one mouse click. Visit www.hrblock .com to learn more about the various versions of the At Home software. Use this information to write your 50-word summary and then email it to your instructor.

TEAM CHALLENGE: An ongoing dilemma for marketers in many industries is trying to offer targeted products and services that meet the needs of specific market segments without creating so many versions that the range of choices overwhelms the consumer. For example, H&R Block can help taxpayers in a variety of ways: several versions of web-based tax software, several versions of downloadable software, professional preparation, and a hybrid service called Best of Both, in which the taxpayer does most of the work using the software and an H&R Block professional helps with advice and verification. Simply helping consumers understand the choices available can become a considerable communication challenge in its own right.

With your team, analyze the company's website at www.hrblock.com in terms of its ability to help a taxpayer understand the various options and choose the one that meets his or her unique needs. For example, are the services clearly distinguished from one another, and can the average taxpayer understand the distinctions being made? What improvements might you suggest? Prepare a brief summary of your analysis as a class presentation or a post on your class blog, as your instructor directs.

TEST YOUR KNOWLEDGE

To review chapter content related to each question, refer to the indicated Learning Objective.

1. What are the three major steps in the writing process? [LO-1]
2. What are the benefits of planning your messages carefully, particularly longer and more complex messages? [LO-1]
3. What two types of purposes do all business messages have? [LO-2]
4. What do you need to know in order to develop an audience profile? [LO-2]
5. What is the value of free writing and other discovery techniques? [LO-3]
6. What three factors determine media richness? [LO-4]
7. What are the main advantages of oral media? Of written media? Of visual media? Of electronic media? [LO-4]
8. How does the topic of a message differ from its main idea? [LO-5]
9. Why is it important to limit the scope of a message? [LO-5]
10. What three elements do you need to consider when choosing between the direct and indirect approaches? [LO-5]

APPLY YOUR KNOWLEDGE

To review chapter content related to each question, refer to the indicated Learning Objective.

1. Some writers argue that planning messages wastes time because they inevitably change their plans as they go along. How would you respond to this argument? Briefly explain. [LO-1]
2. A day after sending an email to all 1,800 employees in your company regarding income tax implications of the company's retirement plan, you discover that one of the sources you relied on for your information plagiarized from other sources. You quickly double-check all the information in your message and confirm that it is accurate. However, you are concerned about using plagiarized information, even though you did nothing wrong. Write a brief email message to your instructor, explaining how you would handle the situation. [LO-3]
3. As a member of the public relations department, which medium (or media) would you recommend using to inform the local community that your toxic-waste cleanup program has been successful? Why? [LO-4]
4. Would you use the direct or indirect approach to ask employees to work overtime to meet an important deadline? Please explain. [LO-5]
5. You have been invited to speak at an annual industry conference. After preparing the outline for your presentation, you see that you've identified 14 different points to support your main idea. Should you move ahead with creating the slides for your presentation or move back and rethink your outline? Why? [LO-5]

PRACTICE YOUR SKILLS

Message for Analysis:
Outlining Your Content [LO-5]

A writer is working on an insurance information brochure and is having trouble grouping the ideas logically into an outline. Using the following information, prepare the outline, paying attention to the appropriate hierarchy of ideas. If necessary, rewrite phrases to make them all consistent.

Accident Protection Insurance Plan

- Coverage is only pennies a day
- Benefit is $100,000 for accidental death on common carrier
- Benefit is $100 a day for hospitalization as result of motor vehicle or common carrier accident
- Benefit is $20,000 for accidental death in motor vehicle accident
- Individual coverage is only $17.85 per quarter; family coverage is just $26.85 per quarter
- No physical exam or health questions
- Convenient payment—billed quarterly
- Guaranteed acceptance for all applicants
- No individual rate increases
- Free, no-obligation examination period
- Cash paid in addition to any other insurance carried
- Covers accidental death when riding as fare-paying passenger on public transportation, including buses, trains, jets, ships, trolleys, subways, or any other common carrier
- Covers accidental death in motor vehicle accidents occurring while driving or riding in or on automobile, truck, camper, motor home, or nonmotorized bicycle

Exercises

Active links for all websites in this chapter can be found on MyBcommLab; see your User Guide for instructions on accessing the content for this chapter. Each activity is labeled according to the primary skill or skills you will need to use. To review relevant chapter content, you can refer to the indicated Learning Objective. In some instances, supporting information will be found in another chapter, as indicated.

1. **Planning: Identifying Your Purpose; Media Skills: Email [LO-2]** Make a list of communication tasks you'll need to accomplish in the next week or so (for example, a homework assignment, an email message to an instructor, a job application, or a speech to a class). For each, determine a general and a specific purpose.

2. **Planning: Identifying Your Purpose [LO-2]** For each of the following communication tasks, state a specific purpose (if you have trouble, try beginning with "I want to . . .").

   a. A report to your boss, the store manager, about the outdated items in the warehouse

   b. A memo to clients about your booth at the upcoming trade show

   c. A letter to a customer who hasn't made a payment for three months

   d. A memo to employees about the department's high phone bills

   e. A phone call to a supplier, checking on an overdue parts shipment

   f. A report to future users of the computer program you have chosen to handle the company's mailing list

3. **Planning: Assessing Audience Needs [LO-2]** For each communication task that follows, write brief answers to three questions: Who is the audience? What is the audience's general attitude toward my subject? What does the audience need to know?

   a. A final-notice collection letter from an appliance manufacturer to an appliance dealer that is 3 months behind on payments, sent 10 days before initiating legal collection procedures

   b. An advertisement for digital cameras

   c. A proposal to top management, suggesting that the four sales regions in the United States be combined into just two regions

   d. Fliers to be attached to doorknobs in the neighborhood, announcing reduced rates for chimney cleaning or repairs

   e. A cover letter sent along with your résumé to a potential employer

   f. A website that describes the services offered by a consulting firm that helps accounting managers comply with government regulations

4. **Planning: Assessing Audience Needs [LO-2]** Choose a fairly simple electronic device (such as a digital music player or digital camera) that you know how to operate well. Write two sets of instructions for operating the device: one set for a reader who has never used that type of device and one set for someone who is generally familiar with that type of machine but has never operated the specific model. Briefly explain how your two audiences affect your instructions.

5. **Planning: Identifying Your Purpose [LO-2]** List five messages you have received lately, such as direct-mail promotions, letters, email messages, phone solicitations, and lectures. For each, determine the general purpose and the specific purpose; then answer the following questions: (1) Was the message well timed? (2) Did the sender choose an appropriate medium for the message? (3) Was the sender's purpose realistic?

6. **Planning: Analyzing the Situation; Media Skills: Electronic Presentations [LO-2]** Go to the PepsiCo website, at www.pepsico.com, and locate the latest annual report. Read the annual report's letter to shareholders. Who is the audience for this message? What is the general purpose of the message? What do you think this audience wants to know from the chairman of PepsiCo? Summarize your answers in a one-page report or five-slide presentation, as your instructor directs.

7. **Planning: Analyzing the Situation; Collaboration: Planning Meetings [LO-2], Chapter 2** How can the material discussed in this chapter also apply to meetings, as discussed in Chapter 2? Outline your ideas in a brief presentation or a post for your class blog.

8. **Planning: Creating an Audience Profile; Collaboration: Team Projects [LO-2], [LO-3], Chapter 2** With a team assigned by your instructor, compare the Facebook pages of three companies in the same industry. Analyze the content on all the available tabs. What can you surmise about the intended audience for each company? Which of the three does the best job of presenting the information its target audience is likely to need? Prepare a brief presentation, including slides that show samples of the Facebook content from each company.

9. **Planning: Analyzing the Situation, Selecting Media; Media Skills: Email [LO-2], [LO-4], Chapter 9** You are the head of public relations for a cruise line that operates out of Miami. You are shocked to read a letter in a local newspaper from a disgruntled passenger, complaining about the service and entertainment on a recent cruise. You need to respond to these publicized criticisms in some way. What audiences will you need to consider in your response? What medium or media should you choose? If the letter had been published in a travel publication widely read by travel agents and cruise travelers, how might your course of action have differed? In an email message to your instructor, explain how you will respond.

10. **Planning: Assessing Audience Needs; Media Skills: Blogging; Communication Ethics: Making Ethical Choices [LO-3], Chapter 1** Your supervisor has asked you to withhold important information that you think should be included in a report you are preparing. Disobeying him could be disastrous for your working relationship and your career. Obeying him could violate your personal code of ethics. What should you do? On the basis of the discussion in Chapter 1, would you consider this situation to be an ethical dilemma or an ethical lapse? Explain your analysis in a brief email message to your instructor.

11. **Planning: Outlining Your Content [LO-5]** Using the improved version of the GNC email message in Figure 4.7, draw an organizational chart similar to the one shown in Figure 4.12. Fill in the main idea, the major points, and the evidence provided in this letter. (*Note:* Your diagram may be smaller than the one shown in Figure 4.12.)

12. **Planning: Limiting Your Scope [LO-5]** Suppose you are preparing to recommend that top management install a new heating system that uses the cogeneration process. The following information is in your files. Eliminate topics that aren't essential and then arrange the other topics so that your report will give top managers a clear understanding of the heating system and a balanced, concise justification for installing it.

- History of the development of the cogeneration heating process
- Scientific credentials of the developers of the process
- Risks assumed in using this process
- Your plan for installing the equipment in the headquarters building
- Stories about the successful use of cogeneration technology in comparable facilities
- Specifications of the equipment that would be installed
- Plans for disposing of the old heating equipment
- Costs of installing and running the new equipment
- Advantages and disadvantages of using the new process
- Detailed 10-year cost projections
- Estimates of the time needed to phase in the new system
- Alternative systems that management might want to consider

13. **Planning: Choosing the Direct or Indirect Approach [LO-5]** Indicate whether the direct or indirect approach would be best in each of the following situations and briefly explain why. Would any of these messages be inappropriate for email? Explain.

   a. A message to the owner of an automobile dealership, complaining about poor service work

   b. A message from a recent college graduate, requesting a letter of recommendation from a former instructor

   c. A message turning down a job applicant

   d. A message announcing that because of high air-conditioning costs, the plant temperature will be held at 78°F during the summer

   e. A message from an advertising agency to a troublesome long-term client, explaining that the agency will no longer be able to work on the client's account

14. **Planning: Choosing the Direct or Indirect Approach** [LO-5] If you were trying to persuade people to take the following actions, how would you organize your argument?

    a. You want your boss to approve your plan for hiring two new people.

    b. You want to be hired for a job.

    c. You want to be granted a business loan.

    d. You want to collect a small amount of money from a regular customer whose account is slightly past due.

    e. You want to collect a large amount of money from a customer whose account is seriously past due.

15. **Planning: Using Storytelling Techniques; Communication Ethics: Providing Ethical Leadership: Media Skills: Podcasting [LO-5], Chapter 1** Research recent incidents of ethical lapses by a business professional or executive in any industry. Choose one example that has a clear story "arc" from beginning to end. Outline a cautionary tale that explains the context of the ethical lapse, the choice the person made, and the consequences of the ethical lapse. Script a podcast (aim for roughly 3 to 5 minutes) that tells the story. If you instructor directs, record your podcast and post to your class blog.

EXPAND YOUR SKILLS

Critique the Professionals

Locate an example of professional communication in any medium that you think would work equally well—or perhaps better—in another medium. Using the media selection guidelines in this chapter and your understanding of the communication process, write a brief analysis (no more than one page) of the company's media choice and explain why your choice would be at least as effective. Use whatever medium your instructor requests for your report and be sure to cite specific elements from the piece and support from the chapter.

Sharpening Your Career Skills Online

Bovée and Thill's Business Communication Web Search, at http://businesscommunicationblog.com/websearch, is a unique research tool designed specifically for business communication research. Use the Web Search function to find a website, video, podcast, or PowerPoint presentation that offers advice on planning a report, speech, or other business message. Write a brief email message to your instructor, describing the item that you found and summarizing the career skills information you learned from it.

5 Writing Business Messages

LEARNING OBJECTIVES After studying this chapter, you will be able to

1 Identify the four aspects of being sensitive to audience needs when writing business messages

2 Explain how establishing your credibility and projecting your company's image are vital aspects of building strong relationships with your audience

3 Explain how to achieve a tone that is conversational but businesslike, explain the value of using plain language, and define active and passive voice

4 Describe how to select words that are not only correct but also effective

5 Define the four types of sentences and explain how sentence style affects emphasis within a message

6 Define the three key elements of a paragraph and list five ways to develop unified, coherent paragraphs

7 Identify the most common software features that help you craft messages more efficiently

MyBcommLab Test your mastery of this chapter and its Learning Objectives. Visit mybcommlab.com to apply what you've learned in Document Makeovers and interactive simulation scenarios.

COMMUNICATION CLOSE-UP AT CREATIVE COMMONS

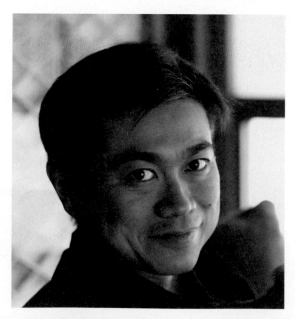

Joi Ito, CEO of Creative Commons, uses a variety of communication vehicles to convince copyright owners to explore new ways of sharing and protecting their creative works.

http://creativecommons.org

Have you ever noticed that tiny © symbol on books, DVDs, music CDs, and other media products? It means that the person or organization that created the item is granted *copyright* protection, the exclusive legal right to produce, distribute, and sell that creation. Anyone who wants to resell, redistribute, or adapt such works usually needs to secure permission from the current copyright holder.

However, what if you *want* people to remix the song you just recorded or use your graphic designs in whatever artistic compositions they might want to create? Or if you want to give away some of your creative works to get your name out there, without giving up all your legal rights to them? Alternatively, suppose you need a few photos or a video clip for a website? Other than for limited personal and educational use, a conventional copyright requires every person to negotiate a contract for every application or adaptation of every piece of work he or she wants to use.

The search for some middle ground between "all rights reserved" and simply giving your work away led Stanford University law professor Lawrence Lessig to co-found Creative Commons. This nonprofit organization's goal is to provide a simple, free, and legal way for musicians, artists, writers, teachers, scientists, and others to collaborate and benefit through the sharing of art and ideas. Instead of the everything-or-nothing approach of traditional copyright, Creative Commons offers a more flexible range of "some rights reserved" options.

Japanese venture capitalist Joichi ("Joi") Ito is now Creative Commons's CEO, bringing an entrepreneur's perspective to the organization's business model. Through a variety of media, Ito continues to promote the benefits of simplifying the legal constraints on sharing and reusing intellectual property, whether for creative expression or scientific research. Millions of Creative Commons licenses have been initiated for musical works, images, short films, educational materials, novels, and more. This approach can't solve the entire dilemma of copyrights in the digital age, and not everyone agrees with the Creative Commons model, but it has created an easier way for creative people to communicate and collaborate.[1]

Adapting to Your Audience: Being Sensitive to Audience Needs

As they work to persuade their audiences to consider new forms of copyright protection, Joi Ito and his colleagues at Creative Commons (profiled in the chapter-opening Communication Close-up) realize it takes more than just a great idea to change the way people think. Expressing ideas clearly and persuasively starts with adapting to one's audience.

Whether consciously or not, audiences greet most incoming messages with a selfish question: "What's in this for me?" If your intended audience members think a message does not apply to them or doesn't meet their needs, they won't be inclined to pay attention to it. Follow the example set by the Creative Commons website, which addresses a diverse audience of artists, lawyers, and business professionals but fine-tunes specific messages for each group of people.

If your readers or listeners don't think you understand or care about their needs, they won't pay attention, plain and simple. You can improve your audience sensitivity by adopting the "you" attitude, maintaining good standards of etiquette, emphasizing the positive, and using bias-free language.

1 **LEARNING OBJECTIVE**

Identify the four aspects of being sensitive to audience needs when writing business messages.

Readers and listeners want to know how your messages will benefit them.

USING THE "YOU" ATTITUDE

Chapter 1 introduced the notion of audience-centered communication and the "you" attitude—speaking and writing in terms of your audience's wishes, interests, hopes, and preferences. On the simplest level, you can adopt the "you" attitude by replacing terms such as *I, me, mine, we, us,* and *ours* with *you* and *yours*:

The "you" attitude is best implemented by expressing your message in terms of the audience's interests and needs.

Instead of This	Write This
Tuesday is the only day that we can promise quick response to purchase order requests; we are swamped the rest of the week.	If you need a quick response, please submit your purchase order requests on Tuesday.
We offer MP3 players with 50, 75, or 100 gigabytes of storage capacity.	You can choose an MP3 player with 50, 75, or 100 gigabytes of storage.

Messages that emphasize "I" and "we" risk sounding selfish and uninterested in the audience. Such messages feel like they are all about the sender, not the receiver.

However, the "you" attitude is more than simply using particular pronouns; it's a matter of genuine interest and concern. You can use *you* 25 times in a single page and still ignore your audience's true concerns. If you're talking to a retailer, try to think like a retailer; if you're dealing with a production supervisor, put yourself in that position; if you're writing to a dissatisfied customer, imagine how you would feel at the other end of the transaction.

Be aware that on some occasions, it's better to avoid using *you*, particularly if doing so will sound overly authoritative or accusing:

MyBcommLab

● Access this chapter's simulation entitled The Communication Process, located at mybcommlab.com.

Avoid using *you* and *yours* when doing so
- Makes you sound dictatorial
- Could make someone else feel unnecessarily guilty
- Is inappropriate for the culture
- Goes against your organization's style

Instead of This	Write This
You failed to deliver the customer's order on time.	The customer didn't receive the order on time.
You must correct all five copies by noon.	All five copies must be corrected by noon.

As you practice using the "you" attitude, be sure to consider the attitudes of other cultures and the policies of your organization. In some cultures, it is improper to single out one person's achievements, because the whole team is responsible for the outcome; in that case, using the pronoun *we* or *our* (when you and your audience are part of the same team) would be more appropriate. Similarly, some companies have a tradition of avoiding references to *you* and *I* in most messages and reports.

MAINTAINING STANDARDS OF ETIQUETTE

You know how it feels to be treated inconsiderately; when that happens, you probably react emotionally and pay less attention to the offending message. By being courteous to members of your audience, you show consideration for them and foster a more successful environment for communication.

Although you may be tempted now and then to be brutally frank, try to express the facts in a kind and thoughtful manner.

On occasions when you experience frustration with coworkers, customers, or others, you may be tempted to say what you think in blunt terms. But venting your emotions rarely improves the situation and can jeopardize your audience's goodwill. Demonstrate your diplomatic skills by controlling your emotions and communicating calmly and politely:

Instead of This	Write This
Once again, you've managed to bring down the entire website through your incompetent programming.	Let's review the last website update to explore ways to improve the process.
You've been sitting on our order for two weeks, and we need it now!	Our production schedules depend on timely delivery of parts and supplies, but we have not yet received the order you promised to deliver two weeks ago. Please respond today with a firm delivery commitment.

Of course, some situations require more diplomacy than others. If you know your audience well, a less formal approach may be more appropriate. However, when you are communicating with people who outrank you or with people outside your organization, an added measure of courtesy is usually needed.

Written communication and most forms of electronic media generally require more tact than oral communication (Figure 5.1). When you're speaking, your words are softened by your tone of voice and facial expression. Plus, you can adjust your approach according to the feedback you get. If you inadvertently offend someone in writing or in a podcast, for example, you don't usually get the immediate feedback you would need to resolve the situation. In fact, you may never know that you offended your audience.

EMPHASIZING THE POSITIVE

You can communicate negative news without being negative.

During your career, you will have many occasions in which you need to communicate bad news. As you rise through the ranks of management, you will encounter situations in which unpleasant news can significantly affect the personal and financial well-being of employees, customers, and investors. However, there is a big difference between *delivering* negative news and *being* negative. When the tone of your message is negative, you put unnecessary strain on business relationships.

Never try to hide negative news, but always be on the lookout for positive points that will foster a good relationship with your audience:[2]

Instead of This	Write This
It is impossible to repair your laptop today.	Your computer can be ready by Tuesday. Would you like a loaner until then?
We wasted $300,000 advertising in that magazine.	Our $300,000 advertising investment did not pay off. Let's analyze the experience and apply the insights to future campaigns.

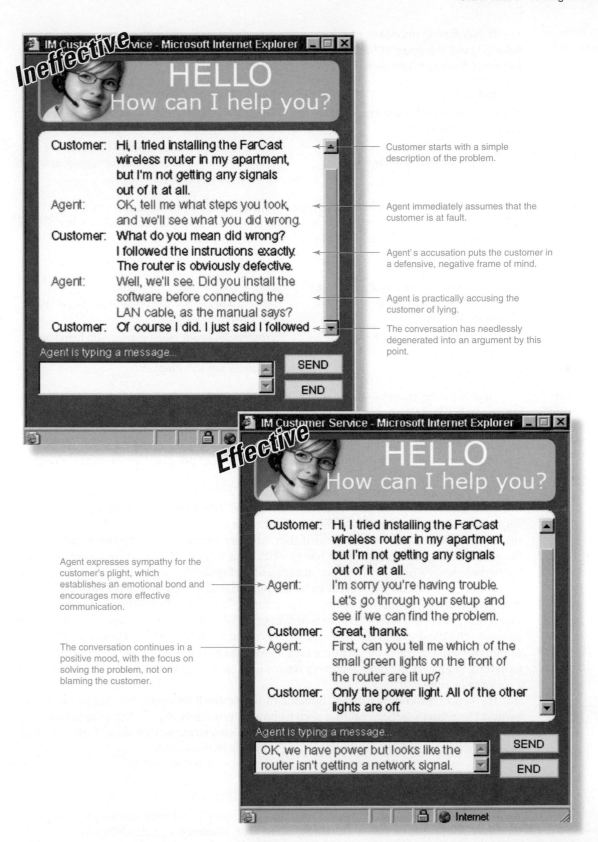

Figure 5.1   Fostering a Positive Relationship with an Audience
In the "ineffective" example, notice how the customer service agent's unfortunate word choices immediately derail this IM exchange. In the "effective" example, a more sensitive approach allows both people to focus on solving the problem.

MyBcommLab

Apply Figure 5.1's key concepts by revising a new document. Go to Chapter 5 in mybcommlab.com and select Document Makeovers.

When you are offering criticism or advice, focus on what the person can do to improve.

If you find it necessary to criticize or correct, don't dwell on the other person's mistakes. Avoid referring to failures, problems, or shortcomings. Focus instead on what the audience members can do to improve the situation:

Instead of This

The problem with this department is a failure to control costs.

You failed to provide all the necessary information on the previous screen.

Write This

The performance of this department can be improved by tightening cost controls.

Please review the items marked in red on the previous screen so that we can process your order as quickly as possible.

Show your audience members how they will benefit from responding to your message in the way you would like them to respond.

If you're trying to persuade audience members to buy a product, pay a bill, or perform a service for you, emphasize what's in it for them. When people recognize the benefits of doing so, they are more likely to respond positively to your appeal:

Instead of This

We will notify all three credit reporting agencies if you do not pay your overdue bill within 10 days.

I am tired of seeing so many errors in the customer service blog.

Write This

Paying your overdue bill within 10 days will prevent a negative entry on your credit record.

Proofreading your blog postings will help you avoid embarrassing mistakes that generate more customer service complaints.

Euphemisms, equivalent words or phrases that express a thought in milder terms, can ease the blow of negative news, but they must be used carefully to avoid annoying or misleading the audience.

In general, try to state your message without using words that may hurt or offend your audience. Look for appropriate opportunities to use **euphemisms**—words or phrases that express a thought in milder terms—that convey your meaning without carrying negative or unpleasant connotations. For example, one common euphemism is referring to people beyond a certain age as "senior citizens," rather than "old people." *Senior* conveys respect in a way that *old* doesn't.

Euphemisms can bring a tone of civility to unpleasant communication, but they *must* be used with great care because they are so easy—and so tempting—to misuse. Euphemisms can be annoying if they force readers to "read between the lines" to get the message, and they can be unethical if they obscure the truth. For instance, one of the toughest messages a manager ever has to write is an internal memo or email announcing immediate layoffs or plans to begin implementing layoffs. This is a difficult situation for everyone involved, and managers can be tempted to resort to euphemisms such as *streamlining, restructuring, improving efficiency, reducing layers,* or *eliminating redundancies* to avoid using the word *layoff*.[3] Doing so might ease the emotional burden on the writer and promote the illusion that the message isn't as negative as it really is. However, these euphemisms can fail the "you" attitude test, as well as the standards of ethical information, by failing to answer the question every reader in these situations has, which is simply: *Am I going to lose my job?*

If you are considering using a euphemism, ask yourself this question: Are you trying to protect the reader's feelings or your own feelings? Even if it is unpleasant, people generally respond better to an honest message delivered with integrity than they do to a sugar-coated message that obscures the truth.

USING BIAS-FREE LANGUAGE

Biased language can perpetuate stereotypes and prejudices.

Bias-free language avoids words and phrases that unfairly and even unethically categorize or stigmatize people in ways related to gender, race, ethnicity, age, disability, or other personal characteristics. Contrary to what some may think, biased language is not simply about "labels." To a significant degree, language reflects the way we think and what we believe, and biased language may well perpetuate the underlying stereotypes and prejudices that it represents.[4] Moreover, because communication is all about perception, simply *being* fair and objective isn't enough. To establish a good relationship with your audience, you must

TABLE 5.1	**Overcoming Bias in Language**	
Examples	**Unacceptable**	**Preferable**

Gender Bias		
Using words containing *man*	Man-made	Artificial, synthetic, manufactured, constructed, human-made
	Mankind	Humanity, human beings, human race, people
	Manpower	Workers, workforce
	Businessman	Executive, manager, businessperson, professional
	Salesman	Sales representative, salesperson
	Foreman	Supervisor
Using female-gender words	Actress, stewardess	Actor, flight attendant
Using special designations	Woman doctor, male nurse	Doctor, nurse
Using *he* to refer to "everyone"	The average worker . . . he	The average worker . . . he or she *OR* Average workers . . . they
Identifying roles with gender	The typical executive spends four hours of his day in meetings.	Most executives spend four hours a day in meetings.
	the consumer . . . she	consumers . . . they
	the nurse/teacher . . . she	nurses/teachers . . . they
Identifying women by marital status	Mrs. Norm Lindstrom	Maria Lindstrom *OR* Ms. Maria Lindstrom
	Norm Lindstrom and Ms. Drake	Norm Lindstrom and Maria Drake *OR* Mr. Lindstrom and Ms. Drake

Racial and Ethnic Bias		
Assigning stereotypes	Not surprisingly, Shing-Tung Yau excels in mathematics.	Shing-Tung Yau excels in mathematics.
Identifying people by race or ethnicity	Mario M. Cuomo, Italian-American politician and ex-governor of New York	Mario M. Cuomo, politician and ex-governor of New York

Age Bias		
Including age when irrelevant	Mary Kirazy, 58, has just joined our trust department.	Mary Kirazy has just joined our trust department.

Disability Bias		
Putting the disability before the person	Disabled workers face many barriers on the job.	Workers with physical disabilities face many barriers on the job.
	An epileptic, Tracy has no trouble doing her job.	Tracy's epilepsy has no effect on her job performance.

also *appear* to be fair.[5] Good communicators make every effort to change biased language (see Table 5.1). Bias can come in a variety of forms:

- **Gender bias.** Avoid sexist language by using the same labels for everyone, regardless of gender. Don't refer to a woman as *chairperson* and then to a man as *chairman*. Use *chair*, *chairperson*, or *chairman* consistently. (Note that it is not uncommon to use *chairman* when referring to a woman who heads a board of directors. Avon's Andrea Jung, Ogilvy & Mather's Shelly Lazarus, and Xerox's Ursula Burns, for example, all refer to themselves as *chairman*.[6]) Reword sentences to use *they* or to use no pronoun at all rather than refer to all individuals as *he*. Note that the preferred title for women in business is *Ms.* unless the individual asks to be addressed as *Miss* or *Mrs.* or has some other title, such as *Dr.*
- **Racial and ethnic bias.** Avoid identifying people by race or ethnic origin unless such a label is relevant to the matter at hand—and it rarely is.

- **Age bias.** As with gender, race, and ethnic background, mention the age of a person only when it is relevant. Words that refer to age carry a variety of positive and negative connotations—and not only when referring to people beyond a certain age. For example, *young* can imply youthfulness, inexperience, or even immaturity, depending on how it's used.
- **Disability bias.** Physical, mental, sensory, or emotional impairments should never be mentioned in business messages unless those conditions are directly relevant to the subject. If you must refer to someone's disability, put the person first and the disability second.[7] For example, by saying "employees with physical handicaps," not "handicapped employees," you focus on the whole person, not the disability. Finally, never use outdated terminology such as *crippled* or *retarded.*

Adapting to Your Audience: Building Strong Relationships

Explain how establishing your credibility and projecting your company's image are vital aspects of building strong relationships with your audience.

People are more likely to react positively to your message when they have confidence in you.

Successful communication relies on a positive relationship between sender and receiver. Establishing your credibility and projecting your company's image are two vital steps in building and fostering positive business relationships.

ESTABLISHING YOUR CREDIBILITY

Audience responses to your messages depend heavily on your **credibility**, a measure of your believability, based on how reliable you are and how much trust you evoke in others. With audiences who already know you, you've already established some degree of credibility, based on past communication efforts. As long as you haven't let people down in the past, they are inclined to accept each new message from you. However, with audiences that don't know you, you need to establish credibility before they'll accept—or perhaps even pay attention to—your messages (see Figure 5.2). To build, maintain, or repair your credibility, emphasize the following characteristics:

To enhance your credibility, emphasize such factors as honesty, objectivity, and awareness of audience needs.

- **Honesty.** Demonstrating honesty and integrity will earn you the respect of your audiences, even if they don't always agree with or welcome your messages.
- **Objectivity.** Show that you can distance yourself from emotional situations and look at all sides of an issue.
- **Awareness of audience needs.** Let your audiences know that you understand what's important to them.
- **Credentials, knowledge, and expertise.** Audiences need to know that you have whatever it takes to back up your message, whether it's education, professional certification, special training, past successes, or simply the fact that you've done your research.
- **Endorsements.** An *endorsement* is a statement on your behalf by someone who is accepted by your audience as an expert.
- **Performance.** Demonstrating impressive communication skills is not enough; people need to know they can count on you to get the job done.
- **Sincerity.** When you offer praise, don't use *hyperbole*, such as "you are the most fantastic employee I could ever imagine." Instead, point out specific qualities that warrant praise.

In addition, audiences need to know that you believe in yourself and your message. If you lack faith in yourself, you're likely to communicate an uncertain attitude that

Figure 5.2   Building Credibility
Lisa Ford is a highly regarded expert in the field of customer service, but she still takes care to communicate her qualifications as a presenter so that potential audience members who aren't familiar with her work can appreciate the expertise she has to offer.

undermines your credibility. In contrast, if you are convinced that your message is sound, you can state your case with authority. Look out for phrases containing words such as *hope* and *trust*, which can drain the audience's confidence in your message:

Instead of This	Write This
We hope this recommendation will be helpful.	We're pleased to make this recommendation.
We trust that you'll want to extend your service contract.	By extending your service contract, you can continue to enjoy top-notch performance from your equipment.

Finally, keep in mind that credibility can take a long time to establish—and it can be wiped out in an instant. An occasional mistake or letdown is usually forgiven, but major lapses in honesty or integrity can destroy your reputation. On the other hand, when you do establish credibility, communication becomes much easier because you no longer have to spend time and energy convincing people that you are a trustworthy source of information and ideas.

PROJECTING YOUR COMPANY'S IMAGE

When you communicate with anyone outside your organization, you represent your company and therefore play a vital role in helping the company build and maintain positive relationships with all its stakeholders. Most successful companies work hard to foster a specific public image, and your external communication efforts need to project that image. As part of this responsibility, the interests and preferred communication style of your company must take precedence over your own views and personal communication style.

Your company's interests and reputation take precedence over your personal communication style.

Many organizations have specific communication guidelines that show everything from the correct use of the company name to preferred abbreviations and other grammatical details. Specifying a desired style of communication is more difficult, however. Observe more experienced colleagues, and never hesitate to ask for editorial help to make sure you're conveying the appropriate tone. For instance, with clients entrusting thousands or millions of dollars to it, an investment firm communicates in a style quite different from that of a clothing retailer. And a clothing retailer specializing in high-quality business attire communicates in a different style than a store catering to the latest trends in casual wear.

Adapting to Your Audience: Controlling Your Style and Tone

3 LEARNING OBJECTIVE

Explain how to achieve a tone that is conversational but businesslike, explain the value of using plain language, and define active and passive voice.

Your communication **style** involves the choices you make to express yourself: the words you select, the manner in which you use those words in sentences, and the way you build paragraphs from individual sentences. Your style creates a certain **tone**, or overall impression, in your messages. You can vary your style to sound forceful or objective, personal or formal, colorful or dry. The right choice depends on the nature of your message and your relationship with the reader.

USING A CONVERSATIONAL TONE

The tone of your business messages can range from informal to conversational to formal (see Table 5.2). When you're communicating with your superiors or with customers, your tone may tend to be more formal and respectful.[8] However, that formal tone might sound distant and cold if used with close colleagues.

TABLE 5.2	Finding the Right Tone
Tone	**Example**
Stuffy: too formal for today's audiences	Dear Ms. Navarro:
	Enclosed please find the information that was requested during our telephone communication of May 14. As was mentioned at that time, Midville Hospital has significantly more doctors of exceptional quality than any other health facility in the state.
	As you were also informed, our organization has quite an impressive network of doctors and other health-care professionals with offices located throughout the state. In the event that you should need a specialist, our professionals will be able to make an appropriate recommendation.
	In the event that you have questions or would like additional information, you may certainly contact me during regular business hours.
	Most sincerely yours,
	Samuel G. Berenz
Conversational: just right for most business communication	Dear Ms. Navarro:
	Here's the information you requested during our phone conversation on Friday. As I mentioned, Midville Hospital has the highest-rated doctors and more of them than any other hospital in the state.
	In addition, we have a vast network of doctors and other health professionals with offices throughout the state. If you need a specialist, they can refer you to the right one.
	If you would like more information, please call any time between 9:00 and 5:00, Monday through Friday.
	Sincerely,
	Samuel G. Berenz
Unprofessional: too casual for business communication	Here's the 411 you requested. IMHO, we have more and better doctors than any other hospital in the state.
	FYI, we also have a large group of doctors and other health professionals w/offices close to U at work/home. If U need a specialist, they'll refer U to the right one.
	Any? just ring or msg.
	L8R,
	S

Compare the three versions of the message in Table 5.2. The first is too formal and stuffy for today's audiences, whereas the third is inappropriately casual for business. The second message demonstrates the **conversational tone** used in most business communication—plain language that sounds businesslike without being stuffy at one extreme or too laid-back and informal at the other extreme. You can achieve a tone that is conversational but still businesslike by following these guidelines:

- **Understand the difference between texting and writing.** The casual, acronym-laden language used in text messaging and instant messaging between friends is not considered professional business writing. Yes, texting style is an efficient way for friends to communicate—particularly taking into account the limitations of a phone keypad—but if you want to be taken seriously in business, you simply cannot write like this on the job.
- **Avoid stale and pompous language.** Most companies now shy away from such dated phrases as "attached please find" and "please be advised that." Similarly, avoid using obscure words, stale or clichéd expressions, and overly complicated sentences to impress others (see Table 5.3).
- **Avoid preaching and bragging.** No one wants to listen to know-it-alls who like to preach or brag. However, if you need to remind your audience of something that should be obvious, try to work in the information casually, perhaps in the middle of a paragraph, where it will sound like a secondary comment rather than a major revelation.
- **Be careful with intimacy.** Business messages should generally avoid intimacy, such as sharing personal details or adopting a casual, unprofessional tone. However, when you have a close relationship with audience members, such as among the members of a close-knit team, a more intimate tone is sometimes appropriate and even expected.
- **Be careful with humor.** Humor can easily backfire and divert attention from your message. If you don't know your audience well or you're not skilled at using humor in a business setting, don't use it at all. Avoid humor in formal messages and when you're communicating across cultural boundaries.

TABLE 5.3	Weeding Out Obsolete Phrases
Obsolete Phrase	**Up-to-Date Replacement**
we are in receipt of	we received
kindly advise	please let me/us know
attached please find	enclosed is or I/we have enclosed
it has come to my attention	I have just learned or [someone] has just informed me
the undersigned	I/we
in due course	(specify a time or date)
permit me to say that	(omit; just say whatever you need to say)
pursuant to	(omit; just say whatever you need to say)
in closing, I'd like to say	(omit; just say whatever you need to say)
we wish to inform you that	(omit; just say whatever you need to say)
please be advised that	(omit; just say whatever you need to say)

USING PLAIN LANGUAGE

What do you think this sentence is trying to say?

> We continually exist to synergistically supply value-added deliverables such that we may continue to proactively maintain enterprise-wide data to stay competitive in tomorrow's world.[9]

Audiences can understand and act on plain language without reading it over and over.

If you don't have any idea what it means, you're not alone. However, this is a real sentence from a real company, written in an attempt to explain what the company does and why. This sort of incomprehensible, buzzword-filled writing is driving a widespread call to use *plain language* (or *plain English* specifically when English is involved).

Plain language presents information in a simple, unadorned style that allows your audience to easily grasp your meaning—language that recipients "can read, understand and act upon the first time they read it."[10] You can see how this definition supports using the "you" attitude and shows respect for your audience. In addition, plain language can make companies more productive and more profitable simply because people spend less time trying to figure out messages that are confusing or aren't written to meet their needs.[11] Finally, plain language helps nonnative speakers read your messages (see "Communication Across Cultures: Can You Connect with a Global Audience on the Web?").

On the Creative Commons website, for instance, licensing terms are available in three versions: a complete "legal code" document that spells out contractual details in specific legal terms that meet the needs of legal professionals, a "human readable" version that explains the licensing terms in nontechnical language that anyone can understand, and a "machine readable" version fine-tuned for search engines and other systems (see Figure 5.3).[12]

COMMUNICATING ACROSS CULTURES

Can You Connect with a Global Audience on the Web?

Reaching an international audience on the web involves more than simply offering translations of the English language. Successful global sites address the needs of international customers in five ways:

1. **Consider the reader's perspective.** Many communication elements that you take for granted may be interpreted differently by audiences in different countries. Should you use the metric system, different notations for times or dates, or even different names for countries? For example, German citizens don't refer to their country by the English word *Germany*; it's *Deutschland* to them. Review the entire online experience and look for ways to improve communication, including such helpful tools as interactive currency converters and translation dictionaries.

2. **Take cultural differences into account.** For instance, because humor is rooted in cultural norms, U.S. humor may not be so funny to readers from other countries. Avoid idioms and references that aren't universally recognized, such as "putting all your eggs in one basket" or "jumping out of the frying pan into the fire."

3. **Keep the message clear.** Choose simple, unambiguous words; construct short, clear, sentences; and write in the active voice whenever possible. Define abbreviations, acronyms, and words an international audience may not be familiar with.

4. **Complement language with visuals.** Use drawings, photos, videos, and other visual elements to support written messages.

5. **Consult local experts.** Seek the advice of local experts about phrases and references that may be expected. Even terms as simple as *homepage* differ from country to country. Spanish readers refer to the "first page," or *pagina inicial*, whereas the French term is "welcome page," or *page d'accueil*.

CAREER APPLICATIONS

1. Visit Sony's Global Headquarters website, at www.sony.net, and find Sony's music websites for Australia (www.sonymusic.com.au), France (www.sonymusic.fr), and Germany (www.sonybmg.de). How does Sony localize each country's site?

2. Compare Sony's international sites to IBM's global webpages, at www.ibm.com/us/, www.ibm.com/au/, www.ibm.com/fr/, and www.ibm.com/de/. How does Sony's approach differ from IBM's? Do both corporations successfully address the needs of a global audience? Write a two-paragraph summary that compares the international sites of the two companies.

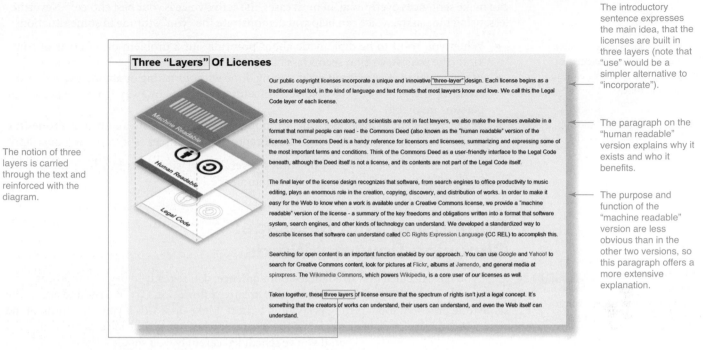

The introductory sentence expresses the main idea, that the licenses are built in three layers (note that "use" would be a simpler alternative to "incorporate").

The notion of three layers is carried through the text and reinforced with the diagram.

The paragraph on the "human readable" version explains why it exists and who it benefits.

The purpose and function of the "machine readable" version are less obvious than in the other two versions, so this paragraph offers a more extensive explanation.

Figure 5.3   Plain Language at Creative Commons
Creative Commons uses this diagram and text to explain the differences among its three versions of content licenses.

SELECTING THE ACTIVE OR PASSIVE VOICE

Your choice of the active or passive voice affects the tone of your message. In **active voice,** the subject performs the action and the object receives the action: "Jodi sent the email message." In **passive voice,** the subject receives the action: "The email message was sent by Jodi." As you can see, the passive voice combines the helping verb *to be* with a form of the verb that is usually similar to the past tense.

Using the active voice helps make your writing more direct, livelier, and easier to read (see Table 5.4). In contrast, the passive voice is often cumbersome, can be unnecessarily vague, and

TABLE 5.4	Choosing Active or Passive Voice
In general, avoid passive voice in order to make your writing lively and direct.	
Dull and Indirect in Passive Voice	**Lively and Direct in Active Voice**
The new procedure was developed by the operations team.	The operations team developed the new procedure.
Legal problems are created by this contract.	This contract creates legal problems.
Reception preparations have been undertaken by our PR people for the new CEO's arrival.	Our PR people have begun planning a reception for the new CEO.
However, passive voice is helpful when you need to be diplomatic or want to focus attention on problems or solutions rather than on people.	
Accusatory or Self-Congratulatory in Active Voice	**More Diplomatic in Passive Voice**
You lost the shipment.	The shipment was lost.
I recruited seven engineers last month.	Seven engineers were recruited last month.
We are investigating the high rate of failures on the final assembly line.	The high rate of failures on the final assembly line is being investigated.

can make sentences overly long. In most cases, the active voice is your best choice.[13] Nevertheless, using the passive voice can help you demonstrate the "you" attitude in some situations:

Use passive sentences to soften bad news, to put yourself in the background, or to create an impersonal tone.

- When you want to be diplomatic about pointing out a problem or an error of some kind (the passive version seems less like an accusation)
- When you want to point out what's being done without taking or attributing either the credit or the blame (the passive version shifts the spotlight away from the person or persons involved)
- When you want to avoid personal pronouns in order to create an objective tone (the passive version may be used in a formal report, for example)

The second half of Table 5.4 illustrates several other situations in which the passive voice helps you focus your message on your audience.

Composing Your Message: Choosing Powerful Words

4 LEARNING OBJECTIVE

Describe how to select words that are not only correct but also effective.

After you have decided how to adapt to your audience, you're ready to begin composing your message. As you write your first draft, let your creativity flow. Don't try to write and edit at the same time or worry about getting everything perfect. Make up words if you can't think of the right word, draw pictures, talk out loud—do whatever it takes to get the ideas out of your head and captured on screen or paper. If you've scheduled carefully, you should have time to revise and refine the material later, before showing it to anyone. In fact, many writers find it helpful to establish a personal rule of *never* showing a first draft to anyone. By working in this "safe zone," away from the critical eyes of others, your mind will stay free to think clearly and creatively.

If you get stuck and feel unable to write, try to overcome writer's block by jogging your brain in creative ways. The introduction is often the hardest part to write, so put it aside and work on whichever parts of the document you're most comfortable with at any given moment. In most cases, you don't need to write the sections in any particular order.[14] Work on nontext elements such as graphics or your cover page. Revisit your purpose and confirm your intent in writing the message. Give yourself a mental break by switching to a different project. Sometimes all you need to do is start writing without worrying about the words you're using or how they will sound to the audience. Words will start flowing, your mind will engage, and the writing will come easier.

A helpful way to view your writing is to look at it in three layers: choosing powerful words, creating effective sentences, and crafting coherent and unified paragraphs. This section deals with words, and the next two cover sentences and paragraphs.

Correctness is the first consideration when choosing words.

Successful writers pay close attention to the correct use of words.[15] If you make grammatical or usage errors, you lose credibility with your audience—even if your message is otherwise correct. Poor grammar implies that you're uninformed, and audiences may choose not to trust an uninformed source. Moreover, poor grammar can imply that you don't respect your audience enough to get things right.

The "rules" of grammar and usage can be a source of worry for writers because some of these rules are complex and some evolve over time. Even professional editors and grammarians occasionally have questions about correct usage, and they sometimes disagree about the answers. For example, the word *data* is the plural form of *datum*, yet some experts now prefer to treat *data* as a singular noun when it's used in nonscientific material to refer to a collection of facts or figures.

If you're not sure of correct grammar or usage, look it up; you'll avoid embarrassing mistakes and learn at the same time.

With practice, you'll become more skilled in making correct choices. If you have doubts about what is correct, you have many ways to find the answer. Check the "Handbook of Grammar, Mechanics, and Usage" at the end of this book, or consult the many special reference books and resources available in libraries, in bookstores, and on the Internet.

Effectiveness is the second consideration when choosing words.

In addition to using words correctly, successful writers and speakers take care to find the most effective words and phrases to convey their meaning. Selecting and using words effectively is often more challenging than using words correctly because it's a matter of judgment and experience. Careful writers continue to work at their craft to find words that communicate with power (see Figure 5.4).

In many cases, *global* is an absolute term and doesn't benefit from a modifier such as *truly*. However, economic globalization is occurring in stages, so *truly* here suggests the point at which globalization is nearly complete. ——

Claim is a powerful word here because it suggests a strong element of doubt. ——

The diplomatic use of passive voice keeps the focus on the issue at hand, rather than on the organizations that are involved.

Two Sides of the Story

Growing interest in the global acceptance of a single set of robust accounting standards comes from all participants in the capital markets. Many multinational companies and national regulators and users support it because they believe that the use of common standards in the preparation of public company financial statements will make it easier to compare the financial results of reporting entities from different countries. They believe it will help investors understand opportunities better. Large public companies with subsidiaries in multiple jurisdictions would be able to use one accounting language company-wide and present their financial statements in the same language as their competitors.

Another benefit some believe is that in a truly global economy, financial professionals including CPAs will be more mobile, and companies will more easily be able to respond to the human capital needs of their subsidiaries around the world.

Nevertheless, many people also believe that U.S. GAAP is the gold standard, and something will be lost with full acceptance of IFRS. However, recent SEC actions and global trends have increased awareness of the need to address possible adoption. According to a survey conducted in the first half of 2008 by Deloitte & Touche among chief financial officers and other financial professionals, U.S. companies have an interest in adopting IFRS and this interest is steadily growing. Thirty percent would consider adopting IFRS now, another 28 percent are unsure or do not have sufficient knowledge to decide, while 42 percent said they would not. Still, an AICPA survey conducted in Fall 2008 among its CPA members shows a significant and positive shift in the number of firms and companies that are starting to prepare for eventual adoption of IFRS. A 55 percent majority of CPAs at firms and companies nationwide said they are preparing in a variety of ways for IFRS adoption, an increase of 14 percentage points over the 41 percent who were preparing for change, according to an April 2008 AICPA survey.

Another concern is that worldwide many countries that claim to be converging to international standards may never get 100 percent compliance. Most reserve the right to carve out selectively or modify standards they do not consider in their national interest, an action that could lead to incompatibility—the very issue that IFRS seek to address.

GAAP and IFRS, Still Differences

Great strides have been made by the FASB and the IASB to converge the content of IFRS and U.S. GAAP. The goal is that by the time the SEC allows or mandates the use of IFRS for U.S. publicly traded companies, most or all of the key differences will have been resolved.

Because of these ongoing convergence projects, the extent of the specific differences between IFRS and U.S. GAAP is shrinking. Yet significant differences do remain. For example:

- IFRS does not permit Last In First Out (LIFO) as an inventory costing method.
- IFRS uses a single-step method for impairment write-downs rather than the two-step method used in U.S. GAAP, making write-downs more likely.
- IFRS has a different probability threshold and measurement objective for contingencies.
- IFRS does not permit curing debt covenant violations after year-end.
- IFRS guidance regarding revenue recognition is less extensive than GAAP and contains relatively little industry-specific instructions.

5

Robust goes beyond simply *strong* to suggest *resilient* and *comprehensive* as well.

Gold standard (a term borrowed from economics) refers to something against which all similar entities are compared, an unsurpassed model of excellence.

In the context of a survey *significant* means more than just *important*; it indicates a statistical observation that is large enough to be more than mere chance. *Positive* indicates the direction of the change and suggests *affirmation* and *progress*.

Carve out is much stronger than *remove* because it could suggest surgical precision if done well or perhaps violent destruction if not done with finesse. In this context, *carve out* is meant to express a concern about countries weakening the international financial standards by modifying them to meet their own needs.

Figure 5.4 Choosing Powerful Words
Notice how careful word choices help this excerpt from a report published by the American Institute of Certified Public Accountants make a number of important points. The tone is formal, which is appropriate for a report with global, public readership. (GAAP refers to accounting standards currently used in the United States; IFRS refers to international standards.)

UNDERSTANDING DENOTATION AND CONNOTATION

A word may have both a denotative and a connotative meaning. The **denotative meaning** is the literal, or dictionary, meaning. The **connotative meaning** includes all the associations and feelings evoked by the word.

The denotative meaning of *desk* is "a piece of furniture with a flat work surface and various drawers for storage." The connotative meaning of *desk* may include thoughts associated with work or study, but the word *desk* has fairly neutral connotations—neither strong nor emotional. However, some words have much stronger connotations than others and should be used with care. For example, the connotations of the word *fail* are negative and can carry strong emotional meaning. If you say that the sales department

Many words have both a *denotative* (explicit, specific) meaning and a *connotative* (implicit, associative) meaning.

failed to meet its annual quota, the connotative meaning suggests that the group is inferior, incompetent, or below some standard of performance. However, the reason for not achieving 100 percent might be an inferior product, incorrect pricing, or some other factor outside the control of the sales department. In contrast, by saying that the sales department achieved 85 percent of its quota, you clearly communicate that the results were less than expected—without triggering all the negative emotions associated with *failure*.

BALANCING ABSTRACT AND CONCRETE WORDS

> The more abstract a word is, the more it is removed from the tangible, objective world that can be perceived with the senses.

Words vary dramatically in their degree of abstraction or concreteness. An **abstract word** expresses a concept, quality, or characteristic. Abstractions are usually broad, encompassing a category of ideas, and they are often intellectual, academic, or philosophical. *Love, honor, progress, tradition,* and *beauty* are abstractions, as are such important business concepts as *productivity, profits, quality,* and *motivation.* In contrast, a **concrete word** stands for something you can touch, see, or visualize. Most concrete terms are anchored in the tangible, material world. *Chair, table, horse, rose, kick, kiss, red, green,* and *two* are concrete words; they are direct, clear, and exact. Incidentally, technology continues to generate new words and new meanings that describe things that don't have a physical presence but are nonetheless concrete: *software, database,* and *website* are all concrete terms as well.

As you can imagine, abstractions tend to cause more trouble for writers and readers than concrete words. Abstractions tend to be "fuzzy" and can be interpreted differently, depending on the audience and the circumstances. The best way to minimize such problems is to blend abstract terms with concrete ones, the general with the specific. State the concept, then pin it down with details expressed in more concrete terms. Save the abstractions for ideas that cannot be expressed any other way. In addition, abstract words such as *small, numerous, sizable, near, soon, good,* and *fine* are imprecise, so try to replace them with terms that are more accurate. Instead of referring to a *sizable loss,* give an exact number.

FINDING WORDS THAT COMMUNICATE WELL

By practicing your writing, learning from experienced writers and editors, and reading extensively, you'll find it easier to choose words that communicate exactly what you want to say. When you compose your business messages, think carefully to find the most powerful words for each situation and to avoid obscure words, clichés, and buzzwords that are turning into clichés (see Table 5.5):

> Try to use words that are powerful and familiar.

- **Choose powerful words.** Choose words that express your thoughts clearly, specifically, and dynamically. If you find yourself using a lot of adjectives and adverbs, you're probably trying to compensate for weak nouns and verbs. Saying that *sales plummeted* is stronger and more efficient than saying *sales dropped dramatically* or *sales experienced a dramatic drop.*
- **Choose familiar words.** You'll communicate best with words that are familiar to both you and your readers. Efforts to improve a situation certainly can be *ameliorative,* but saying they are *helpful* is a lot more effective. Moreover, trying to use an unfamiliar word for the first time in an important document can lead to embarrassing mistakes.

> Avoid clichés, be extremely careful with trendy buzzwords, and use jargon only when your audience is completely familiar with it.

- **Avoid clichés and be careful with buzzwords.** Although familiar words are generally the best choice, avoid *clichés*—terms and phrases so common that they have lost some of their power to communicate. *Buzzwords,* newly coined terms often associated with technology, business, or cultural changes, are slightly more difficult to handle than clichés, but in small doses and in the right situation, they can be useful. The careful

TABLE 5.5	Selected Examples of Finding Powerful Words
Potentially Weak Words and Phrases	**Stronger Alternatives (Effective Usage Depends on the Situation)**
Increase (as a verb)	Accelerate, amplify, augment, enlarge, escalate, expand, extend, magnify, multiply, soar, swell
Decrease (as a verb)	Curb, cut back, depreciate, dwindle, shrink, slacken
Large, small	(use a specific number, such as $100 million)
Good	Admirable, beneficial, desirable, flawless, pleasant, sound, superior, worthy
Bad	Abysmal, corrupt, deficient, flawed, inadequate, inferior, poor, substandard, worthless
We are committed to providing . . .	We provide . . .
It is in our best interest to . . .	We should . . .
Unfamiliar Words	**Familiar Words**
Ascertain	Find out, learn
Consummate	Close, bring about
Peruse	Read, study
Circumvent	Avoid
Unequivocal	Certain
Clichés and Buzzwords	**Plain Language**
An uphill battle	A challenge
Writing on the wall	Prediction
Call the shots	Lead
Take by storm	Attack
Costs an arm and a leg	Expensive
A new ballgame	Fresh start
Fall through the cracks	Be overlooked
Think outside the box	Be creative
Run it up the flagpole	Find out what people think about it
Eat our own dog food	Use our own products
Mission-critical	Vital
Disintermediate	Get rid of
Green light (as a verb)	Approve
Architect (as a verb)	Design
Space (as in, "we compete in the XYZ space")	Market or industry
Blocking and tackling	Basic skills
Trying to boil the ocean	Working frantically but without focus
Human capital	People, employees, workforce
Low-hanging fruit	Tasks that are easy to complete or sales that are easy to close
Pushback	Resistance

use of a buzzword can signal that you're an insider, someone in the know.[16] However, buzzwords quickly become clichés, and using them too late in their "life cycle" can mark you as an outsider desperately trying to look like an insider. When people use clichés and overuse buzzwords, they often sound as though they don't know how to express themselves otherwise and don't invest the energy required for original writing.[17]

- **Use jargon carefully.** *Jargon*, the specialized language of a particular profession or industry, has a bad reputation, but it's not always bad. Using jargon is usually an efficient way to communicate within the specific groups that understand these terms. After all, that's how jargon develops in the first place, as people with similar interests develop ways to communicate complex ideas quickly. For instance, when a recording engineer wants to communicate that a particular piece of music is devoid of reverberation and other sound effects, it's a lot easier to simply describe the track as "dry." Of course, to people who aren't familiar with such insider terms, jargon is meaningless and intimidating—one more reason it's important to understand your audience before you start writing.

As you read for business or pleasure, take note of words that strike you as effective and then try to use those words in your own writing. If you need help finding the right words, try some of the visual dictionaries and thesauruses available online. For example, Visuwords (**www.visuwords.com**) shows words that are similar to or different from a given word and helps you see subtle differences to find the perfect word.[18]

Composing Your Message: Creating Effective Sentences

5 **LEARNING OBJECTIVE**

Define the four types of sentences, and explain how sentence style affects emphasis within a message.

A simple sentence has one main clause.

A compound sentence has two main clauses.

A complex sentence has one main clause and one subordinate clause.

Arranging your carefully chosen words in effective sentences is the next step in creating powerful messages. Start by selecting the best type of sentence to communicate each point you want to make.

CHOOSING FROM THE FOUR TYPES OF SENTENCES

Sentences come in four basic varieties: simple, compound, complex, and compound–complex. A **simple sentence** has one main *clause* (a single subject and a single predicate), although it may be expanded by nouns and pronouns that serve as objects of the action and by modifying phrases. Here's an example with the subject noun underlined once and the predicate verb underlined twice:

> Profits increased in the past year.

A **compound sentence** has two main clauses that express two or more independent but related thoughts of equal importance, usually joined by *and*, *but*, or *or*. In effect, a compound sentence is a merger of two or more simple sentences (independent clauses) that are related. For example:

> Wage rates have declined by 5 percent, and employee turnover has been high.

The independent clauses in a compound sentence are always separated by a comma or by a semicolon (in which case the conjunction—*and*, *but*, *or*—is dropped).

A **complex sentence** expresses one main thought (the independent clause) and one or more subordinate, related thoughts (dependent clauses that cannot stand alone as valid sentences). Independent and dependent clauses are usually separated by a comma. In this example, "Although you may question Gerald's conclusions" is a subordinate thought expressed in a dependent clause:

> Although you may question Gerald's conclusions, you must admit that his research is thorough.

A **compound–complex sentence** has two main clauses, at least one of which contains a subordinate clause:

> <u>Profits</u> <u>have increased</u> in the past year, and although you may question Gerald's conclusions, <u>you</u> <u>must admit</u> that his research is thorough.

A compound–complex sentence has two main clauses and at least one dependent clause.

When constructing sentences, choose the form that matches the relationship of the ideas you want to express. If you have two ideas of equal importance, express them as two simple sentences or as one compound sentence. However, if one of the ideas is less important than the other, place it in a dependent clause to form a complex sentence. For example, although the following compound sentence uses a conjunction to join two ideas, they aren't truly equal:

> The chemical products division is the strongest in the company, and its management techniques should be adopted by the other divisions.

By making the first thought subordinate to the second, you establish a cause-and-effect relationship and emphasize the more important idea (that the other divisions should adopt the chemical division's management techniques):

> Because the chemical products division is the strongest in the company, its management techniques should be adopted by the other divisions.

In addition to selecting the best type for each thought you want to express, using a variety of sentence types throughout a document can make your writing more interesting and effective. For example, if you use too many simple sentences in a row, you may struggle to properly express the relationships among your ideas, and your writing will sound choppy and abrupt. At the other extreme, a long series of compound, complex, or compound–complex sentences can be tiring to read.

Writing is usually more interesting and effective if it balances all four sentence types.

USING SENTENCE STYLE TO EMPHASIZE KEY THOUGHTS

In every message of any length, some ideas are more important than others. You can emphasize these key ideas through your sentence style. One obvious technique is to give important points the most space. When you want to call attention to a thought, use extra words to describe it. Consider this sentence:

> The chairperson called for a vote of the shareholders.

You can emphasize ideas in a sentence by
- Devoting more words to them
- Putting them at the beginning or at the end of the sentence
- Making them the subject of the sentence

To emphasize the importance of the chairperson, you might describe her more fully:

> Having considerable experience in corporate takeover battles, the chairperson called for a vote of the shareholders.

You can increase the emphasis even more by adding a separate, short sentence to augment the first:

> The chairperson called for a vote of the shareholders. She has considerable experience in corporate takeover battles.

You can also call attention to a thought by making it the subject of the sentence. In the following example, the emphasis is on the person:

> I can write letters much more quickly by using a computer.

However, by changing the subject, the computer takes center stage:

> The computer enables me to write letters much more quickly.

Another way to emphasize an idea is to place it either at the beginning or at the end of a sentence:

> **Less emphatic:** We are cutting the price to stimulate demand.
> **More emphatic:** To stimulate demand, we are cutting the price.

You can adjust the emphasis given to a subordinate idea by placing the dependent clause at the beginning, middle, or end of the sentence.

In complex sentences, the placement of the dependent clause hinges on the relationship between the ideas expressed. If you want to emphasize the subordinate idea, put the dependent clause at the end of the sentence (the most emphatic position) or at the beginning (the second most emphatic position). If you want to downplay the idea, put the dependent clause within the sentence:

> **Most emphatic:** The electronic parts are manufactured in Mexico, <u>which has lower wage rates than the United States</u>.
> **Emphatic:** <u>Because wage rates are lower in Mexico than in the United States</u>, the electronic parts are manufactured there.
> **Least emphatic:** Mexico, <u>which has lower wage rates than the United States</u>, was selected as the production site for the electronic parts.

Techniques such as these give you a great deal of control over the way your audience interprets what you have to say.

Composing Your Message: Crafting Unified, Coherent Paragraphs

6 **LEARNING OBJECTIVE**

Define the three key elements of a paragraph, and list five ways to develop unified, coherent paragraphs.

Paragraphs organize sentences related to the same general topic. Readers expect every paragraph to be *unified*—focusing on a single topic—and *coherent*—presenting ideas in a logically connected way. By carefully arranging the elements of each paragraph, you help your readers grasp the main idea of your document and understand how the specific pieces of support material back up that idea.

CREATING THE ELEMENTS OF A PARAGRAPH

Paragraphs vary widely in length and form, but a typical paragraph contains three basic elements: a topic sentence, support sentences that develop the topic, and transitional words and phrases.

Most paragraphs consist of
- A topic sentence that reveals the subject of the paragraph
- Related sentences that support and expand the topic
- Transitions that help readers move between sentences and between paragraphs

Topic Sentence

An effective paragraph deals with a single topic, and the sentence that introduces that topic is called the **topic sentence**. In informal and creative writing, the topic sentence may be implied rather than stated. In business writing, the topic sentence is generally explicit and is often the first sentence in the paragraph. The topic sentence gives readers a summary of the general idea that will be covered in the rest of the paragraph. The following examples show how a topic sentence can introduce the subject and suggest the way the subject will be developed:

> The medical products division has been troubled for many years by public relations problems. [In the rest of the paragraph, readers will learn the details of the problems.]
>
> To get a refund, please supply us with the following information. [The details of the necessary information will be described in the rest of the paragraph.]

In addition to helping your readers, topic sentences help you as a writer because they remind you of the purpose of each paragraph and thereby encourage you to stay focused. In fact, a good way to test the effectiveness of your writing is to prepare a summary version that consists of only the first sentences of all your paragraphs. If this summary communicates the essence of your message in a sensible, compelling way, you've probably done a good job of presenting your information.[19]

Support Sentences

In most paragraphs, the topic sentence needs to be explained, justified, or extended with one or more support sentences. These related sentences must all have a bearing on the general subject and must provide enough specific details to make the topic clear:

> The medical products division has been troubled for many years by public relations problems. Since 2002 the local newspaper has published 15 articles that portray the division in a negative light. We have been accused of everything from mistreating laboratory animals to polluting the local groundwater. Our facility has been described as a health hazard. Our scientists are referred to as "Frankensteins," and our profits are considered "obscene."

The support sentences are all more specific than the topic sentence. Each one provides another piece of evidence to demonstrate the general truth of the main thought. Also, each sentence is clearly related to the general idea being developed, which gives the paragraph unity. A paragraph is well developed if it contains enough information to make the topic sentence understood and convincing, and if it doesn't contain any extraneous, unrelated sentences.

Transitions

Transitions connect ideas by showing how one thought is related to another. They also help alert the reader to what lies ahead so that shifts and changes don't cause confusion. In addition to helping readers understand the connections you're trying to make, transitions give your writing a smooth, even flow.

Depending on the specific need within a document, transitional elements can range in length from a single word to an entire paragraph or more. You can establish transitions in a variety of ways:

Transitional elements include
- Connecting words (conjunctions)
- Repeated words or phrases
- Pronouns
- Words that are frequently paired

- **Use connecting words.** Use conjunctions such as *and*, *but*, *or*, *nevertheless*, *however*, *in addition*, and so on.
- **Echo a word or phrase from a previous paragraph or sentence.** "A system should be established for monitoring inventory levels. *This system* will provide. . . ."
- **Use a pronoun that refers to a noun used previously.** "Ms. Arthur is the leading candidate for the president's position. *She* has excellent qualifications."
- **Use words that are frequently paired.** "The machine has a *minimum* output of. . . . Its *maximum* output is. . . ."

Some transitions serve as mood changers, alerting the reader to a change in mood from the previous material. Some announce a total contrast with what's gone on before, some announce a causal relationship, and some signal a change in time. Here is a list of transitions frequently used to move readers smoothly between clauses, sentences, and paragraphs:

Additional detail: moreover, furthermore, in addition, besides, first, second, third, finally

Cause-and-effect relationship: therefore, because, accordingly, thus, consequently, hence, as a result, so

Comparison: similarly, here again, likewise, in comparison, still

Contrast: yet, conversely, whereas, nevertheless, on the other hand, however, but, nonetheless

Condition: although, if

Illustration: for example, in particular, in this case, for instance
Time sequence: formerly, after, when, meanwhile, sometimes
Intensification: indeed, in fact, in any event
Summary: in brief, in short, to sum up
Repetition: that is, in other words, as mentioned earlier

Consider using a transition whenever it could help the reader understand your ideas and follow you from point to point. You can use transitions inside paragraphs to tie related points together and between paragraphs to ease the shift from one distinct thought to another. In longer reports, a transition that links major sections or chapters may be a complete paragraph that serves as a mini-introduction to the next section or as a summary of the ideas presented in the section just ending. Here's an example:

> Given the nature of this product, our alternatives are limited. As the previous section indicates, we can stop making it altogether, improve it, or continue with the current model. Each of these alternatives has advantages and disadvantages, which are discussed in the following section.

This paragraph makes it clear to the reader that the analysis of the problem (offered in the previous section) is now over and that the document is making a transition to an analysis of the possible solutions (to be offered in the next section).

Figure 5.5 offers several examples of transitions and other features of effective paragraphs.

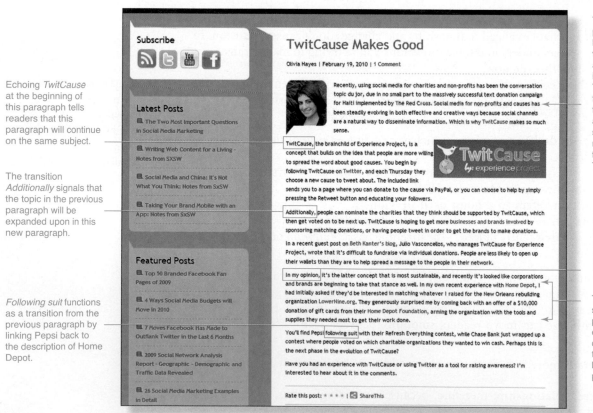

Echoing *TwitCause* at the beginning of this paragraph tells readers that this paragraph will continue on the same subject.

The transition *Additionally* signals that the topic in the previous paragraph will be expanded upon in this new paragraph.

Following suit functions as a transition from the previous paragraph by linking Pepsi back to the description of Home Depot.

The three sentences in this paragraph start with the broad topic (social media for charities and nonprofits) and narrow down the main idea, which is that TwitCause is a good tool for this purpose. (Note that the third sentence is really a fragment, but Hayes is selectively breaking the rules here to emphasize the suitability of TwitCause.)

In my opinion lets readers know she is transitioning from reporting to offering her personal thoughts on the subject at hand.

The second and third sentences in this paragraph provide an example of the observation made in the topic sentence at the beginning of the paragraph.

Figure 5.5 Crafting Unified, Coherent Paragraphs
Olivia Hayes, a copywriter with the social media marketing agency Ignite, demonstrates several aspects of effective writing in this blog post about the Twitter-based social contribution network TwitCause.

MyBcommLab

Apply Figure 5.5's key concepts by revising a new document. Go to Chapter 5 in mybcommlab.com and select Document Makeovers.

CHOOSING THE BEST WAY TO DEVELOP EACH PARAGRAPH

You have a variety of options for developing paragraphs, each of which can convey a specific type of idea. Five of the most common approaches are illustration, comparison or contrast, cause and effect, classification, and problem and solution (see Table 5.6).

In some instances, combining approaches in a single paragraph is an effective strategy. Notice how the example provided for "Problem and solution" in Table 5.6 also includes an element of illustration by listing some of the unique products that could be part of the proposed solution. However, when combining approaches, do so carefully so that you don't lose readers partway through the paragraph.

Five ways to develop paragraphs:
- Illustration
- Comparison or contrast
- Cause and effect
- Classification
- Problem and solution

TABLE 5.6	Five Techniques for Developing Paragraphs	
Technique	**Description**	**Example**
Illustration	Giving examples that demonstrate the general idea	Some of our most popular products are available through local distributors. For example, Everett & Lemmings carries our frozen soups and entrees. The J. B. Green Company carries our complete line of seasonings, as well as the frozen soups. Wilmont Foods, also a major distributor, now carries our new line of frozen desserts.
Comparison or contrast	Using similarities or differences to develop the topic	When the company was small, the recruiting function could be handled informally. The need for new employees was limited, and each manager could comfortably screen and hire her or his own staff. However, our successful bid on the Owens contract means that we will be doubling our labor force over the next six months. To hire that many people without disrupting our ongoing activities, we will create a separate recruiting group within the human resources department.
Cause and effect	Focusing on the reasons for something	The heavy-duty fabric of your Wanderer tent probably broke down for one of two reasons: (1) a sharp object punctured the fabric, and without reinforcement, the hole was enlarged by the stress of pitching the tent daily for a week or (2) the fibers gradually rotted because the tent was folded and stored while still wet.
Classification	Showing how a general idea is broken into specific categories	Successful candidates for our supervisor trainee program generally come from one of several groups. The largest group by far consists of recent graduates of accredited business management programs. The next largest group comes from within our own company, as we try to promote promising staff workers to positions of greater responsibility. Finally, we occasionally accept candidates with outstanding supervisory experience in related industries.
Problem and solution	Presenting a problem and then discussing the solution	Selling handmade toys online is a challenge because consumers are accustomed to buying heavily advertised toys from major chain stores or well-known websites such as Amazon.com. However, if we develop an appealing website, we can compete on the basis of product novelty and quality. In addition, we can provide unusual crafts at a competitive price: a rocking horse of birch, with a hand-knit tail and mane; a music box with the child's name painted on the top; and a real teepee, made by Native American artisans.

In addition, before settling for the first approach that comes to mind, consider the alternatives. Think through various methods before committing yourself, or even write several test paragraphs to see which method works best. By avoiding the easy habit of repeating the same old paragraph pattern time after time, you can keep your writing fresh and interesting.

Using Technology to Compose and Shape Your Messages

Be sure to take advantage of the tools in your word processor or online publishing systems (for websites, blogs, and other documents) to write more efficiently and effectively. The features, functions, and names vary from system to system and version to version, but you'll encounter some combination of the following capabilities:

- **Style sheets, style sets, templates, and themes.** *Style sheets*, *style sets*, *templates*, and *themes* are various ways of ensuring consistency throughout a document and from document to document. These tools also make it easy to redesign an entire document or screen simply by redefining the various styles or selecting a different design theme. Style sheets or sets are collections of formatting choices for words, paragraphs, and other elements. Rather than manually formatting every element, you simply select one of the available styles. Templates usually set overall document parameters such as page size and provide a specific set of styles to use. Templates can be particularly handy if you create a variety of document types, such as letters, calendars, agendas, and so on. Themes tend to address the overall look and feel of the page or screen, including color palettes and background images.
- **Boilerplate and document components.** *Boilerplate* refers to a standard block of text that is reused in multiple documents. Two common examples are company descriptions and executive biographies. Some systems offer the means to store these blocks and drop them into a document as needed, which saves time and ensures consistency. Moving beyond simple text blocks, some systems can store fully formatted document components such as cover pages, sidebars, and *pull quotes* (a piece of text copied from the main body of the document and formatted as a large, eye-catching visual element).
- **Autocorrection or autocompletion.** Some programs can automate text entry and correction using a feature called autocompletion, autocorrection, or something similar. In Microsoft Word, for example, the AutoCorrect feature lets you build a library of actions that automatically fill in longer entries based on the first few characters you type (such as entering a full description of the company after you type the word "boilerplate") or correct common typing errors (such as typing *teh* instead of *the*). Use these features carefully, though. First, they can make changes you might not want in every instance. Second, you may grow to rely on them to clean up your typing, but they won't be there to help when you're using other systems.
- **File merge and mail merge.** Most word processing software makes it easy to combine files, which is an especially handy feature when several members of a team write different sections of a report. Mail merge lets you personalize form letters by automatically inserting names and addresses from a database.
- **Endnotes, footnotes, indexes, and tables of contents.** Your computer can help you track footnotes and endnotes, renumbering them every time you add or delete references. For a report's indexes and table of contents, you can simply flag the items you want to include, and the software assembles the lists for you.

For new articles and advice on writing business messages, visit http://real-timeupdates .com/bct11 and click on Chapter 5. For a reminder of the tasks involved in writing messages, see "Checklist: Writing Business Messages."

✓ Checklist | Writing Business Messages

A. Adapt to your audience.
- Use the "you" attitude.
- Maintain good etiquette through polite communication.
- Emphasize the positive whenever possible.
- Use bias-free language.
- Establish credibility in the eyes of your audience.
- Project your company's preferred image.
- Use a conversational but still professional and respectful tone.
- Use plain language for clarity.

B. Compose your message.
- Choose strong words that communicate efficiently.
- Pay attention to the connotative meaning of your words.
- Balance abstract and concrete terms to convey your meaning accurately.
- Avoid clichés and trendy buzzwords.
- Use jargon only when your audience understands it and prefers it.
- Vary your sentence structure for impact and interest.
- Develop coherent, unified paragraphs.
- Use transitions generously to help your audience follow your message.

COMMUNICATION CHALLENGES AT CREATIVE COMMONS

To achieve their mission of popularizing a new approach to copyrighting songs, artwork, literature, and other creative works, Joi Ito and his staff at Creative Commons need to persuade people that the traditional approach to copyrighting doesn't meet the needs of today's digital society. This is no small challenge: Not only do they need to convince people to reconsider more than 200 years of legal precedent and habit, they also need to communicate with an extremely diverse audience—everyone from lawyers and business managers to artists, writers, musicians, and scientists. After graduating with a business degree, you've joined Creative Commons as a communication intern for a year before entering law school. Apply your knowledge of effective writing to the following scenarios.

INDIVIDUAL CHALLENGE: Visit the licensing section of the Creative Commons website, at http://creativecommons.org/licenses, and read the information on Attribution-NonCommercial-Share Alike, Attribution-NonCommercial, and Attribution-NoDerivatives licenses. Write a brief description that explains how these three licenses differ. Imagine that your audience is a group of music and art majors.

TEAM CHALLENGE: A key aspect of the communication challenge for Creative Commons is translating legal documents into language that musicians, artists, and others with no legal training can easily understand. In a small group, brainstorm ways to rewrite the following paragraph into language for a general audience:

> The above rights may be exercised in all media and formats whether now known or hereafter devised. The above rights include the right to make such modifications as are technically necessary to exercise the rights in other media and formats, but otherwise you have no rights to make adaptations.

Quick Learning Guide

MyBcommLab

If your course uses MyBcommLab, log on to www.mybcommlab.com to access the following study and assessment aids associated with this chapter:

- Video applications
- Real-Time Updates
- Peer review activity
- Pre/post test
- Personalized study plan
- Model documents
- Sample presentations

If you are not using MyBcommLab, you can access Real-Time Updates through http://real-timeupdates.com/bct11.

SUMMARY OF LEARNING OBJECTIVES

1 Identify the four aspects of being sensitive to audience needs when writing business messages. First, the "you" attitude refers to speaking and writing in terms of your audience's wishes, interests, hopes, and preferences rather than your own. Writing with this attitude is essential to effective communication because it shows your audience that you have their needs in mind, not just your own. Second, good etiquette not only indicates respect for your audience but also helps foster a more successful environment for communication by minimizing negative emotional reaction. Third, sensitive communicators understand the difference between delivering negative news and being negative. Without hiding the negative news, they look for way to emphasize positive aspects. Fourth, being sensitive includes taking care to avoid biased language that unfairly and even unethically categorizes or stigmatizes people in ways related to gender, race, ethnicity, age, or disability.

2 Explain how establishing your credibility and projecting your company's image are vital aspects of building strong relationships with your audience. Whether a one-time interaction or a series of exchanges over the course of many months or years, successful communication relies on a positive relationship existing between sender and receiver. Audience responses to your messages depend heavily on your credibility, a measure of your believability, based on how reliable you are and how much trust you evoke in others. When you have established credibility with an audience, communication becomes much easier because you no longer have to spend time and energy convincing people that you are a trustworthy source of information and ideas. Project your company's desired image when communicating with external audiences. You represent your company and therefore play a vital role in helping the company build and maintain positive relationships with all of its stakeholders.

3 Explain how to achieve a tone that is conversational but businesslike, explain the value of using plain language, and define active and passive voice. To achieve a tone that is conversational but still businesslike, avoid obsolete and pompous language, avoid preaching and bragging, be careful with intimacy (sharing personal details or adopting an overly casual tone), and be careful with humor. Plain language is a way of presenting information in a simple, unadorned style so that your audience can easily grasp your meaning. By writing and speaking in plain terms, you demonstrate the "you" attitude and show respect for your audience. In the active voice, the subject performs the action and the object receives the action. In the passive voice, the subject receives the action. The passive voice combines the helping verb *to be* with a form of the verb that is usually in the past tense.

4 Describe how to select words that are not only correct but also effective. To select the best words, first make sure they are correct by checking grammar and usage guides. Then choose words that have few connotations (to reduce the chance of misinterpretation) and no unintended negative connotations (to reduce the chance of offending your audience). Select words that communicate clearly, specifically, and dynamically. Choose words that are strong and familiar, avoid clichés, be extremely careful with buzzwords, and use jargon only when your audience will understand it.

5 Define the four types of sentences, and explain how sentence style affects emphasis within a message. The four types of sentences are *simple* (one main clause), *compound* (two main clauses that express independent but related ideas of equal importance), *complex* (one main clause and one subordinate clause of lesser importance), and *compound–complex* (two main clauses, at least one of which contains a subordinate clause). Sentence style affects emphasis by playing up or playing down specific parts of a sentence. To emphasize a certain point, you can place it at the end of the sentence or make it the subject of the sentence. To deemphasize a point, put it in the middle of the sentence.

6 Define the three key elements of a paragraph, and list five ways to develop unified, coherent paragraphs. The three key elements of a paragraph are a topic sentence that identifies the subject of the paragraph, support sentences that develop the topic and provide examples and evidence, and transitional words and phrases that help readers connect one thought to the next. Effective paragraphs are both *unified* (focused on a single idea) and *coherent* (logically organized). You can develop paragraphs through illustration (giving examples), comparison or contrast (pointing out similarities or differences), cause and effect (giving reasons), classification (discussing categories), and problem and solution (stating a problem and showing how to solve it).

7 **Identify the most common software features that help you craft messages more efficiently.** Common software features that help you craft messages more efficiently include style sheets, style sets, templates, and themes; features to store and use boilerplate and document components; autocorrection or autocompletion; file merge and mail merge; and endnotes, footnotes, indexes, and tables of contents.

KEY TERMS

abstract word Word that expresses a concept, quality, or characteristic; abstractions are usually broad

active voice Sentence structure in which the subject performs the action and the object receives the action

bias-free language Language that avoids words and phrases that categorize or stigmatize people in ways related to gender, race, ethnicity, age, or disability

complex sentence Sentence that expresses one main thought (the independent clause) and one or more subordinate, related thoughts (dependent clauses that cannot stand alone as valid sentences)

compound–complex sentence Sentence with two main clauses, at least one of which contains a subordinate clause

compound sentence Sentence with two main clauses that express two or more independent but related thoughts of equal importance, usually joined by *and*, *but*, or *or*

concrete word Word that represents something you can touch, see, or visualize; most concrete terms are related to the tangible, material world

connotative meaning All the associations and feelings evoked by a word

conversational tone The tone used in most business communication; it uses plain language that sounds businesslike without being stuffy at one extreme or too laid-back and informal at the other extreme

credibility A measure of your believability, based on how reliable you are and how much trust you evoke in others

denotative meaning The literal, or dictionary, meaning of a word

euphemisms Words or phrases that express a thought in milder terms

passive voice Sentence structure in which the subject receives the action

simple sentence Sentence with one main *clause* (a single subject and a single predicate)

style The choices you make to express yourself: the words you select, the manner in which you use those words in sentences, and the way you build paragraphs from individual sentences

tone The overall impression in your messages, created by the style you use

topic sentence Sentence that introduces the topic of a paragraph

transitions Words or phrases that tie together ideas by showing how one thought is related to another

 Checklist

Writing Business Messages

A. Adapt to your audience.
- Use the "you" attitude.
- Maintain good etiquette through polite communication.
- Emphasize the positive whenever possible.
- Use bias-free language.
- Establish credibility in the eyes of your audience.
- Project your company's preferred image.

- Use a conversational but still professional and respectful tone.
- Use plain language for clarity.

B. Compose your message.
- Choose strong words that communicate efficiently.
- Pay attention to the connotative meaning of your words.
- Balance abstract and concrete terms to convey your meaning accurately.

- Avoid clichés and trendy buzzwords.
- Use jargon only when your audience understands it and prefers it.
- Vary your sentence structure for impact and interest.
- Develop coherent, unified paragraphs.
- Use transitions generously to help your audience follow your message.

TEST YOUR KNOWLEDGE

To review chapter content related to each question, refer to the indicated Learning Objective.

1. Do you have to use the word *you* in order to demonstrate the "you" attitude? Why or why not? [LO-1]
2. How does using bias-free language help communicators establish a good relationship with their audiences? [LO-1]
3. Why is it important to establish your credibility when communicating with an audience of strangers? [LO-2]
4. In what three situations is the passive voice appropriate? [LO-3]
5. How does an abstract word differ from a concrete word? [LO-4]
6. How does the denotative meaning of a word differ from its connotative meaning? [LO-4]
7. How can you use sentence style to emphasize key thoughts? [LO-5]
8. How can topic sentences help readers? [LO-6]
9. What functions do transitions serve? [LO-6]
10. What software functions can you use to make it easy to re-use blocks of text across multiple documents? [LO-7]

APPLY YOUR KNOWLEDGE

To review chapter content related to each question, refer to the indicated Learning Objective.

1. Eleven million people in the United States are allergic to one or more food ingredients. Each year, 30,000 of these people end up in the emergency room after suffering allergic reactions, and hundreds of them die. Many of these tragic events are tied to poorly written food labels that either fail to identify dangerous allergens or use scientific terms that most consumers don't recognize.[20] Do food manufacturers have a responsibility to ensure that consumers read, understand, and follow warnings on food products? Explain your answer. [LO-1]
2. When composing business messages, how can you communicate with an authentic voice and project your company's image at the same time? [LO-2]
3. Does using plain language make you come across as less of an expert? Explain your answer. [LO-3]
4. What steps can you take to make abstract concepts such as *opportunity* feel more concrete in your messages? [LO-4]
5. Should you bother using transitions if the logical sequence of your message is obvious? Why or why not? [LO-6]

PRACTICE YOUR SKILLS

Messages for Analysis: Creating a Businesslike Tone [LO-1], [LO-3]

Read the following email draft and then (1) analyze the strengths and weaknesses of each sentence and (2) revise the document so that it follows this chapter's guidelines. The message was written by the marketing manager of an online retailer of baby-related products in the hope of becoming a retail outlet for Inglesina strollers and high chairs. As a manufacturer of stylish, top-quality products, Inglesina (based in Italy) is extremely selective about the retail outlets through which it allows its products to be sold.

> Our e-tailing site, www.BestBabyGear.com, specializes in only the very best products for parents of newborns, infants, and toddlers. We constantly scour the world looking for products that are good enough and well-built enough and classy enough—good enough to take their place alongside the hundreds of other carefully selected products that adorn the pages of our award-winning website, www.bestbabygear.com. We aim for the fences every time we select a product to join this portfolio; we don't want to waste our time with onesey-twosey products that might sell a half dozen units per annum—no, we want every product to be a top-drawer success, selling at least one hundred units per specific model per year in order to justify our expense and hassle factor in adding it to the above mentioned portfolio. After careful consideration, we thusly concluded that your Inglesina lines meet our needs and would therefore like to add it.

Exercises

Active links for all websites in this chapter can be found on MyBcommLab; see your User Guide for instructions on accessing the content for this chapter. Each activity is labeled according to the primary skill or skills you will need to use. To review relevant chapter content, you can refer to the indicated Learning Objective. In some instances, supporting information will be found in another chapter, as indicated.

1. **Writing: Communicating with Sensitivity and Tact [LO-1]** Substitute a better phrase for each of the following:
   a. You claim that
   b. It is not our policy to
   c. You neglected to
   d. In which you assert
   e. We are sorry you are dissatisfied
   f. You failed to enclose
   g. We request that you send us
   h. Apparently you overlooked our terms
   i. We have been very patient
   j. We are at a loss to understand

2. **Writing: Demonstrating the "You" Attitude [LO-1]** Rewrite these sentences to reflect your audience's viewpoint:
   a. Your email order cannot be processed; we request that you use the order form on our website instead.
   b. We insist that you always bring your credit card to the store.
   c. We want to get rid of all our 15-inch LCD screens to make room in our warehouse for the new 19-, 23-, and 35-inch monitors. Thus, we are offering a 25 percent discount on all sales of 15-inch models this week.
   d. I am applying for the position of bookkeeper in your office. I feel my grades prove that I am bright and capable, and I think I can do a good job for you.

e. As requested, we are sending the refund for $25.

f. If you cared about doing a good job, you would've made the extra effort required to learn how to use the machinery properly.

g. Your strategy presentation this morning absolutely blew me away; there's no way we can fail with all the brilliant ideas you've pulled together—I'm so glad you're running the company now!

h. Regarding your email message from September 28 regarding the slow payment of your invoice, it's important for you to realize that we've just undergone a massive upgrade of our accounts payable system and payments have been delayed for everybody, not just you.

i. I know I'm late with the asset valuation report, but I haven't been feeling well and I just haven't had the energy needed to work through the numbers yet.

j. With all the online news sources available today, I can't believe you didn't know that MyTravel and Thomas Cook were in merger talks—I mean, you don't even have to get up from your computer to learn this!

3. Writing: Emphasizing the Positive [LO-1] Revise these sentences to be positive rather than negative:

a. To avoid damage to your credit rating, please remit payment within 10 days.

b. We don't offer refunds on returned merchandise that is soiled.

c. Because we are temporarily out of Baby Cry dolls, we won't be able to ship your order for 10 days.

d. You failed to specify the color of the blouse that you ordered.

e. You should have realized that waterbeds will freeze in unheated houses during winter. Therefore, our guarantee does not cover the valve damage, and you must pay the $9.50 valve-replacement fee (plus postage).

4. Writing: Using Unbiased Language [LO-1] Rewrite each of the following to eliminate bias:

a. For an Indian, Maggie certainly is outgoing.

b. He needs a wheelchair, but he doesn't let his handicap affect his job performance.

c. A pilot must have the ability to stay calm under pressure, and then he must be trained to cope with any problem that arises.

d. Candidate Renata Parsons, married and the mother of a teenager, will attend the debate.

e. Senior citizen Sam Nugent is still an active salesman.

5. Writing: Establishing Your Credibility; Microblogging Skills [LO-2], Chapter 7 Search LinkedIn for the profile of an expert in any industry or profession. Now imagine that you are going to introduce this person as a speaker at a convention. You will make an in-person introduction at the time of the speech, but you decide to introduce him or her the day before on Twitter. Write four tweets: one that introduces the expert and three that cover three key supporting points that will enhance the speaker's credibility in the minds of potential listeners. Make up any information you need to complete this assignment, then email the text of your proposed tweets to your instructor.

6. Writing: Using Plain Language; Communication Ethics: Making Ethical Choices, [LO-3], Chapter 1 Your company has been a major employer in the local community for years, but shifts in the global marketplace have forced some changes in the company's long-term direction. In fact, the company plans to reduce local staffing by as much as 50 percent over the next 5 to 10 years, starting with a small layoff next month. The size and timing of future layoffs have not been decided, although there is little doubt that more layoffs will happen at some point. In the first draft of a letter aimed at community leaders, you write that "this first layoff is part of a continuing series of staff reductions anticipated over the next several years." However, your boss is concerned about the vagueness and negative tone of the language and asks you to rewrite that sentence to read "this layoff is part of the company's ongoing efforts to continually align its resources with global market conditions." Do you think this suggested wording is ethical, given the company's economic influence in the community? Explain your answer in an email message to your instructor.

7. Writing: Using Plain Language; Media Skills: Blogging [LO-3] Download the Securities and Exchange Commission's (SEC's) *A Plain English Handbook*, from www.sec.gov/pdf/handbook.pdf. In one or two sentences, summarize what the SEC means by the phrase *plain English*. Now scan the SEC's introduction to mutual funds at www.sec.gov/investor/pubs/inwsmf.htm. Does this information follow the SEC's plain English guidelines? Cite several examples that support your assessment. Post your analysis on your class blog.

8. Writing: Creating Effective Sentences: Media Skills: Social Networking [LO-4], Chapter 7 If you are interested in business, chances are you've had an idea or two for starting a company. If you haven't yet, go ahead and dream up an idea now. Make it something you are passionate about, something you could really throw yourself into. Now write a four-sentence summary that could appear on the Info tab on a Facebook profile. Make sure the first sentence is a solid topic sentence, and make sure the next three sentences offer relevant evidence and examples. Feel free to make up any details you need. Email your summary to your instructor or post it on your class blog.

 Learn the basics of creating a company profile on Facebook. Visit http://real-timeupdates.com/bct11, click on "Learn More" and then click on "Facebook Screencast."

9. Writing: Choosing Powerful Words [LO-4] Write a concrete phrase for each of these vague phrases:

a. Sometime this spring

b. A substantial savings

c. A large number attended

d. Increased efficiency

e. Expanded the work area

f. Flatten the website structure

10. **Writing: Choosing Powerful Words [LO-4]** List terms that are stronger than the following:
    a. Ran after
    b. Seasonal ups and downs
    c. Bright
    d. Suddenly rises
    e. Moves forward

11. **Writing: Choosing Powerful Words [LO-4]** As you re-write these sentences, replace the clichés and buzzwords with plain language (if you don't recognize any of these terms, you can find definitions online):
    a. Being a jack-of-all-trades, Dave worked well in his new general manager job.
    b. Moving Leslie into the accounting department, where she was literally a fish out of water, was like putting a square peg into a round hole, if you get my drift.
    c. My only takeaway from the offsite was that Laird threw his entire department under the bus for missing the deadline.
    d. I've love to help with that project, but I'm bandwidth-constrained.
    e. The board green-lighted our initiative to repurpose our consumer products for the commercial space.

12. **Writing: Choosing Powerful Words [LO-4]** Suggest short, simple words to replace each of the following:
    a. Inaugurate
    b. Terminate
    c. Utilize
    d. Anticipate
    e. Assistance
    f. Endeavor
    g. Ascertain
    h. Procure
    i. Consummate
    j. Advise
    k. Alteration
    l. Forwarded
    m. Fabricate
    n. Nevertheless
    o. Substantial

13. **Writing: Choosing Powerful Words [LO-4]** Write up-to-date, less-stuffy versions of these phrases; write *none* if you think there is no appropriate substitute or "delete" if the phrase should simply be deleted:
    a. As per your instructions
    b. Attached herewith
    c. In lieu of
    d. In reply I wish to state
    e. Please be advised that

14. **Writing: Choosing Powerful Words; Communication Ethics: Making Ethical Choices [LO-4], Chapter 1** Under what circumstances would you consider the use of terms that are high in connotative meaning to be ethical? When would you consider it to be unethical? Explain your reasoning.

15. **Writing: Creating Effective Sentences [LO-5]** Rewrite each sentence so that it is active rather than passive:
    a. The raw data are entered into the customer relationship management system by the sales representative each Friday.
    b. High profits are publicized by management.
    c. The policies announced in the directive were implemented by the staff.
    d. Our computers are serviced by the Santee Company.
    e. The employees were represented by Janet Hogan.

16. **Writing: Crafting Unified, Coherent Paragraphs; Media Skills: Email [LO-6], Chapter 7** Suppose that end-of-term frustrations have produced this email message to Professor Anne Brewer from a student who believes he should have received a B in his accounting class. If this message were re-cast into three or four clear sentences, the teacher might be more receptive to the student's argument. Rewrite the message to show how you would improve it:

    I think that I was unfairly awarded a C in your accounting class this term, and I am asking you to change the grade to a B. It was a difficult term. I don't get any money from home, and I have to work mornings at the Pancake House (as a cook), so I had to rush to make your class, and those two times that I missed class were because they wouldn't let me off work because of special events at the Pancake House (unlike some other students who just take off when they choose). On the midterm examination, I originally got a 75 percent, but you said in class that there were two different ways to answer the third question and that you would change the grades of students who used the "optimal cost" method and had been counted off 6 points for doing this. I don't think that you took this into account, because I got 80 percent on the final, which is clearly a B. Anyway, whatever you decide, I just want to tell you that I really enjoyed this class, and I thank you for making accounting so interesting.

17. **Writing: Crafting Unified, Coherent Paragraphs [LO-6]** In the following paragraph, identify the topic sentence and the related sentences (those that support the idea of the topic sentence):

    Sync is a snap with Auto-Sync. By default, iTunes automatically copies your entire music library to iPod and deletes songs on iPod that are not listed in iTunes. Or you can use Playlist Sync and select the playlists you want to sync with your iPod. If you have more songs in your iTunes library than you can fit on your iPod, let iTunes create a playlist to fill your iPod, or just update your iPod by dragging over individual songs.[21]

    Now add a topic sentence to this paragraph:

    Our analysis of the customer experience should start before golfers even drive through the front gate here at Glencoe Meadows; it should start when they phone in or log onto our website to reserve tee times. When they do arrive, the first few stages in the process are also vital: the condition of the grounds leading up to the club house, the reception they receive when they drop off their clubs, and the ease of parking. From that point, how well are we doing with check-in at the pro shop, openings at the driving range, and timely scheduling at the first tee? Then there's everything associated with playing the course itself and returning to the club house at the end of the round.

18. **Writing: Crafting Unified, Coherent Paragraphs; Collaboration: Evaluating the Work of Others [LO-6], Chapter 6** Working with four other students, divide the following five topics among yourselves and each write one paragraph on your selected topic. Be sure each student uses a different technique when writing his or her paragraph: One student should use the illustration technique, one the comparison or contrast technique, one a discussion of cause and effect, one the classification technique, and one a discussion of problem and solution. Then exchange paragraphs within the team and pick out the main idea and general purpose of the paragraph one of your teammates wrote. Was everyone able to correctly identify the main idea and purpose? If not, suggest how the paragraph could be rewritten for clarity.

   a. Types of digital cameras (or dogs or automobiles) available for sale

   b. Advantages and disadvantages of eating at fast-food restaurants

   c. Finding that first full-time job

   d. Good qualities of my car (or house, or apartment, or neighborhood)

   e. How to make a dessert (or barbecue a steak or make coffee)

19. **Writing: Using Transitions [LO-6]** Add transitional elements to the following sentences to improve the flow of ideas. (*Note:* You may need to eliminate or add some words to smooth out your sentences.)

   a. Steve Case saw infinite possibilities in online business. Steve Case was determined to turn his vision into reality. The techies scoffed at his strategy of building a simple Internet service for ordinary people. Case doggedly pursued his dream. He analyzed other online services. He assessed the needs of his customers. He responded to their desires for an easier way to access information over the Internet. In 1992, Steve Case named his company America Online (AOL). Critics predicted the company's demise. By the end of the century, AOL was a profitable powerhouse. An ill-fated merger with Time Warner was a financial disaster and led to Case's ouster from the company.

   b. Facing some of the toughest competitors in the world, Harley-Davidson had to make some changes. The company introduced new products. Harley's management team set out to rebuild the company's production process. New products were coming to market and the company was turning a profit. Harley's quality standards were not on par with those of its foreign competitors. Harley's costs were still among the highest in the industry. Harley made a U-turn and restructured the company's organizational structure. Harley's efforts have paid off.

   c. Whether you're indulging in a doughnut in New York or California, Krispy Kreme wants you to enjoy the same delicious taste with every bite. The company maintains consistent product quality by carefully controlling every step of the production process. Krispy Kreme tests all raw ingredients against established quality standards. Every delivery of wheat flour is sampled and measured for its moisture content and protein levels. Krispy Kreme blends the ingredients. Krispy Kreme tests the doughnut mix for quality. Krispy Kreme delivers the mix to its stores. Financial critics are not as kind to the company as food critics have been. Allegations of improper financial reporting have left the company's future in doubt.

20. **Writing: Using Technology to Compose Messages; Designing for Readability [LO-7], Chapter 6** Team up with another student and choose some form of document or presentation software that allows you to create templates or another form of "master design." (Microsoft Word, Microsoft PowerPoint, Google Docs, or their equivalents are good choices for this assignment.) Your task is to design a report template for a company that you either know about firsthand or whose general communication style you are able to analyze from its website and other materials. You can start your template from scratch or adapt an existing template, but if you adapt another template, make sure the final design is largely your own. Chapter 6 offers information on document design.

EXPAND YOUR SKILLS

Critique the Professionals

Locate an example of professional communication from a reputable online source. Choose a paragraph that has at least three sentences. Evaluate the effectiveness of this paragraph at three levels, starting with the paragraph structure. Is the paragraph unified and cohesive? Does it have a clear topic sentence and sufficient support to clarify and expand on that topic? Second, evaluate each sentence. Are the sentences easy to read and easy to understand? Did the writer vary the types and lengths of sentences to produce a smooth flow and rhythm? Is the most important idea presented prominently in each sentence? Third, evaluate at least six word choices. Did the writer use these words correctly and effectively? Using whatever medium your instructor requests, write a brief analysis of the piece (no more than one page), citing specific elements from the piece and support from the chapter.

Sharpening Your Career Skills Online

Bovée and Thill's Business Communication Web Search, at http://businesscommunicationblog.com/websearch is a unique research tool designed specifically for business communication research. Use the Web Search function to find a website, video, PDF document, or PowerPoint presentation that offers advice on writing effective sentences. Write a brief email message to your instructor, describing the item that you found and summarizing the career skills information you learned from it.

6

Completing Business Messages

LEARNING OBJECTIVES After studying this chapter, you will be able to

1 Discuss the value of careful revision and describe the tasks involved in evaluating your first drafts and the work of other writers

2 List four techniques you can use to improve the readability of your messages

3 Describe eight steps you can take to improve the clarity of your writing, and give four tips on making your writing more concise

4 List four principles of effective design, and explain the role of major design elements in document readability

5 Explain the importance of proofreading, and give eight tips for successful proofreading

6 Discuss the most important issues to consider when distributing your messages

MyBcommLab Test your mastery of this chapter and its Learning Objectives. Visit mybcommlab.com to apply what you've learned in Document Makeovers and interactive simulation scenarios.

COMMUNICATION CLOSE-UP AT JEFFERSON RABB WEB DESIGN

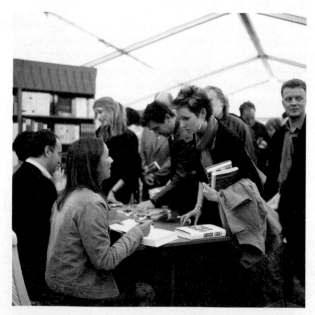

Authors such as Monica Ali still rely on personal contact with readers to promote books, but websites—particularly interactive, multimedia websites—have become an increasingly important element in book promotion.

www.jeffersonrabb.com

As a composer, game designer, photographer, programmer, and website developer, Jefferson Rabb epitomizes the "multi" in multimedia. For all the technical and creative skills he brings, however, Rabb's work never loses sight of audiences and their desire to be informed and entertained when they visit a website.

Rabb's career history includes stints at MTV.com and Sephora.com, but most of his current work as an independent designer involves projects in the publishing industry. The best-selling authors he has helped bring to the web include Dan Brown, Gary Shteyngart, Jhumpa Lahiri, Laura Hillenbrand, and Anita Shreve.

For every project, Rabb starts his design work with an in-depth analysis of the audience. The questions he asks about site visitors include their familiarity with the author's work, the range of their reading interests, and their general demographics. He also wants to know whether a site needs to serve book reviewers, bookstore buyers, and other industry professionals, in addition to readers.

With some insight into who the target visitors are, Rabb puts himself in their place and imagines the knowledge and experiences they hope to gain during their visits. These needs can vary from biographical information about the author to multimedia exhibits (such as video interviews and photographs depicting locations mentioned in a book) to complex games that extend a novel's storylines. Rabb makes a point to find compelling visual connections between a book and a website, too, such as basing the design of the site for Shteyngart's

Super Sad True Love Story on the portable communication device featured in the story. Completing the multimedia experience, he often composes music to create a specific mood that reflects the themes of a book.[1]

Your business communication efforts may not always be as elaborate as Rabb's, but you can always apply his strategy of combining methodical analysis with creative design and implementation. This chapter addresses the third step in the three-step writing process, completing your messages—which includes the important tasks of revising, producing, proofreading, and distributing your messages.

Revising Your Message: Evaluating the First Draft

After you've completed a first draft, you may be tempted to breathe a sigh of relief, send the message on its way, and move on to the next project. Resist the temptation. Successful communicators recognize that the first draft is rarely as tight, clear, and compelling as it needs to be. Careful revision can mean the difference between a rambling, unfocused message and a lively, direct message that gets results. The third step of the three-step writing process involves four key tasks: revising your message to achieve optimum quality and then producing, proofreading, and distributing it.

The revision task can vary somewhat, depending on the medium and the nature of your message. For informal messages to internal audiences, particularly when using instant messaging, text messaging, email, or blogging, the revision process is often as simple as quickly looking over your message to correct any mistakes before sending or posting it. However, don't fall into the common trap of thinking that you don't need to worry about grammar, spelling, clarity, and other fundamentals of good writing when you use these media. These qualities can be *especially* important in electronic media, particularly if these messages are the only contact your audience has with you. Audiences are likely to equate the quality of your writing with the quality of your thinking. Poor-quality messages create an impression of poor-quality thinking and can cause confusion, frustration, and costly delays.

With more complex messages, try to put your draft aside for a day or two before you begin the revision process so that you can approach the material with a fresh eye. Then start with the "big picture," making sure that the document accomplishes your overall goals before moving to finer points, such as readability, clarity, and conciseness. Compare the letters in Figures 6.1 and 6.2 on the next two pages for an example of how careful revision improves a customer letter.

EVALUATING YOUR CONTENT, ORGANIZATION, STYLE, AND TONE

When you begin the revision process, focus your attention on content, organization, style, and tone. To evaluate the content of your message, answer these questions:

- Is the information accurate?
- Is the information relevant to the audience?
- Is there enough information to satisfy the readers' needs?
- Is there a good balance between general information (giving readers enough background information to appreciate the message) and specific information (giving readers the details they need to understand the message)?

When you are satisfied with the content of your message, you can review its organization. Answer another set of questions:

- Are all the points covered in the most logical order?
- Do the most important ideas receive the most space, and are they placed in the most prominent positions?
- Would the message be more convincing if it were arranged in another sequence?
- Are any points repeated unnecessarily?
- Are details grouped together logically, or are some still scattered through the document?

With the content in place and effectively organized, next consider whether you have achieved the right tone for your audience. Is your writing formal enough to meet the

---

1 LEARNING OBJECTIVE

Discuss the value of careful revision, and describe the tasks involved in evaluating your first drafts and the work of other writers.

First drafts are rarely as effective as they could be, so take the time to improve them through revision.

In any medium, readers tend to equate the quality of your writing with the quality of your thinking.

If you have time, put aside your draft for a day or two before you begin the revision process.

MyBcommLab

- Access this chapter's simulation entitled The Communication Process, located at mybcommlab.com.

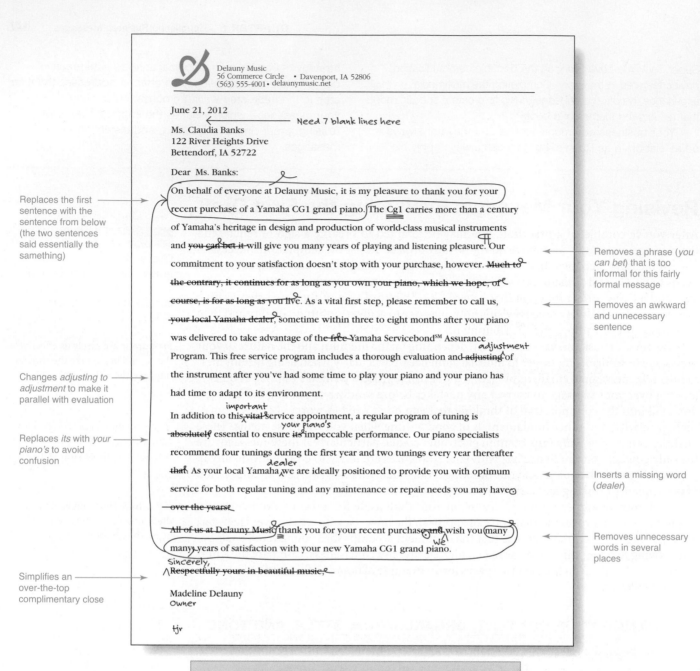

Figure 6.1 Improving a Customer Letter Through Careful Revision

Careful revision makes this draft shorter, clearer, and more focused. These *proofreading symbols* (see Appendix C) are still widely used when printed documents are edited and revised. However, in many instances you'll use the electronic markup features in your word processor or other software, as shown later in this chapter, on page 154.

Delauny Music
56 Commerce Circle   • Davenport, IA 52806
(563) 555-4001 • delaunymusic.net

June 21, 2012

Ms. Claudia Banks
122 River Heights Drive
Bettendorf, IA 52722

Dear Ms. Banks:

Thank you for your recent purchase. We wish you many years of satisfaction with your new Yamaha CG1 grand piano. The CG1 carries more than a century of Yamaha's heritage in design and production of world-class musical instruments and will give you many years of playing and listening pleasure.

Our commitment to your satisfaction doesn't stop with your purchase, however. As a vital first step, please remember to call us sometime within three to eight months after your piano was delivered to take advantage of the Yamaha Servicebond℠ Assurance Program. This free service program includes a thorough evaluation and adjustment of the instrument after you've had some time to play your piano and your piano has had time to adapt to its environment.

In addition to this important service appointment, a regular program of tuning is essential to ensure your piano's impeccable performance. Our piano specialists recommend four tunings during the first year and two tunings every year thereafter. As your local Yamaha dealer, we are ideally positioned to provide you with optimum service for both regular tuning and any maintenance or repair needs you may have.

Sincerely,

Madeline Delauny

Madeline Delauny
Owner

tjr

Figure 6.2   Revised Customer Letter
This revised letter provides the requested information more clearly, in a more organized fashion, with a friendlier style, and with precise mechanics.

audience's expectations, without being too formal or academic? Is it too casual for a serious subject? Does your message emphasize the audience's needs over your own?

Spend a few extra moments on the beginning and end of your message; these sections usually have the greatest impact on the audience. Be sure that the opening is relevant, interesting, and geared to the reader's probable reaction. In longer messages, ensure that the first few paragraphs establish the subject, purpose, and organization of the material. Review the conclusion to be sure that it summarizes the main idea and leaves the audience with a positive impression.

> The beginning and end of a message usually have the greatest impact on your readers, so make sure they are clear, concise, and compelling.

EVALUATING, EDITING, AND REVISING THE WORK OF OTHERS

At many points in your career, you will be asked to evaluate, edit, or revise the work of others. Whether you're suggesting improvements or actually making the improvements yourself (as you might on a wiki site, for example), you can make a contribution by using all the skills are learning in Chapters 4 through 6.

Evaluating and revising the work of others is an important responsibility.

Before you dive into someone else's work, recognize the dual responsibility that doing so entails. First, unless you've been specifically asked to rewrite something in your own style or to change the emphasis of the message, remember that your job is to help the other writer succeed at his or her task, not to impose your writing style or pursue your own agenda. In other words, make sure your input focuses on making the piece more effective, not on making it more like something you would've written. Second, make sure you understand the writer's intent before you begin suggesting or making changes. If you try to edit or revise without knowing what the writer hoped to accomplish, you run the risk of making the piece less effective, not more. With those thoughts in mind, answer the following questions as you evaluate someone else's writing:

- What is the purpose of this document or message?
- Who is the target audience?
- What information does the audience need?
- Does the document provide this information in a well-organized way?
- Does the writing demonstrate the "you" attitude toward the audience?
- Is the tone of the writing appropriate for the audience?
- Can the readability be improved?
- Is the writing clear? If not, how can it be improved?
- Is the writing as concise as it could be?
- Does the design support the intended message?

You can read more about using these skills in the context of wiki writing in Chapter 14.

Revising to Improve Readability

List four techniques you can use to improve the readability of your messages.

Readability formulas can give you a helpful indication, but they can't measure everything that affects readability.

After confirming the content, organization, style, and tone of your message, make a second pass to improve *readability*. Most professionals are inundated with more reading material than they can ever hope to consume, and they'll appreciate your efforts to make your documents easier to read. You'll benefit from this effort, too: If you earn a reputation for creating well-crafted documents that respect the audience's time, people will pay more attention to your work.

You may be familiar with one of the many indexes that have been developed over the years in an attempt to measure readability. For example, the Flesch-Kincaid Grade Level score computes reading difficulty relative to grade-level achievement, with, for instance, a score of 10 suggesting that a document can be read and understood by the average 10th grader. Most business documents score in the 8–11 range. Technical documents often score in the 12–14 range. A similar scoring system, the Flesch Reading Ease score, ranks documents on a 100-point scale; the higher the score, the easier the document is to read. If these measurements aren't built into your word processing software, you can find a number of calculators for various indexes at websites such as **www.editcentral.com**.

Readability indexes offer a useful reference point, but they are limited by what they are able to measure: word length, number of syllables, sentence length, and paragraph length. They can't measure any of the other factors that affect readability, such as document design, the "you" attitude, clear sentence structure, smooth transitions, and proper word usage. Compare these two paragraphs:

> Readability indexes offer a useful reference point, but they are all limited by what they are able to measure: word length, number of syllables, sentence length, and paragraph length. They can't measure any of the other factors that affect readability, from "you" orientation to writing clarity to document design.

> Readability indexes can help. But they don't measure everything. They don't measure whether your writing clarity is good. They don't measure whether your document design is good or not. Reading indexes are based on word length, syllables, sentences, and paragraphs.

The second paragraph scores much better on both grade level and reading ease, but it is choppy, unsophisticated, and poorly organized. As a general rule, then, don't assume that a piece of text is readable if it scores well on a readability index—or that it is difficult to read if it doesn't score well.

Beyond using shorter words and simpler sentences, you can improve the readability of a message by making the document interesting and easy to skim. Most business audiences—particularly influential senior managers—tend to skim documents, looking for key ideas, conclusions, and recommendations. If they determine that a document contains valuable information or requires a response, they will read it more carefully when time permits. Four techniques will make your message easier to read and easier to skim: varying sentence length, using shorter paragraphs, using lists and bullets instead of narrative, and adding effective headings and subheadings.

> The effort to make your documents more readable will pay for itself in greater career success.

VARYING YOUR SENTENCE LENGTH

Varying the length of your sentences is a creative way to make your messages interesting and readable. By choosing words and sentence structure with care, you can create a rhythm that emphasizes important points, enlivens your writing style, and makes information more appealing to your reader. For example, a short sentence that highlights a conclusion at the end of a substantial paragraph of evidence makes your key message stand out. Try for a mixture of sentences that are short (up to 15 words or so), medium (15–25 words), and long (more than 25 words).

> To keep readers' interest, use a variety of long, medium, and short sentences.

Each sentence length has its advantages. Short sentences can be processed quickly and are easier for nonnative speakers and translators to interpret. Medium-length sentences are useful for showing the relationships among ideas. Long sentences are often the best for conveying complex ideas, listing multiple related points, or summarizing or previewing information.

Of course, each sentence length also has disadvantages. Too many short sentences in a row can make your writing choppy. Medium sentences lack the punch of short sentences and the informative power of longer sentences. Long sentences can be difficult to understand because they contain more information and usually have a more complicated structure. Because readers can absorb only a few words per glance, longer sentences are also more difficult to skim. By choosing the best sentence length for each communication need and remembering to mix sentence lengths for variety, you'll get your points across while keeping your messages lively and interesting.

KEEPING YOUR PARAGRAPHS SHORT

Large blocks of text can be visually daunting, particularly on screen, so the optimum paragraph length is short to medium in most cases. Unless you break up your thoughts somehow, you'll end up with lengthy paragraphs that are guaranteed to intimidate even the most dedicated reader. Short paragraphs, generally 100 words or fewer (this paragraph has 84 words), are easier to read than long ones, and they make your writing look inviting. You can also emphasize ideas by isolating them in short, forceful paragraphs.

> Long paragraphs are visually intimidating and can be difficult to read.

However, don't go overboard with short paragraphs. In particular, be careful to use one-sentence paragraphs only occasionally and only for emphasis. Also, if you need to divide a subject into several pieces in order to keep paragraphs short, be sure to help your readers keep the ideas connected by guiding them with plenty of transitional elements.

USING LISTS TO CLARIFY AND EMPHASIZE

An effective alternative to using conventional sentences is to set off important ideas in a list—a series of words, names, or other items. Lists can show the sequence of your ideas, heighten their impact visually, and increase the likelihood that a reader will find key points. In addition, lists help simplify complex subjects, highlight main points, break up a page or

> Lists are effective tools for highlighting and simplifying material.

screen visually, ease the skimming process for busy readers, and give readers a breather. Compare these two treatments of the same information:

Narrative	**List**
Owning your own business has many potential advantages. One is the opportunity to pursue your own personal passion. Another advantage is the satisfaction of working for yourself. As a sole proprietor, you also have the advantage of privacy because you do not have to reveal your financial information or plans to anyone.	Owning your own business has three advantages: • Opportunity to pursue personal passion • Satisfaction of working for yourself • Financial privacy

You can separate list items with numbers, letters, or bullets (a general term for any kind of graphical element that precedes each item). Bullets are generally preferred over numbers, unless the list is in some logical sequence or ranking or you need to refer to specific list items elsewhere in the document. For example, the following three steps need to be performed in the order indicated, and the numbers make that clear:

1. Find out how many employees would like on-site day-care facilities.
2. Determine how much space the day-care center would require.
3. Estimate the cost of converting a conference room for the on-site facility.

Lists are easier to locate and read if the entire numbered or bulleted section is set off by a blank line before and after, as the preceding examples demonstrate. Furthermore, make sure to introduce lists clearly so that people know what they're about to read. One way to introduce lists is to make them a part of the introductory sentence:

The board of directors met to discuss the revised annual budget. To keep expenses in line with declining sales, the directors voted to

● Cut everyone's salary by 10 percent
● Close the employee cafeteria
● Reduce travel expenses

Another way to introduce a list is to precede it with a complete introductory sentence, followed by a colon:

The decline in company profit is attributable to four factors:

● Slower holiday sales
● Increased transportation and fuel costs
● Higher employee wages
● Slower inventory turnover

Regardless of the format you choose, the items in a list should be parallel; that is, they should all use the same grammatical pattern. For example, if one list item begins with a verb, every item should begin with a verb. If one item is a noun phrase, every one should be a noun phrase:

Nonparallel List Items **(a mix of verb and noun phrases)**	**Parallel List Items** **(all verb phrases)**
• Improve our bottom line • Identification of new foreign markets for our products • Global market strategies • Issues regarding pricing and packaging size	• Improving our bottom line • Identifying new foreign markets for our products • Developing our global market strategies • Resolving pricing and packaging issues

TABLE 6.1	Achieving Parallelism
Method	**Example**
Parallel words	The letter was approved by Clausen, Whittaker, Merlin, and Carlucci.
Parallel phrases	We are gaining market share in supermarkets, in department stores, and in specialty stores.
Parallel clauses	I'd like to discuss the issue after Vicki gives her presentation but before Marvin shows his slides.
Parallel sentences	In 2010 we exported 30 percent of our production. In 2011 we exported 50 percent.

Parallel forms are easier to read and skim. You can create parallelism by repeating the pattern in words, phrases, clauses, or entire sentences (see Table 6.1).

ADDING HEADINGS AND SUBHEADINGS

A **heading** is a brief title that tells readers about the content of the section that follows. **Subheadings** are subordinate to headings, indicating subsections with a major section. Headings and subheadings serve these important functions:

- **Organization.** Headings show your reader at a glance how the document is organized. They act as labels to group related paragraphs together and organize lengthy material into shorter sections.
- **Attention.** Informative, inviting, and in some cases intriguing headings grab the reader's attention, make the text easier to read, and help the reader find the parts he or she needs to read—or skip.
- **Connection.** Using headings and subheadings together helps readers see the relationship between main ideas and subordinate ones so that they can understand your message more easily. Moreover, headings and subheadings visually indicate shifts from one idea to the next.

> Use headings and subheadings to show the organization of your material, draw the reader's attention to key points, and show connections between ideas.

Headings fall into two categories. **Descriptive headings**, such as "Cost Considerations," identify a topic but do little more. **Informative headings**, such as "Redesigning Material Flow to Cut Production Costs," guide readers to think in a certain way about the topic. They are also helpful in guiding your work as a writer, especially if written in terms of questions you plan to address in your document. Well-written informative headings are self-contained, which means readers can read just the headings and subheadings and understand them without reading the rest of the document. For example, "Introduction" conveys little information, whereas the heading "Staffing Shortages Cost the Company $150,000 Last Year" provides a key piece of information and captures the reader's attention. Whatever types of headings you choose, keep them brief and use parallel construction throughout the document.

> Informative headings are generally more helpful than descriptive ones.

Editing for Clarity and Conciseness

After you've reviewed and revised your message for readability, your next step is to make sure your message is as clear and as concise as possible.

3 LEARNING OBJECTIVE

Describe eight steps you can take to improve the clarity of your writing, and give four tips on making your writing more concise.

EDITING FOR CLARITY

Make sure every sentence conveys the message you intend and that readers can extract that meaning without needing to read it more than once. To ensure clarity, look closely at your paragraph organization, sentence structure, and word choices. Perhaps a sentence is so complicated that readers can't unravel it. You might have chosen a word that is so

> Clarity is essential to getting your message across accurately and efficiently.

vague that readers can interpret it in several ways. Sentence B may not be a logical sequel to sentence A, or an important word may be used incorrectly.[2]

See Table 6.2 for examples of the following tips:

- **Break up overly long sentences.** If you find yourself stuck in a long sentence, you're probably trying to make the sentence do more than it can reasonably do, such as expressing two dissimilar thoughts or peppering the reader with too many pieces of supporting evidence at once. (Did you notice how difficult this long sentence was to read?)

TABLE 6.2	Revising for Clarity	
Issues to Review	**Ineffective**	**Effective**
Overly Long Sentences		
Taking compound sentences too far	The magazine will be published January 1, and I'd better meet the deadline if I want my article included because we want the article to appear before the trade show.	The magazine will be published January 1. I'd better meet the deadline because we want the article to appear before the trade show.
Hedging Sentences		
Overqualifying sentences	I believe that Mr. Johnson's employment record seems to show that he may be capable of handling the position.	Mr. Johnson's employment record shows that he is capable of handling the position.
Unparallel Sentences		
Using dissimilar construction for similar ideas	Mr. Simms had been drenched with rain, bombarded with telephone calls, and his boss shouted at him.	Mr. Sims had been drenched with rain, bombarded with telephone calls, and shouted at by his boss.
	To waste time and missing deadlines are bad habits.	Wasting time and missing deadlines are bad habits.
Dangling Modifiers		
Placing modifiers close to the wrong nouns and verbs	Walking to the office, a red sports car passed her. [suggests that the car was walking to the office]	A red sports car passed her while she was walking to the office.
	Reduced by 25 percent, Europe had its lowest semiconductor output in a decade. [suggests that Europe shrank by 25 percent]	Europe reduced semiconductor output by 25 percent, its lowest output in a decade.
Long Noun Sequences		
Stringing too many nouns together	The window sash installation company will give us an estimate on Friday.	The company that installs window sashes will give us an estimate on Friday.
Camouflaged Verbs		
Changing verbs and nouns into adjectives	The manager undertook implementation of the rules.	The manager implemented the rules.
	Verification of the shipments occurs weekly.	We verify shipment weekly.
Changing verbs into nouns	reach a conclusion about	conclude
	give consideration to	consider
Sentence Structure		
Separating subject and predicate	A 10% decline in market share, which resulted from quality problems and an aggressive sales campaign by Armitage, the market leader in the Northeast, was the major problem in 2010.	The major problem in 2010 was a 10% loss of market share, which resulted from quality problems and an aggressive sales campaign by Armitage, the market leader in the Northeast.
Separating adjectives, adverbs, or prepositional phrases from the words they modify	Our antique desk lends an air of strength and substance with thick legs and large drawers.	With its thick legs and large drawers, our antique desk lends an air of strength and substance.
Awkward References	The Law Office and the Accounting Office distribute computer supplies for legal secretaries and beginning accountants, respectively.	The Law Office distributes computer supplies for legal secretaries; the Accounting Office distributes those for beginning accountants.

- **Rewrite hedging sentences.** *Hedging* means pulling back from making a confident, definitive statement about a topic. Granted, sometimes you have to write *may* or *seems* to avoid stating a judgment as a fact. However, when you hedge too often or without good reason, you come across as being unsure of what you're saying.

  If you qualify or hedge too often, you undermine your credibility.

- **Impose parallelism.** When you have two or more similar ideas to express, make them parallel by using the same grammatical construction. Parallelism shows that the ideas are related, of similar importance, and on the same level of generality.

- **Correct dangling modifiers.** Sometimes a modifier is not just an adjective or an adverb but an entire phrase modifying a noun or a verb. Be careful not to leave this type of modifier *dangling*, with no connection to the subject of the sentence.

- **Reword long noun sequences.** When multiple nouns are strung together as modifiers, the resulting sentence can be hard to read. See if a single well-chosen word will do the job. If the nouns are all necessary, consider moving one or more to a modifying phrase, as shown in Table 6.2.

- **Replace camouflaged verbs.** Watch for words that end in *-ion, -tion, -ing, -ment, -ant, -ent, -ence, -ance,* and *-ency.* These endings often change verbs into nouns and adjectives, requiring you to add a verb in order to get your point across.

  Camouflaged verbs are verbs that have been changed into nouns; they often increase the length of a sentence without adding any value.

- **Clarify sentence structure.** Keep the subject and predicate of a sentence as close together as possible. When the subject and predicate are far apart, readers may need to read the sentence twice to figure out who did what. Similarly, adjectives, adverbs, and prepositional phrases usually make the most sense when they're placed as close as possible to the words they modify.

  Subject and predicate should be placed as close together as possible, as should modifiers and the words they modify.

- **Clarify awkward references.** If you want readers to refer to a specific point in a document, avoid vague references such as *the above-mentioned, as mentioned above, the aforementioned, the former, the latter,* and *respectively.* Use a specific pointer such as "as described in the second paragraph on page 22."

| Missing the Message with Prescription Medications

Few messages in life are as important as the instructions for prescription medications. Yet, according to the American Academy of Pediatrics, nearly half of all parents fail to correctly follow the information contained on the labels of medications prescribed for their children. Errors also abound among elderly patients, who often need to take multiple medications every day. Blaming the parents and patients for these errors may be tempting, but evidence suggests that the labels themselves are responsible for many mistakes.

Experts cite such communication problems as confusing terminology, information overload, and poor prioritization—emphasizing nonessential information such as the name of the pharmacy at the expense of truly critical information, such as the correct dosage, drug interaction warnings, or even the name of the medication itself. The situation can get even worse in households where two or more people have prescriptions, creating the possibility of patients accidentally taking the wrong medication. Moreover, the information now included with many medications is split among the label on the bottle, the box the bottle comes in, and a government-mandated printed insert. Ironically, those inserts are meant to clarify important information for the patient, but many patients toss them aside rather than read what can be several pages of dense, tiny type and unfamiliar terminology.

Fortunately, some improvements are taking place. After her grandmother accidentally took some of her grandfather's pills, graphic designer Deborah Adler decided that a major change was needed. Overhauling the round pill bottle that has been in use and unchanged for 60 years, Adler and industrial designer Klaus Rosburg crafted a new design that features a large, flat labeling surface that wraps over the top of the bottle. The label makes vital information—particularly the name of the drug, the patient's name, and dosage instructions—easy to find and easy to read. Color-coded bands can be attached as well to help various members of a household identify the right bottles. Adler's design, named ClearRx, is now in use at Target pharmacies nationwide.

CAREER APPLICATIONS

1. Why is information prioritization so important with medicine labels?

2. Aside from medications, what other situations have you encountered in your life in which confusing labels, signs, instructions, or other messages created health or safety hazards? Choose one of these situations and write a brief description of the poor communication and your advice on how it could have been improved.

✔ **Checklist** | **Revising Business Messages**

A. Evaluate content, organization, style, and tone.
- Make sure the information is accurate, relevant, and sufficient.
- Check that all necessary points appear in logical order.
- Verify that you present enough support to make the main idea convincing and compelling.
- Be sure the beginning and ending of the message are effective.
- Make sure you've achieved the right tone for the audience and the situation.

B. Review for readability.
- Consider using a readability index but be sure to interpret the answer carefully.
- Use a mix of short, medium, and long sentences.
- Keep paragraphs short.

- Use bulleted and numbered lists to emphasize key points.
- Make the document easy to skim with headings and subheadings.

C. Edit for clarity.
- Break up overly long sentences and rewrite hedging sentences.
- Impose parallelism to simplify reading.
- Correct dangling modifiers.
- Reword long noun sequences and replace camouflaged verbs.
- Clarify sentence structure and awkward references.

D. Edit for conciseness.
- Delete unnecessary words and phrases.
- Shorten long words and phrases.
- Eliminate redundancies.
- Rewrite sentences that start with "It is" or "There are."

EDITING FOR CONCISENESS

Improving clarity often makes messages shorter, but you can make them shorter still by using some specific revision techniques.

Efforts to improve clarity often reduce overall word count, so at this point you've probably eliminated most of the excess verbiage in your document. The next step is to examine the text with the specific goal of reducing the number of words you use. Readers appreciate conciseness and are more likely to read your documents if you have a reputation for efficient writing. See Table 6.3 for examples of the following tips:

Early drafts often have words and phrases that don't add anything and can easily be cut out.

- **Delete unnecessary words and phrases.** To test whether a word or phrase is essential, try the sentence without it. If the meaning doesn't change, leave it out.
- **Shorten long words and phrases.** Short words and phrases are generally more vivid and easier to read than long ones. Also, by using infinitives (the "to" form of a verb) in place of some phrases, you can often shorten sentences while making them clearer.
- **Eliminate redundancies.** In some word combinations, the words say the same thing. For instance, "visible to the eye" is redundant because *visible* is enough without further clarification; "to the eye" adds nothing.
- **Recast "It is/There are" starters.** If you start a sentence with an indefinite pronoun such as *it* or *there*, odds are the sentence could be shorter and more active. For instance, "We believe . . ." is a stronger opening than "It is believed that . . ." because it is shorter and because it identifies who is doing the believing.

As you rewrite, concentrate on how each word contributes to an effective sentence and on how each sentence helps build a coherent paragraph. For a reminder of the tasks involved in revision, see "Checklist: Revising Business Messages."

USING TECHNOLOGY TO REVISE YOUR MESSAGE

When it's time to revise and polish your message, software features can help you add, delete, and move text, using functions such as *cut and paste* (taking a block of text out of one section of a document and pasting it in somewhere else) and *search and replace* (finding words or phrases and changing them if you need to). Be careful using the "replace all" option; it can result in unintended errors. For example, finding *power* and replacing all occurrences with *strength* will also change the word *powerful* to *strengthful*, which isn't a word.

Revision marks and commenting features are great ways to track the revision process when multiple reviewers are involved.

Software tools such as *revision marks* (look for a feature called *track changes* or something similar) and *commenting* keep track of proposed editing changes electronically and provide a history of a document's revisions. In Microsoft Word, for example, revisions appear in a different text color than the original text (see Figure 6.3 on page 156), giving you a chance to review changes before accepting or rejecting them. Adobe Acrobat lets

TABLE 6.3	**Revising for Conciseness**	
Issues to Review	**Ineffective**	**Effective**
Unnecessary Words and Phrases		
Using wordy phrases	for the sum of	for
	in the event that	if
	prior to the start of	before
	in the near future	soon
	at this point in time	now
	due to the fact that	because
	in view of the fact that	because
	until such time as	when
	with reference to	about
Using too many relative pronouns	Cars that are sold after January will not have a six-month warranty.	Cars sold after January will not have a six-month warranty.
	Employees who are driving to work should park in the underground garage.	Employees driving to work should park in the underground garage. OR Employees should park in the underground garage.
Using too few relative pronouns	The project manager told the engineers last week the specifications were changed.	The project manager told the engineers last week that the specifications were changed. The project manager told the engineers that last week the specifications were changed.
Long Words and Phrases		
Using overly long words	During the preceding year, the company accelerated productive operations.	Last year the company sped up operations.
	The action was predicated on the assumption that the company was operating at a financial deficit.	The action was based on the belief that the company was losing money.
Using wordy phrases rather than infinitives	If you want success as a writer, you must work hard.	To succeed as a writer, you must work hard.
	He went to the library for the purpose of studying.	He went to the library to study.
	The employer increased salaries so that she could improve morale.	The employer increased salaries to improve morale.
Redundancies		
Repeating meanings	absolutely complete	complete
	basic fundamentals	fundamentals
	follows after	follows
	free and clear	free
	refer back	refer
	repeat again	repeat
	collect together	collect
	future plans	plans
	return back	return
	important essentials	essentials
	end result	result
	actual truth	truth
	final outcome	outcome
	uniquely unusual	unique
	surrounded on all sides	surrounded
Using double modifiers	modern, up-to-date equipment	modern equipment
It Is/There Are Starters	It would be appreciated if you would sign the lease today.	Please sign the lease today.
Starting sentences with *It* or *There*	There are five employees in this division who were late to work today.	Five employees in this division were late to work today.

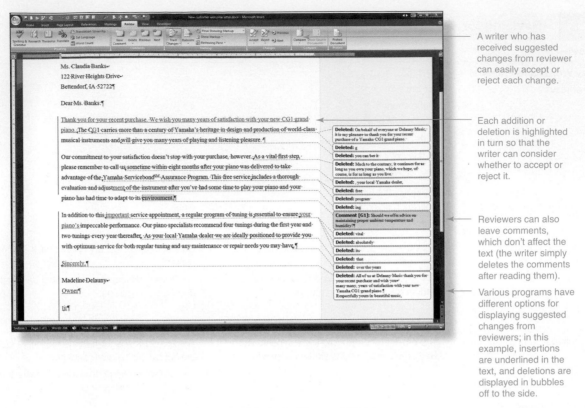

A writer who has received suggested changes from reviewer can easily accept or reject each change.

Each addition or deletion is highlighted in turn so that the writer can consider whether to accept or reject it.

Reviewers can also leave comments, which don't affect the text (the writer simply deletes the comments after reading them).

Various programs have different options for displaying suggested changes from reviewers; in this example, insertions are underlined in the text, and deletions are displayed in bubbles off to the side.

Figure 6.3 Revision Marks in Microsoft Word
Microsoft Word, the most commonly used word processor in business offices, offers handy tools for reviewing draft documents. In this example, text to be added is shown in red, and text to be deleted is shown in balloons in the right margin. The writer can then choose to accept or reject each suggested change.

you attach comments to PDF files (see Figure 6.4). (Note that Adobe Acrobat is not the same product as the free Adobe Reader.) Using revision marks and commenting features is also a great way to keep track of editing changes made by team members. Both Word and Acrobat let you use different colors for each reviewer, so you can keep everyone's comments separate.

Spell checkers, grammar checkers, and computerized thesauruses can all help with the revision process, but they can't take the place of good writing and editing skills.

In addition to the many revision tools, four software functions can help bring out the best in your documents. First, a *spell checker* compares your document with an electronic dictionary, highlights unrecognized words, and suggests correct spellings. Spell checkers are wonderful for finding typos, but they are no substitute for good spelling skills. For example, if you use *their* when you mean to use *there*, your spell checker won't notice because *their* is spelled correctly. Plus, some of the "errors" that the spell checker indicates may actually be proper names, technical words, words that you misspelled on purpose, web addresses, or simply words the spell checker doesn't know. It's up to you to decide whether each flagged word should be corrected or left alone, to find the errors that your spell checker has overlooked, and to catch problems that the spell checker itself might introduce (such as inserting unwanted hyphens or suggesting incorrect word replacements).

Second, a computer *thesaurus* (either within your software or on a website such as http://thesaurus.com) offers alternatives to a particular word. The best uses of a thesaurus are to find fresh, interesting words when you've been using the same word too many times and to find words that most accurately convey your intended meaning. Don't use a thesaurus simply to find impressive-sounding words, however, and don't assume that all the alternatives suggested are correct for each situation.

Third, a *grammar checker* tries to do for your grammar what a spell checker does for your spelling. Because the program doesn't have a clue about what you're trying to say, it can't tell whether you've said it clearly or completely. However, grammar checkers can highlight items you should consider changing, such as passive voice, long sentences, and words that tend to be misused.

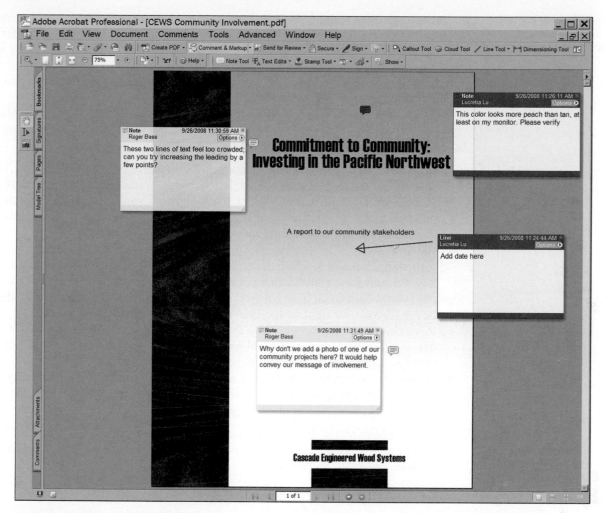

Figure 6.4 Comments Attached to a PDF File
Adobe Acrobat lets reviewers attach comments to any document in PDF format, even if it was originally created using software that the reviewers don't have.

Fourth, a *style checker* can monitor your word and sentence choices and suggest alternatives that might produce more effective writing. For instance, the style-checking options in Microsoft Word range from basic issues, such as spelling out numbers and using contractions, to more subjective matters, such as sentence structure and the use of technical terminology.

By all means, use any software tools that you find helpful when revising your documents. Just remember that it's unwise to rely on them to do all your revision work, and you're responsible for the final product.

Producing Your Message

Now it's time to put your hard work on display. The *production quality* of your message—the total effect of page or screen design, graphical elements, typography, and so on—plays an important role in the effectiveness of your message. A polished, inviting design not only makes your material easier to read but also conveys a sense of professionalism and importance.[3]

DESIGNING FOR READABILITY

Design affects readability in two important ways. First, if used carefully, design elements can improve the effectiveness of your message. If used poorly, design elements can act as barriers, blocking your communication. For example, people age 65 and over are the

4 LEARNING OBJECTIVE

List four principles of effective design, and explain the role of major design elements in document readability.

Production quality affects readability and audience perceptions of you and your message.

Document design sends strong nonverbal signals. Make sure they are positive and appropriate signals.

fastest-growing segment of online consumers in the United States, but many websites don't take into account the natural changes that occur in eyesight as people age. Older people often find it difficult to read the small type that is common on websites—and many websites make the mistake of preventing viewers from enlarging type size in their browsers.[4] Second, the visual design sends a nonverbal message to your readers, influencing their perceptions of the communication before they read a single word.

Effective design helps you establish the tone of your document and helps guide your readers through your message (see Figure 6.5). To achieve an effective design, pay careful attention to the following design elements:

Aim for consistent design within each message and from message to message.

- **Consistency.** Throughout each message, be consistent in your use of margins, typeface, type size, and space. Also be consistent when using recurring design elements, such as vertical lines, columns, and borders. In many cases, you'll want to be consistent from message to message as well; that way, audiences who receive multiple messages from you recognize your documents and know what to expect.
- **Balance.** Balance is an important but subjective issue. One document may have a formal, rigid design in which the various elements are placed in a grid pattern, whereas another may have a less formal design in which elements flow more freely across the page—and both could be in balance. Like the tone of your language, visual balance can be too formal, just right, or too informal for a given message.

Simple designs are usually more effective than more complex designs.

- **Restraint.** Strive for simplicity in design. Don't clutter your message with too many design elements, too much highlighting, too many colors, or too many decorative touches. Let "simpler" and "fewer" be your guiding concepts.
- **Detail.** Pay attention to details that affect your design and thus your message. For instance, extremely wide columns of text can be difficult to read; in many cases a better solution is to split the text into two narrower columns.

Even without special training in graphic design, you can make your printed and electronic messages more effective by understanding the use of white space, margins and line justification, typefaces, and type styles.

Figure 6.5   Designing for Readability
This blog uses a clean, restrained design that is more than adequate for its purpose, which is sharing ideas on project management strategies and techniques.

Apply Figure 6.5's key concepts by revising a new document. Go to Chapter 6 in mybcommlab.com and select Document Makeovers.

White Space

Any space that doesn't contain text or artwork, both in print and online, is considered **white space**. (Note that "white space" isn't necessarily white; it is simply blank.) These unused areas provide visual contrast and important resting points for your readers. White space includes the open area surrounding headings, margins, paragraph indents, space around images, vertical space between columns, and horizontal space between paragraphs or lines of text. To increase the chance that readers will read your messages, be generous with white space; it makes pages and screens feel less intimidating and easier to read.[5]

White space separates elements in a document and helps guide the reader's eye.

Margins and Justification

Margins define the space around text and between text columns. In addition to their width, the look and feel of margins is influenced by the way you arrange lines of text, which can be set (1) *justified* (which means they are *flush*, or aligned vertically, on both the left and the right), (2) flush left with a *ragged-right* margin, (3) flush right with a *ragged-left* margin, or (4) centered. This paragraph is justified, whereas the paragraphs in Figure 6.2 on page 147 are flush left with a ragged-right margin.

Magazines, newspapers, and books often use justified type because it can accommodate more text in a given space. However, justified type needs to be used with care. First, it creates a denser look because the uniform line lengths decrease the amount of white space along the right margin. Second, it produces a more formal and less personalized look. Third, unless it is used with some skill and attention, justified type can be more difficult to read because it can produce large gaps between words and excessive hyphenation at the ends of lines. The publishing specialists who create magazines, newspapers, and books have the time and skill needed to carefully adjust character and word spacing to eliminate these problems. (In some cases, sentences are even rewritten in order to improve the appearance of the printed page.) Because most business communicators don't have that time or skill, it's best to avoid justified type in most business documents.

In contrast to justified type, flush-left, ragged-right type creates a more open appearance on the page, producing a less formal and more contemporary look. Spacing between words is consistent, and only long words that fall at the ends of lines are hyphenated.

Centered type is rarely used for text paragraphs but is commonly used for headings and subheadings. Flush-right, ragged-left type is rarely used in business documents.

Most business documents use a flush-left margin and a ragged-right margin.

Typefaces

Typeface refers to the physical design of letters, numbers, and other text characters. (*Font* and *typeface* are often used interchangeably, although strictly speaking, a font is a set of characters in a given typeface.) Typeface influences the tone of your message, making it look authoritative or friendly, businesslike or casual, classic or modern, and so on (see Table 6.4). Be sure to choose fonts that are appropriate for your message; many of the fonts on your computer are not appropriate for business use.

TABLE 6.4	**Typeface Purposes and Personalities**	
Serif Typefaces (Best for Text)	Sans Serif Typefaces (Best for Headlines; Some Work Well for Text)	Specialty Typefaces (For Decorative Purposes Only)
Bookman Old Style	**Arial**	ANNA
Century Schoolbook	**Eras Bold**	Bauhaus
Courier	Franklin Gothic Book	*Edwardian*
Garamond	Frutiger	*Lucida Handwriting*
Rockwell	Gill Sans	Old English
Times Roman	Verdana	**STENCIL**

The classic style of document design uses a sans serif typeface for headings and a serif typeface for regular paragraph text; however, many contemporary documents now use all sans serif.

Serif typefaces have small crosslines (called serifs) at the ends of each letter stroke. Serif typefaces such as Times New Roman are commonly used for regular paragraph text (as in this book), but they can look busy and cluttered when set in large sizes for headings.

Sans serif typefaces have no serifs (*sans* is French for "without"). The visual simplicity of sans serif typefaces such as Helvetica and Arial makes them ideal for the larger sizes used in headlines. Sans serif faces can be difficult to read in long blocks of text, however, unless they are formatted with generous amounts of *leading* (pronounced *ledding*), or spacing between lines.

For most documents, generally avoid using more than two typefaces, although if you want to make captions or another special text element stand out, you can use a third font for that.[6] You can't go too far wrong with a sans serif typeface (such as Arial) for heads and subheads and a serif typeface (such as Times New Roman) for text and captions. Using too many typefaces clutters a document and can produce an amateurish look.

Type Styles

Type style refers to any modification that lends contrast or emphasis to type, including boldface, italic, underlining, color, and other highlighting and decorative styles. Using boldface type for subheads breaks up long expanses of text. You can also boldface individual words or phrases to draw more attention to them. For example, the key terms in each chapter in this book are set in bold. Italic type also creates emphasis, although not as pronounced as boldface. Italic type has specific uses as well, such as highlighting quotations and indicating foreign words, irony, humor, book and movie titles, and unconventional usage.

Avoid using any type style in ways that might interfere with reading.

As a general rule, avoid using any style in a way that slows your audience's progress through the message. For instance, underlining or using all-uppercase letters can interfere with a reader's ability to recognize the shapes of words, and shadowed or outlined type can seriously hinder legibility. Also, avoid overusing any type style. For example, putting too many words in boldface dilutes the impact of the special treatment by creating too many focal points in the paragraph.

Type size is an important consideration as well. For most printed business messages, use a size of 10 to 12 points for regular text and 12 to 18 points for headings and subheadings (1 point is approximately 1/72 inch). Resist the temptation to reduce type size too much in order to squeeze in extra text or to enlarge it to fill up space. Type that is too small is hard to read, whereas extra-large type looks unprofessional. Be particularly careful with small type online. Small type that looks fine on a medium-resolution screen can be hard to read on both low-resolution screens (because these displays can make letters look jagged or fuzzy) and high-resolution screens (because these monitors reduce the apparent size of the type even further).

DESIGNING MULTIMEDIA DOCUMENTS

A **multimedia document** contains a combination of text, graphics, photographs, audio, animation, video, and interactivity (such as hyperlinks that access webpages or software programs). Most electronic media now support multiple media formats, so you have a variety of options for creating multimedia documents. For example, you can add photos to a word processor file, audio commentary to a PDF, video clips to a blog posting, and animation to webpages.

As rich media, multimedia documents can convey large amounts of information quickly, engage people in multiple ways, express emotions, and allow recipients to personalize the communication process to their own needs. However, these documents are more difficult to create than documents that contain only text and static images. To design and create multimedia documents, you need to consider the following factors:

Multimedia documents can be powerful communication vehicles, but they require more time, tools, and skills to create.

- **Creative and technical skills.** Depending on what you need to accomplish, creating and integrating multimedia elements can require some creative and technical skills. Fortunately, many basic tasks, such as adding photographs or video clips to a webpage, have gotten much easier in recent years. And even if you don't have the advantage of formal training in design, by studying successful examples, you can start to get a feel for what works and what doesn't.

- **Tools.** The hardware and software tools needed to create and integrate media elements are now widely available and generally affordable. For example, with simpler and less expensive consumer versions of professional photo and video editing software, you can often perform all the tasks you need for business multimedia (see Figure 6.6).
- **Time and cost.** The time and cost of creating multimedia documents has dropped dramatically in recent years. However, you still need to consider these elements—and exercise good judgment when deciding whether to include multimedia and how much to include. Make sure the time and money you plan to spend will be paid back in communication effectiveness.
- **Content.** To include various media elements in a document, you obviously need to create or acquire them. If you have the skills, time, and tools, you might be able to create graphics or other media elements. If not, you'll need to find these items and secure the right to use them. Millions of graphics, photos, video clips, and other elements are available online, but you need to make sure you can legally use each item. One good option is to search Creative Commons (www.creativecommons.org) for multimedia elements available for use at no charge but with various restrictions (such as giving the creator credit).
- **Message structure.** Multimedia documents often lack a rigid linear structure from beginning to end, which means you need to plan for readers to take multiple, individualized paths through the material. In other words, a conventional outline is often inadequate. Chapter 13 discusses the challenge of *information architecture*, the structure and navigational flow of websites and other multimedia documents.
- **Compatibility.** Some multimedia elements require specific software to be installed on the recipient's viewing device. Another challenge is the variety of screen sizes and resolutions, from large, high-resolution computer monitors to tiny, low-resolution mobile phone displays. Make sure you understand the demands your message will place on the audience.

Make sure you have the legal right to use any media elements that you include in your documents.

Figure 6.6 Multimedia Tools
Software such as Adobe Photoshop Elements makes it easy for anyone with basic computer skills to create and modify content for multimedia documents. A simple *cropping* operation on a photo is shown here.

USING TECHNOLOGY TO PRODUCE YOUR MESSAGE

Production tools vary widely, depending on the software and systems you're using. Some IM and email systems offer limited formatting and production capabilities, whereas most word processors now offer some capabilities that rival those of professional publishing software for many day-to-day business needs. *Desktop publishing* software such as Adobe InDesign goes beyond word processing, offering more advanced and precise layout capabilities that meet the technical demands of publication-quality printing. (These programs are used mainly by design professionals.)

For online content, web publishing systems make it easy to produce great-looking webpages quickly. Similarly, most blogging systems now simplify the production of blog content, letting you rapidly post new material without worrying too much about design or production. Multimedia production tools such as Microsoft Producer let you combine slides, audio commentary, video clips, and other features into computer-based presentations that once cost thousands of dollars to create.

Learning to use the basic features of your communication tools will help you produce better messages in less time.

No matter what system you're using, become familiar with the basic formatting capabilities. A few hours of exploration on your own or an introductory training course can help you dramatically improve the production quality of your documents. Depending on the types of messages you're creating, you'll benefit from being proficient with the following features:

- **Templates, themes, and stylesheets.** As Chapter 5 notes, you can save a tremendous amount of time by using templates, themes, and stylesheets. Many companies provide these tools to their employees to ensure a consistent look and feel for all print and online documents.
- **Page setup.** Use page setup to control margins, orientation (*portrait* is vertical; *landscape* is horizontal), and the location of *headers* (text and graphics that repeat at the top of every page) and *footers* (similar to headers but at the bottom of the page).
- **Column formatting.** Most business documents use a single column of text per page, but multiple columns can be an attractive format for documents such as newsletters. Columns are also handy for formatting long lists.
- **Paragraph formatting.** Take advantage of paragraph formatting controls to enhance the look of your documents. For instance, you can offset quotations by increasing margin width around a single paragraph, subtly compress line spacing to fit a document on a single page, or use hanging indents to offset the first line of a paragraph.
- **Numbered and bulleted lists.** Let your software do the busywork of formatting numbered and bulleted lists. It can also automatically renumber lists when you add or remove items.
- **Tables.** Tables are great for displaying any information that lends itself to rows and columns, including calendars, numeric data, comparisons, and multicolumn bulleted lists. Use paragraph and font formatting thoughtfully within tables for the best look.
- **Pictures, text boxes, and objects.** Print and online publishing software lets you insert a wide variety of pictures (using industry-standard formats such as JPEG and GIF). *Text boxes* are small blocks of text that stand apart from the main text and can be placed anywhere on the page; they are great for captions, callouts, margin notes, and so on. *Objects* can be anything from a spreadsheet to a sound clip to an engineering drawing. Similarly, blogging systems, wikis, and other web development tools let you insert a variety of pictures, audio and video clips, and other multimedia elements.

By improving the appearance of your documents with these tools, you'll improve your readers' impressions of you and your messages, too.

FORMATTING FORMAL LETTERS AND MEMOS

Formal business letters usually follow certain design conventions, as the letter in Figure 6.2 (see page 147) illustrates. Most business letters are printed on *letterhead stationery*, which includes the company's name, address, and other contact information. The first element to appear after the letterhead is the date, followed by the inside address, which identifies the person receiving the letter. Next is the salutation, usually in the form of *Dear Mr.* or *Ms. Last Name*. The message comes next, followed by the complimentary close, usually *Sincerely* or *Cordially*. And last comes the signature block: space for the signature, followed by the sender's printed name and title. Your company will probably have a standard format to follow for letters, possibly along with a template in Microsoft Word or whatever word processor is standard in the organization. For in-depth information on letter formats, see Appendix A, "Format and Layout of Business Documents."

Like letters, business memos usually follow a preset design (see Figure 6.7). Memos have largely been replaced by electronic media in many companies, but if they are still in use at the firm you join, the company may have a standard format or template for you to use. Most memos begin with a title such as *Memo, Memorandum,* or *Interoffice Correspondence.* Following that are usually four headings: *Date, To, From,* and *Subject.* (*Re:,* short for *Regarding,* is sometimes used instead of *Subject.*) Memos usually don't use a salutation, complimentary close, or signature, although signing your initials next to your name on the *From* line is standard practice in most companies. Bear in mind that memos are often distributed without sealed envelopes, so they are less private than most other message formats.

Letters typically have the following elements:
- Preprinted letterhead stationery
- Date
- Inside address
- Salutation
- Complimentary close
- Signature block

Memos are usually identified by a title such as *Memo* or *Memorandum.*

Uses standard company memo stationery with title indicating that this is a memo

Uses four standard headings for memos

Does not begin with a salutation

Does not include a complimentary close or a signature block

Figure 6.7 A Typical Business Memo
This document shows the elements usually included in a formal business memo.

Proofreading Your Message

Proofreading is the quality inspection stage for your documents, your last chance to make sure that your document is ready to carry your message—and your reputation—to the intended audience. Even a small mistake can doom your efforts, so take proofreading seriously.

Look for two types of problems: (1) undetected mistakes from the writing, design, and layout stages and (2) mistakes that crept in during production. For the first category, you can review format and layout guidelines in Appendix A on page A-1 and brush up on writing basics with the Handbook of Grammar, Mechanics, and Usage on page H-1. The second category can include anything from computer glitches such as missing fonts to broken web links to problems with the ink used in printing. Be particularly vigilant with complex documents and complex production processes that involve teams of people and multiple computers. Strange things can happen as files move from computer to computer, especially when lots of fonts and multimedia elements are involved.

A methodical approach to proofreading will help you find the problems that need to be fixed.

Resist the temptation to treat proofreading as a casual scan up and down the page or screen. Instead, approach it as a methodical procedure in which you look for specific problems that may occur. Use these techniques from professional proofreaders to help ensure high-quality output:

- **Make multiple passes.** Go through the document several times, focusing on a different aspect each time. For instance, look for content errors the first time and layout errors the second time.
- **Use perceptual tricks.** You've probably experienced the frustration of reading over something a dozen times and still missing an obvious error that was staring you right in the face. This happens because your brain has developed a wonderful skill of subconsciously supplying missing pieces and correcting mistakes when it "knows" what is *supposed* to be on the page. To keep your brain from tricking you, you need to trick it by changing the way you process the visual information. Try (1) reading each page backward, from the bottom to the top, (2) placing your finger under each word and reading it silently, (3) making a slit in a sheet of paper that reveals only one line of type at a time, and (4) reading the document aloud and pronouncing each word carefully.
- **Double-check high-priority items.** Double-check the spelling of names and the accuracy of dates, addresses, and any number that could cause grief if incorrect (such as telling a potential employer that you'd be happy to work for $5,000 a year when you meant to say $50,000).

- **Give yourself some distance.** If possible, don't proofread immediately after finishing a document; let your mind wander off to new topics and then come back fresh later on.
- **Be vigilant.** Avoid reading large amounts of material in one sitting and try not to proofread when you're tired.
- **Stay focused.** Concentrate on what you're doing. Try to block out distractions and focus as completely as possible on your proofreading task.
- **Review complex electronic documents on paper.** Some people have trouble proofreading webpages, online reports, and other electronic documents on-screen. If you have trouble, try to print the materials so you can review them on paper.
- **Take your time.** Quick proofreading is not careful proofreading.

The amount of time you need to spend on proofing depends on the length and complexity of the document and the situation. A typo in an email message to your team may not be a big deal, but a typo in a financial report, a contract, or a medical file certainly could be serious. As with every other task in the writing process, practice helps—you become more familiar with what errors to look

Checklist Proofing Business Messages

A. Look for writing errors.
- Typographical mistakes
- Misspelled words
- Grammatical errors
- Punctuation mistakes

B. Look for missing elements.
- Missing text sections
- Missing exhibits (drawings, tables, photographs, charts, graphs, online images, and so on)
- Missing source notes, copyright notices, or other reference items

C. Look for design, formatting, and programming mistakes.
- Incorrect or inconsistent font selections
- Problems with column sizing, spacing, and alignment
- Incorrect margins
- Incorrect special characters
- Clumsy line and page breaks
- Problems with page numbers
- Problems with page headers and footers
- Lack of adherence to company standards
- Inactive or incorrect links
- Missing files

for and more skilled in identifying those errors. See "Checklist: Proofing Business Messages" for a handy list of items to review during proofing.

Distributing Your Message

With the production finished, you're ready to distribute your message. As with every other aspect of business communication, your options for distribution multiply with every advance in technology. In some cases, the choice is obvious: Just click the Send button in your email program or the Publish button on your blog. In other cases, such as when you have a 100-page report with full-color graphics or a massive multimedia file, you need to plan the distribution carefully so that your message is received by everyone who needs it. When choosing a means to distribute messages, consider the following factors:

6 **LEARNING OBJECTIVE**

Discuss the most important issues to consider when distributing your messages.

- **Cost.** Cost isn't a concern for most messages, but for lengthy reports or multimedia productions, it may well be. Printing, binding, and delivering reports can be expensive, so weigh the cost versus the benefits before you decide. Be sure to consider the nonverbal message you send regarding cost as well. Overnight delivery of a printed report could look responsive in one situation but wasteful in another, for example.

- **Convenience.** How much work is involved for you and your audience? For instance, sending huge files may be fine on a fast office network, but receiving such files can be a major headache for remote colleagues trying to download them over slower wireless networks. If you're sending large files as attachments, consider you can use a file-compression utility to shrink the file, but make sure your recipients have the means to expand the files upon arrival. For extremely large files, consider recordable media such as CDs or a file-hosting site such as MediaFire (www.mediafire.com).

Make sure your delivery method is convenient for your audience members.

- **Time.** How soon does the message need to reach the audience? Don't waste money on overnight delivery if the recipient won't read the report for a week. And speaking of time, don't mark any messages, printed or electronic, as "urgent" if they aren't truly urgent.

- **Security and privacy.** The convenience offered by electronic communication needs to be weighed against security and privacy concerns. For the most sensitive messages, your company will probably restrict both the people who can receive the messages and the means you can use to distribute them. In addition, most computer users are wary of opening attachments these days. Instead of sending word processor files, you can use Adobe Acrobat or an equivalent product to convert your documents to PDF files (which are more immune to viruses).

Chapter 7 offers more advice on distributing podcasts, blogs, and other messages in electronic formats. For news on the latest news on revision, proofreading, and other topics related to this chapter, visit http://real-timeupdates.com/bct11 and click on Chapter 6.

MyBcommLab

CHAPTER OUTLINE

Revising Your Message: Evaluating the First Draft
  Evaluating Your Content, Organization, Style, and Tone
  Evaluating, Editing, and Revising the Work of Others

Revising to Improve Readability
  Varying Your Sentence Length
  Keeping Your Paragraphs Short
  Using Lists to Clarify and Emphasize
  Adding Headings and Subheadings

Editing for Clarity and Conciseness
  Editing for Clarity
  Editing for Conciseness
  Using Technology to Revise Your Message

Producing Your Message
  Designing for Readability
  Designing Multimedia Documents
  Using Technology to Produce Your Message
  Formatting Formal Letters and Memos

Proofreading Your Message

Distributing Your Message

SUMMARY OF LEARNING OBJECTIVE

1 **Discuss the value of careful revision, and describe the tasks involved in evaluating your first drafts and the work of other writers.** Revision is a vital step in producing effective business messages; even if the first draft conveys the necessary information, chances are it can be made tighter, clearer, and more compelling—making it more successful for you. Careful revision also helps you locate and correct errors that can reduce the effectiveness of messages and damage your reputation as a communicator.

When evaluating your first drafts, check the *content* (is the content accurate, relevant, complete, and well-balanced between general and specific information?), the *organization* (are your points grouped and sequenced logically, with focus on the most important ideas?), and the *tone* (is the tone appropriate for the audience and the specific situation?).

2 **List four techniques you can use to improve the readability of your messages.** Four techniques that help improve readability are varying sentence length, keeping paragraphs short, using lists, and adding headings and subheadings. Varying sentence length helps keep your writing fresh and dynamic while giving you a chance to emphasize the most important points. Paragraphs, on the other hand, are usually best kept short to make it easier for readers to consume your information in manageable chunks. Lists are effective devices for delineating sets of items, steps in a procedure, or other collections of related information. Headings and subheadings organize your message, call attention to important information, and help readers make connections between related pieces of information.

3 **Describe eight steps you can take to improve the clarity of your writing, and give four tips on making your writing more concise.** To clarify your writing, (1) break up overly long sentences, (2) rewrite hedging sentences, (3) impose parallelism, (4) correct dangling modifiers, (5) reword long noun sequences, (6) replace camouflaged verbs, (7) clarify sentence structure, and (8) clarify awkward references. To make messages more concise, (1) delete unnecessary words and phrases, (2) shorten overly long words and phrases, (3) eliminate redundancies, and (4) recast sentences that begin with "It is" and "There are."

4 **List four principles of effective design, and explain the role of major design elements in document readability.** Four important principles of effective design are *consistency* (using design elements in a consistent and predictable way throughout a document), *balance* (creating a balanced effect on page or screen, whether that balance is dynamic and informal or symmetrical and formal), *restraint* (striving for visual simplicity to avoid drawing attention away from your ideas), and *detail* (making sure that details are handled correctly so that errors or design misjudgments don't detract from your message).

The major design elements for textual messages include white space, margins, typefaces, and type styles. White space provides contrast and gives readers a resting point. Margins define the space around the text and contribute to the amount of white space. Margins can affect both readability and the overall visual appeal of your messages. Typefaces influence the tone of the message and should be chosen carefully for each use to ensure maximum readability. Type styles such as boldface, italics, and underlining provide contrast or emphasis.

5 **Explain the importance of proofreading, and give eight tips for successful proofreading.** Proofreading is essential because it is your final opportunity to verify the quality of your communication efforts and to make sure that no errors in writing, design, or production will undo all the hard work you've put in. Proofreading should be more than just a quick glance through the document. Use the techniques the pros use to make sure your documents are top quality: (1) Make multiple passes, looking for specific types of problems each time; (2) use perceptual tricks such as reading aloud or reading backward to prevent your brain from fooling you by filling in pieces or correcting errors; (3) double-check high-priority items such as names, dates, addresses, and financial data; (4) give yourself some distance by putting the document aside for a few hours or even a few days if possible; (5) stay vigilant by proofing only small sections at a time and not proofing when you are tired; (6) stay focused on your work; (7) review complex electronic documents on paper if possible; and (8) take your time.

6 **Discuss the most important issues to consider when distributing your messages.** Consider cost, convenience, time, security, and privacy when choosing the method to distribute your messages. Cost isn't a major issue for most messages, although production, printing, and distribution of lengthy or complex reports can be a concern. In general, balance the cost with the importance and urgency of the message. Make sure the distribution method is convenient for your audience. For example, attaching a document to an email message might be easy for you, but that might not be the best approach for a given audience. As with cost, balance the time factor with your needs and the needs of your audience. Finally, consider security and privacy issues before distributing documents that contain sensitive or confidential information. Your company may have restrictions on the type of information that can be distributed through various media and channels.

KEY TERMS

descriptive headings Headings that simply identify a topic

heading A brief title that tells readers about the content of the section that follows

informative headings Headings that guide readers to think in a certain way about the topic

multimedia document Electronic document that contains a combination of text, graphics, photographs, audio, animation, video, and interactivity

sans serif typefaces Typefaces whose letters lack serifs: This is sans serif type

serif typefaces Typefaces with small crosslines (called serifs) at the ends of letter strokes: This is serif type.

subheadings Titles that are subordinate to headings, indicating subsections with a major section

typeface The physical design of letters, numbers, and other text characters (*font* and *typeface* are often used

interchangeably, although strictly speaking, a font is a set of characters in a given typeface)

type style Any modification that lends contrast or emphasis to type, including boldface, italic, underlining, color, and other highlighting and decorative styles

white space Space (of any color) in a document or screen that doesn't contain any text or artwork

 Checklist

Revising Business Messages

A. Evaluate content, organization, style, and tone.
- Make sure the information is accurate, relevant, and sufficient.
- Check that all necessary points appear in logical order.
- Verify that you present enough support to make the main idea convincing and compelling.
- Be sure the beginning and ending of the message are effective.
- Make sure you've achieved the right tone for the audience and the situation.

B. Review for readability.
- Consider using a readability index but be sure to interpret the answer carefully.
- Use a mix of short, medium, and long sentences.
- Keep paragraphs short.
- Use bulleted and numbered lists to emphasize key points.
- Make the document easy to skim with headings and subheadings.

C. Edit for clarity.
- Break up overly long sentences and rewrite hedging sentences.
- Impose parallelism to simplify reading.
- Correct dangling modifiers.
- Reword long noun sequences and replace camouflaged verbs.
- Clarify sentence structure and awkward references.

D. Edit for conciseness.
- Delete unnecessary words and phrases.
- Shorten long words and phrases.
- Eliminate redundancies.
- Rewrite sentences that start with "It is" or "There are."

 Checklist

Proofing Business Messages

A. Look for writing errors.
- Typographical mistakes
- Misspelled words
- Grammatical errors
- Punctuation mistakes

B. Look for missing elements.
- Missing text sections
- Missing exhibits (drawings, tables, photographs, charts, graphs, online images, and so on)
- Missing source notes, copyright notices, or other reference items

C. Look for design, formatting, and programming mistakes.
- Incorrect or inconsistent font selections
- Problems with column sizing, spacing, and alignment
- Incorrect margins
- Incorrect special characters
- Clumsy line and page breaks
- Problems with page numbers
- Problems with page headers and footers
- Lack of adherence to company standards
- Inactive or incorrect links
- Missing files

COMMUNICATION CHALLENGES AT JEFFERSON RABB WEB DESIGN

Jefferson Rabb's web business is doing so well that he has hired you to help with a variety of writing and design tasks. Use what you've learned in this chapter about revising messages and designing for readability.

INDIVIDUAL CHALLENGE: The writer Alexander McCall Smith, one of Rabb's clients, is so prolific that summarizing his career is a challenge—and

being a best-selling novelist is only one aspect of his varied life's work. Review his biography at www.randomhouse.com/features/mccallsmith (click "About the Author"), which currently runs about 650 words. Rewrite the bio so that it will fit on a book referral website that limits author bios to 200 words.

TEAM CHALLENGE: With a team of classmates assigned by your instructor, visit three of the book websites on which Rabb has worked. You can find links from his website at www.jeffersonrabb.com. Evaluate and compare the sites' readability based on the advice given in the chapter regarding white space, margins, typefaces, and type styles. Prepare a class presentation of your analysis.

TEST YOUR KNOWLEDGE

To review chapter content related to each question, refer to the indicated Learning Objective.

1. What are the three main tasks involved in revising a business message? [LO-1]
2. What are your two primary responsibilities when editing or revising the work of another writer? [LO-1]
3. What are the relative advantages of short, medium, and long sentences? [LO-2]
4. What functions do headings serve? [LO-2]
5. What are some ways you can make a document more concise? [LO-3]
6. What are hedging sentences, and why should they be avoided unless truly necessary? [LO-4]
7. How do readers benefit from white space? [LO-4]
8. Why is proofreading an important part of the writing process? [LO-5]
9. What perceptual tricks can you use to improve your chances of spotting errors during proofreading? [LO-5]
10. What factors should you consider when choosing a distribution method for your messages (other than for systems where you don't have a choice)? [LO-6]

APPLY YOUR KNOWLEDGE

To review chapter content related to each question, refer to the indicated Learning Objective.

1. Why is it helpful to put your first draft aside for a while before you begin the editing process? [LO-1]
2. Why is it important to spend extra time reviewing and polishing the beginning and end of a message? [LO-1]
3. How does Target's decision to adopt the ClearRx medicine labeling and packaging system (see "Missing the Message

with Prescription Medication" on page 153) fit the definition of ethical communication from Chapter 1? [LO-3]
4. Why should you limit the number of typefaces and type styles in most business documents? [LO-4]
5. How can you demonstrate good business sense in the choices you make regarding message distribution? [LO-6]

PRACTICE YOUR SKILLS

Message for Analysis 6.A:
Revising to Improve Readability [LO-2]

Analyze the strengths and weaknesses of this message, then revise it so that it follows the guidelines in Chapters 4 through 6:

As an organization, the North American Personal Motorsports Marketing Association has committed ourselves to helping our members—a diverse group comprising of dealers of motorcycles, all-terrain vehicles, Snowmobiles, and personal watercraft—achieve their business objectives. Consequently, our organization, which usually goes under the initials NAPMMA, has the following aims, goals, and objectives. Firstly, we endeavor to aid or assist our members in reaching their business objectives. Second, NAPMMA communicates ("lobbying" in slang terms) with local, state, and national governmental agencies and leaders on issues of importance to our members. And lastly, we educate the motorsports public, that being current motorsports vehicle owners, and prospective owners of said vehicles, on the safe and enjoyable operation of they're vehicles.

Message for Analysis 6.B:
Designing for Readability [LO-4]

To access this message, visit http://real-timeupdates.com/bct11, click on "Student Assignments," select Chapter 6, and then select Page 168, Message 6.B. Download and open the Microsoft Word document. Using the various page, paragraph, and font formatting options available in your word processor, modify the formatting of the document so that its visual tone matches the tone of the message.

Message for Analysis 6.C:
Evaluating the Work of Another Writer [LO-1]

To access this message, visit **http://real-timeupdates.com/bct11**, click on "Student Assignments," select Chapter 6, and then select Page 169, Message 6.C. Download and open the Microsoft Word document. Using your knowledge of effective writing and the tips on page 147 for evaluating the work of other writers, evaluate this message. After you set Microsoft Word to track changes, make any necessary corrections. Insert comments, as needed, to explain your changes to the author.

Exercises

Active links for all websites in this chapter can be found on MyBcommLab; see your User Guide for instructions on accessing the content for this chapter. Each activity is labeled according to the primary skill or skills you will need to use. To review relevant chapter content, you can refer to the indicated Learning Objective. In some instances, supporting information will be found in another chapter, as indicated.

1. **Evaluating the Work of Other Writers [LO-1]** Find a blog post (at least three paragraphs long) on any business-related topic. Evaluate it using the 10 questions on page 148. Email your analysis to your instructor, along with a permalink (a permanent link to this specific post, rather than to the blog overall) to the blog post.

2. **Revising for Readability (Sentence and Paragraph Length) [LO-2]** Rewrite the following paragraph to vary the length of the sentences and to shorten the paragraph so it looks more inviting to readers:

   Although major league baseball remains popular, more people are attending minor league baseball games because they can spend less on admission, snacks, and parking and still enjoy the excitement of America's pastime. Connecticut, for example, has three AA minor league teams, including the New Haven Ravens, who are affiliated with the St. Louis Cardinals; the Norwich Navigators, who are affiliated with the New York Yankees; and the New Britain Rock Cats, who are affiliated with the Minnesota Twins. These teams play in relatively small stadiums, so fans are close enough to see and hear everything, from the swing of the bat connecting with the ball to the thud of the ball landing in the outfielder's glove. Best of all, the cost of a family outing to see rising stars play in a local minor league game is just a fraction of what the family would spend to attend a major league game in a much larger, more crowded stadium.

3. **Revising for Readability (Using Lists) [LO-2]** Rewrite the following paragraph using a parallel bulleted list and one introductory sentence:

   Our forensic accounting services provide the insights needed to resolve disputes, recover losses, and manage risk intelligently. One of our areas of practice is insurance claims accounting and preparation services, designed to help you maximize recovery of insured value. Another practice area is dispute advisory, in which we can assist with discovery, expert witness testimony, and economic analysis. A third practice: construction consulting. This service helps our clients understand why large-scale construction projects fail to meet schedule or budget requirements. Fourth, we offer general investigative and forensic accounting services, including fraud detection and proof of loss analysis.[7]

4. **Revising for Readability (Sentence Length) [LO-2]** Break the following sentences into shorter ones by adding more periods and revise as needed for smooth flow:

   a. The next time you write something, check your average sentence length in a 100-word passage, and if your sentences average more than 16 to 20 words, see whether you can break up some of the sentences.

   b. Don't do what the village blacksmith did when he instructed his apprentice as follows: "When I take the shoe out of the fire, I'll lay it on the anvil, and when I nod my head, you hit it with the hammer." The apprentice did just as he was told, and now he's the village blacksmith.

   c. Unfortunately, no gadget will produce excellent writing, but using a yardstick like the Fog Index gives us some guideposts to follow for making writing easier to read because its two factors remind us to use short sentences and simple words.

   d. Know the flexibility of the written word and its power to convey an idea, and know how to make your words behave so that your readers will understand.

   e. Words mean different things to different people, and a word such as *block* may mean city block, butcher block, engine block, auction block, or several other things.

5. **Editing for Conciseness (Unnecessary Words) [LO-3]** Cross out unnecessary words in the following phrases:

   a. Consensus of opinion

   b. New innovations

   c. Long period of time

   d. At a price of $50

   e. Still remains

6. **Editing for Conciseness (Long Words) [LO-3]** Revise the following sentences, using shorter, simpler words:

   a. The antiquated calculator is ineffectual for solving sophisticated problems.

   b. It is imperative that the pay increments be terminated before an inordinate deficit is accumulated.

   c. There was unanimity among the executives that Ms. Jackson's idiosyncrasies were cause for a mandatory meeting with the company's personnel director.

   d. The impending liquidation of the company's assets was cause for jubilation among the company's competitors.

e. The expectations of the president for a stock dividend were accentuated by the preponderance of evidence that the company was in good financial condition.

7. **Editing for Conciseness (Lengthy Phrases)[LO-3]** Use infinitives as substitutes for the overly long phrases in these sentences:

a. For living, I require money.

b. They did not find sufficient evidence for believing in the future.

c. Bringing about the destruction of a dream is tragic.

8. **Editing for Conciseness (Lengthy Phrases)[LO-3]** Rephrase the following in fewer words:

a. In the near future

b. In the event that

c. In order that

d. For the purpose of

e. With regard to

f. It may be that

g. In very few cases

h. With reference to

i. At the present time

j. There is no doubt that

9. **Editing for Conciseness (Lengthy Phrases) [LO-3]** Revise to condense these sentences to as few words as possible:

a. We are of the conviction that writing is important.

b. In all probability, we're likely to have a price increase.

c. Our goals include making a determination about that in the near future.

d. When all is said and done at the conclusion of this experiment, I'd like to summarize the final windup.

e. After a trial period of three weeks, during which time she worked for a total of 15 full working days, we found her work was sufficiently satisfactory so that we offered her full-time work.

10. **Editing for Conciseness (Unnecessary Modifiers)[LO-3]** Remove all the unnecessary modifiers from these sentences:

a. Tremendously high pay increases were given to the extraordinarily skilled and extremely conscientious employees.

b. The union's proposals were highly inflationary, extremely demanding, and exceptionally bold.

11. **Editing for Clarity (Hedging) [LO-3]** Rewrite these sentences so that they no longer contain any hedging:

a. It would appear that someone apparently entered illegally.

b. It may be possible that sometime in the near future the situation is likely to improve.

c. Your report seems to suggest that we might be losing money.

d. I believe Nancy apparently has somewhat greater influence over employees in the e-marketing department.

e. It seems as if this letter of resignation means you might be leaving us.

12. **Editing for Clarity (Indefinite Starters)[LO-3]** Rewrite these sentences to eliminate the indefinite starters:

a. There are several examples here to show that Elaine can't hold a position very long.

b. It would be greatly appreciated if every employee would make a generous contribution to Mildred Cook's retirement party.

c. It has been learned in Washington today from generally reliable sources that an important announcement will be made shortly by the White House.

d. There is a rule that states that we cannot work overtime without permission.

e. It would be great if you could work late for the next three Saturdays.

13. **Editing for Clarity (Parallelism)[LO-3]** Revise these sentences in order to present the ideas in parallel form:

a. Mr. Hill is expected to lecture three days a week, to counsel two days a week, and must write for publication in his spare time.

b. She knows not only accounting, but she also reads Latin.

c. Both applicants had families, college degrees, and were in their thirties, with considerable accounting experience but few social connections.

d. This book was exciting, well written, and held my interest.

e. Don is both a hard worker and he knows bookkeeping.

14. **Editing for Clarity (Awkward References)[LO-3]** Revise the following sentences to delete the awkward references:

a. The vice president in charge of sales and the production manager are responsible for the keys to 34A and 35A, respectively.

b. The keys to 34A and 35A are in executive hands, with the former belonging to the vice president in charge of sales and the latter belonging to the production manager.

c. The keys to 34A and 35A have been given to the production manager, with the aforementioned keys being gold embossed.

d. A laser printer and an inkjet printer were delivered to John and Megan, respectively.

e. The walnut desk is more expensive than the oak desk, the former costing $300 more than the latter.

15. **Editing for Clarity (Dangling Modifiers)[LO-3]** Rewrite these sentences to clarify the dangling modifiers:

a. Full of trash and ripped-up newspapers, we left Dallas on a plane that apparently hadn't been cleaned in days.

b. Lying on the shelf, Ruby found the operations manual.

c. With leaking plumbing and outdated wiring, I don't think we should buy that property.

d. Being cluttered and filthy, Sandy took the whole afternoon to clean up her desk.

e. After proofreading every word, the letter was ready to be signed.

16. **Editing for Clarity (Noun Sequences)[LO-3]** Rewrite the following sentences to eliminate the long strings of nouns:

   a. The focus of the meeting was a discussion of the bank interest rate deregulation issue.

   b. Following the government task force report recommendations, we are revising our job applicant evaluation procedures.

   c. The production department quality assurance program components include employee training, supplier cooperation, and computerized detection equipment.

   d. The supermarket warehouse inventory reduction plan will be implemented next month.

   e. The State University business school graduate placement program is one of the best in the country.

17. **Editing for Clarity (Sentence Structure)[LO-3]** Rearrange the following sentences to bring the subjects closer to their verbs:

   a. Trudy, when she first saw the bull pawing the ground, ran.

   b. It was Terri who, according to Ted, who is probably the worst gossip in the office (Tom excepted), mailed the wrong order.

   c. William Oberstreet, in his book *Investment Capital Reconsidered*, writes of the mistakes that bankers through the decades have made.

   d. Judy Schimmel, after passing up several sensible investment opportunities, despite the warnings of her friends and family, invested her inheritance in a jojoba plantation.

   e. The president of U-Stor-It, which was on the brink of bankruptcy after the warehouse fire, the worst tragedy in the history of the company, prepared a press announcement.

18. **Editing for Clarity (Camouflaged Verbs) [LO-3]** Rewrite each sentence so that the verbs are no longer camouflaged:

   a. Adaptation to the new rules was performed easily by the employees.

   b. The assessor will make a determination of the tax due.

   c. Verification of the identity of the employees must be made daily.

   d. The board of directors made a recommendation that Mr. Ronson be assigned to a new division.

   e. The auditing procedure on the books was performed by the vice president.

19. **Completing: Designing for Readability; Media Skills: Blogging [LO-4], Chapter 7** Compare the home pages of Bloomberg (**www.bloomberg.com**) and MarketWatch (**www.marketwatch.com**), two websites that cover financial markets. What are your first impressions of these two sites? How do their overall designs compare in terms of information delivery and overall user experience? Choose three pieces of information that a visitor to these sites would be likely to look for, such as a current stock price, news from international markets, and commentary from market experts. Which site makes it easier to find this information? Why? Present your analysis in a post for your class blog.

20. **Communication Ethics: Making Ethical Choices; Media Skills: Blogging[LO-3], Chapter 7** The time and energy required for careful revision can often benefit you or your company directly, such as by increasing the probability that website visitors will buy your products. But what about situations in which the quality of your writing and revision work really doesn't stand to benefit you directly? For instance, assume that you are putting a notice on your website, informing the local community about some upcoming construction to your manufacturing plant. The work will disrupt traffic for nearly a year and generate a significant amount of noise and air pollution, but knowing the specific dates and times of various construction activities will allow people to adjust their commutes and other activities to minimize the negative impact on their daily lives. However, your company does not sell products in the local area, so the people affected by all this are not potential customers. Moreover, providing accurate information to the surrounding community and updating it as the project progresses will take time away from your other job responsibilities. Do you have an ethical obligation to keep the local community informed with accurate, up-to-date information? Why or why not?

21. **Proofreading [LO-5]** Proofread the following email message and revise it to correct any problems you find:

   Our final company orrientation of the year will be held on Dec. 20. In preparation for this sesssion, please order 20 copies of the Policy handbook, the confindentiality agreenemt, the employee benefits Manual, please let me know if you anticipate any delays in obtaining these materials.

EXPAND YOUR SKILLS

Critique the Professionals

Identify a company website that in your opinion violates one or more of the principles of good design discussed on page 158. Using whatever medium your instructor requests, write a brief analysis of the site (no more than one page), citing specific elements from the piece and support from the chapter.

Sharpening Your Career Skills Online

Bovée and Thill's Business Communication Web Search, at http://businesscommunicationblog.com/websearch, is a unique research tool designed specifically for business communication research. Use the Web Search function to find a website, video, PDF document, or PowerPoint presentation that offers advice on effective proofreading. Write a brief email message to your instructor, describing the item that you found and summarizing the career skills information you learned from it.

PART 3 | Crafting Brief Messages

Most of your communication on the job will be through brief messages, from Twitter updates and blog posts to formal letters that might run to several pages. Learning how to write these messages effectively is key to maintaining productive working relationships with colleagues and customers. Start by adapting what you already know about electronic media to the professional challenges of business communication. Then learn specific techniques for crafting routine, positive, negative, and persuasive messages—techniques that will help you in everything from getting a raise to calming an angry customer to promoting your next great idea.

LEARNING OBJECTIVES After studying this chapter, you will be able to

1 Identify the electronic media available for short messages, list nine compositional modes used in electronic media, and discuss the challenges of communicating through social media

2 Describe the use of social networks, user-generated content sites, community Q&A sites, and community participation sites in business communication

3 Describe the evolving role of email in business communication and explain how to adapt the three-step writing process to email messages

4 Describe the business benefits of instant messaging (IM) and identify guidelines for effective IM in the workplace

5 Describe the role of blogging and microblogging in business communication today and explain how to adapt the three-step writing process to blogging

6 Explain how to adapt the three-step writing process to podcasting

MyBcommLab Test your mastery of this chapter and its Learning Objectives. Visit mybcommlab.com to apply what you've learned in Document Makeovers and interactive simulation scenarios.

COMMUNICATION CLOSE-UP AT SOUTHWEST AIRLINES

Southwest Airlines's multimedia, multiauthor blog, Nuts About Southwest, features a variety of entertaining writers from around the company.

www.blogsouthwest.com

Southwest Airlines's blog is usually a love fest—or a "luv" fest, to use one of the company's favorite words. In fact, the blog's official name is Nuts About Southwest. A typical post might highlight the community service efforts of a group of employees or congratulate a team of Southwest mechanics for winning gold at the Aviation Maintenance Olympics. Devoted customers post enthusiastic comments on nearly every article, and many seem to have bonded in virtual friendship with the 30 Southwest employees who take turns writing the blog.

Bill Owen probably didn't expect a bubbly reception to a rather workaday post titled "Why can't I make reservations further in advance?" in which he calmly explained why the company usually didn't let customers make reservations as far into the future as other airlines do. But he probably wasn't expecting the response he *did* get, either. In his words, "Talk about sticking your head in a hornet's nest!" Instead of the usual dozen or so happy responses to a typical post, he received several hundred responses—many of which expressed disappointment, unhappiness, and downright anger. Customers described one scenario after another in which they had a real need to book travel further in advance than Southwest allowed, and many complained that the policy was forcing them to fly other airlines. Some Southwest employees chimed in, too, expressing their frustration with not being able to meet customer needs at times.

After bravely and patiently addressing specific customer responses over a period of several months, Owen responded with a new post titled "I blogged. You flamed. We changed." In this message, he explained that the company had listened and was changing its scheduling policies to better accommodate customer needs.

In fact, feedback from blog readers is so important that Southwest considers the blog a "customer service laboratory" that helps the company learn how to better serve its customers.[1]

Electronic Media for Business Communication

Bill Owen from Southwest Airlines (profiled in the chapter-opening Communication Close-up) might've used any number of media to convey the company's message about reservation policies. However, the choice of a blog post is significant because it represents a fundamental change in business communication and the relationships between companies and their stakeholders, a change enabled by the rapid growth of social media (see Figure 7.1).

1 LEARNING OBJECTIVE

Identify the electronic media available for short messages, list nine compositional modes used in electronic media, and discuss the challenges of communicating through social media.

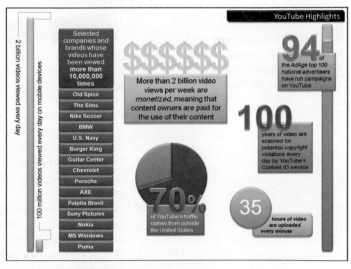

Figure 7.1 The Rise of Social Media

This infographic shows the rapid rise and wide reach of the current Big Four in social media: Facebook, Twitter, LinkedIn and YouTube.

The range of options for short business messages continues to grow with innovations in electronic and social media.

MyBcommLab

- Access this chapter's simulation entitled Crafting Messages for Electronic Media, located at mybcommlab.com.

The considerable range of electronic media available for brief business messages continues to grow as communication technologies evolve:

- **Social networking and community participation websites.** Social networking sites such as Facebook and LinkedIn, user-generated content (UGC) sites such as Flickr and YouTube, community Q&A sites, and a variety of social bookmarking and tagging sites provide an enormous range of communication tools, including status updates, user comments, personal profiles, instant messaging, and integrated email capability.
- **Email.** Conventional email has long been a vital medium for business communication, although it is replaced in many instances by other tools that provide better support for instant communication and real-time collaboration.
- **Instant messaging (IM).** IM usage now rivals email in many companies. IM offers even greater speed than email, as well as simple operation and fewer problems with unwanted messages or security and privacy problems.
- **Text messaging.** Phone-based text messaging has a number of applications in business communication, including order and status updates, marketing and sales messages, electronic coupons, and customer service.[2]
- **Blogging and microblogging.** The ability to update content quickly and easily makes blogs a natural medium when communicators want to get messages out in a hurry. Microblogging systems, including public systems such as Twitter as well as private internal systems, are also being used widely in business for everything from research to customer service to live *backchannels* during presentations and conferences (see page 485).
- **Podcasting.** You may be familiar with podcasts as the online equivalent of recorded radio or video broadcasts (video podcasts are often called *vidcasts* or *vodcasts*). Businesses are now using podcasts to replace or supplement conference calls, newsletters, training courses, and other communication activities.
- **Online video.** Now that YouTube and similar websites have made online video available to hundreds of millions of web users, video has been transformed from a fairly specialized tool to a mainstream business communication medium. More than half of the world's largest companies now have their own *branded channels* on YouTube, for example.[3]

The lines between these media often get blurry as systems expand their capabilities or people use them in new ways (see "Business Communication 2.0: Walking Around with the Entire Internet in Your Hands"). For example, Facebook Messages integrates IM, text messages, and email capabilities, in addition to being a social networking system.[4] Similarly, some people consider Twitter to be a social network, and it certainly offers some of that capability. However, because blog-like messaging is Twitter's core function, this chapter classifies it as a microblogging system.

Most of your business communication is likely to be via electronic means, but don't overlook the benefits of printed messages. (For more on formatting printed letters and memos, see Chapter 6 and Appendix A.) Here are several situations in which you should consider using a printed message rather than electronic alternatives:

Even with the widespread use of electronic media, printed memos and letters still play an important role in business communication.

- **When you want to make a formal impression.** For special messages, such as sending congratulations or condolences, the formality of printed documents usually makes them a much better choice than electronic messages.
- **When you are legally required to provide information in printed form.** Business contracts and government regulations sometimes require that information be provided on paper.
- **When you want to stand out from the flood of electronic messages.** If your audience's computers are overflowing with Twitter updates, email, and IM, sometimes a printed message can stand out enough to get noticed.
- **When you need a permanent, unchangeable, or secure record.** Letters and memos are reliable. Once printed, they can't be erased with a single keystroke or surreptitiously modified the way some electronic messages can be. Letters also offer greater security because they can be sealed in envelopes to be kept away from prying eyes.

BUSINESS COMMUNICATION 2.0

Walking Around with the Entire Internet in Your Hands

Although strictly speaking not a separate medium, the *mobile web*—the capability of connecting to the Internet with smartphones and other mobile devices—is expanding rapidly for business communication. As two indications of the growth of mobile access, YouTube serves up more than 100 million videos a day to mobile devices, and more than 40 percent of Facebook's half-billion-plus members interact with the social network using their mobile devices.[5]

Beyond just the unwired web, though, a growing variety of location-based information services help personalize communication, down to a specific time and place. For example, the ability to scan coded labels such as barcodes or the similar *Quick Response (QR) codes* attached to printed materials, products, or stores and other buildings (or the ability to pick up radio signals from new *near-field communication* tags) gives smartphone users a way to get more information—from the companies themselves and from other consumers providing reviews on social websites.[6]

The combination of mobile phone service, social networking, and GPS navigation has given rise to a new form of communication known as *location-based social networking* through services such as Foursquare and Loopt. Location-based networking promises to become an important business communication medium because mobile consumers are a significant economic force—through the purchases they make directly and through their ability to influence other consumers.

CAREER APPLICATIONS

1. When potential customers can show up on a business's doorstep with the Internet literally in their hands, what effect might this development have on the company's communication efforts?
2. How can businesses use Foursquare and other location-based services to build stronger relationships with customers and potential customers?

Again, most of your on-the-job communication is going to be through electronic media. This chapter focuses on electronic media for brief business messages, while the report writing chapters (Chapters 13 through 15) address writing for the web and wikis.

COMPOSITIONAL MODES FOR ELECTRONIC MEDIA

As electronic media continue to evolve, business professionals often need to keep learning the operational details of new systems. As you practice using electronic media in this course, focus on the principles of social media communication and the fundamentals of planning, writing, and completing messages, rather than on the specific details of any one medium or system.[7]

Fortunately, the basic communication skills required usually transfer from one system to another. You can succeed with written communication in virtually all electronic media by using one of nine *compositional modes*:

- **Conversations.** IM is a great example of a written medium that mimics spoken conversation. With IM, the ability to think, compose, and type relatively quickly is important to maintaining the flow of an electronic conversation.
- **Comments and critiques.** One of the most powerful aspects of social media is the opportunity for interested parties to express opinions and provide feedback. Sharing helpful tips and insightful commentary is also a great way to build your personal brand. To be an effective commenter, focus on short chunks of information that a broad spectrum of other site visitors will find helpful.
- **Orientations.** The ability to help people find their way through an unfamiliar system or new subject is a valuable writing skill, and a talent that readers greatly appreciate. Unlike summaries (see next item), orientations don't give away the key points in the collection of information but rather tell readers where to find those points and how to navigate through the collection.
- **Summaries.** At the beginning of an article or webpage, a summary functions as a miniature version of the document, giving readers all the key points while skipping over details (see Figure 7.2 on the next page). In some instances, this is all a reader needs. At

Communicating successfully with electronic media requires a wide range of writing approaches.

The heading "At a Glance" signals the presence of a summary.

The location of the summary in a prominent, isolated position ensures that most site visitors will see it.

The bullet points in the summary function as informative headings.

Figure 7.2   Writing Summaries for Electronic Media
This "At a Glance" sidebar serves as a helpful summary of Google's AdSense program, while also promoting the program's benefits.

the end of an article or webpage, a summary functions as a review, reminding readers of the key points they've just read.

- **Reference material.** One of the challenges of planning and writing reference material is that people typically don't read such material in a linear sense but rather search through to find particular data points, trends, or other specific elements. Making the information accessible via search engines is an important step. However, readers don't always know which search terms will yield the best results, so include an orientation and organize the material in logical ways with clear headings that promote skimming.

- **Narratives.** The storytelling techniques covered in Chapter 4 (see page 105) can be effective in a wide variety of situations. Narratives work best when they have an intriguing beginning that piques readers' curiosity, a middle section that moves quickly through the challenges that an individual or company faced, and an inspiring or instructive ending that gives readers information they can apply in their own lives and jobs.

With Twitter and other super-short messaging systems, the ability to write a compelling *teaser* is an important skill.

- **Teasers.** Teasers intentionally withhold key pieces of information as a way to pull readers or listeners into a story or other document. Teasers are widely used in marketing and sales messages, such as a bit of copy on the outside of an envelope that promises important information on the inside. In electronic media, the space limitations and URL linking capabilities of Twitter and other microblogging systems make them a natural tool for the teaser approach. Be sure that the *payoff*, the information a teaser links to, is valuable and legitimate. You'll quickly lose credibility if readers think they are being tricked into clicking through to information they don't really want.

- **Status updates and announcements.** If you use social media frequently, much of your writing will involve status updates and announcements. Being mindful of a criticism frequently leveled at personal users of social media will help you be a more effective business user of these media—post only those updates that readers will find useful, and include only the information they need.

- **Tutorials.** Given the community nature of social media, the purpose of many messages is to share how-to advice. Becoming known as a reliable expert is a great way to build customer loyalty for your company while enhancing your own personal value.

As you approach a new communication task using electronic media, ask yourself what kind of information audience members are likely to need and then choose the appropriate compositional mode. Of course, many of these modes are also used in written media, but over time you may find yourself using all of them in various electronic and social media contexts.

CREATING CONTENT FOR SOCIAL MEDIA

No matter what media or compositional mode you are using for a particular message, writing for social media requires a different approach than traditional media. As Chapter 1 points out in the discussion of Business Communication 2.0, social media change the relationship between sender and receiver. Because the relationship has changed, the nature of the messages needs to change as well. Whether you're writing a blog or posting a product demonstration video to YouTube, consider these tips for creating successful content for social media:[8]

- **Remember that it's a conversation, not a lecture or a sales pitch.** One of the great appeals of social media is the feeling of conversation, of people talking *with* one another instead of one person talking *at* everyone else. For all its technological sophistication, in an important sense social media is a new spin on the age-old practice of *word of mouth* communication. As more and more people gain a voice in the marketplace, companies that try to maintain the old "we talk, you listen" mindset are likely to be ignored in the social media landscape.
- **Write informally but not carelessly.** Write as a human being, not as a cog in a faceless corporate machine. At the same time, don't get sloppy; no one wants to slog through misspelled words and half-baked sentences, looking for a message.
- **Create concise, specific, and informative headlines.** Avoid the temptation to engage in clever wordplay with headlines. This advice applies to all forms of business communication, of course, but it is essential for social media. Readers, especially those who might potentially spread your name and your ideas around the web, don't want to spend the time and energy required to figure out what your witty headlines mean. Search engines won't know what they mean, either, so fewer people will find your content.
- **Get involved and stay involved.** Social media understandably make some businesspeople nervous because they don't permit a high level of control over messages. Companies and individual executives can and do get criticized all the time in social media. However, don't hide from criticism. Take the opportunity to correct misinformation or explain how mistakes will be fixed.
- **If you need to promote something, do so indirectly.** Just as you wouldn't hit people with a company sales pitch during an informal social gathering, refrain from blatant promotional efforts in social media. For example, instead of listing selling features of a product, tell a story about how the product changed someone's life.

A momentary lapse of concentration while using social media can cause tremendous career or company damage.

- **Be transparent and honest.** Honesty is always essential, of course, but a particular issue that has tripped up a few companies in recent years is hiding behind an online blogging persona—either a fictitious character whose writing is actually done by a corporate marketing specialist or a real person who fails to disclose an affiliation with a corporate sponsor.
- **Think before you post!** The ease and vast reach of social media present numerous etiquette, ethical, and legal risks. Individuals and companies have been sued for Twitter updates, employees have been fired for Facebook wall postings, vital company secrets have been leaked, and business and personal relationships have been strained by careless messages. Unless you are sending messages through a private channel, assume that every message will be read by people far beyond your original audience.

REAL-TIME UPDATES
Learn More by Listening to This Podcast

Violating ethical expectations in social media

Follow this discussion of how an electronics company violated the spirit of community in social commerce. Go to http://real-timeupdates.com/bct11 and click on "Learn More." If you are using MyBcommLab, you can access Real-Time Updates within each chapter or under Student Study Tools.

REAL-TIME UPDATES
Learn More by Reading This Article

Integrating social media in a global corporation

IBM's Social Computing Guidelines offer practical advice for any company that wants to incorporate social media. Go to http://real-timeupdates.com/bct11 and click on "Learn More." If you are using MyBcommLab, you can access Real-Time Updates within each chapter or under Student Study Tools.

Managing communication in a social media environment is challenging, for several reasons:

- The number of channels to monitor and manage
- The personnel costs associated with staffing social media channels
- Frequent changes in technologies and consumer behavior
- Difficulties in finding the right degree of control

Remember that Twitter is a publishing platform; unless you set your account to private, anyone can see and search for your tweets—and every public tweet from every Twitter user is being archived by the Library of Congress.[9]

MANAGING COMMUNICATION IN A SOCIAL MEDIA ENVIRONMENT

Social media offer a range of potential benefits, but managing business communication in this rapidly changing environment is not a simple task, for a number of reasons. First, the communication effort is more complex, with more internal and external channels to staff and monitor. Managers need to make sure that outgoing messages are consistent, that incoming messages are addressed in a timely fashion, that problems and opportunities don't fall through the cracks between all the various communication channels, and that all channels are used appropriately and legally.[10] Simply keeping track of all the messages a company sends out—which is required for regulatory compliance in some industries—is such a challenge that new systems are being developed to capture and archive these vast and growing communication streams.[11]

Second, with more media information channels that require attention, the cost structure of business communication can change dramatically. For instance, companies shifting some of their marketing communication efforts from traditional advertising vehicles to social media may find themselves spending less on media but more on personnel in order to have enough employees available to monitor and respond to social media traffic.[12] If companies are unable to add staff to handle social media work, they need to find ways to shift workloads around so that social media do not become an unsustainable burden.

Third, media tools and consumer behavior can evolve so quickly and so unpredictably that companies must be prepared to experiment continuously, adapt ideas that work, and abandon bad ideas—or good ideas that have outlived their usefulness. At the same time, companies must avoid slipping into a purely reactive mode, jumping on every hot idea and trend without integrating their efforts in an overall strategic framework.

Fourth, companies need to have social media guidelines for their employees that strike a balance between too much control and too little. On the one hand, companies that go too far in trying to control their messages or their employees' use of social media won't reap the full benefits. On the other hand, not enough control can lead to chaotic inefficiency, mixed messages that confuse customers, and the risk of exposing information that needs to be kept secret for strategic or even legal reasons. Xerox provides a good example of encouraging employees to take full advantage of social media while avoiding potential problems: Through training and personal coaching efforts, the company helps employees set up and manage social media channels with appropriate business purposes. As Celeste Simmons, Xerox's social program marketing manager, explains, "Our goal is to enable social media usage, not restrict it."[13]

Social Networking and Community Participation Websites

2   LEARNING OBJECTIVE

Describe the use of social networks, user-generated content sites, community Q&A sites, and community participation sites in business communication.

Social networks, online services that enable individual and organizational members to form connections and share information, have become a major force in business communication in recent years. For example, Facebook is now the most-visited website on the Internet, and a number of companies, such as Adidas, Red Bull, and Starbucks, have millions of fans on their Facebook pages.[14] This section takes a look at the business communication uses of social networks and a range of related technologies, including *user-generated content (UGC) sites, community Q&A sites,* and *community participation sites.*

SOCIAL NETWORKS

The business world currently has a complicated relationship with the idea of social networks. Some companies embrace them wholeheartedly and encourage employees to use them to reach out to customers. Other companies ban employees from using them at work, particularly networks such as Facebook that weren't originally designed for business use (unlike LinkedIn, for example). No matter what an individual company's take on the topic might be, few observers would deny that social networking is already a major force in business communication and promises to get even bigger as networks grow in size and offer more communication features. In addition to connecting hundreds of millions of consumers to each other and to the companies they buy from, social networks are likely to become the primary communication system for a significant portion of the workforce over the next few years.[15]

Businesses now use several types of social networks, including public, general-purpose networks (Facebook being the most significant of these); public, business-oriented networks (LinkedIn is the largest of these); and a variety of specialized networks. This last group includes networks that help small-business owners get support and advice, those that connect entrepreneurs with investors, and those such as Segway Social and Specialized (see next page) created by individual companies to enhance the sense of community among their customer bases. Some companies have built private social networks for internal use only. For example, the defense contractor Lockheed Martin created its Unity network, complete with a variety of social media applications, to meet the expectations of younger employees accustomed to social media and to capture the expert knowledge of older employees nearing retirement.[16]

> Business communicators make use of a wide range of social networks, in addition to the well-known Facebook.

Business Communication Uses of Social Networks

With their ability to reach virtually unlimited numbers of people through a variety of electronic formats, social networks are a great fit for many business communication needs (see Table 7.1 on page 184). In fact, a significant majority of consumers now want the businesses they patronize to use social networking for distributing information and interacting with customers—and companies that aren't active in social networking risk getting left behind.[17]

In addition to the collaboration uses discussed in Chapter 2, here are some of the key business applications of social networks:

- **Gathering market intelligence.** With hundreds of millions of people expressing themselves via social media, you can be sure that smart companies are listening. For example, *sentiment analysis* is an intriguing research technique in which companies track social networks and other media with automated language-analysis software that tries to take the pulse of public opinion and identify influential opinion makers. Social media can be "an incredibly rich vein of market intelligence," says Margaret Francis of San Francisco's Scout Labs (www.scoutlabs.com).[18]

> Social networks are vital tools for distributing information as well as gathering information about the business environment.

- **Recruiting new employees and finding business partners.** Companies use social networks to find potential employees, short-term contractors, subject-matter experts, product and service suppliers, and business partners. On LinkedIn, for example, members can recommend each other based on current or past business relationships, which helps remove the uncertainty of initiating business relationships with complete strangers.

- **Sharing product information.** Businesses don't invest time and money in social networking simply to gain fans. The ultimate goal is profitable, sustainable relationships with customers, and attracting new customers is one of the primary reasons businesses use networks and other social media.[19] However, the traditional notions of marketing and selling need to be adapted to the social networking environment because customers and potential customers don't join a network merely to be passive recipients of advertising messages. They want to participate, to connect with fellow enthusiasts, to share knowledge about products, to communicate with company insiders, and to influence the decisions that affect the products they value. This notion of interactive participation is the driving force behind **conversation marketing**, in which companies *initiate* and *facilitate* conversations in a networked community of customers and other interested parties.

> Product promotion can be done on social networks, but it needs to be done in a low-key, indirect way.

(continued on page 184)

Business Communicators Innovating with Social Media

Companies in virtually every industry have been adopting social media and experimenting with new ways to connect with customers and other stakeholders. From offering helpful tips on using products to helping customers meet each other, these companies show the enormous range of possibilities that new media bring to business communication.

General-Purpose Social Networks: Business Focus

Most everyone is familiar with Facebook these days, and thousands of companies are active on the world's most popular social network. However, a number of social networks exist just for businesses and business professionals, including LinkedIn, the largest of the business networks. Kelly Financial Resources, part of the Kelly Services staffing company, maintains a profile on LinkedIn, as do several hundred of its employees.

Specialized Social Networks: Business Focus

"Biznik is a social network designed for use by entrepreneurs and small business people to aid them in connecting and collaborating with their peers and contemporaries," explains Biznik's Andrew Lippert. A great example of these groups is The Marketing Crowd. "This Biznik group consists of professionals in the marketing profession who connect with one another and discuss issues relevant to their industry. The group is an online extension of their community, which facilitates their interaction and the development of real relationships supporting and benefiting the group members' professional careers and businesses."

Specialized Social Networks: Consumer Focus

A number of companies now host their own social networking sites, where product enthusiasts interact by sharing personal stories, offering advice, and commenting on products and company news—all brief-message functions that replace more traditional media options. For example, Specialized, a major bicycle manufacturer based in Morgan Hill, California, hosts the Specialized Riders Club (www.specializedriders.com), where customers can interact with each other and the professional riders the company sponsors. Similarly, the Segway Social network connects owners of these unique personal vehicles, including helping teams organize for Segway polo matches and other events.

User-Generated Content

Many companies now encourage *user-generated content* as a way to engage their stakeholders and provide additional value through shared expertise. The online shoe and apparel retailer Zappos, for example, invites customers to create and upload videos that communicate their experiences with Zappos and its products.

Value-Added Content via Blogging

One of the best ways to become a valued member of a network is to provide content that is useful to others in the network. The Quizzle personal finance blog offers a steady stream of articles and advice that help people manage their finances.

Value-Added Content via Online Video

Lie-Nielsen Toolworks of Warren, Maine, uses its YouTube channel to offer valuable information on choosing and using premium woodworking tools. By offering sought-after information for both current and potential customers free of charge, these videos help Lie-Nielsen foster relationships with the worldwide woodworking community and solidify its position as one of the leaders in this market. Animal Planet, Best Western, and Taco Bell are among the many other companies that make effective use of branded channels on YouTube.

Idea Generation Through Community Feedback

Starbucks has collected tens of thousands of ideas for new products and service enhancements through its community website, My Starbucks Idea. The company makes the clear request: "You know better than anyone else what you want from Starbucks. So tell us."

TABLE 7.1	Business Uses of Social Networking Technology
Business Challenge	**Example of Social Networking in Action**
Supporting customers	Allowing customers to develop close relationships with product experts within the company
Integrating new employees	Helping new employees navigate their way through the organization, finding experts, mentors, and other important contacts
Easing the transition after reorganizations and mergers	Helping employees connect and bond after internal staff reorganizations or mergers with other organizations
Overcoming structural barriers in communication channels	Bypassing the formal communication system in order to deliver information where it is needed in a timely fashion
Assembling teams	Identifying the best people, both inside the company and in other companies, to collaborate on projects
Fostering the growth of communities	Helping people with similar—or complementary—interests and skills find each other in order to provide mutual assistance and development
Solving problems	Finding "pockets of knowledge" within the organization—the expertise and experience of individual employees
Preparing for major meetings and events	Giving participants a way to meet before an event takes place, helping to ensure that the meeting or event becomes more productive more quickly
Accelerating the evolution of teams	Accelerating the sometimes slow process of getting to know one another and identifying individual areas of expertise
Maintaining business relationships	Giving people an easy way to stay in contact after meetings and conferences
Sharing and distributing information	Making it easy for employees to share information with people who may need it and for people who need information to find employees who might have it
Finding potential customers, business partners, and employees	Identifying strong candidates by matching user profiles with current business needs and linking from existing member profiles

- **Fostering brand communities.** Social networking is playing an important role in the rapid spread of **brand communities**, groups of people united by their interest in and ownership or use of particular products (see Figure 7.3). These communities can be formal membership organizations, such as the Harley Owners Group, or informal networks of people with similar interests. They can be fairly independent from the company behind the brand or can have the active support and involvement of company management.[20] A strong majority of consumers now trust their peers more than any other source of product information—including conventional advertising techniques—so formal and informal brand communities are becoming an essential information source in consumer buying decisions.[21]

Strategies for Business Communication on Social Networks

Social networks offer lots of communication options, but with those opportunities comes a certain degree of complexity. Moreover, the norms and practices of business social networking continue to evolve. Follow these guidelines to make the most of social networks for both personal branding and company communication:[22]

Communicating on social networks is complicated and requires a thoughtful, well-integrated strategy.

- **Choose the best compositional mode for each message, purpose, and network.** As you visit various social networks, take some time to observe the variety of message types you see in different parts of each website. For example, the informal status update mode works well for Facebook Wall posts but would be less effective for company overviews and mission statements.

Figure 7.3   Business Communication on Social Networks
The energy drink company Red Bull has one of the largest fan bases on Facebook, giving the company the opportunity to connect with millions of enthusiastic customers.

- **Join existing conversations, in addition to starting your own.** Search for online conversations that are already taking place. Answer questions, solve problems, and respond to rumors and misinformation.
- **Anchor your online presence in your hub.** Although it's important to join those conversations and be visible where your stakeholders are active, it's equally important to anchor your presence at your own central *hub*—a web presence that you own and control. This can be a combination of a conventional website, a blog, and a company-sponsored online community, for example.[23] Use the hub to connect the various pieces of your online "self" (as an individual or a company) to make it easier for people to find and follow you. For example, you can link to your blog from your LinkedIn profile, or automatically post your blog entries into the Notes tab on your Facebook page.
- **Facilitate community building.** Make it easy for customers and other audiences to connect with the company and with each other. For example, you can use the group feature on Facebook, LinkedIn, and other social networks to create and foster special-interest groups within your networks. Groups are a great way to connect people who are interested in specific topics, such as owners of a particular product.
- **Restrict conventional promotional efforts to the right time and right place.** Persuasive communication efforts are still valid for specific communication tasks, such as regular advertising and the product information pages on a website, but efforts to inject blatant "salespeak" into social networking conversations will usually be rejected by the audience.
- **Maintain a consistent personality.** Each social network is a unique environment with particular norms of communication.[24] For instance, as a business-oriented network, LinkedIn has a more formal "vibe" than Facebook. However, while adapting to the

expectations of each network, be sure to maintain a consistent personality.[25] The computer giant HP uses the same (fairly formal-sounding) company overview on LinkedIn and Facebook, while posting Wall updates on Facebook that are "chattier" and more in keeping with the tone expected by Facebook visitors.[26]

See "Writing Promotional Messages for Social Media" in Chapter 10 (page 298) for more tips on writing messages for social networks and other social media.

USER-GENERATED CONTENT SITES

YouTube is now a major channel for business communicators, hosting everything from product demonstration videos to television commercials.

Watching entertaining video clips on YouTube is a favorite pastime for millions of web surfers. However, YouTube, Flickr, and other **user-generated content (UGC) sites**, on which users rather than website owners contribute most or all of the content, have also become serious business tools. In fact, a recent survey suggested that video company profiles on YouTube have more measurable impact than company profiles on Facebook, LinkedIn, and other prominent sites.[27]

Video (including screencasts) is a powerful medium for product demonstrations, interviews, industry news, training, facility tours, and other uses. Moreover, the business communication value of sites such as YouTube goes beyond the mere ability to deliver content. The social aspects of these sites, including the ability to vote for, comment on, and share material, encourage enthusiasts to spread the word about the companies and products they endorse.[28]

Creating compelling and useful content is the key to leveraging the reach of social networks.

As with other social media, the keys to effective user-generated content are making it valuable and making it easy. First, provide content that people want to see and to share with colleagues. A video clip that explains how to use a product more effectively will be more popular than a clip that talks about how amazing the company behind the product is. Also, keep videos short, generally no longer than 3 to 5 minutes if possible.[29]

Second, make material easy to find, consume, and share. For example, a *branded channel* on YouTube (see the Lie-Nielsen Toolworks screen on page 183) lets a company organize all its videos in one place, making it easy for visitors to browse the selection or subscribe to get automatic updates of future videos. Sharing features let fans share videos through email or their accounts on Twitter, Facebook, and other platforms.

COMMUNITY Q&A SITES

Community Q&A sites, on which visitors answer questions posted by other visitors or by representatives of companies, are a contemporary twist on the early ethos of computer networking, which was people helping each other. (Groups of like-minded people connected online long before the World Wide Web was even created.) Community Q&A sites include dedicated customer support communities such as those hosted on Get Satisfaction (http:// getsatisfaction.com), public sites such as Yahoo! Answers (http://answers.yahoo.com) and Quora (www.quora.com), and member-only sites such as LinkedIn Answers (www .linkedin.com/answers).

Community Q&A sites offer great opportunities for building your personal brand.

Responding to questions on Q&A sites can be a great way to build your personal brand, to demonstrate your company's commitment to customer service, and to counter misinformation about your company and its products. Keep in mind that when you respond to an individual query on a community Q&A site, you are also "responding in advance" to every person in the future who comes to the site with the same question. In other words, you are writing a type of reference material in addition to corresponding with the original questioner, so keep the long time frame and wider audience in mind.

COMMUNITY PARTICIPATION WEBSITES

Community participation websites pool the inputs of multiple users in order to benefit the community as a whole.

Some of the more intriguing developments in business communication are taking place in a diverse group of **community participation websites**, designed to pool the inputs of multiple users in order to benefit the community as a whole (see Figure 7.4). These include *social bookmarking* or *content recommendation sites* such as Delicious (http://delicious.com), Digg (www.digg.com), and StumbleUpon (www.stumbleupon.com); *group buying sites*

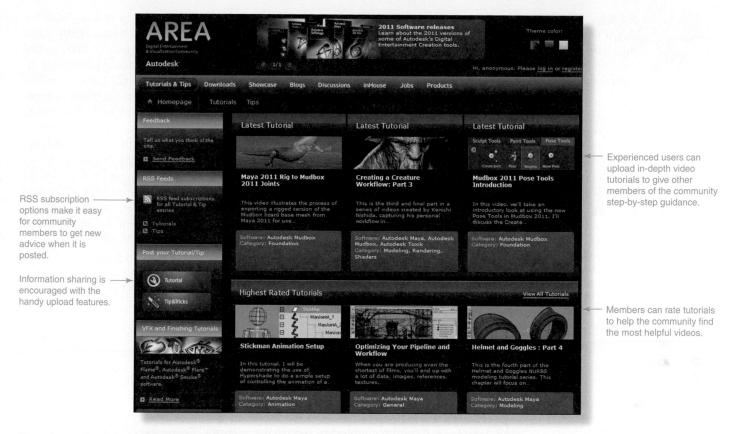

RSS subscription options make it easy for community members to get new advice when it is posted.

Information sharing is encouraged with the handy upload features.

Experienced users can upload in-depth video tutorials to give other members of the community step-by-step guidance.

Members can rate tutorials to help the community find the most helpful videos.

Figure 7.4   Community Participation Sites
The software company Autodesk hosts this community participation website for customers who work in the fields of digital entertainment and visualization. Users share quick tips, advice, and in-depth tutorials about using Autodesk software in video games, animations, product designs, and other creative projects.

such as Groupon (www.groupon.com); *crowdsourcing sites* such as InnoCentive (www .innocentive.com) that invite people to submit or collaborate on research challenges and product designs; and *product and service review* websites that compile reviews from people who have purchased products or patronized particular businesses.

As one example of the way these sites are changing business communication, Yelp (www.yelp.com) has become a major influence on consumer behavior at a local level by aggregating millions of reviews of stores, restaurants, and other businesses in large cities across the United States[30] With the voice of the crowd affecting consumer behavior, businesses need to (a) focus on performing at a high level so that customers reward them with positive reviews and (b) get involved on Yelp (the site encourages business owners to tell potential customers about themselves as well). These efforts could pay off much more handsomely than advertising and other conventional communication efforts.

Email

Email had a long head start on other forms of electronic communication and has been a primary medium for many companies. Over the years, email began to be used (and occasionally misused) for many communication tasks, simply because it was the only widely available electronic medium for written messages and millions of users were comfortable with it. However, newer tools such as instant messaging, blogs, microblogs, social networks, and shared workspaces are taking over specialized tasks for which they are better suited.[31] For example, email is usually not the best choice for conversations (IM is one of the better alternatives for this) or project management updates (blogs, wikis, and various purpose-built systems are often better for this).

3 LEARNING OBJECTIVE

Describe the evolving role of email in business communication, and explain how to adapt the three-step writing process to email messages.

REAL-TIME UPDATES
Learn More by Watching This
PowerPoint Presentation

Take a crash course in email etiquette

Learn career-enhancing tips on using email in professional settings. Go to http://real-timeupdates.com/bct11 and click on "Learn More." If you are using MyBcommLab, you can access Real-Time Updates within each chapter or under Student Study Tools.

In a sense, email can seem out of step in a world of instantaneous and open communication, where many users are accustomed to rapid-fire updates from Twitter, public forums on social networks, and never-ending streams of incoming information.[32] However, email still has compelling advantages that will keep it in steady use in many companies, even as it evolves and becomes integrated with other electronic media. First, email is universal. Anybody with an email address can reach anybody else with an email address, no matter which systems the senders and receivers are on. You don't need to join a special group or be friended by anyone in order to correspond. Second, email is still the best medium for many private, short- to medium-length messages. Unlike microblogs and IM, for instance, midsize messages are easy to compose and easy to read on email. Third, email's noninstantaneous nature is an advantage when used properly. Many business messages don't need the rapid update rates of IM or Twitter, and the implied urgency of those systems can be a productivity-sapping interruption. Email allows senders to compose substantial messages in private and on their own schedule, and it allows recipients to read those messages at their leisure.

> Email can seem a bit "old school" in comparison to social networks and other technologies, but it is still one of the more important business communication media.

PLANNING EMAIL MESSAGES

The biggest complaints about email are that there is just too much of it and too many messages are of little or no value. You can help with this problem during the planning step by making sure every message has a useful, business-related purpose, and when you're ready to distribute each message, don't "cc" (courtesy copy) additional recipients unless those other people really and truly need to receive the message. For instance, suppose you send a message to your boss and cc five colleagues because you want everyone to see that you're giving the boss some good information. Those five people now not only have to read your message but also might feel compelled to reply so that the boss doesn't think they're being negligent. Then everyone will start replying to those replies, and on and on. What should have been a single exchange between you and your boss quickly multiplies into a flurry of messages that wastes everybody's time.

> Do your part to stem the flood of email by making sure you don't send unnecessary messages or cc people who don't really need to see particular messages.

Be aware that many companies now have formal email policies that specify how employees can use email, including restrictions against using company email service for personal messages and sending material that might be deemed objectionable. In addition, many employers now monitor email, either automatically with software programmed to look for sensitive content or manually via security staff actually reading selected email messages. Regardless of formal policies, though, every email user has a responsibility to avoid actions that could cause trouble, from downloading virus-infected software to sending objectionable photographs. *Email hygiene* refers to all the efforts that companies are making to keep email clean and safe—from spam blocking and virus protection to content filtering.[33]

> Email presents considerable legal hazards, and many companies have formal email policies.

Finally, be sure to respect the chain of command. In many companies, any employee can email anyone else, including the president and CEO. However, take care that you don't abuse this freedom. For instance, don't send a complaint straight to the top just because it's easy to do so. Your efforts will be more effective if you follow the organizational hierarchy and give each person a chance to address the situation in turn.

> Respect the chain of command in your company when sending email messages.

WRITING EMAIL MESSAGES

When you approach email writing on the job, recognize that business email is a more formal medium than you are probably accustomed to with email for personal communication (see Figure 7.5). The expectations of writing quality for business email are higher than for personal email, and the consequences of bad writing or poor judgment can be much more serious. For example, email messages and other electronic documents have the same legal weight as printed documents, and they are often used as evidence in lawsuits and criminal investigations.[34]

> Business email messages are more formal than the email messages you send to family and friends.

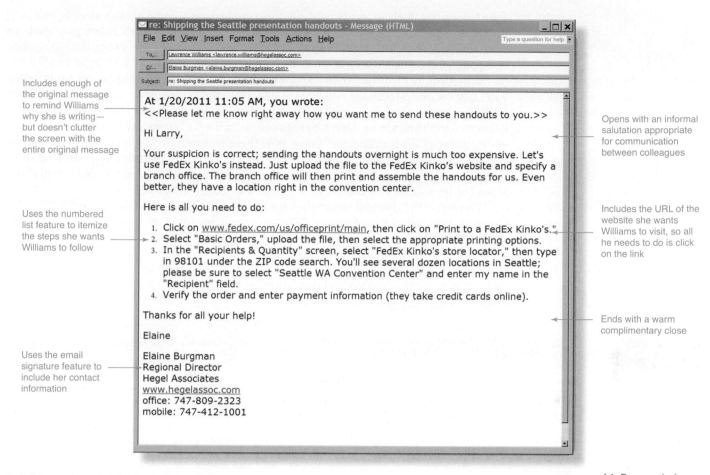

Includes enough of the original message to remind Williams why she is writing—but doesn't clutter the screen with the entire original message

Opens with an informal salutation appropriate for communication between colleagues

Uses the numbered list feature to itemize the steps she wants Williams to follow

Includes the URL of the website she wants Williams to visit, so all he needs to do is click on the link

Ends with a warm complimentary close

Uses the email signature feature to include her contact information

Figure 7.5   Email for Business Communication

In this response to an email query from a colleague, Elaine Burgman takes advantage of her email system's features to create an efficient and effective message.

MyBcommLab

Apply Figure 7.5's key concepts by revising a new document. Go to Chapter 7 in mybcommlab.com and select Document Makeovers.

The email subject line might seem like a small detail, but it is actually one of the most important parts of an email message because it helps recipients decide which messages to read and when to read them. To capture your audience's attention, make your subject lines informative and compelling. Go beyond simply describing or classifying your message; use the opportunity to build interest with keywords, quotations, directions, or questions.[35]

> A poorly written subject line could lead to a message being deleted or ignored.

For example, "July sales results" accurately describes the content of the message, but "July sales results: good news and bad news" is more intriguing. Readers will want to know why some news is good and some is bad.

In addition, many email programs display the first few words or lines of incoming messages, even before the recipient opens them. As noted by social media public relations expert Steve Rubel, you can "tweetify" the opening lines of your email messages to make them stand out. In other words, choose the first few words carefully to grab your reader's attention.[36] Think of the first sentence as an extension of your subject line.

COMPLETING EMAIL MESSAGES

Particularly for important messages, taking a few moments to revise and proofread might save you hours of headaches and damage control. The more important the message, the more carefully you need to revise. Also, favor simplicity when it comes to producing your email messages. A clean, easily readable font, in black on a white background, is sufficient for nearly all email messages. Take advantage of your email system's ability to include an **email signature**, a small file that automatically includes such items as your full name, title, company, and contact information at the end of your messages.

Think twice before hitting "Send." A simple mistake in your content or distribution can cause major headaches.

When you're ready to distribute your message, pause to verify what you're doing before you click "Send." Make sure you've included everyone necessary—and no one else. Don't click "Reply all" when you mean to click only "Reply." The difference could be embarrassing or even career threatening. Don't include people in the "cc" (courtesy copy) or "bcc" (blind courtesy copy) fields unless you know how these features work. (Everyone who receives the message can see who is on the cc line but not who is on the bcc line.) Also, don't set the message priority to "high" or "urgent" unless your message is truly urgent. And if you intend to include an attachment, be sure that it is indeed attached.

To review the tips and techniques for successful email, see Table 7.2 and "Checklist: Creating Effective Email Messages" or click on Chapter 7 at http://real-timeupdates .com/bct11.

TABLE 7.2	**Tips for Effective Email Messages**
Tip	**Why It's Important**
When you request information or action, make it clear what you're asking for, why it's important, and how soon you need it; don't make your reader write back for details.	People will be tempted to ignore your messages if they're not clear about what you want or how soon you want it.
When responding to a request, either paraphrase the request or include enough of the original message to remind the reader what you're replying to.	Some businesspeople get hundreds of email messages a day and may need reminding what your specific response is about.
If possible, avoid sending long, complex messages via email.	Long messages are easier to read as attached reports or web content.
Adjust the level of formality to the message and the audience.	Overly formal messages to colleagues can be perceived as stuffy and distant; overly informal messages to customers or top executives can be perceived as disrespectful.
Activate a signature file, which automatically pastes your contact information into every message you create.	A signature saves you the trouble of retyping vital information and ensures that recipients know how to reach you through other means.
Don't let unread messages pile up in your in-basket.	You'll miss important information and create the impression that you're ignoring other people.
Never type in all caps.	ALL CAPS ARE INTERPRETED AS SCREAMING.
Don't overformat your messages with background colors, multicolored type, unusual fonts, and so on.	Such messages can be difficult and annoying to read on screen.
Remember that messages can be forwarded anywhere and saved forever.	Don't let a moment of anger or poor judgment haunt you for the rest of your career.
Use the "return receipt requested" feature only for the most critical messages.	This feature triggers a message back to you whenever someone receives or opens your message; many consider this an invasion of privacy.
Make sure your computer has up-to-date virus protection.	One of the worst breaches of "netiquette" is infecting other computers because you haven't bothered to protect your own system.
Pay attention to grammar, spelling, and capitalization.	Some people don't think email needs formal rules, but careless messages make you look unprofessional and can annoy readers.
Use acronyms sparingly.	Shorthand such as IMHO (in my humble opinion) and LOL (laughing out loud) can be useful in informal correspondence with colleagues, but avoid using them in more formal messages.

✓ Checklist | Creating Effective Email Messages

A. Planning email messages:
- Make sure every email message you send is necessary.
- Don't cc or bcc anyone who doesn't really need to see the message.
- Follow company email policy; understand the restrictions your company places on email usage.
- Practice good email hygiene by not opening suspicious messages, keeping virus protection up to date, and following other company guidelines.
- Follow the chain of command.

B. Writing email messages:
- Remember that business email is more formal than personal email.
- Recognize that email messages carry the same legal weight as other business documents.
- Pay attention to the quality of your writing and use correct grammar, spelling, and punctuation.

- Make your subject lines informative by clearly identifying the purpose of your message.
- Make your subject lines compelling by wording them in a way that intrigues your audiences.
- Use the first few words of the email body to catch the reader's attention.

C. Completing email messages:
- Revise and proofread carefully to avoid embarrassing mistakes.
- Keep the layout of your messages simple and clean.
- Use an email signature file to give recipients your contact information.
- Double-check your recipient list before sending.
- Don't mark messages as "urgent" unless they truly are urgent.

Instant Messaging and Text Messaging

While email is here to stay as a business medium, its disadvantages—including viruses, spam, and rampant overuse—are driving many people to explore alternatives.[37] One of the most popular of those alternatives is **instant messaging (IM)**, in which users' messages appear on each other's screens instantly, without the need to be opened individually, as with email. For both routine communication and exchanges during online meetings, IM is now widely used throughout the business world and is beginning to overtake and even replace email for internal communication in many companies.[38] IM capabilities are also being embedded into other communication media, including email and social networks, further extending the reach of this convenient technology.[39] Business-grade IM systems offer a range of capabilities, including basic chat, *presence awareness* (the ability to quickly see which people are at their desks and available to IM), remote display of documents, video capabilities, remote control of other computers, automated newsfeeds from blogs and websites, and automated *bot* (derived from the word *robot*) capabilities in which a computer can carry on simple conversations.[40]

Phone-based **text messaging**, also known as *short messaging service* (*SMS*), has long been popular in other parts of the world, where it was widely available for years before it caught on in North America. Text-messaging applications in business include marketing (alerting customers about new sale prices, for example), customer service (such as airline flight status, order status, package tracking, and appointment reminders), security (for example, authenticating mobile banking transactions), crisis management (such as updating all employees working at a disaster scene), and process monitoring (alerting computer technicians to system failures, for example).[41] With text messaging being integrated into systems such as Facebook Messages and GMail, it is likely to find even more widespread use in business communication.

The advice offered here applies primarily to IM but is relevant to text messaging as well.

UNDERSTANDING THE BENEFITS AND RISKS OF IM

The benefits of IM include the possibility of rapid response to urgent messages, lower cost than phone calls, ability to mimic conversation more closely than email, and availability on a wide range of devices and systems.[42] In addition, because it more closely resembles

4 LEARNING OBJECTIVE

Describe the business benefits of instant messaging (IM), and identify guidelines for effective IM in the workplace.

IM is taking the place of email for routine communication in many companies.

Phone-based text messaging is finding more business applications as it becomes more tightly integrated with email and other communication systems.

IM offers many benefits:
- Rapid response
- Low cost
- Ability to mimic conversation
- Wide availability

one-on-one conversation, IM doesn't get misused as a one-to-many broadcast method as often as email does.[43]

Of course, wherever technology goes, trouble seems to follow. The potential drawbacks of IM include security problems (computer viruses, network infiltration, and the possibility that sensitive messages might be intercepted by outsiders), the need for *user authentication* (making sure that online correspondents are really who they appear to be), the challenge of logging messages for later review and archiving, incompatibility between competing IM systems, and *spim* (unsolicited commercial messages, similar to email spam). Fortunately, with the growth of *enterprise instant messaging* (*EIM*), or IM systems designed for large-scale corporate use, many of these problems are being overcome. However, security remains a significant concern for corporate IM systems.[44]

ADAPTING THE THREE-STEP PROCESS FOR SUCCESSFUL IM

Although instant messages are often conceived, written, and sent within a matter of seconds, the principles of the three-step process still apply:

Although you don't plan individual instant messages in the usual way, view important IM exchanges as conversations with specific goals in mind.

- **Planning instant messages.** View every IM exchange as a conversation; while you may not deliberately plan every individual statement you make or question you pose, take a moment to plan the overall exchange. If you're requesting something, think through exactly what you need and the most effective way to ask for it. If someone is asking you for something, consider his or her needs and your ability to meet them before you respond. And although you rarely organize instant messages in the sense of creating an outline, try to deliver information in a coherent, complete way that minimizes the number of individual messages required.

- **Writing instant messages.** As with email, the appropriate writing style for business IM is more formal than the style you may be accustomed to with personal IM or text messaging. You should generally avoid IM acronyms (such as *FWIW* for "for what it's worth" or *HTH* for "hope that helps") except when communicating with close colleagues. In the IM exchange in Figure 7.6, notice how the participants communicate quickly and rather informally but still maintain good etiquette and a professional tone. This style is even more important if you or your staff use IM to communicate with customers and other outside audiences.

- **Completing instant messages.** One of the biggest attractions of IM is that the completing step is so easy. You don't have to produce the message in the usual sense, and distribution is as simple as clicking the Send button. However, don't skip over the revising and proofreading tasks. Quickly scan each message before you send it, to make sure you don't have any missing or misspelled words and that your message is clear and complete.

Regardless of the system you're using, you can make IM more efficient and effective by following these tips:[45]

Understand the guidelines for successful business IM before you begin to use it.

- Unless a meeting is scheduled, make yourself unavailable when you need to focus on other work.
- If you're not on a secure system, don't send confidential information.
- Be extremely careful about sending personal messages—they have a tendency to pop up on other people's computers at embarrassing moments.
- Don't use IM for important but impromptu meetings if you can't verify that everyone concerned will be available.
- Unless your system is set up for it, don't use IM for lengthy, complex messages; email is better for those.
- Try to avoid carrying on multiple IM conversations at once, to minimize the chance of sending messages to the wrong people or making one person wait while you tend to another conversation.
- Follow all security guidelines designed to keep your company's information and systems safe from attack.

To review the advice for effective IM in the workplace, see "Checklist: Using IM Productively" or click on Chapter 7 at http://real-timeupdates.com/bct11.

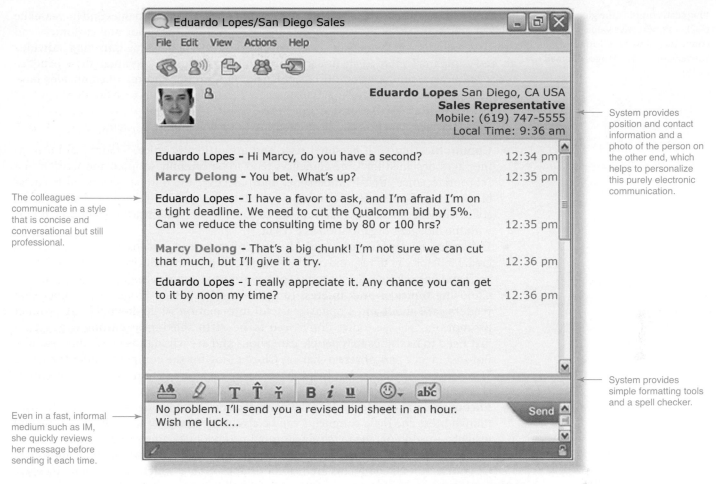

System provides position and contact information and a photo of the person on the other end, which helps to personalize this purely electronic communication.

The colleagues communicate in a style that is concise and conversational but still professional.

Even in a fast, informal medium such as IM, she quickly reviews her message before sending it each time.

System provides simple formatting tools and a spell checker.

Figure 7.6 Instant Messaging for Business Communication
Instant messaging is widely used in business, but you should not use the same informal style of communication you probably use for IM with your friends and family.

MyBcommLab

Apply Figure 7.6's key concepts by revising a new document. Go to Chapter 7 in mybcommlab.com and select Document Makeovers.

✓ Checklist | Using IM Productively

- Pay attention to security and privacy issues and be sure to follow all company guidelines.
- Treat IM as a professional communication medium, not an informal, personal tool; avoid using IM slang with all but close colleagues.

- Maintain good etiquette, even during simple exchanges.
- Protect your own productivity by making yourself unavailable when you need to focus.
- In most instances, don't use IM for confidential messages, complex messages, or personal messages.

Blogging and Microblogging

A **blog** (short for *weblog*) is an easily updatable online journal that can combine the global reach and reference value of a conventional website with the conversational exchanges of email or IM. Blogging first began to catch on in business communication because blogs provided a much easier way for senders to update and distribute fresh content and for receivers to get new information automatically (through *feeds* or *newsfeeds*, of which *RSS* is the best known). Blogging also began to take on a more personal and informal tone than

5 LEARNING OBJECTIVE

Describe the role of blogging and microblogging in business communication today, and explain how to adapt the three-step writing process to blogging.

Blogs can combine the global reach and reference value of a conventional website with the conversational exchanges of email or IM.

regular business websites, which helped "put a human face" on companies and increase the lines of communication between experts and executives on the inside and customers and other stakeholders on the outside. Another important role of blogging is making individuals and companies more easily findable through search engines.[46] With all these benefits, blogs are now a common tool in business communication, and many companies have multiple bloggers, writing either as a team on an individual blog (as with Southwest) or on their own blogs (as with Xerox, see page 21).

Good business bloggers pay close attention to several important elements:

- **Communicating with personal style and an authentic voice.** Traditional business messages designed for large audiences tend to be carefully scripted and written in a "corporate voice" that is impersonal and objective. In contrast, successful business blogs such as Southwest Airlines's are written by individuals and exhibit their personal style. Audiences relate to this fresh approach and often build closer emotional bonds with the blogger's organization as a result.
- **Delivering new information quickly.** The ability to post new material as soon as you create it helps you to respond quickly when needed (such as during a crisis), and it lets your audiences know that an active conversation is taking place.
- **Choosing topics of peak interest to audiences.** Successful blogs cover topics that readers care about and emphasize useful information while downplaying product promotion.[47] These topics don't need to be earth shaking or cutting edge—they just need to be things that people care about and are willing to spend time reading. For instance, a pair of researchers at Clorox blog for the company under the name "Dr. Laundry," dispensing helpful advice on removing stains and tackling other household chores.[48]

Most business blogs invite readers to leave comments.

- **Encouraging audiences to join the conversation.** Not all blogs invite comments, although most do. These comments can be a valuable source of news, information, and insights. In addition, the relatively informal nature of blogging seems to make it easier for company representatives to let their guards down and converse with their audiences. Of course, not all comments are helpful or appropriate, which is why many bloggers *moderate* comments, previewing them before allowing them to be displayed.

Table 7.3 offers a number of specific suggestions for successful business blogging.

UNDERSTANDING THE BUSINESS APPLICATIONS OF BLOGGING

The business applications of blogs include a wide range of internal and external communication tasks.

Blogs are a potential solution whenever you have a continuing stream of information to share with an online audience—and particularly when you want the audience to have the opportunity to respond. Here are some of the many ways businesses are using blogs:[49]

- **Anchoring the social media presence.** As noted on page 185, the multiple threads of any social media program should be anchored in a central hub that the company or individual owns and controls. Blogs make an ideal social media hub.
- **Project management and team communication.** Using blogs is a good way to keep project teams up to date, particularly when team members are geographically dispersed. For instance, the trip reports that employees file after visiting customers or other external parties can be enhanced vividly with *mobile blogs*, or *moblogs*. Thanks to the convenience of camera phones and other multimedia wireless devices, employees on the go can send text, audio, images, and video to their colleagues. Conversely, mobile employees can also stay in touch with their team blogs by using handheld devices.
- **Company news.** Companies can use blogs to keep employees informed about general business matters, from facility news to benefit updates. Blogs also serve as online community forums, giving everyone in the company a chance to raise questions and voice concerns by using the commenting feature.
- **Customer support.** Building on the tradition of online customer support forums that have been around since the earliest days of the Internet, customer support blogs answer questions, offer tips and advice, and inform customers about new products.

TABLE 7.3	Tips for Effective Business Blogging
Tip	**Why It's Important**
Don't blog without a clear plan.	Without a clear plan, your blog is likely to wander from topic to topic and fail to build a sense of community with your audience.
Post frequently; the whole point of a blog is fresh material.	If you won't have a constant supply of new information or new links, create a traditional website instead.
Make it about your audience and the issues that are important to them.	Readers want to know how your blog will help them, entertain them, or give them a chance to communicate with others who have similar interests.
Write in an authentic voice; never create an artificial character who supposedly writes a blog.	*Flogs*, or fake blogs, violate the spirit of blogging, show disrespect for your audience, and will turn audiences against you as soon as they uncover the truth. Fake blogs used to promote products are now illegal in some countries.
Link generously—but carefully.	Providing interesting links to other blogs and websites is a fundamental aspect of blogging, but make sure the links will be of value to your readers and don't point to inappropriate material.
Keep it brief.	Most online readers don't have the patience to read lengthy reports. Rather than writing long, report-style posts, write brief posts that link to in-depth reports on your website.
Don't post anything you wouldn't want the entire world to see.	Future employers, government regulators, competitors, journalists, and community critics are just a few of the people who might eventually see what you've written.
Don't engage in blatant product promotion.	Readers who think they're being advertised to will stop reading.
Take time to write compelling, specific headlines for your postings.	Readers usually decide within a couple of seconds whether to read your postings; boring or vague headlines will turn them away instantly.
Pay attention to spelling, grammar, and mechanics.	No matter how smart or experienced you are, poor-quality writing undermines your credibility with intelligent audiences.
Respond to criticism openly and honestly.	Hiding sends the message that you don't have a valid response to the criticism. If your critics are wrong, patiently explain why you think they're wrong. If they are right, explain how you'll fix the situation.
Listen and learn.	If you don't take the time to analyze the comments people leave on your blog or the comments other bloggers make about you, you're missing out on one of the most valuable aspects of blogging.
Respect intellectual property.	Improperly using material you don't own is not only unethical but can be illegal as well.
Be scrupulously honest and careful with facts.	Honesty is an absolute requirement for every ethical business communicator, of course, but you need to be extra careful online because inaccuracies (both intentional and unintentional) are likely to be discovered quickly and shared widely.
If you review products on your blog, disclose any beneficial relationships you have with the companies that make those products.	Bloggers who receive free products or other compensation from companies whose products they write about are now required to disclose the nature of these relationships.

- **Public relations and media relations.** Many company employees and even high-ranking executives now share company news with both the general public and journalists via their blogs.
- **Recruiting.** Using a blog is a great way to let potential employees know more about your company, the people who work there, and the nature of the company culture (see Figure 7.7 on page 197). Conversely, companies can scan blogs and microblogs to find promising candidates. For instance, University of Oregon student Megan Soto caught the attention of the public relations and social media agency LaunchSquad after she wrote about one of the firm's clients on her Twitter account. LaunchSquad managers then studied her blog writing, which impressed them enough to invite her to interview, after which they hired her.[50]

BUSINESS COMMUNICATION 2.0

Help! I'm Drowning in Social Media!

Anyone who has sampled today's social media offerings has probably experienced this situation: You find a few fascinating blogs, a few interesting people to follow on Twitter, a couple of podcast channels with helpful business tips, and then wham—within a few hours of signing up, your computer is overflowing with updates. Even if every new item is useful (which is unlikely), you receive so many that you can't stay ahead of the incoming flood. Between Twitter updates, newsfeeds, email, instant messaging, and social networks—not to mention a desk phone and a mobile phone—today's business professionals could easily spend their entire days just trying to keep up with incoming messages and never get any work done.

To keep social media from turning into a source of stress and information anxiety, consider these tips:

- **Understand what information you really need in order to excel in your current projects and along your intended career path.** Unfortunately, taking this advice is even trickier than it sounds because you can't always know what you need to know, so you can't always predict which sources will be helpful. However, don't gather information simply because it is interesting or entertaining; collect information that is useful or at least potentially useful.

- **Face the fact that you cannot possibly handle every update from every potentially interesting and helpful source.** You have to set priorities and make tough choices to protect yourself from information overload.
- **Add new information sources slowly.** Give yourself a chance to adjust to the flow and judge the usefulness of each new source.
- **Prune your sources vigorously and frequently.** Bloggers run out of things to say; your needs and interests change; higher-priority sources appear.
- **Remember that information is an enabler, a means to an end.** Collecting vast amounts of information won't get you a sweet promotion with a big raise. *Using* information creatively and intelligently will.

CAREER APPLICATIONS

1. How can you determine whether a social media source is worth paying attention to?
2. Should you allow any information source to interrupt your work flow during the day (even just to signal that a new message is available)? Why or why not?

- **Policy and issue discussions.** Executive blogs in particular provide a public forum for discussing legislation, regulations, and other broad issues of interest to an organization.
- **Crisis communication.** Using blogs is an efficient way to provide up-to-the-minute information during emergencies, correct misinformation, or respond to rumors.
- **Market research.** Blogs can be a clever mechanism for soliciting feedback from customers and experts in the marketplace. In addition to using their own blogs for research, today's companies need to monitor blogs that are likely to discuss them, their executives, and their products. Negative product reviews, rumors, and other information can spread across the globe in a matter of hours, and managers need to know what the online community is saying—whether it's positive or negative. *Reputation analysts* such as Evolve24 (www.evolve24.com) have developed ways to automatically monitor blogs and other online sources to see what people are saying about their corporate clients and evaluate risks and opportunities in the global online conversation.[51]
- **Brainstorming.** Online brainstorming via blogs offers a way for people to toss around ideas and build on each others' contributions.
- **Employee engagement.** Blogs can enhance communication across all levels of a company. For example, as part of a program to align its corporate culture with changes in the global beverage market, Coca-Cola solicited feedback via blog comments from more than 20,000 employees.[52]

Blogs are an ideal medium for *viral marketing*, the spread of promotional messages from one audience member to another.

- **Viral marketing.** Bloggers often make a point of providing links to other blogs and websites that interest them, giving marketers a great opportunity to have their messages spread by enthusiasts. *Viral marketing* refers to the transmission of messages in much the same way that biological viruses are transmitted from person to person. (Although the term is used frequently, viral marketing is not really an accurate metaphor. Real viruses spread from host to host on their own, whereas these virtual "viruses" are

GE uses the background image on its Twitter page to provide a small amount of customized information (in this case, the list of GE divisions whose job openings are posted via this Twitter account).

Most of the job postings include hashtag terms (see page 199) to help people who have set up recurring searches on specific job titles, cities, and other terms.

Note that while this Twitter account doesn't have a huge number of followers, anyone can find the information by searching or monitoring for hashtag terms.

Figure 7.7   Recruiting on Twitter
GE is just one of many companies now recruiting on Twitter.

spread *voluntarily* by their "hosts." The distinction is critical, because you need to give people a good reason—good content, in other words—to pass along your message.)

- **Influencing traditional media news coverage.** According to social media consultant Tamar Weinberg, "the more prolific bloggers who provide valuable and consistent content are often considered experts in their subject matter" and are often called upon when journalists need insights into various topics.[53]
- **Community building.** Blogging is a great way to connect people with similar interests, and popular bloggers often attract a community of readers who connect with one another through the commenting function.

The possibilities of blogs are almost unlimited, so be on the lookout for new ways to use them to foster positive relationships with colleagues, customers, and other important audiences.

ADAPTING THE THREE-STEP PROCESS FOR SUCCESSFUL BLOGGING

The three-step writing process is easy to adapt to blogging tasks. The planning step is particularly important if you're considering starting a blog, because you're planning an entire communication channel, not just a single message. Pay close attention to your audience, your purpose, and your scope:

- **Audience.** Except for team project blogs and other efforts with an obvious and well-defined audience, defining the target audience for a blog can be challenging. You want an audience large enough to justify the time you'll be investing but narrow enough that you can provide a clear focus for the blog. For instance, if you work for a firm that develops computer games, would you focus your blog on "hardcore" players, the type who spend thousands of dollars on super-fast PCs optimized for video games, or would you broaden the reach to include all video gamers? The decision often comes down to business strategy.

Before you launch a blog, make sure you have a clear understanding of your target audience, the purpose of your blog, and the scope of subjects you plan to cover.

Posts articles that interest her readers and encourage them to engage with her

Describes a contest conducted on her Twitter account

Posts comments from some of her Twitter followers, which helps to build the sense of community among her fans

Uses giveaways and other techniques to build her audience on various social media sites

Offers discounts to readers of her blog, which adds financial value to the sense of being part of her community

Category listing makes it easy for readers to find posts of interest

Figure 7.8   Elements of an Effective Business Blog
Amy Reed, owner of Pittsburgh's Chickdowntown clothing store, uses her blog and a variety of other social media tools to build a sense of community among her customers and to promote the store in a way that is compelling without being obtrusive.

- **Purpose.** A business blog needs to have a business-related purpose that is important to your company and to your chosen audience (see Figure 7.8). Moreover, the purpose has to "have legs"—that is, it needs to be something that can drive the blog's content for months or years—rather than focus on a single event or an issue of only temporary interest. For instance, if you're a technical expert, you might create a blog to give the audience tips and techniques for using your company's products more effectively—a never-ending subject that's important to both you and your audience. This would be the general purpose of your blog; each posting would have a specific purpose within the context of that general purpose. Finally, if you are not writing an official company blog but rather blogging as an individual employee, make sure you understand your employer's blogging guidelines. As with email and IM, more and more companies are putting policies in place to prevent employee mistakes with blogging.[54]
- **Scope.** Defining the scope of your blog can be a bit tricky. You want to cover a subject area that is broad enough to offer discussion possibilities for months or years but narrow enough to have an identifiable focus. For instance, GM's FastLane blog (http://fastlane.gmblogs.com/) is about GM automobiles only—not GM's stock price, labor negotiations, or other topics. Moreover, the scope of your blog needs to remain fairly stable so that you can build an audience over time. If you start out discussing product support but then shift to talking about your company's advertising programs, you'll probably lose readers along the way.

Careful planning needs to continue with each message. Unless you're posting to a restricted-access blog, such as an internal blog on a company intranet, you can never be sure who might see your posts. Other bloggers might link to them months or years later.

Use a comfortable, personal writing style. Blog audiences don't want to hear from your company; they want to hear from *you*. Bear in mind, though, that comfortable does not mean careless. Sloppy writing damages your credibility. Successful blog content also needs to be interesting, valuable to readers, and as brief as possible.[55] In addition, although audiences expect you to be knowledgeable in the subject area your blog covers, you don't need to know everything about a topic. If you don't have all the information yourself, provide links to other blogs and websites that supply relevant information. In fact, *media curation*, selecting content that will be useful and interesting to your target audience, in much the same way that museum curators decide which pieces of art to display, is one of the most valuable aspects of blogging.

Write blog postings in a comfortable—but not careless—style.

As with email subject lines, compelling headlines for blog posts are an essential tool to draw in readers. A headline needs to grab the reader's attention in a split second by promising something useful, surprising, challenging, or otherwise different from what the reader already knows. Headlines should be as short as possible and suggest that the information in the post will be easy to read and use. "List" headlines that cut right to the heart of something readers care about, such as "10 Reasons You Didn't Get that Promotion" or "Seven Ways to Save Money with Your Smartphone," are particularly popular among bloggers.

Completing messages for your blog is usually quite easy. Evaluate the content and readability of your message, proofread to correct any errors, and post using your blogging system's tools. Be sure to include one or more *newsfeed options* (often called RSS newsfeeds) so that your audience can automatically receive headlines and summaries of new blog posts. Whatever blogging system you are using can provide guidance on setting up newsfeeds. Finally, make your material easier to find by **tagging** it with descriptive words. Visitors to your blog who want to read everything you've written about recruiting just click on that word to see all your posts on that subject. Tagging can also help audiences locate your posts on blog trackers such as Technorati (http://technorati.com) and on social bookmarking sites.

MICROBLOGGING

A **microblog** is a variation on blogging in which messages are restricted to specific character counts. Twitter (http://twitter.com) is the best known of these systems, but many others exist. Some companies have private microblogging systems for internal use only; these systems are sometimes referred to as *enterprise microblogging* or *internal micromessaging.*[56]

Many of the concepts of regular blogging apply to microblogging as well, although the severe length limitations call for a different approach to composition. The current limit on Twitter, for instance, is 140 characters, including spaces, and if you include a URL, the limit for the rest of the message is 120 characters.

Microblog messages often involve short summaries or teasers that provide links to more information. In fact, Twitter updates are frequently used to announce or promote new posts on regular blogs. In addition, microblogs tend to have a stronger social networking aspect that make it easier for writers and readers to forward messages and for communities to form around individual writers.[57]

Like regular blogging, microblogging quickly caught on with business users and is now a mainstream business medium. Microblogs are used for virtually all of the blog applications mentioned on pages 194–197. In addition, microblogs are frequently used for providing company updates, offering coupons and notice of sales, presenting tips on product usage, sharing relevant and interesting information from experts, serving as the backchannel in meetings and presentations (see page 485 for more on backchannels), and interacting with customers individually (see Figure 7.9 on the next page).

Like Facebook and YouTube, Twitter quickly became an important business communication medium.

As microblogging evolves, the technology is gaining features that continue to enhance its value as a business communication medium. On Twitter, for instance, the ability to tag and search for specific words by means of a *hashtag* (the # symbol followed by a unique term) makes it easy for people to track topics of interest. For example, to establish a

REAL-TIME UPDATES
Learn More by Reading This Article

Tweets from the boss: CEOs on Twitter

See how a number of CEOs are putting microblogging to work for their companies. Go to http://real-timeupdates.com/bct11 and click on "Learn More." If you are using MyBcommLab, you can access Real-Time Updates within each chapter or under Student Study Tools.

Retweets a message from another Twitter user (Patagonia is active in a variety of environmental efforts, so this message reflects its core values)

Responds to queries from other Twitter users

Figure 7.9   Customer Service on Twitter
The outdoor clothing and equipment supplier Patagonia uses Twitter both as a general communication tool and as a way to interact with individual customers to answer questions and solve problems.

backchannel for a conference, you can create a unique hashtag (such as #WBSDCC, the hashtag used by Warner Brothers during a recent San Diego Comic-Con convention[58]) to help people follow messages on a particular subject. *Retweeting*, the practice of forwarding messages from other Twitter users, is the microblogging equivalent of sharing other content from other bloggers via media curation.

"Checklist: Blogging for Business" on the next page summarizes some of the key points to remember when creating and writing a business blog. You can also visit http://real-timeupdates.com/bct11 and click on Chapter 7 for the latest advice on blogging.

Podcasting

6   **LEARNING OBJECTIVE**

Explain how to adapt the three-step writing process to podcasting.

Podcasting is the process of recording audio or video files and distributing them online. Although podcasting is not used as widely as blogging and some other electronic media, it does offer a number of interesting possibilities for business communication.

UNDERSTANDING THE BUSINESS APPLICATIONS OF PODCASTING

Podcasting can be used to deliver a wide range of audio and video messages.

The most obvious use of podcasting is to replace existing audio and video messages, such as one-way teleconferences in which a speaker provides information without expecting to

✓ **Checklist**   **Blogging for Business**

- Consider creating a blog or microblog account whenever you have a continuing stream of information to share with an online audience.
- Identify an audience that is broad enough to justify the effort but narrow enough to have common interests.
- Identify a purpose that is comprehensive enough to provide ideas for a continuing stream of posts.
- Consider the scope of your blog carefully; make it broad enough to attract an audience but narrow enough to keep you focused.

- Communicate with a personal style and an authentic voice but don't write carelessly.
- Deliver new information quickly.
- Choose topics of peak interest to your audience.
- Encourage audiences to join the conversation.
- Consider using Twitter or other microblog updates to alert readers to new posts on your regular blog.

engage in conversation with the listeners. Training is another good use of podcasting; you may have already taken a college course via podcasts. Marketing departments can replace expensive printed brochures with video podcasts that demonstrate new products in action. Sales representatives who travel to meet with potential customers can listen to audio podcasts or view video podcasts to get the latest information on their companies' products. Human resources departments can offer video tours of their companies to entice new recruits. Podcasts are also an increasingly common feature on blogs, letting audiences listen to or watch recordings of their favorite bloggers. Some services can even transcribe blogs into podcasts and vice versa.[59]

ADAPTING THE THREE-STEP PROCESS FOR SUCCESSFUL PODCASTING

Although it might not seem obvious at first, the three-step writing process adapts quite nicely to podcasting. First, focus the planning step on analyzing the situation, gathering the information you'll need, and organizing your material. One vital planning step depends on whether you intend to create podcasts for limited use and distribution (such as a weekly audio update to your virtual team) or to create a **podcasting channel** with regular recordings on a consistent theme, designed for a wider public audience. As with planning a blog, if you intend to create a podcasting channel, be sure to think through the range of topics you want to address over time to verify that you have a sustainable purpose.[60]

The three-step process adapts quite well to podcasting.

As you organize the content for a podcast, pay close attention to previews, transitions, and reviews. These steering devices are especially vital in audio recordings because audio lacks the "street signs" (such as headings) that audiences rely on in print media. Moreover, scanning back and forth to find specific parts of an audio or video message is much more difficult than with textual messages, so you need to do everything possible to make sure your audience successfully receives and interprets your message on the first try.

Steering devices such as transitions, previews, and reviews are vital in podcasts.

One of the attractions of podcasting is the conversational, person-to-person feel of the recordings, so unless you need to capture exact wording, speaking from an outline and notes rather than a prepared script is often the best choice. However, no one wants to listen to rambling podcasts that take several minutes to get to the topic or struggle to make a point, so don't try to make up your content on the fly. Effective podcasts, like effective stories, have a clear beginning, middle, and end.

Plan your podcast content carefully; editing is more difficult with podcasts than with textual messages.

The completing step is where podcasting differs most dramatically from written communication, for the obvious reason that you are recording and distributing audio or video

Figure 7.10 **The Podcasting Process**
Creating a podcast requires a few easy steps, and basic podcasts can be created using free or low-cost hardware and software.

files. Particularly for more formal podcasts, start by revising your script or thinking through your speaking notes before you begin to record. The closer you can get to recording your podcasts in one take, the more productive you'll be.

Figure 7.10 illustrates the basic process of recording and distributing podcasts, but the process can vary depending on such factors as the production quality you need to achieve and whether you plan to record in a studio setting or on the go (using a mobile phone or digital recorder to capture your voice).

Most personal computers, smartphones, and other devices now have basic audio recording capability, including built-in microphones, and free editing software is available online (at http://audacity.sourceforge.net, for example). If you need higher production quality or greater flexibility, you'll need additional pieces of hardware and software, such as an audio processor (to filter out extraneous noise and otherwise improve the audio signal), a mixer (to combine multiple audio or video signals), a better microphone, more sophisticated recording and editing software, and perhaps some physical improvements in your recording location to improve the acoustics. You can find more information at Podcast Alley (www.podcastalley.com/forum) and Podcast Bunker (www.podcastbunker.com; click on "Podcasting Tips & Tools").

> For basic podcasts, your computer and perhaps even your smartphone might have the hardware you already need, and you can download free recording software.

Podcasts can be distributed in several ways, including through media stores such as iTunes, by dedicated podcast hosting services, or on a blog with content that supports the podcast channel. If you distribute your podcast on a blog, you can provide additional information and use the commenting feature of the blog to encourage feedback from your audience.[61]

For a quick review of the key points of business podcasting, see "Checklist: Planning and Producing Business Podcasts." For news on the latest developments in podcasting, visit http://real-timeupdates.com/bct11 and click on Chapter 7.

REAL-TIME UPDATES
Learn More by Watching this Video

Step-by-step advice for recording your first podcast

You'll be podcasting in no time, which includes step-by-step instructions for using the free Audacity audio recording software. Go to http://real-timeupdates.com/bct11 and click on "Learn More." If you are using MyBcommLab, you can access Real-Time Updates within each chapter or under Student Study Tools.

✓ **Checklist** | **Planning and Producing Business Podcasts**

- Consider podcasting whenever you have the opportunity to replace existing audio or video messages.
- If you plan a podcast channel with a regular stream of new content, make sure you've identified a theme or purpose that is rich enough to sustain your effort.
- Pay close attention to previews, transitions, and reviews to help prevent your audience from getting lost.

- Decide whether you want to improvise or speak from a written script.
- If you improvise, do enough planning and organization to avoid floundering and rambling in search of a point.
- Remember that editing is much more difficult to do with audio or video than with textual media and plan your content and recording carefully.

COMMUNICATION CHALLENGES AT SOUTHWEST AIRLINES

You recently joined the corporate communications group at Southwest Airlines, and one of your responsibilities is overseeing the Nuts About Southwest blog. Study the scenarios that follow and apply what you learned about blogging in this chapter to choose the best course of action.

INDIVIDUAL CHALLENGE: Pressure is building to stop the practice of moderating the blog by reviewing reader comments and selecting which ones will appear on the blog. You've received a number of adamant messages saying that Nuts About Southwest won't be a "real" blog until anyone is allowed to write any sort of comment without being "censored" by the company. However, you know that every blog is vulnerable to rude, inappropriate, and irrelevant comments, and you don't want Nuts About Southwest to turn into a free-for-all shouting match. You also want to avoid the all-too-common problem of a comment thread wandering way off topic and thereby aggravating everyone who is trying to follow the original discussion. Write a brief statement to be included in the blog's User's Guide, explaining the company's reasons for continuing to moderate comments.

TEAM CHALLENGE: One member of the blogging team is about to retire, so you need to recruit another employee to take her place on the blog. You earlier sent out a companywide email message asking interested candidates to submit a sample blog entry. Each entry should start with a brief paragraph introducing the writer. With a team of fellow students, discuss the style of these four entries. Which of the following seems like the most compatible style for Nuts About Southwest? Summarize your recommendation in an email message to your instructor.

- **From Candidate A:** Hi everyone! I'm Janice McNathan, and I couldn't be more excited to be joining the Nuts About Southwest blog cuz—hey, I'm nuts! I've worked at some goofball companies before, but nobody has as much fun as the loonies here at Southwest, so I know I'm going to have a great time writing for this blog!

- **From Candidate B:** Howdy folks, Charlie Parker here. No, not the famous jazz musician! I'm just a lowly fuel inventory auditor here in Dallas. Pretty much, I keep tabs on the fuel that goes into our planes and I make sure we get the best deals possible and all the paperwork stays in order. I can't promise any exciting stories of adventure like the pilots and other people write here, but I'll keep my eyes peeled around the airport here, and maybe something interesting will come up.

- **From Candidate C:** I'm Rick Munoz, and I've always wanted to be a professional writer. My career sort of took a detour, though, and I wound up as a programmer who works behind the scenes at the Southwest website. I really appreciate this opportunity to hone my craft, and who knows—maybe this will be the break I need to make it as a "real" writer. You'll be able to say "I knew that guy before he became famous!"

- **From Candidate D:** Excuse me while I wipe the grease off my hands; I don't want to mess up this shiny new keyboard! Hi, I'm Kristal Yan, an airframe and powerplant mechanic at Southwest's facility in Oakland, California. I've been an avid reader of Nuts About Southwest since it started, and I really look forward to participating in this wonderful worldwide conversation. I hope to provide some interesting observations from a mechanic's perspective, and I hope you'll feel free to ask any questions you may have about how we keep Southwest's planes running smoothly and safely.

MyBcommLab

If your course uses MyBcommLab, log on to **www.mybcommlab.com** to access the following study and assessment aids associated with this chapter:

- Video applications
- Real-Time Updates
- Peer review activity
- Pre/post test
- Personalized study plan
- Model documents
- Sample presentations

If you are not using MyBcommLab, you can access Real-Time Updates through **http://real-timeupdates.com/bct11**.

SUMMARY OF LEARNING OBJECTIVES

1 **Identify the electronic media available for short messages, list nine compositional modes used in electronic media, and discuss the challenges of communicating through social media.** Electronic media for short business messages include social networking and community participation websites, email, instant messaging (IM), text messaging, blogging and microblogging, podcasting, and online video. The nine compositional modes used in electronic communication are conversations, comments and critiques, orientations, summaries, reference materials, narratives, teasers, status updates and announcements, and tutorials.

Because social media technologies and expectations change the relationship between sender and receiver, the nature of the messages between them needs to change as well. Seven guidelines for effective social media content are (1) remember that it's a conversation, not a lecture; (2) write informally but not carelessly; (3) create concise, specific, and informative headlines that aren't "cute" or clever; (4) get involved and stay involved with online conversation about your products and your company; (5) if you need to promote something, do so indirectly; (6) be transparent and honest; and (7) think before you post to avoid embarrassing or expensive mistakes.

Managing business communication in the social media environment is not a simple task, for a number of reasons. First, the communication effort is more complex, with more internal and external channels to staff and monitor. Second, with more media information channels that require time and attention from company personnel, the cost structure of business communication can change dramatically. Third, media tools and consumer behavior can evolve so quickly and so unpredictably that companies must be prepared to experiment continuously, adapt ideas that work, and abandon bad ideas or good ideas that have outlived their usefulness. Fourth, companies need to have social media guidelines for their employees that strike a balance between too much control and too little.

2 **Describe the use of social networks, user-generated content sites, community Q&A sites, and community participation sites in business communication.** Businesses now use a variety of social networks, including well-known public networks such as Facebook and business-oriented networks such as LinkedIn, as well as a variety of specialized networks, single-company networks for customers, and internal employee-only networks. The business communication applications of social networks are important and diverse; major uses include collaborating, gathering market intelligence, recruiting employees and connecting with business partners, marketing, and fostering brand communities. User-generated content sites such as YouTube allow companies to host media items (such as videos) that customers and other stakeholders can view, comment on, and share. Community Q&A sites give individuals the opportunity to build their personal brands by providing expertise, and they give companies the chance to address customer complaints and correct misinformation. Community participation websites, which pool the inputs of multiple users in order to benefit the community as a whole, include social bookmarking or content recommendation sites, group buying sites, crowdsourcing sites, and product and service review websites.

3 **Describe the evolving role of email in business communication, and explain how to adapt the three-step writing process to email messages.** As the earliest widely available electronic written medium, email was applied to a broad range of communication tasks—some it was well suited for and some it wasn't. Over time, newer media such as instant messaging, blogs, and social networks have been taking over some of these tasks, but email remains a vital medium that is optimum for many private, short- to medium-length messages.

The three-step process adapts easily to email communication. One of the most important planning decisions in crafting email is making sure every message has a valuable purpose. Any key planning decision is to follow the chain of command in your organization in most instances; emailing over your boss's head is a good way to stir up resentment. When writing email messages, bear in mind that the expectations of writing quality and formality are higher in business email. Also, pay close attention to the wording of an email message's subject line; it often determines whether and when recipients open and read the message. Effective subject lines are both informative (concisely identifying what the message is about) and compelling (giving readers a reason to read the message). Completing email messages is straightforward. Proof and revise messages (particularly important ones), stick with a clean design, make use of the email signature feature, and make sure you distribute the message to the right people.

4 **Describe the business benefits of instant messaging (IM), and identify guidelines for effective IM in the workplace.** The benefits of IM include its capability for rapid response to urgent messages, lower cost than phone calls and email, ability to mimic conversation more closely than email, and availability on a wide range of devices.

As with email, business IM needs to be treated as a professional medium to ensure safe and effective communication. Be courteous in your use of IM to avoid interrupting others unnecessarily. Make yourself unavailable when you need to focus on other work, refrain from sending confidential information if you're not on a secure system, refrain from sending personal messages at work, avoid using IM for lengthy and complex messages, avoid carrying on multiple IM conversations at once, avoid IM slang with anyone other than close colleagues, and follow security guidelines.

5 **Describe the role of blogging and microblogging in business communication today, and explain how to adapt the three-step writing process to blogging.** Blogs are used in numerous ways in business today, such as for project management and team communication, company news, customer support, public relations and media relations, employee recruiting, policy and issue discussions, crisis communication, market research, brainstorming, employee engagement, viral marketing, influencing traditional media news coverage, and community building. Microblogs such as Twitter are used for many of the same purposes as conventional blogging, along with electronic coupons, sale announcements, and one-on-one customer service queries. Microblogs can also serve as the backchannel during meetings and presentations.

The three-step process adapts readily to blogging. In planning, pay particular care to defining your audience, identifying the overall purpose of your blog and specific purposes of each post, and establishing a scope that is narrow enough to be focused but broad enough to afford a steady supply of topics. In writing, be sure to write in a personal, authentic style, without slipping into overly familiar or careless writing. Completing involves the usual tasks of proofing and revising, along with the particular tasks needed to distribute your posts via newsfeeds.

6 **Explain how to adapt the three-step writing process to podcasting.** Although you'll be recording audio or video when creating podcasts, rather than writing messages, using the three-step process is an effective way to develop podcasts. Focus the planning step on analyzing the situation, gathering the information you'll need, and organizing your material. If you plan to create a series of podcasts on a given theme (the equivalent of starting a radio or TV show), make sure you've identified a range of topics extensive enough to keep your podcasts going over time. As you organize and begin to think about the words or images you'll use as content, pay close attention to previews, transitions, and reviews so that audiences don't get lost while listening or watching. Before you record, think through what you plan to say or shoot so that you don't ramble while trying to make your key points. Finally, consider the necessary level of production quality; good-quality podcasts usually require some specialized hardware and software.

KEY TERMS

blog An easily updatable online journal; short for *weblog*

brand communities Groups of people united by their interest in and ownership or use of particular products

community participation websites Websites designed to pool the inputs of multiple users in order to benefit the community as a whole

community Q&A sites Websites on which visitors answer questions posted by other visitors or by representatives of companies

conversation marketing Communication in which companies initiate and facilitate conversations in a networked community of customers and other interested parties

email signature A small file that automatically includes such items as your full name, title, company, and contact information at the end of your messages

instant messaging (IM) Communication system in which users' messages appear on each other's screens instantly, without the need to be opened individually, as with email

microblog A variation on blogging in which messages are restricted to specific character counts; Twitter is the best-known example

podcasting The process of recording audio or video files and distributing them online

podcasting channel Series of regular recordings on a consistent theme

social networks Online services that enable individual and organizational members to form connections and share information

tagging Attaching descriptive terms to blog posts and other articles to facilitate searching

text messaging Phone-based messaging capability, also known as *short messaging service (SMS)*

user-generated content (UGC) sites Websites on which users rather than website owners contribute most or all of the content

TEST YOUR KNOWLEDGE

To review chapter content related to each question, refer to the indicated Learning Objective.

1. What are the situations in which a printed memo or letter might be preferable to an electronic message? [LO-1]
2. How do the compositional modes of orientations, summaries, and teasers differ? [LO-1]
3. How can businesses make use of social networks for business communication? [LO-2]
4. What does it mean to anchor your social media presence in a hub? [LO-2]
5. Why are subject lines important in email messages? [LO-3]
6. What advantages does email maintain over other electronic media? [LO-3]
7. What are the benefits of using IM in business communication? [LO-4]
8. Why does a personal style of writing help blogs build stronger relationships with audiences? [LO-5]
9. How can blogs help with viral marketing efforts? [LO-5]
10. Why is it important to have a long-term, sustainable purpose in mind before you launch a blog or podcast channel? [LO-5], [LO-6]

APPLY YOUR KNOWLEDGE

To review chapter content related to each question, refer to the indicated Learning Objective.

1. Given the strict limits on length, should all your microblogging messages function as teasers that link to more detailed information on a blog or website? Why or why not? [LO-1]
2. Is leveraging your connections on social networks for business purposes ethical? Why or why not? [LO-2]
3. If one of the benefits of blogging and microblogging is the personal, intimate style of writing, is it a good idea to limit your creativity by adhering to conventional rules of grammar, spelling, and mechanics? Why or why not? [LO-5]
4. In your work as a video game designer, you know that eager players search the web for any scrap of information they can find about upcoming releases. In fact, to build interest, your company's public relations department carefully doles out small bits of information in the months before a new title hits the market. However, you and others in the company are also concerned about competitors getting their hands on all this "prerelease" information. If they learn too much too soon, they can use the information to improve their own products more quickly. You and several other designers and programmers maintain blogs that give players insights into game design techniques and that occasionally share tips and tricks. You have thousands of readers, and you believe that your blog helps build customer loyalty. The company president wants to ban blogging entirely so that bloggers don't accidentally share too much prerelease information about upcoming games. Would this be a wise move? Why or why not? [LO-5]
5. Is the communication power of Twitter limited to 140-character messages? Explain your response. [LO-5]

PRACTICE YOUR SKILLS

Message for Analysis 7.A: Media Skills: IM, Creating a Businesslike Tone [LO-4]

Review this IM exchange and explain how the customer service agent could have handled the situation more effectively.

Agent: Thanks for contacting Home Exercise Equipment. What's up?

Customer: I'm having trouble assembling my home gym.

Agent: I hear that a lot! LOL

Customer: So is it me or the gym?

Agent: Well, let's see <g>. Where are you stuck?

Customer: The crossbar that connects the vertical pillars doesn't fit.

Agent: What do you mean doesn't fit?

Customer: It doesn't fit. It's not long enough to reach across the pillars.

Agent: Maybe you assembled the pillars in the wrong place. Or maybe we sent the wrong crossbar.

Customer: How do I tell?

Agent: The parts aren't labeled so could be tough. Do you have a measuring tape? Tell me how long your crossbar is.

Message for Analysis 7.B: Media Skills: Blogging, Creating a Businesslike Tone [LO-5]

Revise this blog post based on what you've learned in this chapter.

[headline]

We're DOOMED!!!!!

[post]

I was at the Sikorsky plant in Stratford yesterday, just checking to see how things were going with the assembly line retrofit we did for them last year. I think I saw the future, and it ain't pretty. They were demo'ing a prototype robot from Motoman that absolutely blows our stuff out of the water. They wouldn't let me really see it, but based on the 10-second glimpse I got, it's smaller, faster, and more maneuverable than any of our units. And when I asked about the price, the guy just grinned. And it wasn't the sort of grin designed to make me feel good.

I've been saying for years that we need to pay more attention to size, speed, and maneuverability instead of just relying on our historical strengths of accuracy and payload capacity, and you'd have to be blind not to agree that this experience proves me right. If we can't at least show a design for a better unit within two or three months, Motoman is going to lock up the market and leave us utterly in the dust.

Believe me, being able to say "I told you so" right now is not nearly as satisfying as you might think!!

Message for Analysis 7.C: Media Skills: Podcasting, Planning: Outlining Your Content [LO-6]

To access this message, visit http://real-timeupdates.com/bct11, click on "Student Assignments," select Chapter 7, and then select page 206, Message 7.C. and listen to this podcast. Identify at least three ways in which the podcast could be improved and draft a brief email message that you could send to the podcaster, giving your suggestions for improvement.

Exercises

Active links for all websites in this chapter can be found on MyBcommLab; see your User Guide for instructions on accessing the content for this chapter. Each activity is labeled according to the primary skill or skills you will need to use. To review relevant chapter content, you can refer to the indicated Learning Objective. In some instances, supporting information will be found in another chapter, as indicated.

1. **Collaboration: Working in Teams; Planning: Selecting Media [Chapter 2] [LO-1]** For each of these message needs, choose a medium that you think would work effectively and explain your choice. (More than one medium could work in some cases; just be able to support your particular choice.)
   a. A technical support service for people trying to use their digital music players
   b. A message of condolence to the family of an employee who passed away recently
   c. A message from the CEO of a small company to the employees of the firm, explaining that she is leaving the company to join a competitor
   d. A series of observations on the state of the industry, intended mostly for professionals within the industry
   e. A series of messages, questions, and answers surrounding the work of a team working on a confidential company project

2. **Media Skills: Social Networking [LO-2]** Pick a company in any industry that interests you. Imagine you are doing strategic planning for this firm, and identify one of your company's key competitors. (Hint: You can use the free listings on www.hoovers.com to find several top competitors for most medium and large companies in the United States; click on the Competition tab.) Now search through social media sources to find three strategically relevant pieces of information about this competitor, such as the hiring of a new executive, the launch of a major new product, or a significant problem of some kind. In a post on your class blog, identify the information you found and the sources you used. (If you can't find useful information, pick another firm or try another industry.)

3. **Media Skills: Writing Email Subject Lines [LO-3]** Using your imagination to make up whatever details you need, revise the following email subject lines to make them more informative:
   a. New budget figures
   b. Marketing brochure—your opinion
   c. Production schedule

4. **Media Skills: Email [LO-3]** The following email message contains numerous errors related to what you've learned about planning and writing business messages. Using the information it contains, write a more effective version.

TO: Felicia August <]fb_august@evertrust.com>]
SUBJECT: Those are the breaks, folks

Some of you may not like the rules about break times; however, we determined that keeping track of employees while they took breaks at times they determined rather than regular breaks at prescribed times was not working as well as we would have liked it to work. The new rules are not going to be an option. If you do not follow the new rules, you could be docked from your pay for hours when you turned up missing, since your direct supervisor will not be able to tell whether you were on a "break" or not and will assume that you have walked away from your job. We cannot be responsible for any errors that result from your inattentiveness to the new rules. I have already heard complaints from some of you and I hope this memo will end this issue once and for all. The decision has already been made.

Starting Monday, January 1, you will all be required to take a regular 15-minute break in the morning and again in the afternoon, and a regular thirty-minute lunch at the times specified by your supervisor, NOT when you think you need a break or when you "get around to it."

There will be no exceptions to this new rule!

Felicia August
Manager
Billing and accounting

5. **Media Skills: IM, Creating a Businesslike Tone [LO-4]** Your firm, which makes professional paint sprayers, uses IM extensively for internal communication and frequently for external communication with customers and suppliers. Several customers have recently forwarded copies of messages they've received from your staff, asking if you know how casually some employees are treating this important medium. You decide to revise parts of several messages to show your staff a more appropriate writing style. Rewrite these sentences, making up any information you need, to convey a more businesslike style and tone. (Look up the acronyms online if you need to.)
   a. IMHO, our quad turbo sprayer is best model 4U.
   b. No prob; happy2help!
   c. FWIW, I use the L400 myself & it rocks
   d. Most cust see 20–30% reduct in fumes w/this sprayer—of course, YMMV.

6. **Media Skills: Blogging, Creating a Businesslike Tone [LO-5]** The members of the project team of which you are the leader have enthusiastically embraced blogging as a communication medium. Unfortunately, as emotions heat up during the project, some of the blog posts are getting too casual, too personal, and even sloppy. Because your boss and other managers around the company also read this project blog, you don't want the team to look unprofessional in anyone's eyes. Revise the following blog post so that it communicates in a more businesslike manner while retaining the informal, conversational tone of a blog. (Be sure to correct any spelling and punctuation mistakes you find as well.)

Well, to the profound surprise of absolutely nobody, we are not going to be able meet the June 1 commitment to ship 100 operating tables to Southeast Surgical Supply. (For those of you who have been living in a cave the past six month, we have been fighting to get our hands on enough high-grade chromium steel to meet our production schedule.) Sure enough, we got news, this morning that we will only get enough for 30 tables. Yes, we look like fools for not being able to follow through on promises we made to the customer, but no, this didn't have to happpen. Six month's ago, purchasing warned us about shrinking supplies and suggested we advance-buy as much as we would need for the next 12 months, or so. We naturally tried to followed their advice, but just as naturally were shot down by the bean counters at corporate who trotted out the policy about never buying more than three months worth of materials in advance. Of course, it'll be us—-not the bean counters who'll take the flak when everybody starts asking why revenues are down next quarter and why Southeast is talking to our friends at Crighton Manuf!!! Maybe, some day this company will get its head out of the sand and realize that we need to have some financial flexibility in order to compete.

7. **Media Skills: Microblogging [LO-5]** Busy knitters can go through a lot of yarn in a hurry, so most keep a sharp eye out for sales. You're on the marketing staff of Knitting-Warehouse, and you like to keep your loyal shoppers up to date with the latest deals. Visit the "Sale Items!" section of the Knitting-Warehouse website at **www.knitting-warehouse.com**, select any product that catches your eye, and write a Twitter update the describes the product and the sale. Be sure to include a link back to the website so your Twitter followers can learn more. (Unless you are working on a private Twitter account that is accessible only by your instructor and your classmates, don't actually send this Twitter update. Email it to your instructor instead.)

8. **Media Skills: Podcasting, Planning: Outlining Your Content [LO-6]** You began recording a weekly podcast to share information with your large and far-flung staff. After a month, you ask for feedback from several of your subordinates, and you're disappointed to learn that some people stopped listening to the podcast after the first couple weeks. Someone eventually admits that many staffers feel the recordings are too long and rambling, and the information they contain isn't valuable enough to justify the time it takes to listen. You aren't pleased, but you want to improve. An assistant transcribes the introduction to last week's podcast so you can review it. You immediately see two problems. Revise the introduction based on what you've learned in this chapter.

So there I am, having lunch with Selma Gill, who just joined and took over the Northeast sales region from Jackson Stroud. In walks our beloved CEO with Selma's old boss at Uni-Plex; turns out they were finalizing a deal to co-brand our products and theirs and to set up a joint distribution program in all four domestic regions. Pretty funny, huh? Selma left Uni-Plex because she wanted to sell our products instead, and now she's back selling her old stuff, too. Anyway, try to chat with her when you can; she knows the biz inside and out and probably can offer insight into just about any sales challenge you might be running up against. We'll post more info on the co-brand deal next week; should be a boost for all of us. Other than those two news items, the other big news this week is the change in commission reporting. I'll go into the details in a minute, but when you log onto the intranet, you'll now see your sales results split out by product line and industry sector. Hope this helps you see where you're doing well and where you might beef things up a bit. Oh yeah, I almost forgot the most important bit. Speaking of our beloved CEO, Thomas is going to be our guest of honor, so to speak, at the quarterly sales meeting next week and wants an update on how petroleum prices are affecting customer behavior. Each district manager should be ready with a brief reports. After I go through the commission reporting scheme, I'll outline what you need to prepare.

EXPAND YOUR SKILLS

Locate the YouTube channel page of any company you find interesting and assess its social networking presence using the criteria for effective communication discussed in this chapter and your own experience using social media. What does this company do well with its YouTube channel? How might it improve? Using whatever medium your instructor requests, write a brief analysis of the company's YouTube presence (no more than one page), citing specific elements from the piece and support from the chapter.

Sharpening Your Career Skills Online

Bovée and Thill's Business Communication Web Search, at **http://businesscommunicationblog.com/websearch**, is a unique research tool designed specifically for business communication research. Use the Web Search function to find a website, video, PDF document, podcast, or PowerPoint presentation that offers advice on using social media in business. Write a brief email message to your instructor, describing the item that you found and summarizing the career skills information you learned from it.

CASES

SOCIAL NETWORKING SKILLS

1. Media Skills: Social Networking; Media Skills: Microblogging [LO-2] [LO-5]   Foursquare (http://foursquare.com/) is one of the leading providers of location-based social networking services. Millions of people use Foursquare for social engagement and friendly competition, and many business owners are starting to recognize the marketing potential of having people that are on the move in local areas, broadcasting their locations and sharing information about stores, restaurants, clubs, and other merchants. (Review the highlight box "Walking Around with the Entire Internet in Your Hands" on page 177 for more on the mobile-local web.)

Your task: Review the information on Foursquare's Merchant Platform at http://foursquare.com/business/venues. Now write four brief messages, no more than 140 characters long (including spaces). The first should summarize the benefits to stores, restaurants, and other "brick and mortar" businesses of participating in Foursquare, and the next three messages should convey three compelling points that support that overall benefit statement. If your class is set up with private Twitter accounts, use your private account to send your messages. Otherwise, email your four messages to your instructor or post them on your class blog, as your instructor directs.

SOCIAL NETWORKING SKILLS

2. Media Skills: Social Networking; Online Etiquette [LO-2], Chapter 2   Employees who take pride in their work are a practically priceless resource for any business. However, pride can sometimes manifest itself in negative ways when employees come under criticism—and public criticism is a fact of life in social media. Imagine that your company has recently experienced a rash of product quality problems, and these problems have generated some unpleasant and occasionally unfair criticism on a variety of social media sites. Someone even set up a Facebook page specifically to give customers a place to vent their frustrations.

You and your public relations team jumped into action, responding to complaints with offers to provide replacement products and help customers who have been affected by the quality problems. Everything seemed to be going as well as could be expected, when you were checking a few industry blogs one evening and discovered that a couple of engineers in your company's product design lab have been responding to complaints on their own. They identified themselves as company employees and defended their product design, blaming the company's production department and even criticizing several customers for lacking the skills needed to use such a sophisticated product. Within a matter of minutes, you see their harsh comments being retweeted and reposted on multiple sites, only fueling the fire of negative feedback against your firm. Needless to say, you are horrified.

Your task: You manage to reach the engineers by private message and tell them to stop posting messages, but you realize you have a serious training issue on your hands. Write a post for the internal company blog that advises employees on how to respond appropriately when they are representing the company online. Use your imagination to make up any details you need.

SOCIAL NETWORKING SKILLS
PRESENTATION SKILLS

3. Media Skills: Social Networking; Media Skills: Presentations [LO-2], Chapters 16–17   Daniel Gordon, the fourth-generation jeweler who is CEO of Samuel Gordon Jewelers in Oklahoma City, has turbocharged the century-old company with social media. During some of the roughest economic times in memory, the company's revenues and foot traffic have grown steadily while its advertising costs have dropped by 90 percent. Gordon is an active social media user, using a variety of media tools to educate jewelry buyers, let customers know about new products, and guide customers through the process of selecting wedding rings and other significant jewelry purchases.

Your task: With a team of classmates, study the company's website (www.samuelgordons.com/) and its social media presence (you can find various social media links on the website). You can read more about the company's social media strategy by visiting http://real-timeupdates.com/bct11, clicking on "Student Assignments" and selecting "Chapter 7 Case 3." Now identify a business near your college that could benefit from a similar social media strategy. Devise a social media strategy that could help this company expand its customer base and forger stronger links with the local community. Prepare a brief class presentation that describes the business and explains your proposed strategy. (Your instructor may ask you to undertake this as a service project, in which you meet with the company owner and present your proposed social media strategy.)

SOCIAL NETWORKING SKILLS

4. Media Skills: Social Networking [LO-2]   Social media can be a great way to, well, socialize during your college years, but employers are increasingly checking up on the online activities of potential hires to avoid bringing in employees who may reflect poorly on the company.

Your task: Team up with another student and review each other's public presence on Facebook, Twitter, Flickr, blogs, and any other website that an employer might check during the interview and recruiting process. Identify any photos, videos, messages, or other material that could raise a red flag when an employee is evaluating a job candidate. Write your teammate an email message that lists any risky material.

EMAIL SKILLS

5. Media Skills: Email; Career Management: Personal Branding [LO-3], Prologue   You've been laboring all summer at an internship, learning how business is conducted. You've done work nobody else wanted to do, but that's okay. Even the smallest tasks can make a good impression on your future résumé.

This morning, your supervisor asks you to write a description of the job you've been doing. "Include everything, even the filing," she suggests, "and address it to me in an email message." She says a future boss might assign such a task prior to a performance review. "You can practice describing your work without exaggeration—or too much modesty," she says, smiling.

Your task: Using good techniques for short messages and relying on your real-life work experience, write an email that will impress your supervisor. Make up any details you need.

EMAIL SKILLS   PORTFOLIO BUILDER

6. Media Skills: Email; Message Strategies: Marketing and Sales Messages [LO-3] Chapter 10 One-quarter of all motor vehicle accidents that involve children under age 12 are side-impact crashes—and these crashes result in higher rates of injuries and fatalities than those with front or rear impacts.[62]

Your task: You work in the consumer information department at Britax, a leading manufacturer of car seats. Your manager has asked you to prepare an email message that can be sent out whenever parents request information about side-impact crashes and the safety features of Britax seats. Start by researching side-impact crashes at www.britaxusa.com (click on "Safety Center" and then "Side Impact Protection Revealed"). Write a three-paragraph message that explains the seriousness of side-impact crashes, describes how injuries and fatalities can be minimized in these crashes, and describes how Britax's car seats are designed to help protect children in side-impact crashes.

EMAIL SKILLS

7. Media Skills: Email [LO-3] The physical difference between the women who model clothes and women who buy them has long been a point of contention for shoppers—and a point of concern for health advocates who say that top fashion models have become too thin in recent years. Not only is the super-thin look unhealthy for the models, but critics says it encourages eating disorders among girls and women who aspire to look like them.

Some industry insiders admit that the images portrayed in fashion advertising are often unrealistic. Designer and television host Tim Gunn says the problem starts with an unrealistic assumption in the illustration stage, when designers are sketching new clothes. "The way in which we illustrate [a model's body] is seven heads high, which isn't normal. We're always striving to have the same look of the illustration on the runway, and it's impossible. You have a few—forgive me—freaky people who can approximate that size and shape, but this look is not part of the real world."

Models weren't always much thinner than the general population, and in at least a few instances, the public and the fashion industry have rebelled about these unreal body images. For example, several years ago, La Maison Simons, a Canadian retailer, pulled its back-to-school catalog following complaints that its models were too thin; the company replaced the catalog and issued an apology. Ken Downing, fashion director at the upscale American retailer Neiman-Marcus, explains, "Any retailer has to consider [its] customer and who [it's] trying to appeal to. There are models of all shapes and sizes, and the people who do the advertising and marketing really have to be conscious that they're portraying healthy, beautiful women of many ages and many colors from many backgrounds."[63]

Your task: Imagine that you're the director of catalog operations at La Maison Simons, and you want to make sure that the embarrassing episode with the back-to-school catalog isn't repeated. Write a brief email to the catalog staff, outlining the company's new policy of using only models with healthy body mass indexes. (Make up any information you need to draft the message.) You can visit the company's website, at www.simons.ca, to learn more about its products, and you can research body mass index at a variety of health-related websites.

EMAIL SKILLS

8. Media Skills: Email [LO-3] You certainly appreciate your company's "virtual team" policy of letting employees live wherever they want and using technology to communicate and collaborate. The company is headquartered in a large urban area, but you get to live in the mountains, only a step or two away from some of the best fly fishing in the world. Most of the time, this approach to work couldn't get any better.

However, the lack of face-to-face contact with your colleagues definitely has disadvantages. For example, when a teammate seems to be upset about something, you wish you could go for a walk with the person and talk it out rather than rely on phone calls, email, or IM. In the past couple weeks, Chris Grogan, the graphic designer working with you on a new e-commerce website project, seems to be complaining about everything. His negative attitude is starting to wear down the team's enthusiasm at a critical point in the project. In particular, he has complained several times that no one on the team seems to care about his design work which is rarely mentioned in team teleconferences, and no one asks him about it. That part is true, actually, but the reason is that there is nothing wrong with his work—some critical technical issues unrelated to the graphic design are consuming everyone's attention.

Your task: After a couple unsuccessful attempts at encouraging Grogan over the phone, you decide to write a brief email message to assure him of the importance of his work on this project and the quality of his efforts. Let him know that graphic design is a critical part of the project's success and that as soon as those technical issues are resolved and the project is completed, everyone will have a chance to appreciate his contribution to the project. Make up whatever details you need to craft your message.

EMAIL SKILLS

9. Media Skills: Email; Message Strategies: Negative Messages [LO-3] Chapter 9 Many companies operate on the principle that the customer is always right, even when the customer *isn't* right. They take any steps necessary to ensure happy customers, lots of repeat sales, and a positive reputation among potential buyers. Overall, this is a smart and successful approach to business. However, most companies eventually encounter a nightmare customer who drains so much time, energy, and profits that the only sensible option is to refuse the customer's business. For example, the nightmare customer might be someone who constantly berates you and your employees, repeatedly makes outlandish demands for refunds and discounts, or simply requires so much help that you not only lose money on this person but also no longer have enough time to help your other customers. "Firing" a customer is an unpleasant step that should be taken only in the most extreme cases and only after other remedies have been attempted (such as talking with the customer about the problem), but it is sometimes necessary for the well-being of your employees and your company.

Your task: If you are currently working or have held a job in the recent past, imagine that you've encountered just such a customer. If you don't have job experience to call on, imagine that you work in a retail location somewhere around campus or in your neighborhood. Identify the type of behavior this imaginary customer exhibits and the reasons the behavior can no longer be accepted. Write a brief email message to the customer to explain that you will no longer be able to accommodate him or her as a customer. Calmly explain why you have had to reach this difficult decision. Maintain a professional tone and keep your emotions in check.

EMAIL SKILLS   TEAM SKILLS

10. Media Skills: Email; Collaboration: Team Projects [LO-3] Chapter 2 For the first time in history (aside from special situations such as major wars), more than half—51 percent—of all U.S. adult women now live without a spouse. (In other words, they live alone, with roommates, or as part of an unmarried couple.) Twenty-five percent have never married, and 26 percent are divorced, widowed, or married but living apart from their spouses. In the 1950s and into the 1960s, only 40 percent of women lived without a spouse, but every decade since, the percentage has increased. In your work as a consumer trend specialist for Seymour Powell (www.seymourpowell.com), a product design firm based in London that specializes in the home, personal, leisure, and transportation sectors, it's your business to recognize and respond to demographic shifts such as this.

Your task: With a small team of classmates, brainstorm possible product opportunities that respond to this trend. In an email message to be sent to the management team at Seymour Powell, list your ideas for new or modified products that might sell well in a society in which more than half of all adult women live without a spouse. For each idea, provide a one-sentence explanation of why you think the product has potential.[64]

IM SKILLS

11. Media Skills: IM; Compositional Modes: Tutorials [LO-1] [LO-4] High-definition television can be a joy to watch—but, oh, what a pain to buy. The field is littered with competing technologies and arcane terminology that is meaningless to most consumers. Moreover, it's nearly impossible to define one technical term without invoking two or three others, leaving consumers swimming in an alphanumeric soup of confusion. The manufacturers themselves can't even agree on which of the *18* different digital TV formats truly qualify as "high definition." As a sales support manager for Crutchfield, www.crutchfield .com, a leading online retailer of audio and video systems, you understand the frustration buyers feel; your staff is deluged daily by their questions.

Your task: To help your staff respond quickly to consumers who ask questions via Crutchfield's online IM chat service, you are developing a set of "canned" responses to common questions.

When a consumer asks one of these questions, a sales advisor can simply click on the ready-made answer. Start by writing concise, consumer-friendly definitions of the following terms: *resolution*, *HDTV*, *1080p*, and *HDMI*. Explore the Learning Center on the Crutchfield website to learn more about these terms. Answers .com and CNET.com are two other handy sources.[65]

IM SKILLS

12. Media Skills: IM; Collaboration: Working in Teams [LO-4] Instant messaging is frequently used in customer support situations where a customer needs help selecting, using, or troubleshooting a problem. In this activity, two two-person teams will use IM to simulate problem solving by helping classmates discuss important academic or life decisions. One team will be the "clients," who are struggling with the decisions, and the other will be the "advisors," who coach them toward solutions.

Your task: First choose a free IM/chat system such as Google Talk, Facebook chat, or any other system on which you can communicate privately in real time. Now choose two decision-making scenarios from your school or personal lives, such as deciding on a major, choosing whether to work during the upcoming summer or attend class, figuring out where to live next year, or any other decision that you're willing to have the group discuss and then later discuss in front of the whole class. Choose decisions that are complicated enough to support an IM conversation lasting at least five minutes.

Decide which team will be the advisors and which will be the clients and move the teams to separate locations (make sure you have Internet access). In each team, one person will be the communicator first, and the other will be the observer, monitoring how well the IM conversation progresses and making note of any confusion, inefficiencies, or other issues.

When you're set up in your separate locations, begin the IM exchange with the communicator from the client team asking the advisor for help with a decision. The advisor should ask probing questions to find out what the client really wants to gain from the decision and help him or her work through the various alternatives. Discuss the decision scenario for at least five minutes. The observers should take notes but should not be involved in the IM exchange in any way.

After working through one of the decision scenarios, swap roles inside each team so that the observer becomes the communicator and vice versa. Now work through the second decision scenario.

Afterward, meet as a full team after the role playing and compare notes about how well each conversation went, how well the technology supported the communicators' needs, and what you might do differently in a business context to ensure smooth communication and customer satisfaction. Be prepared to discuss your observations and conclusions with the rest of the class.

BLOGGING SKILLS

13. Media Skills: Blogging; Compositional Modes: Tutorials [LO-5] Studying abroad for a semester or a year can be a rewarding experience in many ways—improving your language skills, experiencing another culture, making contacts in the international business arena, and building your self-confidence.

Your task: Write a post for your class blog that describes your college's study abroad program and summarizes the steps involved in applying for international study. If your school doesn't offer study-abroad opportunities, base your post on the program offered at another institution in your state.

BLOGGING SKILLS   PORTFOLIO BUILDER

14. Media Skills: Blogging [LO-5] U.S. automakers haven't had much good news to share lately. GM, in particular, has been going through a rough time, entering bankruptcy, shedding assets, and relying on bailouts from the U.S. and Canadian governments to stay in business. The news isn't entirely bleak, however. Chevrolet, one of the brands in the GM automotive stable, has just introduced the Volt, a gas/electric hybrid that might finally give drivers a viable alternative to the wildly popular Toyota Prius.

Your task: Working with a team assigned by your instructor, write a post for GM's dealer-only blog that describes the new Volt and the benefits it offers car owners. Include at least one photo and one link to the Volt section of GM's website. You can learn more about the Volt at Chevy's website, www.chevrolet.com.

BLOGGING SKILLS

15. Media Skills: Blogging [LO-5] Comic-Con International is an annual convention that highlights a wide variety of pop culture and entertainment media, from comic books and collectibles to video games and movies. From its early start as a comic book convention that attracted several hundred fans and publishing industry insiders, Comic-Con has become a major international event with more than 125,000 attendees.

Your task: Several readers of your pop culture blog have been asking for your recommendation about visiting Comic-Con in San Diego next summer. Write a two- or three-paragraph posting for your blog that explains what Comic-Con is and what visitors can expect to experience at the convention. Be sure to address your posting to fans, not industry insiders. You can learn more at www.comic-con.org.[66]

BLOGGING SKILLS

16. Media Skills: Blogging [LO-5] As the travel director for a global management consulting firm, your responsibilities range from finding the best travel deals to helping new employees learn the ins and outs of low-risk, low-stress travels. One of the ways in which you dispense helpful advice is through an internal blog.

Your task: Research advice for safe travel and identify at least six tips that every employee in your company should know. Write a brief blog post that introduces and identifies the six tips.

BLOGGING SKILLS

17. Media Skills: Blogging [LO-5] You work for PreVisor, one of many companies that offer employee screening and testing services. PreVisors's offerings include a variety of online products and consulting services, all designed to help employers find and develop the best possible employees.

To help explain the value of its products and services, PreVisor publishes a variety of customer *case studies* on its website. Each case study describes the staffing challenges a particular company faces, the solution PreVisor was able to provide, and the results the company experienced after using PreVisor products or services.

Your task: Select one of the customer case studies on the PreVisor website (www.previsor.com/results/clients). Write a post that could appear on PreVisor's blog, summarizing the challenges, solutions, and results in no more than 100 words. Include a link to the complete case study on the PreVisor website.

BLOGGING SKILLS

18. Media Skills: Blogging [LO-5] The fact that 97 percent of American youth ages 12 to 17 play video games is not much of a surprise, but more than a few nongaming adults might be surprised to learn that game playing might not be quite the social and civic catastrophe it is sometimes made out to be. A recent study by the Pew Internet & American Life Project puts at least a few cracks in the stereotyped image of gamers being loners who live out violent fantasies while learning few if any skills that could make them positive members of society.[67]

Your task: Imagine that you're on the public relations staff at the Entertainment Software Association (ESA), an industry group that represents the interests of video game companies. You'd like to share the results of the Pew survey with parents to help ease their concerns. Visit http://real-timeupdates.com/bct11, click on "Student Assignments" and then "Chapter 7, page 212, Case 18." Download this PDF file, which is a summary of the Pew results. Find at least three positive aspects of video game playing and write a brief message that could be posted on an ESA public affairs blog.

MICROBLOGGING SKILLS

19. Media Skills: Microblogging [LO-5] Consumers looking for beauty, health, and lifestyle magazines have an almost endless array of choices, but even in this crowded field, Logan Olson found her own niche. Olson, who was born with congenital heart disease, suffered a heart attack at age 16 that left her in a coma and caused serious brain damage. The active and outgoing teen had to relearn everything from sitting up to feeding herself. As she recovered, she looked for help and advice in conquering such daily challenges as finding fashionable clothes that were easier to put on and makeup that was easier to apply. Mainstream beauty magazines didn't seem to offer any information for young women with disabilities, so she started her own magazine. Oprah Winfrey has *Oprah*, and Logan Olson has *Logan*. The magazine not only gives young women tips on buying and using a variety of products but lets women with disabilities know there are others like them, facing and meeting the same challenges.

Your task: Write a 120-character message suggesting a gift subscription to *Logan* magazine as a nice birthday gift for any young woman who might benefit from the magazine. Assume that your readers are not familiar with *Logan*. (Limiting your message to 120 characters allows room for a 20-character URL, which you don't need to include in your message.) You can learn more about *Logan* at www.loganmagazine.com or on Facebook (search for Logan Magazine).[68] If your class is set up with private Twitter accounts, use your private account to send your message. Otherwise, email it to your instructor.

MICROBLOGGING SKILLS

20. Media Skills: Microblogging; Compositional Modes: Teasers [LO-1], [LO-5] Twitter updates are a great way to alert people to helpful articles, videos, and other online resources.

Your task: Find an online resource (it can be a website quiz, a YouTube video, a PowerPoint presentation, a newspaper article, or anything else appropriate) that offers some great tips to help college students prepare for job interviews. Write a teaser of no more than 120 characters that hints at the benefits other students can get from this resource. If your class is set up with private Twitter accounts, use your private account to send your message. Otherwise, email it to your instructor. Be sure to include the URL; if you're using a private Twitter account, the system should shorten it to 20 characters to keep you within the 140-character limit.

MICROBLOGGING SKILLS

21. Media Skills: Microblogging; Compositional Modes: Updates and Announcements [LO-1], [LO-5] JetBlue is known for its innovations in customer service and customer communication, including its pioneering use of the Twitter microblogging system. Nearly two million JetBlue fans and customers follow the company on Twitter to get updates on flight status during weather disruptions, facility upgrades, and other news.[69]

Your task: Write a message of no more than 120 characters that announces the limited-time availability of flights and travel packages—flights plus hotel rooms, for example—at JetBlue's store on eBay. (Limiting your message to 120 characters allows room for a 20-character URL, which you don't need to include in your message.) The key selling point is that travelers may be able to purchase flights they want at steep discounts. If your class is set up with private Twitter accounts, use your private account to send your message. Otherwise, email it to your instructor.

PODCASTING SKILLS

22. Media Skills: Podcasting; Message Strategies: Marketing and Sales Messages [LO-6] Chapter 10 What product do you own (or use regularly) that you can't live without? It could be something as seemingly minor as a favorite pen or something as significant as a medical device that you literally can't live without. Now imagine you're a salesperson for this product; think about how you would sell it to potential buyers. How would you describe it and how would you explain the benefits of owning it? After you've thought about how you would present the product to others, imagine that you've been promoted to sales manager, and it is your job to train other people to sell the product.

Your task: Write the script for a brief podcast (200 to 300 words) that summarizes for your sales staff the most important points to convey about the product. Imagine that they'll listen to your podcast while driving to a customer's location or preparing for the day's activity in a retail store (depending on the nature of the product). Be sure to give your staffers a concise overview message about the product and several key support points.

PODCASTING SKILLS

23. Media Skills: Podcasting; Career Management: Personal Branding [LO-6], Prologue While writing the many letters and email messages that are part of the job search process, you find yourself wishing that you could just talk to some of these companies so your personality could shine through. Well, you've just gotten that opportunity. One of the companies that you've applied to has emailed you back, asking you to submit a two-minute podcast, introducing yourself and explaining why you would be a good person to hire.

Your task: Identify a company that you'd like to work for after graduation and select a job that would be a good match for your skills and interests. Write a script for a two-minute podcast (roughly 250 words). Introduce yourself and the position you're applying for, describe your background, and explain why you think you're a good candidate for the job. Make up any details you need. If your instructor asks you to do so, record the podcast and submit the file.

PODCASTING SKILLS   PORTFOLIO BUILDER

24. Media Skills: Podcasting; Message Strategies: Marketing and Sales Messages [LO-6] Chapter 10 With any purchase decision, from a restaurant meal to a college education, recommendations from satisfied customers are often the strongest promotional messages.

Your task: Write a script for a one- to two-minute podcast (roughly 150 to 250 words), explaining why your college or university is a good place to get an education. Your audience is high school juniors and seniors. You can choose to craft a general message, something that would be useful to all prospective students, or you can focus on a specific academic discipline, the athletic program, or some other important aspect of your college experience. Either way, make sure your introductory comments make it clear whether you are offering a general recommendation or a specific recommendation. If your instructor asks you to do so, record the podcast and submit the file electronically.

PODCASTING SKILLS

25. Media Skills: Podcasting; Message Strategies: Persuasive Business Messages [LO-6] Chapter 10 Every organization, no matter how successfully it operates, can find ways to improve its customer service.

Your task: Write a script for a one- to two-minute podcast (roughly 150 to 250 words), identifying at least one way in which your college experience could have been or still could be improved through specific changes in policies, programs, facilities, or other elements. Your audience is the school's administration. Offer constructive criticism and specific arguments about why your suggestions would help you—and possibly other students as well. Be sure to focus on meaningful and practical opportunities for improvement. If your instructor asks you to do so, record the podcast and submit the file electronically.

Writing Routine and Positive Messages

LEARNING OBJECTIVES After studying this chapter, you will be able to

1 Outline an effective strategy for writing routine business requests

2 Describe three common types of routine requests

3 Outline an effective strategy for writing routine replies and positive messages

4 Describe six common types of routine replies and positive messages

MyBcommLab Test your mastery of this chapter and its Learning Objectives. Visit mybcommlab.com to apply what you've learned in Document Makeovers and interactive simulation scenarios.

COMMUNICATION CLOSE-UP AT GET SATISFACTION

Get Satisfaction uses Web 2.0 tools such as community Q&A websites to address the widespread frustration with traditional approaches to customer support.

http://getsatisfaction.com

For about as long as online communication has been possible, frustrated customers have been going online to complain about faulty products, confusing instructions, and poor service. When Web 2.0 tools hit the scene a few years ago, giving even nontechnical consumers a ready voice, the stream of "I need help!" messages turned into a full-time flood. On product review and shopping websites, enthusiast blogs, and various "complaint sites," consumers can vent their frustrations and ask for help when they feel they aren't getting satisfaction from the companies with which they do business.

These various websites can occasionally provide answers, but they suffer from four fundamental drawbacks. First, they are randomly scattered all over the Web, so many consumers are never quite sure where to look for help. Second, the right experts from the right companies often aren't involved, meaning that customers often have to rely on each other—which sometimes works but sometimes doesn't. Third, even companies that make a valiant effort to keep their customers satisfied know that everyone can benefit if customers can share ideas, learn from one another, and participate in ongoing conversation. Fourth, companies often find that multiple customers have the same routine questions, but communicating with every customer individually can be time-consuming and expensive.

The San Francisco–based company Get Satisfaction is working to address all these issues. CEO Thor Muller explains that the company is "creating a kind of social network designed for companies and customers to communicate with each other." Consumers can post questions or complaints and request email notification whenever a response is posted. If someone else has already posted the same complaint, all a visitor needs to do is ask to be notified when the issue is resolved, saving time for the people asking and answering questions. Consumers can also suggest ideas for new products and services or improvements to existing offerings.

On the other side of the relationship, employees from companies that sell products and services can register as official representatives to answer questions, solve problems, and solicit feedback. As both knowledgeable consumers and company representatives provide answers and solutions, the responses voted most useful rise to the top, ensuring that visitors always get the most helpful information available. Companies that use Get Satisfaction's services can deploy customer service capabilities on Facebook, Twitter, and their own company blogs to try to capture as many customer service conversations as possible.

As Muller explains, "When customers start to converge and talk, for many companies this is gold—real engagement with current or future customers." The idea certainly seems to be catching on, with nearly 50,000 companies now using Get Satisfaction to help their customers get satisfaction from the products and services they buy.[1]

Strategy for Routine Requests

Get Satisfaction's Thor Muller (profiled in the chapter-opening Communication Close-up) knows that much of the vital communication between a company and its customers is about routine matters, from product operation hints and technical support to refunds and ordering glitches. These messages fall into two groups: routine requests, in which you ask for information or action from another party, and a variety of routine and positive messages. Chapter 9 covers messages in which you convey negative information, and Chapter 10 addresses persuasive messages.

Making requests is a routine part of business. In most cases, your audience will be prepared to comply, as long as you're not being unreasonable or asking people to do something they would expect you to do yourself. By applying a clear strategy and tailoring your approach to each situation, you'll be able to generate effective requests quickly.

Like all other business messages, a routine request has three parts: an opening, a body, and a close. Using the direct approach, open with your main idea, which is a clear statement of your request. Use the body to give details and justify your request. Finally, close by requesting specific action.

STATING YOUR REQUEST UP FRONT

Begin routine requests by placing your initial request first; up front is where it stands out and gets the most attention. Of course, getting right to the point should not be interpreted as license to be abrupt or tactless:

- **Pay attention to tone.** Even though you expect a favorable response, the tone of your initial request is important. Instead of demanding action ("Send me the latest personnel cost data"), soften your request with words such as *please* and *I would appreciate*.
- **Assume that your audience will comply.** An impatient demand for rapid service isn't necessary. You can generally assume that your readers will comply with your request when they clearly understand the reason for it.
- **Be specific.** State precisely what you want. For example, if you request the latest market data from your research department, be sure to say whether you want a 1-page summary or 100 pages of raw data.

EXPLAINING AND JUSTIFYING YOUR REQUEST

Use the body of your message to explain your request. Make the explanation a smooth and logical outgrowth of your opening remarks. If possible, point out how complying with the request could benefit the reader. For instance, if you would like some assistance interpreting complex quality-control data, you might point out how a better understanding of quality-control issues would improve customer satisfaction and ultimately lead to higher profits for the entire company.

Whether you're writing a formal letter or a simple instant message, you can use the body of your request to list a series of questions. These questions help organize your

1 LEARNING OBJECTIVE

Outline an effective strategy for writing routine business requests.

For routine requests and positive messages
- State the request or main idea
- Give necessary details
- Close with a cordial request for specific action

Take care that your direct approach doesn't come across as abrupt or tactless.

MyBcommLab
- Access this chapter's simulation entitled Routine Messages located at mybcommlab.com.

✓ Checklist | Writing Routine Requests

A. State your request up front.
- Write in a polite, undemanding, personal tone.
- Use the direct approach because your audience will probably respond favorably to your request.
- Be specific and precise in your request.

B. Explain and justify your request.
- Justify the request or explain its importance.
- Explain any potential benefits of responding.

- Ask the most important questions first.
- Break complex requests into individual questions that are limited to only one topic each.

C. Request specific action in a courteous close.
- Make it easy to comply by including appropriate contact information.
- Express your gratitude.
- Clearly state any important deadlines for the request.

---

message and help your audience identify the information you need. Just keep in mind a few basics:

If you have multiple requests or questions, start with the most important one.

- **Ask the most important questions first.** If cost is your main concern, you might begin with a question such as "What is the cost for shipping the merchandise by air versus truck?" Then you might want to ask more specific but related questions about, say, discounts for paying early.
- **Ask only relevant questions.** To help expedite the response to your request, ask only questions that are central to your main request. Doing so will generate an answer sooner and make better use of the other person's time.
- **Deal with only one topic per question.** If you have an unusual or complex request, break it down into specific, individual questions so that the reader can address each one separately. Don't put the burden of untangling a complicated request on your reader. This consideration shows respect for your audience's time, and it probably will get you a more accurate answer in less time.

REQUESTING SPECIFIC ACTION IN A COURTEOUS CLOSE

Close request messages with
- *A request for some specific action*
- *Information about how you can be reached*
- *An expression of appreciation*

Close your message with three important elements: (1) a specific request, (2) information about how you can be reached (if it isn't obvious), and (3) an expression of appreciation or goodwill. When you ask readers to perform a specific action, ask for a response by a specific date or time, if appropriate (for example, "Please send the figures by May 5 so that I can return first-quarter results to you before the May 20 conference."). Plus, by including your phone number, email address, office hours, and other contact information, you help readers respond easily.

Conclude your message by sincerely expressing your goodwill and appreciation. However, don't thank the reader "in advance" for cooperating; many people find that presumptuous. And if the reader's reply warrants a word of thanks, send it after you've received the reply. To review, see "Checklist: Writing Routine Requests."

Common Examples of Routine Requests

2 **LEARNING OBJECTIVE**

Describe three common types of routine requests.

Many of the routine messages you'll be writing will likely fall into a few main categories: asking for information and action, asking for recommendations, and making claims and requesting adjustments.

ASKING FOR INFORMATION AND ACTION

When you need to know about something, elicit an opinion from someone, or request a simple action, you usually need only ask. In essence, simple requests say

- What you want to know or what you want the reader to do
- Why you're making the request
- Why it may be in your reader's interest to help you

If your reader is able to do what you want, such a straightforward request will get the job done quickly. Use the direct approach by opening with a clear statement of your reason for writing. In the body, provide whatever explanation is needed to justify your request. Then close with a specific description of what you expect and include a deadline, if appropriate (see Figure 8.1 on the next page). In some situations, readers might be unwilling to respond unless they understand how the request benefits them, so be sure to include this information in your explanation. You can assume some shared background when communicating about a routine matter to someone in the same company.

In contrast to requests sent internally, those sent to people outside the organization usually adopt a more formal tone, as in the following example:

> Routine requests can be handled with simple, straightforward messages, but more complicated requests can require additional justification and explanation.

Dear Bioverse:

Please provide additional information on distribution opportunities for your Healthy Ponds product line, as mentioned on your website. Enviro Domestic is a 20-year-old firm with a well-established design, retail, and service presence in the Oklahoma City area, and we believe your bioremediation products would make a compelling addition to our offerings.

→ Makes overall request in polite question form (no question mark)

→ Identifies the writer's affiliation and reason for writing

In particular, we would appreciate answers to the following questions:

→ Specifies exactly what the writer wishes to know to assist the recipient in responding

1. Do you offer exclusive regional distribution contracts?
2. Do you offer factory training for sales and service specialists?
3. Do you plan to expand beyond water bioremediation solutions into other landscaping products?

Please let us hear from you by February 15.

→ Closes with a polite request and a specific answer deadline

A more complex request might require not only greater detail but also information on how responding will benefit the reader.

ASKING FOR RECOMMENDATIONS

The need to inquire about people arises often in business. For example, before extending credit or awarding contracts, jobs, promotions, or scholarships, companies often ask applicants to supply references: a list of people who can vouch for their ability, skills, integrity, character, and fitness for the job. Before you volunteer someone's name as a reference, ask permission to do so. Some people don't want you to use their names, perhaps because they don't know enough about you to feel comfortable writing a letter or because they or their employers have a policy of not providing recommendations.

> Always ask for permission before using someone as a reference.

Because requests for recommendations and references are routine, you can organize your inquiry using the direct approach. Open your message by clearly stating why the recommendation is needed (if it's not for a job, be sure to explain what it is for) and that you would like your reader to write the letter. If you haven't had contact with the person for some time, use the opening to trigger the reader's memory of the relationship you had, the dates of association, and any special events that might bring a clear and favorable picture of you to mind. Consider including an updated résumé if you've had significant career advancement since your last contact.

> Refresh the memory of any potential references you haven't been in touch with for a while.

Close your message with an expression of appreciation and the full name and address of the person to whom the letter should be sent. When asking for an immediate recommendation, you should also mention the deadline. Always

REAL-TIME UPDATES

Learn More by Reading This PDF

The right way to ask for recommendations on LinkedIn

Follow LinkedIn's etiquette guide for students and recent graduations to increase your response rate and to maintain positive networking connections. Go to http://real-timeupdates.com/bct11 and click on "Learn More." If you are using MyBcommLab, you can access Real-Time Updates within each chapter or under Student Study Tools.

Analyze the Situation
Verify that the purpose is to request information from company managers.

Gather Information
Gather accurate, complete information about local competitive threats.

Select the Right Medium
Choose email for this internal message, which also allows the attachment of a Word document to collect the information.

Organize the Information
Clarify that the main idea is collecting information that will lead to a better competitive strategy, which will in turn help the various district managers.

Adapt to Your Audience
Show sensitivity to audience needs with a "you" attitude, politeness, positive emphasis, and bias-free language. The writer already has credibility, as manager of the department.

Compose the Message
Maintain a style that is conversational but still businesslike, using plain English and appropriate voice.

Revise the Message
Evaluate content and review readability; avoid unnecessary details.

Produce the Message
Simple email format is all the design this message needs.

Proofread the Message
Review for errors in layout, spelling, and mechanics.

Distribute the Message
Deliver the message via the company's email system.

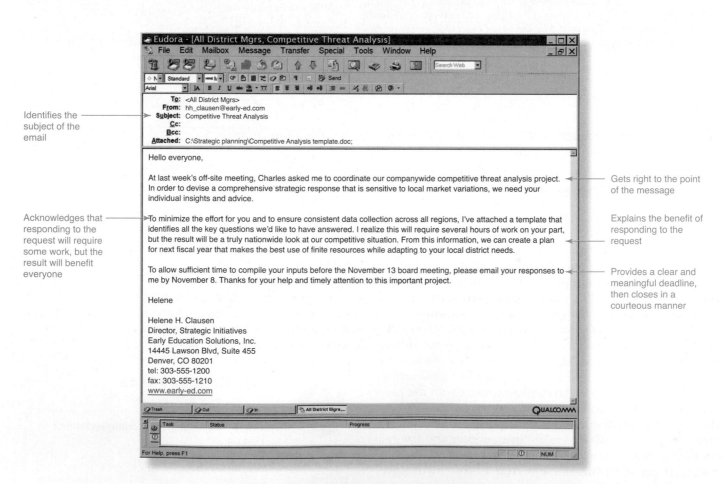

Identifies the subject of the email

Acknowledges that responding to the request will require some work, but the result will benefit everyone

Gets right to the point of the message

Explains the benefit of responding to the request

Provides a clear and meaningful deadline, then closes in a courteous manner

Figure 8.1   Effective Message Requesting Action
In this email request to district managers across the country, Helene Clausen asks them to fill out an attached information collection form. Although the request is not unusual and responding to it is part of the managers' responsibility, Clausen asks for their help in a courteous manner and points out the benefits of responding.

> ## ✔ Checklist | Making Claims and Requesting Adjustments
>
> - Maintain a professional tone, even if you're extremely frustrated.
> - Open with a straightforward statement of the problem.
> - Provide specific details in the body.
> - Present facts honestly and clearly.
> - Politely summarize the desired action in the closing.
> - Clearly state what you expect as a fair settlement or ask the reader to propose a fair adjustment.
> - Explain the benefits of complying with the request, such as your continued patronage.

be sure to enclose a stamped, preaddressed envelope as a convenience to the other party. Figure 8.2 on the next page provides an example of a request that follows these guidelines.

MAKING CLAIMS AND REQUESTING ADJUSTMENTS

If you're dissatisfied with a company's product or service, you can opt to make a **claim** (a formal complaint) or request an **adjustment** (a settlement of a claim). In either case, it's important to maintain a professional tone in all your communication, no matter how angry or frustrated you are. Keeping your cool will help you get the situation resolved sooner.

> When making a claim
> - Explain the problem and give details
> - Provide backup information
> - Request specific action

In most cases, and especially in your first message, assume that a fair adjustment will be made and use a direct request. Open with a straightforward statement of the problem. In the body, give a complete, specific explanation of the details; provide any information an adjuster would need to verify your complaint. In your close, politely request specific action or convey a sincere desire to find a solution. And, if appropriate, suggest that the business relationship will continue if the problem is solved satisfactorily. Be prepared to back up your claim with invoices, sales receipts, canceled checks, dated correspondence, and any other relevant documents. Send copies and keep the originals for your files.

> Be prepared to document any claims you make with a company. Send copies and keep the original documents.

If the remedy is obvious, tell your reader exactly what you expect from the company, such as exchanging incorrectly shipped merchandise for the right item or issuing a refund if the item is out of stock. In some cases, you might ask the reader to resolve a problem. However, if you're uncertain about the precise nature of the trouble, you could ask the company to make an assessment and then advise you on how the situation could be fixed. Supply your contact information so that the company can discuss the situation with you, if necessary. Compare the ineffective and effective versions in Figure 8.3 on page 221 for an example of making a claim.

A rational, clear, and courteous approach is best for any routine request. To review the tasks involved in making claims and requesting adjustments, see "Checklist: Making Claims and Requesting Adjustments."

Strategy for Routine and Positive Messages

Just as you'll make numerous requests for information and action throughout your career, you'll also respond to routine requests and send a variety of routine and positive messages. You have several goals for such messages: to communicate the information or the good news, to answer all questions, to provide all required details, and to leave your reader with a good impression of you and your firm.

> **3 | LEARNING OBJECTIVE**
>
> Outline an effective strategy for writing routine replies and positive messages.

Because readers will generally be interested in what you have to say, you can usually use the direct approach with a routine reply or positive message. Place your main idea (the positive reply or the good news) in the opening, use the body to explain all the relevant details, and close cordially—perhaps highlighting a benefit to your reader.

> Use a direct approach for routine messages.

Analyze the Situation
Verify that the purpose is to request a recommendation letter from a college professor.

Gather Information
Gather information on classes and dates to help the reader recall you and to clarify the position you seek.

Select the Right Medium
The letter format gives this message an appropriate level of formality, although many professors prefer to be contacted by an email.

Organize the Information
Messages like this are common and expected, so a direct approach is fine.

Adapt to Your Audience
Show sensitivity to audience needs with a "you" attitude, politeness, positive emphasis, and bias-free language.

Compose the Message
Style is respectful and businesslike, while still using plain English and appropriate voice.

Revise the Message
Evaluate content and review readability; avoid unnecessary details.

Produce the Message
Simple letter format is all the design this message needs.

Proofread the Message
Review for errors in layout, spelling, and mechanics.

Distribute the Message
Deliver the message via postal mail or email if you have the professor's email address.

1181 Ashport Drive
Tate Springs, TN 38101
March 14, 2011

Professor Lyndon Kenton
School of Business
University of Tennessee, Knoxville
Knoxville, TN 37916

Dear Professor Kenton:

I recently interviewed with Strategic Investments and have been called for a second interview for their Analyst Training Program (ATP). They have requested at least one recommendation from a professor, and I immediately thought of you. May I have a letter of recommendation from you?

Opens by stating the purpose of the letter and making the request, assuming the reader will want to comply with the request

As you may recall, I took BUS 485, Financial Analysis, from you in the fall of 2009. I enjoyed the class and finished the term with an "A." Professor Kenton, your comments on assertiveness and cold-calling impressed me beyond the scope of the actual course material. In fact, taking your course helped me decide on a future as a financial analyst.

Includes information near the opening to refresh the reader's memory about this former student

My enclosed résumé includes all my relevant work experience and volunteer activities. I would also like to add that I've handled the financial planning for our family since my father passed away several years ago. Although I initially learned by trial and error, I have increasingly applied my business training in deciding what stocks or bonds to trade. This, I believe, has given me a practical edge over others who may be applying for the same job.

Refers to résumé in the body and mentions experience that could set applicant apart from other candidates

If possible, Ms. Blackmon in Human Resources needs to receive your letter by March 30. For your convenience, I've enclosed a preaddressed, stamped envelope.

Gives a deadline for response and includes information about the person expecting the recommendation

Mentions the preaddressed, stamped envelope to encourage a timely response

I appreciate your time and effort in writing this letter of recommendation for me. It will be great to put my education to work, and I'll keep you informed of my progress. Thank you for your consideration in this matter.

Sincerely,

Joanne Tucker

Joanne Tucker

Enclosure

Figure 8.2 Effective Letter Requesting a Recommendation
This writer uses the direct approach when asking for a recommendation from a former professor. Note how she takes care to refresh the professor's memory because she took the class a year and a half ago. She also indicates the date by which the letter is needed and points to the enclosure of a stamped, preaddressed envelope.

Figure 8.3 Ineffective and Effective Versions of a Claim
Note the difference in tone and information content in these two versions. The ineffective version is emotional and unprofessional, whereas the effective version communicates calmly and clearly.

MyBcommLab

Apply Figure 8.3's key concepts by revising a new document. Go to Chapter 8 in mybcommlab.com and select Document Makeovers.

STARTING WITH THE MAIN IDEA

With the direct approach, open with a clear and concise expression of the main idea or good news.

By opening routine and positive messages with the main idea or good news, you're preparing your audience for the details that follow. Make your opening clear and concise. Although the following introductory statements make the same point, one is cluttered with unnecessary information that buries the purpose, whereas the other is brief and to the point:

Instead of This

I am pleased to inform you that after careful consideration of a diverse and talented pool of applicants, each of whom did a thorough job of analyzing Trask Horton Pharmaceuticals's training needs, we have selected your bid.

Write This

Trask Horton Pharmaceuticals has accepted your bid to provide public speaking and presentation training to the sales staff.

The best way to write a clear opening is to have a clear idea of what you want to say. Ask yourself, "What is the single most important message I have for the audience?"

PROVIDING NECESSARY DETAILS AND EXPLANATION

Use the body to explain your point completely so that your audience won't be confused or doubtful about your meaning. As you provide the details, maintain the supportive tone established in the opening. This tone is easy to continue when your message is entirely positive, as in this example:

Your educational background and internship have impressed us, and we believe you would be a valuable addition to Green Valley Properties. As discussed during your interview, your salary will be $4,300 per month, plus benefits. Please plan to meet with our benefits manager, Paula Sanchez, at 8 a.m. on Monday, March 21. She will assist you with all the paperwork necessary to tailor our benefit package to your family situation. She will also arrange various orientation activities to help you acclimate to our company.

Try to embed any negative information in a positive context.

However, if your routine message is mixed and must convey mildly disappointing information, put the negative portion of your message into as favorable a context as possible:

Instead of This

No, we no longer carry the Sportsgirl line of sweaters.

Write This

The new Olympic line has replaced the Sportsgirl sweaters that you asked about. Olympic features a wider range of colors and sizes and more contemporary styling.

In this example, the more complete description is less negative and emphasizes how the recipient can benefit from the change. Be careful, though: You can use negative information in this type of message *only* if you're reasonably sure the audience will respond positively. Otherwise, use the indirect approach (discussed in Chapter 9).

If you are communicating with a customer, you might also want to use the body of your message to assure the customer of the wisdom of his or her purchase selection (without being condescending or self-congratulatory). Using such favorable comments, often known as *resale*, is a good way to build customer relationships. These comments are commonly included in acknowledgments of orders and other routine announcements to customers, and they are most effective when they are relatively short and specific:

The KitchenAid mixer you ordered is our best-selling model. It should meet your cooking needs for many years.

> ✓ **Checklist** | Writing Routine Replies and Positive Messages
>
> **A. Start with the main idea.**
> - Be clear and concise.
> - Identify the single most important message before you start writing.
>
> **B. Provide necessary details and explanation.**
> - Explain your point completely to eliminate any confusion or lingering doubts.
> - Maintain a supportive tone throughout.
>
> - Embed negative statements in positive contexts or balance them with positive alternatives.
> - Talk favorably about the choices the customer has made.
>
> **C. End with a courteous close.**
> - Let your readers know that you have their personal well-being in mind.
> - If further action is required, tell readers how to proceed and encourage them to act promptly.

ENDING WITH A COURTEOUS CLOSE

Your message is more likely to succeed if your readers are left feeling that you have their best interests in mind. You can accomplish this task either by highlighting a benefit to the audience or by expressing appreciation or goodwill. If follow-up action is required, clearly state who will do what next. See "Checklist: Writing Routine Replies and Positive Messages" to review the primary tasks involved in this type of business message.

Make sure audience members understand what to do next and how that action will benefit them.

Common Examples of Routine and Positive Messages

Most routine and positive messages fall into six main categories: answers to requests for information and action, grants of claims and requests for adjustment, recommendations, routine information, good-news announcements, and goodwill messages.

4 | **LEARNING OBJECTIVE**

Describe six common types of routine replies and positive messages.

ANSWERING REQUESTS FOR INFORMATION AND ACTION

Every professional answers requests for information and action from time to time. If the response to a request is a simple yes or some other straightforward information, the direct approach is appropriate. A prompt, gracious, and thorough response will positively influence how people think about you and the organization you represent (see Figure 8.4 on the next page).

When you're answering requests and a potential sale is involved, you have three main goals: (1) to respond to the inquiry and answer all questions, (2) to leave your reader with a good impression of you and your firm, and (3) to encourage the future sale. The following message meets all three objectives:

> Here is the brochure "Entertainment Unlimited" that you requested. This booklet describes the vast array of entertainment options available to you with an Ocean Satellite Device (OSD).
>
> On page 12 you'll find a list of the 338 channels that the OSD brings into your home. You'll have access to movie, sports, and music channels; 24-hour news channels; local channels; and all the major television networks. OSD gives you a clearer picture and more precise sound than those old-fashioned dishes that took up most of your yard—and OSD uses only a small dish that mounts easily on your roof.
>
> More music, more cartoons, more experts, more news, and more sports are available to you with OSD than with any other cable or satellite connection in this region. It's all there, right at your fingertips.
>
> Just call us at 1-800-786-4331, and an OSD representative will come to your home to answer your questions. You'll love the programming and the low monthly cost. Call us today!

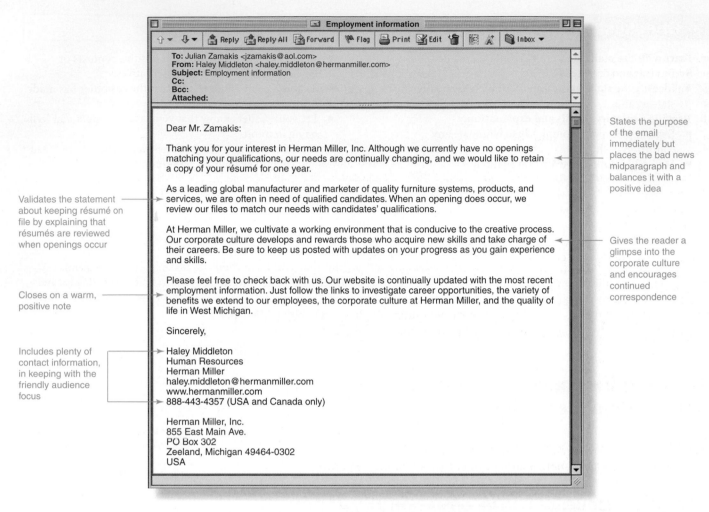

Validates the statement about keeping résumé on file by explaining that résumés are reviewed when openings occur

Closes on a warm, positive note

Includes plenty of contact information, in keeping with the friendly audience focus

States the purpose of the email immediately but places the bad news midparagraph and balances it with a positive idea

Gives the reader a glimpse into the corporate culture and encourages continued correspondence

Figure 8.4 **Effective Response to an Information Request**
This email message answers an information request regarding job openings and provides additional information about the company and some encouragement to the applicant.

GRANTING CLAIMS AND REQUESTS FOR ADJUSTMENT

Even the best-run companies make mistakes, from shipping the wrong order to billing a customer's credit card inaccurately. In other cases, a customer or a third party might be responsible for a mistake, such as misusing a product or damaging a product in shipment. Each of these events represents a turning point in your relationship with your customer. If you handle the situation well, your customer is likely to be even more loyal than before because you've proven that you're serious about customer satisfaction. However, if a customer believes that you mishandled a complaint, you'll make the situation even worse. Dissatisfied customers often take their business elsewhere without notice and tell numerous friends and colleagues about the negative experience. A transaction that might be worth only a few dollars by itself could cost you many times that amount in lost business. In other words, every mistake is an opportunity to improve a relationship.

Your response to a customer complaint depends on your company's policies for resolving such issues and your assessment of whether the company, the customer, or some third party is at fault.

Responding to a Claim When Your Company Is at Fault

Before you respond after your company has made a mistake, make sure you know your company's policies, which might dictate specific legal and financial steps to be taken. For serious problems that go beyond routine errors, your company should have a *crisis management plan* that outlines communication steps both inside and outside the organization (see Chapter 9).

Most routine responses should take your company's specific policies into account and do the following:

- Acknowledge receipt of the customer's claim or complaint.
- Sympathize with the customer's inconvenience or frustration.
- Take (or assign) personal responsibility for setting matters straight.
- Explain precisely how you have resolved, or plan to resolve, the situation.
- Take steps to repair the relationship.
- Follow up to verify that your response was correct.

In addition to taking these positive steps, maintain a professional demeanor. Don't blame anyone in your organization by name; don't make exaggerated, insincere apologies; don't imply that the customer is at fault; and don't promise more than you can deliver. See how this message acknowledges the problem, describes the action being taken, and works to rebuild the customer relationship:

> Maintain a sincere, professional tone when responding to a complaint.

> Your email message concerning your recent Klondike order has been forwarded to our director of order fulfillment. Your complete satisfaction is our goal, and a customer service representative will contact you within 24 hours to assist with the issues raised in your letter.
>
> In the meantime, please accept the enclosed $5 gift certificate as a token of our appreciation for your business. Whether you're skiing or driving a snowmobile, Klondike Gear offers you the best protection from wind, snow, and cold—and Klondike has been taking care of customers' outdoor needs for over 27 years.
>
> Thank you for taking the time to write to us. Your input helps us better serve you and all our customers.

Responding to a Claim When the Customer Is at Fault

Communication about a claim is a delicate matter when the customer is clearly at fault. If you refuse the claim, you may lose your customer—as well as many of the customer's friends and colleagues, who will hear only one side of the dispute. You must weigh the cost of making the adjustment against the cost of losing future business from one or more customers. Some companies have strict guidelines for responding to such claims, whereas others give individual employees and managers some leeway in making case-by-case decisions.

If you choose to grant a claim, you can simply open with the good news, being sure to specify exactly what you're agreeing to do. The body of the message is tricky because you want to discourage such claims in the future by steering the customer in the right direction. For example, customers sometimes misuse products or fail to follow the terms of service agreements, such as forgetting to cancel hotel reservations at least 24 hours in advance and thereby incurring the cost of one night's stay. Even if you do grant a particular claim, you don't want to imply that you will grant similar claims in the future. The challenge is to diplomatically remind the customer of proper usage or procedures without being condescending ("Perhaps you failed to read the instructions carefully") or preachy ("You should know that wool shrinks in hot water"). Close in a courteous manner that expresses your appreciation for the customer's business (see Figure 8.5 on the next page).

> To grant a claim when the customer is at fault, try to discourage future mistakes without insulting the customer.

Responding to a Claim When a Third Party Is at Fault

Sometimes neither your company nor your customer is at fault. For example, ordering a book from Amazon involves not only Amazon but also a delivery service such as UPS or the U.S. Postal Service, the publisher and possibly a distributor of the book, a credit card issuer, and a company that processes credit card transactions. Any one of these other partners might be at fault in the event of a problem, but the customer is likely to blame Amazon because that is the entity primarily responsible for the transaction.

No general scheme applies to every case involving a third party, so evaluate the situation carefully and know your company's policies before responding. For instance, an online retailer and the companies that manufacture its merchandise might have an agreement which specifies that the manufacturers automatically handle all complaints about product

> When a third party is at fault, your response depends on your company's agreements with that organization.

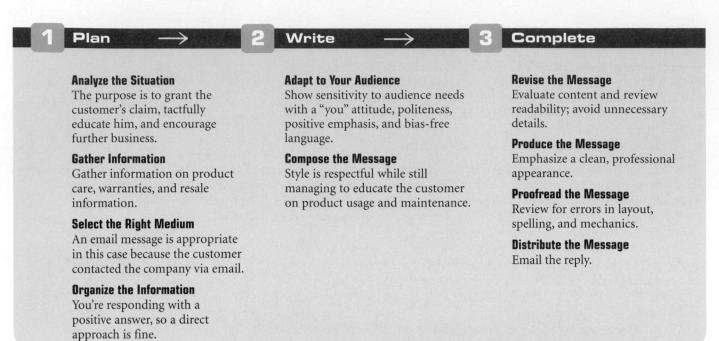

1 Plan → **2 Write** → **3 Complete**

Analyze the Situation
The purpose is to grant the customer's claim, tactfully educate him, and encourage further business.

Gather Information
Gather information on product care, warranties, and resale information.

Select the Right Medium
An email message is appropriate in this case because the customer contacted the company via email.

Organize the Information
You're responding with a positive answer, so a direct approach is fine.

Adapt to Your Audience
Show sensitivity to audience needs with a "you" attitude, politeness, positive emphasis, and bias-free language.

Compose the Message
Style is respectful while still managing to educate the customer on product usage and maintenance.

Revise the Message
Evaluate content and review readability; avoid unnecessary details.

Produce the Message
Emphasize a clean, professional appearance.

Proofread the Message
Review for errors in layout, spelling, and mechanics.

Distribute the Message
Email the reply.

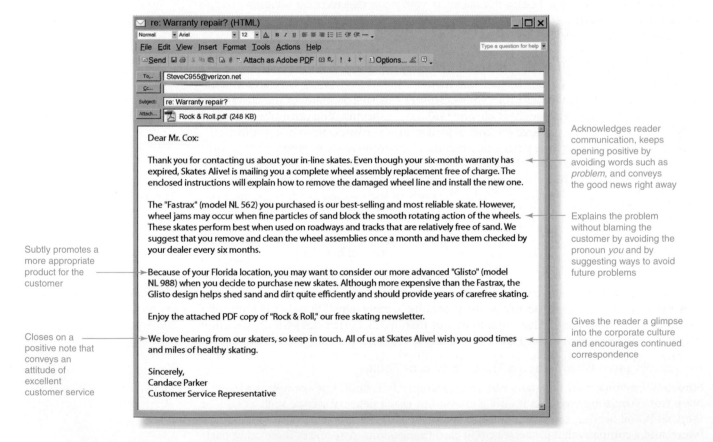

Subtly promotes a more appropriate product for the customer

Closes on a positive note that conveys an attitude of excellent customer service

Acknowledges reader communication, keeps opening positive by avoiding words such as *problem*, and conveys the good news right away

Explains the problem without blaming the customer by avoiding the pronoun *you* and by suggesting ways to avoid future problems

Gives the reader a glimpse into the corporate culture and encourages continued correspondence

re: Warranty repair? (HTML)

To... SteveC955@verizon.net
Cc...
Subject: re: Warranty repair?
Attach... Rock & Roll.pdf (248 KB)

Dear Mr. Cox:

Thank you for contacting us about your in-line skates. Even though your six-month warranty has expired, Skates Alive! is mailing you a complete wheel assembly replacement free of charge. The enclosed instructions will explain how to remove the damaged wheel line and install the new one.

The "Fastrax" (model NL 562) you purchased is our best-selling and most reliable skate. However, wheel jams may occur when fine particles of sand block the smooth rotating action of the wheels. These skates perform best when used on roadways and tracks that are relatively free of sand. We suggest that you remove and clean the wheel assemblies once a month and have them checked by your dealer every six months.

Because of your Florida location, you may want to consider our more advanced "Glisto" (model NL 988) when you decide to purchase new skates. Although more expensive than the Fastrax, the Glisto design helps shed sand and dirt quite efficiently and should provide years of carefree skating.

Enjoy the attached PDF copy of "Rock & Roll," our free skating newsletter.

We love hearing from our skaters, so keep in touch. All of us at Skates Alive! wish you good times and miles of healthy skating.

Sincerely,
Candace Parker
Customer Service Representative

Figure 8.5 Responding to a Claim When the Buyer Is at Fault
In the interest of positive customer relationships, this company agreed to provide replacement parts for a customer's in-line skates, even though the product is outside its warranty period. (For the sake of clarity, the content of the customer's original email message is not reproduced here.)

✓ Checklist Granting Claims and Adjustment Requests

A. Responding when your company is at fault
- Be aware of your company's policies in such cases before you respond.
- For serious situations, refer to the company's crisis management plan.
- Start by acknowledging receipt of the claim or complaint.
- Take or assign personal responsibility for resolving the situation.
- Sympathize with the customer's frustration.
- Explain how you have resolved the situation (or plan to).
- Take steps to repair the customer relationship.
- Verify your response with the customer and keep the lines of communication open.

B. Responding when the customer is at fault
- Weigh the cost of complying with or refusing the request.
- If you choose to comply, open with the good news.
- Use the body of the message to respectfully educate the customer about steps needed to avoid a similar outcome in the future.
- Close with an appreciation for the customer's business.

C. Responding when a third party is at fault
- Evaluate the situation and review your company's policies before responding.
- Avoid placing blame; focus on the solution.
- Regardless of who is responsible for resolving the situation, let the customer know what will happen to resolve the problem.

quality. However, regardless of who eventually resolves the problem, if customers contact you, you need to respond with messages that explain how the problem will be solved. Pointing fingers is unproductive and unprofessional; resolving the situation is the only issue customers care about. See "Checklist: Granting Claims and Adjustment Requests" to review the tasks involved in these kinds of business messages.

PROVIDING RECOMMENDATIONS

When writing a letter of recommendation, your goal is to convince readers that the person being recommended has the characteristics necessary for the job, project assignment, scholarship, or other objective the person is seeking. A successful recommendation letter contains a number of relevant details (see Figure 8.6 on the next page):

- The candidate's full name
- The position or other objective the candidate is seeking
- The nature of your relationship with the candidate
- Facts and evidence relevant to the candidate and the opportunity
- A comparison of this candidate's potential with that of peers, if available (for example, "Ms. Jonasson consistently ranked in the top 10 percent of her class")
- Your overall evaluation of the candidate's suitability for the opportunity

Be aware that recommendation letters have become a complex legal matter in recent years (see "Can You Get Sued for Writing—or Not Writing—a Recommendation Letter?"), so be sure to check your company's policies before writing a recommendation. Also, keep in mind that every time you write a recommendation, you're putting your own reputation on the line. If the person's shortcomings are so pronounced that you don't think he or she is a good fit for the job, the only choice is to not write the letter at all. Unless your relationship with the person warrants an explanation, simply suggest that someone else might be in a better position to provide a recommendation.

> Recommendation letters are vulnerable to legal complications, so consult with your company's legal department before writing one.

SHARING ROUTINE INFORMATION

Many messages involve sharing routine information, such as project updates and order status notifications. Use the opening of these routine messages to state the purpose and briefly

REAL-TIME UPDATES
Learn More by Reading This Article

Get expert tips on writing (or requesting) a letter of recommendation

Find helpful advice on employment recommendations, academic recommendations, and character references. Go to http://real-timeupdates.com/bct11 and click on "Learn More." If you are using MyBcommLab, you can access Real-Time Updates within each chapter or under Student Study Tools.

Specifies duration and nature of relationship in the body to give weight to the evaluation

Closes by inviting reader to discuss the candidate further

Clearly states candidate's full name and the main point of the letter in the opening

Begins the close by summarizing the supportive evaluation

Figure 8.6 **Effective Recommendation Letter**
This letter clearly states the nature of the writer's relationship to the candidate and provides specific examples to support the writer's endorsements.

MyBcommLab

Apply Figure 8.6's key concepts by revising a new document. Go to Chapter 8 in mybcommlab.com and select Document Makeovers.

When writing routine informational messages
- State the purpose at the beginning and briefly mention the nature of the information you are providing
- Provide the necessary details
- End with a courteous close

If a policy change or other announcement could have a profound negative effect on the audience, the indirect approach covered in Chapter 9 is usually preferred.

mention the nature of the information you are providing. Provide the necessary details in the body and end your message with a courteous close (see Figure 8.7 on page 230).

Most routine communications are neutral. That is, they stimulate neither a positive nor a negative response from readers. For example, when you send departmental meeting announcements and reminder notices, you'll generally receive a neutral response from your readers (unless the purpose of the meeting is unwelcome). Simply present the factual information in the body of the message and don't worry too much about the reader's attitude toward the information.

Some routine informative messages may require additional care. For instance, policy statements or procedural changes may be good news for a company, perhaps by saving money. However, it may not be obvious to employees that such savings may make additional employee resources available or even lead to pay raises. In instances in which the reader may not initially view the information positively, use the body of the message to highlight the potential benefits from the reader's perspective. (For situations in which negative news will have a profound effect on the recipients, consider the indirect techniques discussed in Chapter 9.)

COMMUNICATION MISCUES	Can You Get Sued for Writing—or Not Writing— a Recommendation Letter?

Recommendation letters are classified as routine messages, but with all the legal troubles they can cause employers these days, they've become anything but routine. Over the years, employees have won lawsuits that charged former employers with defamation related to job recommendations. In addition to defamation charges—which can be successfully defended if the "defamatory" statements are proven to be true—employers have been sued for retaliation by ex-employees who believed that negative letters were written expressly for purposes of revenge. And as if that weren't enough, employers have even sued each other over recommendation letters when the recipient of a letter believed the writer failed to disclose important negative information.

No wonder many companies now refuse to divulge anything more than job titles and dates of employment. But even that doesn't always solve the problem: Ex-employees have been known to sue for retaliation when their employers refused to write on their behalf. As you can imagine, this refusal to write recommendations creates worries for hiring companies. If they can't get any real background information on job candidates, they risk hiring employees who lack the necessary skills or who are disruptive or even dangerous in the workplace.

For companies that let managers write recommendations, what sort of information should or should not be included? Even though the majority of states now have laws protecting companies against recommendation-related lawsuits when the employer acts in good faith, individual cases vary so much that no specific guidelines can ever apply to all cases. However, answering the following questions before drafting a recommendation letter will help you avoid trouble:

- Does the party receiving this personal information have a legitimate right to it?
- Does all the information I've presented relate directly to the job or benefit being sought?
- Have I put the candidate's case as strongly and as honestly as I can?
- Have I avoided overstating the candidate's abilities or otherwise misleading the reader?
- Have I based all my statements on firsthand knowledge and provable facts?

No matter what the circumstances, experts also advise that you always consult your human resources or legal department for advice.

CAREER APPLICATIONS

1. A former employee was often late for work but was an excellent and fast worker who got along well with everyone. Do you think it's important to mention the tardiness to potential employers? If so, how would you handle it?
2. Step outside yourself for a moment and write a letter of recommendation about you from a former employer's perspective. Make sure your letter embodies honesty, integrity, and prudence.

ANNOUNCING GOOD NEWS

To develop and maintain good relationships, smart companies recognize that it's good business to spread the word about positive developments. Such developments can include opening new facilities, hiring a new executive, introducing new products or services, or sponsoring community events. Because good news is always welcome, use the direct approach.

Good-news announcements are often communicated in a **news release**, also known as a *press release*, a specialized document used to share relevant information with the news media. (News releases are also used to announce negative news, such as plant closings.) In most companies, news releases are usually prepared or at least supervised by specially trained writers in the public relations department. The content follows the customary pattern for a positive message: good news followed by details and a positive close. However, traditional news releases have a critical difference: You're not writing directly to the ultimate audience (such as the readers of a newspaper); you're trying to interest an editor or a reporter in a story, and that person will then write the material that is eventually read by the larger audience. To write a successful news release, keep the following points in mind:[2]

A news release, also known as a press release, is a standardized way to share information with the news media.

- Above all else, make sure your information is newsworthy and relevant to the specific publications or websites to which you are sending it.
- Focus on one subject; don't try to pack a single news release with multiple, unrelated news items.
- Put your most important idea first. Don't force editors to hunt for the news.
- Be brief: Break up long sentences and keep paragraphs short.

Number and bullet lists help readers skim information quickly.

The filtering functions built into Facebook help website visitors find specific note pages.

These links serve the dual purposes of giving credit to the information sources used and providing readers with easy access to additional information.

Figure 8.7 Routine Informational Message
Many companies use the Notes tab on their Facebook pages to share routine informational messages with their customers and other parties.

- Eliminate clutter, such as redundancy and extraneous facts.
- Be as specific as possible.
- Minimize self-congratulatory adjectives and adverbs; if the content of your message is newsworthy, the media professionals will be interested in the news on its own merits.
- Follow established industry conventions for style, punctuation, and format.

Until recently, news releases were crafted in a way to provide information to reporters, who would then write their own articles if the subject matter was interesting to their readers. Thanks to the Internet and social media, however, the nature of the news release is changing. Many companies now view it as a general-purpose tool for communicating directly with customers and other audiences, creating *direct-to-consumer news releases* (see Figure 8.8). As media expert David Meerman Scott puts it, "Millions of people read press releases directly, unfiltered by the media. You need to be speaking directly to them."[3]

Many companies now release news directly to the public, rather than relying on the news media to share it.

The newest twist on news releases is the *social media release*, which has several advantages over the traditional release. First, the social media release emphasizes bullet-point content over narrative paragraphs so that bloggers, editors, and others can assemble their own stories, rather than being forced to rewrite the material in a traditional release. Second, as an electronic-only document (a specialized webpage, essentially), the social media release offers the ability to include videos and other multimedia elements. Third, social bookmarking buttons make it easy for people to help publicize the content.[4]

The "one-two punch" of a heading followed by a subheading is common in news releases; the two work together to convey the main idea of the document.

The release uses the "inverted pyramid" approach, in which the most important points are addressed at the beginning of the message, and then subsequent paragraphs offer successively more detailed information.

Video is offered in two formats, one that can be embedded in a website and one that can be downloaded from here.

Photographs are also available for journalists who want to include them in their articles.

Website and social media links give journalists and consumers access to more information.

Figure 8.8 Announcing Positive News
This multimedia news release from Procter & Gamble, the company that makes Pampers diapers, provides an extensive textual message as well as photos and videos that journalists and bloggers can use in any stories that they write about the Gifts to Grow promotional program.

FOSTERING GOODWILL

All business messages should be written with an eye toward fostering goodwill among business contacts, but some messages are written primarily and specifically to build goodwill. You can use these messages to enhance your relationships with customers, colleagues, and other businesspeople by sending friendly—even unexpected—notes with no direct business purpose.

Effective goodwill messages must be sincere and honest. Otherwise, you'll appear to be interested in personal gain rather than in benefiting customers, fellow workers, or your organization. To come across as sincere, avoid exaggerating and back up any compliments with specific points. In addition, readers often regard more restrained praise as being more sincere. Consider the following example:

Goodwill is the positive feeling that encourages people to maintain a business relationship.

Make sure your compliments are both sincere and honest.

Instead of This	Write This
Words cannot express my appreciation for the great job you did. Thanks. No one could have done it better. You're terrific! You've made the whole firm sit up and take notice, and we are ecstatic to have you working here.	Thanks again for taking charge of the meeting in my absence and doing such an excellent job. With just an hour's notice, you managed to pull the legal and public relations departments together so that we could present a united front in the negotiations. Your dedication and communication abilities have been noted and are truly appreciated.

Even though the second version is longer, it is a more effective message because it is specific and sincere.

Taking note of significant events in someone's personal life helps foster the business relationship.

Sending Congratulations

One prime opportunity for sending goodwill messages is to congratulate individuals or companies for significant business achievements (see Figure 8.9). Other reasons for sending congratulations include the highlights in people's personal lives, such as weddings, births, graduations, and success in nonbusiness competitions. Obviously, the nature of your relationship with a recipient determines the ranges of appropriate subjects for congratulations.

Sending Messages of Appreciation

An effective message of appreciation documents a person's contributions.

An important managerial quality is the ability to recognize the contributions of employees, colleagues, suppliers, and other associates. Your praise does more than just make the person feel good; it encourages further excellence. Moreover, a message of appreciation may become an important part of someone's personnel file. So when you write a message of appreciation, try to specifically mention the person or people you want to praise. The brief message that follows expresses gratitude and reveals the happy result:

> Thank you and everyone on your team for the heroic efforts you took to bring our servers back up after last Friday's flood. We were able to restore business right on schedule first thing Monday morning. You went far beyond the level of contractual service in restoring our data center within 16 hours. I would especially like to highlight the contribution of networking specialist Julienne Marks, who worked for 12 straight hours to reconnect our Internet service. If I can serve as a reference in your future sales activities, please do not hesitate to ask.

Hearing a sincere thank you can do wonders for morale.[5] Moreover, in today's electronic media environment, a handwritten thank-you note can be a particularly welcome acknowledgment.[6]

Opens with a positive and sincere expression of congratulations

Reminds the recipient of their previous meeting and offers specific points about the recipient's worthiness in a way that compliments without exaggerating

Closes on an upbeat note that keeps the focus on the recipient

Congratulations on your financing - Message (HTML)

This message has not been sent.

To... 'ricky.penrose@millersfall.com'
Cc...
Subject: Congratulations on your financing

Hello Ricky,

I just heard from Vivian Albers that you and your partners received full funding from San Marino Capital. Congratulations!

Although we passed on your presentation earlier this year, I was convinced that your unique business model and solid management team were worthy of first-round financing from an investment group with the right mix of connections and experience. I've known Vivian and her colleagues at San Marino for more than twenty years, so I can speak from experience when I say you have joined forces with one of the best firms in the business.

I wish you all the best as you start that wild ride toward your initial product launch. I'll be cheering you on from the sidelines.

Sincerely,
Roger DeCairn

DeCairn & Smythe
(405) 555-2379
www.dsinvestors.biz

Figure 8.9   Goodwill Messages
Goodwill messages serve a variety of business functions. In this email message, investor Roger DeCairn congratulates an entrepreneur who had previously sought start-up capital from his firm but later secured funding from another firm. The message may ultimately benefit DeCairn and his company by building goodwill, but it doesn't serve an immediate business purpose.

Offering Condolences

In times of serious trouble and deep sadness, well-written condolences and expressions of sympathy can mean a great deal to people who've experienced loss. This type of message is difficult to write, but don't let the difficulty of the task keep you from responding promptly.

Open a condolence message with a brief statement of sympathy, such as "I am deeply sorry to hear of your loss" in the event of a death, for example. In the body, mention the good qualities or the positive contributions made by the deceased. State what the person meant to you or your colleagues. In closing, you can offer your condolences and your best wishes. Here are a few general suggestions for writing condolence messages:[7]

REAL-TIME UPDATES
Learn More by Reading This Article

Simple rules for writing effective thank-you notes

These tips are easy to adapt to any business or social occasions in which you need to express appreciation. Go to http://real-timeupdates.com/bct11 and click on "Learn More." If you are using MyBcommLab, you can access Real-Time Updates within each chapter or under Student Study Tools.

The primary purpose of condolence messages is to let the audience know that you and the organization you represent care about the person's loss.

- **Keep reminiscences brief.** Recount a memory, if appropriate, but don't dwell on the details of the loss.
- **Write in your own words.** Write as if you were speaking privately to the person. Don't quote "poetic" passages or use stilted or formal phrases.
- **Be tactful.** Mention your shock and dismay but remember that bereaved and distressed loved ones take little comfort in lines such as "Richard was too young to die" or "Starting all over again will be so difficult." Try to strike a balance between superficial expressions of sympathy and painful references to a happier past or the likelihood of a bleak future.
- **Take special care.** Be sure to spell names correctly and be accurate in your review of facts. Write and deliver your message promptly.
- **Write about special qualities of the deceased.** You may have to rely on reputation to do this, but let the grieving person know you valued his or her loved one.
- **Considerer mentioning special attributes or resources of the bereaved person.** If you know that the bereaved person has attributes or resources that will be a comfort in the time of loss, such as personal resilience, religious faith, or a circle of close friends, mentioning these can make the reader feel more confident about handling the challenges he or she faces.

Supervisor George Bigalow sent the following condolence letter to his administrative assistant, Janice Case, after learning of the death of Janice's husband:

> My sympathy to you and your children. All your friends at Carter Electric were so sorry to learn of John's death. Although I never had the opportunity to meet him, I do know how special he was to you. Your tales of your family's camping trips and his rafting expeditions were always memorable.

To review the tasks involved in writing goodwill messages, see "Checklist: Sending Goodwill Messages." For the latest information on writing routine and positive messages, visit http://real-timeupdates.com/bct11.

✓ Checklist   Sending Goodwill Messages

- Be sincere and honest.
- Don't exaggerate or use vague, grandiose language; support positive statements with specific evidence.
- Use congratulatory messages to build goodwill with clients and colleagues.
- Send messages of appreciation to emphasize how much you value the work of others.
- When sending condolence messages, open with a brief statement of sympathy followed by an expression of how much the deceased person meant to you or your firm (as appropriate); close by offering your best wishes for the future.

Quick Learning Guide

MyBcommLab

CHAPTER OUTLINE

SUMMARY OF LEARNING OBJECTIVES

1 Outline an effective strategy for writing routine business requests. When writing a routine request, open by stating your specific request. Use the body to justify your request and explain its importance. Close routine requests by asking for specific action (including a deadline, if appropriate) and expressing goodwill. A courteous close contains three important elements: (1) a specific request, (2) information about how you can be reached (if it isn't obvious), and (3) an expression of appreciation or goodwill.

2 Describe three common types of routine requests. The most common types of routine messages are asking for information or action, asking for recommendations, and making claims and requesting adjustments. Requests for information or action should explain what you want to know or what you want readers to do, why you're making the request, and why it may be in your readers' interest to help you (if applicable). Requests for recommendations should open by stating what it is you are requesting and asking the recipient to write the message in question. The body should list all the information the recipient would need to write the recommendation (refer to an attached résumé, if applicable). The close should contain an expression of appreciation and a deadline, if applicable. To make a claim (a formal complaint about a product or service) or request an adjustment (a settlement of a claim), open with a straightforward statement of the problem, use the body to give a complete explanation of the situation, and close with a polite request to resolve the situation.

3 Outline an effective strategy for writing routine replies and positive messages. The direct approach works well for routine replies and positive messages because recipients will generally be interested in what you have to say. Place your main idea (the positive reply or the good news) in the opening. Use the body to explain all the relevant details, and close cordially, perhaps highlighting a benefit to your reader.

4 Describe six common types of routine replies and positive messages. Most routine and positive messages fall into six categories: answers to requests for information and action, grants of claims and requests for adjustment, recommendations, informative messages, good-news announcements, and goodwill messages. Providing answers to requests for information or action is a simple task, often assisted with form responses that can be customized as needed. Granting claims and requests for adjustments is more complicated, and the right response depends on whether the company, the customer, or a third party was at fault. Recommendations also require a careful approach to avoid legal complications; some companies prohibit managers from writing recommendation letters or providing anything beyond basic employment history. Informative messages are often simple and straightforward, but some require extra care if the information affects recipients in a significant way. Good-news announcements are often handled by news releases, which used to be sent exclusively to members of the news media but are now usually made available to the public as well. Finally, goodwill messages, meant to foster positive business relationships, include congratulations, thank-you messages, and messages of condolence. To make goodwill messages effective, make them honest, sincere, and factual.

KEY TERMS

adjustment The settlement of a claim
claim A formal complaint made in response to dissatisfaction over a product or service

news release Also known as a *press release*, a specialized document traditionally used to share relevant information with the

local or national news media; today, many companies issue news releases directly to the public as well

Checklist

Writing Routine Requests

A. State your request up front.
- Write in a polite, undemanding, personal tone.
- Use the direct approach because your audience will probably respond favorably to your request.
- Be specific and precise in your request.

B. Explain and justify your request.
- Justify the request or explain its importance.
- Explain any potential benefits of responding.
- Ask the most important questions first.
- Break complex requests into individual questions that are limited to only one topic each.

C. Request specific action in a courteous close.
- Make it easy to comply by including appropriate contact information.
- Express your gratitude.
- Clearly state any important deadlines for the request.

Checklist

Making Claims and Requesting Adjustments

- Maintain a professional tone, even if you're extremely frustrated.
- Open with a straightforward statement of the problem.
- Provide specific details in the body.
- Present facts honestly and clearly.
- Politely summarize the desired action in the closing.
- Clearly state what you expect as a fair settlement or ask the reader to propose a fair adjustment.
- Explain the benefits of complying with the request, such as your continued patronage.

Checklist

Writing Routine Replies and Positive Messages

A. Start with the main idea.
- Be clear and concise.
- Identify the single most important message before you start writing.

B. Provide necessary details and explanation.
- Explain your point completely to eliminate any confusion or lingering doubts.
- Maintain a supportive tone throughout.
- Embed negative statements in positive contexts or balance them with positive alternatives.
- Talk favorably about the choices the customer has made.

C. End with a courteous close.
- Let your readers know that you have their personal well-being in mind.
- If further action is required, tell readers how to proceed and encourage them to act promptly.

Checklist

Sending Goodwill Messages

- Be sincere and honest.
- Don't exaggerate or use vague, grandiose language; support positive statements with specific evidence.
- Use congratulatory messages to build goodwill with clients and colleagues.
- Send messages of appreciation to emphasize how much you value the work of others.
- When sending condolence messages, open with a brief statement of sympathy followed by an expression of how much the deceased person meant to you or your firm (as appropriate); close by offering your best wishes for the future.

Checklist

Granting Claims and Adjustment Requests

A. Responding when your company is at fault.
- Be aware of your company's policies in such cases before you respond.
- For serious situations, refer to the company's crisis management plan.
- Start by acknowledging receipt of the claim or complaint.
- Take or assign personal responsibility for resolving the situation.
- Sympathize with the customer's frustration.
- Explain how you have resolved the situation (or plan to).
- Take steps to repair the customer relationship.
- Verify your response with the customer and keep the lines of communication open.

B. Responding when the customer is at fault.
- Weigh the cost of complying with or refusing the request.
- If you choose to comply, open with the good news.
- Use the body of the message to respectfully educate the customer about steps needed to avoid a similar outcome in the future.
- Close with an appreciation for the customer's business.

C. Responding when a third party is at fault.
- Evaluate the situation and review your company's policies before responding.
- Avoid placing blame; focus on the solution.
- Regardless of who is responsible for resolving the situation, let the customer know what will happen to resolve the problem.

COMMUNICATION CHALLENGES AT GET SATISFACTION

After reading the many helpful responses you, as a representative of your company, posted on the Get Satisfaction website, Thor Muller invited you to join the Get Satisfaction team as a customer service specialist; your job is to communicate with the companies that use Get Satisfaction's online services. Take what you've learned in this chapter and put it to good use as you address the following challenges. (Search for a few companies or product names on **http:// getsatisfaction.com** to get a feel for how the system works.)

INDIVIDUAL CHALLENGE: When people are frustrated with a problem and are trying to discuss it via a lean medium such as online postings, emotions can sometimes boil over. You've been monitoring a conversation between a representative for one of the companies that uses Get Satisfaction and one of its customers. Over the past couple of days, their online conversation has turned into an ugly argument, with accusations of incompetence and even dishonesty flying back and forth. Although the situation doesn't involve Get Satisfaction directly, you think it reflects poorly on your company—and it certainly isn't doing anybody any good to let this "flame war" keep raging. Write a brief post (which you can email to your instructor) that acknowledges the frustration both sides are obviously feeling and offer to act as an intermediary to help get the problem resolved. Make up any information you need in order to complete the message.

TEAM CHALLENGE: Get Satisfaction has just made available an upgrade to its website software in *beta release* form (a free version of software that companies encourage people to use as a way to see if anything needs to be changed or fixed before the official product is released). However, the company hasn't yet announced how much the new upgrade is going to cost when it is officially released, so not surprisingly, more than a few interested customers have written questions about the anticipated

price. Small-business owners in particular want to know if a less-expensive version (perhaps with fewer features) will be available to small companies. When you asked your boss for help in answering this question, he suggested that you send the following response:

> To be as open and transparent about our pricing thinking as possible, I have to be up front: We can't speak to exact pricing yet, because we're still working on those details. We didn't want that to hold up release/use/testing of these new features, which is why we're releasing them on a "try first" beta basis right now, with the caveat that pricing will be a factor in the future for those companies who choose to continue using them.
>
> What we can say is that we are *very* committed to two things:
>
> 1) Making sure that it's a pricing structure that does in fact work both for small companies and large ones, and that if there is a tiered structure, that it scales according to a reliable set of figures/metrics that reflect those size differences.
>
> 2) Always offering a free version that has a minimum level of utility for those companies that can't for whatever reason pay.
>
> We're pretty excited about the new tools and the new functionality and want to see them spread as far and as wide as possible, so that's a significant consideration as we look to our pricing plan as well. But, you know, we've got to pay the bills somehow.
>
> Further updates as events warrant.[8]

This answer provides as much information as the company can release right now, but you think it can be more concise. (It is currently about 200 words.) In teams, as designated by your instructor, have each team member independently revise this message to make it no longer than 100 words. After everyone on the team has written a new draft, have each person share his or her version with the rest of the team. As a team, decide which version is best and then email it to your instructor.

TEST YOUR KNOWLEDGE

To review chapter content related to each question, refer to the indicated Learning Objective.

1. What information should be included in a routine request? [LO-1]
2. Should you use the direct or indirect approach for most routine messages? Why? [LO-1]
3. Where in a routine message should you state your actual request? [LO-1]
4. What information should you include in a request for a recommendation? [LO-2]
5. How does a claim differ from an adjustment? [LO-2]
6. What is resale information? [LO-3]
7. How does the question of fault affect what you say in a message granting a claim? [LO-4]
8. What is the appropriate strategy for responding to a request for a recommendation about a job candidate whose performance was poor? [LO-4]
9. How can you avoid sounding insincere when writing a goodwill message? [LO-4]
10. What are the guidelines for writing condolence messages? [LO-4]

APPLY YOUR KNOWLEDGE

To review chapter content related to each question, refer to the indicated Learning Objective.

1. Why is it good practice to explain why replying to a request could benefit the reader? [LO-1]
2. You have a complaint against one of your suppliers, but you have no documentation to back it up. Should you request an adjustment anyway? Why or why not? [LO-2]
3. The latest issue of a local business newspaper names 10 area executives who have exhibited excellent leadership skills in the past year. You are currently searching for a job, and a friend suggests that you write each executive a congratulatory letter and mention in passing that you are looking for new career opportunities and would appreciate the opportunity for an interview. Is this a smart strategy? Why or why not? [LO-4]
4. You've been asked to write a letter of recommendation for an employee who worked for you some years ago. You recall that the employee did an admirable job, but you can't remember any specific information at this point. Should you write the letter anyway? Explain. [LO-4]
5. Your company's error cost an important business customer a new client; you know it, and your customer knows it. Do you apologize, or do you refer to the incident in a positive light without admitting any responsibility? Briefly explain. [LO-4]

PRACTICE YOUR SKILLS

Messages for Analysis

Read the following messages and then (1) analyze the strengths and weaknesses of each sentence and (2) revise each document so that it follows this chapter's guidelines.

Message 8.A: Message Strategies: Routine Requests [LO-2]

I'm fed up with the mistakes that our current accounting firm makes. I run a small construction company, and I don't have time to double-check every bookkeeping entry and call the accountants a dozen times when they won't return my messages. Please explain how your firm would do a better job than my current accountants. You have a good reputation among homebuilders, but before I consider hiring you to take over my accounting, I need to know that you care about quality work and good customer service.

Message 8.B: Message Strategies: Requesting an Adjustment [LO-2]

At a local business-supply store, I recently purchased your Negotiator Pro for my computer. I bought the CD because I saw your ad for it in Macworld magazine, and it looked as if it might be an effective tool for use in my corporate seminar on negotiation.

Unfortunately, when I inserted it in my office computer, it wouldn't work. I returned it to the store, but because I had already opened it, they refused to exchange it for a CD that would work or give me a refund. They told me to contact you and that you might be able to send me a version that would work with my computer.

You can send the information to me at the letterhead address. If you cannot send me the correct disc, please refund my $79.95. Thanks in advance for any help you can give me in this matter.

Message 8.C: Message Strategies: Responding to Claims and Requests for Adjustments [LO-4]

We read your letter, requesting your deposit refund. We couldn't figure out why you hadn't received it, so we talked to our maintenance engineer, as you suggested. He said you had left one of the doors off the hinges in your apartment in order to get a large sofa through the door. He also confirmed that you had paid him $5.00 to replace the door since you had to turn in the U-Haul trailer and were in a big hurry.

This entire situation really was caused by a lack of communication between our housekeeping inspector and the maintenance engineer. All we knew was that the door was off the hinges when it was inspected by Sally Tarnley. You know that our policy states that if anything is wrong with the apartment, we keep the deposit. We had no way of knowing that George just hadn't gotten around to replacing the door.

But we have good news. We approved the deposit refund, which will be mailed to you from our home office in Teaneck, New Jersey. I'm not sure how long that will take, however. If you don't receive the check by the end of next month, give me a call.

Next time, it's really a good idea to stay with your apartment until it's inspected, as stipulated in your lease agreement. That way, you'll be sure to receive your refund when you expect it. Hope you have a good summer.

Message 8.D: Message Strategies:
Providing Recommendations [LO-4]

Your letter to Kunitake Ando, president of Sony, was forwarded to me because I am the human resources director. In my job as head of HR, I have access to performance reviews for all of the Sony employees in the United States. This means, of course, that I would be the person best qualified to answer your request for information on Nick Oshinski.

In your letter of the 15th, you asked about Nick Oshinski's employment record with us because he has applied to work for your company. Mr. Oshinski was employed with us from January 5, 1998, until March 1, 2008. During that time, Mr. Oshinski received ratings ranging from 2.5 up to 9.6, with 10 being the top score. As you can see, he must have done better reporting to some managers than to others. In addition, he took all vacation days, which is a bit unusual. Although I did not know Mr. Oshinski personally, I know that our best workers seldom use all the vacation time they earn. I do not know if that applies in this case.

In summary, Nick Oshinski performed his tasks well depending on who managed him.

Exercises

Active links for all websites in this chapter can be found on MyBcommLab; see your User Guide for instructions on accessing the content for this chapter. Each activity is labeled according to the primary skill or skills you will need to use. To review relevant chapter content, you can refer to the indicated Learning Objective. In some instances, supporting information will be found in another chapter, as indicated.

1. **Message Strategies: Routine Requests; Revising for Conciseness [LO-1] Chapter 6** Critique the following closing paragraphs. How would you rewrite each to be concise, courteous, and specific?

   a. I need your response sometime soon so I can order the parts in time for your service appointment. Otherwise, your air-conditioning system may not be in tip-top condition for the start of the summer season.

   b. Thank you in advance for sending me as much information as you can about your products. I look forward to receiving your package in the very near future.

   c. To schedule an appointment with one of our knowledgeable mortgage specialists in your area, you can always call our hotline at 1-800-555-8765. This is also the number to call if you have more questions about mortgage rates, closing procedures, or any other aspect of the mortgage process. Remember, we're here to make the home-buying experience as painless as possible.

2. **Message Strategies: Routine Responses; Media Skills: Email [LO-3], Chapter 7** Revise the following short email messages so that they are more direct and concise; develop a subject line for each revised message.

   a. I'm contacting you about your recent email request for technical support on your cable Internet service. Part of the problem we have in tech support is trying to figure out exactly what each customer's specific problem is so

that we can troubleshoot quickly and get you back in business as quickly as possible. You may have noticed that in the online support request form, there are a number of fields to enter your type of computer, operating system, memory, and so on. While you did tell us you were experiencing slow download speeds during certain times of the day, you didn't tell us which times specifically, nor did you complete all the fields telling us about your computer. Please return to our support website and resubmit your request, being sure to provide all the necessary information; then we'll be able to help you.

   b. Thank you for contacting us about the difficulty you had collecting your luggage at Denver International Airport. We are very sorry for the inconvenience this has caused you. As you know, traveling can create problems of this sort regardless of how careful the airline personnel might be. To receive compensation, please send us a detailed list of the items that you lost and complete the following questionnaire. You can email it back to us.

   c. Sorry it took us so long to get back to you. We were flooded with résumés. Anyway, your résumé made the final 10, and after meeting three hours yesterday, we've decided we'd like to meet with you. What is your schedule like for next week? Can you come in for an interview on June 15 at 3:00 p.m.? Please get back to us by the end of this workweek and let us know if you will be able to attend. As you can imagine, this is our busy season.

   d. We're letting you know that because we use over a ton of paper a year and because so much of that paper goes into the wastebasket to become so much more environmental waste, starting Monday, we're placing white plastic bins outside the elevators on every floor to recycle that paper and in the process, minimize pollution.

3. **Message Strategies: Routine and Positive Messages; Revising for Conciseness [LO-3], Chapter 6** Rewrite the following sentences so that they are direct and concise. If necessary, break your answer into two sentences.

   a. We wanted to invite you to our special 40% off by-invitation-only sale; the sale is taking place on November 9.

   b. We wanted to let you know that we are giving a tote bag and a voucher for five iTunes downloads with every $50 donation you make to our radio station.

   c. The director planned to go to the meeting that will be held on Monday at a little before 11 a.m.

   d. In today's meeting, we were happy to have the opportunity to welcome Paul Eccelson, who reviewed the shopping cart function on our website and offered some great advice; if you have any questions about these new forms, feel free to call him at his office.

4. **Message Strategies: Responding to Claims and Requests for Adjustments [LO-4]** Your company markets a line of automotive accessories for people who like to "tune" their cars for maximum performance. A customer has just written a furious email, claiming that a supercharger he purchased from your website didn't deliver the extra engine power he expected. Your company has a standard refund process to handle situations such as this, and you have the information you need to inform the customer about that. You also have information

that could help the customer find a more compatible super-charger from one of your competitors, but the customer's email message is so abusive that you don't feel obligated to help. Is this an appropriate response? Why or why not?

 Learn how to set up a Twitter account and begin tweeting. Visit http://real-timeupdates.com/bct11, click on "Student Assignments" and then click on "Twitter Screencast."

5. **Message Strategies: Writing Positive Messages; Media Skills: Microblogging [LO-4], Chapter 7** Locate an online announcement for a new product that you find interesting or useful. Read enough about the product to be able to describe it to someone else in your own words and then writer four Twitter tweets: one to introduce the product to your followers and three follow-on tweets that describe three particularly compelling features or benefits of the product.

6. **Message Strategies: Goodwill Messages [LO-4]** Visit the Workplace eCards section of the Blue Mountain site, at www.bluemountain.com, and analyze one of the electronic greeting cards bearing a goodwill message of appreciation for good performance. Under what circumstances would you send this electronic message? How could you personalize it for the recipient and the occasion? What would be an appropriate close for this message?

EXPAND YOUR SKILLS

Critique the Professionals

Locate an online example of a news release in which a company announces good news, such as a new product, a notable executive hire, an expansion, strong financial results, or an industry award. Analyze the release using the bullet list on pages 229–230 as a guide. In what ways did the writer excel? What aspects of the release could be improved? Using whatever medium your instructor requests, write a brief analysis of the piece (no more than one page), citing specific elements from the piece and support from the chapter.

Sharpening Your Career Skills Online

Bovée and Thill's Business Communication Web Search, at http://businesscommunicationblog.com/websearch, is a unique research tool designed specifically for business communication research. Use the Web Search function to find a website, video, PDF document, podcast, or PowerPoint presentation that offers advice on writing goodwill messages such as thank-you notes or congratulatory letters. Write a brief email message to your instructor, describing the item that you found and summarizing the career skills information you learned from it.

CASES

Routine Requests

BLOGGING SKILLS

1. Message Strategies: Requesting Information [LO-2] You are writing a book about the advantages and potential pitfalls of using online collaboration systems for virtual team projects. You would like to include several dozen real-life examples from people in a variety of industries. Fortunately, you publish a highly respected blog on the subject, with several thousand regular readers.

Your task: Write a post for your blog that asks readers to submit brief descriptions of their experiences using collaboration tools for team projects. Ask them to email stories of how well a specific system or approach worked for them. Explain that they will receive an autographed copy of the book as thanks, but they will need to sign a release form if their stories are used. In addition, emphasize that you would like to use real names—of people, companies, and software—but you can keep the anecdotes anonymous if readers require. To stay on schedule, you need to have these stories by May 20.

EMAIL SKILLS

2. Message Strategies: Requesting a Recommendation [LO-2] One of your colleagues, Katina Vander, was recently promoted to department manager and now serves on the company's strategic planning committee. At its monthly meeting next week, the committee will choose an employee to lead an important market research project that will help define the company's product portfolio for the next five years.

You worked side by side with Vander for five years, so she knows your abilities well and has complimented your business insights on many occasions. You know that because she has only recently been promoted to manager, she needs to build credibility among her peers and will therefore be cautious about making such an important recommendation. On the other hand, making a stellar recommendation for such an important project would show that she has a good eye for talent—an essential leadership trait.

Your task: Write an email message to Vander, telling her that you are definitely interested in leading the project and asking her to put in a good word for you with the committee. Mention four attributes that you believe would serve you well in the role: a dozen years of experience in the industry, an engineering degree that helps you understand the technologies involved in product design, a consistent record of excellent or exceptional ratings in annual employee evaluations, and the three years you spent working in the company's customer support group, which gave you a firsthand look at customer satisfaction and quality issues. Make up any additional details you need to write the message.

EMAIL SKILLS

3. Message Strategies: Requesting a Recommendation [LO-2] After five years of work in the human resources department at Cell Genesys (a company that is developing cancer treatment drugs), you were laid off in a round of cost-cutting moves that rippled through the biotech industry in recent years. The good news is that you found stable employment in the grocery distribution industry. The bad news is that in the three years since you left Cell Genesys, you have truly missed working in the exciting biotechnology field and having the opportunity to be a part of something as important as helping people recover from life-threatening diseases. You know that careers in biotech are uncertain, but you have a few dollars in the bank now, and you're willing to ride that rollercoaster again.

Your task: Draft an email to Calvin Morris, your old boss at Cell Genesys, reminding him of the time you worked together and asking him to write a letter of recommendation for you.[9]

IM SKILLS

4. Message Strategies: Requesting Information [LO-2] Thank goodness your company, Diagonal Imports, chose the Sametime enterprise instant messaging software produced by IBM Lotus. Other products also allow you to carry on real-time exchanges with colleagues on the other side of the planet, but Sametime supports bidirectional machine translation, and you're going to need it.

The problem is that production on a popular line of decorative lighting appliances produced at your Chinese manufacturing plant inexplicably came to a halt last month. As the product manager in the United States, you have many resources you could call on to help, such as new sources for faulty parts. But you can't do anything if you don't know the details. You've tried telephoning top managers in China, but they're evasive, telling you only what they think you want to hear.

Finally, your friend Kuei-chen Tsao has returned from a business trip. You met her during your trip to China last year. She doesn't speak English, but she's the line engineer responsible for this particular product: a fiber-optic lighting display that features a plastic base with a rotating color wheel. As the wheel turns, light emitted from the spray of fiber-optic threads changes color in soothing patterns. Product #3347XM is one of Diagonal's most popular items, and you have orders from novelty stores around the United States waiting to be filled. Kuei-chen should be able to explain the problem, determine whether you can help, and tell you how long before regular shipping resumes.

Your task: Write the first of what you hope will be a productive instant message exchange with Kuei-chen. Remember that your words will be machine translated.[10]

TEXT MESSAGING SKILLS

5. Message Strategies: Requesting Information [LO-2] The vast Consumer Electronics Show (CES) is the premier promotional event in the industry. More than 130,000 industry insiders from all over the world come to see the exciting new products on display from nearly 1,500 companies—everything from video game gadgets to Internet-enabled refrigerators with built-in computer screens. You've just stumbled on a video game controller that has a built-in webcam to allow networked gamers to see and hear each other while they play. Your company also makes game controllers, and you're worried that your customers will flock to this new controller-cam. You need to know how much buzz is circulating around the show: Have people seen it? What are they saying about it? Are they excited about it?

Your task: Compose a text message to your colleagues at the show, alerting them to the new controller-cam and asking them to listen for any buzz it might be generating among the attendees at the Las Vegas Convention Center and the several surrounding hotels where the show takes place. Here's the catch: Your text-messaging service limits messages to 160 characters, including spaces and punctuation, so your message can't be any longer than this.[11]

EMAIL SKILLS

6. Message Strategies: Requesting an Adjustment [LO-2] Love at first listen is the only way to describe the way you felt when you discovered SongThrong.com. You enjoy dozens of styles of music, from Afrobeat and Tropicalia to mainstream pop and the occasional blast of industrial metal, and SongThrong.com has them all for only $9.99 a month. You can explore every genre imaginable, listening to as many tracks as you like for a fixed monthly fee. The service sounded too good to be true—and sadly, it was. The service was so unreliable that you began keeping note of when it was unavailable. Last month, it was down for all or part of 12 days—well over a third of the month. As much as you like it, you've had enough.

Your task: Write an email to support@songthrong.com, requesting a full refund. To get the $9.99 monthly rate, you prepaid for an entire year ($119.88), and you've been a subscriber for two months now. You know the service has been out for at least part of time on 12 separate days last month, and while you didn't track outages during the first month, you believe it was about the same number of days.

LETTER WRITING SKILLS

7. Message Strategies: Requesting an Adjustment [LO-2] As a consumer, you've probably bought something that didn't work right or paid for a service that did not turn out the way you expected. Maybe it was a pair of jeans with a rip in a seam that you didn't find until you got home or a watch that broke a week after you bought it. Or maybe your family hired a lawn service to do some yard work—and no one from the company showed up on the day promised; and when the gardeners finally appeared, they did not do what they'd been hired for but did other things that wound up damaging valuable plants.

Your task: Choose an incident from your own experience and write a claim letter, asking for a refund, repair, replacement, or other adjustment. You'll need to include all the details of the transaction, plus your contact address and phone number. If you can't think of such an experience, make up details for an imaginary situation. If your experience is real, you might want to mail the letter. The reply you receive will provide a good test of your claim-writing skills.

EMAIL SKILLS

8. Message Strategies: Requesting Action [LO-2] You head up the corporate marketing department for a nationwide chain of clothing stores. The company has decided to launch a new store-within-a-store concept, in which a small section of each store will showcase "business casual" clothing. To ensure a successful launch of this new strategy, you want to get input from the best retailing minds in the company. You also know it's important to get regional insights from around the country, because a merchandising strategy that works in one area might not succeed in another.

Your task: Write an email message to all 87 store managers, asking them to each nominate one person to serve on an advisory team (managers can nominate themselves if they are local market experts). Explain that you want to find people with at least five years of retailing experience, a good understanding of the local business climate, and thorough knowledge of the local retail competition. In addition, the best candidates will be good team players who are comfortable collaborating long distance, using virtual meeting technologies. Also, explain that while you are asking each of the 87 stores to nominate someone, the team will be limited to no more than eight people. You've met many of the store managers, but not all of them, so be sure to introduce yourself at the beginning of the message.

Routine Messages

EMAIL SKILLS

9. Message Strategies: Granting Claims [LO-4] Your company sells flower arrangements and gift baskets. Holidays are always a rush, and the overworked staff makes the occasional mistake. Last week, somebody made a big one. As a furious email message from a customer named Anders Ellison explains, he ordered a Valentine's Day bouquet for his wife, but the company sent a bereavement arrangement instead.

Your task: Respond to Ellison's email message, apologizing for the error, promising to refund all costs that Ellison incurred, informing him that the correct arrangement will arrive tomorrow (and he won't be charged anything for it), and offering Ellison his choice of any floral arrangement or gift basket for free on his wife's birthday.

EMAIL SKILLS

10. Message Strategies: Granting Claims [LO-4] Like many of the staff at Razer (www.razerzone.com), you are an avid game player. You can therefore sympathize with a customer who got so excited during a hotly contested game that he slammed his Razer Anansi keyboard against his chair in celebration. Razer products are built for serious action, but no keyboard can withstand a blow like that. However, in the interest of building goodwill among the online gaming community, your manager has approved a free replacement. This sort of damage is rare enough that the company isn't worried about unleashing a flood of similar requests.

Your task: Respond to Louis Hapsberg's email request for a replacement, in which he admitted to inflicting some abuse on this keyboard. Explain, tongue in cheek, that the company is "rewarding" him with a free keyboard in honor of his massive gaming win, but gently remind him that even the most robust electronic equipment needs to be used with care.

BLOGGING SKILLS

11. Message Strategies: Providing Routine Information; Compositional Modes: Tutorials [LO-4] Austin, Texas, advertising agency GSD&M Idea City brainstorms new advertising ideas using a process it calls *dynamic collaboration*. A hand-picked team of insiders and outsiders is briefed on the project and given a key question or two to answer. The team members then sit down at computers and anonymously submit as many responses as they can within five minutes. The project moderators then pore over these responses, looking for any sparks that can ignite new ways of understanding and reaching out to consumers.

Your task: For these brainstorming sessions, GSD&M recruits an eclectic mix of participants from inside and outside the agency—figures as diverse as economists and professional video gamers. To make sure everyone understands the brainstorming guidelines, prepare a message to be posted on the project blog. In your own words, convey the following four points as clearly and succinctly as you can:

- **Be yourself.** We want input from as many perspectives as possible, which is why we recruit such a diverse array of participants. Don't try to get into what you believe is the mindset of an advertising specialist; we want you to approach the given challenge using whatever analytical and creative skills you normally employ in your daily work.
- **Create, don't edit.** Don't edit, refine, or self-censor while you're typing during the initial five-minute session. We don't care if your ideas are formatted beautifully, phrased poetically, or even spelled correctly. Just crank 'em out as quickly as you can.
- **It's about the ideas, not the participants.** Just so you know up front, all ideas are collected anonymously. We can't tell who submitted the brilliant ideas, the boring ideas, or the already-tried-that ideas. So while you won't get personal credit, you can also be crazy and fearless. Go for it!
- **The winning ideas will be subjected to the toughest of tests.** Just in case you're worried about submitting ideas that could be risky, expensive, or difficult to implement—don't fret. As we narrow down the possibilities, the few that remain will be judged, poked, prodded, and assessed from every angle. In other words, let us worry about containing the fire; you come up with the sparks.[12]

PODCASTING SKILLS   PORTFOLIO BUILDER

12. Message Strategies: Providing Routine Information; Media Skills: Podcasting [LO-4] As a training specialist in Winnebago Industry's human resources department, you're always on the lookout for new ways to help employees learn vital job skills. While watching a production worker page through a training manual while learning how to assemble a new recreational vehicle, you get what seems to be a great idea: Record the assembly instructions as audio files that workers can listen to while performing the necessary steps. With audio instructions, they wouldn't need to keep shifting their eyes between the product and the manual—and constantly losing their place. They could focus on the product and listen for each instruction. Plus, the new system wouldn't cost much at all; any computer can record the audio files, and you'd simply make them available on an intranet site for download into iPods or other digital music players.

Your task: You immediately run your new idea past your boss, who has heard about podcasting but doesn't think it has any place in business. He asks you to prove the viability of the idea by recording a demonstration. Choose a process that you engage in yourself—anything from replacing the strings on a guitar to sewing a quilt to changing the oil in a car—and write a brief (one page or less) description of the process that could be recorded as an audio file. Think carefully about the limitations of the audio format as a replacement for printed text (for instance, do you need to tell people to pause the audio while they perform a time-consuming task?). If directed by your instructor, record your instructions as a podcast.

BLOGGING SKILLS   PORTFOLIO BUILDER

13. Message Strategies: Providing Routine Information [LO-4] You are normally an easygoing manager who gives your employees a lot of leeway in using their own personal communication styles. However, the weekly staff meeting this morning pushed you over the edge. People were interrupting one another, asking questions that had already been answered, sending text messages during presentations, and exhibiting just about every other poor listening habit imaginable.

Your task: Review the advice in Chapter 2 on good listening skills and then write a post for the internal company blog. Emphasize the importance of effective listening and list at least five steps your employees can take to become better listeners.

Routine Replies

EMAIL SKILLS   PORTFOLIO BUILDER

14. Message Strategies: Routine Responses [LO-4] Walmart has grown to international success because it rarely fails to capitalize on a marketing scheme, and its website is no exception. To make sure the website remains effective and relevant, the webmaster asks various people to check out the site and give their feedback. As administrative assistant to Walmart's director of marketing, you have just received a request from the webmaster to visit Walmart's website and give your feedback.

Your task: Visit www.walmart.com and browse through the site, considering the language, layout, graphics, and overall ease of use. In particular, look for aspects of the site that might be confusing or frustrating—annoyances that could prompt shoppers to abandon their quests and head to a competitor such as Target. Summarize your findings and recommendations in an email message that could be sent to the webmaster.

EMAIL SKILLS

15. Message Strategies: Routine Responses [LO-4] As the owner of Paradise Sportswear in Hawaii, Robert Hedin found himself in a battle against the Earth itself when red dirt started seeping into his warehouse and ruining his inventory. Fortunately, a friend suggested that he turn his troubles into opportunities, and he came up with Red Dirt Shirts, all made with dye created from the troublesome local dirt. Hedin's Red Dirt Sportswear designs turned out to be so popular, that he added a new line, Lava Blues, made with real Hawaiian lava rock.

"You can make 500 shirts with a bucket of dirt," says Hedin with a grin as he shows you around the operation on your first day.

Recently, Hedin decided to finally give in to all the requests he's received from retail outlets on the mainland. Buyers kept coming to the islands on vacation, discovering Hedin's "natural"

sportswear in local stores, and begging him to set up a deal. For a long time, his answer was no; he simply couldn't handle the extra work.

But now Hedin's hired you as a sales representative to help him slowly expand distribution on the mainland, starting with one store: Surf's Up, far away from ocean surf in Chicago, Illinois. He figures that with less competition than he'd find on either coast, his island-influenced sportswear will be a big hit in Chicago, especially in the dead of winter.

Your task: Write a positive response to the email received from Surf's Up buyer Ronald Draeger, who says he fell in love with the Paradise clothing concept while on a surfing trip to Maui. Let him know he'll have a temporary, four-month exclusive and that you'll be sending a credit application and other materials by snail mail.[13]

EMAIL SKILLS

16. Message Strategies: Routine Responses [LO-4] You are director of customer services at Highway Bytes, which markets a series of small, handlebar-mounted computers for bicyclists. These Cycle Computers do everything, from computing speed and distance traveled to displaying street maps. Serious cyclists love them, but your company is growing so fast that you can't keep up with all the customer service requests you receive every day. Your boss wants not only to speed up response time but also to reduce staffing costs and allow your technical experts the time they need to focus on the most difficult and important questions.

You've just been reading about automated response systems, and you quickly review a few articles before discussing the options with your boss. Artificial intelligence researchers have been working for decades to design systems that can actually converse with customers, ask questions, and respond to requests. Some of today's systems have vocabularies of thousands of words and the ability to understand simple sentences. For example, *chatterbots* are automated bots that can actually mimic human conversation.

Unfortunately, even though chatterbots hold a lot of promise, human communication is so complex that a truly automated customer service agent could take years to perfect (and may even prove to be impossible). However, the simplest automated systems are called *autoresponders*, or *on-demand email*. They are fast and extremely inexpensive. They have no built-in intelligence, so they do nothing more than send back the same reply to every message they receive.

You explain to your boss that although some of the messages you receive require the attention of your product specialists, many are simply requests for straightforward information. In fact, the customer service staff already answers some 70 percent of email queries with three ready-made attachments:

- **Installing Your Cycle Computer.** This attachment gives customers advice on installing the cycle computer the first time or reinstalling it on a new bike. In most cases, the computer and wheel sensor bolt directly to the bike without modification, but certain bikes do require extra work.
- **Troubleshooting Your Cycle Computer.** This attachment provides a step-by-step guide to figuring out what might be wrong with a malfunctioning cycle computer.

Most problems are simple, such as dead batteries or loose wires, but others are beyond the capabilities of your typical customer.

- **Upgrading the Software in Your Cycle Computer.** This attachment tells customers how to attach the cycle computer to their home or office PC and download new software from Highway Bytes.

Your boss is enthusiastic when you explain that you can program your current email system to look for specific words in incoming messages and then respond, based on what it finds. For example, if a customer message contains the word *installation*, you can program the system to reply with the *Installing Your Cycle Computer* attachment. This reconfigured system should be able to handle a sizable portion of the hundreds of emails your customer service group gets every week.

Your task: First, draft a list of keywords that you want your email system to look for. You need to be creative and spend some time with a thesaurus. Identify all the words and word combinations that could identify a message as pertaining to one of the three subject areas. For instance, the word *attach* would probably indicate a need for the installation material, whereas *new software* would most likely suggest a need for the upgrade attachment.

Second, draft three short email messages, one to accompany each of the ready-made attachments, explaining that the attached document answers the most common questions on a particular subject (installation, troubleshooting, or upgrading). Your messages should invite recipients to write back if the attached document doesn't solve the problem—and don't forget to provide the email address: support2@highwaybytes.com.

Third, draft a fourth message to be sent out whenever your new system is unable to figure out what the customer is asking for. Simply thank the customer for writing and explain that the query will be passed on to a customer service specialist who will respond shortly.

EMAIL SKILLS

17. Message Strategies: Providing Recommendations [LO-4] You enjoy your duties as manager of the women's sportswear department at Clovine's—a chain of moderate to upscale department stores in south Florida. You especially enjoy being able to recommend someone for a promotion. Today, you received an email message from Rachel Cohen, head buyer for women's apparel. She is looking for a smart, aggressive employee to become assistant buyer for the women's sportswear division. Clovine's likes to promote from within, and Rachel is asking all managers and supervisors for likely candidates. You have just the person she's looking for.

Jennifer Ramirez is a salesclerk in the designer sportswear boutique of your main store in Miami, and she has caught your attention. She's quick, friendly, and good at sizing up a customer's preferences. Moreover, at recent department meetings, she has shared some insightful observations about fashion trends in south Florida.

Your task: Write an email reply to Rachel Cohen, head buyer, women's sportswear, recommending Jennifer Ramirez and evaluating her qualifications for the promotion. Rachel can check with the human resources department about Jennifer's educational and employment history; you're mainly interested in conveying your positive impression of Jennifer's potential for advancement.

LETTER WRITING SKILLS   **TEAM** SKILLS

18. Message Strategies: Providing Recommendations [LO-4] As a project manager at Orbitz, one of the largest online travel services in the world, you've seen plenty of college interns in action. However, few have impressed you as much as Maxine "Max" Chenault. For one thing, she learned how to navigate the company's content management system virtually overnight and always used it properly, whereas other interns sometimes left things in a hopeless mess. She asked lots of intelligent questions about the business. You've been teaching her blogging and website design principles, and she's picked them up rapidly. Moreover, she is always on time, professional, and eager to assist. Also, she didn't mind doing mundane tasks.

On the downside, Chenault is a popular student. Early on, you often found her busy on the phone planning her many social activities when you needed her help. However, after you had a brief talk with her, this problem vanished.

You'll be sorry to see Chenault leave when she returns to school in the fall, but you're pleased to respond when she asks you for a letter of recommendation. She's not sure where she'll apply for work after graduation or what career path she'll choose, so she asks you to keep the letter fairly general.

Your task: Working with a team of your classmates, discuss what should and should not be in the letter. Prepare an outline based on your discussion and then draft the letter.

 Learn how to add Notes to your Facebook page. Visit http://real-timeupdates.com/bct11, click on "Student Assignments" and then click on "Facebook Screencast."

SOCIAL NETWORKING SKILLS

19. Message Strategies: Writing Routine Informative Messages; Composition Modes: Summarizing [LO-4] As energy costs trend ever upward and more people become attuned to the environmental and geopolitical complexities of petroleum-based energy, interest in solar, wind, and other alternative energy sources continues to grow. In locations with high *insolation*, a measure of cumulative sunlight, solar panels can be cost-effective solutions over the long term. However, the upfront costs are still daunting for most homeowners. To help lower the entry barrier, the Foster City, California–based firm SolarCity now lets homeowners lease solar panels for monthly payments that are less than their current electricity bills.[14]

Your task: Visit www.solarcity.com, click on "Residential," and then click "SolarLease" to read about the leasing program. Next, study SolarCity's presence on Facebook (www.facebook.com/solarcity) to get a feel for how the company presents itself in a social networking environment. Now assume that you have been assigned the task of writing a brief summary of the SolarLease program that will appear on the Notes tab of SolarCity's Facebook page. In your own language and in 200 words or less, write an introduction to the SolarLease program and email it to your instructor.

Positive Messages

BLOGGING SKILLS

20. Message Strategies: Good News Messages [LO-4]
Amateur and professional golfers in search of lower scores want to find clubs that are optimized for their individual swings. This process of *club fitting* has gone decidedly high tech in recent years, with fitters using Doppler radar, motion-capture video, and other tools to evaluate golfers' swing and ball flight characteristics. Hot Stix Golf (www.hotstixgolf.com) is a leader in this industry, having fitted more than two hundred professionals and thousands of amateurs.[15]

Your task: Imagine that you are the communications director at the Indian Wells Golf Resort (www.indianwellsgolfresort.com) in Indian Wells, California. Your operation has just signed a deal with Hot Stix to open a fitting center on site. Write a three-paragraph message that could be posted on the resort blog. The first paragraph should announce the news that the Hot Stix center will open in six months, the second should summarize the benefits of club fitting, and the third should offer a brief overview of the services that will be available at the Indian Wells Hot Stix Center. Information on club fitting can be found on the Hot Stix website; make up any additional information you need to complete the post.

BLOGGING SKILLS   PORTFOLIO BUILDER

21. Message Strategies: Good-News Messages [LO-4]
You and your staff in the public relations (PR) department at Epson of America were delighted when the communication campaign you created for the new PictureMate Personal Photo Lab was awarded the prestigious Silver Anvil award by the Public Relations Society of America. Now you'd like to give your team a pat on the back by sharing the news with the rest of the company.

Your task: Write a one-paragraph message for the PR department blog (which is read by people throughout the company but is not accessible outside the company) announcing the award. Take care not to "toot your own horn" as the manager of the PR department. Use the opportunity to compliment the rest of the company for designing and producing such an innovative product. You can read more about the Personal Photo Lab at www.epson.com/picturemate.[16]

LETTER WRITING SKILLS

22. Message Strategies: Goodwill Messages [LO-4]
You've been working for two years as administrative assistant to Ron Glover, vice president of global workforce diversity at IBM in Armonk, New York. Chana Panichpapiboon has been with Glover even longer than you have, and, sadly, her husband was killed (along with 19 others) in a bus accident yesterday. The bus skidded on icy pavement into a deep ravine, tipping over and crushing the occupants before rescue workers could get to them.

You met Surin last year at a company banquet. You can still picture his warm smile and the easy way he joked with you and others over chicken Florentine, even though you were complete strangers to him. He was only 32 years old, and he left Chana two children, a 12-year-old boy, Arsa, and a 10-year-old girl, Veera. His death is a terrible tragedy.

Normally, you'd write a condolence letter immediately. But Chana is a native of Thailand, and so was Surin. You know you'd better do a little research first. Is Chana Buddhist or Catholic? Is there anything about the typical Western practice of expressing sympathy that might be inappropriate? Offensive?

After making some discreet inquiries among Chana's closest friends at work, you've learned that she is Theravada Buddhist, as are most people in Thailand. From a reference work in the company library about doing business around the world, you've gleaned only that, in the beliefs of many people in Thailand, "the person takes precedence over rule or law" and "people gain their social position as a result of karma, not personal achievement," which means Chana may believe in reincarnation. But the book also says that Theravada Buddhists are free to choose which precepts of their religion, if any, they will follow. So Chana's beliefs are still a mystery.

You do know that her husband was very important to her and much loved by all their family. That, at least, is universal. And you're toying with a phrase you once read, "The hand of time lightly lays, softly soothing sorrow's wound." Is it appropriate?

Your task: You've decided to handwrite the condolence note on a blank greeting card you've found that bears a peaceful, "Eastern-flavor" image. You know you're risking a cultural gaffe, but at least you won't commit the greater offense of not writing at all. Choose the most sincere wording you can, which should resonate through any differences in custom or tradition.[17]

BLOGGING SKILLS   PORTFOLIO BUILDER

23. Message Strategies: Good-News Messages [LO-4]
In both print and online communication, it's hard to escape the impact of Adobe Systems, the company behind Acrobat, Photoshop, Flash, InDesign and other programs used to create and share textual and visual content. Even as its impact on the communication professions continues to increase, though, Adobe works to decrease its impact on the natural environment. The company invests in a variety of techniques and technologies to reduce its energy usage, and Adobe was the first company ever to receive the Platinum Certification from the U.S. Green Building Council.

Your task: Write a one- or two-paragraph post for an internal blog at Adobe, letting employees know how well the company is doing in its efforts to reduce energy usage and thanking employees for the energy-saving ideas they've submitted and the individual efforts they've made to reduce, reuse, and recycle. You can learn more about the company's efforts and accomplishments at www.adobe.com/corporateresponsibility/environmental.html.[18]

LETTER WRITING SKILLS

24. Message Strategies: Condolence Messages [LO-4]
As chief administrator for the underwriting department of Aetna Health Plans in Walnut Creek, California, you're facing a difficult task. One of your best underwriters, Hector Almeida, recently lost his wife in an automobile accident (he and his teenage daughter weren't with her at the time). Because you're the boss, everyone in the close-knit department is looking to you to communicate the group's sympathy and concern.

Someone suggested a simple greeting card that everyone could sign, but that seems so impersonal for someone you've worked with every day for nearly five years. So you decided to write a personal note on behalf of the whole department. Although you met Hector's wife, Rosalia, at a few company functions, you knew her mostly through Hector's frequent references to her. You didn't know her well, but you do know important things about her life, which you can celebrate in the letter.

Right now, he's devastated by the loss. But if anyone can overcome this tragedy, Hector can. He's always determined to get a job done, no matter what obstacles present themselves, and he does it with an upbeat attitude. That's why everyone in the office likes him so much.

You also plan to suggest that when he returns to work, he might like to move his schedule up an hour so that he'll have more time to spend with his daughter, Lisa, after school. It's your way of helping make things a little easier for them during this period of adjustment.

Your task: Write the letter to Hector Almeida, who lives at 47 West Ave., #10, Walnut Creek, CA 94596. (Feel free to make up any details you need.)[19]

SOCIAL NETWORKING SKILLS

25. Message Strategies: Goodwill Messages [LO-4] As the largest employer in Loganville, your construction company provides jobs, purchasing activity, and tax receipts that make up a vital part of the city's economy. In your role as CEO, however, you realize that the relationship between your company and the community is mutually beneficial, and the company could not survive without the efforts of its employees, the business opportunities offered by a growing marketplace, and the physical and legal infrastructure that the government provides.

The company's dependence on the community was demonstrated in a moving and immediate way last weekend, when a powerful storm pushed the Logan River past flood stage and threatened to inundate your company's office and warehouse facilities. More than two hundred volunteers worked alongside your employees through the night to fill and stack sandbags to protect your buildings, and the city council authorized the deployment of heavy equipment and additional staff to help in the emergency effort. As you watched the water rise nearly 10 feet high behind the makeshift dike, you realized that the community came together to save your company.

Your task: Write a Wall post for your company's Facebook page, thanking the citizens and government officials of Loganville for their help in protecting the company's facilities during the storm. Use your creativity to make up any details you need to write a 100- to 200-word message.

Writing Negative Messages

LEARNING OBJECTIVES   After studying this chapter, you will be able to

1 Apply the three-step writing process to negative messages

2 Explain how to use the direct approach effectively when conveying negative news

3 Explain how to use the indirect approach effectively when conveying negative news

4 Explain the importance of maintaining high standards of ethics and etiquette when delivering negative messages

5 Describe successful strategies for sending negative messages on routine business matters

6 List the important points to consider when conveying negative organizational news

7 Describe successful strategies for sending negative employment-related messages

MyBcommLab Test your mastery of this chapter and its Learning Objectives. Visit mybcommlab.com to apply what you've learned in Document Makeovers and interactive simulation scenarios.

COMMUNICATION CLOSE-UP AT CHARGIFY

Chargify, which offers online billing services to other companies, caused a ruckus among its own customer base when it raised prices without giving any advance notice.

http://chargify.com

If you've ever purchased anything online using a credit or debit card, you've used some form of an automated billing system. From a consumer's point of view, where all you do is fill in a form and a charge eventually shows up on your monthly statement, billing looks fairly simple. However, a lot of tasks need to be done behind the scenes to make billing work, and they need to be done accurately, quickly, and securely. Many e-commerce companies therefore turn to specialists such as Boston-based Chargify to handle this vital business function.

Chargify charges its e-commerce clients flat monthly fees based on the number of customers *they* have. This tiered pricing plan keeps costs low for e-commerce startups who still have few revenue-generating customers. Up until late 2010, the lowest tier in Chargify's pricing plan had an extremely attractive price point—it was free.

The idea behind the free tier was to attract e-commerce companies still in their startup phase; as they grew, they would advance into the higher tiers and become paying clients. However, Chargify discovered that many companies in the free tier grew very slowly, if they grew at all, and Chargify wound up supporting a lot of users that weren't bringing in any revenue.

To bring in enough money to support the dependable, sustainable company that its clients needed, Chargify co-founder David Hauser realized he needed to raise prices, and that included charging lowest-tier clients for the first time. The company announced its new pricing structure in October 2010—and immediately came under attack from many of its clients for the price increases, for the lack of any advance notice, and for Chargify's refusal to "grandfather" existing customers under their original pricing plans. Some called the company "greedy" or "stupid," and a few went so far as to accuse it of bait-and-switch tactics. As bloggers and commentators across the Internet piled on, the technology news site TechCrunch summed up with the situation with an article that began, "It's been a rough day for Chargify. . . ."

After spending two long days responding to criticisms on Twitter, industry blogs, and other venues, Hauser wrote an unusually frank blog post titled "How to Break the Trust of Your Customers in Just One Day: Lessons Learned from a Major

Mistake." He said the company made "a massive mistake" in the way it handled the changes to its pricing model. By failing to alert customers well in advance of the change, he continued, Chargify "broke a trust that we had developed with our customers over a long period of time, and will take much to repair. We should have communicated our need and desire to remove free plans and provided more information about how this would happen, and over a period of time leading up to the change."

The kinds of services Chargify provides take money to deliver, and the price increases were necessary, but everyone involved agrees that the situation was not handled well. Hauser and his team will continue to learn new lessons as they expand Chargify, but you can bet they won't initiate any new price increases without giving their customers plenty of warning.[1]

Using the Three-Step Writing Process for Negative Messages

David Hauser and the rest of the executive team at Chargify (profiled in the chapter-opening Communication Close-up) are experienced and successful entrepreneurs, but even they discovered how tricky it can be to share unexpected and unwelcome news with audiences that have a lot riding on the information. Communicating negative information is a fact of life for all business professionals, whether it's saying no to a request, sharing unpleasant or unwelcome information, or issuing a public apology. With the techniques you'll learn in this chapter, however, you can communicate unwelcome news successfully while minimizing unnecessary stress for everyone involved.

Depending on the situation, you can have as many as five distinct goals when you need to convey negative information: (1) to convey the bad news, (2) to gain acceptance for the bad news, (3) to maintain as much goodwill as possible with your audience, (4) to maintain a good image for your organization, and (5) if appropriate, to reduce or eliminate the need for future correspondence on the matter. Five goals are clearly a lot to accomplish in one message, so careful planning and execution are critical with negative messages.

STEP 1: PLANNING A NEGATIVE MESSAGE

When planning negative messages, you can't avoid the fact that your audience does not want to hear what you have to say. To minimize the damage to business relationships and to encourage the acceptance of your message, analyze the situation carefully to better understand the context in which the recipient will process your message.

Be sure to consider your purpose thoroughly—whether it's straightforward (such as rejecting a job applicant) or more complicated (such as drafting a negative performance review, in which you not only give the employee feedback on past performance but also help the person develop a plan to improve future performance). With a clear purpose and your audience's needs in mind, identify and gather the information your audience requires in order to understand and accept your message. Negative messages can be intensely personal to the recipient, and in many cases, recipients have a right to expect a thorough explanation of your answer.

Selecting the right medium is critical. For instance, bad news for employees should be delivered in person whenever possible, to guard their privacy, demonstrate respect, and give them an opportunity to ask questions. Doing so isn't always possible or feasible, though, so you will have times when you need to share important negative information through written or electronic media.

Defining your main idea in a negative message is often more complicated than simply saying no. For instance, if you need to respond to a hardworking employee who requested

1 **LEARNING OBJECTIVE**

Apply the three-step writing process to negative messages.

Negative messages can have as many as five goals:
- Give the bad news
- Ensure acceptance of the bad news
- Maintain reader's goodwill
- Maintain organization's good image
- Minimize or eliminate future correspondence on the matter, as appropriate

Analysis, investigation, and adaptation help you avoid alienating your readers.

When preparing negative messages, choose the medium with care.

Figure 9.1   Choosing the Indirect or Direct Approach for Negative Messages
Analyze the situation carefully before choosing your approach to organizing negative messages.

a raise, your message might go beyond saying no to explaining how she can improve her performance by working smarter, not just harder.

Appropriate organization helps readers accept your negative news.

Finally, the organization of a negative message requires particular care. One of the most critical planning decisions is choosing whether to use the direct or indirect approach (see Figure 9.1). A negative message using the direct approach opens with the bad news, proceeds to the reasons for the situation or the decision, and ends with a positive statement aimed at maintaining a good relationship with the audience. In contrast, the indirect approach opens with the reasons behind the bad news before presenting the bad news itself.

You need to consider a variety of factors when choosing between direct and indirect approaches for negative messages.

To help decide which approach to take in any situation you encounter, ask yourself the following questions:

- **Will the bad news come as a shock?** The direct approach is fine for many business situations in which people understand the possibility of receiving bad news. However, if the bad news might come as a shock to readers, use the indirect approach to help them prepare for it.
- **Does the reader prefer short messages that get right to the point?** For example, if you know that your boss always wants messages that get right to the point, even when they deliver bad news, use the direct approach.
- **How important is this news to the reader?** For minor or routine scenarios, the direct approach is nearly always best. However, if the reader has an emotional investment in the situation or the consequences to the reader are considerable, the indirect approach is often better.
- **Do you need to maintain a close working relationship with the reader?** The indirect approach lets you soften the blow of bad news and preserve a positive business relationship.
- **Do you need to get the reader's attention?** If someone has ignored repeated messages, the direct approach can help you get his or her attention.
- **What is your organization's preferred style?** Some companies have a distinct communication style, ranging from blunt and direct to gentle and indirect.

MyBcommLab

- Access this chapter's simulation entitled Negative Messages, located at mybcommlab.com.

STEP 2: WRITING A NEGATIVE MESSAGE

When you are adapting a negative message to your audience, pay close attention to effectiveness and diplomacy. After all, your audience does not want to hear bad news or might disagree strongly with you, so messages perceived as being unclear or unkind will amplify the audience's stress. "Continuing with a Clear Statement of the Bad News" on page 253 has advice on conveying unpleasant news with care and tact. Cultural expectations also play a role, from the organizational culture within a company to the regional variations around the world.

TABLE 9.1	Choosing Positive Words
Examples of Negative Phrasings	**Positive Alternatives**
Your request *doesn't make any sense*.	Please clarify your request.
The *damage won't be fixed* for a week.	The item will be repaired next week.
Although it wasn't *our fault*, there will be an *unavoidable delay* in your order.	We will process your order as soon as we receive an aluminum shipment from our supplier, which we expect to happen within 10 days.
You are clearly *dissatisfied*.	I recognize that the product did not live up to your expectations.
I was *shocked* to learn that you're *unhappy*.	Thank you for sharing your concerns about your shopping experience.
Unfortunately, we haven't received it.	The item hasn't arrived yet.
The enclosed statement is *wrong*.	Please verify the enclosed statement and provide a correct copy.

The disappointing nature of negative messages requires that you maintain your audience focus and be as sensitive as possible to audience needs. For example, internal audiences often have expectations regarding negative messages that differ from those of external audiences. In some cases, the two groups can interpret the news in different or even opposite ways. Employees will react negatively to news of an impending layoff, for instance, but company shareholders might welcome the news as evidence that management is trying to control costs. In addition, if a negative message such as news of a layoff is being sent to internal and external audiences, employees will expect not only more detail but also to be informed before the public is told.

> Compared to external audiences, internal audiences often expect more detail in negative messages.

Negative messages to outside audiences require attention to the diverse nature of the audience and the concern for confidentiality of internal information. A single message might have a half-dozen audiences, all with differing opinions and agendas. You may not be able to explain things to the level of detail that some of these people want if doing so would release proprietary information such as future product plans.

> You may need to adjust the content of negative messages for various external audiences.

If your credibility hasn't already been established with the audience, lay out your qualifications for making the decision in question. Recipients of negative messages who don't think you are credible are more likely to challenge your decision or reject your message. And, as always, projecting and protecting your company's image are prime concerns; if you're not careful, a negative answer could spin out of control into negative feelings about your company.

When you use language that conveys respect and avoids an accusing tone, you protect your audience's pride. This kind of communication etiquette is always important, but it demands special care with negative messages. Moreover, you can ease the sense of disappointment by using positive words rather than negative, counterproductive ones (see Table 9.1).

STEP 3: COMPLETING A NEGATIVE MESSAGE

The need for careful attention to detail continues as you complete your message. Revise your content to make sure everything is clear, complete, and concise—bearing in mind that even small flaws are magnified as readers react to your negative news. Produce clean, professional documents and proofread carefully to eliminate mistakes. Finally, be especially sure that your negative messages are delivered promptly and successfully. Delaying when you need to convey negative news can be a serious breach of etiquette.

Using the Direct Approach for Negative Messages

A negative message using the direct approach opens with the bad news, proceeds to the reasons for the situation or the decision, and ends with a positive statement aimed at maintaining a good relationship with the audience. Depending on the circumstances, the message

> **2   LEARNING OBJECTIVE**
>
> Explain how to use the direct approach effectively when conveying negative news.

Use the direct approach when your negative answer or information will have minimal personal impact.

may also offer alternatives or a plan of action to fix the situation under discussion. Stating the bad news at the beginning can have two advantages: (1) It makes a shorter message possible, and (2) it allows the audience to reach the main idea of the message in less time.

OPENING WITH A CLEAR STATEMENT OF THE BAD NEWS

No matter what the news is, come right out and say it. However, even if the news is likely to be devastating, maintain a calm, professional tone that keeps the focus on the news and not on individual failures or other personal factors. Also, if necessary, remind the reader why you're writing.

PROVIDING REASONS AND ADDITIONAL INFORMATION

The amount of detail you should provide depends on your relationship with the audience.

In most cases, you follow the direct opening with an explanation of why the news is negative. The extent of your explanation depends on the nature of the news and your relationship with the reader. For example, if you want to preserve a long-standing relationship with an important customer, a detailed explanation could well be worth the extra effort such a message would require.

However, you will encounter some situations in which explaining negative news is neither appropriate nor helpful, such as when the reasons are confidential, excessively complicated, or irrelevant to the reader. To maintain a cordial working relationship with the reader, you might want to explain why you can't provide the information.

Should you apologize when delivering bad news? The answer isn't quite as simple as one might think, partly because the notion of *apology* is hard to pin down. To some people, it simply means an expression of sympathy that something negative has happened to another person. At the other extreme, it means admitting fault and taking responsibility for specific compensations or corrections to atone for the mistake.

After an explosion that killed one employee and worried local residents about the potential release of toxic chemicals, Bayer CropScience plant manager Nick Crosby said that "We are truly sorry for the serious issues caused by the incident at our facility . . . we understand the anxiety in the community resulting from the incident." He also apologized to people living near the Institute, West Virginia, plant for failing to clarify that there was no danger of toxic emissions. "We could have communicated, and we should have communicated, much better with the community that night."[2]

Some experts have advised that a company should never apologize, even when it knows it has made a mistake, as the apology might be taken as a confession of guilt that could be used against the company in a lawsuit. However, several states have laws that specifically prevent expressions of sympathy from being used as evidence of legal liability. In fact, judges, juries, and plaintiffs tend to be more forgiving of companies that express sympathy for wronged parties; moreover, an apology can help repair a company's reputation. Recently, some prosecutors have begun pressing executives to publicly admit guilt and apologize as part of the settlement of criminal cases—unlike the common tactic of paying fines but refusing to admit any wrongdoing.[3]

Apologies can have legal ramifications, but refusing to apologize out of fear of admitting guilt can damage a company's relationships with its stakeholders.

The best general advice in the event of a serious mistake or accident is to immediately and sincerely express sympathy and offer help if appropriate, without admitting guilt; then seek the advice of your company's lawyers before elaborating. As one survey concluded, "The risks of making an apology are low, and the potential reward is high."[4]

If you do apologize, make it a real apology. Don't say "I'm sorry if anyone was offended" by what you did—this statement implies that you're not sorry at all and that it's the other party's fault for being offended.[5]

Note that you can also express sympathy with someone's plight without suggesting that you are to blame. For example, if a business customer damaged a product through misuse and suffered a financial loss as a result of not being able to use the product, you can say something along the lines of "I'm sorry to hear of your difficulties." This demonstrates sensitivity without accepting blame.

CLOSING ON A RESPECTFUL NOTE

After you've explained the negative news, close the message in a manner that respects the impact the negative news is likely to have on the recipient. If appropriate, consider offering your readers an alternative solution if you can and if doing so is a good use of your time. Look for opportunities to include positive statements, but avoid creating false hopes or writing in a way that seems to suggest that something negative didn't just happen to the recipient. Ending on a false positive can leave readers feeling "disrespected, disregarded, or deceived."[6]

In many situations, an important aspect of a respectful close is describing the actions being taken to avoid similar mistakes in the future. Offering such explanations can underline the sincerity of an apology because doing so signals that the person or organization is serious about not repeating the error. When the credit rating agency Standard & Poor's issued a statement expressing regret for its role in the 2007–2008 subprime mortgage meltdown that helped throw the economy into a deep recession, the company also described the changes it was making "to restore investor confidence in our ratings," as company president Deven Sharma explained.[7]

Using the Indirect Approach for Negative Messages

The indirect approach helps readers prepare for the bad news by presenting the reasons for it first. However, the indirect approach is *not* meant to obscure bad news, delay it, or limit your responsibility. Rather, the purpose of this approach is to ease the blow and help readers accept the situation. When done poorly, the indirect approach can be disrespectful and even unethical. But when done well, it is a good example of audience-oriented communication crafted with attention to ethics and etiquette. Showing consideration for the feelings of others is never dishonest.

OPENING WITH A BUFFER

Messages using the indirect approach open with a **buffer**: a neutral, noncontroversial statement that establishes common ground with the reader (refer to Figure 9.1). A good buffer can express your appreciation for being considered (if you're responding to a request), assure the reader of your attention to the request, or indicate your understanding of the reader's needs. A good buffer also needs to be relevant and sincere. In contrast, a poorly written buffer might trivialize the reader's concerns, divert attention from the problem with insincere flattery or irrelevant material, or mislead the reader into thinking your message actually contains good news.

Consider these possible responses to a manager of the order-fulfillment department who requested some temporary staffing help from your department (a request you won't be able to fulfill):

> Our department shares your goal of processing orders quickly and efficiently.

Establishes common ground with the reader and validates the concerns that prompted the original request—without promising a positive answer

> As a result of the last downsizing, every department in the company is running shorthanded.

Establishes common ground, but in a negative way that downplays the recipient's concerns

> You folks are doing a great job over there, and I'd love to be able to help out.

Potentially misleads the reader into concluding that you will comply with the request

> Those new state labor regulations are driving me crazy over here; how about in your department?

Trivializes the reader's concerns by opening with an irrelevant issue

Only the first of these buffers can be considered effective; the other three are likely to damage your relationship with the other manager—and lower his or her opinion of

3 **LEARNING OBJECTIVE**

Explain how to use the indirect approach effectively when conveying negative news.

Use the indirect approach when some preparation will help your audience accept your bad news.

A well-written buffer establishes common ground with the reader.

TABLE 9.2	Types of Buffers	
Buffer Type	**Strategy**	**Example**
Agreement	Find a point on which you and the reader share similar views.	We both know how hard it is to make a profit in this industry.
Appreciation	Express sincere thanks for receiving something.	Your check for $127.17 arrived yesterday. Thank you.
Cooperation	Convey your willingness to help in any way you realistically can.	Employee Services is here to assist all associates with their health insurance, retirement planning, and continuing education needs.
Fairness	Assure the reader that you've closely examined and carefully considered the problem, or mention an appropriate action that has already been taken.	For the past week, we have had our bandwidth monitoring tools running around the clock to track your actual upload and download speeds.
Good news	Start with the part of your message that is favorable.	We have credited your account in the amount of $14.95 to cover the cost of return shipping.
Praise	Find an attribute or an achievement to compliment.	The Stratford Group clearly has an impressive record of accomplishment in helping clients resolve financial reporting problems.
Resale	Favorably discuss the product or company related to the subject of the letter.	With their heavy-duty, full-suspension hardware and fine veneers, the desks and file cabinets in our Montclair line have long been popular with value-conscious professionals.
Understanding	Demonstrate that you understand the reader's goals and needs.	So that you can more easily find the printer with the features you need, we are enclosing a brochure that describes all the Epson printers currently available.

you. Table 9.2 shows several types of effective buffers you could use to tactfully open a negative message.

Poorly written buffers mislead or insult the reader.

Given the damage that a poorly composed buffer can do, consider every buffer carefully before you send it. Is it respectful? Is it relevant? Does it avoid any chance of misleading the reader? Does it provide a smooth transition to the reasons that follow? If you can answer yes to every question, you can proceed confidently to the next section of your message. However, if a little voice inside your head tells you that your buffer sounds insincere or misleading, it probably is, in which case you'll need to rewrite it.

PROVIDING REASONS AND ADDITIONAL INFORMATION

Phrase your reasons to signal the negative news ahead.

An effective buffer serves as a transition to the next part of your message, in which you build up the explanations and information that will culminate in your negative news. An ideal explanation section leads readers to your conclusion before you come right out and say it. In other words, before you actually say no, the reader has followed your line of reasoning and is ready for the answer. By giving your reasons effectively, you help maintain focus on the issues at hand and defuse the emotions that always accompany significantly bad news. In the blog post that announced Chargify's new pricing model (see page 246), for example, CEO Lance Walley explained how the company's costs had risen as it worked to improve the reliability and security of its services.[8]

As you lay out your reasons, guide your reader's response by starting with the most positive points first and moving forward to increasingly negative ones. Be concise, but provide enough detail for the audience to understand your reasons. You need to convince your audience that your decision is justified, fair, and logical. If appropriate, you can use the explanation section to suggest how the negative news might in fact benefit your reader in some way—but only if that is true and only if you can do so without offending your audience.

Don't hide behind "company policy" when you deliver bad news; present logical answers instead.

Avoid hiding behind company policy to cushion your bad news. If you say, "Company policy forbids our hiring anyone who does not have two years' supervisory experience," you imply that you won't consider anyone on his or her individual merits. Skilled and sympathetic communicators explain company policy (without referring to it as "policy") so that the audience can try to meet the requirements at a later time. Consider this response to an employee:

> Because these management positions are quite challenging, the human relations department has researched the qualifications needed to succeed in them. The findings show that the two most important qualifications are a bachelor's degree in business administration and two years' supervisory experience.

Shows the reader that the decision is based on a methodical analysis of the company's needs and not on some arbitrary guideline

Establishes the criteria behind the decision and lets the reader know what to expect

This paragraph does a good job of stating reasons for the refusal:

- It provides enough detail to logically support the refusal.
- It implies that the applicant is better off avoiding a program in which he or she might fail.
- It shows that the company's policy is based on experience and careful analysis.
- It doesn't offer an apology for the decision because no one is at fault.
- It avoids negative personal expressions (such as "You do not meet our requirements").

Well-written reasons are
- Detailed
- Tactful
- Individualized
- Unapologetic if no one is at fault
- Positive

Even valid, well-thought-out reasons won't convince every reader in every situation. However, if you've done a good job of laying out your reasoning, you've done everything you can to prepare the reader for the main idea, which is the negative news itself.

CONTINUING WITH A CLEAR STATEMENT OF THE BAD NEWS

After you've thoughtfully and logically established your reasons and readers are prepared to receive the bad news, you can use three techniques to convey the negative information as clearly and as kindly as possible. First, deemphasize the bad news:

- Minimize the space or time devoted to the bad news—without trivializing it or withholding any important information.
- Subordinate bad news in a complex or compound sentence ("My department is already shorthanded, so I'll need all my staff for at least the next two months"). This construction presents the bad news in the middle of the sentence, the point of least emphasis.
- Embed bad news in the middle of a paragraph or use parenthetical expressions ("Our profits, which are down, are only part of the picture").

To handle bad news
- Deemphasize the bad news visually and grammatically
- Use a conditional statement, if appropriate
- Tell what you did do, not what you didn't do

However, keep in mind that it's possible to abuse deemphasis. For instance, if the primary point of your message is that profits are down, it would be inappropriate to marginalize that news by burying it in the middle of a sentence. State the negative news clearly and then make a smooth transition to any positive news that might balance the story.

Second, use a conditional (*if* or *when*) statement to imply that the audience could have received, or might someday receive, a favorable answer ("When you have more managerial experience, you are welcome to reapply"). Such a statement could motivate applicants to improve their qualifications.

Third, emphasize what you can do or have done rather than what you cannot do. Say "We sell exclusively through retailers, and the one nearest you that carries our merchandise is . . ." rather than "We are unable to serve you, so please call your nearest dealer." Also, by implying the bad news, you may not need to actually state it ("The five positions have been filled with people whose qualifications match those uncovered in our research"). By focusing on the facts and implying the bad news, you make the impact less personal.

When implying bad news, however, be sure your audience will be able to grasp the entire message—including the bad news. Withholding negative information or overemphasizing positive information is unethical and unfair to your reader. If an implied message

Don't disguise bad news when you emphasize the positive.

might lead to uncertainty, state your decision in direct terms. Just be sure to avoid overly blunt statements that are likely to cause pain and anger:

Instead of This	Write This
I *must refuse* your request.	I will be out of town on the day you need me.
We *must deny* your application.	The position has been filled.
I *am unable* to grant your request.	Contact us again when you have established . . .
We *cannot afford to* continue the program.	The program will conclude on May 1.
Much as I would like to attend . . .	Our budget meeting ends too late for me to attend.
We *must turn down* your extension request.	Please send in your payment by June 14.

CLOSING ON A RESPECTFUL NOTE

As in the direct approach, the close in the indirect approach offers an opportunity to emphasize your respect for your audience, even though you've just delivered unpleasant news. Express best wishes without being falsely upbeat. If you can find a positive angle that's meaningful to your audience, by all means consider adding it to your conclusion. However, don't try to pretend that the negative news didn't happen or that it won't affect the reader. Suggest alternative solutions if such information is available. If you've asked readers to decide between alternatives or to take some action, make sure that they know what to do, when to do it, and how to do it. Whatever type of conclusion you use, follow these guidelines:

- **Avoid a negative or uncertain conclusion.** Don't belabor the bad news. Refrain from expressing any doubt that your reasons will be accepted. (Avoid statements such as "I trust our decision is satisfactory.")
- **Manage future correspondence.** Encourage additional communication *only* if you're willing to discuss the situation further. (If you're not, avoid statements such as "If you have further questions, please write.")
- **Be optimistic about the future, as appropriate.** Don't anticipate problems that haven't occurred yet. (Avoid statements such as "Should you have further problems, please let us know.")
- **Be sincere.** Steer clear of clichés that are insincere in view of the bad news. (If you can't help, don't say, "If we can be of any help, please contact us.")

Keep in mind that the close is the last thing audience members have to remember you by. Even though they're disappointed, leave them with the impression that they were treated with respect.

Maintaining High Standards of Ethics and Etiquette

All business messages demand attention to ethics and etiquette, of course, but these considerations take on special importance when you are delivering bad news—for several reasons. First, a variety of laws and regulations dictate the content and delivery of many business messages with potentially negative content, such as the release of financial information by a public company. Second, negative messages can have a significant negative impact on the lives of those receiving them. Even if the news is conveyed legally and conscientiously, good ethical practice demands that these situations be approached with care and sensitivity. Third, emotions often run high when negative messages are involved, for both the sender and the receiver. Senders need to manage their own emotions and consider the emotional state of their audiences.

For example, in a message announcing or discussing workforce cutbacks, you have the emotional needs of several stakeholder groups to consider. The employees who lost their jobs are likely to experience fear about their futures and possibly a sense of betrayal.

Margin notes:

A positive close
- Builds goodwill
- Offers a suggestion for action
- Provides a look toward the future

4   LEARNING OBJECTIVE

Explain the importance of maintaining high standards of ethics and etiquette when delivering negative messages.

The employees who kept their jobs are likely to feel anxiety about the long-term security of their jobs, the ability of company management to turn things around, and the level of care and respect the company has for its employees. These "survivors" may also feel guilty about keeping their jobs while some colleagues lost theirs. Outside the company, investors, suppliers, and segments of the community affected by the layoffs (such as retailers and homebuilders) will have varying degrees of financial interest in the outcome of the decision. Writing such messages requires careful attention to all these needs, while balancing respect for the departing employees with a positive outlook on the future. The challenge of sending—and receiving—negative messages fosters a tendency to delay, downplay, or distort the bad news (see "Ethics Detective: Solving the Case of the Deceptive Soft Sell").[9] However, doing so may be unethical, if not illegal. In recent years, numerous companies have been sued by shareholders, consumers, employees, and government regulators for allegedly withholding or delaying negative information in such areas as company finances, environmental hazards, and product safety. In many of these cases, the problem was slow, incomplete, or inaccurate communication between the company and external stakeholders. In others, problems stemmed from a reluctance to send or receive negative news within the organization.

Effectively sharing bad news within an organization requires commitment from everyone involved. Employees must commit to sending negative messages when necessary and to doing so in a timely fashion, even when that is unpleasant or difficult. Conversely, managers must commit to maintaining open communication channels, truly listening when employees have negative information to share, and not punishing employees who deliver bad news.

Employees who observe unethical or illegal behavior within their companies and are unable to resolve the problems through normal channels may have no choice but to resort to **whistleblowing**, expressing their concerns internally through company ethics hot lines or—externally through social media or the news media if they perceive no other options. The decision to "blow the whistle" on one's own employer is rarely easy or without consequences; more than 80 percent of whistleblowers in one survey said they were punished in some way for coming forward with their concerns.[10] Although whistleblowing is sometimes characterized as "ratting on" colleagues or managers, it has an essential function. According to international business expert Alex MacBeath, "Whistleblowing can be an invaluable way to alert management to poor business practice within the workplace. Often whistleblowing can be the only way that information about issues such as rule breaking,

Sharing bad news effectively requires commitment from everyone in the organization.

ETHICS DETECTIVE Solving the Case of the Deceptive Soft Sell

You and your colleagues are nervous. Sales have been declining for months, and you see evidence of budget tightening all over the place—the fruit and pastries have disappeared from the coffee stations, accountants are going over expense reports with magnifying glasses, and managers are slow to replace people who leave the company. Instant messages fly around the office; everyone wants to know if anyone has heard anything about layoffs.

The job market in your area is weak, and you know you might have to sell your house—in one of the weakest housing markets in memory—and move your family out of state to find another position in your field. If your job is eliminated, you're ready to cope with the loss, but you need as much time as possible. You breathe a sigh of relief when the following item from the CEO appears on the company's internal blog:

> With news of workforce adjustments elsewhere in our industry, we realize many of you are concerned about

the possibility here. I'd like to reassure all of you that we remain confident in the company's fundamental business strategy, and the executive team is examining all facets of company operations to ensure our continued financial strength.

The message calms your fears. Should it?

ANALYSIS
A month later, the CEO announces a layoff of 20 percent of the company's workforce—nearly 700 people. You're shocked by the news because you felt reassured by the blog posting from last month. In light of what happened, you retrieve a copy of the newsletter and reread the CEO's message. Does it seem ethical now? Why or why not? If you had been in charge of writing this newsletter item and your hands were tied because you couldn't come out and announce the layoffs yet, how would you have rewritten the message?

✓ Checklist | Creating Negative Messages

A. Choose the better approach.
- Consider using the direct approach when the audience is aware of the possibility of negative news, when the reader is not emotionally involved in the message, when you know that the reader would prefer the bad news first, when you know that firmness is necessary, and when you want to discourage a response.
- Consider using the indirect approach when the news is likely to come as a shock or surprise, when your audience has a high emotional investment in the outcome, and when you want to maintain a good relationship with the audience.

B. For the indirect approach, open with an effective buffer.
- Establish common ground with the audience.
- Validate the request, if you are responding to a request.
- Don't trivialize the reader's concerns.
- Don't mislead the reader into thinking the coming news might be positive.

C. Provide reasons and additional information.
- Explain why the news is negative.
- Adjust the amount of detail to fit the situation and the audience.

- Avoid explanations when the reasons are confidential, excessively complicated, or irrelevant to the reader.
- If appropriate, state how you plan to correct or respond to the negative news.
- Seek the advice of company lawyers if you're unsure what to say.

D. Clearly state the bad news.
- State the bad news as positively as possible, using tactful wording.
- To help protect readers' feelings, deemphasize the bad news by minimizing the space devoted to it, subordinating it, or embedding it.
- If your response might change in the future if circumstances change, explain the conditions to the reader.
- Emphasize what you can do or have done rather than what you can't or won't do.

E. Close on a respectful note.
- Express best wishes without being falsely positive.
- Suggest actions readers might take, if appropriate, and provide them with necessary information.
- Encourage further communication only if you're willing to discuss the situation further.

---

criminal activity, cover-ups, and fraud can be brought to management's attention before serious damage is suffered."[11] Recognizing the value of this feedback, many companies have formal reporting mechanisms that give employees a way to voice ethical and legal concerns to management. Various government bodies have also instituted protections for whistleblowers, partly in recognition of the role that workers play in food safety and other vital areas.[12]

> Negative situations can put your sense of self-control and business etiquette to the test.

Finally, recognize that some negative news scenarios will test your self-control and tempt you to respond with a personal attack. Customer service employees often undergo training specifically to help them keep their own emotions on an even keel when they are on the receiving end of anger or criticism from upset customers.[13] However, keep in mind that negative messages can have a lasting impact on the people who receive them and the people who send them. As a communicator, you have a responsibility to minimize the negative impact of your negative messages through careful planning and sensitive, objective writing. As much as possible, focus on the actions or conditions that led to the negative news, not on personal shortcomings or character issues. Develop a reputation as a professional who can handle the toughest situations with dignity.

For a reminder of successful strategies for creating negative messages, see "Checklist: Creating Negative Messages."

Sending Negative Messages on Routine Business Matters

5 LEARNING OBJECTIVE

Describe successful strategies for sending negative messages on routine business matters.

Professionals and companies receive a wide variety of requests and proposals and cannot respond positively to every single one. In addition, mistakes and unforeseen circumstances can lead to delays and other minor problems that occur in the course of business. Occasionally, companies must send negative messages to suppliers and other parties. Whatever the purpose, crafting routine negative responses and messages quickly and graciously is an important skill for every businessperson.

MAKING NEGATIVE ANNOUNCEMENTS ON ROUTINE BUSINESS MATTERS

Many negative messages are written in response to requests from an internal or external correspondent, but on occasion managers need to make unexpected announcements of a negative nature. For example, a company might decide to consolidate its materials purchasing with fewer suppliers and thereby need to tell several firms it will no longer be buying from them. Internally, management may need to announce the elimination of an employee benefit or other changes that employees will view negatively.

Although such announcements happen in the normal course of business, they are generally unexpected. Accordingly, except in the case of minor changes, the indirect approach is usually the better choice. Follow the steps outlined for indirect messages: open with a buffer that establishes some mutual ground between you and the reader, advance your reasoning, announce the change, and close with as much positive information and sentiment as appropriate under the circumstances.

Negative announcements on routine business matters usually should be handled with the indirect approach because the news is unexpected.

REJECTING SUGGESTIONS AND PROPOSALS

Managers receive a variety of suggestions and proposals, both solicited and unsolicited, from internal and external sources. For an unsolicited proposal from an external source, you may not even need to respond if you don't already have a working relationship with the sender. However, if you need to reject a proposal that you solicited, you owe the sender an explanation, and because the news will be unexpected, the indirect approach is better. In general, the closer your working relationship, the more thoughtful and complete you need to be in your response. For example, if you are rejecting a proposal from an employee, explain your reasons fully and carefully so that the employee can understand why the proposal was not accepted and so that you don't damage an important working relationship.

REFUSING ROUTINE REQUESTS

When you are unable to meet a request, your primary communication challenge is to give a clear negative response without generating negative feelings or damaging either your personal reputation or the company's. As simple as such messages may appear to be, they can test your skills as a communicator because you often need to deliver negative information while maintaining a positive relationship with the other party.

The direct approach works best for most routine negative responses. It not only helps your audience get your answer quickly and move on to other possibilities but also helps you save time, because messages with the direct approach are often easier to write than those with the indirect approach.

The indirect approach works best when the stakes are high for you or for the receiver, when you or your company has an established relationship with the person making the request, or when you're forced to decline a request that you might have said yes to in the past (see Figure 9.2 on the next page).

When turning down an invitation or a request for a favor, consider your relationship with the reader.

Consider the following points as you develop your routine negative messages:

- Manage your time carefully; focus on the most important relationships and requests.
- If the matter is closed, don't imply that it's still open by using phrases such as "Let me think about it and get back to you" as a way to delay saying no.
- Offer alternative ideas if you can, particularly if the relationship is important.
- Don't imply that other assistance or information might be available if it isn't.

If you aren't in a position to offer additional information or assistance, don't imply that you are.

HANDLING BAD NEWS ABOUT TRANSACTIONS

Bad news about transactions is always unwelcome and usually unexpected. When you send such messages, you have three goals: (1) modify the customer's expectations, (2) explain how you plan to resolve the situation, and (3) repair whatever damage might have been done to the business relationship.

The specific content and tone of each message can vary widely, depending on the nature of the transaction and your relationship with the customer. Telling an individual consumer

Some negative messages regarding transactions carry significant financial and legal ramifications.

Analyze the Situation

Verify that the purpose is to decline a request and offer alternatives; audience is likely to be surprised by the refusal.

Gather Information

Determine audience needs and obtain the necessary information.

Select the Right Medium

For formal messages, printed letters on company letterhead are best.

Organize the Information

The main idea is to refuse the request so limit your scope to that; select the indirect approach based on the audience and the situation.

Adapt to Your Audience

Adjust the level of formality based on your degree of familiarity with the audience; maintain a positive relationship by using the "you" attitude, politeness, positive emphasis, and bias-free language.

Compose the Message

Use a conversational but professional style and keep the message brief, clear, and as helpful as possible.

Revise the Message

Evaluate content and review readability to make sure the negative information won't be misinterpreted; make sure your tone stays positive without being artificial.

Produce the Message

Maintain a clean, professional appearance on company letterhead.

Proofread the Message

Review for errors in layout, spelling, and mechanics.

Distribute the Message

Deliver your message using the chosen medium.

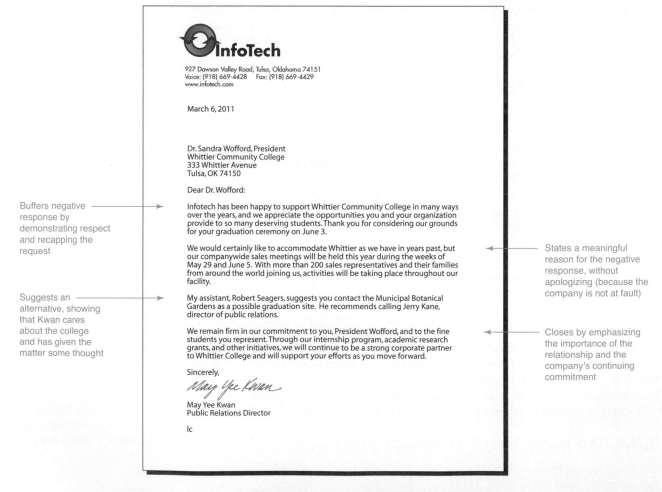

Figure 9.2 Effective Message Declining a Routine Request

May Yee Kwan's company has a long-standing relationship with the college Sandra Wofford represents and wants to maintain that positive relationship, but she can't meet this particular request. To communicate negative news, she therefore uses an indirect approach. If Kwan and Wofford shared a closer relationship (if they worked together in a volunteer organization, for instance), the direct approach might have been more appropriate.

that his new sweater will be arriving a week later than you promised is a much simpler task than telling GM that 30,000 transmission parts will be a week late, especially if you know the company will be forced to idle a multimillion-dollar production facility as a result.

If you haven't done anything specific to set the customer's expectations—such as promising delivery within 24 hours—the message simply needs to inform the customer of the situation, with little or no emphasis on apologies (see Figure 9.3).

> Your approach to bad news about business transactions depends on what you've done previously to set the customer's expectations.

If you did set the customer's expectations and now find that you can't meet them, your task is more complicated. In addition to resetting those expectations and explaining how you'll resolve the problem, you should include an apology as part of your message. The scope of the apology depends on the magnitude of the mistake. For the customer who ordered the sweater, a simple apology followed by a clear statement of when the sweater will arrive would probably be sufficient. For larger business-to-business transactions, the customer may want an explanation of what went wrong to determine whether you'll be able to perform as you promise in the future.

> If you've failed to meet expectations that you set for the customer, you should include an element of apology.

To help repair the damage to the relationship and encourage repeat business, many companies offer discounts on future purchases, free merchandise, or other considerations. Even modest efforts can go a long way to rebuilding a customer's confidence in your company. However, you don't always have a choice. Business-to-business purchasing contracts often include performance clauses that legally entitle the customer to discounts or other

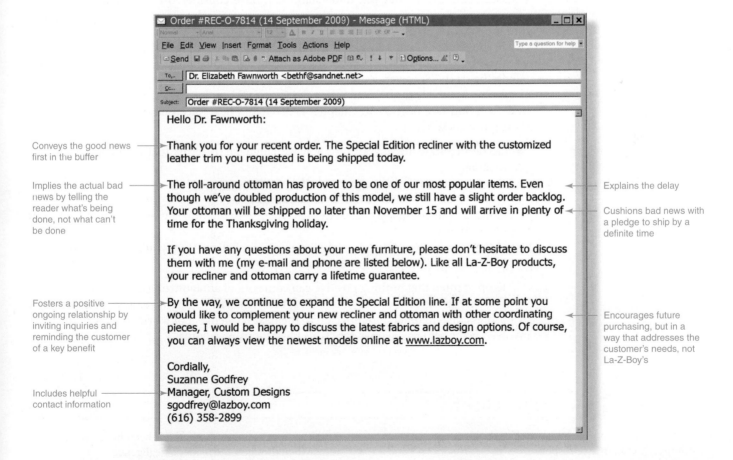

Figure 9.3 Effective Negative Message Regarding a Transaction
This message, which is a combination of good and bad news, uses the indirect approach—with the good news serving as a buffer for the bad news. In this case, the customer wasn't promised delivery by a certain date, so the writer simply informed the customer when to expect the rest of the order. The writer also took steps to repair the relationship and encourage future business with her firm.

MyBcommLab

Apply Figure 9.3's key concepts by revising a new document. Go to Chapter 9 in mybcommlab.com and select Document Makeovers.

✔ Checklist | Handling Bad News About Transactions

- Reset the customer's expectations regarding the transaction.
- Explain what happened and why, if appropriate.
- Explain how you will resolve the situation.

- Repair any damage done to the business relationship, perhaps offering future discounts, free merchandise, or other considerations.
- Offer a professional, businesslike expression of apology if your organization made a mistake.

---

restitution in the event of late delivery. To review the concepts covered in this section, see "Checklist: Handling Bad News About Transactions."

REFUSING CLAIMS AND REQUESTS FOR ADJUSTMENT

Use the indirect approach in most cases of refusing a claim.

Customers who make a claim or request an adjustment tend to be emotionally involved, so the indirect approach is usually the better choice. To avoid accepting responsibility for the unfortunate situation and avoid blaming or accusing the customer, pay special attention to the tone of your letter. A tactful and courteous message can build goodwill even while denying the claim (see Figure 9.4).

When refusing a claim
- Demonstrate your understanding of the complaint
- Explain your refusal
- Suggest alternative action

When refusing a claim, avoid language that might have a negative impact on the reader. Instead, demonstrate that you understand and have considered the complaint carefully. Then, even if the claim is unreasonable, rationally explain why you are refusing the request. End the message on a respectful and action-oriented note.

If you deal with enough customers over a long enough period, chances are you'll get a request that is particularly outrageous. You might even be positive that the person is not telling the truth. However, you need to control your emotions and approach the situation as calmly as possible to avoid saying or writing anything that the recipient might interpret as defamation (see page 27 in Chapter 1). To avoid being accused of defamation, follow these guidelines:

You can help avoid committing defamation by not responding emotionally or abusively.

- Refrain from using any kind of abusive language or terms that could be considered defamatory.
- Provide accurate information and stick to the facts.
- Never let anger or malice motivate your messages.
- Consult your company's legal advisers whenever you think a message might have legal consequences.
- Communicate honestly and make sure that you believe what you're saying is true.
- Emphasize a desire for a good relationship in the future.

Keep in mind that nothing positive can come out of antagonizing a customer, even one who has verbally abused you or your colleagues. Reject the claim or request for adjustment in a professional manner and move on to the next challenge. For a brief review of the tasks involved when refusing claims, see "Checklist: Refusing Claims."

✔ Checklist | Refusing Claims

- Use the indirect approach because the reader is expecting or hoping for a positive response.
- Indicate your full understanding of the nature of the complaint.
- Explain why you are refusing the request, without hiding behind company policy.
- Provide an accurate, factual account of the transaction.

- Emphasize ways things should have been handled rather than dwell on the reader's negligence.
- Avoid any appearance of defamation.
- Avoid expressing personal opinions.
- End with a positive, friendly, helpful close.
- Make any suggested action easy for readers to comply with.

1 Plan →	2 Write →	3 Complete

Analyze the Situation

Verify that the purpose is to refuse a warranty claim and offer repairs; audience's likely reaction will be disappointment and surprise.

Gather Information

Gather information on warranty policies and procedures, repair services, and resale information.

Select the Right Medium

Choose the best medium for delivering your message; for formal messages, printed letters on company letterhead are best.

Organize the Information

Your main idea is to refuse the claim and promote an alternative solution; select an indirect approach based on the audience and the situation.

Adapt to Your Audience

Adjust the level of formality based on degree of familiarity with the audience; maintain a positive relationship by using the "you" attitude, politeness, positive emphasis, and bias-free language.

Compose the Message

Use a conversational but professional style and keep the message brief, clear, and as helpful as possible.

Revise the Message

Evaluate content and review readability to make sure the negative information won't be misinterpreted; make sure your tone stays positive without being artificial.

Produce the Message

Emphasize a clean, professional appearance appropriate for a letter on company stationery.

Proofread the Message

Review for errors in layout, spelling, and mechanics.

Distribute the Message

Deliver your message using the chosen medium; make sure the reader receives any necessary support documents as well.

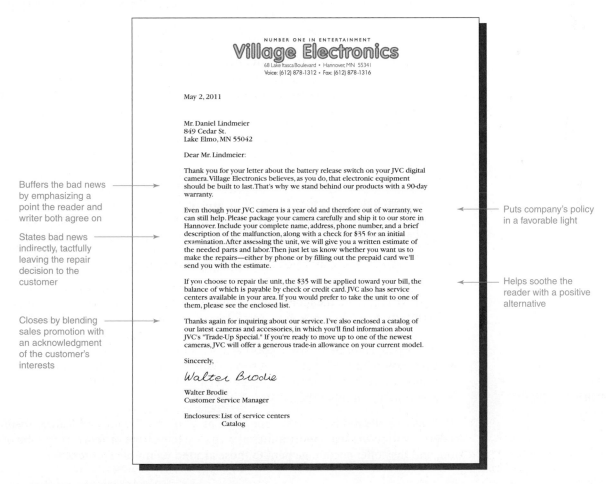

Figure 9.4 Effective Message Refusing a Claim

Daniel Lindmeier, who purchased a digital video camera from Village Electronics a year ago, wrote to say that the unit doesn't work properly and to inquire about the warranty. He incorrectly believed that the warranty covers one year, when it actually covers only three months. In this response, Walter Brodie uses an indirect approach to convey the bad news and to offer additional helpful information.

Sending Negative Organizational News

The messages described in the previous section deal with internal matters or individual interactions with external parties. From time to time, managers must also share negative information with the public at large, and sometimes respond to negative information as well. Most of these scenarios have unique challenges that must be addressed on a case-by-case basis, but the general advice offered here applies to all of them. One key difference among all these messages is whether you have time to plan the announcement. The following section addresses negative messages that you do have time to plan for, and the section after that, "Communicating in a Crisis," offers advice on communication during emergencies.

COMMUNICATING UNDER NORMAL CIRCUMSTANCES

Negative organizational messages to external audiences can require extensive planning.

Businesses must convey a range of negative messages regarding their ongoing operations. As you plan such messages, take extra care to consider all your audiences and their unique needs. Keep in mind that a significant negative event such as a plant closing can affect hundreds or thousands of people in many organizations. Employees need to find new jobs, get training in new skills, or perhaps get emergency financial help. School districts may have to adjust budgets and staffing levels if many of your employees plan to move in search of new jobs. Your customers need to find new suppliers. Your suppliers may need to find other customers of their own. Government agencies may need to react to everything from a decrease in tax revenues to an influx of people seeking unemployment benefits.

When making negative announcements, follow these guidelines:

- **Match your approach to the situation.** A modest price increase won't shock most customers, so the direct approach is fine. However, canceling a product that people count on is another matter, so building up to the news via the indirect approach might be better.
- **Consider the unique needs of each group.** As the plant closing example illustrates, various people have different information needs.

Give people as much time as possible to react to negative organizational news.

- **Give each audience enough time to react as needed.** One of the key mistakes Chargify made (see page 246) in announcing its new pricing model was failing to let customers know ahead of time that monthly prices would be increasing.
- **Give yourself enough time to plan and manage a response.** Chances are you're going to be hit with complaints, questions, or product returns after you make your announcement, so make sure you're ready with answers and additional follow-up information.
- **Look for positive angles but don't exude false optimism.** If eliminating a seldom-used employee benefit means employees will save money, by all means promote that positive angle. On the other hand, laying off 10,000 people does not give them "an opportunity to explore new horizons." It's a traumatic event that can affect employees, their families, and their communities for years. The best you may be able to do is to thank people for their past support and wish them well in the future.

Ask for legal help and other assistance if you're not sure how to handle a significant negative announcement.

- **Seek expert advice if you're not sure.** Many significant negative announcements have important technical, financial, or legal elements that require the expertise of lawyers, accountants, or other specialists.

Negative situations will test your skills as a communicator and leader. Inspirational leaders try to seize such opportunities as a chance to reshape or reinvigorate the organization, and they offer encouragement to those around them (see Figure 9.5).

COMMUNICATING IN A CRISIS

Some of the most critical instances of business communication occur during crises, which can include industrial accidents, crimes or scandals involving company employees, on-site

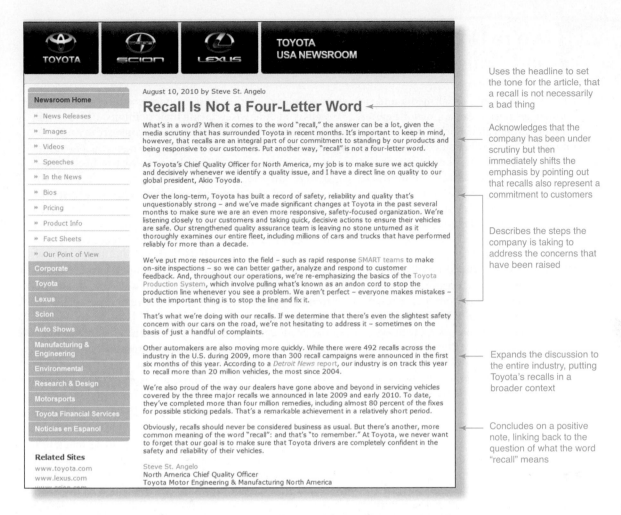

Figure 9.5 Using Negative Situations as Opportunities to Convey Positive Information
Situations that involve negative news are sometimes opportunities in disguise. After Toyota had issued several vehicle recalls and been subjected to quite a bit of media scrutiny regarding product quality, the company's chief quality officer took the opportunity to discuss the meaning of a product recall.

hostage situations, terrorist attacks, information theft, product tampering incidents, and financial calamities. During a crisis, customers, employees, local communities, and others will demand information. In addition, rumors can spread unpredictably and uncontrollably (see "Business Communication 2.0: We're Under Attack! Responding to Rumors and Criticism in a Social Media Environment"). You can also expect the news media to descend quickly, asking questions of anyone they can find.

Although you can't predict these events, you can prepare for them. Analysis of corporate crises over the past several decades reveals that companies that respond quickly with the information people need tend to fare much better in the long run than those that go into hiding or release inconsistent or incorrect information.[14]

The key to successful communication efforts during a crisis is having a **crisis management plan**. In addition to defining operational procedures to deal with the crisis, this plan outlines communication tasks and responsibilities, which can include everything from media contacts to news release

Anticipation and planning are key to successful communication in a crisis.

REAL-TIME UPDATES
Learn More by Watching This Video

Take some of the sting out of delivering bad news

No one likes to deliver bad news, but these techniques can make it easier for you and the recipient. Go to http://real-timeupdates .com/bct11 and click on "Learn More." If you are using MyBcommLab, you can access Real-Time Updates within each chapter or under Student Study Tools.

BUSINESS COMMUNICATION 2.0	We're Under Attack! Responding to Rumors and Criticism in a Social Media Environment

For all the benefits they bring to business, social media and other communication technologies have created a major new challenge: responding to online rumors and attacks on a company's reputation. Consumers and other stakeholders can now communicate through blogs, Twitter, YouTube, Facebook, advocacy sites such as www.walmartwatch.com, community participation websites such as www.epinions.com and www.planetfeedback.com, company-specific sites such as www.verizonpathetic.com, community Q&A sites such as http://getsatisfaction.com, and numerous e-commerce shopping sites that encourage product reviews.

Customers who feel they have been treated unfairly like these sites because they can use the public exposure as leverage. Many companies appreciate the feedback from these sites, too, and many actively seek out complaints to improve their products and operations. However, false rumors and unfair criticisms can spread around the world in a matter of minutes and endanger company reputations. Responding to rumors and countering negative information requires an ongoing effort and case-by-case decisions about which messages require a response. Follow these four steps:

- **Engage early, engage often.** Perhaps the most important step in responding to negative information has to be done *before* the negative information appears, and that is to engage with communities of stakeholders as a long-term strategy. Companies that have active, mutually beneficial relationships with customers and other interested parties are less likely to be attacked unfairly online and more likely to survive such attacks if they do occur. In contrast, companies that ignore constituents or jump into "spin doctoring" mode when a negative situation occurs don't have the same credibility as companies that have done the long, hard work of fostering relationships within their physical and online communities.
- **Monitor the conversation.** If people are interested in what your company does, chances are they are blogging, tweeting, podcasting, posting videos, writing on Facebook walls, and otherwise sharing their opinions. Use the available technologies to listen to what people are saying.
- **Evaluate negative messages.** When you encounter negative messages, resist the urge to fire back immediately. Instead, evaluate the source, the tone, and the content of the message and then choose a response that fits the situation. For example, the Public Affairs Agency of the U.S. Air Force groups senders of negative messages into four categories: "trolls" (those whose only intent is to stir up conflict), "ragers" (those who are just ranting or telling jokes), "the misguided" (those who are spreading incorrect information), and "unhappy customers" (those who have had a negative experience with the Air Force).
- **Respond appropriately.** After you have assessed a negative message, make the appropriate response based on an overall public relations plan. The Air Force, for instance, doesn't respond to trolls or ragers, responds to misguided messages with correct information, and responds to unhappy customers with efforts to rectify the situation and reach a reasonable solution.

Whatever you do, don't assume that a positive reputation doesn't need to be diligently guarded and defended. Everybody has a voice now, and some of those voices don't care to play by the rules of ethical communication.

CAREER APPLICATIONS

1. A legitimate complaint about your restaurant on Yelp also contains a statement that your company "doesn't care about its customers." How should you respond?
2. A few bloggers are circulating false information about your company, but the problem is not widespread—yet. Should you jump on the problem now and tell the world the rumor is false, even though most people haven't heard it yet? Explain your answer.

templates (see Table 9.3). The plan should clearly specify which people are authorized to speak for the company, provide contact information for all key executives, and include a list of the news outlets and social media tools that will be used to disseminate information.

Sending Negative Employment Messages

7 **LEARNING OBJECTIVE**

Describe successful strategies for sending negative employment-related messages.

Most managers must convey bad news about or to individual employees from time to time. Recipients have an emotional stake in your message, so taking the indirect approach is usually advised. In addition, use great care in choosing media for these messages. For instance, email and other written forms let you control the message and avoid personal confrontation, but one-on-one conversations are more sensitive and facilitate questions and answers.

TABLE 9.3	How to Communicate in a Crisis

WHEN A CRISIS HITS:

Do	Don't
Prepare for trouble ahead of time by identifying potential problems, appointing and training a response team, and preparing and testing a crisis management plan.	Don't blame anyone for anything.
Get top management involved immediately.	Don't speculate in public.
Set up a news center for company representatives and the media that is equipped with phones, computers, and other electronic tools for preparing news releases and online updates. At the news center, take the following steps:	Don't refuse to answer questions.
	Don't release information that will violate anyone's right to privacy.
• Issue frequent news updates, and have trained personnel available to respond to questions around the clock.	Don't use the crisis to pitch products or services.
• Provide complete information packets to the media as soon as possible.	Don't play favorites with media representatives.
• Prevent conflicting statements and provide continuity by appointing a single person trained in advance to speak for the company.	
• Tell receptionists and other employees to direct all phone calls to the designated spokesperson in the news center.	
• Provide updates when new information is available via blog postings, microblog updates, text messaging, Facebook, and other appropriate media.	
Tell the whole story—openly, completely, and honestly. If you are at fault, apologize.	
Demonstrate the company's concern by your statements and your actions.	

REFUSING REQUESTS FOR EMPLOYEE REFERENCES AND RECOMMENDATION LETTERS

When sending refusals to prospective employers who have requested information about past employees, your message can be brief and direct:

> Our human resources department has authorized me to confirm that Yolanda Johnson worked for Tandy, Inc., for three years, from June 2007 to July 2009. Best of luck as you interview applicants.

Implies that company policy prohibits the release of any more information but does provide what information is available

Ends on a positive note

This message doesn't need to say, "We cannot comply with your request." It simply gives the reader all the information that is allowable.

Refusing an applicant's direct request for a recommendation letter is another matter. Any refusal to cooperate may seem to be a personal slight and a threat to the applicant's future. Diplomacy and preparation help readers accept your refusal:

> Thank you for letting me know about your job opportunity with Coca-Cola. Your internship there and the MBA you've worked so hard to earn should place you in an excellent position to land the marketing job.
>
> Although we do not send out formal recommendations here at PepsiCo, I can certainly send Coca-Cola a confirmation of your employment dates. And if you haven't considered this already, be sure to ask several of your professors to write evaluations of your marketing skills. Best of luck to you in your career.

Uses the indirect approach since the other party is probably expecting a positive response

Announces that the writer cannot comply with the request, without explicitly blaming it on "policy"

Offers to fulfill as much of the request as possible and offers an alternative

Ends on a positive note

This message tactfully avoids hurting the reader's feelings because it makes positive comments about the reader's recent activities, implies the refusal, suggests an alternative, and uses a polite close.

REFUSING SOCIAL NETWORKING RECOMMENDATION REQUESTS

One of the greatest values offered by business social networks is the opportunity for members to make introductions and recommendations. However, the situation with recommendations in a social networking environment is more complicated than with a traditional recommendation letter because the recommendations you make become part of your online profile. With a traditional letter, only a few hiring managers might read your recommendations, but on a network such as LinkedIn, other network members (or even the general public, in some instances) can see whom you've recommended and what you've written about these people. Much more so than with traditional letters, then, the recommendations you make in a social network become part of your brand.[15] Moreover, networks make it easy to find people and request recommendations, so chances are you will get more requests than you would have otherwise—and sometimes from people you don't know well.

Social networks have created new challenges in recommendation requests, but they also offer more flexibility in responding to these requests.

Fortunately, social networks give you a bit more flexibility when it comes to responding to these requests. You can simply ignore or delete the request, and some people make it personal policy to ignore requests from networkers they don't know. Of course, if you do know a person, ignoring a request could create an uncomfortable situation, so you will need to decide each case based on your relationship with the requester. Another option is to refrain from making recommendations at all, and just letting people know this policy when they ask. Whatever you decide, remember that it is your choice.[16]

If you choose to make recommendations and want to respond to a request, you can write as much or as little information about the person as you are comfortable sharing. Unlike an offline recommendation, you don't need to write a complete letter. You can write a briefer statement, even just a single sentence that focuses on one positive aspect.[17] This flexibility allows you to respond positively in those situations in which you have mixed feelings about a person's overall abilities.

REJECTING JOB APPLICATIONS

Poorly written rejection letters tarnish your company's reputation and can even invite legal troubles.

Application rejection messages are routine communications, but saying no is never easy, and recipients are emotionally invested in the decision. Moreover, companies must be aware of the possibility of employment discrimination lawsuits, which have been on the rise in recent years.[18] Of course, having fair and nondiscriminatory hiring practices is essential, but rejections must also be written in a way that doesn't inadvertently suggest any hint of discrimination. Expert opinions differ on the level of information to include in a rejection message, but the safest strategy is to avoid sharing any explanations for the company's decision and to avoid making or implying any promises of future consideration (see Figure 9.6):[19]

- **Personalize the email message or letter by using the recipient's name.** For example, mail merge makes it easy to insert each recipient's name into a form letter.
- **Open with a courteous expression of appreciation for having applied.** In a sense, this is like the buffer in an indirect message because it gives you an opportunity to begin the conversation without immediately and bluntly telling the reader that his or her application has been rejected.
- **Convey the negative news politely and concisely.** The passive voice is helpful in this situation because it shifts focus away from the people involved and thereby depersonalizes the response. For example, "Your application was not among those selected for an interview," is less blunt than the active phrase "We have rejected your application."
- **Avoid explaining why an applicant was rejected or why other applicants were chosen instead.** Although it was once more common to offer such explanations, and some experts still advocate this approach, the simplest strategy from a legal standpoint is to avoid offering reasons for the decision. Avoiding explanations lowers the possibility that an applicant will perceive discrimination in the hiring decision or be tempted to challenge the reasons given.
- **Don't state or imply that the application will be reviewed at a later date.** Saying that "we will keep your résumé on file for future consideration" can create false hopes for the recipient and leave the company vulnerable to legal complaints if a future hiring decision is made without actually reviewing this candidate's application again. If the candidate might be a good fit for another position in the company in the future, you can suggest he or she reapply if a new job opening is posted.
- **Close with positive wishes for the applicant's career success.** A brief statement such as "We wish you success in your career" is sufficient.

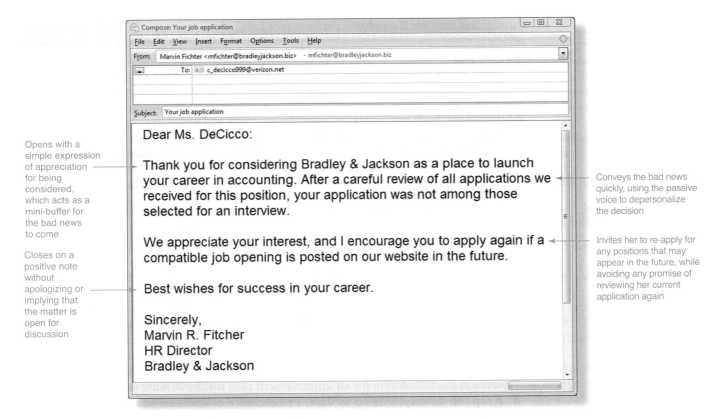

Opens with a simple expression of appreciation for being considered, which acts as a mini-buffer for the bad news to come

Closes on a positive note without apologizing or implying that the matter is open for discussion

Conveys the bad news quickly, using the passive voice to depersonalize the decision

Invites her to re-apply for any positions that may appear in the future, while avoiding any promise of reviewing her current application again

Figure 9.6   Effective Message Rejecting a Job Applicant
This message rejecting a job applicant takes care to avoid making or implying any promises about future opportunities, beyond inviting the person to apply for positions that may appear in the future. Note that this would not be appropriate if the company did not believe the applicant was a good fit for the company in general.

MyBcommLab

Apply Figure 9.6's key concepts by revising a new document. Go to Chapter 9 in mybcommlab.com and select Document Makeovers.

Naturally, you should adjust your tactics to the circumstances. A simple and direct message is fine when someone has only submitted a job application, but rejecting a candidate who has made it at least partway through the interview process requires greater care. Personal contact has already been established through the interview process, so a phone call may be more appropriate.

GIVING NEGATIVE PERFORMANCE REVIEWS

The main purpose of a **performance review** is to improve employee performance by (1) emphasizing and clarifying job requirements, (2) giving employees feedback on their efforts toward fulfilling those requirements, and (3) guiding continued efforts by developing a plan of action, which includes rewards and opportunities. Performance reviews help companies set organizational standards and communicate organizational values.[20] Documentation of performance problems can also protect a company from being sued for unlawful termination.[21]

An important goal of any performance evaluation is to give the employee a plan of action for improving his or her performance.

With pay raises and promotion opportunities often depending on how employees are rated in this process, annual reviews often are a stressful occurrence for managers and workers alike. The worst possible outcome in an annual review is a negative surprise, such as when an employee has been working toward different goals than the manager expects or has been underperforming throughout the year but didn't receive any feedback or improvement coaching along the way.[22] In some instances, failing to confront performance problems in a timely fashion can make a company vulnerable to lawsuits.[23]

To avoid negative surprises, managers should meet with employees to agree on clear goals for the upcoming year and then provide regular feedback and coaching as needed

By giving employees clear goals and regular feedback, you can help avoid unpleasant surprises in a performance review.

troubles. Analyze the approach the company took; was it the most effective strategy possible? Did the company apologize, if doing so would have been appropriate under the circumstances, and does the apology seem sincere? Does the tone of the message match the seriousness of the situation? Does the message end on a positive note, as appropriate? Using whatever medium your instructor requests, write a brief analysis of the message (no more than one page), citing specific elements from the piece and support from the chapter.

Sharpening Your Career Skills Online

Bovée and Thill's Business Communication Web Search, at http://businesscommunicationblog.com/websearch, is a unique research tool designed specifically for business communication research. Use the Web Search function to find a website, video, PDF document, podcast, or PowerPoint presentation that offers advice on writing messages that convey negative information. Write a brief email message to your instructor, describing the item that you found and summarizing the career skills information you learned from it.

CASES

Negative Messages on Routine Business Matters

EMAIL SKILLS

1. Message Strategies: Rejecting Suggestions and Proposals [LO-5]　Walter Joss is one of the best employees in your department, a smart and hard worker with a keen mind for business. His upbeat attitude has helped the entire department get through some rough times recently, and on a personal level, his wise counsel helped you grow into a leadership role when you were promoted to marketing manager several years ago.

You generally welcome Joss's input on the department's operations, and you have implemented several of his ideas to improve the company's marketing efforts. However, the proposal he emailed you yesterday was not his best work, to put it mildly. He proposed that the company dump the advertising agency it has used for a decade and replace it with some new agency you've never heard of. The only reasons he offered were that the agency "had become unresponsive" and that a "smaller agency could meet our needs better." He failed to address any of the other criteria that are used to select advertising agencies, such as costs, creative skills, technical abilities, geographic reach, research capabilities, and media experience.

This is the first you've heard any criticism of the agency, and in fact, their work was helped your company increase sales every year.

Your task:　Draft an email message to Joss, rejecting his proposal. (Note that in a real-life setting, you would want to discuss this with Joss in person, rather than through email, but use email for the purposes of this exercise.)

EMAIL SKILLS

2. Message Strategies: Making Routine Negative Announcements [LO-5]　You've been proud of many things your gardening tool company has accomplished as it grew from just you working in your basement shop to a nationally known company that employs over 200 people. However, nothing made you prouder than the company's Helping Our Hometown Grow program, in which employees volunteer on company time to help residents in your city start their own vegetable gardens, using tools donated by the company. Nearly 50 employees participated

directly, helping some 500 families supplement their grocery budgets with home-grown produce. Virtually everyone in the company contributed, though, because employees who didn't volunteer to help in the gardens pitched in to cover the work responsibilities of the volunteers.

Sadly, ten years after you launched the program, you have reached the inescapable conclusion that the company can no longer afford to keep the program going. With consumers around the country still struggling with the aftereffects of a deep recession, sales have been dropping for the past three years—even as lower cost competitors step up their presence in the market. To save the program, you would have to lay off several employees, but your employees come first.

Your task:　Write an email to the entire company, announcing the cancellation of the program.

TELEPHONE SKILLS

3. Message Strategies: Making Routine Negative Announcements [LO-5]　Vail Products of Toledo, Ohio, manufactured a line of beds for use in hospitals and other institutions that have a need to protect patients who might otherwise fall out of bed and injure themselves (including patients with cognitive impairments or patterns of spasms or seizures). These "enclosed bed systems" use a netted canopy to keep patients in bed rather than the traditional method of using physical restraints such as straps or tranquilizing drugs. The intent is humane, but the design is flawed: At least 30 patients have become trapped in the various parts of the mattress and canopy structure, and 8 of them have suffocated.

Working with the U.S. Food and Drug Administration (FDA), Vail issued a recall on the beds, as manufacturers often do in the case of unsafe products. However, the recall is not really a recall. Vail will not be replacing or modifying the beds, nor will it accept returns. Instead, the company is urging institutions to move patients to other beds, if possible. Vail has also sent out revised manuals and warning labels to be placed on the beds. The company also announced that it is ceasing production of enclosed beds.

Your task:　A flurry of phone calls from concerned patients, family members, and institutional staff is overwhelming the support staff. As a writer in Vail's corporate communications office, you've been asked to draft a short script to be recorded on the company's phone system. When people call the main number, they'll hear "Press 1 for information regarding the recall of Model 500, Model

1000, and Model 2000 enclosed beds." After they press 1, they'll hear the message you're about to write, explaining that although the action is classified as a recall, Vail will not be accepting returned beds, nor will it replace any of the affected beds. The message should also assure customers that Vail has already sent revised operating manuals and warning labels to every registered owner of the beds in question. The phone system has limited memory, and you've been directed to keep the message to 75 words or less.[27]

EMAIL SKILLS   PORTFOLIO BUILDER

4. Message Strategies: Rejecting Suggestions and Proposals; Communication Ethics: Making Ethical Choices [LO-5] A not-so-secret secret is getting more attention than you'd really like after an article in *BusinessWeek* gave the world an inside look at how much money you and other electronics retailers make from extended warranties (sometimes called service contracts). The article explained that typically half of the warranty price goes to the salesperson as a commission and that only 20 percent of the total amount customers pay for warranties eventually goes to product repair.

You also know why extended warranties are such a profitable business. Many electronics products follow a predictable pattern of failure: a high failure rate early in their lives, then a "midlife" period during which failures go way down, and concluding with an "old age" period when failure rates ramp back up again (engineers refer to the phenomenon as the *bathtub curve* because it looks like a bathtub from the side—high at both ends and low in the middle). The early failures are usually covered by manufacturers' warranties, and the extended warranties you sell are designed to cover that middle part of the life span. In other words, many extended warranties cover the period of time during which consumers are *least* likely to need them and offer no coverage when consumers need them *most*. (Consumers can actually benefit from extended warranties in a few product categories, including laptop computers and plasma televisions. Of course, the more sense the warranty makes for the consumer, the less financial sense it makes for your company.)[28]

Your task: Worried that consumers will stop buying so many extended warranties, your boss has directed you to put together a sales training program that will help cashiers sell the extended warranties even more aggressively. The more you ponder this challenge, though, the more you're convinced that your company should change its strategy so it doesn't rely on profits from these warranties so much. In addition to offering questionable value to the consumer, the warranties risk creating a consumer backlash that could lead to lower sales of all your products. You would prefer to voice your concerns to your boss in person, but both of you are traveling on hectic schedules for the next week. You'll have to write an email instead. Draft a brief message, explaining why you think the sales training specifically and the warranties in general are both bad ideas.

MICROBLOGGING SKILLS

5. Message Strategies: Making Routine Negative Announcements [LO-5] JetBlue was one of the first companies to incorporate the Twitter microblogging service into its customer communications, and thousands of fliers and fans now follow the airline's Twittering staff members. Messages include announcements about fare sales (such as limited-time auctions on eBay or special on-site sales at shopping malls), celebrations of company milestones (such as the opening of the carrier's new terminal at New York's JFK airport), schedule updates, and even personalized responses to people who Twitter with questions or complaints about the company.[29]

Your task: Write a Tweet alerting JetBlue customers to the possibility that Hurricane Isaac might disrupt flight schedules from August 13 through August 15. Tell them that decisions about delays and cancellations will be made on a city-by-city basis and will be announced on Twitter and the company's website. The URL will take 20 characters, so you have 120 characters (including spaces) for your message.

BLOGGING SKILLS   PORTFOLIO BUILDER

6. Message Strategies: Making Routine Negative Announcements [LO-5] Marketing specialists usually celebrate when target audiences forward their messages to friends and family—essentially acting as unpaid advertising and sales representatives. In fact, the practice of viral marketing is based on this hope. For one Starbucks regional office, however, viral marketing started to make the company just a bit sick. The office sent employees in the Southeast an email coupon for a free iced drink and invited them to share the coupon with family and friends. To the surprise of virtually no one who understands the nature of online life, the email coupon multiplied rapidly, to the point that Starbucks stores all around the country were quickly overwhelmed with requests for free drinks. The company decided to immediately terminate the free offer, a month ahead of the expiration date on the coupon.[30]

Your task: Write a one-paragraph message that can be posted on the Starbucks website and at individual stores, apologizing for the mix-up and explaining that the offer is no longer valid.

EMAIL SKILLS

7. Message Strategies: Rejecting Suggestions and Proposals [LO-5] Lee Valley Tools (www.leevalley.com) sells high-quality woodworking tools across Canada through its retail stores and around the world through its website and catalogs. While weekend hobbyists can pick up a mass-produced hand plane (a tool for smoothing wood) for $20 or $30 at the local hardware store, serious woodworkers pay five or ten times that much for one of Lee Valley's precision Veritas planes. For the price, they get top-quality materials, precision manufacturing, and innovative designs that help them do better work in less time.

Lee Valley sells both its own Veritas brand tools as well as 5,000 tools made by other manufacturers. One of those companies has just emailed you to ask if Lee Valley would like to carry a new line of midrange hand planes that would cost more than the mass-market, hardware-store models but less than Lee Valley's own Veritas models. Your job is to filter requests such as this, rejecting those that don't meet Lee Valley's criteria and forwarding those that do to the product selection committee for further analysis. After one quick read of this incoming email message, you realize there is no need to send this idea to the committee. While these planes are certainly of decent quality, they achieve their lower cost through lower-quality steel that won't hold an edge as long and through thinner irons (the element that holds the cutting edge) that will be more prone to vibrate during use and thus produce a rougher finish. These planes have a market, to be sure, but they're not a good fit for Lee Valley's top-of-the-line product portfolio. Moreover, the planes don't offer any innovations in terms of ease of use or any other product attribute.[31]

Your task: Reply to this email message, explaining that the planes appear to be decent tools, but they don't fit Lee Valley's strategy of offering only the best and most innovative tools. Support your decision with the three criteria described above. Choose the direct or indirect approach carefully, taking into consideration your company's relationship with this other company.

EMAIL SKILLS

8. Message Strategies: Refusing Claims and Requests for Adjustment [LO-5] Like many other software companies, the Swiss company Fookes Software (www.fookes.com) lets potential customers download free evaluation copies of its software before deciding to purchase. By using the free trial versions, people can verify that the software meets their needs and is compatible with their PCs. Because it allows potential buyers to try products for 30 days before purchasing, the company does not provide refunds except in the case of accidental duplicate orders. Here is the company's refund policy, as shown on its website:

> All of Fookes Software's products can be evaluated, **free of charge**, through a trial mode or separate trial version that can be downloaded directly from our web site. Use the trial **before you purchase** to ensure that the full product will be compatible with your computer systems and satisfy your requirements. If you do not, you accept that the product may not meet your needs and that this will not justify a refund or chargeback. If you experience an issue with our software, then please contact our customer support service for help in solving the problem.
>
> **All sales are final** and refunds are provided only for accidental duplicate orders. Refunds will only be made to the credit card or PayPal account through which the original purchase was made. An administration fee may apply in such cases to cover processing costs and third-party commissions.
>
> Ordering a software license signifies your acceptance of this Refund Policy.

In addition, the ordering page on the website asks potential buyers to read the refund policy before ordering and provides a link to the policy page.

This morning you received an email message from a customer who purchased a copy of Album Express, a software package that helps people organize photos in attractive online albums and slide shows. After purchasing the program, the customer discovered that his admittedly outdated computer has only 16 MB of memory, which is not enough to run the software effectively. He is now requesting a refund of the purchase price of $24.95. The website clearly states that Album Express requires at least 32 MB of memory, but the customer's email doesn't mention whether he read this.[32]

Your task: Write an email message, denying the customer's request for a refund.

LETTER WRITING SKILLS   PORTFOLIO BUILDER

9. Message Strategies: Negative Announcements on Routine Matters [LO-5] You're a marketing manager for Stanton, one of the premier suppliers of DJ equipment (turntables,

amplifiers, speakers, mixers, and related accessories). Your company's latest creation, the FinalScratch system, has been flying off retailers' shelves. Both professional and amateur DJs love the way that FinalScratch gives them the feel of working with vinyl records by letting them control digital music files from any analog turntable or CD player while giving them access to the endless possibilities of digital music technology. (For more information about the product, go to www.stantondj.com.) Sales are strong everywhere except in Music99 stores, a retail chain in the Mid-Atlantic region. You suspect the cause: The owners of this chain refused to let their salespeople attend the free product training you offered when FinalScratch was introduced, claiming their people were smart enough to train themselves.

To explore the situation, you head out from Stanton headquarters in Hollywood, Florida, on an undercover shopping mission. After visiting a few Music99 locations, you're appalled by what you see. The salespeople in these stores clearly don't understand the FinalScratch concept, so they either give potential customers bad information about it or steer them to products from your competitors. No wonder sales are so bad at this chain.

Your task: You're tempted to pull your products out of this chain immediately, but you know how difficult and expensive it is to recruit new retailers in this market. However, this situation can't go on; you're losing thousands of dollars of potential business every week. Write a letter to Jackson Fletcher, the CEO of Music99 (14014 Preston Pike, Dover, DE 19901), expressing your disappointment in what you observed and explaining that the Music99 sales staff will need to agree to attend product training or else your company's management team will consider terminating the business relationship. You've met Mr. Fletcher in person once and talked to him on the phone several times, and you know him well enough to know that he will not be pleased by this ultimatum. Music99 does a good job selling other Stanton products—and he'll probably be furious to learn that you were "spying" on his sales staff.[33]

PODCASTING SKILLS

10. Message Strategies: Negative Announcements on Routine Matters [LO-5] An employee concierge seemed like a great idea when you added it as an employee benefit last year. The concierge handles a wide variety of personal chores for employees, everything from dropping off dry cleaning to ordering event tickets to sending flowers. Employees love the service, and you know that the time they save can be devoted to work or family activities. Unfortunately, profits are way down, and concierge usage is up—up so far that you'll need to add a second concierge to keep up with the demand. As painful as it will be for everyone, you decide that the company needs to stop offering the service.

Your task: Script a brief podcast, announcing the decision and explaining why it was necessary. Make up any details you need. If your instructor asks you to do so, record your podcast and submit the file.

EMAIL SKILLS   PORTFOLIO BUILDER

11. Message Strategies: Negative Announcements on Routine Matters [LO-5] You can certainly sympathize with employees when they complain about having their email and instant messages monitored, but you're implementing a company policy that all employees agree to abide by when they join the company. Your firm, Webcor Builders of San Mateo, California, is one of the estimated 60 percent of U.S. companies with such monitoring systems in place. More and more companies use these systems (which typically operate by scanning messages for keywords that suggest confidential, illegal, or otherwise inappropriate content) in an attempt to avoid instances of sexual harassment and other problems.

As the chief information officer, the manager in charge of computer systems in the company, you're often the target when employees complain about being monitored. Consequently, you know you're really going to hear it when employees learn that the monitoring program will be expanded to personal blogs as well.

Your task: Write an email message to be distributed to the entire workforce, explaining that the automated monitoring program is about to be expanded to include employees' personal blogs. Explain that, while you sympathize with employee concerns regarding privacy and freedom of speech, it is the management team's responsibility to protect the company's intellectual property and the value of the company name. Therefore, employees' personal blogs will be added to the monitoring system to ensure that employees don't intentionally or accidentally expose company secrets or criticize management in a way that could harm the company.[34]

LETTER WRITING SKILLS

12. Message Strategies: Negative Announcements on Routine Matters [LO-5] Your company, PolicyPlan Insurance Services, is a 120-employee insurance claims processor based in Milwaukee. PolicyPlan has engaged Midwest Sparkleen for interior and exterior cleaning for the past five years. Midwest Sparkleen did exemplary work for the first four years, but after a change of ownership last year, the level of service has plummeted. Offices are no longer cleaned thoroughly, you've had to call the company at least six times to remind them to take care of spills and other messes that they're supposed to address routinely, and they've left toxic cleaning chemicals in a public hallway on several occasions. You have spoken with the owner about your concerns twice in the past three months, but his assurances that service would improve have not resulted in any noticeable improvements. When the evening cleaning crew forgot to lock the lobby door last Thursday—leaving your entire facility vulnerable to theft from midnight until 8 a.m. Friday morning—you decided it was time for a change.

Your task: Write a letter to Jason Allred, owner of Midwest Sparkleen, 4000 South Howell Avenue, Milwaukee, WI, 53207, telling him that PolicyPlan will not be renewing its annual cleaning contract with Midwest Sparkleen when the current contract expires at the end of this month. Cite the examples identified above, and keep the tone of your letter professional.

BLOGGING SKILLS   PORTFOLIO BUILDER

13. Message Strategies: Negative Announcements on Routine Matters [LO-5] Like many other companies these days, the accounting firm Ernst & Young is fighting a brain drain, as experienced executives and professionals leave midcareer to pursue charitable interests, devote more time to family matters, or pursue a variety of other dreams or obligations. The problem

is particularly acute among women, because on average they step off the career track more often than men do. As general manager of the largest division in the company, you've been tapped to draft a set of guidelines to make it easier for employees who've taken some time off to move back into the company.

However, as soon as word gets out about what you're planning, several of your top performers, people who've never left the company for personal time off—or "taken the off-ramp," in current buzzword speak—march into your office to complain. They fear that encouraging the "off-rampers" to return isn't fair to the employees who've remained loyal to the firm, as they put it. One goes as far as to say that anyone who leaves the company doesn't deserve to be asked back. Two others claim that the additional experience and skills they've gained as they continued to work should guarantee them higher pay and more responsibilities than employees who took time off for themselves.

Your task: As unhappy as these several employees are, the program needs to be implemented if Ernst & Young hopes to bring "off-rampers" back into the company—thereby making sure they don't go to work for competitors instead. However, you also can't afford to antagonize the existing workforce; if the people who've already complained are any indication, you have a sizable morale problem on your hands. You decide that your first step is to clearly explain why the program is necessary, including how it will benefit everyone in the company by making Ernst & Young more competitive. Write a short posting for the company's internal blog, explaining that, despite the objections some employees have raised, the firm is going ahead with the program as planned. Balance this news (which some employees will obviously view as negative) with positive reassurances that all current employees will be treated fairly in terms of both compensation and promotion opportunities. Close with a call for continued communication on this issue, inviting people to meet with you in person or to post their thoughts on the blog.[35]

Negative Organizational News

SOCIAL NETWORKING SKILLS

14. Message Strategies: Negative Organizational Announcements [LO-6] Caught in a perfect storm of online retailing, downloadable e-books, low-cost mass merchandisers, a fragmented audience with multiple entertainment options, and the worst recession in memory, the giant Borders bookstore chain was forced to file for bankruptcy protection in 2011.

Your task: Download the Borders press release at http://real-timeupdates.com/bct11 (click on "Student Assignments," and then "Chapter 9, Page 277, Case 14"). Review the information, and then write a 100- to 150-word summary of the bankruptcy announcement that could be posted on the company's Facebook page.

BLOGGING SKILLS

15. Message Strategies: Negative Organizational Announcements [LO-6] XtremityPlus is known for its outlandish extreme-sports products, and the Looney Launch is no exception. Fulfilling the dream of every childhood daredevil, the Looney Launch is an aluminum and fiberglass contraption that quickly unfolds to create the ultimate bicycle jump. The product has been selling as fast as you can make it, even though it comes plastered with warning labels proclaiming that its use is inherently dangerous.

As XtremityPlus's CEO, you were nervous about introducing this product, and your fears were just confirmed: You've been notified of the first lawsuit by a parent whose child broke several bones after crash-landing off a Looney Launch.

Your task: Write a post for your internal blog, explaining that the Looney Launch is being removed from the market immediately. Tell your employees to expect some negative reactions from enthusiastic customers and retailers but explain that (a) the company can't afford the risk of additional lawsuits; and (b) even for XtremityPlus, the Looney Launch pushes the envelope a bit too far. The product is simply too dangerous to sell in good conscience.

EMAIL SKILLS

16. Message Strategies: Negative Organizational Announcements [LO-6] Now it's time to follow up the internal employee message about the Looney Launch (see Case 15) with a message to the retailers that carry the product.

Your task: Write an email message to retailers, explaining that the Looney Launch is being removed from the market and explaining why you've reached this decision. Apologize for the temporary disruption this will cause to their businesses but emphasize that it's the right decision from both legal and social perspectives. Thank them for their continuing efforts to sell XtremityPlus products and assure them that your company will continue to offer exciting and innovative products for extreme-sports enthusiasts.

BLOGGING SKILLS

17. Message Strategies: Negative Organizational Announcements [LO-6] As the U.S. economy continued to sag after receiving multiple blows from the housing and financial sectors, plant closures were a common tragedy across many industries. Shaw Industries, the world's largest manufacturer of carpeting, was among those suppliers to the housing industry that suffered as fewer houses were built or remodeled.

Your task: Write a brief message for Shaw's corporate blog, covering the following points:

- With more than $5 billion in annual sales, Shaw Industries is the world's number one carpet manufacturer.
- Shaw's Milledgeville, Georgia, plant makes yarn used in the manufacture of carpeting.
- The continuing struggles in the new-housing market and the inability of many current homeowners to afford remodeling projects have lowered demand for carpet. With less demand for carpet, the Milledgeville plant can no longer operate at a profit.
- Shaw is forced to close the Milledgeville plant and lay off all 150 employees at the plant.
- The plant will close in three to four weeks from the current date.
- As openings become available in other Shaw facilities, the company hopes to be able to place some of the workers in those jobs.

- Georgia Labor Commissioner Michael Thurmond promised to help the affected employees. "The layoff at Shaw Industries in Milledgeville will create a difficult situation for the workers and their families, and I want them to know they're not alone in dealing with this problem. Our staff will work closely with the laid-off workers, company officials, and local elected officials in determining how to best assist the affected employees."
- Assistance to be provided by the State of Georgia includes career counseling, unemployment benefits, and job retraining.[36]

EMAIL SKILLS

18. Message Strategies: Negative Organizational Announcements [LO-6] People who live for an adrenaline rush can find a way to go fast from Canada's Bombardier Recreational Products. Bombardier is one of the world's top makers of snowmobiles, personal watercraft, engines for motorboats, and all-terrain vehicles (ATVs)—all designed for fast fun.

Because it sends customers hurtling across snow, water, or land at high speeds, Bombardier takes safety quite seriously. However, problems do arise from time to time, requiring a rapid response with clear communication to the company's customer base. Bombardier recently became aware of a potentially hazardous situation with the "race-ready" version of its Can-Am DS 90 X ATVs. This model is equipped with a safety device called a tether engine shutoff switch, in which a cord is connected to a special switch that turns off the engine in the event of an emergency. On the affected units, pulling the cord might not shut off the motor, which is particularly dangerous if the rider falls off—the ATV will continue on its own until the engine speed returns to idle.

Your task: Write an email message that will be sent to registered owners of 2008 and 2009 DS 90 X ATVs that include the potentially faulty switch. Analyze the situation carefully as you choose the direct or indirect approach for your message. Explain that the tether engine shutoff switch may not deactivate the engine when it is pulled in an emergency situation. To prevent riders from relying on a safety feature that might not work properly, Bombardier, in cooperation with transportation safety authorities in the United States and Canada, is voluntarily recalling these models to have the tether switch removed. Emphasize the serious nature of the situation by explaining that if the rider is ejected and the engine shutoff switch does not work properly, the ATV will run away on its own, potentially resulting in significant injuries or deaths. Owners should stop riding their vehicles immediately and make an appointment with an authorized dealer to have the switch removed. The service will be performed at no charge, and customers will receive a $50 credit voucher for future purchases of Bombardier accessories. Include the following contact information: **www.can-am.brp.com** and 1-888-638-5397.[37]

BLOGGING SKILLS   PORTFOLIO BUILDER

19. Message Strategies: Communicating in a Crisis [LO-6] One of your company's worst nightmares has just come true. EQ Industrial Services (EQIS), based in Wayne, Michigan, operates a number of facilities around the country that dispose of, recycle, and transport hazardous chemical wastes. Last night, explosions and fires broke out at the company's Apex, North Carolina, facility, forcing the evacuation of 17,000 local residents.

Your task: It's now Friday, the day after the fire. Write a brief post for the company's blog, covering the following points:

- A fire broke out at the Apex facility at approximately 10 P.M. Thursday.
- No one was in the facility at the time.
- Because of the diverse nature of the materials stored at the plant, the cause of the fire is not yet known.
- Rumors that the facility stores extremely dangerous chlorine gas and that the fire was spreading to other nearby businesses are not true.
- Special industrial firefighters hired by EQIS have already brought the fire under control.
- Residents in the immediate area were evacuated as a precaution, and they should be able to return to their homes tomorrow, pending permission from local authorities.
- Several dozen residents were admitted to local hospitals with complaints of breathing problems, but most have been released already; about a dozen emergency responders were treated as well.
- At this point (Friday afternoon), tests conducted by the North Carolina State Department of Environment and Natural Resources "had not detected anything out of the ordinary in the air."

Conclude by thanking the local police and fire departments for their assistance and directing readers to EQIS's toll-free hot line for more information.[38]

BLOGGING SKILLS

20. Message Strategies: Responding to Rumors and Public Criticism [LO-6] Spreading *FUD*—fear, uncertainty, and doubt—about other companies is one of the less-honorable ways of dealing with competition in the business world. For example, someone can start a "whisper campaign" in the marketplace, raising fears that a particular company is struggling financially. Customers who don't want to risk future instability in their supply chains might then shift their purchasing away from the company, based on nothing more than the false rumor.

Your task: Find the website of any company that you find interesting and imagine that you are the CEO and that the company is the subject of an online rumor about impending bankruptcy. Explore the website to get a basic feel for what the company does. Making up any information you need, write a post for the company's blog, explaining that the rumors of bankruptcy are false and that the company is on solid financial ground and plans to keep serving the industry for many years to come. (Be sure to review "We're Under Attack! Responding to Rumors and Criticism in a Social Media Environment" on page 264 for tips.)

SOCIAL NETWORKING SKILLS

21. Message Strategies: Responding to Rumors and Public Criticism [LO-6] The consumer reviews on Yelp (www.yelp .com) can be a promotional boon to any local business—provided the reviews are positive, of course. Negative reviews, fair or not, can affect a company's reputation and drive away potential customers. Fortunately for business owners, sites like Yelp give them the means to respond to reviews, whether they want to apologize for poor service, offer some form of compensation, or correct misinformation in a review.

Your task: Search Yelp for a negative review (one or two stars) on any business in any city. Find a review that has some substance to it, not just a simple, angry rant. Now imagine that you are the owner of that business, and write a reply that could be posted via the "Add Owner Comment" feature. Use information you can find on Yelp about the company and fill in any details by using your imagination. Remember that your comment will be visible to everyone who visits Yelp. (Be sure to review "We're Under Attack! Responding to Rumors and Criticism in a Social Media Environment" on page 264 for tips.)

Negative Employment Messages

SOCIAL NETWORKING **SKILLS**   EMAIL **SKILLS**

22. Message Strategies: Refusing Requests for Recommendations [LO-7] You're delighted to get a message from an old friend and colleague, Heather Lang. You're delighted right up to the moment you read her request that you write a recommendation about her web design and programming skills for your LinkedIn profile. You would do just about anything for Lang—anything except recommend her web design skills. She is a master programmer whose technical wizardry saved more client projects than you can count, but when it comes to artistic design, Lang simply doesn't have "it." From gaudy color schemes to unreadable type treatment to confusing layouts, her design sense is as weak as her technical acumen is strong.

Your task: First, write a brief email to Lang, explaining that you would be most comfortable highlighting her technical skills because that is where you believe her true strengths lie. Second, write a two-sentence recommendation that you could include in your LinkedIn profile, recommending Lang's technical skills. Make up or research any details you need.

TELEPHONE SKILLS

23. Message Strategies: Terminating Employment [LO-7] As the human resources manager at Alion Science and Technology, a military research firm in McLean, Virginia, you were thrilled when one of the nation's top computer visualization specialists accepted your job offer. Claus Gunnstein's skills would have made a major contribution to Alion's work in designing flight simulators and other systems. Unfortunately, the day after he accepted the offer, Alion received news that a major Pentagon contract had been canceled. In addition to letting several dozen current employees know that the company will be forced to lay them off, you need to tell Gunnstein that Alion has no choice but to rescind the job offer.

Your task: Outline the points you'll need to make in a telephone call to Gunnstein. Pay special attention to your opening and closing statements. (You'll review your plans for the phone call with Alion's legal staff to make sure everything you say follows employment law guidelines; for now, just focus on the way you'll present the negative news to Gunnstein. Feel free to make up any details you need.)[39]

EMAIL SKILLS

24. Message Strategies: Refusing Requests for Recommendations [LO-7] Tom Weiss worked in the office at Opal Pools and Patios for four months under your supervision (you're office manager). On the basis of what he told you he could do, you started him off as a file clerk. However, his organizational skills proved inadequate for the job, so you transferred him to logging in accounts receivable, where he performed almost adequately. Then he assured you that his "real strength" was customer relations, so you moved him to the complaint department. After he spent three weeks making angry customers even angrier, you were convinced that no place in your office was appropriate for his talents. Five weeks ago, you encouraged him to resign before being formally fired.

Today's email brings a request from Weiss, asking you to write a letter recommending him for a sales position with a florist shop. You can't assess Weiss's sales abilities, but you do know him to be an incompetent file clerk, a careless bookkeeper, and an insensitive customer service representative. Someone else is more likely to deserve the sales job, so you decide that you have done enough favors for Tom Weiss for one lifetime and plan to refuse his request.

Your task: Write an email reply to Weiss, indicating that you have chosen not to write a letter of recommendation for him.

MEMO WRITING SKILLS PORTFOLIO BUILDER

25. Message Strategies: Negative Performance Reviews [LO-7] Elaine Bridgewater, the former professional golfer you hired to oversee your golf equipment company's relationship with retailers, knows the business inside and out. As a former touring pro, she has unmatched credibility. She also has seemingly boundless energy, solid technical knowledge, and an engaging personal style. Unfortunately, she hasn't been quite as attentive as she needs to be when it comes to communicating with retailers. You've been getting complaints about voicemail messages gone unanswered for days, confusing emails that require two or three rounds of clarification, and reports that are haphazardly thrown together. As valuable as Bridgewater's other skills are, she's going to cost the company sales if this goes on much longer. The retail channel is vital to your company's survival, and she's the employee most involved in this channel.

Your task: Draft a brief (one page maximum) informal performance appraisal and improvement plan for Bridgewater. Be sure to compliment her on the areas in which she excels but don't shy away from highlighting the areas in which she needs to improve, too: punctual response to customer messages; clear writing; and careful revision, production, and proofreading. Use what you've learned in this course so far to supply any additional advice about the importance of these skills.

Writing Persuasive Messages | 10

LEARNING OBJECTIVES After studying this chapter, you will be able to

1 Apply the three-step writing process to persuasive messages

2 Describe an effective strategy for developing persuasive business messages and identify the three most common categories of persuasive business messages

3 Describe an effective strategy for developing marketing and sales messages

4 Explain how to modify your approach when writing promotional messages for social media

5 Identify steps you can take to avoid ethical lapses in marketing and sales messages

MyBcommLab Test your mastery of this chapter and its Learning Objectives. Visit mybcommlab.com to apply what you've learned in Document Makeovers and interactive simulation scenarios.

COMMUNICATION CLOSE-UP AT CAFEMOM

CafeMom uses social media to replicate the in-person experience of parents sharing information, advice, and emotional support.

www.cafemom.com

Few roles in life require more information and insight than parenting. From prenatal care to early childhood development to education to socialization issues, parents are in continuous learning mode as their children grow. Parents also need to learn about themselves as they grow in their roles, from balancing work and home life to nurturing their own relationships. At the same time, parenting can be one of the most isolating experiences for people, often making it difficult for them to acquire the information and support they need to succeed as parents.

Two lifelong friends, actor and activist Andrew Shue and entrepreneur Michael Sanchez, pondered this age-old challenge and saw the web as a solution. The pair co-founded CafeMom, an online community and information resource that helps mothers find answers, insights, and each other.

Information resources and social networks abound on the web, and like any other web start-up, CafeMom faced the challenge of standing apart from the crowd and growing its membership large enough to create a viable business. One of the keys to its success is clear, audience-focused messages that make a compelling case for joining CafeMom. Using straightforward statements such as "CafeMom is an online community where thousands of moms come together every day to connect with each other" and "Whatever you're going through, chances are another mom has been there and can help," the company communicates the features of its various online services and the benefits of joining.

The persuasive communication effort certainly seems to have been successful: CafeMom is now the largest social networking community for mothers and continues to expand as more mothers join in search of helpful insights and friendly support from their peers.[1]

Using the Three-Step Writing Process for Persuasive Messages

Apply the three-step writing process to persuasive messages.

Persuasion is the attempt to change someone's attitudes, beliefs, or actions.

Professionals such as Michael Sanchez, CEO of CafeMom (profiled in the chapter-opening Communication Close-up), understand that successful businesses rely on persuasive messages in both internal and external communication. Whether you're trying to convince your boss to open a new office in Europe or encourage potential customers to try your products, you need to call on your abilities of **persuasion**—the attempt to change an audience's attitudes, beliefs, or actions.[2] As with every other type of business message, the three-step writing process improves persuasive messages.

STEP 1: PLANNING A PERSUASIVE MESSAGE

Having a great idea or a great product is not enough; you need to be able to convince others of its merits.

In today's information-saturated business environment, having a great idea or a great product is no longer enough. Every day, untold numbers of good ideas go unnoticed and good products go unsold simply because the messages meant to promote them aren't compelling enough to be heard above the competitive noise. Creating successful persuasive messages in these challenging situations demands careful attention to all four tasks in the planning step, starting with an insightful analysis of your purpose and your audience.

Analyzing the Situation

Clarifying your purpose is an essential step with persuasive messages.

In defining your purpose, make sure you're clear about what you really hope to achieve. Suppose you want to persuade company executives to support a particular research project. But what does "support" mean? Do you want them to pat you on the back and wish you well? Or do you want them to give you a staff of five researchers and a $1 million annual budget?

Effective persuasive messages are closely aligned with audience motivations, those forces that drive people to satisfy their needs.

The best persuasive messages are closely connected to your audience's desires and interests (see Figure 10.1).[3] Consider these important questions: Who is my audience? What are my audience members' needs? What do I want them to do? How might they resist? Are there alternative positions I need to examine? What does the decision maker consider to be the most important issue? How might the organization's culture influence my strategy?

Demographics include characteristics such as age, gender, occupation, income, and education.

To understand and categorize audience needs, you can refer to specific information, such as **demographics** (the age, gender, occupation, income, education, and other quantifiable characteristics of the people you're trying to persuade) and **psychographics** (personality, attitudes, lifestyle, and other psychological characteristics). When analyzing your audiences, take into account their cultural expectations and practices so that you don't undermine your persuasive message by using an inappropriate appeal or by organizing your message in a way that seems unfamiliar or uncomfortable to your readers.

If you aim to change someone's attitudes, beliefs, or actions through a persuasive message, it is vital to understand his or her **motivation**—the combination of forces that drive people to satisfy their needs. Table 10.1 on page 284 lists some of the needs that psychologists have identified or suggested as being important in influencing human motivation. Obviously, the more closely a persuasive message aligns with a recipient's existing motivation, the more effective the message is likely

REAL-TIME UPDATES
Learn More by Watching This Video

Persuasion skills for every business professional

Persuasion is an essential business skill, no matter what career path you follow. This video offers great tips for understanding, practicing, and applying persuasive skills. Go to http://real-timeupdates.com/bct11 and click on "Learn More." If you are using MyBcommLab, you can access Real-Time Updates within each chapter or under Student Study Tools.

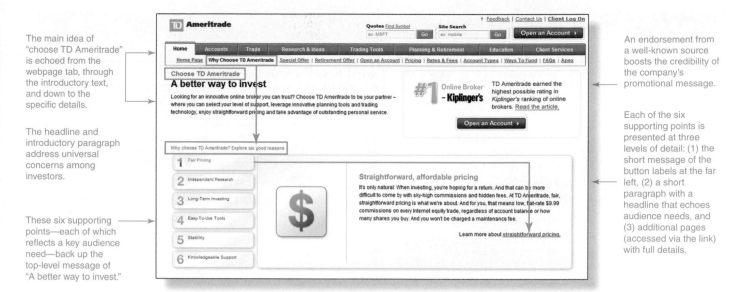

The main idea of "choose TD Ameritrade" is echoed from the webpage tab, through the introductory text, and down to the specific details.

The headline and introductory paragraph address universal concerns among investors.

These six supporting points—each of which reflects a key audience need—back up the top-level message of "A better way to invest."

An endorsement from a well-known source boosts the credibility of the company's promotional message.

Each of the six supporting points is presented at three levels of detail: (1) the short message of the button labels at the far left, (2) a short paragraph with a headline that echoes audience needs, and (3) additional pages (accessed via the link) with full details.

Figure 10.1 **Appealing to Audience Needs**
On this expertly written and designed webpage, TD Ameritrade echoes back the concerns that individual investors are likely to have when selecting a stockbroker. Notice how well the writing moves the reader from the high-level message to six individual supporting points—each of which is a major audience need—and then on to more detailed information. The clean, focused design is equally effective and works in close harmony with the text. The layout guides the reader's eye from the upper left corner, downward to the six key support points, and then across to the right for additional layers of detail.

to be. For example, if you try to persuade consumers to purchase a product on the basis of its fashion appeal, that message will connect with consumers who are motivated by a desire to be in style but probably won't connect with consumers driven by functional or financial concerns.

> Psychographics include characteristics such as personality, attitudes, and lifestyle.

Gathering Information

Once your situation analysis is complete, you need to gather the information necessary to create a compelling persuasive message. You'll learn more about the types of information to include in persuasive business messages and marketing and sales messages later in this chapter. Chapter 11 presents advice on how to find the information you need.

Selecting the Right Medium

Persuasive messages can be found in virtually every communication medium, from instant messages and podcasts to radio advertisements and skywriting. In fact, advertising agencies employ media specialists whose only jobs are to analyze the media options available and select the most cost-effective combination for each client and each advertising campaign (see Figure 10.2 on page 285).

In some situations, various members of your audience might prefer different media for the same message. Some consumers like to do all their car shopping in person, whereas others do most of their car-shopping research online. Some people don't mind promotional emails for products they're interested in; others resent every piece of commercial email they receive. If you can't be sure you can reach most or all of your audience through a single medium, you need to use two or more, such as following up an email campaign with printed letters.

Social media (see Chapter 7) provide some exciting options for persuasive messages, particularly marketing and sales messages. However, as "Writing Promotional Messages for Social Media" on page 298 explains, messages in these media require a unique approach.

Another important area of development is combining personal attention with technological reach and efficiency. For example, a customer support agent can carry on multiple instant messaging conversations at once, responding to one customer while other customers

You may need to use multiple media to reach your entire audience.

TABLE 10.1	Human Needs That Influence Motivation
Need	**Implications for Communication**
Basic physiological requirements: The needs for food, water, sleep, oxygen, etc.	Everyone has these needs, but the degree of attention an individual gives to them often depends on whether the needs are being met; for instance, an advertisement for sleeping pills will have greater appeal to someone suffering from insomnia than to someone who has no problem sleeping.
Safety and security: The needs for protection from bodily harm, to know that loved ones are safe, and for financial security, protection of personal identity, career security, and other assurances	These needs influence both consumer and business decisions in a wide variety of ways; for instance, advertisements for life insurance often encourage parents to think about the financial security of their children and other loved ones.
Affiliation and belonging: The needs for companionship, acceptance, love, and popularity	The need to feel loved, accepted, or popular drives a great deal of human behavior, from the desire to be attractive to potential mates to wearing the clothing style that a particular social group is likely to approve.
Power and control: The need to feel in control of situations or to exert authority over others	You can see many examples appealing to this need in advertisements: *Take control of your life*, *your finances*, *your future*, *your career*, and so on. Many people who lack power want to know how to get it, and people who have power often want others to know they have it.
Achievement: The need to feel a sense of accomplishment— or to be admired by others for accomplishments	This need can involve both *knowing* (when people experience a feeling of accomplishment) and *showing* (when people are able to show others that they've achieved success); advertising for luxury consumer products frequently appeals to this need.
Adventure and distraction: The need for excitement or relief from daily routine	People vary widely in their need for adventure; some crave excitement—even danger—while others value calmness and predictability. Some needs for adventure and distraction are met *virtually*, such as through horror movies, thriller novels, and violent video games.
Knowledge, exploration, and understanding: The need to keep learning	For some people, learning is usually a means to an end, a way to fulfill some other need; for others, acquiring new knowledge is the goal.
Aesthetic appreciation: The desire to experience beauty, order, and symmetry	Although this need may seem "noncommercial" at first glance, advertisers appeal to it frequently, from the pleasing shape of a package to the quality of the gemstones in a piece of jewelry.
Self-actualization: The need to "be all that one can be," to reach one's full potential as a human being	Psychologists Kurt Goldstein and Abraham Maslow popularized self-actualization as the desire to make the most of one's potential, and Maslow identified it as one of the higher-level needs in his classic hierarchy; even if people met most or all of their other needs, they would still feel the need to self-actualize. An often-quoted example of appealing to this need is the U.S. Army's one-time advertising slogan "Be all you can be."
Helping others: The need to believe that one is making a difference in the lives of other people	This need is the central motivation in fundraising messages and other appeals to charity.

are typing messages. Even perceptions of human interaction created by animated *avatars* such as IKEA's "Anna" (www.ikea.com) can create a more sociable experience for shoppers, which can make websites more effective as a persuasive medium.[4]

Organizing Your Information

The most effective main ideas for persuasive messages have one thing in common: They are about the receiver, not the sender. For instance, if you're trying to convince others to join you in a business venture, explain how it will help them, not how it will help you.

Limit your scope to include only the information needed to help your audience take the next step toward making a favorable decision.

Limiting your scope is vital. If you seem to be wrestling with more than one main idea, you haven't zeroed in on the heart of the matter. If you try to craft a persuasive message without focusing on the one central problem or opportunity your audience truly cares about, chances are you won't be able to persuade successfully.[5]

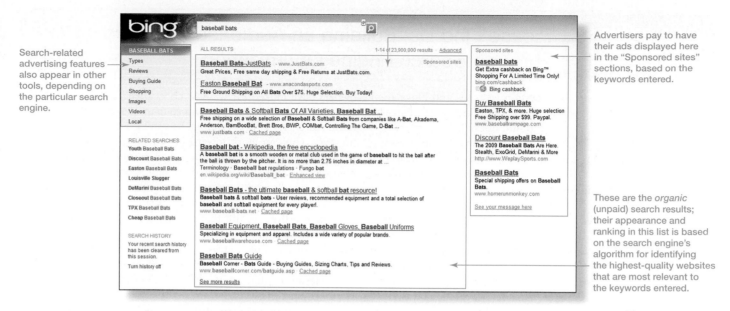

Search-related advertising features also appear in other tools, depending on the particular search engine.

Advertisers pay to have their ads displayed here in the "Sponsored sites" sections, based on the keywords entered.

These are the *organic* (unpaid) search results; their appearance and ranking in this list is based on the search engine's algorithm for identifying the highest-quality websites that are most relevant to the keywords entered.

Figure 10.2 Media Choices: Search Engine Marketing
Search engines now play a central role in online promotion, both as search tools and as an advertising medium themselves. See "Please Find Us: Building an Audience Through Search Engine Optimization" on page 286 for more information.

Because the nature of persuasion is to convince people to change their attitudes, beliefs, or actions, most persuasive messages use the indirect approach. That means you'll want to explain your reasons and build interest before asking for a decision or for action—or perhaps even before revealing your purpose. In contrast, when you have a close relationship with your audience and the message is welcome or at least neutral, the direct approach can be effective.

> Use the direct approach if your audience is ready to hear your proposal.

For persuasive business messages, the choice between the direct and indirect approaches is also influenced by the extent of your authority, expertise, or power in an organization. For instance, if you are a highly regarded technical expert with years of experience, you might use the direct approach in a message to top executives. In contrast, if you aren't well known and therefore need to rely more on the strength of your message than the power of your reputation, the indirect approach will probably be more successful.

> For persuasive business messages, the choice of approach is influenced by your position (or authority within the organization) relative to your audience's.

STEP 2: WRITING A PERSUASIVE MESSAGE

Encourage a positive response to your persuasive messages by (1) using positive and polite language, (2) understanding and respecting cultural differences, (3) being sensitive to organizational cultures, and (4) taking steps to establish your credibility.

> Persuasive messages are often unexpected or even unwelcome, so the "you" attitude is crucial.

Positive language usually happens naturally with persuasive messages because you're promoting an idea or a product you believe in. However, take care not to inadvertently insult your readers by implying that they've made poor choices in the past.

Be sure to understand cultural expectations as well. For example, a message that seems forthright and direct in a low-context culture might seem brash and intrusive in a high-context culture.

> Make sure your persuasive messages consider the culture of your audience.

Just as social culture affects the success of a persuasive message, so too does the culture within various organizations. Some organizations handle disagreement and conflict in an indirect, behind-the-scenes way, whereas others accept and even encourage open discussion and sharing of differing viewpoints.

BUSINESS COMMUNICATION 2.0

Please Find Us: Building an Audience Through Search Engine Optimization

Have you ever wondered why certain websites and blogs appear at the top of the list when you use an online search engine? Or why a site you might expect to find doesn't show up at all? Such questions are at the heart of one of the most important activities in online communication: *search engine optimization* (SEO). (SEO applies to the *natural* or *organic* search results, not the sponsored, paid results you see above, beside, or below the main search results listing.)

SEO involves three major parties: web users, website owners, and search engine developers such as Google, Yahoo!, and Microsoft. Most web users rely heavily on search engines to find relevant websites for shopping, research, and other online tasks. Website owners rely heavily on search engines to steer potential customers and other valuable visitors their way. To bring these two parties together while building lots of web traffic and advertising opportunities for themselves, search engine developers constantly fine-tune their engines to produce relevant, helpful search results.

And that's where things get interesting. Using sophisticated—and secret—algorithms, search engines rank search results by relevance to the user's inputs terms, starting with the most relevant results at the top of the list. Web users typically choose sites that show up in the first few pages of search results, so site owners naturally want to be ranked as high as possible.

Given the secrecy and the high stakes, the online search business has become something of a cat-and-mouse game in which website owners try to figure out what they can do to improve their rankings, while search engine developers work to improve the quality of results—partly by blocking website owners' attempts to "game" the system. For instance, in the early days of online search, some website owners would embed dozens of popular search terms in their websites, even if those terms had nothing to do with their site content. Search engine developers responded with ways to detect such tactics and penalize sites that use them by either lowering the sites' rankings in the search results or leaving them out entirely.

SEO has become a complex topic as search engines and the web itself have continued to evolve and as motivated website owners have looked for ways to boost their rankings. For instance, Google now evaluates more than 100 factors to determine search rankings. Without becoming an expert in SEO, however, you can work toward improving rankings for your website by focusing on these important areas. First, offer fresh, high-quality, audience-oriented content. Content that doesn't appeal to people won't appeal to search engines, either. Second, use relevant keywords judiciously, particularly in important areas such as the page title that displays at the top of the browser screen. Third, don't try to trick search engines with keyword stuffing, sneaky link redirects, or any other shady schemes. Fourth, encourage links to your site from other high-quality sites with relevant content. According to SEO experts who analyze search results, these links from other sites are crucial because they tell the search engines that other people find your content interesting and useful. Not surprisingly, given the importance of links from other sites, the content sharing encouraged by social media has had a huge impact on SEO in recent years.

You can learn more from Google's Webmaster Guidelines at **www.google.com/support/webmasters** and from Copyblogger at **www.copyblogger.com/seo-copywriting**.

CAREER APPLICATIONS

1. Locate a website for any company that sells products to consumers and write a new title for the site's homepage (the title that appears at the top of a web browser). Make the title short enough to read quickly while still summarizing what the company offers. Be sure to use one or more keywords that online shoppers would likely use when searching for the types of products the company sells.

2. Identify three high-quality websites that would be good ones to link to the site you chose in Question 1. For instance, if you chose a website that sells automotive parts and supplies, one of the three linking sites could be a popular blog that deals with automotive repair. Or if the site you chose sells golf equipment, you might find a sports website that covers the professional golf tours or one that provides information about golf courses around the world.

Finally, when you are trying to persuade a skeptical or hostile audience, credibility is essential. You must convince people that you know what you're talking about and that you're not trying to mislead them. Use these techniques:

Audiences often respond unfavorably to over-the-top language, so keep your writing simple and straightforward.

- Use simple language to avoid suspicions of fantastic claims and emotional manipulation.
- Provide objective evidence for the claims and promises you make.
- Identify your sources, especially if your audience already respects those sources.
- Establish common ground by emphasizing beliefs, attitudes, and background experiences you have in common with the audience.
- Be objective and present fair and logical arguments.
- Display your willingness to keep your audience's best interests at heart.

<table>
<tr><td>

ETHICS DETECTIVE

</td><td>

Solving the Case of the Incredible Credibility

</td></tr>
</table>

As the director of human resources in your company, you're desperate for some help. You want to keep the costs of employee benefits under control while making sure you provide employees with a fair benefits package. However, you don't have time to research all the options for health insurance, wellness programs, retirement plans, family counseling, educational benefits, and everything else, so you decide to hire a consultant. You receive the following message from a consultant interested in working with you:

> I am considered the country's foremost authority on employee health insurance programs. My clients offer universally positive feedback on the programs I've designed for them. They also love how much time I save them—hundreds and hundreds of hours. I am

absolutely confident that I can thoroughly analyze your needs and create a portfolio that realizes every degree of savings possible. I invite you to experience the same level of service that has generated such comments as "Best advice ever!" and "Saved us an unbelievable amount of money."

You'd love to get results like that, but the message almost sounds too good to be true. Is it?

ANALYSIS

The consultant's message contains at least a dozen instances in which this writer's credibility might be questioned. Identify as many as you can, and explain how you would bolster reader confidence by providing additional or different information.

- Persuade with logic, evidence, and compelling narratives, rather than trying to coerce with high-pressure, "hard sell" tactics.
- Whenever possible, try to build your credibility before you present a major proposal or ask for a major decision. That way, audiences don't have to evaluate both you and your message at the same time.[6]

Audiences resist the high-pressure tactics of the "hard sell" and tend to distrust communicators who take this approach.

STEP 3: COMPLETING A PERSUASIVE MESSAGE

The pros know from experience that details can make or break a persuasive message, so they're careful not to skimp on this part of the writing process. For instance, advertisers may have a dozen or more people review a message before it's released to the public.

When you evaluate your content, try to judge your argument objectively and try not to overestimate your credibility. If possible, ask an experienced colleague who knows your audience well to review your draft. Make sure your design elements complement, rather than detract from, your persuasive argument. In addition, meticulous proofreading will help you identify any mechanical or spelling errors that would weaken your persuasive potential. Finally, make sure your distribution methods fit your audience's expectations and preferences.

With the three-step model in mind, you're ready to begin composing persuasive messages, starting with *persuasive business messages* (those that try to convince audiences to approve new projects, enter into business partnerships, and so on), followed by *marketing and sales messages* (those that try to convince audiences to consider and then purchase products and services).

Developing Persuasive Business Messages

Persuasive business messages comprise a broad and diverse category, with audiences that range from a single person in your own department to government agencies, investors, business partners, community leaders, and other external groups. Your success as a businessperson is closely tied to your ability to convince others to accept new ideas, change old habits, or act on your recommendations. As you move into positions of greater responsibility in your career, your persuasive messages could start to influence multimillion-dollar investments and the careers of hundreds or thousands of employees. Obviously, you need to match the increase in your persuasive skills with the care and thoroughness of your analysis and planning so that the ideas you convince others to adopt are sound.

2   LEARNING OBJECTIVE

Describe an effective strategy for developing persuasive business messages, and identify the three most common categories of persuasive business messages.

No matter where your career leads, your success will depend on your ability to craft effective persuasive messages.

STRATEGIES FOR PERSUASIVE BUSINESS MESSAGES

Even if you have the power to compel others to do what you want them to do, persuading them is more effective than forcing them. People who are forced into accepting a decision or plan are less motivated to support it and more likely to react negatively than if they're persuaded.[7] Within the context of the three-step process, effective persuasion involves four essential strategies: framing your arguments, balancing emotional and logical appeals, reinforcing your position, and anticipating objections. (Note that all these concepts in this section apply as well to marketing and sales messages, covered later in the chapter.)

Framing Your Arguments

Using the AIDA model is an effective way to organize most persuasive messages:
- Attention
- Interest
- Desire
- Action

As noted earlier, most persuasive messages use the indirect approach. Experts in persuasive communication have developed a number of indirect models for such messages. One of the best known is the **AIDA model**, which organizes messages into four phases:

- **Attention.** Your first objective is to engage your readers or listeners in a way that encourages them to want to hear about your main idea. Write a brief and compelling sentence, without making extravagant claims or irrelevant points. Look for some common ground on which to build your case (see Figure 10.3). And while you want to be positive and confident, make sure you don't start out with a *hard sell*—a pushy, aggressive opening. Doing so often puts audiences on guard and on the defensive.
- **Interest.** Emphasize the relevance of your message to your audience. Continuing the theme you started with, paint a more detailed picture of the problem you propose to solve with the solution you're offering (whether it's a new idea, a new process, a new product, or whatever).
- **Desire.** Help audience members embrace your idea by explaining how the change will benefit them, either personally or professionally. Reduce resistance by identifying and answering in advance any questions the audience might have. If your idea is complex, you might need to explain how you would implement it. Back up your claims in order to increase audience willingness to take the action you suggest in the next section.
- **Action.** Suggest the action you want readers to take and phrase it in a way that emphasizes the benefits to them or to the organization they represent. Make the action as easy as possible to take, including offering to assist, if appropriate. Be sure to provide all the information the audience needs to take the action, including deadlines and contact details.

The AIDA model and similar plans are ideal for the indirect approach.

The AIDA model is tailor-made for using the indirect approach, allowing you to save your main idea for the action phase. However, you can also use AIDA for the direct approach, in which case you use your main idea as an attention-getter, build interest with your argument, create desire with your evidence, and re-emphasize your main idea in the action phase with the specific action you want your audience to take.

When your AIDA message uses the indirect approach and is delivered by memo or email, keep in mind that your subject line usually catches your reader's eye first. Your challenge is to make it interesting and relevant enough to capture reader attention without revealing your main idea. If you put your request in the subject line, you might just get a quick no before you've had a chance to present your arguments:

Instead of This	Write This
Request for development budget to add automated IM response system	Reducing the cost of customer support inquiries

The AIDA approach has limitations:
- It essentially talks *at* audiences, not *with* them
- It focuses on one-time events not long-term relationships

With either the direct or indirect approach, AIDA and similar models do have limitations. First, AIDA is a unidirectional method that essentially talks *at* audiences, not *with* them. Second, AIDA is built around a single event, such as asking an audience for a decision, rather than on building a mutually beneficial, long-term relationship.[8] AIDA is still a valuable tool for the right purposes, but as you'll read later in the chapter, a conversational approach is more compatible with today's social media.

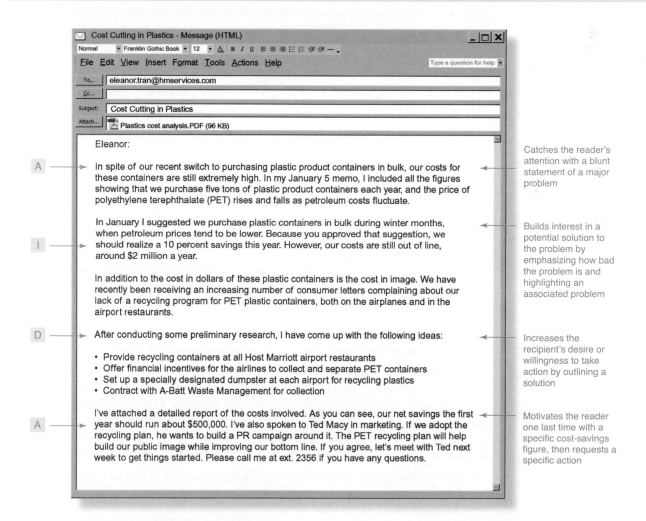

Analyze the Situation
Verify that the purpose is to solve an ongoing problem, so the audience will be receptive.

Gather Information
Determine audience needs and obtain the necessary information on recycling problem areas.

Select the Right Medium
Verify that an email message is appropriate for this communication.

Organize the Information
Limit the scope to the main idea, which is to propose a recycling solution; use the indirect approach to lay out the extent of the problem.

Adapt to Your Audience
Adjust the level of formality based on the degree of familiarity with the audience; maintain a positive relationship by using the "you" attitude, politeness, positive emphasis, and bias-free language.

Compose the Message
Use a conversational but professional style and keep the message brief, clear, and as helpful as possible.

Revise the Message
Evaluate content and review readability to make sure the information is clear and complete without being overwhelming.

Produce the Message
Emphasize a clean, professional appearance.

Proofread the Message
Review for errors in layout, spelling, and mechanics.

Distribute the Message
Verify that the right file is attached and then deliver the message.

Figure 10.3 Persuasive Message Using the AIDA Model
Randy Thumwolt uses the AIDA model in a message about a program that would reduce Host Marriott's annual plastics costs and address consumer complaints about the company's recycling record. Note how Thumwolt "sells the problem" before attempting to sell the solution. Few people are interested in hearing about solutions to problems they don't know about or don't believe exist.

MyBcommLab

Apply Figure 10.3's key concepts by revising a new document. Go to Chapter 10 in mybcommlab.com and select Document Makeovers.

289

REAL-TIME UPDATES
Learn More by Watching This
PowerPoint Presentation

Choose the most effective emotional appeal

Understand the different types of emotional appeals and select the most effective appeal for any marketing or sales message. Go to http://real-timeupdates.com/bct11 and click on "Learn More." If you are using MyBcommLab, you can access Real-Time Updates within each chapter or under Student Study Tools.

Balancing Emotional and Logical Appeals

Imagine you're sitting at a control panel with one knob labeled "logic" and another labeled "emotion." As you prepare your persuasive message, you carefully adjust each knob, tuning the message for maximum impact. Too little emotion, and your audience might not care enough to respond. Too much emotion, and your audience might think you are ignoring tough business questions or even being irrational.

Generally speaking, persuasive business messages rely more heavily on logical appeals than on emotional appeals because the main idea is usually to save money, increase quality, or improve some other practical, measurable aspect of business. To find the optimum balance, consider four factors: (1) the actions you hope to motivate, (2) your readers' expectations, (3) the degree of resistance you need to overcome, and (4) how far you feel empowered to go in order to sell your point of view.[9]

> Emotional appeals attempt to connect with the reader's feelings or sympathies.

Emotional Appeals   As its name implies, an **emotional appeal** calls on audience feelings and sympathies rather than facts, figures, and rational arguments. For instance, you can make use of the emotion surrounding certain words. The word *freedom* evokes strong feelings, as do words such as *success, prestige, compassion, security,* and *comfort.* Such words can help put your audience members in a positive frame of mind and help them accept your message. However, emotional appeals in business messages usually aren't effective by themselves because the audience wants proof that you can solve a business problem. Even if your audience members reach a conclusion based primarily on emotions, they'll look to you to provide logical support as well.

> Logical appeals are based on the reader's notions of reason; these appeals can use analogy, induction, or deduction.

Logical Appeals   A **logical appeal** calls on reasoning and evidence. The basic approach with a logical appeal is to make a claim based on a rational argument, supported by solid evidence. When appealing to your audience's logic, you might use three types of reasoning:

- **Analogy.** With analogy, you reason from specific evidence to specific evidence. For instance, to convince management to buy a more robust firewall to protect your company's computer network, you might use the analogy of "circling the wagons," as when covered wagons crossing the continent gathered in a circle every night to form a safe space within.
- **Induction.** With inductive reasoning, you work from specific evidence to a general conclusion. To convince your team to change to a new manufacturing process, for example, you could point out that every company that has adopted it has increased profits, so it must be a smart idea.
- **Deduction.** With deductive reasoning, you work from a generalization to a specific conclusion. To persuade your boss to hire additional customer support staff, you might point to industry surveys that show how crucial customer satisfaction is to corporate profits.

> Logical flaws include hasty generalizations, circular reasoning, attacks on opponents, oversimplifications, false assumptions of cause and effect, faulty analogies, and illogical support.

Every method of reasoning is vulnerable to misuse, both intentional and unintentional, so verify your rational arguments carefully. For example, in the case of the manufacturing process, are there any other factors that affect the integrity of your reasoning? What if that process works well only for small companies with few products, and your firm is a multinational behemoth with 10,000 products? To guard against faulty logic, follow these guidelines:[10]

- **Avoid hasty generalizations.** Make sure you have plenty of evidence before drawing conclusions.
- **Avoid circular reasoning.** *Circular reasoning* is a logical fallacy in which you try to support your claim by restating it in different words. The statement "We know temporary workers cannot handle this task because temps are unqualified for it" doesn't prove anything because the claim and the supporting evidence are essentially identical. It doesn't prove *why* the temps are unqualified.
- **Avoid attacking an opponent.** If your persuasive appeal involves countering a competitive appeal made by someone else, make sure you attack the argument your opponent is making, not his or her character or qualifications.

- **Avoid oversimplifying a complex issue.** Make sure you present all the factors and don't reduce a wide range of choices to a simple "either/or" scenario if that isn't the case.
- **Avoid mistaken assumptions of cause and effect.** If you can't isolate the impact of a specific factor, you can't assume it's the cause of whatever effect you're discussing. The weather improves in spring, and people start playing baseball in spring. Does good weather cause baseball? No. There is a *correlation* between the two—meaning the data associated with them tend to rise and fall at the same time, but there is no *causation*—no proof that one causes the other. The complexity of many business situations makes cause and effect a particular challenge. You lowered prices, and sales went up. Were lower prices the cause of the increased sales? Perhaps, but the increase in sales might have been caused by a better advertising campaign, a competitor's delivery problems, or some other factor.
- **Avoid faulty analogies.** Be sure that the two objects or situations being compared are similar enough for the analogy to hold. For instance, the analogy between circling the wagons and using a network firewall isn't entirely valid because circling the wagons is a temporary move, and computer networks need permanent protection.
- **Avoid illogical support.** Make sure the connection between your claim and your support is truly logical and not based on a leap of faith, a missing premise, or irrelevant evidence.

Reinforcing Your Position

After you've worked out the basic elements of your argument, step back and look for ways to bolster the strength of your position. Are all your claims supported by believable evidence? Would a quotation from a recognized expert help make your case?

Next, examine your language. Can you find more powerful words to convey your message? For example, if your company is in serious financial trouble, talking about *fighting for survival* is a more powerful emotional appeal than talking about *ensuring continued operations*. As with any other powerful tool, though, use vivid language and abstractions carefully and honestly.

Choose your words carefully and use abstractions to enhance emotional content.

In addition to examining individual word choices, consider using metaphors and other figures of speech. If you want to describe a quality-control system as being designed to detect every possible product flaw, you might call it a "spider web" to imply that it catches everything that comes its way. Similarly, anecdotes (brief stories) can help your audience grasp the meaning and importance of your arguments. Instead of just listing the number of times the old laptop computers in your department have failed, you could describe how you lost a sale when your computer broke down during a critical sales presentation.

Beyond specific words and phrases, look for other factors that can reinforce your position. When you're asking for something, your audience members will find it easier to grant your request if they stand to benefit from it as well.

Anticipating Objections

Even the most compelling ideas and proposals can be expected to encounter some initial resistance. The best way to deal with audience resistance is to anticipate as many objections as you can and address them in your message before your audience can even bring them up. For instance, if you know that your proposal to switch to lower-cost materials will raise concerns about product quality, address this issue head-on in your message. If you wait until people raise the concern after reading your message, they may gravitate toward another firm before you have a chance to address their concerns. By bringing up such potential problems right away, you also demonstrate a broad appreciation of the issue and imply confidence in your message.[11] This anticipation is particularly important in written messages, when you don't have the opportunity to detect and respond to objections on the spot.

Even powerful persuasive messages can encounter resistance from the audience.

To uncover potential audience objections, try to poke holes in your own theories and ideas before your audience does. Then find solutions to the problems you've uncovered. If possible, ask your audience members for their thoughts on the subject before you put together your argument; people are more likely to support solutions they help create.

Keep three things in mind when anticipating objections. First, you don't always have to explicitly discuss a potential objection. You could simply mention that the lower-cost materials have been tested and approved by the quality-control department. Second, if you expect a hostile audience, one biased against your plan from the beginning, present all sides of the story. As you cover each option, explain the pros and cons. You'll gain additional credibility if you present these options before presenting your recommendation or decision.[12] Third, successful persuasion is often a process of give-and-take, particularly in the case of persuasive business messages, where you don't always get everything you asked for in terms of budgets, investments, and other commitments. Be open to compromise.

To review the steps involved in developing persuasive messages, refer to "Checklist: Developing Persuasive Messages."

> Present all sides of an issue when you expect to encounter strong resistance.

COMMON EXAMPLES OF PERSUASIVE BUSINESS MESSAGES

Throughout your career, you'll have numerous opportunities to write persuasive messages within your organization, such as reports suggesting more efficient operating procedures or memos requesting money for new equipment. Similarly, you may produce a variety of persuasive messages for people outside the organization, such as websites shaping public opinions or letters requesting adjustments that go beyond a supplier's contractual obligations. In addition, some of the routine requests you studied in Chapter 8 can become persuasive messages if you want a nonroutine result or believe that you haven't received fair treatment. Most of these messages can be divided into persuasive requests for action, persuasive presentations of ideas, and persuasive claims and requests for adjustment.

Persuasive Requests for Action

> Most persuasive business messages involve a request for action.

The bulk of your persuasive business messages will involve requests for action. In some cases, your request will be anticipated or will require minimal effort on the recipient's part, so the direct approach is fine. In others, you'll need to introduce your intention indirectly. Open with an attention-getting device and show readers that you know something about their concerns, such as maintaining customer satisfaction. Use the interest and desire sections of

---

✓ Checklist Developing Persuasive Messages

A. Get your reader's attention.
- Open with an audience benefit, a stimulating question, a problem, or an unexpected statement.
- Establish common ground by mentioning a point on which you and your audience agree.
- Show that you understand the audience's concerns.

B. Build your reader's interest.
- Expand and support your opening claim or promise.
- Emphasize the relevance of your message to your audience.

C. Increase your reader's desire.
- Make audience members want to change by explaining how the change will benefit them.
- Back up your claims with relevant evidence.

D. Motivate your reader to take action.
- Suggest the action you want readers to take.
- Stress the positive results of the action.
- Make the desired action clear and easy.

E. Balance emotional and logical appeals.
- Use emotional appeals to help the audience accept your message.
- Use logical appeals when presenting facts and evidence for complex ideas or recommendations.
- Avoid faulty logic.

F. Reinforce your position.
- Provide additional evidence of the benefits of your proposal and your own credibility in offering it.
- Use abstractions, metaphors, and other figures of speech to bring facts and figures to life.

G. Anticipate objections.
- Anticipate and answer potential objections.
- Present the pros and cons of all options if you anticipate a hostile reaction.

your message to demonstrate that you have good reasons for making such a request and to cover what you know about the situation: the facts and figures, the benefits of helping, and any history or experience that will enhance your appeal. Your goals are (1) to gain credibility and (2) to make your readers believe that helping you will indeed help solve a significant problem. When you've demonstrated that your message is relevant to your readers, you can close with a request for some specific action or decision.

Persuasive Presentations of Ideas

You may encounter situations in which you simply want to change attitudes or beliefs about a particular topic, without asking the audience to decide or do anything—at least not yet. The goal of your first message might be nothing more than convincing your audience to reexamine long-held opinions or admit the possibility of new ways of thinking.

For instance, the World Wide Web Consortium (a global association that defines many of the guidelines and technologies behind the World Wide Web) has launched a campaign called the Web Accessibility Initiative. Although the consortium's ultimate goal is making websites more accessible to people who have disabilities or age-related limitations, a key interim goal is simply making website developers more aware of the need. As part of this effort, the consortium has developed a variety of presentations and documents that highlight the problems many web visitors face.[13]

The ability to persuade others to accept and support your ideas is an essential career skill.

Persuasive Claims and Requests for Adjustments

Most claims and requests for adjustment are routine messages and use the direct approach discussed in Chapter 8. However, consumers and professionals sometimes encounter situations in which they believe they haven't received a fair deal by following normal procedures. These situations require a more persuasive message.

The key ingredients of a good persuasive claim are a complete and specific review of the facts and a confident and positive tone. Keep in mind that you have the right to be satisfied with every transaction. Begin persuasive claims by outlining the problem and continue by reviewing what has been done about it so far, if anything. The recipient might be juggling numerous claims and other demands on his or her attention, so be clear, calm, and complete when presenting your case. Be specific about how you would like to see the situation resolved.

Next, give your reader a good reason for granting your claim. Show how the individual or organization is responsible for the problem and appeal to your reader's sense of fair play, goodwill, or moral responsibility. Explain how you feel about the problem but don't get carried away, don't complain too much, and don't make threats. People generally respond most favorably to requests that are both calm and reasonable. Close on a positive note that reflects how a successful resolution of the situation will repair or maintain a mutually beneficial working relationship.

Sometimes the objective of persuasive messages is simply to encourage people to consider a new idea.

If a routine claim or request did not meet your needs, you may need to craft a more persuasive message to explain why you deserve a more satisfactory response.

Developing Marketing and Sales Messages

Marketing and sales messages use the same basic techniques as other persuasive messages, with the added emphasis of encouraging someone to participate in a commercial transaction. Although the terms *marketing message* and *sales message* are often used interchangeably, they are slightly different: **Marketing messages** usher potential buyers through the purchasing process without asking them to make an immediate decision (see Figure 10.4 on the next page). **Sales messages** take over at that point, encouraging potential buyers to make a purchase decision then and there. Marketing messages focus on such tasks as introducing new brands to the public, providing competitive comparisons, encouraging customers to visit

3   LEARNING OBJECTIVE

Describe an effective strategy for developing marketing and sales messages.

Marketing and sales messages use many of the same techniques as persuasive business messages.

Offers handy links to earlier and later blog posts

Promotes a sale on wedding gowns but does so in a subtle way that doesn't hinder a reader's appreciation of the information offered in the article

Provides links to additional information about wedding dress designers, content that many readers will find helpful as well

Provides links to product selections (organized by designer name)

Figure 10.4   Marketing Versus Sales Messages
This article on the Bridepower blog functions as a marketing message, rather than a sales message. It provides information that is potentially useful for many brides and indirectly promotes products offered elsewhere on the website, but it doesn't encourage shoppers to make a decision right away.

MyBcommLab

Apply Figure 10.4's key concepts by revising a new document. Go to Chapter 10 in mybcommlab.com and select Document Makeovers.

websites for more information, and reminding buyers that a particular product or service is available. In contrast, a sales message makes a specific request for people to place an order for a particular product or service. (The text of marketing and sales messages is usually referred to as "copy," by the way.)

Most marketing and sales messages, particularly in larger companies, are created and delivered by professionals with specific training in marketing, advertising, sales, or public relations. However, as a manager, you may be called on to review the work of these specialists or even to write such messages in smaller companies, and having a good understanding of how these messages work will help you be a more effective manager. The essential steps to address include assessing customer needs; analyzing your competition; determining key selling points and benefits; anticipating purchase objections; applying the AIDA model or a similar organizational plan; adapting your writing to social media, as needed; and maintaining high standards of ethics, legal compliance, and etiquette.

ASSESSING AUDIENCE NEEDS

Understanding the purchase decision from the buyer's perspective is a vital step in framing an effective marketing or sales message.

Successful marketing and sales messages start with an understanding of audience needs. For some products and services, this assessment is a fairly simple matter. For instance, customers compare only a few basic attributes when purchasing paper, including its size, weight, brightness, color, and finish. In contrast, they might consider dozens of features when shopping for real estate, cars, professional services, and other complex purchases. In addition, customer needs often extend beyond the basic product or service. For example, clothes do far more than simply keep you warm. What you wear can also make a statement about who you are, which social groups you want to be associated with (or not), and how you view your relationships with the people around you.

Begin by assessing audience needs, interests, and emotional concerns—just as you would for any other business message. Try to form a mental image of the typical buyer for the product you want to sell. Ask yourself what your audience members might want to know about this product. How can your product help them? Are they driven by price, or is quality more important to them?

ANALYZING YOUR COMPETITION

Marketing and sales messages nearly always compete with messages from other companies trying to reach the same audience. When Nike plans a marketing campaign to introduce a new shoe model to current customers, the company knows that its audience has also been exposed to messages from New Balance, Reebok, and numerous other shoe companies. In crowded markets, writers sometimes have to search for words and phrases that other companies aren't already using. They might also want to avoid themes, writing styles, or creative approaches that are too similar to those of competitors' messages.

Most marketing and sales messages have to compete for the audience's attention.

DETERMINING KEY SELLING POINTS AND BENEFITS

With some insight into audience needs and existing messages from the competition, you're ready to decide which aspects of your product or service to highlight. For all but the simplest products and services, you want to prioritize the items you plan to discuss. You also want to distinguish between the features of the product or service and the benefits that those features offer the customers. As Table 10.2 shows, **selling points** are the most attractive features of a product or service, whereas **benefits** are the particular advantages that readers will realize from those features. Put another way, selling points focus on the product or service, whereas benefits focus on the user.

Selling points focus on the product; benefits focus on the user.

For example, CafeMom doesn't stress the online networking feature of its services; rather, it stresses the opportunity to connect with other moms who have similar concerns and interests—which is the benefit enabled by the networking feature. A common approach to communicating features and benefits is to show them in a list or a table, identifying each feature and describing the benefits it offers.

ANTICIPATING PURCHASE OBJECTIONS

As with persuasive business messages, marketing and sales messages often encounter objections; once again, the best way to handle them is to identify them up front and try to address as many as you can. Objections can include perceptions of high price, low quality, incompatibility, or unacceptable risk. Consumers might worry that a car won't be safe enough for a family, that a jacket will make them look unattractive, or that a hair salon will botch a haircut. Business buyers might worry about disrupting operations or failing to realize the financial returns on a purchase.

Anticipating objections is crucial to effective marketing and sales messages.

TABLE 10.2	**Features Versus Benefits**
Product or Service Feature	**Customer Benefit**
Carrier's Hybrid Heat dual-fuel system combines our Infinity 19 fuel pump with our Infinity 96 furnace.[14]	Carrier's Hybrid Heat dual-fuel system provides the optimum balance of comfort and energy efficiency.
Our marketing communication audit accurately measures the impact of your advertising and public relations efforts.	Find out whether your message is reaching the target audience and whether you're spending your marketing budget in the best possible manner.
The spools in our fly-fishing reels are machined from solid blocks of aircraft-grade aluminum.	Go fishing with confidence: These lightweight reels will stand up to the toughest conditions.

Price can be a particularly tricky issue in any message. Whether you highlight or downplay the price of your product, prepare your readers for it. Words such as *luxurious* and *economical* provide clues about how your price compares with that of competitors. Such words help your readers accept your price when you finally state it.

If price is a major selling point, give it a position of prominence, such as in the headline or as the last item in a paragraph. If price is not a major selling point, you can handle it in several ways: You can leave the price out altogether or deemphasize it by putting the figure in the middle of a paragraph that comes well after you've presented the benefits and selling points. Here's an example:

Emphasizes the rarity of the edition to signal value and thus prepares the reader for the big-ticket price that follows

Embeds the price in the middle of a sentence and ties it in with a reminder of the exclusivity of the offer

> Only 100 prints of this exclusive, limited-edition lithograph will be created. On June 15, they will be made available to the general public, but you can reserve one now for only $350, the special advance reservation price. Simply rush the enclosed reservation card back today so that your order is in before the June 15 publication date.

Whenever price is likely to cause an objection, look for ways to increase the perceived value of the purchase and decrease the perceived cost. For example, to help blunt the impact of the price of a home gym, you might say that it costs less than a year's worth of health club dues—plus, customers save on transportation costs by exercising at home. Of course, any attempts to minimize perceptions of price or other potential negatives must be ethical.

APPLYING AIDA OR A SIMILAR MODEL

Most marketing and sales messages are prepared according to the AIDA model or some variation of it. (But compare this approach with how *conversation marketing* messages are prepared in "Writing Promotional Messages for Social Media" on page 298.) A typical AIDA-organized message begins with an attention-getting introduction, generates interest by describing some of the product's or service's unique features, increases desire by highlighting the benefits that are most appealing to the audience, and closes by suggesting the action the sender would like the audience members to take.

Getting Attention

You can use a wide range of techniques to attract your audience's attention:

You can use a variety of attention-getting devices in marketing and sales messages.

- **Your product's strongest feature or benefit.** "Game on. And on. And on" (promoting the game-playing aspects of Apple's iPod Touch).[15]
- **A piece of genuine news.** "HealthGrades Reveals America's Best Hospitals."[16]
- **A point of common ground with the audience.** "Tough on Dirt, Gentle on the Earth" (promoting the environmentally friendly aspects of Biokleen cleaning products).[17]
- **A personal appeal to the reader's emotions or values.** "Up to 35 mpg. Unlimited Fun" (promoting the fuel efficiency and sporty driving characteristics of the Ford Focus).[18]
- **The promise of insider information.** "France may seem familiar, but nearly everything—from paying taxes to having a baby—is done quite differently. Get the practical answers to nearly 300 questions about making a life in France."[19]
- **The promise of savings.** "Summer Clearance: Nearly 10,000 Books, Savings up to 90%."[20]
- **A sample or demonstration of the product.** "These videos can provide more detail on Mint's unique and award-winning approach to personal financial management."[21]
- **A solution to a problem.** "Fees to check a bag can add $50 to the cost of a round trip. So the FlightWise Carry-On Backpack is designed to fit in all carry-on storage spaces, even underseat, saving you money with every flight."[22]

Of course, words aren't the only attention-getting device at your disposal. Strong, evocative images are common attention-getters. With online messages, you have even more options, including audio, animation, and video. Even more so than in persuasive business messages, it's important to carefully balance emotion and logic in marketing and sales messages (see Figure 10.5).

Without using any images of people, the solitary teacup (left), the multiple glasses of ice tea (center), and the brunch setting suggested by the tea and food (right) convey both the pleasures of a quiet time alone as well as the pleasures of sharing tea with friends and family.

The red-orange color of the tea, enhanced with the glow of backlighting through the translucent liquid, speaks of warmth and comfort.

Complementary colors suggest freshness and elegance, adding to the emotional appeal.

The text uses the storytelling technique to explain the creation of Bigelow's signature Constant Comment tea flavor and does so in a way that highlights the emotional appeal of drinking tea.

Figure 10.5   Emotional and Logical Appeals
Bigelow Tea uses an effective combination of visual and textual messages in this emotional appeal.

Building Interest

Use the interest section of your message to build on the intrigue you created with your opening. This section should also offer support for any claims or promises you made in the opening. For instance, after opening with the headline, "Game on. And on. And on," the Apple iPod touch web presentation continues with the following:[23]

To build interest, expand on and support the promises in your attention-getting opening.

> **Get your game on with friends across the room or across the globe.**
>
> Games for iPod touch are made to take advantage of its built-in technologies such as the accelerometer, Multi-Touch, Wi-Fi, and Bluetooth wireless technology. The result is truly immersive gameplay—whether you're playing alone or with others in multiplayer mode. And with an App Store that offers thousands of games ready to download and play, the fun of iPod touch never ends.

This paragraph highlights key game-related features of the iPod touch and the key benefit ("truly immersive gameplay") that those features enable. The paragraph also addresses a potential objection that some readers might have, which is the number of games available for the device. At this point, anyone interested in portable gaming devices is probably intrigued enough to keep reading, and the website continues with deeper levels of information on each of the key features.

Increasing Desire

To build desire for a product, a service, or an idea, continue to expand on and explain how accepting it will benefit the recipient. Think carefully about the sequence of support points and use plenty of subheadings, hyperlinks, and other devices to help people quickly find the information they need. For example, after reading this much about the iPod touch, some

Add details and audience benefits to increase desire for the product or service.

users might want to know more about specific technical points such as the accelerometer, the speed and quality of the graphics, or software apps available. The iPod touch product page continues with detailed discussions of various product features and benefits, and it also offers numerous links to pages with other kinds of support information. The ability to provide flexible access to information is just one of the reasons the web is such a powerful medium for marketing and sales. As the TD Ameritrade webpage in Figure 10.1 shows, the ability to provide flexible access to information is just one of the reasons the web is such a powerful medium for marketing and sales.

Throughout the body of your message, remember to keep the focus on the audience, not on your company or your product. When you talk about product features, remember to stress the benefits and talk in terms that make sense to users. For instance, rather than going into a technical description of what an accelerometer is, the webpage offers several examples of what it does, such as how in racing games it turns the iPod into a virtual steering wheel.[24]

As you work to build reader interest, be careful not to get so enthusiastic that you lose credibility. If Apple said that the video viewing experience on the iPod touch was as "satisfying as watching a full-size TV," most people would scoff at the notion of comparing a 3.5-inch display with a full-size television.

To increase desire, as well as boost your credibility, provide support for your claims. Creative writers find many ways to provide support, including testimonials from satisfied users, articles written by industry experts, competitive comparisons, product samples and free demonstrations, independent test results, and movies or computer animations that show a product in action. YouTube and other video hosting sites in particular have been a boon to marketers because they offer an easy, inexpensive way to demonstrate products. You can also highlight guarantees that demonstrate your faith in your product and your willingness to back it up.

> *Avoid being so enthusiastic that you lose credibility.*

Motivating Action

> *After you've generated sufficient interest and desire, you're ready to persuade readers to take the preferred action.*

After you have raised interest and built up the reader's desire for your product or service, you're ready to ask your audience to take action. Whether you want people to pick up the phone to place an order or visit your website to download a free demo version of your software, try to persuade them to do it right away with an effective *call to action*. You might offer a discount to the first 1,000 people who order, put a deadline on the offer, or simply remind shoppers that the sooner they order, the sooner they'll be able to enjoy the product's benefits (see Figure 10.6). Even potential buyers who want the product can get distracted or forget to respond, so encouraging immediate action is important. Make the response action as simple and as risk-free as possible. If the process is confusing or time-consuming, you'll lose potential customers.

Writing Promotional Messages for Social Media

4 **LEARNING OBJECTIVE**

Explain how to modify your approach when writing promotional messages for social media.

> *Social commerce involves the use of social media in buying, selling, and customer support.*

> *Promoting products and services through social media requires a more conversational approach.*

The AIDA model and similar approaches have been successful with marketing and sales messages for decades, but communicating with customers in the social media landscape requires a different approach. As earlier chapters emphasize, potential buyers in a social media environment are no longer willing to be passive recipients in a structured, one-way information delivery process or to rely solely on promotional messages from marketers. This notion of interactive participation is the driving force behind **conversation marketing**, in which companies initiate and facilitate conversations in a networked community of customers, journalists, bloggers, and other interested parties. The term **social commerce** encompasses any aspect of buying and selling products and services or supporting customers through the use of social media.

Given this shift from unidirectional talks to multidirectional conversations, marketing and sales professionals must adapt their approach to planning, writing, and completing persuasive messages. Follow these guidelines:[25]

- **Facilitate community building.** Make sure customers and other audiences can connect with your company and each other. Accomplishing this goal can be as simple as activating the commenting feature on a blog, or it may involve having a more elaborate social commerce system.

Encourages trainers to become ACE-certified

Helps trainers find courses that will expand their knowledge and skills

Offers to help trainers build their businesses

Offers information about a major national conference on physical fitness

Encourages the general public to sign up for regular email updates

Figure 10.6   The Call to Action in a Persuasive Message
Notice how many calls to action are built into the homepage of the American Council on Exercise's website. ACE is a not-for-profit organization committed to encouraging physical fitness through safe and effective exercise. In pursuit of that goal, it offers certification and training for people who want to become personal trainers, and it helps consumers find certified trainers.

- **Listen at least as much as you talk.** Listening is just as essential for online conversations as it is for in-person conversations. Of course, trying to stay on top of a social media universe composed of millions of potential voices is no easy task. A variety of automated tools can help, from free alerts on search engines to sophisticated linguistic monitoring systems.
- **Initiate and respond to conversations within the community.** Through content on your website, blog postings, social network profiles and messages, newsletters, and other tools, make sure you provide the information customers need in order to evaluate your products and services. Use an objective, conversational style; people in social networks want useful information, not "advertising speak."
- **Provide information that people want.** Whether through industry-insider news, in-depth technical guides to using your products, video tutorials, or brief answers to questions posted on community Q&A sites, fill the information gaps about your company and its products (see Figure 10.4). This strategy of *content marketing* helps you build trusted relationships with potential buyers by repeatedly demonstrating that you understand and care about meeting their needs.[26]
- **Identify and support your champions.** In marketing, *champions* are enthusiastic fans of your company and its products. Champions are so enthusiastic that they help spread your message (through their blogs, for instance), defend you against detractors, and help other customers use your products. As Michael Zeisser of Liberty Interactive put it,

"We concluded that we could succeed only by being genuinely useful to the individuals who initiate or sustain virtual word-of-mouth conversations."[27]

- **Be authentic; be transparent; be real.** Trying to fool the public through fake blogs and other tactics is not only unethical (and possibly illegal) but almost guaranteed to eventually backfire in a world where people have unprecedented access to information. Similarly, trying to tack social media onto a consumer-hostile business is likely to fail as soon as stakeholders see through the superficial attempt to "be social." In contrast, social media audiences respond positively to companies that are open and conversational about themselves, their products, and subjects of shared interest.

- **Don't rely on the news media to distribute your message.** In traditional public relations efforts, marketers have to persuade the news media to distribute their messages to consumers and other audiences by producing news stories. These media are still important, but you can also speak directly to these audiences through blogs and other electronic tools.

- **Integrate conventional marketing and sales strategies at the right time and in the right places.** AIDA and similar approaches are still valid for specific communication tasks, such as conventional advertising and the product promotion pages on your website.

For the latest information on using social media for persuasive communication, visit http://real-timeupdates.com/bct11 and click on Chapter 10.

Maintaining High Standards of Ethics, Legal Compliance, and Etiquette

5   LEARNING OBJECTIVE

Identify steps you can take to avoid ethical lapses in marketing and sales messages.

The word *persuasion* has negative connotations for some people, especially in a marketing or sales context. They associate persuasion with dishonest and unethical practices that lead unsuspecting audiences into accepting unworthy ideas or buying unneeded products.

However, effective businesspeople view persuasion as a positive force, aligning their own interests with what is best for their audiences. They influence audience members by providing information and aiding understanding, which allows audiences the freedom to choose.[28] To maintain the highest standards of business ethics, always demonstrate the "you" attitude by showing honest concern for your audience's needs and interests.

Marketing and sales messages are covered by a wide range of laws and regulations.

As marketing and selling grow increasingly complex, so do the legal ramifications of marketing and sales messages. In the United States, the Federal Trade Commission (www .ftc.gov) has the authority to impose penalties (ranging from cease-and-desist orders to multimillion-dollar fines) against advertisers who violate federal standards for truthful advertising. Other federal agencies have authority over advertising in specific industries, such as transportation and financial services. Individual states have additional laws that apply. The legal aspects of promotional communication can be quite complex, varying from state to state and from country to country, and most companies require marketing and salespeople to get clearance from company lawyers before sending messages.

Moreover, communicators must stay on top of changing regulations, such as the latest laws governing unsolicited bulk email ("spam"), disclosure requirements for bloggers who review products, privacy, and data security. Two of the latest ethical concerns that could produce new legislation are *behavioral targeting*, which tracks the online behavior of website visitors and serves up ads based on what they appear to be interested in, and *remarketing*, in which behaviorally targeted ads follow users even as they move on to other websites.[29]

For all marketing and sales efforts, pay close attention to the following legal considerations:[30]

- **Marketing and sales messages must be truthful and nondeceptive.** The FTC considers messages to be deceptive if they include statements that are likely to mislead reasonable customers and the statements are an important part of the purchasing decision. Failing to include important information is also considered deceptive. The FTC also looks at *implied claims*—claims you don't explicitly make but that can be inferred from what you do or don't say.

Figure 10.7   Backing Up Promotional Claims with Solid Evidence
Merck, the company that makes the hair-loss treatment Propecia, takes care to back up its product claims with solid evidence, out of respect for its audience and to ensure compliance with regulations regarding marketing and sales messages. The series of photos available through the "Evidence of Regrowth" link provides additional visual confirmation of the product's benefits.

- **You must back up your claims with evidence.** According to the FTC, offering a money-back guarantee or providing letters from satisfied customers is not enough; you must still be able to support claims for your product with objective evidence such as a survey or scientific study (see Figure 10.7). If you claim that your food product lowers cholesterol, you must have scientific evidence to support that claim.
- **"Bait and switch" advertising is illegal.** Trying to attract buyers by advertising a product that you don't intend to sell—and then trying to sell them another (and usually more expensive) product—is illegal.
- **Marketing messages and websites aimed at children are subject to special rules.** For example, online marketers must obtain consent from parents before collecting personal information about children under age 13.
- **Marketing and sales messages are considered binding contracts in many states.** If you imply or make an offer and then can't fulfill your end of the bargain, you can be sued for breach of contract.
- **In most cases, you can't use a person's name, photograph, or other identity without permission.** Doing so is considered an invasion of privacy. You can use images of people considered to be public figures as long as you don't unfairly imply that they endorse your message.

Meeting your ethical and legal obligations will go a long way toward maintaining good communication etiquette as well. However, you may still face etiquette decisions within ethical and legal boundaries. For instance, you can produce a marketing campaign that complies with all applicable laws and yet is offensive or insulting to your audience. Taking an audience-centered approach, involving respect for your readers and their values, should help you avoid any such etiquette missteps.

Technology also gives communicators new ways to demonstrate sensitivity to user needs. One example is automated RSS newsfeeds from blogs, alerting customers to information in which they've expressed an interest. *Opt-in* email newsletters are another technology that shows the "you" attitude at work. Unlike the unwelcome spam messages that litter email inboxes these days, opt-in messages are sent only to those people who have specifically requested information.

Maintaining high ethical standards is a key aspect of good communication etiquette.

Communication technologies such as opt-in email can help you be sensitive to audience needs.

Quick Learning Guide

MyBcommLab

If your course uses MyBcommLab, log on to www.mybcommlab.com to access the following study and assessment aids associated with this chapter:

- Video applications
- Real-Time Updates
- Peer review activity
- Pre/post test
- Personalized study plan
- Model documents
- Sample presentations

If you are not using MyBcommLab, you can access Real-Time Updates through http://real-timeupdates.com/bct11.

CHAPTER OUTLINE

Using the Three-Step Writing Process for Persuasive Messages

Step 1: Planning a Persuasive Message
Step 2: Writing a Persuasive Message
Step 3: Completing a Persuasive Message

Developing Persuasive Business Messages

Strategies for Persuasive Business Messages
Common Examples of Persuasive Business Messages

Developing Marketing and Sales Messages

Assessing Audience Needs
Analyzing Your Competition
Determining Key Selling Points and Benefits
Anticipating Purchase Objections
Applying AIDA or a Similar Model

Writing Promotional Messages for Social Media

Maintaining High Standards of Ethics, Legal Compliance, and Etiquette

SUMMARY OF LEARNING OBJECTIVES

1 **Apply the three-step writing process to persuasive messages.** To plan persuasive messages, carefully clarify your purpose to make sure you focus on a single goal. Understand audience needs, which can involve research to identify relevant demographic and psychographic variables and to assess audience motivations. Persuasive messages usually ask people to give up time, money, or other resources, so gathering the right information to convince readers of the benefits of responding is essential. Media choices need to be considered carefully, particularly with marketing and sales messages in a social media landscape. For organizing persuasive messages, you will usually want to choose the indirect approach in order to establish awareness and interest before asking the audience to take action.

When writing persuasive messages, use positive and polite language, understand and respect cultural differences, be sensitive to organizational cultures when writing persuasive business messages, and take steps to establish your credibility. Seven common ways to establish credibility in persuasive messages are using simple language, supporting your claims, identifying your sources, establishing common ground, being objective, displaying good intentions, and avoiding the hard sell.

The steps for completing persuasive messages are the same as for other types of messages, but accuracy and completeness are especially important because they send signals about your credibility—a crucial element in persuasive messages.

2 **Describe an effective strategy for developing persuasive business messages, and identify the three most common categories of persuasive business messages.** Within the context of the three-step process, effective persuasion involves four essential strategies: framing your arguments, balancing emotional and logical appeals, reinforcing your position, and anticipating objections. One of the most commonly used methods for framing a persuasive argument is the AIDA model, in which you open your message by getting the audience's attention; build interest with facts, details, and additional benefits; increase desire by providing more evidence and answering possible objections; and motivate a specific action.

Persuasive business messages combine emotional appeals (which call on feelings and sympathies) and logical appeals (which call on reason, using analogy, induction, or deduction). To reinforce your position, look for ways to add convincing evidence, quotations from experts, or other support material.

By identifying potential objections and addressing them as you craft your message, you can help prevent audience members from gravitating toward negative answers before you have the opportunity to ask them for a positive response. You can often resolve these issues before the audience has a chance to go on the defensive.

The most common types of these messages are (1) persuasive requests for action, in which you ask the recipient to make a decision or engage in some activity; (2) persuasive presentations of ideas, in which you aren't necessarily looking for a decision or action but rather would like the audience to consider a different way of looking at a particular topic; and (3) persuasive claims and requests for adjustments, in which you believe that you have not received fair treatment under an organization's standard policies and would like the recipient to give your case fresh consideration.

3 **Describe an effective strategy for developing marketing and sales messages.** Marketing and sales messages use the same basic techniques as other persuasive messages, with the added emphasis of encouraging someone to participate in a commercial transaction. Marketing messages do this indirectly, whereas sales messages do it directly. The basic strategy for creating these messages includes assessing audience needs; analyzing your competition; determining key selling points and benefits; anticipating purchase objections; applying the AIDA model; adapting your writing to social media, if appropriate; and maintaining high standards of ethical and legal compliance.

4 **Explain how to modify your approach when writing promotional messages for social media.** To use social media for promotional communication, start by engaging audiences with efforts to build networked communities of potential buyers and other interested parties. Listen to conversations taking place about your company and its products. Initiate and respond to conversations within these communities, being sure to use an objective, conversational style. Provide the information that interested parties want. Identify and support the enthusiastic product champions who want to help spread your message. Be authentic and transparent in all your communication. Speak directly to customers so you don't have to rely on the news media. Finally, continue to use the AIDA model or similar approaches, but only at specific times and places.

5 **Identify steps you can take to avoid ethical lapses in marketing and sales messages.** Effective and ethical persuasive communicators focus on aligning their interests with the interests of their audiences. They help audiences understand how their proposals will provide benefits to the audience, using language that is persuasive without being manipulative. They choose words that are less likely to be misinterpreted and take care not to distort the truth. Throughout, they maintain a "you" attitude with honest concern for the audience's needs and interests. By following applicable laws and regulations, marketers can avoid many ethical problems.

KEY TERMS

AIDA model Message sequence that involves attention, interest, desire, and action

benefits The particular advantages that readers will realize from a product's selling points

conversation marketing Approach in which companies initiate and facilitate conversations in a networked community of customers, journalists, bloggers, and other interested parties

demographics Quantifiable characteristics of a population, including age, gender, occupation, income, and education

emotional appeal Persuasive approach that calls on audience feelings and sympathies rather than facts, figures, and rational arguments

logical appeal Persuasive approach that calls on reasoning and evidence

marketing messages Promotional messages that usher potential buyers through the purchasing process without asking them to make an immediate decision

motivation The combination of forces that drive people to satisfy their needs

persuasion The attempt to change an audience's attitudes, beliefs, or actions

psychographics Psychological characteristics of an audience, including personality, attitudes, and lifestyle

sales messages In contrast to marketing messages, sales messages encourage potential buyers to make a purchase decision then and there

selling points The most attractive features of a product or service

social commerce Encompasses any aspect of buying and selling products and services or supporting customers through the use of social media

 Checklist

Developing Persuasive Messages

A. **Get your reader's attention.**
   - Open with an audience benefit, a stimulating question, a problem, or an unexpected statement.
   - Establish common ground by mentioning a point on which you and your audience agree.
   - Show that you understand the audience's concerns.

B. **Build your reader's interest.**
   - Expand and support your opening claim or promise.
   - Emphasize the relevance of your message to your audience.

C. **Increase your reader's desire.**
   - Make audience members want to change by explaining how the change will benefit them.
   - Back up your claims with relevant evidence.

D. **Motivate your reader to take action.**
   - Suggest the action you want readers to take.

   - Stress the positive results of the action.
   - Make the desired action clear and easy.

E. **Balance emotional and logical appeals.**
   - Use emotional appeals to help the audience accept your message.
   - Use logical appeals when presenting facts and evidence for complex ideas or recommendations.
   - Avoid faulty logic.

F. **Reinforce your position.**
   - Provide additional evidence of the benefits of your proposal and your own credibility in offering it.
   - Use abstractions, metaphors, and other figures of speech to bring facts and figures to life.

G. **Anticipate objections.**
   - Anticipate and answer potential objections.
   - Present the pros and cons of all options if you anticipate a hostile reaction.

COMMUNICATION CHALLENGES AT CAFEMOM

You're the vice president of member services at CafeMom, reporting to CEO Michael Sanchez. In addition to developing new online services, a key part of your job responsibility is crafting messages that describe the new services and persuade members to try them. Use what you've learned in this chapter and in your own experiences as a consumer (and as a parent, if applicable) to address these challenges.

INDIVIDUAL CHALLENGE: You asked one of your staffers to write a benefit statement to communicate the advantages of the Groups section of the CafeMom website, which lets members find and join any of the thousands of existing groups or create new groups focused on just about any topic imaginable. She emails the following sentence: "We've worked hard to define and create a powerful online group capability; you can search far and wide on the Web, but you won't find anything as great as what we've created." Write an email message in response, explaining why it's important to make marketing messages about the customer, not about the company. Include a revised version that illustrates this vital aspect of the "you" attitude. You can learn more about the Groups feature at the CafeMom website, **www.cafemom.com/groups**.

TEAM CHALLENGE: A common challenge in marketing communication is distilling a long list of features to a single compelling message that can serve as the product's "headline." With your team, review this list of features and benefits:

- The experiences of thousands of moms are now aggregated in a single place online.
- Connect with moms like you; search for moms by personal and family challenges, interests, age of kids, or location.
- Get and give support; find support and swap advice with other moms on a wide range of topics that matter most to you.
- Post questions online and get input from mothers who've been there before.
- Joining CafeMom is absolutely free.
- Setting up your own personal profile is fast and easy.
- Join groups who share your likes and concerns.
- Write as much or as little as you want to share in your personal profile.
- You have complete control over the privacy of your information.

Brainstorm three one-sentence possibilities that could serve as the headline for a webpage promoting CafeMom and then choose the most compelling of the three options. Don't assume that every feature or benefit in the list needs to be incorporated in your high-level message.

TEST YOUR KNOWLEDGE

To review chapter content related to each question, refer to the indicated Learning Objective.

1. What role do demographics and psychographics play in audience analysis during the planning of a persuasive message? [LO-1]
2. What are four of the many ways you can build credibility with an audience when planning a persuasive message? [LO-1]
3. What is the AIDA model, and what are its limitations? [LO-2]
4. How do emotional appeals differ from logical appeals? [LO-2]
5. What three types of reasoning can you use in logical appeals? [LO-2]
6. What is conversation marketing? [LO-4]
7. What is social commerce? [LO-4]
8. What is likely to happen if you don't anticipate audience objections when crafting your messages? [LO-2], [LO-3]

9. How do benefits differ from features? [LO-3]
10. How does ethical behavior contribute to positive etiquette in persuasive messages? [LO-5]

APPLY YOUR KNOWLEDGE

To review chapter content related to each question, refer to the indicated Learning Objective.

1. Why is it essential to understand your readers' likely motivations before writing a persuasive message? [LO-1]
2. Why is it important to present both sides of an argument when writing a persuasive message to a potentially hostile audience? [LO-2]
3. Are emotional appeals ethical? Why or why not? [LO-2]
4. What is likely to happen if a promotional message starts immediately with a call to action? Why? [LO-3]
5. Why do the AIDA model and similar approaches need to be modified when writing persuasive messages in social media? [LO-4]

PRACTICE YOUR SKILLS

Messages for Analysis

For Message 10.A and Message 10.B, read the following documents and then (1) analyze the strengths and weaknesses of each sentence and (2) revise each document so that it follows this chapter's guidelines.

Message 10.A: Message Strategies: Persuasive Claims and Requests for Adjustment [LO-2]

Dear TechStar Computing:

I'm writing to you because of my disappointment with my new multimedia PC display. The display part works all right, but the audio volume is set too high and the volume knob doesn't turn it down. It's driving us crazy. The volume knob doesn't seem to be connected to anything but simply spins around. I can't believe you would put out a product like this without testing it first.

I depend on my computer to run my small business and want to know what you are going to do about it. This reminds me of every time I buy electronic equipment from what seems like any company. Something is always wrong. I thought quality was supposed to be important, but I guess not.

Anyway, I need this fixed right away. Please tell me what you want me to do.

Message 10.B: Message Strategies: Sales Messages [LO-3]

We know how awful dining hall food can be, and that's why we've developed the "Mealaweek Club." Once a week, we'll deliver food to your dormitory or apartment. Our meals taste great. We have pizza, buffalo wings, hamburgers and curly fries, veggie roll-ups, and more!

When you sign up for just six months, we will ask what day you want your delivery. We'll ask you to fill out your selection of meals. And the rest is up to us. At "Mealaweek," we deliver! And payment is easy. We accept MasterCard and Visa or a personal check. It will save money especially when compared with eating out.

Just fill out the enclosed card and indicate your method of payment. As soon as we approve your credit or check, we'll begin delivery. Tell all your friends about Mealaweek. We're the best idea since sliced bread!

Message 10.C: Media Skills: Podcasting [LO-2]

To access this message, visit **http://real-timeupdates.com/bct11**, click on "Student Assignments," and select "Chapter 10, page 305, Message 10.C." Download and listen to this podcast. Identify at least three ways in which the podcast could be more persuasive and draft a brief email message that you could send to the podcaster with your suggestions for improvement.

Exercises

Active links for all websites in this chapter can be found on MyBcommLab; see your User Guide for instructions on accessing the content for this chapter. Each activity is labeled according to the primary skill or skills you will need to use. To review relevant chapter content, you can refer to the indicated Learning Objective. In some instances, supporting information will be found in another chapter, as indicated.

1. **Choosing a Message Strategy: [LO-1], Chapters 8–9** Now that you've explored routine, positive, negative, and persuasive messages, review the following message scenarios and identify which of the four message strategies would be most appropriate for the situation. Offer a brief justification for your choices. (Depending on the particular circumstances, a scenario might lend itself to more than one type of message; just be sure to offer compelling reasons for your choices.)

   a. An unsolicited message to your department manager, explaining why you believe that the company's experiment with self-managed work teams has not been successful

   b. An unsolicited message to your department manager, explaining why you believe that the company's experiment with self-managed work teams has not been successful and suggesting that one of the more experienced employees (such as yourself) should be promoted to supervisor

   c. A message to a long-time industrial customer, explaining that a glitch in your accounting system resulted in the customer being overcharged on its last five orders, apologizing for the problem, and assuring the customer that you will refund the overcharged amount immediately

   d. A news release announcing that your company plans to invite back 50 employees who were laid off earlier in the year

2. **Message Strategies: Persuasive Business Messages; Collaboration: Team Projects [LO-2]** With another student, analyze the persuasive email message to Eleanor Tran at Host Marriott (Figure 10.3) by answering the following questions:

   a. What techniques are used to capture the reader's attention?

   b. Does the writer use the direct or indirect organizational approach? Why?

   c. Is the subject line effective? Why or why not?

   d. Does the writer use an emotional or a logical appeal? Why?

   e. What reader benefits are included?

   f. How does the writer establish credibility?

   g. What tools does the writer use to reinforce his position?

3. **Message Strategies: Persuasive Business Messages, Marketing and Sales Messages: Media Skills: Email [LO-2], [LO-3]** Compose effective subject lines for the following persuasive email messages:

   a. A recommendation was sent by email to your branch manager to install wireless networking throughout the facility. Your primary reason is that management has encouraged more teamwork, but teams often congregate in meeting rooms, the cafeteria, and other places that lack network access—without which they can't do much of the work they are expected to do.

   b. A message to area residents, soliciting customers for your new business, "Meals à la Car," a carryout dining service that delivers from most of the local restaurants. All local restaurant menus are on the Internet. Mom and Dad can dine on egg rolls and chow mein while the kids munch on pepperoni pizza.

c. An email message to the company president, asking that employees be allowed to carry over their unused vacation days to the following year. Apparently, many employees canceled their fourth-quarter vacation plans to work on the installation of a new company computer system. Under their current contract, vacation days not used by December 31 can't be carried over to the following year.

4. **Communication Ethics: Making Ethical Choices [LO-2], [LO-5]** Your boss has asked you to post a message on the company's internal blog, urging everyone in your department to donate money to the company's favorite charity, an organization that operates a summer camp for children with physical challenges. You wind up writing a lengthy posting, packed with facts and heartwarming anecdotes about the camp and the children's experiences. When you must work that hard to persuade your audience to take an action such as donating money to a charity, aren't you being manipulative and unethical? Explain.

5. **Message Strategies: Marketing and Sales Messages (Customer Benefits) [LO-3]** Determine whether the following sentences focus on features or benefits; rewrite as necessary to focus all the sentences on benefits.
   a. All-Cook skillets are coated with a durable, patented nonstick surface.
   b. You can call anyone and talk as long as you like on Saturdays and Sundays with our new FamilyTalk wireless plan.
   c. With 8-millisecond response time, the Samsung LN-S4095D 40-inch LCD TV delivers fast video action that is smooth and crisp.[31]

6. **Message Strategies: Marketing and Sales Messages [LO-3]** The daily mail often brings a selection of sales messages. Find a direct-mail package from your mailbox that includes a sales letter. Then answer the following questions to help analyze and learn from the approach used by the communication professionals who prepare these glossy sales messages. Your instructor might also ask you to share the package and your observations in a class discussion.
   a. Who is the intended audience?
   b. What are some of the demographic and psychographic characteristics of the intended audience?
   c. What is the purpose of the direct-mail package? Has it been designed to solicit a phone-call response, make a mail-order sale, obtain a charitable contribution, or do something else?
   d. What technique was used to encourage you to open the envelope?
   e. Did the letter writer follow the AIDA model or something similar? If not, explain the letter's organization.
   f. What emotional appeals and logical arguments does the letter use?
   g. What selling points and consumer benefits does the letter offer?
   h. Did the letter and the rest of the package provide convincing support for the claims made in the letter? If not, what is lacking?

EXPAND YOUR SKILLS

Critique the Professionals

Visit the Facebook pages of six companies in several industries. How do the companies make use of their Wall? Do any of the companies use Wall posts to promote their products? Compare the material on the Info tabs. Which company has the most compelling information here? How about the use of custom tabs; which company does the best job of using this Facebook feature? Using whatever medium your instructor requests, write a brief analysis of the message (no more than one page), citing specific elements from the piece and support from the chapter.

Sharpening Your Career Skills Online

Bovée and Thill's Business Communication Web Search, at http://businesscommunicationblog.com/websearch, is a unique research tool designed specifically for business communication research. Use the Web Search function to find a website, video, PDF document, podcast, or PowerPoint presentation that offers advice on writing persuasive messages (either persuasive business messages or marketing and sales messages). Write a brief email message to your instructor, describing the item that you found and summarizing the career skills information you learned from it.

CASES

Persuasive Business Messages

 Learn how to set up a Twitter account and begin tweeting. Visit http://real-timeupdates.com/bce5, click on "Student Assignments" and then click on "Twitter Screencast."

MICROBLOGGING SKILLS

1. Message Strategies: Persuasive Business Messages [LO-3] You've been trying for months to convince your boss, company CEO Will Florence, to start using Twitter. You've told him that top executives in numerous industries now use Twitter as a way to connect with customers and other stakeholders without going through the filters and barriers of formal corporate communications, but he doesn't see the value.

Your task: You come up with the brilliant plan to demonstrate Twitter's usefulness using Twitter itself. First, find three executives from three companies who are on Twitter (choose any companies and executive you find interesting). Second, study their tweets to get a feel for the type of information they share. Third, if you don't already have a Twitter account set up for this class, set one up for the purposes of this exercise (you can deactivate later). Fourth, write four tweets to demonstrate the value of executive microblogging: one that summarizes the value of having a company CEO use Twitter and three support tweets, each one summarizing how your three real-life executive role models use Twitter.

BLOGGING SKILLS   TEAM SKILLS

2. Message Strategies: Persuasive Business Messages [LO-3]

As a strong advocate for the use of social media in business, you are pleased by how quickly people in your company have taken up blogging, wiki writing, and other new-media activities. You are considerably less excited by the style and quality of what you see in the writing of your colleagues. Many seem to have interpreted "authentic and conversational" to mean "anything goes." Several of the Twitter users in the company seem to have abandoned any pretense of grammar and spelling. A few managers have dragged internal disagreements about company strategy out into public view, arguing with each other through comments on various industry-related forums. Production demonstration videos have been posted to the company's YouTube channel virtually unedited, making the whole firm look unpolished and unprofessional. The company CEO has written some blog posts that bash competitors with coarse and even crude language.

You pushed long and hard for greater use of these tools, so you feel a sense of responsibility for this situation. In addition, you are viewed by many in the company as the resident expert on social media, so you have some "expertise authority" on this issue. On the other hand, you are only a first-level manager, with three levels of managers above you, so while you have some "position authority" as well, you can hardly dictate best practices to the managers above you.

Your task: Working with two other students, write a post for the company's internal blog (which is not viewable outside the company), outlining your concerns about these communication practices. Use the examples mentioned above, and make up any additional details you need. Emphasize that while social media communication is often less formal and more flexible than traditional business communication, it shouldn't be unprofessional. You are thinking of proposing a social media training program for everyone in the company, but for this message you just want to bring attention to the problem.

LETTER WRITING SKILLS

3. Message Strategies: Persuasive Business Messages [LO-3]

The coffee shop across the street from your tiny apartment is your haven away from home—great beverages, healthy snacks, an atmosphere that is convivial but not so lively that you can't focus on your homework, and free wireless. It lacks only one thing: some way to print out your homework and other files when you need hardcopies. Your college's libraries and computer labs provide printers, but you live three miles from campus, and it's a long walk or an inconvenient bus ride.

Your task: Write a letter to the owner of the coffee shop, encouraging her to set up a printing service to complement the free wireless access. Propose that the service run at break-even prices, just enough to pay for paper, ink cartridges, and the cost of the printer itself. The benefit to the shop would be enticing patrons to spend more time—and therefore more of their coffee and tea money—in the shop. You might also mention that you had to take the bus to campus in order to print this letter, so you bought your afternoon latté somewhere else.

EMAIL SKILLS   PORTFOLIO BUILDER

4. Message Strategies: Persuasive Business Messages [LO-2]

As someone who came of age in the "post email" world of blogs, wikis, social networks, and other Web 2.0 technologies, you were rather disappointed to find your new employer solidly stuck in the age of email. You use email, of course, but it is only one of the tools in your communication toolbox. From your college years, you have hands-on experience with a wide range of social media tools, having used them to collaborate on school projects, to become involved in your local community, to learn more about various industries and professions, and to research potential employers during your job search. (In fact, without social media, you might never have heard about your current employer in the first place.) Moreover, your use of social media on the job has already paid several important dividends, including finding potential sales contacts at several large companies, connecting with peers in other companies to share ideas for working more efficiently, and learning about some upcoming legislative matters in your state that could profoundly hamper your company's current way of doing business.

You hoped that by setting an example through your own use of social media at work, your new colleagues and company management would quickly adopt these tools as well. However, just the opposite has happened. Waiting in your email in-box this morning was a message from the CEO, announcing that the company is now cutting off access to social networking websites and banning the use of any social media at work. The message says that using company time and company computers for socializing is highly inappropriate and might be considered grounds for dismissal in the future if the problem gets out of hand.

Your task: You are stunned by the message. You fight the urge to fire off a hotly worded reply to straighten out the CEO's misperceptions. Instead, you wisely decide to send a message to your immediate superior first, explaining why you believe the new policy should be reversed. Using your boss's favorite medium (email, of course!), write a persuasive message, explaining why Facebook, Twitter, and other social networking technologies are valid—and valuable—business tools. Bolster your argument with examples from other companies and advice from communication experts. (To access a list of links to get your research started, visit http://real-timeupdates.com/bct11, click on "Student Assignments," and select Chapter 10, page 307, Case 4.)

EMAIL SKILLS

5. Message Strategies: Persuasive Claims and Requests for Adjustment [LO-2]

It's hard to go through life without becoming annoyed at the way some things work. You have undoubtedly been dissatisfied with a product you've bought, a service you've received, or an action of some elected official or government agency.

Your task: Write a three- to five-paragraph persuasive email message request, expressing your dissatisfaction in a particular case. Specify the action you want the reader to take.

IM SKILLS

6. Message Strategies: Requests for Action [LO-2]   At IBM, you're one of the coordinators for the annual Employee Charitable Contributions Campaign. Since 1978, the company has helped employees contribute to more than 2,000 health and human service agencies. These groups may offer child care; treat substance abuse; provide health services; or fight illiteracy, homelessness, and hunger. Some offer disaster relief or care for the elderly. All deserve support. They're carefully screened by IBM, one of the largest corporate contributors of cash, equipment, and people to nonprofit organizations and educational institutions in the United States and around the world. As your literature states, the program "has engaged our employees more fully in the important mission of corporate citizenship."

During the winter holidays, you target agencies that cater to the needs of displaced families, women, and children. It's not difficult to raise enthusiasm. The prospect of helping children enjoy the holidays—children who otherwise might have nothing—usually awakens the spirit of your most distracted workers. But some of them wait until the last minute and then forget.

They have until December 16 to come forth with cash contributions. To make it in time for holiday deliveries, they can also bring in toys, food, and blankets through Tuesday, December 20. They shouldn't have any trouble finding the collection bins; they're everywhere, marked with bright red banners. But some will want to call you with questions or (you hope) to make credit card contributions: 800-658-3899, ext. 3342.

Your task: It's December 14. Write a 75- to 100-word instant message, encouraging last-minute holiday gifts.[32]

EMAIL SKILLS

7. Message Strategies: Persuasive Claims and Requests for Adjustment [LO-2]   Last week you ordered new design software for your boss, Martin Soderburgh, at ArtAlive, the small art consulting business where you work. As he requested, you used his Visa card to order Adobe InDesign and Adobe Photoshop from an Internet vendor, PurelySoftware.

When you didn't receive the usual email order confirmation, you called the company's toll-free number. The operator said the company's website was having problems, and he took a second order over the phone: $649 for Adobe InDesign, $564 for Adobe Photoshop, including tax and shipping. Four days later, ArtAlive received two shipments of the software, and your boss's credit card was charged $1,213 twice, for a total of $2,426.

Your task: Strictly speaking, you did authorize both orders. But you understood during the phone call that the first order was canceled, although you have no written proof. Write a persuasive email message requesting an immediate credit to your boss's Visa account and a postage-paid return label for the duplicate order.[33]

MEMO WRITING SKILLS

8. Message Strategies: Requests for Action [LO-2]   This morning as you drove to your job as food services manager at the Pechanga Casino Entertainment Center in Temecula, California, you were concerned to hear on the radio that the local Red Cross chapter put out a call for blood because national supplies have fallen dangerously low. During highly publicized disasters, people are emotional and eager to help out by donating blood. But in calmer times, only 5 percent of eligible donors think of giving blood. You're one of those few.

Not many people realize that donated blood lasts only 72 hours. Consequently, the mainstay of emergency blood supplies must be replenished in an ongoing effort. No one is more skilled, dedicated, or efficient in handling blood than the American Red Cross, which is responsible for half the nation's supply of blood and blood products.

Donated blood helps victims of accidents and disease, as well as surgery patients. Just yesterday you were reading about a girl named Melissa, who was diagnosed with multiple congenital heart defects and underwent her first open-heart surgery at one week old. Now five, she's used well over 50 units of donated blood, and she wouldn't be alive without them. In a thank-you letter, her mother lauded the many strangers who had "given a piece of themselves" to save her precious daughter—and countless others. You also learned that a donor's pint of blood can benefit up to four other people.

Today, you're going to do more than just roll up your own sleeve. You know the local Red Cross chapter takes its blood donation equipment to corporations, restaurants, beauty salons—any place willing to host public blood drives. What if you could convince the board of directors to support a blood drive at the casino? The slot machines and gaming tables are usually full, hundreds of employees are on hand, and people who've never visited before might come down to donate blood. The positive publicity will boost Pechanga's community image, too. With materials from the Red Cross, you're confident you can organize Pechanga's hosting effort and handle the promotion. (Last year, you headed the casino's successful Toys for Tots drive.)

To give blood, one must be healthy, be at least 17 years old (with no upper age limit), and weigh at least 110 pounds. Donors can give every 56 days. You'll be urging Pechanga donors to eat well, drink water, and be thoroughly rested before donating.[34]

Your task: Write a memo persuading the Pechanga board of directors to host a public Red Cross blood drive. You can learn more about what's involved in hosting a blood drive at www.redcrossblood.org (click on "Hosting a Blood Drive"). Ask the board to provide water, orange juice, and snacks for donors. You'll organize food service workers to handle the distribution, but you'll need the board's approval to let your team volunteer during work hours. Use a combination of logical and emotional appeals.

EMAIL SKILLS   PORTFOLIO BUILDER

9. Message Strategies: Requests for Action [LO-2]   Your new company, WorldConnect Language Services, started well and is going strong. However, to expand beyond your Memphis, Tennessee, home market, you need a one-time infusion of cash to open branch offices in other cities around the Southeast. At the Entrepreneur's Lunch Forum you attended yesterday, you learned about several *angels*, as they are called in the investment community—private individuals who invest money in small companies in exchange for a share of ownership. One such angel, Melinda Sparks, told the audience that she is looking for investment opportunities outside of high technology, where angels often invest their money. She also indicated that she looks for entrepreneurs who know their industries and markets well, who are passionate about the value they bring to the marketplace, who are committed to growing their businesses, and who have a solid plan for how they will spend an investor's money. Fortunately, you meet all of her criteria.

Your task: Draft an email message to Sparks, introducing yourself and your business and asking for a meeting at which you can present your business plan in more detail. Explain that your Memphis office was booked to capacity within two months of opening, thanks to the growing number of international business professionals looking for translators and interpreters. You've researched the entire Southeast region and identified at least 10 other cities that could support a language services office such as yours. Making up whatever other information you need, draft a four-paragraph message following the AIDA model, ending with a request for a meeting within the next four weeks.

BLOGGING SKILLS   PORTFOLIO BUILDER

10. Message Strategies: Persuasive Presentation of Ideas [LO-2]   Like most other companies today, your firm makes extensive use of the web for internal and external communication. However, after reading about the Web Accessibility Initiative (WAI), you've become concerned that your company's various websites haven't been designed to accommodate people with disabilities or age-related limitations. Fortunately, as one of the company's top managers, you have a perfect forum for letting everyone in the company know how important accessible web design is: Your internal blog is read by the vast majority of employees and managers throughout the company.

Your task: Visit the WAI website, at www.w3.org/WAI, and read the two articles "Introduction to Web Accessibility" (look in the "Introducing Accessibility" section) and "Developing a Web Accessibility Business Case for Your Organization" (in the "Managing Accessibility" section). Using the information you learn in these articles, write a post for your blog that emphasizes how important it is for your company's websites to be made more accessible. You don't have direct authority over the company's web developers, so it would be inappropriate for you to request them to take any specific action. Your goal is simply to raise awareness and encourage everyone to consider the needs of the company's online audiences. Don't worry about the technical aspects of web accessibility; focus instead on the benefits of improving accessibility.[35]

EMAIL SKILLS

11. Message Strategies: Persuasive Claims and Requests for Adjustment [LO-2]   You thought it was strange that no one called you on your new mobile phone, even though you had given your family members, friends, and boss your new number. Two weeks after getting the new phone and agreeing to a $49 monthly fee, you called the service provider, InstantCall, just to see if everything was working. Sure enough, the technician discovered that your incoming calls were being routed to an inactive number. You're glad she found the problem, but then it took the company nearly two more weeks to fix it. When you called to complain about paying for service you didn't receive, the customer service agent suggests you send an email to Judy

Hinkley at the company's regional business office to request an adjustment.

Your task: Decide how much of an adjustment you think you deserve under the circumstances and then send an email message to Hinkley to request the adjustment to your account. Write a summary of events in chronological order, supplying exact dates for maximum effectiveness. Make up any information you need, such as problems that the malfunctioning service caused at home or at work.

LETTER WRITING SKILLS

12. Message Strategies: Persuasive Claims and Requests for Adjustment [LO-2]   As a professional photographer, you travel the world for business, leaving from your home base in Williamstown, Massachusetts. Last month it was a trip to Australia, and you thought you'd finally found a way around the "no-locks-on-checked-baggage" rules.

After the World Trade Center attacks of September 11, 2001, the U.S. Travel Security Administration (TSA) forbade airline passengers to check locked luggage. TSA inspectors want easy access so that they can open and check bags for security purposes. But because you carry so much expensive equipment, including numerous camera bags, you've been nervous about the safety of your belongings—not to mention the loss of privacy.

So you were relieved when you read Joe Sharkey's "On the Road" column in the *New York Times* just before your trip. The columnist extolled a newly announced TSA program allowing airline travelers to lock their luggage *if they use special TSA-approved locks*, certified by a company called Travel Sentry. You immediately went to the Brookstone store in Albany after reading its web advertisement for "The luggage locks security won't cut off. Our Easycheck™ locks are certified by Travel Sentry™ and feature a secure system accepted and recognized by the Transportation Security Administration (TSA). Airport security personnel can now inspect and re-lock your bags quickly and easily." You bought eight locks, at $20 for each set of two.

When you left the Albany airport, TSA inspectors assured you that they had a master key for these locks, just as Sharkey's column had promised they would. But when you got to Melbourne after changing planes in Chicago and Los Angeles, you were stunned to discover the condition of your luggage. One bag was missing the new lock entirely; another was missing the lock and had a rip all along the seam—perhaps from an irritated inspector? Inside a third bag you found its broken Easycheck lock, with a terse TSA inspection notice reminding you that locked baggage is not allowed. On the return trip you tried again, using three of your remaining locks on camera bags. They arrived with no locks and no inspection notices.

You've now called the airports in Chicago and Cleveland, where TSA inspectors told you they'd "never heard of the program." Brookstone will replace the broken lock, but the woman on the phone was not sure about the ones that went missing entirely because you have nothing left to bring into the store except your receipt.

Your task: After 10 minutes of listening to music while on hold for the TSA, you've abandoned the idea of making a phone complaint to the government agency. You're going to write a letter to Brookstone (120 Washington Ave., Albany, NY

12203), requesting damages for the ripped luggage (a 24-inch Expandable Ballistic Suitor, $320) and a refund for all eight locks ($80). Six of them were ruined or missing, and your last two are essentially useless.[36]

Marketing and Sales Messages: Conventional Media

LETTER WRITING SKILLS   PORTFOLIO BUILDER

13. Message Strategies: Marketing and Sales Messages LO-4]   Like all other states, Kentucky works hard to attract businesses that are considering expanding into the state or relocating entirely from another state. The Kentucky Cabinet for Economic Development is responsible for reaching out to these companies and overseeing the many incentive programs the state offers to new and established businesses.

Your task: As the communication director of the Kentucky Cabinet for Economic Development, you play the lead role in reaching out to companies that want to expand or relocate to Kentucky. Visit www.thinkkentucky.com and download the *Kentucky Facts* brochure (look under the "Why Kentucky" link). Identify the major benefits the state uses to promote Kentucky as a great place to locate a business. Summarize these reasons in a one-page form letter that will be sent to business executives throughout the country. Be sure to introduce yourself and your purpose in the letter, and close with a compelling call to action (have them reach you by telephone at 800-626-2930 or by email at econdev@ky.gov). As you plan your letter, try to imagine yourself as the CEO of a company and consider what a complex choice it would be to move to another state.[37]

LETTER WRITING SKILLS   PORTFOLIO BUILDER

14. Message Strategies: Marketing and Sales Messages [LO-3]   Water polo is an active sport that provides great opportunities for exercise and for learning the collaborative skills involved in teamwork. You can learn more at www.usawaterpolo.org.

Your task: Write a one-page letter to parents of 10- to 14-year-old boys and girls, promoting the health and socialization benefits of water polo and encouraging them to introduce their children to the sport through a local club. Tell them they can learn more about the sport and find a club in their area by visiting the USA Water Polo website.

WEB WRITING SKILLS

15. Message Strategies: Marketing and Sales Messages [LO-3]   Natalie Sisson bills herself as the "Suitcase Entrepreneur," and she's living proof that one can live an adventurous life and build a thriving business—she had been traveling the world since she left her native New Zealand in 2006. She offers business and social media coaching, and she recently compiled her social media advice in a PDF e-book, *The Entrepreneur's Social Media Workout.*

Your task: Sisson has been offering her social media e-book for free to anyone who subscribes to her email newsletter. However, as the assistant she recently hired, you convinced her the book

was valuable enough on its own to warrant a small purchase price. She decided to give it a try and set the price at $10.00, with one catch: you need to write the website copy to promote the e-book.

First, visit http://real-timeupdates.com/bct11, click on "Student Assignments" and then "Chapter 10, page 310, Case 15" to download the e-book. Then visit Sisson's website at http://womanzworld.com to learn more about her business experiences. Now write webpage copy (at least 200 words but no more than 400) to promote the e-book and encourage people to place an order.

EMAIL SKILLS

16. Message Strategies: Marketing and Sales Messages [LO-3]   The oud (rhymes with "mood") is a popular musical instrument in many cultures from northern Africa to southwest Asia, enjoying the same status in these countries as the guitar enjoys in Europe and the Americas. The oud, which dates back to the seventh century, was also the ancestor of the European-style lute that had its heyday during the Renaissance.

Many guitar players are familiar with the lute, but probably fewer with the oud. As the marketing director for Your World Instruments (www.yourworldinstruments.com) you'd like to encourage guitar players to consider the oud. Some might want to just explore another musical heritage. Others might want to expand their sonic palettes, so to speak, giving their music a broader range of sounds.

Your task: Write a brief email message that encourages guitar players to try something new. Or something old, more precisely. The people to whom you will be writing have heard from the company before, many are past customers, and all have opted-in to the email list. The call to action is encouraging these musicians to click through to the website to watch videos of expert oud players and to learn more about these storied instruments.[38]

WEB WRITING SKILLS   TEAM SKILLS
PORTFOLIO BUILDER

17. Message Strategies: Marketing and Sales Messages [LO-3]   You never intended to become an inventor, but you saw a way to make something work more easily, so you set to work. You developed a model, found a way to mass-produce it, and set up a small manufacturing studio in your home. You know that other people are going to benefit from your invention. Now all you need to do is reach that market.

Your task: Team up with other students assigned by your instructor and imagine a useful product that you might have invented—perhaps something related to a hobby or sporting activity. List the features and benefits of your imaginary product, and describe how it helps customers. Then write the copy for a webpage that would introduce and promote this product, using what you've learned in this chapter and making up details as you need them. As your instructor indicates, submit the copy as a word processor file or as a webpage using basic HTML formatting.

PODCASTING SKILLS

18. Message Strategies: Marketing and Sales Messages [LO-3]   Your new podcast channel, School2Biz, offers advice to business students making the transition from college to career.

You provide information on everything from preparing résumés to interviewing to finding a place in the business world and building a successful career. As you expand your audience, you'd eventually like to turn School2Biz into a profitable operation (perhaps by selling advertising time during your podcasts). For now, you're simply offering free advice.

Your task: You've chosen Podcast Bunker (www.podcastbunker .com) as the first website on which to promote School2Biz. This site lets podcasters promote their feeds with brief text listings, such as this description of Toolmonger Tool Talk: "Chuck and Sean from the web's first tool blog, Toolmonger.com, keep you up-to-date on the newest hand and power tools, and answer your home improvement, automotive, and tool-related questions."

As your instructor directs, either write a 50-word description of your new podcast that can be posted on Podcast Bunker or record a 30-second podcast describing the new service. Make up any information you need to describe School2Biz. Be sure to mention who you are and why the information you present is worth listening to.[39]

EMAIL SKILLS   PORTFOLIO BUILDER

19. Message Strategies: Marketing and Sales Messages [LO-3]   The great thing about Insure.com is that no one is obligated to buy a thing, which makes your job in the company's marketing department easier. Free of charge, consumers can log on to your website, ask for dozens of insurance quotes, and then go off and buy elsewhere. They can look at instant price-comparison quotes from more than 200 insurers, covering every kind of insurance from term life and medical to private passenger auto insurance. All rates are guaranteed up-to-the-day accurate against a $500 reward. And so far the online service has received positive press from *Nation's Business, Kiplinger's Personal Finance, Good Housekeeping, The Los Angeles Times, Money, U.S. News & World Report,* and *Forbes.*

Insure.com generates revenues primarily from the receipt of commissions and fees paid by insurers based on the volume of business produced. Customers can purchase insurance from the company of their choice via the Insure.com website at www .insure.com, or they can call a toll-free number to speak to one of the company's representatives. The reps are paid salaries versus commissions and do not directly benefit by promoting one insurance company's product over another.

And all this is free. Too bad more people don't know about your services.

Your task: It's your job to lure more insurance customers to Insure .com. You've decided to use direct email marketing (using a list of consumers who have inquired about rates in the past but never committed to purchase anything). Write an email sales message promoting the benefits of Insure.com's services. Be sure your message is suited to email format, with an appropriate subject heading.[40]

LETTER WRITING SKILLS   PORTFOLIO BUILDER

20. Message Strategies: Marketing and Sales Messages [LO-3]   Kelly Services is a large staffing company based in Troy, Michigan. Client firms turn to Kelly to strategically balance their workloads and workforces during peaks and valleys of demand, to handle special projects, and to evaluate employees prior to making a full-time hiring decision. Facing the economic pressures of global competition, many companies now rely on a dynamic combination of permanent employees and temporary contractors hired through service providers such as Kelly. In addition to these staffing services, Kelly offers project services (managing both short- and long-term projects) and outsourcing and consulting services (taking over entire business functions).

Your task: Write a one-page sales letter that would be sent to human resources executives at large U.S.-based corporations describing Kelly's three groups of business services. For current information, visit the Kelly website at www.kellyservices.com and look in the "Business Services" section.[41]

WEB WRITING SKILLS   PORTFOLIO BUILDER

21. Message Strategies: Marketing and Sales Messages [LO-3]   After a shaky start as the technology matured and advertisers tried to figure out this new medium, online advertising has finally become a significant force in both consumer and business marketing. Companies in a wide variety of industries are shifting some of the ad budgets from traditional media such as TV and magazines to the increasing selection of advertising possibilities online—and more than a few companies now advertise almost exclusively online. That's fine for companies that sell advertising time and space online, but your job involves selling advertising in print magazines that are worried about losing market share to online publishers.

Online advertising has two major advantages that you can't really compete with: interactivity and the ability to precisely target individual audience members. On the other hand, you have several advantages going for you, including the ability to produce high-color photography, the physical presence of print (such as when a magazine sits on a table in a doctor's waiting room), portability, guaranteed circulation numbers, and close reader relationships that go back years or decades.

Your task: You work as an advertising sales specialist for the Time Inc. division of Time Warner, which publishes more than 100 magazines around the world. Write a brief persuasive message about the benefits of magazine advertising; the statement will be posted on the individual websites of Time Inc.'s numerous magazines, so you can't narrow in on any single publication. Also, Time Inc. coordinates its print publications with an extensive online presence (including thousands of paid online ads), so you can't bash online advertising, either.[42]

Marketing and Sales Messages: Social Media

BLOGGING SKILLS

22. Message Strategies: Marketing and Sales Messages; Media Skills: Blogging [LO-4], Chapter 7   Other than possibly wrinkling their noses at that faint smell that wafts out of the plastic bags when they bring clothes home from the dry cleaner, many consumers probably don't pay much attention to the process that goes on behind the scenes at their neighborhood cleaner. However, traditional dry cleaning is a chemically intense process—so much so that these facilities require special environmental permits and monitoring by government agencies.

At Kansas City's Hangers Cleaners, the process is different— much different. The company's innovative machines use safe liquid carbon dioxide (CO_2) and specially developed detergents to clean clothes. The process requires no heat (making it easier on clothes) and has no need for the toxic, combustible perchloroethylene used in conventional dry cleaning (making it safer for employees and the environment). Customers can tell the difference, too. As one put it, "Since I started using Hangers, my clothes are softer, cleaner and they don't have that chemical smell."

Your task: Because many consumers aren't familiar with traditional dry cleaning, they don't immediately grasp why Hangers's method is better for clothes, employees, and the environment. Write a post for the company blog, explaining why Hangers is different. Limit yourself to 400 words. You can learn more about the company and its unique process at www.hangerskc.com.[43]

SOCIAL NETWORKING SKILLS

23. Message Strategies: Marketing and Sales Messages; Media Skills: Social Networking [LO-4], Chapter 7 Curves is a fitness center franchise that caters to women who may not feel at home in traditional gyms. With its customer-focused and research-based approach, Curves has become a significant force in the fitness industry and one of the most successful franchise operations in history.[44]

Your task: Read the Overview and History sections at www.curves.com/about-curves. Imagine that you are adapting this material for the Info tab on the company's Facebook page. Write a "Company Overview" (95–100 words) and a "Mission" statement (45–50 words).

SOCIAL NETWORKING SKILLS
TEAMWORK SKILLS

24. Message Strategies: Marketing and Sales Messages; Media Skills: Social Networking [LO-4], Chapter 7 You chose your college or university based on certain expectations, and you've been enrolled long enough now to have some idea about whether those expectations have been met. In other words, you are something of an expert about the "consumer benefits" your school can offer prospective students.

Your task: In a team of four students, interview six other students who are not taking this business communication course. Try to get a broad sample of demographics and psychographics, including students in a variety of majors and programs. Ask these students (1) why they chose this college or university and

(2) whether the experience has met their expectations so far. To ensure the privacy of your respondents, do not record their names with their answers. Each member of the team should then answer these same two questions, so that you have responses from a total of ten students.

After compiling the responses (you might use Google Docs or a similar collaboration tool so that everyone on the team has easy access to the information), analyze them as a team to look for any recurring "benefit themes." Is it the quality of the education? Research opportunities? Location? The camaraderie of school sporting events? The chance to meet and study with fascinating students from a variety of backgrounds? Identify two or three strong benefits that your college or university can promise— and deliver—to prospective students.

Now nominate one member of the team to draft a short marketing message that could be posted on the Notes tab of your school's Facebook page. The message should include a catchy title that makes it clear the message is a student's perspective on why this is a great place to get a college education. When the draft is ready, the other members of the team should review it individually. Finally, meet as a team to complete the message.

MICROBLOGGING SKILLS

25. Message Strategies: Marketing and Sales Messages; Media Skills: Microblogging [LO-4], Chapter 7 Effective microblogging messages emphasize clarity and conciseness— and so do effective sales messages.

Your task: Find the website of any product that can be ordered online (any product you find interesting and that is appropriate to use for a class assignment). Adapt the information on the website, using your own words, and write four tweets to promote the product. The first should get your audience's attention (with an intriguing benefit claim, for example), the second should build audience interest by providing some support for the claim you made in the first message, the third should increase readers' desire to have the product by layering on one or two more buyer benefits, and the fourth should motivate readers to take action to place an order. Your first three tweets can be up to 140 characters, but the fourth should be limited to 120 to accommodate a URL (you don't need to include the URL in your message, however).

If your class is set up with private Twitter accounts, use your private account to send your messages. Otherwise, email your four messages to your instructor or post them on your class blog, as your instructor directs.

PART 4 Supporting Messages with Quality Information

CHAPTER 11 Finding, Evaluating, and Processing Information

CHAPTER 12 Designing Visual Communication

Follow a straightforward process for finding and analyzing information, and your readers will learn to trust your messages because they'll know you support your conclusions and recommendations with reliable information. The second major way to support your messages is with clear and compelling visuals. In fact, the visual presentation of information is one of the most exciting developments in business communication today. Even if you have no background in design, by following a few basic principles you can create powerful images to bolster your written messages.

Finding, Evaluating, and Processing Information

LEARNING OBJECTIVES After studying this chapter, you will be able to

1 Describe an effective process for conducting business research

2 Define *secondary research* and explain how to evaluate, locate, and document information sources

3 Define *primary research* and outline the steps involved in conducting surveys and interviews

4 Describe the major tasks involved in processing research results

5 Explain how to summarize research results and present conclusions and recommendations

MyBcommLab Test your mastery of this chapter and its Learning Objectives. Visit mybcommlab.com to apply what you've learned in Document Makeovers and interactive simulation scenarios.

COMMUNICATION CLOSE-UP AT TESCO

British retail giant Tesco relies on extensive audience research to plan and craft its consumer messages.

www.tesco.com

Most consumers enjoy the benefits of stiff price competition among their local grocery stores, but the competition is anything but enjoyable for grocery retailers. In the United States, the average grocery store's after-tax profit margin hovers around 1 percent. With so little room for error, grocers need to stay on top of consumer behavior to make sure they offer the right mix of products at the right prices.

Tesco, the leading grocery retailer in the United Kingdom, is not only surviving but thriving in this tough industry. Under the leadership of Richard Brasher, the company's top marketing executive in the United Kingdom, Tesco devotes considerable effort to acquiring and processing information about its customers, information that is used in a variety of documents to drive both strategic and tactical decisions.

For example, when demographic research indicated a growing number of immigrants from Poland to the UK, the store reached out to Polish-speaking consumers to learn more about their wants and needs. After a successful experiment in a few stores, Tesco expanded its Polish foods selection to roughly a hundred other stores. In another instance, the marketing team couldn't figure out why flowers and wine had become such hot sellers during a particular week at the beginning of summer that didn't coincide with any regular holidays. Analysis of sales data revealed that families were buying these items as gifts for their children's teachers at the end of the school year, so the company responded by making sure these items were stocked in plentiful supply during that week.

Tesco is now busy applying its information-driven approach to the competitive U.S. market. After studying the market for two decades, the company made its move in 2007 and now has more than 50 Fresh & Easy Neighborhood Markets in California, Nevada, and Arizona. True to form, Tesco is emphasizing research and information every step of the way in every facet of the business. When the company approached the Phoenix-based dessert manufacturer Berto's Gelato and

Sorbet about carrying its premium gelato in Fresh & Easy stores, Berto's CEO Ed DeBartolo was amazed at the amount of information the company demanded. Tesco even sent auditors and food scientists to the Berto's facility to conduct their own research. DeBartolo so admires Tesco's emphasis on information that he has applied the giant retailer's methods to all the products his company makes. And, he says, "I want to be a Tesco supplier for life."[1]

Planning Your Research

Whether you're planning a simple blog posting or an entire business plan, you can follow the lead of Tesco (profiled in the chapter-opening Communication Close-up) and make sure your reporting, analysis, and recommendations are supported with solid research. Figure 11.1 outlines a five-step research process that will help you gather and use information efficiently; you'll learn more about these steps in the following sections.

With so much information now online, it's tempting just to punch some keywords into a search engine and then grab the first few results that show up. However, effective and efficient research requires a more thoughtful approach. Your favorite search engine might not be able to reach the webpages that have the information you need, the information might not be online at all, it might be online but not under the search terms you've used, or the information might not even exist in any form.

To maximize your chances of finding useful information and to minimize the time you spend looking for it, follow these planning steps: Familiarize yourself with the subject so that you can frame insightful questions, identify the most critical gaps in your information, and then prioritize your research needs. However, before launching any research project, be sure to take a moment or two to consider the ethics and etiquette of your approach.

MAINTAINING ETHICS AND ETIQUETTE IN YOUR RESEARCH

Your research tactics can affect both the people from whom you gather information and the people who use your results. To avoid ethical lapses, keep the following points in mind:

- **Don't force a specific outcome by skewing your research.** Approach your research with an open mind and a willingness to accept whatever you find, even if it's not what you expect or want to see.
- **Respect the privacy of your research participants.** Privacy is a contentious issue today. Businesses believe they have a right to protect their confidential information from competitors, and consumers believe they have a right to protect their personal information from businesses.

1 LEARNING OBJECTIVE

Describe an effective process for conducting business research.

Audiences expect you to support your business messages with solid research.

Researching without a plan wastes time and usually produces unsatisfactory results.

Take precautions to avoid ethical lapses in your research.

Privacy is a contentious issue in the research field today.

1 Plan	2 Locate data and information	3 Process data and information	4 Apply your findings	5 Manage information
▪ Maintain research ethics and etiquette ▪ Familiarize yourself with the subject; develop a problem statement ▪ Identify information gaps ▪ Prioritize research needs	▪ Evaluate sources ▪ Collect secondary information at the library, online, or elsewhere ▪ Document your sources ▪ Collect primary information through surveys and interviews	▪ Quote, paraphrase, or summarize textual information ▪ Analyze numerical information	▪ Summarize findings ▪ Draw conclusions ▪ Make recommendations	▪ Make research results available to others via your company's knowledge management system

Figure 11.1   The Research Process
By following a methodical research process, you can save time and money while uncovering better information.

- **Document sources and give appropriate credit.** Whether you are using published documents, personal interviews, or company records, citing your sources not only is fair to the people who created and provided the information but also helps your audience members confirm your information or explore it in more detail, if they so choose.
- **Respect the intellectual property and digital rights of your sources.** For example, your research might turn up a great new way to sell services online, but that doesn't mean you're free to implement that process. It might be protected by one of the many patents that have been granted in recent years for business process models.
- **Don't extract more from your sources than they actually provide.** In other words, don't succumb to the temptation to put words in a source's mouth. For instance, if an industry expert says that a sales increase is possible, don't quote him or her as saying that a sales increase is probable.
- **Don't misrepresent who you are or what you intend to do with the research results.** One classic example of ethical lapses in this area is known as *sugging*, short for *selling under the guise of research*. For example, a firm might appear to be conducting a survey when it is in fact using the questions to identify hot sales leads. Another unethical variation on sugging is following up a real survey with sales calls, using information that respondents shared in the belief that they were only participating in a survey.[2]

Research etiquette deserves careful attention, too. For example, respect the time of anyone who agrees to be interviewed or to be a research participant and maintain courtesy throughout the interview or research process. For more information on research ethics and etiquette, review the *Code of Standards and Ethics for Survey Research* published by the Council of America Survey Research Organizations, at www.casro.org/codeofstandards.cfm.

FAMILIARIZING YOURSELF WITH THE SUBJECT

Give yourself some unstructured time at the beginning of the project to explore the general subject area, perhaps by reading industry publications and blogs, visiting competitors' websites, and interviewing experts within your organization. Scan the tables of contents and indexes of books on the subject. Some of the newest online search tools can be quite helpful in this regard; see "Innovations in Research Technology" on page 324.

When you have a basic grasp of the subject area, develop a **problem statement** that defines the problem or purpose of your research—the decision you need to make or the conclusion you need to reach at the end of the process. You may find it easier to phrase the problem as a question, such as "How can we improve customer satisfaction?" or "Does Apple's new system pose a competitive threat to us?"

IDENTIFYING INFORMATION GAPS

Your problem statement frames the purpose of your research, but it often doesn't tell you what specific information you need to find. Your next task is to dig deeper to discover the specific *information gaps* that need to be filled through research. You or someone in your company may already have some of the information you need, and you don't want to waste time or money gathering information you already have.

For instance, the question "How can we improve customer satisfaction?" is too vague because many separate factors contribute to customer satisfaction. To get useful information, you would break this topic down into specific issues, such as product reliability and customer service skills. Digging further, you may discover that you don't need to research product reliability because the company already tracks data on product repairs. However, if no one has ever measured the employees' customer service skills, you would identify that as a definite information gap.

PRIORITIZING RESEARCH NEEDS

Prioritizing your research needs is important because you won't have the time or money to answer every question you might have. Moreover, if you'll be using interviewers or surveys, you'll need to limit the number of questions you ask so that you don't consume more time

---

Don't automatically assume that you can use all the ideas and information you find online.

MyBcommLab

- Access this chapter's simulation entitled How to Find, Interpret, and Use Business Data Effectively, located at mybcommlab.com.

Avoid false starts and blind alleys by familiarizing yourself with new subject areas before you start your research.

The problem statement defines the purpose of your research and guides your investigation.

Focus your research by identifying the most important gaps in your information.

You usually won't have enough time or money to answer every question that comes to mind, so setting priorities is a must.

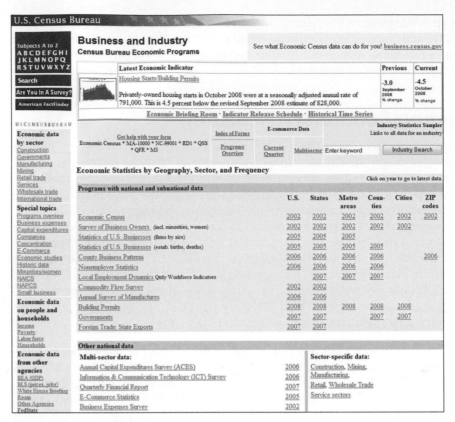

Figure 11.2   Getting Information from Reliable Sources
The U.S. Census Bureau is a trusted source of many types of facts and figures about the people and businesses in the United States.

- **Are all claims supported with evidence?** Are opinions presented as facts? Does the writer make broad claims, such as "most people believe . . ." without citing any surveys to prove his or her point?
- **Do the source's claims stand up to logical scrutiny?** Finally, step back and ask whether the information makes sense. If that little voice in your head says that something sounds suspicious, listen!

You probably won't have time to conduct a thorough background check on all your sources, so focus your efforts on the most important or most suspicious pieces of information.

LOCATING SOURCES

Start your research by conducting secondary research first.

Even if you intend to eventually conduct primary research, start with a review of any available secondary research. Inside the company, you might be able to find a variety of documents prepared for other projects that offer helpful information. Be sure to ask whether your company has a *knowledge management system.* (See "Managing Information" on page 333 for more on this topic.) Outside the company, you can choose from a wide range of print and online resources, some of which are included in Table 11.1. (Of course, the list in Table 11.1 represents a tiny fraction of the secondary resources available.)[3] For instance, if you want to know more about a specific company, one of the first things you'll need to find out is whether the company is public (sells shares of stock to the general public) or private. Public corporations, which are required to submit extensive financial reports to government agencies, generally have more information available than private companies.

REAL-TIME UPDATES
Learn More by Reading This Article

10 reasons you should not cite Wikipedia in your research

Find out how the popular encyclopedia can be useful in research— but why you should not rely on it as a primary source. Go to http:// real-timeupdates.com/bct11 and click on "Learn More." If you are using MyBcommLab, you can access Real-Time Updates within each chapter or under Student Study Tools.

than people are willing to give. One simple way to prioritize is to divide your questions into "need to know" and "nice to know" and then toss out all the "nice to know" questions. If you start with a technique such as information gap analysis, you will get a clear idea of the information you truly need to collect.

Conducting Secondary Research

With a clear plan and careful prioritization, you're ready to conduct research—and the first step is to see whether anyone else has already done some or all of the research you need. Consulting research that was done previously for another purpose is considered **secondary research**. The sources for such information include print and online periodicals, online databases, books, and other research reports. (Some companies specialize in reports on particular industries, companies, technologies, market regions, and other subjects.) Don't let the name *secondary* fool you, though. You want to start with secondary research because it can save you considerable time and money, although you may have to pay to see someone else's results. In contrast, **primary research** (see page 325) is new research done specifically for the current project. Primary sources include surveys, interviews, observations, and experiments.

2   LEARNING OBJECTIVE

Define *secondary research* and explain how to evaluate, locate, and document information sources.

Primary research contains information that you gather specifically for a new research project; secondary research contains information that others have gathered for other purposes.

EVALUATING SOURCES

No matter where you're searching, it is your responsibility to separate quality information from unreliable junk, so you don't taint your results or damage your reputation. Social media have complicated this challenge by making many new sources of information available. On the positive side, independent sources communicating through blogs, wikis, Twitter, user-generated content sites, and podcasting channels can provide valuable and unique insights, often from experts whose voices might never be heard otherwise. On the negative side, these nontraditional information sources often lack the editorial boards and fact checkers commonly used in traditional publishing. You cannot assume that the information you find in blogs and other sources is accurate, objective, and current. Answer the following questions about each piece of material:

Evaluate your sources carefully to avoid embarrassing and potentially damaging mistakes.

- **Does the source have a reputation for honesty and reliability?** Naturally, you'll feel more comfortable using information from an established source that has a reputation for accuracy (see Figure 11.2 on page 318). But don't let your guard down completely; even the finest reporters and editors can make mistakes. For sources that are new or relatively unknown, your safest bet is to corroborate anything you learn with information from several other sources.
- **Is the source potentially biased?** The individual or organization providing the information might have a particular bias or point of view regarding the information and its context. Such bias is neither inherently bad nor unethical, but you need to be aware of it so that you can interpret the information you find.
- **What is the purpose of the material?** Was the material designed to inform others of new research, advance a position, or stimulate discussion? Was it designed to promote or sell a product? Be sure to distinguish among advertising, advocating, and informing.
- **Is the author credible?** Find out whether the person or the publisher is well known in the field. Is the author an amateur? Merely someone with an opinion?
- **Where did the source get its information?** Many sources of secondary information get their material from other secondary sources, removing you even further from the original data.
- **Can you verify the material independently?** Verification can uncover biases or mistakes—which is particularly important when the information goes beyond simple facts to include projections, interpretations, and estimates. If you can't verify critical information, let your audience know that.
- **Is the material current?** Make sure you are using the most current information available by checking the publication or posting date.
- **Is the material complete?** Have you accessed the entire document or only a selection from it? If it's a selection, which parts were excluded? Do you need more detail?

Let your readers know if you were unable to verify critical pieces of information obtained in your research.

TABLE 11.1 | **Important Resources for Business Research**

COMPANY, INDUSTRY, AND PRODUCT RESOURCES (URLs are provided for online resources)

AnnualReports.com (www.annualreports.com). Free access to annual reports from thousands of public companies.

Brands and Their Companies/Companies and Their Brands. Contains data on more than 430,000 consumer products and 100,000 manufacturers, importers, marketers, and distributors. Also available as an online database; ask at your library.

CNN/Money (http://money.cnn.com). News, analysis, and financial resources covering companies, industries, and world markets.

D&B Directories. A variety of directories, including *America's Corporate Families* (ownership connections among companies), *Business Rankings* (25,000 leading companies), *Directory of Service Companies* (more than 50,000 companies in the service sector), and *Industrial Guide* (more than 120,000 manufacturing companies).

Hoover's Handbook of American Business. Profiles of 750 influential public and private corporations.

Hoover's Online (www.hoovers.com). Database of millions of companies worldwide, including in-depth coverage of thousands of leading companies around the world. Basic information available free; in-depth information requires a subscription.

Manufacturing and Distribution USA. Data on thousands of companies in the manufacturing, wholesaling, and retailing sectors.

NAICS Codes (www.census.gov/eos/www/naics). North American Industry Classification System.

Reference USA. Concise information on millions of U.S. companies; subscription database.

SEC filing (www.sec.gov/edgar.shtml). SEC filings, including 10Ks, 10Qs, annual reports, and prospectuses for U.S. public firms.

Standard & Poor's NetVantage. Comprehensive range of directories and databases focusing on publicly traded companies and their industries and markets.

ThomasNet (www.thomasnet.com). Information on thousands of U.S. manufacturers, indexed by company name and product.

RESEARCH DIRECTORIES AND INDEXES

Books in Print. Database indexes nearly 20 million book, audio book, and video titles from around the world. Available in print and professional online versions.

Directories in Print. Information on more than 15,000 business and industrial directories.

Encyclopedia of Associations. Index of thousands of associations, listed by broad subject category, specific subject, association, and location. Available as an online database as well.

Reader's Guide to Periodical Literature. Classic index of general-interest magazines, categorized by subject and author; also available in electronic format, including a version with the full text of thousands of articles.

TRADEMARKS AND PATENTS

Official Gazette of the United States Patent and Trademark Office (www.uspto.gov).Weekly publication (one for trademarks and one for patents) providing official record of newly assigned trademarks and patents, product descriptions, and product names.

United States Patent and Trademark Office (www.uspto.gov). Trademark and patent information records.

STATISTICS AND OTHER BUSINESS DATA

Bureau of Economic Analysis (www.bea.gov). Large collection of economic and government data.

Europa—The European Union Online (http://europa.eu/index_en.htm). A portal that provides up-to-date coverage of current affairs, legislation, policies, and EU statistics.

FedStats (www.fedstats.gov). Access to a full range of statistics and information from more than 70 U.S. government agencies.

Key Business Ratios (Dun & Bradstreet). Industry, financial, and performance ratios.

Information Please Almanac. Compilation of broad-range statistical data, with strong focus on labor force.

Annual Statement Studies. Industry, financial, and performance ratios published by the Risk Management Association.

Statistical Abstract of the United States (www.census.gov). Annual compendium of U.S. economic, social, political, and industrial statistics.

The World Almanac and Book of Facts. Facts on economic, social, educational, and political events for major countries.

U.S. Bureau of Labor Statistics (www.bls.gov). Extensive national and regional information on labor and business, including employment, industry growth, productivity, the Consumer Price Index (CPI), and the overall U.S. economy.

U.S. Census Bureau (www.census.gov). Demographic data and analysis on consumers and businesses based on census results.

COMMERCIAL DATABASES (Require subscriptions; check with your school library)

ABI/INFORM Trade & Industry. Access to more than 750 periodicals and newsletters that focus on specific trades or industries.

Business Source Premier (Ebsco). Access to a variety of databases on a wide range of disciplines from leading information providers.

ProQuest Dialog. Hundreds of databases that include areas such as business and finance, news and media, medicine, pharmaceuticals, reference, social sciences, government and regulation, science and technology, and more.

ProQuest. Thousands of periodicals and newspapers with extensive archives.

HighBeam Research. Thousands of full-text newspaper, magazine, and newswire sources, plus maps and photographs.

Gale Business & Company Resource Center. A comprehensive research tool designed for undergraduate and graduate students, job searchers, and investors; offers a wide variety of information on companies and industries.

LexisNexis. Several thousand databases covering legal, corporate, government, and academic subjects.

If your company doesn't have an in-house research librarian, consider beginning your search for secondary information at the nearest public or university library.

Finding Information at the Library

Libraries offer information and resources you can't find anywhere else—including research librarians who can show you how to plan and conduct effective searches.

Public, corporate, and university libraries offer an enormous array of business books, electronic databases, newspapers, periodicals, directories, almanacs, and government publications. Some of these printed sources provide information that is not available online, and some of the online sources provide information that is available by subscription. Don't assume that you can find everything you need through your own online research. Libraries are also where you'll find one of your most important resources: librarians. Reference librarians are skilled in research strategies and can often help you find obscure information you can't find on your own. They can also direct you to many sources of business information. Also, many library websites now have a business portal, with links to helpful resources and advice on finding information.

Whether you're trying to locate information in printed materials or in databases, each type of resource serves a special function:

- **Newspapers and periodicals.** Libraries offer access to a wide variety of popular magazines, general business magazines, *trade journals* (which provide information about specific professions and industries), and *academic journals* (which provide research-oriented articles from researchers and educators). Check the library's website or ask a librarian to see which periodicals are available in print or electronic formats.
- **Business books.** Although less timely than newspapers and periodicals, business books provide in-depth coverage of a variety of business topics. Many libraries now offer online access to their card catalogs so you can see if they have specific titles in their collections.
- **Directories.** Thousands of directories are published in print and electronic formats in the United States, and many include membership information for all kinds of professions, industries, and special-interest groups.
- **Almanacs and statistical resources.** Almanacs are handy guides to factual and statistical information about countries, politics, the labor force, and so on. One of the most extensive, the *Statistical Abstract of the United States*, published annually by the U.S. Department of Commerce, contains statistics about occupations, government, population, health, business, crime, and the environment (also available online at www .census.gov).

Local, state, and federal government agencies publish a huge array of information that is helpful to business researchers.

- **Government publications.** Information on laws, court decisions, tax questions, regulatory issues, and other governmental concerns is often available in collections of government documents. A librarian can direct you to the information you want.
- **Electronic databases.** Databases offer vast collections of searchable information, often in specific areas, such as business, law, science, technology, and education. Some libraries offer remote online access to some or all databases; for others, you need to visit in person.

Finding Information Online

Much of the information online has not been subjected to the same quality controls common in traditional offline publishing.

The Internet can be a tremendous source of business information, provided that you know how to approach a search, where to look, and how to use the tools available (see Figure 11.3). Roughly speaking, the tools fall into two categories: those you can use to actively *search* for existing information and those you can use to *monitor* selected sources for new information. (Some tools can perform both functions.)

To be a successful online researcher, you need to expand your toolkit beyond the popular search engines.

Online Search Tools The most familiar search tools are general-purpose **search engines**, such as Google and Bing, which scan millions of websites to identify individual webpages that contain a specific word or phrase and then attempt to rank the results from most useful to least useful. Search engines have the advantage of scanning millions or billions of individual webpages, and the best engines use powerful ranking algorithms to present the pages that are probably the most relevant to your search request. Table 11.2 on page 322 lists some of the most popular search engines, directories, metacrawlers, and specialized search tools available today.

Today's search engines are powerful tools, but they still have important limitations.

For all their ease and power, conventional search engines have three primary shortcomings: (1) no human editors are involved to evaluate the quality or ranking of the search results; (2) various engines use different search techniques, so they often find different material; and

Google Book Search   information architecture   [Search Books]   My library | Sign in

About this book | Preview this book | **Information Architecture for the World Wide Web** By Louis Rosenfeld, Peter Morville

Page 34   ◄ ►   reading   [Go]

« Summary

Page 33
... berrypicking techniques for the online search interface" (in Online Review, vol.13, no.5, 1989), is required **reading** for every information architect. ...

Page 85
Yet the statistics closer to the top of the page don't merit the same treatment, as most readers could visually distinguish these without actually **reading** ...

Page 227
Sorry, this page's content is restricted.

Page 228
... **reading** ...

Page 232
Sorry, this page's content is restricted.

Page 259
Sorry, this page's content is restricted.

Page 267
Sorry, this page's content is restricted.

Page 294
Sorry, this page's content is restricted.

Page 321
Information architecture is not something you can pick up by **reading** a couple of books and taking a class. We apologize for the soapbox rant, ...

Page 338
... many minutes per day an employee would save, or how many more sales a redesigned shopping cart would convert, we are

Figure 3-4. The "berry-picking" model of how users move through an information system

The berry-picking diagram looks messy, much more so than the "too-simple" model. It should; that's the way our minds often work. After all, we're not automatons.

If the berry-picking model is common to your site's users, you'll want to look for ways to support moving easily from search to browse and back again. Yahoo! provides one such integrated approach to consider: you can search within the subcategories you find through browsing, as shown in Figure 3-5. And you can browse through categories that you find by searching, as shown in Figure 3-6.

Another useful model is the "pearl-growing" approach. Users start with one or a few good documents that are exactly what they need. They want to get "more like this one." To meet this need, Google and many other search engines allow users to do just that: Google provides a command called "Similar pages" next to each search result. A similar approach is to allow users to link from a "good" document to documents indexed with the same keywords. In sites that contain scientific papers and other documents that are heavy with citations, you can find other papers that share many of the same citations as yours or that have been co-cited with the one you like. These are all architectural approaches for getting "more like this one."

Corporate portals often utilize a "two-step" model. Confronted with an intranet consisting of links to perhaps hundreds of departmental subsites, users want to first

Figure 11.3   Google Book Search
The ability to search through printed texts electronically is a significant advantage for researchers in all subject areas.

(3) search engines can't reach all the content on some websites (this part of the Internet is sometimes called the *hidden Internet* or the *deep Internet*).

A variety of tools are available to overcome the three main weaknesses of general-purpose search engines, and you should consider using one or more of them in your business research. First, "human-powered search engines" such as Mahalo (www.mahalo.com) offer manually compiled results for popular search queries that aim to provide more accurate and more meaningful information, although for a much narrower range of topics than a regular search engine.[4] Similarly, **web directories**, such as the Open Directory Project (www.dmoz.org) and Internet Public Library (www.ipl.org) use human editors to categorize and evaluate websites. A variety of other directories focus on specific media types, such as blogs or podcasts.

Second, *metacrawlers* or *metasearch engines* (such as Bovée and Thill's Web Search, at http://businesscommunicationblog.com/websearch) help overcome the differences among search engines by formatting your search request for multiple search engines, making it easy to find a broader range of results. With a few clicks, you can compare results from multiple search engines to make sure you are getting a broad view of the material.

Third, **online databases** help address the challenge of the hidden Internet by offering access to newspapers, magazines, journals, electronic copies of books, and other resources often not available with standard search engines. Some of these databases offer free access to the public, but others require a subscription (check with your library). Also, a variety of

REAL-TIME UPDATES
Learn More by Reading This Article

See your way into the hidden Internet

These innovative search tools can access valuable information beyond the reach of conventional search engines. Go to http://real-timeupdates.com/bct11 and click on "Learn More." If you are using MyBcommLab, you can access Real-Time Updates within each chapter or under Student Study Tools.

Web directories benefit from having human editors evaluate and select websites.

Metacrawlers can save you time by using multiple search engines at once.

Online databases give you access to some the most important resources that search engines usually can't reach: millions of newspaper, magazine, and journal articles.

TABLE 11.2	The Broad Spectrum of Online Search Tools		
General-Purpose Search Engines			
AOL Search	http://search.aol.com	Bing	www.bing.com
AlltheWeb	www.alltheweb.com	Google	www.google.com
AltaVista	www.altavista.com	Yahoo! Search	http://search.yahoo.com
Ask.com	www.ask.com		
Metacrawlers, Clustering Engines, and Hybrid Sites			
Bovée & Thill Web Search	http://businesscommunicationblog.com/websearch/	Search.com	www.search.com
Dogpile	www.dogpile.com	SurfWax	www.surfwax.com
ixquick	www.ixquick.com	WebBrain	www.webbrain.com
Mamma	www.mamma.com	WebCrawler	www.webcrawler.com
MetaCrawler	www.metacrawler.com	ZapMeta	www.zapmeta.com
Web Directories and Online Libraries			
About	www.about.com	Internet Public Library	www.ipl.org
Answers.com	www.answers.com	Library of Congress	www.loc.gov/rr/business
CEOExpress	http://ceoexpress.com	Library Spot	www.libraryspot.com
Digital Librarian	www.digital-librarian.com/business.html	Open Directory Project	www.dmoz.com
Google Directory	www.google.com/dirhp	Questia (requires subscription)	www.questia.com
INFOMINE	http://infomine.ucr.edu	USA.gov (U.S. government portal)	www.usa.gov
News Search Engines and Social Tagging Sites			
10 × 10	http://tenbyten.org	NewsNow	www.newsnow.co.uk
Delicious	http://delicious.com	Newseum	www.newseum.org
Digg	www.digg.com	WorldNews	www.wn.com
Google News	http://news.google.com	Yahoo! News	http://news.yahoo.com
Blog, Video, and Podcast Search Engines and Directories			
American Rhetoric (speeches)	www.americanrhetoric.com	Podcast Alley	www.podcastalley.com
Bing videos	www.bing.com/videos	Podcast Bunker	www.podcastbunker.com
blinkx	www.blinkx.com	Podcast Network	www.thepodcastnetwork.com
Bloglines	www.bloglines.com	podscope	www.podscope.com
BlogPulse	www.blogpulse.com	Technorati	www.technorati.com
Google Blog search	http://blogsearch.google.com	Yahoo! Video search	http://video.search.yahoo.com
Google Video search	http://video.google.com	YouTube	www.youtube.com
Periodical and Book Search Engines			
Google Scholar search	http://scholar.google.com	Google Book search	http://books.google.com

specialized search engines now exist to reach various parts of the hidden Internet (see the Real-Time Updates item on the previous page).

To stay up to date on a research topic, subscribe to RSS feeds, search engine alerts, or Twitter updates from knowledgeable individuals.

Online Monitoring Tools   One of the most powerful aspects of online research is the ability to automatically monitor selected sources for new information so that you can get new information without doing manual searches repeatedly. The possibilities include subscribing to newsfeeds from blogs and websites, following people on Twitter and other microblogs, setting up alerts on search engines and online databases, and using specialized monitors such as TweetBeep (http://tweetbeep.com) and TweetDeck (www.tweetdeck.com) to track tweets that mention specific companies or other terms.

Exercise some care when setting up monitoring tools, however, because it's easy to get overwhelmed by the flood of information. Remember that you can always go back and search your information sources if you need to gather additional information.

Search Tips   Search engines, metacrawlers, and databases offer a variety of ways to find information. Unfortunately, no two of them work in exactly the same way, and you have to learn how to use each one most effectively. This learning may take a few extra minutes at the beginning of your research, but it could save you hours of lost time later on—and save you from embarrassing oversights.

The most basic form of searching is a *keyword search*, in which the engine or database attempts to find items that include all the words you enter. A *Boolean search* expands on this capability by using search operators that let you define a query with greater precision. Common operators include AND (the search must include both words before and after the AND), OR (the search can include either or both words), and NOT (the search ignores items with whatever word comes after NOT). For example:

- *corporate AND profits* finds webpages or database entries that contain both *corporate* and *profits.*
- *corporate OR profits* finds items that contain either *corporate* or *profits* but not necessarily both.
- *corporate NOT profits* finds items that contain *corporate* but excludes all those that contain the word *profits.*

Boolean searches can also include operators that let you find a particular word in close proximity to other words or use *wildcards* to find similar spellings (such as *profit, profits,* and *profitability*).

As a simpler alternative to Boolean searches, some search engines and databases offer *natural language searches,* which let you ask questions in normal, everyday English. (Natural language is what humans speak, as opposed to the languages computers speak.) For example, "Which video game companies are the most profitable?" is a natural language query. Be aware that some search tools let you choose keyword, Boolean, or natural language searches, so make sure you know which method you're using.

Several search tools offer *forms-based searches* that help you create powerful queries without needing to learn any special techniques.[5] As the name implies, you simply fill out an online form that typically lets you specify parameters such as date ranges, words to include or exclude, language, Internet domain name, and even file and media types. To access these forms, click on "advanced search" or a similar option.

To make the best use of any search engine or database, keep the following points in mind:

- **Think before you search.** The neatly organized results you get from a search engine can create the illusion that the Internet is a neatly organized warehouse of all the information in the universe, but the reality is far different. The Internet is an incomplete, unorganized hodge-podge of millions of independent websites with information that ranges in value from priceless to utter rubbish. After you have identified what you need to know, spend a few moments thinking about where that information might be found, how it might be structured, and what terms various websites might use to describe it.
- **Read the instructions.** You can usually find a Help or Support page that explains both basic and advanced functions, with advice on how to use a particular tool most effectively.
- **Pay attention to the details.** Details can make all the difference in a search. For example, if you use multiple words in your search phrase, Bing advises you to put the most important words first because word order affects search results.[6]
- **Review the search and display options carefully.** When searching in databases, for instance, pay close attention to whether you are searching in the title, author, subject, or document field and whether the search is limited to full-text documents or full text plus

REAL-TIME UPDATES
Learn More by Reading This Article

A practical guide to selecting the best online search tools

Different research projects require different search tools, and this article provides great advice for selecting search tools based on the requirements of each project. Go to http://real-timeupdates.com/bct11 and click on "Learn More." If you are using MyBcommLab, you can access Real-Time Updates within each chapter or under Student Study Tools.

Make sure you know how each search engine, directory, database, or metacrawler works; they work in different ways, and you can get unpredictable results if you don't know how each one operates.

Search engine results can create the illusion that the Internet is a complete, well-organized warehouse of reliable information; it is not.

abstracts. Each choice will return different results. And when the results are displayed, verify the presentation order; results might be sorted by date or by relevance.

- **Try variations of terms.** If you can't find what you're looking for, try abbreviations (*CEO, CPA*), synonyms (*man, male*), related terms (*child, adolescent, youth*), different spellings (*dialog, dialogue*), singular and plural forms (*woman, women*), nouns and adjectives (*manager, management, managerial*), and open and compound forms (*online, on line, on-line*). Some search engines search for such synonyms automatically.
- **Adjust the scope of your search, if needed.** If a search yields little or no information, broaden your search by specifying fewer terms. Conversely, if you're inundated with too many hits, use more terms to narrow your search. For example, *Apple* yields many more hits than *Apple iPod*, which yields many more than *Apple iPod nano*.
- **Look beyond the first few pages of results.** Don't assume that the highest-ranking results are the best sources for you. In general, materials that haven't been optimized for search engines won't rank as highly, but they may be far better for your purposes.

Take advantage of the latest research technologies, including desktop and enterprise search engines, research and content managers, social bookmarking sites, newsfeeds, and new types of search engines.

Innovations in Research Technology   Search technologies continue to evolve rapidly, so look for new ways to find the information you need. Some tools search or monitor specific media or channels in better ways, whereas others approach search in new ways. For instance, Yolink (**www.yolink.com**) finds webpages like a regular search engine does but also searches through documents and webpages that are linked to those first-level results.[7]

Other powerful search tools include *desktop search engines* that search all the files on your personal computer, *enterprise search engines* (see Figure 11.4) that search all the computers on a company's network, *research and content managers* such as the free Zotero browser extension (**www.zotero.com**), and *social tagging* or *bookmarking sites* such as Digg (**http://digg.com**) and Delicious (**http://delicious.com**).

For more on the latest developments in online research tools, visit **http://realtimeupdates.com/bct11** and click on Chapter 11.

DOCUMENTING YOUR SOURCES

Proper documentation of the sources you use is an ethical responsibility—and an important resource for your readers.

Documenting the sources you use in your writing serves three important functions: It properly and ethically credits the person who created the original material; it shows your audience that you have sufficient support for your message; and, as mentioned earlier, it

Figure 11.4   Enterprise Search Engines
Enterprise search engines can do deep searches across an entire corporate network to help employees find a wide variety of information resources.

helps your readers explore your topic in more detail, if desired. Your results might be used by people long after you conducted the research, and these people won't always have the opportunity to query you in person for more information.

Be sure to take advantage of source documentation tools whenever you can, to help ensure that you accurately track all your sources. Most word-processing programs can automatically track and number endnotes for you, and you can use the "table of authorities" feature to create a bibliography of all the sources you've used. A wide variety of *citation management* or *reference management* tools are available with popular web browsers.

You may document your sources through footnotes, endnotes, or some similar system (see Appendix B, "Documentation of Report Sources"). Whatever method you choose, documentation is necessary for books, articles, tables, charts, diagrams, song lyrics, scripted dialogue, letters, speeches, and anything else you take from someone else, including ideas and information that you've re-expressed through paraphrasing or summarizing.

However, you do not have to cite a source for general knowledge or for specialized knowledge that's generally known among your readers. For example, almost everyone knows that Nike is a large sporting goods company and that computers are pervasive in business today. You can say so on your own authority, even if you've read an article in which the author says the same thing.

Chapter 1 notes that copyright law covers the expression of creative ideas, and copyrights can apply to a wide range of materials, including reports and other documents, web content, movies, musical compositions, lectures, computer programs, and even choreographed dance routines. Copyright protection is initiated the moment the expression is put into fixed form. Copyright law does not protect such elements as titles, names, short phrases, slogans, familiar symbols, or lists of ingredients or contents. It also doesn't protect ideas, procedures, methods, systems, processes, concepts, principles, discoveries, or devices, although it does cover their description, explanation, or illustration.[8] (Note that many of the entities that aren't covered under copyright law are covered under other legal protections, such as patents for devices and processes and trademarks for slogans.)

> Copyright protections may prevent you from using some materials without obtaining permission from the copyright holder.

Merely crediting the source is not always enough. According to the *fair use doctrine*, you can use other people's work only as long as you don't unfairly prevent them from benefiting as a result. For example, if you reproduce someone else's copyrighted questionnaire in a report you're writing, even if you identify the source thoroughly, you may be preventing the author from selling a copy of that questionnaire to your readers.

In general, avoid relying to a great extent on someone else's work. However, when you can't avoid it, contact the copyright holder (usually the author or publisher) for permission to reprint. You'll often be asked to pay a fee.

For more information on copyrights, visit www.copyright.gov or www.creative commons.org.

Conducting Primary Research

If secondary research can't provide the information and insights you need, your next choice is to gather the information yourself with primary research. The two most common primary research methods are surveys and interviews, the focus of this section. Other primary techniques include *observations* and *experiments*, such as Tesco's test-marketing study with Polish foods (see page 314).

 3   LEARNING OBJECTIVE

Define *primary research* and outline the steps involved in conducting surveys and interviews.

> Surveys and interviews are the most common primary research tools.

GATHERING INFORMATION WITH SURVEYS

Surveys can provide invaluable insights on a wide variety of business topics, but they are useful only when they're reliable and valid. A survey is *reliable* if it produces identical results when repeated. A survey is *valid* if it measures what it's intended to measure. To conduct a survey that generates reliable and valid results, you need to choose research participants carefully and develop an effective set of questions. (A good research handbook can guide you through the process of selecting a sufficient number of representative participants. For important surveys on strategically important topics with lots at stake, you're usually better off hiring a research specialist who knows how to avoid errors during planning, execution, and analysis.)

For a survey to produce valid results, it must be based on a representative sample of the population of interest.

When selecting the people who'll participate in your survey, the most critical task is getting a representative sample of the population in question. For instance, if you want to know how U.S. consumers feel about a particular product or company, you can't just randomly survey people in the local mall and assume that their answers represent the opinions of everyone in the country. Different types of consumers shop at different times of the day and on different days of the week, some consumers don't shop at malls regularly, and many who do won't stop to talk with researchers.

To develop an effective survey questionnaire, start with the information gaps you identified earlier and then break these points into specific questions, choosing an appropriate type of question for each point. (Figure 11.5 shows various types of survey questions.) The following guidelines will help you produce results that are both valid and reliable:[9]

- Provide clear instructions to make sure people can answer every question correctly.
- Don't ask for information that people can't be expected to remember, such as how many times they went grocery shopping in the past year.
- Keep the questionnaire short and easy to answer; don't expect people to give you more than 10 or 15 minutes of their time.
- Whenever possible, formulate questions that provide answers that are easy to analyze. Numbers and facts are easier to summarize than opinions, for instance.

Provide clear instructions in questionnaires to prevent incorrect or ambiguous answers.

- Avoid *leading questions* that could bias your survey. If you ask, "Do you prefer that we stay open in the evenings for customer convenience?" you'll no doubt get a "yes." Instead, ask, "What time of day do you normally do your shopping?"
- Avoid ambiguous descriptors such as "often" or "frequently." Such terms mean different things to different people.
- Avoid compound questions such as "Do you read books and magazines?" People who read one but not the other won't know whether to answer yes or no.
- Make the survey *adaptive*. With an online survey, you can program the software to branch automatically based on audience inputs. Not only does this sort of real-time adaptation deliver better answers, but it reduces frustration for survey respondents as well.[10]

COMMUNICATION MISCUES　The Art of the Question

Poorly worded questions can produce unintended and unforeseen results. For example, assume that you receive regular surveys from the human resources department in your company, dealing with such issues as productivity, employee satisfaction, and employee benefits. This month's survey contains the following questions:

1. How would you rate the food in the company cafeteria? (Choose one.)

   Fantastic
   Nutritious
   Delicious
   Filling
   A good value for the money

2. What is your opinion of the improved insurance sign-up process we instituted last month?

3. If the dental benefits plan were modified relative to the current plan, wherein employees are expected to pay a $20 copayment at the time of each visit, with benefits subject to the normal companywide 80 percent co-insurance standard, provided the co-insurance ratio did not drop, would you continue to participate in the plan if copayment were increased to $50 but counterbalanced by a reduction in your monthly payroll deduction amount? _____ yes _____ no

4. Division supervisors continue to report problems with employees reporting for work late. Do the employees in your department tend to report for work

   Always on time
   Mostly on time
   Usually on time
   Occasionally late
   Frequently late

5. How many times did you personally report for work late last year?

6. Do you ever feel poorly trained or insufficiently motivated in your job? _____ yes _____ no

CAREER APPLICATIONS

1. Which of these questions might result in unusable information? Why?

2. How would you help the human resources manager rewrite the questions to improve the quality of information they generate?

QUESTION TYPE	EXAMPLE
Open-ended	How would you describe the flavor of this ice cream?
Either-or	Do you think this ice cream is too rich? _____ Yes _____ No
Multiple choice	Which description best fits the taste of this ice cream? (Choose only one.) a. Delicious b. Too fruity c. Too sweet d. Too intense e. Bland f. Stale
Scale	Please mark an X on the scale to indicate how you perceive the texture of this ice cream. Too light Light Creamy Too creamy
Checklist	Which of the following ice cream brands do you recognize? (Check all that apply.) _____ Ben & Jerry's _____ Breyers _____ Carvel _____ Dreyer's _____ Häagen-Dazs
Ranking	Rank these flavors in order of your preference, from 1 (most preferred) to 5 (least preferred): _____ Vanilla _____ Cherry _____ Strawberry _____ Chocolate _____ Coconut
Short-answer	In the past 2 weeks, how many times did you buy ice cream in a grocery store? _____ In the past 2 weeks, how many times did you buy ice cream in an ice cream shop? _____

Figure 11.5   Types of Survey Questions
For each question you have in your survey, choose the type of question that will elicit the most useful answers.

MyBcommLab

Apply Figure 11.5's key concepts by revising a new document. Go to Chapter 11 in mybcommlab.com and select Document Makeovers.

Before you conduct your survey, test it on a sample group first to identify questions that might be confusing or that might generate answers you don't expect (see "Communication Miscues: The Art of the Question").

Be sure to test your survey before using it.

You have probably noticed simple polls and surveys on many websites. Online surveys (see Figure 11.6 on page 328) offer a number of advantages, including speed, cost, and the ability to adapt the question set along the way based on a respondent's answers. However, they must be designed and administered as carefully as offline surveys. For example, you can't assume that the results from a survey on your company's website reflect the attitudes, beliefs, or behaviors of the population as a whole, because the visitors to your website are almost guaranteed not to be an accurate cross-section of the entire population.

Online surveys are relatively quick and inexpensive, but they require the same care in planning and analysis as offline surveys.

Figure 11.6 **Online Survey Tools**
Online survey systems such as this one, offered by Object Planet, make it easy to create, administer, and analyze surveys.

GATHERING INFORMATION WITH INTERVIEWS

Getting in-depth information straight from an expert or an individual concerned about an issue can be a great method for collecting primary information. Interviews can dig deeper than the "hands-off" approach of surveys, and skilled interviewers can also watch for nonverbal signals that provide additional insights. Interviews can take a variety of formats, from email exchanges to group discussions. For example, Tesco invites thousands of customers to visit its stores every year for meetings known as Customer Question Time, when it asks customers how the company can serve them better.[11]

> Interviews are easy to conduct but require careful planning to produce useful results.

Be aware that the answers you receive in an interview are influenced by the types of questions you ask, by the way you ask them, and by each subject's cultural and language background. Potentially significant factors include the person's race, gender, age, educational level, and social status.[12]

Ask **open-ended questions** (such as "Why do you believe that South America represents a better opportunity than Europe for this product line?") to solicit opinions, insights, and information. Ask **closed questions** to elicit a specific answer, such as yes or no. However, don't use too many closed questions in an interview, or the experience will feel more like a simple survey and won't take full advantage of the interactive interview setting.

> Choose question types that will generate the specific types of information you need.

Think carefully about the sequence of your questions and the subject's potential answers so you can arrange questions in an order that helps uncover layers of information. Also, consider providing the person with a list of questions at least a day or two before the interview, especially if you'd like to quote your subject in writing or if your questions might require your subject to conduct research or think extensively about the answers. If you want to record the interview, ask the person ahead of time and respect his or her wishes. During the interview, be alert to new topics that you might not have considered while planning the interview, and pursue them if they will shed light on your research questions.

As soon as possible after the interview, take a few moments to write down your thoughts, go over your notes, and organize your material. Look for important themes, helpful facts or statistics, and direct quotes. If you recorded the interview, *transcribe* it (take down word for word what the person said) or take notes from the recording just as you would while listening to someone in person.

Face-to-face interviews give you the opportunity to gauge reactions to your questions and observe the nonverbal signals that accompany the answers, but interviews don't necessarily have to take place in person. For example, email interviews give subjects a chance to think through their responses thoroughly rather than rush to fit the time constraints of a face-to-face interview.[13] Also, email interviews might be the only way you will be able to access some experts.

In addition to individual interviews, business researchers can also use a form of group interview known as the **focus group**. In this format, a moderator guides a group through a series of discussion questions while the rest of the research team members observe through a one-way mirror. The key advantage of focus groups is the opportunity to learn from group dynamics as the various participants bounce ideas and questions off each other. Allowing a group to discuss topics and problems in this manner can uncover much richer information than can a series of individual interviews.[14]

As a reminder of the tasks involved in interviews, see "Checklist: Conducting Effective Information Interviews."

Face-to-face interviews give you the opportunity to gauge nonverbal responses.

Processing Data and Information

After you've collected all the necessary secondary and primary information, the next step is to transform it into the specific content you need. For simple projects, you may be able to insert your material directly into your report, presentation, or other application. However, when you have gathered a significant amount of information or raw data, you need to process the material before you can use it. This step can involve quoting, paraphrasing, or summarizing textual material; analyzing numeric data; drawing conclusions; and making recommendations.

4 LEARNING OBJECTIVE

Describe the major tasks involved in processing research results.

After you have collected your research results, the next step is to convert this into usable information.

QUOTING, PARAPHRASING, AND SUMMARIZING

You can use textual information from secondary sources in three ways. *Quoting* a source means you reproduce the material exactly as you found it (giving full credit to the source, of course). Use direct quotations when the original language will enhance your argument or when rewording the passage would reduce its impact. However, be careful with direct quotes: Using too many creates a choppy patchwork of varying styles and gives the impression that all you've done is piece together the work of other people. When quoting sources, set off shorter passages with quotation marks and set off longer passages (generally, five lines or more) as separate, indented paragraphs.

You can often maximize the impact of secondary material in your own writing by *paraphrasing* it—restating it in your own words and with your own sentence structures.[15] Paraphrasing helps you maintain consistent tone, present information using vocabulary more familiar to your audience, and avoid the choppy feel of too many quotations. Of course, you still need to credit the originator of the information, through a footnote, endnote, or in-text citation.

Quoting a source means reproducing the content exactly and indicating who created the information originally.

Paraphrasing is expressing someone else's ideas in your own words.

MyBcommLab

- Apply these key concepts by revising a new document. Go to Chapter 11 in mybcommlab.com and select Document Makeovers.

✓ Checklist   Conducting Effective Information Interviews

- Learn about the person you will be interviewing.
- Formulate your main idea to ensure effective focus.
- Choose the length, style, and organization of the interview.
- Select question types to elicit the specific information you want.
- Design each question carefully to collect useful answers.

- Limit the number of questions you ask.
- During the interview, be alert to new topics that you might want to probe.
- Consider recording the interview if the subject permits.
- Review your notes as soon as the interview ends.

To paraphrase effectively, follow these tips:[16]

- Read and reread the original passage until you fully understand its meaning.
- Restate the central ideas of the original passage using your own words.
- Check your version against the source to verify that you have not altered the meaning.
- Use quotation marks to identify any unique terms or phrases you have borrowed exactly from the source.
- Record the source accurately so that you can give proper credit if you use this material in your report.

Summarizing is similar to paraphrasing but distills the content into fewer words.

Summarizing is similar to paraphrasing but presents the gist of the material in fewer words than the original. An effective summary identifies the main ideas and major support points from your source material but leaves out minor details, examples, and other information that is less critical to your audience. Like quotations and paraphrases, summaries also require complete documentation of sources.

Of course, all three approaches require careful attention to ethics. When quoting directly, take care not to distort the original intent of the material by quoting selectively or out of context. If an interview subject said, "This market could grow dramatically next year if we invest heavily in new products," using only the phrase "this market could grow dramatically next year" in a report would be unethical.

When paraphrasing and summarizing, take care not to distort the original intent as you express the ideas in your own words and sentences. Remember that the goal is to help your audience relate to material that supports your message. Double-check your writing to make sure you didn't subconsciously skew the other writer's message to fit your own needs (see "Ethics Detective: Solving the Case of the Imaginary Good News").

ANALYZING NUMERIC DATA

Research often produces numeric data—everything from sales figures to population statistics to survey answers. By themselves, these numbers might not provide the insights you or your audience require. Are sales going up or going down? Are the age groups that represent your target markets growing or shrinking? What percentage of employees surveyed are so dissatisfied that they're ready to look for new jobs? These are the insights managers need in order to make good business decisions.

Gaining Insights

Mean, median, and mode provide insight into sets of data.

Even without advanced statistical techniques, you can use simple arithmetic to extract powerful insights from sets of research data. Three common and useful measures are shown in Table 11.3. The **mean** (which is what most people refer to when they use the term *average*) is the sum of all the items in the group divided by the number of items in that group. The **median** is the "middle of the road," or the midpoint of a series (with an equal number of items above and below). The **mode** is the number that occurs more often than any other

TABLE 11.3 | **Three Types of Data Measures: Mean, Median, and Mode**

Wilson	$ 3,000	
Green	5,000	
Carrick	6,000	
Cho	7,000	—— Mean
Keeble	7,500	—— Median
Lopes	8,500	
O'Toole	8,500	Mode
Mannix	8,500	
Caruso	9,000	
Total	$63,000	

ETHICS DETECTIVE
Solving the Case of the Imaginary Good News

To deal with a growing problem of employee turnover, your company recently hired a research firm to survey employees to find out why more of them have been leaving than in past years. You and a colleague were assigned to work with the consultants and present their findings to upper management. Neither one of you welcomed the assignment because you suspect you'll have to present information that is critical of the management team.

As you feared, the researchers deliver a mixture of news that is mostly negative:

- Seventy-eight percent of employees believe management cares more about profits than people.
- Fifty-five percent aren't sure what's expected of them anymore.
- Forty percent believe wages at the company have not kept up with the industry average.
- Thirty-eight percent think management has done a good job of responding to competitive advances.
- Fifty-two percent expect to finish their careers at the company.
- Eighty percent believe the economy is too slow to support a productive job search.

While you're poring over the report, trying to figure out how you'll present the information tomorrow, an instant message from the CEO pops up on your partner's computer, asking for a quick summary of the results. She types the following and then asks you to review it before she sends it:

> As you'd expect in a no-holds-barred investigation like this, the researchers did uncover some areas for improvements. The good news: Only 20 percent of the workforce is even considering other options, and we could reasonably expect that only a fraction of that group will leave anytime soon.

ANALYSIS

You read your partner's summary twice, but something doesn't feel quite right. Does it present an accurate summary of the research? Why or why not? What's likely to happen when you present the complete research results to the CEO after first sending this IM?

---

in a sample. It's the best answer to a question such as "What is the usual amount?" Each of these three measures can give you different insights into a set of data.

Next, look at the data to spot **trends**—definite patterns taking place over time, including growth, decline, and cyclical trends that vary between growth and decline. By examining data over a period of time, you can detect patterns and relationships that help you answer important questions.

Statistical measures and trends identify *what* is happening. To help you understand *why* those things are happening, look at **causation** (the cause-and-effect linkage between two factors, where one of them causes the other to happen) and **correlation** (the simultaneous change in two variables that you're measuring, such as customer satisfaction dropping when product reliability drops). Bear in mind that causation can be easy to assume but difficult to prove. The drop in customer satisfaction might have been caused by a new accounting system that fouled up customer invoices. To prove causation, you need to be able to isolate the suspected cause as the *only* potential source of the change in the measured effect. However, eliminating all but one possible cause isn't always feasible, so you often have to apply careful judgment to correlations. Researchers frequently explore the relationships between subsets of data using a technique called *cross-tabulation*. For instance, if you're trying to figure out why total sales rose or fell, you might look separately at sales data by age, gender, location, and product type.

> Trends identify patterns that tend to repeat over time.

> *Causation* shows cause-and-effect relationships; *correlation* indicates simultaneous changes in two variables that may not necessarily be causally related.

Guarding Against Mistakes and Misinterpretations

Numbers are easy to manipulate with spreadsheets and other computer tools, so be sure to guard against computational errors and misinterpretation of results. Double-check all calculations, and document the operation of any spreadsheets you plan to share with colleagues. Common spreadsheet mistakes to watch for include errors in math formulas, references to unintended cells in the spreadsheet (resulting in the inclusion of data you don't want or the exclusion of data you do want), and failures to verify the specific operation of the spreadsheet's built-in math functions.

In addition to watching for computer errors, step back and look at your entire set of data before proceeding with any analysis. Do the numbers make sense, based on what you

> Watch out for errors that might have crept in during collection and processing of data.

know about the subject? Are any data points suspicious? If the production numbers you've been measuring have never varied more than 10 percent month to month and then suddenly jumped 50 percent last month, is that new number real or an erroneous measurement?

Even when your data points are accurate and your analysis is technically correct, it's still possible to misinterpret or misrepresent the results. Many analysis errors require statistical expertise to identify and fix, but even without advanced skills, you can take these precautions:

- **Avoid faulty comparisons.** Make sure you compare "apples to apples" and not "apples to oranges," as the saying goes.
- **Don't push research results beyond their limits.** The temptation to extract insights and assurances that aren't really there can be quite strong, particularly in situations of great uncertainty. For instance, if you're about to recommend that your company invest millions of dollars in developing a new product, based on your consumer research, you're likely to "see" every possible justification in the data. If possible, have a trusted colleague review your data to see whether he or she extracts the same conclusions.
- **Steer clear of misleading presentations.** As you'll see in Chapter 12, even valid data can be presented in invalid ways, and it's your responsibility to make sure the visual presentation of your data is accurate.

Applying Your Findings

5 LEARNING OBJECTIVE

Explain how to summarize research results and present conclusions and recommendations.

A summary is an unbiased presentation of information regarding a particular topic, without attempts to draw conclusions or make recommendations.

After all your planning, research, and processing, you're finally ready to apply your findings. This step can involve summarizing your results, drawing conclusions based on your results, and making recommendations.

SUMMARIZING YOUR RESEARCH

A research summary is an unbiased condensation of the information uncovered in your research. ("Summary" in this context means a summary of your entire research project, not just a summary of secondary source material.) Summaries should not include opinions, conclusions, or recommendations. Summarizing is not always a simple task, and your readers will judge your ability to separate significant issues from less-significant details. Identify the main idea and the key support points; separate them from details, examples, and other supporting evidence (see Table 11.4). Focus your efforts on your audience, highlighting the

TABLE 11.4	**Summarizing Effectively**		
Original Material (116 Words)		45-Word Summary	22-Word Summary
Our facilities costs spiraled out of control last year. The 23 percent jump was far ahead of every other cost category in the company and many times higher than the 4 percent average rise for commercial real estate in the Portland metropolitan area. The rise can be attributed to many factors, but the major factors include repairs (mostly electrical and structural problems at the downtown office), energy (most of our offices are heated by electricity, the price of which has been increasing much faster than for oil or gas), and last but not least, the loss of two sublease tenants whose rent payments made a substantial dent in our cost profile for the past five years.		**Our facilities costs jumped 23 percent last year,** far ahead of every other cost category in the company and many times higher than the 4 percent local average. The major factors contributing to the increase are repairs, energy, and the loss of two sublease tenants.	**Our facilities costs jumped 23 percent last year,** primarily because of rising repair and energy costs and the loss of sublease income.
Main idea			
Major support points			
Details			

information that is most important to the person who assigned the project or to those who will be reading the report.

However, focusing on the audience doesn't mean conveying only the information your audience wants to hear. A good summary might contain nothing but bad news, if that's what your research uncovered. Even if the summary isn't pleasant, effective managers always appreciate and respect honest, complete, and perceptive information from their employees.

DRAWING CONCLUSIONS

A **conclusion** is a logical interpretation of the facts and other information in a report. Reaching good conclusions based on the evidence at hand is one of the most important skills you can develop in your business career. For a conclusion to be sound, it must meet two criteria. First, it must be based strictly on the information in your report. You shouldn't introduce any new information in your conclusion. (If something is that important, it belongs in the body of the report.) Also, you can't ignore any of the information you've presented, even if it doesn't support your conclusion. Second, the conclusion must be logical, meaning it must follow accepted patterns of inductive or deductive reasoning. Conclusions that are based on unproven premises, appeal to emotion, make hasty generalizations, or contain any other logical fallacies are not valid.

Remember that your personal values or the organization's values may also influence your conclusions; just be sure that you're aware of how these biases can affect your judgment. If a bias affects your conclusion, you should explain it to your audience. Also, don't expect all team members to examine the evidence and arrive at the same conclusion. One of the reasons for bringing additional people into a decision is to gain their unique perspectives and experiences.

Even though conclusions need to be logical, they may not automatically or obviously flow from the evidence. Many business decisions require assumptions, judgment calls, and creative thinking—in fact, the ability to see patterns and possibilities that others can't see is one of the hallmarks of innovative business leaders.

> A conclusion is a logical interpretation of research results.

MAKING RECOMMENDATIONS

Whereas a conclusion interprets information, a **recommendation** suggests what to do about the information. The following example illustrates the difference between a conclusion and a recommendation:

> A recommendation is a suggested course of action.

Conclusion	Recommendation
On the basis of its track record and current price, I believe that this company is an attractive buy.	I recommend that we offer to buy the company at a 10 percent premium over the current market value of its stock.

To be credible, recommendations must be based on logical analysis and sound conclusions. They must also be practical and acceptable to your readers, the people who have to make your recommendations work. Finally, when making a recommendation, be certain that you have adequately described the steps that come next. Don't leave your readers wondering what they need to do in order to act on your recommendation.

MANAGING INFORMATION

Conducting your research well does more than provide strong support for your own writing projects. Your individual research projects are also an important contribution to your organization's collective knowledge base. To organize information and make it readily available to everyone in the company, many firms use some form of **knowledge management (KM)**, a set of technologies, policies, and procedures that let colleagues capture and share information throughout an organization. In recent years, social media tools have been enhancing the flexibility and capability of KM systems, making it easier for more people to contribute to and benefit from shared knowledge.[17]

> Knowledge management systems help organizations share research results and other valuable information and insights.

Quick Learning Guide

MyBcommLab

CHAPTER OUTLINE

SUMMARY OF LEARNING OBJECTIVES

1 Describe an effective process for conducting business research. Begin the research process with careful planning to make sure you familiarize yourself with the subject area, identify the most important information gaps you face, and prioritize the questions you need to ask to fill those gaps. Then locate the required data and information, using primary and secondary research as needed. Process the results of your research, analyzing both textual and numeric information to extract averages, trends, and other insights. Apply your findings by summarizing information for someone else's benefit, drawing conclusions based on what you've learned, or developing recommendations. Finally, manage information effectively so that you and others can retrieve it later and reuse it in other projects.

2 Define *secondary research*, and explain how to evaluate, locate, and document information sources. Secondary research involves collecting information that was originally gathered for another research project or another effort. Secondary research is generally done before primary research, to save time and money in the event someone else has already gathered the information needed.

Information should come from a credible source that has a reputation for being honest and reliable; the source should also be unbiased. The purpose of the material should be known, and the author should be credible. The information should include references to sources (if obtained elsewhere), and it should be independently verifiable. The material should be current, complete, and supported with evidence. Finally, the information should seem logical.

The tasks involved in locating secondary sources of data and information can vary widely depending on the project, but much of your efforts will involve finding information in a corporate, public, or university library or finding information online. Libraries offer an enormous array of business books, electronic databases, newspapers, periodicals, directories, almanacs, and government publications. Some of these printed sources provide information that is not available online, and some of the online sources provide information that is available by subscription. Librarians can be a huge help when you need advice on structuring an investigation or finding specific sources.

Finding information online is often more complicated than simply plugging a few terms into a search engine. General-purpose search engines are sophisticated tools, but even when they are used wisely, they are not able to find everything on the Internet. Moreover, with no human reviewers to evaluate the quality or ranking of the search results, you can't always be sure of the quality of what you find. Human-powered search engines, web directories, metacrawlers, and online databases all complement the capabilities of general-purpose search engines. Use online monitoring tools to be alerted to new materials on topics of interest.

To make the best use of any search engine or database, think about your information needs carefully before you start searching, read and understand the instructions for using each online research tool, pay attention to the details because even minor aspects of searching can influence results dramatically, review search and display options carefully to optimize results, try variations on your search terms if you can't find what you're looking for, and try narrower or broader searches to adjust the scope of what you're looking for.

3 Define *primary research*, and outline the steps involved in conducting surveys and interviews. Primary research is research that is being conducted for the first time, and the two most common methods are surveys and interviews. Conducting a survey involves selecting a representative set of respondents from the population you are studying, developing a questionnaire using carefully written and sequenced questions, and administering the actual survey to collect information. Conducting an interview starts with learning about the person(s) you plan to interview and then formulating your main idea to make sure your interview will stay focused. Choose the length, style, and organization of the interview and then select question types to elicit the sort of information you want, with each question designed to collect useful answers. Limit your questions to the most important queries. Record the interview, if the person allows, and review your notes as soon as the interview ends.

4 Describe the major tasks involved in processing research results. In most cases, you need to process your research results in some fashion before applying them in reports and presentations. The three basic ways to process verbal information are *quoting* (using someone else's words directly, with appropriate attribution), *paraphrasing* (restating someone else's words in your own language), and *summarizing* (creating a shorter version of an original piece of writing). Processing numeric data can involve a variety of statistical analysis techniques. Three basic computations are the *mean* (what people mean when they say "average"), the *median* (the midpoint in a series, indicating an equal number of lesser and greater values), and the *mode* (the most frequently occurring value in a series). Processing results can also involve looking for trends and distinguishing causal relationships from correlations and mere coincidences.

5 **Explain how to summarize research results and present conclusions and recommendations.** Research results can be applied in several ways, depending on the purpose of the report or presentation. A *summary* is an unbiased condensation of the information uncovered in your research. It filters out details and presents only the most important ideas. A *conclusion* is your analysis of what the findings mean (an interpretation of the facts). A *recommendation* is your opinion (based on reason and logic) about the course of action that should be taken.

KEY TERMS

causation Cause-and-effect linkage between two factors, where one of them causes the other to happen

closed questions Questions with a fixed range of possible answers

conclusion A logical interpretation of the facts and other information in a report

correlation The simultaneous change in two variables

focus group A form of group research interview

knowledge management (KM) Set of technologies, policies, and procedures that let colleagues capture and share information throughout an organization

mean Equal to the sum of all the items in the group divided by the number of items in that group; what people refer to when they use the term *average*

median The midpoint of a series, with an equal number of items above and below

mode The number that occurs more often than any other in a sample

online databases Online compilations of newspapers, magazines, journals, and other information sources

open-ended questions Questions without simple, predetermined answers; used to solicit opinions, insights, and information

primary research New research done specifically for the current project

problem statement Defines the problem or purpose of your research

recommendation A suggested course of action

search engines Online search tools that identify individual webpages that contain specific words or phrases you've asked for

secondary research Research done previously for another purpose

trends Repeatable patterns taking place over time

web directories Online lists of websites selected by human editors

 Checklist

Conducting Effective Information Interviews

- Learn about the person you will be interviewing.
- Formulate your main idea to ensure effective focus.
- Choose the length, style, and organization of the interview.

- Select question types to elicit the specific information you want.
- Design each question carefully to collect useful answers.
- Limit the number of questions you ask.

- During the interview, be alert to new topics that you might want to probe.
- Consider recording the interview if the subject permits.
- Review your notes as soon as the interview ends.

1 Plan	2 Locate data and information	3 Process data and information	4 Apply your findings	5 Manage information
▪ Maintain research ethics and etiquette ▪ Familiarize yourself with the subject; develop a problem statement ▪ Identify information gaps ▪ Prioritize research needs	▪ Evaluate sources ▪ Collect secondary information at the library, online, or elsewhere ▪ Document your sources ▪ Collect primary information through surveys and interviews	▪ Quote, paraphrase, or summarize textual information ▪ Analyze numerical information	▪ Summarize findings ▪ Draw conclusions ▪ Make recommendations	▪ Make research results available to others via your company's knowledge management system

Figure 11.1 The Research Process
By following a methodical research process, you can save time and money while uncovering better information.

COMMUNICATION CHALLENGES AT TESCO

As a market development manager working for Richard Brasher, Tesco's top marketing executive in the United Kingdom, you are responsible for a variety of research, planning, and customer communication projects. Using what you've learned in this chapter about effective research methods, craft solutions to these two challenges.

INDIVIDUAL CHALLENGE: Tesco has created several online stores (see www.tesco.com) and would like to expand the number of consumers who order goods and services online.

What information would you need in order to devise a plan to attract more online shoppers?

TEAM CHALLENGE: Shoppers often make numerous purchase decisions in the store rather than arrive with a preset list of specific brands to purchase. Brasher would like more information on why consumers choose one brand over another while standing in front of an array of products on the shelf. Is it the brand name? Something about the packaging? The price? Other factors? With your team, brainstorm ways to collect this information from at least 500 shoppers. Be sure to consider the practical considerations of data collection as well as privacy concerns. Summarize your plan in a short report for your instructor.

TEST YOUR KNOWLEDGE

To review chapter content related to each question, refer to the indicated Learning Objective.

1. What are the five steps in the research process? [LO-1]
2. What is the purpose of identifying information gaps before starting research? [LO-1]
3. Should you conduct secondary research first or primary research? Why? [LO-2]
4. How can online monitoring tools help you with research? [LO-2]
5. What is the *hidden Internet*? [LO-2]
6. What does it mean to make a survey adaptive? [LO-3]
7. What is paraphrasing, and what is its purpose? [LO-4]
8. What is the difference between the mean, median, and mode? [LO-4]
9. What are the characteristics of a sound conclusion? [LO-5]
10. How does a conclusion differ from a recommendation? [LO-5]

APPLY YOUR KNOWLEDGE

To review chapter content related to each question, refer to the indicated Learning Objective.

1. Why is it important to plan your research effort? [LO-1]
2. Companies occasionally make mistakes that expose confidential information, such as when employees lose laptop computers containing sensitive data files or webmasters forget to protect confidential webpages from search engine indexes. If you conducted a Google search that turned up competitive information on webpages that were clearly intended to be private, what would you do? Explain your answer. [LO-1]
3. Why must you be careful when citing information from online sources? [LO-2]

4. One of your employees submitted a report, comparing the market opportunities for two product ideas your company might develop. The report concludes that because the first idea yielded 340,000 hits in a Google search whereas the second idea yielded only 128,000 Google hits, the first idea clearly has more sales potential. Is this a valid conclusion? Why or why not? [LO-4]
5. While analyzing last year's sales data, you notice that sales were 10 to 15 percent higher than average during August, September, and November. The marketing department invested heavily in a search engine advertising campaign from August through December. Can you conclude that the advertising campaign caused the increase in sales? Why or why not? [LO-5]

PRACTICE YOUR SKILLS

Message for Analysis: Primary Research: Conducting Interviews [LO-4]

The following set of interview questions was prepared for a manager of Whirlpool Corporation. The goal of the interview was to learn some basic information about Whirlpool's meeting practices. Read the questions and then (1) critique them, as a whole, indicating what you like or dislike about this series of questions, and (2) select five questions and revise them to make them more effective.

1. What is your position in the company?
2. To whom do you report?
3. Do you attend or run many meetings?
4. Do your meetings start on time? Run late?
5. Do you distribute or receive a meeting agenda several days in advance of the meeting?
6. Do you like your job?
7. Do you travel a lot for your job?

8. Has your company cut back on travel expenditures? If so, how and why?

9. Does your company use videoconferencing or online meetings as an alternative to travel?

10. Does your company own its own videoconferencing equipment?

11. Are virtual meetings more or less effective than face-to-face meetings?

12. How long have you worked for Whirlpool?

13. Is Sears your largest retail customer?

14. How often does your management team meet with the managers of Sears?

15. Does your company produce only household appliances?

16. How do you keep your meetings on track?

17. Does someone prepare written minutes of meetings? Are the minutes distributed to meeting members?

Exercises

Active links for all websites in this chapter can be found on MyBcommLab; see your User Guide for instructions on accessing the content for this chapter. Each activity is labeled according to the primary skill or skills you will need to use. To review relevant chapter content, you can refer to the indicated Learning Objective. In some instances, supporting information will be found in another chapter, as indicated.

1. **Planning Your Research; Collaboration: Team Projects [LO-1]** In a team assigned by your instructor, decide how you would structure a research project to answer the following questions. Identify any shortcomings in the approaches you have chosen.
   a. Has the litter problem on campus been reduced since the cafeteria began offering fewer take-out choices this year than in past years?
   b. Has the school attracted more transfer students since it waived the formal application process and allowed students at other colleges simply to send their transcripts and a one-page letter of application?
   c. Have the number of traffic accidents at the school's main entrance been reduced since a traffic light was installed?
   d. Has student satisfaction with the campus bookstore improved now that students can order their books online and pick them up at several convenient campus locations?

2. **Planning a Research Project [LO-1]** You and your business partners are considering buying several franchises in the fast-food business. You are all experienced managers or entrepreneurs, but none of you has experience in franchising. Visit www.amazon.com and search for books on this subject. Explore some of the books that you find by reading reviews and using the "search inside" feature.
   a. Use the information you find to develop a list of subquestions to help you narrow your focus.
   b. Write down the names of three books you might purchase to further aid your research.
   c. Summarize how a search like this can assist you with your research efforts and identify any risks of using this technique.

3. **Planning a Research Project [LO-1]** Analyze any recent school or work assignment that required you to conduct research. How did you approach your investigation? Did you rely mostly on sources of primary information or mostly on sources of secondary information? Now that you have studied this chapter, can you identify two ways to improve the research techniques you used during that assignment? Briefly explain.

4. **Conducting Secondary Research (Company and Industry Data) [LO-2]** Using online or printed sources, find the following information. Be sure to properly cite your sources, using the formats discussed in Appendix B.
   a. Contact information for the American Management Association
   b. Median weekly earnings of men and women by occupation
   c. Current market share for Perrier water
   d. Performance ratios for office supply retailers
   e. Annual stock performance for Hewlett-Packard
   f. Number of franchise outlets in the United States
   g. Composition of the U.S. workforce by profession

5. **Conducting Secondary Research (Finding Sources) [LO-2]** Businesspeople have to know where to look for secondary information when they conduct research. Identify five periodicals or online resources in each the following professions:
   a. Marketing and advertising
   b. Insurance
   c. Telecommunications
   d. Accounting

6. **Conducting Secondary Research (Documenting Sources) [LO-2]** Select five business articles from sources such as journals, books, newspapers, or websites. Develop a resource list, using Appendix B as a guideline.

7. **Conducting Secondary Research (Evaluating Sources) [LO-2]** Break into small groups and surf the Internet to find websites that provide business information such as company or industry news, trends, analysis, facts, or performance data. Using the criteria discussed under "Evaluating Sources" on page 317, evaluate the credibility of the information presented at these websites.

8. **Conducting Secondary Research (Online Monitoring); Media Skills: Microblogging [LO-2], Chapter 7** Select a business topic that interests you and configure a Twitter monitoring tool such as TweetBeep (http://tweetbeep.com) or TweetDeck (www.tweetdeck.com) to track tweets on this topic. After you've found at least a dozen tweets, identify three that provide potentially useful information and describe them in a brief email message to your instructor.

9. **Conducting Secondary Research (Company Data) [LO-2]** Select any publicly traded company and find the following information:
   a. Names of the company's current officers
   b. List of the company's products or services (summarized by product lines or divisions, if the company offers many products and services)
   c. Current issues in the company's industry
   d. Outlook for the company's industry as a whole

10. **Conducting Secondary Research (Industry Issues) [LO-2]** You'd like to know if it's a good idea to buy banner advertisements on other websites to drive more traffic to your company's website. You're worried about the expense and difficulty of running an experiment to test banner effectiveness, so you decide to look for some secondary data. Identify three secondary sources that might offer helpful data on this question.

11. **Conducting Primary Research (Surveys) [LO-3]** You work for a movie studio that is producing a young director's first motion picture, the story of a group of unknown musicians finding work and making a reputation in a competitive industry. Unfortunately, some of your friends leave the first complete screening, saying that the 182-minute movie is simply too long. Others said they couldn't imagine any sequences to cut out. Your boss wants to test the movie on a regular audience and ask viewers to complete a questionnaire that will help the director decide whether edits are needed and, if so, where. Design a questionnaire that you can use to solicit valid answers for a report to the director about how to handle the audience members' reactions to the movie.

12. **Conducting Primary Research (Interviews) [LO-3]** Plan an informational interview with a professional working in your chosen field of study. Plan the structure of the interview and create a set of interview questions. Conduct the interview. Using the information you gathered, write a memo to another student, describing the tasks, advantages, and disadvantages of jobs in this field of study. (Assume that your reader is a person who also plans to pursue a career in this field of study.)

13. **Conducting Primary Research (Interviews) [LO-3]** You're conducting an information interview with a manager in another division of your company. Partway through the interview, the manager shows clear signs of impatience. How should you respond? What might you do differently to prevent this from happening in the future? Explain your answers.

14. **Processing Data and Information [LO-4]** Select an article from a business periodical such as *Bloomberg Businessweek*,

Fortune, or *Forbes*. Read the article and highlight the article's key points. Summarize the article in fewer than 100 words, paraphrasing the key points.

15. **Processing Data and Information [LO-4]** Your boss has asked you to analyze and report on your division's sales for the first nine months of this year. Using the following data from company invoices, calculate the mean for each quarter and all averages for the year to date. Then identify and discuss the quarterly sales trends.

January	$24,600	June	$26,800
February	$25,900	July	$29,900
March	$23,000	August	$30,500
April	$21,200	September	$26,600
May	$24,600		

EXPAND YOUR SKILLS

Critique the Professionals

Find a recent example of a significant business blunder, such as a new product that failed in the marketplace. Based on what you can learn about the episode, how might better research have helped the company in question avoid the blunder? Using whatever medium your instructor requests, write a brief conclusion of your analysis.

Sharpening Your Career Skills Online

Bovée and Thill's Business Communication Web Search, at http://businesscommunicationblog.com/websearch, is a unique research tool designed specifically for business communication research. Use the Web Search function to find a website, video, PDF document, podcast, or PowerPoint presentation that offers advice on using online search tools in business research. Write a brief email message to your instructor, describing the item that you found and summarizing the career skills information you learned from it.

Designing Visual Communication | 12

LEARNING OBJECTIVES After studying this chapter, you will be able to

1 Explain the power of business images, discuss six principles of graphic design that help ensure effective visuals, and explain how to avoid ethical lapses when using visuals

2 Explain how to choose which points in your message to illustrate

3 Describe the most common options for presenting data in a visual format

4 Describe the most common options for presenting information, concepts, and ideas

5 Explain how to integrate visuals with text and list three criteria to review in order to verify the quality of your visuals

MyBcommLab Test your mastery of this chapter and its Learning Objectives. Visit mybcommlab.com to apply what you've learned in Document Makeovers and interactive simulation scenarios.

COMMUNICATION CLOSE-UP AT XPLANE

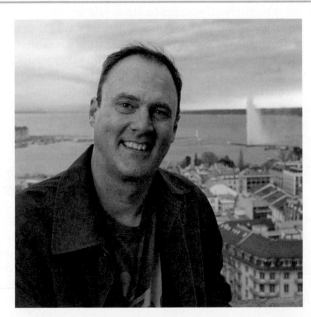

Founder Dave Gray helped establish Xplane as one of the world's most innovative information design consultancies.

www.xplane.com

As its name suggests, Xplane is in the business of simplicity. According to CEO Aric Wood, "There's a reason the best business plans are sketched on napkins. Simple drawings are easier to understand than a 120-page document." Emphasizing *visual thinking*, Xplane distills complex business situations down to their simplest elements to make sure clients can understand the essential elements of a problem or opportunity, devise appropriate solutions, and communicate those results to diverse audiences.

Using eclectic teams of artists, writers, and business experts, Xplane applies visual thinking to some of the most difficult problems businesses face, including streamlining mergers and acquisitions, launching new ventures, educating investors, ensuring collaboration with external business partners, and training employees on complicated business processes. After a solution has been reached, Xplane's information designers create highly visual media pieces to help audiences grasp both the big picture and essentials details. (You can see an example of Xplane's work in Figure 4.4 on page 95.)

Xplane uses its techniques on its own problems and challenges, too. When the Portland, Oregon–based firm expanded into Europe through a new office in Spain, it used visual thinking to analyze the challenge of adopting Xplane's methods to European business practices.

The company's website emphasizes that "communication isn't a message sent. It's a message received." Clients are clearly receiving the message: Xplane's ever-expanding portfolio now includes projects for such A-list organizations as Apple, *Bloomberg Businessweek*, Lexus, Nokia, *Rolling Stone*, and the U.S. Marine Corps.[1]

Understanding Visual Communication

1   LEARNING OBJECTIVE

Explain the power of business images, discuss six principles of graphic design that help ensure effective visuals, and explain how to avoid ethical lapses when using visuals.

MyBcommLab

● Access this chapter's simulation entitled Designing Visual Communication, located at mybcommlab.com.

Like words, visuals often carry connotative or symbolic meanings.

Project teams from Xplane (profiled in the chapter-opening Communication Close-up) look for new ways to connect and explore business ideas through creative visuals, often helping clients see important concepts and relationships that aren't obvious using text alone. Although the primary focus of this course is written messages, visual communication has become an important skill for today's business professionals and managers. This chapter helps you appreciate the power of images and the visual evolution of business communication. It then explains how to identify which points in your messages to illustrate, how to select the best visual for each of those points, and how to create effective visuals in any medium, from memos to reports to webpages to electronic presentations.

THE POWER OF IMAGES

Well-designed visual elements can enhance the communication power of textual messages and, in some instances, even replace textual messages. Visuals can often convey some message points (such as spatial relationships, correlations, procedures, and emotions) more effectively and more efficiently than words. Generally speaking, in a given amount of time, effective images can convey much more information than text.[2] In the numbers-oriented world of work, people rely heavily on trend lines, distribution curves, and other visual presentations of numeric quantities. Visuals attract and hold people's attention, helping your audience understand and remember your message. Busy readers often jump to visuals to try to get the gist of a message, and attractive visuals can draw readers more deeply into your reports and presentations. Using pictures is also an effective way to communicate with the diverse audiences that are common in today's business environment.

In addition to their direct information value, visuals often convey connotative meaning as well. As you read in Chapter 5, many words and phrases carry connotative meanings, which are all the mental images, emotions, and other impressions that the word or phrase evokes in audience members. A significant part of the power—and risk—of visual elements derives from their connotative meanings. Even something as simple as a watermark symbol embedded in letterhead stationery can boost reader confidence in the message that is printed on the paper.[3] Many colors, shapes, and other design elements have **visual symbolism**, and their symbolic, connotative meaning can evolve over time and mean different things in different cultures (see Figure 12.1). Being aware of these symbolic meanings and using them to your advantage are important aspects of being an effective business communicator.

Because they have so much power to communicate, visuals must be carefully planned, competently created, and seamlessly integrated with text. An awkward sentence or grammatical error deep within a report might not be noticed by the majority of readers, but a poorly chosen or clumsily implemented visual will be noticed by most—and can confuse or alienate audiences and damage your credibility. You don't need to be a professional designer to use visuals effectively, but you do need to be aware of some basic design principles if you want to avoid making high-visibility mistakes. This chapter gives you enough background to begin creating your own business visuals, and with some practice, you'll be able to craft effective visuals for nearly any communication project you might encounter.

Figure 12.1   Visual Symbolism
A red cross (with equal-length arms) on a white background is the well-known symbol of the Red Cross relief organization. It is also used to indicate the medical branches of many nations' military services. The red cross symbol is based on the flag of Switzerland (where the first Red Cross organization was formed), which over the course of hundreds of years developed from battle flags that originally used the Christian cross symbol. Although the Red Cross emblem is not based directly on the Christian symbol, the organization uses a red crescent in countries where Islam is the dominant religion and is known as the Red Crescent. To avoid any association with religious symbols, the International Federation of Red Cross and Red Crescent Societies (the global umbrella organization for all national Red Cross and Red Crescent organizations) recently adopted the Red Crystal as its new symbol.

THE VISUAL EVOLUTION IN BUSINESS COMMUNICATION

Several technological and social factors are contributing to the increasing use and importance of visuals in business communication. The process of creating and working with visual elements used to be the domain of experts with complex and expensive tools. However, digital technology has changed this situation dramatically. Digital cameras that can produce high-quality images and video are inexpensive, and the software needed to create diagrams, process photos, edit video, and prepare other visual elements continues to get both easier and more powerful all the time. Design and production tasks that used to take days can now be completed in hours or even minutes. As technologies such as wireless networking advance, business communicators will continue to reach wider audiences in less time, using equipment that costs less and requires fewer skills.[4]

While technology has been putting visual design and production into the hands of everyday business communicators in recent years, audience skills and expectations have been evolving as well. Two changes in particular could affect your communication efforts in the coming years. First, U.S. government research indicates that only half of the adult population in the United States now has the literacy skills considered necessary for success in today's workplace.[5] In other words, depending on the nature of your work, you could find yourself communicating with audiences whose skills could prevent them from successfully reading your documents. Visuals could play a vital role in communicating your messages to audiences with lower reading skills. Second, as technology has multiplied the ways in which communicators can create visuals and as people grow up and live in a more visual, media-saturated environment, audiences may well expect messages to be more visual.

As a result of these changes in both the tools and the communication environment, **visual literacy**, the ability to create effective images and to correctly interpret such images, has become a key business skill.[6] Whether you are using visuals to reach an audience with limited reading skills or to magnify the impact of your written messages, knowing how to help your audience see what you see will enable you to become a more effective communicator.

> Thanks to advances in technology and changing audience expectations, business communication is becoming more visual.

> Visual literacy is the ability to create and interpret visuals successfully.

VISUAL DESIGN PRINCIPLES

Just as creating effective sentences and paragraphs requires working knowledge of the principles of good writing, creating effective visuals requires some knowledge of the principles of good design. Even though few businesspeople have the opportunity to formally study the "language" of line, mass, space, size, color, pattern, and texture, anyone can learn enough of the basic concepts to craft effective basic visuals.

When you encounter visuals that you find appealing or unappealing, effective or ineffective, stop and ask yourself

REAL-TIME UPDATES
Learn More by Reading This PDF

See why visual design is a lot more than just "eye candy"

The visual design of a website is more than mere decoration—it is an essential, functional part of the website and a key factor in the communication process. Go to http://real-timeupdates.com/bct11 and click on "Learn More." If you are using MyBcommLab, you can access Real-Time Updates within each chapter or under Student Study Tools.

what caused your response. Did a particular design grab you and practically force you to pay attention, or did you pass right by with hardly a notice? Did one chart reveal its information quickly and easily, while another made you spend time decoding its confusing message? Did one photo appeal to you at an emotional level and therefore draw you into a document, whereas another was off-putting and caused you to lose interest in the document? By thinking about your own reactions to visual designs, you can become a more effective designer yourself.

As you consider your reactions to various designs and create designs of your own, you'll begin to see how six fundamental principles help distinguish ineffective and effective designs:

- **Consistency.** Audiences view a series of visuals as a whole and assume that design elements will be consistent from one page to the next. Think of consistency as *visual parallelism*, in the same way that textual parallelism helps audiences understand and compare a series of ideas.[7] You can achieve visual parallelism in a variety of ways, including through consistent use of color, shape, size, texture, position, scale, or typeface.
- **Contrast.** To emphasize differences, depict items in contrasting colors, shapes, or sizes. For example, to highlight the difference between two quantities in a pie chart, don't use two shades of blue; instead, use blue for one and yellow or some other dramatically contrasting color for the other.
- **Balance.** Balance can be either *formal*, in which the elements in the images are arranged symmetrically around a central point or axis, or *informal*, in which elements are not distributed evenly, but stronger and weaker elements are arranged in a way that achieves an overall effect of balance. A common approach to informal balance is weighing one visually dominant element against several smaller or weaker elements.[8] Generally speaking, formal balance is more calming and serious, whereas informal balance tends to feel more dynamic and engaging.
- **Emphasis.** Audiences usually assume that the dominant element in a design is the most important, so make sure that the visually dominant element really does represent the most important information. You can do so through color, position, size, or placement, for example. Conversely, be sure to visually downplay less important items. For instance, avoid using strong colors for minor support points, and deemphasize background features such as the grid lines on a chart.
- **Convention.** Visual communication is guided by a variety of generally accepted rules or conventions, just as written communication is guided by an array of spelling, grammar, punctuation, and usage conventions. These conventions dictate virtually every aspect of design.[9] Moreover, many conventions are so ingrained that people don't even realize they are following these rules. For example, if English is your native language, you assume that ideas progress across the page from left to right because that's the direction in which English text is written. However, if you are a native Arabic or Hebrew speaker, you might automatically assume that flow on a page or screen is from right to left because that is the direction in which those languages are written. Similarly, Japanese audiences are used to reading publications from back to front, right to left. Flouting conventions often causes breakdowns in communication, but in some cases, it can be done to great effect.[10] For instance, flipping an organization chart upside down to put the customers at the top, with frontline employees directly beneath them and on down to the chief executive at the bottom, can be an effective way to emphasize that customers come first and that the managers are responsible for supporting employees in their efforts to satisfy customers.
- **Simplicity.** As a general rule, simple is better when it comes to visuals for business communication (see Figure 12.2). Remember that you're conveying information, not decorating an apartment or creating artwork. Limit the number of colors and design elements you use, and take care to avoid *chartjunk*, a term coined by visual communication specialist Edward R. Tufte for decorative elements that clutter documents and potentially confuse readers without adding any relevant information.[11] Computers make it far too easy to add chartjunk, from clip art illustrations to three-dimensional charts that display only two dimensions of data.

Creating effective visuals requires basic knowledge of the principles of good design.

Nearly every aspect of visual design is governed by conventions that set audience expectations.

(a)

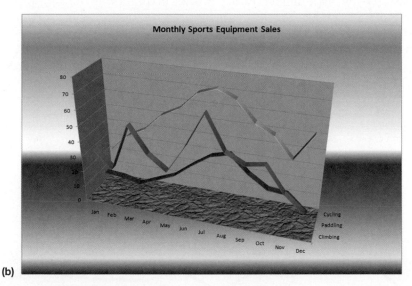

(b)

Figure 12.2 The Power of Simplicity
These two graphs contain the same information, but Figure 12.2a is much easier to interpret. None of the additional elements in Figure 12.2b add any information value—and they make the graph harder to interpret. Adding a false third dimension to two-dimensional information such as these sales figures is a common mistake.

THE ETHICS OF VISUAL COMMUNICATION

Power always comes with responsibility—and the potential power of visuals places an ethical burden on every business communicator. Ethical problems, both intentional and unintentional, can range from photos that play on racial or gender stereotypes to images that imply cause-and-effect relationships that may not exist to graphs that distort data (see Figure 12.3 on page 344).

Altering the scale of items in a visual is just one of many ways to emphasize or deemphasize certain aspects of information. For example, to increase the perceived size of a product, an advertiser might show a close-up of it being held by someone with smaller-than-average hands. Conversely, a large hand would make the product seem smaller.

You can work to avoid ethical lapses in your visuals by following these guidelines:[12]

- **Consider all possible interpretations—and misinterpretations.** Try to view your visuals from your audience members' perspective; will their biases, beliefs, or backgrounds lead them to different conclusions than you've intended? For instance, assume that you want to show how easy your product is to use, and the photograph you've chosen just happens to show a woman operating the product. Will anyone conclude that what you really mean to say is that your product is so simple that "even a woman can use it"?

Remember that the power to communicate with visuals comes with the responsibility to communicate ethically.

You can take many steps to emphasize or deemphasize specific elements in your visuals, but make sure you don't inadvertently commit an ethical lapse while doing so.

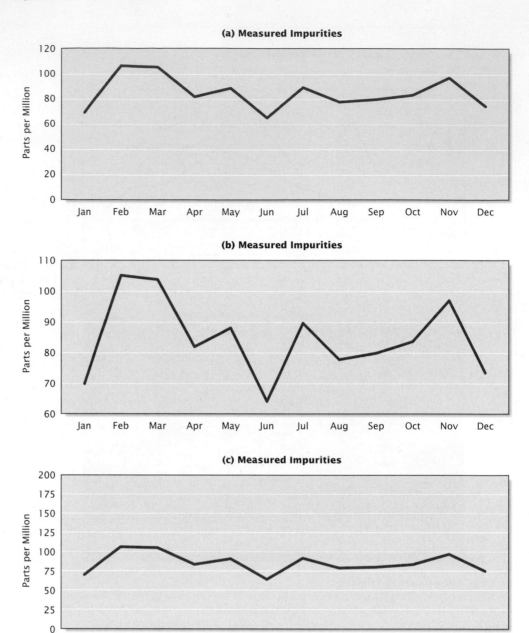

Figure 12.3   Influencing Perception Through Visual Design

Figure 12.3a shows impurities measured over the course of a 12-month period; the vertical scale is set from 0 to 120, sufficient to cover the range of variations in the data. However, what if you wanted to make the variations from month to month look more severe? Less severe? Figure 12.3b, with the scale "zoomed in" to a narrow range of 60 to 110, makes the variations look much more dramatic. The result could be a stronger emotional impact on the reader, creating the impression that these impurities are out of control. In contrast, Figure 12.3c expands the scale from 0 to 200, which minimizes the appearance of the variations in the data. This graph is visually "calmer," creating the opposite impression, that there's really nothing to worry about. The data shown in all three graphs are identical, but the graphs send three different messages to the reader. Are any of the graphs unethical? That depends on the communicator's intent and whether it inhibits the audience's ability to make informed decisions.

ETHICS DETECTIVE | Solving the Case of the Hidden Numbers

You've been assigned to present the results of an industrywide study of the effects of insecticide. Your audience consists of the department heads in your company, whose experience and educational backgrounds vary widely, from chemical engineering to insurance to law. You're convinced you need to keep your report as simple and as jargon-free as possible.

You're not a scientific expert on insecticides, but your supervisor has introduced you to a scientist who works for a trade association that represents chemical producers, including your firm. The scientist is familiar with the study you'll be reporting on, and she has experience in communicating technical subjects to diverse audiences. You jumped at the chance to have such a knowledgeable person review your presentation for technical accuracy, but you're uncomfortable with some of her feedback. In particular, you question her advice to replace the following line chart, which shows the number of insecticide poisonings and deaths by age.

The scientist suggests that this chart is too busy and too difficult for nonspecialists to understand. As an alternative, she provides a bar chart that selects four specific ages from the entire range. She says this chart communicates the same basic idea as the line chart but is much easier to read.

ANALYSIS

You agree with the scientist that the line chart is visually busy and takes more effort to process, but something bothers you about the bar chart. Does it present the insecticide situation accurately and honestly? Why or why not?

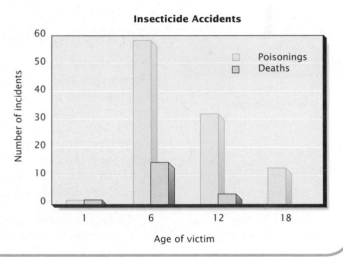

- **Provide context.** Even when they are completely accurate, visuals can show only a partial view of reality. Part of your responsibility as a communicator is to provide not only accurate visuals but enough background information to help audiences interpret the visual information correctly.
- **Don't hide or minimize negative information that runs counter to your argument.** Obscuring information prevents your audiences from making fully informed decisions regarding your content.
- **Don't exaggerate information that supports your argument.** Similarly, you have a responsibility not to oversell information in support of your argument. You should also resist the temptation to alter or enhance photographs and other images in order to support your arguments.
- **Don't oversimplify complex situations.** By their very nature, visuals tend to present simplified views of reality. This is usually a benefit and one of the key reasons for using visuals. However, take care not to mislead an audience by hiding complications that are important to the audience's understanding of the situation.

Visuals can't always speak for themselves; make sure your audience has enough context to interpret your visuals correctly.

- **Don't imply cause-and-effect relationships without providing proof that they exist.** For example, if you create a line chart that shows how increasing sales seem to track increasing advertising expenditures, you can claim a correlation but not necessarily a causal relationship between the two. You can claim a causal relationship (meaning that the increase in advertising spending caused the increase in sales) only if you can isolate advertising spending as the *only* factor that can account for the increase in sales.
- **Avoid emotional manipulation or other forms of coercion.** For instance, a photograph of an unhappy child being treated as a social outcast because he or she doesn't own the trendiest new toys could be considered an unethical way to persuade parents to buy those products for their children.

The ways in which you aggregate data for display can affect the messages and meanings that your audience extracts from your visuals.

- **Be careful with the way you aggregate data.** Preparing charts, graphs, and tables that present data often involves decisions about *aggregating*, or grouping, data. The decisions you make about aggregating data can have a profound effect on the message your audience receives (see "Ethics Detective: Solving the Case of the Hidden Numbers"). For example, if you aggregate daily production levels to show only a single data point for each week, you might be obscuring important variations that happen from day to day.

Identifying Points to Illustrate

2 **LEARNING OBJECTIVE**

Explain how to choose which points in your message to illustrate.

To help identify which parts of your message can benefit from visuals, step back and consider the flow of your message from the audience's point of view. Which parts of the message are likely to seem complex, open to misinterpretation, or even just a little bit dull? Are there any connections between ideas that might not be obvious if they are addressed only in text? Is there a lot of numeric data or other discrete factual content that would be difficult to read if presented in paragraph form? Is there a chance that the main idea won't "jump off the page" if it's covered only in text?

If you answer yes to any of these questions, you probably need one or more visuals. When you're deciding which points to present visually, think of the five Cs:

Effective visuals are clear, complete, concise, connected, and compelling.

- **Clear.** The human mind is extremely adept at processing visual information, whether it's something as simple as the shape of a stop sign or as complicated as the floor plan for a new factory. If you're having difficultly conveying an idea in words, consider whether a visual element will do the job instead.
- **Complete.** Visuals, particularly tables, often serve to provide the supporting details for a main idea or recommendation. A table or another visual can provide these details without getting in the way of your main message.
- **Concise.** You've probably heard the expression "A picture is worth a thousand words." If a particular section of your message seems to require extensive description or explanation, see whether there's a way to convey this information visually. With a picture working in conjunction with text, you may be able to reduce your word count considerably.
- **Connected.** A key purpose of many business messages is showing connections of some sort—similarities or differences, correlations, cause-and-effect relationships, and so on. Whenever you want readers to see such a connection, determine whether a chart, a diagram, or another illustration might help.
- **Compelling.** Will one or more illustrations make your message more persuasive, more interesting, more likely to get read? You rarely want to insert visuals simply for decorative purposes, of course, but even if a particular point can be expressed equally well via text or visuals, consider adding the visual in order to make your report or presentation more compelling.

As you identify which points in your document would benefit from a visual, make sure that each visual you decide on has a clear purpose (see Table 12.1).

TABLE 12.1	When to Use Visuals
Purpose	**Application**
To clarify	Support text descriptions of "graphic" topics: quantitative or numeric information, explanations of trends, descriptions.
To simplify	Divide complicated descriptions into components that can be depicted with conceptual models, flowcharts, organization charts, or diagrams.
To emphasize	Call attention to particularly important points by illustrating them with line, bar, and pie charts.
To summarize	Review major points in the narrative by providing a chart or table that sums up the data.
To reinforce	Present information in visual form to supplement descriptions in text.
To attract	Make material seem more interesting by decorating the cover or title page and by breaking up the text with visual aids.
To impress	Build confidence by using visual forms to convey authenticity and precision.
To unify	Depict the relationships among various elements of a whole.

Selecting Visuals for Presenting Data

After you have identified which points would benefit most from visual presentation, your next decision is choosing which type of visual to use for each message point. As you can see in Figure 12.4 on the next page, you have many choices for business graphics, which can be roughly divided into those for presenting data and those for presenting information, concepts, and ideas.

For some content, the decision is usually obvious. For example, to present a large set of numeric values or detailed textual information, a table is the obvious choice in most cases. However, if you're presenting data broken down geographically, a color-coded map might be more effective, to show overall patterns rather than individual data points. Also, certain visuals are used more commonly for certain applications, as you'll see in the following sections.

Business professionals have a tremendous number of choices for presenting data, from general-purpose line, bar, and pie charts to specialized charts for product portfolios, financial analysis, and other professional functions. The visuals most commonly used to present data include tables; line and surface charts; bar charts, pictograms, and Gantt charts; scatter and bubble diagrams; and pie charts. (Note that most people use the terms *chart* and *graph* interchangeably.)

3 | LEARNING OBJECTIVE

Describe the most common options for presenting data in a visual format.

You have many types of visuals to choose from, and each is best suited to particular communication tasks.

TABLES

When you need to present detailed, specific information, choose a **table**, a systematic arrangement of data in columns and rows. Tables are ideal when your audience needs information that would be either difficult or tedious to handle in the main text.

Most tables contain the standard parts illustrated in Figure 12.5 on page 349 . Every table includes vertical columns and horizontal rows, with useful headings along the top and side. For printed documents, you can adjust font size and column and row spacing to fit a considerable amount of information on the page and still maintain readability. For online documents, you'll need to reduce the number of columns and rows to make sure your tables are easily readable online. Tables for electronic presentations usually need to be the simplest of all because you can't expect audiences to read detailed information from the screen.

Although complex information may require formal tables that are set apart from the text, you can present some

Printed tables can display extensive amounts of data, but tables for websites and presentations need to be simpler.

REAL-TIME UPDATES
Learn More by Reading This Article

Quickly peruse dozens of data and information display techniques

This "periodic table of visualization methods" shows dozens of ways to display data, information, concepts, strategies, and more. Go to http://real-timeupdates.com/bct11 and click on "Learn More." If you are using MyBcommLab, you can access Real-Time Updates within each chapter or under Student Study Tools.

Communication Challenge	Effective Visual Choice

Presenting Data

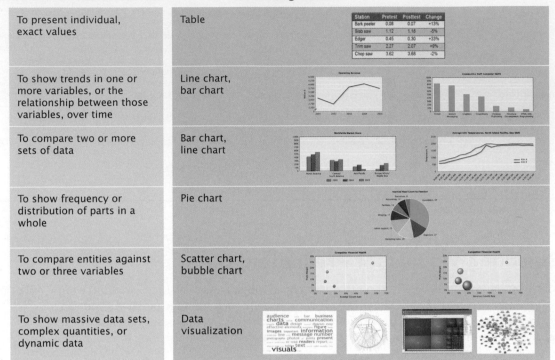

To present individual, exact values	Table
To show trends in one or more variables, or the relationship between those variables, over time	Line chart, bar chart
To compare two or more sets of data	Bar chart, line chart
To show frequency or distribution of parts in a whole	Pie chart
To compare entities against two or three variables	Scatter chart, bubble chart
To show massive data sets, complex quantities, or dynamic data	Data visualization

Presenting Information, Concepts, and Ideas

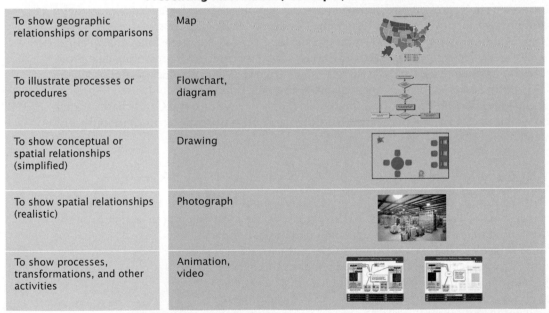

To show geographic relationships or comparisons	Map
To illustrate processes or procedures	Flowchart, diagram
To show conceptual or spatial relationships (simplified)	Drawing
To show spatial relationships (realistic)	Photograph
To show processes, transformations, and other activities	Animation, video

Figure 12.4 Selecting the Best Visual
For each point you want to illustrate, make sure you choose the most effective type of visual.

	Multicolumn Heading			Single-Column Heading
	Column Subheading	Column Subheading	Column Subheading	
Row Heading	xxx*	xxx	xxx	xxx
Row Heading	xxx	xxx	xxx	xxx
Row Subheading	xxx	xxx	xxx	xxx
Row Subheading	xxx	xxx	xxx	xxx
Row Heading	xxx	xxx	xxx	xxx
Row Heading	xxx	xxx	xxx	xxx
TOTALS	xxx	xxx	xxx	xxx

Figure 12.5 Parts of a Table
Here are the standard parts of a table. No matter which design you choose, make sure the layout is clear and that individual rows and columns are easy to follow.
Source: (In the same format as a text footnote; see Appendix B)
*Footnotes (Used to explain any entries in the table; can be designed with superscript numbers, letters, or symbols)

MyBcommLab

Apply Figure 12.5's key concepts by revising a new document. Go to Chapter 12 in mybcommlab.com and select Document Makeovers.

data more simply within the text. You make the table, in essence, a part of the paragraph, typed in tabular format. Such text tables are usually introduced with a sentence that leads directly into the tabulated information. Here's an example:[13]

Here is how five leading full-service restaurant chains compare in terms of number of locations and annual revenue:

	OSI Restaurant Partners	DineEquity	Carlson	Brinker	Darden
Major Chain(s)	Outback Steakhouse, Carrabba's	Applebee's, IHOP	Friday's, Pick Up Stix	Chili's, Maggiano's	Red Lobster, Olive Garden
Locations	1,470	3,300	990	1,550	1,800
Revenue ($ Million)	$3,600	$1,414	N/A	$2,859	7,113

Source: Hoover's Online [accessed 25 February 2011] www.hoovers.com; "America's Largest Private Companies," Forbes [accessed 25 February 2011] www.forbes.com; company financial reports accessed on Google Finance [accessed 25 February 2011] www.google.com/finance.

When you prepare tables, follow these guidelines to make your tables easy to read:

- Use common, understandable units and clearly identify the units you're using, whether it's dollars, percentages, price per ton, or some other units.
- Express all items in a column in the same unit and round off for simplicity whenever doing so won't eliminate essential details.
- Label column headings clearly, and use a subheading if necessary.
- Separate columns or rows with lines or extra space to make the table easy to follow; in complex tables, consider highlighting every other row or column in a pale, contrasting color.
- Provide totals or averages of columns or rows when relevant.
- Document the source of the data, using the same format as a text footnote (see Appendix B).

Tables can contain numerals, words, symbols, or other facts and figures. Word tables are particularly appropriate for presenting survey findings or for comparing various items against a specific standard.

LINE AND SURFACE CHARTS

Line charts are commonly used to show trends over time or the relationship between two or more variables.

A **line chart** illustrates trends over time or plots the relationship of two or more variables. In line charts showing trends, the vertical, or *y*, axis shows the amount, and the horizontal, or *x*, axis shows the time or other quantity against which the amount is being measured. Both axes often start at zero in the lower-left corner, but you can exercise a fair amount of flexibility with both axes in order to present your data as clearly as possible. For instance, to show both positive and negative values (such as profit and loss), you can have the *y* axis span from a negative value up to a positive value, with zero somewhere in between. Of course, you should always avoid distorting the data in ways that could mislead your audience, as noted in the section "The Ethics of Visual Communication," on page 343.

If you need to compare two or more sets of data, you can plot them on the same chart for instant visual comparison (see Figure 12.6). Two or three lines on a single chart are usually easy to read, but beyond that, things can get confusing, particularly if the lines cross.

By their very nature, line charts often raise the question "What happens next?" For instance, if you present sales data for the past 12 months, your audience may well ask what you think will happen in the next 12 months. Predicting the future is always risky, but you can use your spreadsheet's forecasting tools to extend a line into the future, using a statistical technique known as *regression analysis*. Check your spreadsheet's Help function for more information on using its *linear regression*, *trend line*, or *forecasting* functions. However, when using these tools, be aware that all they can do is extract patterns from past data and extend them into the future. They don't have any awareness of the "real-life" factors that shaped that past data—and they may or may not produce that same pattern in the future.

Spreadsheet forecasting functions can help predict future values based on past values shown in a line chart.

A **surface chart**, also called an **area chart**, is a form of line chart with a cumulative effect; all the lines add up to the top line, which represents the total (see Figure 12.7). This presentation helps you illustrate changes in the composition of something over time. One common use is to show how sales of individual products contribute to the company's overall revenue.[14] When preparing a surface chart, put the most important segment on the bottom and build up from there.

BAR CHARTS, PICTOGRAMS, AND GANTT CHARTS

You can create bar charts in a wide variety of formats; choose the form that best illustrates the data and relationships in your message.

A **bar chart** portrays numbers by the height or length of its rectangular bars, making a series of numbers easy to read or understand. (Vertical bar charts are sometimes called *column charts*.) Bar charts are particularly valuable when you want to

- Compare the sizes of several items at one time
- Show changes in one item over time
- Indicate the composition of several items over time
- Show the relative sizes of components of a whole

Average Kiln Temperatures, North Island Facility, Day Shift

Figure 12.6 Line Chart
This line chart compares the temperatures measured inside two cement kilns from 8:00 A.M. to 5:00 P.M.

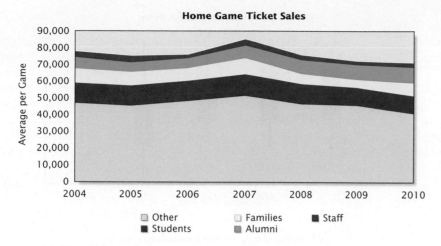

Figure 12.7   Surface Chart
Surface, or area, charts can show a combination of trends over time and the individual contributions of the components of a whole.

As the charts in Figure 12.8 show, bar charts can appear in various forms. *Grouped* bar charts compare more than one set of data, using a different color or pattern for each set. *Deviation* bar charts identify positive and negative values, or winners and losers. *Segmented* bar charts, also known as *stacked* bar charts, show how individual components contribute to a total number, using a different color or pattern for each component. *Combination* bar

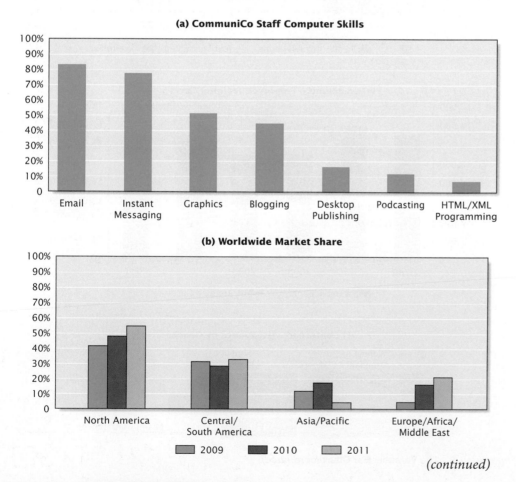

(continued)

Figure 12.8   The Versatile Bar Chart
Here are six of the dozens of variations possible with bar charts: *singular* (12.8a), *grouped* (12.8b), *deviation* (12.8c), *segmented* (12.8d), *combination* (12.8e), and *paired* (12.8f).

(c) CommuniCo Stock Price

(d) CommuniCo Preferred Communication Media

(e) CommuniCo Employee Training Costs

(f) Conference Attendance by Gender

Figure 12.8   **The Versatile Bar Chart** *(continued)*

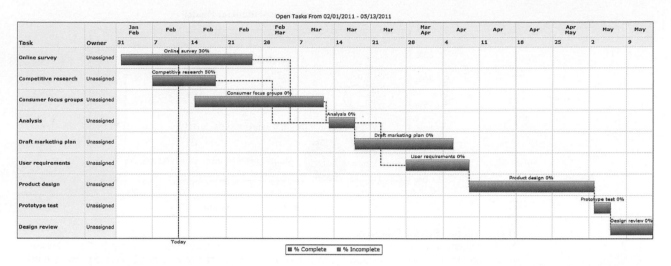

Figure 12.9   Gantt Chart
A Gantt chart is a specialized bar chart that uses bars to show durations of tasks and lines to show dependencies between tasks, such as when one task cannot be started before another one is completed.

MyBcommLab

Apply Figure 12.9's key concepts by revising a new document. Go to Chapter 12 in mybcommlab.com and select Document Makeovers.

and line charts compare quantities that require different intervals. *Paired* bar charts show the correlations between two items.

Figure 12.8 also suggests how creative you can be with bar charts. You might align the bars either vertically or horizontally, or you might use bar charts to show both positive and negative quantities. No matter what you do, however, be sure to space the bars evenly and place them in a logical order, such as chronological or alphabetical.

You can also convert the bars of a bar chart into lines of symbols, so that the number or length of the symbols indicates the relative value of each item. A chart that portrays data as symbols instead of words or numbers is known as a **pictogram**. The chief value of pictograms is their novelty and ability to convey a more literal, visual message, but they can be more difficult to read if not designed with care and can present a less professional tone than a straightforward bar chart.

Closely related to the bar chart is the **time line chart**, which shows how much time is needed to complete each task in a given project. When you want to track progress toward completing a project, you can use a type of time line chart known as a **Gantt chart** (see Figure 12.9).

SCATTER AND BUBBLE DIAGRAMS

If you need to compare several entities (companies, markets, employees, and so on) on two variables, such as revenue and profit margin, use a **scatter diagram**, also known as an **XY diagram**. This diagram is similar to a line chart in the sense that one variable is plotted along the *x* (horizontal) axis and another along the *y* (vertical) axis. However, in a scatter diagram, individual points are plotted, not continuous lines. The **bubble diagram** expands to three variables, with the size of the bubble representing the third variable (see Figure 12.10 on page 354).

Scatter diagrams compare entities against two variables; bubble diagrams compare them against three.

PIE CHARTS

A **pie chart** is a commonly used tool for showing how the parts of a whole are distributed. Although pie charts are popular and can quickly highlight the dominant parts of a whole, they are often not as effective as bar charts or tables. For example, comparing percentages accurately is often difficult with a pie chart but can be fairly easy with a bar chart (see Figure 12.11 on page 354). Making pie charts easier to read with accuracy can require labeling each slice with data values, in which case a table might serve the purpose more effectively.[15]

Pie charts are used frequently in business reports, but in many instances they are not as helpful to readers as bar charts and other types of visuals would be.

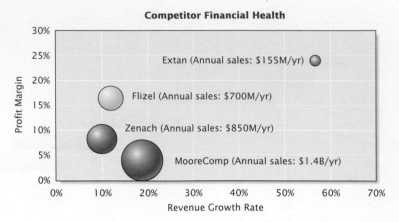

Figure 12.10 **Bubble Diagram**
A bubble diagram shows three variables: distance along the *x* and *y* axes, plus the diameter of each bubble. In this case, the rate of revenue growth is plotted on the *x* axis, profit margin is plotted on the *y* axis, and the size of the bubbles represents annual revenues. For instance, MooreComp has the greatest revenues but the lowest profit margin, although it is growing faster than two of its three competitors.

DATA VISUALIZATION

Data visualization tools can overcome the limitations of conventional charts and other display types.

Conventional charts and graphs are limited in several ways: Most types can show only a limited number of data points before becoming too cluttered to interpret, they often can't show complex relationships among data points, and they can represent only numeric data. As computer technologies continue to generate massive amounts of data that can be combined and connected in endless ways, a diverse class of display capabilities known as **data visualization** work to overcome all these drawbacks.

Unlike conventional charts, data visualization tools are more about uncovering broad meaning and finding hidden connections.

Unlike charts and graphs, data visualization is less about clarifying individual data points and more about extracting broad meaning from giant masses of data or putting the data in context.[16] For instance, the Facebook "friend wheel" in Figure 12.12b on the next page offers a visual sense of this particular Facebook user's network by showing which of his friends are friends of each other and thereby indicating "clustering" within the network (work friends, social friends, and so on). The diagram doesn't attempt to show quantities, but rather the overall nature of the network.

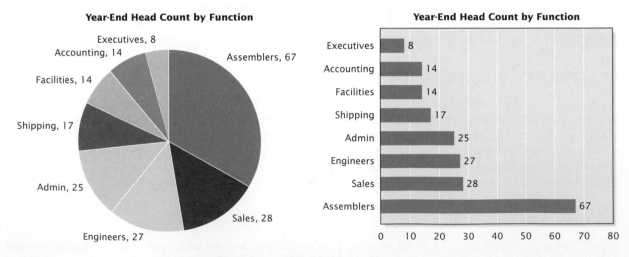

Figure 12.11 **Pie Charts Versus Bar Charts**
Pie charts are used frequently, but they aren't necessarily the best choice for many data presentations. This pie chart does make it easy to see that assemblers are the largest employee category, but other comparisons of slice sizes (such as Sales, Engineers, and Admin) are not as easy to make and require a numerical rather than a visual comparison. In contrast, the bar chart gives a quick visual comparison of every data point.

(a) Website Linkage Map. This interactive network diagram shows the most active links to and from Apple's homepage (**www.apple.com**). *Website linkage map by TouchGraph.com*

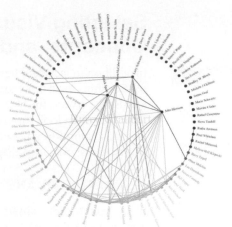

(b) Facebook Friend Wheel. This network diagram shows how the connections of Barry Graubart (an executive with an e-commerce company) are connected with one another.

audience avoid bar business charts color communication create data design detailed diagram easy effective elements example figure help images important information instance line maps message number photographs photos pie points present product professional re read readers report sales shows size sure tables text textual used usually value video visuals ways

(c) Tag Cloud. This "word chart" shows the relative frequency of the 50 most-used words in this chapter (other than common words such as and, or, and the).

(d) Interactive Data Display. This interactive display conveys two company performance variables at once (sales and profits) for a large data set by using the size and color of the individual blocks.

Figure 12.12 Data Visualization
The range of data visualization displays is virtually endless; here are a few of the many different ways to display complex sets of data.

In addition to displaying large data sets and linkages within data sets, other kinds of visualization tools combine data with textual information to communicate complex or dynamic data much faster than conventional presentations can. For example, a *tag cloud* shows the relative frequency of terms, or tags (user-applied content labels), in an article, a blog, a website, survey data, or another collection of text.[17] Figure 12.12 shows a few of the many data visualization tools now available.

REAL-TIME UPDATES
Learn More by Reading This Article

Data visualization gateway: A comprehensive collection for business communicators

This unique web resource offers links to a vast array of data visualization techniques and examples. Go to http://real-timeupdates.com/bct11 and click on "Learn More." If you are using MyBcommLab, you can access Real-Time Updates within each chapter or under Student Study Tools.

Selecting Visuals for Presenting Information, Concepts, and Ideas

4　**LEARNING OBJECTIVE**

Describe the most common options for presenting information, concepts, and ideas.

In addition to facts and figures, you'll need to present other types of information, from spatial relationships to abstract ideas. As Dave Gray and his colleagues at Xplane demonstrate, using words isn't always the best way to communicate information, concepts, or ideas, so these professionals often look for visual solutions to complement or even replace textual information. The most common types of visuals for these applications include flowcharts and organization charts; maps; drawings, diagrams, infographics, and photographs; and animation and video.

FLOWCHARTS AND ORGANIZATION CHARTS

Use flowcharts to show a series of steps in a process or other sequential relationships.

If you need to show physical or conceptual relationships rather than numeric ones, you might want to use a flowchart or an organization chart. A **flowchart** (see Figure 12.13) illustrates a sequence of events from start to finish. It is particularly helpful when illustrating processes and procedures in which there are decision points, loops, and other complexities. For general business purposes, you don't need to be too concerned about the specific shapes, although do keep them consistent. However, be aware that there is a formal flowchart "language" in which each shape has a specific meaning (diamonds are decision points, rectangles are process steps, and so on). If you're communicating with computer programmers and others who are accustomed to formal flowcharting, make sure you use the correct symbols, to avoid confusion. Graphics programs that have flowchart symbols usually label their functions, making it easy to use the right ones.

Use organization charts to depict the interrelationships among the parts of a whole.

As the name implies, an **organization chart** illustrates the positions, units, or functions of an organization and the way they interrelate (refer to Figure 1.3 on page 8 for an

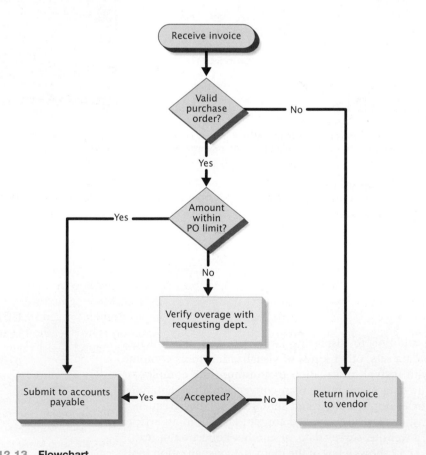

Figure 12.13　Flowchart
Flowcharts show sequences of events and are most valuable when the process or procedure has a number of decision points and variable paths.

Figure 12.14   Geographic Information Displays
Businesses use geographic information systems (GIS) in a variety of ways. By overlaying maps and aerial or satellite imagery with descriptive data, companies can use these displays for such purposes as planning sales campaigns, optimizing transportation routing, and selecting retail or production sites.

example). These charts aren't limited to organizational structures, of course; as you saw in Chapter 4, they can also be used to outline messages.

MAPS

Maps can show location, distance, points of interest (such as competitive retail outlets), and geographic distribution of data, such as sales by region or population by state. In addition to presenting facts and figures, maps are useful for showing market territories, distribution routes, and facilities locations.

Use maps for such tasks as representing statistics by geographic area or showing spatial relationships.

When combined with databases and aerial or satellite photography in *geographic information systems (GIS)*, maps become extremely powerful visual reporting tools (see Figure 12.14). As one example, retailing specialists can explore the demographic and psychographic makeup of neighborhoods within various driving distances from a particular store location. Using such information, managers can plan everything from new building sites to delivery routes to marketing campaigns.

DRAWINGS, DIAGRAMS, INFOGRAPHICS, AND PHOTOGRAPHS

The opportunities to use drawings, diagrams, and photographs are virtually endless. Simple drawings can show the network of suppliers in an industry, the flow of funds through a company, or the process for completing the payroll each week. More complex diagrams can convey technical topics such as the operation of a machine or repair procedures. Diagrams that contain enough visual and textual information to function as independent, standalone documents are sometimes called **infographics**. Figure 4.4 on page 95 and Figure 7.1 on page 175 are good examples.

Use drawings and diagrams to show how something works or how it is made or used; drawings are sometimes better than photographs because they let you focus on the most important details.

Word processors and presentation software now offer fairly advanced drawing capabilities, but for more precise and professional illustrations, you may need a specialized package such as Microsoft Visio, Adobe Illustrator, or Google SketchUp. Moving a level beyond those programs, *computer-aided design* (CAD) systems such as Autodesk's AutoCAD can produce extremely detailed architectural and engineering drawings.

Photographs offer both functional and decorative value, and nothing can top a photograph when you need to show exact appearances. Because audiences expect photographs

Use photographs for visual appeal and to show exact appearances.

to show literal visual truths, you must take care when using image processing tools such as Adobe Photoshop.

To use photographs successfully, consider these guidelines:

- **Consider whether a diagram would be more effective than a photograph.** Photographs are often unmatched in their ability to communicate spatial relationships, sizes, shapes, and other physical parameters, but sometimes they communicate too much information. For example, to show how to adjust a specific part of a complicated machine, a photo can be confusing because it shows all the parts within the camera's view. A simplified diagram is often more effective because it allows you to emphasize the specific parts that are relevant to the problem at hand.

- **Learn how to use basic image processing functions.** For most business reports, websites, and presentations, you won't need to worry about more advanced image processing functions and special effects. However, you need to know such basic operations such as the difference between resizing (changing the size of an image without removing any parts of it) and cropping (cutting away parts of the image).

- **Make sure the photographs have communication value.** Except for covers, title slides, and other special uses, it's usually best to avoid including photographs simply for decorative value.

Make sure you have the right to use photographs you find online.

- **Be aware of copyrights and model permissions.** Just as with textual information you find online, you can't simply insert online photographs into your documents. Unless they are specifically offered for free, you have to assume that someone owns the photos and is entitled to payment or at least a photo credit. In addition, professional photographers are careful to have any person who poses in photos sign a model release form, which gives the photographer permission to use the person's image.

ANIMATION AND VIDEO

Computer animation and video are among the most specialized forms of business visuals; when they are appropriate and done well, they offer unparalleled visual impact (see Figure 12.15). At a simple level, you can animate shapes and text within electronic presentations (see Chapter 17). At a more sophisticated level, software such as Adobe Flash enables the creation of multimedia files that include computer animation, digital video, and other elements.

Branded channels on YouTube have become an important business communication outlet.

The combination of low-cost digital video cameras and video-sharing websites such as YouTube has spurred a revolution in business video applications in recent years. Product demonstrations, company overviews, promotional presentations, and training seminars are among the most popular applications of business video. *Branded channels* on YouTube, such as the Lie-Nielsen example presented on page 183 in Chapter 7, allow companies to present their videos as an integrated collection in a customized user interface.

Producing and Integrating Visuals

5 **LEARNING OBJECTIVE**

Explain how to integrate visuals with text and list three criteria to review in order to verify the quality of your visuals.

Now that you understand the communication power of visuals and have chosen the best visuals to illustrate key points in your report, website, or presentation, it's time to get creative. This section offers advice on creating visuals, integrating them with your text, and verifying the quality of your visual elements.

CREATING VISUALS

Computer software offers a variety of graphical tools but doesn't automatically give you the design sensibility that is needed for effective visuals.

Learning how to use your computer tools will help you save enormous amounts of time and produce better results.

Computers make it easy to create visuals, but they also make it easy to create ineffective, distracting, and even downright ugly visuals. However, by following the basic design principles discussed on pages 341–342, you can create all the basic visuals you need—visuals that are both attractive and effective.

Whether you're using the charting functions offered in a spreadsheet or the design features of a specialized graphics program, take a few minutes to familiarize yourself with the software's quirks and capabilities. For important visuals, try to have a professional designer set up a template for the various types of visuals you and your colleagues need to create. In addition to helping ensure an effective design, using templates saves you the time of making numerous design decisions every time you create a chart or graphic.

Readers who want to learn more about F5's solutions for secure remote access can get a presentation on that specific topic; the diagram then animates to show how that solution works.

Figure 12.15 Interactive, Animated Diagram
Clearly drawn diagrams help audiences grasp complex ideas quickly. Extending this capability with interactivity and animation, as F5 Networks did with this networking visual, can make a diagram even more audience-focused by letting website visitors choose the information most relevant to their individual needs. You can interact with the diagram yourself at **www.f5.com/flash/product-demo/**.

No matter which tools you're using, take care to match the style and quality of your visuals with the subject matter and the situation at hand. The style of your visuals communicates a subtle message about your relationship with the audience. A simple sketch might be fine for a working meeting but inappropriate for a formal presentation or report. On the other hand, elaborate, full-color visuals may be viewed as extravagant for an informal report but may be entirely appropriate for a message to top management or influential outsiders.

> A visual's level of sophistication should match the communication situation.

INTEGRATING VISUALS WITH TEXT

For maximum effectiveness and minimum disruption for the reader, visual elements need to be carefully integrated with the text of your message. In some instances, visual elements are somewhat independent from the text, as in the *sidebars* that occasionally accompany magazine articles. Such images are related to the content of the main story, but they aren't referred to by a specific title or figure number. This sort of treatment is often used in promotional materials such as brochures and advertisements.

For reports and most other business documents, however, visuals are tightly integrated with the text so that readers can move back and forth between text and visuals with as little disruption as possible. Successful integration involves four decisions: maintaining a balance between visuals and text, referring to visuals in the text, placing the visuals in a document, and writing titles and other descriptions.

Maintaining a Balance Between Illustrations and Words

Strong visuals enhance the descriptive and persuasive power of your writing, but putting too many visuals into a report can distract your readers. If you're constantly referring to tables, drawings, and other visual elements, the effort to switch back and forth from words

> Maintain a balance between text and visuals and place your visuals so that they help emphasize your key points.

REAL-TIME UPDATES
Learn More by Reading This PDF

Jumpstart your visual creativity

The notion that visual creativity is a skill that only artists have—or should care about—is simply not true. Go to http://real-timeupdates.com/bct11 and click on "Learn More." If you are using MyBcommLab, you can access Real-Time Updates within each chapter or under Student Study Tools.

Make sure your visuals match the needs, expectations, and interpretation skills of your audience.

To tie visuals to text, introduce them in the text and place them near the points they illustrate.

Help your readers understand why each visual is important.

to visuals can make it difficult for readers to maintain focus on the thread of your message. The space occupied by visuals can also disrupt the flow of text on the page or screen.

As always, take into account your readers' specific needs. If you're addressing an audience with multiple language backgrounds or widely varying reading skills, you can shift the balance toward more visual elements to help get around any language barriers. The professional experience, education, and training of your audience should influence your approach as well. For instance, detailed statistical plots and mathematical formulas are everyday reading material for quality-control engineers but not for most salespeople or top executives.

Referencing Visuals

Unless a visual element clearly stands on its own, it should be clearly referred to by number in the text of your report. Some report writers refer to all visuals as "exhibits" and number them consecutively throughout the report; many others number tables and figures separately (everything that isn't a table is regarded as a figure). In a long report with numbered sections, illustrations may have a double number (separated by a period or a hyphen) representing the section number and the individual illustration number within that section. Whatever scheme you use, make sure it's clear and easy to follow.

Help your readers understand the significance of visuals by referring to them before readers encounter them in the document or on the screen. The following examples show how you can make this connection in the text:

> Figure 1 summarizes the financial history of the motorcycle division over the past five years, with sales broken into four categories.
>
> Total sales were steady over this period, but the mix of sales by category changed dramatically (see Figure 2).
>
> The underlying reason for the remarkable growth in our sales of youth golf apparel is suggested by Table 4, which shows the growing interest in junior golf around the world.

When describing the data shown in your visuals, be sure to emphasize the main point you are trying to make. Don't make the mistake of simply repeating the data to be shown. Paragraphs that do are guaranteed to put the reader to sleep:

> Among those who replied to the survey, 17.4 percent earn less than $8 per hour; 26.4 percent earn $8 to $12; 25.7 percent, $13 to $20; 18.0 percent, $20 to $30; 9.6 percent, $30 to $49; and 2.9 percent, $50 and over.

The visual will (or at least should) provide all these details; there is no need to repeat them in the text. Instead, use round numbers that sum up the message:

> As Table 4.2 shows, more than two-thirds of the respondents earn less than $20 per hour.

Placing Visuals

Place each visual as close as possible to its in-text reference to help readers understand the illustration's relevance and to minimize the effort of reading.

Try to position your visuals so that your audience won't have to flip back and forth (in printed documents) or scroll (on-screen) between the visuals and the text. Ideally, it's best to place each visual within, beside, or immediately after the paragraph it illustrates so that readers can consult the explanation and the visual at the same time. This scheme works well both in print and online. If at all possible, avoid bunching visuals at the end of a section or the end of a document; doing so asks a lot of the reader. (Bunching is unavoidable in some cases, such as when multiple visuals accompany a single section of text—as in this chapter, for instance.) Word-processing, desktop-publishing, and web-design programs let you place graphical elements virtually anywhere you wish, so take advantage of this flexibility.

Writing Titles, Captions, and Legends

Titles, captions, and legends help connect your visual and textual messages and ensure a seamless reading experience. A **title** identifies the content and purpose of the visual, along with whatever label and number you're using to refer to the visual. A **descriptive title** simply identifies the topic of the illustration, whereas an **informative title** calls attention to the conclusion that ought to be drawn from the data. Here's an example of the difference:

A descriptive title simply identifies the topic of an illustration; an informative title helps the reader understand the conclusion to be drawn from the illustration.

Descriptive Title	Informative Title
Relationship Between Petroleum Demand and Refinery Capacity in the United States	Refinery Capacity Declines as Petroleum Demand Continues to Grow

An informative title saves readers the work of interpreting the visual to extract the main idea from it. Regardless of whether your titles and legends are informative or descriptive, phrase them consistently throughout a document.

A **caption** usually offers additional discussion of the visual's content and can be up to several sentences long, if appropriate. Captions can also alert readers that additional discussion is available in the accompanying text. A **legend** helps readers "decode" the visual by explaining what various colors, symbols, or other design choices mean (several of the figures in this chapter use legends, for example). Legends aren't necessary for simple graphs, such as a line chart or bar chart with only one series of data, but they are invaluable with more complex graphics.

VERIFYING THE QUALITY OF YOUR VISUALS

Visuals have a particularly strong impact on your readers and on their perceptions of you and your work, so verifying the quality of your visuals is an essential step. Ask yourself three questions about every visual element:

- **Is the visual accurate?** Be sure to check for mistakes such as typographical errors, inconsistent color treatment, confusing or undocumented symbols, and misaligned elements. Also verify that information in visuals and text matches. For data presentations, particularly if you're producing charts with a spreadsheet, verify any formulas used to generate the numbers and make sure you've selected the right numbers for each chart. For flowcharts, organization charts, diagrams, photos, and other visuals make sure each visual delivers your message accurately and that you have inserted the correct image files.

Review each visual to make sure it doesn't intentionally or unintentionally distort the meaning of the underlying information.

- **Is the visual properly documented?** As with the textual elements in your reports and presentations, visuals based on other people's research, information, and ideas require full citation. (Even if the graphical design is entirely yours, any underlying information taken from other sources needs to be documented.) Also, try to anticipate any questions or concerns your audience may have and address them with additional information, as needed. For instance, if you're presenting the results of survey research, many readers will want to know who participated in the survey, how many people responded, and when the questions were asked. You could answer these questions with a note in the caption along the lines of "652 accountants, surveyed the week of January 17." Similarly, if you found a visual in a secondary source, list that source on or near the graphic to help readers assess the information. Alternatively, you can list sources in an appendix.
- **Is the visual honest?** As a final precaution, step back and verify that your visuals communicate truthful messages. Make sure they don't hide information the audience needs, imply conclusions that your information doesn't support, or play on audience emotions in manipulative or coercive ways.

For a review of the important points to remember when creating visuals, see "Checklist: Creating Effective Visuals." For more information on visual communication, including design principles, ethical matters, and the latest tools for creating and displaying visuals, visit http://real-timeupdates .com/bct11 and click on Chapter 12.

REAL-TIME UPDATES
Learn More by Reading This Article

Understand why some visuals work and some don't

Learn from the insightful analysis of more than a dozen commonly used displays for data and information, along with redesigned visuals that address the identified problems. Go to http:// real-timeupdates.com/bct11 and click on "Learn More." If you are using MyBcommLab, you can access Real-Time Updates within each chapter or under Student Study Tools.

MyBcommLab

CHAPTER OUTLINE

Understanding Visual Communication
The Power of Images
The Visual Evolution in Business Communication
Visual Design Principles
The Ethics of Visual Communication

Identifying Points to Illustrate

Selecting Visuals for Presenting Data
Tables
Line and Surface Charts
Bar Charts, Pictograms, and Gantt Charts
Scatter and Bubble Diagrams
Pie Charts
Data Visualization

Selecting Visuals for Presenting Information, Concepts, and Ideas
Flowcharts and Organization Charts
Maps
Drawings, Diagrams, Infographics, and Photographs
Animation and Video

Producing and Integrating Visuals
Creating Visuals
Integrating Visuals with Text
Verifying the Quality of Your Visuals

SUMMARY OF LEARNING OBJECTIVES

1 Explain the power of business images, discuss six principles of graphic design that help ensure effective visuals, and explain how to avoid ethical lapses when using visuals. Well-designed visual elements can enhance the communication power of textual messages and, in some instances, even replace textual messages. Visuals can often convey some message points (such as spatial relationships, correlations, procedures, and emotions) more effectively and more efficiently than words. In the numbers-oriented world of work, readers rely heavily on trend lines, distribution curves, and other visual presentations of numeric quantities. Visuals attract and hold people's attention, helping your audience understand and remember your message. Visuals are also an effective way to communicate with diverse audiences.

When preparing visuals, (1) use elements of design consistently so you don't confuse your audience; (2) use color and other elements to show contrast effectively; (3) strive for a visual balance, either formal or informal, that creates a feel that is appropriate for your overall message; (4) use design choices to draw attention to key elements and to visually downplay less important items; (5) understand and follow design conventions that your audience expects (even if the expectation is subconscious), although you can consider unconventional design choices if they promise to convey your message more effectively; and (6) strive for simplicity in all your visuals, making design decisions that enhance the reception and understanding of information rather than obscure or confuse it.

Communicators are responsible for avoiding both intentional and unintentional ethical lapses when using visual elements. They can work to avoid these lapses by (1) considering all possible interpretations—and misinterpretations—of their messages and avoiding design choices that could lead to unwanted interpretations; (2) providing sufficient context, whether visual or verbal, for audiences to understand the meaning and significance of visuals; (3) not hiding or minimizing negative information that runs counter to their arguments; (4) not exaggerating information that supports their arguments; (5) not oversimplifying complex situations by hiding complications that are relevant to the audience's understanding; (6) not implying cause-and-effect relationships without providing proof that they exist; (7) avoiding emotional manipulation or other forms of coercion; and (8) being careful with the way they aggregate data.

2 Explain how to choose which points in your message to illustrate. To decide which points to illustrate, first step back and consider the overall flow of your message from the audience's point of view. Identify elements of the message that might be complex, vulnerable to misinterpretation, or even dull. Look for connections between ideas that should be highlighted or extensive collections of data and other discrete factual content that might be difficult to read in textual format.

3 Describe the most common options for presenting data in a visual format. The visuals most commonly used to present data include tables, line and surface charts, bar charts, pictograms, Gantt charts, scatter and bubble diagrams and pie charts. You will probably use line, bar, and pie charts most often in your business communication efforts. Moving beyond basic display formats, designers continue to invent new data visualization tools to present large or complex sets of data.

4 Describe the most common options for presenting information, concepts, and ideas. Among the most commonly used visual formats in business communication are flowcharts (which depict a sequence of events in a process), organization charts (which show the relationships among people or elements in an organization), various types of maps (including data-driven map displays made possible by geographic information systems), drawings (which are often used instead of photographs because they can focus attention on specific parts of an object), diagrams (used to convey designs, interrelated ideas, and other complex entities), infographics (hybrid elements that contain enough textual and visual information to function as standalone documents), photographs (used when realism or emotional impact is important), computer animation (which can range from simple motions in presentation software such as Microsoft PowerPoint to richly complex short "films"), and video (used for everything from résumé supplements to product demonstrations).

5 **Explain how to integrate visuals with text, and list three criteria to review in order to verify the quality of your visuals.** To integrate visuals with text, strive for a balance between text and visuals, refer to visuals clearly, place visuals to maximize the smooth flow of reading, and write helpful titles, captions, and legends. To verify the quality of your visuals, make sure every visual is accurate (there are no mistakes or missing information), properly documented (the creator of any underlying data used in the visual has been given complete credit), and honest (the visual honestly reveals the real meaning of the underlying data or information).

KEY TERMS

area chart Another name for a surface chart

bar chart Chart that portrays quantities by the height or length of its rectangular bars

bubble diagram Chart that expands the scatter diagram idea to three variables, with the size of the bubble representing the third variable

caption Brief commentary or explanation that accompanies a visual

data visualization A diverse class of displays that can show enormous sets of data in a single visual or show text and other complex information visually

descriptive title Title that simply identifies the topic of an illustration

flowchart Process diagram that illustrates a sequence of events from start to finish

Gantt chart The best known type of time line chart

infographics Diagrams that contain enough visual and textual information to function as independent, standalone documents

informative title Title that highlights the conclusion to be drawn from the data

legend A "key" that helps readers decode a visual by explaining what various colors, symbols, or other design choices mean

line chart Chart that illustrates trends over time or plots the relationship of two or more variables

organization chart Diagram that illustrates the positions, units, or functions of an organization and their relationships

pictogram Chart that portrays data as symbols instead of words or numbers

pie chart Circular chart that shows how the parts of a whole are distributed

scatter diagram Chart that plots discrete data points, with one variable along the x

(horizontal) axis and another along the y (vertical) axis

surface chart Form of line chart with a cumulative effect; all the lines add up to the top line, which represents the total

table A systematic arrangement of data in columns and rows

time line chart Chart that shows how much time is needed to complete each task in a project

title Identifies the content and purpose of a visual

visual literacy The ability to create effective images and to correctly interpret such images

visual symbolism The connotative (as opposed to the denotative, or literal) meaning of visuals

XY diagram Another name for a scatter diagram

 Checklist

Creating Effective Visuals

- Emphasize visual consistency to connect parts of a whole and minimize audience confusion.
- Avoid arbitrary changes of color, texture, typeface, position, or scale.
- Highlight contrasting points through color, position, and other design choices.
- Decide whether you want to achieve formal or informal balance.
- Emphasize dominant elements and de-emphasize less important pieces in a design.
- Understand and follow (at least most of the time) the visual conventions your audience expects.

- Strive for simplicity and clarity; don't clutter your visuals with meaningless decoration.
- Follow the guidelines for avoiding ethical lapses.
- Carefully consider your message, the nature of your information, and your audience to choose which points to illustrate.
- Select the proper types of graphics for the information at hand and for the objective of the message.
- Be sure the visual contributes to overall understanding of the subject.

- Understand how to use your software tools to maximize effectiveness and efficiency.
- Integrate visuals and text by maintaining a balance between illustrations and words, clearly referring to visuals within the text, and placing visuals carefully.
- Use titles, captions, and legends to help readers understand the meaning and importance of your visuals.
- Verify the quality of your visuals by checking for accuracy, proper documentation, and honesty.

✔ Checklist | Creating Effective Visuals

- Emphasize visual consistency to connect parts of a whole and minimize audience confusion.
- Avoid arbitrary changes of color, texture, typeface, position, or scale.
- Highlight contrasting points through color, position, and other design choices.
- Decide whether you want to achieve formal or informal balance.
- Emphasize dominant elements and de-emphasize less important pieces in a design.
- Understand and follow (at least most of the time) the visual conventions your audience expects.
- Strive for simplicity and clarity; don't clutter your visuals with meaningless decoration.
- Follow the guidelines for avoiding ethical lapses.
- Carefully consider your message, the nature of your information, and your audience to choose which points to illustrate.

- Select the proper types of graphics for the information at hand and for the objective of the message.
- Be sure the visual contributes to overall understanding of the subject.
- Understand how to use your software tools to maximize effectiveness and efficiency.
- Integrate visuals and text by maintaining a balance between illustrations and words, clearly referring to visuals within the text, and placing visuals carefully.
- Use titles, captions, and legends to help readers understand the meaning and importance of your visuals.
- Verify the quality of your visuals by checking for accuracy, proper documentation, and honesty.

COMMUNICATION CHALLENGES AT XPLANE

Your passion for tackling complex problems led you to a position in Xplane's Portland, Oregon, home office after graduation. Using the principles of visual communication you learned in this chapter, tackle the following challenges. For inspiration, refer to Figure 4.4 on page 95 or visit Xplane's website, at www.xplane.com/work/solutions, to see other examples.

INDIVIDUAL CHALLENGE: Using a flowchart as the foundation, create a visual guide to planning a fun weekend. In addition to labeling the individual shapes (see Figure 12.13 on page 356),

feel free to add as many additional notes and other graphic elements as you need—but make sure your guide is clear and easy to use. If possible, create the piece electronically or scan it and create a PDF file that you can submit to your instructor.

TEAM CHALLENGE: As part of a team of three or four students, create a visual guide to getting into college that could help high schoolers plan and manage their way through this complicated process. Start by listing all the steps required to research colleges, take necessary tests, apply for financial aid, and so on. Then choose a visual metaphor that you can use to organize your information—a ladder, a road map, a treasure map, whatever works for you. Use this image as the foundation of your visual guide and then add labels and blocks of text to complete your work. If possible, create the piece electronically or scan it and create a PDF file that you can submit to your instructor.

TEST YOUR KNOWLEDGE

To review chapter content related to each question, refer to the indicated Learning Objective.

1. What type of data visual would you use to compare one part with a whole? [LO-3]
2. What type of data visual would you use to present detailed, exact values? [LO-3]
3. Why is simplicity important in business visuals? [LO-1]
4. What type of data visual would you use to illustrate trends over time? [LO-3]
5. When would you use a bubble diagram instead of a scatter diagram? [LO-3]
6. For what purposes are Gantt charts used? [LO-3]
7. Why might you use a simplified line drawing instead of a full-color digital photograph in a particular application? [LO-4]
8. In what important ways do infographics differ from other business visuals? [LO-4]
9. What is the purpose of adding titles, captions, and legends to visuals in reports? [LO-5]
10. How do you check a visual for quality? [LO-5]

APPLY YOUR KNOWLEDGE

To review chapter content related to each question, refer to the indicated Learning Objective.

1. What similarities do you see between visuals and nonverbal communication? Explain your answer. [LO-1]

2. After studying the designs of corporate websites, Penn State University professor S. Shyam Sundar discovered quite an interesting phenomenon: The more interactive and engaging a website is, the more likely visitors are to "buy into whatever is being advocated" on the site. In other words, if two websites have identical content, the site with greater interactivity and more "bells and whistles" would be more persuasive.[18] Is it ethical to increase the persuasive power of a website simply by making it more interactive? Why or why not? [LO-1]
3. You're writing a report for the director of human resources on implementing team-based management throughout your company. You want to emphasize that since the new approaches were implemented six months ago, absenteeism and turnover have been sharply reduced in all but two departments. How do you visually present your data in the most favorable light while maintaining honest communication? Explain. [LO-1]
4. In addition to telling readers why an illustration is important, why else should you refer to it in the text of your document? [LO-5]
5. When you read a graph, how can you be sure that the visual impression you are receiving is an accurate reflection of reality? Explain. [LO-5]

PRACTICE YOUR SKILLS

Messages for Analysis

Message 12.A: Presenting Data (Bar Charts) [LO-1], [LO-3]

Examine the bar charts in Figure 12.16 and point out any problems or errors you notice.

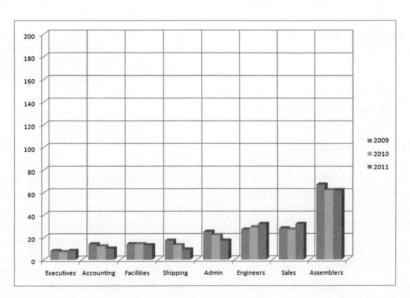

Figure 12.16 **Bar Chart for Analysis**

Message 12.B: Presenting Data (Line Charts) [LO-1], [LO-3]
Examine the line chart in Figure 12.17 and point out any problems or errors you notice.

Figure 12.17 Line Chart for Analysis

Exercises

1. **Applying Visual Design Principles [LO-1]** Review one of the client stories in the portfolio section of the Xplane website (www.xplane.com/portfolio). Briefly describe how a visual was used to address a business problem and why a visual approach worked better in this instance than a conventional text approach would've worked.

2. **Applying Visual Design Principles [LO-1]** From online sources, find three visual presentations of data, information, or concepts. Which of the three presents its data or information most clearly? What design choices promote this level of clarity? What improvements would you make to the other visuals to make them clearer?

3. **Communication Ethics [LO-1]** Using a spreadsheet, create a bar chart or line chart, using data you find online or in a business publication. Alter the horizontal and vertical scales in several ways to produce different displays of the original data. How do the alterations distort the information? How might a reader detect whether a chart's scale has been altered?

4. **Presenting Data (Bar and Pie Charts) [LO-3]** As a market researcher for a statewide chain of car dealerships, you're examining car and truck ownership and lease patterns among single drivers in various age groups. By discovering which age groups have the highest percentages of owners, you will be better able to target advertising that promotes the leasing option. Using the information that follows, prepare a bar chart comparing the number of owners with the number of people who lease in each age category. Be sure to label your chart and include combined totals for owners and lessees ("total drivers"). Then prepare a pie chart showing the proportion of owners and lessees in the one age group that you think holds the most promise for leasing a new vehicle. Write a sentence that prepares your company's management for the information shown in the pie chart.

Age Group	Number of Owners (in Thousands)	Number of Lessees (in Thousands)
18–24	1,830	795
25–29	1,812	1,483
30–34	1,683	1,413
35–44	1,303	1,932
45–54	1,211	1,894
55–64	1,784	1,435
65–74	3,200	1,142
75+	3,431	854

5. **Presenting Data (Line Charts) [LO-3]** The pet food manufacturer you work for is interested in the results of a recent poll of U.S. pet-owning households. Look at the cat ownership statistics that follow and decide on the most appropriate scale for a chart; then create a line chart of the trends in cat ownership. What conclusions do you draw from the trend you've charted? Draft a paragraph or two discussing the results of this poll and the potential consequences for the pet food business. Support your conclusions by referring readers to your chart.

   In 1995, 22 million U.S. households owned cats. In 2000, 24 million households owned cats. In 2005, 28 million households owned a cat. In 2010, 32 million households owned cats.

6. **Presenting Data (Bar Charts) [LO-3]** Team up with a classmate to design charts based on a comparison of the total tax burden of the U.S. taxpayer with that of people in other nations (see the data at the top of the next page). One teammate should sketch a horizontal or vertical bar chart, and the other should sketch a pictogram from the estimates that follow. Then exchange charts and analyze how well each conveys the situation of the U.S. taxpayer. Would the bar chart look best with vertical or horizontal bars? Why? What scale is best? How does the symbol used in the pictogram enhance or obscure the meaning or impact of the data? What suggestions can each student make for improving the other's visual aid?

Estimates show that Swedish taxpayers spend 51 percent of their incomes on taxes, British taxpayers spend 48 percent, French taxpayers spend 37 percent, Japanese taxpayers spend 28 percent, and U.S. taxpayers spend 27 percent.

7. **Presenting Data (Line Charts) [LO-3]** Here are last year's sales figures for the appliance and electronics megastore where you work. Construct a line chart that will help you explain to the store's general manager seasonal variations in each department.

STORE SALES (IN $ THOUSANDS)

Month	Home Electronics	Computers	Appliances
January	$68	$39	$36
February	72	34	34
March	75	41	30
April	54	41	28
May	56	42	44
June	49	33	48
July	54	31	43
August	66	58	39
September	62	58	36
October	66	44	33
November	83	48	29
December	91	62	24

8. **Presenting Data (Line Charts) [LO-3]** Re-create the line chart in Figure 12.6 on page 350 as a bar chart and as a pie chart. Which of these three formats does the best job of conveying the information? Are any of the formats definitely inappropriate for this information? Explain your answers.

9. **Presenting Data (Data Visualization) [LO-3]** Explore several of the data visualization tools available through the Bovée & Thill Data Visualization Gateway. (Go to http://real-timeupdates.com/bct11 and click on "Learn More." If you are using MyBcommLab, you can access Real-Time Updates within each chapter or under Student Study Tools.) Select one that has the potential to help business managers make decisions. Write a post for your class blog, explaining how this tool could assist with decision making. Be sure to include a link to the site where you found it.

10. **Presenting Information, Concepts, and Ideas (Photographs) [LO-4]** As directed by your instructor, team up with other students, making sure that at least one of you has a digital camera or camera phone capable of downloading images to your word-processing software. Find a busy location on campus or in the surrounding neighborhood, someplace with lots of signs, storefronts, pedestrians, and traffic. Scout out two different photo opportunities, one that maximizes the visual impression of crowding and clutter, and one that minimizes this impression. For the first, assume that you are someone who advocates reducing the crowding and clutter, so you want to show how bad it is. For the second, assume that you are a real estate agent or someone else who is motivated to show people that even though the location offers lots of shopping, entertainment, and other attractions, it's actually a rather calm and quiet neighborhood. Insert the two images in a word-processing document and write a caption for each that emphasizes the two opposite messages just described. Finally, write a brief paragraph, discussing the ethical implications of what you've just done. Have you distorted reality or just presented it in ways that work to your advantage? Have you prevented audiences from gaining the information they would need to make informed decisions?

11. **Selecting the Right Type of Visual [LO-3], [LO-4]** You're preparing the annual report for FretCo Guitar Corporation. For each of the following types of information, select the right chart or visual to illustrate the text. Explain your choices.
   a. Data on annual sales for the past 20 years
   b. Comparison of FretCo sales, product by product (electric guitars, bass guitars, amplifiers, acoustic guitars), for this year and last year
   c. Explanation of how a FretCo acoustic guitar is manufactured
   d. Explanation of how the FretCo Guitar Corporation markets its guitars
   e. Data on sales of FretCo products in each of 12 countries
   f. Comparison of FretCo sales figures with sales figures for three competing guitar makers over the past 10 years

12. **Presenting Information, Concepts, and Ideas (Maps) [LO-4]** You work for C & S Holdings, a company that operates coin-activated, self-service car washes. Research shows that the farther customers live from a car wash, the less likely they are to visit. You know that 50 percent of customers at each of your car washes live within a 4-mile radius of the location, 65 percent live within 6 miles, 80 percent live within 8 miles, and 90 percent live within 10 miles. C & S's owner wants to open two new car washes in your city and has asked you to prepare a report, recommending locations. Using a map of your city, choose two possible locations for car washes and create a visual depicting the customer base surrounding each location.

13. **Presenting Information, Concepts, and Ideas (Organization Charts) [LO-4]** Create an organization chart for your college or university. Start with the school's website to learn the various offices and departments.

14. **Selecting the Right Type of Visual [LO-3], [LO-4]** With a team of two or three other students, brainstorm and then sketch at least three types of charts you can use to compare the populations of all 50 states in the United States. You can use any of the graphic ideas presented in this chapter, as well as any ideas or examples you find from other sources.

EXPAND YOUR SKILLS

Critique the Professionals

Find an infographic or data visualization display online that presents some form of business-related data. Analyze its communication effectiveness using the criteria on page 342. Summarize your conclusions in a post on your class blog or an email to your instructor. Be sure to include a link to the visual.

Sharpening Your Career Skills Online

Bovée and Thill's Business Communication Web Search, at http://businesscommunicationblog.com/websearch, is a unique research tool designed specifically for business communication research. Use the Web Search function to find a website, video, PDF document, podcast, or PowerPoint presentation that offers advice on creating effective visuals for documents and presentations. Write a brief email message to your instructor, describing the item that you found and summarizing the career skills information you learned from it.

PART 5   Planning, Writing, and Completing Reports and Proposals

CHAPTER 13   Planning Reports and Proposals

CHAPTER 14   Writing Reports and Proposals

CHAPTER 15   Completing Reports and Proposals

Printed and online reports (including entire websites) are the major leagues of business communication. These are the tools you use to analyze complex problems, educate audiences, address opportunities in the marketplace, win contracts, and even launch new companies through compelling business plans. Adapt what you've learned so far to the particular challenges of long-format messages, including some special touches that can make formal reports stand out from the crowd.

COMMUNICATION CLOSE-UP AT **MYCITYWAY**

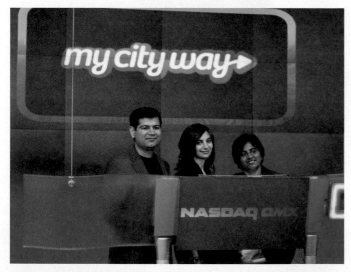

MyCityWay's effective use of a business plan helped secure financing that allowed the company to expand far beyond its initial New York City market.

http://mycityway.com

Any experienced entrepreneur will tell you there's a big difference between having a great idea for a business and actually building a successful business. Many things have to go right, from creating a compelling product or service to finding the right employees to getting enough money to launch, expand, and sustain operations.

For Archana Patchirajan, Sonpreet Bhatia, and Puneet Mehta, the adventure started with the NYC BigApps competition. This contest is sponsored by the city of New York as a way to encourage entrepreneurs to create better ways for people to use the NYC Data Mine, a huge trove of data created by all the government departments and agencies in the city.

The three partners jumped on the opportunity with NYC Way, a mobile application that helps people "navigate and explore" the city, whether they are residents looking for apartment deals or visitors looking for a great restaurant. One key aspect of the BigApps competition is that entrepreneurs must put their apps online for people to try out. By the time the contest ended, 100,000 people were using NYC Way.

Patchirajan, Bhatia, and Mehta clearly had a hit product on their hands. The next challenge was to turn it into a thriving business. As with most startups, that meant getting money to expand operations. The competition garnered the new firm, MyCityWay, priceless publicity and a small amount of *seed funding* that let the team set up offices and begin hiring.

Momentum continued to build as they enhanced the product and several hundred thousand more people began using it. After a successful launch in the New York City market, the next step was to conquer the world. That would require a significant infusion of capital, and to attract that, the three founders knew they needed a formal *business plan* to show potential investors why MyCityWay would be a smart place to invest their money.

With their Wall Street backgrounds, Patchirajan, Bhatia, and Mehta understood the fundamentals of business finance, which gave them a good foundation for their plan. They also got smart advice on what today's investors are looking for: short, compelling documents that strike a balance between providing enough information to be persuasive and providing so much information that potential investors balk at reading it. With so many plans crossing their desks day after day, most venture capitalists and other investors don't have the time to slog through 50 or 60 pages of details to judge whether a company might be worth pursuing as an investment candidate. They want to be captivated in a matter of seconds and persuaded to learn more in a matter of minutes.

MyCityWay clearly found the right balance with its plan, as a second round of funding brought in $1 million in capital and then luxury carmaker BMW invested $5 million as part of its "BMW i" program, which promotes the development of innovative automotive materials and technologies. By early 2011, the company had apps for several dozen cities around the world and was launching a new city app about every week. Thanks to a great product and a compelling business plan, MyCityWay is now well on its way to becoming a global player in the world of mobile information.[1]

Applying the Three-Step Writing Process to Reports and Proposals

Whether they are printed documents or online resources, **reports** are written accounts that objectively communicate information about some aspect of a business. **Informational reports** offer data, facts, feedback, and other types of information, without analysis or recommendations. **Analytical reports** offer both information and analysis and can also include recommendations. **Proposals** are a special category of reports that combine information delivery and persuasive communication.

The nature of these reports can vary widely, depending on the circumstances. Some of the reports you write will be voluntary, launched at your own initiative and following whatever structure you find most effective. Other reports will be in response to a manager's or customer's request, and you may or may not receive guidance regarding the organization and content. You'll also write reports that follow strict, specific guidelines for content and layout.

Your audience will sometimes be internal, which gives you more freedom to discuss sensitive information. At other times, your audience might include customers, investors, community members, or news media, any of which can create additional demands as you present company information to such external groups.

Finally, your reports will vary widely in length and complexity. You may write one-page memo- or letter-format reports that are simple and straightforward. Or you may write reports that cover complicated subjects, that run into hundreds or even thousands of pages, and that involve multiple writers.

No matter what the circumstances, these reports require all the skills and knowledge that you've gained throughout this course and will continue to gain on the job. View every business report as an opportunity to demonstrate your understanding of business challenges and your ability to contribute to your organization's success.

By adapting the three-step writing process (see Figure 13.1 on the next page), you can reduce the time required to write effective reports and still produce documents that make lasting and positive impressions on your audiences. The concepts are the same as those you explored in Chapters 4 through 6 and applied to shorter messages in Chapters 7 through 10. However, the emphasis on specific tasks can vary considerably. For instance, planning can take days or weeks for a complex report or proposal.

Part 5 offers in-depth coverage of the three-step writing process for reports and proposals. This chapter discusses planning, Chapter 14 discusses writing, and Chapter 15 covers completing reports and proposals. Because much of the writing process has already been covered in Chapters 4 through 6, Chapters 13 through 15 focus on aspects that require special attention for longer messages. These chapters also address the challenge of planning and creating conventional website content.

ANALYZING THE SITUATION

The complexity of most reports and the magnitude of the work involved heighten the need to analyze the situation carefully. With an email or another short message, you can change

1 LEARNING OBJECTIVE

Adapt the three-step writing process to reports and proposals.

The purpose and content of business reports varies widely; in some cases you'll follow strict guidelines, but in others the organization and format will be up to you.

Many of your reports will be written for internal audiences, but you're also likely to write reports for a wide range of outside readers.

MyBcommLab

- Access this chapter's simulation entitled Business Reports, located at mybcommlab.com.

Given the length and complexity of many reports, it's crucial to define your purpose clearly so you don't waste time with avoidable rework.

1 Plan →	**2** Write →	**3** Complete
Analyze the Situation Clarify the problem or opportunity at hand, define your purpose, develop an audience profile, and develop a work plan. **Gather Information** Determine audience needs and obtain the information necessary to satisfy those needs; conduct a research project, if necessary. **Select the Right Medium** Choose the best medium for delivering your message; consider delivery through multiple media. **Organize the Information** Define your main idea, limit your scope, select the direct or indirect approach, and outline your content using an appropriate structure for an informational report, an analytical report, or a proposal.	**Adapt to Your Audience** Be sensitive to audience needs with a "you" attitude, politeness, positive emphasis, and bias-free language. Build a strong relationship with your audience by establishing your credibility and projecting your company's image. Control your style with a tone and voice appropriate to the situation. **Compose the Message** Choose strong words that will help you create effective sentences and coherent paragraphs throughout the introduction, body, and close of your report or proposal.	**Revise the Message** Evaluate content and review readability, then edit and rewrite for conciseness and clarity. **Produce the Message** Use effective design elements and suitable layout for a clean, professional appearance; seamlessly combine text and graphical elements. **Proofread the Message** Review for errors in layout, spelling, and mechanics. **Distribute the Message** Deliver your report using the chosen medium; make sure all documents and all relevant files are distributed successfully.

Figure 13.1   Three-Step Writing Process for Reports and Proposals
The three-step writing process becomes even more valuable with reports and proposals. By guiding your work at each step, the process helps you make the most of the time and energy you invest.

direction halfway through the first draft and perhaps lose only a few minutes of work. In contrast, if you change direction halfway through a major report, you could lose days or weeks. To minimize that chance, pay special attention to your statement of purpose. In addition, for anything beyond the simplest reports, take the time to prepare a work plan before you start writing.

Defining Your Purpose

In some cases, you'll be told the purpose of the report; in others, it's up to you to identify the purpose.

Informational reports often address a predetermined need and must meet specific audience expectations. For example, you may be asked to write reports that verify your company's compliance with government regulations, that summarize sales, or that monitor a process—all of which have audiences who expect certain information in a certain format. With other informational reports, you will need to uncover audience needs before you can define the optimum purpose.

Analytical reports and proposals are almost always written in response to a perceived problem or a perceived opportunity. A clear statement of this problem or opportunity helps frame the communication challenge by identifying *what* you're going to write about, but it's insufficient to guide your writing efforts. To plan effectively, address the problem or opportunity with a clear **statement of purpose** that defines *why* you are preparing the report (see Table 13.1).

The most useful way to phrase your purpose statement is to begin with an infinitive phrase (*to* plus a verb). Using an infinitive phrase encourages you to take control and decide where you're going before you begin. When you choose an infinitive phrase (such as *to inform, to confirm, to analyze, to persuade,* or *to recommend*), you pin down your general goal in preparing the report. Consider these examples for informational reports:

To update clients on the progress of the research project (progress report)

To develop goals and objectives for the coming year (strategic plan)

To identify customers and explain how the company will serve them (marketing plan)

To submit monthly sales statistics to management (operating report)

To summarize what occurred at the annual sales conference (personal activity report)

To explain building access procedures (policy implementation report)

To submit required information to the Securities and Exchange Commission (compliance report)

Your statement of purpose for an analytical report often needs to be more comprehensive than a statement for an informational report. Linda Moreno, the cost accounting manager for Electrovision, a high-tech company based in Los Gatos, California, was recently asked to find ways of reducing employee travel and entertainment costs. (Her complete report appears in Chapter 15.) Because Moreno was supposed to suggest specific ways to solve a problem, she phrased her statement of purpose accordingly:

... to analyze the T&E [travel and entertainment] budget, evaluate the impact of recent changes in airfares and hotel costs, and suggest ways to tighten management's control over T&E expenses.

If Moreno had been assigned an informational report instead, she might have stated her purpose differently:

To summarize Electrovision's spending on travel and entertainment

You can see from these two examples how much influence the purpose statement has on the scope of your report. If Moreno's manager had expected her to suggest ways to reduce costs but Moreno had collected only cost data, her report would have failed to meet expectations. Because she was assigned an analytical report rather than an informational report, Moreno had to go beyond merely collecting data; she had to draw conclusions and make recommendations.

Proposals must also be guided by a clear and specific statement of purpose to help you focus on crafting a persuasive message. Here are several examples:

To secure funding in next year's capital budget for a new conveyor system in the warehouse (funding proposal)

To get management approval to reorganize the North American salesforce (general project proposal)

To secure $2 million in venture capital funding to complete design and production of the new line of titanium mountain bikes (investment proposal as part of a business plan)

To convince CommuniCo to purchase a trial subscription to our latest database offering (sales proposal)

TABLE 13.1 Problem Statements Versus Purpose Statements

Problem Statement	Statement of Purpose
Our company's market share is steadily declining.	To explore new ways of promoting and selling our products and to recommend the approaches most likely to stabilize our market share
Our current computer network lacks sufficient bandwidth and cannot be upgraded to meet our future needs.	To analyze various networking options and to recommend the system that will best meet our company's current and future needs
We need $2 million to launch our new product.	To convince investors that our new business would be a sound investment so that we can obtain desired financing
Our current operations are too decentralized and expensive.	To justify the closing of the Newark plant and the transfer of East Coast operations to a single Midwest location in order to save the company money

Preparing Your Work Plan

A detailed work plan saves time and often produces more effective reports.

You're already accustomed to some schedule pressure with school reports. This is good practice for your business career, in which you'll be expected to produce quality reports quickly and efficiently. Carefully thinking out a work plan is the best way to make sure you produce good work on schedule. By identifying all the tasks that must be performed, you ensure that nothing is overlooked.

If you are preparing a work plan for yourself, it can be relatively informal: a simple list of the steps you plan to take and an estimate of their sequence and timing. However, for more complicated projects, particularly those that involve multiple team members, you'll want to prepare a formal, detailed work plan that can guide the performance of many tasks over a span of time. For consultants and others whose work output is a formal report, the work plan can also become the basis for a contract if the proposal is accepted. A formal work plan might include the following elements (especially the first two):

- **Statement of the problem or opportunity.** The problem statement clarifies the challenge you face, helps you (and anyone working with you) stay focused on the core issues, and helps everyone avoid the distractions that are likely to arise along the way.
- **Statement of the purpose and scope of your investigation.** The purpose statement describes what you plan to accomplish and therefore also defines the boundaries of your work. Delineating which subjects you will cover and which you won't is especially important for complex investigations.
- **Discussion of tasks to be accomplished.** For simple reports, the list of tasks to be accomplished will be short and probably obvious. However, longer reports and complex investigations require an exhaustive list so that you can reserve time with customers, with executives, or for outside services, such as market researchers or print shops.
- **Description of any additional products or activities that will result from your investigation.** In many cases, the only outcome of your efforts will be the report itself. In other cases, you'll need to produce something or perform some task in addition to completing the report. Make such expectations clear at the outset.
- **Review of project assignments, schedules, and resource requirements.** Indicate who will be responsible for what, when tasks will be completed, and how much the investigation will cost. If more than one person will be involved, you may also want to include a brief section on coordinating report writing and production, such as whether you'll use a wiki to develop the report content. If constraints on time, money, personnel, or data are likely to affect the quality of the report, identify these limitations up front.
- **Plans for following up after delivering the report.** Follow-up can be as simple as making sure people received the information they need or as complex as conducting additional research to evaluate the results of proposals included in your report. Even informal follow-up can help you improve your future reports and communicate that you care about your work's effectiveness and its impact on the organization.
- **Working outline.** Some work plans include a tentative outline of the report, as does the plan in Figure 13.2.

GATHERING INFORMATION

Some reports require formal research projects in order to gather all the necessary information.

The amount of information needed in many reports and proposals requires careful planning—and may even require a separate research project just to get the data and information you need. As Chapter 11 emphasizes, you should prioritize your information needs before you start and focus on the most important questions. Whenever possible, try to reuse or adapt existing information to save time.

SELECTING THE RIGHT MEDIUM

In some situations, you may be required to use a specific medium for your reports.

In addition to the general media selection criteria discussed in Chapter 4, consider several points for reports and proposals. First, for many reports and proposals, audiences have specific media requirements, and you might not have a choice. For instance, executives in many corporations now expect to review many reports via their in-house intranets, sometimes in conjunction with an *executive dashboard* (see Figure 13.3 on page 376), a customized online

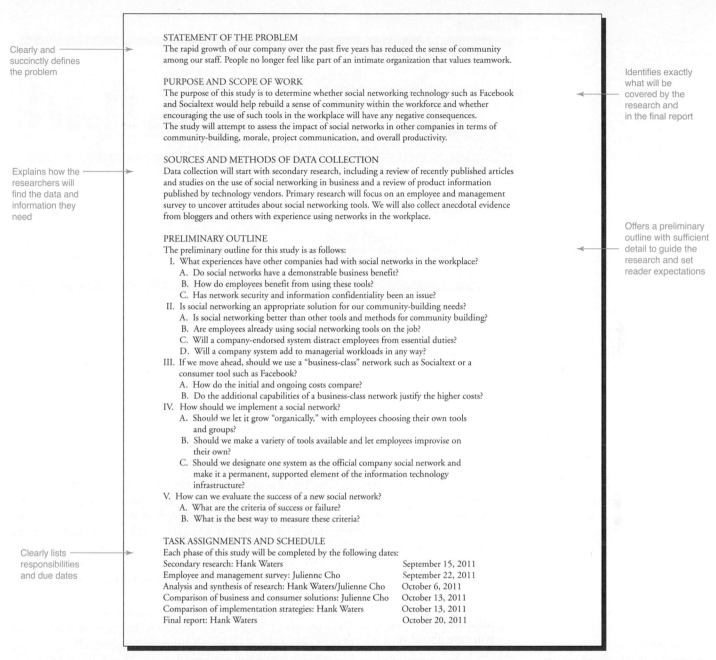

Clearly and succinctly defines the problem

Explains how the researchers will find the data and information they need

Clearly lists responsibilities and due dates

Identifies exactly what will be covered by the research and in the final report

Offers a preliminary outline with sufficient detail to guide the research and set reader expectations

STATEMENT OF THE PROBLEM

The rapid growth of our company over the past five years has reduced the sense of community among our staff. People no longer feel like part of an intimate organization that values teamwork.

PURPOSE AND SCOPE OF WORK

The purpose of this study is to determine whether social networking technology such as Facebook and Socialtext would help rebuild a sense of community within the workforce and whether encouraging the use of such tools in the workplace will have any negative consequences. The study will attempt to assess the impact of social networks in other companies in terms of community-building, morale, project communication, and overall productivity.

SOURCES AND METHODS OF DATA COLLECTION

Data collection will start with secondary research, including a review of recently published articles and studies on the use of social networking in business and a review of product information published by technology vendors. Primary research will focus on an employee and management survey to uncover attitudes about social networking tools. We will also collect anecdotal evidence from bloggers and others with experience using networks in the workplace.

PRELIMINARY OUTLINE

The preliminary outline for this study is as follows:
I. What experiences have other companies had with social networks in the workplace?
   A. Do social networks have a demonstrable business benefit?
   B. How do employees benefit from using these tools?
   C. Has network security and information confidentiality been an issue?
II. Is social networking an appropriate solution for our community-building needs?
   A. Is social networking better than other tools and methods for community building?
   B. Are employees already using social networking tools on the job?
   C. Will a company-endorsed system distract employees from essential duties?
   D. Will a company system add to managerial workloads in any way?
III. If we move ahead, should we use a "business-class" network such as Socialtext or a consumer tool such as Facebook?
   A. How do the initial and ongoing costs compare?
   B. Do the additional capabilities of a business-class network justify the higher costs?
IV. How should we implement a social network?
   A. Should we let it grow "organically," with employees choosing their own tools and groups?
   B. Should we make a variety of tools available and let employees improvise on their own?
   C. Should we designate one system as the official company social network and make it a permanent, supported element of the information technology infrastructure?
V. How can we evaluate the success of a new social network?
   A. What are the criteria of success or failure?
   B. What is the best way to measure these criteria?

TASK ASSIGNMENTS AND SCHEDULE

Each phase of this study will be completed by the following dates:

Secondary research: Hank Waters	September 15, 2011
Employee and management survey: Julienne Cho	September 22, 2011
Analysis and synthesis of research: Hank Waters/Julienne Cho	October 6, 2011
Comparison of business and consumer solutions: Julienne Cho	October 13, 2011
Comparison of implementation strategies: Hank Waters	October 13, 2011
Final report: Hank Waters	October 20, 2011

Figure 13.2 Work Plan for a Report
A formal work plan such as this is a vital tool for planning and managing complex writing projects. The preliminary outline here helps guide the research; the report writers may well modify the outline when they begin writing the report.

MyBcommLab

Apply Figure 13.2's key concepts by revising a new document. Go to Chapter 13 in mybcommlab.com and select Document Makeovers.

presentation of highly summarized business information. Second, consider how your audience members want to provide feedback on your report or proposal. Do they prefer to write comments on a printed document or edit a wiki article? Third, will people need to search through your document electronically or update it in the future? Fourth, bear in mind that your choice of medium sends a message. For instance, a routine sales report dressed up in expensive multimedia will look like a waste of valuable company resources.

ORGANIZING YOUR INFORMATION

The length and complexity of most reports and proposals require extra emphasis on clear, reader-oriented organization. Your readers might have the patience to struggle through

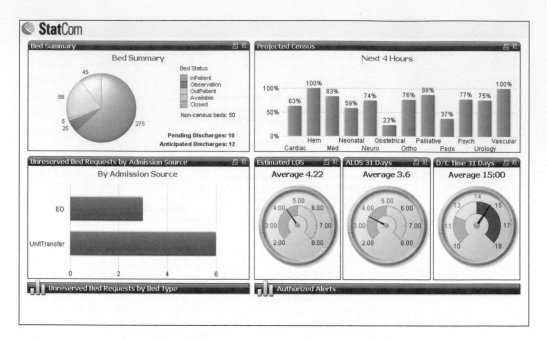

Figure 13.3   Executive Dashboards
To help managers avoid information overload, many companies now use executive dashboards to present carefully filtered highlights of key performance parameters. Dashboards are essentially super-summarized reports. The latest generation of software makes it easy to customize screens to show each manager the specific summaries he or she needs to see.

Most business reports use the direct approach.

a short, disorganized email message but not through a poorly organized 200-page report. As Chapter 4 discusses, when an audience is likely to be receptive or at least open-minded, use the direct approach: Lead with a summary of your key findings, conclusions, recommendations, or proposal, whichever is relevant. This "up-front" arrangement is by far the most popular and convenient for business reports. It saves time and makes the rest of the report easier to follow. For those who have questions or want more information, later parts of the report provide complete findings and supporting details. The direct approach also produces a more forceful report. You sound sure of yourself when you state your conclusions confidently at the outset.

At times, however, confidence may be misconstrued as arrogance. If you're a junior member of a status-conscious organization, or if your audience is skeptical or hostile, consider the indirect approach: Introduce your complete findings and discuss all supporting details before presenting your conclusions and recommendations. The indirect approach gives you a chance to prove your points and gradually overcome your audience's reservations. By deferring the conclusions and recommendations to the end of your report, you imply that you've weighed the evidence objectively. You also imply that you're subordinating your judgment to that of the audience, whose members are capable of drawing their own conclusions when they have access to all the facts.

Use the indirect approach when you need to build support for your main idea or you want to avoid coming across as arrogant.

Although the indirect approach has advantages, some readers will always be in a hurry to get to the answer and will immediately flip to the recommendations anyway, thus defeating your purpose. Therefore, consider length before choosing the direct or indirect approach. In general, the longer the message, the less effective an indirect approach is likely to be.

Long reports sometimes combine direct and indirect approaches, building support for interim conclusions or recommendations along the way.

Because both direct and indirect approaches have merit, businesspeople often combine them. They reveal their conclusions and recommendations as they go along rather than put them either first or last. Figure 13.4 presents the introductions from two reports that follow the same general outline. In the direct version, a series of statements summarizes the conclusion reached in relation to each main topic in the outline. In the indirect version, the same topics are introduced in the same order but without drawing any conclusions about them. Instead, the conclusions appear within the body of the report.

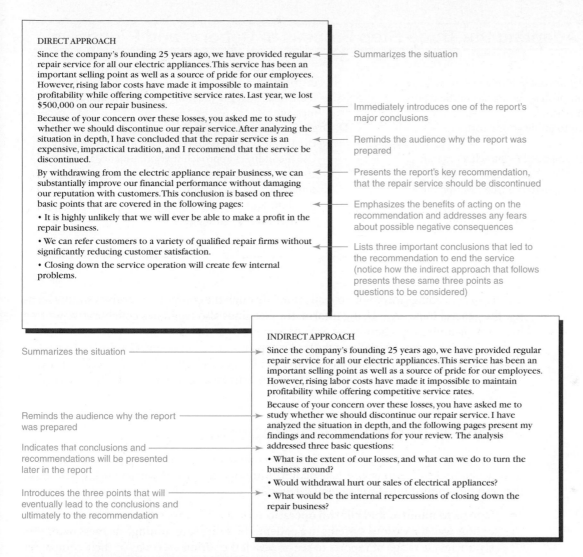

DIRECT APPROACH

Since the company's founding 25 years ago, we have provided regular repair service for all our electric appliances. This service has been an important selling point as well as a source of pride for our employees. However, rising labor costs have made it impossible to maintain profitability while offering competitive service rates. Last year, we lost $500,000 on our repair business.

Because of your concern over these losses, you asked me to study whether we should discontinue our repair service. After analyzing the situation in depth, I have concluded that the repair service is an expensive, impractical tradition, and I recommend that the service be discontinued.

By withdrawing from the electric appliance repair business, we can substantially improve our financial performance without damaging our reputation with customers. This conclusion is based on three basic points that are covered in the following pages:

• It is highly unlikely that we will ever be able to make a profit in the repair business.

• We can refer customers to a variety of qualified repair firms without significantly reducing customer satisfaction.

• Closing down the service operation will create few internal problems.

— Summarizes the situation

— Immediately introduces one of the report's major conclusions

— Reminds the audience why the report was prepared

— Presents the report's key recommendation, that the repair service should be discontinued

— Emphasizes the benefits of acting on the recommendation and addresses any fears about possible negative consequences

— Lists three important conclusions that led to the recommendation to end the service (notice how the indirect approach that follows presents these same three points as questions to be considered)

Summarizes the situation ———

Reminds the audience why the report ——— was prepared

Indicates that conclusions and ——— recommendations will be presented later in the report

Introduces the three points that will ——— eventually lead to the conclusions and ultimately to the recommendation

INDIRECT APPROACH

Since the company's founding 25 years ago, we have provided regular repair service for all our electric appliances. This service has been an important selling point as well as a source of pride for our employees. However, rising labor costs have made it impossible to maintain profitability while offering competitive service rates.

Because of your concern over these losses, you have asked me to study whether we should discontinue our repair service. I have analyzed the situation in depth, and the following pages present my findings and recommendations for your review. The analysis addressed three basic questions:

• What is the extent of our losses, and what can we do to turn the business around?

• Would withdrawal hurt our sales of electrical appliances?

• What would be the internal repercussions of closing down the repair business?

Figure 13.4   Direct Approach Versus Indirect Approach in an Introduction
In the direct version of this introduction, the writer quickly presents the report's recommendation, followed by the conclusions that led to that recommendation. In the indirect version, the same topics are introduced in the same order but no conclusions are drawn about them (the conclusions and the ultimate recommendation appear later, in the body of the report).

Regardless of the format, length, or order of your report, think carefully about how your ideas will be subdivided and developed. Take care to choose the most logical argument structure—one that suits your topic and goals and that makes sense to your audience.

As you outline your content, use informative ("talking") headings rather than simple descriptive ("topical") headings (see Table 13.2). With question or summary form,

TABLE 13.2	Types of Outline Headings		

DESCRIPTIVE (TOPICAL) OUTLINE	INFORMATIVE (TALKING) OUTLINE	
	Question Form	Summary Form
I. Industry Characteristics	I. What is the nature of the industry?	I. Flour milling is a mature industry.
a. Annual sales	a. What are the annual sales?	a. Market is large.
b. Profitability	b. Is the industry profitable?	b. Profit margins are narrow.
c. Growth rate	c. What is the pattern of growth?	c. Growth is modest.
1. Sales	1. Sales growth?	1. Sales growth averages less than 3 percent a year.
2. Profit	2. Profit growth?	2. Profits are flat.

✓ **Checklist**   **Adapting the Three-Step Process to Reports and Proposals**

A. Analyze the situation.
- Clearly define your purpose before you start writing.
- If you need to accomplish several goals in the report, identify them all in advance.
- Prepare a work plan to guide your efforts.

B. Gather information.
- Determine whether you need to launch a separate research project to collect the necessary information.
- Reuse or adapt existing material whenever possible.

C. Select the right medium.
- Base your decision on audience expectations or requirements.

- Consider the need for commenting, revising, distributing, and storing.
- Remember that the medium you choose also sends a message.

D. Organize your information.
- Use the direct approach if your audience is receptive.
- Use the indirect approach if your audience is skeptical.
- Use the indirect approach when you don't want to risk coming across as arrogant.
- Combine approaches if doing so will help build support for your primary message.

---

informative headings force you to really think through the content rather than simply identify the general topic area. Using informative headings also facilitates collaborative writing by reducing ambiguity about what each person needs to write.

For a quick review of adapting the three-step process to long reports, refer to "Checklist: Adapting the Three-Step Process to Reports and Proposals." The following sections provide specific advice on how to plan informational reports, analytical reports, and proposals.

Planning Informational Reports

Informational reports are used to monitor and control operations, to implement policies and procedures, to demonstrate compliance, and to document progress.

Informational reports provide the information that employees, managers, and others need in order to make decisions and take action. Although dozens of particular formats exist, they can be grouped into four general categories:

- **Reports to monitor and control operations.** Just as doctors rely on medical reports to see how well the various systems in a patient's body are functioning, business managers rely on a wide range of reports to see how well the various systems in their companies are functioning. *Plans* establish expectations and guidelines to direct future action (see "Creating Successful Business Plans" on the next page). *Operating reports* provide feedback on a wide variety of an organization's functions, including sales, inventories, expenses, shipments, and other aspects of company operations. *Personal activity reports* provide information regarding an individual's experiences during sales calls, industry conferences, market research trips, and other activities.

- **Reports to implement policies and procedures.** *Policy reports* range from brief descriptions of business procedures to manuals that run dozens or hundreds of pages. *Position papers*, sometimes called *white papers* or *backgrounders*, outline an organization's official position on issues that affect the company's success.

- **Reports to demonstrate compliance.** Even the smallest businesses are required to show that they are in compliance with government regulations of one sort or another. Some compliance reports, such as quarterly and annual tax reports, affect all businesses. Others concern particular industries, companies using hazardous materials, specific professional functions, or other special factors. Compliance reports are usually created in specific formats that must be followed exactly.

Progress reports range from simple, informal updates to comprehensive status reports.

- **Reports to document progress.** Progress reports range from simple updates to comprehensive reports that include such elements as measured progress toward goals, comparisons of budgeted versus actual expenses, and lists of ongoing concerns and risks.

Figure 13.5 shows the major subcategories within each of the major report categories, along with examples of the most common types. Specific titles may vary, depending on the company you're with, but chances are you'll be called on to read nearly every one of these report types—and to write many of them, too.

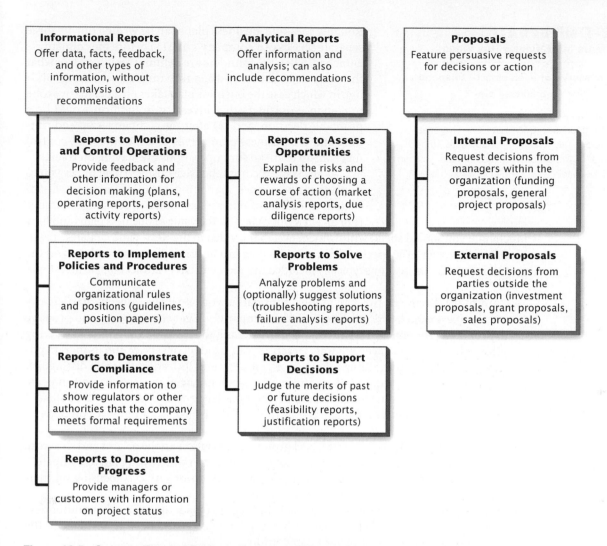

Figure 13.5 Common Types of Business Reports and Proposals
You will have the opportunity to read and write many types of reports in your career; here are some of the most common.

ORGANIZATIONAL STRATEGIES FOR INFORMATIONAL REPORTS

Most informational reports use a **topical organization**, arranging the material by topic in one of the following ways:

- **Comparison.** Showing similarities and differences (or advantages and disadvantages) between two or more entities
- **Importance.** Building up from the least important item to the most important (or from most important to the least, if you don't think your audience will read the entire report)
- **Sequence.** Organizing the steps or stages in a process or procedure
- **Chronology.** Organizing a chain of events in order from oldest to newest or vice versa
- **Geography.** Organizing by region, city, state, country, or other geographic unit
- **Category.** Grouping by topical category, such as sales, profit, cost, or investment

Whichever pattern you choose, use it consistently so that readers can easily follow your discussion from start to finish. Of course, certain reports (such as compliance or monitor-and-control reports) must follow a prescribed flow.

Creating Successful Business Plans

A **business plan** such as the one written by the founders of MyCityWay is a comprehensive document that describes a company's mission, structure, objectives, and operations.

A topical organization is built around the content itself, using such arrangements as comparison, importance, sequence, chronology, spatial orientation, geography, or category.

Formal business plans, particularly those used to solicit outside investment, must meet a specific set of reader expectations.

REAL-TIME UPDATES
Learn More by Watching This Video

Is it necessary—or even smart—to spend months writing a business plan?

Some entrepreneurs don't agree that writing a comprehensive business plan is always a good idea. See what Kevin Ryan has to say in this interview. Go to http://real-timeupdates.com/bct11 and click on "Learn More." If you are using MyBcommLab, you can access Real-Time Updates within each chapter or under Student Study Tools.

Roughly speaking, business plans can be written during three separate phases of a company's life: (1) before the company is launched, when the founders are defining their vision of what the company will be; (2) when the company is seeking funding, in which case the business plan takes on a persuasive tone to convince outsiders that investing in the firm would be a profitable decision; and (3) after the company is up and running and the business plan serves as a monitor-and-control mechanism to make sure operations are staying on track.

At any stage, a comprehensive business plan forces you to think about personnel, marketing, facilities, suppliers, distribution, and a host of other issues vital to a company's success. (For an alternative view on the value of business plans and how much time you should spend writing them, watch the video in the Real-Time Updates "Learn More" on this page.) The specific elements to include in a business plan can vary based on the situation; here are the sections typically included in a plan written to attract outside investors:[2]

- **Summary.** In one or two paragraphs, summarize your business concept, particularly the *business model*, which defines how the company will generate revenue and produce a profit. The summary must be compelling, catching the investor's attention and giving him or her reasons to keep reading. Describe your product or service and its market potential. Highlight some things about your company and its leaders that will distinguish your firm from the competition. Summarize your financial projections and indicate how much money you will need from investors or lenders and where it will be spent.
- **Mission and objectives.** Explain the purpose of your business and what you hope to accomplish.
- **Company and industry.** Give full background information on the origins and structure of your venture and the characteristics of the industry in which you plan to compete.
- **Products or services.** Concisely describe your products or services, focusing on their unique attributes and their appeal to customers.
- **Market and competition.** Provide data that will persuade investors that you understand your target market and can achieve your sales goals. Be sure to identify the strengths and weaknesses of your competitors.
- **Management.** Summarize the background and qualifications of the key management personnel in your company. Include résumés in an appendix.
- **Marketing strategy.** Provide projections of sales volume and market share; outline a strategy for identifying and reaching potential customers, setting prices, providing customer support, and physically delivering your products or services. Whenever possible, include evidence of customer acceptance, such as advance product orders.
- **Design and development plans.** If your product requires design or development, describe the nature and extent of what needs to be done, including costs and possible problems. For new or unusual products, you may want to explain how the product will be manufactured.
- **Operations plan.** Provide information on facilities, equipment, and personnel requirements.
- **Overall schedule.** Forecast important milestones in the company's growth and development, including when you need to be fully staffed and when your products will be ready for the market.
- **Critical risks and problems.** Identify significant negative factors and discuss them honestly.
- **Financial projections and requirements.** Include a detailed budget of start-up and operating costs, as well as projections for income, expenses, and cash flow for the first few years of business. Identify the company's financing needs and potential sources, if appropriate.
- **Exit strategy.** Explain how investors will be able to profit from their investment, such as through a public stock offering, sale of the company, or a buyback of the investors' interest.

Creating a complete business plan requires a considerable amount of work. However, by thinking your way through all these issues, you'll enjoy a smoother launch and a greater chance of success in your new adventure. For more insider advice on writing business plans, see Chapter 15's Communication Close-up on page 424.

Organizing Website Content

Many company websites function as informational reports, offering sections with information about the company, its history, its products and services, its executive team, and other key subjects. While most of what you've already learned about informational reports applies to website writing, the online experience requires some special considerations and practices.

As you begin to plan a website, start by recognizing the unique nature of online communication:

- **Web readers are demanding.** If your site can't meet readers' needs quickly, most people will move to another site that can. Most visitors won't bother to dig for information. They scan navigation buttons, headings, images, and hyperlinks, looking for possibilities. If nothing looks promising, they're gone.[3]
- **Reading online can be difficult.** For most people, reading on a computer monitor is more difficult than reading from the printed page. In fact, studies show that reading speeds are about 25 percent slower on a monitor than on paper.[4] Reading from computer screens can also be tiring on the eyes, even to the point of causing headaches, double vision, blurred vision, and other physical problems.[5]
- **The web is a nonlinear, multidimensional medium.** As a web writer, you can't expect your readers to follow a predefined path. Readers of printed reports can skim and skip through the material, of course, but the general scheme of reading proceeds in a linear fashion from the beginning, through the middle, to the end. In contrast, the navigational flexibility of the web makes it easy for readers to jump around in any direction, as they follow interesting links or search for specific content.

As you move on to define your purpose, bear in mind that most websites have to perform more than one communication function. Consequently, a single website could have a half-dozen purposes or more. Each of these individual purposes needs to be carefully defined and then integrated into an overall statement of purpose for the entire website. Then, as you develop the site, you'll need to clearly identify the specific purpose of each section of the site so that readers always know where to find the information they need.[6]

Just as you probably will have a number of purposes for a single website, you're likely to have a number of audiences as well. The global reach of the web further complicates the audience analysis issue because you may get visitors from all parts of the world. After you've identified your multiple audiences, you need to analyze each group's unique information needs and then find a logical way to organize all that material. Professional website designers often use the term **information architecture** to describe the structure and navigational flow of all the parts of a website. In a sense, the information architecture is a three-dimensional outline of the site, showing (1) the vertical hierarchy of pages from the homepage down to the lower level; (2) the horizontal division of pages across the various sections of the site; and (3) the links that tie all these pages together, both internally (between various pages on the site) and externally (between your site and other websites).

As you develop the site architecture, you can begin to simulate how various audiences will use the site and refine the plan to meet everyone's needs (see Figure 13.6 on the next page). For instance, can potential customers find new product information quickly? And can existing customers get support or warranty information quickly, without wading through pages of promotion for new products? You can also get a sense of how you'll need to assist visitors who enter the site at points other than the homepage, as often happens with search engine links. Accommodating these multiple entry points is one of the most difficult tasks in site design.[7]

Although many websites and website sections function as information reports, the unique nature of online communication requires special consideration.

A typical company website has multiple purposes and multiple audiences that need to be addressed during the planning process.

Map out the various paths that different types of users are likely to take through your website, and then develop content to fit this structure.

General information about the SBA is always available for access but doesn't intrude on the main screen.

Always-visible tabs link to the site's four major areas.

Advice is categorized by business "life stage," making it easy to find articles of interest.

Figure 13.6 Information Architecture
The website of the U.S. Small Business Administration uses clearly defined and labeled navigation choices to help site visitors quickly find the information they need.

To organize a website effectively, keep the following advice in mind:

- **Plan your navigation first.** Don't make the mistake of writing a traditional report and then adding some links to make it a website. To ensure that readers will be able to navigate your material effectively and efficiently, plan your site structure and navigation before you write.[8]
- **Let your readers be in control.** Help your readers get oriented by starting with a homepage that clearly points the way to various sections of the site; then offer plenty of descriptive labels, subheads, and other devices that let readers create their own paths through the site.
- **Break your information into chunks.** Help online readers scan and absorb information by breaking it into self-contained, easily readable chunks that are linked together logically. By doing so, you can provide comprehensive coverage that is easy to consume online.

EFFECTIVE INFORMATIONAL REPORTS: AN EXAMPLE

Effective informational reports are clearly and logically organized, with audience-centered content and generous use of previews and summaries. They are complete, without being unnecessarily long or detailed. One of the tasks your audience expects you to accomplish is to sort out the details and separate major points from minor points. In other words, readers expect you to take the time and effort needed to make the best use of their time. In addition, effective reports are honest and objective but not unduly harsh whenever negative information must be conveyed. Compare the differences between the report versions shown in Figures 13.7 and 13.8.

Planning Analytical Reports

3 LEARNING OBJECTIVE

Discuss three major ways to organize analytical reports.

The purpose of analytical reports is to analyze, to understand, to explain—to think through a problem or an opportunity and figure out how it affects the company and how the company should respond. In many cases, you'll also be expected to make a recommendation based on your analysis. As you saw in Figure 13.5, analytical reports fall into three basic categories:

Figure 13.7   Ineffective Informational Report
While this report looks professional at first glance, it contains a number of weaknesses in tone, content, and formatting. Compare with Figure 13.8 on the next page.

MyBcommLab

Apply Figure 13.7's key concepts by revising a new document. Go to Chapter 13 in mybcommlab.com and select Document Makeovers.

- **Reports to assess opportunities.** Every business opportunity carries some degree of risk and also requires a variety of decisions and actions in order to capitalize on the opportunity. For instance, *market analysis reports* are used to judge the likelihood of success for new products or sales initiatives by identifying potential opportunities as well as competitive threats and other risks. *Due diligence reports* examine the financial aspects of a proposed decision, such as acquiring another company.

- **Reports to solve problems.** Managers often assign *troubleshooting reports* when they need to understand why something isn't working properly and what can be done to fix the situation. A variation, the *failure analysis report*, studies events that happened in the past, with the hope of learning how to avoid similar failures in the future.

- **Reports to support decisions.** *Feasibility reports* are called for when managers need to explore the ramifications of a decision they're about to make (such as replacing an advertising agency or switching materials used in a manufacturing process). *Justification reports* justify a decision that has already been made.

Clarify the problem in an analytical report by determining what you need to analyze, why the issue is important, who is involved, where the trouble is located, and how and when it started.

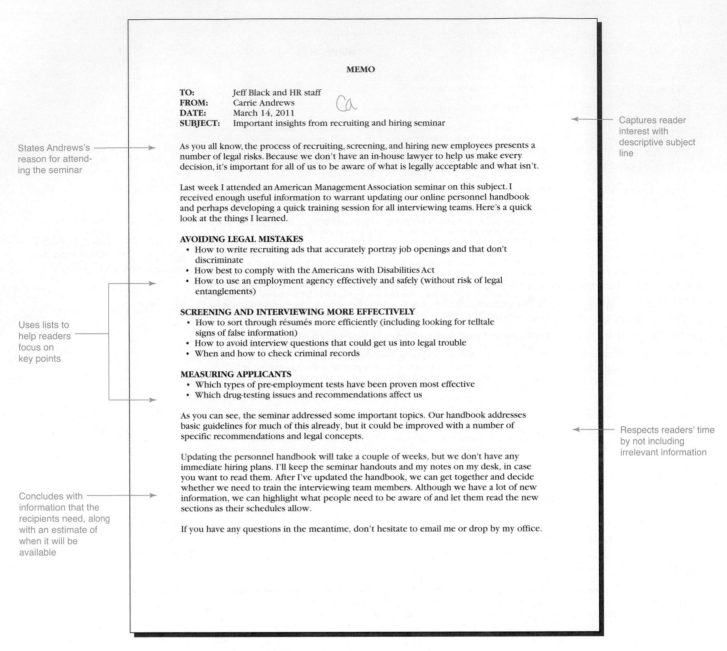

States Andrews's reason for attending the seminar

Uses lists to help readers focus on key points

Concludes with information that the recipients need, along with an estimate of when it will be available

Captures reader interest with descriptive subject line

Respects readers' time by not including irrelevant information

MEMO

TO: Jeff Black and HR staff
FROM: Carrie Andrews
DATE: March 14, 2011
SUBJECT: Important insights from recruiting and hiring seminar

As you all know, the process of recruiting, screening, and hiring new employees presents a number of legal risks. Because we don't have an in-house lawyer to help us make every decision, it's important for all of us to be aware of what is legally acceptable and what isn't.

Last week I attended an American Management Association seminar on this subject. I received enough useful information to warrant updating our online personnel handbook and perhaps developing a quick training session for all interviewing teams. Here's a quick look at the things I learned.

AVOIDING LEGAL MISTAKES
- How to write recruiting ads that accurately portray job openings and that don't discriminate
- How best to comply with the Americans with Disabilities Act
- How to use an employment agency effectively and safely (without risk of legal entanglements)

SCREENING AND INTERVIEWING MORE EFFECTIVELY
- How to sort through résumés more efficiently (including looking for telltale signs of false information)
- How to avoid interview questions that could get us into legal trouble
- When and how to check criminal records

MEASURING APPLICANTS
- Which types of pre-employment tests have been proven most effective
- Which drug-testing issues and recommendations affect us

As you can see, the seminar addressed some important topics. Our handbook addresses basic guidelines for much of this already, but it could be improved with a number of specific recommendations and legal concepts.

Updating the personnel handbook will take a couple of weeks, but we don't have any immediate hiring plans. I'll keep the seminar handouts and my notes on my desk, in case you want to read them. After I've updated the handbook, we can get together and decide whether we need to train the interviewing team members. Although we have a lot of new information, we can highlight what people need to be aware of and let them read the new sections as their schedules allow.

If you have any questions in the meantime, don't hesitate to email me or drop by my office.

Figure 13.8 Effective Informational Report
This version of the report (see Figure 13.7) is much easier to read and presents pertinent information in a clear, concise way.

Writing analytical reports presents a greater challenge than writing informational reports, for three reasons. First, you're doing more than simply delivering information; you're also thinking through a problem or an opportunity and presenting your conclusions. The best writing in the world can't compensate for flawed analysis. Second, when your analysis is complete, you need to present your thinking in a credible manner. Third, analytical reports often convince other people to make significant financial and personnel decisions, so your reports carry the added responsibility of the consequences of these decisions.

In some situations, the problem or opportunity you address in an analytical report may be defined by the person who authorizes the report. In other cases, you will have to define it yourself. Be careful not to confuse a simple topic (quarterly profits) with a problem (the decline in profits over the past six quarters). Moreover, if you're the only person who thinks a particular issue is a problem, your readers won't be interested in your solution unless your report first convinces them that a problem exists. As with marketing and sales messages, sometimes you need to "sell the problem" before you can sell the solution.

To help define the problem that your analytical report will address, answer these questions:

- What needs to be determined?
- Why is this issue important?
- Who is involved in the situation?
- Where is the trouble located?
- How did the situation originate?
- When did it start?

Not all these questions apply in every situation, but asking them helps you define the problem being addressed and limit the scope of your discussion.

Another effective way to tackle a complex problem is to divide it into a series of logical, connected questions, a process sometimes called **problem factoring**. You probably subconsciously approach most problems this way. When your car won't start, what do you do? You use the available evidence to organize your investigation, to start a search for cause-and-effect relationships. For example, if the engine doesn't turn over at all, you might suspect a dead battery. If the engine does turn over but won't fire, you can conclude that the battery is okay, but perhaps you're out of gas. When you speculate on the cause of a problem, you're forming a **hypothesis**, a potential explanation that needs to be tested. By subdividing a problem and forming hypotheses based on available evidence, you can tackle even the most complex situations. With a clear picture of the problem or opportunity in mind, you're ready to consider the best structure for your report.

Whenever you are preparing an analytical report, make sure you are clear in your own mind about whether you are advocating one particular line of thought or objectively exploring all the available options.[9] Even if advocating one position is appropriate in the circumstances, your readers will expect you to have considered the other options so that you can help them understand why your answer is preferred.

> Use problem factoring to divide a complex problem into more manageable pieces.

ORGANIZATIONAL STRATEGIES FOR ANALYTICAL REPORTS

When you expect your audience to agree with you, use the direct approach to focus attention on conclusions and recommendations. When you expect your audience to disagree with you or to be hostile, use the indirect approach to focus attention on the rationale behind your conclusions and recommendations.

The three most common structural approaches for analytical reports are focusing on conclusions (a direct format), focusing on recommendations (another direct format), and focusing on logical arguments (an indirect format). See Table 13.3.

> Before you choose an approach, determine whether your audience is receptive or skeptical.

TABLE 13.3	**Common Ways to Structure Analytical Reports**		
Element	**FOCUS ON CONCLUSIONS OR RECOMMENDATIONS**	**FOCUS ON LOGICAL ARGUMENT**	
		Use 2 + 2 = 4 Model	**Use Yardstick Model**
Reader mindset	Are likely to accept	Hostile or skeptical	Hostile or skeptical
Approach	Direct	Indirect	Indirect
Writer credibility	High	Low	Low
Advantages	Readers quickly grasp conclusions or recommendations	Works well when you need to show readers how you built toward an answer by following clear, logical steps	Works well when you have a list of criteria (standards) that must be considered in a decision; alternatives are all measured against same criteria
Drawbacks	Structure can make topic seem too simple	Can make report longer	Readers must agree on criteria; can be lengthy because of the need to address each criteria for every alternative

Focusing on Conclusions

Focusing on conclusions is often the best approach when you're addressing a receptive audience.

When writing for audiences that are likely to accept your conclusions—either because they've asked you to perform an analysis or they trust your judgment—consider using a direct approach that focuses immediately on your conclusions. This structure communicates the main idea quickly, but it presents some risks. Even if audiences trust your judgment, they may have questions about your data or the methods you used. Moreover, starting with a conclusion may create the impression that you have oversimplified the situation. You're generally better off taking this direct approach in a report only when your credibility is high—when your readers trust you and are willing to accept your conclusions (see Figure 13.9).

Focusing on Recommendations

When readers want to know what you think they should do, organize your report to focus on recommendations.

A slightly different approach is useful when your readers want to know what they ought to do in a given situation (as opposed to what they ought to conclude). You'll often be asked to solve a problem or assess an opportunity rather than just study it. The actions you want your readers to take become the main subdivisions of your report.

When structuring a report around recommendations, use the direct approach as you would for a report that focuses on conclusions. Then unfold your recommendations using a series of five steps:

1. Establish or verify the need for action in the introduction by briefly describing the problem or opportunity.
2. Introduce the benefit that can be achieved, without providing any details.
3. List the steps (recommendations) required to achieve the benefit, using action verbs for emphasis.
4. Explain each step more fully, giving details on procedures, costs, and benefits.
5. Summarize your recommendations.

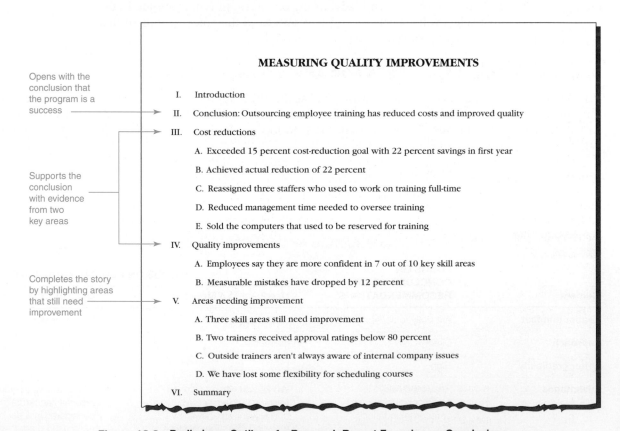

Figure 13.9   Preliminary Outline of a Research Report Focusing on Conclusions
Cynthia Zolonka works on the human resources staff of a bank in Houston, Texas. Her company decided to have an outside firm handle its employee training, and a year after the outsourcing arrangement was established, Zolonka was asked to evaluate the results. Her analysis shows that the outsourcing experiment was a success, and she opens with that conclusion but supports it with clear evidence. Readers who accept the conclusion can stop reading, and those who desire more information can continue.

If your recommendation carries any risks, be sure to clearly address them. Doing so not only makes your report more ethical but also offers you some protection in the event that your recommendation is implemented but doesn't work out as you had hoped. In short, make sure your readers know the potential disadvantages as well as the potential benefits.

Whenever a recommendation carries some element of risk, you owe it to your audience to make this clear.

Focusing on Logical Arguments

When readers are likely to be skeptical or hostile to the conclusion or recommendation you plan to make, use an indirect approach. If you guide people along a logical path toward the answer, they are more likely to accept it when they encounter it. The two most common logical approaches are known as the *2 + 2 = 4 approach* and the *yardstick approach*.

Two common logical patterns arguments are the 2 + 2 = 4 approach (adding everything up) and the yardstick approach (comparing solutions against criteria).

The 2 + 2 + 4 Approach   The **2 + 2 = 4 approach** is so named because it convinces readers of your point of view by demonstrating that everything adds up. The main points in your outline are the main reasons behind your conclusions and recommendations. You support each reason with the evidence you collected during your analysis.

Because of its natural feel and versatility, the 2 + 2 = 4 approach is generally the most persuasive and efficient way to develop an analytical report for skeptical readers. When organizing your own reports, try this structure first. You'll find that many business situations lend themselves nicely to this pattern of logical argumentation.

Start by considering using the 2 + 2 = 4 approach; it's familiar and easy to develop.

The Yardstick Approach   The **yardstick approach** is useful when you need to use a number of criteria to evaluate one or more possible solutions. These criteria become the "yardstick" by which you measure the various alternatives. With this approach, you begin by discussing the problem or opportunity and then list the criteria that will guide the decision. The body of the report then evaluates the alternatives against those criteria. The main points of the outline are either the criteria themselves or the alternatives (see Figure 13.10 on page 388).

The yardstick approach compares a solution or several solutions to a set of predetermined standards.

The yardstick approach is particularly useful for proposals when the audience has provided a list of criteria the solution must meet. Say that your company has been asked to bid on a contract to design and install a factory-floor distribution system for a large corporation. The client has listed the requirements (criteria) for the system, and you've developed a preliminary design to meet them. In the body of your proposal, you could use the client's list of requirements as the main headings and under each one explain how your preliminary design meets the requirement.

The yardstick approach has two potential drawbacks. First, your audience members need to agree with the criteria you're using in your analysis. If they don't, they won't agree with the results of the evaluation. If you have any doubt about their agreement, build consensus before you start your report, if possible, or take extra care to explain why the criteria you're using are the best ones in this particular case. Second, the yardstick approach can get tedious when you have many options to consider or many criteria to compare them against. One way to minimize repetition is to compare the options in tables and then highlight the most unusual or important aspects of each alternative in the text so that you get the best of both worlds. This approach allows you to compare all the alternatives against the same yardstick while calling attention to the most significant differences among them.

EFFECTIVE ANALYTICAL REPORTS: AN EXAMPLE

As national sales manager of a New Hampshire sporting goods company, Binh Phan was concerned about his company's ability to sell to its largest customers. His boss, the vice president of marketing, shared these concerns and asked Phan to analyze the situation and recommend a solution. As Phan says, "We sell to retail chains across the country. Large nationwide chains of superstores have been revolutionizing the industry, but we haven't had as much success with these big customers as we've had with smaller companies that operate strictly on a local or regional basis. With more and more of the industry in the hands of the large chains, we knew we had to fix the situation."

Phan's troubleshooting report appears in Figure 13.11 on pages 389–390. The main idea is that the company should establish separate sales teams for these major accounts rather than continue to service them through the company's four regional divisions. However, Phan knew his plan would be controversial because it requires a big change in the company's organization and in the way sales reps are paid. His thinking had to be clear and easy to follow, so he used the 2 + 2 = 4 approach to focus on his reasons.

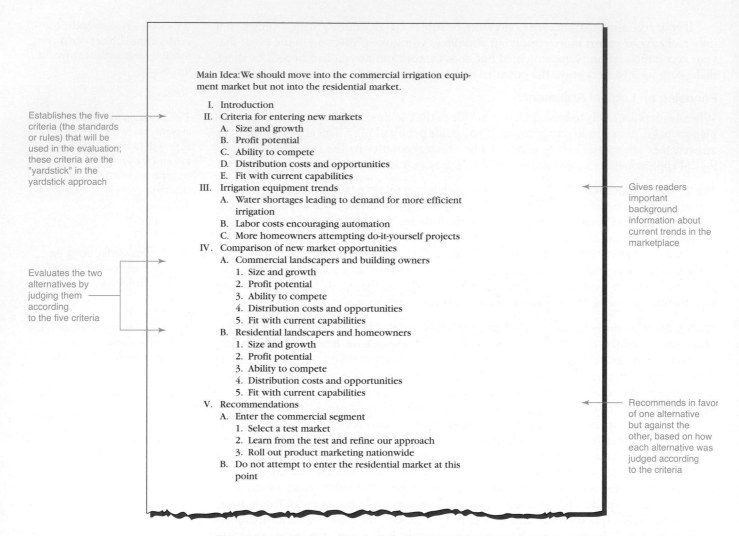

Main Idea: We should move into the commercial irrigation equipment market but not into the residential market.

I. Introduction
II. Criteria for entering new markets
   A. Size and growth
   B. Profit potential
   C. Ability to compete
   D. Distribution costs and opportunities
   E. Fit with current capabilities
III. Irrigation equipment trends
   A. Water shortages leading to demand for more efficient irrigation
   B. Labor costs encouraging automation
   C. More homeowners attempting do-it-yourself projects
IV. Comparison of new market opportunities
   A. Commercial landscapers and building owners
      1. Size and growth
      2. Profit potential
      3. Ability to compete
      4. Distribution costs and opportunities
      5. Fit with current capabilities
   B. Residential landscapers and homeowners
      1. Size and growth
      2. Profit potential
      3. Ability to compete
      4. Distribution costs and opportunities
      5. Fit with current capabilities
V. Recommendations
   A. Enter the commercial segment
      1. Select a test market
      2. Learn from the test and refine our approach
      3. Roll out product marketing nationwide
   B. Do not attempt to enter the residential market at this point

Annotations (left):
Establishes the five criteria (the standards or rules) that will be used in the evaluation; these criteria are the "yardstick" in the yardstick approach

Evaluates the two alternatives by judging them according to the five criteria

Annotations (right):
Gives readers important background information about current trends in the marketplace

Recommends in favor of one alternative but against the other, based on how each alternative was judged according to the criteria

Figure 13.10   Outline of an Analytical Report Using the Yardstick Approach
This outline was prepared by J. C. Hartley, a market analyst for a large Sacramento company that makes irrigation equipment for farms and ranches. "We've been so successful in the agricultural market that we're starting to run out of customers to sell to," says Hartley. "To keep the company growing, we needed to find another market. Two obvious choices to consider were commercial buildings and residences," so she structured her report to compare these two opportunities.

Planning Proposals

4   LEARNING OBJECTIVE

Explain how to choose an organizational strategy when writing a proposal.

Proposals are written for both internal and external audiences. Internal proposals request decisions from managers within the organization, such as proposals to buy new equipment or launch new research projects. Examples of external proposals include *grant proposals*, which request funds from government agencies and other sponsoring organizations, and *sales proposals*, which suggest individualized solutions for potential customers and request purchase decisions.

The most significant factor in planning any proposal is whether the intended recipient has asked you to submit a proposal. *Solicited proposals* are generally prepared at the request of external parties that require a product or a service, but they may also be requested by such internal sources as management or the board of directors. When organizations require complex products, services, or systems, they often prepare a formal invitation to bid on the contract, called a **request for proposals (RFP)**, which includes instructions that specify exactly the type of work to be performed or products to be delivered, along with budgets, deadlines, and other requirements.

Buyers often solicit proposals by publishing a request for proposals (RFP).

To attract a large pool of qualified bidders, organizations send RFPs to firms with good performance records in the field, print them in trade publications, and post them on the

Clarifies who requested the report, when it was requested, and who wrote it

Explains how the information used in the analysis was collected

Describes the first problem and explains how it occurred, without blaming anyone personally

Highlights the serious nature of the problem

Organizational problems are the first "2" in Phan's 2 + 2 = 4 approach

Figure 13.11   Analytical Report Using the 2 + 2 = 4 Approach   *(continued)*
To make his logical argument both clear and compelling, Binh Phan used the 2 + 2 = 4 approach.

web. Federal government RFPs, for instance, can be found through FedBizOpps, at www .cbd-net.com.

To write a proposal in response to an RFP, you begin by reviewing the requirements. Next, you define the scope of the deliverables, determine the methods and procedures to be used, and estimate time requirements, personnel requirements, and costs. Then you put it all in writing—exactly as specified in the RFP, following the precise format it requires and responding meticulously to every point it raises.[10] RFPs can seem surprisingly picky, even to the point of specifying the paper size for the proposal and the number of copies to send, but you must follow every detail.

Unsolicited proposals are created by organizations attempting to obtain business or funding without a specific invitation from a potential client. Such proposals may also be initiated by employees or managers who want to convince company insiders to adopt a program, a policy, or an idea. In other words, with an unsolicited proposal, the writer makes the first move. Even so, an unsolicited proposal should not come as a surprise to the recipient but rather should be the summation of a conversation that has been ongoing with the recipient.[11] This approach helps ensure acceptance, and it gives you an opportunity to explore the recipient's needs and craft your proposal around them.

2

For example, having retail outlets across the lower tier of the country, AmeriSport received pitches from reps out of our West, South, and East regions. Because our regional offices have a lot of negotiating freedom, the three were offering different prices. But all AmeriSport buying decisions were made at the Tampa headquarters, so all we did was confuse the customer. The irony of the current organization is that we're often giving our weakest selling and support efforts to the largest customers in the country.

COMMISSION PROBLEMS

The regional organization problems are compounded by the way we assign commissions and quota credit. Salespeople in one region can invest a lot of time in pursuing a sale, only to have the customer place the order in another region. So some sales rep in the second region ends up with the commission on a sale that was partly or even entirely earned by someone in the first region. Therefore, sales reps sometimes don't pursue leads in their regions, thinking that a rep in another region will get the commission.

For example, Athletic Express, with outlets in 35 states spread across all four regions, finally got so frustrated with us that the company president called our headquarters. Athletic Express has been trying to place a large order for tennis and golf accessories, but none of our local reps seem interested in paying attention. I spoke with the rep responsible for Nashville, where the company is headquartered, and asked her why she wasn't working the account more actively. Her explanation was that last time she got involved with Athletic Express, the order was actually placed from their L.A. regional office, and she didn't get any commission after more than two weeks of selling time.

RECOMMENDATIONS

Our sales organization should reflect the nature of our customer base. To accomplish that goal, we need a group of reps who are free to pursue accounts across regional borders—and who are compensated fairly for their work. The most sensible answer is to establish a national account group. Any customers whose operations place them in more than one region would automatically be assigned to the national group.

In addition to solving the problem of competing sales efforts, the new structure will also largely eliminate the commission-splitting problem because regional reps will no longer invest time in prospects assigned to the national accounts team. However, we will need to find a fair way to compensate regional reps who are losing long-term customers to the national team. Some of these reps have invested years in developing customer relationships that will continue to yield sales well into the future, and everyone I talked to agrees that reps in these cases should receive some sort of compensation. Such a "transition commission" would also motivate the regional reps to help ensure a smooth transition from one sales group to the other. The exact nature of this compensation would need to be worked out with the various sales managers.

3

SUMMARY

The regional sales organization is effective at the regional and local levels but not at the national level. We should establish a national accounts group to handle sales that cross regional boundaries. Then we'll have one set of reps who are focused on the local and regional levels and another set who are pursuing national accounts.

To compensate regional reps who lose accounts to the national team, we will need to devise some sort of payment to reward them for the years of work invested in such accounts. This can be discussed with the sales managers once the new structure is in place.

Brings the first problem to life by complementing the general description with a specific example

Simplifies the reader's task by maintaining a parallel structure for the discussion of the second problem: a general description followed by a specific example

Explains how the new organizational structure will solve both problems

Acknowledges that the recommended solution does create a temporary compensation problem, but expresses confidence that a solution to that can be worked out

Commission problems are the second "2" in Phan's 2 + 2 = 4 approach

Phan concludes the 2 + 2 = 4 approach: organizational problems + commission problems = the need for a new sales structure

Neatly summarizes both the problem and the recommended solution

Figure 13.11   Analytical Report Using the 2 + 2 = 4 Approach *(continued)*

Unsolicited proposals differ from solicited proposals in another important respect: Your audience may not be aware of the problem you are addressing, so your proposal must first convince readers that a problem or an opportunity exists before convincing them that you can address it. Thus, unsolicited proposals generally spend considerable time explaining why readers should take action and convincing them of the benefits of doing so.

Unsolicited proposals require additional persuasive elements because the audience isn't expecting the proposal and might not even be conscious of the problem you propose to solve.

With virtually any proposal, keep in mind that you are always competing for something—money, time, management attention, and so on. Even if yours is the only proposal on the table, you are still competing with all the other choices your audience members could make with their time, money, and attention.

Every proposal competes for something: money, time, attention, and so on.

Proposals can be significant writing projects, particularly when you are responding to a complex RFP. Fortunately, a variety of software products are available to lighten the load considerably. Basic features include the ability to automatically personalize the proposal, ensure proper structure, and organize storage of all your boilerplates (identical sections of text used in every proposal, such as a description of your company). At a more advanced level, semi-automated proposal writing systems can scan RFPs to identify questions and requirements and fill in potential answers from a centralized knowledge base that contains input from all the relevant experts in your company.[12]

ORGANIZATIONAL STRATEGIES FOR PROPOSALS

Your choice of structure for proposals depends on whether the proposal is solicited and, if so, whether you expect readers to be receptive to your specific recommendation. In general, your audience is likely to be more receptive with solicited proposals because the problem and the solution have already been identified. Submit your proposal for the solution specified in the RFP and structure the proposal using the direct approach to focus on your recommendation. As soon as possible within the constraints of the RFP requirements, identify why your solution is unique and deserves close consideration.[13]

ETHICS DETECTIVE   Solving the Case of the Overblown Proposals

As the manager in charge of your company's New Ventures Group, you've read your share of proposals—hundreds, maybe thousands, of them. You've developed a sixth sense about these documents, an ability to separate cautious optimism from self-doubt and distinguish justified enthusiasm from insupportable hype.

Your company invests in promising smaller firms that could grow into beneficial business partners or even future acquisitions. In a typical scenario, a small company invents a new product but needs additional funding to manufacture and market it, so the owners approach you with funding proposals. Because you make the first major decision in this investment process, your choices and recommendations to the board of directors are crucial.

Moreover, the risks are considerable: If one of your recommendations doesn't pan out, the company could lose all the money it invested (often millions), and that's only the start. Failures consume your team's precious time and energy and can even put the company at risk for shareholder lawsuits and other serious headaches. In other words, mistakes in your line of work are costly.

The proposal in front of you today is intriguing. A small company in Oklahoma has designed a product called the Wireless Shopping List, and you think the idea might appeal to upscale homeowners. Small touchscreens are placed around the house, wherever occupants are likely to think of things they need to buy on the next shopping trip: on the refrigerator door, in the media room, in the nursery, in the garage, in the gardening shed. The system collects all these inputs, and on command it prints out a shopping list or downloads it to a PDA. It's a clever idea, but one paragraph in the proposal bothers you:

> Everybody in our test market audience was absolutely stunned when we demonstrated the simulated system. They couldn't believe something like this was even possible. It was so handy and so convenient—everyone said it would change their lives forever. We haven't even specified the price yet, but every single person in the room wanted to place an order, on the spot.

ANALYSIS

This proposal potentially oversells the idea in at least three different ways. Identify them and explain how they could lead you to decline the investment opportunity.

The indirect approach following AIDA or a similar model is often the best way to build your case in an unsolicited proposal.

Depending on the circumstances and your relationship with the recipient, the indirect approach is often better for unsolicited proposals. When writing unsolicited proposals, you must first convince the audience that a problem exists and establish your credibility if you are unknown to the reader. At the same time, you need to give the reader a compelling reason to keep reading a document that he or she didn't request. Follow the AIDA model or a similar approach to grab the reader's attention quickly. For an external proposal, for instance, you might start off with an attention-getter such as "In working with other companies in your industry, our productivity specialists were able to lower their operating costs by as much as 15 percent." Then, to convince the reader that you can back up that claim, present your solution in a logical fashion, with solid evidence, leading up to a request for a decision.

Catches the reader's attention with a compelling promise in subject line

Explains the proposed solution in enough detail to make it convincing, without burdening the reader with excessive detail

Describes the current situation and explains why it should be fixed

Builds reader interest in the proposed solution by listing a number of compelling benefits

MEMO

TO: Jamie Engle
FROM: Shandel Cohen
DATE: July 8, 2011
SUBJECT: Saving $145k/year with an automated email response system

THE PROBLEM:
Expensive and Slow Response to Customer Information Requests

Our new product line has been very well received, and orders have surpassed our projections. This very success, however, has created a shortage of printed brochures, as well as considerable overtime for people in the customer response center. As we introduce upgrades and new options, our printed materials quickly become outdated. If we continue to rely on printed materials for customer information, we have two choices: Distribute existing materials (even though they are incomplete or inaccurate) or discard existing materials and print new ones.

THE SOLUTION:
Automated Email Response System

With minor additions and modifications to our current email system, we can set up an automated system to respond to customer requests for information. This system can save us time and money and can keep our distributed information current.

Automated email response systems have been tested and proven effective. Many companies already use this method to respond to customer information requests, so we won't have to worry about relying on untested technology. Using the system is easy, too: Customers simply send a blank email message to a specific address, and the system responds by sending an electronic copy of the requested brochure.

Benefit #1: Always-Current Information

Rather than discard and print new materials, we would only need to keep the electronic files up to date on the server. We could be able to provide customers and our field sales organization with up-to-date, correct information as soon as the upgrades or options are available.

Benefit #2: Instantaneous Delivery

Almost immediately after requesting information, customers would have that information in hand. Electronic delivery would be especially advantageous for our international customers. Regular mail to remote locations sometimes takes weeks to arrive, by which time the information may already be out of date. Both customers and field salespeople will appreciate the automatic mail-response system.

Benefit #3: Minimized Waste

With our current method of printing every marketing piece in large quantities, we discard thousands of pages of obsolete catalogs, data sheets, and other materials every year. By maintaining and distributing the information electronically, we would eliminate this waste. We would also free up a considerable amount of expensive floor space and shelving that is required for storing printed materials.

(continued)

Figure 13.12   Internal Proposal
Shandel Cohen's internal proposal seeks management's approval to install an automatic mail-response system. Because the company manufactures computers, she knows that her boss won't object to a computer-based solution. Also, since profits are always a concern, her report emphasizes the financial benefits of her proposal.

EFFECTIVE PROPOSALS: AN EXAMPLE

A good proposal explains why a project or course of action is needed, what it will involve, how much it will cost, and how the recipient will benefit. You can see all these elements in Shandel Cohen's internal proposal for an automatic mail-response system (see Figure 13.12).

Cohen manages the customer-response section of the marketing department at a personal computer manufacturer located in the Midwest. Her section sends out product information requested by customers and the field salesforce. Cohen has observed that the demand for information increases when a new product is released and that it diminishes as a product matures. This fluctuating demand causes drastic changes in her section's workload.

"Either we have more work than we can possibly handle," says Cohen, "or we don't have enough to keep us busy. But I don't want to get into a hiring-and-firing cycle." Cohen is also concerned about the amount of printed material that's discarded when products are upgraded or replaced. Her report describes the problem, her proposed solutions, the benefits to the company, and the projected costs, giving her audience all the information needed to make a decision.

For the latest information on planning reports and proposals, visit http://realtimeupdates.com/bct11 and click on Chapter 13.

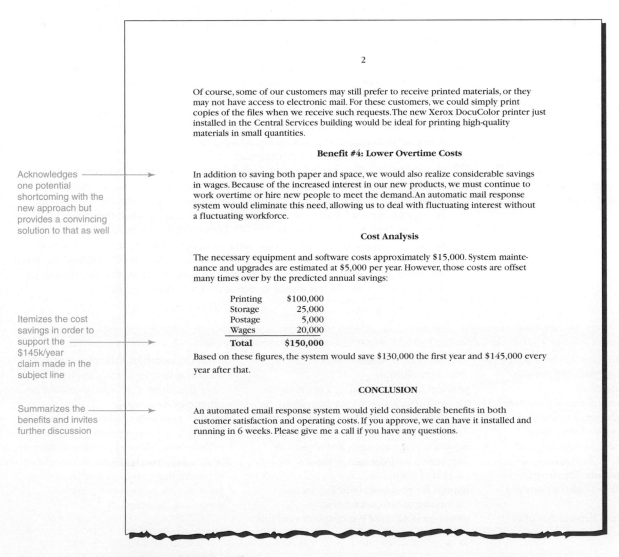

Acknowledges one potential shortcoming with the new approach but provides a convincing solution to that as well

Itemizes the cost savings in order to support the $145k/year claim made in the subject line

Summarizes the benefits and invites further discussion

2

Of course, some of our customers may still prefer to receive printed materials, or they may not have access to electronic mail. For these customers, we could simply print copies of the files when we receive such requests. The new Xerox DocuColor printer just installed in the Central Services building would be ideal for printing high-quality materials in small quantities.

Benefit #4: Lower Overtime Costs

In addition to saving both paper and space, we would also realize considerable savings in wages. Because of the increased interest in our new products, we must continue to work overtime or hire new people to meet the demand. An automatic mail response system would eliminate this need, allowing us to deal with fluctuating interest without a fluctuating workforce.

Cost Analysis

The necessary equipment and software costs approximately $15,000. System maintenance and upgrades are estimated at $5,000 per year. However, those costs are offset many times over by the predicted annual savings:

Printing	$100,000
Storage	25,000
Postage	5,000
Wages	20,000
Total	**$150,000**

Based on these figures, the system would save $130,000 the first year and $145,000 every year after that.

CONCLUSION

An automated email response system would yield considerable benefits in both customer satisfaction and operating costs. If you approve, we can have it installed and running in 6 weeks. Please give me a call if you have any questions.

Figure 13.12 **Internal Proposal** *(continued)*

Quick Learning Guide

MyBcommLab

If your course uses MyBcommLab, log on to www.mybcommlab.com to access the following study and assessment aids associated with this chapter:

- Video applications
- Real-Time Updates
- Peer review activity
- Pre/post test
- Personalized study plan
- Model documents
- Sample presentations

If you are not using MyBcommLab, you can access Real-Time Updates through http://real-timeupdates.com/bct11.

SUMMARY OF LEARNING OBJECTIVES

1 **Adapt the three-step writing process to reports and proposals.** The comprehensive nature of the three-step process is ideal for the work involved in most reports and proposals. Use all the advice you learned in Chapters 4 through 6, with added emphasis on a few specific points for longer documents: (1) Identify your purpose clearly to avoid rework, (2) prepare a work plan to guide the research and writing tasks, (3) determine whether a separate research project might be needed to gather the necessary information, (4) choose the appropriate medium (or media, in some cases) for your audience, and (5) organize your information by selecting the best approach for an informational or analytical report.

2 **List the options for organizing informational reports, identify the parts of a business plan, and explain three important steps in planning website content.** Informational reports focus on the delivery of facts, figures, and other types of information. Most informational reports use a topical organization, arranging material by comparison, importance, sequence, chronology, geography, or category.

Formal business plans—those that are shown to outside audiences such as investors and bankers—typically contain the following elements: a summary of the business concept, the company's mission and objectives, background on the company and the industry in which it competes, descriptions of its products and services, an analysis of target markets and key competitors, a discussion of the management team, a summary of the marketing strategy, design and development plans, an operations plan, a schedule with major milestones, an analysis of critical risks and problems, financial projections and requirements, and a description of the proposed exit strategy.

To help ensure effective organization of both online reports and websites in general, start by planning the structure and navigation paths before writing the content. Next, make sure you let readers be in control. Give them plenty of navigational flexibility so they can create their own paths according to the information they find interesting and useful. Don't force them to follow a rigid page-by-page scheme. Finally, break your information into chunks that can be scanned and absorbed quickly.

3 **Discuss three major ways to organize analytical reports.** The three most common ways to organize analytical reports are by focusing on conclusions, focusing on recommendations, and focusing on logical arguments. The first two are direct approaches; the third is an indirect approach.

4 **Explain how to choose an organizational strategy when writing a proposal.** The most significant factor in planning a proposal is whether the proposal is solicited or unsolicited. Solicited proposals are obviously expected and welcomed by the recipient, but they often must follow a specific organization, particularly when they are submitted in response to a request for proposals (RFP). For unsolicited proposals, the writer has flexibility in choosing the most effective organization, format, and content. However, because unsolicited proposals are unexpected, the writer often needs to explain why the solution offered in the proposal is even necessary for the reader to consider. Because of this, the indirect approach is usually preferred for unsolicited proposals.

KEY TERMS

analytical reports Reports that offer both information and analysis; they can also include recommendations

business plan A comprehensive document that describes a company's mission, structure, objectives, and operations

hypothesis A potential explanation that needs to be tested

information architecture The structure and navigational flow of all the parts of a website

informational reports Reports that offer data, facts, feedback, and other types

of information, without analysis or recommendations

problem factoring Dividing a problem into a series of logical, connected questions

proposals Reports that combine information delivery and persuasive communication

reports Written accounts that objectively communicate information about some aspect of a business

request for proposals (RFP) A formal invitation to bid on a contract

statement of purpose Planning statement that defines why you are preparing the report

topical organization Arranging material according to comparisons, importance, sequence, chronology, spatial orientation, geography, or category

yardstick approach Logical argumentation approach that uses a number of criteria to evaluate one or more possible solutions

2 + 2 = 4 approach Logical argumentation approach that convinces readers of your point of view by demonstrating how everything "adds up"

Checklist

A. Analyze the situation.
- Clearly define your purpose before you start writing.
- If you need to accomplish several goals in the report, identify them all in advance.
- Prepare a work plan to guide your efforts.

B. Gather information.
- Determine whether you need to launch a separate research project to collect the necessary information.
- Reuse or adapt existing material whenever possible.

C. Select the right medium.
- Base your decision on audience expectations or requirements.
- Consider the need for commenting, revising, distributing, and storing.
- Remember that the medium you choose also sends a message.

D. Organize your information.
- Use the direct approach if your audience is receptive.
- Use the indirect approach if your audience is skeptical.
- Use the indirect approach when you don't want to risk coming across as arrogant.
- Combine approaches if doing so will help build support for your primary message.

Informational Reports
Offer data, facts, feedback, and other types of information, without analysis or recommendations

Reports to Monitor and Control Operations
Provide feedback and other information for decision making (plans, operating reports, personal activity reports)

Reports to Implement Policies and Procedures
Communicate organizational rules and positions (guidelines, position papers)

Reports to Demonstrate Compliance
Provide information to show regulators or other authorities that the company meets formal requirements

Reports to Document Progress
Provide managers or customers with information on project status

Analytical Reports
Offer information and analysis; can also include recommendations

Reports to Assess Opportunities
Explain the risks and rewards of choosing a course of action (market analysis reports, due diligence reports)

Reports to Solve Problems
Analyze problems and (optionally) suggest solutions (troubleshooting reports, failure analysis reports)

Reports to Support Decisions
Judge the merits of past or future decisions (feasibility reports, justification reports)

Proposals
Feature persuasive requests for decisions or action

Internal Proposals
Request decisions from managers within the organization (funding proposals, general project proposals)

External Proposals
Request decisions from parties outside the organization (investment proposals, grant proposals, sales proposals)

Figure 13.5 Common Types of Business Reports and Proposals
You will have the opportunity to read and write many types of reports in your career; here are some of the most common.

COMMUNICATION CHALLENGES AT **MYCITYWAY**

You work as Archana Patchirajan's executive assistant in MyCityWay's New York headquarters, where you help her with a variety of communication projects. Use your knowledge of report and proposal writing to address the following challenges.

INDIVIDUAL CHALLENGE: MyCityWay works with a wide variety of local businesses that use the software for brand building campaigns, coupons, and mobile commerce. Recently, several of these companies have called to ask about MyCityWay's relationship with BMW. Most people recognize the BMW name, but relatively few understand the new "BMW i" program. Patchirajan thinks it would be helpful to have a brief overview ready to provide business partners who have questions. Review the information at www.bmw-i.com and draft the outline of an informational report that summarizes the "BMW i" program.

TEAM CHALLENGE: Many companies offer a downloadable one-page "fact sheet" that summarizes the concept of the business, its product lines, unique technologies, target markets, biographies of key executives, and other information of potential interest to various stakeholders. In a team with two or three other students, review the fact sheets (sometimes called a "company overview" or something similar) offered on the websites of three companies in any industry, and then collaborate on a one-page fact sheet for MyCityWay.

TEST YOUR KNOWLEDGE

To review chapter content related to each question, refer to the indicated Learning Objective.

1. What is the major difference between informational and analytical reports? [LO-1]
2. What does a statement of purpose convey? [LO-1]
3. What should you include in the work plan for a complex report or proposal? [LO-1]
4. What elements should be included in a formal business plan? [LO-2]
5. How are reports for monitoring and controlling operations used? [LO-2]
6. What are the seven major ways to organize an informational report? [LO-2]
7. What are the three major ways to organize an analytical report? [LO-3]
8. How does a feasibility report differ from a justification report? [LO-3]
9. What is problem factoring? [LO-3]
10. What is an RFP, and how does it relate to proposal writing? [LO-4]

APPLY YOUR KNOWLEDGE

To review chapter content related to each question, refer to the indicated Learning Objective.

1. Why is it important to identify all the paths that users are likely to take at a website before creating content for a new website? [LO-2]
2. How does planning a website differ from outlining a conventional report? [LO-2]
3. If you want to make a specific recommendation in your report, should you include information that might support a different recommendation? Explain your answer. [LO-3]
4. Assume you were assigned the task of evaluating two firms to provide security for your company's office and factory facilities, then write a report recommending one of the two firms. After a thorough analysis, however, you conclude that neither firm is capable of providing quality service at an acceptable cost. How should you structure your report? [LO-3]
5. In what ways are unsolicited proposals more challenging to write than solicited proposals? [LO-4]

PRACTICE YOUR SKILLS

Message for Analysis:
Comparing Two Report Formats [LO-1]

The Securities and Exchange Commission (SEC) requires all public companies to file a comprehensive annual report (form 10-K) electronically. Many companies post links to these reports on their websites, along with links to other company reports. Visit the website of Dell, at www.dell.com, and find the company's most recent 10-K and Fiscal Year in Review reports. Compare the style and format of the two reports. For which audience(s) is the Year in Review targeted? Who besides the SEC might be interested in the 10-K? Which report do you find easier to read? More interesting? More detailed?

Exercises

Active links for all websites in this chapter can be found on MyBcommLab; see your User Guide for instructions on accessing the content for this chapter. Each activity is labeled according to the primary skill or skills you will need to use. To review relevant chapter content, you can refer to the indicated Learning Objective. In some instances, supporting information will be found in another chapter, as indicated.

1. **Planning: Analyzing the Situation [LO-1]** Sales at The Style Shop, a clothing store for men, have declined for the third month in a row. Your boss is not sure whether this decline is because the economy is weak or if it's because of another unknown reason. She has asked you to investigate the situation and to submit a report to her, highlighting some possible reasons for the decline. Develop a statement of purpose for your report.

2. **Planning: Preparing the Work Plan [LO-1]** South by Southwest (SXSW) is a family of conferences and festivals in Austin, Texas, that showcase some of the world's most creative talents in music, interactive media, and film. In addition to being a major entertainment venue for a week every March, SXSW is also an increasingly important *trade show*, an opportunity for companies to present products and services to potential customers and business partners. You work for a company that makes music training equipment such as an electronic keyboard with an integrated computer screen that guides learners through every step of learning to play a keyboard. Your manager has asked you to look into whether the company should rent an exhibition booth at SXSW next year. Prepare a work plan for an analytical report that will assess the promotional opportunities at SXSW and make a recommendation on exhibiting. Include the statement of purpose, a problem statement for any research you will conduct, a description of what will result from your investigation, the sources and methods of data collection, and a preliminary outline. Visit the SXSW website, at http://sxsw.com, for more information.[14]

3. **Planning: Organizing Reports [LO-1]** For each of the following scenarios, determine whether the direct or indirect approach would be advisable, and explain why.

   a. The monthly financial report prepared by the accounting department for upper management

   b. An accountant fresh out of college who wants to propose a new way to present those monthly financial results to upper management

   c. An unsolicited proposal to provide payroll processing services

   d. An analytical report, requested by the CEO, explaining why the company has been losing money in the eastern sales region for the past two years

   e. An unsolicited proposal to the board of directors, outlining why it makes strategic sense for your company to expand into international markets; the board rejected a similar—but poorly presented—idea last year

4. **Planning: Organizing Reports [LO-1]** Look through recent issues (print or online) of *Bloomberg Businessweek*, *Fortune*, or other business publications for an article that describes how an executive's conclusions about his or her company's current situation or future opportunities led to changes in policy, plans, or products. Construct an outline of the material, first using a direct approach and then using an indirect approach. Which approach do you think the executive would use when reporting these conclusions to stockholders? When reporting to other senior managers? Explain your answers.

5. **Planning: Organizing Reports (Informational Reports) [LO-1]** Assume that your college president has received many student complaints about campus parking problems. You are appointed the chair of a student committee organized to investigate the problems and recommend solutions. The president gives you a file labeled "Parking: Complaints from Students," and you jot down the essence of the complaints as you inspect the contents. Your notes look like this:

- Inadequate student spaces at critical hours
- Poor night lighting near the computer center
- Inadequate attempts to keep resident neighbors from occupying spaces
- Dim marking lines
- Motorcycles taking up full spaces
- Discourteous security officers
- Spaces (often empty) reserved for college officials
- Relatively high parking fees
- Full fees charged to night students even though they use the lots only during low-demand periods
- Vandalism to cars and a sense of personal danger
- Inadequate total space
- Resident harassment of students parking on the street in front of neighboring houses

Prepare an outline for an informational report to be submitted to committee members. Use a topical organization that categorizes this information.

6. **Planning: Organizing Reports (Analytical Reports) [LO-1]** Three years ago, your company (a carpet manufacturer) modernized its Georgia plant in anticipation of increasing demand for carpets. Because of the depressed housing market, the increase in demand for new carpets has been slow to materialize. As a result, the company has excess capacity at both its Georgia and California plants. On the basis of your research, you have recommended that the company close the California plant. The company president, J. P. Lawrence, has asked you to prepare a justification report to support your recommendation. Here are the facts you gathered by interviewing the respective plant managers:

Operational Statistics

- Georgia plant: This plant has newer equipment, has higher productivity, employs 100 nonunion production workers, and ships $12 million in carpets a year. Hourly base wage is $16.
- California plant: California plant employs 80 union production workers and ships $8 million in carpets a year. Hourly base wage is $20.

Financial Implications

- Savings by closing California plant: (1) Increase productivity by 17 percent; (2) reduce labor costs by 20 percent (total labor savings would be $1 million per year; see assumptions); (3) annual local tax savings of $120,000 (Georgia has a more favorable tax climate).
- Sale of Pomona, California, land: Purchased in 1952 for $200,000. Current market value $2.5 million. Net profit (after capital gains tax) over $1 million.
- Sale of plant and equipment: Fully depreciated. Any proceeds a windfall.
- Costs of closing California plant: One-time deductible charge of $250,000 (relocation costs of $100,000 and severance payments totaling $150,000).

Assumptions

- Transfer five workers from California to Georgia.
- Hire 45 new workers in Georgia.
- Lay off 75 workers in California.
- Georgia plant would require a total of 150 workers to produce the combined volume of both plants.

a. Which approach (focus on conclusions, recommendations, or logical arguments) will you use to structure your report to the president? Why?

b. Suppose this report were to be circulated to plant managers and supervisors instead. What changes, if any, might you make in your approach?

c. List some conclusions that you might draw from the preceding information to use in your report.

d. Using the structure you selected for your report to the president, draft a final report outline with first- and second-level informative headings.

7. **Planning Reports and Proposals [LO-2], [LO-3], [LO-4]** Using the information presented in this chapter, identify the report type represented by each of the following examples. In addition, write a brief paragraph about each, explaining who the audience is likely to be, what type of data would be used, and whether conclusions and recommendations would be appropriate.

a. A statistical study of the pattern of violent crime in a large city during the past five years

b. A report prepared by a seed company, demonstrating the benefits of its seed corn for farmers

c. A report prepared by an independent testing agency, evaluating various types of nonprescription cold remedies

d. A trip report submitted at the end of a week by a traveling salesperson

e. A report indicating how 45 acres of undeveloped land could be converted into an industrial park

f. An annual report to be sent to the shareholders of a large corporation

g. A report from a U.S. National Park wildlife officer to Washington, D.C., headquarters showing the status of the California condor (an endangered species)

h. A report outlining the risks of closing a chain of retail stores and moving the entire business online

8. **Planning Website Architecture; Collaboration: Team Projects [LO-2], Chapter 2** With a team of two or three other students, identify a business you might like to start after college and imagine that you are planning the company's website. Brainstorm the various audiences the website would have and the types of information these site visitors would be looking for. With those audience needs in mind, lay out the architecture of the website, identify all the major pages, the content they would offer, and the various links within the site.

9. **Planning Proposals [LO-4]** Follow the step-by-step hints and examples for writing a funding proposal at www .learnerassociates.com/proposal. Review the writing hints and the entire sample proposal online. What details did the author decide to include in appendixes? Why was this material placed in the appendixes and not the main body of the report? According to the author's tips, when is the best time to prepare a project overview?

10. **Planning Informational Reports [LO-2]** You're the vice president of operations for a Florida fast-food chain. In the aftermath of a major hurricane, you're drafting a report on the emergency procedures to be followed by personnel in each restaurant when storm warnings are in effect. Answer who, what, when, where, why, and how and then prepare a one-page outline of your report. Make up any details you need.

11. **Planning Proposals [LO-4]** You're getting ready to launch a new lawn-care business that offers mowing, fertilizing, weeding, and other services. The lawn surrounding a nearby shopping center looks as if it could use better care, so you target that business for your first unsolicited proposal. To help prepare this proposal, write your answers to these questions:

a. What questions will you need to answer before you can write a proposal to solve the reader's problem? Be as specific as possible.

b. What customer benefits will you include in your proposal?

c. Will you use a letter or memo format for your proposal? Explain your answer.

12. **Planning Proposals; Collaboration: Team Projects [LO-4], Chapter 2** Break into small groups and identify an operational problem occurring at your campus, involving one of the following: registration, university housing, food services, parking, or library services. Develop a workable solution to that problem. Finally, develop a list of pertinent facts that your team will need to gather to convince the reader that the problem exists and that your solution will work.

EXPAND YOUR SKILLS

Critique the Professionals

Company websites function as multidimensional informational reports, with numerous sections and potentially endless ways for visitors to navigate through all the various pages. Identify a public corporation that has a fairly complex website. Imagine that you are approaching the website as (a) a potential employee, (b) a potential investor (purchaser of stock), (c) a member of one of the local communities in which this company operators, and (d) a potential customer of the company's products and services. Analyze how easy or difficult it is to find the information that each of these four visitors would typically be looking for. Using whatever medium your instructor requests, write a brief analysis of the information architecture of the website, describing what works well and what doesn't work well.

Sharpening Your Career Skills Online

Bovée and Thill's Business Communication Web Search, at http://businesscommunicationblog.com/websearch, is a unique research tool designed specifically for business communication research. Use the Web Search function to find a website, video, PDF document, or PowerPoint presentation that offers advice on writing effective business proposals. Write a brief email message to your instructor, describing the item that you found and summarizing the career skills information you learned from it.

Writing Reports and Proposals | 14

LEARNING OBJECTIVES   After studying this chapter, you will be able to

1 Explain how to adapt to your audiences when writing reports and proposals

2 Name five characteristics of effective report content and list the topics commonly covered in the introduction, body, and close of formal reports

3 List six strategies to strengthen a proposal argument and list the topics commonly covered in the introduction, body, and close of proposals

4 Identify six characteristics of effective website writing

5 Offer guidelines for becoming a valuable wiki contributor

MyBcommLab Test your mastery of this chapter and its Learning Objectives. Visit mybcommlab.com to apply what you've learned in Document Makeovers and interactive simulation scenarios.

COMMUNICATION CLOSE-UP AT TELLABS

The annual reports written by Tellabs's George Stenitzer go beyond regulatory compliance to helping investors understand the business and its financial performance.

www.tellabs.com

Few reports get as much scrutiny as corporate annual reports, and the feedback from many readers of these reports is not particularly positive.

These compliance reports are required of every company listed on U.S. stock exchanges, and investors pore over them, looking for clues about a company's financial health and prospects. However, investor surveys suggest that many readers don't believe they are getting the information they need in order to make intelligent decisions about investing in a company's stock. Some companies have even been sued in recent years over their annual reports, with investors accusing them of withholding or obscuring vital information.

In this environment of uncertainty and outright mistrust, writers who communicate clearly and openly tend to stand out from the crowd. One such writer is George Stenitzer, vice president of corporate communication for Tellabs, a major producer of equipment for Internet service providers based in Naperville, Illinois. According to one widely respected consultant who assesses the quality of annual reports, Stenitzer's work practically demands to be read, thanks to its brevity, forthright style, full disclosure of important financial information, numerous features that enhance readability, and attractive design.

While annual report writers must comply with a complex array of legal requirements, Stenitzer's view is that accuracy and compliance—while vital—are not enough. He recognizes that many companies still lean in the direction of minimal disclosure, saying just enough to satisfy government regulations, but Stenitzer's goal is to help investors truly understand the nature of Tellabs's business and its financial performance. As he puts it, "The test for investor communications is shifting from technical accuracy and legal compliance to clear communication and investor understanding."

The proof of his approach seems to be borne out in investor surveys. In an environment in which many investors are extremely skeptical of, or even confused by, what they read in annual reports, one of Tellabs's recent annual reports was rated "good" or "very good" by an overwhelming 83 percent of readers.[1]

Writing Reports and Proposals: Adapting to Your Audience

1 **LEARNING OBJECTIVE**

Explain how to adapt to your audiences when writing reports and proposals.

George Stenitzer (profiled in the chapter-opening Communication Close-up) and all other successful report writers will tell you how important the writing stage is in the development of effective reports and proposals. This chapter builds on the writing techniques and ideas you learned in Chapter 5, with issues that are particularly important when preparing longer messages. As with shorter messages, take a few moments before you start writing to make sure you're ready to adapt your approach to your audience.

Like all other messages, reports and proposals are most effective when they are adapted to the needs and interests of their intended audiences. To ensure your own success with reports, be sensitive to audience needs, build strong relationships with your audience, and control your style and tone.

BEING SENSITIVE TO YOUR AUDIENCE'S NEEDS

Long or complex reports demand a lot from readers, making the "you" attitude more important than ever.

Chapter 5 discusses four aspects of audience sensitivity, and all four apply to reports and proposals: adopting the "you" attitude, maintaining a strong sense of etiquette, emphasizing the positive, and using bias-free language. Reports and proposals that are highly technical, complex, or lengthy can put heavy demands on readers, so the "you" attitude takes on special importance with these messages.

In addition, various audience members can have widely different information needs. For instance, if you're reporting on the results of a customer satisfaction survey, the service manager might want every detail, whereas the president might want only a top-level summary. With previews, summaries, appendixes, and other elements, you can meet the needs of a diverse audience—provided that you plan for these elements in advance.

Help your audiences navigate through your reports by providing clear directions to key pieces of content.

Today's readers often lack the time or the inclination to plow through long reports page by page or screen by screen. They typically want to browse quickly, find a section of interest, dive in for details, browse for another section, and so on. If you want readers to understand and accept your message, help them navigate your document by using headings and links, smooth transitions, and previews and reviews.

Headings and Links

As you learned in Chapter 6, headings are brief titles that cue readers about the content of sections that follow. They improve a document's readability and are especially useful for identifying the framework of a report. They also visually indicate shifts from one idea to the next, and when you use a combination of headings and subheadings, you help readers see the relationship between subordinate and main ideas. In addition, busy readers can quickly understand the gist of a document simply by scanning the headings. In online reports, headings serve all these functions, plus they can be used to provide links to other sections and other websites.

Many companies specify a format for headings, either through style guides or document templates. If yours does, use that recommended format. If you are creating your own scheme, make sure the hierarchy of headings and subheadings is clear. If you have three

MyBcommLab

• Access this chapter's simulation entitled Persuasive Business Messages & Proposals, located at mybcommlab.com.

levels of headings in a report, for example, you might use 20 point bold type for the first level headings, 16 points for the second level, and 12 points for the third level:

First level

Second level

Third level

Another option is to put the first level headings in all capital letters or emphasize them using color. The sample report on pages 428–442 in Chapter 15 does both of these, for instance.

Transitions

Successful report writers use transitions (see Chapter 5) to help readers move from one section of a report to the next and from key point to key point within sections. Transitions can be words, sentences, or complete paragraphs. Here's an example:

> . . . As you can see, our profits have decreased by 12 percent over the past eight months.
>
> To counteract this decline in profits, we can explore alternatives. First, we can raise our selling prices. Second, we can work to reduce our manufacturing costs. Third, we can introduce new products that will support higher profit margins. However, each of these alternatives has both advantages and disadvantages.

Transitions connect ideas by helping readers move from one thought to the next.

The phrase *As you can see* alerts readers to the fact that they are reading a summary of the information just presented. The phrase *this decline in profits* refers to the previous paragraph, to let readers know that the text will be saying something else about that topic. The words *first, second*, and *third* help readers stay on track as the three alternatives are introduced, and the word *however* alerts readers to the fact that evaluating the three alternatives requires some additional discussion. Effective transitions such as these can help readers summarize and remember what they've learned so far while giving them a mental framework to process new information.

Previews and Reviews

Preview sections introduce important topics by helping readers get ready for new information; they are particularly helpful when the information is complex, unexpected, or unfamiliar. Think of a preview as an opportunity for readers to arrange their mental file folders before you start giving them information to put in those folders.

Previews help readers prepare for upcoming information, and reviews help them verify and clarify what they've just read.

Review sections come after a body of material and summarize the information just covered. They help readers absorb details while keeping track of the big picture. Long reports and those dealing with complex subjects can often benefit from multiple review sections, one at the end of every major subject block, as well as a more comprehensive review at the very end of a document.

Previews and reviews can be written in sentence format, in bulleted lists, or using a combination of the two. Both are effective, but bullets can increase your document's readability by adding white space to the document design. Consider the following preview, which is written using both formats:

Sentence Format	Bulleted List
The next section discusses the advantages of online advertising. Among them are currency, global reach, affordability, and interactivity.	As the next section shows, online advertising has four advantages: • Currency • Global reach • Affordability • Interactivity

For more on writing effective bullets and lists, see "Using Lists to Clarify and Emphasize" on page 149 in Chapter 6.

BUILDING STRONG RELATIONSHIPS WITH YOUR AUDIENCE

Your reports may continue to be read for months or years after you write them—and reach audiences you never envisioned.

Building relationships with your readers starts with planning how to adapt your style and your language to meet their needs and expectations. Bear in mind that some reports—particularly any reports that can be transmitted online—can take on lives of their own, reaching a wider audience than you ever imagined and being read years after you write them. Consequently, choose your content and language with care. Also, because many companies have specific guidelines for communicating with public audiences, make sure you're aware of these preferences before you start writing.

As discussed in Chapter 5, establishing your credibility is vital to successful communication. To gain your audience's trust, research all sides of your topic and document your findings with credible sources. Also, be aware that setting audience expectations too high can lead to problems with your credibility if you can't deliver everything people expect you to, so take particular care with the introductory sections of important reports.

CONTROLLING YOUR STYLE AND TONE

Adjust the level of formality to match the situation and your audience's expectations.

If you know your readers reasonably well and your report is likely to meet with their approval, you can adopt a fairly informal tone—provided that doing so is acceptable in the situation and in your company's culture. To make your tone less formal, refer to readers as *you*, and refer to yourself as *I* (or *we*, if there are multiple report authors).

A more formal tone is usually appropriate for longer reports, especially those that deal with controversial or complex information. You'll also want to use a more formal tone when your report will be sent to other parts of the organization or to outsiders, such as customers, suppliers, or members of the community (see Figure 14.1).

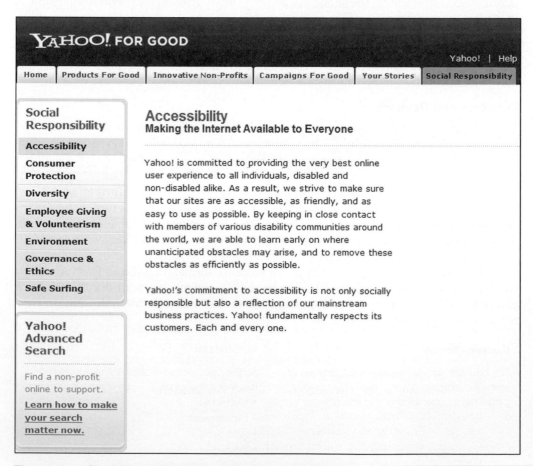

Figure 14.1   Choosing the Right Tone for Business Reports
Yahoo! is known for a playful, informal tone in its advertising and in most communication with customers, but the company's tone is more formal when communicating with the public on more serious matters.

If the situation calls for a more formal tone, use the impersonal journalism style, eliminating all references to *you* and *I* (including *we*, *us*, and *our*). When you use an impersonal style, you impose a controlled distance between you and your readers. Your tone is not only objective but also businesslike and unemotional. Be careful to avoid jokes, and minimize the use of similes, metaphors, and overly colorful language.

However, when crafting a more formal tone, take care not to go overboard, or you'll end up sounding stiff or dull. In addition, don't inadvertently slip into the passive voice. You can avoid this potential weakness by making the report content itself the actor in a sentence. For example, to convert "I think we should buy TramCo" to a more formal tone, you could write "The financial analysis clearly shows that buying TramCo is the best alternative."

Composing Reports and Proposals: Drafting Report Content

With a clear picture of how you need to adapt to your audience, you're ready to begin composing your first draft. Before you put those first words down on paper, though, review your outline one last time. Verify that the organization you've chosen makes sense, given everything you've learned about your topic so far. Also, review the wording of the headings and subheadings to make sure they establish the right tone. For a hard-hitting, direct tone, use informative phrasing ("Quality Problems Result in Nearly 500 Customer Defections Every Year"). For an objective, indirect tone, use descriptive phrasing ("Effects of Product Quality on Customer Retention").

Writing lengthy reports and proposals can be a huge task, so be sure to take advantage of technological tools to help throughout the process. In addition to the tools described under "Using Technology to Compose and Shape Your Messages" on page 136, look for opportunities to use *linked and embedded documents* to incorporate graphics, spreadsheets, databases, and other elements produced in other software programs. For instance, in Microsoft Office, you can choose to either *link* to another file (which ensures that changes in that file are reflected in your file) or *embed* another file (which doesn't include this automatic updating feature).

Like other written business communications, reports and proposals have three main sections: an introduction (or *opening*), a body, and a close. The content and length of each section vary with the type and purpose of the document, the document's organizational structure, the length and depth of the material, the document's degree of formality, and your relationship with your audience.

An effective *introduction* accomplishes at least four things:

- Puts the report or proposal in a broader context by tying it to a problem or an assignment
- Introduces the subject or purpose of the report or proposal and indicates why the subject is important
- Previews the main ideas and the order in which they'll be covered
- Establishes the tone of the document and the writer's relationship with the audience

In the *body*, the middle section in your report or proposal, you present, analyze, and interpret the information gathered during your investigation. If appropriate, the body also contains the detailed proof necessary to support your conclusions and recommendations (see Figure 14.2 on the next page).

The *close*, the final section of your report or proposal, has three important functions:

- Emphasizes the main points of the message and briefly reiterates the logic behind any conclusions or recommendations you've made
- Summarizes the benefits to the reader if the document suggests a change or some other course of action
- Brings all the action items together in one place and gives details about who should do what, when, where, and how

---

Sidebar notes:

2 | **LEARNING OBJECTIVE**

Name five characteristics of effective report content, and list the topics commonly covered in the introduction, body, and close of formal reports.

Before you start writing, review your outline one more time and verify the wording of your headings and subheadings.

The introduction needs to provide context for the reader, introduce the subject, preview main ideas, and establish the tone of the document.

The body of a report presents, analyzes, and interprets the information you gathered during your investigation.

The close of your report should emphasize the main message, summarize audience benefits, gather together all the action items (if any), and indicate responsibilities for each one.

Reminds readers of the origin and purpose of the report

Presents logical reasons for recommending that the firm expand its website to include e-commerce

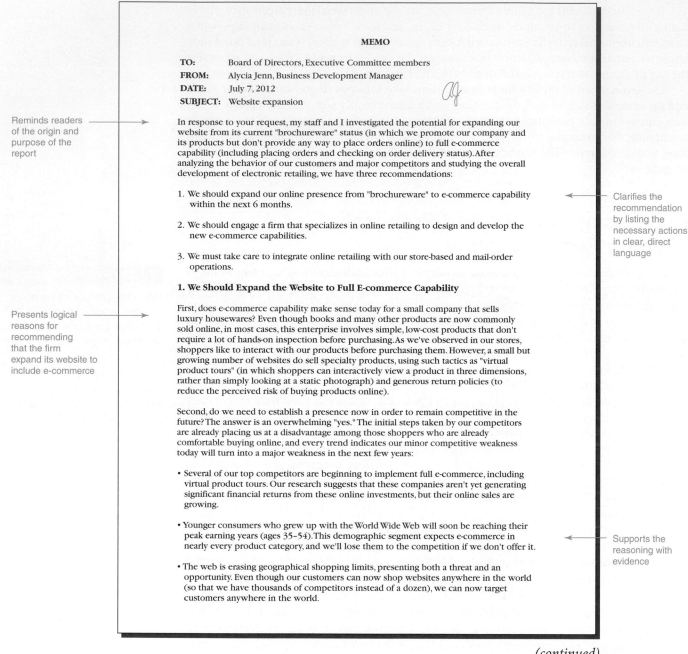

MEMO

TO: Board of Directors, Executive Committee members
FROM: Alycia Jenn, Business Development Manager
DATE: July 7, 2012
SUBJECT: Website expansion

In response to your request, my staff and I investigated the potential for expanding our website from its current "brochureware" status (in which we promote our company and its products but don't provide any way to place orders online) to full e-commerce capability (including placing orders and checking on order delivery status). After analyzing the behavior of our customers and major competitors and studying the overall development of electronic retailing, we have three recommendations:

1. We should expand our online presence from "brochureware" to e-commerce capability within the next 6 months.

2. We should engage a firm that specializes in online retailing to design and develop the new e-commerce capabilities.

3. We must take care to integrate online retailing with our store-based and mail-order operations.

1. We Should Expand the Website to Full E-commerce Capability

First, does e-commerce capability make sense today for a small company that sells luxury housewares? Even though books and many other products are now commonly sold online, in most cases, this enterprise involves simple, low-cost products that don't require a lot of hands-on inspection before purchasing. As we've observed in our stores, shoppers like to interact with our products before purchasing them. However, a small but growing number of websites do sell specialty products, using such tactics as "virtual product tours" (in which shoppers can interactively view a product in three dimensions, rather than simply looking at a static photograph) and generous return policies (to reduce the perceived risk of buying products online).

Second, do we need to establish a presence now in order to remain competitive in the future? The answer is an overwhelming "yes." The initial steps taken by our competitors are already placing us at a disadvantage among those shoppers who are already comfortable buying online, and every trend indicates our minor competitive weakness today will turn into a major weakness in the next few years:

• Several of our top competitors are beginning to implement full e-commerce, including virtual product tours. Our research suggests that these companies aren't yet generating significant financial returns from these online investments, but their online sales are growing.

• Younger consumers who grew up with the World Wide Web will soon be reaching their peak earning years (ages 35–54). This demographic segment expects e-commerce in nearly every product category, and we'll lose them to the competition if we don't offer it.

• The web is erasing geographical shopping limits, presenting both a threat and an opportunity. Even though our customers can now shop websites anywhere in the world (so that we have thousands of competitors instead of a dozen), we can now target customers anywhere in the world.

Clarifies the recommendation by listing the necessary actions in clear, direct language

Supports the reasoning with evidence

(continued)

Figure 14.2   Effective Problem-Solving Report Focusing on Recommendations
In this report recommending that her firm expand its website to full e-commerce capability, Alycia Jenn uses the body of her report to provide enough information to support her argument, without burdening her high-level readership with a lot of tactical details.

The close might be the only part of your report some readers have time for, so make sure it conveys the full weight of your message.

Research shows that the final section of a report or proposal leaves a strong lasting impression. The close gives you one last chance to make sure that your report says what you intended.[2] In fact, readers who are in a hurry might skip the body of the report and read only the summary, so make sure it carries a strong, clear message.

Your credibility and prospects for the future are on the line with every business report you write, so make sure your content is

Effective report content is accurate, complete, balanced, clear, logical, and properly documented.

• **Accurate.** Information presented in a report must be factually correct. When writing reports, be sure to double-check your facts and references in addition to checking for typos. If an audience ever gets the inkling that your information is shaky, they'll start to view all your work with a skeptical eye.

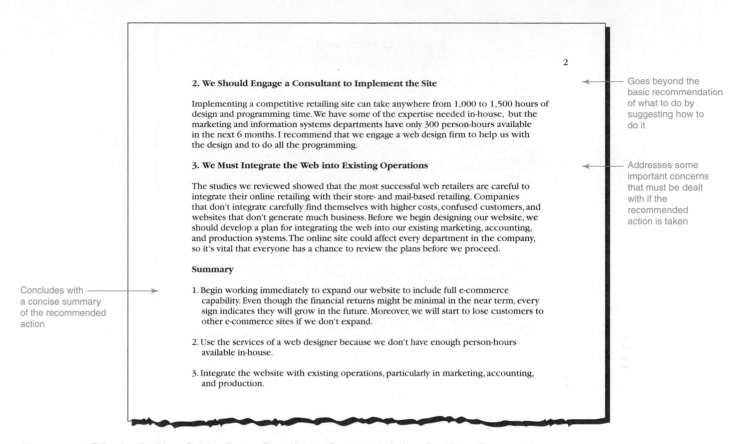

Figure 14.2 **Effective Problem-Solving Report Focusing on Recommendations** *(continued)*

- **Complete.** To help audiences make informed decisions, include all the information necessary for readers to understand the situation, problem, or proposal. Support all key assertions, using an appropriate combination of illustrations, explanations, and facts.[3] Tell your readers what they need to know—no more, no less—and present the information in a way that is geared to their needs. In a recent Tellabs annual report, for example, George Stenitzer and his team provided a concise and easily understandable overview of the company's complex and technical product line. Rather than burying the audience under technical details, the product overview clearly identifies how the company's products deliver the benefits that Internet users want and how the products offer business advantages to Tellabs's customers. The subject matter is presented in a way that any investor interested in the company's stock can comprehend.[4]
- **Balanced.** It's important to present all sides of the issue fairly and equitably and to include all the essential information, even if some of it doesn't support your line of reasoning. Omitting relevant information or facts can bias your report.
- **Clear and logical.** Save your readers time by making sure your sentences are uncluttered, contain well-chosen words, and proceed logically. To help your readers move from one point to the next, make your transitions clear and logical. For a successful report, identify the ideas that belong together and organize them in a way that's easy to understand.[5]
- **Documented properly.** If you use primary and secondary sources for your report or proposal, be sure to properly document and give credit to your sources, as Chapter 11 explains.

Keeping these points in mind will help you draft an effective introduction, body, and close for your report (see Figure 14.3 on the next page).

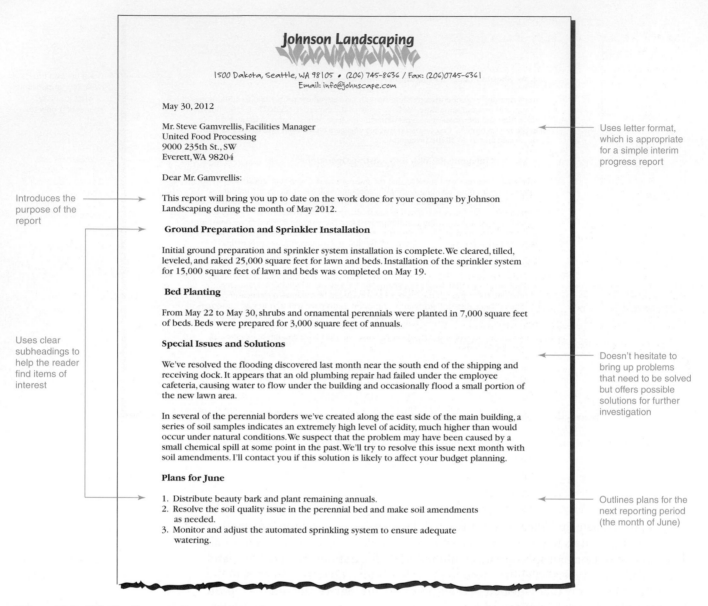

Figure 14.3   Effective Progress Report (Excerpt)

Note how Carlyce Johnson offers her client a complete but concise update of her company's landscaping services. In addition to providing routine information, she also informs the client of progress on two problem areas, one that her firm has been able to resolve and one that they've just discovered. Johnson does the right thing by telling the client about the problems as early as possible, giving the client time to react and plan.

MyBcommLab

Apply Figure 14.3's key concepts by revising a new document. Go to Chapter 14 in mybcommlab.com and select Document Makeovers.

REPORT INTRODUCTION

Carefully select the elements to include in your introduction; don't include anything your audience doesn't need.

The specific elements you should include in a report's introduction depend on the nature and length of the report, the circumstances in which you're writing the report, and your relationship with the audience. An introduction could contain all of the following topics, although you'll want to pick and choose the best ones to include with each report you write:

- **Authorization.** When, how, and by whom the report was authorized; who wrote it; and when it was submitted. This material is especially important when no *letter of transmittal* is included.
- **Problem/opportunity/purpose.** The reason for the report's existence and what is to be accomplished as a result of your having written the report.

- **Scope.** What is and what isn't going to be covered in the report. The scope indicates the report's size and complexity; it also helps with the critical job of setting the audience's expectations.
- **Background.** The historical conditions or factors that led up to the report. This section enables readers to understand how the problem, situation, or opportunity developed and what has been done about it so far.
- **Sources and methods.** The primary and secondary sources of information used. As appropriate, this section explains how samples were selected, how questionnaires (which should be included in an appendix with any cover letters) were constructed, what follow-up was done, and so on. This section builds reader confidence in the work and in the sources and methods used.
- **Definitions.** A list of terms that might be unfamiliar to your audience, along with brief definitions. This section is unnecessary if readers are familiar with the terms you've used in your report—and they all agree on what the terms mean, which isn't always the case. Terms may also be defined where they appear in the body, in explanatory notes, or in a glossary.
- **Limitations.** Factors beyond your control that affect report quality, such as budget limitations, schedule constraints, or limited access to information or people. However, don't apologize for or try to explain away avoidable errors (such as having put off the report until the last minute).
- **Report organization.** The organization of the report, along with a rationale for following this plan, if appropriate. This section is a road map that helps readers understand what's coming at each turn of the report and why.

In a relatively brief report, these topics may be discussed in only a paragraph or two. Here's an example of a brief indirect opening, taken from the introduction of a memo on why a new line of luggage has failed to sell well. The writer's ultimate goal is to recommend a shift in marketing strategy:

> Sales performance of the Venturer line can be improved. In the two years since its introduction, this product line has achieved a sales volume lower than we expected, resulting in a drain on the company's overall earnings. The purpose of this report is to review the luggage-buying habits of consumers in all markets where the Venturer line is sold, so that we can determine where to put our marketing emphasis.

This paragraph quickly introduces the subject (disappointing sales), tells why the problem is important (drain on earnings), and indicates the main points to be addressed in the body of the report (review of markets where the Venturer line is sold), without revealing what the conclusions and recommendations will be.

In a much longer formal report, the discussion of these topics may span several pages and constitute a significant section of the report.

REPORT BODY

The body of a report can require some tough decisions about which elements to include and how much detail to offer. You should provide only enough detail in the body to support your conclusions and recommendations; you can put additional information in appendixes. The following topics are commonly covered in a report body:

- Explanations of a problem or an opportunity
- Facts, statistical evidence, and trends
- Results of studies or investigations
- Discussion and analyses of potential courses of action
- Advantages, disadvantages, costs, and benefits of a particular course of action
- Procedures or steps in a process
- Methods and approaches
- Criteria for evaluating alternatives and options
- Conclusions and recommendations (in direct reports)
- Supporting reasons for conclusions or recommendations

The report body should contain only enough information to convey your message convincingly; don't overload the body with excessive details.

For analytical reports using the direct approach, you can state your conclusions or recommendations in the introduction and use the body to provide your evidence and support (as illustrated in Figures 14.2 and 14.3). If you're using the indirect approach, you can use the body to discuss your logic and reserve your conclusions or recommendations until the close.

REPORT CLOSE

The nature of your close depends on the type of report (informational, analytical, or proposal) and the approach (direct or indirect).

The content and length of a report's close depend primarily on your choice of direct or indirect approach. If you're using the direct approach, you can end with a summary of key points, listed in the order in which they appear in the report body. If you're using the indirect approach, you can use the close to present your conclusions or recommendations if you didn't end the body with them. However, don't introduce new facts in your close; audience members should have all the information they need by the time they reach this point.

If your report is intended to prompt others to action, use the close to spell out exactly what should happen next. If you'll be taking all the actions yourself, make sure your readers understand this fact so that they know what to expect from you (see Figure 14.4).

In a short report, the close may be only a paragraph or two. In a long report, however, the close might have separate sections for conclusions, recommendations, and actions.

Figure 14.4   Clarifying Expectations in the Close
Roger Watson's personal activity report for July is a good example of efficiently conveying key information points, including a concise plan of action in the close. Note the use of hyperlinks to maps, photos, and a related report, all of which are stored on the same secure intranet site.

Separate sections help your reader locate this material and focus on each element. Such an arrangement also gives you a final opportunity to emphasize important content.

If you have multiple conclusions, recommendations, or actions, you may want to number and list them. An appropriate lead-in to such a list might be "The findings of this study lead to the following conclusions." A statement that could be used for a list of recommendations might be "Based on the conclusions of this study, we make the following recommendations." A statement that could be used for actions might be "In order to accomplish our goals on time, we must complete the following actions before the end of the year."

For long reports, you may need to divide your close into separate sections for conclusions, recommendations, and actions.

Composing Reports and Proposals: Drafting Proposal Content

If you're writing an unsolicited proposal, you have some latitude in the scope and organization of content. However, the scope and organization of a solicited proposal are usually governed by the request for proposals. Most RFPs spell out precisely what you should cover and in what order. This uniformity lets the recipient evaluate competing proposals in a systematic way.

The general purpose of any proposal is to persuade readers to do something, such as purchase goods or services, fund a project, or implement a program. Thus, your writing approach for a proposal is similar to that used for persuasive sales messages (see Chapter 10). Your proposal must sell your audience on your ideas, product, service, methods, and company. As with any other persuasive message, you can use the AIDA model to gain attention, build interest, create desire, and motivate action (of course, you may need to adapt it if you're responding to an RFP or working within some other constraints). Here are some additional strategies to strengthen your persuasive argument:[6]

- **Demonstrate your knowledge.** Everything you write should show the reader that you have the knowledge and experience to solve the problem or address the opportunity outlined in your proposal.
- **Provide concrete information and examples.** Avoid vague, unsupported generalizations such as "We are losing money on this program." Instead, provide quantifiable details such as the amount of money being lost, how, why, and so on. Explain how much money your proposed solution will save. Spell out your plan and give details on how the job will be done.
- **Research the competition.** Find out what alternatives your audience might choose over your proposal so that you can emphasize why your solution is the optimum choice. In some cases, potential customers face a "buy or build" decision, in which they must choose between buying a solution from an external party and building it themselves. In these cases, you are effectively competing against your target customers.
- **Prove that your proposal is workable.** Your proposal must be appropriate and feasible for your audience. It should be consistent with your audience's capabilities. For instance, your proposal would be pointless if it recommended a plan of action that requires three times the number of available employees or twice the available budget.
- **Adopt the "you" attitude.** Relate your product, service, or personnel to the reader's exact needs, either as stated in the RFP for a solicited proposal or as discovered through your own investigation for an unsolicited proposal.
- **Package your proposal attractively.** Make sure your proposal is letter perfect, inviting, and readable. Readers will prejudge the quality of your products or services by the proposal you submit. Errors, omissions, and inconsistencies will work against you—and may even cost you important career and business opportunities.

Proposals in various industries often have their own special challenges as well. For instance, management consultants have to convince every potential client that they have the

3 **LEARNING OBJECTIVE**

List six strategies to strengthen a proposal argument, and list the topics commonly covered in the introduction, body, and close of proposals.

The AIDA model you learned in Chapter 10 works well for proposals, although you may need to adapt it if you're responding to an RFP.

Business proposals need to provide more than just attractive ideas—readers look for evidence of practical, achievable solutions.

REAL-TIME UPDATES
Learn More by Watching This PowerPoint Presentation

Need clarification about plagiarism?

Get helpful tips for avoiding plagiarism when researching and writing reports. Go to http://real-timeupdates.com/bct11 and click on "Learn More." If you are using MyBcommLab, you can access Real-Time Updates within each chapter or under Student Study Tools.

skills and knowledge to solve the client's problem—without giving away the answer for free in the proposal. In other industries, such as transportation services, bidders may be asked to compute hundreds or thousands of individual pricing scenarios. Hands-on experience goes a long way when you're deciding what to include and exclude in a report; whenever possible, get advice from a senior colleague who's been through it before.

PROPOSAL INTRODUCTION

The introduction presents and summarizes the problem you want to solve or the opportunity you want to pursue, along with your proposed solution. The introduction orients readers to the remainder of the report. If your proposal is solicited, its introduction should refer to the RFP so that readers know which RFP you're responding to. If your proposal is unsolicited, your introduction should mention any factors that led you to submit your proposal, such as prior conversations with members of the recipient organization's staff. The following topics are commonly covered in a proposal introduction:

- **Background or statement of the problem or opportunity.** Briefly reviews the reader's situation and establishes a need for action. Bear in mind that readers may not perceive a problem or an opportunity the same way you do. In unsolicited proposals, you need to convince them that a problem or an opportunity exists before you can convince them to accept your solution. In a way that is meaningful to your reader, discuss the current situation and explain how things could be better. Emphasize how your goals align with your audience's goals.
- **Solution.** Briefly describes the solution you propose and highlights your key selling points and their benefits, showing how your proposal will help readers meet their business objectives. The heading for this section might be "Preliminary Analysis," "Overview of Approach," or some other wording that identifies this section as a preview of your solution.
- **Scope.** States the boundaries of the proposal, defining what you will and will not do. This section is sometimes called "Delimitations."
- **Organization.** Orients the reader to the remainder of the proposal and calls attention to the major divisions of information.

In short proposals, your discussion of these topics will be brief—perhaps only a sentence or two for each one. For long, formal proposals, each of these topics may warrant separate subheadings and several paragraphs of discussion.

PROPOSAL BODY

The proposal's body gives complete details on the proposed solution and specifies what the anticipated results will be. Because a proposal is by definition a persuasive message, your audience expects you to promote your offering in a confident, professional manner. Even when you're expressing an idea that you believe in passionately, be sure to maintain an objective tone so that you don't risk overselling your message.

In addition to providing facts and evidence to support your conclusions, an effective body covers this information:

- **Proposed solution.** Describes what you have to offer: your concept, product, or service. This section may also be titled "Technical Proposal," "Research Design," "Issues for Analysis," or "Work Statement." Focus on the strengths of your offer that are relevant to your readers' needs, and point out any advantages that you have over your competitors.
- **Work plan.** Sometimes called the *statement of work*, this describes how you'll accomplish what must be done, unless you'll be providing a standard, off-the-shelf item. (Note that *work plan* in this context describes the work you'll perform if your proposal is accepted, not the work plan you may have written to help guide the writing of the proposal itself.) Explain the steps you'll take, their timing, the methods or resources you'll use, and the person(s) responsible. Specifically include when the work will begin, how it will be divided into stages, when you will finish, and whether any follow-up is involved. If appropriate, include a time line or Gantt chart highlighting any critical dates.

In an unsolicited proposal, your introduction may need to convince readers that a problem or opportunity exists.

Readers understand that a proposal is a persuasive message, so they're willing to accommodate a promotional style—as long as it is professional and focused on their needs.

The work plan indicates exactly how you will accomplish the solution presented in the proposal.

For solicited proposals, make sure your dates match those specified in the RFP. Keep in mind that if your proposal is accepted, the work plan is contractually binding, so don't promise to deliver more than you can realistically achieve within the stated time period.

- **Statement of qualifications.** Describes your organization's experience, personnel, and facilities—all in relation to reader needs. The qualifications section can be an important selling point, and it deserves to be handled carefully. You can supplement your qualifications by including a list of client references but get permission ahead of time to use these references.
- **Costs.** Covers pricing, reimbursable expenses, discounts, and cost factors. Coverage can vary widely, from a single price amount to detailed breakdowns by part number, service category, and so on. If you're responding to an RFP, follow its instructions. In other cases, your firm probably has a policy for discussing costs, including how much detail to provide.

In an informal proposal, discussion of some or all of these elements may be grouped together and presented in a letter format, as in the proposal shown in Figure 14.5 on pages 412–413. In a formal proposal, the discussion of these elements will be quite long and thorough. The format may resemble the format of long reports with multiple parts, as Chapter 15 discusses.

PROPOSAL CLOSE

The final section of a proposal generally summarizes the key points, emphasizes the benefits that readers will realize from your solution, summarizes the merits of your approach, restates why you and your firm are the ones to perform the service or provide the products in question, and asks for a decision from the readers. The close is your last opportunity to persuade readers to accept your proposal. In both formal and informal proposals, make this section relatively brief, assertive (but not brash or abrupt), and confident.

The close is your last chance to convince the reader of the merits of your proposal, so make doubly sure it's clear, compelling, and audience-oriented.

Drafting Online Content

In addition to the other advice in this chapter about report writing, paying attention to six key aspects of web writing will help make your web content more effective. First, take special care to build trust with your intended audiences, because careful readers can be skeptical of online content. Make sure your content is accurate, current, complete, and authoritative. Indicate the date material was originally posted and again when it is updated, so that readers can judge how current your content is. Don't promise value-added content and then present thinly disguised promotional materials.

Second, adapt your content for a global audience. Translating content is expensive, however, and *localizing* it so that it reflects not only the native language of your readers but their cultural norms, weights, measures, time, money, and so on is even more expensive. Some companies compromise by localizing the homepage and key secondary pages while keeping the deeper, more detailed content in its original language.

Third, present your information in a concise, skimmable format. Studies show that web readers typically read only a fraction of the words on a page—about 20 percent on the average—and the percentage goes down the longer the webpage gets.[7] Effective websites use a variety of means to help readers skim pages quickly, including lists, careful use of color and boldface, informative headings ("clever" headings with lots of wordplay are more annoying than effective), and helpful summaries. Wherever you can, use the *inverted pyramid* style, in which you cover the most important information briefly at first and then gradually reveal successive layers of detail—letting readers choose to see those additional layers if they want to.

Fourth, write headlines that answer the questions your target readers have in mind when they go looking for content.[8] For example, homeowners looking to sell their houses want to get the highest possible price. If you've written a report that offers advice on this subject, consider a title along the lines of "Selling Your Home? Five Steps to Maximize

 4 LEARNING OBJECTIVE

Identify six characteristics of effective website writing.

Localizing web content involves translating the content and adapting it to local cultural norms and practices.

Make online reports and website content easy to skim; most people read only a fraction of the content.

REAL-TIME UPDATES
Learn More by Reading This Article

Get a head start on writing great headlines

Headlines can make or break a website; see what works in this free series of articles. Go to http://real-timeupdates.com/bct11 and click on "Learn More." If you are using MyBcommLab, you can access Real-Time Updates within each chapter or under Student Study Tools.

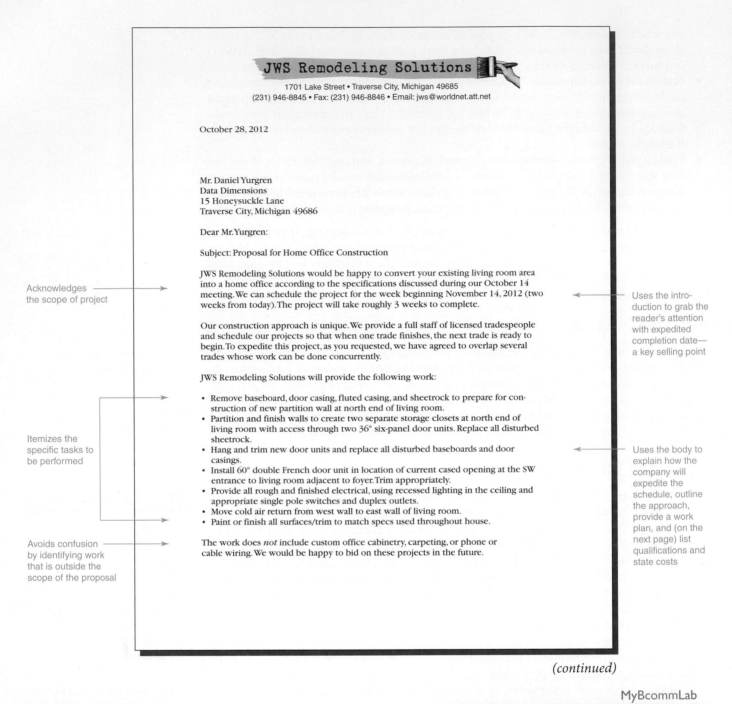

JWS Remodeling Solutions

1701 Lake Street • Traverse City, Michigan 49685
(231) 946-8845 • Fax: (231) 946-8846 • Email: jws@worldnet.att.net

October 28, 2012

Mr. Daniel Yurgren
Data Dimensions
15 Honeysuckle Lane
Traverse City, Michigan 49686

Dear Mr. Yurgren:

Subject: Proposal for Home Office Construction

JWS Remodeling Solutions would be happy to convert your existing living room area into a home office according to the specifications discussed during our October 14 meeting. We can schedule the project for the week beginning November 14, 2012 (two weeks from today). The project will take roughly 3 weeks to complete.

Our construction approach is unique. We provide a full staff of licensed tradespeople and schedule our projects so that when one trade finishes, the next trade is ready to begin. To expedite this project, as you requested, we have agreed to overlap several trades whose work can be done concurrently.

JWS Remodeling Solutions will provide the following work:

- Remove baseboard, door casing, fluted casing, and sheetrock to prepare for construction of new partition wall at north end of living room.
- Partition and finish walls to create two separate storage closets at north end of living room with access through two 36" six-panel door units. Replace all disturbed sheetrock.
- Hang and trim new door units and replace all disturbed baseboards and door casings.
- Install 60" double French door unit in location of current cased opening at the SW entrance to living room adjacent to foyer. Trim appropriately.
- Provide all rough and finished electrical, using recessed lighting in the ceiling and appropriate single pole switches and duplex outlets.
- Move cold air return from west wall to east wall of living room.
- Paint or finish all surfaces/trim to match specs used throughout house.

The work does *not* include custom office cabinetry, carpeting, or phone or cable wiring. We would be happy to bid on these projects in the future.

(continued)

Annotations (left side):

Acknowledges the scope of project

Itemizes the specific tasks to be performed

Avoids confusion by identifying work that is outside the scope of the proposal

Annotations (right side):

Uses the introduction to grab the reader's attention with expedited completion date—a key selling point

Uses the body to explain how the company will expedite the schedule, outline the approach, provide a work plan, and (on the next page) list qualifications and state costs

MyBcommLab

Figure 14.5   Solicited Proposal
This informal solicited proposal in letter format provides the information the customer needs to make a purchase. Note that by signing the proposal and returning it, the customer will enter into a legal contract to pay for the services described.

Apply Figure 14.5's key concepts by revising a new document. Go to Chapter 14 in mybcommlab.com and select Document Makeovers.

Your Selling Price" or "Get the Best Price for Your House." These headlines are also packed with the keywords people are likely to type into a search engine. In contrast, headlines such as "Push It to the Limit" or "Home $weet Home" would mean next to nothing to human readers and search engines alike. For more on search engine optimization, see "Please Find Us: Building an Audience Through Search Engine Optimization" on page 286 .

Effective links in online reports let readers know exactly what to expect before they click on them.

Fifth, whenever you include links in your material, write link text that is descriptive and unambiguous so that readers know where the link will take them. For example, in the report about selling a house, a good link to a next page for the article might be "Step Two: Spruce Up Your Landscaping." Use meaningful key words at the beginning of links so that readers can quickly identify items of interest.[9] As with headlines, don't hide the meaning with clever

Mr. Daniel Yurgren   Page 2   October 28, 2012

JWS Remodeling Solutions has been in business in the Michigan area for over 17 years. We have a strong reputation for being a quality builder. We take great pride in our work and we treat all projects with the same high-level attention, regardless of their size or scope. Our tradespeople are all licensed, insured professionals with years of experience in their respective crafts. Enclosed is a copy of our company brochure discussing our qualifications in greater detail, along with a current client list. Please contact any of the names on this list for references. — *Increases desire by highlighting qualifications*

Helps reader accept the cost total by breaking it down into specific categories → The total cost for this project is $6,800, broken down as follows:

Materials and supplies	$3,800
Labor	2,700
Disposal fees	300
Total	$6,800

An initial payment of $3,800 is due upon acceptance of this proposal. The remaining $3,000 is due upon completion of the work.

If you would like to have JWS Remodeling Solutions complete this work, please sign one copy of this letter and return it to us with your deposit in the enclosed envelope. We currently anticipate no construction delays, since the materials needed for your job are in stock and our staff of qualified workers is available during the period mentioned. If you have any questions regarding the terms of this proposal, please call me.

Sincerely,

Jordan W. Spurrier
President

Enclosures (3)

Accepted by:

Makes letter a binding contract, if signed →

_____   _____
Daniel Yurgren   Date

Figure 14.5   Solicited Proposal *(continued)*

wordplay. If a link takes readers to another website or launches a video or a podcast, make that clear as well so that website visitors aren't surprised when they click the link.

Sixth, make your website a "living" document by adding fresh content and deleting reports and articles that are out of date or no longer relevant to your target audience. Over time, websites can accumulate many pages of outdated information that get in the way and send a negative message about the company's efforts to stay on top of user needs.[10] Fresh content is also a key factor in search engine ranking algorithms.[11]

Collaborating on Wikis

As Chapter 2 points out, using wikis is a great way for teams and other groups to collaborate on writing projects, from brief articles to long reports and reference works. The benefits of wikis are compelling, but they do require a unique approach to writing.

5 LEARNING OBJECTIVE

Offer guidelines for becoming a valuable wiki contributor.

BUSINESS COMMUNICATION 2.0

Hey, You! Hands Off My Content!

As many customer communication efforts evolve from the old promotional mindset to Business Communication 2.0 conversations, blog and website content is becoming more important than ever. In fact, content is so important that *content marketing* has become a major communication effort for many entrepreneurs and companies. With this strategy, website owners offer valuable content free of charge in the form of reports, articles, videos, and other materials.

Customer-focused content is vital for several reasons. First, it helps break down the barriers between companies and potential customers. Few people enjoy reading sales pitches, but many people will take the opportunity to read or watch material that offers information of value to them. Second, helpful content allows individuals and organizations to demonstrate their knowledge and expertise. If you want to establish yourself as an expert in your field, offering some useful articles or reports is more or less expected these days. Third, content is vital to being found online, whether it's through social media sharing or conventional search engines. For example, websites that offer a steady stream of fresh content that (a) appears to be about the topics web searchers are looking for and (b) is linked to by other websites and blogs—indicating that these people find it useful—will rank higher in search results than websites with stale, sparse, uninteresting content. Fourth, advertising-supported sites benefit from great content because it increases traffic and therefore increases their ad revenues.

Of course, creating useful content takes time. A solo entrepreneur might invest a hundred hours a year or more writing articles and reports to share with potential clients, and larger companies can easily spend thousands of hours a year. Time is money, as they say, and these time investments can equate to many thousands of dollars spent by an individual and tens or hundreds of thousands of dollars by a good-sized company.

Unfortunately, valuable content is also incredibly easy to steal. One swipe of a mouse down the screen, a couple of clicks, and presto—an article or report that you might've labored over for days is now attracting potential customers on somebody else's website. And thanks to RSS newsfeeds, content thieves can automatically *scrape* websites and blogs, taking whatever new content is posted as soon as it appears.

(Note that posting the first few sentences of someone else's article, giving full credit, and providing a link back to the originator's website is accepted practice and actually helps content creators by offering them wide exposure. Copying entire articles and failing to give credit is definitely not acceptable.)

Fortunately, content creators also have some powerful tools at their disposal. They can search for stolen content (using unique phrases from an article or report) using a standard search engine or take advantage of several web services designed to find copied content, including Plagium (http://plagium.com), FairShare (https://fairshare.attributor.com), and Copyscape (www.copyscape.com). Finding content thieves can take some work, but considering the cost of creating content and the value it has, the effort is usually worthwhile.

CAREER APPLICATIONS

1. Would it be ethical to copy an entire article or report from another website and post it on your site if you give credit to the person who wrote it? Why or why not?
2. What advantages does value-added content have over conventional advertising methods for building customer relationships?

UNDERSTANDING THE WIKI PHILOSOPHY

Becoming an effective wiki collaborator requires a shift in your mindset from the approach you use for individual writing.

To be a valuable wiki contributor, keep these points in mind:[12]

- Writers need to let go of traditional expectations of authorship, including individual recognition and control. The value of a wiki stems from the collective insight of all its contributors.
- Team members sometimes need to be encouraged to edit and improve each other's work.
- Writers should use page templates and other formatting options to make sure the content fits the same style as the rest of the wiki.
- Many wikis provide both editing and commenting capabilities, and participants should use the appropriate tool for each. In other words, don't insert comments or questions into the main content; use the "talk page" or other commenting features if you want to discuss the content.
- New users should take advantage of the *sandbox*, if available; this is a "safe," nonpublished section of the wiki where team members can practice editing and writing.

Wikis usually have guidelines to help new contributors integrate their work into the group's ongoing effort. Be sure to read and understand these guidelines; don't be afraid to ask for help.

ADAPTING THE THREE-STEP PROCESS FOR SUCCESSFUL WIKI WRITING

You can easily adapt the three-step writing process for wikis, depending on whether you are creating a new wiki, adding new material to an existing wiki, or revising existing material on a wiki.

If you are creating a new wiki, think through your long-term purpose carefully, just as you would with a new blog or podcast channel (see Figure 14.6). Will the wiki be a one-time project (creating a report, for example) or an ongoing effort (such as maintaining "help" files for a software program)? Who will be allowed to add or modify content? Will you or someone else serve as editor, reviewing all additions and changes? What rules and guidelines will you establish to guide the growth of the wiki? What security measures might be required? For instance, the PlayStation development team at Sony uses a wiki to keep top managers up to date on new products, and because this information is highly confidential, access to the wiki is tightly controlled.[13]

If you are adding a page or an article to an existing wiki, figure out how this new material fits in with the existing structure of the wiki. Find out whether any similar material already exists; it might be better to expand an existing article or add a subpage than to create a new item. Also, learn the wiki's preferred style for handling incomplete articles. For example, on the wiki that contains the user documentation for the popular WordPress blogging software, contributors are discouraged from adding new pages until the content is "fairly complete and accurate." Writers are instead encouraged to insert incomplete pages (usually called "stubs" in wiki parlance) and rough drafts under their personal pages until they are ready to be added to the main wiki content.[14]

> Whenever you add content to a wiki, make sure it fits in smoothly with the organization of the existing content.

If you are revising or updating an existing wiki article, use the checklist on page 148 in Chapter 6 to evaluate the content before you make changes. If you don't agree with published content and plan to revise it, you can use the wiki's discussion facility to share your concerns with other contributors. A well-run wiki encourages discussions and even robust disagreements, as long as everyone remains civil and respectful.

To review the tasks involved in writing reports and proposals, see "Checklist: Composing Business Reports and Proposals."

For the latest information on writing business reports and proposals, visit http://real-timeupdates.com/bct11 and click on Chapter 14.

Figure 14.6 IBM Business Partner Wiki
IBM created this wiki to facilitate collaboration with its external business partners.
Reprint Courtesy of International Business Machines Corporation, © 2011 International Business Machines Corporation.

Quick Learning Guide

MyBcommLab

If your course uses MyBcommLab, log on to www.mybcommlab.com to access the following study and assessment aids associated with this chapter:

- Video applications
- Real-Time Updates
- Peer review activity
- Pre/post test
- Personalized study plan
- Model documents
- Sample presentations

If you are not using MyBcommLab, you can access Real-Time Updates through http://real-timeupdates.com/bct11.

CHAPTER OUTLINE

Writing Reports and Proposals: Adapting to Your Audience
- Being Sensitive to Your Audience's Needs
- Building Strong Relationships with Your Audience
- Controlling Your Style and Tone

Composing Reports and Proposals: Drafting Report Content
- Report Introduction
- Report Body
- Report Close

Composing Reports and Proposals: Drafting Proposal Content
- Proposal Introduction
- Proposal Body
- Proposal Close

Drafting Online Content

Collaborating on Wikis
- Understanding the Wiki Philosophy
- Adapting the Three-Step Process for Successful Wiki Writing

SUMMARY OF LEARNING OBJECTIVES

1 **Explain how to adapt to your audiences when writing reports and proposals.** Adapt to your audience by demonstrating sensitivity to their needs (adopting the "you" attitude, maintaining a strong sense of etiquette, emphasizing the positive, and using bias-free language), building a strong relationship with your audience (making sure your writing reflects the desired image of your organization and building your credibility), and controlling your style and tone to achieve the appropriate degree of formality, given the nature of the material and your relationship with the audience.

Effective reports help readers navigate the document by using three elements: (1) headings (and links for online reports), which set off important ideas and provide the reader with clues as to the report's framework and shifts in discussion; (2) transitions, which tie together ideas and keep readers moving along; and (3) previews and reviews, which prepare readers for new information and summarize previously discussed information.

2 **Name five characteristics of effective report content, and list the topics commonly covered in the introduction, body, and close of formal reports.** Effective report content is accurate if it is factually correct and error free. It is complete if it includes all necessary information and supports all key assertions. It is balanced if it presents all sides of an argument. It is clear and logical if it is well written and organized logically. It is properly documented if credit is given to all primary and secondary sources of information used.

The introduction highlights who authorized the report, the purpose and scope of a report, necessary background material, the sources or methods used to gather information, important definitions, any limitations, and the order in which the various topics are covered. The body can discuss such details as problems, opportunities, facts, evidence, trends, results of studies or investigations, analysis of potential courses of action and their advantages and disadvantages, process procedures and steps, methods and approaches, evaluation criteria for options, conclusions, recommendations, and supporting reasons. The close summarizes key points, restates conclusions and recommendations, if appropriate, and lists action items.

3 **List six strategies to strengthen a proposal argument, and list the topics commonly covered in the introduction, body, and close of proposals.** To strengthen your argument, you should demonstrate your knowledge, provide concrete examples, research the competition, prove that your proposal is workable, adopt a "you" attitude, and make your proposal attractive and error free.

The most common elements in the introduction of a proposal are background information or a statement of the problem or opportunity, an overview of the proposed solution, a delineation of the scope of the proposal, and a description of how the proposal is organized. The body can contain a full description of the proposed solution, a work plan with schedules and other key implementation information, a statement of the firm's qualifications, and a breakdown of project costs. The close usually contains a summary of key points, a brief reminder of the benefits readers will realize from the solution and the merits of the proposed approach, a quick summary of qualifications, and a call to action in terms of a request for a decision.

4 **Identify six characteristics of effective website writing.** First, effective web content builds trust with often-skeptical online audiences by being accurate, current, complete, and authoritative. Second, as much as possible, the content is adapted to global audiences, including localizing for specific languages and cultural norms. Third, good web content is easy to scan quickly because online readers often take a quick look at a webpage to see if anything promises to meet their information needs. Fourth, effective online reports and other content feature clearly worded headlines that answer the questions site visitors have in mind and include keywords that search engines are likely to be looking for as well. Fifth, successful websites use carefully worded links that clearly describe what readers can expect when they click on each link. Sixth, a steady supply of fresh content creates ongoing value for readers and signals your intention to stay on top of audience needs.

5 **Offer guidelines for becoming a valuable wiki contributor.** To become a valuable wiki contributor, let go of traditional expectations of authorship, including individual recognition and control; don't be afraid to edit and improve existing content; use page templates and other formatting options to make sure your content is formatted in the same style as the rest of the wiki; keep edits and comments separate by using the "talk page" to discuss content, rather than inserting comments directly into the text; take advantage of the sandbox to learn how to use the wiki's writing and editing tools; and understand and follow the wiki's contributor guidelines.

Checklist

A. Review and fine-tune your outline.
- Match your parallel headings to the tone of your report.
- Understand how the introduction, body, and close work together to convey your message.

B. Help readers find their way.
- Provide headings to improve readability and clarify the framework of your ideas.
- Create transitions that tie together ideas and show how one thought relates to another.
- Preview important topics to help readers get ready for new information.
- Review information to help readers absorb details and keep the big picture in mind.

C. Draft report content.
- Use the introduction to establish the purpose, scope, and organization of your report.

- Use the body to present and interpret the information you gathered.
- Use the close to summarize major points, discuss conclusions, or make recommendations.

D. Draft proposal content.
- Use the introduction to discuss the background or problem, your solution, the scope, and organization.
- Use the body to persuasively explain the benefits of your proposed approach.
- Use the close to emphasize reader benefits and summarize the merits of your approach.

E. Draft online content.
- Establish your credibility with information that is accurate, current, complete, and authoritative.
- Adapt your content to local audiences as much as possible.

- Compose compelling, web-friendly content in the inverted pyramid style.
- Write clear, informative headlines that help readers and search engines find your content.
- Create user-friendly links that clearly identify where the reader will be taken upon clicking.

F. Collaborate on wikis.
- Adopt the wiki philosophy, starting with letting go of traditional expectations of authorship and control.
- Encourage everyone to contribute.
- Use wiki capabilities wisely.
- Carefully think through the purpose of new wikis before creating them.
- Before adding content to an existing wiki, make sure it will fit the organization of the existing content.
- Evaluate wiki articles carefully before editing them.

✓ Checklist Composing Business Reports and Proposals

A. Review and fine-tune your outline.
- Match your parallel headings to the tone of your report.
- Understand how the introduction, body, and close work together to convey your message.

B. Help readers find their way.
- Provide headings to improve readability and clarify the framework of your ideas.
- Create transitions that tie together ideas and show how one thought relates to another.
- Preview important topics to help readers get ready for new information.
- Review information to help readers absorb details and keep the big picture in mind.

C. Draft report content.
- Use the introduction to establish the purpose, scope, and organization of your report.
- Use the body to present and interpret the information you gathered.
- Use the close to summarize major points, discuss conclusions, or make recommendations.

D. Draft proposal content.
- Use the introduction to discuss the background or problem, your solution, the scope, and organization.
- Use the body to persuasively explain the benefits of your proposed approach.

- Use the close to emphasize reader benefits and summarize the merits of your approach.

E. Draft online content.
- Establish your credibility with information that is accurate, current, complete, and authoritative.
- Adapt your content to local audiences as much as possible.
- Compose compelling, web-friendly content in the inverted pyramid style.
- Write clear, informative headlines that help readers and search engines find your content.
- Create user-friendly links that clearly identify where the reader will be taken upon clicking.

F. Collaborate on wikis.
- Adopt the wiki philosophy, starting with letting go of traditional expectations of authorship and control.
- Encourage everyone to contribute.
- Use wiki capabilities wisely.
- Carefully think through the purpose of new wikis before creating them.
- Before adding content to an existing wiki, make sure it will fit the organization of the existing content.
- Evaluate wiki articles carefully before editing them.

COMMUNICATION CHALLENGES AT TELLABS

You wanted to start your career in corporate communications with an opportunity to learn from one of the best, so you're excited to be on George Stenitzer's team at Tellabs. Using the skills you've been practicing in your course, respond to these challenges.

INDIVIDUAL CHALLENGE: Like many other companies associated with the Internet, Tellabs's business declined when the dot-com boom of the late 1990s began to fizzle out by early 2001. The following excerpt from a recent Tellabs annual report describes the effect this had on the company's operations. (The carriers and service providers referred to are the companies that buy Tellabs's products; material charges are expenses that are significant enough to affect the company's stock price.) As you review these two paragraphs (don't worry about all the technical and financial details), you can see that the first discusses the period from 2001 to 2003, when the company's financial results suffered. The second discusses the upturn that began in 2003 and continued through 2005. Write a transition sentence for the beginning of the second paragraph, signaling to readers that the story is about to change from the negative news of 2001–2003 to the more positive results that began in 2003.

The markets for our products have undergone dynamic change over the last few years. Beginning in 2001, carrier overcapacity, a softening economy and other factors caused our customers to reduce their capital spending significantly. The impact on Tellabs was a dramatic decline in revenue for each of the years 2001 through 2003. In addition, we had manufacturing overcapacity, excess inventories and a cost structure that could not be supported by our smaller revenue base. We responded by closing manufacturing facilities, reducing global head count, consolidating office space, exiting certain product lines and instituting cost controls across the organization. We also reviewed our product portfolio and cut back or stopped development efforts on some products. In addition, at the end of 2003, we moved to outsource the majority of our remaining manufacturing operations to third-party electronics manufacturing services providers to take advantage of their greater purchasing power and other efficiencies. These actions caused us to record material charges in 2001 through 2005 for excess and obsolete inventory and excess purchase commitments, severance costs, facilities shutdown costs, including accelerated depreciation on certain manufacturing and office buildings and equipment due to shortened useful lives, and various contractual obligations. We also recorded charges for other impaired and surplus assets.

Market stability began in 2003 and continued in 2004 and 2005 as service providers invested in their networks at levels at or above 2003. This stability enabled us to post year-over-year revenue growth in 2004 for the first time since fiscal 2000. Growing demand for wireless services, including third-generation (3G) services, drove capital investments by both wireless and wireline service providers and helped drive sales of our transport and managed access products.

TEAM CHALLENGE: Stenitzer's audience-oriented approach to writing extends to the web, through such key elements as

carefully worded hyperlinks that let website visitors know exactly what to expect before they click. He wants to make sure that the links on the Investor Relations page (www.tellabs.com/investors) are as good as they can possibly be. With your team, establish criteria that you believe make effective links and then review the investor pages on four other corporate websites (choose any four companies in any industries that interest you). Create a table that compares the four sites with Tellabs, using the criteria you established. Write a one-paragraph summary of the information in the table, along with a list of any improvements that you think could be made to the Tellabs investor section.

TEST YOUR KNOWLEDGE

To review chapter content related to each question, refer to the indicated Learning Objective.

1. Why is the "you" attitude especially important with long, complex reports? [LO-1]
2. What writing choices can you make to adjust the formality of your reports? [LO-1]
3. Why is it helpful to review your outline one last time before you begin writing a report? [LO-1]
4. What is the function of a report introduction? [LO-2]
5. What information might you include in the close of a report? [LO-2]
6. How do the introductions of solicited and unsolicited proposals differ? [LO-3]
7. Why is the work plan a key component of a proposal? [LO-3]
8. How does giving dates for online content help your readers? [LO-4]
9. How does the inverted pyramid style help online readers? [LO-4]
10. How are the editing and commenting capabilities used differently in a wiki? [LO-5]

APPLY YOUR KNOWLEDGE

To review chapter content related to each question, refer to the indicated Learning Objective.

1. How do previews and reviews work in tandem to help readers? [LO-1]
2. What are the risks of not explaining the purpose of a proposal within the introduction? [LO-3]
3. If a company receives a solicited proposal from a management consulting firm, is it ethical for the company to adopt the recommendations discussed in the proposal even though the company does not hire the submitting firm? Why or why not? [LO-3]
4. Why do experts recommend that online content be shorter than printed content, wherever possible? [LO-4]
5. Why do you need to approach wiki writing with a different attitude than the one you take with conventional writing? [LO-5]

PRACTICE YOUR SKILLS

Messages for Analysis

Message 14.A: Improving a Solicited Proposal [LO-3]

Read the solicited proposal in Figure 14.7. (1) Analyze the strengths and weaknesses of this document and (2) revise the document so that it follows this chapter's guidelines.

 Message 14.B: Revising Web Content with a "You" Attitude [LO-4] [LO-5]

To access this wiki exercise, visit http://real-timeupdates.com/bct11, click on "Student Assignments," and select "Chapter 14, page 419, Message 14.B." Follow the instructions for evaluating the existing content and revising it to make it more reader oriented.

 Message 14.C: Improving the Effectiveness of a Wiki Article [LO-5]

To access this wiki exercise, go to http://real-timeupdates.com/bct11, click on "Student Assignments," and select "Chapter 14, page 419, Message 14.C." Follow the instructions for evaluating the existing content and revising it to make it clear and concise.

Exercises

Active links for all websites in this chapter can be found on MyBcommLab; see your User Guide for instructions on accessing the content for this chapter. Each activity is labeled according to the primary skill or skills you will need to use. To review relevant chapter content, you can refer to the indicated Learning Objective. In some instances, supporting information will be found in another chapter, as indicated.

1. **Writing: Adapting to Your Audience [LO-1]** Review the reports shown in this chapter. Give specific examples of how each of these reports establishes a good relationship with the audience. Consider such things as using the "you" attitude, emphasizing the positive, establishing credibility, being polite, using bias-free language, and projecting a positive company image.
2. **Writing: Adapting to Your Audience [LO-1]** Review a long business article in a journal or newspaper. Highlight examples of how the article uses headings, transitions, and previews and reviews to help the readers find their way.

Memco Construction
187 W. Euclid Avenue, Glenview, IL 60025
www.memco.com
April 19, 2012

Dear Mr. Estes:

PROJECT: IDOT Letting Item #83 Contract No. 79371 DuPage County

Memco Construction proposes to furnish all labor, material, equipment, and supervision to provide Engineered Fill—Class II and IV—for the following unit prices.

Engineered Fill—Class II and IV

Description	Unit	Quantity	Unit Price	Total
Mobilization*	Lump Sum	1	$4,500.00	$4,500.00
Engineered Fill Class II	Cubic Yards	1,267	$33.50	$41,811.00
Engineered Fill Class IV	Cubic Yards	1,394	$38.00	$52,972.00

* Mobilization includes one move-in. Additional move-ins to be billed at $1,100.00 each.

The following items clarify and qualify the scope of our subcontracting work:
1. All forms, earthwork, clearing, etc., to be provided and maintained by others at
   no cost to Memco Construction.
2. General Contractor shall provide location for staging, stockpiling material,
   equipment, and storage at the job site.
3. Memco Construction shall be paid strictly based upon the amount of material
   actually used on the job.
4. All prep work, including geotechnical fabrics, geomembrane liners, etc., to be
   done by others at no cost to Memco Construction.
5. Water is to be available at project site at no charge to Memco Construction.
6. Dewatering to be done by others at no cost to Memco Construction.
7. Traffic control setup, devices, maintenance, and flagmen are to be provided by
   others at no cost to Memco Construction.
8. Memco Construction LLC may withdraw this bid if we do not receive a written
   confirmation that we are the apparent low sub-bidder within 10 days of your
   receipt of this proposal.
9. Our F.E.I.N. is 36-4478095.
10. Bond is not included in above prices. Bond is available for an additional
    1 percent.

If you have any questions, please contact me at the phone number listed below.

Sincerely

Kris Beiersdorf

Kris Beiersdorf
Memco Construction
187 W. Euclid Avenue, Glenview, IL 60025
Office: (847) 352-9742, ext. 30
Fax: (847) 352-6595
Email: Kbeiersdorf@memco.com

Figure 14.7 Solicited Proposal

3. **Writing: Adapting to Your Audience; Communication Ethics: Making Ethical Choices [LO-1], Chapter 1** Your boss has asked you to prepare a feasibility report to determine whether the company should advertise its custom-crafted cabinetry in the weekly neighborhood newspaper. Based on your primary research, you think they should. As you draft the introduction to your report, however, you discover that the survey administered to the neighborhood newspaper subscribers was flawed. Several of the questions were poorly written and misleading. You used the survey results, among other findings, to justify your recommendation. The report is due in three days. What actions might you want to take, if any, before you complete your report?

4. **Message Strategies: Informational Reports [LO-2]** You are writing an analytical report on the U.S. sales of your newest product. Of the following topics, identify where in the report each element should be included—the introduction, body, or close. Briefly explain your decisions.

   a. Regional breakdowns of sales across the country

   b. Date the product was released in the marketplace

   c. Sales figures from competitors selling similar products worldwide

   d. Predictions of how the struggling U.S. economy will affect sales over the next six months

   e. The method used for obtaining the preceding predictions

f. The impact of similar products being sold in the United States by Japanese competitors

g. Your recommendation about whether the company should sell this product internationally

h. Actions that must be completed by year end if the company decides to sell this product internationally

5. **Message Strategies: Analytical Reports [LO-2]** Find an article in a business newspaper or journal (in print or online) that recommends a solution to a problem. Identify the problem, the recommended solution(s), and the supporting evidence provided by the author to justify his or her recommendation(s). Did the author cite any formal or informal studies as evidence? What facts or statistics did the author include? Did the author cite any criteria for evaluating possible options? If so, what were they?

6. **Message Strategies: Analytical Reports [LO-2]** Your boss, Len Chow (vice president of corporate planning), has asked you to research opportunities in the cosmetics industry and to prepare a report that presents your findings and your recommendation for where you think the company should focus its marketing efforts. Here's a copy of your note cards (data were created for this exercise):

Subject: Demand	ref: 1.1
Industrywide sales have grown consistently for several decades, fueled by both a growing population and increased per capita consumption	

Subject: Competition	ref: 1.2
700 companies currently in cosmetics industry	

Subject: Niches	ref: 1.3
Focusing on special niches avoids head-on competition with industry leaders	

Subject: Competition	ref: 1.4
Industry dominated by market leaders: Revlon, Procter & Gamble, Avon, Gillette	

Subject: Demand	ref: 1.5
Industry no longer recession-proof: Past year, sales sluggish; consumer spending is down; most affected were mid- to high-priced brands; consumers traded down to less expensive lines	

Subject: Competition	ref: 1.6
Smaller companies (Neutrogena, Mary Kay, Soft Soap, and Noxell) survive by specializing in niches, differentiating product line, focusing on market segment	

Subject: Demand	ref: 1.7
Consumption of cosmetics relatively flat for past five years	

Subject: Competition	ref: 1.8
Prices are constant while promotion budgets are increasing	

Subject: Niches	ref: 1.9
Men: 50 percent of adult population; account for one-fifth of cosmetic sales; market leaders have attempted this market but failed	

Subject: Demand	ref: 1.10
Cosmetic industry is near maturity, but some segments may vary. Total market currently produces annual retail sales of $14.5 billion: Cosmetics/lotions/fragrances—$5.635 billion; Personal hygiene products—$4.375 billion; Hair-care products—$3.435 billion; shaving products—$1.055 billion	

Subject: Niches	ref: 1.11
Ethnic groups: Some firms specialize in products for African Americans; few firms oriented toward Hispanic, Asian, or Native Americans, which tend to be concentrated geographically	

Subject: Demand	ref: 1.12
Average annual expenditure per person for cosmetics is $158	

Subject: Competition	ref: 1.13
Competition is intensifying, and dominant companies are putting pressure on smaller ones	

Subject: Demand	ref: 1.14
First quarter of current year, demand is beginning to revive; trend expected to continue well into next year	

Subject: Niches	ref: 1.15
Senior citizens: large growing segment of population; account for 6% of cosmetic sales; specialized needs for hair and skin not being met; interested in appearance	

Subject: Demand	ref: 1.16
Demographic trends: (1) Gradual maturing of baby boomer generation will fuel growth by consuming greater quantities of skincare products, hair replenishment and coloring products, and anti-aging products; (2) population is increasing in the South and Southwest, where some brands have strong distribution	

List the main idea of your message (your recommendation), the major points (your conclusions), and supporting evidence. Then construct a final report outline with first- and second-level informative headings focusing on your conclusions. Because Chow requested this report, you can feel free to use the direct approach. Finish by writing a draft of your report to Chow.

7. **Drafting Online Content [LO-4]** Write an effectively worded link for each of the following content sections on a website (make up any information you need):

a. A page that summarizes the company's most recent quarterly financial results

b. A page that lists the phone numbers and email addresses for key contacts within the company

c. A page containing a news release announcing that the company is being investigated by the Securities and Exchange Commission (SEC) for possible accounting irregularities

d. A page that announces the launch of a major new product

EXPAND YOUR SKILLS

Critique the Professionals

Download the latest issue of the *International Trade Update* from http://trade.gov (look under "Publications"). What techniques does the report use to help readers find their way through the document or direct readers to other sources of information? What techniques are used to highlight key points in the document? Are these techniques effective? Using whatever medium your instructor requests, write a brief summary of your analysis.

Sharpening Your Career Skills Online

Bovée and Thill's Business Communication Web Search, at http://businesscommunicationblog.com/websearch, is a unique research tool designed specifically for business communication research. Use the Web Search function to find a website, video,

PDF document, or PowerPoint presentation that offers advice on writing website content. Write a brief email message to your instructor, describing the item that you found and summarizing the career skills information you learned from it.

CASES

Informal Informational Reports

1. Message Strategies: Informational Reports [LO-2]   As you know, the procedural requirements involved in getting a degree or certificate can be nearly as challenging as any course you could take.

Your task: Prepare an interim progress report that details the steps you've taken toward completing your graduation or certification requirements. After examining the requirements listed in your college catalog, indicate a realistic schedule for completing those that remain. In addition to course requirements, include steps such as completing the residency requirement, filing necessary papers, and paying necessary fees. Use a memo format for your report and address it to anyone who is helping or encouraging you through school.

2. Message Strategies: Informational Reports [LO-2]   Success in any endeavor doesn't happen all at once. For example, success in college is built one quarter or semester at a time, and the way to succeed in the long term is to make sure you succeed in the short term. After all, even a single quarter or semester of college involves a significant investment of time, money, and energy.

Your task: Imagine you work for a company that has agreed to send you to college full time, paying all your educational expenses. You are given complete freedom in choosing your courses, as long as you graduate by an agreed-upon date. All your employer asks in return is that you develop your business skills and insights as much as possible so that you can make a significant contribution to the company when you return to full-time work after graduation. To make sure that you are using your time—and your company's money—wisely, the company requires a brief personal activity report at the end of every quarter or semester (whichever your school uses). Write a brief informational report that you can email to your instructor, summarizing how you spent your quarter or semester. Itemize the classes you took, how much time you spent studying and working on class projects, whether you got involved in campus activities and organizations that help you develop leadership or communication skills, and what you learned that you can apply in a business career. (For the purposes of this assignment, your time estimates don't have to be precise.)

WIKI SKILLS   TEAM SKILLS

3. Message Strategies: Informational Reports; Media Skills: Wiki Writing [LO-2], [LO-5]   The use of social networks by employees during work hours remains a controversial topic, with some companies encouraging networking, some at least allowing it, and others prohibiting it.

Your task: Using the free wiki service offered by Zoho (www.zoho.com/wiki/) or a comparable system, collaborate on a report that summarizes the potential advantages and disadvantages of allowing social network usage in the workplace.

WEB WRITING SKILLS   TEAM SKILLS

4. Message Strategies: Online Content; Collaboration: Team Projects [LO-4], Chapter 2   If you're like many other college students, your first year was more than you expected: more difficult, more fun, more frustrating, more expensive, more exhausting, more rewarding—more of everything, positive and negative. Oh, the things you know now that you didn't know then!

Your task: With several other students, identify five or six things you wish you would've realized or understood better before you started your first year of college. These can relate to your school life (such as "I didn't realize how much work I would have for my classes" or "I should've asked for help sooner") and your personal and social life ("I wish I would've been more open to meeting people"). Use these items as the foundation of a brief informational report that you could post on a blog that is read by high school students and their families. Your goal with this report is to help the next generation of students make a successful and rewarding transition to college.

WEB WRITING SKILLS

5. Message Strategies: Online Content [LO-4]   As you probably experienced, trying to keep all the different schools straight in one's mind while researching and applying for colleges can be rather difficult. Applicants and their families would no doubt appreciate a handy summary of your college or university's key points as they relate to the selection and application process.

Your task: Adapt content from your college or university's website to create a one-page "Quick Facts" sheet about your school. Choose the information that you think prospective students and their families would find most useful. (Note that adapting existing content would be acceptable in a real-life scenario like this, because you would be re-using content on behalf of the content owner. Doing so would definitely *not* be acceptable if you were using the content for yourself or for someone other than the original owner.)

Informal Analytical Reports

6. Message Strategies: Analytical Reports [LO-2]   Mistakes can be wonderful learning opportunities if we're honest with ourselves and receptive to learning from the mistake.

Your task: Identify a mistake you've made—something significant enough to have cost you a lot of money, wasted a lot of time, harmed your health, damaged a relationship, created serious problems at work, prevented you from pursuing what could've been a rewarding opportunity, or otherwise had serious consequences. Now figure out why you made that mistake. Did you let emotions get in the way of clear thinking? Did you make a serious financial blunder because you didn't take the time to understand the consequences of a decision? Were you too cautious? Not cautious enough? Perhaps several factors led to a poor decision.

Write a brief analytical report to your instructor that describes the situation and outlines your analysis of why the failure occurred and how you can avoid making a similar mistake in the future. If you can't think of a significant mistake or failure that you're comfortable sharing with your instructor, write about a mistake that a friend or family member made (without revealing the person's identify or potentially causing him or her any embarrassment).

7. Message Strategies: Analytical Reports [LO-2]   Think of a course you would love to see added to the core curriculum at your school. Conversely, if you would like to see a course offered as an elective rather than being required, write your email report accordingly.

Your task: Write a short email proposal, using the 2 + 2 = 4 approach. Prepare your proposal to be submitted to the academic dean by email. Be sure to include reasons supporting your idea.

8. Message Strategies: Analytical Reports [LO-2]   Assume that you will have time for only one course next term.

Your task: List the pros and cons of four or five courses that interest you and use the yardstick method to settle on the course that is best for you to take at this time. Write your report in memo format, addressing it to your academic adviser.

9. Message Strategies: Analytical Reports [LO-2]   Visit any restaurant, including your school cafeteria. The workers and fellow customers will assume that you are an ordinary customer, but you are really a spy for the owner.

Your task: After your visit, write a short letter to the owner, explaining (1) what you did and what you observed, (2) any violations of policy that you observed, and (3) your recommendations for improvement. The first part of your report (what you did and what you observed) will be the longest. Include a description of the premises, inside and out. Tell how long it took for each step in ordering and receiving your meal. Describe the service and food thoroughly. You are interested in both the good and bad aspects of the establishment's décor, service, and food. For the second section (violations of policy), use some common sense. If all the servers but one have their hair covered, you may assume that policy requires hair to be covered; a dirty window or restroom obviously violates policy. The last section (recommendations for improvement) involves professional judgment. What management actions would improve the restaurant?

Proposals

10. Message Strategies: Proposals [LO-3]   One of the banes of apartment living is those residents who don't care about the condition of their shared surroundings. They might leave trash all over the place, dent walls when they move furniture, spill food and beverages in common areas, destroy window screens, and otherwise degrade living conditions for everyone. Landlords obviously aren't thrilled about this behavior, either, because it raises the costs of cleaning and maintaining the facility.

Your task: Assume that you live in a fairly large apartment building some distance from campus. Write an email proposal that you could send to your landlord, suggesting that fostering a sense of stronger community among residents in your building might help reduce incidents of vandalism and neglect. Propose that the little-used storage area in the basement of the building be converted to a community room, complete with a simple kitchen and a large-screen television. By attending Super Bowl parties and other events there, residents could get to know one another and perhaps forge bonds that would raise the level of shared concern for their living environment. You can't offer any proof of this in advance, of course, but share your belief that a modest investment in this room could pay off long term in lower repair and maintenance costs. Moreover, it would be an attractive feature to entice new residents.

11. Message Strategies: Proposals [LO-3]   Select a product you are familiar with and imagine that you are the manufacturer, trying to get a local retail outlet to carry it. Use the Internet and other resources to gather information about the product.

Your task: Write an unsolicited sales proposal in letter format to the owner (or manager) of the store, proposing that the item be stocked. Use the information you gathered to describe some of the product's features and benefits to the store. Then make up some reasonable figures, highlighting what the item costs, what it can be sold for, and what services your company provides (return of unsold items, free replacement of unsatisfactory items, necessary repairs, and so on).

PORTFOLIO BUILDER

12. Message Strategies: Proposals [LO-3]   As a sales manager for Air-Trak, one of your responsibilities is writing sales proposals for potential buyers of your company's Air-Trak tracking system. The system uses the global positioning system (GPS) to track the location of vehicles and other assets. For example, the dispatcher for a trucking company can simply click a map display on a computer screen to find out where all the company's trucks are at that instant. Air-Trak lists the following as benefits of the system:

- Making sure vehicles follow prescribed routes with minimal loitering time
- "Geofencing," in which dispatchers are alerted if vehicles leave assigned routes or designated service areas
- Route optimization, in which fleet managers can analyze routes and destinations to find the most time- and fuel-efficient path for each vehicle
- Comparisons between scheduled and actual travel
- Enhanced security, protecting both drivers and cargo

Your task: Write a brief proposal in letter format to Doneta Zachs, fleet manager for Midwest Express, 338 S.W. 6th, Des Moines, Iowa, 50321. Introduce your company, explain the benefits of the Air-Trak system, and propose a trial deployment in which you would equip five Midwest Express trucks. For the purposes of this assignment, you don't need to worry about the technical details of the system; focus on promoting the benefits and asking for a decision regarding the test project. (You can learn more about the Air-Trak system at www.air-trak.com.)[15]

Completing Reports and Proposals

LEARNING OBJECTIVES After studying this chapter, you will be able to

1 Describe the challenge of revising reports and proposals

2 Identify the major components of formal reports

3 Identify the major components of formal proposals

4 Describe an effective plan for proofreading reports and proposals

5 Describe the decision process for distributing reports and proposals

6 Identify the elements to include in a request for proposals (RFP)

MyBcommLab Test your mastery of this chapter and its Learning Objectives. Visit mybcommlab.com to apply what you've learned in Document Makeovers and interactive simulation scenarios.

COMMUNICATION CLOSE-UP AT GARAGE TECHNOLOGY VENTURES

Guy Kawasaki, one of the founders of the venture capital firm Garage Technology Ventures, advises entrepreneurs to craft concise, compelling summaries of their businesses before pitching their ideas to investors.

www.garage.com

The "garage" is a well-known metaphor in entrepreneurial circles that dates back at least to the founding of the giant technology company Hewlett-Packard, which was literally started in a garage in the late 1930s by Bill Hewlett and Dave Packard. More than the physical space of a workshop, the garage suggests a mindset, with inspired visionaries working on shoestring budgets in humble surroundings but pouring their hearts and minds into business ideas that can change the world—or at least make a lot of money.

Noted entrepreneur, author, speaker, and investor Guy Kawasaki and his colleagues carry on this tradition with a venture capital firm called, appropriately enough, Garage Technology Ventures. Garage is based in the heart of Silicon Valley: Palo Alto, California (which also happens to be the current and ancestral home of Hewlett-Packard).

Venture capitalists (VCs) invest in young companies, primarily in high-technology fields, and help them through the early growth stages with an eye toward recouping their investments when the company gets big enough to go public or is sold to another company. The personal finance website Motley Fool and the online music service Pandora are among the many firms in which Garage has invested in recent years.

In the Silicon Valley VC culture, the process of presenting a new company to potential investors usually involves a short presentation, "the pitch," that is supported by the executive summary from a business plan. The entire plan might become part of the conversation later, but in the early stages the executive summary has to carry the load by itself.

After listening to thousands of pitches and reading thousands of business plans, the Garage team has a clear idea of what it takes for entrepreneurs to get the attention—and money—of a VC. Garage advises entrepreneurs to keep their executive summaries under 20 pages and to include nine particular elements, starting with "the grab," a compelling one- or two-sentence statement that gets an investor's attention. Following that are the customer problems the entrepreneurs aim to solve, the solution they propose, and the business opportunity that this offering represents. The next three items describe the new company's competitive advantages, its business model (how it will generate revenue), and the key personnel involved in the new venture—including why these are the right people to drive this new company forward. The final two elements are directly about money: "the promise," which is how much investors can expect to earn from their stake in the company, followed by "the ask," how much money the new company wants.

This is a lot of information to pack into a relatively short document, but doing so is essential. If investors don't understand the business model or don't think the start-up team has honed in on a real market opportunity, they won't keep listening. Fortunately, entrepreneurs can tap into the expertise of those who have gone before them and use this advice to craft powerful business plans that get noticed. The Garage team is waiting with enthusiastic encouragement, too. As the company puts it, "We are on your side. So please help us get to know you better by telling your story clearly and concisely."[1]

Revising Reports and Proposals

Experienced business communicators such as Guy Kawasaki (profiled in the chapter-opening Communication Close-up) recognize that the process of writing a report or proposal doesn't end with a first draft. This chapter addresses all four tasks involved in completing longer messages: revising, producing, proofreading, and distributing. Although the tasks covered in this chapter are similar in concept to those you studied for short messages in Chapter 6, the completion stage for reports and proposals can require a lot more work. And as you've probably already experienced while doing school reports, computers, printers, network connections, and other resources have an uncanny knack for going haywire when you're frantic to finish and have no time to spare. When you're completing an important report on the job, try to leave yourself double or even triple the amount of time you think you'll need so that last-minute glitches don't compromise the quality of all your hard work.

Most of the discussion in this chapter applies to *formal* reports and proposals, documents that require an extra measure of polish and professionalism and often include packaging elements not used in informal reports and other documents. Few reports and proposals require every component described in this chapter, but be sure to carefully select the elements you want to include in each of your documents.

The revision process is essentially the same for reports as for any other business message, although it may take considerably more time, depending on the length of your document. Evaluate your organization, style, and tone, making sure that you've said what you want to say and that you've said it in the most logical order and in a way that responds to your audience's needs. Then work to improve the report's readability by varying sentence length, keeping paragraphs short, using lists and bullets, adding headings and subheadings, and making generous use of transitions. Keep revising the content until it is clear, concise, and compelling.

Tight, efficient writing that is easy to skim is always a plus, but it's especially important for impatient online audiences.[2] Review online report content carefully; strip out all information that doesn't directly meet audience needs and condense everything else as much as possible. Audiences will gladly return to sites that deliver quality information quickly—and they'll avoid sites that don't.

1 LEARNING OBJECTIVE

Describe the challenge of revising reports and proposals.

Formal reports have a higher degree of polish and production quality, and they often contain elements not found in informal reports.

MyBcommLab

• Access this chapter's simulation entitled Completing Reports and Proposals, located at mybcommlab.com.

Revising for clarity and conciseness is especially important for online reports because reading online can be difficult.

Producing Formal Reports

When you are satisfied with the quality of your text, you're ready to produce your report by incorporating the design elements discussed in Chapter 6. At this point, you should also start to add charts, graphs, and other visuals, as well as any missing textual elements, such as previews and reviews.

2 LEARNING OBJECTIVE

Identify the major components of formal reports.

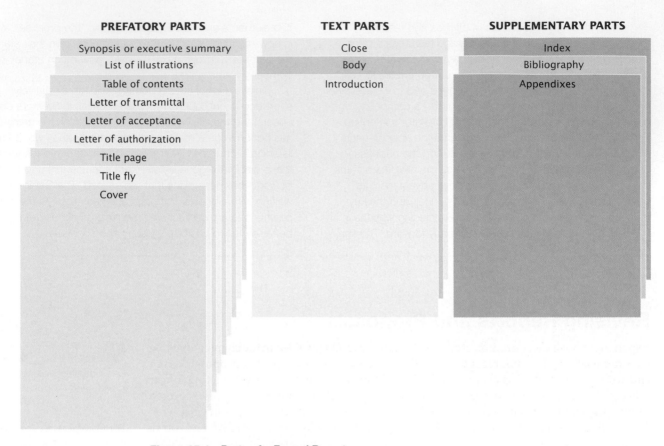

PREFATORY PARTS	TEXT PARTS	SUPPLEMENTARY PARTS
Synopsis or executive summary	Close	Index
List of illustrations	Body	Bibliography
Table of contents	Introduction	Appendixes
Letter of transmittal		
Letter of acceptance		
Letter of authorization		
Title page		
Title fly		
Cover		

Figure 15.1   Parts of a Formal Report
Depending on the level of formality you need to achieve, you can select from these elements to complete a formal report.

In today's leanly staffed companies, you should be prepared to produce formal reports with little or no assistance from design specialists or other professionals.

In some organizations, you'll be able to rely on the help of specialists in design and production, particularly when you are working on important, high-visibility reports. You may also have clerical help available to assist with the mechanical assembly and distribution. However, for most reports in many of today's leanly staffed companies, you should count on doing most or all of the production work yourself.

The parts you include in a report depend on the type of report you are writing, its length, your audience's expectations and requirements, and your organization's preferences. The components listed in Figure 15.1 fall into three categories: prefatory parts, text of the report, and supplementary parts. For an illustration of how the various parts fit together, see Linda Moreno's Electrovision report in "Report Writer's Notebook: Analyzing a Formal Report."

If you want a section to stand out, start it on a new page.

A component of a formal report may start on a new page, but not always. Inserting page breaks consumes more paper and adds to the bulk of your report. On the other hand, starting a section on a new page helps your readers navigate the report and recognize transitions between major sections or features.

When you want a particular section to stand apart, start it on a new page (in the same way that each chapter in this book starts on a new page). Most prefatory parts, such as the table of contents, should also be placed on their own pages. However, the various parts in the report text are often run together. If your introduction is only a paragraph long, don't bother with a page break before moving into the body of your report. If the introduction runs longer than a page, however, a page break can signal the reader that a major shift is occurring in the flow of the report.

REAL-TIME UPDATES
Learn More by Reading This Article

Get practical advice on developing research reports

The Online Writing Lab offers advice on developing all the sections of a typical research report. Go to http://real-timeupdates.com/bct11 and click on "Learn More." If you are using MyBcommLab, you can access Real-Time Updates within each chapter or under Student Study Tools.

PREFATORY PARTS OF THE REPORT

Prefatory parts are front-end materials that provide key preliminary information so that readers can decide whether and how to read the report.[3] Note that many of these parts—such as the table of contents, list of illustrations, and executive summary—are easier to prepare after the text has been completed because they are based on the main text of the report. When your text is complete, you can also use your word-processing software to automatically compile the table of contents and the list of illustrations.

Formal reports can contain a variety of prefatory parts, from a cover page to a synopsis or executive summary.

Cover

Many companies have standard covers for reports, made of heavy paper and imprinted with the company's name and logo. If your company doesn't have such covers, you can usually find something suitable in a good stationery or office supply store. Look for cover stock that is attractive, convenient, and appropriate to the subject matter.

Covers are typically labeled with the report title, the writer's name (optional), and the submission date (also optional). Think carefully about the title. You want it be concise and compelling while still communicating the essence of the subject matter.

Title Fly and Title Page

The **title fly** is a single sheet of paper with only the title of the report on it. It adds a touch of formality, but it isn't really necessary, and it consumes additional paper. The **title page** includes four blocks of information: (1) the title of the report; (2) the name, title, and address of the person, group, or organization that authorized the report (if anyone); (3) the name, title, and address of the person, group, or organization that prepared the report; and (4) the date on which the report was submitted. On some title pages, the second block of information is preceded by the words *Prepared for* or *Submitted to*, and the third block of information is preceded by *Prepared by* or *Submitted by*. In some cases, the title page serves as the cover of the report, especially if the report is relatively short and is intended solely for internal use.

Letter of Authorization and Letter of Acceptance

If you received written authorization to prepare a report, you might want to include that **letter of authorization** (or *memo of authorization*) in your report. If you wrote a **letter of acceptance** (or *memo of acceptance*) in response to that communication, accepting the assignment and clarifying any conditions or limitations, you might also include that letter here, in the report's prefatory parts. In general, letters of authorization and acceptance are included in only the most formal reports. However, consider including one or both if a significant amount of time has passed since you started the project or if you do not have a close working relationship with the audience. These pieces help make sure everyone is clear about the report's intent and the approach you took to create it.

A letter of authorization is a document that instructs you to produce a report; a letter of acceptance is your written agreement to produce the report.

Letter of Transmittal

The **letter of transmittal** (or *memo of transmittal*), a specialized form of a cover letter that is usually positioned right before the table of contents, introduces your report to the audience. This piece says what you would say if you were handing the report directly to the person who authorized it, so the style is often less formal than the rest of the report.

A letter or memo of transmittal introduces your report to your audience.

If your readers are likely to be skeptical of or even hostile to something in your report, the letter of transmittal is a good place to acknowledge their concerns and explain how the report addresses the issues they care about. Also, if you need to convey sensitive information to selected audience members, you can opt to include the letter in just those copies.

Depending on the nature of your report, your letter of transmittal can follow either the direct approach for routine or positive messages described in Chapter 8 or the indirect approach for negative messages described in Chapter 9. Open by introducing the report and summarizing its purpose, with a statement such as "Here is the report you asked me to prepare on . . . " The rest of the introduction includes information about the scope of the report, the methods used to complete the study, limitations, and any special messages you need to convey. If the report does not have a synopsis, the letter of transmittal may summarize the major findings, conclusions, and recommendations.

If you don't include a synopsis, you can summarize the report's content in your letter of transmittal.

REPORT WRITER'S NOTEBOOK | Analyzing a Formal Report

The report presented in the following pages was prepared by Linda Moreno, manager of the cost accounting department at Electrovision, a high-tech company based in Los Gatos, California. Electrovision's main product is optical character recognition equipment, which is used by the U.S. Postal Service for sorting mail. Moreno's job is to help analyze the company's costs. She has this to say about the background of the report:

> For the past three or four years, Electrovision has been on a roll. Our A-12 optical character reader was a real breakthrough, and the post office grabbed up as many as we could make. Our sales and profits kept climbing, and morale was fantastic. Everybody seemed to think that the good times would last forever. Unfortunately, everybody was wrong. When the Postal Service announced that it was postponing all new equipment purchases because of cuts in its budget, we woke up to the fact that we are essentially a one-product company with one customer. At that point, management started scrambling around looking for ways to cut costs until we could diversify our business a bit.
>
> The vice president of operations, Dennis McWilliams, asked me to help identify cost-cutting opportunities in travel and entertainment. On the basis of his personal observations, he felt that Electrovision was overly generous in its travel policies and that we might be able to save a significant amount by controlling these costs more carefully. My investigation confirmed his suspicion.
>
> I was reasonably confident that my report would be well received. I've worked with Dennis for several years and know what he likes: plenty of facts, clearly stated conclusions, and specific recommendations for what should be done next. I also knew that my report would be passed on to other Electrovision executives, so I wanted to create a good impression. I wanted the report to be accurate and thorough, visually appealing, readable, and appropriate in tone.

When writing the analytical report that follows, Moreno based the organization on conclusions and recommendations presented in direct order. The first two sections of the report correspond to Moreno's two main conclusions: that Electrovision's travel and entertainment costs are too high and that cuts are essential. The third section presents recommendations for achieving better control over travel and entertainment expenses. As you review the report, analyze both the mechanical aspects and the way Moreno presents her ideas. Be prepared to discuss the way the various components convey and reinforce the main message.

MyBcommLab

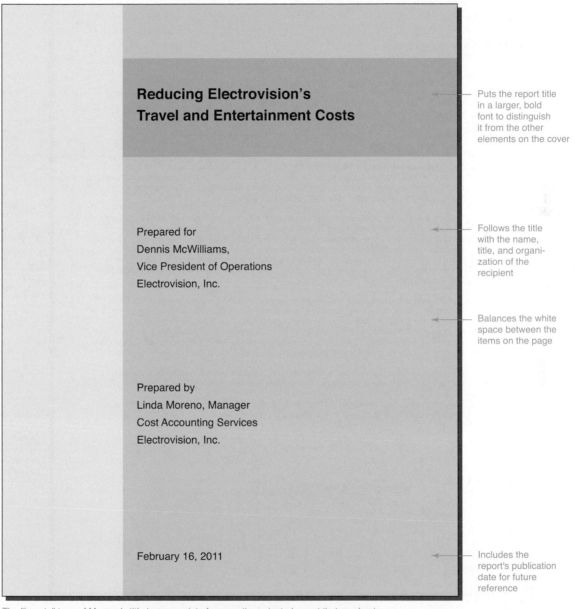

**Reducing Electrovision's
Travel and Entertainment Costs**

Puts the report title in a larger, bold font to distinguish it from the other elements on the cover

Prepared for
Dennis McWilliams,
Vice President of Operations
Electrovision, Inc.

Follows the title with the name, title, and organization of the recipient

Balances the white space between the items on the page

Prepared by
Linda Moreno, Manager
Cost Accounting Services
Electrovision, Inc.

February 16, 2011

Includes the report's publication date for future reference

The "how-to" tone of Moreno's title is appropriate for an action-oriented report that emphasizes recommendations. A more neutral title, such as "An Analysis of Electrovision's Travel and Entertainment Costs," would be more suitable for an informational report.

Uses memo format for transmitting this internal report; otherwise, letter format would be used for transmitting external reports

Uses a conversational style

Acknowledges help that has been received

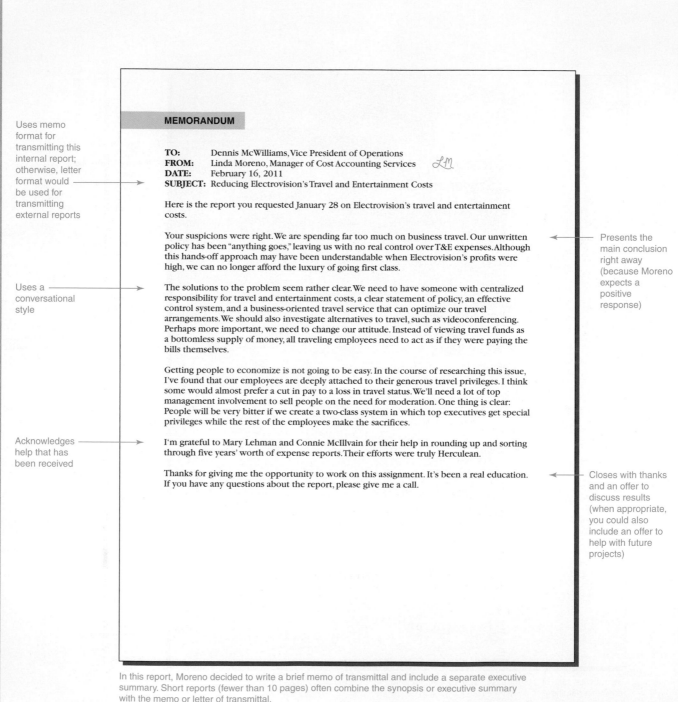

MEMORANDUM

TO: Dennis McWilliams, Vice President of Operations
FROM: Linda Moreno, Manager of Cost Accounting Services *LM*
DATE: February 16, 2011
SUBJECT: Reducing Electrovision's Travel and Entertainment Costs

Here is the report you requested January 28 on Electrovision's travel and entertainment costs.

Your suspicions were right. We are spending far too much on business travel. Our unwritten policy has been "anything goes," leaving us with no real control over T&E expenses. Although this hands-off approach may have been understandable when Electrovision's profits were high, we can no longer afford the luxury of going first class.

The solutions to the problem seem rather clear. We need to have someone with centralized responsibility for travel and entertainment costs, a clear statement of policy, an effective control system, and a business-oriented travel service that can optimize our travel arrangements. We should also investigate alternatives to travel, such as videoconferencing. Perhaps more important, we need to change our attitude. Instead of viewing travel funds as a bottomless supply of money, all traveling employees need to act as if they were paying the bills themselves.

Getting people to economize is not going to be easy. In the course of researching this issue, I've found that our employees are deeply attached to their generous travel privileges. I think some would almost prefer a cut in pay to a loss in travel status. We'll need a lot of top management involvement to sell people on the need for moderation. One thing is clear: People will be very bitter if we create a two-class system in which top executives get special privileges while the rest of the employees make the sacrifices.

I'm grateful to Mary Lehman and Connie McIllvain for their help in rounding up and sorting through five years' worth of expense reports. Their efforts were truly Herculean.

Thanks for giving me the opportunity to work on this assignment. It's been a real education. If you have any questions about the report, please give me a call.

Presents the main conclusion right away (because Moreno expects a positive response)

Closes with thanks and an offer to discuss results (when appropriate, you could also include an offer to help with future projects)

In this report, Moreno decided to write a brief memo of transmittal and include a separate executive summary. Short reports (fewer than 10 pages) often combine the synopsis or executive summary with the memo or letter of transmittal.

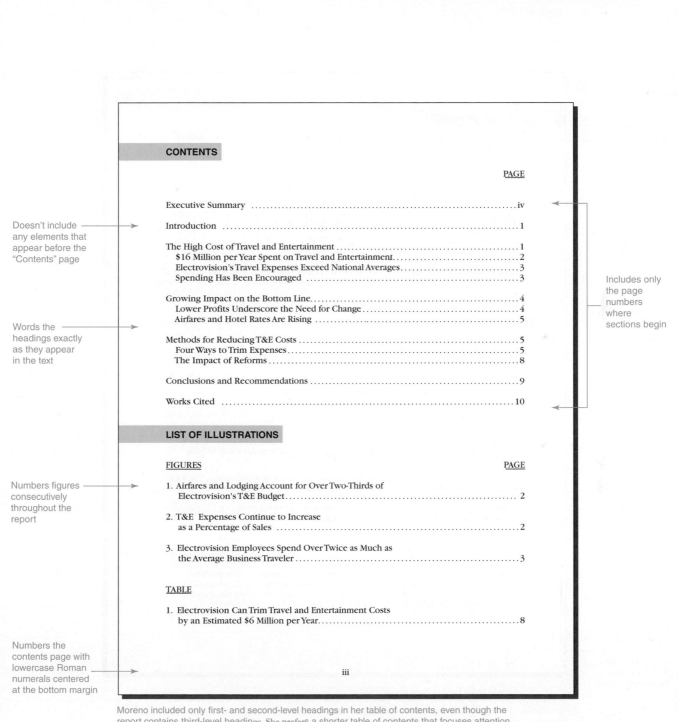

Doesn't include any elements that appear before the "Contents" page

Words the headings exactly as they appear in the text

Numbers figures consecutively throughout the report

Numbers the contents page with lowercase Roman numerals centered at the bottom margin

Includes only the page numbers where sections begin

CONTENTS

LIST OF ILLUSTRATIONS

iii

Moreno included only first- and second-level headings in her table of contents, even though the report contains third-level headings. She prefers a shorter table of contents that focuses attention on the main divisions of thought. She used informative titles, which are appropriate for a report to a receptive audience.

Begins by stating the purpose of the report

Presents the points in the executive summary in the same order as they appear in the report, using subheadings that summarize the content of the main sections of the report

Targets a receptive audience with a hard-hitting tone in the executive summary (a more neutral approach would be better for hostile or skeptical readers)

Executive summary uses the same font and paragraph treatment as the text of the report

Continues numbering the executive summary pages with lowercase Roman numerals

EXECUTIVE SUMMARY

This report analyzes Electrovision's travel and entertainment (T&E) costs and presents recommendations for reducing those costs.

Travel and Entertainment Costs Are Too High

Travel and entertainment is a large and growing expense category for Electrovision. The company spends over $16 million per year on business travel, and these costs have been increasing by 12 percent annually. Company employees make roughly 3,390 trips each year at an average cost per trip of $4,720. Airfares are the biggest expense, followed by hotels, meals, and rental cars.

The nature of Electrovision's business does require extensive travel, but the company's costs are excessive: Our employees spend more than twice the national average on travel and entertainment. Although the location of the company's facilities may partly explain this discrepancy, the main reason for our high costs is a management style that gives employees little incentive to economize.

Cuts Are Essential

Electrovision management now recognizes the need to gain more control over this element of costs. The company is currently entering a period of declining profits, prompting management to look for every opportunity to reduce spending. At the same time, rising airfares and hotel rates are making T&E expenses more significant.

Electrovision Can Save $6 Million per Year

Fortunately, Electrovision has a number of excellent opportunities for reducing T&E costs. Savings of up to $6 million per year should be achievable, judging by the experience of other companies. A sensible travel-management program can save companies as much as 35 percent a year (Gilligan 39–40), and we should be able to save even more, since we purchase many more business-class tickets than the average. Four steps will help us cut costs:

1. Hire a director of travel and entertainment to assume overall responsibility for T&E spending, policies, and technologies, including the hiring and management of a national travel agency.
2. Educate employees on the need for cost containment, both in avoiding unnecessary travel and reducing costs when travel is necessary.
3. Negotiate preferential rates with travel providers.
4. Implement technological alternatives to travel, such as virtual meetings.

As necessary as these changes are, they will likely hurt morale, at least in the short term. Management will need to make a determined effort to explain the rationale for reduced spending. By exercising moderation in their own travel arrangements, Electrovision executives can set a good example and help other employees accept the changes. On the plus side, using travel alternatives such as web conferencing will reduce the travel burden on many employees and help them balance their business and personal lives.

iv

Moreno decided to include an executive summary because her report is aimed at a mixed audience, some of whom are interested in the details of her report and others who just want the "big picture." The executive summary is aimed at the second group, giving them enough information to make a decision without burdening them with the task of reading the entire report.

Her writing style matches the serious nature of the content without sounding distant or stiff. Moreno chose the formal approach because several members of her audience are considerably higher up in the organization, and she did not want to sound too familiar. In addition, her

Uses a color bar to highlight the report title and the first-level headings; a variety of other design treatments are possible as well

REDUCING ELECTROVISION'S TRAVEL AND ENTERTAINMENT COSTS

INTRODUCTION

Electrovision has always encouraged a significant amount of business travel. To compensate employees for the stress and inconvenience of frequent trips, management has authorized generous travel and entertainment (T&E) allowances. This philosophy has been good for morale, but last year Electrovision spent $16 million on travel and entertainment—$7 million more than it spent on research and development.

Opens by establishing the need for action

This year's T&E costs will affect profits even more, due to increases in airline fares and hotel rates. Also, the company anticipates that profits will be relatively weak for a variety of other reasons. Therefore, Dennis McWilliams, Vice President of Operations, has asked the accounting department to explore ways to reduce the T&E budget.

The purpose of this report is to analyze T&E expenses, evaluate the effect of recent hotel and airfare increases, and suggest ways to tighten control over T&E costs. The report outlines several steps that could reduce Electrovision's expenses, but the precise financial impact of these measures is difficult to project. The estimates presented here provide a "best guess" view of what Electrovision can expect to save.

In preparing this report, the accounting department analyzed internal expense reports for the past five years to determine how much Electrovision spends on travel and entertainment. These figures were then compared with average statistics compiled by Dow Jones (publisher of the *Wall Street Journal*) and presented as the Dow Jones Travel Index. We also analyzed trends and suggestions published in a variety of business journal articles to see how other companies are coping with the high cost of business travel.

Mentions sources and methods to increase credibility and to give readers a complete picture of the study's background

THE HIGH COST OF TRAVEL AND ENTERTAINMENT

Although many companies view travel and entertainment as an incidental cost of doing business, the dollars add up. At Electrovision the bill for airfares, hotels, rental cars, meals, and entertainment totaled $16 million last year. Our T&E budget has increased by 12 percent per year for the past five years. Compared to the average U.S. business traveler, Electrovision's expenditures are high, largely because of management's generous policy on travel benefits.

Uses a *running footer* that contains the report title and the page number

In her brief introduction, Moreno counts on topic sentences and transitions to indicate that she is discussing the purpose, scope, and limitations of the study.

$16 Million per Year Spent on Travel and Entertainment

Electrovision's annual budget for travel and entertainment is only 8 percent of sales. Because this is a relatively small expense category compared with such things as salaries and commissions, it is tempting to dismiss T&E costs as insignificant. However, T&E is Electrovision's third-largest controllable expense, directly behind salaries and information systems.

Last year Electrovision personnel made about 3,390 trips at an average cost per trip of $4,720. The typical trip involved a round-trip flight of 3,000 kilometers, meals, and hotel accommodations for two or three days, and a rental car. Roughly 80 percent of trips were made by 20 percent of the staff—top management and sales personnel traveled most, averaging 18 trips per year.

Figure 1 illustrates how the T&E budget is spent. The largest categories are airfares and lodging, which together account for $7 out of $10 that employees spend on travel and entertainment. This spending breakdown has been relatively steady for the past five years and is consistent with the distribution of expenses experienced by other companies.

Places the visual as close as possible to the point it illustrates ⟶

Figure 1
Airfares and Lodging Account for Over
Two-Thirds of Electrovision's T&E Budget

Although the composition of the T&E budget has been consistent, its size has not. As mentioned earlier, these expenditures have increased by about 12 percent per year for the past five years, roughly twice the rate of the company's sales growth (see Figure 2). This rate of growth makes T&E Electrovision's fastest-growing expense item.

Gives each visual a title that clearly indicates what it's about; titles are consistently placed to the left of each visual ⟶

Figure 2
T&E Expenses Continue to Increase as a
Percentage of Sales

Moreno opens the first main section of the body with a topic sentence that introduces an important fact about the subject of the section. Then she orients the reader to the three major points developed in the section.

Electrovision's Travel Expenses Exceed National Averages

Much of our travel budget is justified. Two major factors contribute to Electrovision's high T&E budget:

- With our headquarters on the West Coast and our major customer on the East Coast, we naturally spend a lot of money on cross-country flights.

- A great deal of travel takes place between our headquarters here on the West Coast and the manufacturing operations in Detroit, Boston, and Dallas. Corporate managers and division personnel make frequent trips to coordinate these disparate operations.

However, even though a good portion of Electrovision's travel budget is justifiable, the company spends considerably more on T&E than the average business traveler (see Figure 3).

Figure 3
Electrovision Employees Spend Over Twice as Much as the Average Business Traveler

Source: *Wall Street Journal* and company records

Electrovision

U.S. Average

$0 $500 $1,000 $1,500 $2,000 $2,500

Dollars Spent per Day

The Dow Jones Travel Index calculates the average cost per day of business travel in the United States, based on average airfare, hotel rates, and rental car rates. The average fluctuates weekly as travel companies change their rates, but it has been running at about $1,000 per day for the last year or so. In contrast, Electrovision's average daily expense over the past year has been $2,250—a hefty 125 percent higher than average. This figure is based on the average trip cost of $4,720 listed earlier and an average trip length of 2.1 days.

Spending Has Been Encouraged

Although a variety of factors may contribute to this differential, Electrovision's relatively high T&E costs are at least partially attributable to the company's philosophy and management style. Since many employees do not enjoy business travel, management has tried to make the trips more pleasant by authorizing business-class airfare, luxury hotel accommodations, and full-size rental cars. The sales staff is encouraged to entertain clients at top restaurants and to invite them to cultural and sporting events.

Numbers the visuals consecutively and refers to them in the text by their numbers

Introduces visuals before they appear and indicates what readers should notice about the data

The chart in Figure 3 is simple but effective; Moreno includes just enough data to make her point. Notice how she is as careful about the appearance of her report as she is about the quality of its content.

The cost of these privileges is easy to overlook, given the weakness of Electrovision's system for keeping track of T&E expenses:

- The monthly financial records do not contain a separate category for travel and entertainment; the information is buried under Cost of Goods Sold and under Selling, General, and Administrative Expenses.

- Each department head is given authority to approve any expense report, regardless of how large it may be.

- Receipts are not required for expenditures of less than $100.

- Individuals are allowed to make their own travel arrangements.

- No one is charged with the responsibility for controlling the company's total spending on travel and entertainment.

GROWING IMPACT ON THE BOTTOM LINE

During the past three years, the company's healthy profits have resulted in relatively little pressure to push for tighter controls over all aspects of the business. However, as we all know, the situation is changing. We're projecting flat to declining profits for the next two years, a situation that has prompted all of us to search for ways to cut costs. At the same time, rising airfares and hotel rates have increased the impact of T&E expenses on the company's financial results.

Lower Profits Underscore the Need for Change

The next two years promise to be difficult for Electrovision. After several years of steady increases in spending, the Postal Service is tightening procurement policies for automated mail-handling equipment. Funding for the A-12 optical character reader has been canceled. As a consequence, the marketing department expects sales to drop by 15 percent. Although Electrovision is negotiating several other promising R&D contracts, the marketing department does not foresee any major procurements for the next two to three years.

At the same time, Electrovision is facing cost increases on several fronts. As we have known for several months, the new production facility now under construction in Salt Lake City, Utah, is behind schedule and over budget. Labor contracts in Boston and Dallas will expire within the next six months, and plant managers there anticipate that significant salary and benefits concessions may be necessary to avoid strikes.

Moreover, marketing and advertising costs are expected to increase as we attempt to strengthen these activities to better cope with competitive pressures. Given the expected decline in revenues and increase in costs, the Executive Committee's prediction that profits will fall by 12 percent in the coming fiscal year does not seem overly pessimistic.

Moreno designed her report to include plenty of white space so even those pages that lack visuals are still attractive and easy to read.

Documents the facts to add weight to Moreno's argument

Gives recommendations an objective flavor by pointing out both the benefits and the risks of taking action

Airfares and Hotel Rates Are Rising

Business travelers have grown accustomed to frequent fare wars and discounting in the travel industry in recent years. Excess capacity and aggressive price competition, particularly in the airline business, made travel a relative bargain.

However, that situation has changed as weaker competitors have been forced out and the remaining players have grown stronger and smarter. Airlines and hotels are better at managing inventory and keeping occupancy rates high, which translates into higher costs for Electrovision. Last year saw some of the steepest rate hikes in years. Business airfares (tickets most likely to be purchased by business travelers) jumped more than 40 percent in many markets. The trend is expected to continue, with rates increasing another 5 to 10 percent overall (Phillips 331; "Travel Costs Under Pressure" 30; Dahl B6).

Given the fact that air and hotel costs account for almost 70 percent of our T&E budget, the trend toward higher prices in these two categories will have serious consequences, unless management takes action to control these costs.

METHODS FOR REDUCING T&E COSTS

By implementing a number of reforms, management can expect to reduce Electrovision's T&E budget by as much as 40 percent. This estimate is based on the general assessment made by American Express (Gilligan 39) and on the fact that we have an opportunity to significantly reduce air travel costs by eliminating business-class travel. However, these measures are likely to be unpopular with employees. To gain acceptance for such changes, management will need to sell employees on the need for moderation in T&E allowances.

Four Ways to Trim Expenses

By researching what other companies are doing to curb T&E expenses, the accounting department has identified four prominent opportunities that should enable Electrovision to save about $6 million annually in travel-related costs.

Institute Tighter Spending Controls

A single individual should be appointed director of travel and entertainment to spearhead the effort to gain control of the T&E budget. More than a third of all U.S. companies now employ travel managers ("Businesses Use Savvy Managers" 4). The director should be familiar with the travel industry and should be well versed in both accounting and information technology. The director should also report to the vice president of operations. The director's first priorities should be to establish a written T&E policy and a cost-control system.

Electrovision currently has no written policy on travel and entertainment, a step that is widely recommended by air travel experts (Smith D4). Creating a policy would clarify management's position and serve as a vehicle for communicating the need for moderation.

Moreno creates a forceful tone by using action verbs in the third-level subheadings of this section. This approach is appropriate to the nature of the study and the attitude of the audience. However, in a status-conscious organization, the imperative verbs might sound a bit too presumptuous coming from a junior member of the staff.

At a minimum, the policy should include the following:

Breaks up text with bulleted lists, which not only call attention to important points but also add visual interest

- All travel and entertainment should be strictly related to business and should be approved in advance.

- Except under special circumstances to be approved on a case-by-case basis, employees should travel by coach and stay in mid-range business hotels.

- The T&E policy should apply equally to employees at all levels.

To implement the new policy, Electrovision will need to create a system for controlling T&E expenses. Each department should prepare an annual T&E budget as part of its operating plan. These budgets should be presented in detail so that management can evaluate how T&E dollars will be spent and can recommend appropriate cuts. To help management monitor performance relative to these budgets, the director of travel should prepare monthly financial statements showing actual T&E expenditures by department.

The director of travel should also be responsible for retaining a business-oriented travel service that will schedule all employee business trips and look for the best travel deals, particularly in airfares. In addition to centralizing Electrovision's reservation and ticketing activities, the agency will negotiate reduced group rates with hotels and rental car firms. The agency selected should have offices nationwide so that all Electrovision facilities can channel their reservations through the same company. This is particularly important in light of the dizzying array of often wildly different airfares available between some cities. It's not uncommon to find dozens of fares along commonly traveled routes (Rowe 30). In addition, the director can help coordinate travel across the company to secure group discounts whenever possible (Barker 31; Miller B6).

Specifies the steps required to implement recommendations

Reduce Unnecessary Travel and Entertainment

One of the easiest ways to reduce expenses is to reduce the amount of traveling and entertaining that occurs. An analysis of last year's expenditures suggests that as much as 30 percent of Electrovision's travel and entertainment is discretionary. The professional staff spent $2.8 million attending seminars and conferences last year. Although these gatherings are undoubtedly beneficial, the company could save money by sending fewer representatives to each function and perhaps by eliminating some of the less valuable seminars.

Similarly, Electrovision could economize on trips between headquarters and divisions by reducing the frequency of such visits and by sending fewer people on each trip. Although there is often no substitute for face-to-face meetings, management could try to resolve more internal issues through telephone, electronic, and written communication.

Electrovision can also reduce spending by urging employees to economize. Instead of flying business class, employees can fly coach class or take advantage of discount fares. Rather than ordering a $50 bottle of wine, employees can select a less expensive bottle or dispense with

Moreno takes care not to overstep the boundaries of her analysis. For instance, she doesn't analyze the value of the seminars that employees attend every year, so she avoids any absolute statements about reducing travel to seminars.

alcohol entirely. People can book rooms at moderately priced hotels and drive smaller rental cars.

Obtain Lowest Rates from Travel Providers

Apart from urging employees to economize, Electrovision can also save money by searching for the lowest available airfares, hotel rates, and rental car fees. Currently, few employees have the time or knowledge to seek out travel bargains. When they need to travel, they make the most convenient and comfortable arrangements. A professional travel service will be able to obtain lower rates from travel providers.

Judging by the experience of other companies, Electrovision may be able to trim as much as 30 to 40 percent from the travel budget simply by looking for bargains in airfares and negotiating group rates with hotels and rental car companies. Electrovision should be able to achieve these economies by analyzing its travel patterns, identifying frequently visited locations, and selecting a few hotels that are willing to reduce rates in exchange for guaranteed business. At the same time, the company should be able to save up to 40 percent on rental car charges by negotiating a corporate rate.

The possibilities for economizing are promising; however, making the best travel arrangements often requires trade-offs such as the following:

- The best fares might not always be the lowest. Indirect flights are usually cheaper, but they take longer and may end up costing more in lost work time.

- The cheapest tickets often require booking 14 or even 30 days in advance, which is often impossible for us.

- Discount tickets are usually nonrefundable, which is a serious drawback when a trip needs to be canceled at the last minute.

Replace Travel with Technological Alternatives

Less-expensive travel options promise significant savings, but the biggest cost reductions over the long term might come from replacing travel with virtual meeting technology. Both analysts and corporate users say that the early kinks that hampered online meetings have largely been worked out, and the latest systems are fast, easy to learn, and easy to use (Solheim 26). For example, Webex (a leading provider of webconferencing services) offers everything from simple, impromptu team meetings to major online events with up to 3,000 participants ("Online Meeting Solutions").

One of the first responsibilities of the new travel director should be an evaluation of these technologies and a recommendation for integrating them throughout Electrovision's operations.

Reducing Electrovision's Travel and Entertainment Costs   P a g e   **7**

Points out possible difficulties to show that all angles have been considered and to build confidence in her judgment

Note how Moreno makes the transition from section to section. The first sentence under the second heading on this page refers to the subject of the previous paragraph and signals a shift in thought.

The Impact of Reforms

By implementing tighter controls, reducing unnecessary expenses, negotiating more favorable rates, and exploring alternatives to travel, Electrovision should be able to reduce its T&E budget significantly. As Table 1 illustrates, the combined savings should be in the neighborhood of $6 million, although the precise figures are somewhat difficult to project.

Table 1
Electrovision Can Trim Travel and Entertainment Costs
by an Estimated $6 Million per Year

SOURCE OF SAVINGS	ESTIMATED SAVINGS
Switching from business-class to coach airfare	$2,300,000
Negotiating preferred hotel rates	940,000
Negotiating preferred rental car rates	460,000
Systematically searching for lower airfares	375,000
Reducing interdivisional travel	675,000
Reducing seminar and conference attendance	1,250,000
TOTAL POTENTIAL SAVINGS	**$6,000,000**

To achieve the economies outlined in the table, Electrovision will incur expenses for hiring a director of travel and for implementing a T&E cost-control system. These costs are projected at $115,000: $105,000 per year in salary and benefits for the new employee and a one-time expense of $10,000 for the cost-control system. The cost of retaining a full-service travel agency is negligible, even with the service fees that many are now passing along from airlines and other service providers.

The measures required to achieve these savings are likely to be unpopular with employees. Electrovision personnel are accustomed to generous T&E allowances, and they are likely to resent having these privileges curtailed. To alleviate their disappointment

- Management should make a determined effort to explain why the changes are necessary.

- The director of corporate communication should be asked to develop a multifaceted campaign that will communicate the importance of curtailing T&E costs.

- Management should set a positive example by adhering strictly to the new policies.

- The limitations should apply equally to employees at all levels in the organization.

Uses informative title in the table, which is consistent with the way headings are handled in this report and is appropriate for a report to a receptive audience

Uses complete sentences to help readers focus immediately on the point of the table

Includes financial estimates to help management envision the impact of the suggestions, even though estimated savings are difficult to project

Note how Moreno calls attention in the first paragraph to items in the following table, without repeating the information in the table.

Uses a descriptive heading for the last section of the text (in informational reports, this section is often called "Summary"; in analytical reports, it is called "Conclusions" or "Conclusions and Recommendations")

Summarizes conclusions in the first two paragraphs—a good approach because Moreno organized her report around conclusions and recommendations, so readers have already been introduced to them

Emphasizes the recommendations by presenting them in list format

CONCLUSIONS AND RECOMMENDATIONS

Electrovision is currently spending $16 million per year on travel and entertainment. Although much of this spending is justified, the company's costs are high relative to competitors' costs, mainly because Electrovision has been generous with its travel benefits.

Electrovision's liberal approach to travel and entertainment was understandable during years of high profitability; however, the company is facing the prospect of declining profits for the next several years. Management is therefore motivated to cut costs in all areas of the business. Reducing T&E spending is particularly important because the bottom-line impact of these costs will increase as airline fares increase.

Electrovision should be able to reduce T&E costs by as much as 40 percent by taking four important steps:

1. *Institute tighter spending controls.* Management should hire a director of travel and entertainment who will assume overall responsibility for T&E activities. Within the next six months, this director should develop a written travel policy, institute a T&E budget and a cost-control system, and retain a professional, business-oriented travel agency that will optimize arrangements with travel providers.

2. *Reduce unnecessary travel and entertainment.* Electrovision should encourage employees to economize on T&E spending. Management can accomplish this by authorizing fewer trips and by urging employees to be more conservative in their spending.

3. *Obtain lowest rates from travel providers.* Electrovision should also focus on obtaining the best rates on airline tickets, hotel rooms, and rental cars. By channeling all arrangements through a professional travel agency, the company can optimize its choices and gain clout in negotiating preferred rates.

4. *Replace travel with technological alternatives.* With the number of computers already installed in our facilities, it seems likely that we could take advantage of desktop videoconferencing and other distance-meeting tools. Technological alternatives won't be quite as feasible with customer sites, since these systems require compatible equipment at both ends of a connection, but such systems are certainly a possibility for communication with Electrovision's own sites.

Because these measures may be unpopular with employees, management should make a concerted effort to explain the importance of reducing travel costs. The director of corporate communication should be given responsibility for developing a plan to communicate the need for employee cooperation.

Moreno doesn't introduce any new facts in this section. In a longer report she might have divided this section into subsections, labeled "Conclusions" and "Recommendations," to distinguish between the two.

Lists references alphabetically by the author's last name, and when the author is unknown, by the title of the reference (see Appendix B for additional details on preparing reference lists)

WORKS CITED

Barker, Julie. "How to Rein in Group Travel Costs." *Successful Meetings* Feb. 2011: 31. Print.

"Businesses Use Savvy Managers to Keep Travel Costs Down." *Christian Science Monitor* 17 July 2008: 4. Print.

Dahl, Jonathan. "2000: The Year Travel Costs Took Off." *Wall Street Journal* 29 Dec. 2007: B6. Print.

Gilligan, Edward P. "Trimming Your T&E Is Easier Than You Think." *Managing Office Technology* Nov. 2008: 39–40. Print.

Miller, Lisa. "Attention, Airline Ticket Shoppers." *Wall Street Journal* 7 July 2007: B6. Print.

Phillips, Edward H. "Airlines Post Record Traffic." *Aviation Week & Space Technology* 8 Jan. 2007: 331. Print.

"Product Overview: Cisco WebEx Meeting Center," *Webex.com*. 2011. WebEx, n.d. 2 February 2011. Web.

Rowe, Irene Vlitos. "Global Solution for Cutting Travel Costs." *European Business* 12 Oct. 2008: 30. Print.

Smith, Carol. "Rising, Erratic Airfares Make Company Policy Vital." *Los Angeles Times* 2 Nov. 2007: D4. Print.

Solheim, Shelley. "Web Conferencing Made Easy." *eWeek* 22 Aug. 2008: 26. Web.

"Travel Costs Under Pressure." *Purchasing* 15 Feb. 2007: 30. Print.

Moreno's list of references follows the style recommended in the *MLA Style Manual*. The box below shows how these sources would be cited following APA style.

REFERENCES

Barker, J. (2011, February). How to rein in group travel costs. *Successful Meetings,* 31.

Businesses use savvy managers to keep travel costs down. (2008, July 17). *Christian Science Monitor,* 4.

Dahl, J. (2007, December 29). 2000: The year travel costs took off. *Wall Street Journal,* B6.

Gilligan, E. (2008, November). Trimming your T&E is easier than you think. *Managing Office Technology,* 39–40.

Miller, L. (2007, July 7). Attention, airline ticket shoppers. *Wall Street Journal,* B6.

Phillips, E. (2007, January 8). Airlines post record traffic. *Aviation Week & Space Technology,* 331.

Rowe, I. (2008, October 12). Global solution for cutting travel costs. *European,* 30.

Smith, C. (2007, November 2). Rising, erratic airfares make company policy vital. *Los Angeles Times,* D4.

Solheim, S. (2008, August 22). Web conferencing made easy. *eWeek,* 26.

Travel costs under pressure. (2007, February 15). *Purchasing,* 30.

WebEx.com. (2011). *Product Overview: Cisco WebEx Meeting Center.* Retrieved 2 February 2011, from http://www.webex.com/product-overview/index.html

In the body of the letter, you may also highlight important points or sections of the report, make comments on side issues, give suggestions for follow-up studies, and offer any details that will help readers understand and use the report. You may also want to acknowledge help given by others. The conclusion of the transmittal letter often includes a note of thanks for having been given the report assignment, an expression of willingness to discuss the report, and an offer to assist with future projects.

Table of Contents

The table of contents (often titled simply "Contents") indicates in outline form the coverage, sequence, and relative importance of the information in the report. The headings used in the text of the report are the basis for the table of contents. Depending on the length and complexity of the report, you may need to decide how many levels of headings to show in the contents; it's a trade-off between simplicity and completeness. Contents that show only first-level heads are easy to scan but could frustrate people looking for specific subsections in the report. Conversely, contents that show every level of heading—down to fourth or fifth level in detailed reports—identify all the sections but can intimidate readers and blur the focus by detracting from your most important message points. Where the detailed table of contents could have dozens or even hundreds of entries, consider including two tables: a high-level table that shows only major headings, followed by a detailed table that includes everything (as this and many other textbooks do). No matter how many levels you include, make sure readers can easily distinguish between them.

Also, take extra care to verify that your table of contents is accurate, consistent, and complete. Even minor errors could damage your credibility if readers turn to a given page and don't find what they expect to see there, or if they find headings that seem similar to those in the table of contents but aren't worded quite the same. To ensure accuracy, construct the table of contents after your report is complete, thoroughly edited, and proofed. This way, the headings and subheadings aren't likely to change or move from page to page. And if at all possible, use the automatic features in your word-processing software to generate the table of contents. Doing so helps improve accuracy by eliminating typing mistakes, and it keeps your table current in the event that you have to repaginate or revise headings late in the process.

> To save time and reduce errors, use the table of contents generator in your word-processing software.

If you will be creating a PDF file of the report for electronic distribution, you can make life easier for your readers by making the entries in the table of contents clickable links.

List of Illustrations

If you have more than a handful of illustrations in your report, or if you want to call attention to them, include a list of illustrations after the table of contents. For simplicity's sake, some reports refer to all visuals as *illustrations* or *exhibits*. In other reports, as in Moreno's Electrovision report, tables are labeled separately from other types of visuals, which are called *figures*. Regardless of the system you use, be sure to include titles and page numbers.

If you have enough space on a single page, include the list of illustrations directly beneath the table of contents. Otherwise, put this list on the page after the contents page. When tables and figures are numbered separately, they should also be listed separately.

Synopsis or Executive Summary

A **synopsis** is a brief overview (one page or less) of a report's most important points, designed to give readers a quick preview of the contents (see Figure 15.2 on the next page). It's often included in long informational reports dealing with technical, professional, or academic subjects and can also be called an **abstract**. Because it's a concise representation of an entire report, it may be distributed separately to a wide audience; interested readers can then request a copy of the entire report. A synopsis or an abstract is not a lengthy element, but take your time with it. In a sense, it's an advertisement for the entire report, so you want it to represent the report accurately.

> A synopsis is a brief preview of the most important points in your report.

The phrasing of a synopsis can be either informative or descriptive. An informative synopsis presents the main points of the report in the order in which they appear in the text. A descriptive synopsis, on the other hand, simply tells what the report is about, using

Report title establishes the ACA's stance, that it is sensitive to climate change concerns and is taking steps to address those concerns.

This brief synopsis (see page 443) offers a brief overview of the report's most important points.

issue backgrounder

FOCUS

The Paint and Coatings Industry:
Addressing Climate Change Proactively

Efforts to control greenhouse gas (GHG) emissions as a means of addressing climate change have taken center stage of late. While states have been leading the way, the debate has now taken hold at the federal level. On the regulatory side, the U.S. Environmental Protection Agency (EPA) has proposed a plan to establish a nationwide system for reporting GHG emissions — a program that could serve as the basis for a federal cap on the buildup of carbon dioxide (CO_2) and other gases linked to global warming, which is the subject of recently drafted legislation.

One thing is certain: the promulgation of state, federal and international measures to curb GHG emissions will affect almost every sector of the U.S. economy, particularly energy production and consumption, agriculture, manufacturing, transportation and construction. While the U.S. paint and coatings industry has a relatively small carbon footprint, it is important to note that, for years, the paint and coatings industry has aggressively looked for strategies to produce products in an environmentally conscious way, without compromising product performance. What's more, the U.S. paint and coatings industry has also partnered with EPA through the American Coatings Association (ACA), as a participant in EPA's Sector Strategies Program, to seek out cost-effective methods for minimizing industry's impact on the environment.

THIS ACA *ISSUE BACKGROUNDER* REVIEWS THE LATEST EFFORTS TO REDUCE GHG EMISSIONS AT BOTH THE STATE AND NATIONAL LEVEL. IT DEMONSTRATES THE PAINT AND COATINGS INDUSTRY'S STRIDES IN MINIMIZING ITS ENVIRONMENTAL IMPACT, AS WELL AS ITS SUPPORT AND PREFERENCE FOR A NATIONAL PROGRAM BASED ON A REASONABLE THRESHOLD FOR EMISSIONS LIMITS THAT WOULD PREEMPT COMPETING STATE PROGRAMS FOR GHG REDUCTIONS.

June 2009 • Vol. 17 • No. 2

A MINIMAL AND MINIMIZED FOOTPRINT

The paint and coatings industry has taken proactive steps toward reducing its carbon footprint, turning to more energy efficient technologies and reformulation: The introduction of high solids, low volatile organic compound (VOC) and hazardous air pollutant (HAP) paints; the use of low vapor pressure solvents; and the increasing use of powder coatings, have all significantly reduced emissions and energy use from our manufacturing processes, as well as end user processes. Business conditions have also led to dramatic changes in our manufacturing process.

One example is smaller batch sizes. The predominance of smaller batch sizes — which means paints are being made in one container and not transferred — eliminates emissions from transfer/ loading and cleaning operations during manufacturing and decreases energy consumption. In addition, many coating manufacturing companies have reduced emissions and energy use ⟶

This subheading makes two strong statements, that the industry already has a comparatively small carbon footprint and that it has already taken steps to minimize it.

Notice the effective use of topic sentences.

○ A Minimal and Minimized Footprint
○ The National Scene
○ States Paving The Way
○ Conclusion
○ Contact

inside

This modified table of contents offers an overview of what can be found inside this four-page report.

Figure 15.2   Synopsis and Other Report Features
This *backgrounder* report from the American Coatings Association (ACA) shows an effective brief synopsis and several other report features.

MyBcommLab

Apply Figure 15.2's key concepts by revising a new document. Go to Chapter 15 in mybcommlab.com and select Document Makeovers.

only moderately greater detail than the table of contents; the actual findings of the report are omitted. Here are examples of statements from each type:

Informative Synopsis

Sales of super-premium ice cream make up 11 percent of the total ice cream market.

Descriptive Synopsis

This report contains information about super-premium ice cream and its share of the market.

The way you handle a synopsis reflects the approach you use in the text. If you're using the indirect approach in your report, you're better off with a descriptive synopsis because an informative synopsis "gives away the ending" of your report. No matter which type of synopsis you use, be sure to present an accurate picture of the report's contents.[4]

Many report writers prefer to include an **executive summary** instead of a synopsis or an abstract. Whereas a synopsis is a "prose table of contents" that outlines the main points of the report, an executive summary is a fully developed "mini" version of the report itself. An executive summary is more comprehensive than a synopsis; many contain headings, well-developed transitions, and even visual elements. They are usually organized in the same way as the report, using a direct or an indirect approach, depending on the audience's receptivity.

An executive summary is a "mini" version of your report.

Executive summaries are intended for readers who lack the time or motivation to study the complete text. As a general rule, keep the length of an executive summary proportionate to the length of the report. A brief business report may have only a one-page or shorter executive summary. Longer business reports may have a two- or three-page summary. Anything longer, however, might cease to be a summary.[5]

Many reports require neither a synopsis nor an executive summary. Length is usually the determining factor. Most reports of fewer than 10 pages either omit such a preview or combine it with the letter of transmittal. However, if your report is over 20 or 30 pages long, you'll probably want to include either a synopsis or an executive summary as a convenience for readers. Which one you provide depends on the traditions of your organization.

TEXT OF THE REPORT

The heart of a report is composed of three main parts: the introduction, body, and close. Chapter 14 describes the content of these sections in more detail, but here are a few considerations to bear in mind as you prepare a formal report:

No matter how many separate elements are in a formal report, the heart of the report is still the introduction, body, and close.

- **Introduction.** A good introduction prepares your readers to follow and comprehend the information that follows. It invites audience members to continue reading by telling them what the report is about, why they should be concerned, and how the report is organized. If your report has a synopsis or an executive summary, minimize redundancy by balancing the introduction with the material in your summary, as Linda Moreno does in her Electrovision report. For example, Moreno's executive summary is fairly detailed, so she keeps her introduction brief.
- **Body.** This section contains information that supports your conclusions and recommendations as well as your analysis, logic, and interpretation of the information. See the body of Linda Moreno's Electrovision report for an example of the types of supporting details commonly included in this section.
- **Close.** The close of your report should summarize your main ideas, highlight your conclusions or recommendations (if any), and list any courses of action that you expect readers to take or that you will be taking yourself. This section may be labeled "Summary" or "Conclusions and Recommendations." In reports that use the direct approach, the close is relatively brief. In contrast, with the indirect approach, you may be using this section to present your conclusions and recommendations for the first time, in which case this section might be fairly extensive.

SUPPLEMENTARY PARTS OF THE REPORT

Supplementary parts follow the text of the report and provide information for readers who seek more detailed discussion. For online reports, you can put supplements on separate webpages and allow readers to link to them from the main report pages. Supplements are more common in long reports than in short ones, and they typically include appendixes, a bibliography, and an index.

Appendixes

An **appendix** contains materials related to the report but not included in the text because they are too long or perhaps not relevant to everyone in the audience. If your company has an intranet, shared workspaces, or other means of storing and accessing information online, consider putting your detailed supporting evidence there and referring readers to those sources for more detail.

Use an appendix for materials that are too lengthy or detailed for the body or not directly relevant to all audience members.

The content of report appendixes varies widely, including any sample questionnaires and cover letters, sample forms, computer printouts, statistical formulas, financial statements and spreadsheets, copies of important documents, and multipage illustrations that would break up the flow of text. You might also include a glossary as an appendix or as a separate supplementary part.

If you have multiple categories of supporting material, give each type a separate appendix. An appendix is usually identified with a letter and a short, descriptive title. All appendixes should be mentioned at appropriate places in the text and listed in the table of contents.

Bibliography

A bibliography fulfills your ethical obligation to credit your sources, and it allows readers to consult those sources for more information.

To fulfill your ethical and legal obligation to credit other people for their work and to assist readers who want to research your topic further, include a **bibliography**, a list of the secondary sources you consulted when preparing your report. In her Electrovision report, Linda Moreno labeled her bibliography "Works Cited" because she listed only the works that were mentioned in the report. You might call this section "References" if it includes works consulted but not mentioned in your report. Moreno uses the author–date system to format her bibliographic sources. An alternative is to use numbered footnotes (at the bottom of the page) or endnotes (at the end of the report). For more information on citing sources, see Appendix B, "Documentation of Report Sources."

In addition to providing a bibliography, some authors prefer to cite references in the report text. Acknowledging your sources in the body of your report demonstrates that you have thoroughly researched your topic. Furthermore, mentioning the names of well-known or important authorities on the subject helps build credibility for your message. Such source references should be handled as smoothly as possible. One approach, especially for internal reports, is simply to mention a source in the text:

> According to Dr. Lewis Morgan of Northwestern Hospital, hip replacement operations account for 7 percent of all surgeries performed on women age 65 and over.

However, if your report will be distributed to outsiders, include additional information on where you obtained the data. You are probably familiar with citation methods suggested by the Modern Language Association (MLA) or the American Psychological Association (APA). *The Chicago Manual of Style* is a reference often used by typesetters and publishers. All these sources encourage the use of in-text citations (inserting the author's last name and a year of publication or a page number directly in the text).

Index

If your report is lengthy, an index can help readers locate specific topics quickly.

An **index** is an alphabetical list of names and subjects mentioned in a report, along with the pages on which they occur (see the indexes in this book for examples). If you think your readers will need to access specific points of information in a lengthy report, consider including an index that lists all key topics, product names, markets, or important persons— whatever is relevant to your subject matter. As with your table of contents, accuracy in an index is critical. The good news is that you can also use your word-processing software to compile the index. Just be sure to update the index (and any other automatically generated elements, such as the table of contents) right before you produce and distribute your report.

Producing Formal Proposals

3 **LEARNING OBJECTIVE**

Identify the major components of formal proposals.

Formal proposals must have a high degree of polish and professionalism.

Proposals addressed to external audiences, including potential customers and investors, are nearly always formal. For smaller projects and situations in which you already have a working relationship with the audience, a proposal can be less formal and skip some of the components described in this section.

Formal proposals contain many of the same components as other formal reports (see Figure 15.3). The difference lies mostly in the text, although a few of the prefatory parts are also different. With the exception of an occasional appendix, most proposals have few

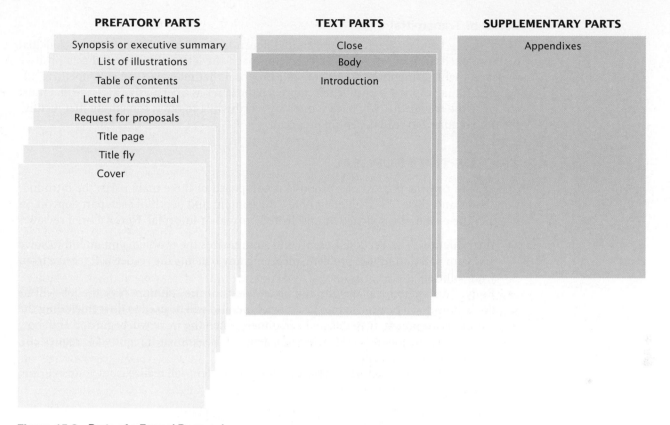

Figure 15.3   Parts of a Formal Proposal
As with formal reports, you can select from a variety of components to complete a formal proposal.

supplementary parts. As always, if you're responding to an RFP, follow its specifications to the letter, being sure to include everything it asks for and nothing it doesn't ask for.

PREFATORY PARTS OF THE PROPOSAL

The cover, title fly, title page, table of contents, and list of illustrations are handled the same way in a formal proposal as in other formal reports. However, you'll want to handle other prefatory parts a bit differently, such as a copy of the RFP, the synopsis or executive summary, and the letter of transmittal.

Copy of or Reference to the RFP

RFPs usually have specific instructions for referring to the RFP itself in your proposal because the organizations that issue RFPs need a methodical way to track all their active RFPs and the incoming responses. Some organizations require that you include a copy of the entire RFP in your proposal; others simply want you to refer to the RFP by name or number. Just make sure you follow the instructions in every detail. If the RFP offers no specific instructions, use your best judgment, based on the length of the RFP and whether you received a printed copy or accessed it online.

An RFP may require you to include a copy of the RFP in your prefatory section; be sure to follow instructions carefully.

Synopsis or Executive Summary

Although you may include a synopsis or an executive summary for your reader's convenience when your proposal is quite long, these components are often less useful in a formal proposal than they are in a formal report. If your proposal is unsolicited, your transmittal letter will already have caught the reader's interest, making a synopsis or an executive summary redundant. It may also be less important if your proposal is solicited because the reader is already committed to studying your proposal to find out how you intend to satisfy the terms of a contract. The introduction of a solicited proposal would provide an adequate preview of the contents.

Letter of Transmittal

The way you handle the letter of transmittal depends on whether the proposal is solicited or unsolicited. If the proposal is solicited, approach the letter of transmittal as a positive message, highlighting those aspects of your proposal that may give you a competitive advantage. If the proposal is unsolicited, approach the letter as a persuasive message that must convince the reader that you have something worthwhile to offer, something that justifies the time required to read the entire proposal.

TEXT OF THE PROPOSAL

Just as with reports, the text of a proposal is composed of three main parts: the introduction, body, and close. As Chapter 14 notes, the content and depth of each part depend on whether the proposal is solicited or unsolicited, formal or informal. Here's a brief review:[6]

- **Introduction.** This section presents and summarizes the problem you intend to solve and your solution to that problem, including any benefits the reader will receive from your solution.
- **Body.** This section explains the complete details of the solution: how the job will be done, how it will be broken into tasks, what method will be used to do it (including the required equipment, material, and personnel), when the work will begin and end, how much the entire job will cost (including a detailed breakdown, if required or requested), and why you are qualified.
- **Close.** This section emphasizes the benefits that readers will realize from your solution, and it urges readers to act.

Figure 15.4 provides an example of an informal proposal.

Proofreading Reports and Proposals

4 LEARNING OBJECTIVE

Describe an effective plan for proofreading reports and proposals.

After you have assembled all the components of your report or proposal, revised the entire document's content for clarity and conciseness, and designed the document to ensure readability and a positive impression on your readers, you have essentially produced your document in its final form. Now you need to review it thoroughly one last time, looking for inconsistencies, errors, and missing components. Proofing can catch minor flaws that might diminish your credibility—and major flaws that might damage your career.

Proofreading the textual part of your report is essentially the same as proofreading any other business message—you check for typos, spelling errors, and mistakes in punctuation. However, reports often have elements that may not be included in other messages, so don't forget to proof your visuals thoroughly and make sure they are positioned correctly. If you need specific tips on proofreading documents, look back at Chapter 6 for some reminders on what to look for when proofreading text and how to proofread like a pro.

Ask for proofreading assistance from someone who hasn't been involved in the development of your proposal; he or she might see errors that you've been overlooking.

Whenever possible, arrange for someone with "fresh eyes" to proofread the report, somebody who hasn't been involved with the text so far. At this point in the process, you are so familiar with the content that your mind will fill in missing words, fix misspelled words, and subconsciously compensate for other flaws, without your even being aware of it. Someone else might see mistakes that you've passed over a dozen times without noticing. An ideal approach is to have two people review it, one who is an expert in the subject matter and one who isn't. The first person can ensure its technical accuracy, and the second can ensure that a wide range of readers will understand it.[7]

Distributing Reports and Proposals

5 LEARNING OBJECTIVE

Describe the decision process for distributing reports and proposals.

All the distribution issues explored in Chapter 6 apply to reports and proposals, but pay particular attention to the length and complexity of your documents. For physical distribution, consider spending the few extra dollars for a professional courier or package delivery service, if that will help your document stand apart from the crowd. The online tracking

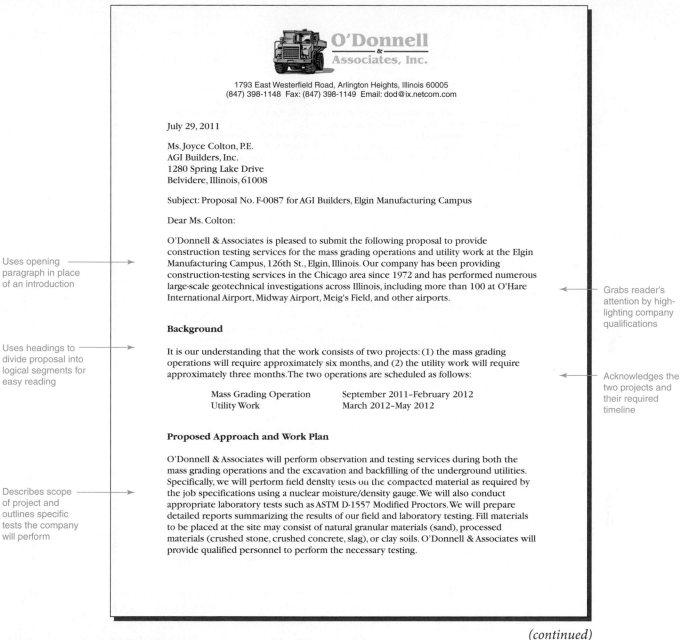

Uses opening paragraph in place of an introduction

Uses headings to divide proposal into logical segments for easy reading

Describes scope of project and outlines specific tests the company will perform

Grabs reader's attention by highlighting company qualifications

Acknowledges the two projects and their required timeline

(continued)

Figure 15.4 Informal Solicited Proposal
This proposal was submitted by Dixon O'Donnell, vice president of O'Donnell & Associates, a geotechnical engineering firm that conducts a variety of environmental testing services. As you review this document, pay close attention to the specific items addressed in the proposal's introduction, body, and close.

offered by FedEx, UPS, and other services can verify that your document arrived safely. On the other hand, if you've prepared the document for a single person or small group, delivering it in person can be a nice touch. In addition to answering any immediate questions about it, you can promote the results in person—reminding the recipient of the benefits contained in your report or proposal.

For electronic distribution, unless your audience specifically requests a word-processor file, provide documents as PDF files. Many people are reluctant to open word-processor files these days, particularly from outsiders, given the greater vulnerability of such files to macro viruses and other contaminations. Moreover, using PDF files lets you

Using portable document format (PDF) is a safe and common way to distribute reports electronically.

Figure 15.4   **Informal Solicited Proposal (continued)**

control how your document is displayed on your audience's computer, ensuring that your readers see your document as you intended. In addition, making documents available as downloadable PDF files is almost universally expected these days, if only for the sake of convenience.

If your company or client expects you to distribute your reports via a web-based content management system, intranet, or extranet, be sure to upload the correct file(s) to the correct online location. Verify the onscreen display of your report after you've posted it, too; make sure graphics, charts, links, and other elements are in place and operational.

When you've completed your formal report or proposal and sent it off to your audience, your next task is to wait for a response. If you don't hear from your readers within a week or two, you might want to ask politely whether the report arrived. (Some RFPs specify a response time frame. In such a case, *don't* pester the recipient ahead of schedule, or you'll hurt your chances.) In hope of stimulating a response, you might ask a question about the report,

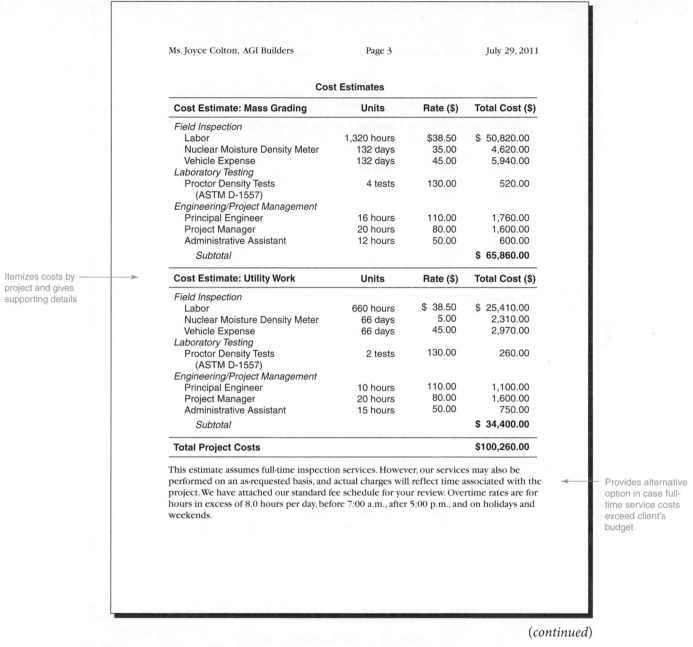

Cost Estimates

Itemizes costs by project and gives supporting details

Cost Estimate: Mass Grading	Units	Rate ($)	Total Cost ($)
Field Inspection			
Labor	1,320 hours	$38.50	$ 50,820.00
Nuclear Moisture Density Meter	132 days	35.00	4,620.00
Vehicle Expense	132 days	45.00	5,940.00
Laboratory Testing			
Proctor Density Tests	4 tests	130.00	520.00
(ASTM D-1557)			
Engineering/Project Management			
Principal Engineer	16 hours	110.00	1,760.00
Project Manager	20 hours	80.00	1,600.00
Administrative Assistant	12 hours	50.00	600.00
Subtotal			**$ 65,860.00**

Cost Estimate: Utility Work	Units	Rate ($)	Total Cost ($)
Field Inspection			
Labor	660 hours	$ 38.50	$ 25,410.00
Nuclear Moisture Density Meter	66 days	5.00	2,310.00
Vehicle Expense	66 days	45.00	2,970.00
Laboratory Testing			
Proctor Density Tests	2 tests	130.00	260.00
(ASTM D-1557)			
Engineering/Project Management			
Principal Engineer	10 hours	110.00	1,100.00
Project Manager	20 hours	80.00	1,600.00
Administrative Assistant	15 hours	50.00	750.00
Subtotal			**$ 34,400.00**

Total Project Costs			**$100,260.00**

This estimate assumes full-time inspection services. However, our services may also be performed on an as-requested basis, and actual charges will reflect time associated with the project. We have attached our standard fee schedule for your review. Overtime rates are for hours in excess of 8.0 hours per day, before 7:00 a.m., after 5:00 p.m., and on holidays and weekends.

Provides alternative option in case full-time service costs exceed client's budget

(continued)

Figure 15.4   Informal Solicited Proposal *(continued)*

such as "How do you think accounting will react to the proposed budget increase?" You might also offer to answer any questions or provide additional information. To review the ideas presented in this chapter, see "Checklist: Producing Formal Reports and Proposals."

Writing Requests for Proposals

At some point in your career, you might be the one receiving proposals, and learning how to request effective proposals will simplify the process considerably. Various organizations handle RFPs in different ways. When writing an RFP, remember that it is more than just a request; it's an informational report that provides potential bidders with the information they need to craft effective proposals. Writing an RFP demands careful consideration because it starts a process that leads to a proposal, a contract, and eventually the delivery

6   LEARNING OBJECTIVE

Identify the elements to include in a request for proposals (RFP).

When writing an RFP, be sure to give potential respondents all the information they need to craft a meaningful response to your request.

Uses brief close to emphasize qualifications and ask for client decision

Ms. Joyce Colton, AGI Builders   Page 4   July 29, 2011

Authorization

With a staff of over 30 personnel, including registered professional engineers, resident engineers, geologists, construction inspectors, laboratory technicians, and drillers, we are convinced that O'Donnell & Associates is capable of providing the services required for a project of this magnitude.

If you would like our firm to provide the services as outlined in this proposal, please sign this letter and return it to us along with a certified check in the amount of $10,000 (our retainer) by August 14, 2011. Please call me if you have any questions regarding the terms of this proposal or our approach.

Provides deadline and makes response easy

Sincerely,

Dixon O'Donnell

Dixon O'Donnell
Vice President

Enclosures

Accepted for AGI BUILDERS, INC.

Makes letter a binding contract, if signed

By_____   Date _____

Figure 15.4   Informal Solicited Proposal *(continued)*

of a product or the performance of a service. In other words, mistakes at the RFP stage can ripple throughout the process and create costly headaches for everyone involved.

An RFP's specific content will vary widely from industry to industry, but all RFPs should include some combination of the following elements:[8]

- **Company background.** Give potential bidders some background information on your organization, your business priorities, and other information they might need in order to respond in an informed manner.
- **Project description.** Put your requirements in context; are you seeking bids for routine supplies or services, or do you need a major computer system?
- **Requirements.** The requirements section should spell out everything you expect from potential vendors; don't leave anything to unstated assumptions. Will potential vendors provide key equipment, or will you? Will you expect vendors to work under confidentiality restrictions, such as a nondisclosure agreement? Who will pay if costs

---

✓ **Checklist** | **Producing Formal Reports and Proposals**

A. Prefatory parts.
- Use your company's standard report covers, if available.
- Include a concise, descriptive title on the cover.
- Include a title fly only if you want an extra-formal touch.
- On the title page, list (1) report title; (2) name, title, and address of the group or person who authorized the report; (3) name, title, and address of the group or person who prepared the report; and (4) date of submission.
- Include a copy of the letter of authorization, if appropriate.
- If responding to an RFP, follow its instructions for including a copy or referring to the RFP by name or tracking number.
- Include a letter of transmittal that introduces the report.
- Provide a table of contents in outline form, with headings worded exactly as they appear in the body of the report.
- Include a list of illustrations if the report contains a large number of them.
- Include a synopsis (brief summary of the report) or an executive summary (a condensed, "mini" version of the report) for longer reports.

B. Text of the report.
- Draft an introduction that prepares the reader for the content that follows.
- Provide information that supports your conclusions, recommendations, or proposals in the body of the report.
- Don't overload the body with unnecessary detail.
- Close with a summary of your main idea.

C. Supplementary parts.
- Use appendixes to provide supplementary information or supporting evidence.
- List in a bibliography any secondary sources you used.
- Provide an index if your report contains a large number of terms or ideas and is likely to be consulted over time.

---

run higher than expected? Will you require ongoing service or support? Providing this information can be a lot of work, but again, overlooking anything at this point is likely to create considerable problems once the project gets rolling.

- **Decision criteria.** Let bidders know how you'll be making the decision. Is quality more important than cost? Will you consider only certain types of vendors or only those that use certain processes or technologies? Will you entertain bids from companies that have never worked in your particular industry? The answers to such questions not only help bidders determine whether they're right for your project but also help them craft proposals that meet your needs.
- **Proposal requirements.** Explain exactly what you expect to see in the proposal itself—which sections, what media, how many copies, and so on.
- **Submission and contact information.** A well-written RFP answers most potential questions, and it also tells people when, where, and how to respond. In addition, effective RFPs always give bidders the name of a contact within the organization who can answer detailed questions.

A smart approach to managing RFPs can minimize the work involved for everyone and maximize the effectiveness of the RFP. First, identify your decision criteria and then brainstorm the information you need to measure against those criteria. Don't ask bidders to submit information about every aspect of their operations if such details aren't relevant to your decision. Making such unreasonable demands is unfair to bidders, will unnecessarily complicate your review process, and will discourage some potentially attractive bidders from responding.

Second, to get quality responses that match your unique business needs, give bidders plenty of time to respond. Successful companies are usually busy responding to other RFPs and working on other projects, and you can't expect them to drop everything to focus solely on your RFP.

Third, if your company generates numerous RFPs, tracking proposals can become a full-time job. Consider establishing an online system for tracking responses automatically.[9]

MyBcommLab

If your course uses MyBcommLab, log on to www.mybcommlab.com to access the following study and assessment aids associated with this chapter:

- Video applications
- Real-Time Updates
- Peer review activity
- Pre/post test
- Personalized study plan
- Model documents
- Sample presentations

If you are not using MyBcommLab, you can access Real-Time Updates through http://real-timeupdates.com/bct11.

SUMMARY OF LEARNING OBJECTIVES

1 **Describe the challenge of revising reports and proposals.** Revising reports and proposals involves the same tasks you practiced in Chapter 6—evaluating content, style, organization, and tone; reviewing for readability; and editing for clarity and conciseness. However, the length and complexity of longer documents make revision even more important, because long, unwieldy reports are an unwelcome burden to readers. If you're creating material for online publishing, take extra care to make it as short as possible. Online readers are particularly demanding, and some won't make the effort to read long, dense material.

2 **Identify the major components of formal reports.** Report components can be divided into prefatory parts, text parts, and supplementary parts. *Prefatory parts*, which present and package your report, can include a synopsis (a brief overview of an entire report) or executive summary (a "mini" version of the report), a list of illustrations, the table of contents, a letter of transmittal, a letter of acceptance, a letter of authorization, a title page, a title fly, and a cover. *Text parts* include the standard message elements of introduction, body, and close. *Supplementary parts* can include an index, a bibliography, and one or more appendixes.

3 **Identify the major components of formal proposals.** Like a formal report, a formal proposal consists of prefatory parts, text parts, and supplementary parts. *Prefatory parts* that package and present the proposal include a synopsis or an executive summary, a list of illustrations, a table of contents, a letter of transmittal, a copy of or reference to the RFP (for solicited proposals), a title page, a title fly, and a cover. *Text parts* include the standard introduction, body, and close. Proposals typically don't have a significant number of *supplementary parts*, other than possibly an appendix or two that provide supporting information.

4 **Describe an effective plan for proofreading reports and proposals.** The process of proofreading is essentially the same as with shorter messages, but the length and complexity of reports and proposals makes proofreading more challenging. For example, be sure to proof all the visuals and make sure they are positioned correctly. An ideal plan for proofreading reports is to ask two people who weren't involved in writing it to review it, one checking for technical accuracy and one verifying that the content will be understood by everyone in the target audience.

5 **Describe the decision process for distributing reports and proposals.** All the distribution issues explored in Chapter 6 apply to reports and proposals, but pay particular attention to the length and complexity of these longer documents. The manner in which you deliver reports and proposals sends a signal about your professionalism and understanding of audience expectations. Express delivery through a package delivery service can be a sensible investment for important proposals, for example, not only for expediency but so that you can verify receipt. For electronic delivery, you should generally convert your documents to PDF files, which are welcomed more readily by most users than word-processor files. When responding to an RFP, always follow its instructions for delivering your proposal.

6 **Identify the elements to include in a request for proposals (RFP).** The content of RFPs varies widely from industry to industry and project to project, but most include background on the company, a description of the project, solution requirements, the criteria that will be used to make selection decisions, expectations for submitted proposals, and any relevant submission and contact information.

abstract Name usually given to a synopsis that accompanies long technical, professional, or academic reports

appendix Supplementary section that contains materials related to the report but not included in the text because they are too long or perhaps not relevant to everyone in the audience

bibliography A list of the secondary sources consulted in the preparation of a report

executive summary A complete but summarized version of the report; may contain headings, well-developed transitions, and even visual elements

index An alphabetical list of names and subjects mentioned in a report, along with the pages on which they occur

letter of acceptance Message written in response to a letter of authorization

letter of authorization Written authorization to prepare a report

letter of transmittal A specialized form of cover letter that introduces a report to the audience

synopsis A brief overview (one page or less) of a report's most important points, designed to give readers a quick preview of the contents

title fly A single sheet of paper with only the title of the report on it

title page Page that includes the report title; the name, title, and address of the person or organization that authorized the report (if anyone); the name, title, and address of the person or organization that prepared the report; and the date on which the report was submitted

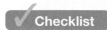

Checklist

Producing Formal Reports and Proposals

A. Prefatory parts.
- Use your company's standard report covers, if available.
- Include a concise, descriptive title on the cover.
- Include a title fly only if you want an extra-formal touch.
- On the title page, list (1) report title; (2) name, title, and address of the group or person who authorized the report; (3) name, title, and address of the group or person who prepared the report; and (4) date of submission.
- Include a copy of the letter of authorization, if appropriate.
- If responding to an RFP, follow its instructions for including a copy or referring to the RFP by name or tracking number.

- Include a letter of transmittal that introduces the report.
- Provide a table of contents in outline form, with headings worded exactly as they appear in the body of the report.
- Include a list of illustrations if the report contains a large number of them.
- Include a synopsis (brief summary of the report) or an executive summary (a condensed, "mini" version of the report) for longer reports.

B. Text of the report.
- Draft an introduction that prepares the reader for the content that follows.

- Provide information that supports your conclusions, recommendations, or proposals in the body of the report.
- Don't overload the body with unnecessary detail.
- Close with a summary of your main idea.

C. Supplementary parts.
- Use appendixes to provide supplementary information or supporting evidence.
- List in a bibliography any secondary sources you used.
- Provide an index if your report contains a large number of terms or ideas and is likely to be consulted over time.

Figure 15.1 **Parts of a Formal Report**
Depending on the level of formality you need to achieve, you can select from these elements to complete a formal report.

COMMUNICATION CHALLENGES AT GARAGE TECHNOLOGY VENTURES

You recently joined Guy Kawasaki and the rest of the team at Garage Technology Ventures in Palo Alto. Part of your responsibilities include screening executive summaries of business plans submitted by start-up companies seeking financing. Review the criteria discussed in the chapter-opening vignette on page 424 to address the following challenges.

INDIVIDUAL CHALLENGE: You've just received an intriguing executive summary from a start-up company whose technology reduces the cost of providing Internet service by nearly 30 percent, an amount that would spark interest from just about every Internet service provider in the world. The financial projections in the executive summary are realistic—and quite positive. Even if this investment panned out only half as well as the numbers suggest, it would bring in a sizable amount of cash when the company eventually goes public. The technological solution is sound, too; you used to work as a network engineer, and these people know what they're doing. There is just one problem: the submission is entirely anonymous. The document describes, in vague terms, four experienced technical and business specialists but without giving their names

or their specific work experiences. A note attached to the plan apologizes for the secrecy but says the four principles in the new firm can't reveal themselves until they get financing and can therefore leave their current jobs. Do you reject the submission or pass it on to Kawasaki and the other managing directors for their consideration? Explain your answer.

TEAM CHALLENGE: Review these "grabs" presented in three executive summaries. Discuss their strengths and weaknesses and decide which one of the three you would forward to Kawasaki and the other directors.

Company A: Pardon our bullish tone, but this is the best investment opportunity you are likely to see this year. As one of our board members recently said, we are already on track to out-Apple Apple and out-Google Google.

Company B: Cooling the huge data centers that power the Internet costs millions of dollars and consumes massive amounts of energy. Our low-temperature server technology pays for itself in less than a year by reducing energy bills and extending the life of data center hardware.

Company C: Our travel-search website has already proven so popular that last month we had 140,000 site visitors. By the way, we have interest from three other investment firms, so our advice would be to jump on this opportunity!

TEST YOUR KNOWLEDGE

To review chapter content related to each question, refer to the indicated Learning Objective.

1. What are the tasks involved in revising a report or proposal? [LO-1]
2. What information is typically included on the title page of a report? [LO-2]
3. What is the difference between a letter of authorization and a letter of acceptance? [LO-2]
4. What is a letter of transmittal, and where is it positioned within a report? [LO-2]
5. When are executive summaries useful? [LO-2]
6. What are three supplementary parts often included in formal reports? [LO-2]
7. What types of material does an appendix contain? [LO-2]
8. What is the equivalent of a letter of authorization for a proposal? [LO-3]
9. How should you refer to the RFP in a solicited proposal? [LO-3]
10. Why does writing an RFP require such careful thought? [LO-6]

APPLY YOUR KNOWLEDGE

To review chapter content related to each question, refer to the indicated Learning Objective.

1. Is an executive summary a persuasive message? Explain your answer. [LO-2]
2. Under what circumstances would you include more than one table of contents in a report? [LO-2]
3. If you included a bibliography in your report, would you also need to include in-text citations? Please explain. [LO-2]
4. How would you report on a confidential survey in which employees rated their managers' capabilities? Both employees and managers expect to see the results. Would you give the same report to employees and managers? What components would you include or exclude for each audience? Explain your choices. [LO-2]
5. If you were submitting a solicited proposal to build a small shopping center, would you include as references the names and addresses of other clients for whom you recently built similar facilities? Where in the proposal would you include these references? Why? [LO-3]

PRACTICE YOUR SKILLS

Message for Analysis

Message 15.A: Executive Summaries [LO-2]

To access this document for this exercise, go to http://real-timeupdates.com/bct11, click on "Student Assignments," and select "Chapter 15, page 457, Message 15.A." Download this PDF file, which is the executive summary of *Dietary Guidelines for Americans*, a publication from the U.S. Center for Nutrition Policy and Promotion. Using the information in this chapter, analyze the executive summary and offer specific suggestions for revising it.

Exercises

Active links for all websites in this chapter can be found on MyBcommLab; see your User Guide for instructions on accessing the content for this chapter. Each activity is labeled according to the primary skill or skills you will need to use. To review relevant chapter content, you can refer to the indicated Learning Objective. In some instances, supporting information will be found in another chapter, as indicated.

1. **Revising for Clarity and Conciseness [LO-1]** The following sentence appears in your first draft of a report that analyzes perceived shortcomings in your company's employee health benefits:

   Among the many criticisms and concerns expressed by the workforce, at least among the 376 who responded to our online survey (out of 655 active employees), the issues of elder care, health insurance during retirement, and the increased amount that employees are being forced to pay every month as the company's contribution to health insurance coverage has declined over the past two years were identified as the most important.

   Revise this 69-word sentence to make it shorter, more direct, and more powerful.

2. **Producing Formal Reports; Collaboration: Team Projects [LO-2], Chapter 2** You and a classmate are helping Linda Moreno prepare her report on Electrovision's travel and entertainment costs (see "Report Writer's Notebook" on page 428). This time, however, the report is to be informational rather than analytical, so it will not include recommendations. Review the existing report and determine what changes would be needed to make it an informational report. Be as specific as possible. For example, if your team decides the report needs a new title, what title would you use? Now draft a transmittal memo for Moreno to use in conveying this informational report to Dennis McWilliams, Electrovision's vice president of operations.

3. **Producing Formal Reports [LO-2]** You are president of the Friends of the Library, a nonprofit group that raises funds and provides volunteers to support your local library. Every February, you send a report of the previous year's activities and accomplishments to the County Arts Council, which provides an annual grant of $1,000 toward your group's summer reading festival. Now it's February 6, and you've completed your formal report. Here are the highlights:

   - Back-to-school book sale raised $2,000.
   - Holiday craft fair raised $1,100.
   - Promotion and prizes for summer reading festival cost $1,450.
   - Materials for children's program featuring local author cost $125.
   - New reference databases for library's career center cost $850.
   - Bookmarks promoting library's website cost $200.

   Write a letter of transmittal to Erica Maki, the council's director. Because she is expecting this report, you can use the direct approach. Be sure to express gratitude for the council's ongoing financial support.

4. **Producing Formal Reports [LO-2]** Government reports vary in purpose and structure. Read through the Department of Education's report "Helping Your Child Become a Reader," available at www.ed.gov. What is the purpose of this document? Does the title communicate this purpose? What type of report is this, and what is the report's structure? Which prefatory and supplementary parts are included? Now analyze the visuals. What types of visuals are included in this report? Are they all necessary? Are the titles and legends sufficiently informative? How does this report take advantage of the online medium to enhance readability?

5. **Distributing Reports; Communication Ethics: Resolving Ethical Dilemmas [LO-5], Chapter 1** You submitted what you thought was a masterful report to your boss over three weeks ago. The report analyzes current department productivity and recommends several steps that you think will improve employee output without increasing individual workloads. Brilliant, you thought. But you haven't heard a word from your boss. Did you overstep your boundaries by making recommendations that might imply that she has not been doing a good job? Did you overwhelm her with your ideas? You'd like some feedback. In your last email to her, you asked if she had read your report. So far you've received no reply. Then yesterday, you overheard the company vice president talk about some productivity changes in your department. The changes were ones that you recommended in your report. Now you're worried that your boss submitted your report to senior management and will take full credit for your terrific ideas. What, if anything, should you do? Should you confront your boss about this? Should you ask to meet with the company vice president? Discuss this situation with your teammates and develop a solution to this sticky situation. Present your solution to the class, explaining the rationale behind your decision.

EXPAND YOUR SKILLS

Critique the Professionals

Browse the websites of several companies to find a download-able PDF file of a report, white paper, company backgrounder, product overview, or other document at least two pages long. Evaluate the design and production quality of this document. Does the layout enhance the message or distract your attention from it? It what ways do design elements convey the company's brand image? Does the document strike you as "under-designed" or "over-designed" for its intended purpose? Using whatever medium your instructor requests, write a brief summary of your analysis. Be sure to include a link to the document.

Sharpening Your Career Skills Online

Bovée and Thill's Business Communication Web Search, at http://businesscommunicationblog.com/websearch, is a unique research tool designed specifically for business communication research. Use the Web Search function to find a website, video, PDF document, or PowerPoint presentation that offers advice on producing formal reports and proposals. Write a brief email message to your instructor, describing the item that you found and summarizing the career skills information you learned from it.

CASES

Short Formal Reports Requiring No Additional Research

PORTFOLIO BUILDER

1. Message Strategies: Informational Reports As the newest member of the corporate training division of Paper Products, Inc., you have been asked to investigate and analyze the merits of creating online courses for the company's employees. The president of your company thinks e-learning might be a good employee benefit as well as a terrific way for employees to learn new skills that they can use on the job. You've already done your research, and here's a copy of your notes:

Online courses open up new horizons for working adults, who often find it difficult to juggle conventional classes with jobs and families.
Adults over 25 now represent nearly half of higher-ed students; most are employed and want more education to advance their careers.
Some experts believe that online learning will never be as good as face-to-face instruction.
Online learning requires no commute and is appealing for employees who travel regularly.
Enrollment in courses offered online by postsecondary institutions is expected to increase from 4 million students in 2009 to 7 million students in 2014.
E-learning is a cost-effective way to get better-educated employees.
More than one-third of the $50 billion spent on employee training every year is spent on e-learning.
At IBM, some 200,000 employees received education or training online last year, and 75 percent of the company's Basic Blue course for new managers is online. E-learning cut IBM's training bill by $350 million last year—mostly because online courses don't require travel.
There are no national statistics, but a recent report from the *Chronicle of Higher Education* found that institutions are seeing dropout rates that range from 20 to 50 percent for online learners. The research does not adequately explain why the dropout rates for e-learners are higher.

A recent study of corporate online learners reported that employees want the following things from their online courses: college credit or a certificate; active correspondence with an online facilitator who has frequent virtual office hours; access to 24-hour, seven-day-a-week technical support; and the ability to start a course anytime.
Corporate e-learners said that their top reason for dropping a course was lack of time. Many had trouble completing courses from their desktops because of frequent distractions caused by co-workers. Some said they could only access courses through the company's intranet, so they couldn't finish their assignments from home.
Besides lack of time, corporate e-learners cited the following as e-learning disadvantages: lack of management oversight, lack of motivation, problems with technology, lack of student support, individual learning preferences, poorly designed courses, substandard/inexperienced instructors.
A recent study by GE Capital found that finishing a corporate online course was dependent on whether managers gave reinforcement on attendance, how important employees were made to feel, and whether employee progress in the course was tracked.
Sun Microsystems found that interactivity can be a critical success factor for online courses. Company studies showed that only 25 percent of employees finish classes that are strictly self-paced. But 75 percent finish when given similar assignments and access to tutors through email, phone, or online discussion groups.
Company managers must supervise e-learning just as they would any other important initiative.
For online learning to work, companies must develop a culture that takes online learning just as seriously as classroom training.
For many e-learners, studying at home is optimal. Whenever possible, companies should offer courses through the Internet or provide intranet access at home. Having employees studying on their own time will more than cover any added costs.
Corporate e-learning has flared into a $2.3 billion market, making it one of the fastest-growing segments of the education industry.
Rather than fly trainers to 7,000 dealerships, General Motors University now uses interactive satellite broadcasts to teach salespeople the best way to highlight features of the new Buick.
Fast and cheap, e-training can shave companies' training costs while it saves employees' travel time.

Pharmaceutical companies such as Merck are conducting live, interactive classes over the web, allowing sales reps to learn about the latest product information at home rather than fly to a conference center.
McDonald's trainers can log into Hamburger University to learn such skills as how to assemble a made-to-order burger or properly place a drink on a tray.
One obstacle to the spread of online corporate training is the mismatch between what employees really need—customized courses that are tailored to a firm's products and its unique corporate culture—and what employers can afford.
Eighty percent of companies prefer developing their own online training courses in-house. But creating even one customized e-course can take months, involve armies of experts, and cost anywhere from $25,000 to $50,000. Thus, most companies either stick with classroom training or buy generic courses on such topics as how to give performance appraisals, understanding basic business ethics, and so on. Employers can choose from a wide selection of noncustomized electronic courses.
For online learning to be effective, content must be broken into short "chunks" with lots of pop quizzes, online discussion groups, and other interactive features that let students demonstrate what they've learned. For instance, Circuit City's tutorial on digital camcorders consists of three 20-minute segments. Each contains audio demonstrations of how to handle customer product queries, tests on terminology, and "try-its" that propel trainees back onto the floor to practice what they've learned.
Dell expects 90 percent of its learning solutions to be totally or partially technology enabled.
The Home Depot has used e-training to cut a full day from the time required to train new cashiers.
Online training has freed up an average of 17 days every year for Black & Decker's sales representatives.

Your task: Write a short (three to five pages) memo report to the director of human resources, Kerry Simmons, presenting the advantages and disadvantages of e-learning and making a recommendation about whether Paper Products, Inc., should invest time and money in training its employees this way. Be sure to organize your information so that it is clear, concise, and logically presented. Simmons likes to read the "bottom line" first, so be direct: Present your recommendation up-front and support your recommendation with your findings.[10]

PORTFOLIO BUILDER

2. Message Strategies: Analytical Reports   You've been in your new job as human resources director for only a week, and already you have a major personnel crisis on your hands. Some employees in the marketing department got their hands on a confidential salary report, only to learn that, on average, marketing employees earn less than engineering employees. In addition, several top performers in the engineering group make significantly more money than anybody in marketing. The report was passed around the company instantly by email, and now everyone is discussing the situation. You'll deal with the data security issue later; for now, you need to address the dissatisfaction in the marketing group.

Case Table 15.1 lists the salary and employment data you were able to pull from the employee database. You also had the opportunity to interview the engineering and marketing directors to get their opinions on the pay situation; their answers are listed in Case Table 15.2.

Your task: The CEO has asked for a short report, summarizing the data and information you have on engineering and marketing salaries. Feel free to offer your own interpretation of the situation as well (make up any information you need), but keep in mind that as a new manager with almost no experience in the company, your opinion might not have a lot of influence.

PORTFOLIO BUILDER

3. Message Strategies: Analytical Reports   Spurred on in part by the success of numerous television shows and even entire cable networks devoted to remodeling, homeowners across the country are redecorating and rebuilding like never before. Many people are content with superficial changes, such as new paint or new accessories, but some are more ambitious. These homeowners want to move walls, add rooms, redesign kitchens, convert garages to home theaters—the big stuff.

With many consumer trends, publishers try to create magazines that appeal to carefully identified groups of potential readers and the advertisers who'd like to reach them. The do-it-yourself (DIY) market is already served by numerous magazines, but you see an opportunity in those homeowners who tackle the heavy-duty projects. Case Tables 15.3 through 15.5 summarize the results of some preliminary research you asked your company's research staff to conduct.

CASE TABLE 15.1   Selected Employment Data for Engineers and Marketing Staff

Employment Statistic	Engineering Department	Marketing Department
Average number of years of work experience	18.2	16.3
Average number of years of experience in current profession	17.8	8.6
Average number of years with company	12.4	7.9
Average number of years of college education	6.9	4.8
Average number of years between promotions	6.7	4.3
Salary range	$58–165K	$45–85K
Median salary	$77K	$62K

CASE TABLE 15.2 **Summary Statements from Department Director Interviews**

Question	Engineering Director	Marketing Director
1. Should engineering and marketing professionals receive roughly similar pay?	In general, yes, but we need to make allowances for the special nature of the engineering profession. In some cases, it's entirely appropriate for an engineer to earn more than a marketing person.	Yes.
2. Why or why not?	Several reasons: (1) Top engineers are extremely hard to find, and we need to offer competitive salaries; (2) the structure of the engineering department doesn't provide as many promotional opportunities, so we can't use promotions as a motivator the way marketing can; (3) many of our engineers have advanced degrees, and nearly all pursue continuing education to stay on top of the technology.	Without marketing, the products the engineers create wouldn't reach customers, and the company wouldn't have any revenue. The two teams make equal contributions to the company's success.
3. If we decide to balance pay between the two departments, how should we do it?	If we do anything to cap or reduce engineering salaries, we'll lose key people to the competition.	If we can't increase payroll immediately to raise marketing salaries, the only fair thing to do is freeze raises in engineering and gradually raise marketing salaries over the next few years.

CASE TABLE 15.3 **Rooms Most Frequently Remodeled by DIYers**

Room	Percentage of Homeowners Surveyed Who Have Tackled or Plan to Tackle at Least a Partial Remodel
Kitchen	60
Bathroom	48
Home office/study	44
Bedroom	38
Media room/home theater	31
Den/recreation room	28
Living room	27
Dining room	12
Sun room/solarium	8

CASE TABLE 15.4 **Average Amount Spent on Remodeling Projects**

Estimated Amount	Percentage of Surveyed Homeowners
Under $5K	5
$5–10K	21
$10–20K	39
$20–50K	22
More than $50K	13

CASE TABLE 15.5 **Tasks Performed by Homeowner on a Typical Remodeling Project**

Task	Percentage of Surveyed Homeowners Who Perform or Plan to Perform Most or All of This Task Themselves
Conceptual design	90
Technical design/architecture	34
Demolition	98
Foundation work	62
Framing	88
Plumbing	91
Electrical	55
Heating/cooling	22
Finish carpentry	85
Tile work	90
Painting	100
Interior design	52

Your task: You think the data show a real opportunity for a "big projects" DIY magazine, although you'll need more extensive research to confirm the size of the market and refine the editorial direction of the magazine. Prepare a brief analytical report that presents the data you have, identifies the opportunity or opportunities you've found (suggest your own ideas based on the tables), and requests funding from the editorial board to pursue further research.

Short Formal Reports Requiring Additional Research

PORTFOLIO BUILDER

4. Message Strategies: Analytical Reports   Like any other endeavor that combines hardnosed factual analysis and creative freethinking, the task of writing business plans generates a range of opinions.

Your task: Find at least six sources of advice on writing successful business plans (focus on start-up businesses that are likely to seek outside investors). Use at least two books, two magazine or journal articles, and two websites or blogs. Analyze the advice you find and identify points where most or all the experts agree and points where they don't agree. Wherever you find points of significant disagreement, identify which opinion you find most convincing and explain why. Summarize your findings in a brief formal report.

TEAM SKILLS   PORTFOLIO BUILDER

5. Message Strategies: Analytical Reports   Anyone looking at the fragmented 21st-century landscape of media and entertainment options might be surprised to learn that poetry was once a dominant medium for not only creative literary expression but philosophical, political, and even scientific discourse. Alas, such is no longer the case.

Your task: With a team of fellow students, your challenge is to identify opportunities to increase sales of poetry—any kind of poetry, in any medium. The following suggestions may help you get started:

- Research recent bestsellers in the poetry field and try to identify why they have been popular.
- Interview literature professors, professional poets, librarians, publishers, and bookstore personnel.
- Conduct surveys and interviews to find out why consumers don't buy more poetry.
- Attend a few poetry slams or readings and talk to the participants about their poetry buying needs and habits.
- Review professional journals that cover the field of poetry, including *Publishers Weekly* and *Poets & Writers*, from both business and creative standpoints.

Summarize your recommendations in a brief formal report; assume that your target readers are executives in the publishing industry.

PORTFOLIO BUILDER

6. Message Strategies: Analytical Reports   After 15 years in the corporate world, you're ready to strike out on your own. Rather than building a business from the ground up, however, you think that buying a franchise is a better idea. Unfortunately, some of the most lucrative franchise opportunities, such as the major fast-food chains, require significant start-up costs—some more than a half-million dollars. Fortunately, you've met several potential investors who seem willing to help you get started in exchange for a share of ownership. Between your own savings and money from these investors, you estimate that you can raise from $350,000 to $600,000, depending on how much ownership share you want to concede to the investors.

You've worked in several functional areas already, including sales and manufacturing, so you have a fairly well-rounded business résumé. You're open to just about any type of business, too, as long as it provides the opportunity to grow; you don't want to be so tied down to the first operation that you can't turn it over to a hired manager and expand into another market.

Your task: To convene a formal meeting with the investor group, you need to first draft a report that outlines the types of franchise opportunities you'd like to pursue. Write a brief report, identifying five franchises that you would like to explore further. (Choose five based on your own personal interests and the criteria already identified.) For each possibility, identify the nature of the business, the financial requirements, the level of support the company provides, and a brief statement of why you could run such a business successfully (make up any details you need). Be sure to carefully review the information you find about each franchise company to make sure you can qualify for it. For instance, McDonald's doesn't allow investment partnerships to buy franchises, so you won't be able to start up a McDonald's outlet until you have enough money to do it on your own.

For a quick introduction to franchising, see How Stuff Works (www.howstuffworks.com/franchising). You can learn more about the business of franchising at Franchising.com (www.franchising.com) and search for specific franchise opportunities at Francorp Connect (www.francorpconnect.com). In addition, many companies that sell franchises, such as Subway, offer additional information on their websites.

PORTFOLIO BUILDER

7. Message Strategies: Informational Reports   Health care costs are a pressing concern at every level in the economy, from individual households up through companies of all sizes on up to state and federal governments. Many companies that want to continue offering or to start offering some level of health insurance to their employees are struggling with a cost spiral that seems out of control.

Your task: Identify five ways that companies are reducing the cost of providing health care insurance for their employees (other than eliminating this benefit entirely). Compile your findings in a brief report that includes at least one real-life example for each of the five ways.

PORTFOLIO BUILDER

8. Message Strategies: Analytical Reports.   After several false starts over the past few years, tablet computers seem to have finally caught on among business users. In addition to Apple's popular iPad, seemingly every computer company on the planet is looking to get a share of this market. Will they be a passing fad? A cool toy or a serious business tool?

Your task: Prepare a short analytical report that compares the advantages and disadvantages of tablet computers for traveling salespeople.

Long Formal Reports Requiring No Additional Research

PORTFOLIO BUILDER

9. Message Strategies: Informational Reports As a researcher in your state's consumer protection agency, you're frequently called on to investigate consumer topics and write reports for the agency's website. Thousands of consumers have arranged the purchase of cars online, and millions more do at least some of their research online before heading to a dealership. Some want to save time and money, some want to be armed with as much information as possible before talking to a dealer, while others want to completely avoid the often-uncomfortable experience of negotiating prices with car salespeople. In response, a variety of online services have emerged to meet these consumer needs. Some let you compare information on various car models, some connect you to local dealers to complete the transaction, and some complete nearly all of the transaction details for you, including negotiating the price. Some search the inventory of thousands of dealers, whereas others search only a single dealership or a network of affiliated dealers. In other words, a slew of new tools are available for car buyers, but it's not always easy to figure out where to go and what to expect. That's where your report will help.

By visiting a variety of car-related websites and reading magazine and newspaper articles on the car-buying process, you've compiled a variety of notes related to the subject:

- **Process overview.** The process is relatively straightforward and fairly similar to other online shopping experiences, with two key differences. In general, a consumer identifies the make and model of car he or she wants, and then the online car-buying service searches the inventories of car dealers nationwide and presents the available choices. The consumer chooses a particular car from that list, and the service handles the communication and purchase details with the dealer. When the paperwork is finished, the consumer then visits the dealership and picks up the car. The two biggest differences with online auto buying are that (1) you can't actually complete the purchase over the Internet (in most cases, you must visit a local dealer to pick up the car and sign the papers, although in some cities, a dealer or a local car-buying service will deliver it to your home), and (2) in most states, it's illegal to purchase a new car from anyone other than a franchise dealer (i.e., you can't buy directly from the manufacturer, the way you can buy a Dell computer directly from Dell, for instance).
- **Information you can find online (not all information is available at all sites).** The information you can find online includes makes, models, colors, options, option packages (often, specific options are available only as part of a package; you need to know these constraints before you select your options), photos, specifications (everything from engine size to interior space), fuel efficiency estimates, performance data, safety information, predicted resale value, reviews, comparable models, insurance costs, consumer ratings, repair and reliability histories, available buyer incentives and rebates, true ownership costs (including fuel, maintenance, repairs, etc.), warranty information, loan and lease payments, and maintenance requirements.

- **Advantages of shopping online.** Advantages of shopping online include shopping from the comfort and convenience of home, none of the dreaded negotiating at the dealership (in many cases), the ability to search far and wide for a specific car (even nationwide, on many sites), rapid access to considerable amounts of data and information, and reviews from both professional automotive journalists and other consumers. In general, online auto shopping reduces a key advantage that auto dealers used to have: control of most of the information in the purchase transaction. Now consumers can find out how reliable each model is, how quickly it will depreciate, how often it is likely to need repairs, what other drivers think of it, how much the dealer paid the manufacturer for it, and so on.
- **Changing nature of the business.** The relationship between dealers and third-party websites (such as CarsDirect .com and Vehix.com) continues to evolve. At first, the relationship was antagonistic, as some third-party sites and dealers frequently competed for the same customers, and each side made bold proclamations about driving the other out of business. However, the relationship is more collaborative in many cases now, with dealers realizing that some third-party sites already have wide brand awareness and nationwide audiences. As the percentage of new car sales that originate via the Internet continues to increase, dealers are more receptive to working with third-party sites.
- **Comparing information from multiple sources.** Consumers shouldn't rely solely on the information from a single website. Each site has its own way of organizing information, and many have their own ways of evaluating car models and connecting buyers with sellers.
- **Understanding what each site is doing.** For instance, some search thousands of dealers, regardless of ownership connections. Others, such as AutoNation, search only affiliated dealers. A search for a specific model might yield only a half-dozen cars on one site but dozens of cars on another site. Find out who owns the site and what their business objectives are, if you can; this will help you assess the information you receive.
- **Leading websites.** Consumers can check out a wide variety of websites, some of which are full-service operations, offering everything from research to negotiation; others provide more specific and limited services. For instance, CarsDirect (www.carsdirect.com) provides a full range of services, whereas Carfax (www.carfax.com) specializes in uncovering the repair histories of individual used cars. Case Table 15.6 lists some of the leading car-related websites.

Your task: Write an informational report, based on your research notes. The purpose of the report is to introduce consumers to the basic concepts of integrating the Internet into their car-buying activities and to educate them about important issues.[11]

PORTFOLIO BUILDER

10. Message Strategies: Informational Reports Your company is the largest private employer in your metropolitan area, and the 43,500 employees in your workforce have a tremendous impact on local traffic. A group of city and county transportation officials recently approached your CEO with a request to explore ways to reduce this impact. The CEO has assigned you the task of analyzing the workforce's transportation habits and attitudes as a first step toward identifying potential solutions. He's willing to consider anything from subsidized bus passes to company-owned shuttle buses to telecommuting, but the decision requires a thorough understanding of employee transportation needs. Case Tables 15.7 through 15.11 summarize data you collected in an employee survey.

CASE TABLE 15.6   Leading Automotive Websites

Site	URL
AutoAdvice	www.autoadvice.com
Autobytel	www.autobytel.com
Autos.com	www.autos.com
AutoVantage	www.autovantage.com
Autoweb	www.autoweb.com
CarBargains	www.carbargains.com
Carfax	www.carfax.com
CarPrices.com	www.carprices.com
Cars.com	www.cars.com
CarsDirect	www.carsdirect.com
CarSmart	www.carsmart.com
Consumer Reports	www.consumerreports.org
eBay Motors	www.motors.ebay.com
Edmunds	www.edmunds.com
iMotors	www.imotors.com
IntelliChoice	www.intellichoice.com
InvoiceDealers	www.invoicedealers.com
JDPower	www.jdpower.com
Kelley Blue Book	www.kbb.com
MSN Autos	http://autos.msn.com
PickupTrucks.com	www.pickuptrucks.com
The Car Connection	www.thecarconnection.com
Vehix.com	www.vehix.com
Yahoo! Autos	http//autos.yahoo.com

CASE TABLE 15.7   Employee Carpool Habits

Frequency of Use: Carpooling	Portion of Workforce
Every day, every week	10,138 (23%)
Certain days, every week	4,361 (10%)
Randomly	983 (2%)
Never	28,018 (64%)

CASE TABLE 15.8   Use of Public Transportation

Frequency of Use: Public Transportation	Portion of Workforce
Every day, every week	23,556 (54%)
Certain days, every week	2,029 (5%)
Randomly	5,862 (13%)
Never	12,053 (28%)

CASE TABLE 15.9   Effect of Potential Improvements to Public Transportation

Which of the Following Would Encourage You to Use Public Transportation More Frequently (check all that apply)	Portion of Respondents
Increased perceptions of safety	4,932 (28%)
Improved cleanliness	852 (5%)
Reduced commute times	7,285 (41%)
Greater convenience: fewer transfers	3,278 (18%)
Greater convenience: more stops	1,155 (6%)
Lower (or subsidized) fares	5,634 (31%)
Nothing could encourage me to take public transportation	8,294 (46%)

Note: This question was asked of respondents who use public transportation randomly or never, a subgroup that represents 17,915 employees, or 41 percent of the workforce.

CASE TABLE 15.10   Distance Traveled to/from Work

Distance You Travel to Work (one way)	Portion of Workforce
Less than 1 mile	531 (1%)
1–3 miles	6,874 (16%)
4–10 miles	22,951 (53%)
11–20 miles	10,605 (24%)
More than 20 miles	2,539 (6%)

CASE TABLE 15.11   Is Telecommuting an Option?

Does the Nature of Your Work Make Telecommuting a Realistic Option?	Portion of Workforce
Yes, every day	3,460 (8%)
Yes, several days a week	8,521 (20%)
Yes, random days	12,918 (30%)
No	18,601 (43%)

Your task: Present the results of your survey in an informational report, using the data provided in Case Tables 15.7 through 15.11.

Long Formal Reports Requiring Additional Research

PORTFOLIO BUILDER

11. Message Strategies: Informational Reports The partners in your accounting firm have agreed to invest some of the company's profits in the stock market. A previous team effort identified two leading companies in each of five different industries:

- Boeing; Lockheed Martin (aerospace, defense)
- Hewlett-Packard; Dell (computers and software)
- Barnes & Noble; Amazon (retailing)
- UPS; FedEx (delivery and logistics)

The partners have already done an in-depth financial analysis of all 10 firms, and they have asked you to look for more qualitative information, such as

- Fundamental philosophical differences in management styles, launch and handling of products and services, marketing of products and services, and approach to e-commerce that sets one rival company apart from the other
- Future challenges that each competitor faces
- Important decisions made by the two competitors and how those decisions affected their company
- Fundamental differences in each company's vision of its industry's future (for instance, do they both agree on what consumers want, what products to deliver, and so on?)
- Specific competitive advantages of each rival
- Past challenges each competitor has faced and how each met those challenges
- Strategic moves made by one rival that might affect the other
- Company success stories
- Brief company background information
- Brief comparative statistics, such as annual sales, market share, number of employees, number of stores, types of equipment, number of customers, sources of revenue, and so on

Your task: Select two competitors from the preceding list (or another list provided by your instructor) and write a long formal informational report comparing how the two companies are addressing the topics outlined by the partners. Of course, not every topic will apply to each company, and some will be more important than others—depending on the companies you select.

The partners will invest in only one of the two companies in your report. (*Note:* Because these topics require considerable research, your instructor may choose to make this a team project.)

PORTFOLIO BUILDER

12. Message Strategies: Analytical Reports As a college student and an active consumer, you may have considered one or more of the following questions at some point in the past few years:

a. What criteria distinguish the top-rated MBA programs in the country? How well do these criteria correspond to the needs and expectations of business? Are the criteria fair for students, employers, and business schools?

b. Which of three companies you might like to work for has the strongest corporate ethics policies?

c. What will the music industry look like in the future? What's next after online stores such as Apple iTunes and digital players such as the iPod?

d. Which industries and job categories are forecast to experience the greatest growth—and therefore the greatest demands for workers—in the next 10 years?

e. What has been the impact of Starbucks's aggressive growth on small, independent coffee shops? On midsized chains or franchises? In the United States or in another country?

f. How large is the "industry" of major college sports? How much do the major football or basketball programs contribute—directly or indirectly—to other parts of a typical university?

g. How much have minor league sports—baseball, hockey, arena football—grown in small- and medium-market cities? What is the local economic impact when these municipalities build stadiums and arenas?

Your task: Answer one of these questions, using secondary research sources for information. Be sure to document your sources in the correct form. Make conclusions and offer recommendations where appropriate.

PORTFOLIO BUILDER

13. Message Strategies: Analytical Reports An observer surveying the current consumer electronics landscape and seeing Apple products everywhere might be surprised to learn that during part of the company's history, it was regarded by some as a fairly minor player in the computer industry—and at times a few pundits even wondered whether the company would survive.

Your task: In a two- to three-page report, identify the reasons Apple has been successful and explain how other companies can apply Apple's strategies and tactics to improve their business results.

Formal Proposals

PORTFOLIO BUILDER

14. Message Strategies: Proposals Presentations can make or break both careers and businesses. A good presentation can bring in millions of dollars in new sales or fresh investment capital. A bad presentation might cause a number of troubles, from turning away potential customers to upsetting fellow employees to derailing key projects. To help business professionals plan, create, and deliver more effective presentations, you offer a three-day workshop that covers the essentials of good presentations:

- Understanding your audience's needs and expectations
- Formulating your presentation objectives
- Choosing an organizational approach
- Writing openings that catch your audience members' attention
- Creating effective graphics and slides
- Practicing and delivering your presentation
- Leaving a positive impression on your audience
- Avoiding common mistakes with Microsoft PowerPoint
- Making presentations online using webcasting tools
- Handling questions and arguments from the audience
- Overcoming the top 10 worries of public speaking (including How can I overcome stage fright? and I'm not the performing type; can I still give an effective presentation?)

Here is some additional information about the workshop:

- **Workshop benefits:** Students will learn how to prepare better presentations in less time and deliver them more effectively.
- **Who should attend:** Top executives, project managers, employment recruiters, sales professionals, and anyone else who gives important presentations to internal or external audiences.
- **Your qualifications:** 18 years of business experience, including 14 years in sales and 12 years in public speaking. Experience speaking to audiences as large as 5,000 people. More than a dozen speech-related articles published in professional journals. Have conducted successful workshops for nearly 100 companies.
- **Workshop details:** Three-day workshop (9 A.M. to 3:30 P.M.) that combines lectures, practice presentations, and both individual and group feedback. Minimum number of students: 6. Maximum number of students per workshop: 12.
- **Pricing:** The cost is $3,500, plus $100 per student. 10 percent discount for additional workshops.

- **Other information:** Each attendee will have the opportunity to give three practice presentations that will last from three to five minutes. Everyone is encouraged to bring PowerPoint files containing slides from actual business presentations. Each attendee will also receive a workbook and a digital video recording of his or her final class presentation. You'll also be available for phone or email coaching for six months after the workshop.

Your task: Identify a company in your local area that might be a good candidate for your services. Learn more about the company by visiting its website so you can personalize your proposal. Using the information listed earlier in this exercise, prepare a sales proposal that explains the benefits of your training and what students can expect during the workshop.

PORTFOLIO BUILDER

15. Message Strategies: Proposals For years, a controversy has been brewing over the amount of junk food and soft drinks being sold through vending machines in local schools. Schools benefit from revenue-sharing arrangements, but many parents and health experts are concerned about the negative effects of these snacks and beverages. You and your brother have almost a decade of experience running espresso and juice stands in malls and on street corners, and you'd love to find some way to expand your business into schools. After a quick brainstorming session, the two of you craft a plan that makes good business sense while meeting the financial concerns of school administrators and the nutritional concerns of parents and dietitians. Here are the notes from your brainstorming session:

- Set up portable juice bars on school campuses, offering healthy fruit and vegetable drinks along with simple healthy snacks.
- Offer schools 30 percent of profits in exchange for free space and long-term contracts.
- Provide job training opportunities for students (during athletic events, etc.).
- Provide detailed dietary analysis of all products sold.
- Establish a nutritional advisory board composed of parents, students, and at least one certified health professional.
- Assure schools and parents that all products are safe (e.g., no stimulant drinks, no dietary supplements, and so on).
- Support local farmers and specialty food preparers by buying locally and giving these vendors the opportunity to test market new products at your stands.

Your task: Based on the ideas listed, draft a formal proposal to the local school board, outlining your plan to offer healthier alternatives to soft drinks and prepackaged snack foods. Invent any details you need to complete your proposal.

PORTFOLIO BUILDER

16. Message Strategies: Proposals   Seems like everybody in the firm is frustrated. On the one hand, top executives complain about the number of lower-level employees who want promotions but just don't seem to "get it" when it comes to dealing with customers and the public, recognizing when to speak out and when to be quiet, knowing how to push new ideas through the appropriate channels, and performing other essential but difficult-to-teach tasks. On the other hand, ambitious employees who'd like to learn more feel that they have nowhere to turn for career advice from people who've been there. In between, a variety of managers and midlevel executives are overwhelmed by the growing number of mentoring requests they're getting, sometimes from employees they don't even know.

You've been assigned the challenge of proposing a formal mentoring program—and a considerable challenge it is:

- The number of employees who want mentoring relationships far exceeds the number of managers and executives willing and able to be mentors. How will you select people for the program?
- The people most in demand for mentoring also tend to be some of the busiest people in the organization.
- After several years of belt tightening and staff reductions, the entire company feels overworked; few people can imagine adding another recurring task to their seemingly endless to-do lists.
- What's in it for the mentors? Why would they be motivated to help lower-level employees?
- How will you measure success or failure of the mentoring effort?

Your task: Identify potential solutions to the issues (make up any information you need) and draft a proposal to the executive committee for a formal, companywide mentoring program that would match selected employees with successful managers and executives.

PART 6 Designing and Delivering Oral and Online Presentations

CHAPTER 16 Developing Oral and Online Presentations

CHAPTER 17 Enhancing Presentations with Slides and Other Visuals

Presentations give you the opportunity to put all your communication skills on display, from audience analysis and research to the design of presentation materials to public speaking. Learn how to plan effective presentations, overcome the anxieties that every speaker feels, respond to questions from the audience, and embrace the Twitter-enabled backchannel. Discover some tips and techniques for succeeding with online presentations, an increasingly common mode of communication in today's environment. Complement your talk with compelling visual materials and learn how to create presentation slides that engage and excite your audience.

16

Developing Oral and Online Presentations

LEARNING OBJECTIVES After studying this chapter, you will be able to

1 Describe the tasks involved in analyzing the situation for a presentation and organizing a presentation

2 Explain how to adapt to your audience and develop an effective opening, body, and close for a presentation

3 Discuss five steps for delivering a successful presentation

4 Explain the growing importance of the backchannel in presentations and list six steps for giving effective presentations online

MyBcommLab Test your mastery of this chapter and its Learning Objectives. Visit mybcommlab.com to apply what you've learned in Document Makeovers and interactive simulation scenarios.

COMMUNICATION CLOSE-UP AT **PRINCIPATO-YOUNG ENTERTAINMENT**

Talent agent Peter Principato coaches his comedian clients to hone their presentations before pitching movie and TV show ideas to studio executives.

The business of being funny can be profoundly unfunny these days, particularly for comedians who want to break into movies and television shows. Fewer movies are being made, and the audience for television and online shows is so fragmented that trying to build a fan base is an uphill struggle. Making the situation even worse for comedians, many of whom are writers at heart, is the seemingly unstoppable growth of reality shows, which require neither writers nor actors in any conventional sense.

Talent agent Peter Principato knows this landscape as well as anyone, and as he puts it, "There's less and less real estate every year." Studios are increasingly reluctant to "green light" projects, particularly with the young and not-quite-top-of-the-marquee talent that is the specialty of Principato-Young Entertainment, the Beverly Hills company he co-founded with producer Paul Young. But comedy is in Principato's blood, so he works overtime to make his clients successful, even in this challenging environment.

In the entertainment industry, the road to success often starts with "the pitch," a brief presentation to one or more studio executives by an individual writer, actor, director, or producer or by a team of these people. If the executive is intrigued by the concept, it might be discussed further within the studio, and eventually a decision will be made about funding production.

With so much riding on this brief presentation, you can imagine that it's a high-anxiety event for the presenters, and making pitches is a vital communication skill. In fact, the ability to pitch effectively is so important that it has its own slang term: being "good in a room."

Pitches can fall flat for a number of reasons, whether the concept is just not a good fit for a particular studio, the idea is so unusual that the executives are unwilling to risk investing in it, or the pitch is just poorly presented. A presenter may fail by being unable to summarize what a new show or movie idea is all about, by smothering the executives in too many details, or by trying too hard to sell the concept.

The pointers Principato gives his clients constitute good advice for presentations in any industry, but they're vital in the entertainment industry. First, come up with a single compelling sentence that describes the show or movie. If presenters can't do this, chances are they haven't thought the idea out well enough, or the idea is so complicated that it would be too risky or too expensive to attempt. This one-line summary is essential for another reason, in that the first studio executive to hear the pitch will usually need to share it with other executives or potential financiers before a decision can be made. A catchy, succinct idea is a lot easier to repeat than a rambling, confused concept.

Second, expand on that one sentence with a single paragraph that builds interest by substantiating the concept

and helping the listener envision what the show or movie would be like. Third, for a proposed series, explain how the concept would play out, week by week, by describing several episodes. Fourth, fill in the "big picture," such as by describing how the show would look on screen or by rounding out the main characters.

You've probably noticed how this advice follows the classic AIDA model of getting attention, building interesting, increasing desire, and asking for a decision, which is what makes Principato's advice valuable for just about any profession.

The funny business is tough and getting tougher, but Principato is clearly doing something right. Principato-Young continues to expand and attract more of the young comedians who might be box office stars for the next several decades. And his love of comedy and comedians continues to motivate Principato himself. As he describes it, having his job "is like getting to hang out with your favorite band."[1]

Planning a Presentation

You might not pitch the next Oscar winner to a studio executive as Peter Principato hopes to do (profiled in the chapter-opening Communication Close-up), but wherever your career takes you, oral presentations will offer important opportunities to put all your communication skills on display, including research, planning, writing, visual design, and interpersonal and nonverbal communication. Presentations also let you demonstrate your ability to think on your feet, grasp complex business issues, and handle challenging situations—all attributes that executives look for when searching for talented employees to promote.

If the thought of giving a speech or presentation makes you nervous, keep three points in mind. First, everybody gets nervous when speaking in front of groups. Second, being nervous is actually a good thing; it means you care about the topic, your audience, and your career success. Third, with practice, you can convert those nervous feelings into positive energy that helps you give more compelling presentations. You can take control of the situation by using the three-step writing process to prepare for successful presentations (see Figure 16.1 on the next page).

Planning oral presentations is much like planning any other business message: You analyze the situation, gather information, select the right medium, and organize the information. Gathering information for oral presentations is essentially the same as it is for written communication projects. The other three planning tasks have some special applications when it comes to oral presentations; they are covered in the following sections.

On the subject of planning, be aware that preparing a professional-quality business presentation can take a considerable amount of time. Nancy Duarte, whose design firm has years of experience creating presentations for corporations, offers this rule of thumb: depending on how much research you need to do and how much production work your slides need, for a one-hour presentation that uses 30 slides, allow 36 to 90 hours to research, conceive, create, and practice.[2] Not every one-hour presentation justifies a week or two of preparation, of course, but the important presentations that can make your career or your company certainly can.

 1   LEARNING OBJECTIVE

Describe the tasks involved in analyzing the situation for a presentation and organizing a presentation.

Oral presentations involve all of your communication skills, and they let you demonstrate your business acumen as well.

Feeling nervous is normal before a presentation; the good news is there are positive steps you can take to reduce your anxiety.

Creating a high-quality presentation for an important event can take many days, so be sure to allow enough time.

 REAL-TIME UPDATES
Learn More by Watching This Video

Dealing with the difficult four

Get advice on dealing with four difficult audience members: the Resister, the Expert, the Dominator, and the Rambler. Go to http://real-timeupdates.com/bct11 and click on "Learn More." If you are using MyBcommLab, you can access Real-Time Updates within each chapter or under Student Study Tools.

1 Plan →	**2** Write →	**3** Complete
Analyze the Situation Define your purpose and develop a profile of your audience, including their likely emotional states and language preferences.	**Adapt to Your Audience** Adapt your content, presentation style, and room setup to the audience and the specific situation. Be sensitive to audience needs and expectations with a "you" attitude, politeness, positive emphasis, and bias-free language. Plan to establish your credibility as required.	**Revise the Message** Evaluate your content and speaking notes.
Gather Information Determine audience needs and obtain the information necessary to satisfy those needs.		**Master Your Delivery** Choose your delivery mode and practice your presentation.
Select the Right Medium Choose the best medium or combination of media for delivering your presentation, including handouts and other support materials.	**Compose Your Presentation** Outline an attention-getting introduction, body, and close. Prepare supporting visuals and speaking notes.	**Prepare to Speak** Verify facilities and equipment, including online connections and software setups. Hire an interpreter if necessary.
Organize the Information Define your main idea, limit your scope and verify timing, select the direct or indirect approach, and outline your content.		**Overcome Anxiety** Take steps to feel more confident and appear more confident on stage.

Figure 16.1   The Three-Step Process for Developing Oral and Online Presentations
Although you rarely "write" a presentation or speech in the sense of composing every word ahead of time, the tasks in the three-step writing process adapt quite well to the challenge of planning, creating, and delivering both oral and online presentations.

ANALYZING THE SITUATION

The purpose of most business presentations is to inform or persuade; you may also give presentations designed primarily to collaborate with others.

As with written communications, analyzing the situation for an oral presentation involves defining your purpose and developing an audience profile. The purpose of most of your presentations will be to inform or to persuade, although you may occasionally need to make a collaborative presentation, such as when you're leading a problem-solving or brainstorming session. Given the time limitations of most presentations and the live nature of the event, make sure your purpose is crystal clear so that you make the most of the opportunity and show respect for your listeners' time and attention.

Knowing your audience's state of mind will help you adjust both your message and your delivery.

When you develop your audience profile, try to anticipate the likely emotional state of your audience members. Figure 16.2 offers tips for dealing with a variety of audience mindsets.

You also need to determine whether your audience is comfortable listening to the language you speak. Listening to an unfamiliar language is much more difficult than reading that language, so an audience that might be able to read a written report might not be able to understand an oral presentation covering the same material (see "Communicating Across Cultures: Making Sure Your Message Doesn't Get Lost in Translation").

Learn as much as you can about the setting and circumstances of your presentation, from the size of the audience to seating arrangements to potential interruptions.

Also consider the specific circumstances in which you'll be making your presentation. Will you speak to five people in a conference room, where you can control everything from light to sound to temperature? Or will you be demonstrating a product on the floor of a trade show, where you might have from 1 to 100 listeners and little control over the environment? Will everyone be in the same room, or will some or all of your audience

Supportive: Reward their goodwill with a presentation that is clear, concise, and upbeat; speak in a relaxed, confident manner.

Interested but neutral: Build your credibility as you present compelling reasons to accept your message; address potential objections as you move forward; show confidence but a willingness to answer questions and concerns.

Uninterested: Use the techniques described in this chapter to get their attention and work hard to hold it throughout; find ways to connect your message with their personal or professional interests; be well organized and concise.

Worried: Don't dismiss their fears or tell them they are mistaken for feeling that way; if your message will calm their fears, use the direct approach; if your message will confirm their fears, consider the indirect approach to build acceptance.

Hostile: Recognize that angry audiences care deeply but might not be open to listening; consider the indirect approach to find common ground and to diffuse anger before sharing your message; work to keep your own emotions under control.

Figure 16.2   Planning for Various Audience Mindsets
Try to assess the emotional state of your audience ahead of time so you can plan your presentation approach accordingly.

participate from remote locations via the Internet? What equipment will you have at your disposal?

For in-person presentations, pay close attention to seating arrangements. The four basic formats have distinct advantages and disadvantages:

- **Classroom or theater seating**, in which all chairs or desks face forward, helps keep attention focused on the speaker and is usually the best method for accommodating large audiences. However, this arrangement inhibits interaction among audience members, so it is not desirable for brainstorming or other collaborative activities.
- **Conference table seating**, in which people sit along both sides of a long table and the speaker stands at one end, is a common arrangement for smaller meetings. It promotes interaction among attendees, but it tends to isolate the speaker at one end of the room.
- **Horseshoe, or "U"-shaped, seating**, in which tables are arranged in the shape of a "U," improves on conference table seating by allowing the speaker to walk between the tables to interact with individual audience members.
- **Café seating**, in which people sit in groups at individual tables, is best for breakout sessions and other small-group activities. However, this arrangement is less than ideal for anything more than short presentations because it places some in the audience with their backs to the speaker, making it awkward for both them and the presenter.

If you can't control the seating arrangement, at least be aware of what it is so you can adjust your plans if needed.

All these variables can influence not only the style of your presentation but the content. For instance, in a public environment full of distractions and uncertainties, you're probably better off keeping your content simple and short because chances are you won't be able to keep everyone's attention for the duration of your presentation.

Table 16.1 on the next page offers a summary of the key steps in analyzing an audience for oral presentations. For even more insight into audience evaluation (including emotional and cultural issues), consult a good public-speaking textbook.

MyBcommLab

- Access this chapter's simulation entitled Developing Oral and Online Presentations, located at mybcommlab.com.

TABLE 16.1	Analyzing an Audience for Oral Presentations
Task	**Actions**
To determine audience size and composition	• Estimate how many people will attend and whether they will all attend in person, online, or a mix of both. • Find out if they share professional interests or other affiliations that can help you establish common ground with them. • Analyze demographic and psychographic variables to see any significant differences or similarities should influence the content and style of your presentation.
To predict the audience's probable reaction	• Analyze why audience members are attending the presentation. • Predict the mood that people will be in when you speak to them: supportive, interested but neutral, uninterested, apprehensive, or hostile. • Find out what kind of backup information will impress and influence the audience: technical data, historical information, financial data, demonstrations, samples, and so on. • Consider whether the audience has any biases that might work against you. • Anticipate possible objections or questions.
To gauge the audience's level of understanding	• Analyze whether everybody has the same background and experience. • Determine what the audience already knows about the subject. • Decide what background information the audience will need to better understand the subject. • Consider whether the audience is familiar with your vocabulary. • Analyze what the audience expects from you. • Think about the mix of general concepts and specific details you will need to present.

SELECTING THE RIGHT MEDIUM

Expect to give many online presentations in your career.

The task of selecting the right medium might seem obvious. After all, you are speaking, so it's an oral medium. However, you have an array of choices these days, ranging from live, in-person presentations to *webcasts* or *webinars* (online presentations or seminars that people either view live or download later from your website), *screencasts* (recordings of activity on computer displays with audio voiceover), or *twebinars* (online events that combine a webinar with the use of Twitter as a *backchannel*—see page 485—for real-time conversation[3]).

COMMUNICATING ACROSS CULTURES

Making Sure Your Message Doesn't Get Lost in Translation

When speaking to an international audience, keep in mind that audience members' language fluency might vary widely. So take special care to ensure clear communication:

- **Speak slowly and distinctly.** The most common complaint of international audiences is that English speakers talk too fast. Articulate each word carefully, emphasize consonants for clarity, and pause frequently.
- **Repeat key words and phrases.** When audiences are not very familiar with your language, they need to hear important information more than once. Also, they may not be familiar with synonyms, so word key points in the same way throughout your presentation.
- **Aim for clarity.** Keep your message simple. Eliminate complex sentence structure, abbreviations, and acronyms. Replace two-word verbs with one-word alternatives (such as *review* instead of *look over*). Such verbs are confusing because the definition of each separate word differs from the meaning of the two words combined. Similarly, avoid slang and cultural idioms, such as *once in a blue moon*, which may be unfamiliar to an international audience. If you use words or phrases from the audience's native language, make sure you understand them fully.

- **Communicate with body language.** Emphasize and clarify verbal information with gestures and facial expressions. For instance, smile to emphasize positive points and use gestures to illustrate the meaning of words such as *up*, *down*, or *under*.
- **Support your spoken message with visuals.** Simple, clear visuals, from flip charts to electronic slides, can help you describe your key points. If possible, prepare captions in both English and your audience's native language.

CAREER APPLICATIONS

1. One of the most important changes speakers need to make when addressing audiences in other cultures is to avoid colloquial figures of speech. Replace such phrases (for example, "hit one out of the park," "go for broke," "get your ducks in a row") with wording that is more likely to be understood by nonnative English speakers or audiences in other countries.
2. Make a list of 10 two-word verbs. How does the meaning of each separate word differ from the definition of the combined words? Replace each two-word verb with a single, specific word that will be clearer to an international audience.

Explore these options early in your planning efforts so that you can take full advantage of the ones at your disposal. For example, to reach an international audience, you might want to conduct a live presentation with a question-and-answer session for the on-site audience and post a video archive of this meeting on your website for audience members in other time zones.

ORGANIZING YOUR PRESENTATION

Organizing a presentation involves the same tasks as organizing a written message: Define your main idea, limit your scope, select the direct or indirect approach, and outline your content. As you work through these tasks, keep in mind that oral media have certain limitations. When reading written reports, audiences can skip back and forth, backing up if they miss a point or become confused and jumping ahead if they aren't interested in a particular part or are already familiar with the content. However, audiences for live presentations are more or less trapped in your time frame and sequence. Aside from interrupting you, they have no choice but to listen to your content in the exact order in which you present it.

Defining Your Main Idea

If you've ever heard a speaker struggle to get his or her point across ("What I really mean to say is . . ."), you know how frustrating such an experience can be for an audience. To avoid that struggle, identify the most important message you want audience members to take away with them. Then compose a one-sentence summary that links this idea to your audience's frame of reference, much as an advertising slogan points out how a product can benefit consumers. Here are some examples:

If you can't express your main idea in a single sentence, you probably haven't defined it clearly enough.

> Convince management that reorganizing the technical support department will improve customer service and reduce employee turnover.
>
> Convince the board of directors that we should build a new plant in Texas to eliminate manufacturing bottlenecks and improve production quality.
>
> Address employee concerns regarding a new health-care plan by showing how the plan will reduce costs and improve the quality of their care.

Each of these statements puts a particular slant on the subject, one that directly relates to the audience's interests. Make sure your purpose is based on a clear understanding of audience needs so that you can deliver information your audience truly cares about.[4] For example, a group of new employees will be much more responsive to your discussion of plant safety procedures if you focus on how the procedures can save lives and prevent injuries rather than on how they will save the company money or conform to government regulations.

Limiting Your Scope

Limiting your scope is important with any message, but it's particularly vital with presentations, for two reasons. First, for most presentations, you must work within strict time limits. For example, at DEMO and TechCrunch, two influential conferences in which entrepreneurs present their business plans to potential investors, presentations are limited to six and eight minutes, respectively.[5] To accomplish in six or eight minutes the complex task of introducing your company and convincing people to invest in it, you must distill your message down to its essential points. No matter what the time constraints, if you overestimate the amount of material you can cover within your allotted time, you're left with only unpleasant alternatives: rushing through your presentation, skipping some of the information you've so carefully prepared, or trying to steal a few minutes from the next presenter. At the other extreme, if you don't have enough material prepared to fill your time slot, you might be left standing in front of the audience trying to ad lib information you haven't prepared.

Limiting your scope is important for two reasons: to ensure that your presentation fits the allotted time and to make sure you respect your audience members' time and attention.

Second, you can count on having audience attention for only a finite amount of time, and you'll lose the audience if you try to cover too much material. For example, studies show that audience attention levels and retention rates drop sharply after 20 minutes.[6] In other words, even if you are not given a time limit, keep your presentation as short as possible, taking only as much of the audience's time as you need to accomplish your purpose.

The only sure way to know how much material you can cover in a given time is to practice your presentation after you complete it. As an alternative, if you're using conventional structured slides (see page 496) you can figure on 3 or 4 minutes per slide as a rough guide.[7] For instance, if you have 20 minutes, plan on being able to cover only 6 or 7 slides. Of course, be sure to factor in time for introductions, coffee breaks, demonstrations, question-and-answer sessions, and anything else that takes away from your speaking time.

If you're having trouble meeting a time limit or just want to keep your presentation as short as possible, consider a hybrid approach in which you present your key points in summary form and give people printed handouts with additional detail.[8] By the way, whenever you're up against a time or space constraint, try to view it as a creative challenge. Such limitations can force you to focus on the most essential message points that are important to your audience.[9] (See Case 3 on page 517 for the special twist on time-constrained presentations known as *pecha-kucha*.)

The only sure way to measure the length of your presentation is to complete a practice run.

Choosing Your Approach

With a well-defined main idea to guide you and a clear idea about the scope of your presentation, you can begin to arrange your message. If you have 10 minutes or less to deliver your message, organize your presentation much as you would a brief written message: Use the direct approach if the subject involves routine information or good news; use the indirect approach if the subject involves negative news or persuasion. Plan to spend a minute or two during your introduction to arouse interest and to give a preview of what's to come. For the body of the presentation, be prepared to explain the who, what, when, where, why, and how of your subject. In the final few moments, review the points you've made, and close with a statement that will help your audience remember the subject of your speech (see Figure 16.3).

Organize a short presentation the same way you would a brief written message; organize a longer presentation as you would a report.

Longer presentations are organized like reports. If the purpose is to inform, use the direct approach and a structure imposed naturally by the subject: importance, sequence, chronology, spatial orientation, geography, or category (as discussed in Chapter 13). If your purpose is to analyze, persuade, or collaborate, organize your material around conclusions and recommendations or around a logical argument. Use the direct approach if the audience is receptive and the indirect approach if you expect resistance.

As you develop your presentation, keep in mind that oral reports have one important advantage over written reports: You can adjust your outline on the fly if you need to. Identify the critical points in your presentation and ask yourself some "what if" questions to address possible audience reactions. For instance, if you're worried that the audience might not agree with the financial assumptions you've made, you might prepare a detailed analysis that you can include in your presentation in case you sense that a negative reaction is building or if someone openly questions you about it. As you'll see in Chapter 17, presentation software such as Microsoft PowerPoint makes it easy to adjust your presentation as you move along, allowing you to skip over any parts you decide not to use or to insert backup material at the last minute.

Simplicity is critical in the organization of presentations.

Regardless of the length of your presentation, remember that simplicity of organization is especially valuable in oral communication. If listeners lose the thread of your presentation, they'll have a hard time catching up and following your message in the remainder of your speech. Explain at the beginning how you've organized your material and try to limit the number of main points to three or four.

No matter what the length, look for opportunities to integrate storytelling (see page 105) into the structure of your presentation. The dramatic tension (not knowing what will happen to the "hero") at the heart of effective storytelling is a great way to capture and keep the audience's attention.

Progress Update: August 2012

Purpose: To update the Executive Committee on our product development schedule

    I. Review goals and progress.

        A. Mechanical design:

            1. Goal: 100%

            2. Actual: 80%

            3. Reason for delay: Unanticipated problems with case durability

        B. Software development:

            1. Goal: 50%

            2. Actual: 60%

        C. Material sourcing:

            1. Goal: 100%

            2. Actual: 45% (and materials identified are at 140% of anticipated costs)

            3. Reason for delay: Purchasing is understaffed and hasn't been able to research sources adequately.

    II. Discuss schedule options.

        A. Option 1: Reschedule product launch date.

        B. Option 2: Launch on schedule with more expensive materials.

   III. Suggest goals for next month.

   IV. Q&A

Figure 16.3   Effective Outline for a 10-Minute Progress Report
Here is an outline of a short presentation that updates management on the status of a key project; the presenter has some bad news to deliver, so she opted for an indirect approach to lay out the reasons for the delay before sharing the news of the schedule slip.

MyBcommLab

Apply Figure 16.3's key concepts by revising a new document. Go to Chapter 16 in mybcommlab.com and select Document Makeovers.

Preparing Your Outline

A presentation outline helps you organize your message, and it serves as the foundation for delivering your speech. Prepare your outline in several stages:[10]

- State your purpose and main idea and then use these to guide the rest of your planning.
- Organize your major points and subpoints in logical order, expressing each major point as a single, complete sentence.
- Identify major points in the body first and then outline the introduction and close.
- Identify transitions between major points or sections and then write these transitions in full-sentence form.
- Prepare your bibliography or source notes; highlight those sources you want to identify by name during your talk.
- Choose a compelling title. Make it brief, action oriented, and focused on what you can do for the audience.[11]

Many speakers like to prepare both a detailed *planning outline* (see Figure 16.4 on page 476) and a simpler *speaking outline* that provides all the cues and reminders they need to present their material. To prepare an effective speaking outline, follow these steps:[12]

- Start with the planning outline and then strip away anything you don't plan to say directly to your audience.
- Condense points and transitions to key words or phrases.
- Add delivery cues, such as places where you plan to pause for emphasis or use visuals.
- Arrange your notes on numbered cards or use the notes capability in your presentation software.

In addition to planning your speech, a presentation outline helps you plan your speaking notes as well.

You may find it helpful to create a simpler speaking outline from your planning outline.

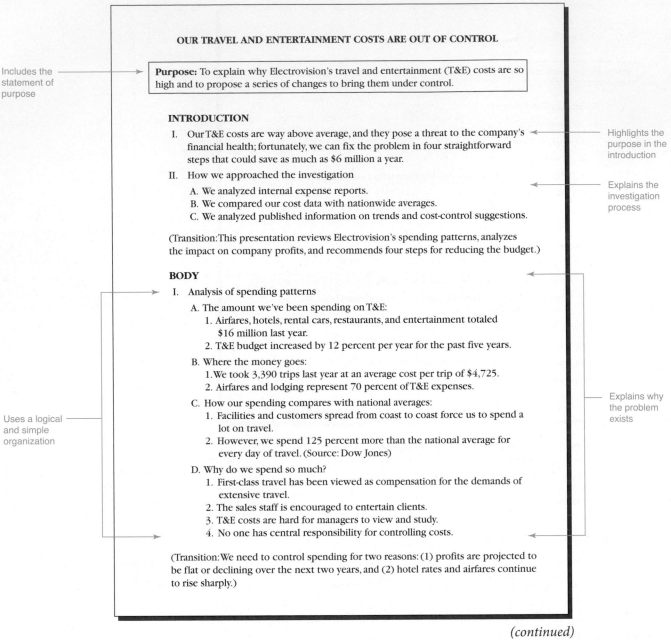

Includes the statement of purpose

Highlights the purpose in the introduction

Explains the investigation process

Uses a logical and simple organization

Explains why the problem exists

OUR TRAVEL AND ENTERTAINMENT COSTS ARE OUT OF CONTROL

Purpose: To explain why Electrovision's travel and entertainment (T&E) costs are so high and to propose a series of changes to bring them under control.

INTRODUCTION

I. Our T&E costs are way above average, and they pose a threat to the company's financial health; fortunately, we can fix the problem in four straightforward steps that could save as much as $6 million a year.

II. How we approached the investigation
   A. We analyzed internal expense reports.
   B. We compared our cost data with nationwide averages.
   C. We analyzed published information on trends and cost-control suggestions.

(Transition: This presentation reviews Electrovision's spending patterns, analyzes the impact on company profits, and recommends four steps for reducing the budget.)

BODY

I. Analysis of spending patterns
   A. The amount we've been spending on T&E:
      1. Airfares, hotels, rental cars, restaurants, and entertainment totaled $16 million last year.
      2. T&E budget increased by 12 percent per year for the past five years.
   B. Where the money goes:
      1. We took 3,390 trips last year at an average cost per trip of $4,725.
      2. Airfares and lodging represent 70 percent of T&E expenses.
   C. How our spending compares with national averages:
      1. Facilities and customers spread from coast to coast force us to spend a lot on travel.
      2. However, we spend 125 percent more than the national average for every day of travel. (Source: Dow Jones)
   D. Why do we spend so much?
      1. First-class travel has been viewed as compensation for the demands of extensive travel.
      2. The sales staff is encouraged to entertain clients.
      3. T&E costs are hard for managers to view and study.
      4. No one has central responsibility for controlling costs.

(Transition: We need to control spending for two reasons: (1) profits are projected to be flat or declining over the next two years, and (2) hotel rates and airfares continue to rise sharply.)

(continued)

Figure 16.4 Effective Outline for a 30-Minute Presentation
This outline (based on Linda Moreno's report in Chapter 15) clearly identifies the purpose and the distinct points to be made in the introduction, body, and close. Notice also how she wrote her major transitions in full sentence form to be sure she can clearly phrase these critical passages when it's time to speak.

MyBcommLab

Apply Figure 16.4's key concepts by revising a new document. Go to Chapter 16 in mybcommlab.com and select Document Makeovers.

Developing a Presentation

2 LEARNING OBJECTIVE

Explain how to adapt to your audience and develop an effective opening, body, and close for a presentation.

Although you usually don't write out a presentation word for word, you still engage in the writing process—developing your ideas, structuring support points, phrasing your transitions, and so on. Depending on the situation and your personal style, the eventual presentation might follow your initial words closely, or you might express your thoughts in fresh, spontaneous language. This section covers the tasks of adapting to your audience and composing your presentation; Chapter 17 covers the task of creating slides to accompany your talk.

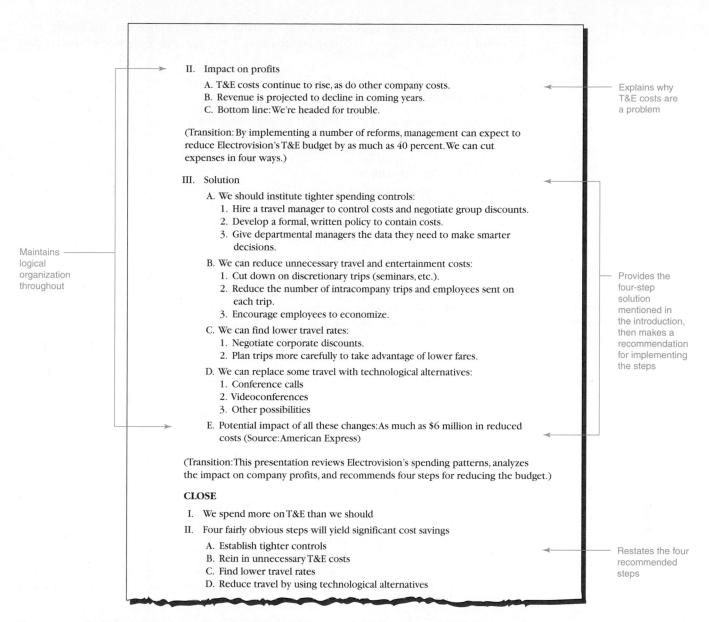

II.   Impact on profits

    A. T&E costs continue to rise, as do other company costs.
    B. Revenue is projected to decline in coming years.
    C. Bottom line: We're headed for trouble.

(Transition: By implementing a number of reforms, management can expect to reduce Electrovision's T&E budget by as much as 40 percent. We can cut expenses in four ways.)

III.   Solution

    A. We should institute tighter spending controls:
      1. Hire a travel manager to control costs and negotiate group discounts.
      2. Develop a formal, written policy to contain costs.
      3. Give departmental managers the data they need to make smarter decisions.
    B. We can reduce unnecessary travel and entertainment costs:
      1. Cut down on discretionary trips (seminars, etc.).
      2. Reduce the number of intracompany trips and employees sent on each trip.
      3. Encourage employees to economize.
    C. We can find lower travel rates:
      1. Negotiate corporate discounts.
      2. Plan trips more carefully to take advantage of lower fares.
    D. We can replace some travel with technological alternatives:
      1. Conference calls
      2. Videoconferences
      3. Other possibilities
    E. Potential impact of all these changes: As much as $6 million in reduced costs (Source: American Express)

(Transition: This presentation reviews Electrovision's spending patterns, analyzes the impact on company profits, and recommends four steps for reducing the budget.)

CLOSE

I.   We spend more on T&E than we should

II.   Four fairly obvious steps will yield significant cost savings

    A. Establish tighter controls
    B. Rein in unnecessary T&E costs
    C. Find lower travel rates
    D. Reduce travel by using technological alternatives

Marginal annotations (left): Maintains logical organization throughout

Marginal annotations (right): Explains why T&E costs are a problem / Provides the four-step solution mentioned in the introduction, then makes a recommendation for implementing the steps / Restates the four recommended steps

Figure 16.4   Effective Outline for a 30-Minute Presentation *(continued)*

ADAPTING TO YOUR AUDIENCE

Your audience's size, the venue (in person or online), your subject, your purpose, your budget, the time available for preparation, and the time allotted for your talk all influence the style of your presentation. If you're speaking to a small group, particularly people you already know, you can use a casual style that encourages audience participation. A small conference room, with your audience seated around a table, may be appropriate. Use simple visuals and invite your audience to interject comments. Deliver your remarks in a conversational tone, using notes to jog your memory if necessary.

If you're addressing a large audience or if the event is important, establish a more formal atmosphere. During formal presentations, speakers are often on a stage or platform, standing behind a lectern and using a microphone so that their remarks can be heard throughout the room or captured for broadcasting or webcasting.

When you deliver an oral presentation to people from other cultures, you may need to adapt the content of your presentation. It is also important to take into account any

Marginal note: Adapting to your audience addresses a number of issues, from speaking style to technology choices.

cultural preferences for appearance, mannerisms, and other customs. An interpreter or event host can suggest appropriate changes for a specific audience or particular occasion.

COMPOSING YOUR PRESENTATION

Like written documents, oral presentations are composed of distinct elements: the introduction, the body, and the close.

Presentation Introduction

A good introduction arouses the audience's interest in your topic, establishes your credibility, and prepares the audience for what will follow. That's a lot to pack into the first few minutes of your presentation, so give yourself plenty of time to prepare the words and visuals you'll use to get your presentation off to a great start.

If your audience isn't likely to be naturally interested in your topic, your introduction will need to build interest by relating the subject to their personal concerns.

Arousing Audience Interest Some subjects are naturally more interesting to some audiences than others. If you will be discussing a matter of profound significance that will personally affect the members of your audience, chances are they'll listen, regardless of how you begin. All you really have to do is announce your topic, and you'll have their attention. Other subjects call for more imagination. Here are six ways to arouse audience interest:[13]

- **Unite the audience around a common goal.** Invite listeners to help solve a problem, capitalize on an opportunity, or otherwise engage in the topic of your presentation.
- **Tell a story.** Well-told stories are naturally interesting and can be compelling. Of course, make sure your story illustrates an important and relevant point.
- **Pass around an example.** Psychologists say that you can get people to remember your points by appealing to their senses. A great way to do so is to pass around an example. If your company is in the textile business, let the audience handle some of your fabrics. If you sell chocolates, give everybody a taste.
- **Ask a question.** Asking questions will get the audience actively involved in your presentation and, at the same time, will give you information about them and their needs.
- **Share a startling statistic.** An intriguing, unexpected, or shocking detail can often grab the attention of your listeners.
- **Use humor.** Opening with an amusing observation about yourself, the subject matter of the presentation, or the circumstances surrounding the presentation can be an effective way to lighten the "pre-presentation jitters" for you and the audience or to make an emotional connection with your listeners. However, humor must be used with great care. Make sure any comments are relevant, appropriate, and not offensive to anyone in the audience. In general, avoid humor when you and the audience don't share the same native language or culture; it's too easy for humor to fall flat or backfire.

Regardless of which technique you choose, make sure you can give audience members a reason to care and to believe that the time they're about to spend listening to you will be worth their while.[14]

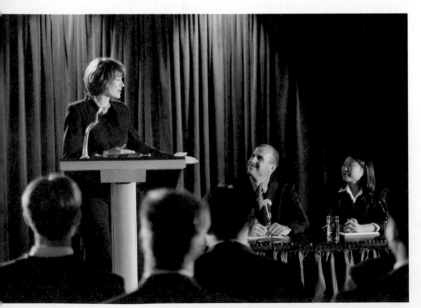

If you will be introduced by a master of ceremonies or another speaker, that person may be able to briefly itemize your qualifications as a way to build your credibility with the audience.

Building Your Credibility In addition to grabbing the audience's attention, your introduction needs to establish your credibility. If you're a well-known expert in the subject matter or have earned your audience's trust in other situations, you're already ahead of the game.

However, if you have no working relationship with your audience or if you're speaking in an area outside your known expertise, you need to establish credibility and do so quickly; people tend to decide within a few minutes whether you're worth listening to.[15]

Techniques for building credibility vary, depending on whether you will be introducing yourself or having someone else introduce you. If a master of ceremonies, a conference chair, or another person will introduce you, he or she can present your credentials so that you won't appear boastful. However, make sure that the person introducing you doesn't exaggerate your qualifications; your credibility will probably go down rather than up if this happens.

If someone else will be introducing you to the audience, you can ask this person to present your credentials.

If you will be introducing yourself, keep your comments simple. At the same time, don't be afraid to mention your accomplishments. Your listeners will be curious about your qualifications, so tell them briefly who you are and why you're the right person to be giving this presentation. Here's an example:

> I'm Karen Whitney, a market research analyst with Information Resources Corporation. For the past five years, I've specialized in studying high-technology markets. Your director of engineering, John LaBarre, has asked me to talk to you about recent trends in computer-aided design so that you'll have a better idea of how to direct your research efforts.

This speaker establishes credibility by tying her credentials to the purpose of her presentation, without boasting. By mentioning her company's name, her specialization and position, and the name of the audience's boss, she lets her listeners know immediately that she is qualified to tell them something they need to know. She connects her background to their concerns.

Previewing Your Message In addition to arousing audience interest and establishing your credibility, a good introduction gives your audience members a preview of what's ahead, helping them understand the structure and content of your message. A report reader can learn these things by looking at the table of contents and scanning the headings, but in a presentation, you need to provide that framework with a preview.

Use the preview to help your audience understand the importance, the structure, and the content of your message.

Your preview should summarize the main idea of your presentation, identify major supporting points, and indicate the order in which you'll develop those points. Tell your listeners in so many words, "This is the subject, and these are the points I will cover." Once you've established the framework, you can be confident that the audience will understand how the individual facts and figures are related to your main idea as you move into the body of your presentation. If you are using an indirect approach, your preview can discuss the nature of your main idea without disclosing it.

Presentation Body

The bulk of your speech or presentation is devoted to a discussion of the main supporting points from your outline. Whether you're using the direct or indirect approach, make sure the organization of your presentation is clear and your presentation holds the audience's attention.

Connecting Your Ideas In written documents, you can show how ideas are related on the page or screen by using a variety of design clues, such as headings, paragraph indentations, and lists. However, with oral communication—particularly when you aren't using visuals for support—you have to rely primarily on words to link various parts and ideas.

For links between sentences and paragraphs, use transitional words and phrases: *therefore, because, in addition, in contrast, moreover, for example, consequently, nevertheless,* or *finally.* To link major sections of a presentation, use complete sentences or paragraphs, such as "Now that we've reviewed the problem, let's take a look at some solutions." Every time you shift topics, be sure to stress the connection between ideas. Summarize what's been said and then preview what's to come. You might also want to call attention to the

Use transitions to repeat key ideas and help the audience follow along, particularly in longer presentations.

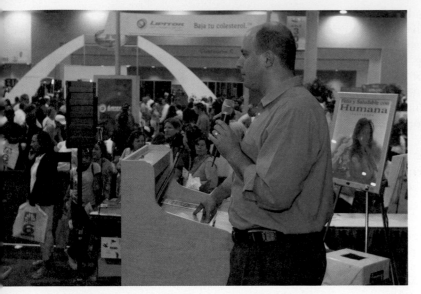

When attempting to hold an audience's attention, public speakers sometimes face distractions in the background. It takes a focused speaker to overcome such physical interruptions and get his or her message across.

transitions by using gestures, changing your tone of voice, or introducing a visual, as Chapter 17 points out.

Holding Your Audience's Attention   After you've successfully captured your audience's attention in your introduction, you need to work to keep it throughout the body of your presentation. In addition to the general challenge of keeping readers interested, you have to compensate for another inescapable fact of oral presentations: Your audience can think and read faster than you can speak. And with online presentations, where people in remote locations are sitting alone at their computers, they may be tempted by numerous distractions. Here are a few helpful tips for keeping the audience tuned into your message:

- **Relate your subject to your audience's needs.** People are naturally most interested in things that affect them personally.
- **Anticipate your audience's questions.** Try to anticipate as many questions as you can and address these questions in the body of your presentation. You'll also want to prepare and reserve additional material to use during the question-and-answer period, in case the audience asks for greater detail.

> The most important way to hold an audience's attention is to show how your message relates to their individual needs and concerns.
>
> Plan your close carefully so that your audience leaves with your main idea fresh in their minds.

- **Use clear, vivid language.** If your presentation will involve abstract ideas, show how those abstractions connect with everyday life. Use familiar words, short sentences, and concrete examples. Be sure to use some variety as well; repeating the same words and phrases puts people to sleep.
- **Explain the relationship between your subject and familiar ideas.** Show how your subject is related to ideas that audience members already understand and give people a way to categorize and remember your points.[16] Be sure to make connections that your listeners are sure to get, too. For example, when Peter Principato and his team were recently brainstorming how to present a young writer/director to studio executives, Principato rejected the suggestion of comparing him to Charlie Kaufman. Kaufman is revered among comedy insiders, but Principato wasn't sure a mainstream television executive would understand the reference.[17]
- **Ask for opinions or pause occasionally for questions or comments.** Audience feedback helps you determine whether your listeners understand a key point before you launch into another section. Asking questions or providing comments also gives your audience members a chance to switch for a time from listening to participating, which helps them engage with your message and develop a sense of shared ownership.
- **Illustrate your ideas with visuals.** As Chapter 17 discusses, you might want to develop visuals for your presentation and coordinate them with your delivery. Visuals enliven your message, help you connect with audience members, and help people remember your message more effectively.

Presentation Close

The close of a speech or presentation has two critical jobs to accomplish: making sure your listeners leave with the key points from your talk clear in their minds and in the appropriate emotional state. For example, if the purpose of your presentation was to warn company managers that their out-of-control spending threatens the company's survival, you want them to leave with that message ringing in their ears—and with enough concern for the problem to stimulate changes in their behavior.

Restating Your Main Points   Use the close to succinctly restate your main points, emphasizing what you want your listeners to do or to think. For example, to close a presentation on your company's executive compensation program, you could repeat your specific recommendations and then conclude with a memorable statement to motivate your audience to take action:

> We can all be proud of the way our company has grown. However, if we want to continue that growth, we need to adjust our executive compensation program to reflect competitive practices. If we don't, our best people will look for opportunities elsewhere. To review, our research has shown that we need to do four things to improve executive compensation:
>
> - Increase the overall level of compensation
> - Install a cash bonus program
> - Offer a variety of stock-based incentives
> - Improve our health insurance and pension benefits
>
> By making these improvements, we can attract and keep the level of talent we need to take on our industry's largest competitors.

Such repetition of key ideas greatly improves the chance that your audience will hear your message in the way you intended.

Ending with Clarity and Confidence   If you've been successful with the introduction and body of your presentation, your listeners now have the information they need, and they're in the right frame of mind to put that information to good use. Now you're ready to end on a strong note that confirms expectations about any actions or decisions that will follow the presentation—and to bolster the audience's confidence in you and your message one final time.

> Plan your final statement carefully so you can end on a strong, positive note.

Some presentations require the audience to reach a decision or agree to take specific action, in which case the close provides a clear wrap-up. If the audience agrees on an issue covered in the presentation, briefly review the consensus. If they don't agree, make the lack of consensus clear by saying something like, "We seem to have some fundamental disagreement on this question." Then be ready to suggest a method of resolving the differences.

> If you need to have the audience make a decision or agree to take action, make sure the responsibilities for doing so are clear.

If you expect any action to occur as a result of your speech, be sure to explain who is responsible for doing what. List the action items and, if possible within the time available, establish due dates and assign responsibility for each task.

Make sure your final remarks are memorable and expressed in a tone that is appropriate to the situation. If your presentation is a persuasive request for project funding, you might emphasize the importance of this project and your team's ability to complete it on schedule and within budget. Expressing confident optimism will send the message that you believe in your ability to perform.

> Make sure your final remarks are memorable and have the right emotional tone.

Whatever final message is appropriate, think through your closing remarks carefully before stepping in front of the audience. You don't want to wind up on stage with nothing to say but "Well, I guess that's it."

Delivering a Presentation

With an outline, speaking notes, and any visual aids you plan to use (see Chapter 17 for those), you're almost ready to deliver your presentation. This section covers five essential topics that will help you prepare for and deliver engaging and effective presentations, starting with choosing your presentation method.

> **3 LEARNING OBJECTIVE**
>
> Discuss five steps for delivering a successful presentation.

CHOOSING YOUR PRESENTATION METHOD

Depending on the circumstance of your presentation, you can choose from a variety of delivery methods:

- **Memorizing.** Except for extremely short speeches, trying to memorize an entire presentation is not a good idea. In the best of circumstances, you'll probably sound stilted; in the worst, you might forget your lines. Besides, you'll often need to address audience questions during your speech, so you need to be flexible enough to adjust your speech as you go. However, memorizing a quotation, an opening paragraph, and some strong finishing remarks can bolster your confidence and strengthen your delivery.

- **Reading.** In a few instances, you may want to read your speech from a prepared script. For instance, policy statements and legal documents are sometimes read in full because the wording can be critical. However, unless you're required or expected to read your presentation verbatim, reading is not a good choice. If you read from a prepared script, chances are you won't speak as naturally as you would otherwise, and the result will be a monotonous, uninspiring presentation.[18] After all, if all you're doing is reading, why not just write a report and let your audience members read it themselves? If you must read your speech for some reason, practice enough so that you can still make periodic eye contact with your audience and make sure the printout of your speech is easy to read.

Speaking from carefully prepared notes is the best delivery mode for nearly all presentations.

- **Speaking from an outline or notes.** Speaking with the help of an outline or note cards is nearly always the easiest and most effective delivery mode. The outline or notes guide you through the flow of the speech while giving you the freedom to speak naturally and spontaneously, to maintain eye contact with your listeners, and to respond and improvise as circumstances warrant. If you print note cards, use heavy note cards instead of regular paper. They're quieter and easier to flip through as you talk.

- **Impromptu speaking.** From time to time, you may be called upon unexpectedly to give an *impromptu* or *extemporaneous* speech on the spot, without the benefit of any planning or practice. Take a few seconds to identify the one key idea you want to share with the audience. That idea alone may be enough to meet the audience's expectations, or it might be enough to get you started and allow you to piece together additional ideas on the fly. Then think about a structure that would help convey that idea. Telling a brief story can be particularly effective in these situations because the structure helps you organize what you want to say, even as you're speaking. If you are asked to speak on a topic and simply don't have the information at hand, don't try to fake it. Instead, offer to get the information to the audience after the meeting or ask if anyone else in the room can respond. Finally, before you even enter the meeting or other setting, if there is a chance you might be called on to say a few words, you can "prepare for the surprise" by thinking through what you might say in response to potential questions.[19]

Regardless of which delivery mode you use, be sure that you're thoroughly familiar with your subject. Knowing what you're talking about is the best way to build your self-confidence. If you stumble, get interrupted, or suffer equipment failures, your expertise will help you get back on track.

PRACTICING YOUR DELIVERY

The more you practice, the more confidence you'll have in yourself and your material.

Practice is key to the success with presentations, no matter how much experience you have. Apple co-founder and CEO Steve Jobs, who is widely admired for his new-product presentations and has decades of experience speaking in front of huge crowds, still spends hours practicing his delivery.[20]

Practice helps ensure that you appear polished and confident, and it lets you verify the operation of visuals and equipment. A test audience can tell you if your slides are understandable and whether your delivery is effective. If you are unable to pull together a test audience, record yourself on video to check your voice, timing, phrasing, and physical gestures.

A day or two before you're ready to step on stage for an important talk, make sure you and your presentation are ready:

Make sure you're comfortable with the equipment you'll be expected to use; you don't want to be fumbling with controls while the audience is watching and waiting.

- Can you present your material naturally, without reading your slides?
- Could you still make a compelling and complete presentation if you experience an equipment failure and have to proceed without using your slides at all?
- Is the equipment working, and do you know how to work it?
- Is your timing on track?
- Can you easily pronounce all the words you plan to use?
- Have you anticipated likely questions and objections?

With experience, you'll get a feel for how much practice is enough in any given situation. Practicing helps keep you on track, helps you maintain a conversational tone with your audience, and boosts your confidence and composure.

You'll know you've practiced enough when you can present the material at a comfortable pace and in a natural, conversational tone.

PREPARING TO SPEAK

In addition to knowing your material thoroughly and practicing your delivery, make sure that your location is ready, you have everything you'll need, and you're prepared to address audiences from other cultures, if that applies.

Whenever you can, scout the location for your presentation in advance. Check the seating arrangement to make sure it's appropriate for your needs and the audience's. Verify the availability and operation of all the equipment and supplies you're counting on, from the projection system to simple but vital necessities such as flip charts and marking pens. If you're using electronic slides, make sure you know how to get the file from your computer or other device to the projection system.

If possible, visit the speaking venue ahead of time to familiarize yourself with the facilities and the equipment.

If you're addressing audience members who speak a different native language, consider using an interpreter. Working with an interpreter does constrain your presentation somewhat. For instance, you must speak slowly enough for the interpreter to keep up with you. Send your interpreter a copy of your speaking notes and your visuals as far in advance of your presentation as possible. If your audience is likely to include persons with hearing impairments, be sure to team up with a sign-language interpreter as well.

When you deliver an oral presentation to people from other cultures, take into account cultural differences in appearances, mannerisms, and other customs. Your interpreter or host will be able to suggest appropriate changes for a specific audience or occasion.

OVERCOMING ANXIETY

Recognize that nervousness is an indication that you care about your audience, your topic, and the occasion. These techniques will help you convert anxiety into positive energy:[21]

Preparation is the best antidote for anxiety; it gives you confidence that you know your material and that you recover from any glitches you might encounter.

- **Stop worrying about being perfect.** Everyone makes mistakes, whether it's tripping over a hard-to-pronounce word or literally tripping while on stage. Successful speakers focus on making an authentic connection with their listeners, rather than on trying to deliver a note-perfect presentation.
- **Prepare more material than necessary.** Combined with having a genuine interest in your topic, having extra knowledge will reduce your anxiety.
- **Practice.** The more familiar you are with your material, the less panic you'll feel.
- **Visualize your success.** Visualize mental images of yourself in front of the audience, feeling confident, prepared, and able to handle any situation that might arise.[22] Remember that your audience wants you to succeed, too.
- **Remember to breathe.** Tension can lead people to breathe in a rapid and shallow fashion, which can create a lightheaded feeling. Breathe slowly and deeply to maintain a sense of calm and confidence.
- **Be ready with your opening line.** Have your first sentence memorized and on the tip of your tongue.
- **Be comfortable.** Dress appropriately but as comfortably as possible. Drink plenty of water ahead of time to hydrate your voice (bring a bottle of water with you, too).
- **Take a three-second break.** If you sense that you're starting to race, pause and arrange your notes or perform some other small task while taking several deep breaths. Then start again at your normal pace. If you feel that you're losing your audience, try to pull them back by asking for comments or questions.
- **Concentrate on your message and your audience, not on yourself.** When you're busy thinking about your subject and observing your audience's response, you tend to forget your fears.
- **Maintain eye contact with friendly audience members.** Eye contact not only makes you appear sincere, confident, and trustworthy but can give you positive feedback as well.
- **Keep going.** Things usually get better as you move along, with each successful minute giving you more and more confidence.

COMMUNICATION MISCUES Disasters Will Happen—Are You Ready?

You've researched your topic, analyzed your audience, prepared a compelling message, crafted eye-catching visuals, and practiced until you're running like a smooth machine. You're ready to go.

Then you wake up with a sore throat and half a voice. You grab a few lozenges, hope for the best, and drive to the conference facility in plenty of time to set up your equipment. Oops, somebody forgot to tell you that your presentation has been moved up by an hour, and your audience is already in the room waiting for you. You scramble to turn on your laptop and get it connected to the projector, only to discover that you forgot the power cord and your battery is low. But that won't be a problem: Your laptop is dead anyway. Feeling smart, you pull out a CD-ROM with a backup copy of your PowerPoint slides and ask to use one of the several laptops you see scattered around the room. Nice idea, but they're equipped only with USB flash drives, so your CD is useless. The audience is getting restless; a few people get up to leave. You keep hoping you'll wake up from this bad dream so that your great day can really start. Sorry. This *is* your day.

Ask any business speaker with a few years of experience, and you'll hear all these horror stories and a few more. People who've driven to the wrong conference center, hit themselves in the head with a microphone, tripped over wires, started with a sure-fire joke that generated nothing but cold stares, or been rendered speechless by tough questions. Hoping you'll be spared isn't an effective response. You must be prepared for when—not if—something goes wrong.

If you assume that something *will* go wrong at some point, you can make peace with the possibility and focus on backup planning. Experts suggest that you make a list of every major problem you might encounter and imagine how you'll respond when these calamities strike you on the day of a big presentation. As much as possible, create a backup plan, such as calling ahead to reserve a second projector in the event that yours gets lost in transit. You won't be able to put backup resources in place for every possible glitch, but by at least thinking through the possibilities, you can decide how you'll respond. When disaster does strike, you'll look like a polished pro instead of a befuddled novice.

CAREER APPLICATIONS

1. If you spy trouble ahead in your presentation, such as noticing that your laptop battery is about to go dead or that you somehow have an old copy of the presentation file, should you tell your audience what's wrong? Or should you try to "wing it"? Explain your answer.

2. What steps can you take to make absolutely sure that you have a usable backup copy of your electronic presentation slides outside your office? Why is this important?

No one enjoys mistakes, equipment failures, and other troubles, but they are survivable. To learn how several experienced presenters have overcome some serious glitches, see "Communication Miscues: Disasters Will Happen—Are You Ready?"

Nonverbal signals tell the audience how you're feeling, so pay attention to the signals you send.

Confident delivery starts as soon as you become the focus of attention, before you even begin to speak, so don't rush. As you approach the front of the room, walk with confidence, breathe deeply, and stand up straight. Face your audience, adjust the microphone and other equipment, as needed, count to three slowly, and then scan the audience. When you find a friendly face, make eye contact and smile. Look away, count to three again, and then begin your presentation.[23] If you are nervous, this slow, controlled beginning will help you establish rapport and appear more confident. Make sure your nonverbal signals send a message of confidence.

Your posture is important in projecting more confidence. Stand tall, with your weight on both feet and your shoulders back. Avoid gripping the lectern or other physical structure. Use your hands to emphasize your remarks with appropriate gestures. Meanwhile, vary your facial expressions to make the message more dynamic.

Finally, think about the sound of your voice. Studies indicate that people who speak with lower pitches at a slightly faster-than-average rate are perceived as being more credible.[24] Try to sound poised and confident, varying your pitch and speaking rate to add emphasis. For instance, slow down slightly when you're making an important point.[25] Speak clearly and crisply, articulating all the syllables, and sound enthusiastic about what you're saying. Use silence instead of meaningless filler words such as *um, you know, okay,* and *like.* Silence adds dramatic punch and gives the audience time to think about your message.

HANDLING QUESTIONS RESPONSIVELY

The question-and-answer (Q&A) period is often one of the most important parts of a presentation. Answering questions gives you a chance to obtain important information, to emphasize your main idea and supporting points, and to build enthusiasm for your point of view. When you're speaking to high-ranking executives in your company, the Q&A period may consume most of the time allotted for your presentation.[26]

Whether or not you can establish ground rules for Q&A depends on the audience and the situation. If you're presenting to a small group of upper managers or potential investors, for example, you will probably have no say in the matter: Audience members will likely ask as many questions as they want, whenever they want, to get the information they need. On the other hand, if you are presenting to your peers or a large public audience, establish some guidelines, such as the number of questions allowed per person and the overall time limit for questions.

Don't assume that you can handle whatever comes up without some preparation.[27] Learn enough about your audience members to get an idea of their concerns and think through answers to potential questions.

When people ask questions, pay attention to nonverbal signals to help determine what each person really means. Repeat the question to confirm your understanding and to ensure that the entire audience has heard it. If the question is vague or confusing, ask for clarification; then give a simple, direct answer.

If you are asked a difficult or complex question, avoid the temptation to sidestep it. Offer to meet with the questioner afterward if the issue isn't relevant to the rest of the audience or if giving an adequate answer would take too long. If you don't know the answer, don't pretend that you do. Instead, offer to get a complete answer as soon as possible or ask if someone else can offer information on the topic.

Be on guard for audience members who use questions to make impromptu speeches or to take control of your presentation. Without offending anyone, find a way to stay in control. You might admit that you and the questioner have differing opinions and, before calling on someone else, offer to get back to the questioner after you've done more research.[28]

If a question ever puts you on the hot seat, respond honestly but keep your cool. Look the person in the eye, answer the question as well as you can, and keep your emotions under control. Defuse hostility by paraphrasing the question and asking the questioner to confirm that you've understood it correctly. Maintain a businesslike tone of voice and a pleasant expression.[29]

When the time allotted for your presentation is almost up, prepare the audience for the end by saying something like, "We have time for one more question." After you reply to that last question, summarize the main idea of the presentation and thank people for their attention. Conclude with the same confident demeanor you've had from the beginning.

> Don't leave the question-and-answer period to chance: anticipate likely questions and think through your answers.

> If you don't have the complete answer to an important question, offer to provide it after the presentation.

> If you ever face hostile questions, respond honestly and directly while keeping your cool.

> No matter how the presentation has gone, conclude in a strong, confident manner.

Incorporating Technology in Your Presentation

Like much of the rest of business communication, presentations have been high-tech affairs in many companies. Two aspects you will most likely encounter on the job are the backchannel and online presentations.

> **4** | LEARNING OBJECTIVE
>
> Explain the growing importance of the backchannel in presentations, and list six steps for giving effective presentations online.

EMBRACING THE BACKCHANNEL

Many business presentations these days involve more than just the spoken conversation between the speaker and his or her audience. Using Twitter and other electronic media, audience members often carry on their own parallel communication during a presentation via the **backchannel**, which presentation expert Cliff Atkinson defines as "a line of communication created by people in an audience to connect with others inside or outside the room, with or without the knowledge of the speaker."[30] Chances are you've participated in a backchannel already, such as when texting with your classmates or live-blogging during a lecture.

The backchannel presents both risks and rewards for business presenters. On the negative side, for example, listeners can research your claims the instant you make them and spread the word quickly if they think your information is shaky. The backchannel also gives contrary audience members more leverage, which can lead to presentations spinning out of control. On the plus side, listeners who are excited about your message can build support for it, expand on it, and spread it to a much larger audience in a matter of seconds. You can also get valuable feedback during and after presentations.[31]

> Twitter and other social media are dramatically changing business presentations by making it easy for all audience members to participate in the *backchannel*.

REAL-TIME UPDATES
Learn More by Watching This Video

Maximize the rewards of the backchannel and minimize the risks

This webinar hosted by author Cliff Atkinson outlines the principles of the social media backchannel and analyzes a real-life presentation where the backchannel spurred an audience revolt and what presenters can learn from this. Go to http://real-timeupdates.com/bct11 and click on "Learn More." If you are using MyBcommLab, you can access Real-Time Updates within each chapter or under Student Study Tools.

Resist the urge to ignore or fight the backchannel; instead, learn how to use it to your advantage.

By embracing the backchannel, rather than trying to fight it or ignore it, presenters can use this powerful force to their advantage. Follow these tips to make the backchannel work for you:[32]

- **Integrate social media into the presentation process.** For example, you can set up a formal backchannel yourself using tools such as BackNoise (http://backnoise.com); create a website for the presentation so that people can access relevant resources during or after the presentation; create a Twitter hashtag that everyone can use when sending tweets; or display the Twitterstream during Q&A so that everyone can see the questions and comments on the backchannel.
- **Monitor and ask for feedback.** Using a free service such as Tweetdeck, which organizes tweets by hashtag and other variables, you can monitor in real time what the people in the audience are writing about. To avoid trying to monitor the backchannel while speaking, you can schedule "Twitter breaks," during which you review comments and respond as needed.
- **Review comments to improve your presentation.** After a presentation is over, review comments on audience members' Twitter accounts and blogs to see which parts confused them, which parts excited them, and which parts seemed to have little effect (based on few or no comments).
- **Automatically tweet key points from your presentation while you speak.** Add-ons for presentation software can send out prewritten tweets as you show specific slides during a presentation. By making your key points readily available, you make it easy for listeners to retweet and comment on your presentation.
- **Establish expectations with the audience.** Explain that you welcome audience participation but that to ensure a positive experience for everyone, comments should be civil, relevant, and productive.

GIVING PRESENTATIONS ONLINE

In some companies, online presentations have already become a routine matter, conducted via internal groupware, virtual meeting systems, or webcast systems designed specifically for online presentations. Your audience members will view your presentations on a variety of devices, from smartphones to individual computer screens to large-screen monitors in specially built conferencing facilities.

Online presentations give you a way to reach more people in less time, but they require special preparation and skills.

The benefits of online presentations are considerable, including the opportunity to communicate with a geographically dispersed audience at a fraction of the cost of travel and the ability for a project team or an entire organization to meet at a moment's notice. However, the challenges for a presenter can be significant, thanks to that layer of technology between you and your audience. Many of those "human moments" that guide and encourage the speaker through an in-person presentation won't travel across the digital divide. For instance, presenters may struggle to discern whether listeners are bored or confused because their view of them is often confined to small video images.

To ensure successful online presentations, keep the following advice in mind:

- **Consider sending preview study materials ahead of time.** Doing so allows audience members to familiarize themselves with any important background information. Also, by using a free service such as SlideShare (www.slideshare.net), you can distribute your presentation slides to either public or private audiences, and you can record audio narrative to make your presentations function on their own.[33] Some presenters advise against giving out your slides ahead of time, however, because doing so gives away the ending of your presentation. If time allows, you can prepare preview materials that don't include your entire slide set.
- **Rehearse using the system live, if at all possible.** Presenting online has all the challenges of other presentations, with the additional burden of operating the presentation

system while you are talking. Practice with at least one test viewer so you're comfortable using the system.[34]

- **Keep your presentation as simple as possible.** Break complicated slides down into multiple slides if necessary and keep the direction of your discussion clear so that no one gets lost.
- **Ask for feedback frequently.** Except on the most advanced telepresence systems, you won't have as much of the visual feedback that alerts you when audience members are confused, and many online viewers will be reluctant to call attention to themselves by interrupting you to ask for clarification. Setting up a backchannel via Twitter or as part of your online meeting system will help in this regard.
- **Consider the viewing experience from the audience members' point of view.** Will they be able to see what you think they can see? For instance, webcast video is often displayed in a small window on-screen, so viewers may miss important details.
- **Allow plenty of time for everyone to get connected and familiar with the screen they're viewing.** Build extra time into your schedule to ensure that everyone is connected and ready to start.

Online presentations let you reach a wider audience, but the lack of direct contact forces you to take a more active role in engaging your audience.

With online presentations, you often can't rely on nonverbal signals to sense audience confusion or disagreement, so check in with your listeners frequently to see if they have questions.

Last but not least, don't get lost in the technology. Use these tools whenever they'll help but remember that the most important aspect of any presentation is getting the audience to receive, understand, and embrace your message.

For a reminder of the steps to take in developing an oral presentation, refer to "Checklist: Developing Oral and Online Presentations." For the latest advice on planning presentations, visit http://real-timeupdates.com/bct11 and click on Chapter 16.

✓ Checklist   Developing Oral and Online Presentations

A. Planning your presentation.
- Analyze the situation by defining your purpose and developing an audience profile.
- Select the right medium.
- Organize your presentation by defining the main idea, limiting the scope, choosing your approach, and preparing your outline.

B. Developing your presentation.
- Adapt to your audience by tailoring your style and language.
- Compose your presentation by preparing an introduction, a body, and a close.
- Use your introduction to arouse audience interest, build your credibility, and preview your message.
- Use the body to connect your ideas and hold your audience's attention.
- Close with confidence and clarity, restating your main points and describing the next steps.

C. Delivering your presentation.
- Choose a presentation method, which should be speaking from an outline or notes in nearly all situations.
- Practice until you can deliver your material naturally, without reading your slides.

- Prepare to speak by verifying the operation of all the equipment you'll need to use.
- Determine whether you should use an interpreter.
- Overcome anxiety by preparing thoroughly.
- Handle questions responsively.

D. Embracing the backchannel.
- Integrate social media into the presentation process.
- Monitor and ask for feedback.
- Review comments to improve your presentation.
- Automatically tweet key points from your presentation while you speak.
- Establish expectations with the audience.

E. Giving presentations online.
- Consider sending preview study materials ahead of time.
- Rehearse using the system live, if at all possible.
- Keep your presentation as simple as possible.
- Ask for feedback frequently.
- Consider the viewing experience from the audience members' point of view.
- Allow plenty of time for everyone to get connected and familiar with the screen they're viewing.

Quick Learning Guide

MyBcommLab

If your course uses MyBcommLab, log on to www.mybcommlab.com to access the following study and assessment aids associated with this chapter:

- Video applications
- Real-Time Updates
- Peer review activity
- Pre/post test
- Personalized study plan
- Model documents
- Sample presentations

If you are not using MyBcommLab, you can access Real-Time Updates through http://real-timeupdates.com/bct11.

CHAPTER OUTLINE

Planning a Presentation
Analyzing the Situation
Selecting the Right Medium
Organizing Your Presentation

Developing a Presentation
Adapting to Your Audience
Composing Your Presentation

Delivering a Presentation
Choosing Your Presentation Method
Practicing Your Delivery
Preparing to Speak
Overcoming Anxiety
Handling Questions Responsively

Incorporating Technology in Your Presentation
Embracing the Backchannel
Giving Presentations Online

SUMMARY OF LEARNING OBJECTIVES

1 **Describe the tasks involved in analyzing the situation for a presentation and organizing a presentation.** Although you rarely want to write out a presentation word for word, the three-step writing process is easy to adapt to presentations. The steps you take in planning presentations are generally the same as with any other business message: analyze the situation, gather information, select the right medium, and organize the information. The purpose of most business presentations is to inform or to persuade, although you may occasionally need to make a collaborative presentation. When you develop your audience profile, anticipate the likely emotional state of your audience members and plan to diffuse emotional situations if needed.

Organizing a presentation requires the same general tasks as organizing a written message (define your main idea, limit your scope, select the direct or indirect approach, and outline your content), but pay special attention to the demands a presentation puts on listeners. They are largely captive to your timing and sequence, so make doubly sure you have a clear purpose, and limit your scope to convey your main idea and necessary supporting points within your allotted time frame. At the same time, take advantage of the flexibility you have with speeches and presentations to adjust the flow and level of detail on the fly if you sense that the audience wants different information than you originally planned. After you complete your *planning outline*, consider simplifying it to create a *speaking outline* to guide you during your presentation.

2 **Explain how to adapt to your audience and develop an effective opening, body, and close for a presentation.** To adapt to your audience, assess your audience's size, the venue (in person or online), your subject, your purpose, your budget, and time available for preparation, and the time allotted for your presentation. Determine whether you need to adjust your presentation or engage an interpreter when addressing audiences from other cultures, and assess the specific circumstances in which you'll be making your presentation.

You rarely write out a presentation in full, but plan your word and phrase choices so you can speak in a way that delivers planned messages in a spontaneous way. This step also includes creating whatever visual support materials you plan to use.

An effective introduction arouses audience interest in your topic, builds your credibility, and gives your audience a preview of your message. If your topic doesn't naturally interest the audience, you need to work extra hard in your introduction (and throughout the presentation) to relate the material to the audience in as personal a manner as possible. If you can't demonstrate credibility in your subject area, you can "borrow" credibility from recognized experts by incorporating their insights and opinions into your presentation (giving proper credit, of course). Previewing your message in the introduction helps the audience members recognize the importance of your material and gives them a chance to prepare for it by understanding how you plan to present it.

The bulk of your speech or presentation is devoted to a discussion of the main supporting points from your outline. Throughout the body of your talk, take care to connect your supporting points so that listeners can follow your thinking. Also work to hold your audience's attention by relating your subject to their needs, anticipating their questions, using clear and vivid language, relating your subject to familiar ideas, asking for questions or comments, and illustrating your ideas with visuals.

The close of a speech or presentation has two critical jobs to accomplish: making sure your listeners leave with the key points from your talk clear in their minds and in the appropriate emotional state.

3 **Discuss five steps for delivering a successful presentation.** First, choose the best delivery method, which is speaking naturally and spontaneously from notes or a speaking outline in nearly all instances. Second, practice until you can deliver your material naturally, without reading your slides. Third, prepare to speak by making sure that your location is ready, you have everything you'll need, and you're prepared to address audiences from other cultures, if that applies. Fourth, work to overcome anxiety before and during your presentation by letting go of worrying about being perfect, preparing more material than necessary, visualizing your success, remembering to breathe, being ready with your opening line, making yourself comfortable, taking a three-second break if you sense that you're starting to race, concentrating on your message and your audience rather than on yourself, maintaining eye contact with friendly audience members, and keeping going even if you stumble. Fifth, handle questions responsively by determining whether you can set boundaries for the Q&A period, prepare answers to potential questions, pay attention to nonverbal signals and be sure to respond to all questions, don't let questioners take control of the presentation, face hostile questions head-on without getting defensive, and alert the audience when the Q&A period is almost over.

④ Explain the growing importance of the backchannel in presentations, and list six steps for giving effective presentations online. The backchannel is a parallel conversation taking place among audience members and other interested parties using Twitter and other media. To take advantage of the backchannel, you can integrate social media into your presentation, monitor and ask for feedback, review point by point comments to improve your presentation, automatically tweet key points from your presentation while you speak, and establish expectations with the audience.

To ensure a successful online presentation, consider sending preview materials ahead of time, keep your content and presentation as simple as possible, ask for feedback frequently, consider the viewing experience from the audience's side, and give participants time to get connected.

 Checklist

Developing Oral and Online Presentations

A. Planning your presentation.
- Analyze the situation by defining your purpose and developing an audience profile.
- Select the right medium.
- Organize your presentation by defining the main idea, limiting the scope, choosing your approach, and preparing your outline.

B. Developing your presentation.
- Adapt to your audience by tailoring your style and language.
- Compose your presentation by preparing an introduction, a body, and a close.
- Use your introduction to arouse audience interest, build your credibility, and preview your message.
- Use the body to connect your ideas and hold your audience's attention.
- Close with confidence and clarity, restating your main points and describing the next steps.

C. Delivering your presentation.
- Choose a presentation method, which should be speaking from an outline or notes in nearly all situations.
- Practice until you can deliver your material naturally, without reading your slides.
- Prepare to speak by verifying the operation of all the equipment you'll need to use.
- Determine whether you should use an interpreter.
- Overcome anxiety by preparing thoroughly.
- Handle questions responsively.

D. Embracing the backchannel.
- Integrate social media into the presentation process.
- Monitor and ask for feedback.
- Review comments to improve your presentation.
- Automatically tweet key points from your presentation while you speak.
- Establish expectations with the audience.

E. Giving presentations online.
- Consider sending preview study materials ahead of time.
- Rehearse using the system live, if at all possible.
- Keep your presentation as simple as possible.
- Ask for feedback frequently.
- Consider the viewing experience from the audience members' point of view.
- Allow plenty of time for everyone to get connected and familiar with the screen they're viewing.

COMMUNICATION CHALLENGES AT **PRINCIPATO-YOUNG ENTERTAINMENT**

You share Peter Principato's love of comedy, and now you get to learn from his decades of experience in the business. You've joined Principato-Young as his assistant, replacing the former assistant, who was just promoted to a talent manager with her own list of clients. That is the same career path you hope to pursue, so this opportunity seems perfect. Practice your presentation skills with these two challenges.

INDIVIDUAL CHALLENGE: Distilling something as complicated as a movie or a TV series down to a single sentence is a skill that will serve you well in any profession. Choose three of your all-time favorite movies and write a one-sentence "pitch" for each one, imagining yourself as the writer or director who is trying to convince a studio to spend millions of dollars to produce it.

TEAM CHALLENGE: In a team assigned by your instructor, pick a TV or web-based comedy program (something appropriate to discuss in class). Get a feel for the show, including its style, content, and characters—and what makes it distinct in the crowded marketplace. Now imagine you're turning back the clock to a year or so before this show started, and it's your job to pitch it to a studio executive who will make the decision to fund its production. Develop a five-minute pitch, following Principato's advice of leading with a memorable one-sentence introduction about what the show is, expanding on that with a one-paragraph introduction (be sure to identify the key characters), followed by ideas for a few episodes (you can use actual episodes for this). Be prepared to pitch your show to the class.

TEST YOUR KNOWLEDGE

To review chapter content related to each question, refer to the indicated Learning Objective.

1. What skills do business presentations give you the opportunity to practice and demonstrate? [LO-1]
2. What are the two most common purposes for giving presentations? [LO-1]
3. Why do you have to limit your scope when planning a presentation? [LO-1]
4. How can outlines help you with the writing and delivery of a presentation? [LO-1]
5. What three goals should you accomplish during the introduction of a presentation? [LO-2]
6. How can you get and keep the audience's attention? [LO-2]
7. How does the delivery method of impromptu speaking differ from the delivery method of speaking from notes? [LO-3]
8. As a speaker, what nonverbal signals can you send to appear more confident? [LO-3]
9. What can speakers do to maintain control during the question-and-answer period of a presentation? [LO-3]
10. What is the backchannel? [LO-4]

APPLY YOUR KNOWLEDGE

To review chapter content related to each question, refer to the indicated Learning Objective.

1. How might the audience's attitude affect the amount of audience interaction during or after a presentation? Explain your answer. [LO-1]

2. What role can entertainment play in an effective presentation? [LO-2]
3. From the speaker's perspective, what are the advantages and disadvantages of responding to questions from the audience throughout a presentation rather than just afterward? From the listener's perspective, which approach would you prefer? Why? [LO-3]
4. Letting go of the idea that you have to be perfect can reduce your anxiety before a presentation. However, is it possible to create ethical problems by being too relaxed about your message and your performance? Explain your answer. [LO-3]
5. What are the possible consequences of ignoring the backchannel during a presentation to a public audience (such as at a convention)? [LO-4]

PRACTICE YOUR SKILLS

Messages for Analysis

Message 16.A: Analyzing the Structure of a Presentation [LO-1]

Find the transcript of a business-oriented speech or presentation by searching online for "speech transcription" or "presentation transcription." You can also browse www.americanrhetoric.com, which has thousands of transcriptions from speeches on a variety of subjects. Examine both the introduction and the close and analyze how these two sections work together to emphasize the main idea. Does the speaker want the audience to take any specific actions? To change any particular beliefs or feelings?

Next, identify the transitional sentences or phrases that clarify the speech's structure for the listener, especially those that help the speaker shift between supporting points. Using these transitions as clues, list the main message and supporting points; then indicate how each transitional phrase links the current supporting point to the succeeding one. Finally, prepare a brief (two- to three-minute) oral presentation summarizing your analysis for your class.

Message 16.B: Did the Introduction Get Your Attention? [LO-2]

To access this message, visit http://real-timeupdates.com/bct11, click on "Student Assignments," and select "Chapter 16, page 491, Message 16.B." Download and listen to this podcast, which is the introduction of a presentation to college seniors. Identify at least two techniques the speaker uses to try to grab your attention.

Exercises

Active links for all websites in this chapter can be found on MyBcommLab; see your User Guide for instructions on accessing the content for this chapter. Each activity is labeled according to the primary skill or skills you will need to use. To review relevant chapter content, you can refer to the indicated Learning Objective. In some instances, supporting information will be found in another chapter, as indicated.

1. **Presentations: Planning and Developing [LO-1], [LO-2]** With a team of three other students, prepare a detailed outline (including descriptions of any visuals you would plan to use) for a 10-minute presentation on the advantages of attending your college or university. The presentation would be delivered by someone from the admissions office, and the audience would be visiting high school students and their family members. After completing the outline together, each team member should individually develop a 60-second introduction to the presentation. Meet again, have each team member give his or her introduction, and then discuss which was most effective and why. Be prepared to discuss your conclusion with the class.

2. **Presentations: Planning and Developing [LO-1], [LO-2]** Browse through the following topics to see which ones interest you:

    a. What I expect to learn in this course

    b. Past public speaking experiences: the good, the bad, and the ugly

    c. I would be good at teaching _____.

    d. I am afraid of _____.

    e. It's easy for me to _____.

    f. I get angry when _____.

    g. I am happiest when I _____.

    h. People would be surprised if they knew that I _____.

    i. My favorite older person

    j. My favorite charity

    k. My favorite place

    l. My favorite sport

    m. My favorite store

    n. My favorite television show

    o. The town you live in suffers from a great deal of juvenile vandalism. Explain to a group of community members why juvenile recreational facilities should be built instead of a juvenile detention complex.

    p. You are speaking to the Humane Society. Support or oppose the use of animals for medical research purposes.

    q. You are talking to civic leaders of your community. Try to convince them to build an art gallery.

    r. You are speaking to a first-grade class at an elementary school. Explain why they should brush their teeth after meals.

    s. You are speaking to a group of traveling salespeople. Convince them that they should wear their seatbelts while driving.

    t. You are speaking to a group of elderly people. Convince them to adopt an exercise program.

    u. Energy issues (supply, conservation, alternative sources, national security, global warming, pollution, etc.)

    v. Financial issues (banking, investing, family finances, etc.)

    w. Government (domestic policy, foreign policy, social security taxes, welfare, etc.)

    x. Interesting new technologies (virtual reality, geographic information systems, nanotechnology, bioengineering, etc.)

    y. Politics (political parties, elections, legislative bodies and legislation, the presidency, etc.)

    z. Sports (amateur and professional, baseball, football, golf, hang gliding, hockey, rock climbing, tennis, etc.)

    Choose a topic and prepare a brief speech or presentation (5–10 minutes), with or without visuals, as your instructor indicates.

3. **Presentations: Planning, Developing, and Delivering [LO-1], [LO-2], [LO-3]** Identify a company whose prospects look bright over the next few years because of highly competitive products, strong leadership, fundamental changes in the market, or any other significant reason. Prepare a five-minute speech, without visuals, explaining why you think this company is going to do well in the near future.

4. **Presentations: Planning, Developing, and Delivering [LO-1], [LO-2], [LO-3]** In the following table, rate yourself on each of the elements of the presentation process.

Then examine your ratings to identify where you are strongest and where you can improve, using the tips in this chapter.

Elements of the Presentation Process	Always	Frequently	Occasionally	Never
1. I start by defining my purpose.				
2. I analyze my audience before writing an oral presentation.				
3. I match my presentation length to the allotted time.				
4. I begin my oral presentations with an attention-getting introduction.				
5. I look for ways to build credibility as a speaker.				
6. I cover only a few main points in the body of my presentation.				
7. I use transitions to help listeners follow my ideas.				
8. I review main points and describe next steps in the close.				
9. I practice my presentation beforehand.				
10. I prepare in advance for questions and objections.				
11. I conclude oral presentations by summarizing my main idea.				

5. **Presentations: Mastering Delivery [LO-3]** Watch any talk that interests you at the TED website, www.ted.com/talks, and compare the speaker's delivery with this chapter's "Checklist: Developing Oral and Online Presentations." Write a two-page report, analyzing the speaker's performance and suggesting improvements.

6. **Presentations: Mastering Delivery; Communication Ethics: Making Ethical Choices [LO-3], Chapter 1** Think again about the presentation you observed and analyzed in the previous exercise. How could the speaker have used nonverbal signals to unethically manipulate the audience's attitudes or actions?

7. **Presentations: Using the Backchannel; Collaboration: Team Projects [LO-4], Chapter 2** In a team of six students, develop a 10-minute slide presentation on any topic that interests you. Nominate one person to give the presentation; the other five will participate via a Twitter backchannel. Create a webpage that holds at least one downloadable file that will be discussed during the presentation, and set up a backchannel on BackNoise (http://backnoise.com) or a similar service. Practice using the backchannel, including using a hashtag for the meeting and having the presenter ask for audience feedback during a "Twitter break." Be ready to discuss your experience with the entire class. For information on getting started on Twitter, visit http://real-timeupdates.com/bct11, click on "Learn More," and then click on "Twitter Screencast."

EXPAND YOUR SKILLS

Critique the Professionals

Find a product demonstration video on YouTube for any product that is appropriate to discuss in class. (Find a video that is at least two minutes long and was produced by the company that makes the product, not by a customer or other outside party.) Study the effectiveness of the demonstration, including the use of visuals, the presenter's speech and mannerisms. Did you find the demonstration compelling? Why or why not? If not, what would've made it more compelling? Using whatever medium your instructor requests, write a brief summary of your analysis. Be sure to include a link to the video.

Sharpening Your Career Skills Online

Bovée and Thill's Business Communication Web Search, at http://businesscommunicationblog.com/websearch, is a unique research tool designed specifically for business communication research. Use the Web Search function to find a website, video, PDF document, podcast, or PowerPoint presentation that offers advice on public speaking or presentations in business. Write a brief email message to your instructor, describing the item that you found and summarizing the career skills information you learned from it.

Enhancing Presentations with Slides and Other Visuals   **17**

LEARNING OBJECTIVES   After studying this chapter, you will be able to

1 Explain the role of visuals in business presentations and list the types of visuals commonly used

2 Explain the difference between structured and free-form slides and suggest when each design strategy is more appropriate

3 Outline the decisions involved in selecting color, artwork, and typefaces to create effective slide designs

4 Explain how to create effective slide content

5 Explain the role of navigation slides, support slides, and handouts

MyBcommLab Test your mastery of this chapter and its Learning Objectives. Visit mybcommlab.com to apply what you've learned in Document Makeovers and interactive simulation scenarios.

COMMUNICATION CLOSE-UP AT **PRESENTATION ZEN**

Restraint, simplicity, and naturalness are some of the key elements of Zen-inspired design. Garr Reynolds, author of *Presentation Zen* and a popular blog of the same name, advises presenters to adopt these principles in the design and delivery of slide presentations.

www.presentationzen.com

Nobody wants to give a boring presentation, and certainly nobody wants to sit through a boring presentation. In spite of best intentions, however, presentation expert Garr Reynolds claims that "most presentations remain mind-numbingly dull, something to be endured by presenter and audience alike." He aims to help improve this unfortunate situation by example and through his many books, blogs, and seminars.

Reynolds, an American who has lived, worked, and taught in Japan for many years, believes the solution to better presentations lies in adapting some of the principles of the Zen school of Buddhism. However, it isn't the spiritual practices of Zen that he wants to infuse into presentations, but rather some of the overall approach and aesthetic sense of Zen—particularly the three principles of restraint, simplicity, and naturalness. His approach reflects these ideals through *restrained preparation*, *simple designs*, and *natural delivery*.

Most people can grasp the notions of restraint and naturalness, but simplicity is sometimes misunderstood. From a design and communication perspective, simplicity is not about "dumbing down" but rather about rising up—rising above the details and stripping away the distractions to focus on the essential elements of an idea or a problem. This approach to design leads to slides that look dramatically different from conventional presentation slides.

Reynolds's advice for restrained preparation starts with walking away from your computer, to "plan analog" as he puts it, with just a notepad and a pen or pencil. This low-tech approach to planning offers several advantages. First, it helps you avoid falling into the trap of thinking that your *slides* are the presentation. The *message* is the heart of your presentation, and slides are simply one possible medium for expressing that message. Moreover, starting away from your computer is a good reminder that a presentation, even one with dazzling multimedia and special effects, is still a speech or a conversation that is supported by visuals. In other words, it involves primarily an oral medium, not an electronic medium.

Second, by figuring out your message before firing up your presentation software, you're not mentally locked into the single medium of electronic slides. With insight into audience needs and a well-defined message in place, you can then consider all your options and select whatever combination of media is best for the situation. You might discover, for example, that getting your listeners involved would help build consensus for your message. By incorporating another medium, such as flip charts or a whiteboard, you can record questions and suggestions from the audience during a few minutes of brainstorming.

Third, presentation software has so many features and functions that it is easy to get caught up in these "bells and whistles" and thereby lose sight of your audience and lose track of your purpose. By having a clear, audience-focused message in mind before you start creating slides, you can focus on building effective slides to carry your message.

This restrained, audience-focused planning promotes Reynolds's next goal of simple, uncluttered slides. You will often find that the simplest way to convey a given message point is also the most effective. A few carefully chosen words, sometimes with a compelling image but sometimes without, are usually all you need to support the spoken message you will share at that moment in the presentation. To keep viewers focused on your message, avoid distracting them with anything that does not support that message. When it comes to editing and revising your slides, Reynolds says, "You must be ruthless."

In turn, simple slides with few words can encourage a more natural delivery by forcing you out from behind your slides, so to speak. If your slides are packed with every detail of your presentation, you can wind up being a bystander at your own presentation as both you and the audience read all that information. In contrast, if you know your material and you've practiced thoroughly, you will be able to speak much more fluidly and naturally, without relying on your slides. The result will be much more like a natural conversation, in which the connection is between you and your audience, not between your audience and your slides.[1]

(For a video summary of Reynolds's popular book *Presentation Zen*, see the Real-Time Updates "Learn More" link below.)

Planning Your Presentation Visuals

1 **LEARNING OBJECTIVE**

Explain the role of visuals in business presentations, and list the types of visuals commonly used.

By following the three-step development process in Chapter 16, you'll have a well-crafted, audience-focused message. The techniques in this chapter, which reflect the advice offered by experts such as Garr Reynolds (profiled in the chapter-opening Communication Close-up) will help you enhance the delivery of that message with creative and effective visuals.

Visuals can improve the quality and impact of any presentation by creating interest, illustrating points that are difficult to explain with words alone, adding variety, and increasing the audience's ability to absorb and remember information. Behavioral research has shown that visuals can improve learning by up to 400 percent because humans can process visuals 60,000 times faster than text.[2]

Remember that the purpose of visuals is to support your spoken message, not replace it.

For all the communication power of visuals, however, don't make the mistake of thinking that your visuals *are* a presentation. Particularly when using presentation software such as Microsoft PowerPoint, Apple Keynote, or Google Presentations, communicators sometimes fall into the trap of letting the slides take center stage. Remember that your message is the presentation, not your visuals; your visuals are there to help support and clarify what you have to say.[3]

REAL-TIME UPDATES
Learn More by Watching This Video

Get a quick video tour of Garr Reynolds's *Presentation Zen*

Fellow designer Matt Helmke offers a succinct overview of Reynolds's groundbreaking book. Go to http://real-timeupdates .com/bct11 and click on "Learn More." If you are using MyBcommLab, you can access Real-Time Updates within each chapter or under Student Study Tools.

SELECTING THE TYPE OF VISUALS TO USE

You can select from a variety of visuals to enhance presentations, each with unique advantages and disadvantages:

- **Electronic slides.** Electronic slides created with Microsoft PowerPoint, Apple Keynote, or similar programs are the visuals of choice in most business situations today. Electronic presentations have a number of advantages: they are relatively easy to create and edit (at least for simple slides), slides can be made more engaging with images and various multimedia elements, slides are easy to incorporate into online meetings and webcasts, and you can record self-running presentations or screencasts for trade shows, websites, and other uses. The primary disadvantages are the amount of time that developing slides can consume, the equipment requirements, the potential complexity involved in creating more advanced presentations, and the risk that your hardware or software won't cooperate when it's show time.

- **Overhead transparencies.** Overhead transparencies are the very definition of old school, but they do have advantages. They can be created with nothing more than a marking pen, they don't require the latest computer or projection equipment, you can write on them during a presentation, and they never malfunction. On the downside, they're limited to static displays, they're virtually impossible to edit once you've printed them, and you or a partner are forced to stand next to the projector throughout your entire presentation.

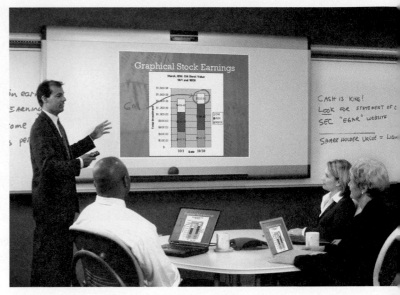

Electronic whiteboards let you capture notes and feedback during presentations and then print or email them to audience members.

- **Chalkboards and whiteboards.** Chalkboards and whiteboards are effective tools for recording points made during small-group sessions. With electronic whiteboards, you can print and email copies of whatever is written, too.

- **Flip charts.** Flip charts are another dependable low-tech tool for meetings and presentations. They are great for recording comments and questions during a presentation or for creating a "group memory" during brainstorming sessions, keeping track of all the ideas the team generates.

- **Other visuals.** Be creative when choosing visuals to support your presentation. A video of a focus group talking about your company can have a lot more impact than a series of slides that summarize what the group said. In technical or scientific presentations, a sample of a product or material lets your audience experience your subject directly. Designers and architects use mock-ups and models to help people envision what a final creation will look like. You might also want to incorporate other software in your presentation, such as a live spreadsheet to show financial data or a computer-aided design program to show a new product's design. If you're demonstrating the use of a software program, you can create a screencast that shows the software in action. Screencasting software also lets you add on-screen annotations and record an audio track to explain what is happening on-screen.

This chapter focuses on electronic presentations, the mainstay of business presentations today, although most of these design tips apply to other visuals as well.

In most businesses, electronic presentations are now the presentation visual of choice, although they're certainly not the only option.

MyBcommLab

- Access this chapter's simulation entitled Business Presentations, located at mybcommlab.com.

VERIFYING YOUR DESIGN PLANS

After you have chosen the medium or media for your visuals, think through your presentation plan carefully before you start creating anything. Discerning audience members—the sort of people who can influence the direction of your career—are not easily fooled by visual razzle-dazzle. If your analysis is shaky or your conclusions are suspect, an over-the-top visual production won't help your presentation succeed. Review the plan for each visual and ask yourself how it will help your audience understand and appreciate your message.

Next, make sure your presentation style is appropriate for the subject matter, the audience, and the setting (see Figure 17.1 on page 496). Take the time to double-check any cultural assumptions that might be inappropriate. Are you highlighting with a color that has negative emotional connotations in your audience's culture? Would your materials be too playful for a serious audience? Too serious for an audience that values creativity?

When it comes time to make design choices, from selecting fonts to deciding whether to include a photo, remember the advice from Chapter 16 and designers such as Garr

Think through your presentation outline carefully before designing your visuals.

Figure 17.1   Presentation Style
Presentation software makes it easy to create an endless variety of visual styles. Compare the staid, "quiet" style on the left with the more dynamic style on the right.

Reynolds: Let simplicity be your guide. Doing so has several advantages. First, creating simple materials often takes less time, and time is the most precious commodity in today's business environment. Second, simple visuals reduce the chances of distraction and misinterpretation. Third, the more complex your presentation, the more likely something might go wrong.

Finally, use your time wisely. Presentation software seems to encourage experimentation and fiddling around with details and special effects, which can eat up hours and hours of time you probably don't have. Based on your audience and situation, decide up-front how much visual design is sufficient for your purpose and then stop when you get there. Use the time you'll save to rehearse your presentation—practice is far more important than minor design issues on your slides.

Choosing Structured or Free-Form Slides

Explain the difference between structured and free-form slides, and suggest when each design strategy is more appropriate.

Structured slides are usually based on templates that give all the slides in a presentation the same general look; free-form slides typically don't follow any set design plan.

Free-form slides often have far less content per slide than structured designs, which can require many more slides to cover a presentation of equal length.

Structured slides are usually the best choice for project updates and other routine information presentations, particularly if the slides are intended to be used only once.

Perhaps the most important design choice you face when creating slides is whether to use conventional **structured slides** or the looser, **free-form slides** that many presentation specialists now advocate. Compare the two rows of slides in Figure 17.2. The structured slides in the top row follow the same basic format throughout the presentation; in fact, they're based directly on the templates built into PowerPoint. The free-form slides in the bottom row don't follow a rigid structure—and most definitely not a template. However, choosing a free-form design strategy does not mean you can just randomly change the design from one slide to the next. Effectively designed slides should still be unified by design elements such as color and typeface selections, as Figures 17.2c and 17.2d show. Also, note how Figure 17.2d combines visual and textual messages to convey the point about listening without criticizing. This complementary approach of pictures and words is a highlight of free-form design.

Because the amount of content varies so dramatically between the two design approaches, the number of slides in a presentation can also vary dramatically. For instance, someone using structured slides might have 5 or 6 slides for a 20-minute presentation and spend 3 or 4 minutes on each one. In contrast, someone using free-form slides for the same presentation might have 60–80 slides or more and spend only 15 or 20 seconds on each one. In the extreme, a 20-minute free-form presentation could have *hundreds* of slides, with individual slides often displayed for less than a second.[4] Of course, this is only a general assessment. Don't feel that you need to create dozens of slides when using a free-form design; create only as many slides as you need to support your spoken message.

STRUCTURED SLIDES

Both design strategies have advantages and disadvantages, and one or the other can be a better choice for specific situations. Structured slides have the advantage of being fast and

Figure 17.2a

Figure 17.2b

Figure 17.2c

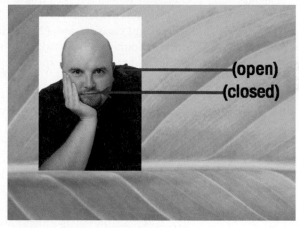

Figure 17.2d

Figure 17.2 Structured Versus Free-Form Slide Design
Compare the rigid, predictable design of the two slides in the top row with the free-form designs in the bottom row. Although the two free-form slides don't follow the same design structure, they are visually linked by color and font choices. As you compare these two styles, you can imagine how the free-form designs will require more slides to cover the same subject and require the speaker to convey more of the message. (Note that Figure 17.2d is a lighthearted but effective way of conveying the first bullet point in Figure 17.2b.)

easy to create: You simply choose an overall design theme for the presentation, select a template for a new slide, and start typing. Given the speed and ease of creating them, structured slides can be a more practical choice for routine presentations such as project status updates. Of course, making things easier on the presenter won't necessarily make them easier for the audience, but if you're in a schedule crunch, going the structured route might save the day because at least you'll have *something* ready to show.

Also, because more information can usually be packed on each slide, structured slides can be more effective at conveying complex ideas or sets of interrelated data to the right audiences. For example, if you are talking to a group of executives who must decide where to make budget cuts across the company's eight divisions, at some point in the presentation they probably will want to see summary data for all eight divisions on a single slide for easy comparison. Such a slide would be overcrowded by the usual definition, but this might be the only practical way to get a "big picture" view of the situation. (The best solution is probably some high-level, summary slides supported by a detailed handout, as page 499 explains.)

Finally, structured slides can be more effective as stand-alone documents that people can read on their own, without a presenter. However, such slides are really a different type of message delivery vehicle altogether—essentially a report in bullet-point form—and they are *not* effective as presentation visuals and often not terribly effective as reports, either. See the discussion of "slideuments" on page 499 for more on this problem.

REAL-TIME UPDATES
Learn More by Watching This Video

**Way beyond bullet points: A stunning
example of free-form slide design**

See how a creative mind can transform electronic slides into
something far more compelling than conventional bullet points. Go
to http://real-timeupdates.com/bct11 and click on "Learn More." If
you are using MyBcommLab, you can access Real-Time Updates
within each chapter or under Student Study Tools.

The primary disadvantage of structured design is the mind-numbing effect of text-heavy slides that all look alike. Slide after slide of dense, highly structured bullet points with no visual relief can overload the audience, particularly if the presenter stuffs too many bullet points on a slide, writes the bullet points as complete sentences, or simply reads the bullet points to the audience. Multimedia expert Richard Mayer of the University of California, Santa Barbara, explains that this problem is the result of presenters focusing on delivering information without considering how the audience can convert that information to usable meaning.[5]

Structured slide designs, which can lead to screen after screen of identical-looking bullet points, can be boring and overwhelming.

FREE-FORM SLIDES

The goal of free-form slide design is to overcome the drawbacks of text-heavy structured design by fulfilling three criteria that Mayer and other researchers have identified as important for successful presentations: (1) providing complementary information through both textual and visual means; (2) limiting the amount of information delivered at any one time to prevent cognitive overload; and (3) helping viewers process information by identifying priorities and connections, such as by highlighting the most important data points in a graph.[6] (Of course, well-designed structured slides can also meet these criteria, but the constraints of prebuilt templates make doing so more of a challenge.) With appropriate imagery, free-form designs can also create a more dynamic and engaging experience for the audience. Given their ability to excite and engage, free-form designs are particularly good for motivational, educational, and persuasive presentations—particularly when the slides will be used multiple times and therefore compensate for the extra time and effort often required to create them.

Well-designed free-form slides help viewers understand, process, and remember the speaker's message while keeping the focus on what the speaker is saying.

In addition to these benefits, however, free-form slides have several potential disadvantages. First, effectively designing slides with both visual and textual elements is more creatively demanding and more time-consuming than simply typing text into preformatted templates. The emphasis on visual content also requires more images, which take time to find.

Second, because far less textual information tends to be displayed on-screen, the speaker is responsible for conveying more of the content. Ideally, of course, this is how a presentation *should* work, but presenters sometimes find themselves in less than ideal circumstances, such as being asked to fill in for a colleague on short notice. In any event, keep in mind that free-form slide designs require more preparation and more practice on the part of the speaker.

A key disadvantage of free-form slide designs is the time and effort often required to create them.

Third, if not handled carefully, dividing information into smaller chunks can make it difficult to present complex subjects in a cohesive, integrated manner. For instance, if you're discussing a business problem that has five interrelated causes, it might be helpful to insert a conventional bullet-point slide as a summary and reminder after discussing each problem on its own.

Designing Effective Slides

3   LEARNING OBJECTIVE

Outline the decisions involved in selecting color, artwork, and typefaces to create effective slide designs.

Microsoft's PowerPoint software holds a curious distinction in the business world: Virtually everyone seems to use it—and virtually everyone seems to hate it. This is an exaggeration, to be sure, but enough people have grown weary of sleep-inducing slide presentations for "death by PowerPoint" to become a common complaint.

The problem is not with PowerPoint itself (or with Apple Keynote or any other presentation program). The software is just a tool, and like all other tools, it can be used well or poorly. Granted, some of the features in presentation software practically encourage bad design choices, but those choices are still up to the user. In any event, when the software is used poorly for whatever reason, the result can be cluttered slides that are difficult to understand and sleep-inducing presentations that are difficult to follow.

"Death by PowerPoint" is a common complaint; however, the problem isn't with the tools but how they are used.

Businesspeople don't start out with the intention to create bad slides, of course. However, a lack of design awareness, inadequate training, schedule pressures, and the instinctive response of doing things the way they've always been done can lead to ineffective slides. For instance, presenters often reuse slides from other presentations to save time, which means that a poorly designed slide can take on a life of its own and propagate throughout a company.

One reason for ineffective slides is the practice of using slide sets as standalone documents that can be read on their own, without a presenter. As mentioned earlier, these "slideument" hybrids that try to function as both presentation visuals and printed documents don't work well as either: They have too much information to be effective visuals and too little to be effective reports (in addition to being clumsy to read). Entrepreneur David S. Rose is among those who go so far as to say that slides by themselves should be more or less useless to an audience without the speaker, because good slides are there to support the speaker.[7]

Unfortunately, slideuments appear to be fairly common, partly because some presenters are in the habit of overstuffing their slides and partly because some audience members expect to be able to read or view slides on their own if they miss a live presentation. The emergence of websites such as SlideShare (see "Business Communication 2.0: Presentations Get Social" on page 506) might be contributing to the phenomenon, too, by making it so easy to share slide sets. Garr Reynolds suggests yet another cause as well: industry conferences that require speakers to submit their slides to be included in attendee handout packages.[8]

Presenters can avoid the pitfalls of slideuments, but doing so usually requires some extra work. As "Creating Effective Handouts" on page 510 explains, the ideal solution is to create an effective slide set and a separate handout document that provides additional details and supporting information. This way, you can optimize each piece to do the job it is really meant to do. An alternative is to use the notes field in your presentation software to include your speaking notes for each slide. Anyone who gets a copy of your slides can at least follow along by reading your notes, although you will probably need to edit and embellish them to make them understandable by others.

> Resist the temptation to create "slideuments," slide sets crammed with so much information that they are sometimes read as reports; these hybrid slide set/reports aren't good at either task.

SELECTING DESIGN ELEMENTS

As you design and create slides, always keep the audience's experience in mind: What will it be like to view this slide while listening to a speaker? Chapter 12 highlights six principles of effective design: consistency, contrast, balance, emphasis, convention, and simplicity. Pay close attention to these principles as you select the design elements for your slides (covered in this section) and create content for each slide (covered in the following section).

> To design effective slides, remember the six principles of effective design: consistency, contrast, balance, emphasis, convention, and simplicity (review Chapter 12 for a refresher).

Color

Color is a critical design element, far more than mere decoration. It grabs the viewer's attention, emphasizes important ideas, creates contrast, and isolates slide elements. Color sends a powerful nonverbal message, too, whether it's elegance, technical sophistication, fiscal prudence, or hipster trendiness. You can study this effect as you view various websites or advertisements, for instance. A palette of cool grays and blues "says" something different than a palette of warm oranges and browns, which says something different than a palette of hot pink and lime green.

Color can also play a key role in the overall acceptance of your message. Research shows that color visuals can account for 60 percent of an audience's acceptance or rejection of an idea. Color can increase willingness to read by up to 80 percent, and it can enhance learning and improve retention by more than 75 percent.[9]

Your color choices can also stimulate various emotions, as Table 17.1 suggests. For instance, if you want to excite your audience, add some warm colors, such as red and orange, to your slides. If you want to achieve a more relaxed and receptive environment, blue is a better choice.[10] Remember, color may have a different meaning in certain cultures, so if you are creating slides for international audiences, research these cultural differences.

When selecting color, limit your choices to a few compatible ones and keep in mind that some colors work better together than others. Contrasting colors, for example, increase readability, so when selecting color for backgrounds, titles, and text, avoid choosing colors that are close in hue, such as brown on green or blue on purple.[11] If you'll be presenting in

> Color is much more than mere decoration: It provides emphasis, isolation, and contrast; it increases readability and retention; it sends powerful nonverbal signals; and it can stimulate desired emotional responses.

TABLE 17.1	Color and Emotion	
Color	**Selected Emotional Associations in U.S. Business Culture (Can Vary in Other Cultures, Sometimes Significantly)**	**Best Uses**
Blue	Peaceful, soothing, tranquil, cool, trusting	Background for presentation slides (usually dark blue); safe and conservative
White	Neutral, innocent, pure, wise	Font color of choice for most presentation slides that have a dark background
Yellow	Warm, bright, cheerful, enthusiastic	Text bullets and subheadings on a dark background
Red	Passionate, dangerous, active, painful	To promote action or stimulate the audience; seldom used as a background. ("In the red" specifically refers to financial losses.)
Green	Assertive, prosperous, envious, relaxed	Highlight and accent color. (Green symbolizes money in the United States but not in other countries.)

a dark room, use dark colors such as blue for the background, a midrange of brightness for illustrations, and light colors for text. If you are presenting in well-lit rooms, reverse the colors: Use light colors for the background and dark colors for text. If you have some reason to change colors between slides, don't switch back and forth from very dark to very bright; the effect is jarring to the audience's eyes.[12]

Artwork

Every slide has two layers or levels of visual elements: the background and foreground. The *background* is the equivalent of paper in a printed report and often stays the same from slide to slide, particularly with structured designs. The *foreground* contains the unique text and graphic elements that make up each individual slide.

> The background should stay in the background, not compete with the foreground.

Generally speaking, the less your background does, the better. As presentation designer Nancy Duarte explains, the background "should be open, spacious, and simple."[13] Cluttered or flashy backgrounds tend to distract from your message. The background needs to stay in the background; it shouldn't compete with the foreground elements. Be careful when using the design templates that come with your software. Many have backgrounds that are too busy, and some are too playful for business use. Bear in mind that you don't *need* to use a background at all, other than perhaps a solid color to set type and images against.

> Artwork can be either decorative or functional; use decorative artwork only if it supports the message of the slide in question.

In the background, all artwork is essentially decorative. In the foreground, artwork can be either functional or decorative. *Functional artwork* includes photos, technical drawings, charts, and other visual elements containing information that is part of your message. In contrast, *decorative artwork* doesn't deliver textual or numerical information, and it may or may not be helpful. Decorative artwork can be helpful if it establishes an appropriate emotional tone or amplifies the message of a slide, partly because simple, high-impact images are easier to remember than text.[14] However, decorative artwork is unhelpful if it doesn't add value, is off topic, conveys an unprofessional image, or pulls viewer attention away from the essential elements on a slide (see Figure 17.3). Decorative artwork is usually the least important element of any slide, but it often causes the most trouble. *Clip art*, collections of drawings that you can insert in slides and other documents, is probably the biggest troublemaker of them all. You can find thousands of pieces of free clip art in presentation software or online, but few of them have any information value and many give your slides an unprofessional, cartoony appearance.

Typefaces and Type Styles

> Many of the typefaces available on your computer are difficult to read when projected, so they aren't good choices for presentation slides.

When selecting typefaces and type styles for slides, follow these guidelines:

- Avoid script or decorative typefaces, except for limited, special uses.
- Use serif typefaces with care and only with larger text (see Figure 17.4).

Figure 17.3a

Figure 17.3b

Figure 17.3   Effective and Ineffective Artwork
Slide artwork can carry your message, support your message, or totally get in the way. Figure 17.3a could be an effective way to introduce a talk about teamwork, with one ant helping its "teammate" out of a tough spot. If this image were created using clip art, it would probably be too cartoony for a professional presentation. However, this image has a sophisticated, almost elegant, look in spite of the fact that it features ants. The slide in Figure 17.3b is a disaster. The visual confusion created by the clutter and mixed styles of artwork will distract the audience and obscure the message.

- Limit the number of typefaces to one or two per slide.
- When using thinner typefaces, use boldface so that letters won't look washed out.
- Avoid most italicized type; it is usually difficult to read when projected.
- Avoid all-capitalized words and phrases.
- Allow extra white space between lines of text.
- Be consistent with typefaces, type styles, colors, and sizes.

When selecting type sizes, consider the room(s) in which you'll be presenting. The farther the audience is from the screen, the larger your type needs to be in order to be readable from everywhere in the room. Venture capitalist and investor Guy Kawasaki (see page 424), who has sat through hundreds and hundreds of PowerPoint presentations, suggests using no type smaller than 30 points. Doing so not only ensures readable slides but forces you to distill every idea down to its essential core, simply because you won't have

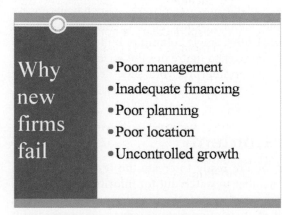

Figure 17.4a Times New Roman (serif) font

Figure 17.4b Calibri (sans serif) font

Figure 17.4   Selecting Typefaces for Projection
Serif typefaces can be more difficult to read on-screen, particularly at the smaller type sizes used for bullet points (Figure 17.4a). Italicized type can also be more difficult to read on-screen. As Figure 17.4b shows, sans serif typefaces are usually a better choice for slide text; they are cleaner and easier to read from a distance.

Figure 17.5a Slide master for bullet slides   Figure 17.5b Example of how content is displayed

Figure 17.5 **Presentation Slide Master**
The slide master feature in PowerPoint and other presentation programs makes it easy to create consistent slides. Simply adjust the master as you need, and all the slides of that type in your presentation will change accordingly. Note that many slide design templates contain more levels of bullet points than you would ever want to use for normal presentation purposes.

room to be wordy.[15] After you have selected your fonts and type styles, test them for readability by viewing sample slides from your audience's viewing location. If you don't have access to the conference room, a clever way to test readability at your computer is to stand back as many feet from the screen as your screen size in inches (17 feet for a 17-inch screen, for example). If the slides are readable at this distance, you're probably in good shape.[16]

MAINTAINING DESIGN CONSISTENCY

Design inconsistencies confuse and annoy audiences; don't change colors and other design elements randomly throughout your presentation.

Audiences start to assign meaning to visual elements beginning with your first slide. For instance, if the first slide presents the most important information in dark red, 36-point, Gill Sans typeface, your audience will expect the same type treatment for the most important information on the remaining slides as well. Don't force viewers to repeatedly figure out the meaning of design elements by making arbitrary changes from slide to slide.

Fortunately, presentation software makes consistency easy to achieve, particularly for structured slide designs. You simply adjust the *slide master* using the colors, fonts, and other design elements you've chosen; these choices will then automatically show up on every slide in the presentation (see Figure 17.5). In addition, you can maintain consistency by choosing a predefined layout from those available in your software—which helps ensure that bulleted lists, charts, graphics, and other elements show up in predictable places on each slide. Something as simple as switching from a single column of bullet points to two columns can cause problems for readers, as they try to figure out the meaning of the new arrangement. The less work readers have to do to interpret your slide designs, the more attention they can pay to your message.

Creating Effective Slide Content

 LEARNING OBJECTIVE

Explain how to create effective slide content.

With some design fundamentals in mind, you're ready to create the textual and visual content for your slides. For every slide, remember to watch out for information overload. When slides have too much content—textual, visual, or both—particularly for several slides in a row, viewers can't process the incoming information fast enough to make sense of it and eventually tune out. In the words of Jim Confalone of New York's ProPoint Graphics, the presentation "becomes like wallpaper." Keep your slides clear and easy to grasp, and pace the flow of information at a speed that lets people connect your ideas from one slide to the next.[17]

SLIDE TEXT

To choose effective words and phrases, think of the text on your slides as a guide to the content, not the content itself. One of the most common mistakes with slide text—and one of the chief criticisms leveled at structured slide designs in general—is stuffing slides with too much text. Doing so creates several problems: It overloads the audience with too much information too fast, it takes attention away from the speaker by forcing people to read more, and it requires the presenter to use smaller type—which in turn makes the slides even harder to read. Keep in mind that slide text is not supposed to display your entire speaking script or highlight every point you intend to make.[18]

In a sense, slide text serves as the headings and subheadings for your presentation. Accordingly, choose words and short phrases that help your audience follow the flow of ideas, without forcing them to read in depth. You primarily want your audience to *listen*, not to *read*. Use your slides to highlight key points, summarize and preview your message, signal major shifts in thought, illustrate concepts, or help create interest in your spoken message. If the audience can benefit from additional information, provide those details in handouts (see page 510).

When writing content for text slides, keep your message short and simple (see Figure 17.6 on the next page):

- Limit each slide to one thought, concept, or idea (without dividing things so far that the audience has trouble seeing the big picture).
- Limit text content to four or five lines with four or five words per line. For selected slides, it might make sense to exceed these limits, but do so infrequently.
- Don't show a large number of text-heavy slides in a row; give the audience some visual relief.
- Write short, bulleted phrases rather than long sentences.
- Use sentences only when you need to share a quotation or some other text item verbatim.[19]
- Phrase list items in parallel grammatical form to facilitate quick reading.
- Use the active voice.
- Include short, informative titles.
- When combining visuals with text, the more information the visual can convey, the less work your text needs to do.

Use your slides as guides to the content, not as the content themselves.

No matter which design strategy you use, limit the amount of information on each slide to avoid overloading your viewers.

SLIDE TABLES AND GRAPHICS

Just as text needs to be simplified for projection, so do many charts, graphs, tables, and other visual elements. Detailed visuals that might look fine on the printed page can be too dense and complicated for presentations. Don't make the audience study your charts and graphs in order to get the message. Follow these guidelines:

- **Reduce the detail.** Eliminate anything that is not absolutely essential to the message. If necessary, break information into more than one slide. If a deeper level of detail is helpful or necessary, hand out printed visuals that people can review during or after the presentation.
- **Simplify.** For example, if a bar chart is segmented by week, don't write "Week of 12/01," "Week of 12/08," and so on. Use the "Week of" label once and then just include the dates. Similarly, you might be able to remove the vertical scale from the left side of the chart and just show individual values above each bar.[20]
- **Shorten numbers.** If doing so doesn't hide essential details, you can round off numbers such as $12,500.72 to $12 or $12.5 and then label the axis to indicate thousands.
- **Limit the amount of data shown.** Line graphs look busy when they have more than two or three lines, bar charts look crowded with more than five or six bars, and tables are difficult to read if they have too many rows or columns.

Many graphics that work well in printed form need to be simplified for use in presentations because they are too dense and too complicated to be easily viewed on-screen.

REAL-TIME UPDATES
Learn More by Watching This Video

Five easy tips to add a professional finish to your slides

Learn some simple techniques pros use to create and edit high-quality images for PowerPoint presentations. Go to http://real-timeupdates.com/bct11 and click on "Learn More." If you are using MyBcommLab, you can access Real-Time Updates within each chapter or under Student Study Tools.

Figure 17.6a

Figure 17.6b

Figure 17.6c

Figure 17.6d

Figure 17.6 Writing Text for Slides
Effective text slides are clear, simple guides that help the audience understand and remember the speaker's message. Notice the progression toward simplicity in these slides: Figure 17.6a is a paragraph that would distract the audience for an extended period of time. Figure 17.6b offers concise, readable bullets, although too many slides in a row in this structured design would become tedious. Figure 17.6c distills the message down to a single thought that is complete on its own but doesn't convey all the information from the original and would need embellishment from the speaker. Figure 17.6d pushes this to the extreme, with only the core piece of the message to serve as an "exclamation point" for the spoken message. Figure 17.6c, and especially Figure 17.6d, could be more even more powerful with a well-chosen visual that illustrates the idea of following the flow.

MyBcommLab

Apply Figure 17.6's key concepts by revising a new document. Go to Chapter 17 in mybcommlab.com and select Document Makeovers.

- **Highlight key points.** Use arrows, boldface type, and color to direct your audience's eyes to the main point of a visual. Summarize the intent of the graphic in one clear title, such as "Earnings up by 15%."
- **Adjust the size and design.** Modify the size of a graphic to accommodate the size of a slide. Leave plenty of white space so that audience members can view and interpret content from a distance. Use colors that stand out from the slide's background and choose a typeface for labels that is clear and easy to read.

Although you can animate just about everything in an electronic presentation, resist the temptation to do so—make sure each animation has a purpose.

ANIMATION AND MULTIMEDIA

Today's presentation software offers a wide array of options for livening up your slides, including sound, animation, video clips, transition effects from one slide to the next, and hyperlinks to websites and other resources. As with every other visual element, the key is to make sure that any effects you use support your message. Always consider the impact that all these effects will have on your audience members and their desire to understand your message.[21]

Animation and special effects can be grouped into four categories: functional animation, transitions and builds, hyperlinks, and multimedia. These capabilities are briefly discussed in the following sections; to learn more about using them, consult the Help menu in your software.

Functional Animation

PowerPoint and other presentation packages offer a mind-boggling set of tools for moving and changing things on screen. You can have a block of text cartwheel in from outer space, change colors, change font and font size, spin around in circles, blink on and off, wave back and forth, crawl around the screen following a predefined path, and then disappear one letter at a time, like some sort of erasing typewriter. You *can* do all this, but *should* you?

Just as static graphic elements can be either functional or decorative, so too can animated elements. For instance, having each bullet point fly in from the left side of the screen doesn't add any functional value to your communication effort. In contrast, a highlight arrow or color bar that moves around the screen to emphasize specific points in a technical diagram can be an effective use of animation and a welcome alternative to a laser pointer. You can control every aspect of the animation, so it's easy to coordinate the movement with the points you're making in your presentation. Using carefully controlled functional animation is also a great way to demonstrate sequences and procedures. For a training session on machinery repair, for example, you can show a schematic diagram of the machinery and walk your audience through each step of the troubleshooting process, highlighting each step on-screen as you address it verbally. Again, use animation in support of your message, not simply for animation's sake.

Transitions and Builds

In addition to animating specific elements on your slides, you can choose from various options for adding motion between slides. These **slide transitions** control how one slide replaces another on-screen. Subtle transitions can ease your viewers' gaze from one slide to the next—such as having the current slide gently fade out before the next one fades in. However, many of the transitions currently available (such as checkerboards, pinwheels, and spinning "newsflashes") are like miniature animated shows themselves and are therefore distracting. These pointless transition effects not only disrupt the flow of your presentation, they can make the whole thing seem amateurish. If you use a transition effect, use the same one throughout the presentation (so that audiences don't wonder if there is some significance to a new transition at some point during the presentation) and choose the effect carefully. Aim for a smooth, subtle effect that is easy on the eye. And unless a sound effect is somehow integral to the message, there is no reason to add audio to a transition.

Use subtle transition animations between slides to ease the viewer from one slide to the next; most of the transitions available in presentation software are too distracting.

Builds are much more useful than transitions, at least when used with care and thought. These effects control the release of text, graphics, and other elements on individual slides. For instance, with builds you can make a list of bullet points appear one at a time rather than having all of them appear on a slide at once, which makes it difficult to focus on a single point. This controlled release of information helps draw audience members' attention to the point being discussed and keeps them from reading ahead.

As with transitions, stick with the subtle, basic options for builds. The point of a build is to release information in a controlled fashion, not to distract or entertain the audience. Another useful option is to change the color of bullet points as you discuss each one. For instance, if your primary text color is a strong blue, you might have the text in each bullet point change to a light gray after you've finished talking about it. This subtle approach keeps the audience's attention focused on the bullet point you are currently discussing.

Using carefully designed builds can be a great way to reveal information in easy-to-process pieces.

After you've assigned builds to your slides, you can control the build activity with a mouse or a remote control device. Experiment with the options in your software to find the most effective build scheme. In addition to building up text, you can build up graphical elements. For instance, to discuss monthly sales of three products over the past year, you can have a line graph of the first product appear by itself while you discuss it, and then you can click the mouse to display the second product's sales line, then the third.

Presentations Get Social

When you're looking for creative inspiration, collaboration, or feedback, don't limit yourself to the people in your office. With a presentation sharing website such as SlideShare (www.slideshare.net), you can learn from and collaborate with the entire world. Sometimes described as "YouTube for Power-Point," SlideShare offers free storage and controlled access for presentation slides; it now hosts thousands of presentations, with more added every day.

If you'd like to find presentations on just about any topic imaginable, you can search for slides by keyword, browse by category, select popular topics from a tag cloud, or sort by popularity. For inspiration and design ideas, simply browse until something catches your eye. You can view any publicly available presentation in the viewer window right on the SlideShare website or download presentations to your computer (if the person who uploaded the presentation you select allows it to be downloaded).

If you want to share your slides, you can upload presentations as a guest or create a profile much as you can on a social networking site. With your profile established, you can continue to add new presentations to your *slidespace* and expand your online community by adding new contacts. As with Flickr and some other content-sharing sites, SlideShare lets you set various levels of access permission, from "your eyes only" to selected contacts to the entire world. This controlled-sharing aspect is a great way to share slides with conference attendees, business partners, and team members. You can also embed your presentations in your blog so all your blog visitors can see them, or embed them on an intranet so that only your coworkers can see them.

In the spirit of community, SlideShare offers tools to alert your followers on Twitter and your contacts on LinkedIn and other social networking sites. With SlideShare, your friends, fans, and customers can see your inspiring content as soon as you publish it.

CAREER APPLICATIONS

1. Visit SlideShare and find two presentations on the same business topic, such as public relations, financial matters, leadership, or even giving presentations. View and compare the two presentations in terms of content. Which presentation is clearer? More credible? More convincing? What specific steps did this presenter take to ensure clarity and confidence?
2. Now compare those two presentations in terms of their visual design. Do their designs help or hinder the communication effort? If you see any weaknesses, what improvements would you suggest?

Hyperlinks

You can increase the flexibility of your presentation slides with hyperlinks that let you jump to different slides, websites, or other software screens with the click of a mouse.

Hyperlinks and action buttons can be quite handy when you need flexibility in your presentations or want to share different kinds of files with the audience. A **hyperlink** instructs your computer to jump to another slide in your presentation, to a website, or to another program entirely. Depending on your presentation software, hyperlinks can be simple underlined text, invisible *hotspots* in graphical elements, or clearly labeled *action buttons*.

Using hyperlinks is also a great way to customize your presentations. For instance, if you work in sales and call on a variety of customers, you can't be sure what sort of situation you'll encounter at each customer's site. You might be prepared to give an in-depth technical presentation to a group of engineers, only to have the company president walk in and request a brief financial overview instead. Or you might prepare a set of detailed technical slides but not show them unless the audience asks detailed questions.

Another challenging situation is finding out at the last minute that you have less time than you thought you had to make your presentation. With some foresight and planning, you won't need to rush through your entire presentation or scramble on the spot to find the most important slides. Instead, you can simply click an action button labeled "Five-minute overview" and jump right to the two or three most important slides in your presentation.

Figure 17.7 Adapting a Presentation on the Fly
With hyperlinks that jump to various slides throughout a presentation, you can easily adapt your presentation in response to audience needs. In this simple presentation, for example, the speaker can jump to detailed discussions about engineering, marketing, or finance with one click of the mouse.

With hyperlinks, you can even switch from the indirect approach to the direct approach or vice versa, based on the response you're getting from your audience. By building in links that accommodate these various scenarios, you can adjust your presentation at a moment's notice—and look polished and professional while you do it (see Figure 17.7). Obviously, building a slide set with this capability requires time and insight into the presentation scenarios you are likely to encounter.

Multimedia Elements

Multimedia elements offer the ultimate in active presentations. Using audio and video clips can be an effective way to complement your live message, such as including a recorded message from a company executive or scenes from a customer focus group. Just be sure to keep these elements brief and relevant, as supporting points for your presentation, not as replacements for it.

Video clips can add memorable, engaging content to your presentations—as long as they are relevant, interesting, and brief.

Completing Slides and Support Materials

Just as you would review any message for content, style, tone, readability, clarity, and conciseness, you should apply the same quality control to your slides and other visuals. As you look over your presentation for the final time, make sure that all visuals are

- **Readable.** Can text be read from the back of the room? Does the text stand out from the background?
- **Consistent.** Are colors and design elements used consistently?
- **Simple.** Is each slide and the entire presentation as simple as possible? Can you eliminate any slides?
- **Audience centered.** Are the message and the design focused on the audience?
- **Clear.** Is the main point of a slide obvious? Easy to understand? Can the audience grasp the main point in just a few seconds?[22]
- **Concise and grammatical.** Is text written in concise phrases? Are bulleted phrases grammatically parallel?
- **Focused.** Does each slide cover only one thought, concept, or idea (or summarize a group of related ideas)? Does the slide grab the viewer's attention in the right place and

5 LEARNING OBJECTIVE

Explain the role of navigation slides, support slides, and handouts.

Review each slide carefully to make sure it is clear and readable.

support the key points of the message? Are arrows, symbols, or other techniques used to draw the audience's attention to the key sections of a chart or diagram?

- **Fully operational.** Have you verified every slide in your presentation? Do all the animations and other special effects work as you intended?

Remember, you want the audience to listen to you, not study the slides, so make sure your slides are not distracting in any way.

Use the slide sorter view to verify and modify the organization of your slides.

Presentation software can help you during the editing and revision process. As Figure 17.8 shows, using the *slide sorter* makes it easy to add and delete slides, reposition them, and check for design consistency. You can also use this view to preview animation and transition effects and experiment with design elements. For instance, if you want to experiment with a different background design or different font, select a new design element and preview it in your slides. If you choose to keep the new design, execute the "apply all" command to update all existing slides and to change the slide master, which will apply the design changes to any new slides you create. Note that you can also use the slide sorter view as a *storyboard* to plan your presentation.[23]

With your slides working properly and in clear, logical order, you're just a few steps away from being ready. Now is a good time to think about a backup plan. What will you do if your laptop won't turn on or the projector dies? Can you get by without your slides? For important presentations, consider having backup equipment on standby, loaded with your presentation, and ready to go. At the very least, have enough printed handouts ready to give the audience so that, as a last resort, you can give your presentation "on paper."

CREATING NAVIGATION AND SUPPORT SLIDES

Now that the content slides are ready, enhance your presentation with a few additional slides that add "finish" to your presentation and provide additional information to benefit your audience:

- **Title slide(s).** Make a good first impression on your audience with one or two title slides, the equivalent of a report's cover and title page (see Figures 17.9a and 17.9b). A title slide should contain the title of your presentation (and subtitle, if appropriate), your name, your department affiliation (for internal audiences), and your company affiliation (for external audiences). You may also include the presentation date and an

Figure 17.8   Slide Sorter View
Examining thumbnails of slides on one screen is the best way to check the overall design of your final product. The slide sorter also makes it easy to review the order and organization of your presentation; you can even use this screen to storyboard your presentation before creating slides.

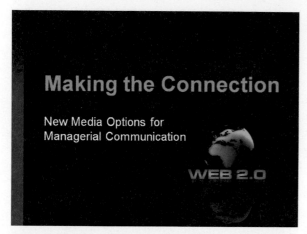

Figure 17.9a Title slide

Figure 17.9b Title slide 2

Figure 17.9c Agenda

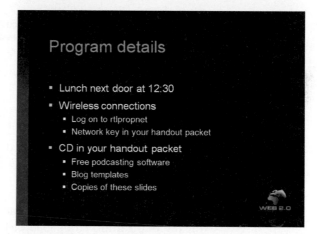

Figure 17.9d Program details

MyBcommLab

Figure 17.9   Navigation and Support Slides
You can use a variety of navigation and support slides to introduce yourself and
your presentation, to let the audience know what your presentation covers, and
to provide essential details.

Apply Figure 17.9's key concepts by revising a new
document. Go to Chapter 17 in mybcommlab.com
and select Document Makeovers.

appropriate graphic element. Depending on the amount of information you need to
convey at this point, two title slides might be appropriate: one focusing on the topic of
the presentation and a second slide with your affiliation and other information. This
second slide can also be used to introduce the speaker and list his or her credentials.

- **Agenda and program details.** You can use these slides to communicate the agenda for
your presentation and any additional information that your audience might need. Because
presentations pull your audience members away from their daily routines and work
responsibilities, people can have questions about anything from break times or lunch
plans to the password needed to log onto the facility's wireless network (see Figures 17.9c
and 17.9d). By answering these questions at the beginning of your presentation, you'll
minimize disruptions later and help the audience stay focused on your message.

- **Navigation slides.** To tell your audience where you're going and where you've been,
you can use a series of **navigation slides** based on your outline or agenda. This technique is most useful in longer presentations with several major sections. As you complete each section, repeat the slide but indicate which material has been covered and
which section you are about to begin (see Figure 17.10 on the next page). This sort
of slide is sometimes referred to as a *moving blueprint.* You can then use the original
slide again in the close of your presentation to review the points you've covered. As an
alternative to the repeating agenda slide, you can insert a simple *bumper slide* at each
major section break, announcing the title of the section you're about to begin.[24]

Navigation slides help your
audience keep track of what you've
covered already and what you plan
to cover next.

Figure 17.10a "Muting" topics already covered

Figure 17.10b Highlighting the next topic

Figure 17.10 **Blueprint Slides**
Here are two of the ways you can use a *blueprint slide* as a navigational aid to help your audience stay on track with the presentation. Figure 17.10a visually "mutes" and checks off the sections of the presentation that have already been covered. In contrast, Figure 17.10b uses a sliding highlight box to indicate the next section to be covered.

CREATING EFFECTIVE HANDOUTS

View handouts as an integral part of your presentation strategy so that they work in harmony with your slides and spoken message.

Use handout materials to support the points made in your presentation and to offer the audience additional information on your topic.

Handouts, any printed materials you give the audience to supplement your talk, should be considered an integral part of your presentation strategy. Plan them in tandem with your presentation so that you use each medium as effectively as possible. Your presentation should paint the big picture, convey and connect major ideas, set the emotional tone, and rouse the audience to action (if that is relevant to your talk). Your handouts can then carry the rest of the information load, so to speak, providing the supporting details that audience members can consume at their own speed, on their own time. You won't need to worry about stuffing every detail into your slides. because you have the more appropriate medium of printed documents to do that. As Garr Reynolds puts it, "Handouts can set you free."[25]

Possibilities for good handout materials include the following:[26]

- **Complex charts and diagrams.** Charts and tables that are too unwieldy for the screen or that demand thorough analysis make good handouts.
- **Articles and technical papers.** Magazine articles that supplement the information in your presentation make good handout materials, as do technical papers that provide in-depth coverage of the material you've highlighted in your presentation.
- **Case studies.** Summaries of business case studies can make good supplemental reading material.
- **Recommended resources.** Lists of websites, bloggers, and other online resources related to your topic can be useful. For each source, provide a URL and a one- or two-sentence summary of its content.
- **Copies of presentation slides.** In many cases, audiences like to have print versions of the slides used by a speaker, containing the speaker's comments about each slide and blank lines for note taking. Use the page and print setup options in your software to choose the more useful arrangement.

Timing the distribution of handouts depends on the content of your handouts, the nature of your presentation, and your personal preference. Some speakers prefer to distribute handout copies of their slides before the presentation begins so that the audience can take notes. Doing so can be risky, however, particularly if you've organized your talk with the indirect approach, because the audience can read ahead and reach the conclusion and recommendations before you're able to build up to them yourself. Other speakers simply advise the audience of the types of information they are including in handouts but delay distributing anything until they have finished speaking.

For a quick review of the key steps in creating effective visuals, see "Checklist: Enhancing Presentations with Visuals." For the latest information on presentation design, visit http://real-timeupdates.com/bct11 and click on Chapter 17.

✓ Checklist   Enhancing Presentations with Visuals

A. Plan your presentation visuals.
- Make sure you and your message, not your visuals, remain the focus of your presentation.
- Select your visuals carefully to support your message; use a combination of visuals if needed.
- Review your plan for each visual to make sure it truly supports your message.
- Follow effective design principles, with an emphasis on accuracy and simplicity.
- Use your time wisely so that you have plenty of time to practice your presentation.

B. Choose structured or free-form slides.
- Structured slides using bullet-point templates are easy to create, require little design time or skill, and can be completed in a hurry. Best uses: routine, internal presentations.
- Primary disadvantages of structured slides are mind-numbing repetition of bullet-point format and the common tendency of stuffing too much information on them.
- Free-form slides make it easier to combine textual and visual information, to create a more dynamic and engaging experience, and to maintain a conversational connection with the audience. Best uses: motivational, educational, and persuasive presentations.
- Primary disadvantages of structured slides are the time, skill, and imagery required; added responsibilities for the speaker; and possibility of fragmenting complex topics.

C. Design effective slides.
- Avoid the temptation to create "slideuments," slides that are so packed with information that they can be read as standalone documents.
- Use color to emphasize important ideas, create contrast, isolate visual elements, and convey intended nonverbal signals.
- Limit color to a few compatible choices and use them consistently.
- Make sure your slide background doesn't compete with the foreground.

- Use decorative artwork sparingly and only to support your message.
- Emphasize functional artwork—photos, technical drawings, charts, and other visual elements containing information that is part of your message.
- Choose typefaces that are easy to read on-screen; limit the number of typefaces and use them consistently.
- Use slide masters to maintain consistency throughout your presentation.

D. Create effective slide content.
- Write content that will be readable from everywhere in the room.
- Write short, active, parallel phrases that support, not replace, your spoken message.
- Avoid complete sentences unless you need to quote verbatim.
- Limit the amount of text so that your audience can focus on listening, not reading.
- Simplify print graphics for use on slides but don't oversimplify.
- Use functional animation when it can support your message.
- Make sure slide transitions are subtle, if used at all.
- Use builds carefully to control the release of information.
- Use hyperlinks and action buttons to add flexibility to your presentation.
- Incorporate multimedia elements that can help engage your audience and deliver your message.

E. Complete slides and support materials.
- Review every slide carefully to ensure accuracy, consistency, and clarity.
- Make sure that all slides are fully operational.
- Use the slide sorter to verify and adjust the sequence of slides, if needed.
- Have a backup plan in case your electronic presentation plan fails.
- Create navigation and support slides.
- Create handouts to give the audience additional information and to minimize the amount of information you need to put on your slides.

Quick Learning Guide

MyBcommLab

If your course uses MyBcommLab, log on to www.mybcommlab.com to access the following study and assessment aids associated with this chapter:

- Video applications
- Real-Time Updates
- Peer review activity
- Pre/post test
- Personalized study plan
- Model documents
- Sample presentations

If you are not using MyBcommLab, you can access Real-Time Updates through http://real-timeupdates.com/bct11.

CHAPTER OUTLINE

Planning Your Presentation Visuals
Selecting the Type of Visuals to Use
Verifying Your Design Plans

Choosing Structured or Free-Form Slides
Structured Slides
Free-Form Slides

Designing Effective Slides
Selecting Design Elements
Maintaining Design Consistency

Creating Effective Slide Content
Slide Text
Slide Tables and Graphics
Animation and Multimedia

Completing Slides and Support Materials
Creating Navigation and Support Slides
Creating Effective Handouts

SUMMARY OF LEARNING OBJECTIVES

1 Explain the role of visuals in business presentations, and list the types of visuals commonly used. Visuals create interest, illustrate and clarify important points, add variety, and help the listener absorb the information you're presenting. In most businesses today, electronic slide presentations are the most common tool, but you might also use overhead transparencies, chalkboards and whiteboards (including electronic whiteboards), flip charts, product samples, models, video, and various software programs.

2 Explain the difference between structured and free-form slides, and suggest when each design strategy is more appropriate. Structured slides follow the same design plan for most or all the slides in a presentation. They are often created by using the templates provided with PowerPoint and other electronic presentation programs. Structured slides tend to convey most of their information through bullet points. In contrast, free-form slides do not follow any set design scheme from slide to slide, although they can and should use color, font selection, and other design choices to create a unified feel across a presentation. Free-form slides often have just a single statement on each slide, requiring many more slides to cover the same amount of material as the typical structured design.

The ease and speed with which structured slides can be created make them most useful for routine presentations such as project update meetings, particularly for internal audiences and in situations in which the slide deck will be used only once. They can also be useful when the audience needs to see a number of information points on screen simultaneously in order to make comparisons. Given their ability to excite and engage, free-form designs are particularly good for motivational, educational, and persuasive presentations—particularly when the slides will be used multiple times and therefore compensate for the extra time and effort often required to create them.

3 Outline the decisions involved in selecting color, artwork, and typefaces to create effective slide designs. Color is a critical design element because it can grab the viewer's attention, emphasize important ideas, create contrast, isolate particular slide elements, stimulate emotions, and send powerful nonverbal messages such as elegance or technical sophistication. Color also affects the acceptance and retention of messages. When selecting color, limit your choices to a few compatible ones and use them consistently.

Slides have two layers of visual elements, the *background* (which should be as unobtrusive as possible) and the *foreground*, which carries the information content of the slide. Artwork on the background and foreground can be divided into *functional*, which conveys information directly, and *decorative*, which does not. Well-designed functional artwork is always useful and a great way to convey message points quickly. Decorative artwork can be useful if it supports the message point on a slide, but it can be distracting otherwise.

Typefaces and type styles need careful consideration to ensure that they are easily readable from every point in the presentation room. Clean, sans serif typefaces are usually the best choice, although serif typefaces can be useful when used in large sizes. In general, avoid decorative typefaces except for limited, special purposes.

4 Explain how to create effective slide content. Slide content can be divided into three groups: text, tables and graphics, and animation and multimedia. To choose effective words and phrases, think of the text on your slides as a guide to the content, not the content itself. For all-text slides, try to limit the content to four or five lines, with four or five words per line, and use short phrases rather than full sentences.

To create effective tables and graphics, keep in mind that visuals for projection need to be simpler than those used for print documents. If necessary, create simplified versions for your slides and provide the full-detail versions in a printed handout.

Like artwork, animation can be functional or decorative. Functional animation can be a powerful way to demonstrate processes and procedures. Decorative animation is nearly always a distraction and should be avoided. Slide transitions, which control how one slide replaces another on screen, are a form of animation. Except for subtle transitions such as a gentle fade to black, avoid using most of the transitions that come with your software. Builds, on the other hand, can be extremely helpful by letting you control the release of individual text points or graphical elements on a slide.

Hyperlinks instruct your computer to jump to another slide in your presentation, to a website, or to another program entirely. They can be handy for designing flexibility into your presentations and for sharing other types of files with the audience.

Audio, video, and other multimedia files can complement your live message, but make sure they support your message rather than replace it.

5 **Explain the role of navigation slides, support slides, and handouts.** In addition to the slides that convey your content, you can create one or more *title slides* to introduce your presentation (and yourself, if necessary), *agenda and program detail slides* that tell viewers what to expect during the presentation and provide information to help them plan their time, and *navigation slides* that help you and your audience keep track of where you are in the presentation. Particularly for longer presentations, a *moving blueprint* slide is a great way to show the audience what has been covered so far and what is still to come.

Handouts should be considered an integral part of your presentation, working in conjunction with your slides and spoken message to provide audience members with additional details, supporting documents, and other material too detailed to include in the presentation itself.

Checklist

Enhancing Presentations with Visuals

A. Plan your presentation visuals.
- Make sure you and your message, not your visuals, remain the focus of your presentation.
- Select your visuals carefully to support your message; use a combination of visuals if needed.
- Review your plan for each visual to make sure it truly supports your message.
- Follow effective design principles, with an emphasis on accuracy and simplicity.
- Use your time wisely so that you have plenty of time to practice your presentation.

B. Choose structured or free-form slides.
- Structured slides using bullet-point templates are easy to create, require little design time or skill, and can be completed in a hurry. Best uses: routine, internal presentations.
- Primary disadvantages of structured slides are mind-numbing repetition of bullet-point format and the common tendency of stuffing too much information on them.
- Free-form slides make it easier to combine textual and visual information, to create a more dynamic and engaging experience, and to maintain a conversational connection with the audience. Best uses: motivational, educational, and persuasive presentations.

- Primary disadvantages of structured slides are the time, skill, and imagery required; added responsibilities for the speaker; and possibility of fragmenting complex topics.

C. Design effective slides.
- Avoid the temptation to create "slideuments," slides that are so packed with information that they can be read as standalone documents.
- Use color to emphasize important ideas, create contrast, isolate visual elements, and convey intended nonverbal signals.
- Limit color to a few compatible choices and use them consistently.
- Make sure your slide background doesn't compete with the foreground.
- Use decorative artwork sparingly and only to support your message.
- Emphasize functional artwork—photos, technical drawings, charts, and other visual elements containing information that is part of your message.
- Choose typefaces that are easy to read on-screen; limit the number of typefaces and use them consistently.
- Use slide masters to maintain consistency throughout your presentation.

D. Create effective slide content.
- Write content that will be readable from everywhere in the room.
- Write short, active, parallel phrases that support, not replace, your spoken message.

- Avoid complete sentences unless you need to quote verbatim.
- Limit the amount of text so that your audience can focus on listening, not reading.
- Simplify print graphics for use on slides but don't oversimplify.
- Use functional animation when it can support your message.
- Make sure slide transitions are subtle, if used at all.
- Use builds carefully to control the release of information.
- Use hyperlinks and action buttons to add flexibility to your presentation.
- Incorporate multimedia elements that can help engage your audience and deliver your message.

E. Complete slides and support materials.
- Review every slide carefully to ensure accuracy, consistency, and clarity.
- Make sure that all slides are fully operational.
- Use the slide sorter to verify and adjust the sequence of slides, if needed.
- Have a backup plan in case your electronic presentation plan fails.
- Create navigation and support slides.
- Create handouts to give the audience additional information and to minimize the amount of information you need to put on your slides.

COMMUNICATION CHALLENGES AT PRESENTATION ZEN

Garr Reynolds was impressed enough with your student project portfolio and part-time work to hire you as a communication associate. You will work from your home in California, assisting him on various projects and eventually meeting with his U.S. clients.

INDIVIDUAL CHALLENGE: Reynolds gave you an intriguing assignment your first day on the job. He is developing some presentations, website content, and a printed brochure for an energy technology company doing some advanced research in wind and tidal power. He asked you to propose a color palette to use for all these materials. Using any software program you're comfortable with (you can use a word processor if you don't have access to a graphics program) choose five standard colors or mix your own. Reynolds wants one dark color to use for slide backgrounds, one contrasting color that could be used for type on the dark background, and three compatible accent colors to use for various purposes. One restriction: you can't use green. The client feels that green is becoming overused in the renewable energy industry and wants to stand out by using different colors. Create a couple of simple slides in PowerPoint, Keynote, or Google Docs showing how your color palette could be used.

TEAM CHALLENGE: With a team of classmates, search Creative Commons (http://creativecommons.org) for attractive photos that could be used on slides to help illustrate or emphasize the following message points in a presentation:

- Trends in health-care costs
- Competition
- High levels of employee engagement (the energy, enthusiasm, and effort employees put into their work)
- Consumer hyperchoice (situations in which shoppers have such an overwhelming array of choices in a given product category that making purchase decisions becomes difficult and stressful)
- Scalability (the ease with which a business process or an entire company can be expanded to handle a greater number of transactions)

For each message point, find three candidates and then decide as a team which one conveys the point most effectively and in the most appropriate style for a fairly formal business presentation. Create a slide show in which you show the photos and explain how each one conveys the concept in question. Make sure you follow the usage and attribution guidelines for any photos you find online.

TEST YOUR KNOWLEDGE

To review chapter content related to each question, refer to the indicated Learning Objective.

1. What is a screencast? [LO-1]
2. What are your options for supporting a presentation with visuals aids? [LO-1]
3. How do structured and free-form slide designs differ from one another? [LO-2]
4. What should the role of the background be in a slide? [LO-3]
5. What is the recommended number of fonts to use per slide? [LO-4]
6. What is the difference between decorative and functional artwork and animation? [LO-4]
7. How do slide transitions differ from builds? [LO-4]
8. How is a moving blueprint slide used in a presentation? [LO-5]
9. How does the slide sorter view facilitate the editing process for an electronic presentation? [LO-5]

APPLY YOUR KNOWLEDGE

To review chapter content related to each question, refer to the indicated Learning Objective.

1. Would you choose a structured or free-form design plan for a presentation about upcoming changes in international accounting regulations? Why? [LO-2]
2. What is the fundamental problem with "slideuments"? [LO-2]
3. How can you use slide masters to enhance the effectiveness of your slides? [LO-3]
4. Is it ethical to use design elements and special effects to persuade an audience? Why or why not? [LO-3]
5. How does Guy Kawasaki's "30-point rule" for fonts help ensure readable and memorable slide content? [LO-3]
6. If you are giving a presentation to company management that uses the indirect approach to recommend that the company consolidate its manufacturing operations (a traumatic change that would result in the loss of hundreds of jobs, including a dozen management positions), would it be wise to hand out copies of your slides at the beginning of the presentation? Why or why not? [LO-5]

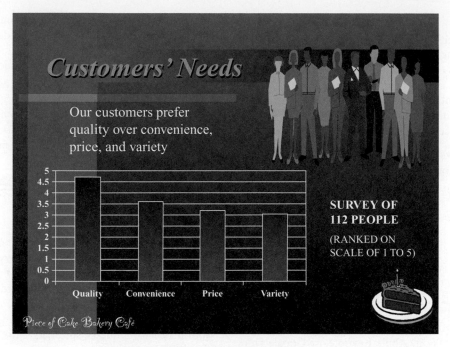

Figure 17.11   **Piece of Cake Bakery Customer Survey**

PRACTICE YOUR SKILLS

Messages for Analysis

Message 17.A: Improving a Slide

Examine the slide in Figure 17.11 and point out any problems you notice. How would you correct these problems?

Message 17.B: Modifying for Presentation

Examine the graph in Figure 17.12 and explain how to modify it for an electronic presentation, using the guidelines discussed in this chapter.

Message 17.C: Analyzing the Animation

To access this PowerPoint presentation, visit http://real-time updates.com/bct11, click on "Student Assignments," and select "Chapter 17, page 515, Message 17.C." Download and watch the presentation in slide show mode (after you select Slide Show from the View menu, simply click your mouse to advance through the slides). After you've watched the presentation, identify at least three ways in which various animations, builds, and transitions either enhanced or impeded your understanding of the subject matter.

Figure 17.12   **CommuniCo Employee Training Costs**

Exercises

Active links for all websites in this chapter can be found on MyBcommLab; see your User Guide for instructions on accessing the content for this chapter. Each activity is labeled according to the primary skill or skills you will need to use. To review relevant chapter content, you can refer to the indicated Learning Objective. In some instances, supporting information will be found in another chapter, as indicated.

1. **Designing Effective Slides [LO-2]** Find a business-related slide presentation on SlideShare (www.slideshare.net) and analyze the design. Do you consider it structured or free form? Does the design help the audience understand and remember the message? Why or why not? What improvements would you suggest to the design? Is the slide set understandable on its own?

2. **Designing Effective Slides [LO-3]** Think about a company you might like to start after graduation and imagine that you are giving a 20-minute presentation to potential investors. Review the design templates or themes available in whatever presentation software you have available, such as Microsoft PowerPoint, Apple Keynote, or Google Docs. Choose a template and color palette that best supports the message you want to convey to these financiers. Write a one-page report or brief blog post that includes a sample slide using this theme and color palette and an explanation of how this design supports your message.

3. **Creating Effective Slide Content [LO-4]** Look through recent issues of several business periodicals for an article that discusses issues a specific company or industry is facing. Based on the information in the article and the guidelines discussed in this chapter, create three to five presentation slides summarizing these issues.

4. **Creating Effective Slide Content [LO-4]** Convert Table 2.2 on page 41 to presentation slides so that the content is easily readable in a large conference room. Decide whether to use free-form or structured slides and decide how much content will be on the slides and how much will be spoken by the presenter. Provide speaker's notes along with your slides.

5. **Completing Slides and Support Materials [LO-5]** Find a business-oriented presentation on SlideShare (www.slideshare.net) that could use better navigation slides. Download the presentation and write at least three navigation slides that would help viewers follow the flow of the presentation.

EXPAND YOUR SKILLS

Critique the Professionals

Dave Paradi, author of *The Visual Slide Revolution*, specializes in helping presenters transform text-heavy slides into more readable and more effective visuals. Visit his YouTube channel at www.youtube.com/thinkoutsidetheslide, watch several of his "PowerPoint Slide Makeover" videos, and select the one that you find most helpful or enlightening. Using whatever medium your instructor requests, summarize the changes Paradi made to the slide in question and explain in your own words why these changes made the slide more effective.

Sharpening Your Career Skills Online

Bovée and Thill's Business Communication Web Search, at http://businesscommunicationblog.com/websearch, is a unique research tool designed specifically for business communication research. Use the Web Search function to find a website, video, PDF document, podcast, or PowerPoint presentation that offers advice on creating slides and other presentation visuals. Write a brief email message to your instructor, describing the item that you found and summarizing the career skills information you learned from it.

CASES

PRESENTATION SKILLS

1. Planning, Designing, and Creating Presentation Slides [LO-1], [LO-2], [LO-3], [LO-4] Read the Communication Close-up at Southwest Airlines on page 174 in Chapter 7 and decide whether free-form or structured slides would be the most effective way to present this story to an audience of customer service agents to help them understand the power of social media.

Your task: Using whichever design approach you think is better, create a brief presentation (slides and speaking notes) to tell the story.

PRESENTATION SKILLS   TEAM SKILLS

2. Planning, Designing, and Creating Presentation Slides [LO-1], [LO-2], [LO-3], [LO-4] Changing a nation's eating habits is a Herculean task, but the physical and financial health of the United States depends on it. You work for the USDA Center for Nutrition Policy and Promotion (www.cnpp.usda.gov), and it's your job to educate people on the dangers of unhealthy eating and the changes they can make to eat more balanced and healthful diets.

Your task: Visit http://real-timeupdates.com/bct11, click on "Student Assignments," select "Chapter 17, page 516, Case 2," and download the *Dietary Guidelines for Americans.* (If you worked on Message for Analysis 15.A on page 457, you've already seen the executive summary from this document.) With your team, develop a presentation no longer than 15 minutes, using free-form slides, that conveys the key points from Chapter 3 of the *Guidelines,* "Food and Food Components to Reduce." The objectives of your presentation are to alert people to the dangers of excessive consumption of the five components discussed in the chapter and to let them know what healthy levels of consumptions are. This chapter has a lot of information, but you don't need to pack it all into your slides; you can assume that the chapter will be available as a handout to anyone who attends your presentation. Create as many slides as you need, along with speaking notes that someone outside your team could use to give the presentation. You can use images from the *Guidelines* PDF, the websites of the U.S. Department of Agriculture and the U.S. Department of Health and Human Services, or a non-government source such as Creative Commons (http://creativecommons.org). Make sure you follow the usage and attribution guidelines for any photos you find on non-government sites.

PRESENTATION SKILLS

3. Planning, Designing, and Creating Presentation Slides [LO-1], [LO-2], [LO-3], [LO-4] *Pecha-kucha* is a style of presentation that might be the ultimate in creative constraint: The speaker is limited to 20 slides, each of which is displayed for exactly 20 seconds before automatically advancing. Pecha-kucha Nights, which are open to the public, are now put on in cities all over the world. Visit www.pecha-kucha.org for more information on these events or to view some archived presentations.

Your task: Select one of the subjects from Exercise 2 on page 491 in Chapter 16 and develop a *pecha-kucha* style presentation with 20 slides, each designed to be displayed for 20 seconds. Use the slide timing capabilities in your presentation software to control the pace. Make sure you practice before presenting to your class so that you can hit the precise timing requirements.[27]

PRESENTATION SKILLS
SOCIAL NETWORKING SKILLS

4. Planning, Designing, and Creating Presentation Slides [LO-1], [LO-2], [LO-3], [LO-4] You know those times when you're craving Thai food or the perfect fruit smoothie, but you don't know where to go? Or when you're out shopping or clubbing and want to let your friends know where you are? Foursquare's location-based services (https://foursquare.com/) connect you with friends and companies that offer products and services of interest.

Your task: Create a brief presentation explaining the Foursquare concept and its features and benefits. List two Foursquare competitors and give a brief assessment of which of the three you would recommend to your classmates.[28]

PRESENTATION SKILLS
TEAM SKILLS   PORTFOLIO BUILDER

5. Planning, Designing, and Creating Presentation Slides [LO-1], [LO-2], [LO-3], [LO-4] In your job as a business development researcher for a major corporation, you're asked to gather and process information on a wide variety of subjects. Management has gained confidence in your research and analysis skills and would now like you to begin making regular presentations at management retreats and other functions. Topics are likely to include the following:

- Offshoring of U.S. jobs
- Foreign ownership of U.S. firms
- Employment issues involving workers from other countries
- Tax breaks offered by local and state governments to attract new businesses
- Economic impact of environmental regulations

Your task: With a team assigned by your instructor, choose one of the topics from the list and conduct enough research to familiarize yourself with the topic. Identify at least three important issues that anyone involved with this topic should know about. Prepare a 10-minute presentation that introduces the topic, comments on its importance to the U.S. economy, and discusses the issues you've identified. Assume that your audience is a cross-section of business managers who don't have any particular experience in the topic you've chosen.

PRESENTATION SKILLS   PORTFOLIO BUILDER

6. Planning, Designing, and Creating Presentation Slides [LO-1], [LO-2], [LO-3], [LO-4] Depending on the sequence your instructor chose for this course, you've probably covered at least a dozen chapters at this point and learned or improved many valuable skills. Think through your progress and identify five business communication skills that you've either learned for the first time or developed during this course.

Your task: Create a six-slide presentation, with a title slide and five slides that describe each of the five skills you've identified. Be sure to explain how each skill could help you in your career. Use any visual style that you feel is appropriate for the assignment.

PRESENTATION SKILLS   TEAM SKILLS

7. Planning, Designing, and Creating Presentation Slides; Collaboration: Team Projects [LO-1], [LO-3], [LO-4], Chapter 2 Garr Reynolds offers an excellent brief introduction to effective slide design in his "Top Ten Slide Tips" at www.garrreynolds.com/presentation/slides.html.

Your task: With a team of two or three other students, create a free-form slide presentation that covers Reynolds's ten tips. Be sure to give Reynolds credit for his information and ideas. You may include a few brief quotations from him, but for the most part, express his ideas in your own words. Illustrate his points as you see fit with visuals that you create yourselves or use with appropriate attribution from a source such as Creative Commons (http://creativecommons.org) or Morguefile (www.morguefile.com). Make sure you follow the usage and attribution terms for any photos you find online. (For these two sites, the terms should be listed for any photo you find.)

PRESENTATION SKILLS   PORTFOLIO BUILDER

8. Planning, Designing, and Creating Presentation Slides [LO-1], [LO-3], [LO-4]   In its competitive battles with AT&T, Sprint, and other carriers, Verizon seeks to attract and keep not just customers but top employees. Engineers and technicians obviously play a vital role in a technology company such as Verizon, but the firm also needs specialists in everything from accounting to public relations to real estate.

Your task: Prepare a brief presentation that Verizon recruiters could use at job fairs and other venues to entice both new graduates and experienced professionals to consider joining the company. Choose a structured or free-form design and then create an appropriate number of slides for a presentation that is at least 10 minutes but no longer than 15 (not including a question-and-answer period). Assume that the audience members have heard of Verizon but don't have any in-depth knowledge about the company. You can learn more about the company and the benefits of working there by visiting www22.verizon.com/jobs.

PART 7   Writing Employment Messages and Interviewing for Jobs

CHAPTER 18   Building Careers and Writing Résumés

CHAPTER 19   Applying and Interviewing for Employment

The same techniques you use to succeed in your career can also help you launch and manage that career. Understand the employer's perspective on the hiring process so that you can adapt your approach and find the best job in the shortest possible time. Learn the best ways to craft a résumé and the other elements in your job search portfolio. Understand the interviewing process to make sure you're prepared for every stage and every type of interview.

Building Careers and Writing Résumés

LEARNING OBJECTIVES After studying this chapter, you will be able to

1 List eight key steps to finding the ideal opportunity in today's job market

2 Explain the process of planning your résumé, including how to choose the best résumé organization

3 Describe the tasks involved in writing your résumé and list the major sections of a traditional résumé

4 Characterize the completing step for résumés, including the six most common formats in which you can produce a résumé

MyBcommLab Test your mastery of this chapter and its Learning Objectives. Visit mybcommlab.com to apply what you've learned in Document Makeovers and interactive simulation scenarios.

COMMUNICATION CLOSE-UP AT ATK

ATK's Carl Willis oversees the company's efforts to use advanced statistical analysis to predict workforce needs.

www.atk.com

One could say ATK is in the business of accuracy. Whether it's rocket motors for NASA, missiles and munitions for the U.S. Army, or ammunition for law enforcement and sporting uses, customers depend on ATK for accuracy and overall performance. Failure is not an option, because as the company says, "Our customers' lives depend on the products we make."

Over the past few years, the multifaceted Minneapolis aerospace and defense company has been applying that obsession with accuracy and performance to one of the toughest problems any business faces: attracting, hiring, and keeping the quality employees who make business success possible. Along the way, ATK is one of a small but growing cadre of firms revolutionizing the practice of human resources (HR).

In the eyes of some professionals in finance, manufacturing, sales, and other data-driven functional areas, HR suffers from a "reputational deficit," to put it politely. Most other functional areas have long since adopted information technology to improve decision making and demonstrate their contribution to the bottom line. However, HR is still viewed by some as a "soft" function that might do a fine job of processing employee paperwork but can't really prove how well it's doing the critical job of finding the right employees and making sure they stay on board. The information systems being used tend to focus on recordkeeping, compliance verification, and other important but not terribly strategic tasks.

Carl Willis, ATK's vice president of human resources, oversees the company's efforts in the emerging field of *predictive workforce analytics*, the use of statistical modeling to help a company keep its business needs and employee skill sets in alignment. Balancing this complex equation of supply and demand is particularly vital for a company such as ATK, where many jobs are highly specialized and the departure of a single employee can sometimes cause significant problems. ATK's system is so advanced that it can predict the "flight risk" of individual employees, and it was able to predict with remarkable accuracy the number of employees who would take early retirement before a particular retirement benefit was set to expire. By predicting such events with accuracy, a company can ramp up hiring and focus on specific types of skills it will need to bring in.

At a broader level, the aerospace and defense sector is facing a shortage of key talent in the near future, as its aging workforce heads into retirement. ATK is counting on predictive analytics to help it characterize the skills required to perform those jobs and identify new employees who can provide them when the time comes.

With these tools in hand, a new generation of HR professionals is poised to make a more strategic contribution, armed with the data to prove it.[1]

Finding the Ideal Opportunity in Today's Job Market

The efforts made by ATK (profiled in the chapter-opening Communication Close-Up) show the importance that top companies place on finding the right employees and the investments they are willing to make in both personnel and technology to attract and keep valuable talent. Whether you'll be looking for your first professional job on graduation or you're already in mid-career, you need to put as much thought and care into finding the right job as employers put into finding the right employees.

Identifying and landing the ideal job can be a long and difficult process, particularly in tough employment markets. Fortunately, the skills you're developing in this course will give you a competitive advantage. This section offers a general job-search strategy with advice that applies to just about any career path you might want to pursue. As you craft your personal strategy, keep these two guidelines in mind:

- **Get organized.** Your job search could last many months and involve multiple contacts with dozens of companies. You need to keep all the details straight to make sure you don't miss opportunities or make mistakes such as losing someone's email address or forgetting an appointment.
- **Start now and stick to it.** Even if you are a year or more away from graduation, now is not too early to get started with some of the essential research and planning tasks. If you wait until the last minute, you will miss opportunities and you won't be as prepared as the candidates you'll be competing against.

WRITING THE STORY OF YOU

Take the time you have now to explore the possibilities, to find your passion, and to identify appealing career paths. If you haven't yet, read the career-planning Prologue that starts on page xxxi, and particularly the "What Do You Want to Do?" section on page xxxiii, to help identify the nature of the work you'd like to do, if not a specific profession.

Next, using the advice on creating a personal brand on page xxxvi, begin writing the "story of you," the things you are passionate about, the skills you possess, your ability to help an organization reach its goals, the path you've been on so far, and the path you want to follow in the future. Think in terms of an image or a theme you'd like to project. Are you academically gifted? An effective leader? A well-rounded professional with wide-ranging talents? A creative problem solver? A technical wizard? Writing your story is a valuable planning exercise that helps you think about where you want to go and how to present yourself to target employers.

LEARNING TO THINK LIKE AN EMPLOYER

Now that you know your side of the hiring equation a little better, switch sides and look at it from an employer's perspective. To begin with, recognize that companies take risks with every hiring decision—the risk that the person hired doesn't meet expectations and the risk

1   LEARNING OBJECTIVE

List eight key steps to finding the ideal opportunity in today's job market.

If you haven't already, read the Prologue, "Building a Career with Your Communication Skills," before studying this chapter.

MyBcommLab

- Access this chapter's simulation entitled Cover Letters and Résumés, located at mybcommlab.com.

What's your story? Employers will want to know where you've been and where you want to go.

Employers judge their recruiting success by *quality of hire,* and you can take steps to be—and look like—a high-quality hire.

that they let a better candidate slip through their fingers. Many companies judge the success of their recruiting efforts by *quality of hire,* a measure of how closely new employees meet the company's needs.[2] What steps can you take to present yourself as the low-risk, high-reward choice, as someone who can make a meaningful contribution to the organization?

Your perceived ability to perform the job is obviously an essential part of your potential quality as a new hire. However, hiring managers consider more than just your ability to handle the responsibilities you'll be given. They want to know if you'll be reliable and motivated, if you're somebody who "gets it" when it comes to being a professional in today's workplace. A great way to get inside the heads of corporate recruiters is to "eavesdrop" on their professional conversations by reading periodicals such as *Workforce Management* (www.workforce.com) and blogs such as Fistful of Talent (www.fistfuloftalent.com) and The HR Capitalist (www.hrcapitalist.com).

Follow the online conversations of professional recruiters to learn what their hot-button issues are.

RESEARCHING INDUSTRIES AND COMPANIES OF INTEREST

Learning more about professions, industries, and individual companies is easy to do with the library and online resources available to you. Don't limit your research to easily available sources, however. Companies are likely to be impressed by creative research, such as interviewing their customers to learn more about how the firm does business. "Detailed research, including talking to our customers, is so rare it will almost guarantee you get hired," explains the recruiting manager at Alcon Laboratories.[3]

Table 18.1 lists some of the many websites where you can learn more about companies and find job openings. Start with The Riley Guide, www.rileyguide.com, which offers advice for online job searches as well as links to hundreds of specialized websites that post

TABLE 18.1	**Selected Job-Search Websites**	
Website*	**URL**	**Highlights**
Riley Guide	www.rileyguide.com	Vast collection of links to both general and specialized job sites for every career imaginable; don't miss this one—it could save you hours of searching
TweetMyJobs.com	http://tweetmyjobs.com	The largest Twitter job board, with thousands of channels segmented by geography, job type, and industry
CollegeRecruiter.com	www.collegerecruiter.com	Focused on opportunities for graduates with less than three years of work experience
Monster	http://home.monster.com	One of the most popular job sites, with hundreds of thousands of openings, many from hard-to-find small companies; extensive collection of advice on the job search process
MonsterCollege	http://college.monster.com	Focused on job searches for new college grads; your school's career center site probably links here
CareerBuilder	www.careerbuilder.com	One of the largest job boards; affiliated with more than 150 newspapers around the country
Jobster	www.jobster.com	Uses social networking to link employers with job seekers
USAJOBS	www.usajobs.opm.gov	The official job search site for the U.S. government, featuring everything from jobs for economists to astronauts to border patrol agents
IMDiversity	www.imdiversity.com	Good resource on diversity in the workplace, with job postings from companies that have made a special commitment to promoting diversity in their workforces
Dice.com	www.dice.com	One of the best sites for high-technology jobs
Net-Temps	www.net-temps.com	Popular site for contractors and freelancers looking for short-term assignments
Internship Programs.com	http://internshipprograms.com	Posts listings from companies looking for interns in a wide variety of professions
Simply Hired Indeed	www.simplyhired.com www.indeed.com	Specialized search engines that look for job postings on hundreds of websites worldwide; they find many postings that aren't listed on job board sites such as Monster

Note: This list represents only a small fraction of the hundreds of job-posting sites and other resources available online; be sure to check with your college's career center for the latest information.

openings in specific industries and professions. Your college's career center placement office probably maintains an up-to-date list as well.

To learn more about contemporary business topics, peruse some of these leading business periodicals and newspapers with significant business sections (in some cases, you may need to go through your library's online databases to gain full access):

Wall Street Journal: http://online.wsj.com/public/us
New York Times: www.nyt.com
USA Today: www.usatoday.com
BusinessWeek: www.businessweek.com
Business 2.0: http://money.cnn.com/magazines/business2
Fast Company: www.fastcompany.com
Fortune: http://money.cnn.com/magazines/fortune
Forbes: www.forbes.com

Employers expect you to be familiar with important developments in their industries, so stay on top of business news.

In addition, thousands of bloggers, microbloggers, and podcasters offer news and commentary on the business world. To identify some that you might find helpful, start with directories such as Technorati (http://technorati.com/business) for blogs or Podcast Alley (www.podcastalley.com; select the "Business" genre) for podcasts. AllTop (http://alltop.com) is another good resource for finding people who write about topics that interest you. In addition to learning more about professions and opportunities, this research will help you get comfortable with the jargon and buzzwords currently in use in a particular field—including essential *keywords* to use in your résumé (see "Composing Your Résumé" on page 531).

TRANSLATING YOUR GENERAL POTENTIAL INTO A SPECIFIC SOLUTION FOR EACH EMPLOYER

An important aspect of the quality-of-hire challenge is trying to determine how well a candidate's attributes and experience will translate to the challenges of a specific position. As Jim Schaper, CEO of the Alpharetta, Georgia, software company Infor Global Solutions, puts it, "We try to determine if newly minted graduates can apply knowledge they've already gained."[4] Customizing your résumé to each job opening is an important step in showing employers that you will be a good fit. From your initial contact all the way through the interviewing process, in fact, you will have opportunities to impress recruiters by explaining how your general potential translates to the specific needs of the position.

An essential task in your job search is presenting your skills and accomplishments in a way that is relevant to the employer's business challenges.

For example, instead of following up with just a simple thank-you note after interviewing with Detroit-based InStar Services, Mary Berman offered a plan showing how she could help the company during her first 60 days on the job.[5] Berman could offer such a plan because she researched the company to know what its needs were and she understands her own capabilities well enough to match them to the company's needs.

TAKING THE INITIATIVE TO FIND OPPORTUNITIES

When it comes to finding the right opportunities, the easiest ways are not always the most productive ones. The major job boards such as Monster and classified services such as Craigslist might have thousands of openings—but many thousands of job seekers are looking at and applying for these same openings. Moreover, posting job openings on these sites is often a company's last resort, after it has exhausted other possibilities.

Don't hesitate to contact interesting companies even if they haven't advertised job openings to the public yet—they might be looking for somebody just like you.

Instead of searching through the same job openings as everyone else, take the initiative and go find opportunities. Identify the companies you want to work for and focus your efforts on them. Get in touch with their human resources departments (or individual managers if possible), describe what you can offer the company, and ask to be considered if any

REAL-TIME UPDATES
Learn More by Reading This Article

100 Twitter tools for job searchers

From specialized search tools to job listing feeds in specific professions, these Twitter tools can help you navigate today's job market. Go to http://real-timeupdates.com/bct11 and click on "Learn More." If you are using MyBcommLab, you can access Real-Time Updates within each chapter or under Student Study Tools.

opportunities come up.[6] Your message might appear right when a company is busy looking for someone but hasn't yet advertised the opening to the outside world.

BUILDING YOUR NETWORK

Networking is the process of making informal connections with mutually beneficial business contacts. Networking takes place wherever and whenever people communicate: at industry functions, at social gatherings, at alumni reunions—and all over the Internet, from LinkedIn to Facebook to Twitter. Networking is more essential than ever, because the vast majority of job openings are never advertised to the general public. To avoid the time and expense of sifting through thousands of applications and the risk of hiring complete strangers, most companies prefer to ask their employees for recommendations first.[7] The more people who know you, the better chance you have of being recommended for one of these hidden job openings.

> Start thinking like a networker now; your classmates could turn out to be some of your most important business contacts.

Start building your network now, before you need it. Your classmates could end up being some of your most valuable contacts, if not right away then possibly later in your career. Then branch out by identifying people with similar interests in your target professions, industries, and companies. Read news sites, blogs, and other online sources. Follow industry leaders on Twitter. You can also follow individual executives at your target companies to learn about their interests and concerns.[8] Connect with people on LinkedIn and Facebook, particularly in groups dedicated to particular career interests. Depending on the system and the settings on individual users' accounts, you may be able to introduce yourself via private messages. Just make sure you are respectful of people and don't take up much of their time.[9]

Participate in student business organizations, especially those with ties to professional organizations. Visit *trade shows* to learn about various industries and rub shoulders with people who work in those industries.[10] Don't overlook volunteering; you not only meet people but also demonstrate your ability to solve problems, manage projects, and lead others. You can do some good while creating a network for yourself.

Remember that networking is about people helping each other, not just about other people helping you. Pay close attention to networking etiquette: Try to learn something about the people you want to connect with, don't overwhelm others with too many messages or requests, be succinct in all your communication efforts, don't give out other people's names and contact information without their permission to do so, never email your résumé to complete strangers, don't assume you can send your résumé to everyone you meet, and remember to say thank you every time someone helps you.[11]

> Networking is a mutually beneficial activity, so look for opportunities to help others in some way.

To become a valued network member, you need to be able to help others in some way. You may not have any influential contacts yet, but because you're actively researching a number of industries and trends in your own job search, you probably have valuable information you can share via your social networks, blog, or Twitter account. Or you might simply be able to connect one person with another who can help. The more you network, the more valuable you become in your network—and the more valuable your network becomes to you.

Finally, be aware that your online network reflects on who you are in the eyes of potential employers, so exercise some judgment in making connections. Also, some employers are beginning to contact people in a candidate's network for background information, even if the candidate doesn't list those people as references.[12]

SEEKING CAREER COUNSELING

Your college's career center probably offers a wide variety of services, including individual counseling, job fairs,

REAL-TIME UPDATES
Learn More by Watching This Video

Tweet your way to a sweet job

This simple introduction to Twitter focuses on using the microblogging service for career networking. Go to http://real-timeupdates.com/bct11 and click on "Learn More." If you are using MyBcommLab, you can access Real-Time Updates within each chapter or under Student Study Tools.

on-campus interviews, and job listings. Counselors can give you advice on career planning and provide workshops in job search techniques, résumé preparation, job readiness training, interview techniques, self-marketing, and more.[13] You can also find career planning advice online. Many of the websites listed in Table 18.1 offer articles and online tests to help you choose a career path, identify essential skills, and prepare to enter the job market.

REAL-TIME UPDATES
Learn More by Reading This Article

Follow these people to a new career

Alison Doyle maintains a great list of career experts to follow on Twitter. Go to http://real-timeupdates.com/bct11 and click on "Learn More." If you are using MyBcommLab, you can access Real-Time Updates within each chapter or under Student Study Tools.

AVOIDING MISTAKES

While you're making all these positive moves to show employers you will be a quality hire, take care to avoid the simple blunders that can torpedo a job search, such as not catching mistakes in your résumé, misspelling the name of a manager you're writing to, showing up late for an interview, tweeting something unprofessional, failing to complete application forms correctly, asking for information that you can easily find yourself on a company's website, or making any other error that could flag you as someone who is careless, clueless, or disrespectful.

Don't let a silly mistake knock you out of contention for a great job.

To understand why even a minor mistake can hurt your chances, look at the situation from a recruiter's point of view. At KeyBank, for instance, a recruiter typically has 25 to 30 open positions at any given time.[14] If a hundred people are applying for each position—and the number can be much higher in a slow job market—a single recruiter could be considering 2,500 to 3,000 candidates at once. As recruiters work to narrow down the possibilities, even a minor mistake on your part can give them a reason to bump you out of the candidate pool.

Planning a Résumé

Although you will create many messages during your career search, your résumé will be the most important document in this process. You will be able to use it directly in many instances, adapt it to a variety of uses such an e-portfolio, and reuse pieces of it in social networking profiles and online application forms.

Writing a résumé is one of those projects that really benefits from multiple planning, writing, and completing sessions spread out over several days or weeks. You are trying to summarize a complex subject (yourself!) and present a compelling story to complete strangers in a brief document. Follow the three-step writing process (see Figure 18.1 on the next page) and give yourself plenty of time.

2   LEARNING OBJECTIVE

Explain the process of planning your résumé, including how to choose the best résumé organization.

ANALYZING YOUR PURPOSE AND AUDIENCE

A **résumé** is a structured summary of a person's education, employment background, and job qualifications. Before you begin writing a résumé, make sure you understand its true function—as a brief, persuasive business message intended to stimulate an employer's interest in meeting you and learning more about you (see Table 18.2 on page 526). In other words, the purpose of a résumé is not to get you a job but rather to get you an interview.[15]

Once you view your résumé as a persuasive business message, it's easier to decide what should and shouldn't be in it.

As you conduct your research on various professions, industries, companies, and individual managers, you will have a better perspective on your target readers and their information needs. Learn as much as you can about the individuals who may be reading your résumé. Many professionals and managers are bloggers, Twitter users, and LinkedIn members, for example, so you can learn more about them online even if you've never met them. Any bit of information can help you craft a more effective message.

Thanks to Twitter, LinkedIn, and other social media, you can often learn valuable details about individual managers in your target employers.

By the way, if employers ask to see your "CV," they're referring to your *curriculum vitae*, the term used instead of *résumé* in academic professions and in many countries outside the United States. Résumés and CVs are essentially the same, although CVs can be much more detailed. If you need to adapt a U.S.-style résumé to CV format, or vice versa, career expert Alison Doyle offers advice on her website, **www.alisondoyle.com.**

1 Plan →	**2** Write →	**3** Complete
Analyze the Situation Recognize that the purpose of your résumé is to get an interview, not to get a job. **Gather Information** Research target industries and companies so that you know what they're looking for in new hires; learn about various jobs and what to expect; learn about the hiring manager, if possible. **Select the Right Medium** Start with a traditional paper résumé and develop scannable, electronic plain-text, PDF, and online versions, as needed. Consider using PowerPoint and video for your e-portfolio. **Organize the Information** Choose an organizational model that highlights your strengths and downplays your shortcomings; use the chronological approach unless you have a strong reason not to.	**Adapt to Your Audience** Plan your wording carefully so that you can catch a recruiter's eye within seconds; translate your education and experience into attributes that target employers find valuable. **Compose the Message** Write clearly and succinctly, using active, powerful language that is appropriate to the industries and companies you're targeting; use a professional tone in all communications.	**Revise the Message** Evaluate content and review readability and then edit and rewrite for conciseness and clarity. **Produce the Message** Use effective design elements and suitable layout for a clean, professional appearance; seamlessly combine text and graphical elements. When printing, use quality paper and a good printer. **Proofread the Message** Review for errors in layout, spelling, and mechanics; mistakes can cost you interview opportunities. **Distribute the Message** Deliver your résumé, carefully following the specific instructions of each employer or job board website.

Figure 18.1   Three-Step Writing Process for Résumés
Following the three-step writing process will help you create a successful résumé in a short time. Remember to pay particular attention to the "you" attitude and presentation quality; your résumé will probably get tossed aside if it doesn't speak to audience needs or if it contains mistakes.

GATHERING PERTINENT INFORMATION

If you haven't been building an employment portfolio thus far, you may need to do some research on yourself. Gather all the pertinent personal history you can think of, including the dates, duties, and accomplishments from any previous jobs you've held. Collect relevant educational experience that adds to your qualifications—formal degrees, skills

TABLE 18.2	**Fallacies and Facts About Résumés**
Fallacy	**Fact**
The purpose of a résumé is to list all your skills and abilities.	The purpose of a résumé is to kindle employer interest and generate an interview.
A good résumé will get you the job you want.	All a résumé can do is get you in the door.
Your résumé will always be read carefully and thoroughly.	In most cases, your résumé needs to make a positive impression within 30 or 45 seconds; only then will someone read it in detail. Moreover, it will likely be screened by a computer looking for keywords first—and if it doesn't contain the right keywords, a human being may never see it.
The more good information you present about yourself in your résumé, the better, so stuff your résumé with every positive detail you can think of.	Recruiters don't need that much information about you at the initial screening stage, and they probably won't read it.
If you want a really good résumé, have it prepared by a résumé service.	You have the skills needed to prepare an effective résumé, so prepare it yourself—unless the position is especially high level or specialized. Even then, you should check carefully before using a service.

certificates, academic awards, or scholarships. Also, gather any relevant information about school or volunteer activities that might be relevant to your job search, including offices you have held in any club or professional organization, presentations given, and online or print publications. You probably won't use every piece of information you come up with, but you'll want to have it at your fingertips before you begin composing your résumé.

SELECTING THE BEST MEDIUM

You should expect to produce your résumé in several media and formats. "Producing Your Résumé" on page 537 explores the various options.

ORGANIZING YOUR RÉSUMÉ AROUND YOUR STRENGTHS

Although you will see a number of ways to organize a résumé, most are some variation of chronological, functional, or a combination of the two. The right choice depends on your background and your goals, as the following sections explain.

The Chronological Résumé

In a **chronological résumé**, the work experience section dominates and is placed immediately after your contact information and introductory statement. The chronological approach is the most common way to organize a résumé, and many employers prefer this format because it presents your professional history in a clear, easy-to-follow arrangement.[16] If you're just graduating from college and have limited professional experience, you can vary this chronological approach by putting your educational qualifications before your experience.

The chronological résumé is the most common approach, but it might not be right for you at this stage in your career.

Develop your work experience section by listing your jobs in reverse chronological order, beginning with the most recent position and giving the most space to the most recent positions. For each job, start by listing the employer's name and location, your official job title, and the dates you held the position (write "to present" if you are still in your most recent position). Next, in a short block of text, highlight your accomplishments in a way that is relevant to your readers. This may require "translating" the terminology used in a particular industry or profession into terms that are more meaningful to your target readers. If the general responsibilities of the position are not obvious from the job title, provide a little background to help readers understand what you did. See Figures 18.2 and 18.3 on pages 528 and 529 for examples of ineffective and effective approaches.

The Functional Résumé

A **functional résumé**, sometimes called a *skills résumé*, emphasizes your skills and capabilities, identifying employers and academic experience in subordinate sections. This arrangement stresses individual areas of competence rather than job history. The functional approach also has three advantages: (1) Without having to read through job descriptions, employers can see what you can do for them, (2) you can emphasize earlier job experience, and (3) you can deemphasize any lengthy unemployment or lack of career progress. However, you should be aware that because the functional résumé can obscure your work history, many employment professionals are suspicious of it.[17] If you don't believe the chronological format will work for you, consider the combination résumé instead.

The functional résumé is often considered by people with limited or spotty employment history, but many employers are suspicious of this format.

The Combination Résumé

A **combination résumé** meshes the skills focus of the functional format with the job history focus of the chronological format (see Figure 18.4 on page 530). The chief advantage of this format is that it allows you to focus attention on your capabilities when you don't have a long or steady employment history, without raising concerns that you might be hiding something about your past.

If you don't have a lot of work history to show, consider a combination résumé to highlight your skills while still providing a chronological history of your employment.

As you look at a number of sample résumés, you'll probably notice many variations on the three basic formats presented here. Study these other options in light of the effective communication principles you've learned in this course and the unique circumstances of

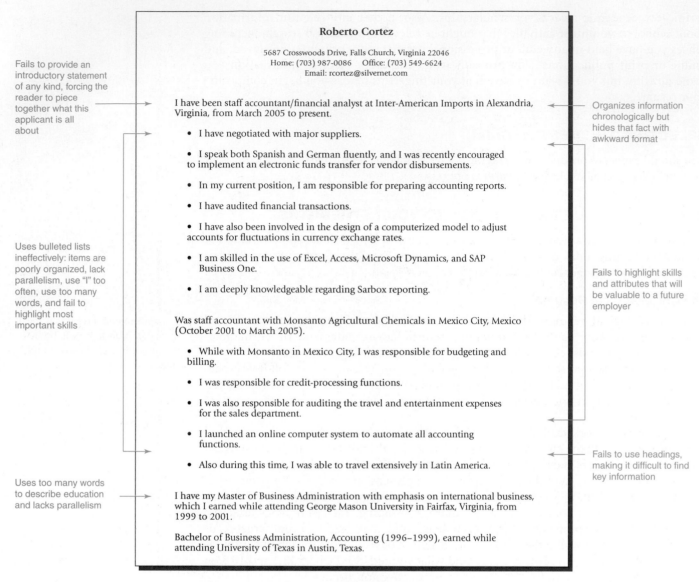

Fails to provide an introductory statement of any kind, forcing the reader to piece together what this applicant is all about

Uses bulleted lists ineffectively: items are poorly organized, lack parallelism, use "I" too often, use too many words, and fail to highlight most important skills

Uses too many words to describe education and lacks parallelism

Organizes information chronologically but hides that fact with awkward format

Fails to highlight skills and attributes that will be valuable to a future employer

Fails to use headings, making it difficult to find key information

Roberto Cortez

5687 Crosswoods Drive, Falls Church, Virginia 22046
Home: (703) 987-0086   Office: (703) 549-6624
Email: rcortez@silvernet.com

I have been staff accountant/financial analyst at Inter-American Imports in Alexandria, Virginia, from March 2005 to present.

- I have negotiated with major suppliers.

- I speak both Spanish and German fluently, and I was recently encouraged to implement an electronic funds transfer for vendor disbursements.

- In my current position, I am responsible for preparing accounting reports.

- I have audited financial transactions.

- I have also been involved in the design of a computerized model to adjust accounts for fluctuations in currency exchange rates.

- I am skilled in the use of Excel, Access, Microsoft Dynamics, and SAP Business One.

- I am deeply knowledgeable regarding Sarbox reporting.

Was staff accountant with Monsanto Agricultural Chemicals in Mexico City, Mexico (October 2001 to March 2005).

- While with Monsanto in Mexico City, I was responsible for budgeting and billing.

- I was responsible for credit-processing functions.

- I was also responsible for auditing the travel and entertainment expenses for the sales department.

- I launched an online computer system to automate all accounting functions.

- Also during this time, I was able to travel extensively in Latin America.

I have my Master of Business Administration with emphasis on international business, which I earned while attending George Mason University in Fairfax, Virginia, from 1999 to 2001.

Bachelor of Business Administration, Accounting (1996–1999), earned while attending University of Texas in Austin, Texas.

Figure 18.2   Ineffective Chronological Résumé
This chronological résumé exhibits a wide range of problems. The language is self-centered and unprofessional, and the organization forces the reader to dig out essential details—and today's recruiters don't have the time or the patience for that. Compare this with the improved version in Figure 18.3.

your job search. If you find one that seems like the best fit for your unique situation, by all means use it.

ADDRESSING AREAS OF CONCERN

Many people have gaps in their careers or other issues that could be a concern for employers. Here are some common issues and suggestions for handling them in a résumé:[18]

Frequent job changes and gaps in your work history are two of the more common issues that employers may perceive as weaknesses.

- **Frequent job changes.** If you've had a number of short-term jobs of a similar type, such as independent contracting and temporary assignments, try to group them under a single heading. Also, if past job positions were eliminated as a result of layoffs or mergers, find a subtle way to convey that information (if not in your résumé, then in your cover letter). Reasonable employers understand that many professionals have been forced to job hop by circumstances beyond their control.

- **Gaps in work history.** Mention relevant experience and education you gained during employment gaps, such as volunteer or community work.

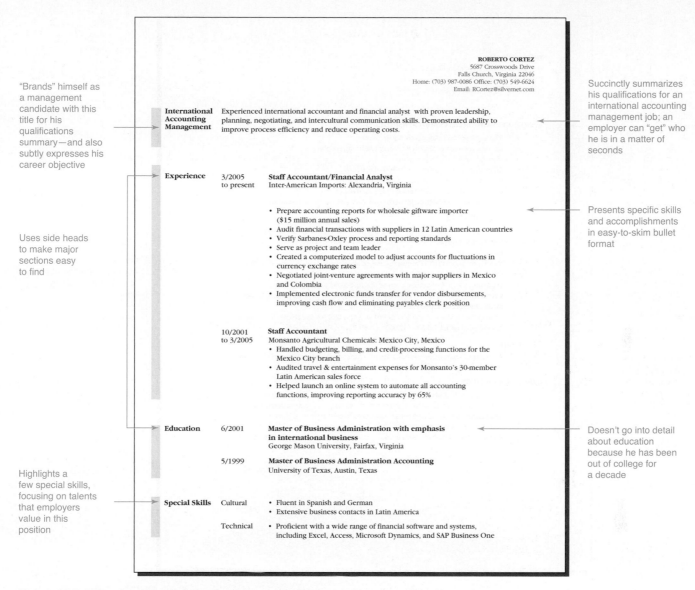

Roberto Cortez resume annotations:

"Brands" himself as a management candidate with this title for his qualifications summary—and also subtly expresses his career objective

Uses side heads to make major sections easy to find

Highlights a few special skills, focusing on talents that employers value in this position

Succinctly summarizes his qualifications for an international accounting management job; an employer can "get" who he is in a matter of seconds

Presents specific skills and accomplishments in easy-to-skim bullet format

Doesn't go into detail about education because he has been out of college for a decade

Figure 18.3   Effective Chronological Résumé
This version does a much better job of presenting the candidate's ability to contribute to a new employer.
Notice in particular how easy it is to scan through this résumé to find sections of interest.

- **Inexperience.** Mention related volunteer work and membership in professional groups. List relevant course work and internships.
- **Overqualification.** Tone down your résumé, focusing exclusively on the experience and skills that relate to the position.
- **Long-term employment with one company.** Itemize each position held at the firm to show both professional growth and career growth within the organization and increasing responsibilities along the way.
- **Job termination for cause.** Be honest with interviewers and address their concerns with proof, such as recommendations and examples of completed projects.
- **Criminal record.** You don't necessarily need to disclose a criminal record or time spent incarcerated on your résumé, but you may be asked about it on job application forms. Laws regarding what employers may ask (and whether they can conduct a criminal background check) vary by state and profession, but if you are asked and the question applies to you, you are legally bound to answer truthfully. Use the interview process to explain any mitigating circumstances and to emphasize your rehabilitation and commitment to being a law-abiding, trustworthy employee.[19]

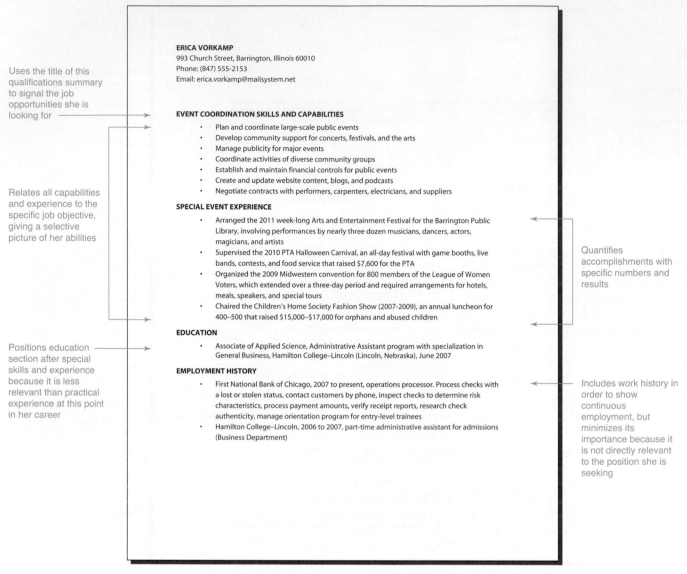

Uses the title of this qualifications summary to signal the job opportunities she is looking for

Relates all capabilities and experience to the specific job objective, giving a selective picture of her abilities

Positions education section after special skills and experience because it is less relevant than practical experience at this point in her career

ERICA VORKAMP
993 Church Street, Barrington, Illinois 60010
Phone: (847) 555-2153
Email: erica.vorkamp@mailsystem.net

EVENT COORDINATION SKILLS AND CAPABILITIES

- Plan and coordinate large-scale public events
- Develop community support for concerts, festivals, and the arts
- Manage publicity for major events
- Coordinate activities of diverse community groups
- Establish and maintain financial controls for public events
- Create and update website content, blogs, and podcasts
- Negotiate contracts with performers, carpenters, electricians, and suppliers

SPECIAL EVENT EXPERIENCE

- Arranged the 2011 week-long Arts and Entertainment Festival for the Barrington Public Library, involving performances by nearly three dozen musicians, dancers, actors, magicians, and artists
- Supervised the 2010 PTA Halloween Carnival, an all-day festival with game booths, live bands, contests, and food service that raised $7,600 for the PTA
- Organized the 2009 Midwestern convention for 800 members of the League of Women Voters, which extended over a three-day period and required arrangements for hotels, meals, speakers, and special tours
- Chaired the Children's Home Society Fashion Show (2007-2009), an annual luncheon for 400–500 that raised $15,000–$17,000 for orphans and abused children

EDUCATION

- Associate of Applied Science, Administrative Assistant program with specialization in General Business, Hamilton College–Lincoln (Lincoln, Nebraska), June 2007

EMPLOYMENT HISTORY

- First National Bank of Chicago, 2007 to present, operations processor. Process checks with a lost or stolen status, contact customers by phone, inspect checks to determine risk characteristics, process payment amounts, verify receipt reports, research check authenticity, manage orientation program for entry-level trainees
- Hamilton College–Lincoln, 2006 to 2007, part-time administrative assistant for admissions (Business Department)

Quantifies accomplishments with specific numbers and results

Includes work history in order to show continuous employment, but minimizes its importance because it is not directly relevant to the position she is seeking

Figure 18.4 **Combination Résumé**
With her limited work experience in her field of interest (event coordinator), Erica Vorkamp opted for a combination résumé to highlight her skills. Her employment history is complete and easy to find, but it isn't featured to the same degree as the other elements. Notice how she uses the title of the introductory statement to identify the job opportunities she is looking for.

MyBcommLab

Apply Figure 18.4's key concepts by revising a new document. Go to Chapter 18 in mybcommlab.com and select Document Makeovers.

Writing a Résumé

3 **LEARNING OBJECTIVE**

Describe the tasks involved in writing your résumé, and list the major sections of a traditional résumé.

If you're uncomfortable writing your own résumé, see if you can trade with a classmate and write each other's résumé.

As you follow the three-step process to develop your résumé, keep four points in mind. First, treat your résumé with the respect it deserves. A single mistake or oversight can cost you interview opportunities. Second, give yourself plenty of time. Don't put off preparing your résumé until the last second and then try to write it in one sitting. Third, learn from good models. You can find sample résumés online at college websites and on job boards such as Monster and CareerBuilder. Fourth, don't get frustrated by the conflicting advice you'll read about résumés. Résumés are as much art as science, and there is more than one way to be successful with them. Consider the alternatives and choose the approach that makes the most sense to you, given everything you know about successful business communication.

If you feel uncomfortable writing about yourself, you're not alone. Many people, even accomplished writers, find it difficult to write their own résumés. If you get stuck, find a classmate or friend who is also writing a résumé and swap projects for a while. By working on each other's résumés, you might be able to speed up the process for both of you.

KEEPING YOUR RÉSUMÉ HONEST

Estimates vary, but one comprehensive study uncovered lies about work history in more than 40 percent of the résumés tested.[20] And dishonest applicants are getting bolder all the time—going so far as to buy fake diplomas online, pay computer hackers to insert their names into prestigious universities' graduation records, and sign up for services that offer phony employment verification.[21]

Applicants with integrity know they don't need to stoop to lying. If you are tempted to stretch the truth, bear in mind that professional recruiters have seen every trick in the book, and frustrated employers are working aggressively to uncover the truth. Nearly all employers do some form of background checking, from contacting references and verifying employment to checking criminal records and sending résumés through verification services.[22] Employers are also beginning to craft certain interview questions specifically to uncover dishonest résumé entries.[23]

More than 90 percent of companies that find lies on résumés refuse to hire the offending applicants, even if that means withdrawing formal job offers.[24] And if you do sneak past these filters and get hired, you'll probably be exposed on the job when you can't live up to your own résumé. Given the networked nature of today's job market, lying on a résumé could haunt you for years—and could force you to keep lying throughout your career to hide the original misrepresentations on your résumé.[25]

ADAPTING YOUR RÉSUMÉ TO YOUR AUDIENCE

The importance of adapting your résumé to your target readers' needs and interests cannot be overstated. In a competitive job market, the more you look like a good fit, the better your chances will be of securing interviews. Address your readers' business concerns by showing how your capabilities meet the demands and expectations of the position and of the organization as a whole. For example, if you are applying for work in public relations (PR), you would need to know that an internal corporate PR department and an independent PR agency perform many of the same tasks, but the outside agency must also sell its services to multiple clients. Consequently, it needs employees who are skilled at attracting and keeping paying customers, in addition to being skilled at PR.

Adapting to your readers can mean customizing your résumé, sometimes for each job opening. However, the effort can pay off in more interviewing opportunities.

Use what you've learned about your target readers to express your experience using the terminology of the hiring organization. For instance, military experience can help you develop many skills that are valuable in business, but military terminology can sound like a foreign language to people who aren't familiar with it. Isolate the important general concepts and present them in common business language. Similarly, educational achievements in other countries might not align with the standard U.S. definitions of high schools, community colleges, technical and trade schools, and universities. If necessary, include a brief statement explaining how your degree or certificate relates to U.S. expectations—or how your U.S. degree relates to expectations in other countries, if you're applying for work abroad.

COMPOSING YOUR RÉSUMÉ

Write your résumé using a simple and direct style. Use short, crisp phrases instead of whole sentences and focus on what your reader needs to know. Avoid using the word *I*, which can sound both self-involved and repetitive by the time you outline all your

REAL-TIME UPDATES
Learn More by Watching This Video

Learn to use LinkedIn's résumé builder

See how to build and customize a résumé on LinkedIn and then use it on other social networking sites. Go to http://real-timeupdates.com/bct11 and click on "Learn More." If you are using MyBcommLab, you can access Real-Time Updates within each chapter or under Student Study Tools.

Résumé fraud has reached epidemic proportions, but employers are fighting back with more rigorous screening techniques.

Translate your past accomplishments into a compelling picture of what you can do for employers in the future.

Military service and other specialized experiences may need to be "translated" into terms more readily understandable by your target readers.

Draft your résumé using short, crisp phrases built around strong verbs and nouns.

skills and accomplishments. Instead, start your phrases with strong action verbs such as these:[26]

accomplished	assumed	coordinated	explored	initiated
achieved	budgeted	created	forecasted	installed
administered	chaired	demonstrated	generated	introduced
approved	changed	developed	identified	investigated
arranged	compiled	directed	implemented	joined
assisted	completed	established	improved	launched
maintained	participated	recommended	set up	supervised
managed	performed	reduced	simplified	systematized
motivated	planned	reorganized	sparked	targeted
operated	presented	resolved	streamlined	trained
organized	proposed	saved	strengthened	transformed
oversaw	raised	served	succeeded	upgraded

For instance, you might say, "Created a campus organization for students interested in entrepreneurship" or "Managed a fast-food restaurant and four employees." Whenever you can, quantify the results so that your claims don't come across as empty puffery. Don't just say you're a team player or detail oriented—show you are by offering concrete proof.[27] Here are some examples of phrasing accomplishments using active statements that show results:

Avoid Weak Statements	Use Active Statements That Show Results
Responsible for developing a new filing system	Developed a new filing system that reduced paperwork by 50 percent
I was in charge of customer complaints and all ordering problems	Handled all customer complaints and resolved all product order discrepancies
I won a trip to Europe for opening the most new customer accounts in my department	Generated the highest number of new customer accounts in my department
Member of special campus task force to resolve student problems with existing cafeteria assignments	Assisted in implementing new campus dining program that balances student wishes with cafeteria capacity

Providing specific supporting evidence is vital but make sure you don't go overboard with small details.[28]

In addition to clear writing with specific examples, the particular words and phrases you use throughout your résumé are critically important. The majority of résumés are now subjected to *keyword searches* in an applicant tracking system or other database, in which a recruiter searches for résumés most likely to match the requirements of a particular job. Résumés that don't match the requirements closely may never be seen by a human reader, so it is essential to use the words and phrases that a recruiter is most likely to search for. (Although most experts used to advise including a separate *keyword summary* as a stand-alone list, the trend nowadays is to incorporate your keywords into your introductory statement and other sections of your résumé.)[29]

Identifying these keywords requires some research, but you can uncover many of them while you are researching various industries and companies (see page 522). The trick is to study job descriptions carefully and to understand your target audience's needs. In contrast to the action verbs that catch a human reader's attention, keywords that catch a computer's attention are usually nouns that describe the specific skills, attributes, and experiences an

Include relevant keywords in your introductory statement, work history, and education sections.

employer is looking for in a candidate. Keywords can include the business and technical terms associated with a specific profession, industry-specific jargon, names or types of products or systems used in a profession, job titles, and college degrees.[30] Follow the Real-Time Updates link on this page to see a helpful list of ideas for compiling keywords for your career search.

Finally, beware of clichés that are used on so many résumés and social media profiles that they've probably lost most of their impact. For example, LinkedIn recently identified these 10 buzzwords and phrases as the most overused: *extensive experience, innovative, motivated, results-oriented, dynamic, proven track record, team player, fast-paced, problem solver,* and *entrepreneurial*.[31] Instead of *saying* you are all these things, *show* how you are, using solid evidence.

REAL-TIME UPDATES
Learn More by Reading This Article

Find the keywords that will light up your résumé

This list of tips and tools will help you find the right keywords to customize your résumé for every opportunity. Go to http://real-timeupdates.com/bct11 and click on "Learn More." If you are using MyBcommLab, you can access Real-Time Updates within each chapter or under Student Study Tools.

Name and Contact Information

Your name and contact information constitute the heading of your résumé; include the following:

- Name
- Physical address (both permanent and temporary, if you're likely to move during the job search process; however, if you're posting a résumé in an unsecured location online, leave off your physical address for security purposes)
- Phone number(s)
- Email address
- The URL of your personal webpage, e-portfolio, or social media résumé (if you have one)

Be sure to provide complete and accurate contact information; mistakes in this section of the résumé are surprisingly common.

Be sure that everything in your résumé heading is well organized and clearly laid out on the page.

If the only email address you have is through your current employer, get a free personal email address from one of the many services that offer them. It's not fair to your current employer to use company resources for a job search, and it sends a bad signal to potential employers. Also, if your personal email address is anything like precious.princess@something.com or PsychoDawg@something.com, get a new email address for your business correspondence.

Get a professional-sounding email address for business correspondence (such as *firstname.lastname@something.com*), if you don't already have one.

Introductory Statement

Of all the parts of a résumé, the brief introductory statement that follows your name and contact information probably generates the most disagreement. You can put one of three things here:[32]

- **Career objective.** A career objective identifies either a specific job you want to land or a general career track you would like to pursue. Some experts advise against including a career objective because it can categorize you so narrowly that you miss out on interesting opportunities, and it is essentially about fulfilling your desires, not about meeting the employer's needs. In the past, most résumés included a career objective, but in recent years more job seekers are using a qualifications summary or a career summary. However, if you have little or no work experience in your target profession, a career objective might be your best option. If you do opt for an objective, word it in a way that relates your qualifications to employer needs (see Figure 18.6 on page 540). Avoid such self-absorbed statements as "A fulfilling position that provides ample opportunity for career growth and personal satisfaction."
- **Qualifications summary.** A qualifications summary offers a brief view of your key qualifications. The goal is to let a reader know within a few seconds what you can deliver. You can title this section generically as "Qualifications Summary" or "Summary of Qualifications," or if you have one dominant qualification, you can use that as the title (see the career summary in Figure 18.5 on page 538 for an example). Consider using a qualifications summary if you have one or more important qualifications but don't

You can choose to open with a career objective, a qualifications summary, or a career summary.

If you have a reasonably focused skill set but don't yet have a long career history, a qualifications summary is probably the best type of introductory statement for you.

REAL-TIME UPDATES
Learn More by Reading This Article

**Watch a résumé pro rework
an introductory statement**

Whichever style of introductory statement you choose to include, it must be concise, concrete, and reader-focused. Follow the revisions in this real-life example to see how to craft an effective statement. Go to http://real-timeupdates.com/bct11 and click on "Learn More." If you are using MyBcommLab, you can access Real-Time Updates within each chapter or under Student Study Tools.

yet have a long career history. Also, if you haven't been working long but your college education has given you a dominant professional "theme," such as multimedia design or statistical analysis, you can craft a qualifications summary that highlights your educational preparedness.

- **Career summary.** A career summary offers a brief recap of your career, with the goal of presenting increasing levels of responsibility and performance. A career summary can be particularly useful for executives who have demonstrated the ability to manage increasingly larger and more complicated business operations—a key consideration when companies look to hire upper-level managers.

Education

If you are early in your career, your education is probably your strongest selling point.

If you're still in college or have recently graduated, education is probably your strongest selling point. Present your educational background in depth, choosing facts that support your "theme." Give this section a heading such as "Education," "Technical Training," or "Academic Preparation," as appropriate. Then, starting with the most recent, list the name and location of each school you have attended, the month and year of your graduation (say "anticipated graduation in _____" if you haven't graduated yet), your major and minor fields of study, significant skills and abilities you've developed in your course work, and the degrees or certificates you've earned. If you're still working toward a degree, include in parentheses the expected date of completion. Showcase your qualifications by listing courses that have directly equipped you for the job you are seeking and indicate any scholarships, awards, or academic honors you've received.

The education section should also include relevant training sponsored by business or government organizations. Mention high school or military training only if the associated achievements are pertinent to your career goals.

Whether you list your grade point average depends on the job you want and the quality of your grades. If you don't show your GPA on your résumé—and there's no rule saying you have to—be prepared to answer questions about it during the interview process because many employers will assume that your GPA is not spectacular if you didn't list it on your résumé. If you choose to show a grade point average, be sure to mention the scale, especially if it isn't a four-point scale. If your grades are better within your major than in other courses, you can also list your GPA as "Major GPA" and include only those courses within your major.

Work Experience, Skills, and Accomplishments

When you describe past job responsibilities, identify the skills and knowledge that you can apply to a future job.

Like the education section, the work experience section should focus on your overall theme in a way that shows how your past can contribute to an employer's future. Use keywords to call attention to the skills you've developed on the job and to your ability to handle increasing responsibility.

List your jobs in reverse chronological order, starting with the most recent. Include military service and any internships and part-time or temporary jobs related to your career objective. Include the name and location of the employer, and if readers are unlikely to recognize the organization, briefly describe what it does. When you want to keep the name of your current employer confidential, you can identify the firm by industry only ("a large video game developer"). If an organization's name or location has changed since you worked there, state the current name and location and include the old information preceded by "formerly . . ." Before or after each job listing, state your job title and give the years you worked in the job; use the phrase "to present" to denote current employment. Indicate whether a job was part time.

Devote the most space to jobs that are related to your target position.

Devote the most space to the jobs that are related to your target position. If you were personally responsible for something significant, be sure to mention it. Facts about your skills and accomplishments are the most important information you can give a prospective employer, so quantify them whenever possible.

One helpful exercise is to write a 30-second "commercial" for each major skill you want to highlight. The commercial should offer proof that you really do possess the skill. For your résumé, distill the commercials down to brief phrases; you can use the more detailed proof statements in cover letters and as answers to interview questions.[33]

If you have a number of part-time, temporary, or entry-level jobs that don't relate to your career objective, you have to use your best judgment when it comes to including or excluding them. Too many minor and irrelevant work details can clutter your résumé, particularly if you've been in the professional workforce for a few years. However, if you don't have a long employment history, including these jobs shows your ability and willingness to keep working.

Activities and Achievements

Include activities and achievements outside of a work context only if they make you a more attractive job candidate. For example, traveling, studying, or working abroad and fluency in multiple languages could weigh heavily in your favor with employers who do business internationally.

> Include personal accomplishments if they suggest special skills or qualities that are relevant to the jobs you're seeking.

Because many employers are involved in their local communities, they tend to look positively on applicants who are active and concerned members of their communities as well. Consider including community service activities that suggest leadership, teamwork, communication skills, technical aptitude, or other valuable attributes.

You should generally avoid indicating membership or significant activity in religious or political organizations (unless, of course, you're applying to such an organization) because doing so might raise concerns for people with differing beliefs or affiliations. However, if you want to highlight skills you developed while involved with such a group, you can refer to it generically as a "not-for-profit organization."

Finally, if you have little or no job experience and not much to discuss outside of your education, indicating involvement in athletics or other organized student activities lets employers know that you don't spend all your free time hanging around your apartment playing video games. Also consider mentioning publications, projects, and other accomplishments that required relevant business skills.

Personal Data and References

In nearly all instances, your résumé should not include any personal data beyond the information described in the previous sections. When applying to U.S. companies, never include any of the following: physical characteristics, age, gender, marital status, sexual orientation, religious or political affiliations, race, national origin, salary history, reasons for leaving jobs, names of previous supervisors, names of references, Social Security number, or student ID number.

> When applying to U.S. companies, your résumé should not include any personal data such as age, marital status, physical description, or Social Security number.

Note that standards can vary in other countries. For example, you might be expected to include your citizenship, nationality, or marital status.[34] However, verify such requirements before including any personal data.

The availability of references is usually assumed, so you don't need to put "References available upon request" at the end of your résumé. However, be sure to have a list of several references ready when you begin applying for jobs. Prepare your reference sheet with your name and contact information at the top. For a finished look, use the same design and layout you use for your résumé. Then list three or four people who have agreed to serve as references. Include each person's name, job title, organization, address, telephone number, email address (if the reference prefers to be contacted by email), and the nature of your relationship.

> Prepare a list of references but don't include them on your résumé.

Completing a Résumé

Completing your résumé involves revising it for optimum quality, producing it in the various forms and media you'll need, and proofreading it for any errors before distributing it or publishing it online. Producing and distributing a résumé used to be fairly straightforward; you printed it on quality paper and mailed or faxed it to employers. However, the advent of **applicant tracking systems** (databases that let managers sort through incoming applications to find the most promising candidates), social media, and other innovations

4 LEARNING OBJECTIVE

Characterize the completing step for résumés, including the six most common formats in which you can produce a résumé.

COMMUNICATION MISCUES | Don't. Just Don't.

Even though employment recruiters might think they've seen it all by now, innovative job applicants still keep finding new ways to get their résumés tossed into the recycling bin. Here are a few examples for your amusement—and warning, if you're inclined to share a little too much information:

- The passing of a beloved pet is never easy, but should grief over a departed cat keep someone out of the workforce for three months? That's how one job applicant explained a three-month gap in his employment history.
- One applicant's résumé arrived in an envelope that had a picture of a car on it, along with an explanation saying it would be a gift for the hiring manager.
- A person's family medical history is obviously important to him or her, but it's not something to put on a résumé, as one job seeker did, for reasons unknown.
- In a valiant effort to cram as many mistakes as possible onto a single page, one creative candidate included a full body photo of herself—in thigh-high boots, no less—and used oversized, fluorescent pink paper. This résumé

probably did look pretty as it fluttered off a recruiter's desk into the recycling bin.

- Expressing strong interest in a job is good, but not if that interest is expressed like this: "to keep my parole officer from putting me back in jail."
- One applicant's mother was proud of her, to be sure, but including a letter from her with a résumé made the applicant look like, well, a child.

These cringe-inducing blunders are worth more than a quick chuckle: They're a great reminder of why it is crucial to understand the purpose of a résumé and the effect a résumé has on hiring managers.

CAREER APPLICATIONS

1. Is it a good idea to "show some personality" in your résumé? Explain your answer.
2. How should you handle the employment section of your résumé if you really did take three months off work to grieve the loss of a pet?

---

has dramatically changed the nature of résumé production and distribution. Be prepared to produce several versions of your résumé, in multiple formats and multiple media.

Even if most or all of your application efforts take place online, starting with a traditional paper résumé is still useful, for several reasons. First, a traditional printed résumé is a great opportunity to organize your background information and identify your unique strengths. Second, the planning and writing tasks involved in creating a conventional résumé will help you generate blocks of text that you can reuse in multiple ways throughout the job search process. Third, you'll never know when someone might ask for your résumé during a networking event or other in-person encounter, and you don't want to let that interest fade in the time it might take for the person to get to your information online.

Most of your application efforts will take place online, but starting with a traditional paper résumé is still useful.

REVISING YOUR RÉSUMÉ

Ask professional recruiters to list the most common mistakes they see on résumés, and you'll hear the same things over and over again. Keep your résumé out of the recycling bin by avoiding these flaws:

Avoid the common errors that will get your résumé excluded from consideration.

- Too long or too wordy
- Too short or sketchy
- Difficult to read
- Poorly written
- Displaying weak understanding of the business world in general or of a particular industry or company
- Poor-quality printing or cheap paper
- Full of spelling and grammar errors
- Boastful
- Gimmicky design

If your employment history is brief, keep your résumé to one page.

The ideal length of your résumé depends on the depth of your experience and the level of the positions for which you are applying. As a general guideline, if you have fewer than 10 years of professional experience, try to keep a conventional printed résumé to one page. Recruiters appreciate brevity, and presenting yourself in a single page shows your ability to write concise, focused, audience-oriented messages.[35] For online résumé formats, you can always provide links to additional information. If you have more experience and are applying for a higher-level position, you may need to prepare a somewhat longer résumé.[36] For highly technical positions, longer résumés are often the norm as well because the qualifications for such jobs can require more description.

PRODUCING YOUR RÉSUMÉ

No matter how many media and formats you eventually choose for producing your résumé, a clean, professional-looking design is a must. Unless you have some experience in graphic design and you're applying in a field such as advertising or retail merchandising, where visual creativity is viewed as an asset, resist the urge to "get creative" with your résumé layout.[37] Recruiters and hiring managers want to skim your essential information in a matter of seconds, and anything that distracts or delays them will work against you. Moreover, complex layouts can confuse an applicant tracking system, which can result in your information getting garbled.

> Effective résumé designs are simple, clean, and professional— not gaudy, "clever," or cute.

Fortunately, good résumé design is not difficult to achieve. As you can see in Figures 18.3 and 18.4, good designs feature simplicity, order, effective use of white space, and clear typefaces. Make subheadings easy to find and easy to read, placing them either above each section or in the left margin. Use lists to itemize your most important qualifications. Color is not necessary by any means, but if you add color, make it subtle and sophisticated, such as a thin horizontal line under your name and address. The most common way to get into trouble with résumé design is going overboard (see Figure 18.5 on the next page).

Depending on the companies you apply to, you might want to produce your résumé in as many as six formats (all are explained in the following sections):

> Be prepared to produce several versions of your résumé in multiple media.

- Printed traditional résumé
- Printed scannable résumé
- Electronic plain-text file
- Microsoft Word file
- Online résumé, also called a multimedia résumé or social media résumé
- PDF file

Unfortunately, there is no single format or medium that works for all the situations you will encounter, and employer expectations continue to change as technology evolves. Find out what each employer or job posting website expects, and provide your résumé in that specific format.

As you produce your résumé in various formats, you will encounter the question of whether to include a photograph of yourself on or with your résumé. For print or electronic documents that you will be submitting to employers or job websites, the safest advice is to avoid photos. The reason is that seeing visual cues of the age, ethnicity, and gender of candidates early in the selection process exposes employers to complaints of discriminatory hiring practices. In fact, some employers won't even look at résumés that include photos, and some applicant tracking systems automatically discard résumés with any kind of extra files.[38] However, photographs are acceptable for social media résumés and other online formats where you are not actually submitting a résumé to an employer.

> Do not include or enclose a photo in résumés that you send to employers or post on job websites.

In addition to these six main formats, some applicants create PowerPoint presentations or videos to supplement a conventional résumé. Two key advantages of a PowerPoint supplement are flexibility and multimedia capabilities. For instance, you can present a menu of choices on the opening screen and allow viewers to click through to sections of interest. (Note that most of the things you can accomplish with PowerPoint can be done with an online résumé, which is probably more convenient for most readers.)

A video résumé can be a compelling supplement as well, but be aware that some employment law experts advise employers not to view videos, at least not until after candidates have been evaluated solely on their credentials. The reason for this caution is the same as with photographs. In addition, videos are more cumbersome to evaluate than paper or electronic résumés, and some recruiters refuse to watch them.[39] However, not all companies share this concern over videos, so you'll have to research their individual preferences. In fact, Zappos (see page 548) actually encourages applicant videos and provides a way to upload videos on its job application webpage.[40]

Uses inappropriate design elements in an attempt to grab the reader's attention; name and contact information should not be "decorated" in any way

Uses an unconventional format for the phone number, which only looks amateurish

Distracts the reader with large background images (the E and V initials)

Uses unconventional indentations, which force the reader to try to figure out the meaning of the different levels

Fails to use bullet point symbols and white space to separate list items

Uses far too much space for contact information, which then crowds the rest of the document

Includes an inappropriate email address

Fails to use adequate white space between headings and text sections, making reading more difficult

Crams too much information into too little space; the lack of white space makes the body of the résumé extremely difficult to read

Uses a font that some readers will consider too casual for an important business document

Introducing: Erica Vorkamp

Address
993 Church Street, Barrington, Illinois 60010

Phone
847/884/2153

Email
live2party@mailsystem.net

1. OBJECTIVE
An event coordinator position in which my broad mix of skills in planning, supervision, and communication will benefit a growing, customer-oriented company
2. SKILLS AND CAPABILITIES
Plan and coordinate large-scale public events
　　Develop community support for concerts, festivals, and the arts
　　　Manage publicity for major events
　　　　Coordinate activities of diverse community groups
　　　Establish and maintain financial controls for public events
　　Create and update website content, blogs, and podcasts
Negotiate contracts with performers, carpenters, electricians, and suppliers
3. SPECIAL EVENT EXPERIENCE
Arranged the 2009 week-long Arts and Entertainment Festival for the Barrington Public Library, involving performances by nearly three dozen musicians, dancers, actors, magicians, and artists
Supervised the 2008 PTA Halloween Carnival, an all-day festival with game booths, live bands, contests, and food service that raised $7,600 for the PTA
Organized the 2007 Midwestern convention for 800 members of the League of Women Voters, which extended over a three-day period and required arrangements for hotels, meals, speakers, and special tours
Chaired the Children's Home Society Fashion Show (2005-2007), an annual luncheon for 400–500 that raised $15,000–$17,000 for orphans and abused children
4. EDUCATION
Associate of Applied Science, Administrative Assistant program with specialization in General Business, Hamilton College–Lincoln (Lincoln, Nebraska), June 2005
5. EMPLOYMENT HISTORY
First National Bank of Chicago, 2005 to present, operations processor; processed checks with a lost/stolen status, contacted customers by phone, inspected checks to determine risk characteristics, processed payment amounts, verified receipt reports, researched check authenticity, managed orientation program for entry-level trainees
Hamilton College–Lincoln, 2004 to 2005, part-time administrative assistant for admissions (Business Department)

Figure 18.5   Ineffective Résumé Design
This résumé tries too hard to be creative and eye-catching, resulting in a document that is difficult to read—and that probably won't get read. Recruiters have seen every conceivable design gimmick, so don't try to stand out from the crowd with unusual design. Instead, provide compelling, employer-focused information that is easy to find.

MyBcommLab

Apply Figure 18.5's key concepts by revising a new document. Go to Chapter 18 in mybcommlab.com and select Document Makeovers.

Producing a Traditional Printed Résumé

Use high-quality paper when printing your résumé.

The traditional paper résumé still has a place in this world of electronic job searches, if only to have a few copies ready whenever one of your networking contacts asks for one. Avoid basic, low-cost white bond paper intended for general office use and gimmicky papers with borders and backgrounds. Choose a heavier, higher-quality paper designed specifically for résumés and other important documents. White or slightly off-white is the best color choice. This paper is more expensive than general office paper, but you don't need much, and it's a worthwhile investment.

When you're ready to print your résumé, use a well-maintained, quality printer. Don't tolerate any streaks, stray lines, or poor print quality. You wouldn't walk into an interview looking messy, so make sure your résumé doesn't look that way, either.

Printing a Scannable Résumé

You might encounter a company that prefers *scannable résumés*, a type of printed résumé that is specially formatted to be compatible with optical scanning systems that convert printed documents to electronic text. These systems were quite common just a few years ago, but their use appears to be declining rapidly as more employers prefer email delivery or website application forms.[41] A scannable résumé differs from the traditional format in two major ways: it should always include a keyword summary, and it should be formatted in a simpler fashion that avoids underlining, special characters, and other elements that can confuse the scanning system. If you need to produce a scannable résumé, search online for "formatting a scannable résumé" to get detailed instructions.

Some employers still prefer résumés in scannable format, but most now want electronic submissions.

Creating a Plain-Text File of Your Résumé

A *plain-text file* (sometimes known as an ASCII text file) is an electronic version of your résumé that has no font formatting, no bullet symbols, no colors, no lines or boxes, or other special formatting. The plain-text version can be used in two ways. First, you can include it in the body of an email message, for employers who want email delivery but don't want file attachments. Second, you can copy and paste the sections into the application forms on an employer's website.

A plain-text version is easy to create with your word processor. Start with the file you used to create your résumé, use the "Save As" choice to save it as "plain text" or whichever similarly labeled option your software has, and verify the result by using a basic text editor (such as Microsoft Notepad). If necessary, reformat the page manually, moving text and inserting space as needed. For simplicity's sake, left-justify all your headings rather than trying to center them manually.

A plain-text version of your résumé is simply a computer file without any of the formatting that you typically apply using a word processor.

Make sure you verify the plain-text file that you create with your word processor; it might need a few manual adjustments using a text editor such as NotePad.

Creating a Word File of Your Résumé

In some cases, an employer or job-posting website will want you to upload a Microsoft Word file or attach it to an email message. (Although there are certainly other word processors on the market, Microsoft Word is the de facto standard in business these days.) This method of transferring information preserves the design and layout of your résumé and saves you the trouble of creating a plain-text version. However, before you submit a Word file to anyone, make sure your computer is free of viruses. Infecting a potential employer's computer will not make a good first impression.

Some employers and websites want your résumé in Microsoft Word format; make sure your computer is thoroughly scanned for viruses first, however.

Creating a PDF Version of Your Résumé

Creating a PDF file is a simple procedure, but you need the right software. Adobe Acrobat (not the free Adobe Reader) is the best-known program, but many others are available, including some free versions. You can also use Adobe's online service, at http://createpdf.adobe.com, to create PDFs without buying software.

Creating an Online Résumé

A variety of terms are used to describe online résumés, including *personal webpage, e-portfolio, social media résumé,* and *multimedia résumé.* Whatever the terminology used on a particular site, all these formats provide the opportunity to expand on the information contained in your basic résumé with links to projects, publications, screencasts, online videos, course lists, social networking profiles, and other elements that give employers a more complete picture of who you are and what you can offer (see Figure 18.6 on the next page).

A good place to start is your college's career center. Ask whether the career center (or perhaps the information technology department) hosts online résumés or e-portfolios for students.

A commercial hosting service is another good possibility for an online résumé. For instance, the free service VisualCV (www.visualcv.com) lets you build an online résumé with video clips and other multimedia elements. This site is a good place to see numerous examples, from students just about to enter the workforce full-time all the way up to corporate CEOs.[42]

Regardless of the approach you take to creating an online résumé, keep these helpful tips in mind:

You have many options for creating an online résumé, from college-hosted e-portfolios to multimedia résumés on commercial websites.

- **Remember that your online presence is a career-management tool.** The way you are portrayed online can work for you or against you, and it's up to you to create a

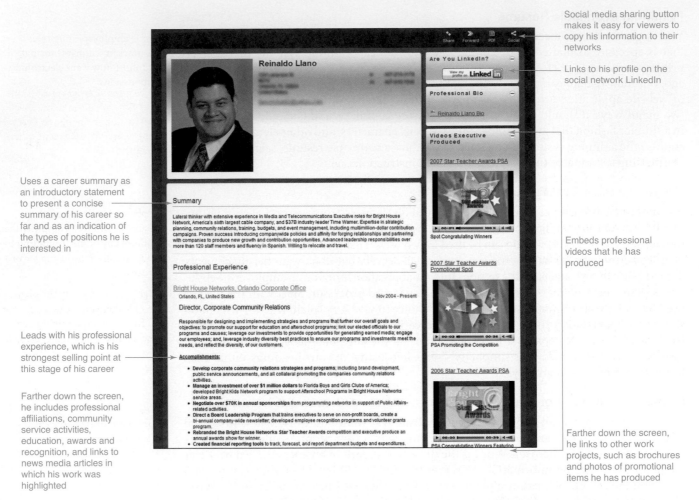

Social media sharing button makes it easy for viewers to copy his information to their networks

Links to his profile on the social network LinkedIn

Uses a career summary as an introductory statement to present a concise summary of his career so far and as an indication of the types of positions he is interested in

Embeds professional videos that he has produced

Leads with his professional experience, which is his strongest selling point at this stage of his career

Farther down the screen, he includes professional affiliations, community service activities, education, awards and recognition, and links to news media articles in which his work was highlighted

Farther down the screen, he links to other work projects, such as brochures and photos of promotional items he has produced

Figure 18.6   Online Résumé
Reinaldo Llano, a corporate communications executive in the media industry, used the résumé hosting website VisualCV to create and present this multimedia/social media résumé.

positive impression. Most employers now conduct online searches to learn more about promising candidates, and 70 percent of those who do have rejected applicants because of information they dug up online.[43]

- **Take advantage of social networking.** Use whatever tools are available to direct people to your online résumé, such as including the URL of your online résumé on the "Info" tab on your Facebook page.
- **During the application process, don't expect or ask employers to retrieve a résumé from your website.** Submit your résumé using whatever method and medium each employer prefers. If employers then want to know more about you, they will likely do a web search on you and find your site, or you can refer them to your site in your résumé or application materials.

PROOFREADING YOUR RÉSUMÉ

Your résumé can't be "pretty good" or "almost perfect"—it needs to be *perfect*, so proofread it thoroughly and ask several other people to verify it, too.

Employers view your résumé as a concrete example of your attention to quality and detail. Your résumé doesn't need to be good or pretty good—it needs to be *perfect*. Although it may not seem fair, just one or two errors in a job application package are enough to doom a candidate's chances.[44]

Your résumé is one of the most important documents you'll ever write, so don't rush or cut corners when it comes to proofreading. Check all headings and lists for clarity and parallelism and be sure that your grammar, spelling, and punctuation are correct. Double-check all dates, phone numbers, email addresses, and other essential data. Ask at least three other people to read it, too. As the creator of the material, you could stare at a mistake for weeks and not see it.

DISTRIBUTING YOUR RÉSUMÉ

How you distribute your résumé depends on the number of employers you target and their preferences for receiving résumés. Employers usually list their requirements on the career pages of their websites, so verify this information and follow it carefully. Beyond that, here are some general distribution tips:

- **Mailing printed résumés.** Take some care with the packaging. Spend a few extra cents to mail these documents in a flat 9 × 12 envelope, or better yet, use a Priority Mail flat-rate envelope, which gives you a sturdy cardboard mailer and faster delivery for just a few more dollars.

- **Emailing your résumé.** Some employers want applicants to include the text of their résumés in the body of an email message; others prefer an attached Microsoft Word file. If you have a reference number or a job ad number, include it in the subject line of your email message.

- **Submitting your résumé to an employer's website.** Many employers, including most large companies, now prefer or require applicants to submit their résumés online. In some instances, you will be asked to upload a complete file. In others, you will need to copy and paste sections of your résumé into individual boxes in an online application form.

- **Posting your résumé on job websites.** You can post your résumé (or create one online, on some sites) on general-purpose job websites such as Monster (http://home.monster .com and http://college.monster.com) and CareerBuilder (www.careerbuilder.com), on more specialized websites such as Jobster (www.jobster.com) or Jobfox (www .jobfox.com), or with staffing services such as Volt (http://jobs.volt.com). Roughly 100,000 job boards are now online, so you'll need to spend some time looking for sites that specialize in your target industries, regions, or professions.[45] Before you upload your résumé to any site, however, learn about its confidentiality protection. Some sites allow you to specify levels of confidentiality, such as letting employers search your qualifications without seeing your personal contact information or preventing your current employer from seeing your résumé. Don't post your résumé to any website that doesn't give you the option of restricting the display of your contact information. Only employers that are registered clients of the service should be able to see your contact information.[46]

When distributing your résumé, pay close attention to the specific instructions provided by every employer, job website, or other recipient.

Don't post a résumé on any public website unless you understand its privacy and security policies.

For a quick summary of the steps to take when planning, writing, and completing your résumé, refer to "Checklist: Writing an Effective Résumé." For the latest information on résumé writing, visit http://real-timeupdates.com/bct11 and click on Chapter 18.

✓ **Checklist** | **Writing an Effective Résumé**

A. Plan your résumé.
- Analyze your purpose and audience carefully to make sure your message meets employers' needs.
- Gather pertinent information about your target companies.
- Select the best medium by researching the preferences of each employer.
- Organize your résumé around your strengths, choosing the chronological, functional, or combination structure. (Be careful about using the functional structure.)

B. Write your résumé.
- Keep your résumé honest.
- Adapt your résumé to your audience to highlight the qualifications each employer is looking for.

- Choose a career objective, qualifications summary, or career summary as your introductory statement—and make it concise, concrete, and reader-focused.
- Use powerful language to convey your name and contact information, introductory statement, education, work experience, skills, work or school accomplishments, and activities and achievements.

C. Complete your résumé.
- Revise your résumé until it is clear, concise, and compelling.
- Produce your résumé in all the formats you might need: traditional printed résumé, scannable, plain-text file, Microsoft Word file, PDF, or online.
- Proofread your résumé to make sure it is absolutely perfect.
- Distribute your résumé using the means that each employer prefers.

MyBcommLab

If your course uses MyBcommLab, log on to www.mybcommlab.com to access the following study and assessment aids associated with this chapter:

- Video applications
- Real-Time Updates
- Peer review activity
- Pre/post test
- Personalized study plan
- Model documents
- Sample presentations

If you are not using MyBcommLab, you can access Real-Time Updates through http://real-timeupdates.com/bct11.

SUMMARY OF LEARNING OBJECTIVES

1 **List eight key steps to finding the ideal opportunity in today's job market.** The eight steps discussed in the chapter are (1) writing the story of you, which involves describing where you have been in your career so far and where you would like to go in the future; (2) learning to think like an employer so you can present yourself as a quality hire; (3) researching industries and companies of interest to identify promising opportunities and to learn the language of the hiring managers; (4) translating your general potential into a specific solution for each employer so that you look like a good fit for each opening; (5) taking the initiative to approach interesting companies even if they haven't yet posted any job openings; (6) building your network so you and your connections can help each other in the job search process; (7) seeking career counseling if appropriate; and (8) avoiding the easily avoidable mistakes that can ruin your chances of getting a job.

2 **Explain the process of planning your résumé, including how to choose the best résumé organization.** Planning a résumé starts with recognizing what it is: a persuasive message designed to get you job interviews. Gathering the necessary information involves learning about target industries, professions, companies, and specific positions, as well as gathering information about yourself. Choosing the best résumé organization depends on your background and your goals. A chronological résumé helps employers easily locate necessary information, highlights your professional growth and career progress, and emphasizes continuity and stability. If you can use the chronological format, you should because it is the approach employers tend to prefer. A functional résumé helps employers easily see what you can do for them, allows you to emphasize earlier job experience, and lets you downplay any lengthy periods of unemployment or a lack of career progress. However, many employers are suspicious of functional résumés for this very reason. The combination approach uses the best features of the other two and is often the best choice for recent graduates.

3 **Describe the tasks involved in writing your résumé, and list the major sections of a traditional résumé.** Adapting to the audience is crucial, because readers are looking to see how well you understand their businesses and can present a solution to their talent needs. The major sections of a traditional résumé are (1) your name and contact information; (2) an introductory statement, which can be a career objective, a qualifications summary, or a career summary; (3) your education; (4) your work experience; and (5) activities and achievements that are professionally relevant. Most résumés do not need to include any personal data.

4 **Characterize the completing step for résumés, including the six most common formats in which you can produce a résumé.** Quality is paramount with résumés, so the tasks of revising and proofing are particularly important. The six common résumé formats are traditional printed résumé, scannable résumé, electronic plain-text file, Microsoft Word file, PDF, and online résumé (which might be called a personal webpage, an e-portfolio, or a social media résumé).

applicant tracking systems Computer systems that capture and store incoming résumés and help recruiters find good prospects for current openings

chronological résumé The most common résumé format; it emphasizes work experience, with past jobs shown in reverse chronological order

combination résumé Format that includes the best features of the chronological and functional approaches

functional résumé Format that emphasizes your skills and capabilities while identifying employers and academic experience in subordinate sections; many recruiters view this format with suspicion

networking The process of making connections with mutually beneficial business contacts

résumé A structured, written summary of a person's education, employment background, and job qualifications

 Checklist

Writing an Effective Résumé

A. Plan your résumé.
- Analyze your purpose and audience carefully to make sure your message meets employers' needs.
- Gather pertinent information about your target companies.
- Select the best medium by researching the preferences of each employer.
- Organize your résumé around your strengths, choosing the chronological, functional, or combination structure. (Be careful about using the functional structure.)

B. Write your résumé.
- Keep your résumé honest.
- Adapt your résumé to your audience to highlight the qualifications each employer is looking for.
- Choose a career objective, qualifications summary, or career summary as your introductory statement—and make it concise, concrete, and reader-focused.
- Use powerful language to convey your name and contact information, introductory statement, education, work experience, skills, work or school accomplishments, and activities and achievements.

C. Complete your résumé.
- Revise your résumé until it is clear, concise, and compelling.
- Produce your résumé in all the formats you might need: traditional printed résumé, scannable, plain-text file, Microsoft Word file, PDF, or online.
- Proofread your résumé to make sure it is absolutely perfect.
- Distribute your résumé using the means that each employer prefers.

TABLE 18.2	Fallacies and Facts About Résumés
Fallacy	**Fact**
The purpose of a résumé is to list all your skills and abilities.	The purpose of a résumé is to kindle employer interest and generate an interview.
A good résumé will get you the job you want.	All a résumé can do is get you in the door.
Your résumé will always be read carefully and thoroughly.	In most cases, your résumé needs to make a positive impression within 30 or 45 seconds; only then will someone read it in detail. Moreover, it will likely be screened by a computer looking for keywords first—and if it doesn't contain the right keywords, a human being may never see it.
The more good information you present about yourself in your résumé, the better, so stuff your résumé with every positive detail you can think of.	Recruiters don't need that much information about you at the initial screening stage, and they probably won't read it.
If you want a really good résumé, have it prepared by a résumé service.	You have the skills needed to prepare an effective résumé, so prepare it yourself—unless the position is especially high level or specialized. Even then, you should check carefully before using a service.

COMMUNICATION CHALLENGES AT ATK

You work as a recruiter in the human resources department at ATK's Minneapolis headquarters, where part of your responsibility involves using the applicant tracking system to identify promising job candidates. Solve these challenges by using what you've learned about presenting oneself effectively on a résumé.

INDIVIDUAL CHALLENGE: One of today's tasks is selecting candidates to be interviewed for a management trainee position. This position involves significant interaction with other departments, so communication skills are vital. The applicant tracking system has turned up two candidates with almost identical qualifications. You have time to interview only one of them, however. Based on the way the two candidates described their education, which one would you invite in for an interview—and why?

a. Morehouse College, Atlanta, GA, 2003–2007. Received BA degree with a major in Business Administration and a minor in Finance. Graduated with a 3.65 grade-point average. Played varsity football and basketball. Worked 15 hours per week in the library. Coordinated the local student chapter of the American Management Association. Member of Alpha Phi Alpha social fraternity.

b. I attended Wayne State University in Detroit, Michigan, for two years and then transferred to the University of Michigan at Ann Arbor, where I completed my studies. My major was economics, but I also took many business management courses, including employee motivation, small business administration, history of business start-ups, and organizational behavior. I selected courses based on the professors' reputation for excellence, and I received mostly As and Bs. Unlike many other college students, I viewed the acquisition of knowledge—rather than career preparation— as my primary goal. I believe I have received a well-rounded education that has prepared me to approach management situations as problem-solving exercises.

TEAM CHALLENGE: To find candidates for an accounting associate position (a job typically filled by college graduates rather than more experienced professionals), you searched the application tracking system and found the following rather unconventional résumé. With one or two other students, decide whether you should (1) invite this candidate for an interview; (2) reject the application without further analysis; (3) review the candidate's web-based e-portfolio, then make a decision about inviting him in for an interview; or (4) compare the candidate's qualifications relative to those of other applicants and invite him in for an interview only if you cannot find several qualified applicants. Explain your choice.

Darius Jaidee
809 N. Perkins Rd, Stillwater, OK 74075
Phone: (405) 369-0098
Email: dariusj@okstate.edu

Career Objective: To build a successful career in financial management

Summary of Qualifications: As a student at the University of Oklahoma, Stillwater, completed a wide variety of assignments that demonstrate skills related to accounting and management. For example:

Planning Skills: As president of the university's foreign affairs forum, organized six lectures and workshops featuring 36 speakers from 16 foreign countries within a nine-month period. Identified and recruited the speakers, handled their travel arrangements, and scheduled the facilities.

Communication Skills: Wrote more than 25 essays and term papers on various academic topics, including at least 10 dealing with business and finance. As a senior, wrote a 20-page analysis of financial trends in the petroleum industry, interviewing five high-ranking executives in accounting and finance positions at ConocoPhillip's refinery in Ponca City, Oklahoma, and company headquarters in Houston, Texas.

Accounting and Computer Skills: Competent in all areas of Microsoft Office, including Excel spreadsheets and Access databases. Assisted with bookkeeping activities in parents' small business, including the conversion from paper-based to computer-based accounting (Peachtree software). Have taken courses in accounting, financial planning, database design, web design, and computer networking.

For more information, including employment history, please access my e-portfolio at http://dariusjaidee.com.

TEST YOUR KNOWLEDGE

To review chapter content related to each question, refer to the indicated Learning Objective.

1. What does *quality of hire* mean? [LO-1]
2. Why is it important to have an organized approach to finding a new job? [LO-1]
3. Why is it important to contribute to any networks you belong to, in addition to looking for assistance for your own career? [LO-1]
4. What is the purpose of a résumé? [LO-2]
5. How does a chronological résumé differ from a functional résumé, and when is each appropriate? [LO-2]
6. Why are some employers suspicious of the functional résumé? [LO-2]

7. Explain the difference between a qualifications summary and a career summary. [LO-3]
8. What are keywords? [LO-3]
9. Should you include personal data on a résumé? Explain your answer. [LO-3]
10. What is a plain-text résumé? [LO-4]

APPLY YOUR KNOWLEDGE

To review chapter content related to each question, refer to the indicated Learning Objective.

1. How can you "think like an employer" if you have no professional business experience? [LO-1]
2. If you were a team leader at a summer camp for children with special needs, should you include this in your employment history if you are applying for work that is unrelated? Explain your answer. [LO-3]
3. Can you use a qualifications summary if you don't yet have extensive professional experience in your desired career? Why or why not? [LO-3]
4. Some people don't have a clear career path when they enter the job market. If you're in this situation, how would your uncertainty affect the way you write your résumé? [LO-3]
5. Between your sophomore and junior years, you quit school for a year to earn the money to finish college. You worked as a loan-processing assistant in a finance company, checking references on loan applications, typing, and filing. Your manager made a lot of the fact that he had never attended college. He seemed to resent you for pursuing your education, but he never criticized your work, so you thought you were doing okay. After you'd been working there for six months, he fired you, saying that you'd failed to be thorough enough in your credit checks. You were actually glad to leave, and you found another job right away at a bank, doing similar duties. Now that you've graduated from college, you're writing your résumé. Will you include the finance company job in your work history? Explain. [LO-3]

PRACTICE YOUR SKILLS

Message for Analysis

Read the following résumé information and then (1) analyze the strengths or weaknesses of the information and (2) revise the résumé so that it follows the guidelines presented in this chapter.

Message 18.A: Writing a Résumé [LO-3]

Sylvia Manchester
765 Belle Fleur Blvd.
New Orleans, LA 70113
(504) 312-9504
smanchester@rcnmail.com

PERSONAL: Single, excellent health, 5'7", 136 lbs.; hobbies include cooking, dancing, and reading.

JOB OBJECTIVE: To obtain a responsible position in marketing or sales with a good company.

EDUCATION: BA degree in biology, University of Louisiana, 1998. Graduated with a 3.0 average. Member of the varsity cheerleading squad. President of Panhellenic League. Homecoming queen.

WORK EXPERIENCE

Fisher Scientific Instruments, 2004 to now, field sales representative. Responsible for calling on customers and explaining the features of Fisher's line of laboratory instruments. Also responsible for writing sales letters, attending trade shows, and preparing weekly sales reports.

Fisher Scientific Instruments, 2001–2003, customer service representative. Was responsible for handling incoming phone calls from customers who had questions about delivery, quality, or operation of Fisher's line of laboratory instruments. Also handled miscellaneous correspondence with customers.

Medical Electronics, Inc., 1998–2001, administrative assistant to the vice president of marketing. In addition to handling typical secretarial chores for the vice president of marketing, I was in charge of compiling the monthly sales reports, using figures provided by members of the field sales force. I also was given responsibility for doing various market research activities.

New Orleans Convention and Visitors Bureau, 1995–1998, summers, tour guide. During the summers of my college years, I led tours of New Orleans for tourists visiting the city. My duties included greeting conventioneers and their spouses at hotels, explaining the history and features of the city during an all-day sightseeing tour, and answering questions about New Orleans and its attractions. During my fourth summer with the bureau, I was asked to help train the new tour guides. I prepared a handbook that provided interesting facts about the various tourist attractions, as well as answers to the most commonly asked tourist questions. The Bureau was so impressed with the handbook they had it printed up so that it could be given as a gift to visitors.

University of Louisiana, 1995–1998, part-time clerk in admissions office. While I was a student in college, I worked 15 hours a week in the admissions office. My duties included filing, processing applications, and handling correspondence with high school students and administrators.

Exercises

Active links for all websites in this chapter can be found on MyBcommLab; see your User Guide for instructions on accessing the content for this chapter. Each activity is labeled according to the primary skill or skills you will need to use. To review relevant chapter content, you can refer to the indicated Learning Objective. In some instances, supporting information will be found in another chapter, as indicated.

1. **Career Management: Researching Career Opportunities [LO-1]** Based on the preferences you identified in your career self-assessment (see page xxxiv in the Prologue) and the academic, professional, and personal qualities you have to offer, perform an online search for a career that matches your interests (starting with the websites listed in Table 18.1). Draft a brief report for your instructor, indicating how the career you select and the job openings you find match your strengths and preferences.

2. **Message Strategies: Writing a Résumé; Collaboration: Team Projects [LO-3], Chapter 2** Working with another student, change the following statements to make them more effective for a résumé by using action verbs.

   a. Have some experience with database design.

   b. Assigned to a project to analyze the cost accounting methods for a large manufacturer.

   c. I was part of a team that developed a new inventory control system.

   d. Am responsible for preparing the quarterly department budget.

   e. Was a manager of a department with seven employees working for me.

   f. Was responsible for developing a spreadsheet to analyze monthly sales by department.

   g. Put in place a new program for ordering supplies.

3. **Message Strategies: Writing a Résumé [LO-3]** Using your team's answers to Exercise 2, make the statements stronger by quantifying them. (Make up any numbers you need.)

4. **Message Strategies: Writing a Résumé; Communication Ethics: Resolving Ethical Dilemmas [LO-3], Chapter 1** Assume that you achieved all the tasks shown in Exercise 2 not as an individual employee but as part of a work team. In your résumé, must you mention other team members? Explain your answer.

5. **Completing a Résumé [LO-4]** Using your revised version of the résumé in Message for Analysis 18.A, create a plain-text file that Sylvia Manchester could use to include in email messages.

6. **Completing a Résumé [LO-4]** Imagine that you are applying for work in a field that involves speaking in front

of an audience, such as sales, consulting, management, or training. Using material you created for any of the exercises or cases in Chapters 16 or 17, record a two- to three-minute video demonstration of your speaking and presentation skills. Record yourself speaking to an audience, if one can be arranged.

EXPAND YOUR SKILLS

Critique the Professionals

Locate an example of an online résumé (a sample or an actual résumé) from VisualCV (www.visualcv.com) or a similar website. Analyze the résumé using the guidelines presented in this chapter. Using whatever medium your instructor requests, write a brief analysis (no more than one page) of the résumé's strengths and weaknesses, citing specific elements from the résumé and support from the chapter. If you are analyzing a real résumé, do not include any personally identifiable data, such as the person's name, email address, or phone number, in your report.

Sharpening Your Career Skills Online

Bovée and Thill's Business Communication Web Search, at http://businesscommunicationblog.com/websearch, is a unique research tool designed specifically for business communication research. Use the Web Search function to find a website, video, PDF document, podcast, or PowerPoint presentation that offers advice on creating an effective résumé. Write a brief email message to your instructor, describing the item that you found and summarizing the career skills information you learned from it.

CASES

CAREER SKILLS   **EMAIL SKILLS**

1. Career Planning: Researching Career Opportunities [LO-1]   Knowing the jargon and "hot button" issues in a particular profession or industry can give you a big advantage when it comes to writing your résumé and participating in job interviews. You can fine-tune your résumé for both human readers and applicant tracking systems, sound more confident and informed in interviews, and present yourself as a professional-class individual with an inquiring mind.

Your task: Imagine a specific job category in a company that has an informative, comprehensive website (to facilitate the research you'll need to do). This doesn't have to be a current job opening, but a position that you know exists or is likely to exist in this company, such as a business systems analyst at Apple or a brand manager at Unilever.

Explore the company's website and other online sources to find the following: (1) A brief description of what this job entails, with enough detail that you could describe it to a fellow student. (2) Some of the terminology used in the profession or the industry, both formal terms that might serve as keywords on your résumé and informal terms and phrases that insiders

are likely to use in publications and conversations. (3) An ongoing online conversation among people in this profession. For example, this might be a LinkedIn Group, a popular industry or professional blog that seems to get quite a few comments, or an industry or professional publication that attracts a lot of comments. (4) At least one significant issue that will affect people in this profession or companies in this industry over the next few years. For example, if your chosen profession involves accounting in a publicly traded corporation, upcoming changes in international financial reporting standards would be a significant issue. Similarly, for a company in the consumer electronics industry, the recycling and disposal of *e-waste* is an issue. Write a brief email message summarizing your findings and explaining how you could use this information on your résumé and during job interviews.

CAREER SKILLS   **EMAIL SKILLS**

2. Career Management: Researching Career Opportunities [LO-1]   Perhaps you won't be able to land your ultimate dream job right out of college, but that doesn't mean you shouldn't start planning right now to make that dream come true.

Your task: Using online job search tools, find a job that sounds just about perfect for you, even if you're not yet qualified for it. It might even be something that would take 10 or 20 years to reach. Don't settle for something that's not quite right—find a job that is so "you" and so exciting that you would jump out of bed every morning, eager to go to work (such jobs really do exist!). Start with the job description you found online and then supplement it with additional research so that you get a good picture of what this job and career path are all about. Compile a list of all the qualifications you would need in order to have a reasonable chance of landing such a job. Now compare this list with your current résumé. Write a brief email message to your instructor that identifies all the areas in which you would need to improve your skills, work experience, education, and other qualifications in order to land your dream job.

CAREER SKILLS

3. Message Strategies: Planning a Résumé [LO-2] Think about yourself. What are some things that come easily to you? What do you enjoy doing? In what part of the country would you like to live? Do you like to work indoors? Outdoors? A combination of the two? How much do you like to travel? Would you like to spend considerable time on the road? Do you like to work closely with others or more independently? What conditions make a job unpleasant? Do you delegate responsibility easily, or do you like to do things yourself? Are you better with words or numbers? Better at speaking or writing? Do you like to work under fixed deadlines? How important is job security to you? Do you want your supervisor to state clearly what is expected of you, or do you like the freedom to make many of your own decisions?

Your task: After answering these questions, gather information about possible jobs that suit your current qualifications by consulting reference materials (from your college library or placement center) and by searching online. Next, choose a location, a company, and a job that interests you. Write a résumé that matches your qualifications and the job description; use whatever format your instructor specifies.

CAREER SKILLS   TEAM SKILLS

4. Planning a Résumé [LO-2] If you haven't begun your professional career yet or you are pursuing a career change, the employment history section on your résumé can sometimes be a challenge to write. A brainstorming session with your wise and creative classmates could help.

Your task: In a team assigned by your instructor, you will help each other evaluate your employment histories and figure out the best way to present your work backgrounds on a résumé. First,

each member of the team should compile his or her work history, including freelance projects and volunteer work if relevant, and share this information with the team. After allowing some time for everyone to review each other's information, meet as a team (in person if you can, or online otherwise). Discuss each person's history, pointing out strong spots and weak spots, and then brainstorm the best way to present each person's employment history.

Note: If there are aspects of your employment history you would rather not share with your teammates, substitute a reasonably similar experience of the same duration.

CAREER SKILLS   TEAM SKILLS

5. Writing a Résumé [LO-3] The introductory statement of a résumé requires some careful thought, both in deciding which of the three types of introductory statement (see page 533) to use and what information to include in it. Getting another person's perspective on this communication challenge can be helpful. In this activity, in fact, someone else is going to write your introductory statement for you, and you will return the favor.

Your task: Pair off with a classmate. Provide each other with the basic facts about your qualifications, work history, education, and career objectives. Then meet in person or online for an informal interview, in which you ask each other questions to flesh out the information you have on each other. Assume that each of you has chosen to use a qualifications summary for your résumé. Now write each other's qualifications summary and then trade them for review. As you read what your partner wrote about you, ask yourself if this feels true to what you believe about yourself and your career aspirations. Do you think it introduces you effectively to potential employers? What might you change about it?

PRESENTATION SKILLS   PORTFOLIO BUILDER

6. Message Strategies: Completing a Résumé [LO-4] Creating presentations and other multimedia supplements can be a great way to expand on the brief overview that a résumé provides.

Your task: Starting with any version of a résumé that you've created for yourself, create a PowerPoint presentation that expands on your résumé information to give potential employers a more complete picture of what you can contribute. Include samples of your work, testimonials from current or past employers and colleagues, videos of speeches you've made, and anything else that tells the story of the professional "you." If you have a specific job or type of job in mind, focus your presentation on that. Otherwise, present a more general picture that shows why you would be a great employee for any company to consider. Be sure to review the information from Chapter 17 about creating professional-quality presentations.

Applying and Interviewing for Employment

LEARNING OBJECTIVES   After studying this chapter, you will be able to

1 Explain the purposes of application letters and describe how to apply the AIDA organizational approach to them

2 Describe the typical sequence of job interviews, the major types of interviews, and what employers look for during an interview

3 List six tasks you need to complete to prepare for a successful job interview

4 Explain how to succeed in all three stages of an interview

5 Identify the most common employment messages that follow an interview and explain when you would use each one

MyBcommLab Test your mastery of this chapter and its Learning Objectives. Visit mybcommlab.com to apply what you've learned in Document Makeovers and interactive simulation scenarios.

COMMUNICATION CLOSE-UP AT ZAPPOS

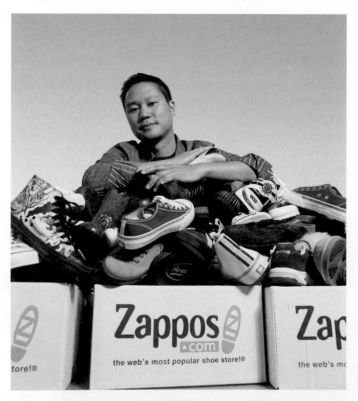

Zappos CEO Tony Hsieh makes sure the company's interviewing process finds the candidates who are compatible with an offbeat customer- and colleague-focused culture.

www.zappos.com

When a company communicates its core values with the help of a cartoon amphibian named Core Values Frog, you can guess the company doesn't quite fit the stuffy corporate stereotype. While it is passionately serious about customer satisfaction and employee engagement, the Las Vegas–based online shoe and clothing retailer Zappos doesn't take itself too seriously. In fact, one of the 10 values the frog promotes is "Create fun and a little weirdness."

Fun and a little weirdness can make a workplace more enjoyable, but CEO Tony Hsieh's commitment to employees runs much deeper than that. The company makes frequent reference to "the Zappos Family," and the ideals of taking care of one another and enjoying time spent together are embraced in numerous ways. These activities can range from parades in the workplace and other goofy events to the Wishez program, in which employees can ask one another to fulfill personal wishes, from lighthearted desires such as getting backstage access at concerts to serious matters such as getting help during tough financial times.

To find employees who will thrive in and protect the unconventional Zappos culture, the company takes an unconventional path when it comes to recruiting and interviewing. For example, in stark contrast to the companies that refuse to look at videos as part of job application packages, Zappos encourages applicants to send videos of themselves and even provides an upload facility on its website's application page.

The interviewing process searches out passionate, free-thinking candidates who fit the culture, from the offbeat antics to the serious commitment to customers and fellow employees. Some of the questions interviewees can expect to encounter include "What was the best mistake you made on the job?" and "On a scale of 1 to 10, how weird are you?"

Speaking of offbeat interviews, the company recently screened software engineering candidates using 30-minute coding challenges, in which the first programmer to solve the problem was "fast-tracked to Vegas" for the next round of interviews. Coding contests are not all that unusual for recruiting programmers, but it's unlikely that many feature an open bar, as the Zappos competition did.

A strong customer- and employee-focused culture, a strong commitment to maintaining that culture, and a recruiting strategy that finds the right people for that culture—this relentless focus on doing business the Zappos way keeps paying off. The company continues to grow and continues to be ranked as one of the best places to work in the United States.[1]

Submitting Your Résumé

Whether you plan to apply to Zappos (profiled in the chapter-opening Communication Close-up) or any other company, your résumé in some form will usually be the centerpiece of your job-search package. However, it needs support from several other employment messages before, during, and after the interview process. These messages can include application letters, job-inquiry letters, application forms, and follow-up notes.

1 **LEARNING OBJECTIVE**

Explain the purposes of application letters, and describe how to apply the AIDA organizational approach to them.

WRITING APPLICATION LETTERS

Whenever you mail, email, hand-deliver, or upload your résumé, you should include an **application letter**, also known as a *cover letter*, to let readers know what you're sending, why you're sending it, and how they can benefit from reading it. (Although this message is often not a printed letter anymore, many professionals still refer to it as a letter.) Take the same care with your application letter that you took with your résumé. A poorly written application letter can prompt employers to skip over your résumé, even if you are a good fit for a job.[2] Staffing specialist Abby Kohut calls the application letter "a writing-skills evaluation in disguise" and emphasizes that even a single error can get you bounced from contention.[3]

The best approach for an application letter depends on whether you are sending a **solicited application letter** to apply for an identified job opening or are *prospecting* with an **unsolicited application letter**—taking the initiative to write to companies even though they haven't announced a job opening that is right for you.[4] In many ways, the difference between the two is like the difference between solicited and unsolicited proposals (see page 388). Figure 19.1 on the next page shows an application message written in response to a posted job opening. The writer knows exactly what qualifications the organization is seeking and can "echo" those attributes back in his message.

Prospecting is more challenging because you don't have the clear target you have with a solicited message. You will need to do more research to identify the qualities that a company would probably seek for the position you hope to occupy (see Figure 19.2 on page 551). Also, search for news items that involve the company, its customers, the profession, or the individual manager to whom you are writing. Using this information in your application letter helps you establish common ground with your reader—and it shows that you are tuned in to what is going on in the industry.

For either type of letter, follow these tips to be more effective:[5]

- Resist the temptation to stand out with gimmicky application letters; impress with knowledge and professionalism instead.
- If the name of an individual manager is at all findable, address your letter to that person, rather than something generic such as "Dear Hiring Manager." Search LinkedIn, the company's website, industry directories, Twitter, and anything else you can think of to find an appropriate name. Ask the people in your network if they know a name. If another applicant finds a name and you don't, you're at a disadvantage.
- Clearly identify the opportunity you are applying for or expressing interest in.
- Show that you understand the company and its marketplace.

Always accompany your résumé with an application message (letter or email) that motivates the recipient to read the résumé.

An unsolicited application letter is more challenging because you must identify the qualities the company would likely be looking for in the position you would like to get.

MyBcommLab

- Access this chapter's simulation entitled Interviewing, located at mybcommlab.com.

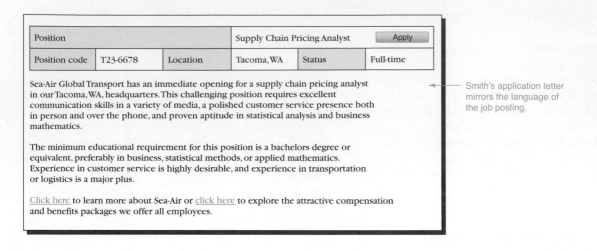

Smith's application letter mirrors the language of the job posting.

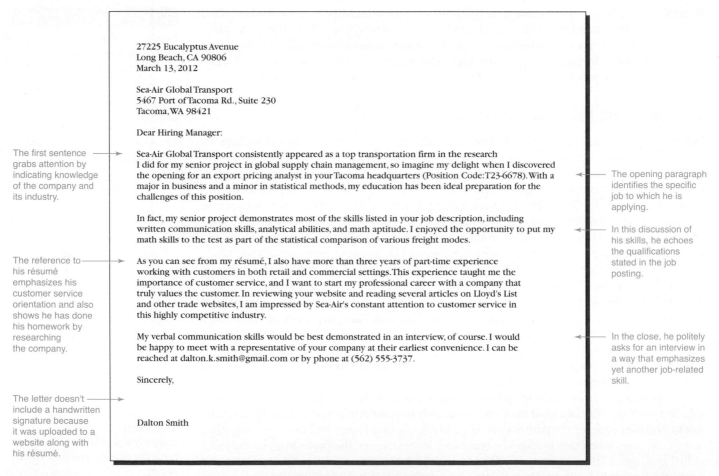

The first sentence grabs attention by indicating knowledge of the company and its industry.

The reference to his résumé emphasizes his customer service orientation and also shows he has done his homework by researching the company.

The letter doesn't include a handwritten signature because it was uploaded to a website along with his résumé.

The opening paragraph identifies the specific job to which he is applying.

In this discussion of his skills, he echoes the qualifications stated in the job posting.

In the close, he politely asks for an interview in a way that emphasizes yet another job-related skill.

Figure 19.1 Solicited Application Message
In this response to an online job posting, Dalton Smith highlights his qualifications while mirroring the requirements specified in the posting. Following the AIDA model, he grabs attention immediately by letting the reader know that he is familiar with the company and the global transportation business.

- Never volunteer salary history or requirements unless an employer has asked for this information.
- Keep it short—no more than three paragraphs. Keep in mind that all you are trying to do at this point is move the conversation forward one step.
- Show some personality, while maintaining a business-appropriate tone. The letter gives you the opportunity to balance the facts-only tone of your résumé.
- Project confidence without being arrogant.

457 Mountain View Rd.
Clear Lake, IA 50428
June 16, 2012

Ms. Patricia Downing, Store Manager
Walmart
840 South Oak
Iowa Falls, IA 50126

Dear Ms. Downing:

Johns gets the reader's attention in the first paragraph by speaking directly to her needs.

You want retail clerks and managers who are accurate, enthusiastic, and experienced. You want someone who cares about customer service, who understands merchandising, and who can work with others to get the job done. When you're ready to hire a manager trainee or a clerk who is willing to work toward promotion, please consider me for the job.

Working as a clerk and then as an assistant manager in a large department store has taught me how to anticipate customer problems and deliver the type of service that keeps customers coming back. Moreover, my recent BA degree in retailing, which encompassed such courses as retailing, marketing, management, and business information systems, will provide your store with a well-rounded associate. (Please refer to my enclosed résumé for more information.) You'll find that I'm interested in every facet of retailing, eager to take on responsibility, and willing to continue learning throughout my career.

The body of the letter points out personal qualities that aren't specifically stated in her résumé.

Close builds the reader's interest by demonstrating knowledge of the company's policy regarding promotion.

I understand that Walmart prefers to promote its managers from within the company, and I would be pleased to start out with an entry-level position until I gain the necessary experience. Do you have any associate positions opening up soon? Could we discuss my qualifications? I will phone you early next Wednesday to arrange a meeting at your convenience.

Johns focuses on the reader and displays the "you" attitude, even though the last paragraph uses the word "I."

Sincerely,

Glenda Johns

Glenda Johns

Enclosure

Figure 19.2   Unsolicited Application Letter
Glenda Johns's experience as a clerk and an assistant manager gives her a good idea of the qualities that Walmart is likely to be looking for in future managers. She uses these insights to craft the opening of her letter.

Because application letters are persuasive messages, the AIDA approach you learned in Chapter 10 is ideal, as the following sections explain.

Getting Attention

The opening paragraph of your application letter has two important tasks to accomplish: (1) clearly stating your reason for writing and (2) giving the recipient a reason to keep reading. Why would a recruiter want to keep reading your letter instead of the hundred others piling up on his or her desk? Because you show some immediate potential for meeting the company's needs. You've researched the company and the position, and you know something about the industry and its current challenges. Consider this opening:

The opening paragraph of your application letter needs to clearly convey the reason you're writing and give the recipient a compelling reason to keep reading.

With the recent slowdown in corporate purchasing, I can certainly appreciate the challenge of new fleet sales in this business environment. With my high energy level and 16 months of new-car sales experience, I believe I can produce the results you listed as vital in the job posting on your website.

This applicant does a smooth job of mirroring the company's stated needs while highlighting his personal qualifications, along with evidence that he understands the broader market. He balances his relative lack of experience with enthusiasm and knowledge of the industry. Table 19.1 highlights some ways you can spark interest and grab attention in your opening paragraph. All these openings demonstrate the "you" attitude, and many indicate how the applicant can benefit the employer.

Building Interest and Increasing Desire

Use the middle section of your application letter to expand on your opening and present a more complete picture of your strengths.

The middle section of your application letter presents your strongest selling points in terms of their potential benefit to the organization, thereby building interest in you and creating a desire to interview you. As with the opening, the more specific you can be in the middle section, the better. And back up your assertions with some convincing evidence of your ability to perform:

Poor

I completed three college courses in business and managerial communication, earning an A in each course, and have worked for the past year at Imperial Construction.

Improved

Using the skills gained from three semesters of college training in business and managerial communication, I developed a collection system for Imperial Construction that reduced annual bad-debt losses by 25 percent. By emphasizing a win–win scenario for the company and its clients with incentives for on-time payment, the system was also credited with improving customer satisfaction.

When writing a solicited letter, be sure to discuss each requirement specified in the advertisement. If you are deficient in any of these requirements, stress other solid selling points to help strengthen your overall presentation.

TABLE 19.1   Tips for Getting Attention in Application Letters

Tip	Example
Unsolicited Application Letters	
Show how your strongest skills will benefit the organization.	If you need a regional sales specialist who consistently meets sales targets while fostering strong customer relationships, please consider my qualifications.
Describe your understanding of the job's requirements and show how well your qualifications fit them.	Your annual report stated that improving manufacturing efficiency is one of the company's top priorities for next year. Through my postgraduate research in systems engineering and consulting work for several companies in the industry, I've developed reliable methods for quickly identifying ways to cut production time while reducing resource use.
Mention the name of a person known to and highly regarded by the reader.	When Janice McHugh of your franchise sales division spoke to our business communication class last week, she said you often need promising new marketing graduates at this time of year.
Refer to publicized company activities, achievements, changes, or new procedures.	Today's issue of the *Detroit News* reports that you may need the expertise of computer programmers versed in robotics when your Lansing tire plant automates this spring.
Use a question to demonstrate your understanding of the organization's needs.	Can your fast-growing market research division use an interviewer with two years of field survey experience, a B.A. in public relations, and a real desire to succeed? If so, please consider me for the position.
Use a catchphrase opening if the job requires ingenuity and imagination.	*Haut monde*—whether referring to French, Italian, or Arab clients, it still means "high society." As an interior designer for your Beverly Hills showroom, not only could I serve and sell to your distinguished clientele, but I could do it in all these languages. I speak, read, and write them fluently.
Solicited Application Letters	
Identify where you discovered the job opening; describe what you have to offer.	Your job posting on Monster.com for a cruise-line social director caught my eye. My eight years of experience as a social director in the travel industry would allow me to serve your new Caribbean cruise division well.

Don't restrict your message to just core job duties. Also highlight personal characteristics that apply to the targeted position, such as your diligence or your ability to work hard, learn quickly, handle responsibility, or get along with people:

> While attending college full time, I worked part-time during the school year and up to 60 hours a week each summer in order to be totally self-supporting while in college. I can offer your organization the same level of effort and perseverance.

Mention your salary requirements at this stage only if the organization has asked you to state them. If you don't know the salary that's appropriate for the position and someone with your qualifications, you can find typical salary ranges at the Bureau of Labor Statistics website, **www.bls.gov**, or a number of commercial websites. If you do state a target salary, tie it to the value you offer:

Don't bring up salary in your application letter unless the recipient has asked you to include your salary requirements.

> For the past two years, I have been helping a company similar to yours organize its database marketing efforts. I would therefore like to receive a salary in the same range (the mid-60s) for helping your company set up a more efficient customer database.

Toward the end of this section, refer the reader to your résumé by citing a specific fact or general point covered there:

> As you can see in the attached résumé, I've been working part time with a local publisher since my sophomore year. During that time, I've used client interactions as an opportunity to build strong customer service skills.

Motivating Action

The final paragraph of your application letter has two important functions: to ask the reader for a specific action (usually an interview) and to facilitate a reply. Offer to come to the employer's office at a convenient time or, if the firm is some distance away, to meet with its nearest representative or arrange a telephone interview. Include your email address and phone number, as well as the best time to reach you. Alternatively, you can take the initiative and say that you will follow up with a phone call. Refer again to your strongest selling point and, if desired, your date of availability:

In the final paragraph of your application letter, respectfully ask for specific action and make it easy for the reader to respond.

> After you have reviewed my qualifications, could we discuss the possibility of putting my marketing skills to work for your company? Because I will be on spring break the week of March 8, I would like to arrange a time to talk then. I will call in late February to schedule a convenient time when we could discuss employment opportunities at your company.

After editing and proofreading your application letter, give it a final quality check by referring to "Checklist: Writing Application Letters." Then send it along with your résumé promptly, especially if you are responding to an advertisement or online job posting.

FOLLOWING UP AFTER SUBMITTING A RÉSUMÉ

Deciding if, when, and how to follow up after submitting your résumé and application letter is one of the trickiest parts of a job search. First and foremost, keep in mind that employers continue to evaluate your communication efforts and professionalism during this phase, so don't say or do anything to leave a negative impression. Second, adhere to whatever instructions the employer has provided. If a job posting says "no calls," for example, don't call. Third, if the job posting lists a *close date*,

REAL-TIME UPDATES
Learn More by Reading This Article

How much are you worth?

Find real-life salary ranges for a wide range of jobs. Go to http://real-timeupdates.com/bct11 and click on "Learn More." If you are using MyBcommLab, you can access Real-Time Updates within each chapter or under Student Study Tools.

✓ Checklist | Writing Application Letters

- Take the same care with your application letter that you took with your résumé.
- If you are *prospecting* using an unsolicited message, do deep research to identify the qualities the company likely wants.
- For solicited messages in response to a posted job opening, word your message in a way that echoes back the qualifications listed in the posting.
- Open the letter by capturing the reader's attention in a businesslike way.
- Use specific language to clearly state your interests and objectives.

- Build interest and desire in your potential contribution by presenting your key qualifications for the job.
- Link your education, experience, and personal qualities to the job requirements.
- Outline salary requirements only if the organization has requested that you provide them.
- Request an interview at a time and place that is convenient for the reader.
- Make it easy to comply with your request by providing your complete contact information and good times to reach you.
- Adapt your style for cultural variations, if required.

---

don't call or write before then, because the company is still collecting applications and will not have made a decision about inviting people for interviews. Wait a week or so after the close date. If no close date is given and you have no other information to suggest a time-line, you can generally contact the company starting a week or two after submitting your résumé.[6] Keep in mind that a single instance of poor etiquette or clumsy communication can undo all your hard work in a job search, so maintain your professional behavior every step of the way.

> Think creatively about a follow-up message to show that you've continued to add to your skills or that you've learned more about the company or the industry.

When you follow up by email or telephone, you can share an additional piece of information that links your qualifications to the position (keep an eye out for late-breaking news about the company, too) and ask a question about the hiring process as a way to gather some information about your status. Good questions to ask include:[7]

- Has a hiring decision been made yet?
- Can you tell me what to expect next in terms of the hiring process?
- What is the company's timeframe for filling this position?
- Could I follow up in another week if you haven't had the chance to contact me yet?
- Can I provide any additional information regarding my qualifications for the position?

Whatever the circumstances, a follow-up message can demonstrate that you're sincerely interested in working for the organization, persistent in pursuing your goals, and committed to upgrading your skills.

If you don't land a job at your dream company on the first attempt, don't give up. You can apply again if a new opening appears, or you can send an updated résumé with a new unsolicited application letter that describes how you have gained additional experience, taken a relevant course, or otherwise improved your skill set. Many leading employers take note of applicants who came close but didn't quite make it and may extend offers when positions open up in the future.[8]

Understanding the Interviewing Process

> **2** LEARNING OBJECTIVE
>
> Describe the typical sequence of job interviews, the major types of interviews, and what employers look for during an interview.

An **employment interview** is a formal meeting during which both you and the prospective employer ask questions and exchange information. The employer's objective is to find the best talent to fill available job openings, and your objective is to find the right match for your goals and capabilities.

> Start preparing early for your interviews—and be sure to consider a wide range of options.

As you get ready to begin interviewing, keep two vital points in mind. First, recognize that the process takes time. Start your preparation and research early; the best job offers usually go to the best-prepared candidates. Second, don't limit your options by looking at only a few companies. By exploring a wide range of firms and positions, you might uncover great opportunities that you would not have found otherwise. You'll increase the odds of getting more job offers, too.

THE TYPICAL SEQUENCE OF INTERVIEWS

Most employers interview an applicant multiple times before deciding to make a job offer. At the most selective companies, you might have a dozen or more individual interviews across several stages.[9] Depending on the company and the position, the process may stretch out over many weeks, or it may be completed in a matter of days.[10]

Employers start with the *screening stage*, in which they filter out applicants who are unqualified or otherwise not a good fit for the position. Screening can take place on your school's campus, at company offices, via telephone (including Skype or another Internet-based phone service), or through a computer-based screening system. Time is limited in screening interviews, so keep your answers short while providing a few key points that differentiate you from other candidates. If your screening interview will take place by phone, try to schedule it for a time when you can be focused and free from interruptions.[11]

> During the screening stage of interviews, use the limited time available to differentiate yourself from other candidates.

The next stage of interviews, the *selection stage*, helps the organization identify the top candidates from all those who qualify. During these interviews, show keen interest in the job, relate your skills and experience to the organization's needs, listen attentively, and ask insightful questions that show you've done your research.

> During the selection stage, continue to show how your skills and attributes can help the company.

If the interviewers agree that you're a good candidate, you may receive a job offer, either on the spot or a few days later by phone, mail, or email. In other instances, you may be invited back for a final evaluation, often by a higher-ranking executive. The objective of the *final stage* is often to sell you on the advantages of joining the organization.

> During the final stage, the interviewer may try to sell you on working for the firm.

COMMON TYPES OF INTERVIEWS

Employers can use a variety of interviewing methods throughout the interviewing process, and you need to recognize the different types and be prepared for each one. These methods can be distinguished by the way they are structured, the number of people involved, and the purpose of the interview.

Structured Versus Unstructured Interviews

In a **structured interview**, the interviewer (or a computer program) asks a series of questions in a predetermined order. Structured interviews help employers identify candidates who don't meet basic job criteria, and they make it easier for the interview team to compare answers from multiple candidates.[12]

> A structured interview follows a set sequence of questions, allowing the interview team to compare answers from all candidates.

In contrast, in an **open-ended interview**, the interviewer adapts his or her line of questioning based on the answers you give and any questions you ask. Even though it may feel like a conversation, remember that it's still an interview, so keep your answers focused and professional.

> In an open-ended interview, the interviewer adapts the line of questioning based on your responses and questions.

Panel and Group Interviews

Although one-on-one interviews are the most common format, some employers use panel or group interviews as well. In a **panel interview**, you meet with several interviewers at once.[13] Try to make a connection with each person on the panel and keep in mind that each person has a different perspective, so tailor your responses accordingly.[14] For example, an upper-level manager is likely to be interested in your overall business sense and strategic perspective, whereas a potential colleague might be more interested in your technical skills and ability to work in a team. In a **group interview**, one or more interviewers meet with several candidates simultaneously. A key purpose of a group interview is to observe how the candidates interact with potential peers.[15]

> In a panel interview, you meet with several interviewers at once; in a group interview, you and several other candidates meet with one or more interviewers at once.

Behavioral, Situational, Working, and Stress Interviews

Perhaps the most common type of interview these days is the **behavioral interview**, in which you are asked to relate specific incidents and experiences from your past.[16] Generic interview questions can often be answered with "canned" responses, but behavioral questions require candidates to use their own experiences and attributes to craft answers. Studies show that behavioral interviewing is a much better predictor of success on the job than traditional interview questions.[17] To prepare for a behavioral interview, review your work

> In a behavioral interview, you are asked to describe how you handled situations from your past.

or college experiences to recall several instances in which you demonstrated an important job-related attribute or dealt with a challenge such as uncooperative team members or heavy workloads. Get ready with responses that quickly summarize the situation, the actions you took, and the outcome of those actions.[18]

A **situational interview** is similar to a behavioral interview except that the questions focus on how you would handle various hypothetical situations on the job. The situations will likely relate to the job you're applying for, so the more you know about the position, the better prepared you'll be.

A **working interview** is the most realistic type of interview: You actually perform a job-related activity during the interview. You may be asked to lead a brainstorming session, solve a business problem, engage in role playing, or even make a presentation.[19]

The most unnerving type of interview is the **stress interview**, during which you might be asked questions designed to unsettle you, or you might be subjected to long periods of silence, criticism, interruptions, and or even hostile reactions by the interviewer. The theory behind this approach is that you'll reveal how well you handle stressful situations, although some experts find the technique of dubious value.[20] If you find yourself in a stress interview, recognize what is happening and collect your thoughts for a few seconds before you respond.

> In situational interviews, you're asked to explain how you would handle various hypothetical situations.

> In a working interview, you actually perform work-related tasks.

> The theory behind stress interviews is to let recruiters see how you handle yourself under pressure.

INTERVIEW MEDIA

Expect to be interviewed through a variety of media. Employers trying to cut travel costs and the demands on staff time now interview candidates via telephone, email, instant messaging, virtual online systems, and videoconferencing, in addition to traditional face-to-face meetings (see Figure 19.3).

To succeed at a telephone interview, make sure you treat it as seriously as an in-person interview. Be prepared with a copy of all the materials you have sent to the employer, including your résumé and any correspondence. In addition, prepare some note cards with key message points you'd like to make and questions you'd like to ask. If possible, arrange to speak on a landline so you don't have to worry about mobile phone reception problems. And remember that you won't be able to use a pleasant smile, a firm handshake, and other nonverbal signals to create a good impression. A positive, alert tone of voice is therefore vital.[21]

Email and IM are also sometimes used in the screening stage. Although you have almost no opportunity to send and receive nonverbal signals with these formats, you do have the major advantage of being able to review and edit each response before you send it.

> Expect to use a variety of media when you interview, from in-person conversations to virtual meetings.

> Treat a telephone interview as seriously as you would an in-person interview.

> When interviewing via email or IM, be sure to take a moment to review your responses before sending them.

Figure 19.3   Finding Real Jobs in a Virtual World
Virtual job fairs, such as the Working Worlds event hosted by Luxembourg's GAX Technologies, allow candidates and recruiters to interact without the time and expense of travel.

Maintain a professional style in your responses, and be sure to ask questions that demonstrate your knowledge of the company and the position.[22]

Many employers use video technology for both live and recorded interviews. For instance, Zappos often uses video interviews on Skype to select the top two or three finalists for each position and then invites those candidates for in-person interviews.[23] With recorded video interviews, an online system asks a set of questions and records the respondent's answers. Recruiters then watch the videos as part of the screening process.[24] Prepare for a video interview as you would for an in-person interview—including dressing and grooming—and take the extra steps needed to become familiar with the equipment and the process. If you're interviewing from home, arrange your space so that the webcam doesn't pick up anything distracting or embarrassing in the background. During any video interview, remember to sit up straight and focus on the camera.

Online interviews can range from simple structured questionnaires and tests to sophisticated job simulations that are similar to working interviews (see Figure 19.4). In the banking industry, for example, Atlanta-based SunTrust and Cleveland-based National City use computerized simulations to see how well candidates can perform job-related tasks and decision-making scenarios. These simulations help identify good candidates, give applicants an idea of what the job is like, and reduce the risk of employment discrimination lawsuits because they closely mimic actual job skills.[25]

REAL-TIME UPDATES
Learn More by Watching This Video

Video interviewing on Skype

Chances are you'll have at least one video interview using Skype or another Internet-based phone service. Watch this video for essential tips on preparing and participating in an online video interview. Go to http://real-timeupdates.com/bct11 and click on "Learn More." If you are using MyBcommLab, you can access Real-Time Updates within each chapter or under Student Study Tools.

In a video interview, speak to the camera as though you are addressing the interviewer in person.

Computer-based virtual interviews range from simple structured interviews to realistic job simulations to meetings in virtual worlds.

WHAT EMPLOYERS LOOK FOR IN AN INTERVIEW

Interviews give employers the chance to go beyond the basic data of your résumé to get to know you and to answer two essential questions. The first is whether you can handle the responsibilities of the position. Naturally, the more you know about the demands of the position, and the more you've thought about how your skills match those demands, the better you'll be able to respond.

Suitability for a specific job is judged on the basis of such factors as
- Academic preparation
- Work experience
- Job-related personality traits

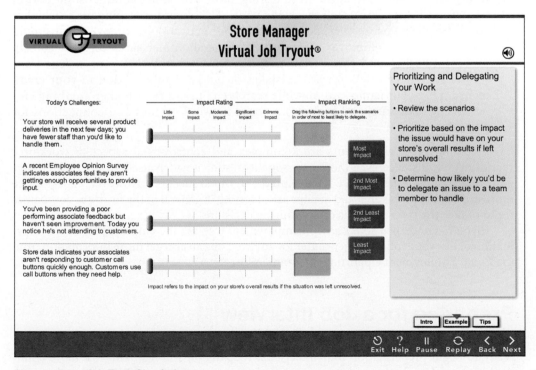

Figure 19.4 Job Task Simulations
Computer-based job simulations are an increasingly popular approach to testing job-related skills.

Compatibility with an organization and a position is judged on the basis of personal background, attitudes, and style.

The second essential question is whether you will be a good fit with the organization and the target position. This line of inquiry includes both a general and a specific aspect. The general aspect concerns your overall personality and approach to work. All good employers want people who are confident, dedicated, positive, curious, courteous, ethical, and willing to commit to something larger than their own individual goals.

The specific aspect involves the fit with a particular company and position. Just like people, companies have different "personalities." Some are intense; others are more laid back. Some emphasize teamwork; others expect employees to forge their own way and even to compete with one another. Expectations also vary from job to job within a company and from industry to industry. An outgoing personality is essential for sales but less so for research, for instance.

PREEMPLOYMENT TESTING AND BACKGROUND CHECKS

Preemployment tests attempt to provide objective, quantitative information about a candidate's skills, attitudes, and habits.

In an effort to improve the predictability of the selection process, many employers now conduct a variety of preemployment evaluations and investigations. Here are types of assessments you are likely to encounter during your job search:[26]

- **Integrity tests.** Integrity tests attempt to measure how truthful and trustworthy a candidate is likely to be.
- **Personality tests.** Personality tests are designed to gauge such aspects as attitudes toward work, interests, managerial potential, dependability, commitment, and motivation.
- **Cognitive tests.** Cognitive tests measure a variety of attributes involved in acquiring, processing, analyzing, using, and remembering information. Typical tests involve reading comprehension, mathematics, problem solving, and decision making.
- **Job knowledge and job skills tests.** These assessments measure the knowledge and skills required to succeed in a particular position. An accounting candidate, for example, might be tested on accounting principles and legal matters (knowledge) and asked to create a simple balance sheet or income statement (skills).
- **Substance tests.** A majority of companies perform some level of drug and alcohol testing. Many employers believe such testing is necessary to maintain workplace safety, ensure productivity, and protect companies from lawsuits, but others view it as an invasion of employee privacy.
- **Background checks.** In addition to testing, most companies conduct some sort of background check, including reviewing your credit record, checking to see whether you have a criminal history, and verifying your education. Moreover, you should assume that every employer will conduct a general online search on you. To help prevent a background check from tripping you up, verify that your college transcripts are current, look for any mistakes or outdated information in your credit record, plug your name into multiple search engines to see whether anything embarrassing shows up, and scour your social network profiles and connections for potential problems.

Preemployment assessments are a complex and controversial aspect of workforce recruiting. For instance, even though personality testing is widely used, some research suggests that current tests are not a reliable predictor of job success.[27] However, expect to see more innovation in this area and greater use of testing in general in the future as companies try to reduce the risks and costs of poor hiring decisions.

If you're concerned about any preemployment test, ask the employer for more information or ask your college career center for advice. You can also get more information from the Equal Employment Opportunity Commission, at www.eeoc.gov.

Preparing for a Job Interview

3 LEARNING OBJECTIVE

List six tasks you need to complete to prepare for a successful job interview.

Now that you're armed with insights into the interviewing and assessment process, you're ready to begin preparing for your interviews. Preparation will help you feel more confident and perform better under pressure, and preparation starts with learning about the organization.

LEARNING ABOUT THE ORGANIZATION AND YOUR INTERVIEWERS

Today's employers expect serious candidates to demonstrate an understanding of the company's operations, its markets, and its strategic and tactical challenges.[28] You've already done some initial research to identify companies of interest, but when you're invited to interview, it's time to dig a little deeper (see Table 19.2). Making this effort demonstrates your interest in the company, and it identifies you as a business professional who knows the importance of investigation and analysis.

In addition to learning about the company and the job opening, learn as much as you can about the managers who will be interviewing you, if you can get their names. Search LinkedIn in particular; many professionals have profiles on the popular business networking site. Think about ways to use whatever information you find during your interview. For example, if an interviewer lists membership in a particular professional organization, you might ask whether the organization is a good forum for people to learn about vital issues in the profession or industry. This question gives the interviewer an opportunity to talk about his or her own interests and experiences for a moment, which builds rapport and might reveal vital insights into the career path you are considering. Just make sure your questions are sincere and not uncomfortably personal.

Interviewers expect you to know some basic information about the company and its industry.

THINKING AHEAD ABOUT QUESTIONS

Planning ahead for the interviewer's questions will help you handle them more confidently and successfully. In addition, you will want to prepare insightful questions of your own.

TABLE 19.2   Investigating an Organization and a Job Opportunity

Where to Look and What You Can Learn
- *Company website, blogs, and social media accounts:* Overall information about the company, including key executives, products and services, locations and divisions, employee benefits, job descriptions
- *Competitors' websites, blogs, and social media accounts:* Similar information from competitors, including the strengths these companies claim to have
- *Industry-related websites and blogs:* Objective analysis and criticism of the company, its products, its reputation, and its management
- *Marketing materials (print and online):* The company's marketing strategy and customer communication style
- *Company publications (print and online):* Key events, stories about employees, new products
- *Your social network contacts:* Names and job titles of potential contacts within a company
- *Periodicals (newspapers and trade journals, both print and online):* In-depth stories about the company and its strategies, products, successes, and failures; you may find profiles of top executives
- *Career center at your college:* Often provides a wide array of information about companies that hire graduates
- *Current and former employees:* Insights into the work environment

Points to Learn About the Organization
- Full name
- Location (headquarters and divisions, branches, subsidiaries, or other units)
- Ownership (public or private; whether it is owned by another company)
- Brief history
- Products and services
- Industry position (whether the company is a leader or a minor player; whether it is an innovator or more of a follower)
- Key financial points (such as stock price and trends, if a public company)
- Growth prospects (whether the company is investing in its future through research and development; whether it is in a thriving industry)

Points to Learn About the Position
- Title
- Functions and responsibilities
- Qualifications and expectations
- Possible career paths
- Salary range
- Travel expectations and opportunities
- Relocation expectations and opportunities

Asking questions of your own is as important as answering the interviewer's questions. Not only do you get vital information, but you show initiative and curiosity.

Planning for the Employer's Questions

Many general interview questions are "stock" queries that you can expect to hear again and again during your interviews. Get ready to face these five at the very least:

- **What is the hardest decision you've ever had to make?** Be prepared with a good example (that isn't too personal), explaining why the decision was difficult, how you made the choice you made, and what you learned from the experience.
- **What is your greatest weakness?** This question seems to be a favorite of some interviewers, although it probably rarely yields useful information. One good strategy is to mention a skill or attribute you haven't had the opportunity to develop yet but would like to in your next position.[29]
- **Where do you want to be five years from now?** This question tests (1) whether you're merely using this job as a stopover until something better comes along and (2) whether you've given thought to your long-term goals. Your answer should reflect

You can expect to face a number of common questions in your interviews, so be sure to prepare for them.

your desire to contribute to the employer's long-term goals, not just your own goals. Whether this question often yields useful information is also a matter of debate, but be prepared to answer it.[30]

- **What didn't you like about previous jobs you've held?** Answer this one carefully: The interviewer is trying to predict whether you'll be an unhappy or difficult employee.[31] Describe something that you didn't like in a way that puts you in a positive light, such as having limited opportunities to apply your skills or education. Avoid making negative comments about former employers or colleagues.
- **Tell me something about yourself.** One good strategy is to *briefly* share the "story of you" (see page 521), quickly summarizing where you have been and where you would like to go—in a way that aligns your interests with the company's. Alternatively, you can focus on a specific skill that you know is valuable to the company, share something business-relevant that you are passionate about, or offer a short summary of what colleagues or customers think about you.[32] Whatever tactic you choose, this is not the time to be shy or indecisive, so be ready with a confident, memorable answer.

Continue your preparation by planning a brief answer to each question in Table 19.3. You can also find typical interview questions at websites such as InterviewUp, www.interviewup.com, where candidates share actual questions they have faced in recent interviews.[33]

Look for ways to frame your responses as brief stories rather than as dry facts or statements.

As you prepare answers, look for ways to frame your responses as brief stories (again, 30 to 90 seconds) rather than simple declarative answers.[34] Cohesive stories tend to stick in the listener's mind more effectively than disconnected facts and statements.

REAL-TIME UPDATES
Learn More by Watching This Video

Study the classics to ace your next interview

No, not Homer and Ovid—classic interview questions. Prepare answers to these old standbys so you can respond with clarity and confidence. Go to http://real-timeupdates.com/bct11 and click on "Learn More." If you are using MyBcommLab, you can access Real-Time Updates within each chapter or under Student Study Tools.

Planning Questions of Your Own

Remember that an interview is a two-way conversation: The questions you ask are just as important as the answers you provide. By asking insightful questions, you can demonstrate your understanding of the organization, you can steer the discussion into areas that allow you to present your qualifications to best advantage, and you can verify for yourself whether this is a good opportunity. Plus, interviewers

TABLE 19.3	**Twenty-Five Common Interview Questions**

Questions About College

1. What courses in college did you like most? Least? Why?
2. Do you think your extracurricular activities in college were worth the time you spent on them? Why or why not?
3. When did you choose your college major? Did you ever change your major? If so, why?
4. Do you feel you did the best scholastic work you are capable of?
5. How has your college education prepared you for this position?

Questions About Employers and Jobs

6. What jobs have you held? Why did you leave?
7. What percentage of your college expenses did you earn? How?
8. Why did you choose your particular field of work?
9. What are the disadvantages of your chosen field?
10. Have you served in the military? What rank did you achieve? What jobs did you perform?
11. What do you think about how this industry operates today?
12. Why do you think you would like this particular type of job?

Questions About Work Experiences and Expectations

13. Do you prefer to work in any specific geographic location? If so, why?
14. What motivates you? Why?
15. What do you think determines a person's progress in a good organization?
16. Describe an experience in which you learned from one of your mistakes.
17. Why do you want this job?
18. What have you done that shows initiative and willingness to work?
19. Why should I hire you?

Questions About Work Habits

20. Do you prefer working with others or by yourself?
21. What type of boss do you prefer?
22. Have you ever had any difficulty getting along with colleagues or supervisors? With instructors? With other students?
23. What would you do if you were given an unrealistic deadline for a task or project?
24. How do you feel about overtime work?
25. How do you handle stress or pressure on the job?

expect you to ask questions and tend to look negatively on candidates who don't have any questions to ask. For a list of good questions that you might use as a starting point, see Table 19.4 on the next page.

BOLSTERING YOUR CONFIDENCE

Interviewing is stressful for everyone, so some nervousness is natural. However, you can take steps to feel more confident. Start by reminding yourself that you have value to offer the employer, and the employer already thinks highly enough of you to invite you to an interview.

If some aspect of your appearance or background makes you uneasy, correct it if possible or offset it by emphasizing positive traits such as warmth, wit, intelligence, or charm. Instead of dwelling on your weaknesses, focus on your strengths. Instead of worrying about how you will perform in the interview, focus on how you can help the organization succeed. As with public speaking, the more prepared you are, the more confident you'll be.

The best way to build your confidence is to prepare thoroughly and address shortcomings as best you can—in other words, take action.

POLISHING YOUR INTERVIEW STYLE

Competence and confidence are the foundation of your interviewing style, and you can enhance them by giving the interviewer an impression of poise, good manners, and good judgment. You can develop an adept style by staging mock interviews with a friend or using an interview

Staging mock interviews with a friend is a good way to hone your style.

TABLE 19.4	Ten Questions to Consider Asking an Interviewer
Question	**Reason for Asking**
1. What are the job's major responsibilities?	A vague answer could mean that the responsibilities have not been clearly defined, which is almost guaranteed to cause frustration if you take the job.
2. What qualities do you want in the person who fills this position?	This will help you go beyond the job description to understand what the company really wants.
3. How do you measure success for someone in this position?	A vague or incomplete answer could mean that the expectations you will face are unrealistic or ill defined.
4. What is the first problem that needs the attention of the person you hire?	Not only will this help you prepare, but it can signal whether you're about to jump into a problematic situation.
5. Would relocation be required now or in the future?	If you're not willing to move often or at all, you need to know those expectations now.
6. Why is this job now vacant?	If the previous employee got promoted, that's a good sign. If the person quit, that might not be such a good sign.
7. What makes your organization different from others in the industry?	The answer will help you assess whether the company has a clear strategy to succeed in its industry and whether top managers communicate this to lower-level employees.
8. How would you define your organization's managerial philosophy?	You want to know whether the managerial philosophy is consistent with your own working values.
9. What is a typical workday like for you?	The interviewer's response can give you clues about daily life at the company.
10. What systems and policies are in place to help employees stay up to date in their professions and continue to expand their skills?	If the company doesn't have a strong commitment to employee development, chances are it isn't going to stay competitive very long.

simulator. Record these mock interviews so you can evaluate yourself. Your college's career center may have computer-based systems for practicing interviews as well (see Figure 19.5).

After each practice session, look for opportunities to improve. Have your mock interview partner critique your performance or critique yourself if you're able to record your

Figure 19.5 Interview Simulators
Experts advise you to practice your interview skills as much as possible. You can use a friend or classmate as a practice partner, or you might be able to use one of the interview simulators now available, such as this system from Perfect Interview. Ask at your career center, or search online for "practice interviews" or "interview simulators."

COMMUNICATING ACROSS CULTURES | Successfully Interviewing Across Borders

Interviewing for a job in another country can be one of the most exciting steps in your career. To succeed, you need to pay especially close attention to the important elements of the interviewing process, including personal appearance, an awareness of what interviewers are really trying to learn about you, and what you should learn about the organization you're hoping to join.

Some countries and cultures place a much higher importance on dress and personal grooming than many employees in the United States are accustomed to; moreover, expectations of personal appearance can vary dramatically from country to country. Ask people who've been to the country before and observe local businesspeople when you arrive. Many people interpret inappropriate dress as more than a simple fashion mistake; they view it as an inability or unwillingness to understand another culture.

Whether or not these things should matter isn't the issue; they do matter, and successful job candidates learn how to respond to different expectations. For instance, business image consultant Ashley Rothschild points out that you could get away with wearing a boldly colored suit in Italy but probably not in Japan. Business professionals do tend to dress formally in Italy, but as a worldwide fashion leader, the country has a broad definition of what is appropriate business attire.

Smart recruiters always analyze both nonverbal signals and verbal messages to judge whether an applicant truly has the qualities necessary for a job. In international employment situations, you'll probably be under even closer scrutiny. Recruiters abroad will want to know if you really have what it takes to succeed in unfamiliar social settings, how your family will handle the transition, and whether you can adapt your personal work style and habits enough to blend in with the hiring organization.

Remember to ask plenty of questions and do your research, both before and after the interview. Some employees view overseas postings as grand adventures, only to collide headfirst with the reality of what it's like to live and work in a completely different culture. For instance, if you've grown accustomed to the independent work style you enjoy in your current job or in school, could you handle a more structured work environment with a hierarchical chain of command? Make sure to get a sense of the culture both within the company and within its social community before you commit to a job in another country.

CAREER APPLICATIONS

1. Explain how you could find out what is appropriate dress for a job interview in South Africa.
2. Would it be appropriate to ask an interviewer to describe the culture in his or her country? Explain your answer.

---

practice interviews, using the list of warning signs shown in Table 19.5. Pay close attention to the length of your planned answers as well. Interviewers want you to give complete answers but they don't want you to take up valuable time or test their patience by chatting about minor or irrelevant details.[35]

In addition to reviewing your answers, evaluate your nonverbal behavior, including your posture, eye contact, facial expressions, and hand gestures and movements. Do you come across as alert and upbeat or passive and withdrawn? Pay close attention to your speaking voice as well. If you tend to speak in a monotone, for instance, practice speaking in a livelier style, with more inflection and emphasis. And watch out for "filler words" such as *uh* and *um*. Many people start sentences with a filler without being conscious of doing so. Train yourself to pause silently for a moment instead as you gather your thoughts and plan what to say.

Evaluate the length and clarity of your answers, your nonverbal behavior, and the quality of your voice.

TABLE 19.5	**Warning Signs: 25 Attributes That Interviewers Don't Like to See**
1. Poor personal appearance	13. Poor scholastic record
2. Overbearing, overaggressive, or conceited demeanor; a "superiority complex"; a know-it-all attitude	14. Unwillingness to start at the bottom; expecting too much too soon
3. Inability to express ideas clearly; poor voice, diction, or grammar	15. Tendency to make excuses
	16. Evasive answers; hedging on unfavorable factors in record
4. Lack of knowledge or experience	17. Lack of tact
5. Poor preparation for the interview	18. Lack of maturity
6. Lack of interest in the job	19. Lack of courtesy and common sense, including answering mobile phones, texting, or chewing gum during the interview
7. Lack of planning for career; lack of purpose or goals	
8. Lack of enthusiasm; passive and indifferent demeanor	20. Being critical of past or present employers
9. Lack of confidence and poise; appearance of being nervous and ill at ease	21. Lack of social skills
	22. Marked dislike for schoolwork
10. Insufficient evidence of achievement	23. Lack of vitality
11. Failure to participate in extracurricular activities	24. Failure to look interviewer in the eye
12. Overemphasis on money; interest only in the best dollar offer	25. Limp, weak handshake

PRESENTING A PROFESSIONAL IMAGE

Dress conservatively and be well groomed for every interview.

Clothing and grooming are important elements of preparation because they reveal something about a candidate's personality, professionalism, and ability to sense the unspoken "rules" of a situation. Inappropriate dress is a common criticism leveled at interviewees, so stand out by looking professional.[36] Your research into various companies, industries, and professions should give you insight into expectations for business attire. If you're not sure what to wear and the company hasn't provided any guidance, refer to Table 2.4 on page 51 for tips on selecting appropriate business attire or ask someone who works in the same industry. And don't be afraid to call the company for advice.

You don't need to spend a fortune on interview clothes, but your clothes must be clean, pressed, and appropriate. The following conservative look will serve you well in most business interview situations:[37]

- Neat, "adult" hairstyle
- Conservative business suit (for women, that means no exposed midriffs, short skirts, or plunging necklines) in a dark solid color or a subtle pattern such as pinstripes
- Solid color shirt for men (white in more conservative professions); coordinated blouse for women
- Conservative tie (classic stripes or subtle patterns) for men
- Limited jewelry (men, especially, should wear very little jewelry)
- No visible piercings other than one or two earrings (for women only)
- No visible tattoos
- Stylish but professional-looking shoes (no extreme high heels or casual shoes)
- Clean hands and nicely trimmed fingernails
- Little or no perfume or cologne (some people are allergic, and many people are put off by strong smells)
- Subtle makeup (for women)
- Exemplary personal hygiene

If you want to be taken seriously, dress and act seriously.

Be ready to go the minute you arrive at the interviewing site; don't fumble around for your résumé or your list of questions.

Remember, an interview is not the place to express your individuality or to let your inner rebel run wild. Send a clear signal that you understand the business world and know how to adapt to it. You won't be taken seriously otherwise.

Make a positive first impression with careful grooming and attire. You don't need to spend a fortune on new clothes, but you do need to look clean, prepared, and professional.

BEING READY WHEN YOU ARRIVE

When you go to your interview, take a small notebook, a pen, a list of the questions you want to ask, several copies of your résumé (protected in a folder), an outline of what you have learned about the organization, and any past correspondence about the position. You may also want to take a small calendar, a transcript of your college grades, a list of references, and a portfolio containing samples of your work, performance reviews, and certificates of achievement.[38] Think carefully if you plan to use a tablet computer or any other device for note taking or reference during an interview. You don't want to waste any of the interviewer's time fumbling with it. Also, turn off your mobile phone; in a recent survey of hiring professionals, answering calls or texting while in an interview was identified as the most common mistake job candidates make during their interviews.[39]

Be sure you know when and where the interview will be held. The worst way to start an interview is to be late, and arriving in a stressed-out state isn't much better. Check the route you will take, but don't rely on time estimates from a bus or subway service or from an online mapping service.

✓ Checklist   Planning for a Successful Job Interview

- Learn about the organization, including its operations, markets, and challenges.
- Learn as much as you can about the people who will be interviewing you, if you can find their names.
- Plan for the employer's questions, including questions about tough decisions you've made, your perceived shortcomings, what you didn't like about previous jobs, and your career plans.
- Plan questions of your own to find out whether this is really the job and the organization for you and to show that you've done your research.
- Bolster your confidence by removing as many sources of apprehension as you can.

- Polish your interview style by staging mock interviews.
- Present a professional appearance with appropriate dress and grooming.
- Be ready when you arrive and bring along a pen, paper, a list of questions, copies of your résumé, an outline of your research on the company, and any correspondence you've had regarding the position.
- Double-check the location and time of the interview and map out the route beforehand.
- Relax and be flexible; the schedule and interview arrangements may change when you arrive.

If you're not familiar with the route, the safest choice is to travel to the location a few days before the interview, if possible, to verify it for yourself. Leave yourself plenty of time for unforeseen problems.

When you arrive, remind yourself that you are fully prepared and confident and then try to relax. You may have to wait, so bring along something business oriented to read. If company literature is available in the lobby, read it while you wait. At every step, show respect for everyone you encounter. If the opportunity presents itself, ask a few questions about the organization or express enthusiasm for the job. Refrain from smoking before the interview (nonsmokers can smell smoke on the clothing of interviewees) and avoid chewing gum or otherwise eating or drinking in the lobby (or at any point during the interview). Anything you do or say while you wait may well get back to the interviewer, so make sure your best qualities show from the moment you enter the premises. To review the steps for planning a successful interview, see "Checklist: Planning for a Successful Job Interview."

Interviewing for Success

At this point, you have a good sense of the overall process and know how to prepare for your interviews. The next step is to get familiar with the three stages that occur in some form in all interviews: the warm-up, the question-and-answer session, and the close.

4   LEARNING OBJECTIVE

Explain how to succeed in all three stages of an interview.

THE WARM-UP

Of the three stages, the warm-up is the most important, even though it may account for only a small fraction of the time you spend in the interview. Studies suggest that many interviewers, particularly those who are poorly trained in interviewing techniques, make up their minds within the first 20 seconds of contact with a candidate.[40] Don't let your guard down if it appears that the interviewer wants to engage in what feels like small talk; these exchanges are every bit as important as structured questions.

The first minute of the interview is crucial, so stay alert and be on your best business behavior.

Body language is crucial at this point. Stand or sit up straight, maintain regular but natural eye contact, and don't fidget. When the interviewer extends a hand, respond with a firm but not overpowering handshake. Repeat the interviewer's name when you're introduced ("It's a pleasure to meet you, Ms. Litton"). Wait until you're asked to be seated or the interviewer has taken a seat. Let the interviewer start the discussion, and be ready to answer one or two substantial questions right away. The following are some common openers:[41]

- Why do you want to work here?
- What do you know about us?
- Tell me a little about yourself.

Recognize that you could face substantial questions as soon as your interview starts, so make sure you are prepared and ready to go.

THE QUESTION-AND-ANSWER STAGE

Questions and answers usually consume the greatest part of the interview. Depending on the type of interview, the interviewer will likely ask about your qualifications, discuss some of the points mentioned in your résumé, and ask about how you have handled particular situations in the past or would handle them in the future. You'll also be asking questions of your own.

Dealing with Questions

Listen carefully to questions before you answer.

Let the interviewer lead the conversation and never answer a question before he or she has finished asking it. Not only is this type of interruption rude, but the last few words of the question might alter how you respond. As much as possible, avoid one-word yes-or-no answers. Use the opportunity to expand on a positive response or explain a negative response. If you're asked a difficult question or the offbeat questions that companies such as Zappos and Google are known to use, pause before responding. Think through the implications of the question. For instance, the recruiter may know that you can't answer a question and only wants to know how you'll respond under pressure.

Whenever you're asked if you have any questions, or whenever doing so naturally fits the flow of the conversation, ask a question from the list you've prepared. Probe for what the company is looking for in its new employees so that you can show how you meet the firm's needs. Also try to zero in on any reservations the interviewer might have about you so that you can dispel them.

COMMUNICATION MISCUES   Make Sure You Don't Talk Yourself out of a Job

Even well-qualified applicants sometimes talk themselves right out of an opportunity by making avoidable blunders during a job interview. Take care to avoid these all-too-common mistakes:

- **Being defensive.** An interview isn't an interrogation, and the interviewer isn't out to get you. Treat interviews as business conversations, an exchange of information in which both sides have something of value to share. You'll give (and get) better information that way.
- **Failing to ask questions.** Interviewers expect you to ask questions, both during the interview and at its conclusion, when they ask if you have any questions. If you have nothing to ask, you come across as someone who isn't really interested in the job or the company. Prepare a list of questions before every interview.
- **Failing to answer questions—or trying to bluff your way through difficult questions.** If you can't answer a question, don't try to talk your way around it or fake your way through it. Remember that sometimes interviewers ask strange questions just to see how you'll respond. What kind of fish would you like to be? How would you go about nailing jelly to the ceiling? Why are manhole covers round? Some of these questions are designed to test your grace under pressure, whereas others are used to get you to think through a logical answer. (Manhole covers are round because a circle is the only shape that can't fall through an open hole of slightly smaller size, by the way.) Don't act like the question is stupid or refuse to answer it. As Lynne Sarikas, director of the MBA Career Center at

Northeastern University, explains, these questions offer an opportunity to "demonstrate quick thinking, poise, creativity, and even a sense of humor."

- **Freezing up.** The human brain seems to have the capacity to just freeze up in stressful situations. An interviewer might have asked you a simple question, or perhaps you are halfway through an intelligent answer, and poof!—all your thoughts disappear and you can't organize words in any logical order. Try to quickly replay the last few seconds of the conversation in your mind to see if you can recapture the conversational thread. If that fails, you're probably better off explaining to the interviewer that your mind has gone blank and asking him or her to repeat the question. Doing so is embarrassing but not as embarrassing as chattering on and on with no idea of what you're saying, hoping you'll stumble back onto the topic.
- **Failing to understand your potential to contribute to the organization.** Interviewers care less about your history than about how you can help their organization in the future. Be sure to understand ahead of time how your skills can help the company meet its challenges.

CAREER APPLICATIONS

1. What should you do if you suddenly realize that something you said earlier in the interview is incorrect or incomplete? Explain your answer.
2. How would you answer the following question: "How do you respond to colleagues who make you angry?" Explain your answer.

Listening to the Interviewer

Paying attention when the interviewer speaks can be as important as giving good answers or asking good questions. Review the tips on listening offered in Chapter 2. The interviewer's facial expressions, eye movements, gestures, and posture may tell you the real meaning of what is being said. Be especially aware of how your answers are received. Does the interviewer nod in agreement or smile to show approval? If so, you're making progress. If not, you might want to introduce another topic or modify your approach.

Paying attention to both verbal and nonverbal messages can help you turn the question-and-answer stage to your advantage.

Handling Potentially Discriminatory Questions

A variety of federal, state, and local laws prohibit employment discrimination on the basis of race, ethnicity, gender, age (at least if you're between 40 and 70), marital status, religion, national origin, or disability. Interview questions designed to elicit information on these topics are potentially illegal.[42] Table 19.6 compares some questions that are acceptable for employers to ask with questions that can land an employer in legal trouble if the questions are asked in order to gather information that can be used to discriminate in the hiring decision.[43]

Federal, state, and local laws prohibit a wide variety of interview questions.

If an interviewer asks a potentially unlawful question, consider your options carefully before you respond. You can answer the question as it was asked, you can ask tactfully whether the question might be prohibited, you can simply refuse to answer it, or you can try to answer "the question behind the question."[44] For example, if an interviewer inappropriately asks whether you are married or have strong family ties in the area, he or she might be trying to figure out if you're willing to travel or relocate—both of which are acceptable questions. Only you can decide which is the right choice based on the situation.

Think about how you might respond if you were asked a potentially unlawful question.

Even if you do answer the question as it was asked, think hard before accepting a job offer from this company if you have alternatives. Was the off-limits question possibly accidental (it happens) and therefore not really a major concern? If you think it was intentional, would you want to work for an organization that condones illegal or discriminatory questions or that doesn't train its employees to avoid them?

If you believe an interviewer's questions to be unreasonable, unrelated to the job, or an attempt to discriminate, you have the option of filing a complaint with the EEOC (www.eeoc.gov) or with the agency in your state that regulates fair employment practices.

TABLE 19.6	Acceptable Versus Potentially Discriminatory Interview Questions
Interviewers May Ask This . . .	**But Not This**
What is your name?	What was your maiden name?
Are you over 18?	When were you born?
Did you graduate from high school?	When did you graduate from high school?
[No questions about race are allowed.]	What is your race?
Can you perform [specific tasks]?	Do you have physical or mental disabilities? Do you have a drug or alcohol problem? Are you taking any prescription drugs?
Would you be able to meet the job's requirement to frequently work weekends?	Would working on weekends conflict with your religion?
Do you have the legal right to work in the United States?	What country are you a citizen of?
Have you ever been convicted of a felony?	Have you ever been arrested?
This job requires that you speak Spanish. Do you?	What language did you speak in your home when you were growing up?

REAL-TIME UPDATES
**Learn More by Watching This
PowerPoint Presentation**

Should you accept? Evaluating a job offer

Explore the many steps needed to determine whether a job offer is right for you, your family, and your future. Go to http://real-timeupdates.com/bct11 and click on "Learn More." If you are using MyBcommLab, you can access Real-Time Updates within each chapter or under Student Study Tools.

THE CLOSE

Like the warm-up, the end of the interview is more important than its brief duration would indicate. These last few minutes are your last opportunity to emphasize your value to the organization and to correct any misconceptions the interviewer might have. Be aware that many interviews will ask whether you have any more questions at this point, so ask one or two from the list you brought or ask a question related to something that came up during the interview.

Concluding Gracefully

Conclude an interview with courtesy and enthusiasm.

You can usually tell when the interviewer is trying to conclude the session. He or she may ask whether you have any more questions, check the time, summarize the discussion, or simply tell you that the allotted time for the interview is up. When you get the signal, be sure to thank the interviewer for the opportunity and express your interest in the organization. If you can do so comfortably, try to pin down what will happen next, but don't press for an immediate decision.

If this is your second or third visit to the organization, the interview may end with an offer of employment. If you have other offers or need time to think about this offer, it's perfectly acceptable to thank the interviewer for the offer and ask for some time to consider it. If no job offer is made, the interview team may not have reached a decision yet, but you may tactfully ask when you can expect to know the decision.

Discussing Salary

If you receive an offer during the interview, you'll naturally want to discuss salary. However, let the interviewer raise the subject. If asked your salary requirements during

---

✓ **Checklist**   ## Making a Positive Impression in Job Interviews

A. Be ready to make a positive impression in the warm-up stage.
- Be alert from the moment you arrive; even initial small talk is part of the interviewing process.
- Greet the interviewer by name, with a smile and direct eye contact.
- Offer a firm (not crushing) handshake if the interviewer extends a hand.
- Take a seat only after the interviewer invites you to sit or has taken his or her own seat.
- Listen for clues about what the interviewer is trying to get you to reveal about yourself and your qualifications.
- Exhibit positive body language, including standing up straight, walking with purpose, and sitting up straight.

B. Convey your value to the organization during the question-and-answer stage.
- Let the interviewer lead the conversation.
- Never answer a question before the interviewer finishes asking it.
- Listen carefully to the interviewer and watch for nonverbal signals.

- Don't limit yourself to simple yes-or-no answers; expand on the answer to show your knowledge of the company (but don't ramble on).
- If you encounter a potentially discriminatory question, decide how you want to respond before you say anything.
- When you have the opportunity, ask questions from the list you've prepared; remember that interviewers expect you to ask questions.

C. Close on a strong note.
- Watch and listen for signs that the interview is about to end.
- Quickly evaluate how well you've done and correct any misperceptions the interviewer might have.
- If you receive an offer and aren't ready to decide, it's entirely appropriate to ask for time to think about it.
- Don't bring up salary but be prepared to discuss it if the interviewer raises the subject.
- End with a warm smile and a handshake and thank the interviewer for meeting with you.

the interview or on a job application, you can say that your requirements are open or negotiable or that you would expect a competitive compensation package.[45]

How far you can negotiate depends on several factors, including market demand for your skills, the strength of the job market, the company's compensation policies, the company's financial health, and whether you have other job offers. Remember that you're negotiating a business deal, not asking for personal favors, so focus on the unique value you can bring to the job. The more information you have, the stronger your position will be.

> Research salary ranges in your job, industry, and geographic region before you try to negotiate salary.

If salary isn't negotiable, look at the overall compensation and benefits package. You may find flexibility in a signing bonus, profit sharing, retirement benefits, health coverage, vacation time, and other valuable elements.[46]

> Negotiating benefits may be one way to get more value from an employment package.

To review the important tips for successful interviews, see "Checklist: Making a Positive Impression in Job Interviews."

INTERVIEW NOTES

Maintain a notebook or simple database with information about each company, interviewers' answers to your questions, contact information for each interviewer, the status of thank-you notes and other follow-up communication, and upcoming interview appointments. Carefully organized notes will help you decide which company is the right fit for you when it comes time to choose from among the job offers you receive.

> Keeping careful records of your job interviews is essential.

For the latest information on interviewing strategies, visit http://real-timeupdates .com/bct11 and click on Chapter 19.

Following Up After the Interview

Staying in contact with a prospective employer after an interview shows that you really want the job and are determined to get it. Doing so also gives you another chance to demonstrate your communication skills and sense of business etiquette. Following up brings your name to the interviewer's attention once again and reminds him or her that you're actively looking and waiting for the decision.

> **5 LEARNING OBJECTIVE**
>
> Identify the most common employment messages that follow an interview, and explain when you would use each one.

Any time you hear from a company during the application or interview process, be sure to respond quickly. Companies flooded with résumés may move on to another candidate if they don't hear back from you within 24 hours.[47]

THANK-YOU MESSAGE

Write a thank-you message within two days of the interview, even if you feel you have little chance of getting the job. In addition to demonstrating good etiquette, a thank-you message gives you the opportunity to reinforce the reasons you are a good choice for the position and lets you respond to any negatives that might've arisen in the interview.[48] Acknowledge the interviewer's time and courtesy, convey your continued interest, reinforce the reasons that you are a good fit for the position, and ask politely for a decision (see Figure 19.6 on the next page).

> A thank-you message is more than a professional courtesy; it's another chance to promote yourself to an employer.

Depending on the company and the relationship you've established with the interviewer, the thank-you message can be handled via letter or email. Be brief and sound positive without sounding overconfident.

MESSAGE OF INQUIRY

If you're not advised of the interviewer's decision by the promised date or within two weeks, you might make an inquiry. A message of inquiry (which can be handled by email if the interviewer has given you his or her email address) is particularly appropriate if you've received a job offer from a second firm and don't want to accept it before you

> Use the model for a direct request when you write an inquiry about a hiring decision.

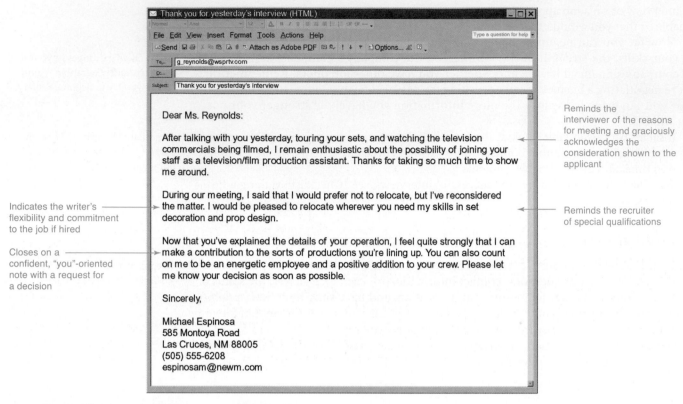

Figure 19.6 Thank-You Message
In three brief paragraphs, Michael Espinosa acknowledges the interviewer's time and consideration, expresses his continued interest in the position, explains a crucial discussion point that he has reconsidered, and asks for a decision.

MyBcommLab

Apply Figure 19.6's key concepts by revising a new document. Go to Chapter 19 in mybcommlab.com and select Document Makeovers.

have an answer from the first. The following message illustrates the general model for a direct request:

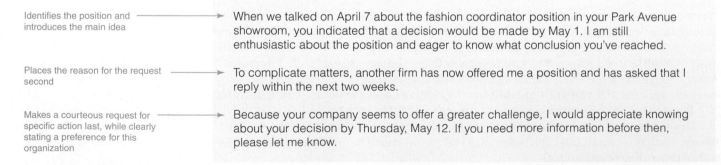

Identifies the position and introduces the main idea → When we talked on April 7 about the fashion coordinator position in your Park Avenue showroom, you indicated that a decision would be made by May 1. I am still enthusiastic about the position and eager to know what conclusion you've reached.

Places the reason for the request second → To complicate matters, another firm has now offered me a position and has asked that I reply within the next two weeks.

Makes a courteous request for specific action last, while clearly stating a preference for this organization → Because your company seems to offer a greater challenge, I would appreciate knowing about your decision by Thursday, May 12. If you need more information before then, please let me know.

REQUEST FOR A TIME EXTENSION

If you receive a job offer while other interviews are still pending, you can ask the employer for a time extension. Open with a strong statement of your continued interest in the job, ask for more time to consider the offer, provide specific reasons for the request, and assure the reader that you will respond by a specific date (see Figure 19.7).

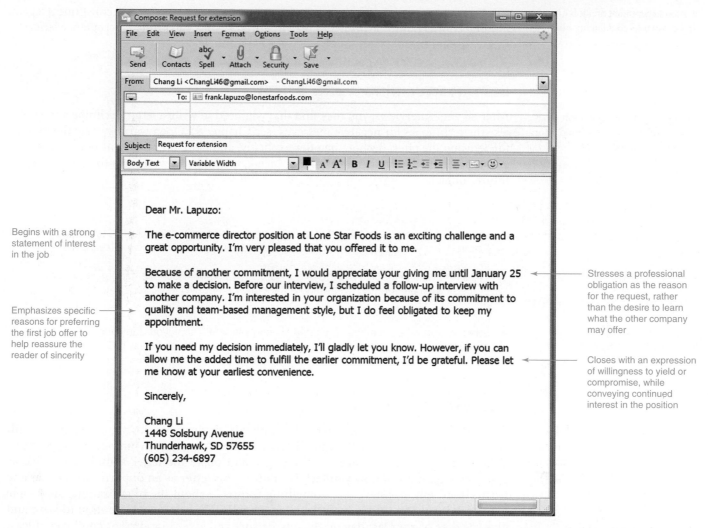

Begins with a strong statement of interest in the job

Emphasizes specific reasons for preferring the first job offer to help reassure the reader of sincerity

Stresses a professional obligation as the reason for the request, rather than the desire to learn what the other company may offer

Closes with an expression of willingness to yield or compromise, while conveying continued interest in the position

Figure 19.7 Request for a Time Extension
If you need to request more time to make a decision about a job offer, make sure to reaffirm that you are still interested in the job.

MyBcommLab

Apply Figure 19.7's key concepts by revising a new document. Go to Chapter 19 in mybcommlab.com and select Document Makeovers.

LETTER OF ACCEPTANCE

When you receive a job offer that you want to accept, reply within five days. Begin by accepting the position and expressing thanks. Identify the job that you're accepting. In the next paragraph, cover any necessary details. Conclude by saying that you look forward to reporting for work. As always, a positive letter should convey your enthusiasm and eagerness to cooperate:

Use the model for positive messages when you write a letter of acceptance.

I'm delighted to accept the graphic design position in your advertising department at the salary of $2,875 per month.

Enclosed are the health insurance forms you asked me to complete and sign. I've already given notice to my current employer and will be able to start work on Monday, January 18.

The prospect of joining your firm is exciting. Thank you for giving me this opportunity, and I look forward to making a positive contribution.

Confirms the specific terms of the offer with a good-news statement at the beginning

Covers miscellaneous details in the middle

Closes with another reference to the good news and a look toward the future

Written acceptance of a job offer can be considered a legally binding contract.

Be aware that a job offer and a written acceptance of that offer can constitute a legally binding contract, for both you and the employer. Before you send an acceptance letter, be sure you want the job.

LETTER DECLINING A JOB OFFER

If you decide to decline a job offer, do so tactfully, using the model for negative messages.

After all your interviews, you may find that you need to write a letter declining a job offer. Use the techniques for negative messages (see Chapter 9): Open warmly, state the reasons for refusing the offer, decline the offer explicitly, and close on a pleasant note, expressing gratitude. By taking the time to write a sincere, tactful letter, you leave the door open for future contact:

Uses a buffer in the opening paragraph → Thank you for your hospitality during my interview at your Durham facility last month. I'm flattered that you would offer me the computer analyst position that we talked about.

Precedes the bad news with tactfully phrased reasons for the applicant's unfavorable decision and leaves the door open → I was fortunate to receive two job offers during my search. Because my desire to work abroad can more readily be satisfied by another company, I have accepted that job offer.

Lets the reader down gently with a sincere and cordial ending → I deeply appreciate the time you spent talking with me. Thank you again for your consideration and kindness.

LETTER OF RESIGNATION

Letters of resignation should always be written in a gracious and professional style that avoids criticism of your employer or your colleagues.

If you get a job offer and are currently employed, you can maintain good relations with your current employer by writing a letter of resignation to your immediate supervisor. Follow the approach for negative messages and make the letter sound as positive as possible, regardless of how you feel. Don't take this letter as an opportunity to vent any frustrations you may have. Say something favorable about the organization, the people you work with, or what you've learned on the job. Then state your intention to leave and give the date of your last day on the job. Be sure you give your current employer at least two weeks' notice:

Uses an appreciative opening to serve as a buffer → My sincere thanks to you and to all the other Emblem Corporation employees for helping me learn so much about serving the public these past two years. You have given me untold help and encouragement.

States reasons before the bad news itself, using tactful phrasing to help keep the relationship friendly, should the writer later want letters of recommendation → You may recall that when you first interviewed me, my goal was to become a customer relations supervisor. Because that opportunity has been offered to me by another organization, I am submitting my resignation. I will miss my friends and colleagues at Emblem, but I want to take advantage of this opportunity.

Discusses necessary details in an extra paragraph → I would like to terminate my work here two weeks from today (June 13) but can arrange to work an additional week if you want me to train a replacement.

Tempers any disappointment with a cordial close → My sincere thanks and best wishes to all of you.

To verify the content and style of your follow-up messages, consult the tips in "Checklist: Writing Follow-Up Messages."

✓ Checklist Writing Follow-Up Messages

A. Thank-you messages.
- Write a brief thank-you letter within two days of the interview.
- Acknowledge the interviewer's time and courtesy.
- Restate the specific job you're applying for.
- Express your enthusiasm about the organization and the job.
- Add any new facts that may help your chances.
- Politely ask for a decision.

B. Messages of inquiry.
- If you haven't heard from the interviewer by the promised date, write a brief message of inquiry.
- Use the direct approach: main idea, necessary details, specific request.

C. Requests for a time extension.
- Request an extension if you have pending interviews and need time to decide about an offer.
- Open on a friendly note.
- Explain why you need more time and express continued interest in the company.
- In the close, promise a quick decision if your request is denied and ask for a confirmation if your request is granted.

D. Letters of acceptance.
- Send this message within five days of receiving the offer.
- State clearly that you accept the offer, identify the job you're accepting, and confirm vital details such as salary and start date.
- Make sure you want the job; an acceptance letter can be treated as a legally binding contract.

E. Letters declining a job offer.
- Use the indirect approach for negative messages.
- Open on a warm and appreciative note and then explain why you are refusing the offer.
- End on a sincere, positive note.

F. Letters of resignation.
- Send a letter of resignation to your current employer as soon as possible.
- Begin with an appreciative buffer.
- In the middle section, state your reasons for leaving and actually state that you are resigning.
- Close cordially.

COMMUNICATION CHALLENGES AT ZAPPOS

You recently joined the human resources department at Zappos headquarters in Las Vegas. Using what you know about interviewing, address these challenges. To learn more about working at Zappos, you can visit http://about.zappos.com/jobs.

INDIVIDUAL CHALLENGE: You're looking for experienced customer support specialists who remain calm when things get chaotic and stressful, who are flexible enough to interact with a wide range of personality types, and who are comfortable communicating over the phone, through IM, and on Twitter. With those requirements in mind, create a list of three or four questions to use during the screening interviews (using Skype video calls) for these candidates.

TEAM CHALLENGE: Seven candidates survived the screening process, and now you're planning the on-site interviews. In a small group, discuss the types of people to include on the interview team (consult a management textbook if you're unfamiliar with positions in a typical corporation): Who should serve as host and handle the warm-up stage? Who should be involved in the question-and-answer stage? Who should handle the close? Justify your choices.

MyBcommLab

CHAPTER OUTLINE

SUMMARY OF LEARNING OBJECTIVES

1 Explain the purposes of application letters, and describe how to apply the AIDA organizational approach to them. The purposes of an application letter are to introduce your résumé, persuade an employer to read it, and request an interview. With the AIDA model, get attention in the opening paragraph by showing how your work skills could benefit the organization, by explaining how your qualifications fit the job, or by demonstrating an understanding of the organization's needs. Build interest and desire by showing how you can meet the job requirements and, near the end of this section, be sure to refer your reader to your résumé. Finally, motivate action by making your request easy to fulfill and by including all necessary contact information.

2 Describe the typical sequence of job interviews, the major types of interviews, and what employers look for during an interview. The typical sequence of interviews involves three stages. During the screening stage, employers filter out unqualified applicants and identify promising candidates. During the selection stage, the pool of applicants is narrowed through a variety of structured and unstructured interviewing methods. In the final stage, employers select the candidates who will receive offers and, if necessary, promote the benefits of joining the company.

Interviews can be distinguished by the way they are structured (structured or unstructured interviews), the number of people involved (one-on-one, panel, or group interviews), and the purpose of the interview (behavioral, situational, working, or stress interviews). The behavioral interview, probably the most common in terms of purpose, requires candidates to use their own experiences and attributes to craft answers. The situational interview is similar, but instead of using incidents from the candidate's past, it explores how the candidate would respond to hypothetical situations in the future.

Employers look for two things during an employment interview. First, they seek evidence that an applicant is qualified for the position. Second, they seek reassurance that an applicant will be a good fit with the "personality" of the organization and the position.

3 List six tasks you need to complete to prepare for a successful job interview. To prepare for a successful job interview, (1) complete the research you started when planning your résumé, (2) think ahead about questions you'll need to answer and questions you'll want to ask, (3) bolster your confidence by focusing on your strengths and preparing thoroughly, (4) polish your interviewing style, (5) present a professional image with businesslike clothing and good grooming, and (6) arrive on time and ready to begin.

4 Explain how to succeed in all three stages of an interview. All employment interviews have three stages. The warm-up stage is the most important because first impressions greatly influence an interviewer's decision. The question-and-answer stage, during which you will answer and ask questions, is the longest. The close is your final opportunity to promote your value to the organization and counter any misconceptions the interviewer may have.

5 Identify the most common employment messages that follow an interview, and explain when you would use each one. Following an interview, send a thank-you message to show appreciation, emphasize your strengths, and politely ask for a decision. Send an inquiry if you haven't received the interviewer's decision by the date promised or within one or two weeks of the interview—especially if you've received a job offer from another firm. You can request a time extension if you need more time to consider an offer. Send a letter of acceptance after receiving a job offer that you want to take. Send a letter declining a job offer when you want to refuse an offer tactfully. Finally, if you are currently employed, send a letter of resignation after you have accepted the offer of another job.

application letter Message that accompanies a résumé to let readers know what you're sending, why you're sending it, and how they can benefit from reading it

behavioral interview Interview in which you are asked to relate specific incidents and experiences from your past

employment interview Formal meeting during which you and an employer ask questions and exchange information

group interview Interview in which one or more interviewers meet with several candidates simultaneously

open-ended interview Interview in which the interviewer adapts his or her line of questioning based on the answers you give and any questions you ask

panel interview Interview in which you meet with several interviewers at once

situational interview Similar to a behavioral interview, except the questions focus on how you would handle various hypothetical situations on the job

solicited application letter Message sent in response to an announced job opening

stress interview Interview in which you might be asked questions designed to unsettle you or subject you to long periods of silence, criticism, interruptions, and or hostile reactions by the interviewer

structured interview Interview in which the interviewer (or a computer) asks a series of prepared questions in a set order

unsolicited application letter Message sent to an organization that has not announced an opening

working interview Interview in which you perform a job-related activity

---

✓ Checklist

Writing Application Letters

- Take the same care with your application letter that you took with your résumé.
- If you are *prospecting* using an unsolicited message, do deep research to identify the qualities the company likely wants.
- For solicited messages in response to a posted job opening, word your message in a way that echoes back the qualifications listed in the posting.
- Open the letter by capturing the reader's attention in a businesslike way.
- Use specific language to clearly state your interests and objectives.
- Build interest and desire in your potential contribution by presenting your key qualifications for the job.
- Link your education, experience, and personal qualities to the job requirements.
- Outline salary requirements only if the organization has requested that you provide them.
- Request an interview at a time and place that is convenient for the reader.
- Make it easy to comply with your request by providing your complete contact information and good times to reach you.
- Adapt your style for cultural variations, if required.

✓ Checklist

Planning for a Successful Job Interview

- Learn about the organization, including its operations, markets, and challenges.
- Learn as much as you can about the people who will be interviewing you, if you can find their names.
- Plan for the employer's questions, including questions about tough

decisions you've made, your perceived shortcomings, what you didn't like about previous jobs, and your career plans.
- Plan questions of your own to find out whether this is really the job and the organization for you and to show that you've done your research.
- Bolster your confidence by removing as many sources of apprehension as you can.
- Polish your interview style by staging mock interviews.
- Present a professional appearance with appropriate dress and grooming.
- Be ready when you arrive and bring along a pen, paper, a list of questions, copies of your résumé, an outline of your research on the company, and any correspondence you've had regarding the position.
- Double-check the location and time of the interview and map out the route beforehand.
- Relax and be flexible; the schedule and interview arrangements may change when you arrive.

✓ Checklist

Making a Positive Impression in Job Interviews

A. **Be ready to make a positive impression in the warm-up stage.**
  - Be alert from the moment you arrive; even initial small talk is part of the interviewing process.
  - Greet the interviewer by name, with a smile and direct eye contact.
  - Offer a firm (not crushing) handshake if the interviewer extends a hand.
  - Take a seat only after the interviewer invites you to sit or has taken his or her own seat.

- Listen for clues about what the interviewer is trying to get you to reveal about yourself and your qualifications.
- Exhibit positive body language, including standing up straight, walking with purpose, and sitting up straight.

B. **Convey your value to the organization during the question-and-answer stage.**
  - Let the interviewer lead the conversation.
  - Never answer a question before the interviewer finishes asking it.
  - Listen carefully to the interviewer and watch for nonverbal signals.
  - Don't limit yourself to simple yes-or-no answers; expand on the answer to show your knowledge of the company (but don't ramble on).
  - If you encounter a potentially discriminatory question, decide how you want to respond before you say anything.
  - When you have the opportunity, ask questions from the list you've prepared; remember that interviewers expect you to ask questions.

C. **Close on a strong note.**
  - Watch and listen for signs that the interview is about to end.
  - Quickly evaluate how well you've done and correct any misperceptions the interviewer might have.
  - If you receive an offer and aren't ready to decide, it's entirely appropriate to ask for time to think about it.
  - Don't bring up salary but be prepared to discuss it if the interviewer raises the subject.
  - End with a warm smile and a handshake and thank the interviewer for meeting with you.

TEST YOUR KNOWLEDGE

To review chapter content related to each question, refer to the indicated Learning Objective.

1. What two message elements can you use when writing a follow-up message after submitting a résumé? [LO-1]
2. How can you apply the AIDA model to an application letter? [LO-1]
3. How does a structured interview differ from an open-ended interview? [LO-2]
4. Why do many employers now use situational or behavioral interviews? [LO-2]
5. Why do employers conduct preemployment testing? [LO-2]
6. Why are the questions you ask during an interview as important as the answers you give to the interviewer's questions? [LO-3]
7. What are the three stages of every interview, and which is the most important? [LO-4]
8. How should you respond if an interviewer at a company where you want to work asks you a question that seems too personal or unethical? [LO-4]
9. What should you say in a thank-you message after an interview? [LO-5]
10. What is the potential legal significance of a letter of acceptance? [LO-5]

APPLY YOUR KNOWLEDGE

To review chapter content related to each question, refer to the indicated Learning Objective.

1. How can you distinguish yourself from other candidates in a screening interview and still keep your responses short and to the point? Explain. [LO-2]
2. How can you prepare for a situational or behavioral interview if you have no experience with the job for which you are interviewing? [LO-2]
3. If you lack one important qualification for a job but have made it past the initial screening stage, how should you prepare to handle this issue during the next round of interviews? Explain your answer. [LO-3]
4. What is an interviewer likely to conclude about you if you don't have any questions to ask during the interview? [LO-3]
5. Why is it important to distinguish unethical or illegal interview questions from acceptable questions? Explain. [LO-4]

PRACTICE YOUR SKILLS

Messages for Analysis

Read the following messages and then (1) analyze the strengths or weaknesses of each document and (2) revise each document so that it follows this chapter's guidelines.

Message 19.A: Writing an Application Letter [LO-1]

I'm writing to let you know about my availability for the brand manager job you advertised. As you can see from my enclosed résumé, my background is perfect for the position. Even though I don't have any real job experience, my grades have been outstanding, considering that I went to a top-ranked business school.

I did many things during my undergraduate years to prepare me for this job:

- Earned a 3.4 out of a 4.0, with a 3.8 in my business courses
- Elected representative to the student governing association
- Selected to receive the Lamar Franklin Award
- Worked to earn a portion of my tuition

I am sending my résumé to all the top firms, but I like yours better than any of the rest. Your reputation is tops in the industry, and I want to be associated with a business that can pridefully say it's the best.

If you wish for me to come in for an interview, I can come on a Friday afternoon or anytime on weekends when I don't have classes. Again, thanks for considering me for your brand manager position.

Message 19.B: Writing Application Follow-up Messages [LO-1]

Did you receive my résumé? I sent it to you at least two months ago and haven't heard anything. I know you keep résumés on file, but I just want to be sure that you keep me in mind. I heard you are hiring health-care managers and certainly would like to be considered for one of those positions.

Since I last wrote you, I've worked in a variety of positions that have helped prepare me for management. To wit, I've become lunch manager at the restaurant where I work, which involved a raise in pay. I now manage a waitstaff of 12 girls and take the lunch receipts to the bank every day.

Of course, I'd much rather be working at a real job, and that's why I'm writing again. Is there anything else you would like to know about me or my background? I would really like to know more about your company. Is there any literature you could send me? If so, I would really appreciate it.

I think one reason I haven't been hired yet is that I don't want to leave Atlanta. So I hope when you think of me, it's for a position that wouldn't require moving. Thanks again for considering my application.

Message 19.C: Thank-You Message [LO-5]

Thank you for the really marvelous opportunity to meet you and your colleagues at Starret Engine Company. I really enjoyed touring your facilities and talking with all the people there. You have quite a crew! Some of the other companies I have visited have been so rigid and uptight that I can't imagine how I would fit in. It's a relief to run into a group of people who seem to enjoy their work as much as all of you do.

I know that you must be looking at many other candidates for this job, and I know that some of them will probably be more experienced than I am. But I do want to emphasize that my two-year hitch in the Navy involved a good deal of engineering work. I don't think I mentioned all my shipboard responsibilities during the interview.

Please give me a call within the next week to let me know your decision. You can usually find me at my dormitory in the evening after dinner (phone: 877-9080).

Message 19.D: Letter of Inquiry [LO-5]

I have recently received a very attractive job offer from the Warrington Company. But before I let them know one way or another, I would like to consider any offer that your firm may extend. I was quite impressed with your company during my recent interview, and I am still very interested in a career there.

I don't mean to pressure you, but Warrington has asked for my decision within 10 days. Could you let me know by Tuesday whether you plan to offer me a position? That would give me enough time to compare the two offers.

Message 19.E: Letter Declining a Job Offer [LO-5]

I'm writing to say that I must decline your job offer. Another company has made me a more generous offer, and I have decided to accept. However, if things don't work out for me there, I will let you know. I sincerely appreciate your interest in me.

Exercises

Active links for all websites in this chapter can be found on MyBcommLab; see your User Guide for instructions on accessing the content for this chapter. Each activity is labeled according to the primary skill or skills you will need to use. To review relevant chapter content, you can refer to the indicated Learning Objective. In some instances, supporting information will be found in another chapter, as indicated.

1. **Career Management: Preparing for Interviews [LO-3]** Google yourself, Bing yourself, scour your social networking profiles, review your Twitter messages, and explore every other possible online source you can think of that might have something about you. If you find anything potentially embarrassing, remove it if possible. Write a summary of your search-and-destroy mission (you can skip any embarrassing details in your report to your instructor!).

2. **Career Management: Researching Target Employers [LO-3]** Select a medium or large company (one that you can easily find information on) where you might like to work. Use Internet sources to gather some preliminary research on the company; don't limit your search to the company's own website.
   1. What did you learn about this organization that would help you during an interview there?
   2. What Internet sources did you use to obtain this information?
   3. Armed with this information, what aspects of your background do you think might appeal to this company's recruiters?
   4. Based on what you've learned about this company's culture, what aspects of your personality should you try to highlight during an interview?

3. **Career Management: Interviewing; Collaboration: Team Projects [LO-4], Chapter 2** Divide the class into two groups. Half the class will be recruiters for a large chain of national department stores, looking to fill manager trainee

positions (there are 16 openings). The other half of the class will be candidates for the job. The company is specifically looking for candidates who demonstrate these three qualities: initiative, dependability, and willingness to assume responsibility.
   1. Have each recruiter select and interview an applicant for 10 minutes.
   2. Have all the recruiters discuss how they assessed the applicant in each of the three desired qualities. What questions did they ask or what did they use as an indicator to determine whether the candidate possessed the quality?
   3. Have all the applicants discuss what they said to convince the recruiters that they possessed each of these qualities.

4. **Career Management: Interviewing [LO-3]** Write a short email to your instructor, discussing what you believe are your greatest strengths and weaknesses from an employment perspective. Next, explain how these strengths and weaknesses would be viewed by interviewers evaluating your qualifications.

5. **Career Management: Interviewing [LO-3]** Prepare written answers to 10 of the questions listed in Table 19.3.

6. **Message Strategies: Employment Messages, Communication Ethics: Resolving Ethical Dilemmas [LO-5], Chapter 1** You have decided to accept a new position with a competitor of your company. Write a letter of resignation to your supervisor, announcing your decision.
   1. Will you notify your employer that you are joining a competing firm? Explain.
   2. Will you use the direct or the indirect approach? Explain.
   3. Will you send your letter by email, send it by regular mail, or place it on your supervisor's desk?

EXPAND YOUR SKILLS

Critique the Professionals

Visit LinkedIn Answers at www.linkedin.com/answers (open a free LinkedIn account if required). In the "Browse" panel, click on "Career and Education" and then "Job Search." Browse both "Open Questions" and "Closed Questions" to find three job-search insights that you didn't know before. Using whatever medium your instructor requests, write a brief summary (no more than one page) of what you learned.

Sharpening Your Career Skills Online

Bovée and Thill's Business Communication Web Search, at http://businesscommunicationblog.com/websearch, is a unique research tool designed specifically for business communication research. Use the Web Search function to find a website, video, PDF document, or PowerPoint presentation that offers advice on interviewing. Write a brief email message to your instructor, describing the item that you found and summarizing the career skills information you learned from it.

CASES

Writing Application Letters

EMAIL SKILLS

1. Message Strategies: Employment Messages (Application Letters) [LO-1] Use one of the websites listed in Table 18.1 on page 522 to find a job opening in your target profession. If you haven't narrowed down to one career field yet, choose a business job for which you will have at least some qualifications at the time of your graduation.

Your task: Write an email message that would serve as your application letter if you were to apply for this job. Base your message on your actual qualifications for the position, and be sure to "echo" the requirements listed in the job description. Include the job description in your email message when you submit it to your instructor.

EMAIL SKILLS

2. Message Strategies: Employment Messages (Application Letters) [LO-1] You've applied yourself with vigor and resolve for four years, and you're just about to graduate with your business degree. While cruising the web to relax one night, you stumble on something called Google Earth. You're hooked instantly by the ability to zoom all around the globe and look at detailed satellite photos of places you've been to or dreamed of visiting. You can even type in the address of your apartment and get an aerial view of your neighborhood. You're amazed at the three-dimensional renderings of major U.S. cities. Plus, the photographs and maps are linked to Google's other search technologies, allowing you to locate everything from ATMs to coffees shops in your neighborhood.

You've loved maps since you were a kid, and discovering Google Earth is making you wish you'd majored in geography. Knowing how important it is to follow your heart, you decide to apply to Google anyway, even though you don't have a strong background in geographic information systems. You do have a ton of passion for maps and a good head for business.

Your task: Visit http://earth.google.com and explore the system's capabilities. (You can download a free copy of the software.) In particular, look at the business and government applications of the technology, such as customized aerial photos and maps for real estate sales, land use and environmental impact analysis, and emergency planning for homeland security agencies. Be sure to visit the Community pages as well, where you can learn more about the many interesting applications of this technology. Draft an application email to Google, asking to be considered for the Google Earth team. Think about how you could help the company develop the commercial potential of this product line and make sure your enthusiasm shines through in the message.

Interviewing

TEAM SKILLS   BLOGGING SKILLS

3. Career Management: Researching Target Employers [LO-3] Research is a critical element of the job-search process. With information in hand, you increase the chance of finding the right opportunity (and avoiding bad choices), and you impress interviewers in multiple ways by demonstrating initiative, curiosity, research and analysis skills, an appreciation for the complex challenges of running a business, and willingness to work to achieve results.

Your task: With a small team of classmates, use online job listings to identify an intriguing job opening that at least one member of the team would seriously consider pursuing as graduation approaches. (You'll find it helpful if the career is related to at least one team member's college major or on-the-job experience so that the team can benefit from some knowledge of the profession in question.) Next, research the company, its competitors, its markets, and this specific position to identify five questions that would (1) help the team member decide if this is a good opportunity and (2) show an interviewer that you've really done your homework. Go beyond the basic and obvious questions to identify current, specific, and complex issues that only deep research can uncover. For example, is the company facing significant technical, financial, legal, or regulatory challenges that threaten its ability to grow or perhaps even survive in the long term? Or is the market evolving in a way that positions this particular company for dramatic growth? In a post for your class blog, list your five questions, identify how you uncovered the issue, and explain why each question is significant.

TEAM SKILLS

4. Career Management: Interviewing [LO-4] Interviewing is a skill that can be improved through practice and observation.

Your task: You and all other members of your class are to write letters of application for an entry-level or management-trainee position that requires an engaging personality and intelligence but a minimum of specialized education or experience. Sign your letter with a fictitious name that conceals your identity. Next, polish (or create) a résumé that accurately identifies you and your educational and professional accomplishments.

Now, three members of the class who volunteer as interviewers divide up all the anonymously written application letters. Then each interviewer selects a candidate who seems the most convincing in his or her letter. At this time, the selected candidates identify themselves and give the interviewers their résumés.

Each interviewer then interviews his or her chosen candidate in front of the class, seeking to understand how the items on the résumé qualify the candidate for the job. At the end of the interviews, the class decides who gets the job and discusses why this candidate was successful. Afterward, retrieve your letter, sign it with the right name, and submit it to the instructor for credit.

TEAM SKILLS

5. Career Management: Interviewing [LO-4] Select a company in an industry in which you might like to work and then identify an interesting position within the company. Study the company and prepare for an interview with that company.

Your task: Working with a classmate, take turns interviewing each other for your chosen positions. Interviewers should take notes during the interview. When the interview is complete, critique each other's performance. (Interviewers should critique how well candidates prepared for the interview and answered the questions; interviewees should critique the quality of the questions asked.) Write a follow-up letter thanking your interviewer and submit the letter to your instructor.

Following Up After an Interview

LETTER WRITING SKILLS

6. Message Strategies: Employment Messages (Request for a Time Extension) [LO-5] Because of a mix-up in your job application scheduling, you accidentally applied for your third-choice job before going after the one you really wanted. What you want to do is work in retail marketing with the upscale department store Neiman Marcus in Dallas; what you have been offered is a job with Longhorn Leather and Lumber, 65 miles away in the small town of Commerce, Texas.

You review your notes. Your Longhorn interview was three weeks ago with the human resources manager, R. P. Bronson, who has just written to offer you the position. The store's address is 27 Sam Rayburn Drive, Commerce, TX 75428. Mr. Bronson notes that he can hold the position open for 10 days. You have an interview scheduled with Neiman Marcus next week, but it is unlikely that you will know the store's decision within this 10-day period.

Your task: Write to Mr. Bronson, requesting a reasonable delay in your consideration of his job offer.

LETTER WRITING SKILLS   EMAIL SKILLS

7. Message Strategies: Employment Messages (Letter Declining a Job Offer) [LO-5] Fortunately for you, your interview with Neiman Marcus (see Case 6) went well, and you've just received a job offer from the company.

Your task: Write a letter to R. P. Pronson at Longhorn Leather and Lumber, declining his job offer, and write an email message to Clarissa Bartle at Neiman Marcus, accepting her job offer. Make up any information you need when accepting the Neiman Marcus offer.

LETTER WRITING SKILLS

8. Message Strategies: Employment Messages (Letters of Resignation) [LO-5] Leaving a job is rarely stress free, but it's particularly difficult when you are parting ways with a mentor who played an important role in advancing your career. A half-dozen years into your career, you have benefited greatly from the advice, encouragement, and professional connections offered by your mentor, who also happens to be your current boss. She seemed to believe in your potential from the very beginning and went out of her way on numerous occasions to help you. You returned the favor by becoming a stellar employee who has made important contributions to the success of the department your boss leads.

Unfortunately, you find yourself at a career impasse. You believe you are ready to move into a management position, but your company is not growing enough to create many opportunities. Worse yet, you joined the firm during a period of rapid expansion, so there are many eager and qualified internal candidates at your career level interested in the few managerial jobs that do become available. You fear it may be years before you get the chance to move up in the company. Through your online networking activities, you found an opportunity with a firm in another industry and have decided to pursue it.

Your task: You have a close relationship with your boss, so you will announce your intention to leave the company in a private, one-on-one conversation. However, you also recognize the need to write a formal letter of resignation, which you will hand to your boss during this meeting. This letter is addressed to your boss, but as formal business correspondence that will become part of your personnel file, it should not be a "personal" letter. Making up whatever details you need, write a brief letter of resignation.

Format and Layout of Business Documents

The format and layout of business documents vary from country to country. In addition, many organizations develop their own variations of standard styles, adapting documents to the types of messages they send and the kinds of audiences they communicate with. The formats described here are the most common approaches used in U.S. business correspondence, but be sure to follow whatever practices are expected at your company.

First Impressions

Your documents tell readers a lot about you and about your company's professionalism. So all your documents must look neat, present a professional image, and be easy to read. Your audience's first impression of a document comes from the quality of its paper, the way it is customized, and its general appearance.

PAPER

To give a quality impression, businesspeople consider carefully the paper they use. Several aspects of paper contribute to the overall impression:

- **Weight.** Paper quality is judged by the weight of four reams (each a 500-sheet package) of letter-size paper. The weight most commonly used by U.S. business organizations is 20-pound paper, but 16- and 24-pound versions are also used.
- **Cotton content.** Paper quality is also judged by the percentage of cotton in the paper. Cotton doesn't yellow over time the way wood pulp does, plus it's both strong and soft. For letters and outside reports, use paper with a 25 percent cotton content. For memos and other internal documents, you can use a lighter-weight paper with lower cotton content. Airmail-weight paper may save money for international correspondence, but make sure it isn't too flimsy.[1]
- **Size.** In the United States, the standard paper size for business documents is 8½ by 11 inches. Standard legal documents are 8½ by 14 inches. Executives sometimes have heavier 7-by-10-inch paper on hand (with matching envelopes) for personal messages such as congratulations.[2] They may also have a box of note cards imprinted with their initials and a box of plain folded notes for condolences or for acknowledging formal invitations.
- **Color.** White is the standard color for business purposes, although neutral colors such as gray and ivory are sometimes used. Memos can be produced on pastel-colored paper to distinguish them from external correspondence. In addition, memos are sometimes produced on various colors of paper for routing to separate departments. Light-colored papers are appropriate, but bright or dark colors make reading difficult and may appear too frivolous.

CUSTOMIZATION

For letters to outsiders, U.S. businesses commonly use letterhead stationery, which may be either professionally printed or designed in-house using word processing templates and graphics. Letterhead typically contains the company name, logo, address, telephone and fax numbers, general email address, website URL, and possibly one or more social media URLs.

In the United States, businesses always use letterhead for the first page of a letter. Successive pages are usually plain sheets of paper that match the letterhead in color and quality. Some companies use a specially printed second-page letterhead that bears only the company's name.

APPEARANCE

Nearly all business documents are produced using an inkjet or laser printer; make sure to use a clean, high-quality printer. Certain documents, however, should be handwritten (such as a short informal memo or a note of condolence). Be sure to handwrite, print, or type the envelope to match the document. However, even a letter on the best-quality paper with the best-designed letterhead may look unprofessional if it's poorly produced. So pay close attention to all the factors affecting appearance, including the following:

- **Margins.** Business letters typically use 1-inch margins at the top, bottom, and sides of the page, although these parameters are sometimes adjusted to accommodate letterhead elements.
- **Line length.** Lines are rarely justified, because the resulting text looks too formal and can be difficult to read.
- **Character spacing.** Use proper spacing between characters and after punctuation. For example, U.S. conventions include leaving one space after commas, semicolons, colons, and sentence-ending periods. Each letter in a person's initials is followed by a period and a single space. However, abbreviations such as U.S.A. or MBA may or may not have periods, but they never have internal spaces.

- **Special symbols.** Take advantage of the many special symbols available with your computer's selection of fonts. In addition, see if your company has a style guide for documents, which may include particular symbols you are expected to use.
- **Corrections.** Messy corrections are unacceptable in business documents. If you notice an error after printing a document with your word processor, correct the mistake and reprint. (With informal memos to members of your own team or department, the occasional small correction in pen or pencil is acceptable, but never in formal documents.)

Letters

All business letters have certain elements in common. Several of these elements appear in every letter; others appear only when desirable or appropriate. In addition, these letter parts are usually arranged in one of three basic formats.

STANDARD LETTER PARTS

The letter in Figure A.1 shows the placement of standard letter parts. The writer of this business letter had no letterhead available but correctly included a heading. All business letters typically include these seven elements.

Heading

The elements of the letterhead make up the heading of a letter in most cases. If letterhead stationery is not available, the heading includes a return address (but no name) and starts 13 lines from the top of the page, which leaves a 2-inch top margin.

Date

If you're using letterhead, place the date at least one blank line beneath the lowest part of the letterhead. Without letterhead, place the date immediately below the return address. The standard method of writing the date in the United States uses the full name of the month (no abbreviations), followed by the day (in numerals, without *st*, *nd*, *rd*, or *th*), a comma,

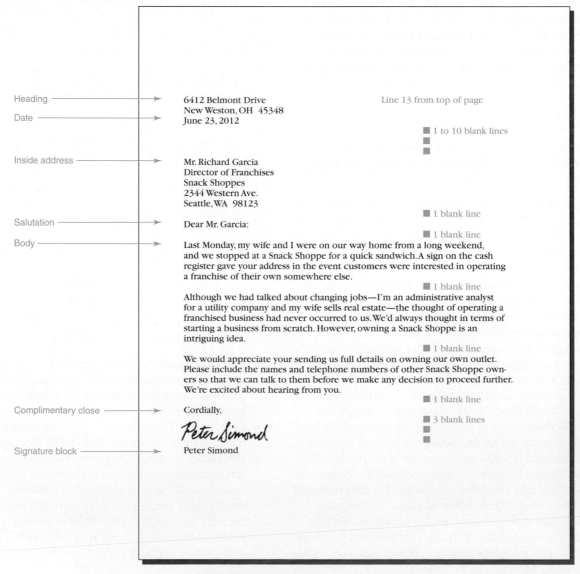

Figure A.1 Standard Letter Parts

TABLE A.1	Common Date Forms		
Convention	Description	Date—Mixed	Date—All Numerals
U.S. standard	Month (spelled out) day, year	July 14, 2012	7/14/12
U.S. government and some U.S. industries	Day (in numerals) month (spelled out) year	14 July 2012	14/7/12
European	Replace U.S. solidus (diagonal line) with periods	14 July 2012	14.7.2012
2012 International standard	Year month day	2012 July 14	2012,7,14

and then the year: July 14, 2012 (7/14/2012). Some organizations follow other conventions (see Table A.1). To maintain the utmost clarity in international correspondence, always spell out the name of the month in dates.[3]

Inside Address

The inside address identifies the recipient of the letter. For U.S. correspondence, begin the inside address at least one line below the date. Precede the addressee's name with a courtesy title, such as *Dr., Mr.,* or *Ms.* The accepted courtesy title for women in business is *Ms.,* although a woman known to prefer the title *Miss* or *Mrs.* is always accommodated. If you don't know whether a person is a man or a woman (and you have no way of finding out), omit the courtesy title. For example, *Terry Smith* could be either a man or a woman. The first line of the inside address would be just *Terry Smith,* and the salutation would be *Dear Terry Smith.* The same is true if you know only a person's initials, as in *S. J. Adams.*

Spell out and capitalize titles that precede a person's name, such as *Professor* or *General* (see Table A.2 on the next page for the proper forms of address). The person's organizational title, such as *Director,* may be included on this first line (if it is short) or on the line below; the name of a department may follow. In addresses and signature lines, don't forget to capitalize any professional title that follows a person's name:

Mr. Ray Johnson, Dean

Ms. Patricia T. Higgins

Assistant Vice President

However, professional titles not appearing in an address or signature line are capitalized only when they directly precede the name:

President Kenneth Johanson will deliver the speech.

Maria Morales, president of ABC Enterprises, will deliver the speech.

The Honorable Helen Masters, senator from Arizona, will deliver the speech.

If the name of a specific person is unavailable, you may address the letter to the department or to a specific position within the department. Also, be sure to spell out company names in full, unless the company itself uses abbreviations in its official name.

Other address information includes the treatment of buildings, house numbers, and compass directions (see Table A.3

on page A-5). The following example shows all the information that may be included in the inside address and its proper order for U.S. correspondence:

Ms. Linda Coolidge, Vice President
Corporate Planning Department
Midwest Airlines
Kowalski Building, Suite 21-A
7279 Bristol Ave.
Toledo, OH 43617

Canadian addresses are similar, except that the name of the province is usually spelled out:

Dr. H. C. Armstrong
Research and Development
Commonwealth Mining Consortium
The Chelton Building, Suite 301
585 Second St. SW
Calgary, Alberta T2P 2P5

The order and layout of address information vary from country to country. So when addressing correspondence for other countries, carefully follow the format and information that appear in the company's letterhead. However, when you're sending mail from the United States, be sure that the name of the destination country appears on the last line of the address in capital letters. Use the English version of the country name so that your mail is routed from the United States to the right country. Then, to be sure your mail is routed correctly within the destination country, use the foreign spelling of the city name (using the characters and diacritical marks that would be commonly used in the region). For example, the following address uses *Köln* instead of *Cologne*:

H. R. Veith, Director	Addressee
Eisfieren Glaswerk	Company name
Blaubachstrasse 13	Street address
Postfach 10 80 07	Post office road
D-5000 Köln I	District, city
GERMANY	Country

For additional examples of international addresses, see Table A.4 on page A-6.

Be sure to use organizational titles correctly when addressing international correspondence. Job designations vary around the world. In England, for example, a managing director is often what a U.S. company would call its chief executive officer or president, and a British deputy is the equivalent of a vice president. In France, responsibilities are

TABLE A.2   Forms of Address

Person	In Address	In Salutation
Personal Titles		
Man	Mr. [first & last name]	Dear Mr. [last name]:
Woman*	Ms. [first & last name]	Dear Ms. [last name]:
Two men (or more)	Mr. [first & last name] and Mr. [first & last name]	Dear Mr. [last name] and Mr. [last name] or Messrs. [last name] and [last name]:
Two women (or more)	Ms. [first & last name] and Ms. [first & last name]	Dear Ms. [last name] and Ms. [last name] or Mses. [last name] and [last name]:
One woman and one man	Ms. [first & last name] and Mr. [first & last name]	Dear Ms. [last name] and Mr. [last name]:
Couple (married with same last name)	Mr. [husband's first name] and Mrs. [wife's first name] [couple's last name]	Dear Mr. and Mrs. [last name]:
Couple (married with different last names)	Mr. [first & last name of husband] Ms. [first & last name of wife]	Dear Mr. [husband's last name] and Ms. [wife's last name]:
Couple (married professionals with same title and same last name)	[title in plural form] [husband's first name] and [wife's first name] [couple's last name]	Dear [title in plural form] [last name]:
Couple (married professionals with different titles and same last name)	[title] [first & last name of husband] and [title] [first & last name of wife]	Dear [title] and [title] [last name]:
Professional Titles		
President of a college or university	[title] [first & last name], President	Dear [title] [last name]:
Dean of a school or college	Dean [first & last name] or Dr., Mr., or Ms. [first & last name], Dean of [title]	Dear Dean [last name]: or Dear Dr., Mr., or Ms. [last name]:
Professor	Professor or Dr. [first & last name]	Dear Professor or Dr. [last name]:
Physician	[first & last name], M.D.	Dear Dr. [last name]:
Lawyer	Mr. or Ms. [first & last name], Attorney at Law	Dear Mr. or Ms. [last name]:
Military personnel	[full rank, first & last name, abbreviation of service designation] (add *Retired* if applicable)	Dear [rank][last name]:
Company or corporation	[name of organization]	Ladies and Gentlemen: or Gentlemen and Ladies:
Governmental Titles		
President of the United States	The President	Dear Mr. or Madam President:
Senator of the United States	The Honorable [first & last name]	Dear Senator [last name]:
Cabinet member	The Honorable [first & last name]	Dear Mr. or Madam Secretary:
Attorney General	The Honorable [first & last name]	Dear Mr. or Madam Attorney General:
Mayor	The Honorable [first & last name], Mayor of [name of city]	Dear Mayor [last name]:
Judge	The Honorable [first & last name]	Dear Judge [last name]:

*Use *Mrs.* or *Miss* only if the recipient has specifically requested that you use one of these titles; otherwise *always* use *Ms.* in business correspondence. Also, never refer to a married woman by her husband's name (e.g., *Mrs. Robert Washington*) unless she specifically requests that you do so.

TABLE A.3	**Inside Address Information**
Description	**Example**
Capitalize building names.	Empire State Building
Capitalize locations within buildings (apartments, suites, rooms).	Suite 1073
Use numerals for all house or building numbers, except the number one.	One Trinity Lane; 637 Adams Ave., Apt. 7
Spell out compass directions that fall within a street address	1074 West Connover St.
Abbreviate compass directions that follow the street address	783 Main St., N.E., Apt. 27

assigned to individuals without regard to title or organizational structure, and in China the title *project manager* has meaning, but the title *sales manager* may not.

To make matters worse, businesspeople in some countries sign correspondence without their names typed below. In Germany, for example, the belief is that employees represent the company, so it's inappropriate to emphasize personal names.[4] Use the examples in Table A.4 as guidelines when addressing correspondence to countries outside the United States.

Salutation

In the salutation of your letter, follow the style of the first line of the inside address. If the first line is a person's name, the salutation is *Dear Mr.* or *Ms. Name*. The formality of the salutation depends on your relationship with the addressee. If in conversation you would say "Mary," your letter's salutation should be *Dear Mary*, followed by a colon. Otherwise, include the courtesy title and last name, followed by a colon. Presuming to write *Dear Lewis* instead of *Dear Professor Chang* demonstrates a disrespectful familiarity that the recipient will probably resent.

If the first line of the inside address is a position title such as *Director of Personnel*, then use *Dear Director*. If the addressee is unknown, use a polite description, such as *Dear Alumnus, Dear SPCA Supporter*, or *Dear Voter*. If the first line is plural (a department or company), then use *Ladies and Gentlemen* (look again at Table A.2). When you do not know whether you're writing to an individual or a group (for example, when writing a reference or a letter of recommendation), use *To whom it may concern*.

In the United States some letter writers use a "salutopening" on the salutation line. A salutopening omits *Dear* but includes the first few words of the opening paragraph along with the recipient's name. After this line, the sentence continues a double space below as part of the body of the letter, as in these examples:

Thank you, Mr. Brown,   *Salutopening Body*
for your prompt payment of your bill.

Congratulations, Ms. Lake!   *Salutopening Body*
Your promotion is well deserved.

Whether your salutation is informal or formal, be especially careful that names are spelled correctly. A misspelled name is glaring evidence of carelessness, and it belies the personal interest you're trying to express.

Body

The body of the letter is your message. Almost all letters are single-spaced, with one blank line before and after the salutation or salutopening, between paragraphs, and before the complimentary close. The body may include indented lists, entire paragraphs indented for emphasis, and even subheadings. If it does, all similar elements should be treated in the same way. Your department or company may select a format to use for all letters.

Complimentary Close

The complimentary close begins on the second line below the body of the letter. Alternatives for wording are available, but currently the trend seems to be toward using one-word closes, such as *Sincerely* and *Cordially*. In any case, the complimentary close reflects the relationship between you and the person you're writing to. Avoid cute closes, such as *Yours for bigger profits*. If your audience doesn't know you well, your sense of humor may be misunderstood.

Signature Block

Leave three blank lines for a written signature below the complimentary close, and then include the sender's name (unless it appears in the letterhead). The person's title may appear on the same line as the name or on the line below:

Cordially,

Raymond Dunnigan

Director of Personnel

Your letterhead indicates that you're representing your company. However, if your letter is on plain paper or runs to a second page, you may want to emphasize that you're speaking legally for the company. The accepted way of doing that is to place the company's name in capital letters, a double

TABLE A.4	International Addresses and Salutations		
Country	**Postal Address**	**Address Elements**	**Salutations**
Argentina	Sr. Juan Pérez Editorial Internacional S.A. Av. Sarmiento 1337, 8° P.C. C1035AAB BUENOS AIRES–CF ARGENTINA	S.A. = Sociedad Anónima (corporation) Av. Sarmiento (name of street) 1337 (building number) 8° - 8th. P = Piso (floor) C (room or suite) C1035AAB (postcode + city) CF = Capital Federal (federal capital)	Sr. = Señor (Mr.) Sra. = Señora (Mrs.) Srta. = Señorita (Miss) Don't use given names except with people you know well.
Australia	Mr. Roger Lewis International Publishing Pty. Ltd. 166 Kent Street, Level 9 GPO Box 3542 SYDNEY NSW 200 AUSTRALIA	Pty. Ltd. – Proprietory Limited (corp.) 166 (building number) Kent Street (name of street) Level (floor) GPO Box (P.O. box) City + state (abbrev.) + postcode	Mr. and Mrs. used on first contact. Ms. not common (avoid use). Business is informal—use given name freely.
Austria	Herrn Dipl.-Ing.J.Gerdenitsch International Verlag Ges.m.b.H. Glockengasse 159 1010 WIEN AUSTRIA	Herrn – To Mr. (separate line) Dipl.-Ing. (engineering degree) Ges.m.b.H. (a corporation) Glockengasse (street name) 159 (building number) 1010 (postcode + city) WIEN (Vienna)	Herr (Mr.) Frau (Mrs.) Fräulein (Miss) obsolete in business, so do not use. Given names are almost never used in business.
Brazil	Ilmo. Sr. Gilberto Rabello Ribeiro Editores Internacionais S.A. Rua da Ajuda, 228–6° Andar Caixa Postal 2574 20040–000 RIO DE JANEIRO–RJ BRAZIL	Ilmo. = Ilustrissimo (honorific) Ilma. = Ilustrissima (hon. female) S.A. – Sociedade Anônima (corporation) Rua = street, da Ajuda (street name) 228 (building number) 6° = 6th. Andar (floor) Caixa Postal (P.O. box) 20040–000 (postcode + city)–RJ (state abbrev.)	Sr. = Senhor (Mr.) Sra. = Senhora (Mrs.) Srta. = Senhorita (Miss) Family name at end, e.g., Senhor Ribeiro (Rabello is mother's family name) Given names readily used in business.
China	Xia Zhiyi International Publishing Ltd. 14 Jianguolu Chaoyangqu BEIJING 100025 CHINA	Ltd. (limited liability corporation) 14 (building number) Jianguolu (street name), lu (street) Chaoyangqu (district name) (city + postcode)	Family name (single syllable) first. Given name (2 syllables) second, sometimes reversed. Use Mr. or Ms. at all times (Mr. Xia).
France	Monsieur LEFÈVRE Alain Éditions Internationales S.A. Siège Social Immeuble Le Bonaparte 64–68, av. Galliéni B.P. 154 75942 PARIS CEDEX 19 FRANCE	S.A. = Société Anonyme (corporation) Siège Social (head office) Immeuble (building + name) 64–68 (building occupies 64, 66, 68) av. = avenue (no initial capital) B.P. = Boîte Postale (P.O. box) 75942 (postcode + city) CEDEX (postcode for P.O. box)	Monsieur (Mr.) Madame (Mrs.) Mademoiselle (Miss) Best not to abbreviate. Family name is sometimes in all caps with given name following.
Germany	Herrn Gerhardt Schneider International Verlag GmbH Schillerstraße 159 44147 DORTMUND GERMANY	Herrn = To Mr. (on a separate line) GmbH (inc.—incorporated) –straße (street—'β' often written 'ss') 159 (building number) 44147 (postcode – city)	Herr (Mr.) Frau (Mrs.) Fräulein (Miss) obsolete in business. Business is formal: (1) do not use given names unless invited, and (2) use academic titles precisely.
India	Sr. Shyam Lal Gupta International Publishing (Pvt.) Ltd. 1820 Rehaja Centre 214, Darussalam Road Andheri East MUMBAI–400049 INDIA	(Pvt.) (privately owned) Ltd. (limited liability corporation) 1820 (possibly office #20 on 18th floor) Rehaja Centre (building name) 214 (building number) Andheri East (suburb name) (city + hyphen + postcode)	Shri (Mr.), Shrimati (Mrs.) but English is common business language, so use Mr., Mrs., Miss. Given names are used only by family and close friends.

(continued)

Country	Postal Address	Address Elements	Salutations
Italy	Egr. Sig. Giacomo Mariotti Edizioni Internazionali S.p.A. Via Terenzio, 2120138 MILANO ITALY	Egr. = Egregio (honorific) Sig. = Signor (not nec. a separate line) S.p.A. = Società per Azioni (corp.) Via (street) 21 (building number) 20138 (postcode + city)	Sig. = Signore (Mr.) Sig.ra = Signora (Mrs.) Sig.a (Ms.) Women in business are addressed as Signora. Use given name only when invited.
Japan	Mr. Taro Tanaka Kokusai Shuppan K.K. 10–23, 5-chome, Minamiazabu Minato-ku TOKYO 106 JAPAN	K.K. = Kabushiki Kaisha (corporation) 10 (lot number) 23 (building number) 5-chome (area #5) Minamiazabu (neighborhood name) Minato-ku (city district) (city + postcode)	Given names not used in business. Use family name + job title. Or use family name + "-san" (Tanaka-san) or more respectfully, add "-sama" or "-dono."
Korea	Mr. Kim Chang-ik International Publishers Ltd. Room 206, Korea Building 33–4 Nonhyon-dong Kangnam-ku SEOUL 135–010 KOREA	English company names common Ltd. (a corporation) 206 (office number inside the building) 33–4 (area 4 of subdivision 33) -dong (city neighborhood name) -ku (subdivision of city) (city + postcode)	Family name is normally first but sometimes placed after given name. A two-part name is the given name. Use Mr. or Mrs. in letters, but use job title in speech.
Mexico	Sr. Francisco Pérez Martínez Editores Internacionales S.A. Independencia No. 322 Col. Juárez 06050 MEXICO D.F.	S.A. – Sociedad Anónima (corporation) Independencia (street name) No. = Número (number) 322 (building number) Col. = Colonia (city district) Juárez (locality name) 06050 (postcode + city) D.F. = Distrito Federal (federal capital)	Sr. = Señor (Mr.) Sra. = Señora (Mrs.) Srta. = Señorita (Miss) Family name in middle: e.g., Sr. Pérez (Martínez is mother's family). Given names are used in business.
South Africa	Mr. Mandla Ntuli International Publishing (Pty.) Ltd. Private Bag X2581 JOHANNESBURG 2000 SOUTH AFRICA	Pty. = Proprietory (privately owned) Ltd. (a corporation) Private Bag (P.O. Box) (city + postcode) or (postcode + city)	Mnr. = Meneer (Mr.) Mev. = Mevrou (Mrs.) Mejuffrou (Miss) is not used in business. Business is becoming less formal, so the use of given names is possible.
United Kingdom	Mr. N. J. Lancaster International Publishing Ltd. Kingsbury House 12 Kingsbury Road EDGEWARE Middlesex HA8 9XG ENGLAND	N. J. (initials of given names) Ltd. (limited liability corporation) Kingsbury House (building name) 12 (building number) Kingsbury Road (name of street/road) EDGEWARE (city—all caps) Middlesex (county—not all caps) HA8 9XG	Mr. and Ms. used mostly. Mrs. and Miss sometimes used in North and by older women. Given names—called Christian names—are used in business after some time. Wait to be invited.

space below the complimentary close, and then include the sender's name and title four lines below that:

Sincerely,
WENTWORTH INDUSTRIES

(Ms.) Helen B. Taylor
President

If your name could be taken for either a man's or a woman's, a courtesy title indicating gender should be included, with or without parentheses. Also, women who prefer a particular courtesy title should include it:

Mrs. Nancy Winters
(Ms.) Juana Flores

Ms. Pat Li
(Mr.) Jamie Saunders

ADDITIONAL LETTER PARTS

Letters vary greatly in subject matter and thus in the identifying information they need and the format they adopt. The letter in Figure A.2 on the next page shows how these additional parts should be arranged. The following elements may be used in any combination, depending on the requirements of the particular letter:

- **Addressee notation.** Letters that have a restricted readership or that must be handled in a special way should include such addressee notations as *PERSONAL, CONFIDENTIAL,* or *PLEASE FORWARD.* This sort of notation appears a double space above the inside address, in all-capital letters.

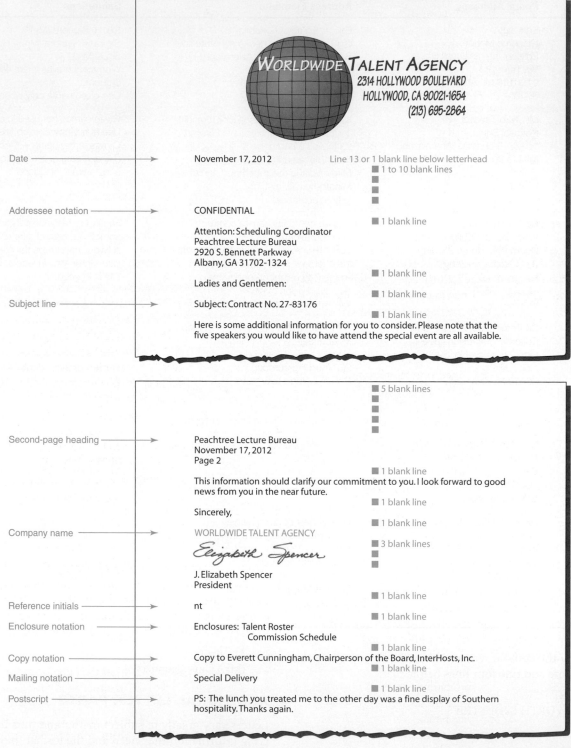

WORLDWIDE TALENT AGENCY
2314 HOLLYWOOD BOULEVARD
HOLLYWOOD, CA 90021-1654
(213) 695-2864

Date →

November 17, 2012

Line 13 or 1 blank line below letterhead
■ 1 to 10 blank lines
■
■
■

Addressee notation →

CONFIDENTIAL

■ 1 blank line

Attention: Scheduling Coordinator
Peachtree Lecture Bureau
2920 S. Bennett Parkway
Albany, GA 31702-1324

■ 1 blank line

Ladies and Gentlemen:

■ 1 blank line

Subject line →

Subject: Contract No. 27-83176

■ 1 blank line

Here is some additional information for you to consider. Please note that the five speakers you would like to have attend the special event are all available.

■ 5 blank lines
■
■
■

Second-page heading →

Peachtree Lecture Bureau
November 17, 2012
Page 2

■ 1 blank line

This information should clarify our commitment to you. I look forward to good news from you in the near future.

■ 1 blank line

Sincerely,

■ 1 blank line

Company name →

WORLDWIDE TALENT AGENCY

■ 3 blank lines
■

Elizabeth Spencer

J. Elizabeth Spencer
President

■ 1 blank line

Reference initials →

nt

■ 1 blank line

Enclosure notation →

Enclosures: Talent Roster
             Commission Schedule

■ 1 blank line

Copy notation →

Copy to Everett Cunningham, Chairperson of the Board, InterHosts, Inc.

■ 1 blank line

Mailing notation →

Special Delivery

■ 1 blank line

Postscript →

PS: The lunch you treated me to the other day was a fine display of Southern hospitality. Thanks again.

Figure A.2   Additional Letter Parts

- **Attention line.** Although not commonly used today, an attention line can be used if you know only the last name of the person you're writing to. It can also direct a letter to a position title or department. Place the attention line on the first line of the inside address and put the company name on the second.[5] Match the address on the envelope with the style of the inside address. An attention line may take any of the following forms or variants of them:

Attention Dr. McHenry

Attention Director of Marketing

Attention Marketing Department

- **Subject line.** The subject line tells recipients at a glance what the letter is about (and indicates where to file the letter for future reference). It usually appears below the salutation, either against the left margin, indented (as a paragraph in the body), or centered. It can be placed above the salutation or at the very top of the page, and it can be underscored. Some businesses omit the word *Subject*, and some organizations replace it with *Re:* or *In re:* (meaning "concerning" or "in the matter of"). The subject line may take a variety of forms, including the following:

  Subject: RainMaster Sprinklers
  About your February 2, 2012, order
  FALL 2012 SALES MEETING
  Reference Order No. 27920

- **Second-page heading.** Use a second-page heading whenever an additional page is required. Some companies have second-page letterhead (with the company name and address on one line and in a smaller typeface). The heading bears the name (person or organization) from the first line of the inside address, the page number, the date, and perhaps a reference number. Leave two blank lines before the body. Make sure that at least two lines of a continued paragraph appear on the first and second pages. Never allow the closing lines to appear alone on a continued page. Precede the complimentary close or signature lines with at least two lines of the body. Also, don't hyphenate the last word on a page. All the following are acceptable forms for second-page headings:

  Ms. Melissa Baker
  May 10, 2012
  Page 2

  Ms. Melissa Baker, May 10, 2012, Page 2

  Ms. Melissa Baker-2-May 10, 2012

- **Company name.** If you include the company's name in the signature block, put it a double space below the complimentary close. You usually include the company's name in the signature block only when the writer is serving as the company's official spokesperson or when letterhead has not been used.

- **Reference initials.** When businesspeople keyboard their own letters, reference initials are unnecessary, so they are becoming rare. When one person dictates a letter and another person produces it, reference initials show who helped prepare it. Place initials at the left margin, a double space below the signature block. When the signature block includes the writer's name, use only the preparer's initials. If the signature block includes only the department, use both sets of initials, usually in one of the following forms: *RSR/sm, RSR:sm,* or *RSR:SM* (writer/preparer). When the writer and the signer are different people, at least the file copy should bear both their initials as well as the typist's: *JFS/RSR/sm* (signer/writer/preparer).

- **Enclosure notation.** Enclosure notations appear at the bottom of a letter, one or two lines below the reference initials. Some common forms include the following:

  Enclosure
  Enclosures (2)
  Enclosures: Résumé
            Photograph
            Brochure

- **Copy notation.** Copy notations may follow reference initials or enclosure notations. They indicate who's receiving a *courtesy copy* (*cc*). Recipients are listed in order of rank or (rank being equal) in alphabetical order. Among the forms used are the following:

  cc: David Wentworth, Vice President
  Copy to Hans Vogel
  748 Chesterton Road
  Snohomish, WA 98290

- **Mailing notation.** You may place a mailing notation (such as *Special Delivery* or *Registered Mail*) at the bottom of the letter, after reference initials or enclosure notations (whichever is last) and before copy notations. Or you may place it at the top of the letter, either above the inside address on the left side or just below the date on the right side. For greater visibility, mailing notations may appear in capital letters.

- **Postscript.** A postscript is presented as an afterthought to the letter, a message that requires emphasis, or a personal note. It is usually the last thing on any letter and may be preceded by *P.S., PS., PS:*, or nothing at all. A second afterthought would be designated *P.P.S.* (post postscript).

LETTER FORMATS

A letter format is the way of arranging all the basic letter parts. Sometimes a company adopts a certain format as its policy; sometimes the individual letter writer or preparer is allowed to choose the most appropriate format. In the United States, three major letter formats are commonly used:

- **Block format.** Each letter part begins at the left margin. The main advantage is quick and efficient preparation (see Figure A.3).
- **Modified block format.** Same as block format, except that the date, complimentary close, and signature block start near the center of the page (see Figure A.4 on page A-11). The modified block format does permit indentions as an option. This format mixes preparation speed with traditional placement of some letter parts. It also looks more balanced on the page than the block format does. (Note: The address and contact information in the left margin of this letter is part of this company's particular stationery design; other designs put this information at the top or bottom of the page.)

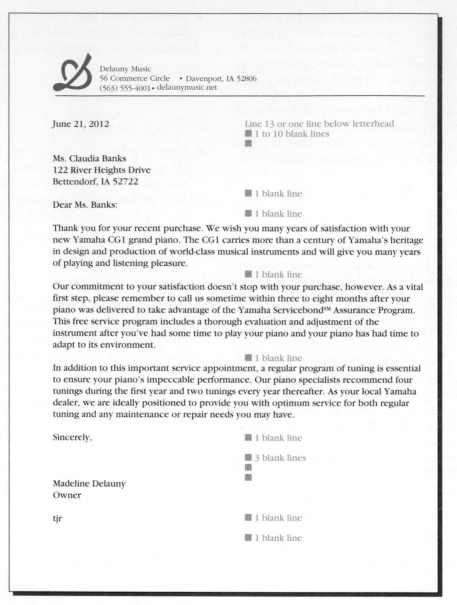

Figure A.3   **Block Letter Format**

- **Simplified format.** Instead of using a salutation, this format often weaves the reader's name into the first line or two of the body and often includes a subject line in capital letters (see Figure A.5 on page A-12). This format does not include a complimentary close, so your signature appears immediately below the body text. Because certain letter parts are eliminated, some line spacing is changed.

These three formats differ in the way paragraphs are indented, in the way letter parts are placed, and in some punctuation. However, the elements are always separated by at least one blank line, and the printed name is always separated from the line above by at least three blank lines to allow space for a signature. If paragraphs are indented, the indention is normally five spaces. The most common formats for intercultural business letters are the block style and the modified block style.

In addition to these three letter formats, letters may also be classified according to their style of punctuation. *Standard*, or *mixed, punctuation* uses a colon after the salutation (a comma if the letter is social or personal) and a comma after the complimentary close. *Open punctuation* uses no colon or comma after the salutation or the complimentary close. Although the most popular style in business communication is mixed punctuation, either style of punctuation may be used with block or modified block letter formats. Because the simplified letter format has no salutation or complimentary close, the style of punctuation is irrelevant.

Envelopes

For a first impression, the quality of the envelope is just as important as the quality of the stationery. Letterhead and envelopes should be of the same paper stock, have the same color ink,

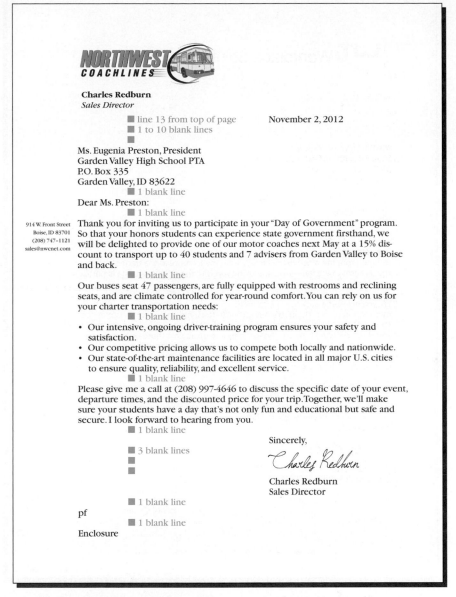

Figure A.4   Modified Block Letter Format

and be imprinted with the same address and logo. Most envelopes used by U.S. businesses are No. 10 envelopes (9½ inches long), which are sized for an 8½-by-11-inch piece of paper folded in thirds. Some occasions call for a smaller, No. 6¾, envelope or for envelopes proportioned to fit special stationery. Figure A.6 on page A-13 shows the two most common sizes.

ADDRESSING THE ENVELOPE

No matter what size the envelope, the address is always single-spaced with all lines aligned on the left. The address on the envelope is in the same style as the inside address and presents the same information. The order to follow is from the smallest division to the largest:

1. Name and title of recipient
2. Name of department or subgroup
3. Name of organization
4. Name of building
5. Street address and suite number, or post office box number
6. City, state, or province, and zip code or postal code
7. Name of country (if the letter is being sent abroad)

Because the U.S. Postal Service uses optical scanners to sort mail, envelopes for quantity mailings, in particular, should be addressed in the prescribed format. Everything is in capital letters, no punctuation is included, and all mailing instructions of interest to the post office are placed above the address area (see Figure A.6). Canada Post requires a similar format, except that only the city is all in capitals, and the postal code is placed on the line below the name of the city. The post office scanners read addresses from the bottom up, so if a letter is to be sent to a post office box rather than to a street address, the street address should appear on the line

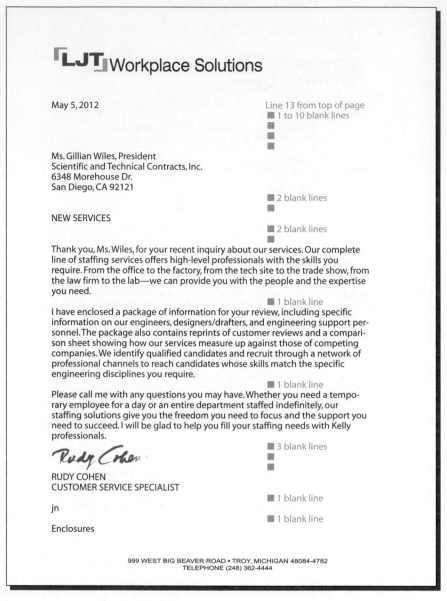

Figure A.5   Simplified Letter Format

above the box number. Figure A.6 also shows the proper spacing for addresses and return addresses.

The U.S. Postal Service and the Canada Post Corporation have published lists of two-letter mailing abbreviations for states, provinces, and territories (see Table A.5 on the next page). Postal authorities prefer no punctuation with these abbreviations. Quantity mailings should always follow post office requirements. For other letters, a reasonable compromise is to use traditional punctuation, uppercase and lowercase letters for names and street addresses, but two-letter state or province abbreviations, as shown here:

Mr. Kevin Kennedy
2107 E. Packer Dr.
Amarillo, TX 79108

Canadian postal codes are alphanumeric, with a three-character "area code" and a three-character "local code" separated by a single space (K2P 5A5). Zip and postal codes should be separated from state and province names by one space. Canadian postal codes may be treated the same or may be put in the bottom line of the address all by itself.

FOLDING TO FIT

The way a letter is folded also contributes to the recipient's overall impression of your organization's professionalism. When sending a standard-size piece of paper in a No. 10 envelope, fold it in thirds, with the bottom folded up first and the top folded down over it (see Figure A.7); the open end should be at the top of the envelope and facing out. Fit smaller stationery neatly into the appropriate envelope simply by folding it in half or in thirds. When sending a standard-size letterhead in a No. 6¾ envelope, fold it in half from top to bottom and then in thirds from side to side.

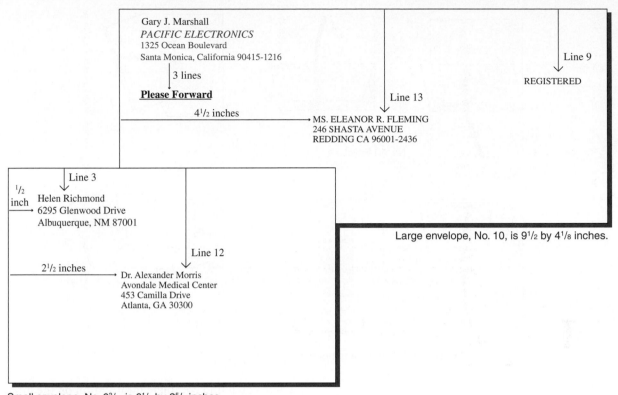

Figure A.6 **Prescribed Envelope Format**

| TABLE A.5 | Two-Letter Mailing Abbreviations for the United States and Canada |

State/ Territory/ Province	Abbreviation	State/ Territory/ Province	Abbreviation	State/ Territory/ Province	Abbreviation
United States		Massachusetts	MA	Tennessee	TN
Alabama	AL	Michigan	MI	Texas	TX
Alaska	AK	Minnesota	MN	Utah	UT
American Samoa	AS	Mississippi	MS	Vermont	VT
Arizona	AZ	Missouri	MO	Virginia	VA
Arkansas	AR	Montana	MT	Virgin Islands	VI
California	CA	Nebraska	NE	Washington	WA
Canal Zone	CZ	Nevada	NV	West Virginia	WV
Colorado	CO	New Hampshire	NH	Wisconsin	WI
Connecticut	CT	New Jersey	NJ	Wyoming	WY
Delaware	DE	New Mexico	NM	**Canada**	
District of Columbia	DC	Maryland	MD	Alberta	AB
Florida	FL	New York	NY	British Columbia	BC
Georgia	GA	North Carolina	NC	Manitoba	MB
Guam	GU	North Dakota	ND	New Brunswick	NB
Hawaii	HI	Northern Mariana	MP	Newfoundland and Labrador	NL
Idaho	ID	Ohio	OH	Northwest Territories	NT
Illinois	IL	Oklahoma	OK	Nova Scotia	NS
Indiana	IN	Oregon	OR	Nunavut	NU
Iowa	IA	Pennsylvania	PA	Ontario	ON
Kansas	KS	Puerto Rico	PR	Prince Edward Island	PE
Kentucky	KY	Rhode Island	RI	Quebec	QC
Louisiana	LA	South Carolina	SC	Saskatchewan	SK
Maine	ME	South Dakota	SD	Yukon Territory	YT

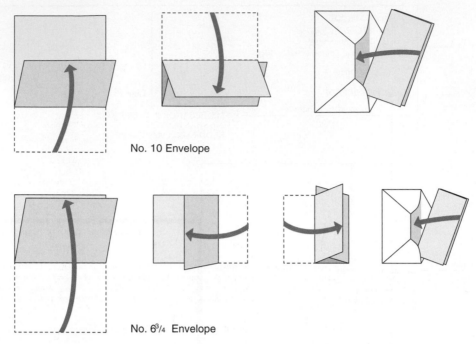

No. 10 Envelope

No. 6³/₄ Envelope

Figure A.7 Folding Standard-Size Letterhead

INTERNATIONAL MAIL

Postal service differs from country to country, so it's always a good idea to investigate the quality and availability of various services before sending messages and packages internationally. Also, compare the services offered by delivery companies such as UPS and FedEx to find the best rates and options for each destination and type of shipment. No matter which service you choose, be aware that international mail requires more planning than domestic mail. For example, for anything beyond simple letters, you generally need to prepare *customs forms* and possibly other documents, depending on the country of destination and the type of shipment. You are responsible for following the laws of the United States and any countries to which you send mail and packages.

The U.S. Postal Service currently offers four classes of international delivery, listed here from the fastest (and most expensive) to the slowest (and least expensive):

- **Global Express Guaranteed** is the fastest option. This service, offered in conjunction with FedEx, provides delivery in one to three business days to more than 190 countries and territories.
- **Express Mail International** guarantees delivery in three to five business days to a limited number of countries, including Australia, China, Hong Kong, Japan, and South Korea.
- **Priority Mail International** offers delivery guarantees of 6 to 10 business days to more than 190 countries and territories.
- **First Class Mail International** is an economical way to send correspondence and packages weighing up to four pounds to virtually any destination worldwide.

To prepare your mail for international delivery, follow the instructions provided at www.usps.com/international.

There you'll find complete information on the international services available through the U.S. Postal Service, along with advice on addressing and packaging mail, completing customs forms, and calculating postage rates and fees. The *International Mail Manual*, also available on this website, offers the latest information and regulations for both outbound and inbound international mail. For instance, you can click on individual country names to see current information about restricted or prohibited items and materials, required customs forms, and rates for various classes of service.[6] Various countries have specific and often extensive lists of items that may not be sent by mail at all or that must be sent using particular postal service options.

Memos

Electronic media have replaced most internal printed memos in many companies, but you may have occasion to send printed memos from time to time. These can be simple announcements or messages, or they can be short reports using the memo format (see Figure A.8).

On your document, include a title such as MEMO or INTEROFFICE CORRESPONDENCE (all in capitals) centered at the top of the page or aligned with the left margin. Also at the top, include the words *To, From, Date,* and *Subject*—followed by the appropriate information—with a blank line between as shown here:

MEMO

TO:
FROM:
DATE:
SUBJECT:

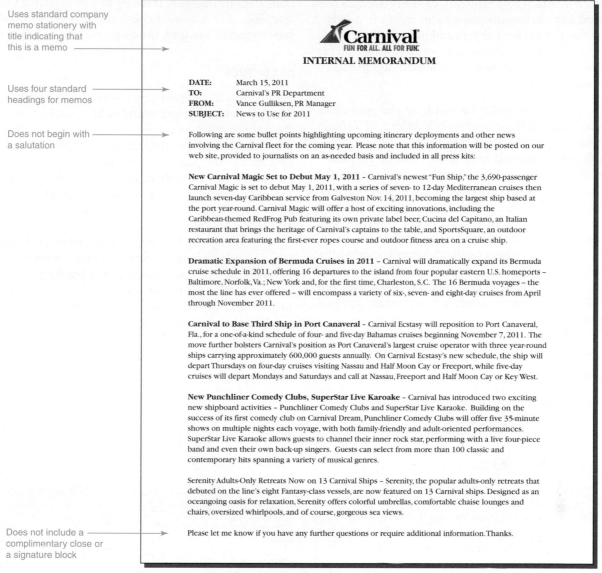

Uses standard company memo stationery with title indicating that this is a memo

Uses four standard headings for memos

Does not begin with a salutation

Does not include a complimentary close or a signature block

Figure A.8   Short Report Using the Memo Format

Sometimes the heading is organized like this:

MEMO

TO: FROM:
DATE: SUBJECT:

The following guidelines will help you effectively format specific memo elements:

- **Addressees.** When sending a memo to a long list of people, include the notation *See distribution list* or *See below* in the *To* position at the top; then list the names at the end of the memo. Arrange this list alphabetically, except when high-ranking officials deserve more prominent placement. You can also address memos to groups of people—*All Sales Representatives, Production Group, New Product Team*.
- **Courtesy titles.** You need not use courtesy titles anywhere in a memo; first initials and last names, first names, or even initials alone are often sufficient. However, use a courtesy title if you would use one in a face-to-face encounter with the person.
- **Subject line.** The subject line of a memo helps busy colleagues quickly find out what your memo is about, so take care to make it concise and compelling.
- **Body.** Start the body of the memo on the second or third line below the heading. Like the body of a letter, it's usually single-spaced with blank lines between paragraphs. Indenting paragraphs is optional. Handle lists, important passages, and subheadings as you do in letters.
- **Second page.** If the memo carries over to a second page, head the second page just as you head the second page of a letter.
- **Writer's initials.** Unlike a letter, a memo doesn't require a complimentary close or a signature, because your name is already prominent at the top. However, you may initial the memo—either beside the name appearing at the top of the memo or at the bottom of the memo.

- **Other elements.** Treat elements such as reference initials and copy notations just as you would in a letter. One difference between letters and memos is that while letters use the term *enclosure* to refer to other pieces included with the letter, memos usually use the word *attachment*.

Memos may be delivered by hand, by the post office (when the recipient works at a different location), or through interoffice mail. Interoffice mail may require the use of special reusable envelopes that have spaces for the recipient's name and department or room number; the name of the previous recipient is simply crossed out. If a regular envelope is used, the words *Interoffice Mail* appear where the stamp normally goes, so that it won't accidentally be stamped and mailed with the rest of the office correspondence.

Informal, routine, or brief reports for distribution within a company are often presented in memo form. Don't include report parts such as a table of contents and appendixes, but write the body of the memo report just as carefully as you'd write a formal report.

Reports

Enhance the effectiveness of your reports by paying careful attention to their appearance and layout. Follow whatever guidelines your organization prefers, always being neat and consistent throughout. If it's up to you to decide formatting questions, the following conventions may help you decide how to handle margins, headings, and page numbers.

MARGINS

All margins on a report page should be at least 1 inch wide. The top, left, and right margins are usually the same, but the bottom margins can be 1½ times deeper. Some special pages also have deeper top margins. Set top margins as deep as 2 inches for pages that contain major titles: prefatory parts (such as the table of contents or the executive summary), supplementary parts (such as the reference notes or bibliography), and textual parts (such as the first page of the text or the first page of each chapter).

If you're going to bind your report at the left or at the top, add half an inch to the margin on the bound edge (see Figure A.9): The space taken by the binding on left-bound reports makes the center point of the text a quarter inch to the right of the center of the paper. Be sure to center headings between the margins, not between the edges of the paper.

HEADINGS

If you don't have a template supplied by your employer, choose a design for headings and subheadings that clearly distinguishes the various levels in the hierarchy. The first-level

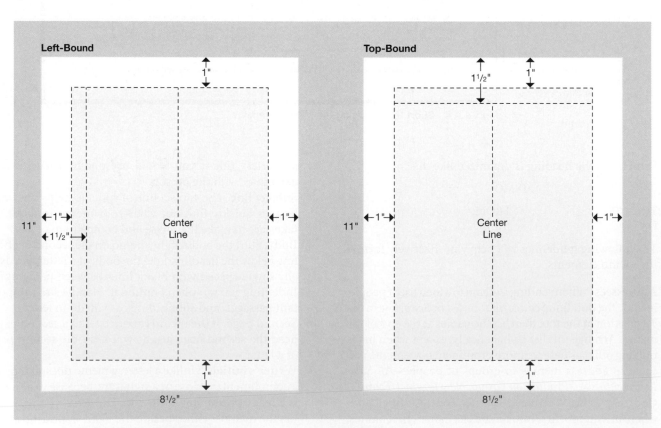

Figure A.9 **Margins for Formal Reports**

headings should be the most prominent, on down to the lowest-level subheading.

PAGE NUMBERS

Every page in a report is counted; however, not all pages show numbers. The first page of the report, normally the title page, is unnumbered. All other pages in the prefatory section are numbered with a lowercase roman numeral, beginning with *ii* and continuing with *iii, iv, v,* and so on. Start number-ing again with arabic numerals (1, 2, and so on) starting at the first page of the body.

You have many options for placing and formatting the page numbers, although these choices are usually made for you in a template. If you're not using a standard company template, position the page number where it is easy to see as the reader flips through the report. If the report will be stapled or otherwise bound along the left side, for instance, the best place for the page number is the upper right or lower right corner.

Documentation of Report Sources

By providing information about your sources, you improve your own credibility as well as the credibility of the facts and opinions you present. Documentation gives readers the means for checking your findings and pursuing the subject further. Also, documenting your report is the accepted way to give credit to the people whose work you have drawn from.

What style should you use to document your report? Experts recommend various forms, depending on your field or discipline. Moreover, your employer or client may use a form different from those the experts suggest. Don't let this discrepancy confuse you. If your employer specifies a form, use it; the standardized form is easier for colleagues to understand. However, if the choice of form is left to you, adopt one of the styles described here. Whatever style you choose, be consistent within any given report, using the same order, punctuation, and format from one reference citation or bibliography entry to the next.

A wide variety of style manuals provide detailed information on documentation. These publications explain the three most commonly used styles:

- American Psychological Association, *Publication Manual of the American Psychological Association*, 6th ed. (Washington, D.C.: American Psychological Association, 2009). Details the author-date system, which is preferred in the social sciences and often in the natural sciences as well.
- *The Chicago Manual of Style*, 16th ed. (Chicago: University of Chicago Press, 2010). Often referred to only as "*Chicago*" and widely used in the publishing industry; provides detailed treatment of source documentation and many other aspects of document preparation.
- Joseph Gibaldi, *MLA Style Manual and Guide to Scholarly Publishing*, 3rd ed. (New York: Modern Language Association, 2008). Serves as the basis for the note and bibliography style used in much academic writing and is recommended in many college textbooks on writing term papers; provides a lot of examples in the humanities.

For more information on these three guides, visit http:// real-timeupdates.com/bct11 and click on Appendix B. Although many schemes have been proposed for organizing the information in source notes, all of them break the information into parts: (1) information about the author (name), (2) information about the work (title, edition, volume number), (3) information about the publication (place, publisher), (4) information about the date, and (5) information on relevant page ranges.

The following sections summarize the major conventions for documenting sources in three styles: *The Chicago Manual of Style* (Chicago), the *Publication Manual of the American Psychological Association* (APA), and the *MLA Style Manual* (MLA).

Chicago Humanities Style

The Chicago Manual of Style recommends two types of documentation systems. The *documentary-note*, or *humanities*, style gives bibliographic citations in notes—either footnotes (when printed at the bottom of a page) or endnotes (when printed at the end of the report). The humanities system is often used in literature, history, and the arts. The other system recommended by *Chicago* is the *author-date* system, which cites the author's last name and the date of publication in the text, usually in parentheses, reserving full documentation for the reference list (or bibliography). For the purpose of comparing styles, this section concentrates on the humanities system, which is described in detail in *Chicago*.

IN-TEXT CITATION— *CHICAGO* HUMANITIES STYLE

To document report sources in text, the humanities system relies on superscripts—arabic numerals placed just above the line of type at the end of the reference:

> Toward the end of his speech, Myers sounded a note of caution, saying that even though the economy is expected to grow, it could easily slow a bit.[10]

The superscript lets the reader know how to look for source information in either a footnote or an endnote (see Figure B.1 on the next page). Some readers prefer footnotes so that they can simply glance at the bottom of the page for information. Others prefer endnotes so that they can read the text without a clutter of notes on the page. Also, endnotes relieve the writer from worrying about how long each note will be and how much space it will take away from the page. Both footnotes and endnotes are handled automatically by today's word processing software.

For the reader's convenience, you can use footnotes for **content notes** (which may supplement your main text with asides about a particular issue or event, provide a cross-reference to another section of your report, or direct the

NOTES

Journal article with volume and issue numbers

1. Jonathan Clifton, "Beyond Taxonomies of Influence," *Journal of Business Communication* 46, no. 1 (2009): 57–79.

Brochure

2. BestTemp Staffing Services, *An Employer's Guide to Staffing Services,* 2d ed. (Denver: BestTemp Information Center, 2008), 31.

Newspaper article, no author

3. "Might Be Harder Than It Looks," *Los Angeles Times,* 30 January 2009, sec. A, p. 22.

Annual report

4. The Walt Disney Company, *2007 Annual Report* (Burbank, Calif.: The Walt Disney Company, 2008), 48.

Magazine article

5. Kerry A. Dolan, "A Whole New Crop" *Forbes,* 2 June 2008, 72–75.

Television broadcast

6. Daniel Han, "Trade Wars Heating Up Around the Globe," *CNN Headline News* (Atlanta: CNN, 5 March 2002).

Internet, World Wide Web

7. "Intel—Company Capsule," Hoover's Online [cited 19 June 2008], 3 screens; available from www.hoovers.com/intel/-ID_13787-/free-co-factsheet.xhtml.

Book, component parts

8. Sonja Kuntz, "Moving Beyond Benefits," in *Our Changing Workforce,* ed. Randolf Jacobson (New York: Citadel Press, 2001), 213–27.

Unpublished dissertation or thesis

9. George H. Morales, "The Economic Pressures on Industrialized Nations in a Global Economy" (Ph.D. diss., University of San Diego, 2001), 32–47.

Paper presented at a meeting

10. Charles Myers, "HMOs in Today's Environment" (paper presented at the Conference on Medical Insurance Solutions, Chicago, Ill., August 2001), 16–17.

Online magazine article

11. Leo Babauta, "17 Tips to Be Productive with Instant Messaging," in *Web Worker Daily* [online] (San Francisco, 2007 [updated 14 November 2007; cited 14 February 2008]); available from http://webworkerdaily.com.

CD-ROM encyclopedia article, one author

12. Robert Parkings, "George Eastman," *The Concise Columbia Encyclopedia* (New York: Columbia University Press, 1998) [CD-ROM].

Interview

13. Georgia Stainer, general manager, Day Cable and Communications, interview by author, Topeka, Kan., 2 March 2000.

Newspaper article, one author

14. Evelyn Standish, "Global Market Crushes OPEC's Delicate Balance of Interests," *Wall Street Journal,* 19 January 2002, sec. A, p. 1.

Book, two authors

15. Miriam Toller and Jay Fielding, *Global Business for Smaller Companies* (Rocklin, Calif.: Prima Publishing, 2001), 102–3.

Government publication

16. U.S. Department of Defense, *Stretching Research Dollars: Survival Advice for Universities and Government Labs* (Washington, D.C.: GPO, 2002), 126.

Figure B.1   Sample Endnotes—Chicago Humanities Style

reader to a related source). Then you can use endnotes for **source notes** (which document direct quotations, paraphrased passages, and visual aids). Consider which type of note is most common in your report, and then choose whether to present these notes all as endnotes or all as footnotes. Regardless of the method you choose for referencing textual information in your report, notes for visual aids (both content notes and source notes) are placed on the same page as the visual.

BIBLIOGRAPHY— *CHICAGO* HUMANITIES STYLE

The humanities system may or may not be accompanied by a bibliography (because the notes give all the necessary bibliographic information). However, endnotes are arranged in order of appearance in the text, so an alphabetical bibliography can be valuable to your readers. The bibliography may be titled *Bibliography, Reference List, Sources, Works Cited* (if you include only those sources you actually cited in your report), or *Works Consulted* (if you include uncited sources as well). This list of sources may also serve as a reading list for those who want to pursue the subject of your report further, so you may want to annotate each entry—that is, comment on the subject matter and viewpoint of the source, as well as on its usefulness to readers. Annotations may be written in either complete or incomplete sentences. (See the annotated list of style manuals earlier in this appendix.) A bibliography may also be more manageable if you subdivide it into categories (a classified bibliography), either by type of reference (such as books, articles, and unpublished material) or by subject

BIBLIOGRAPHY

Journal article with volume and issue numbers	Clifton, Jonathan. "Beyond Taxonomies of Influence." *Journal of Business Communication* 46, no. 1 (2009): 57–79.
Online magazine article	Babauta, Leo. "17 Tips to Be Productive with Instant Messaging," In *Web Worker Daily* [online], San Francisco, 2007 [updated 14 November 2007, cited 14 February 2008]. Available from http://webworkerdaily.com.
Brochure	BestTemp Staffing Services. *An Employer's Guide to Staffing Services.* 2d ed. Denver: BestTemp Information Center, 2008.
Newspaper article, no author	"Might Be Harder Than It Looks." *Los Angeles Times,* 30 January 2009, sec. A, p. 22.
Magazine article	Dolan, Kerry A. "A Whole New Crop," *Forbes,* 2 June 2008, 72–75.
Television broadcast	Han, Daniel. "Trade Wars Heating Up Around the Globe." *CNN Headline News.* Atlanta: CNN, 5 March 2002.
Internet, World Wide Web	"Intel—Company Capsule." *Hoover's Online* [cited 19 June 2008]. 3 screens; Available from www.hoovers.com/intel/-ID_13787-/free-co-factsheet.xhtml.
Book, component parts	Kuntz, Sonja. "Moving Beyond Benefits." In *Our Changing Workforce*, edited by Randolf Jacobson. New York: Citadel Press, 2001.
Unpublished dissertation or thesis	Morales, George H. "The Economic Pressures on Industrialized Nations in a Global Economy." Ph.D. diss., University of San Diego, 2001.
Paper presented at a meeting	Myers, Charles. "HMOs in Today's Environment." Paper presented at the Conference on Medical Insurance Solutions, Chicago, Ill., August 2001.
CD-ROM encyclopedia article, one author	Parkings, Robert. "George Eastman." *The Concise Columbia Encyclopedia.* New York: Columbia University Press, 1998. [CD-ROM].
Interview	Stainer, Georgia, general manager, Day Cable and Communications. Interview by author. Topeka, Kan., 2 March 2000.
Newspaper article, one author	Standish, Evelyn. "Global Market Crushes OPEC's Delicate Balance of Interests." *Wall Street Journal,* 19 January 2002, sec. A, p. 1.
Book, two authors	Toller, Miriam, and Jay Fielding. *Global Business for Smaller Companies.* Rocklin, Calif.: Prima Publishing, 2001.
Government publication	U.S. Department of Defense. *Stretching Research Dollars: Survival Advice for Universities and Government Labs.* Washington, D.C.: GPO, 2002.
Annual report	The Walt Disney Company, *2007 Annual Report,* Burbank, Calif.: The Walt Disney Company, 2008.

Figure B.2   Sample Bibliography—Chicago Humanities Style

matter (such as government regulation, market forces, and so on). Following are the major conventions for developing a bibliography according to *Chicago* style (see Figure B.2):

- Exclude any page numbers that may be cited in source notes, except for journals, periodicals, and newspapers.
- Alphabetize entries by the last name of the lead author (listing last name first). The names of second and succeeding authors are listed in normal order. Entries without an author name are alphabetized by the first important word in the title.
- Format entries as hanging indents (indent second and succeeding lines three to five spaces).
- Arrange entries in the following general order: (1) author name, (2) title information, (3) publication information, (4) date, (5) periodical page range.

- Use quotation marks around the titles of articles from magazines, newspapers, and journals. Capitalize the first and last words, as well as all other important words (except prepositions, articles, and coordinating conjunctions).
- Use italics to set off the names of books, newspapers, journals, and other complete publications. Capitalize the first and last words, as well as all other important words.
- For journal articles, include the volume number and the issue number (if necessary). Include the year of publication inside parentheses and follow with a colon and the page range of the article: *Journal of Business Communication* 46, no. 1 (2009): 57–79. (In this source, the volume is 46, the number is 1, and the page range is 57–79.)
- Use brackets to identify all electronic references: [Online database] or [CD-ROM].

- Explain how electronic references can be reached: Available from www.spaceless.com/WWWVL.
- Give the citation date for online references: Cited 23 August 2010.

APA Style

The American Psychological Association (APA) recommends the author-date system of documentation, which is popular in the physical, natural, and social sciences. When using this system, you simply insert the author's last name and the year of publication within parentheses following the text discussion of the material cited. Include a page number if you use a direct quotation. This approach briefly identifies the source so that readers can locate complete information in the alphabetical reference list at the end of the report. The author-date system is both brief and clear, saving readers time and effort.

IN-TEXT CITATION—APA STYLE

To document report sources in text using APA style, insert the author's surname and the date of publication at the end of a statement. Enclose this information in parentheses. If the author's name is referred to in the text itself, then the name can be omitted from parenthetical material.

> Some experts recommend both translation and back-translation when dealing with any non-English-speaking culture (Clifton, 2009).
>
> Toller and Fielding (2001) make a strong case for small companies succeeding in global business.

Personal communications and interviews conducted by the author would not be listed in the reference list at all. Such citations would appear in the text only.

> Increasing the role of cable companies is high on the list of Georgia Stainer, general manager at Day Cable and Communications (personal communication, March 2, 2009).

LIST OF REFERENCES—APA STYLE

For APA style, list only those works actually cited in the text (so you would not include works for background or for further reading). Following are the major conventions for developing a reference list according to APA style (see Figure B.3):

- Format entries as hanging indents.
- List all author names in reversed order (last name first), and use only initials for the first and middle names.
- Arrange entries in the following general order: (1) author name, (2) date, (3) title information, (4) publication information, (5) periodical page range.
- Follow the author name with the date of publication in parentheses.
- List titles of articles from magazines, newspapers, and journals without underlines or quotation marks.

Capitalize only the first word of the title, any proper nouns, and the first word to follow an internal colon.

- Italicize titles of books, capitalizing only the first word, any proper nouns, and the first word to follow a colon.
- Italicize titles of magazines, newspapers, journals, and other complete publications. Capitalize all the important words in the title.
- For journal articles, include the volume number (in italics) and, if necessary, the issue number (in parentheses). Finally, include the page range of the article: *Journal of Business Communication, 46*(1), 57–79. (In this example, the volume is 46, the number is 1, and the page range is 57–79.)
- Include personal communications (such as letters, memos, email, and conversations) only in text, not in reference lists.
- Electronic references include author, date of publication, title of article, name of publication (if one), volume, date of retrieval (month, day, year), and the source.
- For electronic references, indicate the actual year of publication and the exact date of retrieval.
- For webpages with extremely long URLs, use your best judgment to determine which URL from the site to use. For example, rather than giving the URL of a specific news release with a long URL, you can provide the URL of the "Media relations" webpage.
- APA citation guidelines for social media are still evolving. For the latest information, visit the APA Style Blog at http://blog.apastyle.org/apastyle.
- For online journals or periodicals that assign a digital object identifier (DOI), include that instead of a conventional URL. If no DOI is available, include the URL of the publication's home page (such as http://online.wsj.com for the *Wall Street Journal*).

MLA Style

The style recommended by the Modern Language Association of America is used widely in the humanities, especially in the study of language and literature. Like APA style, MLA style uses brief parenthetical citations in the text. However, instead of including author name and year, MLA citations include author name and page reference.

IN-TEXT CITATION—MLA STYLE

To document report sources in text using MLA style, insert the author's last name and a page reference inside parentheses following the cited material: (Matthews 63). If the author's name is mentioned in the text reference, the name can be omitted from the parenthetical citation: (63). The citation indicates that the reference came from page 63 of a work by Matthews. With the author's name, readers can find complete publication information in the alphabetically arranged list of works cited that comes at the end of the report.

REFERENCES

Journal article with volume and issue numbers

Clifton, J. (2009). Beyond Taxonomies of Influence. *Journal of Business Communication 46* (1), 57.

Online magazine article

Babauta, L. (2007, November 14), 17 tips to be productive with instant messaging. *Web Worker Daily.* Retrieved from http://webworkerdaily.com

Brochure

BestTemp Staffing Services. (2008). *An employer's guide to staffing services* (2d ed.) [Brochure]. Denver: BestTemp Information Center.

Newspaper article, no author

Might be harder than it looks. (2009, January 30). *Los Angeles Times,* p. A22.

Magazine article

Dolan, K. A. (2008, June 2). A whole new crop. *Forbes,* 72–75.

Television broadcast

Han, D. (2002, March 5). Trade wars heating up around the globe. *CNN Headline News.* [Television broadcast]. Atlanta, GA: CNN.

Internet, World Wide Web

Hoover's Online. (2003). *Intel—Company Capsule.* Retrieved June 19, 2008, from http://www.hoovers.com/intel/-ID_13787-/free-co-factsheet.xhtml

Book, component parts

Kuntz, S. (2001). Moving beyond benefits. In Randolph Jacobson (Ed.), *Our changing workforce* (pp. 213–227). New York: Citadel Press.

Unpublished dissertation or thesis

Morales, G. H. (2001). *The economic pressures on industrialized nations in a global economy.* Unpublished doctoral dissertation, University of San Diego.

Paper presented at a meeting

Myers, C. (2001, August). *HMOs in today's environment.* Paper presented at the Conference on Medical Insurance Solutions, Chicago, IL.

CD-ROM encyclopedia article, one author

Parkings, R. (1998). George Eastman. On *The concise Columbia encyclopedia.* [CD-ROM]. New York: Columbia University Press.

Interview

Cited in text only, not in the list of references.

Newspaper article, one author

Standish, E. (2002, January 19). Global market crushes OPEC's delicate balance of interests. *Wall Street Journal,* p. A1.

Book, two authors

Toller, M., & Fielding, J. (2001). *Global business for smaller companies.* Rocklin, CA: Prima Publishing.

Government publication

U.S. Department of Defense. (2002). *Stretching research dollars: Survival advice for universities and government labs.* Washington, DC: U.S. Government Printing Office.

Annual report

The Walt Disney Company. (2008). *2007 Annual Report.* Burbank, Calif.: The Walt Disney Company.

Figure B.3   Sample References—APA Style

Some experts recommend both translation and back-translation when dealing with any non-English-speaking culture (Clifton 57).

Toller and Fielding make a strong case for small companies succeeding in global business (102–03).

LIST OF WORKS CITED—MLA STYLE

The *MLA Style Manual* recommends preparing the list of works cited first so that you will know what information to give in the parenthetical citation (for example, whether to add a short title if you're citing more than one work by the same author, or whether to give an initial or first name if you're citing two authors who have the same last name). The list of works cited appears at the end of your report, contains all the works that you cite in your text, and lists them in alphabetical order. Following are the major conventions for developing a reference list according to MLA style (see Figure B.4 on the next page):

- Format entries as hanging indents.
- Arrange entries in the following general order: (1) author name, (2) title information, (3) publication information, (4) date, (5) periodical page range.
- List the lead author's name in reverse order (last name first), using either full first names or initials. List second and succeeding author names in normal order.
- Use quotation marks around the titles of articles from magazines, newspapers, and journals. Capitalize all important words.

WORKS CITED

Journal article with volume and issue numbers	Clifton, Jonathan. "Beyond Taxonomies of Influence." *Journal of Business Communication* 46, 1 (2009): 57–79.
Online magazine article	Babauta, Leo. "17 Tips to Be Productive with Instant Messaging," *Web Worker Daily* 14 Nov. 2007. 14 Feb. 2008. http://webworkerdaily.com
Brochure	BestTemp Staffing Services. *An Employer's Guide to Staffing Services.* 2d ed. Denver: BestTemp Information Center, 2008.
Newspaper article, no author	"Might Be Harder Than It Looks." *Los Angeles Times,* 30 Jan. 2009: A22.
Magazine article	Dolan, Kerry A. "A Whole New Crop" *Forbes*, 2 June 2008: 72–75.
Television broadcast	Han, Daniel. "Trade Wars Heating Up Around the Globe." *CNN Headline News.* CNN, Atlanta. 5 Mar. 2002.
Internet, World Wide Web	"Intel—Company Capsule." *Hoover's Online.* 2008. Hoover's Company Information. 19 June 2008 http://www.hoovers.com/intel/-ID_13787/free-co-factsheet.xhtml
Book, component parts	Kuntz, Sonja. "Moving Beyond Benefits." *Our Changing Workforce.* Ed. Randolf Jacobson. New York: Citadel Press, 2001. 213–27.
Unpublished dissertation or thesis	Morales, George H. "The Economic Pressures on Industrialized Nations in a Global Economy." Diss. U of San Diego, 2001.
Paper presented at a meeting	Myers, Charles. "HMOs in Today's Environment." Conference on Medical Insurance Solutions. Chicago. 13 Aug. 2001.
CD-ROM encyclopedia article, one author	Parkings, Robert. "George Eastman." *The Concise Columbia Encyclopedia.* CD-ROM. New York: Columbia UP, 1998.
Interview	Stainer, Georgia, general manager, Day Cable and Communications. Telephone interview. 2 Mar. 2000.
Newspaper article, one author	Standish, Evelyn. "Global Market Crushes OPEC's Delicate Balance of Interests." *Wall Street Journal,* 19 Jan. 2002: A1.
Book, two authors	Toller, Miriam, and Jay Fielding. *Global Business for Smaller Companies.* Rocklin, CA: Prima Publishing, 2001.
Government publication	United States. Department of Defense. *Stretching Research Dollars: Survival Advice for Universities and Government Labs.* Washington: GPO, 2002.
Annual report	The Walt Disney Company, *2007 Annual Report.* Calif.: The Walt Disney Company, 2008.

Figure B.4   Sample Works Cited—MLA Style

- Italicize the names of books, newspapers, journals, and other complete publications, capitalizing all main words in the title.
- For journal articles, include the volume number and the issue number (if necessary). Include the year of publication inside parentheses and follow with a colon and the page range of the article: *Journal of Business Communication* 46, 1 (2009): 57. (In this source, the volume is 46, the number is 1, and the page is 57.)
- Electronic sources are less fixed than print sources, and they may not be readily accessible to readers. So citations for electronic sources must provide more information. Always try to be as comprehensive as possible, citing whatever information is available (however, see the note in the right column about extremely long URLs).

- The date for electronic sources should contain both the date assigned in the source (if no date is shown, write "n.d." instead) and the date accessed by the researcher.
- The URL for electronic sources must be as accurate and complete as possible, from access-mode identifier (such as http or ftp) to all relevant directory and file names. If the URL is extremely long, however, use the URL of the website's home page or the URL of the site's search page if you used the site's search function to find the article. Beginning with its 2009 edition, the MLA Style Manual no longer requires writers to include URLs for materials retrieved online. However, follow whatever guidelines your instructor gives you in this regard.
- Also beginning in 2009, MLA style requires you to indicate the medium of publication. For most sources, this will be "Web" or "Print," but you may also cite "CD-ROM" and other media, as appropriate.

Correction Symbols

Instructors often use these short, easy-to-remember correction symbols and abbreviations when evaluating students' writing. You can use them too, to understand your instructor's suggestions and to revise and proofread your own letters, memos, and reports. Refer to the Handbook of Grammar, Mechanics, and Usage (pp. H-1–H-25) for further information.

Content and Style

Acc	Accuracy. Check to be sure information is correct.
ACE	Avoid copying examples.
ACP	Avoid copying problems.
Adp	Adapt. Tailor message to reader.
App	Follow proper organization approach. (Refer to Chapter 4.)
Assign	Assignment. Review instructions for assignment.
AV	Active verb. Substitute active for passive.
Awk	Awkward phrasing. Rewrite.
BC	Be consistent.
BMS	Be more sincere.
Chop	Choppy sentences. Use longer sentences and more transitional phrases.
Con	Condense. Use fewer words.
CT	Conversational tone. Avoid using overly formal language.
Depers	Depersonalize. Avoid attributing credit or blame to any individual or group.
Dev	Develop. Provide greater detail.
Dir	Direct. Use direct approach; get to the point.
Emph	Emphasize. Develop this point more fully.
EW	Explanation weak. Check logic; provide more proof.
Fl	Flattery. Avoid compliments that are insincere.
FS	Figure of speech. Find a more accurate expression.
GNF	Good news first. Use direct order.
GRF	Give reasons first. Use indirect order.
GW	Goodwill. Put more emphasis on expressions of goodwill.
H/E	Honesty/ethics. Revise statement to reflect good business practices.
Imp	Imply. Avoid being direct.
Inc	Incomplete. Develop further.
Jar	Jargon. Use less specialized language.
Log	Logic. Check development of argument.

Neg	Negative. Use more positive approach or expression.
Obv	Obvious. Do not state point in such detail.
OC	Overconfident. Adopt humbler language.
OM	Omission.
Org	Organization. Strengthen outline.
OS	Off the subject. Close with point on main subject.
Par	Parallel. Use same structure.
Pom	Pompous. Rephrase in down-to-earth terms.
PV	Point of view. Make statement from reader's perspective rather than your own.
RB	Reader benefit. Explain what reader stands to gain.
Red	Redundant. Reduce number of times this point is made.
Ref	Reference. Cite source of information.
Rep	Repetitive. Provide different expression.
RS	Resale. Reassure reader that he or she has made a good choice.
SA	Service attitude. Put more emphasis on helping reader.
Sin	Sincerity. Avoid sounding glib or uncaring.
SL	Stereotyped language. Focus on individual's characteristics instead of on false generalizations.
Spec	Specific. Provide more specific statement.
SPM	Sales promotion material. Tell reader about related goods or services.
Stet	Let stand in original form.
Sub	Subordinate. Make this point less important.
SX	Sexist. Avoid language that contributes to gender stereotypes.
Tone	Tone needs improvement.
Trans	Transition. Show connection between points.
UAE	Use action ending. Close by stating what reader should do next.
UAS	Use appropriate salutation.
UAV	Use active voice.
Unc	Unclear. Rewrite to clarify meaning.
UPV	Use passive voice.
USS	Use shorter sentences.
V	Variety. Use different expression or sentence pattern.
W	Wordy. Eliminate unnecessary words.
WC	Word choice. Find a more appropriate word.
YA	"You" attitude. Rewrite to emphasize reader's needs.

Grammar, Mechanics, and Usage

Ab	Abbreviation. Avoid abbreviations in most cases; use correct abbreviation.
Adj	Adjective. Use adjective instead.
Adv	Adverb. Use adverb instead.
Agr	Agreement. Make subject and verb or noun and pronoun agree.
Ap	Appearance. Improve appearance.
Apos	Apostrophe. Check use of apostrophe.
Art	Article. Use correct article.
BC	Be consistent.
Cap	Capitalize.
Case	Use cases correctly.
CoAdj	Coordinate adjective. Insert comma between coordinate adjectives; delete comma between adjective and compound noun.
CS	Comma splice. Use period or semicolon to separate clauses.
DM	Dangling modifier. Rewrite so that modifier clearly relates to subject of sentence.
Exp	Expletive. Avoid expletive beginnings, such as it is, there are, there is, this is, and these are.
F	Format. Improve layout of document.
Frag	Fragment. Rewrite as complete sentence.
Gram	Grammar. Correct grammatical error.
HCA	Hyphenate compound adjective.
lc	Lowercase. Do not use capital letter.
M	Margins. Improve frame around document.
MM	Misplaced modifier. Place modifier close to word it modifies.
NRC	Nonrestrictive clause (or phrase). Separate from rest of sentence with commas.
P	Punctuation. Use correct punctuation.
Par	Parallel. Use same structure.
PH	Place higher. Move document up on page.
PL	Place lower. Move document down on page.
Prep	Preposition. Use correct preposition.
RC	Restrictive clause (or phrase). Remove commas that separate clause from rest of sentence.
RO	Run-on sentence. Separate two sentences with comma and coordinating conjunction or with semicolon.
SC	Series comma. Add comma before *and*.
SI	Split infinitive. Do not separate *to* from rest of verb.
Sp	Spelling error. Consult dictionary.
S-V	Subject-verb pair. Do not separate with comma.
Syl	Syllabification. Divide word between syllables.
WD	Word division. Check dictionary for proper end-of-line hyphenation.
WW	Wrong word. Replace with another word.

Proofreading Marks

Symbol	Meaning	Symbol Used in Context	Corrected Copy
═	Align horizontally	meaningful ͬᵉsult	meaningful result
‖	Align vertically	1. Power cable 2. Keyboard	1. Power cable 2. Keyboard
(bf)	Boldface	Recommendations (bf)	**Recommendations**
≡	Capitalize	Pepsico, Inc.	PepsiCo, Inc.
]⊏	Center	⌐Awards Banquet ⌐	Awards Banquet
◡	Close up space	self- confidence	self-confidence
ℓ	Delete	har/assment and abuse ℓ	harassment
(ds)	Double-space	text in first line text in second line] (ds)	text in first line text in second line
∧	Insert	ͧturquoise͜shirts and white	turquoise and white shirts
∨	Insert apostrophe	our teams goals	our team's goals
∧	Insert comma	a, b͜and c	a, b, and c
=/∧	Insert hyphen	third͜quarter sales	third-quarter sales
⊙	Insert period	Harrigan et al⊙	Harrigan et al.
∨ ∨	Insert quotation marks	This team isn't cooperating.	This "team" isn't cooperating.
#	Insert space	real/estate test/case	real estate test case
(ital)	Italics	Quarterly Report (ital)	*Quarterly Report*
/	Lowercase	TɄLSA, Ⱥouth of here	Tulsa, south of here
⌊__⌋	Move down	⌊Sincerely,⌋	Sincerely,
⊏	Move left	Attention: ⊏Security	Attention: Security
⊐	Move right	February 2, 2010 ⟍⊐	February 2, 2010
⌐ ⌐	Move up	⌐THIRD-QUARTER SALES⌐	THIRD-QUARTER SALES
(STET)	Restore	staff talked openly and frankly ℓ (STET)	staff talked openly
⟩	Run lines together	Manager,⟍ ⌐Distribution	Manager, Distribution
(ss)	Single space	⌐text in first line ⌊text in second line	text in first line text in second line
⬯	Spell out	(COD)	cash on delivery
(sp)	Spell out	(sp)(Assn. of Biochem. Engrs.)	Association of Biochemical Engineers
⌐⌐	Start new line	Marla Fenton,⌐Manager, Distri- bution	Marla Fenton, Manager, Distribution
¶	Start new paragraph	¶⌐The solution is easy to determine but difficult to implement in a competitive environment like the one we now face.	The solution is easy to determine but difficult to implement in a competitive environment like the one we now face.
∿	Transpose	airy,͜light,͜casɄɇl tone	light, airy, casual tone

Handbook of Grammar, Mechanics, and Usage

The rules of grammar, mechanics, and usage provide the guidance every professional needs in order to communicate successfully with colleagues, customers, and other audiences. Understanding and following these rules helps you in two important ways. First, the rules determine how meaning is encoded and decoded in the communication process. If you don't encode your messages using the same rules your readers or listeners use to decode them, chances are your audiences will not extract your intended meaning from your messages. Without a firm grasp of the basics of grammar, mechanics, and usage, you risk being misunderstood, damaging your company's image, losing money for your company, and possibly even losing your job. In other words, if you want to get your point across, you need to follow the rules of grammar, mechanics, and usage. Second, apart from transferring meaning successfully, following the rules tells your audience that you respect the conventions and expectations of the business community.

You can think of *grammar* as the agreed-upon structure of a language, the way that individual words are formed and the manner in which those words are then combined to form meaningful sentences. *Mechanics* are style and formatting issues such as capitalization, spelling, and the use of numbers and symbols. *Usage* involves the accepted and expected way in which specific words are used by a particular community of people—in this case, the community of businesspeople who use English. This handbook can help you improve your knowledge and awareness in all three areas. It is divided into the following sections:

- **Diagnostic Test of English Skills.** Testing your current knowledge of grammar, mechanics, and usage helps you find out where your strengths and weaknesses lie. This test offers 50 items taken from the topics included in this handbook.
- **Assessment of English Skills.** After completing the diagnostic test, use the assessment form to highlight the areas you most need to review.
- **Essentials of Grammar, Mechanics, and Usage.** This section helps you quickly review the basics. You can study the things you've probably already learned but may have forgotten about grammar, punctuation, mechanics (including capitalization, abbreviation, number style, and word division), and vocabulary (including frequently confused words, frequently misused words, frequently misspelled words, and transitional words and phrases). Practice sessions throughout this section help you test yourself and reinforce what you learn. Use this

essential review not only to study and improve your English skills but also as a reference for any questions you may have during this course.

Diagnostic Test of English Skills

Use this test to determine whether you need more practice with grammar, punctuation, mechanics, or vocabulary. When you've answered all the questions, ask your instructor for an answer sheet so that you can score the test. On the Assessment of English Skills form (page H-3), record the number of questions you answered incorrectly in each section.

The following choices apply to items 1–5. Write in each blank the letter of the choice that best describes the part of speech that is underlined.

A. noun
B. pronoun
C. verb
D. adjective
E. adverb
F. preposition
G. conjunction
H. article

_____ 1. The new branch location will be decided <u>by</u> next week.

_____ 2. We must hire only <u>qualified</u>, ambitious graduates.

_____ 3. After their <u>presentation,</u> I was still undecided.

_____ 4. See <u>me</u> after the meeting.

_____ 5. Margaret, pressed for time, turned in <u>unusually</u> sloppy work.

In the blanks for items 6–15, write the letter of the word or phrase that best completes each sentence.

_____ 6. (A. Russ's, B. Russ') laptop was stolen last week.

_____ 7. Speaking only for (A. me, B. myself), I think the new policy is discriminatory.

_____ 8. Of the five candidates we interviewed yesterday, (A. who, B. whom) do you believe is the best choice?

_____ 9. India has increased (A. it's, B. its) imports of corn and rice.

_____ 10. Anyone who wants to be (A. their, B. his or her) own boss should think about owning a franchise.

_____ 11. If the IT department can't (A. lie, B. lay) the fiber-optic cable by March 1, the plant will not open on schedule.

____ 12. Starbucks (A. is, B. are) opening five new stores in San Diego in the next year.

____ 13. The number of women-owned small businesses (A. has, B. have) increased sharply in the past two decades.

____ 14. Greg and Bernyce worked (A. good, B. well) together.

____ 15. They distributed the supplies (A. among, B. between) the six staff members.

The following choices apply to items 16–20. Write in each blank the letter of the choice that best describes the sentence structure problem with each item.

A. sentence fragment
B. comma splice
C. misplaced modifier
D. fused sentence
E. lack of parallelism
F. unclear antecedent

____ 16. The number of employees who took the buyout offer was much higher than expected, now the entire company is understaffed.

____ 17. The leader in Internet-only banking.

____ 18. Diamond doesn't actually sell financial products rather it acts as an intermediary.

____ 19. Helen's proposal is for not only the present but also for the future.

____ 20. When purchasing luxury products, quality is more important than price for consumers.

For items 21–30, circle the letter of the preferred choice in each of the following groups of sentences.

21. A. What do you think of the ad slogan "Have it your way?"
    B. What do you think of the ad slogan "Have it your way"?

22. A. Send copies to Jackie Cross, Uniline, Brad Nardi, Peale & Associates, and Tom Griesbaum, MatchMakers.
    B. Send copies to Jackie Cross, Uniline; Brad Nardi, Peale & Associates; and Tom Griesbaum, MatchMakers.

23. A. They've recorded 22 complaints since yesterday, all of them from long-time employees.
    B. They've recorded 22 complaints since yesterday; all of them from long-time employees.

24. A. We are looking for two qualities in applicants: experience with computers and an interest in people.
    B. We are looking for two qualities in applicants; experience with computers and an interest in people.

25. A. At the Center for the Blind the clients we serve have lost vision, due to a wide variety of causes.
    B. At the Center for the Blind, the clients we serve have lost vision due to a wide variety of causes.

26. A. Replace your standard lightbulbs with new, compact fluorescent bulbs.
    B. Replace your standard lightbulbs with new, compact, fluorescent bulbs.
    C. Replace your standard lightbulbs with new compact fluorescent bulbs.

27. A. Blue Cross of California may have changed its name to Anthem Blue Cross but the company still has the same commitment to California.
    B. Blue Cross of California may have changed its name to Anthem Blue Cross, but the company still has the same commitment to California.

28. A. Only eight banks in this country—maybe nine can handle transactions of this magnitude.
    B. Only eight banks in this country—maybe nine—can handle transactions of this magnitude.

29. A. Instead of focusing on high-growth companies, we targeted mature businesses with only one or two people handling the decision making
    B. Instead of focusing on high growth companies, we targeted mature businesses with only one or two people handling the decision-making.

30. A. According to board president Damian Cabaza "having a crisis communication plan is a high priority."
    B. According to board president Damian Cabaza, "Having a crisis communication plan is a high priority."

For items 31–40, select the best choice from among those provided.

31. A. At her previous employer, Mary-Anne worked in Marketing Communications and Human Resources.
    B. At her previous employer, Mary-Anne worked in marketing communications and human resources.

32. A. By fall, we'll have a dozen locations between the Mississippi and Missouri rivers.
    B. By Fall, we'll have a dozen locations between the Mississippi and Missouri Rivers.

33. A. The Board applauded President Donlan upon her reelection for a fifth term.
    B. The board applauded president Donlan upon her reelection for a fifth term.
    C. The board applauded President Donlan upon her re-election for a fifth term.

34. A. If you want to travel to France, you need to be au courant with the business practices.
    B. If you want to travel to France, you need to be "au courant" with the business practices.

35. A. As the company's CEO, Thomas Spurgeon handles all dealings with the FDA.
    B. As the company's C.E.O., Thomas Spurgeon handles all dealings with the F.D.A.

36. A. The maximum speed limit in most states is 65 mph.
    B. The maximum speed limit in most states is 65 m.p.h.

37. A. Sales of graphic novels increased nine percent between 2008 and 2009.
    B. Sales of graphic novels increased 9 percent between 2008 and 2009.

38. A. Our store is open daily from nine a.m. to seven P.M.
    B. Our store is open daily from 9:00 A.M. to 7:00 P.M.

39. A. The organizing meeting is scheduled for July 27, and the event will be held in January 2012.
    B. The organizing meeting is scheduled for July 27th, and the event will be held in January, 2012.

40. A. We need six desks, eight file cabinets, and 12 trashcans.
   B. We need 6 desks, 8 file cabinets, and 12 trashcans.

For items 41–50, write in each blank the letter of the word that best completes each sentence.

_____ **41.** Will having a degree (A. affect, B. effect) my chances for promotion?

_____ **42.** Try not to (A. loose, B. lose) this key; we will charge you a fee to replace it.

_____ **43.** I don't want to discuss my (A. personal, B. personnel) problems in front of anyone.

_____ **44.** Let us help you choose the right tie to (A. complement, B. compliment) your look.

_____ **45.** The repairman's whistling (A. aggravated, B. irritated) all of us in accounting.

_____ **46.** The bank agreed to (A. loan, B. lend) the Smiths $20,000 for their start-up.

_____ **47.** The credit card company is (A. liable, B. likely) to increase your interest rate if you miss a payment.

_____ **48.** The airline tries to (A. accommodate, B. accomodate) disabled passengers.

_____ **49.** Every company needs a policy regarding sexual (A. harrassment, B. harassment).

_____ **50.** Use your best (A. judgment, B. judgement) in selecting a service provider.

Assessment of English Skills

In the space provided, record the number of questions you answered incorrectly.

Questions	Skills Area	Number of Incorrect Answers
1–5	Parts of speech	_____
6–15	Usage	_____
16–20	Sentence structure	_____
21–30	Punctuation	_____
31–40	Mechanics	_____
41–50	Vocabulary	_____

If you had more than two incorrect answers in any of the skills areas, focus on those areas in the appropriate sections of this handbook.

Essentials of Grammar, Mechanics, and Usage

The following sentence looks innocent, but is it really?

> We sell tuxedos as well as rent.

You sell tuxedos, but it's highly unlikely that you sell rent—which is what this sentence says. Whatever you're selling, some people will ignore your message because of a blunder like this. The following sentence has a similar problem:

> Vice President Eldon Neale told his chief engineer that he would no longer be with Avix, Inc., as of June 30.

Is Eldon or the engineer leaving? No matter which side the facts are on, the sentence can be read the other way. Now look at this sentence:

> The year before we budgeted more for advertising sales were up.

Confused? Perhaps this is what the writer meant:

> The year before, we budgeted more for advertising. Sales were up.

Or maybe the writer meant this:

> The year before we budgeted more for advertising, sales were up.

These examples show that even short, simple sentences can be misunderstood because of errors on the part of the writer. As you've learned in numerous courses over your schooling, an English sentence consists of the parts of speech being combined with punctuation, mechanics, and vocabulary to convey meaning. Making a point of brushing up on your grammar, punctuation, mechanics, and vocabulary skills will help ensure that you create clear, effective business messages.

1.0 Grammar

Grammar is the study of how words come together to form sentences. Categorized by meaning, form, and function, English words fall into various parts of speech: nouns, pronouns, verbs, adjectives, adverbs, prepositions, conjunctions, articles, and interjections. You will communicate more clearly if you understand how each of these parts of speech operates in a sentence.

1.1 NOUNS

A **noun** names a person, a place, a thing, or an idea. Anything you can see or detect with one of your senses has a noun to name it. Some things you can't see or sense are also nouns—ions, for example, or space. So are things that exist as ideas, such as accuracy and height. (You can see that something is accurate or that a building is tall, but you can't see the idea of accuracy or the idea of height.) These names for ideas are known as **abstract nouns**. The simplest nouns are the names of things you can see or touch: _car_, _building_, _cloud_, _brick_; these are termed **concrete nouns**. A few nouns, such as _algorithm_, _software_, and _code_, are difficult to categorize as either abstract or concrete but can reasonably be considered concrete even though they don't have a physical presence.

1.1.1 Proper Nouns and Common Nouns

So far, all the examples of nouns have been **common nouns**, referring to general classes of things. The word *building* refers to a whole class of structures. Common nouns such as *building* are not capitalized.

If you want to talk about one particular building, however, you might refer to the Glazier Building. The name is capitalized, indicating that *Glazier Building* is a **proper noun**.

Here are three sets of common and proper nouns for comparison:

Common	Proper
city	Kansas City
company	Blaisden Company
store	Books Galore

1.1.2 Nouns as Subject and Object

Nouns may be used in sentences as subjects or objects. That is, the person, place, thing, or idea that is being or doing (subject) is represented by a noun. So is the person, place, idea, or thing that is being acted on (object). In the following sentence, the nouns are underlined:

The <u>web designer</u> created the <u>homepage</u>.

The web designer (subject) is acting in a way that affects the homepage (object). The following sentence is more complicated:

The <u>installer</u> delivered the <u>carpet</u> to the <u>customer</u>.

Installer is the subject. *Carpet* is the object of the main part of the sentence (acted on by the installer), and *customer* is the object of the phrase *to the customer*. Nevertheless, both *carpet* and *customer* are objects.

1.1.3 Plural Nouns

Nouns can be either singular or plural. The usual way to make a plural noun is to add *s* or *es* to the singular form of the word:

Singular	Plural
file	files
tax	taxes
cargo	cargoes

Many nouns have other ways of forming the plural. Some plurals involve a change in a vowel (*mouse/mice, goose/geese, woman/women*), the addition of *en* or *ren* (*ox/oxen, child/children*), the change from *y* to *ies* (*city/cities, specialty/specialties*), or the change from *f* to *v* (*knife/knives, half/halves;* some exceptions: *fifes, roofs*). Some words of Latin origin offer a choice of plurals (*phenomena/phenomenons, indexes/indices, appendixes/appendices*). It's always a good idea to consult a dictionary if you are unsure of the correct or preferred plural spelling of a word.

The plurals of compound nouns are usually formed by adding *s* or *es* to the main word of the compound (*fathers-in-law, editors-in-chief, attorneys-at-law*).

Some nouns are the same whether singular or plural (*sleep, deer, moose*). Some nouns are plural in form but singular in use (*ethics, measles*). Some nouns are used in the plural only (*scissors, trousers*).

Letters, numbers, and words used as words are sometimes made plural by adding an apostrophe and an *s* (*A's, Ph.D.'s, I's*). However, if no confusion would be created by leaving off the apostrophe, it is common practice to just add the *s* (*1990s, RFPs, DVDs*).

1.1.4 Possessive Nouns

A noun becomes possessive when it's used to show the ownership of something. Then you add *'s* to the word:

the man's car   the woman's apartment

However, ownership does not need to be legal:

the secretary's desk   the company's assets

Also, ownership may be nothing more than an automatic association:

a day's work   the job's prestige

An exception to the rule about adding *'s* to make a noun possessive occurs when the word is singular and already has two "s" sounds at the end. In cases like the following, an apostrophe is all that's needed:

crisis' dimensions   Mr. Moses' application

When the noun has only one "s" sound at the end, however, retain the *'s:*

Chris's book   Carolyn Nuss's office

With compound (hyphenated) nouns, add *'s* to the last word:

Compound Noun	Possessive Noun
mother-in-law	mother-in-law's
mayor-elect	mayor-elect's

To form the possessive of plural nouns, just begin by following the same rule as with singular nouns: add *'s*. However, if the plural noun already ends in an *s* (as most do), drop the one you've added, leaving only the apostrophe:

the clients' complaints   employees' benefits

To denote joint possession by two or more proper nouns, add the *'s* to the last name only (*Moody, Nation, and Smith's* ad agency). To denote individual possession by two or more persons, add an *'s* to each proper noun (*Moody's, Nation's, and Smith's* ad agencies).

1.1.5 Collective Nouns

Collective nouns encompass a group of people or objects: *crowd, jury, committee, team, audience, family, couple, herd, class*. They are often treated as singular nouns. (For more on collective nouns, see Section 1.3.4, Subject–Verb Agreement.)

1.2 PRONOUNS

A **pronoun** is a word that stands for a noun; it saves repeating the noun:

> Employees have some choice of weeks for vacation, but *they* must notify the HR office of *their* preference by March 1.

The pronouns *they* and *their* stand in for the noun *employees*. The noun that a pronoun stands for is called the **antecedent** of the pronoun; *employees* is the antecedent of *they* and *their*.

When the antecedent is plural, the pronoun that stands in for it has to be plural; *they* and *their* are plural pronouns because *employees* is plural. Likewise, when the antecedent is singular, the pronoun has to be singular:

> We thought the contract had expired, but we soon learned that *it* had not.

1.2.1 Multiple Antecedents

Sometimes a pronoun has a double (or even a triple) antecedent:

> Kathryn Boettcher and Luis Gutierrez went beyond *their* sales quotas for January.

If taken alone, *Kathryn Boettcher* is a singular antecedent. So is *Luis Gutierrez*. However, when together they are the plural antecedent of a pronoun, so the pronoun has to be plural. Thus the pronoun is *their* instead of *her* or *his*.

1.2.2 Unclear Antecedents

In some sentences the pronoun's antecedent is unclear:

> Sandy Wright sent Jane Brougham *her* production figures for the previous year. *She* thought they were too low.

To which person does the pronoun *her* refer? Someone who knew Sandy and Jane and knew their business relationship might be able to figure out the antecedent for *her*. Even with such an advantage, however, a reader might receive the wrong meaning. Also, it would be nearly impossible for any reader to know which name is the antecedent of *she*.

The best way to clarify an ambiguous pronoun is usually to rewrite the sentence, repeating nouns when needed for clarity:

> Sandy Wright sent her production figures for the previous year to Jane Brougham. Jane thought they were too low.

The noun needs to be repeated only when the antecedent is unclear.

1.2.3 Pronoun Classes

Personal pronouns consist of *I, you, we/us, he/him, she/her, it,* and *they/them.*

Compound personal pronouns are created by adding *self* or *selves* to simple personal pronouns: *myself, ourselves, yourself, yourselves, himself, herself, itself, themselves.* Compound personal pronouns are used either *intensively,* to emphasize the identity of the noun or pronoun (I *myself* have seen the demonstration), or *reflexively,* to indicate that the subject is the receiver of his or her own action (I promised *myself* I'd finish by noon). Compound personal pronouns are used incorrectly if they appear in a sentence without their antecedent:

> Walter, Virginia, and *I* (not *myself*) are the top salespeople.
>
> You need to tell *her* (not *herself*) about the mixup.

Relative pronouns refer to nouns (or groups of words used as nouns) in the main clause and are used to introduce clauses:

> Purina is the brand *that* most dog owners purchase.

The relative pronouns are *which, who, whom, whose,* and *what.* Other words used as relative pronouns include *that, whoever, whomever, whatever,* and *whichever.*

Interrogative pronouns are those used for asking questions: *who, whom, whose, which,* and *what.*

Demonstrative pronouns point out particular persons, places, or things:

> *That* is my desk.   *This* can't be correct.

The demonstrative pronouns are *this, these, that,* and *those.*

Indefinite pronouns refer to persons or things not specifically identified. They include *anyone, someone, everyone, everybody, somebody, either, neither, one, none, all, both, each, another, any, many,* and similar words.

1.2.4 Case of Pronouns

The case of a pronoun tells whether it's acting or acted upon:

> *She* sells an average of five packages each week.

In this sentence, *she* is doing the selling. Because *she* is acting, *she* is said to be in the **nominative case.** Now consider what happens when the pronoun is acted upon:

> After six months, Ms. Browning promoted *her.*

In this sentence, the pronoun *her* is acted upon and is thus said to be in the **objective case.**

Contrast the nominative and objective pronouns in this list:

Nominative	Objective
I	me
we	us
he	him
she	her
they	them
who	whom
whoever	whomever

Objective pronouns may be used as either the object of a verb (such as *promoted*) or the object of a preposition (such as *with*):

> Rob worked with *them* until the order was filled.

In this example, *them* is the object of the preposition *with* because Rob acted upon—worked with—them. Here's a sentence with three pronouns, the first one nominative, the second the object of a verb, and the third the object of a preposition:

> *He* paid *us* as soon as the check came from *them.*

He is nominative; *us* is objective because it's the object of the verb *paid; them* is objective because it's the object of the preposition *from.*

Every writer sometimes wonders whether to use *who* or *whom:*

> (*Who, Whom*) will you hire?

Because this sentence is a question, it's difficult to see that *whom* is the object of the verb *hire.* You can figure out which pronoun to use if you rearrange the question and temporarily try *she* and *her* in place of *who* and *whom:* "Will you hire *she?*" or "Will you hire *her?*" *Her* and *whom* are both objective, so the correct choice is "Whom will you hire?" Here's a different example:

> (*Who, Whom*) logged so much travel time?

Turning the question into a statement, you get:

> He logged so much travel time.

Therefore, the correct statement is:

> Who logged so much travel time?

1.2.5 Possessive Pronouns

Possessive pronouns work like possessive nouns—they show ownership or automatic association:

her job	their preferences
his account	its equipment

However, possessive pronouns are different from possessive nouns in the way they are written. Possessive pronouns never have an apostrophe:

Possessive Noun	**Possessive Pronoun**
the woman's estate	her estate
Roger Franklin's plans	his plans
the shareholders' feelings	their feelings
the vacuum cleaner's attachments	its attachments

The word *its* is the possessive of *it.* Like all other possessive pronouns, *its* has no apostrophe. Some people confuse *its* with *it's,* the contraction of *it is.* (Contractions are discussed in Section 2.9, Apostrophes.)

1.2.6 Pronoun–Antecedent Agreement

Like nouns, pronouns can be singular or plural. Pronouns must agree in number with their antecedents—a singular antecedent requires a singular pronoun:

> The president of the board tendered *his* resignation.

Multiple antecedents require a plural pronoun:

> The members of the board tendered *their* resignations.

A pronoun referring to singular antecedents connected by *or* or *nor* should be singular:

> Neither Sean nor Terry made his quota.

But a pronoun referring to a plural and a singular antecedent connected by *or* or *nor* should be plural:

> Neither Sean nor the twins made *their* quotas.

Formal English prefers the nominative case after the linking verb *to be:*

> It is *I.*   That is *he.*

However, for general usage it's perfectly acceptable to use the more natural "It's me" and "That's him."

1.3 VERBS

A **verb** describes an action or acts as a link between a subject and words that define or describe that subject:

> They all *quit* in disgust.
> Working conditions *were* substandard.

The English language is full of **action verbs**. Here are a few you'll often run across in the business world:

verify	perform	fulfill
hire	succeed	send
leave	improve	receive
accept	develop	pay

You could undoubtedly list many more.

The most common linking verbs are all the forms of *to be:* I *am, was,* or *will be;* you *are, were,* or *will be.* Other words that can serve as linking verbs include *seem, become, appear, prove, look, remain, feel, taste, smell, sound, resemble, turn,* and *grow:*

> It *seemed* a good plan at the time.
>
> She *sounds* impressive at a meeting.
>
> The time *grows* near for us to make a decision.

These verbs link what comes before them in the sentence with what comes after; no action is involved. (See Section 1.7.5 for a fuller discussion of linking verbs.)

An **auxiliary verb** is one that helps another verb and is used for showing tense, voice, and so on. A verb with its helpers is called a **verb phrase.** Verbs used as auxiliaries include *do, did, have, may, can, must, shall, might, could, would,* and *should.*

1.3.1 Verb Tenses

English has three simple verb tenses: present, past, and future.

Present:	Our branches in Hawaii *stock* other items.
Past:	We *stocked* Purquil pens for a short time.
Future:	Rotex Tire Stores *will stock* your line of tires when you begin a program of effective national advertising.

With most verbs (the regular ones), the past tense ends in *ed*, and the future tense always has *will* or *shall* in front of it. But the present tense is more complex, depending on the subject:

	First Person	**Second Person**	**Third Person**
Singular	I stock	you stock	he/she/it stocks
Plural	we stock	you stock	they stock

The basic form, *stock*, takes an additional *s* when *he, she*, or *it* precedes it. (See Section 1.3.4 for more on subject–verb agreement.)

In addition to the three simple tenses, the three **perfect tenses** are created by adding forms of the auxiliary verb *have*. The present perfect tense uses the past participle (regularly the past tense) of the main verb, *stocked*, and adds the present-tense *have* or *has* to the front of it:

(I, we, you, they) *have stocked.*

(He, she, it) *has stocked.*

The past perfect tense uses the past participle of the main verb, *stocked*, and adds the past-tense *had* to the front of it:

(I, you, he, she, it, we, they) *had stocked.*

The future perfect tense also uses the past participle of the main verb, *stocked*, but adds the future-tense *will have*:

(I, you, he, she, it, we, they) *will have stocked.*

Verbs should be kept in the same tense when the actions occur at the same time:

When the payroll checks *came in*, everyone *showed up* for work.

We *have found* that everyone *has pitched* in to help.

When the actions occur at different times, you may change tense accordingly:

The shipment *came* last Wednesday, so if another one *comes* in today, please return it.

The new employee *had been* ill at ease, but now she *has become* a full-fledged member of the team.

1.3.2 Irregular Verbs

Many verbs don't follow some of the standard patterns for verb tenses. The most irregular of these verbs is *to be*:

Tense	Singular	Plural
Present:	I *am*	we *are*
	you *are*	you *are*
	he, she, it *is*	they *are*
Past:	I *was*	we *were*
	you *were*	you *were*
	he, she, it *was*	they *were*

The future tense of *to be* is formed in the same way that the future tense of a regular verb is formed.

The perfect tenses of *to be* are also formed as they would be for a regular verb, except that the past participle is a special form, *been*, instead of just the past tense:

Present perfect:	you have been
Past perfect:	you had been
Future perfect:	you will have been

Here's a sampling of other irregular verbs:

Present	**Past**	**Past Participle**
begin	began	begun
shrink	shrank	shrunk
know	knew	known
rise	rose	risen
become	became	become
go	went	gone
do	did	done

Dictionaries list the various forms of other irregular verbs.

1.3.3 Transitive and Intransitive Verbs

Many people are confused by three particular sets of verbs:

lie/lay   sit/set   rise/raise

Using these verbs correctly is much easier when you learn the difference between transitive and intransitive verbs.

Transitive verbs require a receiver; they "transfer" their action to an object. Intransitive verbs do not have a receiver for their action. Some intransitive verbs are complete in themselves and need no help from other words (prices *dropped*; we *won*). Other intransitive words must be "completed" by a noun or adjective called a **complement**. Complements occur with linking verbs.

Here are some sample uses of transitive and intransitive verbs:

Intransitive	**Transitive**
We should include in our new offices a place to *lie* down for a nap.	The workers will be here on Monday to *lay* new carpeting.
Even the way an interviewee *sits* is important.	That crate is full of stemware, so *set* it down carefully.
Salaries at Compu-Link, Inc., *rise* swiftly.	They *raise* their level of production every year.

The workers *lay* carpeting, you *set down* the crate, they *raise* production; each action is transferred to something. In the intransitive sentences, a person *lies down*, an interviewee *sits*, and salaries *rise* without affecting anything else. Intransitive sentences are complete with only a subject and a verb; transitive sentences are not complete unless they also include an object; or something to transfer the action to.

Tenses are a confusing element of the lie/lay problem:

Present	Past	Past Participle
I *lie*	I *lay*	I *have lain*
I *lay* (something down)	I *laid* (something down)	I *have laid* (something down)

The past tense of *lie* and the present tense of *lay* look and sound alike, even though they're different verbs.

1.3.4 Subject–Verb Agreement

Whether regular or irregular, every verb must agree with its subject, both in person (first, second, or third) and in number (single or plural).

	First Person	Second Person	Third Person
Singular	I *am*	you *are*	he/she/it *is*
	I *write*	you *write*	he/she/it *writes*
Plural	we *are*	you *are*	they *are*
	we *write*	you *write*	they *write*

In a simple sentence, making a verb agree with its subject is a straightforward task:

Hector Ruiz *is* a strong competitor. (third-person singular)

We *write* to you every month. (first-person plural)

Confusion sometimes arises when sentences are a bit more complicated. For example, be sure to avoid agreement problems when words come between the subject and verb. In the following examples, the verb appears in italics, and its subject is underlined:

The <u>analysis</u> of existing documents *takes* a full week.

Even though *documents* is a plural, the verb is in the singular form. That's because the subject of the sentence is *analysis*, a singular noun. The phrase *of existing documents* can be disregarded. Here is another example:

The <u>answers</u> for this exercise *are* in the study guide.

Take away the phrase *for this exercise* and you are left with the plural subject *answers*. Therefore, the verb takes the plural form.

Verb agreement is also complicated when the subject is a collective noun or pronoun or when the subject may be considered either singular or plural. In such cases, you often have to analyze the surrounding sentence to determine which verb form to use:

The <u>staff</u> *is* quartered in the warehouse.

The <u>staff</u> *are* at their desks in the warehouse.

The <u>computers</u> and the <u>staff</u> *are* in the warehouse.

Neither the staff nor the <u>computers</u> *are* in the warehouse.

<u>Every</u> computer *is* in the warehouse.

Many a <u>computer</u> *is* in the warehouse.

Did you notice that words such as *every* use the singular verb form? In addition, when an *either/or* or a *neither/nor* phrase combines singular and plural nouns, the verb takes the form that matches the noun closest to it.

In the business world, some subjects require extra attention. Company names, for example, are considered singular and therefore take a singular verb in most cases—even if they contain plural words:

Stater Brothers *offers* convenient grocery shopping.

In addition, quantities are sometimes considered singular and sometimes plural. If a quantity refers to a total amount, it takes a singular verb; if a quantity refers to individual, countable units, it takes a plural verb:

Three hours *is* a long time.

The eight dollars we collected for the fund *are* tacked on the bulletin board.

Fractions may also be singular or plural, depending on the noun that accompanies them:

One-third of the warehouse *is* devoted to this product line.

One-third of the products *are* defective.

To decide whether to use a singular or plural verb with subjects such as *number* and *variety*, follow this simple rule: If the subject is preceded by *a*, use a plural verb:

A number of products *are* being displayed at the trade show.

If the subject is preceded by *the*, use a singular verb:

The variety of products on display *is* mind-boggling.

For a related discussion, see Section 1.7.1, Longer Sentences.

1.3.5 Voice of Verbs

Verbs have two voices, active and passive. When the subject comes first, the verb is in **active voice**; when the object comes first, the verb is in **passive voice**:

Active: The buyer *paid* a large amount.

Passive: A large amount *was paid* by the buyer.

The passive voice uses a form of the verb *to be*, which adds words to a sentence. In the example, the passive-voice sentence uses eight words, whereas the active-voice sentence uses only six to say the same thing. The words *was* and *by* are unnecessary to convey the meaning of the sentence. In fact, extra words usually clog meaning. So be sure to opt for the active voice when you have a choice.

At times, however, you have no choice:

Several items *have been taken*, but so far we don't know who took them.

The passive voice becomes necessary when you don't know (or don't want to say) who performed the action; the active voice is bolder and more direct.

1.3.6 Mood of Verbs

Verbs can express one of three moods: indicative, imperative, or subjunctive. The **indicative mood** is used to make a statement or to ask a question:

The secretary mailed a letter to each supplier.

<u>Did the secretary mail a letter to each supplier?</u>

Use the **imperative mood** when you wish to command or request:

Please mail a letter to each supplier.

With the imperative mood, the subject is the understood *you*.

The **subjunctive mood** is used to express doubt or a wish or a condition contrary to fact:

If I *were* you, I wouldn't send that email.

The subjunctive is also used to express a suggestion or a request:

I asked that Rosario *be* [not *is*] present at the meeting.

1.3.7 Verbals

Verbals are verbs that are modified to function as other parts of speech. They include infinitives, gerunds, and participles.

Infinitives are formed by placing a *to* in front of the verb (*to go*, *to purchase*, *to work*). They function as nouns. Although many of us were taught that it is "incorrect" to split an infinitive—that is, to place an adverb between the *to* and the verb—that rule is not a hard and fast one. In some cases, the adverb is best placed in the middle of the infinitive to avoid awkward constructions or ambiguous meaning:

Production of steel is expected to *moderately exceed* domestic use.

Gerunds are verbals formed by adding *ing* to a verb (*going*, *having*, *working*). Like infinitives, they function as nouns. Gerunds and gerund phrases take a singular verb:

Borrowing from banks *is* preferable to getting venture capital.

Participles are verb forms used as adjectives. The present participle ends in *ing* and generally describes action going on at the same time as other action:

Checking the schedule, the contractor was pleased with progress on the project.

The past participle is usually the same form as the past tense and generally indicates completed action:

When *completed*, the project will occupy six city blocks.

The **perfect participle** is formed by adding *having* to the past participle:

Having completed the project, the contractor submitted his last invoice.

1.4 ADJECTIVES

An **adjective** modifies (tells something about) a noun or pronoun. Each of the following phrases says more about the noun or pronoun than the noun or pronoun would say alone:

an *efficient* staff   a *heavy* price

brisk trade   *light* web traffic

Adjectives modify nouns more often than they modify pronouns. When adjectives do modify pronouns, however, the sentence usually has a linking verb:

They were *attentive*.   It looked *appropriate*.

He seems *interested*.   You are *skillful*.

1.4.1 Types of Adjectives

Adjectives serve a variety of purposes. **Descriptive adjectives** express some quality belonging to the modified item (*tall*, *successful*, *green*). **Limiting or definitive adjectives**, on the other hand, point out the modified item or limit its meaning without expressing a quality. Types include:

- Numeral adjectives (one, fifty, second)
- Articles (a, an, the)
- Pronominal adjectives: pronouns used as adjectives (his desk, each employee)
- Demonstrative adjectives: this, these, that, those (these tires, that invoice)

Proper adjectives are derived from proper nouns:

Chinese customs   *Orwellian* overtones

Predicate adjectives complete the meaning of the predicate and are introduced by linking verbs:

The location is *perfect*.   Prices are *high*.

1.4.2 Comparative Degree

Most adjectives can take three forms: simple, comparative, and superlative. The simple form modifies a single noun or pronoun. Use the comparative form when comparing two items. When comparing three or more items, use the superlative form:

Simple	Comparative	Superlative
hard	harder	hardest
safe	safer	safest
dry	drier	driest

The comparative form adds *er* to the simple form, and the superlative form adds *est*. (The *y* at the end of a word changes to *i* before the *er* or *est* is added.)

A small number of adjectives are irregular, including these:

Simple	Comparative	Superlative
good	better	best
bad	worse	worst
little	less	least

When the simple form of an adjective has two or more syllables, you usually add *more* to form the comparative and *most* to form the superlative:

Simple	Comparative	Superlative
useful	more useful	most useful
exhausting	more exhausting	most exhausting
expensive	more expensive	most expensive

The most common exceptions are two-syllable adjectives that end in *y*:

Simple	Comparative	Superlative
happy	happier	happiest
costly	costlier	costliest

If you choose this option, change the *y* to *i* and tack *er* or *est* onto the end.

Some adjectives cannot be used to make comparisons because they themselves indicate the extreme. For example, if something is perfect, nothing can be more perfect. If something is unique or ultimate, nothing can be more unique or more ultimate.

1.4.3 Hyphenated Adjectives

Many adjectives used in the business world are actually combinations of words: *up-to-date* report, *last-minute* effort, *fifth-floor* suite, *well-built* engine. As you can see, they are hyphenated when they come before the noun they modify. However, when such word combinations come after the noun they modify, they are not hyphenated. In the following example, the adjectives appear in italics and the nouns they modify are underlined:

> The <u>report</u> is *up to date* because of our team's *last-minute* <u>efforts</u>.

Hyphens are not used when part of the combination is a word ending in *ly* (because that word is usually not an adjective). Hyphens are also omitted from word combinations that are used so frequently that readers are used to seeing the words together:

> We live in a *rapidly shrinking* world.
>
> Our *highly motivated* employees will be well paid.
>
> Please consider renewing your *credit card* account.
>
> Send those figures to our *data processing* department.
>
> Our new intern is a *high school* student.

1.5 ADVERBS

An **adverb** modifies a verb, an adjective, or another adverb:

Modifying a verb:	Our marketing department works *efficiently*.
Modifying an adjective:	She was not dependable, although she was *highly* intelligent.
Modifying another adverb:	When signing new clients, he moved *extremely* cautiously.

An adverb can be a single word (*clearly*), a phrase (*very clearly*), or a clause (*because it was clear*).

1.5.1 Types of Adverbs

Simple adverbs are simple modifiers:

> The door opened *automatically*.
>
> The order arrived *yesterday*.
>
> Top companies were *there*.

Interrogative adverbs ask a question:

> *Where* have you been?

Conjunctive adverbs connect clauses:

> We can't start *until* Maria gets here.
>
> Jorge tried to explain *how* the new software works.

Words frequently used as conjunctive adverbs include *where*, *wherever*, *when*, *whenever*, *while*, *as*, *how*, *why*, *before*, *after*, *until*, and *since*.

Negative adverbs include *not*, *never*, *seldom*, *rarely*, *scarcely*, *hardly*, and similar words. Negative adverbs are powerful words and therefore do not need any help in conveying a negative thought. Avoid using double negatives like these:

> I don't want no mistakes.
>
> (Correct: "I don't want any mistakes," or "I want no mistakes.")
>
> They couldn't hardly read the report.
>
> (Correct: "They could hardly read the report," or "They couldn't read the report.")
>
> They scarcely noticed neither one.
>
> (Correct: "They scarcely noticed either one," or "They noticed neither one.")

1.5.2 Adverb–Adjective Confusion

Many adverbs are adjectives turned into adverbs by adding *ly*: *highly*, *extremely*, *officially*, *closely*, *really*. In addition, many words can be adjectives or adverbs, depending on their usage in a particular sentence:

The *early* bird gets the worm. [adjective]	We arrived *early*. [adverb]
It was a *hard* decision. [adjective]	He hit the wall *hard*. [adverb]

Because of this situation, some adverbs are difficult to distinguish from adjectives. For example, in the following sentences, is the underlined word an adverb or an adjective?

> They worked <u>well</u>.
>
> The baby is <u>well</u>.

In the first sentence, *well* is an adverb modifying the verb *worked*. In the second sentence, *well* is an adjective modifying the noun *baby*. To choose correctly between adverbs and adjectives, remember that linking verbs are used to connect an adjective to describe a noun. In contrast, you would use an adverb to describe an action verb:

Adjective	Adverb
He is a *good* worker. (What kind of worker is he?)	He works *well*. (How does he work?)
It is a *real* computer. (What kind of computer is it?)	It *really* is a computer. (To what extent is it a computer?)

Adjective	Adverb
The traffic is *slow*. (What quality does the traffic have?)	The traffic moves *slowly*. (How does the traffic move?)
This food tastes *bad* without salt. (What quality does the food have?)	This food *badly* needs salt. (How much is it needed?)

1.5.3 Comparative Degree

Like adjectives, adverbs can be used to compare items. Generally, the basic adverb is combined with *more* or *most*, just as long adjectives are. However, some adverbs have one-word comparative forms:

One Item	Two Items	Three Items
quickly	more quickly	most quickly
sincerely	less sincerely	least sincerely
fast	faster	fastest
well	better	best

1.6 OTHER PARTS OF SPEECH

Nouns, pronouns, verbs, adjectives, and adverbs carry most of the meaning in a sentence. Four other parts of speech link them together in sentences: prepositions, conjunctions, articles, and interjections.

1.6.1 Prepositions

A preposition is a word or group of words that describes a relationship between other words in a sentence. A simple preposition is made up of one word: *of, in, by, above, below.* A *compound preposition* is made up of two prepositions: *out of, from among, except for, because of.*

A **prepositional phrase** is a group of words introduced by a preposition that functions as an adjective (an adjectival phrase) or as an adverb (adverbial phrase) by telling more about a pronoun, noun, or verb:

> The shipment will be here *by next Friday*.
> Put the mail *in the out-bin*.

Prepositional phrases should be placed as close as possible to the element they are modifying:

> Shopping *on the Internet* can be confusing for the uninitiated. (*not* Shopping can be confusing for the uninitiated *on the Internet*.)

Some prepositions are closely linked with a verb. When using phrases such as *look up* and *wipe out*, keep them intact and do not insert anything between the verb and the preposition.

You may have been told that it is unacceptable to put a preposition at the end of a sentence. However, that is not a hard-and-fast rule, and trying to follow it can sometimes be a challenge. You can end a sentence with a preposition as long as the sentence sounds natural and as long as rewording the sentence would create awkward wording:

> I couldn't tell what they were interested in.
> What did she attribute it to?
> What are you looking for?

Avoid using unnecessary prepositions. In the following examples, the prepositions in parentheses should be omitted:

> All (of) the staff members were present.
> I almost fell off (of) my chair with surprise.
> Where was Mr. Steuben going (to)?
> They couldn't help (from) wondering.

The opposite problem is failing to include a preposition when you should. Consider these two sentences:

> Sales were over $100,000 for Linda and Bill.
> Sales were over $100,000 for Linda and for Bill.

The first sentence indicates that Linda and Bill had combined sales over $100,000; the second, that Linda and Bill each had sales over $100,000, for a combined total in excess of $200,000. The preposition *for* is critical here.

When the same preposition can be used for two or more words in a sentence without affecting the meaning, only the last preposition is required:

> We are familiar (with) and satisfied with your company's products.

But when different prepositions are normally used with the words, all the prepositions must be included:

> We are familiar with and interested in your company's products.

Some prepositions have come to be used in a particular way with certain other parts of speech. Here is a partial list of some prepositions that have come to be used with certain words:

according to	independent of
agree to (a proposal)	inferior to
agree with (a person)	plan to
buy from	prefer to
capable of	prior to
comply with	reason with
conform to	responsible for
differ from (things)	similar to
differ with (person)	talk to (without interaction)
different from	talk with (with interaction)
get from (receive)	wait for (person or thing)
get off (dismount)	wait on (like a waiter)

If you are unsure of the correct idiomatic expression, check a dictionary.

Some verb–preposition idioms vary depending on the situation: You agree *to* a proposal but *with* a person, *on* a price, or *in* principle. You argue *about* something, *with* a person, and *for* or *against* a proposition. You compare one item *to* another to show their similarities; you compare one item *with* another to show differences.

Here are some other examples of preposition usage that have given writers trouble:

among/between: *Among* is used to refer to three or more (Circulate the memo *among* the staff); *between* is used to refer to two (Put the copy machine *between* Judy and Dan).

as if/like: *As if* is used before a clause (It seems *as if* we should be doing something); *like* is used before a noun or pronoun (He seems *like* a nice guy).

have/of: *Have* is a verb used in verb phrases (They should *have* checked first); *of* is a preposition and is never used in such cases.

in/into: *In* is used to refer to a static position (The file is *in* the cabinet); *into* is used to refer to movement toward a position (Put the file *into* the cabinet).

1.6.2 Conjunctions

Conjunctions connect the parts of a sentence: words, phrases, and clauses. A coordinating conjunction connects two words, phrases, or clauses of equal rank. The simple coordinating conjunctions include *and, but, or, nor, for, yet,* and *so.* Correlative conjunctions are coordinating conjunctions used in pairs: *both/and, either/or, neither/nor, not only/ but also.* Constructions with correlative conjunctions should be parallel, with the same part of speech following each element of the conjunction:

The purchase was *not only* expensive *but also* unnecessary.

The purchase *not only was* expensive *but also was* unnecessary.

Conjunctive adverbs are adverbs used to connect or show relationships between clauses. They include *however, nevertheless, consequently, moreover,* and *as a result.*

A **subordinate conjunction** connects two clauses of unequal rank; it joins a dependent (subordinate) clause to the independent clause on which it depends (for more on dependent and independent clauses, see Section 1.7.1). Subordinate conjunctions include *as, if, because, although, while, before, since, that, until, unless, when, where,* and *whether.*

1.6.3 Articles and Interjections

Only three articles exist in English: *the, a,* and *an.* These words are used, like adjectives, to specify which item you are talking about. *The* is called the *definite article* because it indicates a specific noun; *a* and *an* are called the *indefinite articles* because they are less specific about what they are referring to.

If a word begins with a vowel (soft) sound, use *an;* otherwise, use *a.* It's *a history,* not *an history, a hypothesis,* not *an hypothesis.* Use *an* with an "h" word only if it is a soft "h," as in *honor* and *hour.* Use *an* with words that are pronounced with a soft vowel sound even if they are spelled beginning with a consonant (usually in the case of abbreviations): *an SEC application, an MP3 file.* Use *a* with words that begin with vowels if they are pronounced with a hard sound: *a university, a Usenet account.*

Repeat an article if adjectives modify different nouns: *The red house and the white house are mine.* Do not repeat an article if all adjectives modify the same noun: *The red and white house is mine.*

Interjections are words that express no solid information, only emotion:

Wow!	Well, well!
Oh, no!	Good!

Such purely emotional language has its place in private life and advertising copy, but it only weakens the effect of most business writing.

1.7 SENTENCES

Sentences are constructed with the major building blocks, the parts of speech. Take, for example, this simple two-word sentence:

Money talks.

It consists of a noun (*money*) and a verb (*talks*). When used in this way, the noun works as the first requirement for a sentence, the **subject**, and the verb works as the second requirement, the **predicate**. Without a subject (who or what does something) and a predicate (the doing of it), you have merely a collection of words, not a sentence.

1.7.1 Longer Sentences

More complicated sentences have more complicated subjects and predicates, but they still have a simple subject and a predicate verb. In the following examples, the subject is underlined once, the predicate verb twice:

<u>Marex</u> and <u>Contron</u> enjoy higher earnings each quarter.

Marex [and] *Contron* do something; *enjoy* is what they do.

My <u>interview</u>, coming minutes after my freeway accident, did not impress or move anyone.

Interview is what did something. What did it do? It *did* [not] *impress* [or] *move.*

In terms of usable space, a steel <u>warehouse</u>, with its extremely long span of roof unsupported by pillars, makes more sense.

Warehouse is what *makes.*

These three sentences demonstrate several things. First, in all three sentences, the simple subject and predicate verb are the "bare bones" of the sentence, the parts that carry the core idea of the sentence. When trying to find the subject and predicate verb, disregard all prepositional phrases, modifiers, conjunctions, and articles.

Second, in the third sentence, the verb is singular (*makes*) because the subject is singular (*warehouse*). Even though the plural noun *pillars* is closer to the verb, *warehouse* is the subject. So *warehouse* determines whether the verb is singular or plural. Subject and predicate must agree.

Third, the subject in the first sentence is compound (*Marex* [and] *Contron*). A compound subject, when connected by *and*, requires a plural verb (*enjoy*). Also, the second sentence shows how compound predicates can occur (*did* [not] *impress* [or] *move*).

Fourth, the second sentence incorporates a group of words—*coming minutes after my freeway accident*—containing a form of a verb (*coming*) and a noun (*accident*). Yet, this group of words is not a complete sentence for two reasons:

- Not all nouns are subjects: *Accident* is not the subject of *coming.*
- Not all verbs are predicates: A verb that ends in *ing* can never be the predicate of a sentence (unless preceded by a form of *to be*, as in *was coming*).

Because they don't contain a subject and a predicate, the words *coming minutes after my freeway accident* (called a **phrase**) can't be written as a sentence. That is, the phrase cannot stand alone; it cannot begin with a capital letter and end with a period. So a phrase must always be just one part of a sentence.

Sometimes a sentence incorporates two or more groups of words that do contain a subject and a predicate; these word groups are called **clauses**:

My <u>interview</u>, because it came minutes after my freeway accident, did not impress or move anyone.

The **independent clause** is the portion of the sentence that could stand alone without revision:

My *interview* did not impress or move anyone.

The other part of the sentence could stand alone only by removing *because*.

(because) It came minutes after my freeway accident.

This part of the sentence is known as a **dependent clause**; although it has a subject and a predicate (just as an independent clause does), it's linked to the main part of the sentence by a word (*because*) showing its dependence.

In summary, the two types of clauses—dependent and independent—both have a subject and a predicate. Dependent clauses, however, do not bear the main meaning of the sentence and are therefore linked to an independent clause. Nor can phrases stand alone, because they lack both a subject and a predicate. Only independent clauses can be written as sentences without revision.

1.7.2 Types of Sentences

Sentences come in four main types, depending on the extent to which they contain clauses. A simple sentence has one subject and one predicate; in short, it has one main independent clause:

Boeing is the world's largest aerospace company.

A **compound sentence** consists of two independent clauses connected by a coordinating conjunction (*and, or, but*, etc.) or a semicolon:

Airbus outsold Boeing for several years, but Boeing has recently regained the lead.

A **complex sentence** consists of an independent clause and one or more dependent clauses:

Boeing is betting [independent clause] that airlines will begin using moderately smaller planes to fly passengers between smaller cities [dependent clause introduced by *that*].

A **compound-complex sentence** has two main clauses, at least one of which contains a subordinate (dependent clause):

Boeing is betting [independent clause] that airlines will begin using moderately smaller planes to fly passengers between smaller cities [dependent clause], and it anticipates that new airports will be developed to meet passenger needs [independent clause].

1.7.3 Sentence Fragments

An incomplete sentence (a phrase or a dependent clause) that is written as though it were a complete sentence is called a **fragment**. Consider the following sentence fragments:

Marilyn Sanders, having had pilferage problems in her store for the past year. Refuses to accept the results of our investigation.

This serious error can easily be corrected by putting the two fragments together:

Marilyn Sanders, having had pilferage problems in her store for the past year, refuses to accept the results of our investigation.

The actual details of a situation will determine the best way for you to remedy a fragment problem.

The ban on fragments has one exception. Some advertising copy contains sentence fragments, written knowingly to convey a certain rhythm. However, advertising is the only area of business in which fragments are acceptable.

1.7.4 Fused Sentences and Comma Splices

Just as there can be too little in a group of words to make it a sentence, there can also be too much:

All our mail is run through a postage meter every afternoon someone picks it up.

This example contains two sentences, not one, but the two have been blended so that it's hard to tell where one ends and the next begins. Is the mail run through a meter every afternoon? If so, the sentences should read:

All our mail is run through a postage meter every afternoon. Someone picks it up.

Perhaps the mail is run through a meter at some other time (morning, for example) and is picked up every afternoon;

All our mail is run through a postage meter. Every afternoon someone picks it up.

The order of words is the same in all three cases; sentence division makes all the difference. Either of the last two cases is grammatically correct. The choice depends on the facts of the situation.

Sometimes these so-called **fused sentences** have a more obvious point of separation:

> Several large orders arrived within a few days of one another, too many came in for us to process by the end of the month.

Here, the comma has been put between two independent clauses in an attempt to link them. When a lowly comma separates two complete sentences, the result is called a **comma splice**. A comma splice can be remedied in one of three ways:

- Replace the comma with a period and capitalize the next word: ". . . one another. Too many . . ."
- Replace the comma with a semicolon and do not capitalize the next word: ". . . one another; too many . . ." This remedy works only when the two sentences have closely related meanings.
- Change one of the sentences so that it becomes a phrase or a dependent clause. This remedy often produces the best writing, but it takes more work.

The third alternative can be carried out in several ways. One is to begin the sentence with a subordinating conjunction:

> Whenever several large orders arrived within a few days of one another, too many came in for us to process by the end of the month.

Another way is to remove part of the subject or the predicate verb from one of the independent clauses, thereby creating a phrase:

> Several large orders arrived within a few days of one another, too many for us to process by the end of the month.

Finally, you can change one of the predicate verbs to its *ing* form:

> Several large orders arrived within a few days of one another, too many coming in for us to process by the end of the month.

In many cases, simply adding a coordinating conjunction can separate fused sentences or remedy a comma splice:

> You can fire them, or you can make better use of their abilities.
>
> Margaret drew up the designs, and Matt carried them out.
>
> We will have three strong months, but after that sales will taper off.

Be careful with coordinating conjunctions: Use them only to join simple sentences that express similar ideas.

Also, because they say relatively little about the relationship between the two clauses they join, avoid using coordinating conjunctions too often: *and* is merely an addition sign; *but* is just a turn signal; *or* only points to an alternative. Subordinating conjunctions such as *because* and *whenever* tell the reader a lot more.

1.7.5 Sentences with Linking Verbs

Linking verbs were discussed briefly in the section on verbs (Section 1.3). Here, you can see more fully the way they function in a sentence. The following is a model of any sentence with a linking verb:

> A *(verb)* B.

Although words such as *seems* and *feels* can also be linking verbs, let's assume that the verb is a form of *to be*:

> A *is* B.

In such a sentence, A and B are always nouns, pronouns, or adjectives. When one is a noun and the other is a pronoun, or when both are nouns, the sentence says that one is the same as the other:

> She is president.
>
> Rachel is president.
>
> She is forceful.

Recall from Section 1.3.3 that the noun or adjective that follows the linking verb is called a *complement*. When it is a noun or noun phrase, the complement is called a *predicate nominative*, when the complement is an adjective, it is referred to as a *predicate adjective*.

1.7.6 Misplaced Modifiers

The position of a modifier in a sentence is important. The movement of *only* changes the meaning in the following sentences:

> Only we are obliged to supply those items specified in your contract.
>
> We are obliged only to supply those items specified in your contract.
>
> We are obliged to supply only those items specified in your contract.
>
> We are obliged to supply those items specified only in your contract.

In any particular set of circumstances, only one of those sentences would be accurate. The others would very likely cause problems. To prevent misunderstanding, place such modifiers as close as possible to the noun or verb they modify.

For similar reasons, whole phrases that are modifiers must be placed near the right noun or verb. Mistakes in placement create ludicrous meanings:

> Antia Information Systems bought new computer chairs for the programmers with more comfortable seats.

The anatomy of programmers is not normally a concern of business writers. Obviously, the comfort of the chairs was the issue:

> Antia Information Systems bought programmers the new computer chairs with more comfortable seats.

Here is another example:

> I asked him to file all the letters in the cabinet that had been answered.

In this ridiculous sentence, the cabinet has been answered, even though no cabinet in history is known to have asked a question. *That had been answered* is too far from *letters* and too close to *cabinet*. Here's an improvement:

> I asked him to file in the cabinet all the letters that had been answered.

The term **dangling modifier** is often used to refer to a clause or phrase that because of its position in the sentence seems to modify a word that it is not meant to modify. For instance:

> Lying motionless, co-workers rushed to Barry's aid.

Readers expect an introductory phrase to modify the subject of the main clause. But in this case it wasn't the *co-workers* who were lying motionless but rather *Barry* who was in this situation. Like this example, most instances of dangling modifiers occur at the beginning of sentences. The source of some danglers is a passive construction:

> To find the needed information, the whole book had to be read.

In such cases, switching to the active voice can usually remedy the problem:

> To find the needed information, you will need to read the whole book.

1.7.7 Parallelism

Two or more sentence elements that have the same relation to another element should be in the same form. Otherwise, the reader is forced to work harder to understand the meaning of the sentence. When a series consists of phrases or clauses, the same part of speech (preposition, gerund, etc.) should introduce them. Do not mix infinitives with participles or adjectives with nouns. Here are some examples of nonparallel elements:

> Andersen is hiring managers, programmers, and people who work in accounting. [nouns not parallel]
>
> Andersen earns income by auditing, consulting, and by bookkeeping. [prepositional phrases not parallel]
>
> Andersen's goals are to win new clients, keeping old clients happy, and finding new enterprises. [infinitive mixed with gerunds]

2.0 Punctuation

On the highway, signs tell you when to slow down or stop, where to turn, and when to merge. In similar fashion, punctuation helps readers negotiate your prose. The proper use of punctuation keeps readers from losing track of your meaning.

2.1 PERIODS

Use a period (1) to end any sentence that is not a question, (2) with certain abbreviations, and (3) between dollars and cents in an amount of money.

2.2 QUESTION MARKS

Use a question mark after any direct question that requests an answer:

> Are you planning to enclose a check, or shall we bill you?

Don't use a question mark with commands phrased as questions for the sake of politeness:

> Will you send us a check today.

A question mark should precede quotation marks, parentheses, and brackets if it is part of the quoted or parenthetical material; otherwise, it should follow:

> This issue of *Inc.* has an article titled "What's Your Entrepreneurial IQ?"
>
> Have you read the article "Five Principles of Guerrilla Marketing"?

Do not use the question mark with indirect questions or with requests:

> Mr. Antonelli asked whether anyone had seen Nathalia lately.

Do not use a comma or a period with a question mark; the question mark takes the place of these punctuation marks.

2.3 EXCLAMATION POINTS

Use exclamation points after highly emotional language. Because business writing almost never calls for emotional language, you will seldom use exclamation points.

2.4 SEMICOLONS

Semicolons have three main uses. One is to separate two closely related independent clauses:

> The outline for the report is due within a week; the report itself is due at the end of the month.

A semicolon should also be used instead of a comma when the items in a series have commas within them:

> Our previous meetings were on November 11, 2009; February 20, 2010; and April 28, 2011.

Finally, a semicolon should be used to separate independent clauses when the second one begins with a conjunctive adverb such as *however, therefore,* or *nevertheless* or a phrase such as *for example* or *in that case:*

> Our supplier has been out of part D712 for 10 weeks; however, we have found another source that can ship the part right away.
>
> His test scores were quite low; on the other hand, he has a lot of relevant experience.

Section 4.4 provides more information on using transitional words and phrases.

> Semicolons should always be placed outside parentheses.

Events Northwest has the contract for this year's convention (August 23–28); we haven't awarded the contract for next year yet.

2.5 COLONS

Use a colon after the salutation in a business letter. You should also use a colon at the end of a sentence or phrase introducing a list or (sometimes) a quotation:

> Our study included the three most critical problems: insufficient capital, incompetent management, and inappropriate location.

A colon should not be used when the list, quotation, or idea is a direct object of the verb or preposition. This rule applies whether the list is set off or run in:

> We are able to supply
>
> staples
>
> wood screws
>
> nails
>
> toggle bolts

> This shipment includes 9 DVDs, 12 CDs, and 4 USB flash drives.

Another way you can use a colon is to separate the main clause and another sentence element when the second explains, illustrates, or amplifies the first:

> Management was unprepared for the union representatives' demands: this fact alone accounts for their arguing well into the night.

However, in contemporary usage, such clauses are frequently separated by a semicolon.

Like semicolons, colons should always be placed outside parentheses.

> He has an expensive list of new demands (none of which is covered in the purchase agreement): new carpeting, network cabling, and a new security system.

2.6 COMMAS

Commas have many uses; the most common is to separate items in a series:

> He took the job, learned it well, worked hard, and succeeded.

> Put paper, pencils, and paper clips on the requisition list.

Company style may dictate omitting the final comma in a series. However, if you have a choice, use the final comma; it's often necessary to prevent misunderstanding.

A second place to use a comma is between independent clauses that are joined by a coordinating conjunction (*and*, *but*, or *or*).

> She spoke to the sales staff, and he spoke to the production staff.

> I was advised to proceed, and I did.

A third use for the comma is to separate a dependent clause at the beginning of a sentence from an independent clause:

> Because of our lead in the market, we may be able to risk introducing a new product.

However, a dependent clause at the end of a sentence is separated from the independent clause by a comma only when the dependent clause is unnecessary to the main meaning of the sentence:

> We may be able to introduce a new product, although it may involve some risk.

A fourth use for the comma is after an introductory phrase or word:

> Starting with this amount of capital, we can survive in the red for one year.

> Through more careful planning, we may be able to serve more people.

> Yes, you may proceed as originally planned.

However, with short introductory prepositional phrases and some one-syllable words (such as *hence* and *thus*), the comma is often omitted:

> Before January 1 we must complete the inventory.

> Thus we may not need to hire anyone.

> In July we will complete the move to Tulsa.

Fifth, paired commas are used to set off nonrestrictive clauses and phrases. A **restrictive clause** is one that cannot be omitted without altering the meaning of the main clause, whereas a **nonrestrictive clause** can be:

> The *Time Magazine* website, which is produced by Steve Conley, has won several design awards. [nonrestrictive: the material set off by commas could be omitted]

> The website that is produced by Steve Conley has won several design awards. [restrictive: no commas are used before and after *that is produced by Steve Conley* because this information is necessary to the meaning of the sentence—it specifies which website]

A sixth use for commas is to set off appositive words and phrases. (An **appositive** has the same meaning as the word it is in apposition to.) Like nonrestrictive clauses, appositives can be dropped without changing or obscuring the meaning of the sentence:

> Conley, a freelance designer, also produces the websites for several nonprofit corporations.

Seventh, commas are used between adjectives modifying the same noun (coordinate adjectives):

> She left Monday for a long, difficult recruiting trip.

To test the appropriateness of such a comma, try reversing the order of the adjectives: *a difficult, long recruiting trip*. If the order cannot be reversed, leave out the comma (a *good old friend* isn't the same as an *old good friend*). A comma should not be used when one of the adjectives is part of the noun. Compare these two phrases:

> a distinguished, well-known figure
>
> a distinguished public figure

The adjective–noun combination of *public* and *figure* has been used together so often that it has come to be considered a single thing: *public figure*. So no comma is required.

Eighth, commas are used both before and after the year in sentences that include month, day, and year:

> It will be sent by December 15, 2012, from our Cincinnati plant.

Some companies write dates in another form: 15 December 2012. No commas should be used in that case. Nor is a comma needed when only the month and year are present (December 2012).

Ninth, commas are used to set off a variety of parenthetical words and phrases within sentences, including state names, dates, abbreviations, transitional expressions, and contrasted elements:

> They were, in fact, prepared to submit a bid.
>
> Habermacher, Inc., went public in 1999.
>
> Our goal was increased profits, not increased market share.
>
> Service, then, is our main concern.
>
> The factory was completed in Chattanooga, Tennessee, just three weeks ago.
>
> Joanne Dubiik, M.D., has applied for a loan from First Savings.
>
> I started work here on March 1, 2003, and soon received my first promotion.

Tenth, a comma is used to separate a quotation from the rest of the sentence:

> Your warranty reads, "These conditions remain in effect for one year from date of purchase."

However, the comma is left out when the quotation as a whole is built into the structure of the sentence:

> He hurried off with an angry "Look where you're going."

Finally, a comma should be used whenever it's needed to avoid confusion or an unintended meaning. Compare the following:

> Ever since they have planned new ventures more carefully.
>
> Ever since, they have planned new ventures more carefully.

2.7 DASHES

Use dashes to surround a comment that is a sudden turn in thought:

> Membership in the IBSA—it's expensive but worth it— may be obtained by applying to our New York office.

A dash can also be used to emphasize a parenthetical word or phrase:

> Third-quarter profits—in excess of $2 million—are up sharply.

Finally, use dashes to set off a phrase that contains commas:

> All our offices—Milwaukee, New Orleans, and Phoenix— have sent representatives.

Don't confuse a dash with a hyphen. A dash separates and emphasizes words, phrases, and clauses more strongly than commas or parentheses can; a hyphen ties two words so tightly that they almost become one word.

When using a computer, use the em dash symbol. When typing a dash in email, type two hyphens with no space before, between, or after.

A second type of dash, the en dash, can be produced with computer word processing and page-layout programs. This kind of dash is shorter than the regular dash and longer than a hyphen. It is reserved almost exclusively for indicating "to" or "through" with numbers such as dates and pages: *2011–2012, pages 30–44.*

2.8 HYPHENS

Hyphens are mainly used in three ways. The first is to separate the parts of compound words beginning with such prefixes as *self-, ex-, quasi-,* and *all-*:

> self-assured   quasi-official
>
> ex-wife   all-important

However, do not use hyphens in words that have prefixes such as *pro, anti, non, re, pre, un, inter,* and *extra*:

> prolabor   nonunion
>
> antifascist   interdepartmental

Exceptions occur when (1) the prefix occurs before a proper noun or (2) the vowel at the end of the prefix is the same as the first letter of the root word:

> pro-Republican   anti-American
>
> anti-inflammatory   extra-atmospheric

When in doubt, consult your dictionary.

Hyphens are used in some types of spelled-out numbers. For instance, they are used to separate the parts of a spelled-out number from *twenty-one* to *ninety-nine* and for spelled-out fractions: *two-thirds, one-sixth* (although some style guides say not to hyphenate fractions used as nouns).

Certain compound nouns are formed by using hyphens: *secretary-treasurer, city-state.* Check your dictionary for compounds you're unsure about.

Hyphens are also used in some compound adjectives, which are adjectives made up of two or more words. Specifically, you should use hyphens in compound adjectives that come before the noun:

> an interest-bearing account   well-informed executives

However, you need not hyphenate when the adjective follows a linking verb:

> This account is interest bearing.
>
> Their executives are well informed.

You can shorten sentences that list similar hyphenated words by dropping the common part from all but the last word:

> Check the costs of first-, second-, and third-class postage.

Finally, hyphens may be used to divide words at the end of a typed line. Such hyphenation is best avoided, but when you have to divide words at the end of a line, do so correctly (see Section 3.5). Dictionaries show how words are divided into syllables.

2.9 APOSTROPHES

Use an apostrophe in the possessive form of a noun (but not in a pronoun):

> On his desk was a reply to Bette *Ainsley's* application for the *manager's* position.

Apostrophes are also used in place of the missing letter(s) of a contraction:

Whole Words	Contraction
we will	we'll
do not	don't
they are	they're

2.10 QUOTATION MARKS

Use quotation marks to surround words that are repeated exactly as they were said or written:

> The collection letter ended by saying, "This is your third and final notice."

Remember: (1) When the quoted material is a complete sentence, the first word is capitalized. (2) The final comma or period goes inside the closing quotation marks.

Quotation marks are also used to set off the title of a newspaper story, magazine article, or book chapter:

> You should read "Legal Aspects of the Collection Letter" in *Today's Credit*.

Quotation marks may also be used to indicate special treatment for words or phrases, such as terms that you're using in an unusual or ironic way:

> Our management "team" spends more time squabbling than working to solve company problems.

When you are defining a word, put the definition in quotation marks:

> The abbreviation *etc.* means "and so forth."

When using quotation marks, take care to insert the closing marks as well as the opening ones.

Although periods and commas go inside any quotation marks, colons and semicolons generally go outside them. A question mark goes inside the quotation marks only if the quotation is a question:

> All that day we wondered, "Is he with us?"

If the quotation is not a question but the entire sentence is, the question mark goes outside:

> What did she mean by "You will hear from me"?

For quotes within quotes, use single quotation marks within double:

> As David Pottruck, former co-CEO of Charles Schwab, told it, "I assembled about 100 managers at the base of the Golden Gate Bridge and gave them jackets emblazoned with the phrase 'Crossing the Chasm' and then led them across the bridge."

Otherwise, do not use single quotation marks for anything, including titles of works—that's British style.

2.11 PARENTHESES AND BRACKETS

Use parentheses to surround comments that are entirely incidental or to supply additional information:

> Our figures do not match yours, although (if my calculations are correct) they are closer than we thought.
>
> These kinds of supplements do not require FDA (Food and Drug Administration) approval.

Parentheses are used in legal documents to surround figures in arabic numerals that follow the same amount in words:

> Remittance will be One Thousand Two Hundred Dollars ($1,200).

Be careful to put punctuation marks (period, comma, and so on) outside the parentheses unless they are part of the statement in parentheses. And keep in mind that parentheses have both an opening and a closing mark; both should always be used, even when setting off listed items within text: *(1)*, not *1)*.

Brackets are used for notation, comment, explanation, or correction within quoted material:

> In the interview, multimillionaire Bob Buford said, "One of my major influences was Peter [Drucker], who encourages people and helps them believe in themselves."

Brackets are also used for parenthetical material that falls within parentheses:

> Drucker's magnum opus (*Management: Tasks, Responsibilities, Practices* [Harper & Row, 1979]) has influenced generations of entrepreneurs.

2.12 ELLIPSES

Use ellipsis points, or three evenly spaced periods, to indicate that material has been left out of a direct quotation. Use them only in direct quotations and only at the point where material was left out. In the following example, the first sentence is quoted in the second:

The Dow Jones Industrial Average fell 276.39 points, or 2.6%, during the week to 10292.31.

According to the *Wall Street Journal*, "The Dow Jones Industrial Average fell 276.39 points . . . to 10,292.31."

The number of dots in ellipses is not optional; always use three. Occasionally, the points of an ellipsis come at the end of a sentence, where they seem to grow a fourth dot. Don't be fooled: One of the dots is a period. Ellipsis points should always be preceded and followed by a space.

Avoid using ellipses to represent a pause in your writing; use a dash for that purpose:

At first we had planned to leave for the conference on Wednesday—but then we changed our minds. [not *on Wednesday . . . but then*]

3.0 Mechanics

The most obvious and least tolerable mistakes that a business writer makes are probably those related to grammar and punctuation. However, a number of small details, known as writing mechanics, demonstrate the writer's polish and reflect on the company's professionalism.

When it comes to mechanics, also called *style*, many of the "rules" are not hard and fast. Publications and organizations vary in their preferred styles for capitalization, abbreviations, numbers, italics, and so on. Here, we'll try to differentiate between practices that are generally accepted and those that can vary. When you are writing materials for a specific company or organization, find out the preferred style (such as *The Chicago Manual of Style* or Webster's *Style Manual*). Otherwise, choose a respected style guide. The key to style is consistency: If you spell out the word *percent* in one part of a document, don't use the percent sign in a similar context elsewhere in the same document.

3.1 CAPITALIZATION

With capitalization, you can follow either an "up" style (when in doubt, capitalize: *Federal Government, Board of Directors*) or a "down" style (when in doubt, use lowercase: *federal government, board of directors*). The trend over the last few decades has been toward the down style. Your best bet is to get a good style manual and consult it when you have a capitalization question. Following are some rules that most style guides agree on.

Capital letters are used at the beginning of certain word groups:

- **Complete sentence:** Before hanging up, he said, "We'll meet here on Wednesday at noon."
- **Formal statement following a colon:** She has a favorite motto: Where there's a will, there's a way.
- **Phrase used as sentence:** Absolutely not!
- **Quoted sentence embedded in another sentence:** Scott said, "Nobody was here during lunch hour except me."

- **List of items set off from text:** Three preliminary steps are involved:

Design review
Budgeting
Scheduling

Capitalize proper adjectives and proper nouns (the names of particular persons, places, and things):

Darrell Greene lived in a Victorian mansion.

We sent Ms. Larson an application form, informing her that not all applicants are interviewed.

Let's consider opening a branch in the West, perhaps at the west end of Tucson, Arizona.

As office buildings go, the Kinney Building is a pleasant setting for TDG Office Equipment.

We are going to have to cancel our plans for hiring French and German sales reps.

Larson's name is capitalized because she is a particular applicant, whereas the general term *applicant* is left uncapitalized. Likewise, *West* is capitalized when it refers to a particular place but not when it means a direction. In the same way, *office* and *building* are not capitalized when they are general terms (common nouns), but they are capitalized when they are part of the title of a particular office or building (proper nouns). Some proper adjectives are lowercased when they are part of terms that have come into common use, such as *french fries* and *roman numerals*.

Titles within families or companies as well as professional titles may also be capitalized:

I turned down Uncle David when he offered me a job. I wouldn't be comfortable working for one of my relatives.

We've never had a president quite like President Sweeney.

People's titles are capitalized when they are used in addressing a person, especially in a formal context. They are not usually capitalized, however, when they are used merely to identify the person:

Address the letter to Chairperson Anna Palmer.

I wish to thank Chairperson Anna Palmer for her assistance.

Anna Palmer, chairperson of the board, took the podium.

Also capitalize titles if they are used by themselves in addressing a person:

Thank you, Doctor, for your donation.

Always capitalize the first word of the salutation and complimentary close of a letter:

Dear Mr. Andrews: *Yours* very truly,

The names of organizations are capitalized, of course; so are the official names of their departments and divisions. However, do not use capitals when referring in general terms to a department or division, especially one in another organization:

Route this memo to Personnel.

Larry Tien was transferred to the Microchip Division.

Will you be enrolled in the Psychology Department?

Someone from the personnel department at EnerTech stopped by the booth.

Capitalization is unnecessary when using a word like *company, corporation*, or *university* alone:

The corporation plans to issue 50,000 shares of common stock.

Likewise, the names of specific products are capitalized, although the names of general product types are not:

Apple Inc.   Xerox machine

Tide laundry detergent

When it comes to government terminology, here are some guides to capitalization: (1) Lowercase *federal* unless it is part of an agency name; (2) capitalize names of courts, departments, bureaus, offices, and agencies but lowercase such references as *the bureau* and *the department* when the full name is not used; (3) lowercase the titles of government officers unless they precede a specific person's name: *the secretary of state, the senator, the ambassador, the governor, and the mayor* but *Mayor Gonzalez* (Note: style guides vary on whether to capitalize *president* when referring to the president of the United States without including the person's name); capitalize the names of laws and acts: *the Sherman Antitrust Act, the Civil Rights Act*; (4) capitalize the names of political parties but lowercase the word *party: Democratic party, Libertarian party*.

When writing about two or more geographic features of the same type, it is now accepted practice to capitalize the common noun in addition to the proper nouns, regardless of word order:

Lakes Ontario and Huron

Allegheny and Monongahela Rivers

Corson and Ravenna Avenues

The names of languages, races, and ethnic groups are capitalized: Japanese, Caucasian, Hispanic. But racial terms that denote only skin color are not capitalized: black, white.

When referring to the titles of books, articles, magazines, newspapers, reports, movies, and so on, you should capitalize the first and last words and all nouns, pronouns, adjectives, verbs, and adverbs, and capitalize prepositions and conjunctions with five letters or more. Except for the first and last words, do not capitalize articles:

Economics During the Great War

"An Investigation into the Market for Long-Distance Services"

"What Successes Are Made Of"

When *the* is part of the official name of a newspaper or magazine, it should be treated this way too:

The Wall Street Journal

Style guides vary in their recommendations regarding capitalization of hyphenated words in titles. A general guide is to capitalize the second word in a temporary compound (a compound that is hyphenated for grammatical reasons and not spelling reasons), such as *Law-Abiding Citizen*, but to lowercase the word if the term is always hyphenated, such as *Son-in-law*).

References to specific pages, paragraphs, lines, and the like are not capitalized: *page 73, line 3*. However, in most other numbered or lettered references, the identifying term is capitalized:

Chapter 4   Serial No. 382-2203   Item B-11

Finally, the names of academic degrees are capitalized when they follow a person's name but are not capitalized when used in a general sense:

I received a bachelor of science degree.

Thomas Whitelaw, Doctor of Philosophy, will attend.

Similarly, general courses of study are not capitalized, but the names of specific classes are:

She studied accounting as an undergraduate.

She is enrolled in Accounting 201.

3.2 UNDERSCORES AND ITALICS

Usually a line typed underneath a word or phrase either provides emphasis or indicates the title of a book, magazine, or newspaper. If possible, use italics instead of an underscore. Italics (or underlining) should also be used for defining terms and for discussing words as words:

In this report, *net sales* refers to after-tax sales dollars.

The word *building* is a common noun and should not be capitalized.

Also use italics to set off foreign words, unless the words have become a common part of English:

Top Shelf is considered the *sine qua non* of comic book publishers.

Chris uses a laissez-faire [no italic] management style.

3.3 ABBREVIATIONS

Abbreviations are used heavily in tables, charts, lists, and forms. They're used sparingly in prose. Here are some abbreviation situations to watch for:

- In most cases do not use periods with acronyms (words formed from the initial letter or letters of parts of a term): *CEO, CD-ROM, DOS, YWCA, FDA*; but *Ph.D., M.A., M.D.*
- Use periods with abbreviations such as *Mr., Ms., Sr., Jr., a.m., p.m., B.C.,* and *A.D.*
- The trend is away from using periods with such units of measure as *mph, mm,* and *lb*.
- Use periods with such Latin abbreviations as *e.g., i.e., et al.,* and *etc.* However, style guides recommend that you avoid using these Latin forms and instead use their English equivalents (*for example, that is, and others,* and *and so on,* respectively). If you must use these abbreviations, such as in parenthetical expressions or footnotes, do not put them in italics.

- Some companies have abbreviations as part of their names (*&, Co., Inc., Ltd.*). When you refer to such firms by name, be sure to double-check the preferred spelling, including spacing: *AT&T; Barnes & Noble; Carson Pirie Scott & Company; PepsiCo; Kate Spade, Inc.; National Data Corporation; Siemens Corp.; Glaxo Wellcome PLC; US Airways; U.S. Business Reporter.*
- Most style guides recommend that you spell out *United States* as a noun and reserve *U.S.* as an adjective preceding the noun modified.

One way to handle an abbreviation that you want to use throughout a document is to spell it out the first time you use it, follow it with the abbreviation in parentheses, and then use the abbreviation in the remainder of the document.

3.4 NUMBERS

Numbers may be correctly handled many ways in business writing, so follow company style. In the absence of a set style, however, generally spell out all numbers from one to nine and use arabic numerals for the rest.

There are some exceptions to this general rule. For example, never begin a sentence with a numeral:

> Twenty of us produced 641 units per week in the first 12 weeks of the year.

Use numerals for the numbers one through nine if they're in the same list as larger numbers:

> Our weekly quota rose from 9 to 15 to 27.

Use numerals for percentages, time of day (except with o'clock), dates, and (in general) dollar amounts:

> Our division is responsible for 7 percent of total sales.
>
> The meeting is scheduled for 8:30 a.m. on August 2.
>
> Add $3 for postage and handling.

When using numerals for time, be consistent: It should be *between 10:00 a.m. and 4:30 p.m.*, not *between 10 a.m. and 4:30 p.m.* Expressions such as *4:00 o'clock* and *7 a.m. in the morning* are redundant.

Use a comma in numbers expressing thousands (1,257), unless your company specifies another style. When dealing with numbers in the millions and billions, combine words and figures: 7.3 million, 2 billion.

When writing dollar amounts, use a decimal point only if cents are included. In lists of two or more dollar amounts, use the decimal point either for all or for none:

> He sent two checks, one for $67.92 and one for $90.00.

When two numbers fall next to each other in a sentence, use figures for the number that is largest, most difficult to spell, or part of a physical measurement; use words for the other:

> I have learned to manage a classroom of 30 twelve-year-olds.
>
> She won a bonus for selling 24 thirty-volume sets.
>
> You'll need twenty 3-inch bolts.

In addresses, all street numbers except One are in numerals. So are suite and room numbers and zip codes. For street names that are numbered, practice varies so widely that you should use the form specified on an organization's letterhead or in a reliable directory. All the following examples are correct:

> One Fifth Avenue   297 Ninth Street
>
> 1839 44th Street   11026 West 78 Place

Telephone numbers are always expressed in numerals. Parentheses may separate the area code from the rest of the number, but a slash or a hyphen may be used instead, especially if the entire phone number is enclosed in parentheses:

> 382-8329   (602/382-8329)   602-382-8329

Percentages are always expressed in numerals. The word *percent* is used in most cases, but % may be used in tables, forms, and statistical writing.

Ages are usually expressed in words—except when a parenthetical reference to age follows someone's name:

> Mrs. Margaret Sanderson is seventy-two.
>
> Mrs. Margaret Sanderson, 72, swims daily.

Also, ages expressed in years and months are treated like physical measurements that combine two units of measure: *5 years 6 months.*

Physical measurements such as distance, weight, and volume are also often expressed in numerals: *9 kilometers, 5 feet 3 inches, 7 pounds 10 ounces.*

Decimal numbers are always written in numerals. In most cases, add a zero to the left of the decimal point if the number is less than one and does not already start with a zero:

> 1.38   .07   0.2

In a series of related decimal numbers with at least one number greater than one, make sure that all numbers smaller than one have a zero to the left of the decimal point: 1.20, 0.21, 0.09.

Simple fractions are written in words, but more complicated fractions are expressed in figures or, if easier to read, in figures and words:

> two-thirds   9/32   2 hundredths

Most style guides recommend that you use a comma with numbers consisting of four digits: *2,345*, not *2345.*

When typing ordinal numbers, such as *3rd edition* or *21st century,* your word processing program may automatically make the letters *rd* (or *st, th,* or *nd*) into a superscript. Do yourself a favor and turn that formatting function off in your "Preferences," as superscripts should not be used in regular prose or even in bibliographies.

3.5 WORD DIVISION

In general, avoid dividing words at the end of lines. When you must do so, follow these rules:

- Don't divide one-syllable words (such as *since, walked,* and *thought*), abbreviations (*mgr.*), contractions (*isn't*), or numbers expressed in numerals (*117,500*).

- Divide words between syllables, as specified in a dictionary or word-division manual.
- Make sure that at least three letters of the divided words are moved to the second line: *sin-cerely* instead of *sincere-ly*.
- Do not end a page or more than three consecutive lines with hyphens.
- Leave syllables consisting of a single vowel at the end of the first line (*impedi-ment* instead of *imped-iment*), except when the single vowel is part of a suffix such as *-able, -ible, -ical,* or *-ity* (*re-spons-ible* instead of *re-sponsi-ble*).
- Divide between double letters (*tomor-row*), except when the root word ends in double letters (*call-ing* instead of *cal-ling*).
- Wherever possible, divide hyphenated words at the hyphen only: instead of *anti-inde-pendence,* use *anti-independence.*
- Whenever possible, do not break URLs or email addresses. If you must break a long URL or email address, do not insert a hyphen at the end of the first line.

4.0 Vocabulary

Using the right word in the right place is a crucial skill in business communication. However, many pitfalls await the unwary.

4.1 FREQUENTLY CONFUSED WORDS

Because the following sets of words sound similar, be careful not to use one when you mean to use the other:

Word	Meaning
accede	to comply with
exceed	to go beyond
accept	to take
except	to exclude
access	admittance
excess	too much
advice	suggestion
advise	to suggest
affect	to influence
effect	the result
allot	to distribute
a lot	much or many
all ready	completely prepared
already	completed earlier
born	given birth to
borne	carried
capital	money; chief city
capitol	a government building
cite	to quote
sight	a view
site	a location

Word	Meaning
complement	complete amount; to go well with
compliment	expression of esteem; to flatter
corespondent	party in a divorce suit
correspondent	letter writer
council	a panel of people
counsel	advice; a lawyer
defer	to put off until later
differ	to be different
device	a mechanism
devise	to plan
die	to stop living; a tool
dye	to color
discreet	careful
discrete	separate
envelop	to surround
envelope	a covering for a letter
forth	forward
fourth	number four
holey	full of holes
holy	sacred
wholly	completely
human	of people
humane	kindly
incidence	frequency
incidents	events
instance	example
instants	moments
interstate	between states
intrastate	within a state
later	afterward
latter	the second of two
lead	a metal; to guide
led	guided
lean	to rest at an angle
lien	a claim
levee	embankment
levy	tax
loath	reluctant
loathe	to hate
loose	free; not tight
lose	to mislay
material	substance
materiel	equipment
miner	mineworker
minor	underage person

Word	Meaning
moral	virtuous; a lesson
morale	sense of well-being
ordinance	law
ordnance	weapons
overdo	to do in excess
overdue	past due
peace	lack of conflict
piece	a fragment
pedal	a foot lever
peddle	to sell
persecute	to torment
prosecute	to sue
personal	private
personnel	employees
precedence	priority
precedents	previous events
principal	sum of money; chief; main
principle	general rule
rap	to knock
wrap	to cover
residence	home
residents	inhabitants
right	correct
rite	ceremony
write	to form words on a surface
role	a part to play
roll	to tumble; a list
root	part of a plant
rout	to defeat
route	a traveler's way
shear	to cut
sheer	thin, steep
stationary	immovable
stationery	paper
than	as compared with
then	at that time
their	belonging to them
there	in that place
they're	they are
to	a preposition
too	excessively; also
two	the number
waive	to set aside
wave	a swell of water; a gesture

Word	Meaning
weather	atmospheric conditions
whether	if
who's	contraction of "who is" or "who has"
whose	possessive form of who

In the preceding list, only enough of each word's meaning is given to help you distinguish between the words in each group. For more complete definitions, consult a dictionary.

4.2 FREQUENTLY MISUSED WORDS

The following words tend to be misused for reasons other than their sound. Reference books (including the *Random House College Dictionary*, revised edition; Follett's *Modern American Usage*; and Fowler's *Modern English Usage*) can help you with similar questions of usage:

a lot: When the writer means "many," *a lot* is always two separate words, never one.

aggravate/irritate: *Aggravate* means "to make things worse." Sitting in the smoke-filled room *aggravated* his sinus condition. *Irritate* means "to annoy." Her constant questions *irritated* [not *aggravated*] me.

anticipate/expect: *Anticipate* means "to prepare for": Macy's *anticipated* increased demand for athletic shoes in spring by ordering in November. In formal usage, it is incorrect to use *anticipate* for *expect*: I *expected* (not *anticipated*) a better response to our presentation than we actually got.

compose/comprise: The whole comprises the parts:

> The company's distribution division *comprises* four departments.

It would be incorrect usage to say

> The company's distribution division *is comprised of* four departments.

In that construction, *is composed of* or *consists of* would be preferable. It might be helpful to think of *comprise* as meaning "encompasses" or "contains."

continual/continuous: *Continual* refers to ongoing actions that have breaks:

> Her *continual* complaining will accomplish little in the long run.

Continuous refers to ongoing actions without interruptions or breaks:

> A *continuous* stream of paper came out of the fax machine.

convince/persuade: One is *convinced* of a fact or that something is true; one is *persuaded* by someone else to do something. The use of *to* with *convince* is unidiomatic—you don't convince someone to do something, you persuade them to do it.

correspond with: Use this phrase when you are talking about exchanging letters. Use *correspond to* when you mean "similar to." Use either *correspond with* or *correspond to* when you mean "relate to."

dilemma/problem: Technically, a *dilemma* is a situation in which one must choose between two undesirable alternatives. It shouldn't be used when no choice is actually involved.

disinterested: This word means "fair, unbiased, having no favorites, impartial." If you mean "bored" or "not interested," use uninterested.

etc.: This abbreviated form of the Latin phrase et cetera means "and so on" or "and so forth," so it is never correct to write and etc. The current tendency among business writers is to use English rather than Latin.

example/sample: An example is a model to be followed or one item that represents a group. A sample is a preview of a product or another entity, intended to demonstrate the product's qualities. In statistics, a sample is selected to represent the characteristics of a larger population.

flaunt/flout: To flaunt is to be ostentatious or boastful; to flout is to mock or scoff at.

impact: Avoid using impact as a verb when influence or affect is meant.

imply/infer: Both refer to hints. Their great difference lies in who is acting. The writer implies, the reader infers, sees between the lines.

lay: This word is a transitive verb. Never use it for the intransitive lie. (See Section 1.3.3.)

lend/loan: Lend is a verb; loan is a noun. Usage such as "Can you loan me $5?" is therefore incorrect.

less/fewer: Use less for uncountable quantities (such as amounts of water, air, sugar, and oil). Use fewer for countable quantities (such as numbers of jars, saws, words, pages, and humans). The same distinction applies to much and little (uncountable) versus many and few (countable).

liable/likely: Liable means "responsible for": I will hold you liable if this deal doesn't go through. It is incorrect to use liable for "possible": Anything is likely (not liable) to happen.

literally: Literally means "actually" or "precisely"; it is often misused to mean "almost" or "virtually." It is usually best left out entirely or replaced with figuratively.

many/much: See less/fewer.

regardless: The less suffix is the negative part. No word needs two negative parts, so don't add *ir* (a negative prefix) to the beginning. There is no such word as irregardless.

try: Always follow with *to*, never *and*.

verbal: People in the business community who are careful with language frown on those who use *verbal* to mean "spoken" or "oral." Many others do say "verbal agreement." Strictly speaking, *verbal* means "of words" and therefore includes both spoken and written words. Follow company usage in this matter.

4.3 FREQUENTLY MISSPELLED WORDS

All of us, even the world's best spellers, sometimes have to check a dictionary for the spelling of some words. People who have never memorized the spelling of commonly used words must look up so many that they grow exasperated and give up on spelling words correctly.

Don't expect perfection and don't surrender. If you can memorize the spelling of just the words listed here, you'll need the dictionary far less often and you'll write with more confidence:

absence	convertible
absorption	corroborate
accessible	criticism
accommodate	
accumulate	definitely
achieve	description
advantageous	desirable
affiliated	dilemma
aggressive	disappear
alignment	disappoint
aluminum	disbursement
ambience	discrepancy
analyze	dissatisfied
apparent	dissipate
appropriate	
argument	eligible
asphalt	embarrassing
assistant	endorsement
asterisk	exaggerate
auditor	exceed
	exhaust
bankruptcy	existence
believable	extraordinary
brilliant	
bulletin	fallacy
	familiar
calendar	flexible
campaign	fluctuation
category	forty
ceiling	
changeable	gesture
clientele	grievous
collateral	
committee	haphazard
comparative	harassment
competitor	holiday
concede	
congratulations	illegible
connoisseur	immigrant
consensus	incidentally
convenient	indelible

independent
indispensable
insistent
intermediary
irresistible

jewelry
judgment
judicial

labeling
legitimate
leisure
license
litigation

maintenance
mathematics
mediocre
minimum

necessary
negligence
negotiable
newsstand
noticeable

occurrence
omission

parallel
pastime
peaceable
permanent
perseverance
persistent
personnel
persuade
possesses
precede

predictable
preferred
privilege
procedure
proceed
pronunciation
psychology
pursue

questionnaire

receive
recommend
repetition
rescind
rhythmical
ridiculous

salable
secretary
seize
separate
sincerely
succeed
suddenness
superintendent
supersede
surprise

tangible
tariff
technique
tenant
truly

unanimous
until

vacillate
vacuum
vicious

4.4 TRANSITIONAL WORDS AND PHRASES

The following sentences don't communicate as well as they could because they lack a transitional word or phrase:

> Production delays are inevitable. Our current lag time in filling orders is one month.

A semicolon between the two sentences would signal a close relationship between their meanings, but it wouldn't even hint at what that relationship is. Here are the sentences again, now linked by means of a semicolon, with a space for a transitional word or phrase:

> Production delays are inevitable; _____, our current lag time in filling orders is one month.

Now read the sentence with *nevertheless* in the blank space. Then try *therefore, incidentally, in fact*, and *at any rate* in the blank. Each substitution changes the meaning of the sentence.

Here are some transitional words (conjunctive adverbs) that will help you write more clearly:

accordingly	furthermore	moreover
anyway	however	otherwise
besides	incidentally	still
consequently	likewise	therefore
finally	meanwhile	

The following transitional phrases are used in the same way:

as a result	in other words
at any rate	in the second place
for example	on the other hand
in fact	to the contrary

When one of these words or phrases joins two independent clauses, it should be preceded by a semicolon and followed by a comma:

> The consultant recommended a complete reorganization; moreover, she suggested that we drop several products.

References

PROLOGUE

1. Jeanne C. Meister and Karie Willyerd, "Leading Virtual Teams to Real Results," *Harvard Business Review blogs*, 30 June 2010 [accessed 16 August 2010] http://blogs.hbr.org; *The Small Business Economy, 2009*, U.S. Small Business Administration website [accessed 16 August 2010] www.sba.gov; Malik Singleton, "Same Markets, New Marketplaces," *Black Enterprise*, September 2004, 34; Edmund L. Andrews, "Where Do the Jobs Come From?" *New York Times*, 21 September 2004, E1, E11; Maureen Jenkins, "Yours for the Taking," *Boeing Frontiers Online*, June 2004 [accessed 25 September 2005] www.boeing.com; "Firm Predicts Top 10 Workforce/Workplace Trends for 2004," *Enterprise*, 8–14 December 2003, 1–2; Ricky W. Griffin and Michael W. Pustay, *International Business*, 6th ed. (Upper Saddle River, N.J.: Pearson Prentice Hall, 2010), 21.
2. Vivian Yeo, "India Still Top Choice for Offshoring," *BusinessWeek*, 27 June 2008 [accessed 7 July 2008] www.businessweek.com; Jim Puzzanghera, "Coalition of High-Tech Firms to Urge Officials to Help Keep U.S. Competitive," *San Jose Mercury News*, 8 January 2004 [accessed 14 February 2004] www.ebscohost.com.
3. Courtland L. Bovée and John V. Thill, *Business in Action*, 5th ed. (Upper Saddle River, N.J.: Pearson Prentice Hall, 2010), 18–21; Randall S. Hansen and Katharine Hansen, "What Do Employers Really Want? Top Skills and Values Employers Seek from Job-Seekers," QuintCareers.com [accessed 17 August 2010] www.quintcareers.com.
4. Nancy M. Somerick, "Managing a Communication Internship Program," *Bulletin of the Association for Business Communication* 56, no. 3 (1993): 10–20.
5. Fellowforce website [accessed 17 August 2010] www.fellowforce.com.
6. Jeffrey R. Young, "'E-Portfolios' Could Give Students a New Sense of Their Accomplishments," *The Chronicle of Higher Education*, 8 March 2002, A31.
7. Brian Carcione, e-portfolio [accessed 20 December 2006] http://eportfolio.psu.edu.
8. Mohammed Al-Taee, "Personal Branding," Al-Taee blog [accessed 17 August 2010] http://altaeeblog.com.
9. Pete Kistler, "Seth Godin's 7-Point Guide to Bootstrap Your Personal Brand," Personal Branding blog, 28 July 2010 [accessed 17 August 2010] www.personalbrandingblog; Kyle Lacy, "10 Ways to Building Your Personal Brand Story," Personal Branding blog, 5 August 2010 [accessed 17 August 2010] www.personalbrandingblog; Al-Taee, "Personal Branding"; Scot Herrick, "30 Career Management Tips—Marketing AND Delivery Support Our Personal Brand," Cube Rules blog, 8 September 2007 [accessed 17 August 2010] http://cuberules.com; Alina Tugend, "Putting Yourself Out There on a Shelf to Buy," *New York Times*, 27 March 2009 [accessed 9 August 2009] www.nytimes.com.

CHAPTER 1

1. Toyota Facebook page, [accessed 22 December 2010] www.facebook.com/toyota; Lisa Lacy, "Toyota Pushes 'Auto-Biography' Facebook Campaign," ClickZ, 2 August 2010, [accessed 22 December 2010] www.clickz.com; Alan Ohnsman and Makiko Kitamura, "Is Toyota's Reputation Finished?" *Bloomberg Businessweek*, 28 January 2010, [accessed 22 December 2010] www.businessweek.com.
2. Richard L. Daft, *Management*, 6th ed. (Cincinnati: Thomson South-Western, 2003), 580.
3. Julie Connelly, "Youthful Attitudes, Sobering Realities," *New York Times*, 28 October 2003, E1, E6; Nigel Andrews and Laura D'Andrea Tyson, "The Upwardly Global MBA," *Strategy+Business* 36, 60–69; Jim McKay, "Communication Skills Found Lacking," *Pittsburgh Post-Gazette*, 28 February 2005, [accessed 28 February 2005] www.delawareonline.com.
4. Brian Solis, *Engage!* (Hoboken: John Wiley & Sons, 2010), 11–12; "Majority of Global Companies Face an Engagement Gap," Internal Comms Hub website, 23 October 2007, [accessed 5 July 2008] www.internalcommshub.com; Gary L. Neilson, Karla L. Martin, and Elizabeth Powers, "The Secrets to Successful Strategy Execution," *Harvard Business Review*, June 2008, 61–70; Nicholas Carr, "Lessons in Corporate Blogging," *BusinessWeek*, 18 July 2006, 9; Susan Meisinger, "To Keep Employees, Talk—and Listen—to Them!" *HR Magazine*, August 2006, 10.
5. Daft, *Management*, 147.
6. Don Hellriegel, Susan E. Jackson, and John W. Slocum, Jr., *Management: A Competency-Based Approach* (Cincinnati: Thomson South-Western, 2002), 447.
7. "CEOs to Communicators: 'Stick to Common Sense'," Internal Comms Hub website, 23 October 2007, [accessed 11 July 2008] www.internalcommshub.com; "A Writing Competency Model for Business," BizCom 101.com, 14 December 2007, [accessed 11 July 2008] www.business-writing-courses.com; Sue Dewhurst and Liam FitzPatrick, "What Should Be the Competency of Your IC Team?" white paper, 2007, [accessed 11 July 2008] http://competentcommunicators.com.
8. Philip C. Kolin, *Successful Writing at Work*, 6th ed. (Boston: Houghton Mifflin, 2001), 17–23.
9. Laura L. Myers and Mary L. Tucker, "Increasing Awareness of Emotional Intelligence in a Business Curriculum," *Business Communication Quarterly*, March 2005, 44–51.
10. Pete Cashmore, "10 Web Trends to Watch in 2010," CNN Tech, 3 December 2009 [accessed 6 March 2011] www.cnn.com.
11. Stephanie Armour, "Music Hath Charms for Some Workers—Others It Really Annoys," *USA Today*, 24 March 2006, B1–B2.
12. Paul Martin Lester, *Visual Communication: Images with Messages* (Belmont, Calif.: Thomson South-Western, 2006), 6–8.
13. Michael R. Solomon, *Consumer Behavior: Buying, Having, and Being*, 6th ed. (Upper Saddle River, N.J.: Pearson Prentice Hall, 2004), 65.
14. Anne Field, "What You Say, What They Hear," *Harvard Management Communication Letter*, Winter 2005, 3–5.
15. Chuck Williams, *Management*, 2nd ed. (Cincinnati: Thomson South-Western, 2002), 690.
16. Charles G. Morris and Albert A. Maisto, *Psychology: An Introduction*, 12th ed. (Upper Saddle River, N.J.: Pearson Prentice Hall, 2005), 226–239; Saundra K. Ciccarelli and Glenn E. Meyer, *Psychology* (Upper Saddle River, N.J.: Prentice Hall, 2006), 210–229; Mark H. Ashcraft, *Cognition*, 4th ed. (Upper Saddle River, N.J.: Prentice Hall, 2006), 44–54.

17. Niall Harbison, "Seven Important Social Media Trends for the Next Year," TNW Social Media, 12 September 2010, [accessed 21 December 2010] http://thenextweb.com.

18. Jacques Bughin and Michael Chu, "The Rise of the Networked Enterprise: Web 2.0 Finds Its Payday," *McKinsey Quarterly*, December 2010, [accessed 21 December 2010] www.mckinsey quarterly.com.

19. IBM Corporation, "Capitalizing on Complexity: Insights from the Global Chief Executive Study," May 2010, [accessed 21 December 2010] www.ibm.com.

20. Tara Craig, "How to Avoid Information Overload," *Personnel Today*, 10 June 2008, 31; Jeff Davidson, "Fighting Information Overload," *Canadian Manager*, Spring 2005, 16+.

21. "Are You Addicted to Your BlackBerry?" *Forbes*, 3 April 2008, [accessed 23 July 2008] www.forbes.com; "Employers, Beware: 'Techno Addicts' May Be More Liability Than Boon," Lockergnome.com, 18 August 2006, [accessed 23 August 2006] www.lockergnome.com.

22. "The Top Ten Ways Workers Waste Time Online," 24/7 Wall St., 30 September 2010, [accessed 21 December 2010] http://247wallst .com.

23. Eric J. Sinrod, "Perspective: It's My Internet—I Can Do What I Want," News.com, 29 March 2006, [accessed 12 August 2006] www.news.com.

24. Eric J. Sinrod, "Time to Crack Down on Tech at Work?" News .com, 14 June 2006, [accessed 12 August 2006] www.news.com.

25. Jack Trout, "Beware of 'Infomania,'" *Forbes*, 11 August 2006, [accessed 5 October 2006] www.forbes.com.

26. Steve Lohr, "As Travel Costs Rise, More Meetings Go Virtual," *New York Times*, 22 July 2008, [accessed 23 July 2008] www.nytimes .com.

27. Kolin, *Successful Writing at Work*, 24–30.

28. Nancy K. Kubasek, Bartley A. Brennan, and M. Neil Browne, *The Legal Environment of Business*, 3rd ed. (Upper Saddle River, N.J.: Prentice Hall, 2003), 172.

29. Michael Oliveira, "Netflix Apologizes for Using Actors to Meet Press at Canadian Launch," *Globe and Mail*, 22 September 2010 [accessed 6 March 2011] www.theglobeandmail.com.

30. Word of Mouth Marketing Association, "WOM 101," [accessed 2 June 2010] http://womma.org; Nate Anderson, "FTC Says Stealth Marketing Unethical," *Ars Technica*, 13 December 2006, [accessed 27 January 2008] http://arstechnica.com; "Undercover Marketing Uncovered," CBSnews.com, 25 July 2004, [accessed 11 April 2005] www.cbsnews.com; Stephanie Dunnewind, "Teen Recruits Create Word-of-Mouth 'Buzz' to Hook Peers on Products," *Seattle Times*, 20 November 2004, [accessed 11 April 2005] www.seattletimes.com.

31. Pophal, "Tweet Ethics: Trust and Transparency in a Web 2.0 World."

32. Rich Phillips and John Zarrella, "Live Bombs Haunt Orlando Neighborhood," CNN.com, 1 July 2008, [accessed 24 July 2008] www.cnn.com.

33. Daft, *Management*, 155.

34. Gap, Inc., "Code of Business Conduct," updated 7 December 2009, [accessed 21 December 2010] www.gapinc.com.

35. Based in part on Robert Kreitner, *Management*, 9th ed. (Boston: Houghton Mifflin, 2004), 163.

36. Henry R. Cheeseman, *Contemporary Business and E-Commerce Law*, 4th ed. (Upper Saddle River, N.J.: Prentice Hall, 2003), 841–843.

37. Cheeseman, *Contemporary Business and E-Commerce Law*, 201.

38. John Jude Moran, *Employment Law: New Challenges in the Business Environment*, 2nd ed. (Upper Saddle River, N.J.: Prentice Hall, 2002), 186–187; Kubasek et al., *The Legal Environment of Business*, 562.

39. Cheeseman, *Contemporary Business and E-Commerce Law*, 325.

40. Kubasek et al., *The Legal Environment of Business*, 306.

41. Robert Plummer, "Will Fake Business Blogs Crash and Burn?" BBC News, 22 May 2008, [accessed 3 June 2010] http://news.bbc.co.uk.

42. Tim Arango, "Soon, Bloggers Must Give Full Disclosure," *New York Times*, 5 October 2009, [accessed 7 June 2010] www.nytimes.com.

43. The concept of a four-tweet summary is adapted from Cliff Atkinson, *The Backchannel* (Berkeley, Calif.: New Riders, 2010), 120–121.

CHAPTER 2

1. Evelyn Nussenbaum, "Boosting Teamwork with Wikis," *Fortune Small Business*, 12 February 2008 [accessed 15 August 2008] http://money.cnn.com; Doug Cornelius, "Wikis at the Rosen Law Firm," KM Space blog, 28 February 2008 [accessed 15 August 2008] http://kmspace.blogspot.com; Rosen Law Firm website [accessed 28 December 2010] www.rosen.com.

2. James Manyika, Kara Sprague, and Lareina Yee, "Using Technology to Improve Workforce Collaboration," What Matters (McKinsey & Company), 27 October 2009 [accessed 26 December 2010] http://whatmatters.mckinseydigital.com.

3. Courtland L. Bovée and John V. Thill, *Business in Action*, 5th ed. (Upper Saddle River, N.J.: Pearson Prentice Hall, 2011), 172.

4. "Five Case Studies on Successful Teams," *HR Focus*, April 2002, 18+.

5. Stephen R. Robbins, *Essentials of Organizational Behavior,* 6th ed. (Upper Saddle River, N.J.: Prentice Hall, 2000), 98.

6. Max Landsberg and Madeline Pfau, "Developing Diversity: Lessons from Top Teams," *Strategy + Business*, Winter 2005, 10–12.

7. "Groups Best at Complex Problems," *Industrial Engineer*, June 2006, 14.

8. Nicola A. Nelson, "Leading Teams," *Defense AT&L*, July–August 2006, 26–29; Larry Cole and Michael Cole, "Why Is the Teamwork Buzz Word Not Working?" *Communication World*, February–March 1999, 29; Patricia Buhler, "Managing in the 90s: Creating Flexibility in Today's Workplace," *Supervision*, January 1997, 241; Allison W. Amason, Allen C. Hochwarter, Wayne A. Thompson, and Kenneth R. Harrison, "Conflict: An Important Dimension in Successful Management Teams," *Organizational Dynamics*, Autumn 1995, 201.

9. Geoffrey Colvin, "Why Dream Teams Fail," *Fortune*, 12 June 2006, 87–92.

10. Vijay Govindarajan and Anil K. Gupta, "Building an Effective Global Business Team," *MIT Sloan Management Review*, Summer 2001, 631.

11. Colvin, "Why Dream Teams Fail," 87–92.

12. Tiziana Casciaro and Miguel Sousa Lobo, "Competent Jerks, Lovable Fools, and the Formation of Social Networks," *Harvard Business Review*, June 2005, 92–99.

13. Stephen P. Robbins and David A. DeCenzo, *Fundamentals of Management*, 4th ed. (Upper Saddle River, N.J.: Prentice Hall, 2004), 266–267; Jerald Greenberg and Robert A. Baron, *Behavior in Organizations*, 8th ed. (Upper Saddle River, N.J.: Prentice Hall, 2003), 279–280.

14. B. Aubrey Fisher, *Small Group Decision Making: Communication and the Group Process*, 2nd ed. (New York: McGraw-Hill, 1980), 145–149; Robbins and De Cenzo, *Fundamentals of Management*, 334–335; Richard L. Daft, *Management*, 6th ed. (Cincinnati: Thomson South-Western, 2003), 602–603.

15. Michael Laff, "Effective Team Building: More Than Just Fun at Work," *Training + Development*, August 2006, 24–35.

16. Claire Sookman, "Building Your Virtual Team," *Network World*, 21 June 2004, 91.

17. Jared Sandberg, "Brainstorming Works Best If People Scramble for Ideas on Their Own," *Wall Street Journal*, 13 June 2006, B1.

18. Mark K. Smith, "Bruce W. Tuckman—Forming, Storming, Norming, and Performing in Groups," Infed.org [accessed 5 July 2005] www.infed.org.

19. Robbins and DeCenzo, *Fundamentals of Management*, 258–259.

20. Daft, *Management*, 609–612.

21. Andy Boynton and Bill Fischer, *Virtuoso Teams: Lessons from Teams That Changed Their Worlds* (Harrow, UK: FT Prentice Hall, 2005), 10.

22. Thomas K. Capozzoli, "Conflict Resolution—A Key Ingredient in Successful Teams," *Supervision*, November 1999, 14–16.
23. Jesse S. Nirenberg, *Getting Through to People* (Paramus, N.J.: Prentice Hall, 1973), 134–142.
24. Nirenberg, *Getting Through to People*, 134–142.
25. Nirenberg, *Getting Through to People*, 134–142.
26. Jon Hanke, "Presenting as a Team," *Presentations*, January 1998, 74–82.
27. William P. Galle, Jr., Beverly H. Nelson, Donna W. Luse, and Maurice F. Villere, *Business Communication: A Technology-Based Approach* (Chicago: Irwin, 1996), 260.
28. Mary Beth Debs, "Recent Research on Collaborative Writing in Industry," *Technical Communication*, November 1991, 476–484.
29. Mark Choate, "What Makes an Enterprise Wiki?" CMS Watch website, 28 April 2006 [accessed 18 August 2006] www.cmswatch.com.
30. Choate, "What Makes an Enterprise Wiki?"
31. Rob Koplowitz, "Building a Collaboration Strategy," *KM World*, November/December 2009, 14–15.
32. Eric Knorr and Galen Gruman, "What Cloud Computing Really Means," *InfoWorld* [accessed 11 June 2010] www.infoworld.com; Lamont Wood, "Cloud Computing Poised to Transform Communication," *LiveScience*, 8 December 2009 [accessed 11 June 2010] www.livescience.com.
33. Christopher Carfi and Leif Chastaine, "Social Networking for Businesses & Organizations," white paper, Cerado website [accessed 13 August 2008] www.cerado.com.
34. Richard McDermott and Douglas Archibald, "Harnessing Your Staff's Informal Networks," *Harvard Business Review*, March 2010, 82–89.
35. Tony Hsieh, "Why I Sold Zappos," *Inc.*, 1 June 2010 [accessed 11 June 2010] www.inc.com.
36. Chuck Williams, *Management*, 2nd ed. (Cincinnati: Thomson South-Western, 2002), 706–707.
37. Ron Ashkenas, "Why We Secretly Love Meetings," *Harvard Business Review* blogs, 5 October 2010 [accessed 26 December 2010] http://blogs.hbr.org.
38. Douglas Kimberly, "Ten Pitfalls of Pitiful Meetings," Payroll Manager's Report, January 2010, 1, 11; "Making the Most of Meetings," *Journal of Accountancy*, March 2009, 22.
39. Cyrus Farivar, "How to Run an Effective Meeting," BNET website [accessed 12 August 2008] www.bnet.com.
40. "Better Meetings Benefit Everyone."
41. Manyika, Sprague, and Yee, "Using Technology to Improve Workforce Collaboration."
42. Roger O. Crockett, "The 21st Century Meeting," *BusinessWeek*, 26 February 2007, 72–79.
43. Steve Lohr, "As Travel Costs Rise, More Meetings Go Virtual," *New York Times*, 22 July 2008 [accessed 23 July 2008] www.nytimes.com.
44. "Unlock the Full Power of the Web Conferencing," CEOworld.biz, 20 November 2007 [accessed 30 January 2008] www.ceoworld.biz.
45. IBM Jam Events website [accessed 10 June 2010] www.collaborationjam.com; "Big Blue Brainstorm," *BusinessWeek*, 7 August 2006 [accessed 15 August 2006] www.businessweek.com.
46. "17 Tips for More Productive Conference Calls," AccuConference [accessed 30 January 2008] www.accuconference.com.
47. Augusta M. Simon, "Effective Listening: Barriers to Listening in a Diverse Business Environment," *Bulletin of the Association for Business Communication* 54, no. 3 (September 1991): 73–74.
48. Judi Brownell, *Listening*, 2nd ed. (Boston: Allyn & Bacon, 2002), 9, 10.
49. Carmine Gallo, "Why Leadership Means Listening," *BusinessWeek*, 31 January 2007 [accessed 29 January 2008] www.businessweek.com.
50. Anne Fisher, "The Trouble with MBAs," *Fortune International*, 30 April 2007, 33–34.
51. Dennis M. Kratz and Abby Robinson Kratz, *Effective Listening Skills* (New York: McGraw-Hill, 1995), 45–53; J. Michael Sproule, *Communication Today* (Glenview, Ill.: Scott Foresman, 1981), 69.
52. Brownell, *Listening*, 230–231.
53. Kratz and Kratz, *Effective Listening Skills*, 78–79; Sproule, *Communication Today*.
54. Bill Brooks, "The Power of Active Listening," *American Salesman*, June 2003, 12; "Active Listening," Study Guides and Strategies website [accessed 5 February 2005] www.studygs.net.
55. Bob Lamons, "Good Listeners Are Better Communicators," *Marketing News*, 11 September 1995, 13+; Phillip Morgan and H. Kent Baker, "Building a Professional Image: Improving Listening Behavior," *Supervisory Management*, November 1985, 35–36.
56. Clarke, "Do You Hear What I Hear?"; Dot Yandle, "Listening to Understand," *Pryor Report Management Newsletter Supplement* 15, no. 8 (August 1998): 13.
57. Brownell, *Listening*, 14; Kratz and Kratz, *Effective Listening Skills*, 8–9; Sherwyn P. Morreale and Courtland L. Bovée, *Excellence in Public Speaking* (Orlando, Fla.: Harcourt Brace, 1998), 72–76; Lyman K. Steil, Larry L. Barker, and Kittie W. Watson, *Effective Listening: Key to Your Success* (Reading, Mass.: Addison Wesley, 1983), 21–22.
58. Patrick J. Collins, *Say It with Power and Confidence* (Upper Saddle River, N.J.: Prentice Hall, 1997), 40–45.
59. Morreale and Bovée, *Excellence in Public Speaking*, 296.
60. Dale G. Leathers, *Successful Nonverbal Communication: Principles and Applications* (New York: Macmillan, 1986), 19.
61. Gerald H. Graham, Jeanne Unrue, and Paul Jennings, "The Impact of Nonverbal Communication in Organizations: A Survey of Perceptions," *Journal of Business Communication* 28, no. 1 (Winter 1991): 45–62.
62. Virginia P. Richmond and James C. McCroskey, *Nonverbal Behavior in Interpersonal Relations* (Boston: Allyn & Bacon, 2000), 153–157.
63. Mary Ellen Slayter, "Pamela Meyer on the Science Behind 'Liespotting,'" SmartBlog on Workforce, 14 September 2010 [accessed 27 December 2010] http://smartblogs.com.
64. Slayter, "Pamela Meyer on the Science Behind 'Liespotting.'"
65. Joe Navarro, "Body Language Myths," *Psychology Today*, 25 October 2009 [accessed 11 June 2010] www.psychologytoday.com; Richmond and McCroskey, *Nonverbal Behavior in Interpersonal Relations*, 2–3.
66. John Hollon, "No Tolerance for Jerks," *Workforce Management*, 12 February 2007, 34.
67. Marilyn Pincus, *Everyday Business Etiquette* (Hauppauge, N.Y.: Barron's Educational Series, 1996), 136.
68. Susan G. Hauser, "The Degeneration of Decorum," *Workforce Management*, January 2011, 16–18, 20–21.
69. "Use Proper Cell Phone Etiquette at Work," Kelly Services website [accessed 11 June 2010] www.kellyservices.us.
70. J. J. McCorvey, "How to Create a Cell Phone Policy," *Inc.*, 10 February 2010 [accessed 11 June 2010] www.inc.com; "Use Proper Cell Phone Etiquette at Work."
71. Casperson, *Power Etiquette*, 10–14; Ellyn Spragins, "Introducing Politeness," *Fortune Small Business*, November 2001, 30.
72. Tanya Mohn, "The Social Graces as a Business Tool," *New York Times*, 10 November 2002, sec. 3, 12.
73. Casperson, *Power Etiquette*, 44–46.
74. Casperson, *Power Etiquette*, 109–110.
75. "Are You Practicing Proper Social Networking Etiquette?" *Forbes*, 9 October 2009 [accessed 11 June 2010] www.forbes.com; Pete Babb, "The Ten Commandments of Blog and Wiki Etiquette," *InfoWorld*, 28 May 2007 [accessed 3 August 2008] www.infoworld.com; Judith Kallos, "Instant Messaging Etiquette," NetM@nners blog [accessed 3 August 2008] www.netmanners.com; Michael S. Hyatt, "E-Mail Etiquette 101," From Where I Sit blog, 1 July 2007 [accessed 3 August 2008] www.michaelhyatt.com.

76. Dan Schawbel, "5 Lessons Celebrities Can Teach Us About Facebook Pages," Mashable, 15 May 2009 [accessed 13 June 2010] http://mashable.com.

CHAPTER 3

1. IBM website [accessed 4 January 2011] www.ibm.com; "No. 10 IBM Corp.: Why It's on the DiversityInc Top 50," DiversityInc.com, 13 March 2009 [accessed 4 January 2011] http://diversityinc.com; "IBM Innovation Embraces All Races, Cultures and Genders," Diversity Careers website [accessed 16 August 2008] www.diversitycareers.com; Regina Tosca and Rima Matsumoto, "Diversity and Inclusion: A Driving Force for Growth and Innovation at IBM," 2 February 2007, Hispanic Association on Corporate Responsibility website [accessed 12 February 2007] www.hacr.org; "Executive Corner: Letter from IBM's Vice President, Global Workforce Diversity," IBM website [accessed 12 February 2007] www.ibm.com; "IBM—Diversity as a Strategic Imperative," TWI website [accessed 6 July 2005] www.diversityatwork.com; Cliff Edwards, "The Rewards of Tolerance," BusinessWeek, 15 December 2003 [accessed 6 July 2005] www.businessweek.com; David A. Thomas, "IBM Finds Profit in Diversity," HBS Working Knowledge, 27 September 2004 [accessed 5 July 2005] http://hbswk.hbs.edu; "IBM Diversity Executive to Speak at the University of Virginia," University of Virginia News, 7 November 2003 [accessed 5 July 2005] www.virginia.edu.
2. Michael R. Carrell, Everett E. Mann, and Tracey Honeycutt Sigler, "Defining Workforce Diversity Programs and Practices in Organizations: A Longitudinal Study," Labor Law Journal, Spring 2006, 5–12.
3. "Dimensions of Diversity—Workforce," Merck website [accessed 4 January 2011] www.merck.com.
4. "Top Ten Countries with Which the U.S. Trades," U.S. Census Bureau website [accessed 29 December 2010] www.census.gov.
5. Nancy R. Lockwood, "Workplace Diversity: Leveraging the Power of Difference for Competitive Advantage," HR Magazine, June 2005, special section 1–10.
6. Alan Kline, "The Business Case for Diversity," USBanker, May 2010, 10–11.
7. Podcast interview with Ron Glover, IBM website [accessed 17 August 2008] www.ibm.com.
8. "More Than 300 Counties Now 'Majority–Minority,'" press release, U.S. Census Bureau website, 9 August 2007 [accessed 29 December 2010] www.census.gov; Robert Kreitner, Management, 9th ed. (Boston: Houghton Mifflin, 2004), 84.
9. Linda Beamer and Iris Varner, Intercultural Communication in the Workplace, 2nd ed. (New York: McGraw-Hill Irwin, 2001), xiii.
10. Tracy Novinger, Intercultural Communication, A Practical Guide (Austin, Tex.: University of Texas Press, 2001), 15.
11. Larry A. Samovar and Richard E. Porter, "Basic Principles of Intercultural Communication," in Intercultural Communication: A Reader, 6th ed., edited by Larry A. Samovar and Richard E. Porter (Belmont, Calif.: Wadsworth, 1991), 12.
12. Arthur Chin, "Understanding Cultural Competency," New Zealand Business, December 2010/January 2011, 34–35; Sanjeeta R. Gupta, "Achieve Cultural Competency," Training, February 2009, 16–17; Diane Shannon, "Cultural Competency in Health Care Organizations: Why and How," Physician Executive, September–October 2010, 15–22.
13. Beamer and Varner, Intercultural Communication in the Workplace, 3.
14. "Languages of the United States," Ethnologue website [accessed 29 December 2010] www.ethnologue.com.
15. Philip R. Harris and Robert T. Moran, Managing Cultural Differences, 3rd ed. (Houston: Gulf, 1991), 394–397, 429–430.
16. Lillian H. Chaney and Jeanette S. Martin, Intercultural Business Communication, 2nd ed. (Upper Saddle River, N.J.: Prentice Hall, 2000), 6.
17. Beamer and Varner, Intercultural Communication in the Workplace, 4.
18. Chaney and Martin, Intercultural Business Communication, 2nd ed., 9.
19. Richard L. Daft, Management, 6th ed. (Cincinnati: Thomson South-Western, 2003), 455.
20. Lillian H. Chaney and Jeanette S. Martin, Intercultural Business Communication, 4th ed. (Upper Saddle River, N.J.: Pearson Prentice Hall, 2007), 53.
21. Project Implicit website [accessed 29 December 2010] http://implicit.harvard.edu/implicit.
22. Linda Beamer, "Teaching English Business Writing to Chinese-Speaking Business Students," Bulletin of the Association for Business Communication 57, no. 1 (1994): 12–18.
23. Edward T. Hall, "Context and Meaning," in Intercultural Communication, 6th ed., edited by Larry A. Samovar and Richard E. Porter (Belmont, Calif.: Wadsworth, 1991), 46–55.
24. Daft, Management, 459.
25. Charley H. Dodd, Dynamics of Intercultural Communication, 3rd ed. (Dubuque, Ia.: Brown, 1991), 69–70.
26. Daft, Management, 459.
27. Hannah Seligson, "For American Workers in China, a Culture Clash," New York Times, 23 December 2009 [accessed 1 January 2011] www.nytimes.com.
28. Beamer and Varner, Intercultural Communication in the Workplace, 230–233.
29. Ed Marcum, "More U.S. Businesses Abandon Outsourcing Overseas," Seattle Times, 28 August 2010 [accessed 2 January 2011] www.seattletimes.com.
30. Guo-Ming Chen and William J. Starosta, Foundations of Intercultural Communication (Boston: Allyn & Bacon, 1998), 288–289.
31. Mary A. DeVries, Internationally Yours (New York: Houghton Mifflin, 1994), 194.
32. Robert O. Joy, "Cultural and Procedural Differences That Influence Business Strategies and Operations in the People's Republic of China," SAM Advanced Management Journal, Summer 1989, 29–33.
33. Chaney and Martin, Intercultural Business Communication, 2nd ed., 122–123.
34. Seligson, "For American Workers in China, a Culture Clash."
35. Mansour Javidan, "Forward-Thinking Cultures," Harvard Business Review, July–August 2007, 20.
36. IBM website [accessed 17 August 2008] www.ibm.com; Wendy Harris, "Out of the Corporate Closet," Black Enterprise, May 2007, 64–66; David A. Thomas, "Diversity as Strategy," Harvard Business Review, September 2004, 98–108; Joe Mullich, "Hiring Without Limits," Workforce Management, June 2004, 53–58; Mike France and William G. Symonds, "Diversity Is About to Get More Elusive, Not Less," 7 July 2003, BusinessWeek [accessed 24 January 2005] www.businessweek.com.
37. Novinger, Intercultural Communication: A Practical Guide, 54.
38. Peter Coy, "Old. Smart. Productive." BusinessWeek, 27 June 2005 [accessed 24 August 2006] www.businessweek.com; Beamer and Varner, Intercultural Communication in the Workplace, 107–108.
39. Beamer and Varner, Intercultural Communication in the Workplace, 107–108.
40. Steff Gelston, "Gen Y, Gen X and the Baby Boomers: Workplace Generation Wars," CIO, 30 January 2008 [accessed 2 January 2011] www.cio.com.
41. Tonya Vinas, "A Place at the Table," IndustryWeek, 1 July 2003, 22.
42. Daft, Management, 445.
43. John Gray, Mars and Venus in the Workplace (New York: HarperCollins, 2002), 10, 25–27, 61–63.
44. Chaney and Martin, Intercultural Business Communication, 4th ed., 62.
45. Todd Henneman, "A New Approach to Faith at Work," Workforce Management, October 2004, 76–77.
46. Mark D. Downey, "Keeping the Faith," HR Magazine, January 2008, 85–88.

47. Vadim Liberman, "What Happens When an Employee's Freedom of Religion Crosses Paths with a Company's Interests?" *Conference Board Review*, September/October 2007, 42–48.

48. IBM Accessibility Center [accessed 24 August 2006] www-03.ibm .com/able; AssistiveTech.net [accessed 24 August 2006] www .assistivetech.net; Business Leadership Network website [accessed 24 August 2006] www.usbln.org; National Institute on Disability and Rehabilitation Research website [accessed 24 August 2006] www.ed.gov/about/offices/list/osers/nidrr; Rehabilitation Engineering & Assistive Technology Society of North America website [accessed 24 August 2006] www.resna.org.

49. Daphne A. Jameson, "Reconceptualizing Cultural Identity and its Role in Intercultural Business Communication," *Journal of Business Communication*, July 2007, 199–235.

50. Leslie Knudson, "Diversity on a Global Scale," *HR Management* [accessed 17 August 2008] www.hrmreport.com.

51. Craig S. Smith, "Beware of Green Hats in China and Other Cross-Cultural Faux Pas," *New York Times*, 30 April 2002, C11.

52. Sana Reynolds and Deborah Valentine, *Guide for Internationals: Culture, Communication, and ESL* (Upper Saddle River, N.J.: Pearson Prentice Hall, 2006), 3–11, 14–19, 25.

53. P. Christopher Earley and Elaine Mosakowsi, "Cultural Intelligence," *Harvard Business Review*, October 2004, 139–146.

54. Wendy A. Conklin, "An Inside Look at Two Diversity Intranet Sites: IBM and Merck," *The Diversity Factor*, Summer 2005.

55. Bob Nelson, "Motivating Workers Worldwide," *Global Workforce*, November 1998, 25–27.

56. Mona Casady and Lynn Wasson, "Written Communication Skills of International Business Persons," *Bulletin of the Association for Business Communication* 57, no. 4 (1994): 36–40.

57. Lynn Gaertner-Johnston, "Found in Translation," Business Writing blog, 25 November 2005 [accessed 18 August 2008] www .businesswritingblog.com.

58. Myron W. Lustig and Jolene Koester, *Intercultural Competence*, 4th ed. (Boston: Allyn & Bacon, 2003), 196.

59. "'Can You Spell That for Us Nonnative Speakers?' Accommodation Strategies in International Business Meetings," Pamela Rogerson-Revell, *Journal of Business Communication*, Vol 47, No 4, October 2010, 432–454.

60. Wilfong and Seger, *Taking Your Business Global*, 232.

61. Mark Lasswell, "Lost in Translation," *Business 2.0*, August 2004, 68–70.

62. Sheridan Prasso, ed., "It's All Greek to These Sites," *BusinessWeek*, 22 July 2002, 18.

CHAPTER 4

1. H&R Block website [accessed 9 January 2011] www.hrblock.com; Paula Drum, "I Got People (Online): How H&R Block Connects by Using Social Media," presentation at BlogWell conference, 22 January 2009 [accessed 9 January 2011] www.socialmedia.org; Shel Israel, "Twitterville Notebook: H&R Block's Paula Drum," Global Neighbourhoods blog, 22 December 2008 [accessed 25 January 2009] http://redcouch.typepad.com/weblog; "H&R Block's Paula Drum Talks Up Value of Online 'Presence,'" The Deal website, video interview, 6 June 2008 [accessed 28 August 2008] www.thedeal.com; Shel Israel, "SAP Global Survey: H&R Block's Paula Drum," Global Neighbourhoods blog, 4 April 2008 [accessed 28 August 2008] http://redcouch.typepad.com/weblog; "Tango in Plain English," video [accessed 27 August 2008] www .youtube.com; "H&R Block, Inc.," Hoovers [accessed 27 August 2008] www.hoovers.com; Linda Zimmer, "H&R Block Tangoes into Second Life," Business Communicators of Second Life blog, 17 March 2007 [accessed 27 August 2008] http://freshtakes.typepad .com/sl_communicators; "H&R Block Launches First Virtual Tax Experience in Second Life," press release [accessed 27 August 2008] www.hrblock.com.

2. Linda Duyle, "Get Out of Your Office," *HR Magazine*, July 2006, 99–101.

3. Frank Martin Hein, "Making the Best Use of Electronic Media," *Communication World*, November–December 2006, 20–23.

4. "About Skype," Skype website [accessed 7 January 2011] http:// about.skype.com.

5. Caroline McCarthy, "The Future of Web Apps Will See the Death of E-Mail," Webware blog, 29 February 2008 [accessed 25 August 2008] http://news.cnet.com; Kris Maher, "The Jungle," *Wall Street Journal*, 5 October 2004, B10; Kevin Maney, "Surge in Text Messaging Makes Cell Operators :-)," *USA Today*, 28 July 2005, B1–B2.

6. Presselite website [accessed 28 June 2010] www.presselite.com; Neville Hobson, "Augmented Reality: Overlay Your World," Neville Hobson blog, 27 July 2009 [accessed 28 June 2010] www .nevillehobson.com.

7. Berk and Clampitt, "Finding the Right Path in the Communication Maze."

8. Samantha R. Murray and Joseph Peyrefitte, "Knowledge Type and Communication Media Choice in the Knowledge Transfer Process," *Journal of Managerial Issues*, Spring 2007, 111–133.

9. Raymond M. Olderman, *10 Minute Guide to Business Communication* (New York: Alpha Books, 1997), 19–20.

10. Mohan R. Limaye and David A. Victor, "Cross-Cultural Business Communication Research: State of the Art and Hypotheses for the 1990s," *Journal of Business Communication*, Summer 1991, 277–299.

11. Holly Weeks, "The Best Memo You'll Ever Write," *Harvard Management Communication Letter*, Spring 2005, 3–5.

12. Steve Tobak, "How to Be a Great Storyteller and Win Over Any Audience," BNET, 12 January 2011 [accessed 17 January 2011] www.bnet.com.

13. Debra Askanase, "10 Trends in Sustainable Social Media," Community Organizer 2.0 blog, 13 May 2010 [accessed 8 January 2011] www.communityorganizer20.com.

14. Chip Heath and Dan Heath, *Made to Stick: Why Some Ideas Survive and Others Die* (New York: Random House: 2008), 214.

15. Heath and Heath, *Made to Stick: Why Some Ideas Survive and Others Die*, 206, 214.

16. Randolph T. Barker and Kim Gower, "Strategic Application of Storytelling in Organizations," *Journal of Business Communication*, Vol 47, No 3, July 2010, 295–312.

17. Jennifer Aaker and Andy Smith, "7 Deadly Sins of Business Storytelling," American Express Open Forum [accessed 21 March 2011] www.openforum.com.

CHAPTER 5

1. Creative Commons website [accessed 17 January 2011] www .creativecommons.org; "An Interview with Joi Ito, CEO of Creative Commons," audio interview [accessed 6 September 2008] www.businessweek.com; Kenji Hall, "Online Sharing with Creative Commons," *BusinessWeek*, 15 August 2008 [accessed 6 September 2008] www.businessweek.com; Ariana Eunjung Cha, "Creative Commons Is Rewriting Rules of Copyright," *Washington Post*, 15 March 2005 [accessed 3 August 2005] www .washingtonpost.com; Steven Levy, "Lawrence Lessig's Supreme Showdown," Wired, October 2002 [accessed 3 August 2005] www .wired.com; "Happy Birthday: We'll Sue," Snopes.com [accessed 3 August 2005] www.snopes.com.

2. Annette N. Shelby and N. Lamar Reinsch, Jr., "Positive Emphasis and You Attitude: An Empirical Study," *Journal of Business Communication* 32, no. 4 (1995): 303–322.

3. Quinn Warnick, "A Close Textual Analysis of Corporate Layoff Memos," *Business Communication Quarterly*, September 2010, Vol. 73 No. 3, 322–326.

4. Sherryl Kleinman, "Why Sexist Language Matters," *Qualitative Sociology* 25, no. 2 (Summer 2002): 299–304.

5. Judy E. Pickens, "Terms of Equality: A Guide to Bias-Free Language," *Personnel Journal*, August 1985, 24.

6. Biography of Ursula M. Burns, Xerox website [accessed 16 January 2011] www.xerox.com; biography of Shelly Lazarus, Ogilvy &

Mather website [accessed 16 January 2011] www.ogilvy.com; biography of Andrea Jung, Avon website [accessed 16 January 2011] www.avoncompany.com.

7. Lisa Taylor, "Communicating About People with Disabilities: Does the Language We Use Make a Difference?" *Bulletin of the Association for Business Communication* 53, no. 3 (September 1990): 65–67.

8. Susan Benjamin, *Words at Work* (Reading, Mass.: Addison-Wesley, 1997), 136–137.

9. Stuart Crainer and Des Dearlove, "Making Yourself Understood," *Across the Board*, May/June 2004, 23–27.

10. Plain English Campaign website [accessed 28 June 2010] www.plainenglish.co.uk.

11. Plain Language website [accessed 16 January 2011] www.plainlanguage.gov.

12. Creative Commons website [accessed 16 January 2011] www.creativecommons.org.

13. Susan Jaderstrom and Joanne Miller, "Active Writing," *Office Pro*, November/December 2003, 29.

14. Mary Munter, *Guide to Managerial Communication*, 7th ed. (Upper Saddle River, N.J.: Pearson Prentice Hall, 2006), 41.

15. Portions of this section are adapted from Courtland L. Bovée, *Techniques of Writing Business Letters, Memos, and Reports* (Sherman Oaks, Calif.: Banner Books International, 1978), 13–90.

16. Catherine Quinn, "Lose the Office Jargon; It May Sunset Your Career," *The Age* (Australia), 1 September 2007 [accessed 5 February 2008] www.theage.com.au.

17. Robert Hartwell Fiske, *The Dimwit's Dictionary* (Oak Park, Ill.: Marion Street Press, 2002), 16–20.

18. Visuwords website [accessed 16 January 2011] www.visuwords.com.

19. Beverly Ballaro and Christina Bielaszka-DuVernay, "Building a Bridge over the River Boredom," *Harvard Management Communication Letter*, Winter 2005, 3–5.

20. Food Allergy Initiative website [accessed 5 September 2008] www.foodallergyinitiative.org; Diana Keough, "Snacks That Can Kill; Schools Take Steps to Protect Kids Who Have Severe Allergies to Nuts," *Plain Dealer*, 15 July 2003, E1; "Dawdling over Food Labels," *New York Times*, 2 June 2003, A16; Sheila McNulty, "A Matter of Life and Death," *Financial Times*, 10 September 2003, 14.

21. Apple iTunes website [accessed 23 September 2006] www.apple.com/itunes.

CHAPTER 6

1. Jefferson Rabb website [accessed 22 January 2011] www.jeffersonrabb.com; Joshua Bodwell, "Artful Author Web Sites," Poets & Writers, January/February 2011, 79–84; *Super Sad True Love Story* website [accessed 22 January 2011] http://supersadtruelovestory.com; *Beat the Reaper* website [accessed 22 January 2011] www.beatthereaper.com.

2. William Zinsser, *On Writing Well*, 5th ed. (New York: Harper-Collins, 1994), 9.

3. Deborah Gunn, "Looking Good on Paper," *Office Pro*, March 2004, 10–11.

4. Jennifer Saranow, "Memo to Web Sites: Grow Up!" *Wall Street Journal*, 15 November 2004, R14–R15.

5. Jacci Howard Bear, "Desktop Publishing Rules of Page Layout," About.com [accessed 22 August 2005] www.about.com.

6. Jacci Howard Bear, "Desktop Publishing Rules for How Many Fonts to Use," About.com [accessed 22 August 2005] www.about.com.

7. The writing sample in this exercise was adapted from material on the Marsh Risk Consulting website [accessed 2 October 2006] www.marshriskconsulting.com.

CHAPTER 7

1. Southwest Airlines, Nuts About Southwest blog [accessed 1 February 2011] www.blogsouthwest.com; Bill Owens, "Why Can't I Make Reservations Further in Advance?" Nuts About Southwest blog, 24 January 2007 [accessed 15 May 2007] www.blogsouthwest.com; Bill Owens, "I Blogged. You Flamed. We Changed." Nuts About Southwest blog, 18 April 2007 [accessed 10 May 2007] www.blogsouthwest.com; "Southwest Airlines Is Nuts About Blogging," Southwest Airlines press release, 27 April 2007 [accessed 15 May 2007] www.prnewswire.com.

2. "Ten Ways to Use Texting for Business," *Inc.* [accessed 21 July 2010] www.inc.com; Kate Maddox, "Warrillow Finds 39% of Small-Business Owners Use Text Messaging," BtoB, 1 August 2008 [accessed 15 September 2008] www.btobonline.com; Dave Carpenter, "Companies Discover Marketing Power of Text Messaging," *Seattle Times*, 25 September 2006 [accessed 25 September 2006] www.seattletimes.com.

3. "Burson-Marsteller Fortune Global 10 Social Media Study," The Burson-Marsteller Blog, 23 February 2010 [accessed 30 January 2011] www.burson-marsteller.com.

4. "The New Messages," Facebook.com [accessed 30 January 2011] www.facebook.com.

5. Facebook Press Room [accessed 29 January 2011] www.facebook.com; Adam Ostrow, "A Look Back at the Last 5 Years in Social Media," Mashable, 20 July 2010 [accessed 21 July 2010] www.mashable.com.

6. Peter Koeppel, "How Do I Love Thee, Smartphone?" Adotas, 25 January 2011 [accessed 30 January 2011] www.adotas.com; Jennifer Van Grove, "Why Google's Slapping Decals on Small Businesses," Mashable, 7 December 2009 [accessed 30 January 2011] http://mashable.com; Jennifer Van Grove, "5 Huge Trends in Social Media Right Now," Mashable, 20 August 2010 [accessed 30 January 2011] http://mashable.com.

7. Richard Edelman, "Teaching Social Media: What Skills Do Communicators Need?" in *Engaging the New Influencers; Third Annual Social Media Academic Summit* (white paper) [accessed 7 June 2010] www.newmediaacademicsummit.com.

8. Catherine Toole, "My 7 Deadly Sins of Writing for Social Media—Am I Right?" Econsultancy blog, 19 June 2007 [accessed 16 September 2008] www.econsultancy.com; Muhammad Saleem, "How to Write a Social Media Press Release," Copyblogger [accessed 16 September 2008] www.copyblogger.com; Melanie McBride, "5 Tips for (Better) Social Media Writing," Melanie McBride Online, 11 June 2008 [accessed 16 September 2008] http://melaniemcbride.net.

9. "Social Media Policies Reduce Discovery Risks: Are You Prepared?" Armstrong Teasdale, 3 November 2010 [accessed 2 February 2011] www.jdsupra.com; "The Library of Congress Is Archiving Your Tweets," NPR, 19 July 2010 [accessed 19 July 2010] www.npr.org; Simon Quance, "The Guide to Social Media Etiquette for Businesses," MyCustomer.com, 16 August 2010 [accessed 2 February 2011] www.mycustomer.com; Tony Schwartz, "Digital Incivility: The Unseemly Rise of Rudeness," Harvard Business Review blogs, 14 September 2010 [accessed 2 February 2011] http://blogs.hbr.org; Gillian Shaw, "Twitter Can Be a Legal Minefield: Watch What You Say," Vancouver Sun, 17 October 2009 [accessed 2 February 2011] www.vancouversun.com.

10. Mark Evans, "No Social Media for Us, Thank You," Sysomos blog, 9 February 2011 [accessed 13 February 2011] http://blogs.sysomos.com.

11. Tanzina Vega, "Tools to Help Companies Manage Their Social Media," *New York Times*, 14 November 2010 [accessed 30 January 2011] www.nytimes.com.

12. Paula Drum, "I Got People (Online): How H&R Block Connects by Using Social Media," presentation at BlogWell conference, 22 January 2009 [accessed 9 January 2011] www.socialmedia.org.

13. Nick Wreden, "Social Media Policies for Business," *Baseline*, 7 June 2010 [accessed 30 January 2011] www.baselinemag.com.

14. "Facebook Analytics: Full-on Facebook Tracking and Measurement," Webtrends [accessed 10 July 2010] www.webtrends.com; Facebook statistics page, Facebook.com [accessed 10 July 2010] www.facebook.com; Facebook pages of Adidas, Red Bull, and Starbucks [accessed 11 July 2010] www.facebook.com.

15. "Gartner Says Social-Networking Services to Replace E-Mail as the Primary Vehicle for Interpersonal Communications for 20 Percent of Business Users by 2014," Gartner press release, 11 November 2010 [accessed 30 January 2011] www.gartner.com; Sarah Perez, "Social Networking More Popular Than Voice, SMS by 2015," ReadWriteWeb.com, 15 November 2010 [accessed 30 January 2011] www.readwriteweb.com.

16. Todd Henneman, "At Lockheed Martin, Social Networking Fills Key Workforce Needs While Improving Efficiency and Lowering Costs," *Workforce Management*, March 2010 [accessed 14 July 2010] www.workforce.com.

17. Sheryl Kingstone and Zeus Kerravala, "Social Media Means Serious Business," Yankee Group white paper, June 2010 [accessed 30 January 2011] www.siemens-enterprise.com; Sharon Gaudin, "Companies Not Using Social Nets at Risk, Report Says," *Computerworld*, 15 July 2010 [accessed 21 July 2010] www.computerworld.com.

18. Alex Wright, "Mining the Web for Feelings, Not Facts," *New York Times*, 23 August 2009 [accessed 9 September 2009] www.nytimes.com.

19. Erica Swallow, "How to Use Social Media for Lead Generation," Mashable, 24 June 2010 [accessed 11 July 2010] http://mashable.com.

20. Susan Fournier and Lara Lee, "Getting Brand Communities Right," *Harvard Business Review*, April 2009, 105–111.

21. Patrick Hanlon and Josh Hawkins, "Expand Your Brand Community Online," *Advertising Age*, 7 January 2008, 14–15.

22. Josh Bernoff, "Social Strategy for Exciting (and Not So Exciting) Brands," *Marketing News*, 15 May 2009, 18; Larry Weber, *Marketing to the Social Web* (Hoboken, N.J.: Wiley, 2007), 12–14; David Meerman Scott, *The New Rules of Marketing and PR* (Hoboken, N.J.: Wiley, 2007), 62; Paul Gillin, *The New Influencers* (Sanger, Calif.: Quill Driver Books, 2007), 34–35; Jeremy Wright, *Blog Marketing: The Revolutionary Way to Increase Sales, Build Your Brand, and Get Exceptional Results* (New York: McGraw-Hill, 2006), 263–365.

23. Matt Rhodes, "Build Your Own Community or Go Where People Are? Do Both," FreshNetworks blog, 12 May 2009 [accessed 21 July 2010] www.freshnetworks.com.

24. Brian Solis, *Engage!* (Hoboken, N.J.: Wiley, 2010), 13.

25. Zachary Sniderman, "5 Ways to Clean Up Your Social Media Identity," 7 July 2010, Mashable [accessed 10 July 2010] http://mashable.com.

26. HP company profiles on LinkedIn and Facebook [accessed 21 July 2010] www.facebook.com/hp and www.linkedin.com/hp.

27. Ben Hanna, *2009 Business Social Media Benchmarking Study* (published by Business.com), 2 November 2009, 22.

28. Vanessa Pappas, "5 Ways to Build a Loyal Audience on YouTube," Mashable, 15 June 2010 [accessed 21 July 2010] www.mashable.com.

29. Tamar Weinberg, *The New Community Rules: Marketing on the Social Web* (Sebastapol, Calif.: O'Reilly Media, 2009), 288.

30. "About Us," Yelp [accessed 30 January 2011] www.yelp.com; Lisa Barone, "Keynote Conversation with Yelp Chief Operating Officer Geoff Donaker," 5 October 2010 [accessed 30 January 2011] http://outspokenmedia.com.

31. Reid Goldborough, "More Trends for 2009: What to Expect with Personal Technology," *Public Relations Tactics*, February 2009, 9.

32. Jessica E. Vascellaro, "Why Email No Longer Rules . . ." *Wall Street Journal*, 12 October 2008 [accessed 21 July 2010] http://online.wsj.com.

33. Matt Cain, "Managing E-Mail Hygiene," ZD Net Tech Update, 5 February 2004 [accessed 19 March 2004] www.techupdate.zdnet.com.

34. Hilary Potkewitz and Rachel Brown, "Spread of E-Mail Has Altered Communication Habits at Work," *Los Angeles Business Journal*, 18 April 2005 [accessed 30 April 2006] www.findarticles.com; Nancy Flynn, *Instant Messaging Rules* (New York: AMACOM, 2004), 47–54.

35. Mary Munter, Priscilla S. Rogers, and Jone Rymer, "Business E-Mail: Guidelines for Users," *Business Communication Quarterly*, March 2003, 26+; Renee B. Horowitz and Marian G. Barchilon, "Stylistic Guidelines for E-Mail," *IEEE Transactions on Professional Communication* 37, no. 4 (December 1994): 207–212.

36. Steve Rubel, "Tip: Tweetify the Lead of Your Emails," The Steve Rubel Stream blog, 20 July 2010 [accessed 22 July 2010] www.steverubel.com.

37. "E-Mail Is So Five Minutes Ago," *BusinessWeek* online, 28 November 2005 [accessed 3 May 2006] www.businessweek.com.

38. Robert J. Holland, "Connected—More or Less," Richmond.com, 8 August 2006 [accessed 5 October 2006] www.richmond.com.

39. Douglas MacMillan, "The End of Instant Messaging (As We Know It), *BusinessWeek*, 16 November 2008 [accessed 16 December 2008] www.businessweek.com.

40. Vayusphere website [accessed 22 January 2006] www.vayusphere.com; Christa C. Ayer, "Presence Awareness: Instant Messaging's Killer App," *Mobile Business Advisor*, 1 July 2004 [accessed 22 January 2006] www.highbeam.com; Jefferson Graham, "Instant Messaging Programs Are No Longer Just for Messages," *USA Today*, 20 October 2003, 5D; Todd R. Weiss, "Microsoft Targets Corporate Instant Messaging Customers," *Computerworld*, 18 November 2002, 12; "Banks Adopt Instant Messaging to Create a Global Business Network," *Computer Weekly*, 25 April 2002, 40; Michael D. Osterman, "Instant Messaging in the Enterprise," *Business Communications Review*, January 2003, 59–62; John Pallato, "Instant Messaging Unites Work Groups and Inspires Collaboration," *Internet World*, December 2002, 14+.

41. Jack Aronson, "Use Text Messaging in Your Business," ClickZ, 12 June 2009 [accessed 31 January 2011] www.clickz.com; Paul Mah, "Using Text Messaging in Business," Mobile Enterprise blog, 4 February 2008 [accessed 16 September 2008] http://blogs.techrepublic.com/wireless; Paul Kedrosky, "Why We Don't Get the (Text) Message," *Business 2.0*, 2 October 2006 [accessed 4 October 2006] www.business2.com; Carpenter, "Companies Discover Marketing Power of Text Messaging."

42. Mark Gibbs, "Racing to Instant Messaging," *NetworkWorld*, 17 February 2003, 74.

43. "E-Mail Is So Five Minutes Ago."

44. *SANS Top-20 2007 Security Risks*, SANS Institute [accessed 16 September 2008] www.sans.org; Tom Espiner, "Spim, Splog on the Rise," CNET News, 6 July 2006 [accessed 16 September 2008] http://news.cnet.com; Anita Hamilton, "You've Got Spim!" *Time*, 2 February 2004 [accessed 1 March 2004] www.time.com; Elizabeth Millard, "Instant Messaging Threats Still Rising," Newsfactor.com, 6 July 2005 [accessed 5 October 2006] www.newsfactor.com.

45. Clint Boulton, "IDC: IM Use Is Booming in Business," InstantMessagingPlanet.com, 5 October 2005 [accessed 22 January 2006] www.instantmessagingplanet.com; Jenny Goodbody, "Critical Success Factors for Global Virtual Teams," *Strategic Communication Management*, February/March 2005, 18–21; Ann Majchrzak, Arvind Malhotra, Jeffrey Stamps, and Jessica Lipnack, "Can Absence Make a Team Grow Stronger?" *Harvard Business Review*, May 2004, 131–137; Christine Y. Chen, "The IM Invasion," *Fortune*, 26 May 2003, 135–138; Yudhijit Bhattacharjee, "A Swarm of Little Notes," *Time*, September 2002, A3–A8; Mark Bruno, "Taming the Wild Frontiers of Instant Messaging," *Bank Technology News*, December 2002, 30–31; Richard Grigonis, "Enterprise-Strength Instant Messaging," Convergence.com, 10–15 [accessed March 2003] www.convergence.com; Pallato, "Instant Messaging Unites Work Groups and Inspires Collaboration," 14+.

46. Valeria Maltoni, "Corporate Blogs: How's Your Elevator Pitch These Days?" Conversation Agent blog, 6 July 2010 [accessed 31 January 2011] www.conversationagent.com.

47. Amy Porterfield, "10 Top Business Blogs and Why They Are Successful," Social Media Examiner, 25 January 2011 [accessed 31 January 2011] www.socialmediaexaminer.com.

48. Dr. Laundry blog [accessed 31 January 2011] www.drlaundryblog.com.

49. Debbie Weil, Why Your Blog Is the Hub of Social Media Marketing," Social Media Insights Blog, 12 January 2010 [accessed 31 January 2011] http://debbieweil.com; Ross Dawson, "A List of Business Applications for Blogging in the Enterprise," Trends in the Living Network blog, 7 July 2009 [accessed 31 January 2011] http://rossdawsonblog.com; Fredrik Wackå, "Six Types of Blogs—A Classification," CorporateBlogging.Info website, 10 August 2004 [accessed 5 October 2006] www.corporateblogging.info; Stephen Baker, "The Inside Story on Company Blogs," *BusinessWeek* 14 February 2006 [accessed 15 February 2006] www.businessweek.com; Jeremy Wright, *Blog Marketing* (New York: McGraw-Hill, 2006), 45–56; Paul Chaney, "Blogs: Beyond the Hype!" 26 May 2005 [accessed 4 May 2006] http://radiantmarketinggroup.com.

50. Jake Swearingen, "Four Ways Social Networking Can Build Business," Bnet.com [accessed 11 July 2010] www.bnet.com.

51. Evolve24 website [accessed 31 January 2011] www.evolve24.com.

52. Dianne Culhane, "Blog Logs a Culture Change, *Communication World*, January/February 2008, 40–41.

53. Weinberg, *The New Community Rules: Marketing on the Social Web*, 89.

54. Stephen Baker and Heather Green, "Blogs Will Change Your Business," *BusinessWeek*, 2 May 2005, 57–67.

55. Joel Falconer, "Six Rules for Writing Great Web Content," Blog News Watch, 9 November 2007 [accessed 14 February 2008] www.blognewswatch.com.

56. Dion Hinchcliffe, "Twitter on Your Intranet: 17 Microblogging Tools for Business," ZDNet, 1 June 2009 [accessed 22 July 2010] www.zdnet.com.

57. Hinchcliffe, "Twitter on Your Intranet: 17 Microblogging Tools for Business."

58. "Warner Brothers Television Group Social Media Contacts," The WB website [accessed 9 August 2010] www.thewb.com.

59. "Turn Your Feed into a Podcast," Lifehacker blog, 12 January 2006 [accessed 6 May 2006] www.lifehacker.com.

60. "Set Up Your Podcast for Success," FeedForAll website [accessed 4 October 2006] www.feedforall.com.

61. Shel Holtz, "Ten Guidelines for B2B Podcasts," Webpronews.com, 12 October 2005 [accessed 9 March 2006] www.webpronews.com.

62. Adapted from "Side Impact Protection Explained," Britax website [accessed 18 September 2008] www.britaxusa.com.

63. Adapted from Lisa Marsh, "Why Fashion Loves Skinny," MSN Lifestyle [accessed 17 September 2008] http://lifestyle.msn.com.

64. Adapted from Seymour Powell website [accessed 16 January 2007] www.seymourpowell.com; Sam Roberts, "51% of Women Now Living Without a Spouse," *New York Times*, 16 January 2007 [accessed 16 January 2007] www.nytimes.com.

65. Adapted from Crutchfield website [accessed 3 February 2011] www.crutchfield.com.

66. Adapted from Comic-Con website [accessed 19 July 2010] www.comic-con.org; Tom Spurgeon, "Welcome to Nerd Vegas: A Guide to Visiting and Enjoying Comic-Con International in San Diego, 2006!" The Comics Reporter.com, 11 July 2006 [accessed 16 January 2007] www.comicsreporter.com; Rebecca Winters Keegan, "Boys Who Like Toys," *Time*, 19 April 2007 [accessed 15 May 2007] www.time.com.

67. Adapted from "Major New Study Shatters Stereotypes About Teens and Video Games," MacArthur Foundation, 16 September 2008 [accessed 18 September 2008] www.macfound.org.

68. Adapted from *Logan* website [accessed 3 February 2011] www.loganmagazine.com.

69. JetBlue Twitter page [accessed 3 February 2011] http://twitter.com/JetBlue; "JetBlue Lands on eBay," JetBlue website [accessed 18 September 2008] http://jetblue.com/ebay.

CHAPTER 8

1. Get Satisfaction website [accessed 4 February 2011] http://getsatisfaction.com; Dan Fost, "On the Internet, Everyone Can Hear You Complain," *New York Times*, 25 February 2008 [accessed 2 October 2008] www.nytimes.com.

2. Fraser P. Seitel, *The Practice of Public Relations*, 9th ed. (Upper Saddle River, N.J.: Prentice Hall, 2004), 402–411; *Techniques for Communicators* (Chicago: Lawrence Ragan Communication, 1995), 34, 36.

3. David Meerman Scott, *The New Rules of Marketing and PR* (Hoboken, N.J.: Wiley, 2007), 62.

4. Shel Holz, "Next-Generation Press Releases," CW Bulletin, September 2009 [accessed 9 August 2010] www.iabc.com; Steph Gray, "Baby Steps in Social Media News Releases," Helpful Technology blog, 15 May 2009 [accessed 9 August 2010] http://blog.helpfultechnology.com.

5. Pat Cataldo, "Op-Ed: Saying 'Thank You'; Can Open More Doors Than You Think," Penn State University Smeal College of Business website [accessed 19 February 2008] www.smeal.psu.edu.

6. Jackie Huba, "Five Must-Haves for Thank-You Notes," Church of the Customer Blog, 16 November 2007 [accessed 19 February 2008] www.churchofthecustomer.com.

7. Mary Mitchell, "The Circle of Life—Condolence Letters," LiveandLearn.com [accessed 18 July 2005] www.liveandlearn.com; Donna Larcen, "Authors Share the Words of Condolence," *Los Angeles Times*, 20 December 1991, E11.

8. Adapted from an answer on Get Satisfaction website, 26 September 2008 [accessed 3 October 2008] http://getsatisfaction.com.

9. Adapted from Tom Abate, "Need to Preserve Cash Generates Wave of Layoffs in Biotech Industry," *San Francisco Chronicle*, 10 February 2003 [accessed 18 July 2005] www.sfgate.com.

10. Adapted from Lisa DiCarlo, "IBM Gets the Message—Instantly," Forbes.com, 7 July 2002 [accessed 22 July 2003] www.forbes.com; "IBM Introduces Breakthrough Messaging Technology for Customers and Business Partners," *M2 Presswire*, 19 February 2003 [accessed 24 July 2003] www.proquest.com; "IBM and America Online Team for Instant Messaging Pilot," *M2 Presswire*, 4 February 2003 [accessed 24 July 2003] www.proquest.com.

11. Adapted from CES website [accessed 18 July 2005] www.cesweb.org.

12. Adapted from GSD&M Idea City website [accessed 7 July 2010] www.ideacity.com; Burt Helm, "Wal-Mart, Please Don't Leave Me," *BusinessWeek*, 9 October 2006, 84–89.

13. "Entrepreneurs Across America," *Entrepreneur Magazine* [accessed 12 June 1997] www.entrepreneur.com.

14. Adapted from SolarCity website [accessed 7 July 2010] www.solarcity.com.

15. Adapted from Hot Stix Golf website [accessed 8 February 2011] www.hotstixgolf.com.

16. Adapted from Epson Personal Photo Lab website [accessed 8 February 2011] www.epson.com/picturemate; Public Relations Society of America website [accessed 18 June 2005] www.prsa.org.

17. Adapted from Keith H. Hammonds, "Difference Is Power," *Fast Company*, 36, 258 [accessed 11 July 2000] www.fastcompany.com; Terri Morrison, Wayne A. Conaway, and George A. Borden, Ph.D., *Kiss, Bow, or Shake Hands* (Holbrook, Mass.: Adams Media Corporation, April 1995).

18. Adapted from Adobe website [accessed 8 February 2011] www.adobe.com; Jeff Nachtigal, "It's Easy and Cheap Being Green," *Fortune*, 16 October 2006, 53; "Adobe Wins Platinum Certification Awarded by U.S. Green Building Council," press release, 3 July 2006 [accessed 15 October 2006] www.adobe.com.

19. Adapted from Mitchell, "The Circle of Life—Condolence Letters"; Larcen, "Authors Share the Words of Condolence."

CHAPTER 9

1. Chargify website [accessed 18 February 2011] http://chargify.com; David Hauser, "How to Break the Trust of Your Customers in Just One Day: Lessons Learned from a Major Mistake," David

Hauser blog, 13 October 2010 [accessed 18 February 2011] http://davidhauser.com; Jason Kincaid, "Subscription Billing System Chargify Missteps as It Switches from Freemium to Premium," TechCrunch, 11 October 2010 [accessed 18 February 2011] http://techcrunch.com; Lance Walley, "Chargify News: New Pricing, Features & More," 11 October 2010 [accessed 18 February 2011] http://chargify.com; "Chargify New Pricing" comment thread, Hacker News [accessed 18 February 2011] http://news.ycombinator.com.

2. Ken Ward, Jr., "Bayer Admits 'We Fell Short' in Fire Response, redOrbit, 9 October 2008 [accessed 11 October 2008] www.redorbit.com; "Plant Manager Apologizes for Lack of Communication," Charleston Daily Mail, 11 October 2008 [accessed 11 October 2008] www.dailymail.com.

3. Ian McDonald, "Marsh Can Do $600 Million, but Apologize?" Wall Street Journal, 14 January 2005, C1, C3; Adrienne Carter and Amy Borrus, "What if Companies Fessed Up?" BusinessWeek, 24 January 2005, 59–60; Patrick J. Kiger, "The Art of the Apology," Workforce Management, October 2004, 57–62.

4. Ameeta Patel and Lamar Reinsch, "Companies Can Apologize: Corporate Apologies and Legal Liability," Business Communication Quarterly, March 2003 [accessed 1 December 2003] www.elibrary.com.

5. John Guiniven, "Sorry! An Apology as a Strategic PR Tool," Public Relations Tactics, December 2007, 6.

6. Quinn Warnick, "A Close Textual Analysis of Corporate Layoff Memos," Business Communication Quarterly, September 2010, 322–326.

7. Deven Sharma, "Standard & Poor's Commitment to Reform: Restoring Confidence in the Credit Markets," Standard & Poor's [accessed 13 July 2010] www.standardandpoors.com.

8. Walley, "Chargify News: New Pricing, Features & More."

9. "Advice from the Pros on the Best Way to Deliver Bad News," Report on Customer Relationship Management, 1 February 2003 [accessed 1 December 2003] www.elibrary.com.

10. Ben Levisohn, "Getting More Workers to Whistle," BusinessWeek, 28 January 2008, 18.

11. "Less Than Half of Privately Held Businesses Support Whistleblowing," Grant Thornton website [accessed 13 October 2008] www.internationalbusinessreport.com.

12. Steve Karnowski, "New Food Safety Law Protects Whistleblowers," Bloomberg Businessweek, 11 February 2011 [accessed 14 February 2011] www.businessweek.com.

13. Sue Shellenbarger, "How to Keep Your Cool in Angry Times," Wall Street Journal, 22 September 2010 [accessed 15 February 2011] http://online.wsj.com.

14. Courtland L. Bovée, John V. Thill, George P. Dovel, and Marian Burk Wood, Advertising Excellence (New York: McGraw-Hill, 1995), 508–509; John Holusha, "Exxon's Public-Relations Problem," New York Times, 12 April 1989, D1.

15. Omowale Casselle, "Really, You Want ME to Write YOU a LinkedIn Recommendation," RecruitingBlogs, 22 April 2010 [accessed 15 February 2011] www.recruitingblogs.com.

16. "LinkedIn Profiles to Career Introductions: When You Can't Recommend Your Friend," Seattle Post-Intelligencer Personal Finance blog, 16 November 2010 [accessed 15 February 2011] http://blog.seattlepi.com.

17. Neal Schaffer, "How Should I Deal with a LinkedIn Recommendation Request I Don't Want to Give?" Social Web School, 20 January 2010 [accessed 15 February 2011] http://humancapitalleague.com.

18. Dawn Wolf, "Job Applicant Rejection Letter Dos and Donts—Writing an Appropriate 'Dear John' Letter to an Unsuccessful Applicant," 31 May 2009, Employment Blawg.com [accessed 14 July 2010] www.employmentblawg.com.

19. Wolf, "Job Applicant Rejection Letter Dos and Donts—Writing an Appropriate 'Dear John' Letter to an Unsuccessful Applicant"; "Prohibited Employment Policies/Practices," U.S. Equal Employment Opportunity Commission [accessed 14 July 2010] www.eeoc.gov; Susan M. Heathfield, "Candidate Rejection Letter," About.com [accessed 14 July 2010] http://humanresources.about.com; "Rejection Letters Under Scrutiny: 7 Do's & Don'ts," Business Management Daily, 1 April 2009 [accessed 14 July 2010] www.businessmanagementdaily.com.

20. Judi Brownell, "The Performance Appraisal Interviews: A Multipurpose Communication Assignment," Bulletin of the Association for Business Communication 57, no. 2 (1994), 11–21.

21. Gary Dessler, A Framework for Human Resource Management, 3rd ed. (Upper Saddle River, N.J.: Pearson Prentice Hall, 2004), 198.

22. Kelly Spors, "Why Performance Reviews Don't Work—And What You Can Do About It," Independent Street blog, Wall Street Journal, 21 October 2008 [accessed 14 July 2010] http://blogs.wsj.com.

23. Carrie Brodzinski, "Avoiding Wrongful Termination Suits," National Underwriter Property & Casualty—Risk & Benefits Management, 13 October 2003 [accessed 2 December 2003] www.elibrary.com.

24. Susan Friedfel, "Protecting Yourself in the Performance Review Process," Workforce Management, April 2009 [accessed 14 July 2010] www.workforce.com.

25. Friedfel, "Protecting Yourself in the Performance Review Process."

26. E. Michelle Bohreer and Todd J. Zucker, "Five Mistakes Managers Make When Terminating Employees," Texas Lawyer, 2 May 2006 [accessed 14 July 2010] www.law.com; Deborah Muller, "The Right Things to Do to Avoid Wrongful Termination Claims," Workforce Management, October 2008 [accessed 14 July 2010] www.workforce.com; Maria Greco Danaher, "Termination: Telling an Employee," Workforce Management [accessed 14 July 2010] www.workforce.com.

27. Adapted from "FDA Notifies Public That Vail Products, Inc., Issues Nationwide Recall of Enclosed Bed Systems," FDA press release, 30 June 2005 [accessed 18 August 2005] www.fda.gov.

28. Adapted from "Bathtub Curve," Engineering Statistics Handbook, National Institute of Standards and Technology website [accessed 16 April 2005] www.nist.gov; Robert Berner, "The Warranty Windfall," BusinessWeek, 20 December 2004, 84–86; Larry Armstrong, "When Service Contracts Make Sense," BusinessWeek, 20 December 2004, 86.

29. Adapted from Twitter/JetBlue website [accessed 29 October 2008] http://twitter.com/JetBlue.

30. "Viral Effect of Email Promotion," Alka Dwivedi blog [accessed 19 October 2006] www.alkadwivedi.net; Teresa Valdez Klein, "Starbucks Makes a Viral Marketing Misstep," Blog Business Summit website [accessed 19 October 2006] www.blogbusinesssummit.com.

31. Adapted from Lee Valley website [accessed 29 October 2008] www.leevalley.com.

32. Adapted from Fookes Software website [accessed 28 October 2008] www.fookes.com.

33. Adapted from Stanton website [accessed 18 August 2005] www.stantondj.com.

34. Adapted from Pui-Wing Tam, Erin White, Nick Wingfield, and Kris Maher, "Snooping Email by Software Is Now a Workplace Norm," Wall Street Journal, 9 March 2005, B1+.

35. Adapted from Sylvia Ann Hewlett and Carolyn Buck Luce, "Off-ramps and On-ramps," Harvard Business Review, March 2005, 43–54.

36. Adapted from Rodney Manley, "Milledgeville Plant to Close; 150 to Lose Jobs," Macon.com, 28 January 2009 [accessed 1 February 2009] www.macon.com; Jamie Jones, "Shaw Plant Closing in Milledgeville," The Daily Citizen (Dalton, Georgia), 29 January 2009 [accessed 1 February 2009] www.northwestgeorgia.com.

37. Adapted from "Recall Safety Notice," Bombardier Recreational Products website, 10 September 2008 [accessed 30 October 2008] www.brp.com; Bombardier Recreational Products website [accessed 30 October 2008] www.brp.com.

38. Adapted from Environmental Quality Company press releases [accessed 27 October 2006] www.eqonline.com; "N.C. Residents to Return After Fire," Science Daily, 6 October 2006 [accessed 27 October 2006] www.sciencedaily.com; "Hazardous Waste Plant Fire in N.C. Forces 17,000 to Evacuate," FOXNews.com, 6 October 2006 [accessed 27 October 2006] www.foxnews.com.

39. Adapted from Alion website [accessed 19 August 2005] www.alionscience.com.

CHAPTER 10

1. CafeMom website [accessed 19 February 2011] www.cafemom.com; "ClubMom Introduces the MomNetwork—The Web's First Social Network for Moms," press release, 8 May 2006 [accessed 22 October 2006] www.hcp.com; "Laura Fortner Named Senior Vice President, Business Development at ClubMom," press release, 20 September 2006 [accessed 22 October 2006] http://newyork.dbusinessnews.com.

2. Jay A. Conger, "The Necessary Art of Persuasion," *Harvard Business Review*, May–June 1998, 84–95; Jeanette W. Gilsdorf, "Write Me Your Best Case for . . . ," *Bulletin of the Association for Business Communication* 54, no. 1 (March 1991): 7–12.

3. Mary Cross, "Aristotle and Business Writing: Why We Need to Teach Persuasion," *Bulletin of the Association for Business Communication* 54, no. 1 (March 1991): 3–6.

4. IKEA website [accessed 19 February 2011] www.ikea.com; Liz C. Wang, Julie Baker, Judy A. Wagner, and Kirk Wakefield, "Can a Retail Web Site Be Social?" *Journal of Marketing* 71, no. 3 (July 2007), 143–157.

5. Stephen Bayley and Roger Mavity, "How to Pitch," *Management Today*, March 2007, 48–53.

6. Robert B. Cialdini, "Harnessing the Science of Persuasion," *BusinessWeek*, 4 December 2007 [accessed 4 March 2008] www.businessweek.com.

7. Wesley Clark, "The Potency of Persuasion," *Fortune*, 12 November 2007, 48; W. H. Weiss, "Using Persuasion Successfully," *Supervision*, October 2006, 13–16.

8. Tom Chandler, "The Copywriter's Best Friend," *The Copywriter Underground blog*, 20 December 2006 [accessed 4 March 2008] http://copywriterunderground.com.

9. Raymond M. Olderman, *10-Minute Guide to Business Communication* (New York: Macmillan Spectrum/Alpha Books, 1997), 57–61.

10. John D. Ramage and John C. Bean, *Writing Arguments: A Rhetoric with Readings*, 3rd ed. (Boston: Allyn & Bacon, 1995), 430–442.

11. Philip Vassallo, "Persuading Powerfully: Tips for Writing Persuasive Documents," *Et Cetera*, Spring 2002, 65–71.

12. Dianna Booher, *Communicate with Confidence* (New York: McGraw-Hill, 1994), 102.

13. "Social Factors in Developing a Web Accessibility Business Case for Your Organization," W3C website [accessed 17 July 2010] www.w3.org.

14. Adapted from "What Is the HYBRID HEAT Dual Fuel System by Carrier?" Carrier website [accessed 5 November 2008] www.residential.carrier.com.

15. iPod main product page, Apple website [accessed 17 July 2010] www.apple.com/ipod.

16. "HealthGrades Reveals America's Best Hospitals," 27 February 2008 [accessed 4 March 2008] www.ivanhoe.com.

17. Biokleen home page [accessed 17 July 2010] http://biokleenhome.com.

18. Ford Focus product page, Ford website [accessed 17 July 2010] www.fordvehicles.com.

19. *Living in France* product page, Insider Paris Guides website [accessed 4 March 2008] www.insiderparisguides.com.

20. Barnes & Noble website [accessed 17 July 2010] www.barnesandnoble.com.

21. Mint.com website [accessed 17 July 2010] www.mint.com.

22. FlightWise Carry-on Backpack product page, Lands End website [accessed 17 July 2010] www.landsend.com.

23. iPod touch product page, Apple website [accessed 17 July 2010] www.apple.com/ipodtouch/what-is/gaming-device.html.

24. iPod touch product page.

25. Larry Weber, *Marketing to the Social Web* (Hoboken, N.J.: Wiley, 2007), 12–14; David Meerman Scott, *The New Rules of Marketing and PR* (Hoboken, N.J.: Wiley, 2007), 62; Paul Gillin, *The New Influencers* (Sanger, Calif.: Quill Driver Books, 2007), 34–35; Jeremy Wright, *Blog Marketing: The Revolutionary Way to Increase Sales, Build Your Brand, and Get Exceptional Results* (New York: McGraw-Hill, 2006), 263–365.

26. "Content Marketing 101: How to Build Your Business with Content," Copyblogger [accessed 19 February 2011] www.copyblogger.com.

27. Michael Zeisser, "Unlocking the Elusive Potential of Social Networks," *McKinsey Quarterly*, June 2010 [accessed 17 July 2010] www.mckinseyquarterly.com.

28. Gilsdorf, "Write Me Your Best Case for . . ."

29. Miguel Helft and Tanzina Vega, "Retargeting Ads Follow Surfers to Other Sites," *New York Times*, 29 August 2010 [accessed 19 February 2011] www.nytimes.com.

30. "How to Comply with the Children's Online Privacy Protection Rule," U.S. Federal Trade Commission website [accessed 17 July 2010] www.ftc.gov; "Frequently Asked Advertising Questions: A Guide for Small Business," U.S. Federal Trade Commission website [accessed 17 July 2010] www.ftc.gov.

31. Adapted from Samsung website [accessed 22 October 2006] www.samsung.com.

32. Adapted from IBM website [accessed 15 January 2004] www.ibm.com; "DAS Faces an Assured Future with IBM," IBM website [accessed 16 January 2004] www.ibm.com; "Sametime," IBM website [accessed 16 January 2004] www.ibm.com.

33. Adapted from CNET Shopper.com [accessed 1 October 2001] http://shopper.cnet.com.

34. Adapted from American National Red Cross website [accessed 19 July 2010] www.redcrossblood.org; American Red Cross San Diego Chapter website [accessed 19 July 2010] www.sdarc.org.

35. Adapted from Web Accessibility Initiative, World Wide Web Consortium website [accessed 7 November 2008] www.w3.org.

36. Adapted from Joe Sharkey, "Luggage Lock Plan Revisited, Again," *New York Times*, 6 January 2004 [accessed 6 January 2004] www.nytimes.com; Brookstone website [accessed 13 January 2004] www.brookstone.com.

37. Kentucky Cabinet for Economic Development website [accessed 19 July 2010] www.thinkkentucky.com.

38. Adapted from Your World Instruments website [accessed 21 February 2011] www.yourworldinstruments.com; "Ud," *Encyclopedia Britannica* [accessed 21 February 2011] www.brittanica.com.

39. Adapted from Podcast Bunker website [accessed 19 July 2010] www.podcastbunker.com.

40. Adapted from Insure.com website [accessed 20 February 2011] www.insure.com.

41. Adapted from Kelly Services website [accessed 19 July 2010] www.kellyservices.com.

42. Adapted from Time Inc. website [accessed 19 July 2010] www.timewarner.com.

43. Adapted from Hangers Cleaners (Kansas City) website [accessed 19 July 2010] www.hangerskc.com; Charles Fishman, "The Greener Cleaners," Fast Company website [accessed 11 July 2000] http://fastcompany.com; Micell Technologies website [accessed 1 September 2000] www.micell.com; Cool Clean Technologies, Inc., website [accessed 9 January 2004] www.coolclean.com.

44. Adapted from Curves website [accessed 19 July 2010] www.curves.com.

CHAPTER 11

1. Fresh & Easy website [accessed 24 February 2011] www.freshandeasy.com; Tesco website [accessed 24 February 2011] www.tesco.com; "Competition and Profit," Food Marketing Institute website

[accessed 5 November 2006] www.fmi.org; John E. Forsyth, Nicolo Galante, and Todd Guild, "Capitalizing on Customer Insights," *McKinsey Quarterly*, 2006 Issue 3, 42–53; "Company Spotlight: Tesco PLC," *MarketWatch: Global Round-Up*, July 2006, 76–81; James Quilter, "Tesco Hands Senior Role to Brand Planning Chief," *Marketing*, 2 August 2006, 4; Don Longo, "The British Are Coming," *Progressive Grocer*, 15 April 2006, 66–75.

2. Annie Pettit, "Mugging, Sugging and Now Rugging: I Take a Hard Stance on Privacy," LoveStats blog, 29 January 2010 [accessed 22 February 2011] http://lovestats.wordpress.com.

3. Information for this section was obtained from "Finding Industry Information" [accessed 3 November 1998] www.pitt.edu/~buslibry/industries.htm; Thomas P. Bergman, Stephen M. Garrison, and Gregory M. Scott, *The Business Student Writer's Manual and Guide to the Internet* (Upper Saddle River, N.J.: Prentice Hall, 1998), 67–80; Ernest L. Maier, Anthony J. Faria, Peter Kaatrude, and Elizabeth Wood, *The Business Library and How to Use It* (Detroit: Omnigraphics, 1996), 53–76; Sherwyn P. Morreale and Courtland L. Bovée, *Excellence in Public Speaking* (Fort Worth: Harcourt Brace College Publishers, 1998), 166–171.

4. "Mahalo," CrunchBase [accessed 25 July 2010] www.crunchbase.com.

5. AlltheWeb.com advanced search page [accessed 24 November 2008] www.alltheweb.com; Google advanced search page [accessed 24 November 2008] www.google.com; Live Search website [accessed 24 November 2008] www.live.com.

6. "Search Effectively," Bing [accessed 23 February 2011] www.bing.com.

7. Christina Warren, "Yolink Helps Web Researchers Search Behind Links," Mashable, 24 July 2010 [accessed 26 July 2010] http://mashable.com.

8. "Copyright Office Basics," U.S. Copyright Office website [accessed 2 November 2006] www.copyright.gov.

9. Naresh K. Malhotra, *Basic Marketing Research* (Upper Saddle River, N.J.: Prentice-Hall, 2002), 314–317; "How to Design and Conduct a Study," *Credit Union Magazine*, October 1983, 36–46.

10. Product features page, SurveyMonkey.com [accessed 29 October 2006] www.surveymonkey.com.

11. Tesco website [accessed 25 July 2010] www.tesco.com.

12. Morreale and Bovée, *Excellence in Public Speaking*, 177.

13. Morreale and Bovée, *Excellence in Public Speaking*, 182.

14. A. B. Blankenship and George Edward Breen, *State of the Art Marketing Research* (Lincolnwood, Ill.: NTC Business Books, 1992), 225.

15. Lynn Quitman Troyka, *Simon & Schuster Handbook for Writers*, 6th ed. (Upper Saddle River, N.J.: Simon & Schuster, 2002), 481.

16. "How to Paraphrase Effectively: 6 Steps to Follow," Researchpaper.com [accessed 26 October 1998] www.researchpaper.com.

17. Venkatesh Rao, "Social Media vs. Knowledge Management: A Generational War," *Social Computing*, 17 November 2008 [accessed 23 November 2008] www.socialcomputingmagazine.com; Jeff Kelly, "KM vs. Social Media: Beware the Warmongers," 17 November 2008 [accessed 23 November 2008] www.socialcomputingmagazine.com.

CHAPTER 12

1. Xplane website [accessed 25 February 2011] www.xplane.com; "Small & Global," CNN, 23 June 2008 [accessed 4 December 2008] www.cnn.com; "Visionary Leaders," *Portland Monthly*, October 2007, 82–88.

2. Alexis Gerard and Bob Goldstein, *Going Visual* (Hoboken, N.J.: Wiley, 2005), 18.

3. Charles Kostelnick and Michael Hassett, *Shaping Information: The Rhetoric of Visual Conventions* (Carbondale, Ill.: Southern Illinois University Press, 2003), 177.

4. Gerard and Goldstein, *Going Visual*, 25–27.

5. "Fact Sheet Overview," *2003 National Assessment of Adult Literacy*, National Institute for Literacy [accessed 22 November 2006] www.nifl.gov.

6. Gerard and Goldstein, *Going Visual*, 103–106.

7. Edward R. Tufte, *Visual Explanations: Images and Quantities, Evidence and Narrative* (Cheshire, Conn.: Graphics Press, 1997), 82.

8. Joshua David McClurg-Genevese, "The Principles of Design," *Digital Web Magazine*, 13 June 2005 [accessed 23 November 2006] www.digital-web.com.

9. Kostelnick and Hassett, *Shaping Information: The Rhetoric of Visual Conventions*, 17.

10. Kostelnick and Hassett, *Shaping Information: The Rhetoric of Visual Conventions*, 216.

11. Edward R. Tufte, *The Visual Display of Quantitative Information* (Cheshire, Conn.: Graphic Press, 1983), 113.

12. Based in part on Tufte, *Visual Explanations: Images and Quantities, Evidence and Narrative*, 29–37, 53; Paul Martin Lester, *Visual Communication: Images with Messages*, 4th ed. (Belmont, Calif.: Thomson Wadsworth, 2006), 95–105, 194–196.

13. Data from Hoover's Online [accessed 3 December 2008] www.hoovers.com.

14. Robert L. Harris, *Information Graphics: A Comprehensive Illustrated Reference* (New York: Oxford University Press, 1999), 14.

15. Stephen Few, "Save the Pies for Dessert," *Visual Business Intelligence Newsletter*, August 2007 [accessed 29 July 2010] www.perceptualedge.com.

16. Maria Popova, "Data Visualization: Stories for the Information Age," *BusinessWeek*, 12 August 2009 [accessed 29 July 2010] www.businessweek.com.

17. "Data Visualization: Modern Approaches," Smashing Magazine website, 2 August 2007 [accessed 15 March 2008] www.smashing-magazine.com; "7 Things You Should Know About Data Visualization," Educause Learning Initiative [accessed 15 March 2008] www.educause.edu; TagCrowd website [accessed 15 March 2008] www.tagcrowd.com.

18. "Interactive Web Sites Draw Minds, Shape Public Perception," *ScienceDaily*, 27 May 2008 [accessed 3 December 2008] www.sciencedaily.com.

CHAPTER 13

1. Adapted from MyCityWay website [accessed 5 March 2011] http://mycityway.com; BMW i website [accessed 5 March 2011] www.bmw-i.com; Adam Bluestein and Amy Barrett, "How Business-Plan Competitions Reward Innovation," *Inc.*, 1 July 2010 [accessed 5 March 2011] www.inc.com; Nick Saint, "Mayor Bloomberg Announces First Investment by NYC-Sponsored Venture Fund: MyCityWay," SAI Business Insider, 25 May 2010 [accessed 5 March 2011] www.businessinsider.com; Heidi Brown, "How to Write a Winning Business Plan," *Forbes*, 18 June 2010 [accessed 5 March 2011] www.forbes.com; NYC DataMine website [accessed 5 March 2011] www.nyc.gov.

2. Brown, "How to Write a Winning Business Plan"; Michael Gerber, "The Business Plan That Always Works," *Her Business*, May/June 2004, 23–25; J. Tol Broome, Jr., "How to Write a Business Plan," *Nation's Business*, February 1993, 29–30; Albert Richards, "The Ernst & Young Business Plan Guide," *R & D Management*, April 1995, 253; David Lanchner, "How Chitchat Became a Valuable Business Plan," *Global Finance*, February 1995, 54–56; Marguerita Ashby-Berger, "My Business Plan—And What Really Happened," *Small Business Forum*, Winter 1994–1995, 24–35; Stanley R. Rich and David E. Gumpert, *Business Plans That Win $$$* (New York: Harper & Row, 1985).

3. Jakob Nielsen, "Reading on the Web" [accessed 11 November 2004] www.useit.com/alertbox/9710a.html.

4. Reid Goldsborough, "Words for the Wise," *Link-Up*, September–October 1999, 25–26.

5. Julie Rohovit, "Computer Eye Strain: The Dilbert Syndrome," Virtual Hospital website [accessed 9 November 2004] www.vh.org.

6. Nick Usborne, "Two Pillars of a Successful Site," *Excess Voice*, May 2004 [accessed 8 November 2004] www.excessvoice.com.

7. Shel Holtz, *Writing for the Wired World* (San Francisco: International Association of Business Communicators, 1999), 6–9.

8. Holtz, Writing for the Wired World, 28–29.

9. David A. Garvin and Michael A. Roberto, "What You Don't Know About Making Decisions," Harvard Business School Working Knowledge, 15 October 2001 [accessed 28 February 2011] http://hbswk.hbs.edu.

10. Iris Varner, *Contemporary Business Report Writing*, 2nd ed. (Chicago: Dryden Press, 1991), 170.

11. Curt Kampmeier, "How to Write a Proposal That's Accepted Every Time," *Consulting to Management*, September 2000, 62.

12. Qvidian website [accessed 28 February 2011] www.qvidian.com; Dan MacDougall, "Orchestrating Your Proposal," *Canadian Consulting Engineer*, March–April 2003, 51–56.

13. "Why What You Learned in School About Writing Was Wrong," CapturePlanning.com [accessed 9 December 2008] www.capture-planning.com.

14. Adapted from SXSW website [accessed 2 March 2011] http://sxsw.com; Catherine Holahan and Spencer E. Ante, "SXSW: Where Tech Mingles with Music," *BusinessWeek*, 7 March 2008 [accessed 9 March 2008] www.businessweek.com.

CHAPTER 14

1. Adapted from George Stenitzer profile on LinkedIn [accessed 4 March 2011] www.linkedin.com/in/stenitzer; Tellabs website [accessed 4 March 2011] www.tellabs.com; Sid Cato, "World's Best 2005 Reports," Sid Cato's Office Annual Report Website [accessed 11 November 2006] www.sidcato.com; George Stenitzer, "New Challenges for Annual Reports," Presentation to National Investor Relations Institute, November 2005 [accessed 11 November 2006] www.niri-chicago.org.

2. A. S. C. Ehrenberg, "Report Writing—Six Simple Rules for Better Business Documents," *Admap*, June 1992, 39–42.

3. Michael Netzley and Craig Snow, *Guide to Report Writing* (Upper Saddle River, N.J.: Prentice Hall, 2001), 15.

4. "Tellabs Solutions and Applications," Tellabs 2005 Annual Report [accessed 11 November 2006] www.tellabs.com.

5. David A. Hayes, "Helping Students Grasp the Knack of Writing Summaries," *Journal of Reading* (November 1989): 96–101.

6. Philip C. Kolin, *Successful Writing at Work*, 6th ed. (Boston: Houghton Mifflin, 2001), 552–555.

7. Jakob Nielsen, "How Little Do Users Read?" 6 May 2008, UseIt.com [accessed 11 December 2008] www.useit.com.

8. Brian Clark, "How to Create Compelling Content that Ranks Well in Search Engines," Copyblogger, May 2010 [accessed 8 March 2011] www.copyblogger.com.

9. Jakob Nielsen, "Writing Style for Print vs. Web," Useit.com, 9 June 2008 [accessed 28 July 2010] www.useit.com.

10. Paul Boag, "10 Harsh Truths About Corporate Websites," Smashing Magazine blog, 10 February 2009 [accessed 28 July 2010] www.smashingmagazine.com.

11. Clark, "How to Create Compelling Content that Ranks Well in Search Engines."

12. "Codex: Guidelines," WordPress website [accessed 16 February 2008] http://wordpress.org; Michael Shanks, "Wiki Guidelines," Traumwerk website [accessed 18 August 2006] http://metamedia.stanford.edu/projects/traumwerk/home; Joe Moxley, M.C. Morgan, Matt Barton, and Donna Hanak, "For Teachers New to Wikis," Writing Wiki [accessed 18 August 2006] http://writing-wiki.org; "Wiki Guidelines," Psi [accessed 18 August 2006] http://psi-im.org.

13. Rachael King, "No Rest for the Wiki," *BusinessWeek*, 12 March 2007 [accessed 14 February 2008] www.businessweek.com.

14. "Codex: Guidelines," WordPress website [accessed 28 July 2010] http://wordpress.com.

15. Adapted from Air-Trak website [accessed 26 July 2010] www.air-trak.com.

CHAPTER 15

1. Adapted from "Writing a Compelling Executive Summary," Garage Technology Ventures [accessed 9 March 2011] www.garage.com; "Crafting Your Wow! Statement," Garage Technology Ventures [accessed 9 March 2011] www.garage.com; Guy Kawasaki website [accessed 9 March 2011] www.guykawasaki.com.

2. John Morkes and Jakob Nielsen, "Concise, Scannable, and Objective: How to Write for the Web," UseIt.com [accessed 13 November 2006] www.useit.com.

3. Michael Netzley and Craig Snow, *Guide to Report Writing* (Upper Saddle River, N.J.: Prentice Hall, 2001), 57.

4. Oswald M. T. Ratteray, "Hit the Mark with Better Summaries," *Supervisory Management*, September 1989, 43–45.

5. Netzley and Snow, *Guide to Report Writing*, 43.

6. Alice Reid, "A Practical Guide for Writing Proposals" [accessed 31 May 2001] http://members.dca.net/areid/proposal.htm.

7. Toby B. Gooley, "Ocean Shipping: RFPs That Get Results," *Logistics Management*, July 2003, 47–52.

8. Andrea Obana, "How to Write a Request for Proposal (RFP)," Fine Brand Media website [accessed 22 January 2004] www.finebrand.com; Gooley, "Ocean Shipping: RFPs That Get Results," 47–52.

9. Obana, "How to Write a Request for Proposal (RFP)"; Gooley, "Ocean Shipping: RFPs That Get Results," 47–52; "Writing a Good RFP," *Infrastructure Issues*, September 1998, Mead & Hunt website [accessed 23 January 2004] www.meadhunt.com.

10. Adapted from "Home Depot Says E-Learning Is Paying for Itself," *Workforce Management*, 25 February 2004 [accessed 28 February 2004] www.workforce.com; Robert Celaschi, "The Insider: Training," *Workforce Management*, August 2004, 67–69; Joe Mullich, "A Second Act for E-Learning," *Workforce Management*, February 2004, 51–55; Gail Johnson, "Brewing the Perfect Blend," *Training*, December 2003, 30+; Tammy Galvin, "2003 Industry Report," *Training*, October 2003, 21+; William C. Symonds, "Giving It the Old Online Try," *BusinessWeek*, 3 December 2001, 76–80; Karen Frankola, "Why Online Learners Drop Out," *Workforce*, October 2001, 52–60; Mary Lord, "They're Online and on the Job; Managers and Hamburger Flippers Are Being E-Trained at Work," *U.S. News & World Report*, 15 October 2001, 72–77.

11. Adapted from Ieva M. Augstums, "Buyers Take the Driver's Seat," *Dallas Morning News*, 20 February 2004 [accessed 30 June 2004] www.highbeam.com; Jill Amadio, "A Click Away: Automotive Web Sites Are Revved Up and Ready to Help You Buy," *Entrepreneur*, 1 August 2003 [accessed 30 June 2004] www.highbeam.com; Dawn C. Chmielewski, "Car Sites Lend Feel-Good Info for Haggling," *San Jose Mercury News*, 1 August 2003 [accessed 30 June 2004] www.highbeam.com; Cromwell Schubarth, "Autoheroes Handle Hassle of Haggling," *Boston Herald*, 24 July 2003 [accessed 30 June 2004] www.highbeam.com; Rick Popely, "Internet Doesn't Change Basic Shopping Rules," *Chicago Tribune*, 28 February 2004 [accessed 30 June 2004] www.highbeam.com; Matt Nauman, "Walnut Creek, Calif., Firm Prospers as Online Car Buying Becomes More Popular," *San Jose Mercury News*, 21 June 2004 [accessed 30 June 2004] www.highbeam.com; Cliff Banks, "e-Dealer 100," *Ward's Dealer Business*, 1 April 2004 [accessed 30 June 2004] www.highbeam.com; Cars.com website [accessed 30 June 2004] www.cars.com; CarsDirect website [accessed 30 June 2004] www.carsdirect.com.

CHAPTER 16

1. John Bowe, "Funny 5 Money," *New York Times*, 30 December 2010 [accessed 13 March 2011] www.nytimes.com; Stephanie Palmer Taxy, Good in a Room website [accessed 13 March 2011] www.goodinaroom.com; Mike Fleming, "A Banner Day for Two Former Assistants," Deadline Hollywood, 20 January 2011 [accessed 14 March 2011] www.deadline.com.

2. Nancy Duarte, *Slide:ology: The Art and Science of Creating Great Presentations* (Sebastopol, Calif.: O'Reilly Media, 2008), 13.

3. Amber Naslund, "Twebinar: GE's Tweetsquad," 4 August 2009 [accessed 3 August 2010] www.radian6.com/blog.

4. Irwin Pollack, "Don't Just Give Presentations, Impact Your Audience," *Fort Worth Business Press*, 1 May 2006, 10.

5. Carmine Gallo, "How to Deliver a Presentation Under Pressure," *BusinessWeek*, 18 September 2008 [accessed 15 August 2009] www.businessweek.com.

6. Carmine Gallo, "Loaded for Bore," *BusinessWeek* online, 5 August 2005 [accessed 19 September 2005] www.businessweek.com.

7. Sarah Lary and Karen Pruente, "Powerless Point: Common PowerPoint Mistakes to Avoid," *Public Relations Tactics*, February 2004, 28.

8. Garr Reynolds, *Presentation Zen* (Berkeley, Calif.: New Riders, 2008), 66.

9. Reynolds, *Presentation Zen*, 39–42.

10. Sherwyn P. Morreale and Courtland L. Bovée, *Excellence in Public Speaking* (Fort Worth, Tex.: Harcourt Brace College Publishers, 1998), 234–237.

11. John Windsor, "Presenting Smart: Keeping the Goal in Sight," *Presentations*, 6 March 2008 [accessed 19 March 2008] www.presentations.com.

12. Morreale and Bovée, *Excellence in Public Speaking*, 241–243.

13. Adapted from Eric J. Adams, "Management Focus: User-Friendly Presentation Software," *World Trade*, March 1995, 92.

14. Carmine Gallo, "Grab Your Audience Fast," *BusinessWeek*, 13 September 2006, 19.

15. Walter Kiechel III, "How to Give a Speech," *Fortune*, 8 June 1987, 180.

16. *Communication and Leadership Program* (Santa Ana, Calif.: Toastmasters International, 1980), 44, 45.

17. Bowe, "Funny 5 Money."

18. Steve Adubato, "Throw Away That Script, Use an Outline Instead," *NJBiz*, 23 October 2006, 17.

19. Cheryl Wiles, "Impromptu Speaking," *Harvard Management Communication Letter*, December 2001, 7–8.

20. Peter Burrows and Ronald Grover, "Steve Jobs' Magic Kingdom," *BusinessWeek* online, 6 February 2006 [accessed 25 November 2006] www.businessweek.com.

21. Richard Zeoli, "The Seven Things You Must Know About Public Speaking," *Forbes*, 3 June 2009 [accessed 2 August 2010] www.forbes.com; Morreale and Bovée, *Excellence in Public Speaking*, 24–25.

22. Jennifer Rotondo and Mike Rotondo, Jr., *Presentation Skills for Managers* (New York: McGraw-Hill, 2002), 9.

23. Judy Linscott, "Getting On and Off the Podium," *Savvy*, October 1985, 44.

24. Iris R. Johnson, "Before You Approach the Podium," *MW*, January–February 1989, 7.

25. "Advice from a Voice Coach: Say It and Sell It," *Presentations*, 6 November 2006 [accessed 27 November 2006] www.presentations.com.

26. Rick Gilbert, "Presentation Advice for Boardroom Success," *Financial Executive*, September 2005, 12.

27. Rotondo and Rotondo, *Presentation Skills for Managers*, 151.

28. Teresa Brady, "Fielding Abrasive Questions During Presentations," *Supervisory Management*, February 1993, 6.

29. Robert L. Montgomery, "Listening on Your Feet," *The Toastmaster*, July 1987, 14–15.

30. Cliff Atkinson, *The Backchannel* (Berkeley, Calif.: New Riders, 2010), 17.

31. Atkinson, *The Backchannel*, 51, 68–73.

32. Olivia Mitchell, "10 Tools for Presenting with Twitter," Speaking About Presenting blog, 3 November 2009 [accessed 3 August 2010] www.speakingaboutpresenting.com; Atkinson, *The Backchannel*, 51, 68–73, 99.

33. SlideShare website [accessed 3 August 2010] www.slideshare.net.

34. Geoffrey James, "How to Give an Online Presentation," BNET, 23 February 2011 [accessed 10 March 2011] www.bnet.com.

CHAPTER 17

1. Adapted from Garr Reynolds, *Presentation Zen* (Berkeley, Calif.: New Riders, 2008), 7, 10, 62–66, 103–104; Garr Reynolds, "Top Ten Slide Tips," Garr Reynolds website [accessed 19 March 2011] www.garrreynolds.com; Garr Reynolds, "Presentation Zen: The Video" [accessed 19 March 2011] www.youtube.com.

2. "Polishing Your Presentation," 3M Meeting Network [accessed 8 June 2001] www.mmm.com/meetingnetwork/readingroom/meetingguide_pres.html.

3. Michael Hyatt, "Five Rules to Better PowerPoint Presentations," 21 June 2005, Working Smart blog [accessed 2 December 2006] www.michaelhyatt.com.

4. An example of such a presentation is Dick Hardt's keynote presentation at OSCON 2005; the presentation can be viewed at www.identity20.com/media/OSCON2005.

5. Cliff Atkinson, "The Cognitive Load of PowerPoint: Q&A with Richard E. Mayer," Sociablemedia.com [accessed 22 December 2008] www.sociablemedia.com.

6. Atkinson, "The Cognitive Load of PowerPoint: Q&A with Richard E. Mayer."

7. Reynolds, *Presentation Zen: Simple Ideas on Presentation Design and Delivery*, 66.

8. Reynolds, *Presentation Zen: Simple Ideas on Presentation Design and Delivery*, 68–69.

9. Margo Halverson, "Choosing the Right Colors for Your Next Presentation," 3M Meeting Network [accessed 8 June 2001] www.mmm.com/meetingnetwork/readingroom/meetingguide_right_color.html.

10. Carol Klinger and Joel G. Siegel, "Computer Multimedia Presentations," *CPA Journal*, June 1996, 46.

11. Jon Hanke, "Five Tips for Better Visuals," 3M Meeting Network [accessed 25 May 2007] http://www.3m.com/meetingnetwork/presentations/pmag_better_visuals.html.

12. Hanke, "Five Tips for Better Visuals."

13. Nancy Duarte, *Slide:ology: The Art and Science of Creating Great Presentations* (Sebastopol, Calif.: O'Reilly Media, 2008), 118.

14. Reynolds, *Presentation Zen: Simple Ideas on Presentation Design and Delivery*, 132.

15. Guy Kawasaki, "Rule of Thumb," *Entrepreneur*, May 2008, 44.

16. Duarte, *Slide:ology: The Art and Science of Creating Great Presentations*, 152.

17. Eric Markowitz, "How to Create a Great PowerPoint Presentation," *Inc.*, 7 February 2011 [accessed 17 March 2011] www.inc.com.

18. Claudyne Wilder and David Fine, *Point, Click & Wow* (San Francisco: Jossey-Bass Pfeiffer, 1996), 50.

19. Jerry Weissman, *Presenting to Win: The Art of Telling Your Story* (Upper Saddle River, N.J.: Pearson Prentice Hall, 2006), 124.

20. Weissman, *Presenting to Win*, 144–147.

21. Sarah Lary and Karen Pruente, "Powerless Point: Common PowerPoint Mistakes to Avoid," *Public Relations Tactics*, February 2004, 28.

22. Nancy Duarte, "Avoiding the Road to PowerPoint Hell," *Wall Street Journal*, 22 January 2011 [accessed 16 March 2011] http://online.wsj.com.

23. Cliff Atkinson, *Beyond Bullet Points: Using Microsoft PowerPoint to Create Presentations That Inform, Motivate, and Inspire* (Redmond, Wash.: Microsoft Press, 2005), 16.

24. Weissman, *Presenting to Win*, 162.

25. Reynolds, *Presentation Zen: Simple Ideas on Presentation Design and Delivery*, 66.

26. Ted Simons, "Handouts That Won't Get Trashed," *Presentations*, February 1999, 47–50.

27. Adapted from PechaKucha20x20 website [accessed 4 August 2010] www.pecha-kucha.org; Reynolds, *Presentation Zen: Simple Ideas on Presentation Design and Delivery*, 41.

28. Adapted from Foursquare website [accessed 4 August 2010] http://foursquare.com; Christina Warren, "Foursquare Reaches 100 Millions Checkins," Mashable, 20 July 2010 [accessed 4 August 2010] http://mashable.com.

CHAPTER 18

1. Adapted from *ATK Corporate Profile* [accessed 23 March 2011] www.atk.com; Ed Frauenheim, "Weapons-Maker ATK Practices Personnel Precision," *Workforce Management*, March 2011, 22–23, 26; Ed Frauenheim, "Numbers Game: Companies Utilize Data to Predict Workforce Needs," *Workforce Management*, March 2011, 20–21; OrcaEyes website [accessed 23 March 2011] www.orcaeyes.com.

2. Courtland L. Bovée and John V. Thill, *Business in Action*, 5th ed. (Boston: Pearson Prentice Hall, 2011), 241–242.

3. Anne Fisher, "How to Get Hired by a 'Best' Company," *Fortune*, 4 February 2008, 96.

4. Jim Schaper, "Finding Your Future Talent Stars," *BusinessWeek*, 2 July 2010 [accessed 5 August 2010] www.businessweek.com.

5. Eve Tahmincioglu, "Revamping Your Job-Search Strategy," MSNBC.com, 28 February 2010 [accessed 5 August 2010] www.msnbc.com.

6. Tahmincioglu, "Revamping Your Job-Search Strategy."

7. Jessica Dickler, "The Hidden Job Market," CNNMoney.com, 10 June 2009 [accessed 6 August 2010] http://money.cnn.com.

8. Tara Weiss, "Twitter to Find a Job," *Forbes*, 7 April 2009 [accessed 6 August 2010] www.forbes.com.

9. Miriam Saltpeter, "Using Facebook Groups for Job Hunting," Keppie Careers blog, 13 November 2008 [accessed 6 August 2010] www.keppiecareers.com.

10. Anne Fisher, "Greener Pastures in a New Field," *Fortune*, 26 January 2004, 48.

11. Liz Ryan, "Etiquette for Online Outreach," Yahoo! Hotjobs website [accessed 26 March 2008] http://hotjobs.yahoo.com.

12. Eve Tahmincioglu, "Employers Digging Deep on Prospective Workers," MSNBC.com, 26 October 2009 [accessed 10 August 2010] www.msnbc.com.

13. Career and Employment Services, Danville Area Community College website [accessed 23 March 2008] www.dacc.edu/career; Career Counseling, Sarah Lawrence College website [accessed 23 March 2008] www.slc.edu/occ/index.php; Cheryl L. Noll, "Collaborating with the Career Planning and Placement Center in the Job-Search Project," *Business Communication Quarterly* 58, no. 3 (1995): 53–55.

14. Fay Hansen, "Recruiters Bear a Bigger Load as Hiring Takes Off," *Workforce Management*, May 2010 [accessed 5 August 2010] www.workforce.com.

15. Randall S. Hansen and Katharine Hansen, "What Résumé Format Is Best for You?" QuintCareers.com [accessed 7 August 2010] www.quintcareers.com.

16. Hansen and Hansen, "What Résumé Format Is Best for You?"

17. Katharine Hansen, "Should You Consider a Functional Format for Your Resume?" QuintCareers.com [accessed 7 August 2010] www.quintcareers.com.

18. Kim Isaacs, "Resume Dilemma: Criminal Record," Monster.com [accessed 23 May 2006] www.monster.com; Kim Isaacs, "Resume Dilemma: Employment Gaps and Job-Hopping," Monster.com [accessed 23 May 2006] www.monster.com; Susan Vaughn, "Answer the Hard Questions Before Asked," *Los Angeles Times*, 29 July 2001, W1–W2.

19. John Steven Niznik, "Landing a Job with a Criminal Record," About.com [accessed 12 December 2006] http://jobsearchtech.about.com.

20. "How to Ferret Out Instances of Résumé Padding and Fraud," *Compensation & Benefits for Law Offices*, June 2006, 1+.

21. "Resume Fraud Gets Slicker and Easier," CNN.com [accessed 11 March 2004] www.cnn.com.

22. Cari Tuna and Keith J. Winstein, "Economy Promises to Fuel Résumé Fraud," *Wall Street Journal*, 17 November 2008 [accessed 8 August 2010] http://online.wsj.com; Lisa Takeuchi Cullen, "Getting Wise to Lies," *Time*, 1 May 2006, 59; "Resume Fraud Gets Slicker and Easier"; Employment Research Services website [accessed 18 March 2004] www.erscheck.com.

23. "How to Ferret Out Instances of Résumé Padding and Fraud."

24. Jacqueline Durett, "Redoing Your Résumé? Leave Off the Lies," *Training*, December 2006, 9; "Employers Turn Their Fire on Untruthful CVs," *Supply Management*, 23 June 2005, 13.

25. Cynthia E. Conn, "Integrating Writing Skills and Ethics Training in Business Communication Pedagogy: A Résumé Case Study Exemplar," *Business Communication Quarterly*, June 2008, 138–151; Marilyn Moats Kennedy, "Don't Get Burned by Résumé Inflation," *Marketing News*, 15 April 2007, 37–38.

26. Rockport Institute, "How to Write a Masterpiece of a Résumé," [accessed 24 March 2008] www.rockportinstitute.com.

27. Lora Morsch, "25 Words That Hurt Your Resume," CNN.com, 20 January 2006 [accessed 20 January 2006] www.cnn.com.

28. Liz Ryan, "The Reengineered Résumé," *BusinessWeek*, 3 December 2007, SC12.

29. Katharine Hansen, "Tapping the Power of Keywords to Enhance Your Resume's Effectiveness," QuintCareers.com [accessed 7 August 2010] www.quintcareers.com.

30. Hansen, "Tapping the Power of Keywords to Enhance Your Resume's Effectiveness."

31. Jolie O'Dell, "LinkedIn Reveals the 10 Most Overused Job-Hunter Buzzwords," Mashable, 14 December 2010 [accessed 22 March 2011] http://mashable.com.

32. Dave Johnson, "10 Resume Errors That Will Land You in the Trash," BNET, 22 February 2010 [accessed 22 March 2011] www.bnet.com; Anthony Balderrama, "Resume Blunders That Will Keep You from Getting Hired," CNN.com, 19 March 2008 [accessed 26 March 2008] www.cnn.com; Michelle Dumas, "5 Resume Writing Myths," Distinctive Documents blog, 17 July 2007 [accessed 26 March 2008] http://blog.distinctiveweb.com; Kim Isaacs, "Resume Dilemma: Recent Graduate," Monster.com [accessed 26 March 2008] http://career-advice.monster.com.

33. Karl L. Smart, "Articulating Skills in the Job Search," *Business Communication Quarterly* 67, no. 2 (June 2004): 198–205.

34. "When to Include Personal Data," ResumeEdge.com [accessed 25 March 2008] www.resumeedge.com.

35. Eve Tahmincioglu, "Looking for a Job in 2011? Here's How to Stand Out," MSNBC.com, 3 January 2011 [accessed 24 March 2011] http://today.msnbc.com.

36. "Résumé Length: What It Should Be and Why It Matters to Recruiters," *HR Focus*, June 2007, 9.

37. Rachel Zupek, "Seven Exceptions to Job Search Rules," CNN.com, 3 September 2008 [accessed 29 December 2008] www.cnn.com.

38. John Hazard, "Resume Tips: No Pictures, Please and No PDFs," Career-Line.com, 26 May 2009 [accessed 10 August 2010] www.career-line.com; "25 Things You Should Never Include on a Resume," HR World website 18 December 2007 [accessed 25 March 2008] www.hrworld.com.

39. John Sullivan, "Résumés: Paper, Please," *Workforce Management*, 22 October 2007, 50; "Video Résumés Offer Both Pros and Cons During Recruiting," *HR Focus*, July 2007, 8.

40. Jobs page, Zappos website [accessed 24 March 2011] http://about.zappos.com/jobs.

41. Nancy M. Schullery, Linda Ickes, and Stephen E. Schullery, "Employer Preferences for Résumés and Cover Letters," *Business Communication Quarterly*, June 2009, 163–176.

42. VisualCV website [accessed 10 August 2010] www.visualcv.com.
43. Elizabeth Garone, "Five Mistakes Online Job Hunters Make," *Wall Street Journal*, 28 July 2010 [accessed 10 August 2010] http://online.wsj.com.
44. "10 Reasons Why You Are Not Getting Any Interviews," *Miami Times*, 7–13 November 2007, 6D.
45. Deborah Silver, "Niche Sites Gain Monster-Sized Following," *Workforce Management*, March 2011, 10–11.
46. "Protect Yourself From Identity Theft When Hunting for a Job Online," *Office Pro*, May 2007, 6.

CHAPTER 19

1. Adapted from "Wishez Is Live," Zappos Family blog, 17 November 2010 [accessed 25 March 2011] http://blogs.zappos.com; Tony Hsieh, "Amazon & Zappos, 1 Year Later," Zappos CEO & COO blog, 22 July 2010 [accessed 24 March 2011] http://blogs.zappos.com; Zappos Jobs page [accessed 25 March 2011] http://about.zappos.com/jobs; Todd Raphael, "7 Interview Questions from Zappos," Todd Raphael's World of Talent blog, 22 July 2010 [accessed 25 March 2011] http://community.ere.net; Jeffrey M. O'Brien, "Zappos Knows How to Kick It," Fortune, 22 January 2009 [accessed 25 March 2011] http://about.zappos.com/press-center; "Zappos Family Seattle Coding Challenge and Tech Tweet Up," Zappos Family blog, 22 March 2011 [accessed 25 March 2011] http://blogs.zappos.com.
2. Matthew Rothenberg, "Manuscript vs. Machine," The Ladders, 15 December 2009 [accessed 13 August 2010] www.theladders.com; Joann Lublin, "Cover Letters Get You in the Door, So Be Sure Not to Dash Them Off," *Wall Street Journal*, 6 April 2004, B1.
3. Lisa Vaas, "How to Write a Great Cover Letter," The Ladders, 20 November 2009 [accessed 13 August 2010] www.theladders.com.
4. Allison Doyle, "Introduction to Cover Letters," About.com [accessed 13 August 2010] http://jobsearch.about.com.
5. Doyle, "Introduction to Cover Letters"; Vaas, "How to Write a Great Cover Letter"; Toni Logan, "The Perfect Cover Story," *Kinko's Impress* 2 (2000): 32, 34.
6. Lisa Vaas, "How to Follow Up a Résumé Submission," The Ladders, 9 August 2010 [accessed 12 August 2010] www.theladders.com.
7. Alison Doyle, "How to Follow Up After Submitting a Resume," About.com [accessed 13 August 2010] http://jobsearch.about.com; Vaas, "How to Follow Up a Résumé Submission."
8. Anne Fisher, "How to Get Hired by a 'Best' Company," *Fortune*, 4 February 2008, 96.
9. Fisher, "How to Get Hired by a 'Best' Company."
10. Sarah E. Needleman, "Speed Interviewing Grows as Skills Shortage Looms; Strategy May Help Lock in Top Picks; Some Drawbacks," *Wall Street Journal*, 6 November 2007, B15.
11. Scott Beagrie, "How to Handle a Telephone Job Interview," *Personnel Today*, 26 June 2007, 29.
12. John Olmstead, "Predict Future Success with Structured Interviews," *Nursing Management*, March 2007, 52–53.
13. Fisher, "How to Get Hired by a 'Best' Company."
14. Erinn R. Johnson, "Pressure Sessions," *Black Enterprise*, October 2007, 72.
15. "What's a Group Interview?" About.com Tech Careers [accessed 5 April 2008] http://jobsearchtech.about.com.
16. Fisher, "How to Get Hired by a 'Best' Company."
17. Katherine Hansen, "Behavioral Job Interviewing Strategies for Job-Seekers," QuintCareers.com [accessed 13 August 2010] www.quintcareers.com.
18. Hansen, "Behavioral Job Interviewing Strategies for Job-Seekers."
19. Chris Pentilla, "Testing the Waters," *Entrepreneur*, January 2004 [accessed 27 May 2006] www.entrepreneur.com; Terry McKenna, "Behavior-Based Interviewing," *National Petroleum News*, January

2004, 16; Nancy K. Austin, "Goodbye Gimmicks," *Incentive*, May 1996, 241.
20. William Poundstone, "Beware the Interview Inquisition," *Harvard Business Review*, May 2003, 18+.
21. Peter Vogt, "Mastering the Phone Interview," Monster.com [accessed 13 December 2006] www.monster.com; Nina Segal, "The Global Interview: Tips for Successful, Unconventional Interview Techniques," Monster.com [accessed 13 December 2006] www.monster.com.
22. Segal, "The Global Interview: Tips for Successful, Unconventional Interview Techniques."
23. Barbara Kiviat, "How Skype Is Changing the Job Interview," *Time*, 20 October 2009 [accessed 13 August 2010] www.time.com.
24. HireVue website [accessed 4 April 2008] www.hirevue.com; in2View website [accessed 4 April 2008] www.in2view.biz; Victoria Reitz, "Interview Without Leaving Home," *Machine Design*, 1 April 2004, 66.
25. Gina Ruiz, "Job Candidate Assessment Tests Go Virtual," *Workforce Management*, January 2008 [accessed 14 August 2010] www.workforce.com; Connie Winkler, "Job Tryouts Go Virtual," *HR Magazine*, September 2006, 131–134.
26. Jonathan Katz, "Rethinking Drug Testing," *Industry Week*, March 2010, 16–18; Ashley Shadday, "Assessments 101: An Introduction to Candidate Testing," *Workforce Management*, January 2010 [accessed 14 August 2010] www.workforce.com; Dino di Mattia, "Testing Methods and Effectiveness of Tests," *Supervision*, August 2005, 4–5; David W. Arnold and John W. Jones, "Who the Devil's Applying Now?" *Security Management*, March 2002, 85–88; Matthew J. Heller, "Digging Deeper," *Workforce Management*, 3 March 2008, 35–39.
27. Frederick P. Morgeson, Michael A. Campion, Robert L. Dipboye, John R. Hollenbeck, Kevin Murphy, and Neil Schmitt, "Are We Getting Fooled Again? Coming to Terms with Limitations in the Use of Personality Tests in Personnel Selection," *Personnel Psychology* 60, no. 4 (Winter 2007): 1029–1049.
28. Austin, "Goodbye Gimmicks."
29. Rachel Zupek, "How to Answer 10 Tough Interview Questions," CNN.com, 4 March 2009 [accessed 13 August 2010] www.cnn.com; Barbara Safani, "How to Answer Tough Interview Questions Authentically," The Ladders, 5 December 2009 [accessed 13 August 2010] www.theladders.com.
30. Nick Corcodilos, "How to Answer a Misguided Interview Question," *Seattle Times*, 30 March 2008 [accessed 5 April 2008] www.seattletimes.com.
31. Katherine Spencer Lee, "Tackling Tough Interview Questions," *Certification Magazine*, May 2005, 35.
32. Scott Ginsberg, "10 Good Ways to 'Tell Me About Yourself,'" The Ladders, 26 June 2010 [accessed 13 August 2010] www.theladders.com.
33. InterviewUp website [accessed 13 August 2010] www.interviewup.com.
34. Joe Turner, "An Interview Strategy: Telling Stories," Yahoo! HotJobs [accessed 5 April 2008] http://hotjobs.yahoo.com.
35. "A Word of Caution for Chatty Job Candidates," *Public Relations Tactics*, January 2008, 4.
36. "Employers Reveal Outrageous and Common Mistakes Candidates Made in Job Interviews, According to New Career-Builder Survey," CareerBuilder.com, 12 January 2011 [accessed 24 March 2011] www.careerbuilder.com.
37. Randall S. Hansen, "When Job-Hunting: Dress for Success," QuintCareers.com [accessed 5 April 2008] www.quintcareers.com; Alison Doyle, "Dressing for Success," About.com [accessed 5 April 2008] http://jobsearch.about.com.
38. William S. Frank, "Job Interview: Pre-Flight Checklist," *The Career Advisor* [accessed 28 September 2005] http://careerplanning.about.com.

39. "Employers Reveal Outrageous and Common Mistakes Candidates Made in Job Interviews, According to New CareerBuilder Survey."

40. T. Shawn Taylor, "Most Managers Have No Idea How to Hire the Right Person for the Job," *Chicago Tribune*, 23 July 2002 [accessed 29 September 2005] www.ebsco.com.

41. "10 Minutes to Impress," *Journal of Accountancy*, July 2007, 13.

42. Steven Mitchell Sack, "The Working Woman's Legal Survival Guide: Testing," FindLaw.com [accessed 22 February 2004] www.findlaw.com.

43. Mark Henricks, "3 Interview Questions That Could Cost Your Company $1 Million," BNET, 8 March 2011 [accessed 19 April 2011] www.bnet.com.

44. Todd Anten, "How to Handle Illegal Interview Questions," Yahoo! HotJobs [accessed 7 August 2009] http://hotjobs.yahoo.com.

45. "Negotiating Salary: An Introduction," *InformationWeek* online [accessed 22 February 2004] www.informationweek.com.

46. "Negotiating Salary: An Introduction."

47. Lisa Vaas, "Resume, Meet Technology: Making Your Resume Format Machine-Friendly," The Ladders [accessed 13 August 2010] www.theladders.com.

48. Joan S. Lublin, "Notes to Interviewers Should Go Beyond a Simple Thank You," *Wall Street Journal*, 5 February 2008, B1.

APPENDIX A

1. Mary A. De Vries, Internationally Yours (Boston: Houghton Mifflin, 1994), 9.

2. Patricia A. Dreyfus, "Paper That's Letter Perfect," Money, May 1985, 184.

3. Linda Driskill, Business and Managerial Communication: New Perspectives (Orlando, Fla.: Harcourt Brace Jovanovich, 1992), 470.

4. Lennie Copeland and Lewis Griggs, Going International: How to Make Friends and Deal Effectively in the Global Marketplace, 2nd ed. (New York: Random House, 1985), 24–27.

5. De Vries, Internationally Yours, 8.

6. U.S. Postal Service, "International Mail Manual," Issue 34, 14 May 2007 [accessed 23 October 2007] www.usps.gov.

Acknowledgments

TEXT

26 (Business Communication 2.0: Who's Responsible Here?) Adapted from Joseph Lewczak, "Quiznos/Subway Settlement Poses Legal Threat to Future UGC Promos," *Promo*, 23 March 2010, [accessed 24 December 2010] www.promomagazine.com; United States District Court, District of Connecticut, "Memorandum of Decision Denying Defendants' Motion for Summary Judgment, *Doctor's Associates, Inc., v. Qip Holder LLC and Ifilm Corp.*," 19 February 2010; Louise Story, "Can a Sandwich Be Slandered?" *New York Times*, 29 January 2008, [accessed 1 August 2008] www.nytimes.com; David Ardia, "Slandering Sandwiches and User Submitted Content," Citizen Media Law Project website, 29 January 2008, [accessed 1 August 2008] www.citmedialaw.org; "Doctor's Associates Inc. vs. QIP Holders LLC: Complaint for Injunctive Relief and Damages," 27 October 2006, [accessed 1 August 2008] www.citmedialaw.org; "MTV to Run User Generated Ads," *Marketing*, 15 November 2006, 3. **48 (Checklist: Overcoming Barriers to Effective Listening)** Robert A. Luke, Jr., "Improving Your Listening Ability," *Supervisory Management*, June 1992, 7; Madelyn Burley-Allen, "Listening for Excellence in Communication," *The Dynamics of Behavior Newsletter* 2, no. 2 (Summer 1992): 1; Bob Lamons, "Good Listeners Are Better Communicators," *Marketing News,* 11 September 1995, 13+. **49 (Checklist: Improving Nonverbal Communication Skills)** Gerald H. Graham, Jeanne Unrue, and Paul Jennings, "The Impact of Nonverbal Communication in Organizations: A Survey of Perceptions," *Journal of Business Communication* 28, no. 1 (Winter 1991): 45–62; Dianna Booher, *Communicate with Confidence* (New York: McGraw-Hill, 1994), 363–370. **50 (Communicating Across Cultures: Whose Skin Is This, Anyway?)** Rita Pyrillis, "Body of Work," *Workforce Management*, November 2010 [accessed 29 December 2010] www.workforce.com; Danielle S. Urban, "What to Do About 'Body Art' at Work," *Workforce Management*, March 2010 [accessed 29 December 2010] www.workforce.com; "36% – Tattooed Gen Nexters," Pew Research Center [accessed 29 December 2010] http://pewresearch.org. **69 (Communicating Across Cultures: Us Versus Them: Generational Conflict in the Workplace)** Adapted from Anne Fisher, "When Gen X Runs the Show," *Time*, 14 May 2009 [accessed 4 January 2011] www.time.com; Deloitte, "Generation Y: Powerhouse of the Global Economy," research report, 2009 [accessed 2 January 2011] www.deloitte.com; "Generation Y," Nightly Business Report website, 30 June 2010 [accessed 2 January 2011] www.pbs.org; Sherry Posnick-Goodwin, "Meet Generation Z," *California Educator*, February 2010 [accessed 29 December 2010] www.cta.org; Ernie Stark, "Lost in a Time Warp," *People & Strategy*, Vol. 32 No. 4, 2009, 58–64; Nancy Sutton Bell and Marvin Narz, "Meeting the Challenges of Age Diversity in the Workplace," *The CPA Journal*, February 2007 [accessed 17 August 2008] www.nysscpa.org; Steff Gelston, "Gen Y, Gen X and the Baby Boomers: Workplace Generation Wars," *CIO*, 30 January 2008 [accessed 2 January 2011] www.cio.com; Heather Havenstein, "Generation Y in the Workplace: Digital Natives' Tech Needs Are Changing Companies Forever," *CIO*, 17 September 2008 [accessed 4 January 2011] www.cio.com. **124 (Communicating Across Cultures: Can You Connect with a Global Audience on the Web?)** Adapted from Laura Morelli, "Writing for a Global Audience on the Web," *Marketing News*, 17 August 1998, 16; Yuri and Anna Radzievsky, "Successful Global Web Sites Look Through Eyes of the Audience," *Advertising Age's Business Marketing*, January 1998, 17; Sari Kalin,

"The Importance of Being Multiculturally Correct," *Computerworld*, 6 October 1997, G16–G17; B. G. Yovovich, "Making Sense of All the Web's Numbers," *Editor & Publisher*, November 1998, 30–31; David Wilford, "Are We All Speaking the Same Language?" *The Times*, (London), 20 April 2000, 4. **153 (Communication Miscues: Missing the Message with Prescription Medications)** "ClearRx," Target website [accessed 21 January 2011] www.target.com; "Medications—The Importance of Reading the Label," American Academy of Pediatrics [accessed 9 September 2008] www.medem.com; Sarah Bernard, "The Perfect Prescription," *New York Magazine*, 18 April 2005 [accessed 30 September 2006] www.newyorkmetro.com; "ClearRX at Target Pharmacy," Target website [accessed 30 September 2006] www.target.com. **229 (Communication Miscues: Can You Get Sued for Writing—or Not Writing—a Recommendation Letter?)** Adapted from "How to Write Reference Letters," National Association of Colleges and Employers website [accessed 5 July 2010] www.naceweb.org; Diane Cadrain, "HR Professionals Stymied by Vanishing Job References," *HR Magazine*, November 2004, 31–40; "Five (or More) Ways You Can Be Sued for Writing (or Not Writing) Recommendation Letters," *Fair Employment Practice Guidelines*, July 2006, 1, 3–4; Rochelle Kaplan, "Writing a Recommendation Letter," National Association of Colleges and Employers website [accessed 12 October 2006] www.naceweb.org; Maura Dolan and Stuart Silverstein, "Court Broadens Liability for Job References," *Los Angeles Times*, 28 January 1997, A1, A11; David A. Price, "Good References Pave Road to Court," *USA Today*, 13 February 1997, 11A; Frances A. McMorris, "Ex-Bosses Face Less Peril Giving Honest Job References," *Wall Street Journal*, 8 July 1996, B1, B8; Dawn Gunsch, "Gray Matters: Centralize Control of Giving References," *Personnel Journal*, September 1992, 114, 116–117; Betty Southard Murphy, Wayne E. Barlow, and D. Diane Hatch, "Manager's Newsfront: Job Reference Liability of Employees," *Personnel Journal*, September 1991, 22, 26; Ross H. Fishman, "When Silence Is Golden," *Nation's Business*, July 1991, 48–49. **264 (Business Communication 2.0: We're Under Attack! Responding to Rumors and Criticism in a Social Media Environment)** "When Fans Attack: How to Defend a Brand's Reputation Online," Crenshaw Communications blog, 20 May 2010 [accessed 18 February 2011] http://crenshawcomm.com; David Meerman Scott, "The US Air Force: Armed with Social Media," WebInkNow blog, 15 December 2008 [accessed 14 July 2010] www.webinknow.com; Matt Rhodes, "How to React If Somebody Writes About Your Brand Online," FreshNetworks blog, 9 January 2009 [accessed 14 July 2010] www.freshnetworks.com; Matt Rhodes, "Social Media as a Crisis Management Tool," Social Media Today blog, 21 December 2009 [accessed 8 July 2010] www.socialmediatoday.com; Jack Neff, "What to Do When Social Media Spreads Marketing Myth," *Advertising Age*, 7 September 2009, 4, 24; Augie Ray, "Combating Rumors in Social Media: Sarah Palin and Babygate," Experience: The Blog, 1 September 2008 [accessed 18 October 2008] www.experiencetheblog.com; Michelle Conlin, "Web Attack," *BusinessWeek*, 16 April 2007 [accessed 27 February 2008] www.businessweek.com; Melissa Allison, "Corporations Seek to Clean Up Online Rumors," *Seattle Times*, 4 March 2007 [accessed 4 March 2007] www.seattletimes.com; Charles Wolrich, "Top Corporate Hate Web Sites," *Forbes*, 8 March 2005 [accessed 16 August 2005] www.forbes.com; PlanetFeedback.com [accessed 27 February 2008] www.planetfeedback.com; "Health Related Hoaxes and Rumors," Centers for Disease

Control and Prevention website [accessed 16 August 2005] www.cdc .gov; Snopes.com [accessed 16 August 2005] www.snopes.com; "Pranksters, Activists and Rogues: Know Your Adversaries and Where They Surf," *PR News,* 26 June 2000 [accessed 3 December 2003] www .elibrary.com. **286 (Business Communication 2.0: Please Find Us: Building an Audience Through Search Engine Optimization)** Adapted from "Webmaster Guidelines," Google [accessed 22 February 2011] www.google.com; Brian Clark, "How to Create Compelling Content that Ranks Well in Search Engines," Copyblogger, May 2010 [accessed 22 February 2011] www.copyblogger.com; P.J. Fusco, "How Web 2.0 Affects SEO Strategy," ClickZ, 23 May 2007 [accessed 6 November 2008] www.clickz.com; "Law Firm Marketing Now Dependent on Search Engine Optimization," *Law Office Management & Administration Report,* June 2006, 1, 10–12; *Pandia Search Engine Marketing 101,* Pandia website [accessed 25 March 2007] www.pandia .com; Mike Grehan, "Does Textbook SEO Really Work Anymore?" 17 April 2006, Clickz [accessed 25 March 2007], www.clickz.com; Shari Thurow, "Web Positioning Metrics and SEO," 24 October 2005, Clickz .com [accessed 25 March 2007], www.clickz.com. **414 (Business Communication 2.0: Hey You! Hands Off My Content!)** Adapted from Jonathan Bailey, "How to Find Plagiarism," Plagiarism Today [accessed 7 March 2011] www.plagiarismtoday.com; Jonathan Bailey, "Global Grind Scrapes Blogs, Publishes Them to Google News," Plagiarism Today, 27 April 2010 [accessed 7 March 2011] www.plagiarismtoday .com; "Content Marketing 101: How to Build Your Business With Content," Copyblogger [accessed 7 March 2011] www.copyblogger .com. **472 (Communicating Across Cultures: Making Sure Your Message Doesn't Get Lost in Translation)** Adapted from Ramez Naguib, "International Audiences," Toastmasters International [accessed 13 March 2011] www.toastmasters.org; Patricia L. Kurtz, *The Global Speaker* (New York: AMACOM, 1995), 35–47, 56–68, 75–82, 87–100; David A. Victor, *International Business Communication* (New York: HarperCollins Publishers, 1992), 39–45; Lalita Khosla, "You Say Tomato," *Forbes,* 21 May 2001, 36; Stephen Dolainski, "Are Expats Getting Lost in the Translation?" *Workforce,* February 1997, 32–39. **484 (Communication Miscues: Disasters Will Happen—Are You Ready?)** Adapted from C. Peter Giuliano and Frank J. Currilo, "Going Blank in the Boardroom," *Public Relations Quarterly,* Winter 2003, 35+; Jennifer Rotondo and Mike Rotondo, Jr., *Presentation Skills for Managers* (New York: McGraw-Hill, 2002), 160–162; Mark Merritt, "No More Nightmares," *Presentations,* April 2001, 44+. **506 (Business Communication 2.0: Presentations Get Social)** Adapted from SlideShare website [accessed 12 February 2011] www.slideshare.net; "SlideShare Presentations," LinkedIn website [accessed 28 December 2008] www.linkedin .com; Jason Kincaid, "SlideShare Sends PowerPoint to the Cloud with New Plugin," TechCrunch, 15 December 2008 [accessed 28 December 2008] www.techcrunch.com. **585 (Communicating Across Cultures: Successfully Interviewing Across Borders)** Adapted from Jean-Marc Hachey, "Interviewing for an International Job," excerpt from *The Canadian Guide to Working and Living Overseas,* 3rd ed. [accessed 23 February 2004] www.workingoverseas.com; Rebecca Falkoff, "Dress to Impress the World: International Business Fashion," Monster.com [accessed 23 February 2004] www.monster.com; Mary Ellen Slater, "Navigating the Details of Landing an Overseas Job," *Washington Post,* 11 November 2002, E4. **588 (Communication Miscues: Make Sure You Don't Talk Yourself out of a Job)** Adapted from "Because You Asked: Interviews Get a Little Strange," ManageSmarter, 25 September 2008 [accessed 2 January 2009] www.managesmarter.com; Thomas Pack, "Good Answers to Job Interview Questions," *Information Today,* January 2004, 35+; John Lees, "Make Them Believe You Are the Best," *The Times* (London), 21 January 2004, 3; "Six Interview Mistakes," Monster.com [accessed 23 February 2004] www.monster.com.

FIGURES AND TABLES

xxxvii (Prologue Figure 1) Used with permission of Scott Anderson. 9 (Figure 1.4) Used with permission of FreshBooks. 36 (Figure 2.1) Adapted from B. Aubrey Fisher, *Small Group Decision Making: Communication and the Group Process,* 2nd ed. (New York: McGraw-Hill,

1980), 145–149; Robbins and De Cenzo, *Fundamentals of Management,* 334–335; Richard L. Daft, *Management,* 6th ed. (Cincinnati: Thomson South-Western, 2003), 602–603. **39 (Figure 2.2)** © Copyright 2011. SAP AG. All rights reserved. **40 (Figure 2.3)** Used with permission of WizeHive-Zig Marketing. **45 (Figure 2.6)** Peter Wynn Thompson/The New York Times, Redux Pictures. **45 (Figure 2.7)** Used with permission of Virtual Meetings—Sococo Team Space. **47 (Table 2.3)** Madelyn Burley-Allen, *Listening: The Forgotten Skill,* (New York: Wiley, 1995), 70–71, 119–120; Judi Brownell, *Listening: Attitudes, Principles, and Skills,* (Boston: Allyn and Bacon, 2002); 3, 9, 83, 89, 125; Larry Barker and Kittie Watson, *Listen Up,* (New York: St. Martin's, 2000), 8, 9, 64. **52 (Table 2.5)** Alf Nucifora, "Voice Mail Demands Good Etiquette from Both Sides," *Puget Sound Business Journal,* 5–11 September 2003, 24; Ruth Davidhizar and Ruth Shearer, "The Effective Voice Mail Message," *Hospital Material Management Quarterly,* 45–49; "How to Get the Most Out of Voice Mail," *The CPA Journal,* February 2000, 11; Jo Ind, "Hanging on the Telephone," *Birmingham Post,* 28 July 1999, PS10; Larry Barker and Kittie Watson, *Listen Up* (New York: St. Martin's Press, 2000), 64–65; Lin Walker, *Telephone Techniques,* (New York: Amacom, 1998), 46–47; Dorothy Neal, *Telephone Techniques,* 2nd ed. (New York: Glencoe McGraw-Hill, 1998), 31; Jeannie Davis, *Beyond "Hello"* (Aurora, Colo.: Now Hear This, Inc., 2000), 2–3; "Ten Steps to Caller-Friendly Voice Mail," *Managing Office Technology,* January 1995, 25; Rhonda Finniss, "Voice Mail: Tips for a Positive Impression," *Administrative Assistant's Update,* August 2001, 5. **61 (Figure 3.1)** Economic data from International Monetary Fund website [accessed 4 January 2011] www.imf.org. **62 (Figure 3.2)** Courtesy of Merck. **87 (Figure 4.1)** Adapted from Kevin J. Harty and John Keenan, *Writing for Business and Industry: Process and Product* (New York: Macmillan Publishing Company, 1987), 3–4; Richard Hatch, *Business Writing* (Chicago: Science Research Associates, 1983), 88–89; Richard Hatch, *Business Communication Theory and Technique* (Chicago: Science Research Associates, 1983), 74–75; Center for Humanities, *Writing as a Process: A Step-by-Step Guide* (Mount Kisco, N.Y.: Center for Humanities, 1987); Michael L. Keene, *Effective Professional Writing* (New York: D. C. Heath, 1987), 28–34. **93 (Figure 4.3)** Courtesy, Burton Snowboards. **95 (Figure 4.4)** Used with permission of Supply Chain Simple. **96 (Figure 4.5)** Used with permission of World Voyager Vacations. **102 (Figure 4.9)** Used with permission of Limiting the Scope of a Message from Blue-ray Disc Association. **106 (Figure 4.13)** Courtesy of Patagonia, Inc. **121 (Figure 5.2)** Used with permission of Lisa Ford. **127 (Figure 5.4)** Copyright 2011, American Institute of Certified Public Accountants. All rights reserved. Used with Permission. **134 (Figure 5.5)** Used with permission of Ignite Social Media. **161 (Figure 6.6)** Photo by Ryan Lackey. Adobe product screen shot(s) reprinted with permission from Adobe Systems Incorporated. **163 (Figure 6.7)** Carnival Cruise Lines © 2011. All Rights Reserved. **175 (Figure 7.1)** Adapted from "About Us," LinkedIn [accessed 2 May 2011] http://press.linkedin.com/about/; Ben Parr, "LinkedIn Surpasses 100 Million Users," Mashable, 22 March 2011 [accessed 2 May 2011] http://mashable.com; Franky Branckaute, "Facebook Statistics: The Numbers Game Continues," The Blog Herald blog, 11 August 2010 [accessed 2 May 2011] www.blogherald.com; Stan Schroeder, "Facebook: Facts You Probably Didn't Know," Mashable, 13 May 2010 [accessed 2 May 2011] http://mashable.com; "The 1000 Most-Visited Sites on the Web," Doubleclick Ad Planner, February 2011 [accessed 2 May 2011] www.google.com/adplanner; Willis Wee, "The Facebook Story in an Infographic," Penn Olson blog 2 April 2010 [accessed 2 May 2011] www.penn-olson.com; "Statistics," YouTube [accessed 2 May 2011] www.youtube.com; "LinkedIn by the Numbers," HubSpot Blog, 29 June 2010 [accessed 2 May 2011] http:// blog.hubspot.com; "Top Corporate Brands on Twitter," Fan Page List [accessed 2 May 2011] http://fanpagelist.com; "Top Corporate Brands on Facebook," Fan Page List [accessed 2 May 2011]. **184 (Table 7.1)** Adapted from Christopher Carfi and Leif Chastaine, "Social Networking for Businesses & Organizations," white paper, Cerado website [accessed 13 August 2008] www.cerado.com; Anusorn Kansap, "Social Networking," PowerPoint presentation, Silpakorn University [accessed

14 August 2008] http://real-timeupdates.com; "Social Network Websites: Best Practices from Leading Services," white paper, 28 November 2007, FaberNovel Consulting [accessed 14 August 2008] www.fabernovel.com. http://fanpagelist.com; "Twitter Statistics for 2010," Sysomos, December 2010 [accessed 2 May 2011] www.sysomos.com; Shiva Chettri, "The Meteoric Rise of Twitter," NetChunks, 10 July 2010 [accessed 2 May 2011] www.netchunks.com. **185 (Figure 7.3)** Used with permission of Red Bull. **195 (Table 7.3)** Robert Scoble and Shel Israel, *Naked Conversations* (Hoboken, N.J.: John Wiley & Sons, 2006), 78–81, 190–194; Paul McFedries, *The Complete Idiot's Guide to Creating a Web Page & Blog*, 6th ed. (New York: Alpha, 2004), 206–208; 272–276; Shel Holtz and Ted Demopoulos, *Blogging for Business* (Chicago: Kaplan, 2006), 54–59, 113–114; Denise Wakeman, "Top 10 Blog Writing Tips," Blogarooni.com [accessed 1 February 2006] www.blogarooni.com; Dennis A. Mahoney, "How to Write a Better Weblog," 22 February 2002, A List Apart [accessed 1 February 2006] www.alistapart.com. **197 (Figure 7.7)** Used with permission of GE CounselTrademarks. **198 (Figure 7.8)** Used with permission of chickdowntown.com. **200 (Figure 7.9)** Courtesy of Patagonia, Inc. **224 (Figure 8.4)** Courtesy Herman Miller. **230 (Figure 8.7)** Used with permission of Rubbermaid. **231 (Figure 8.8)** Used with permission of Pampers. **263 (Figure 9.5)** Used with permission of Toyota. **283 (Figure 10.1)** Image Courtesy TD Ameritrade IP Company, Inc. **294 (Figure 10.4)** Used with permission of Bridepower. **296 (Figure 10.5)** Used with permission of R.C. Bigelow, Inc. **299 (Figure 10.6)** Courtesy of the American Council on Exercise® (ACE®) www.acefitness.org. **301 (Figure 10.7)** Reproduced with permission of Merck Sharp & Dohme Corp., subsidiary of Merck & Co., Inc. All rights reserved. PROPECIA® is a registered trademark of Merck Sharp & Dohme Corp. **318 (Figure 11.2)** Used with permission of NPN. **321 (Figure 11.3)** © Google, Inc. **324 (Figure 11.4)** Used with permission from Microsoft®. **355 (Figure 12.12a)** Used with permission by ToughGraph.com. **355 (Figure 12.12b)** Visual Your Facebook Social Network with a Friend Wheel. Courtesy of Facebook. **355 (Figure 12.12d)** Used with permission from Microsoft®. Microsoft Dynamics NAV 2009 can be accessed at: //www.microsoft.com/presspass/gallery. **357 (Figure 12.14)** Image courtesy of Satellite Imaging Corporation. **359 (Figure 12.15)** This has been reproduced by permission of F5 Networks, Inc. © 2011 F5 Networks, Inc. All Rights Reserved. **376 (Figure 13.3)** Used with permission of StatCom. **402 (Figure 14.1)** Reproduced with permission of Yahoo! Inc. © 2011 Yahoo! Inc. YAHOO! and the YAHOO! logo are registered trademarks of Yahoo! Inc. **415 (Figure 14.6)** Reprint Courtesy of International Business Machines Corporation, © 2011 International Business Machines Corporation. **444 (Figure 15.2)** Used with permission of the American Coatings Association, Inc. **500 (Table 17.1)** Adapted from Claudyne Wilder and David Fine, *Point, Click & Wow* (San Francisco: Jossey-Bass Pfeiffer, 1996), 63, 527. **501 (Figure 17.3a)** © Mark Evans. **522 (Table 18.1)** TweetMyJob.com [accessed 10 August 2010] http://tweetmyjob.com; The Riley Guide [accessed 10 August 2010] www.rileyguide.com; SimplyHired website [accessed 10 August 2010] www.simplyhired.com; Indeed website [accessed 10 August 2010] www.indeed.com; CollegeRecruiter.com [accessed 10 August 2010] www.collegerecruiter.com; Jobster website [accessed 10 August 2010] www.jobster.com; InternshipPrograms.com [accessed 10 August 2010] http://internshipprograms.com. **540 (Figure 18.6)** Used with permission of VisualCV. **556 (Figure 19.3)** Used with permission of GAX. **557 (Figure 19.4)** Used with permission of Shaker Consulting Group. **561 (Table 19.3)** Adapted from InterviewUp website [accessed 6 April 2008] www.interviewup.com; *The Northwestern Endicott Report* (Evanston, Ill.: Northwestern University Placement Center). **562 (Table 19.4)** Adapted from Joe Conklin, "Turning the Tables: Six Questions to Ask Your Interviewer," *Quality Progress*, November 2007, 55; Andrea N. Browne, "Keeping the Momentum at the Interview; Ask Questions, Do Your Research, and Be a Team Player," *Washington Post*, 29 July 2007, K1; Marilyn Sherman, "Questions R Us: What to Ask at a Job Interview," *Career World*, January 2004, 20; H. Lee Rust, *Job Search: The Completion Manual for Jobseekers* (New York: merican Management Association,

1979), 56. **562 (Figure 19.5)** Used with permission of Interview Simulators, from Perfect Interview LLC. **563 (Table 19.5)** Adapted from "Employers Reveal Outrageous and Common Mistakes Candidates Made in Job Interviews, According to New CareerBuilder Survey," CareerBuilder.com, 12 January 2011 [accessed 24 March 2011] www.careerbuilder.com; *The Northwestern Endicott Report* (Evanston, Ill.: Northwestern University Placement Center). **567 (Table 19.6)** Adapted from Deanna G. Kucler, "Interview Questions: Legal or Illegal?" *Workforce Management* [accessed 28 September 2005] www.workforce.com; "Illegal Interview Questions," *USA Today*, 29 January 2001 [accessed 28 September 2005] www.usatoday.com; "Dangerous Questions," *Nation's Business*, May 1999, 22.

PHOTOS

Cover Pearson Image Specialist: Corin Skidds; Pearson Image Photographer: Shayle Keating; Additional Images: Altay Kaya/Tischenko Irina/Velychko/Carlos E. Santa Maria/PhotoHappiness/mashe/Shutterstock. **1** Yuri Arcurs/Shutterstock. **2** Used with permission of Toyota. **7** © Corbis Super RF/Alamy. **12** © Exactostock/SuperStock. **18 (top left)** Belkin International, Inc. **18 (bottom left)** EMC Documentum. **18 (top right)** Getty Images—Digital Vision. **18 (middle right)** Cranaial Tap, Inc. **18 (bottom right)** © 2002 Ethan Hill. **19 (top left)** Reprint Courtesy of International Business Machines Corporation, © 2011 International Business Machines Corporation. **19 (bottom left)** ©2010 Biznik, Inc - Biznik is an online community of independent business people interested in helping each other succeed. Blending the best of social media with in-person events Biznik encourages collaboration inspiration, education and ultimately . . . professional relationships that produce more business. (http://biznik.com). **19 (bottom)** Used with permission of Innocentive. **19 (top right)** InstantPresenter. **19 (bottom right)** © 2002 Ethan Hill. **20 (bottom left)** Autodesk, Inc. **20 (top right)** del.icio.us/Ross_Pennick. **20 (middle right)** Used with permission of TouchGraph. **20 (bottom right)** © Peter Christopher/Masterfile. **21 (top left)** CustomerReach. **21 (bottom left)** Marcio Jose Sanchez/AP Wide World Photos. **21 (top right)** Used with permission of Segway, Inc. **21 (bottom right)** Christine Winter, Xerox. **21 (bottom)** Courtesy of Patagonia, Inc. **22** © Radius Images/Alamy. **30** Used with permission of Toyota. **33** Rosen Law Firm. **52** © GlowImages/Alamy. **56** Rosen Law Firm. **60** Courtesy of International Business Machines Corporation. Unauthorized use not permitted. **63** Blend Images/SuperStock. **65** © Blend Images/Alamy. **68** Steve Cole/Getty Images—Photodisc-Royalty Free. **78** © AsiaPix/Alamy. **79** Courtesy of International Business Machines Corporation. Unauthorized use not permitted. **85** ZanyZeus/Shutterstock. **86** Provided courtesy of H & R Block Inc. **94** © Robert Nicholas/Alamy. **110** Provided courtesy of H & R Block Inc. **114** Mizuka Ito/Creative Commons. **137** Mizuka Ito/Creative Commons. **144** © Kathy deWitt/Alamy. **168** © Kathy deWitt/Alamy. **173** Goodluz/Shutterstock. **174** Courtesy Southwest Airlines, Co. **214** © MGPhoto/Alamy. **236** © MGPhoto/Alamy. **246** © D. Hurst/Alamy. **250** Tom Hindman/AP Wide World Photos. **269** © D. Hurst/Alamy. **293** © Image Source/SuperStock. **313** Shutterstock. **314** © Kevin Britland/Alamy. **336** Kevin Britland/Alamy. **339** seangilligan.com/XPLANE. **364** seangilligan.com/XPLANE. **369** koh sze kiat/Shutterstock. **370** Courtesy of Sonpreet Bhatia, Archana Patchirajan and Puneet Mehta Mycity.com. **396** Courtesy of Sonpreet Bhatia, Archana Patchirajan and Puneet Mehta Mycity.com. **399** Courtesy Tellabs. Photo by Robert Seale. **418** Courtesy Tellabs. Photo by Robert Seale. **424** Courtesy of Guy Kawasaki. **428** Masterfile Royalty Free Division. **456** Courtesy of Guy Kawasaki. **467** wavebreakmedia ltd./Shutterstock. **468** Alexander Sibaja/Hulton Archive/Getty Images. **478** Comstock/Superstock Royalty Free. **480** Jeff Greenberg/PhotoEdit Inc. **487** © Flirt/SuperStock. **490** Alexander Sibaja/Hulton Archive/Getty Images. **493** © Li Ding/Alamy. **495** Photo courtesy of PolyVision(R) Corporation. **506** Used with permission of SlideShare Inc. **514** © Li Ding/Alamy. **519** Stephen Coburn/Shutterstock. **520** Courtesy of ATK. **544** Courtesy of ATK. **548** Brad Swonetz/Redux. **560** © Exactostock/SuperStock. **564** © Blend Images/Alamy. **573** Brad Swonetz/Redux.

Brand, Organization, Name, and Website Index

Subject Index

A

a lot, H-23
a/an, H-12
abbreviations, H-20
    for states, A-12, A-13
    punctuation with, A-1
ability differences, in workforce, 70
abstract words, 128, H-3
abstracts, in reports, 443, 455
abusive language, 260
acceptance letters, 570–571
access control, 39
accuracy
    of information, 92, 404
    of visuals, 361
achievement
    congratulating people on, 232
    need for, 284
achievements section, on résumés, 535
acronyms, H-20
    in email, 190
    IM, 192
    in text messages, 123
action
    persuasive requests for, 292–293
    requesting, 216, 218
action buttons, in PowerPoint, 506
action items, in oral presentations, 481
action phase, of AIDA model, 288, 289,
        297–298, 553
action plan, in reports, 408
action verbs, 437, H-7
    on résumés, 532
active listening, 46, 55
active voice, 125–126, 139, H-8
addiction, to information
        technology, 22
address, proper forms of, A-3
addressee notation, A-8
addresses
    for envelopes, A-11–A-13
    for international correspondence, 75
    style for, H-20
adjectives, H-9–H-10, H-11
    excessive use of, 128
    placement of, 152, 153
adjustments
    granting, 224–227
    persuasive requests for, 293
    refusing, 260, 261
    requesting, 219, 221, 234
adventure, need for, 284

adverbs, H-10–H-11, H-25
    excessive use of, 128
    placement of, 152, 153
advertising
    comparative, 26
    deceptive, 27
    of job openings, 523
    in a social media environment,
        182, 184, 185
    on search engines, 285
    stealth marketing, 23
    truth in, 300
    see also Marketing messages
aesthetic appreciation, need for, 284
affiliation needs, 284
age bias, 119, 120
age differences, culture and, 68
agenda
    hidden, 35
    for meetings, 42
    in oral presentations, 509
aggravate/irritate, H-23
aggregators, 20
aging, vision and, 158
agreement
    pronoun-antecedent, H-6
    subject-verb, H-8
AIDA model, 288, 289, 303
    for job application letters, 551–553
    for persuasive requests, 292–293
    for proposals, 409
    for sales messages, 296–298
    for unsolicited proposals, 392
alcohol testing, 558
almanacs, 320
American Psychological Association (APA),
        442, A-19, A-22
among/between, H-12
analogies, faulty, 290–291
analogy, arguing by, 290
analytical reports, 371, 372, 394
    direct approach for, 385, 408
    examples of, 388, 389–390, 428–442
    indirect approach for, 387, 408
    memo format for, 404–405
    organization of, 385–387
    planning of, 382–387
    purpose of, 382
    statement of purpose for, 372, 373
    2 + 2 approach to, 385, 387, 389
    types of, 379, 382–383
    yardstick approach to, 385, 387

animation, 348, 358
    in slide shows, 504–507
announcements
    company, 262
    negative, 257
    in social media, 178
annual reports, 396, 399
antecedents, H-5
anticipate/expect, H-23
anxiety, speech, 483–484
APA style, 442, A-22, A-23
apologizing, 250
    to customers, 225, 259
apostrophes, H-18
    for plurals, H-4
    with possessives, H-4, H-6, H-18
appeals, emotional vs. logical, 290–291
appearance, 50–51
    for job interviews, 563, 564
    as nonverbal communication, 49
    in workplace, 50–51
appendixes, in reports, 407,
        445–446, 455
applicant tracking systems, 535–536, 543
application letters, 549–554, 575
appositives, H-16
appraisals. *See* performance reviews
appreciation, messages of, 232
area charts, 350, 363
Argentina, A-6
arguments
    logical, 290
    persuasive, 4
Arial, 159, 160
articles, H-12
as if/like, H-12
ASCII text, 539
assistive technologies, 70
attachments, file, 165
attacking of opponents, 290
attention
    audience's, 473–474
    in job interviews, 567
    listening and, 47–48
    to nonverbal cues, 49
attention line, A-8–A-9
attention phase, of AIDA model, 288, 289,
        296, 551–552
attention-getters, 297
    for job application letters, 552
    for oral presentations, 478
attitudes, changing, 293